The Routledge Anthology of U.S. Drama

1898–1949

The first half of the twentieth century was a vibrant period for U.S. theatre and performance. As the United States emerged as a significant military, economic, political and cultural power, so its theatre began to distinguish itself from the prevailing European model. The plays and dramatic texts in this anthology demonstrate the vital and volatile relationship between U.S. theatre, its society, and the ways in which that theatre has both supported and challenged prevailing systems of thought and action.

This collection is organized around key thematic perspectives, from colonialism to psychoanalysis, viewing the artistic output of this era through the sociopolitical events and controversies that shaped it. Each play is accompanied by a critical commentary from a leading scholar and a set of archive source materials, including playbills, production photos, reviews, essays, poems, newspaper articles, and official documents. These supplements bring to life the rich and diverse theatre cultures that operated in the United States during this period, and explore the essential ways that these cultural artifacts engaged with the national debates that surrounded them.

The plays themselves both support and challenge the existing canon of U.S. dramatic literature; a selection that speaks not only to aesthetic innovation, but also to the critical moments of political change and national definition that shaped the United States. From Arthur Miller, Tennesee Williams, and Eugene O'Neill to Angelina Grimké, David Belasco, and Mae West, this is the ideal collection for any course in U.S. theatre.

Joshua E. Polster is Associate Professor of Theatre at Emerson College. His publications include *Stages of Engagement: U.S. Theatre and Performance 1898–1949*, *Reinterpreting the Plays of Arthur Miller*, a critical edition of Miller's *A Memory of Two Mondays*, and numerous articles on U.S. theatre.

The Routledge Anthology of U.S. Drama

1898–1949

Edited by
Joshua E. Polster

Routledge
Taylor & Francis Group
NEW YORK AND LONDON

First published 2017
by Routledge
711 Third Avenue, New York, NY 10017

Routledge is an imprint of the Taylor & Francis Group, an informa business

British Library Cataloguing-in-Publication Data
A catalogue record for this book is available from the British Library

Library of Congress Cataloguing-in-Publication Data
The Routledge anthology of U.S. drama, 1898–1949/ edited by Joshua E. Polster.
pages cm
Includes bibliographical references and index.
ISBN 978-1-138-01835-8 (hardback: alk. paper)—ISBN 978-1-138-01836-5 (pbk.: alk. paper) 1. American drama—20th century. I. Polster, Joshua E., editor.
PS634.P63 2016
812′.508—dc23
2015028355

ISBN: 978-1-138-01835-8 (hbk)
ISBN: 978-1-138-01836-5 (pbk)

Typeset in Bembo
by Florence Production Ltd, Stoodleigh, Devon, U.K.

For Kimberly, Oliver, and Ana,
with love and appreciation

Plays and Performances

Icons

The following icons are used throughout the book to indicate what type of content is being presented:

Commentary

Image (photograph or illustration)

Lyrics

Poem

Document (letters, speeches, programs, production material, guidebooks or government papers)

Article (newspaper piece or review)

Essay (book chapter extract or journal article)

Playscript

Contents

Acknowledgments

I would like to thank Nicolás Kanellos, Martha Carpentier, Stephen Marino, Tappan Wilder, and Lincoln Konkle for their help with research; William Condee, Barry Witham, Odai Johnson, Sarah Bryant-Bertail, Susan Abbotson, and Melia Bensussen for their years of support and guidance; as well as the wonderful reference assistants at the Buffalo Bill Center of the West, the Chickasaw Council House Museum, the Iwasaki Library at Emerson College, and the Beebe Library in Wakefield, Massachusetts. I am also indebted to the many artists, critics and scholars used in this work. Finally, a special thank you to Ben Piggott and Routledge for their excellence and encouragement.

The publisher would like to thank the following for permission to reproduce their material:

Excerpt from "Memories of the Indian Wars," in Joy Kasson, *Buffalo Bill's Wild West*, New York: Hill and Wang, 2000. Copyright © 2000 by Joy S. Kasson. Reprinted by permission of Hill and Wang, a division of Farrar, Straus and Giroux, LLC.

"Remember the Maine" by Burlington Hawkeye, in Sidney Witherbee, Ed., *Spanish-American War Songs: A Complete Collection of Newspaper Verse During the Recent War with Spain*, Detroit, MI: Sidney A. Witherbee, 1898.

Buffalo Bill's Wild West and Congress of Rough Riders of the World: Historical Sketches and Programme, New York: Fless & Ridge Printing Company, 1900.

William Winter, "Madame Butterfly," in *The Life of David Belasco*, New York: Moffat, Yard and Company, 1918.

Arthur Groos, "Madame Butterfly: The Story," *Cambridge Opera Journal*, 3: 125–158, 1991. © Cambridge University Press, reproduced with permission.

"Marking Time in Tokyo: The Tea House of the Hundred and One Steps," by Richard Harding Davis, reproduced from *Collier's*, pp 10–11. © 1904, reproduced with permission from JTE Multimedia, LLC.

The Belle of Japan, by F. M. Bostwick, *The Toronto Daily Mail* (December 24, 1892). [ ] encloses additions found in *The Tuapeka Times*, November 30, 1889.

David Belasco, *Madame Butterfly. Representative American Plays*, Ed. Arthur Hobson Quinn, New York: The Century Co., 1921.

Rydell, Robert, "The Pan-American Exposition, Buffalo," *All the World's a Fair: Visions of Empire at American International Expositions, 1876–1916*, Chicago, IL: University of Chicago Press, pp 126–153. © University of Chicago Press, 1984. Reproduced with permission.

Thomas Fleming, *Around the "Pan" with Uncle Hank: His Trip Through the Pan-American Exposition*, New York: The Nut Shell Publishing Company, 1901.

Pictures of the Pan-American Exposition from Thomas Leary and Elizabeth Sholes, in *Buffalo's Pan-American Exposition*, Charleston, SC: Arcadia, 1998. Courtesy of the Buffalo History Museum.

Pan-Am Expo, "The Midway," in *Official Catalogue and Guidebook to the Pan-American Exposition*, Buffalo, NY: Charles Ahrhart, 1901.

Richard Barry, in *Snapshots on the Midway of the Pan-Am Expo*, Robert Allan Reid: Buffalo, NY: 1901.

"Civilization and Discontent in William Vaughn Moody's *The Great Divide*." Reproduced by permission of the author Alex Roe, Artistic Director, Metropolitan Playhouse.

William Vaughn Moody, "An Ode in Time of Hesitation" and "On a Soldier Fallen in the Philippines," in *Selected Poems of William Vaughn Moody*, Ed. Robert Morss Lovett, New York: Houghton Mifflin Company, 1931.

William Vaughn Moody, *The Great Divide*, New York: The Macmillan Company, 1911.

John W. Frick, *Uncle Tom's Cabin on the American Stage and Screen*, New York: Palgrave Macmillan, 2012. Reproduced with permission of Palgrave Macmillan.

Robin Bernstein, "'Never Born': Angelina Weld Grimké's *Rachel* as Ironic Response to Topsy," *The Journal of American Drama and Theatre*, 19 (2): 61–75.

Trees, by Angelina Weld Grimké, in *The Selected Works of Angelina Weld Grimké*. Oxford, U.K.: Oxford University Press, 1991. Republished with permission of Oxford University Press; permission conveyed through Copyright Clearance Center, Inc.

Lawrence E. Mintz, "Humor and Ethnic Stereotypes in Vaudeville and Burlesque," *MELUS*, 21 (4): 19–28, 1996. © Oxford University Press, reproduced with permission.

Madison Grant, "The Competition of Races," in *The Passing of the Great Race*, New York: Charles Scribner's Sons, 1921.

Ed Lowry, from *Vaudeville Humor: The Collected Jokes, Routines, and Skits of Ed Lowry*, Ed. Paul M. Levitt, Carbondale, IL: Southern Illinois University Press, 2002. © 2002 by Paul Michael Levitt, reprinted by permission of the publisher.

Nicolás Kanellos, "Brief History of Hispanic Theater in the United States," in *Handbook of Hispanic Cultures in the United States: Literature and Art*, Volume 1, Eds. Nicolás Kanellos, Francisco A. Lomelí, and Claudio Esteva Fabregat, Houston, TX: Arte Público Press and Instituto de Cooperación lberoamericana . Copyright © 1993 by Arte Público Press and Instituto de Cooperación lberoamericana.

Nicolás Kanellos, Introduction to *I'm Going to Mexico*, in *Herencia: The Anthology of Hispanic Literature of the United States*, Ed. Nicolás Kanellos, Oxford, U.K., and New York: Oxford University Press, 2002. © Oxford University Press, U.S.A., reprinted by permission of the publisher.

"The Immigrants (Los Enganchadados—'The Hooked Ones')," in Manuel Gamio, *Mexican Immigration to the United States*, Chicago, IL: University of Chicago Press, 1930. © University of Chicago Press, 1984. Reproduced with permission.

I'm Going to Mexico, from *Herencia: The Anthology of Hispanic Literature of the United States*, Ed. Nicolás Kanellos, Oxford, U.K., and New York: Oxford University Press, 2002. © Oxford University Press, U.S.A., reprinted by permission of the publisher.

Richard Green, "Prologue" and excerpts from *Te Ata: Chickasaw Storyteller*, Norman, OK: University of Oklahoma Press, 2002. © University of Oklahoma Press. Used with permission.

Vivian Shirley, "Vivian Shirley Learns Culture of Indians," *Philadelphia Evening Public Ledger*, January 19, 1932.

Ben-Zvi, Linda. "'Murder, She Wrote': The Genesis of Susan Glaspell's *Trifles*," *Theatre Journal*, 44 (2): 141–162, 1992. © 1992 by Linda Ben-Zvi. Reprinted with permission of Johns Hopkins University Press.

Articles from the *Des Moines Daily News* reproduced by permission of the estate of Susan Glaspell.

Excerpt from "After Death," by Sarah Townsend, in *Stages of Conflict: A Critical Anthology of Latin American Theatre and Performance*, Eds. Diana Taylor and Sarah J. Townsend, Ann Arbor, MI: University of Michigan Press, 2008. © University of Michigan Press. Used with permission.

Luisa Capetillo, "Preface," in *A Nation of Women: An Early Feminist Speaks Out*, Ed. Felix V. Matos Rodriguez, Houston, TX: Arté Publico Press, 2004. © 2004 Arté Publico Press. Used with permission.

How Poor Women Prostitute Themselves, in *Herencia: The Anthology of Hispanic Literature of the United States*, Ed. Nicolás Kanellos, Oxford, U.K., and New York: Oxford University Press, 2002. © Oxford University Press, U.S.A., reprinted by permission of the publisher.

Marybeth Hamilton, "Mae West Live: *SEX, The Drag*, and 1920s Broadway," *TDR/The Drama Review*, 36 (4, T136–Winter, 1992): 82–100. © 1992 New York University and the Massachusetts Institute of Technology.

Items of New York criminal law reprinted from *Criminal Law and Practice of the State of New York* with permission. Copyright © 1920 Matthew Bender & Company, Inc., a LexisNexis company. All rights reserved.

Legal Papers on *Sex* trial from *Three Plays by Mae West*, Ed. Lillian Schlissel, New York: Routledge, 1997.

Mae West, *Sex*, in *Three Plays by Mae West*, New York: Routledge, 1997. Reproduced with permission of The Mae Company, LLC. All rights reserved.

Ann Jones, excerpt from *Women Who Kill*, New York: The Feminist Press at the City University of New York, 2009, pp. 249–266. Copyright © 2009 by Ann Jones. Reprinted with the permission of The Permissions Company, Inc., on behalf of The Feminist Press at the City University of New York, *www.feministpress.org*

Treadwell's Neologism: Machinal, by Ginger Strand, republished with permission of Johns Hopkins University Press, from *Theatre Journal*, 44 (2, May), 1992; permission conveyed through Copyright Clearance Center, Inc.

"Modern Girls Face Certain Disaster: 'Flappers' Called Saddest Type of All," *El Paso Herald* (El Paso, TX), May 20, 1920.

Articles from the *New York Times* used by permission and protected by the copyright laws of the United States. All rights reserved. The printing, copying, redistribution or retransmission of this content without express written permission is prohibited.

Machinal, by Sophie Treadwell, reproduced by kind permission of The Roman Catholic Church of the Diocese of Tucson.

"Hughes' Move to the Left: *Scottsboro, Limited*," by Susan Duffy, in *Political Plays of Langston Hughes*, Carbondale, IL: Southern Illinois University Press, 2000. Republished with permission of Southern Illinois University Press, permission conveyed through Copyright Clearance Center, Inc.

Hallie Flanagan, "A Theatre is Born," *Theatre Arts Monthly*, 15, 1931. Reproduced by kind permission of the Hallie Flanagan Estate.

"Justice" and "The Town of Scottsboro," in Langston Hughes, *The Collected Poems of Langston Hughes*, Ed. Arnold Rampersad with Assoc. Ed. David Roessel, New York: Alfred A. Knopf. Copyright © 1994 by the Estate of Langston Hughes. Used by permission of Alfred A. Knopf, an imprint of the Knopf Doubleday Publishing Group, a division of Penguin Random House LLC. All rights reserved.

Langston Hughes, *Scottsboro, Limited. Scottsboro Limited: Four Poems and a Play in Verse*. New York: Golden Stair Press, 1932. Reproduced by permission of David Higham Associates.

Excerpt(s) from Harold Clurman, *The Fervent Years*, New York: Alfred A. Knopf. Copyright © 1957 by Harold Clurman. Used by permission of Alfred A. Knopf, an imprint of the Knopf Doubleday Publishing Group, a division of Penguin Random House LLC. All rights reserved.

Stanley Burnshaw, "Review of *Waiting for Lefty*," *New Masses*, January 1, 1935. Reproduced by permission of the estate of Stanley Burnshaw.

Waiting for Lefty copyright © 1935 by Clifford Odets. Used by permission of Grove/Atlantic Inc. Any third party use of this material, outside of this publication, is prohibited.

Excerpt from Lowell Swortzell's *Six Plays for Young People from the Federal Theatre Project: An Introductory Analysis and Six Representative Plays*, New York: Greenwood Press, 1986. Reproduced with permission of ABC-CLIO/Greenwood; permission conveyed through Copyright Clearance Center, Inc.

Lou Lantz quotation from *Free, Adult, Uncensored: The Living History of the Federal Theatre Project*, Washington, DC: New Republic Books, 1978.

Hallie Flanagan, "The Yeast which Makes the Bread Rise: Hallie Flanagan on Drama as Politics," from Hallie Flanagan, "Theater as Social Action," in Piere de Roban, Ed., "First Federal Summer Theater: A Report," *Federal Theatre*, June–July: 36, 1937.

"Statement of Mrs. Hallie Flanagan, National Director, Federal Theater Project," from *Investigation into Un-American Propaganda Activities in the United States—Hearings Before a Special Committee on Un-American Activities, House of Representatives, Seventy Fifth Congress, Third Session on H.Res. 282*, Volume 4, November 19, 22, 23, 28; December 1, 5, 6, 7, 8, 9, and 14, 1938, at Washington, DC (United States Government Printing Office, Washington, DC: 1939).

Oscar Saul and Lou Lantz, *Revolt of the Beavers. Six Plays for Young People from the Federal Theatre Project: An Introductory Analysis and Six Representative Plays*, Ed. Lowell Swortzell, New York: Greenwood Press, 1986. Courtesy of the Federal Theatre Project collection, Collection #C0002, Special Collections and Archives, George Mason University Libraries.

Hallie Flanagan, "States United: One-Third of a Nation," from *Arena: The History of the Federal Theatre*, New York: Duell, Sloan and Pearce, 1940. Reproduced by kind permission of the Hallie Flanagan Estate.

Susan Quinn, "*It Can't Happen Here*," from *Furious Improvisation*, New York: Walker and Company, 2008. © Susan Quinn 2008, *Furious Improvisation*, Walker and Company, an imprint of Bloomsbury Publishing Inc.

"Father Coughlin Praised by a Fascist Newspaper," *New York Times*, January 17, 1939. © The Associated Press. Used with Permission, all rights reserved.

Sinclair Lewis and John C. Moffitt, *It Can't Happen Here: A New Version by Sinclair Lewis, of the Play by John C. Moffitt and Sinclair Lewis from the Lewis Novel*, New York: Dramatists Play Service, 1938. (Note: originally produced by FTP in 1936, but rewritten in 1938—the only extant script.)

Excerpt from Albert Wertheim, *Staging the War: American Drama and World War II*, Bloomington, IN: Indiana University Press, 2004. Used by permission, via Copyright.com

The Selected Letters of Thornton Wilder, Eds. Robin G. Wilder and Jackson R. Bryer, New York: Harper. Letter copyright © 2008 by The Wilder Family LLC. Compilation of the letters and added text copyright © 2008 by Robin G. Wilder and Jackson R. Bryer. Foreword 2008 by Scott Donaldson; reprinted by arrangement with The Wilder Family LLC and The Barbara Hogenson Agency, Inc. All rights reserved.

Rex Stout and Thornton Wilder, "The Strength of a Democracy Under Siege." Interview originally broadcast on NBC Radio on October 30, 1941, on the "Speaking of Liberty" program. Transcribed by Drew Eisenhauer.

The Skin of Our Teeth, by Thornton Wilder, copyright © 1942 by The Wilder Family LLC. Reprinted by arrangement with The Wilder Family LLC and The Barbara Hogenson Agency, Inc. All rights reserved.

Richard Moody, "Hardscrabble Farm and *Watch on the Rhine*," in *Lillian Hellman: Playwright*, New York: Pegasus, 1972.

Franklin Roosevelt's Fireside Chat 14, "On the European War" (November 3, 1939); transcript of published text from http://millercenter.org/president/speeches/detail/3315

American First Committee member Charles Lindbergh's Des Moines Speech (September 11, 1941); from www.pbs.org/wgbh/amex/lindbergh/filmmore/reference/primary/desmoinesspeech.html

Ezra Pound, "Canto 73—Cavalcanti—Republican Dispatches" from *The Cantos of Ezra Pound*, New York: New Directions. Copyright © 1948 by Ezra Pound. Reprinted by permission of New Directions Publishing Corp.

John Clum, "From Summer and Smoke to Eccentricities of a Nightingale: The Evolution of the Queer Alma," *Modern Drama*, 39 (1, Spring 1996. © Graduate Centre for Study of Drama Spring 1996. Reprinted with permission from University of Toronto Press.

On the Dr. Alfred Kinsey Report: James Miller, "Sexual Behavior of the American Male." '47 *Magazine of the Year*, 1 (10).

"Maximum Punishments for Certain Sex Crimes in the U.S.A.," taken from James R. Miller, "Sex Laws of the 48 States," *'48 Magazine of the Year*, 2 (2, 1948).

Summer and Smoke, by Tennessee Williams, from *The Theatre Of Tennessee Williams*, Vol. II, New York: New Directions. Copyright © 1971 by The University of the South. Reprinted by permission of New Directions Publishing Corp.

"O'Neill's Critique of Psychological Discourse and *Iceman*," in Joel Pfister, *Staging Depth: Eugene O'Neill and the Politics of Psychological Discourse*, Chapel Hill, NC: University of North Carolina Press. Copyright © 1995 by the University of North Carolina Press. Used by permission of the publisher. www.uncpress.unc.edu

Letters from Eugene O'Neill taken from the Eugene O'Neill Papers, Yale Collection of American Literature, Beinecke Rare Book and Manuscript Library. Yale University is the owner of the literary property rights in this material. Permission courtesy of the Yale Collection of American Literature.

Schneider, Isidor. "The Iceman Cometh," *New Masses*, 29, 1946.

"Gain in Mental Ills Seen," *New York Times*, August 16, 1946. © The Associated Press. Used with permission; all rights reserved.

Eugene O'Neill , *The Iceman Cometh*, reprinted by permission of ICM Partners. Copyright © 1946 by Eugene O'Neill.

"On Social Plays," in Arthur Miller, *The Theater Essays of Arthur Miller*, Ed. Robert A. Martin, New York: Viking Books. Copyright © 1955, 1978, by Arthur Miller. Used by permission of Viking Books, an imprint of Penguin Publishing Group, a division of Penguin Random House LLC.

Lois Tyson, "The Commodity Comes Home to Roost: Repression, Regression, and Death in Arthur Miller's *Death of a Salesman*," in *Psychological Politics of the American Dream*, Columbus, OH: Ohio State University Press, 1994. Used with permission, all rights reserved.

Arthur Miller, *Death of a Salesman*, New York: Viking Books. Copyright © 1949, renewed © 1977 by Arthur Miller. Used by permission of Viking Books, an imprint of Penguin Publishing Group, a division of Penguin Random House LLC.

Introduction

I RECALL THE EXCITEMENT, as a higher-education student, of entering the university bookstore and looking up required course books. The most exciting texts were those dense anthologies for the humanities and literature classes that were packed, on the thinnest of paper, with centuries of prose, plays, and poetry. There was something magical about having access to such relics. It was a way to not just read of the past, but to return to it, and immerse in, listen to and better understand it. It was also a way to better understand my present, as I connected, despite the intervening years, to the thoughts and feelings of those who were involved in similar situations and conflicts. The world that I was growing in took shape and gained clarity through much of what I read in those immense tomes. The scholarship that preceded the selections in these anthologies was also rich and insightful. It helped me interpret the bygone voices, their sometimes-obscure messages, and informed me of where they came from. As my studies focused on theatre, I became increasingly curious about, not just the plays of the past, but also the cultures that helped to produce them. The relationship and dialogue between these two expressions of humanity always proved critical to better understanding the plays and performances, as well as their integral connection to their specific time and place. This interest in the theatrical works and the sociopolitical contexts from which they derived has carried over into the work before you.

The overall intent of this book is to recapture and share the excitement I had as a student by anthologizing a selection of significant plays and dramatic material, from between 1898 and 1949, that illustrated, discussed, and engaged in some of the major cultural issues and events in the United States, as it emerged, in the twentieth century, as a social, political, economic, and cultural power.

Another means to help generate this excitement is to let the selected plays and performances from various theatre and social communities continue their dialogue with their initial cultures—in particular, with select artifacts that resonate from the same time and place. In doing so, this anthology hopes to demonstrate theatre's integral relationship with society—how theatre has been used as a means to support and challenge prevailing systems of thought and action, and how it is not just a reflection of society, but an active part and participant. Along with the various primary sources, there are secondary sources from leading theatre scholars and artists, studying the aesthetic values of the dramatic work, their social importance, and their connection to the primary sources. This collection uses older as well as new criticism and reaches beyond traditional academic circles for intriguing and fresh insights.

The concept for this project began after reading an article discussing William Vaughn Moody's *The Great Divide*. In the article, the play was described as, "a metaphor of conquest that advocates American imperialism" (Bryan 11). That interpretation is quite valid when one reads the text alone, but it loses its strength when the play is contextualized with primary sources from the same historical context, such as anti-imperialist propaganda and other works by the playwright. When *The Great Divide* was first produced, in 1906, Moody was already a staunch opponent of imperialism and a significant member of the Anti-Imperialists League—whose notable members included former President Grover Cleveland, Mark Twain, Andrew Carnegie, and Samuel Gompers. Moody wrote several poems during the Spanish–American War that lashed out against U.S. imperial actions in Cuba, Puerto Rico, and the Philippines. "On a Soldier Fallen in the Philippines," for instance, is about a soldier who had died aiding the "faithless" nation that conquered and colonized the Philippines: "Let him never dream that his bullet's scream went wide of its island mark, / Home to the heart of his darling land where she stumbled and sinned in the dark" (30–31). "Ode in a Time of Hesitation" also harshly criticizes U.S. imperialism and the "ignoble battle" against the Philippine independence movement led by Emilio Aguinaldo. The U.S. risked severe consequences, Moody argued, if the "island men" were not released from the tyranny of U.S. imperialism: "Take heed! / Blindness we may forgive, but baseness we will smite" (14–26). By structuring *The Great Divide* with Moody's other works, it becomes increasingly difficult to see *The Great Divide* as a play that supports U.S. imperialism. It allows a different reading of the play to emerge, one that, quite possibly, is closer to Moody's intent and to how the play was received at its premier production—as a metaphor of unjust conquest that denounces U.S. imperialism. *The Routledge Anthology of U.S. Drama* attempts to get a deeper reading of all of the selected plays and performative events by interpreting them, not just with scholarship, but also with other artifacts from the cultural context of when they first premiered.

A historic moment is ultimately irrecoverable in its entirety. The actual thoughts and feelings of a theatre audience, for instance, can never be fully retrieved. They, however, can be partly understood through the literary texts that have come down to us in forms such as theatre reviews, letters to the editor, diaries, memoirs, biographies, and scholarly criticism. The meaning of plays and performative events, as well, can be more closely approached when they are juxtaposed with artifacts from the same culture. By linking plays and performances to other traces of their past—expressions of the same historical period—new and preexisting meanings can be discovered. The web of signification spreads far and wide, and many cultural artifacts share, to certain degrees, the concerns of their society. This strategy of new historicism, largely developed by Stephen Greenblatt, allows the reader to engage with theatre beyond the hegemony of theatre scholarship that often determines a play's meaning and allows one to witness how a play substantially and excitingly participates in its sociopolitical context.

Consider, for instance, how *Machinal* intersected with the 1920s sexual revolution, the international backlash against flappers, seen as corrosive to youth, the "Blue Laws" for flappers, and the "show trial" of murderess Ruth Snyder. These events are all cultural texts, written, performed, watched, and interpreted. They are all real-life performances that registered the public concerns of a particular space and time. These performances are evidentiary texts that signify cultural anxieties—some of the same anxieties present in the provided plays. It is no coincidence that these cultural performances, plays, and theatre productions exist in the same space and time. They are all the results of a build-up of pressures, fears, dominant issues, and ideas operant in a society. Juxtaposing these kinds of cultural performance and text with plays and theatrical productions, therefore, can help readers to better understand the dramatic works. It allows one to better hear how Buffalo Bill's Wild West, *Madame Butterfly*, and the Pan-American Exposition were in dialogue with the colonial rhetoric and propaganda of the period. It allows one to understand how the *Uncle Tom* shows, the play *Rachel*, the vaudeville and *revista* skits, and Te Ata folklore performances endorsed or countered ideas, images, and practices on religion, race and ethnicity. It allows one to better imagine how plays such as *Scottsboro, Limited*, *Waiting for Lefty*, *The Revolt of the Beavers*, and *One Third of the Nation* participated in the national debates on how best to navigate the country in a time of economic unrest. This methodology differs from scholarship that restricts plays to a formalist literary analysis, with no attention to cultural context, which greatly limits the social, political, and symbolic power of the plays.

The approach to this anthology is also much indebted to the strategies of semiotics and structuralism.[1] Semiotics—the science of signs—studies the nature, properties, and kinds of signs and sign systems. According to linguist Ferdinand de Saussure, semiotics is "a science that studies the life of signs within a society" (Innis 34). Saussure, whose area of concentration was the linguistic sign, described the sign as having two parts—the linguistic signifier (spoken or written word) and the signified. The signifier is the material aspect of a sign (the word "tree"), and the signified is the mental concept ("treeness"). The connection between the signifier and the signified is completely arbitrary; therefore, the words we assign to meanings are completely arbitrary. For Saussure, there were no fixed, intrinsic meanings or truths in words alone. The meanings of words or any given utterance—defined as *la parole*—are based on their relationships to other words that exist in a system of a language—called *la langue*—which is always going through historical transformations. Language is not a reflection of the world, but a separate system of differences, based on unfixed conventional relationships.

In order to better interpret the plays in this anthology and understand how they resonated with the people and societies from which they came, it is first necessary to see the plays as part of a Saussurian sign. The conceptual worlds of the theatre audience and script readers are the signified, and the plays are the signifiers (the spoken or written play texts). The dialogue between these two components helps to create signification. The meanings of the plays (a literary *parole*) are also partly based on their relationships to the other words that exist in a system of language (*la langue*), such as the literary genre of social dramas. The plays, of course, are not only linguistic signs; they can be textually read—as structuralists Roland Barthes and Claude Lévi-Strauss read them—as cultural signs.

Structuralism is "a way of thinking about the world which is predominantly concerned with the perception and description of structures" (Hawkes 17). Barthes and Lévi-Strauss made the important advancement of applying Saussure's concept of the linguistic sign to culture. Both theorists saw all the components of culture as a language—textual signs that could be read. They felt that Saussure's theory of the linguistic sign could be transferred to all signifying systems, and that culture could make statements and be read or decoded just like a language.[2] By analyzing signs, one can gain a better understanding, not only of the makeup of those signs, but of the interpreter and his/her culture (Barthes 31). Like Saussure, Barthes and Lévi-Strauss asserted that there are no fixed, intrinsic truths in a particular item of culture. The significance of an item is based on its place and relationship to the other items in a structure. Any appearance of culture is a part of a larger cultural system; therefore, if a piece of culture is "structuralized," new layers of meaning can be found. In the same manner, each play and performance in *The Routledge Anthology of U.S. Drama* is structured with artifacts from the historical context of its premiere production to reveal meaning.

Moreover, this anthology is much indebted to Clifford Geertz, the eminent cultural anthropologist best known for his influential social and cultural theory of interpretive (or symbolic) anthropology applied to Indonesian and Moroccan cultures.[3] He practiced anthropology at a time when it was being questioned about its colonial past and its ability to truly provide objective knowledge. Geertz wrote, "proposals for new directions in anthropological theory and method appeared almost by the month, one more clamorous than the next [. . .] I contributed to the merriment with interpretive anthropology" (*Life Among the Anthros* 194). To arrive at this methodology, Geertz applied his education in English, philosophy, and the social sciences, emphasizing deep interdisciplinary readings to help break away from the anthropological emphasis on scientific inquiry and to introduce a more metaphorical and literary style. He had a semiotic concept of, and interpretive approach to, culture, seeing all human behavior as symbolic action: "The concept of culture I espouse [. . .] is essentially a semiotic one. Believing [. . .] that man is an animal suspended in webs of significance he himself has spun, I take culture to be those webs, and the analysis of it to be therefore not an experimental science in search of law but an interpretive one in search of meaning." To Geertz, the point of using a semiotic approach to culture was "to aid us in gaining access to the conceptual world in which our subjects live so that we can, in some extended sense of the term, converse with them" (*Interpretation of Cultures* 5, 24).

Geertz's most famous example of this methodology was his study of the Balinese cockfight, discussed in his essay "Deep Play: Notes on the Balinese Cockfight," included in *The Interpretation of Cultures*. He analyzed the kinship and social ties of the Balinese culture that were constructed, emphasized, and maintained in the cockfight, a form of ritual "deep play" where culture was being read like "an assemblage of texts." He described the cockfight neither as an isolated cultural event, nor as just an imitation, depiction, or expression of culture, but as a carefully prepared example of it: "In focusing activity down to a burning-glass dot, the cockfight is merely being Balinese in the same way in which everything from the monadic encounters of everyday life, through the clanging pointillism of gamelan music, to the visiting-day-of-the-gods temple celebrations are" (443–444). The most fascinating part of Geertz's study of the cockfight is how he was able to alter the common connection between a signifier and its referent—to "cross conceptual wires"—and, by doing so, reveal an already existing layer of meaning: "Any expressive form works (when it works) by disarranging semantic contexts in such a way that properties conventionally ascribed to certain things are unconventionally ascribed to others, which are then seen actually to possess them" (447).

Theatrical productions and performative events are cultural performances, like the Balinese cockfight, that are being actively read by members of the culture; the plays and performances are stories that the members of the culture are telling themselves about themselves. As this conceptual world is immaterial, one must take a different approach to understand how these dramatic works were read. One must examine the culture, not in search of facts or uncontestable conclusions, but in search of interpretations of meaning. One method of searching—by using new historicism, semiotics, and cultural anthropology—is to "unhook" the plays from their common referent and give them the ability to take on new meanings or reveal meanings that may have been already present.[4]

These meanings are not indisputable. As Geertz says, "Cultural analysis is intrinsically incomplete. And, worse than that, the more deeply it goes the less complete it is [. . . To] get somewhere with the matter at hand is to intensify the suspicion, both your own and that of others, that you are not quite getting it right." Therefore, by committing oneself to a semiotic understanding of culture and by using an interpretive approach to study it, one "commit[s] oneself to a view of ethnographic assertion as [. . .] essentially contestable." For Geertz, the essential task of the interpretive anthropologist was "not to answer our deepest questions, but to make available to us answers that others [. . .] have given, and thus to include them in the consultable record of what man has said." There are no conclusions to assert, only interpretations of meaning to discuss. In this way, interpreters are not just speaking for the plays—giving their own readings by looking only within themselves or by assuming that the meanings inherently lie within the texts—but they are listening to and recording what the culture may have already said about them (*Interpretation of Cultures* 29–30).

The Routledge Anthology of U.S. Drama has, as well, an interdisciplinary and interpretive approach that attempts to provide a "new direction" for theatre anthologies and denies any definitive or objective understanding of U.S. theatre. The plays and performative events in this collection, like the Balinese cockfight, are examples of culture—in this case U.S. culture—and not just imitations, depictions, or expressions of it. They are artifacts of U.S. culture, just like a boxing match, a Native American ceremony, or a Democratic national convention. Clifford Geertz also believed that a cultural event could not have meaning in isolation, but only in relation to the other parts of its culture. For this reason, this anthology contextualizes the plays and performances with other extant primary data from their native cultures, as well as with secondary sources from later periods. Doing so will provide deeper reads of these theatrical events. For instance, by "crossing conceptual wires" and connecting *The Great Divide* to Moody's poems, or connecting Tennessee Williams' *Summer and Smoke* to coexisting laws and literature on sexual behavior, one is able to arrive at new meanings or meanings that were already present. These interpretations, again, are disputable, as they are among several possible readings, and, of course, the provided texts and images have been subjectively selected and structured with editorial biases. This anthology, therefore, asks you to read with an open and unassuming mind, to let the plays speak differently to you, as they are contextualized with artifacts and commentaries that may detour from standardized interpretations. Similar to Geertz's work, this anthology attempts to break away from a strict scientific approach in order to introduce a more metaphorical and literary style.

The Routledge Anthology of U.S. Drama also uses specific thematic perspectives to help select, structure, and interpret the reading selections: colonialism, religion, race and ethnicity, gender and sexuality, economic systems, systems of government, queer theory, and psychoanalytic theory. These viewpoints were selected to provide a more multicultural and interdisciplinary approach, and to navigate the material to some of the period's major cultural issues and events where theatre was a strong participant (for instance, the Spanish–American War, the assassination of President McKinley, immigration waves, the devastation of Native American cultures, the Civil Rights Movement, the Feminist Movement, the Communist Revolution, the rise of fascism, and the Second World War).

The task of this anthology is to employ various lenses and strategies throughout the book for a more complex and developed understanding of the connectivity between U.S. theatre, culture, and politics.

It is important to note that the thematic lenses, primary sources, and scholarship are designed to add to the discussions on the plays, and not to substitute or limit other approaches and insights. Readers should be encouraged to look at the plays through multiple perspectives, and this anthology attempts to foster this method of analysis. It is well understood that there are several ways to understand O'Neill's *The Iceman Cometh* or Miller's *Death of a Salesman*, beyond a psychoanalytic lens. (This lens, though, is quite practical, considering the postwar rise in mental illness and psychoanalysis.) Simply put, this anthology provides one more tool among many tools for readers to "work" on a play. Again, by no means should this anthology be understood as the definitive read on these plays or even the definitive collection of plays from this period. Consider this anthology, instead, as a contribution to the many excellent collections that have helped to keep the discussion alive on these important works, their societies, and U.S. theatre.

There are a number of outstanding anthologies on U.S. theatre that cover large periods, such as Stephen Watt and Gary Richardson's comprehensive compilation, *American Drama: Colonial to Contemporary*, or that include a small selection of plays based on particular themes, such as Emily Mann and David Roessel's excellent collection, *Political Stages: Plays That Shaped a Century*. This anthology will contribute to these important books by concentrating solely on the first half of the twentieth century, and by encompassing multiple heterogeneous voices and viewpoints of notable theatre artists and scholars as it moves chronologically through U.S. history. These divergent voices, as a whole, will comprise an important understanding of U.S. theatre and performance and will help to prevent a reductive, homogeneous, and hegemonic perspective of historical and theatrical events. This book aims to demonstrate the complex, heterogeneous nature of U.S. theatre—a theatre that defies any simplistic read—and to be of significant value to readers who rightly demand more diverse multicultural and sociopolitical material.

The time period of this anthology (1898–1949) may appear odd to some readers who are more accustomed, as I was as a student, to collections that cover greater spans of time. Simply put, the greater the period covered, often the less work represented. This collection is intended to provide more focus and depth on the roughly five decades of an exciting period in U.S. and theatre history. The years between 1898 and 1949 formed a significant era in the United States, as it grew into a nation of importance (some would argue an empire), with its politics, economy, military, and arts. It is a period when the U.S. stood more significantly on the world stage and better distinguished itself from its English heritage and, importantly for this book, its British theatrical heritage. It is in this period that U.S. plays started to reflect more of its cultural concerns, even if they were expressed by using or adapting European and Asian styles. Moreover, in this period, theatre still retained its leading role in society as an insightful and engaging communal medium, before television started to dominate the arts and create a more disengaged and private culture. The plays chosen for this anthology are those that engaged in this fertile social, political, and artistic landscape and were in clear dialogue with the nation in a period of unprecedented change.

In particular, the anthology begins with the U.S. involvement in the Cuban War for Independence, which led to the U.S. military victory in the Spanish–American War. This victory brought great change to the nation, as it became a military, economic, political, and cultural power—a power that was articulated in the artifacts and performances of the time. New challenges also emerged, as the United States dealt with tumultuous sociopolitical events brought about by imperialism, industrialism, communism, the massive waves of immigration, and political movements such as U.S. communism, feminism, and civil rights. The theatre of this period excitingly engaged in these momentous issues that helped to shape and define the United States. Great change also occurred in the nation and its theatres shortly after the Allied victory in the Second World War, as the country moved into the Cold War and the postwar U.S. avant-garde movement. This anthology uses these events—the time of the Spanish–American War and the years shortly after the Second World War—as bookends to structure the period of study in this collection and to outline a significant period when the nation, together with its theatre, developed into a political and cultural force.

Within this structure of time, the plays and performative events presented in *The Routledge Anthology of U.S. Drama* are arranged, in addition to thematic perspectives, in chronological order, simply because time matters. These theatrical works are participating in, speaking to, and expressing their unique moment, and to dislocate them from their sequence in time in any manner would greatly impact their signification and power. The same can be said for place. Attention has been given to the specific geographic and sociopolitical context of the selected plays and performances. To read these artistic works without considering their primary sociopolitical contexts can cause readers to misread the dramas and theatrical events, and to have a more reductive interpretation. For instance, to read Mae West's *Sex* without giving attention to New York City's cultural war against the sexual revolution would be to miss the societal tensions that West absorbed and dramatized in her work.

Much can be gained from adhering to a formalist approach or strictly textual analysis. This is an important first step when reading plays, in order to help avoid some of the fallacies rampant in play analysis, such as genetic or biographical fallacies. However, to end with a formalist approach and entirely exclude social and historical forces or the author's biographical information from one's analysis greatly limits the signification and resonance of theatre, and, in truth, takes a good deal of fun away from reading and studying plays and performances. Understanding theatre is a fantastic way to understand history—the events and people, great and small, who helped to comprise it. (This anthology has a macro and micro view of historical events, concentrating on both the global wars and leaders, such as the Spanish–American War and Theodore Roosevelt, and the more regional cultural wars and participants, such as the feminist movement and Luisa Capetillo, that helped to define history.) Moreover, the formalist approach forgets that theatre is a collaborative event made up of more than text. It is a rich and vital collaboration between numerous elements that include—along with the actors, designers, and production team—the sociopolitical forces that helped create, give meaning to, and inform the author, the audience, the dramas, and dramatic productions.

The specific plays in the anthology have been selected to demonstrate this collaboration—how the performing arts have illuminated and engaged in U.S. society. Each of the plays exemplifies different aspects of the nation's cultural concerns and anxieties as it went through significant political and cultural changes and redefined itself during the early twentieth century. For example, *It Can't Happen Here*, *The Skin of our Teeth*, and *Watch on the Rhine* all exhibit national concerns about the rise of fascism and U.S. intervention in what was called the "European War." The selected plays in this collection both support and challenge the existing canon of U.S. dramatic literature. There are, of course, countless other plays that are worthy of study. The reasoning behind the choice of plays is that these texts stand out as essential works that discuss and exemplify the various thematic perspectives that are being applied, along with some of the significant sociopolitical events of the time. The plays chosen for this project have also been selected for their artistic contributions, as well as for their popularity among readers over the years. The plays' aesthetic values and innovations, along with their social importance, are discussed in several of the accompanying articles in order to provide a more complex perspective.

In addition to traditional plays, there are also readings included on key performances and performative events—such as the Buffalo Bill's Wild West shows; the Pan-American Exposition; vaudeville and *revista* skits; Te Ata folklore performances; the trials of Margaret Hossack, Luisa Capetillo, Mae West, Ruth Snyder, and the Scottsboro Boys; Hallie Flanagan's hearing before the House Committee on Un-American Activities (HUAC); Father Coughlin and Franklin Roosevelt's radio addresses; and Charles Lindbergh's Des Moines speech—that demonstrate the important issues of the time, which also intersected with the plays. This anthology focuses on famous and momentous theatrical productions, political trials, hearings, and speeches in performance spaces beyond the traditional stage that demonstrated and encapsulated the cultural concerns and tensions of the periods.

It is also necessary to clarify the importance of having the selected plays together in one anthology, despite their existence online or in other texts. It is how these plays are chronologically ordered, thematically presented, and structured with other plays, primary sources, and scholarship that gives new meaning and value to these works and the anthology as a whole. For instance, though Susan Glaspell's *Trifles* appears in other anthologies, there is no known anthology that includes her reportage on the murder trial that inspired the play. Even if students have previously read *Trifles*, the play takes on new meaning and social value when it is related to the performative event of the Hossack show trial. The scholarship on *Trifles* helps to clarify the relationship between the primary material and the play. This book prefers to let the existing scholarship, extant primary material, and plays speak for themselves, instead of letting them be funneled into a condensed blurb through an editor's perspective, as is generally the case in more conventional anthologies. The organization of this compilation in the manner described allows readers to have a greater understanding and appreciation of primary and secondary research, as well as of U.S. history, U.S. theatre history, and the complex relationship between the two.

Some of the selected plays are commonly included in other anthologies, such as Clifford Odets' *Waiting for Lefty* or Arthur Miller's *Death of a Salesman*. It is the intention of this anthology to provide plays that are a part of the existing canon, as well as plays that challenge the canon. This important mix helps to maintain the well-deserved classics and, at the same time, introduce new material. Many of these renowned plays are still commonly taught in the classroom, and so this anthology intends to continue to provide materials that are still in demand, but in new and exciting ways, with the contextual material. *Death of a Salesman*, for instance, recently experienced an excellent revival on Broadway and, as a result, has enjoyed a resurgence in theatres and classrooms throughout the nation.

Some critics may argue that other plays would have been better selected. Many great plays were reviewed, though several were not included because the anthology follows a strict chronological and thematic structure. As can be seen in the table of contents, this anthology keeps the plays in chronological order and groups them under a specific thematic lens. Use of this model excludes several potential plays. For instance, Zora Neale Hurston's *Color Struck* would be a wonderful and important play to anthologize, but this work premiered in 1925, a period when this book chooses to discuss works that deal with the theme "gender and sexuality." Other possible additions did not work owing to the important relationship between the play and its thematic perspective, primary material, and scholarship. For instance, if *Trifles* were substituted by another of Glaspell's plays, such as *The Inheritors*, then it would not resonate as well with the theme "gender and sexuality," the primary material on the murder trial, and the scholarship. This anthology is interested in how all these materials resonate together, with a specific thematic lens that concentrates on a historic moment. It is this strict attention to play selection, chronology, and thematic perspectives that makes this anthology unique and provides an important contribution to U.S. theatre studies—it goes beyond the "greatest hits" approach of choosing plays from a randomly selected time period, with little concern for history or theory.

The Routledge Anthology of U.S. Drama was designed to be of value to theatre scholars, educators, students, practitioners, and general admirers of theatre and drama, from various cultures in the United States and abroad. In particular, this collection will appeal to teachers and students who cohesively study dramatic literature, theatre history, and theory in undergraduate and graduate dramatic literature courses, dramaturgy courses, theatre history courses, and dramatic theory courses. This book's multi-perspective approach of using various theoretical perspectives, historical approaches, sociopolitical contexts, primary and secondary sources, and dramatic material is most beneficial for today's classrooms, which increasingly demand a more interdisciplinary and multicultural curriculum that incorporates the viewpoints, histories, and cultures of various races, ethnicities, economic classes, genders, sexualities, and political parties. This book, though, will be of value to all readers interested in learning about how theatre has been used as a means to understand and participate in society at the regional and national level and, in extension, how it can continue to be similarly used today—as a vital means to enrich cultures, strengthen communities, and support and challenge cultural systems of thought and action.

Numerous years have passed since my days as a student, and with them have come several transcontinental migrations. During these moves, many belongings were lost, sold, or given away, but the anthologies from my school years still rest on my bookshelves, waiting to be enjoyed anew. I hope you enjoy and are as excited about what you read as I was as a student, and as I was when researching and assembling the excellent works in this collection.

Notes

1. Culture, according to Erika Fischer-Lichte, is created by humans, as opposed to nature, which is created without human participation (129). Everything that has been created by humans is symbolically encoded, because humans construct a signified world where everything seen is a signifier that has a signified meaning—all human production, in short, is a production of signs. The production of signs is one of the main functions of a cultural system, in order to produce meaning and to help define itself. Semiotics, or cultural semiotics, can be understood as a science that studies the functional relationships of sign systems circulating in culture.

2. A signifying system, in this case, is defined as any structured network of signs that carries cultural meanings.
3. Anthropology is the holistic study of humanity. Cultural anthropology, a branch of anthropology, is the study of human cultures based on ethnologic, ethnographic, linguistic, social, and psychological data and methods of analysis. "In ethnography," writes Geertz, "the office of theory is to provide a vocabulary in which what symbolic action has to say about itself [. . .] can be expressed" (*Interpretation of Cultures* 27).
4. "Unhook" is a Geertz term that emphasizes how a signifier can be "unhooked" or detached from what it commonly signified and then be reattributed to form a different signified referent.

Works Consulted

Bryan, Mark Evans. "American Drama, 1900–1915." *A Companion to Twentieth-Century American Drama*. Ed. David Krasner, Malden, MA: Blackwell, 2005.

Barthes, Roland. *Image—Music—Text*. Trans. Stephen Heath. New York: Hill and Wang, 1977.

Fischer-Lichte, Erika. *The Semiotics of Theater*. Bloomington, IN: Indiana University Press, 1992.

Geertz, Clifford. *Life Among the Anthros and Other Essays*. Princeton, NJ: Princeton University Press, 2012.

———. *The Interpretation of Cultures*. New York: Basic Books, 1973.

Hawkes, Terence. *Structuralism and Semiotics*. Berkeley, CA: University of California Press, 1977.

Innis, Robert. Ed. *Semiotics: An Introductory Anthology*. Bloomington, IN: Indiana University Press, 1985.

Moody, William Vaughn. *Selected Poems of William Vaughn Moody*. Ed. Robert Morss Lovett. New York: Houghton Mifflin Company, 1931.

Part 1
Colonialism

COLONIAL AND NATIVE RULE IN PERFORMANCE

1. *Buffalo Bill's Wild West Show and Congress of Rough Riders of the World* (Programs)

Commentary

Sources

Play Programs

1.1 MEMORIES OF THE INDIAN WARS—JOY KASSON

FROM THE TIME OF HIS earliest stage plays, Buffalo Bill of course staked his claims to historical authenticity on the conflict that made him famous, the Indian wars. The relationship between this ostensible subject and the silently invoked Civil War was clearest in a figure prominent in both conflicts: General George Armstrong Custer. A flamboyant Civil War soldier known for his theatrical flirtations with danger, Custer had become a martyred symbol of postbellum military ardor after the Battle of the Little Big Horn in 1876. One meaning of his death was that it offered Americans a chance to revisit the theme of loss and sacrifice. Victor and victim, Custer represented both the modern military machine of the Union and the lost cause of the Confederacy.

William F. Cody had dramatized his association with Custer in *The Red Right Hand* only months after the Battle of the Little Big Horn, and drew on his association with the general in many ways, from the battlefield press dispatches to the display of Yellow Hair's scalp to the engravings in his autobiography and program booklets. An enactment of Custer's Last Stand entered the Wild West repertory as early as 1887, and it was reintroduced to the program halfway through the 1893 season at the Columbian Exposition. Reviews in Chicago and in subsequent seasons told audiences that viewing this re-enactment could make them feel they had witnessed the historical events themselves. "The reproduction of the 'Battle of the Little Big Horn' was wonderfully realistic," wrote a reviewer in 1894. "One sitting in the grand stand need no great stretch of the imagination to bring himself to feel that he was on the plains within eyeshot of the spot where Gen. Custer made his last charge . . . It was a scene long to be remembered, so vividly were the minutest details portrayed of the slaughter of those brave men who were with Custer in his last charge." By remembering the performance, the reviewer implies, the spectator could have the illusion of remembering the event itself and sharing the emotions it provoked.

Furthermore, the Wild West's presentation of the battle gave audiences in opportunity to recast defeat as victory. Although the dramatic enactment portrayed the death of Custer and his men, Buffalo Bill rode onto the stage at the incident's conclusion, counter-factually suggesting a triumphant happy ending. Indeed, the Wild West's version of Custer's Last Stand could be seen as an act of revenge for the Battle of the Little Big Horn. Again and again, reviewers stressed that Indian performers in the Wild West had been, or were believed to have been, actual participants in the battle. Not only did the claim bolster the Wild West's pretensions to authenticity, but it also suggested that the tables were now turned: Indians who had mastered Custer were now under the control of Buffalo Bill. After Wounded Knee, a three-way dynamic emerged. In 1894, a reviewer noted that ten of the Indians in the show "took an active part in the massacre of Gen. Custer and his command," while the cavalrymen who performed beside them, including the "personator" of Custer, had served in the battle of Wounded Knee, where, presumably, the slaughter of Sioux avenged the death of Custer and his men. By alluding to the best-known battle of the Indian wars, which also aroused deep emotions associated with the Civil War, the Wild West encouraged audiences to imagine their own participation in historical memory and, indeed, to rewrite history.

Cody was not alone in evoking the memory of the Battle of the Little Big Horn, of course. Custer's legend penetrated American culture on many fronts, from politics to poetry to biography to popular culture. But it may have been the popularity of Buffalo Bill's enactments of the Battle of the Little Big Horn in the 1890s that helped to inspire the brewer Adolphus Busch to commission a print of Custer's Last Stand to help promote his beer, Bud-weiser as a national brand. Busch had already acquired a massive painting of the subject by Cassilly Adams. He gave that work to Custer's own military unit, the Seventh Cavalry, and arranged to have F. Otto Becker do a lithograph of it, issued in a first-run edition of fifteen thousand in 1896.

The Becker lithograph, which soon hung in saloons all across America and was reissued many times, was seen by millions of people and functioned, like the Wild Wests re-enactments, to rewrite popular historical memory. Although no white participants were known to have survived the Battle of the Little Big Horn, in later days numerous purported eyewitnesses emerged, often basing their stories on the image in the lithograph. One old-timer was said to have pointed out the place where, he said, he lay for two days after the battle: "I was right there," he announced, striking the picture with his cane, "right there under that hoss." Becker's lithograph showed the battle scene as smoky and crowded with figures, not unlike the arena representations of Custer's Last Stand, and it also featured a central vignette of Custer in hand-to-hand battle with a single Indian. Of course, Cody's claim to have struggled in single combat with Yellow Hand was by now well known, from the stage plays to the autobiographical writings: "I know you, Pa-he-haska; if you want to fight, come ahead and fight me." At about the same time the Becker print became widely known, the Wild West used an image of Custer's Last Stand on a poster, and it, too, showed Custer in heroic individual combat. Did a memory of Cody's performance become the basis for a representation of Custer that then became the foundation for the Wild West's version of the same event? A photograph entitled "Death of Custer" shows five performers from Buffalo Bill's Wild West posed against a painted backdrop. As three dead Indians lie at his feet, Custer struggles with a single antagonist, who stabs him. His upraised sword in one hand and pistol in the other, the figure of Custer echoes the echo of Buffalo Bill.

The Wild West offered several other scenes in addition to the Battle of the Little Big Horn that were to be understood as representations of "real" incidents of the Indian wars, including the Battle of Summit Springs, in which Cody helped to rescue a white captive and killed Tall Bull. Still other generic episodes also claimed to be truthful to the facts of border warfare. The attack on the settler's cabin and the rescue of the Deadwood stagecoach shared the scenario of Custer's Last Stand and its emotional power. Exciting battles with Indians appeared to be morally and emotionally authorized because they were understood as white retaliation against Indian aggression. As many commentators have noted, the Wild West's war narratives glorify American conquest and invite spectators to unite in their enmity toward a demonized "other" in the form of the American Indians. Although the final result of the Indian wars was still at issue before Wounded Knee, Buffalo Bill's Wild West always presumed the outcome: the "triumph" of "civilization" over "savagery."

And yet, the participation of American Indians themselves in the enactment of their defeat enabled the Wild West to bathe its war stories in a mellower light. Encouraging audiences to hate "the savages" but love the Indian performers, it suggested an attitude the nation could take—triumphant in war but magnanimous to its former enemy—that suited Americans as memories of the Civil War faded into the distant past. By presenting the Indian wars—indeed, the Indians themselves—as spectacles of memory, the Wild West lent the immediacy and conviction of live performance to the proposition so often advanced in popular fiction and patriotic oratory, that war was a noble undertaking and that heroism and even sacrifice were justified by a righteous cause. As memories of Civil War losses receded and veterans North and South reaffirmed their allegiance to the kind of romantic patriotism that had brought it about, Buffalo Bill's Wild West helped to make war imaginatively appealing once again.

By the end of the century, the Indian wars themselves retreated into the past, and Cody's performances interpreted other military events as memories of the Indian wars. America's war with Spain in 1898 seemed to invite America's most visible symbol of military heroism to cross the border once again from showmanship to military duty. When conflict with Spain loomed on the horizon, Cody tried to make a dramatic intervention, which would have advanced in a new and more powerful way the claim of military leadership he had been making for twenty years. In early April 1898, the *New York World* published a proposal by Cody to raise a troop of American Indians to fight the Spanish in Cuba. Under the headline "How I Could Drive Spaniards from Cuba with 30,000 Indian Braves," Cody sketched a scenario in which the Indian warriors of the past would ride again, this time fighting on the side of the United States Army. Drawing on the very image of the fierce redskin that animated the Wild West performances, Cody proposed to turn those qualities to the advantage of American patriotism. "I wish to say first that every Indian would be loyal to the American flag," he asserted, then proposed that American Indians could be effectively mobilized against Spain. "The American Indian has by no means forgotten how to fight. He is a natural-born fighter, and is just as anxious to go to war now as he ever was, and he would rather fight Spaniards than any other people on earth. Why? Because Spain sent the first white man to America." After naming a number of American Indians he considered great war leaders, from Chief American Horse to Chief Joseph to Geronimo, Cody envisioned an attack on Havana by "shouting Indian braves on horseback, resplendent in brilliant war paint, the eagle feathers on their war bonnets fluttering in the wind." Cody projected the capture of Havana as if it were already an act in Buffalo Bill's Wild West; he imagined war imitating the re-enactment of war and, in particular, modern war replaying the Indian wars. The article was excellent publicity for the Wild West, of course, for however slim were the chances of American Indians being sent to Cuba, that season every reader could go to Ambrose Park and see the scene Cody described being performed twice a day. And the article also sums up the struggle between Cody and the pro-assimilation Indian reformers, who must have been horrified to read Buffalo Bill's claim that Indians were naturally warlike, had not forgotten the old ways, and were eager to resume them. Audiences were apparently happy to participate in Cody's latest military fantasy. A few weeks later, another New York newspaper printed a photograph of a group of Wild West Indian performers listening to one of their leaders, with the caption, "Red Horn Bull Telling Sioux that Uncle Sam May Need Them."

But in 1898, Cody was not able to cross the line between performance and military action as readily as he could in 1890, when he was asked by General Miles to play a part in the aftermath of Wounded Knee. Although Cody told Miles he was willing to go to the battlefield and sent his horses ahead to be ready for him, he was never active in the Spanish–American War. He told reporters in March and April that he was "eager to go" and "ready to start immediately," but the call never came. A newspaper interview in July reported that Cody sat in his tent sporting his decorations—jeweled buffalo heads from Grand Duke Alexis and a watch charm from the Prince of Wales—while wishing he were in Cuba with the American troops: "Buffalo Bill sat a typical American, longing more than anything else for an opportunity to get down to the front with the troops of scouts and rough riders which some time ago he tendered to the government." By the time Miles himself arrived on the scene, the war was almost over; Spanish forces in Cuba surrendered on July 17, just ten days after his arrival. In fact, Cody had been superseded as a national symbol by Lieutenant Colonel Theodore Roosevelt, whose charge on San Juan Hill became a new symbol for American military heroism. But Roosevelt reaped his fame by echoing the vision of war Buffalo Bill had made so familiar: his First Regiment of United States Volunteer Cavalry took on the title of the "Rough Riders," a phrase that had entered the national vocabulary through the Wild West.

Although Buffalo Bill did not go to Cuba, Cody and his managers did bring Cuba to the Wild West, where performances about the Spanish–American War appeared to mesh seamlessly with those of the Indian wars. Cuban war veterans performed in the show as early as March 1898. Newspapers reported that, "Battle-Scarred Cuban Soldiers [were] the Feature of the Wild West Show," and described the crowds as "Wild for Old Glory and the Single Star [the Cuban independence flag]." In June, a performance was disrupted when the audience caught sight of two little girls waving United States and Cuba Libre flags. The "storm of cheering and applause" caused Cody to interrupt the act in the arena, ride toward the grandstand, and order the cowboy band to play "Yankee Doodle," bringing "the enthusiasm of the audience to its highest possible pitch." Gallant as was Cody's response, he could not have been pleased to be upstaged. His advertising took on a more overtly military theme. In August 1898, a flier called the Wild West "the Show that Means Something" and promised "Now Bigger and Better Than Ever, Military Display, Unique, It Stands Alone. Up to the Spirit of the Times, Many New Features Added." The three acts promoted in largest letters were the Rough Riders, Custer's Last Battle, and "Cuban Heroes."

In 1899, the Wild West added to its program an enactment of the Battle of San Juan Hill, complete with "detachments from Roosevelt's Rough Riders." Although Buffalo Bill could no longer present himself as a participant in the war he represented, the program text waxed even more eloquent in its claims to historical accuracy. Nate Salsbury's introductory statement reached new heights of rhetoric, proclaiming that "the historian on horseback has Truth for his amanuensis," and describing the Wild West as

> the grandest and most cosmopolitan Object Teacher ever projected by the exceptional experience and executive genius of man, scrupulously truthful in every respect, with every feature herein or elsewhere announced forthcoming, every historical and personal reference authentic, and every narrative, endorsement and criticism correct in spirit, context and application, as regards incident, person, time and location. It presents, with a colosal perfection and versimilitude utterly impossible under any other management, living spectacles of heroic deeds of patriotic devotion and savage resistance; the pomp and circumstances of royal and republican martial array and wildly picturesque and fearsome panoply; the rush, the rally, the splendid force and action of embattled mounted hosts; artillery in skilled and stirring evolutions.

The program cover took a dramatic turn, portraying a much older-looking Buffalo Bill, as if to quell any possible questions about his absence on the battlefields of 1898. And the text made a strong case for the proposition that the Rough Riders at San Juan Hill were, in a sense, an extension of Buffalo Bill himself: "The powerful, practical, patriotic influence of Buffalo Bill's Wild West and Congress of Rough Riders of the World as a mighty and masterly National Object Teacher was strikingly manifested in the suggestion, formation, and even the popular naming of the most fearless and famous single military organization in all martial annals—Teddy Roosevelt's Regiment of Rough Riders."

Now that the scope of the Wild West included other, more modern wars, further new acts were added. Some of these reflected the United States' dramatically altered world stance after the territorial acquisitions of the Spanish–American War. The 1899 printed program included a section on "Strange People from our New Possessions. Families of Porto Ricans, Sandwich Islanders and Filipinos." The Wild West expanded its international interest beyond the display of horsemanship from around the world to take on a quasi-ethnological mission:

> We have delayed the publication of this historical narrative until the last possible moment, in hopes—which as we go to press we are gratified to be able to announce have been fully realized—that our special agent sent to Porto Rico and the Sandwich and the Philippine Islands would be able to secure the finest representatives of the strange and interesting aboriginals of the West Indies and the intermediate and remote

A photograph of Filipino natives showed the same kind of condescending curiosity about the world's peoples that had led to earlier articles like "An Indian's Religion" and "The Bow and Arrow." An illustration from the same program showing various acts from around the world, including acrobats and jugglers, no doubt reflected this turn toward imperialist thinking as well as the increased influence of James Bailey and his pull toward circus acts. By 1900, Filipino performers were appearing in acts like the relay races, and in 1901, two new international conflicts were represented on the program: the Boer War was recognized through the presence of wounded veterans in the Grand Processional—a commando group of Transvaal Boers, a delegation from the Canadian Strathcona Horse (Mounted Police), and a band of Baden-Powell's Defenders of Mafeking—and the Boxer Rebellion in China was enacted in "Battle of Tien-Tsin," in which Allied forces replaced "the Royal Standard of Paganism" with "the Banners of Civilization." But although the new internationalism appeared to be a turn away from the Wild West's traditional focus on the story of the American frontier, the multiple meanings embodied in its presentation of American Indian performers could be found in its new international perspective as well. Presented as curiosities valued for their differencess, but safely encased in the presumption of remoteness, the international peoples of the Wild West were also viewed, like the buffalo and the American Indians, as memorials of an imaginative world distant in time and space. But no matter how many new narratives were added, the Wild West continued to present every struggle as a memory of the Indian wars and perhaps, covertly, of the Civil War as well.

1.2 REMEMBER THE MAINE—BURLINGTON HAWKEYE

WHENEVER a Spaniard shows his head
Remember the Maine! Remember the Maine!
Take aim quickly and shoot him dead.
Remember the Maine! Remember the Maine!
All honor to our sailor lads who on that night found a watery grave,
Caused by the act of a Spanish knave.
Remember the Maine! Remember the Maine!

Chorus.

Three cheers for the red, white and blue,
Three cheers for our flag and Cuba;
Our army and navy forever,
Three cheers for our flag and Cuba.

But Dewey visited them o'er the sea,
He remembered the Maine! Remembered the Maine!
He was full of fight as he could be,
He remembered the Maine! Remembered the Maine!
He entered their harbor during the night.
He fought them left, he fought them right.
Oh! wasn't that a glorious fight?
He remembered the Maine! Remembered the Maine!

Chorus.

Three cheers for the red, white and blue,
Three cheers for our flag and Dewey, too.
Our army and navy forever,
Three cheers for our flag and Dewey, too.

Then Sampson thought to try his hand.
He remembered the Maine! Remembered the Maine!
And sailed away to "Rico" land.
He remembered the Maine! Remembered the Maine!
He riddled their forts with shot and shell,
How many he killed I cannot tell,
But he did them up I know full well.
He remembered the Maine! Remembered the Maine!

Chorus.

Three cheers for the red, white and blue,
Three cheers for our flag and Sampson, too.
Our army and navy forever,
Three cheers for Sampson, Cuba and Dewey, too.

1.3 A SQUAD OF GENUINE CUBAN INSURGENTS

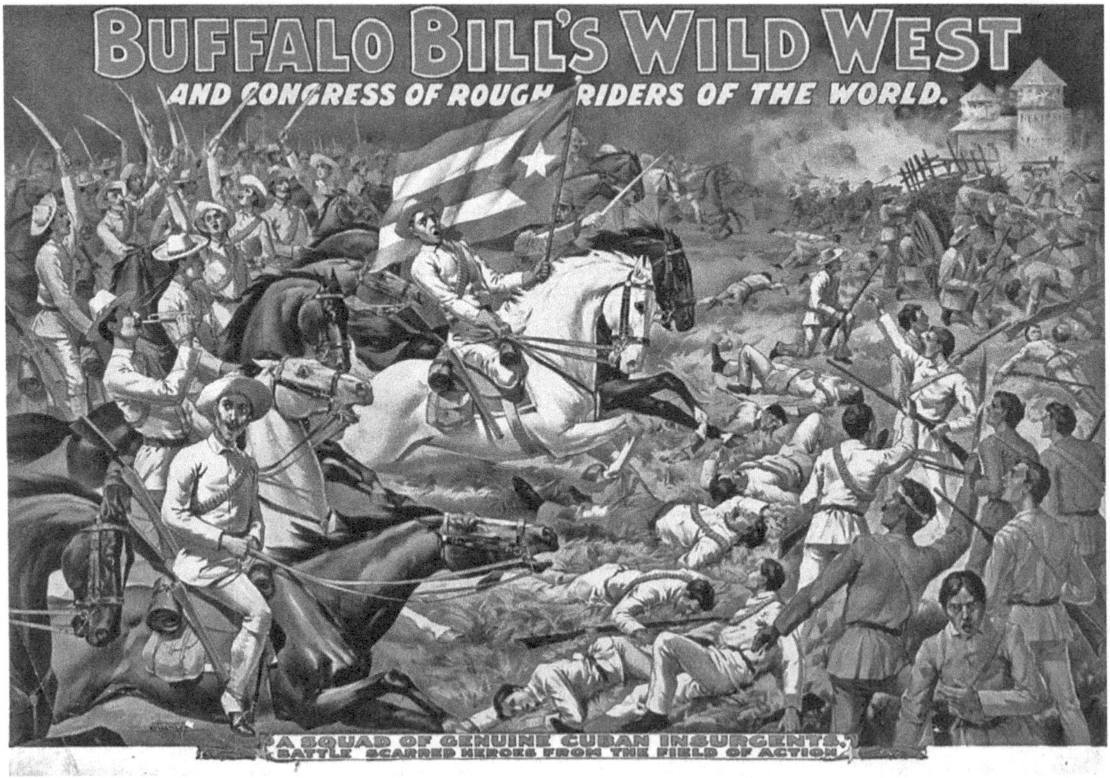

1898 advertisement for Buffalo Bill's Wild West Show. When the U.S. went to war with Spain in 1898, it was partly to help liberate Cuba from Spain's colonial grip. For William Cody, the envisioned good-versus-evil melodrama in Cuba was excellent performance material that fitted nicely with his re-enacted frontier battles and aided the war effort.

1.4 RED HORN BULL TELLING SIOUX THAT UNCLE SAM MAY NEED THEM

NEW YORK HERALD, SUNDAY, APRIL 24, 1898.

RED HORN BULL TELLING SIOUX THAT UNCLE SAM MAY NEED THEM.

"Red Horn Bull Telling Sioux That Uncle Sam May Need Them," from the *New York Herald*, 1898.

Source: Image courtesy of Buffalo Bill Center of the West, Cody, Wyoming, U.S.A.; MS6.3789.999

1.5 BUFFALO BILL'S SHOW—ANON

New York Times, April 3, 1898

Buffalo Bill's Show

ENTERS ON ITS SECOND WEEK at the Garden To-morrow.

Buffalo Bill's Wild West and Congress of Rough Riders of the World will begin the second week of its season at Madison Square Garden to-morrow. The exhibition has attracted enormous audiences, every feature on the programme being full of interest. One of the most attractive features is the military spectacle, "Custer's Last Battle," during which fire scenes and tableaus are shown, the hundreds of Indians and soldiers engaged in the battle giving it an aspect of realism seldom attained.

The appearance of the Cuban Color Guard always excites intense enthusiasm, the veterans bearing the red, white, and blue with the single star. The sports and pastimes so popular among the English and German soldiers are introduced with splendid effect, some of them being seen here for the first time, and all of them creating great amusement.

1.6 HOW I COULD DRIVE SPANIARDS FROM CUBA WITH 30,000 INDIAN BRAVES—WILLIAM F. CODY (BUFFALO BILL)

New York World, 3 April 1898

Buffalo Bill Writes on "How I Could Drive Spaniards From Cuba With 30,000 Indian Braves."

BUFFALO BILL SAYS THERE ARE in the country fully 30,000 Indians who can fight and who would be glad to enlist under Uncle Sam's banner for guerilla warfare in Cuba. Lieut. Emyerich and Lieut.-Col. Delgado, Cuban veterans, say that such a body of galloping, fearless troops could take Havana in one dashing charge. The Indian has a taste for war, and he hates the Spanish for bringing the white man to this continent and for their horrible cruelty to the red men.

In response to your request for a statement regarding the probable conduct and possible usefulness of the American Indian in the event of war, I wish to say first that every Indian would be loyal to the American flag.

There are in the United States to-day fully 30,000 full-blooded Indian warriors and at least 10,000 more youths and aged Indian men who can fight.

With the 30,000 young redmen, mounted on their wiry ponies, acting in conjunction with the insurgents with an adequate amount of artillery, and using the same military tactics that they and their fathers used in fighting the whites in the wild West, I do not think that the Spaniards would last more than sixty days in a land war in Cuba.

Havana is the stronghold of the Spaniards. If Havana were to fall the subjection of the rest of the island, with the help of the gallant insurgents, could be accomplished. The country surrounding Havana is well adapted to the American Indian method of warfare.

From a hurried study of the island defenses of the city and from questioning the veteran insurgents who have just come from Cuba to take part in my Wild West Show, I am led to believe that, with the aid of the six or seven thousand insurgents from Pinar del Rio and Matanzas provinces, who could be easily moved to the region of Havana on short notice, the city could be taken by these armed forces, at least with a naval attack engaging the guns in the forts at the same time.

The most experienced of the Cuban fighters who are with me, men thoroughly acquainted with the region about Havana, assure me that this could be done. Lieut.-Col. Emyerick, who carries eight ugly wounds, is a veteran of two Cuban wars and has fought from one end of the island to the other, has said that the Indians could do it. He also says that he would guarantee to be able to land Indian or any other kind of American troops on any part of the Cuban coast not fortified by the Spaniards.

Lieut.-Col. Delgado, who fought with Gen. Maceo in his last battle and was twice wounded, and Lieut. Mazurro, who composed the Cuban national hymn, and is the head of the Wild West Show's band of insurgents, also say that the Indians, operating in their own peculiar way, would make effective fighters in Cuba, and that 30,000 of them could capture Havana. Others of the wounded veterans have said the same.

These men have been thoroughly impressed by the appearance of the fierce Sioux Indians whom they have met in Madison Square Garden, and have been even more impressed by what they have learned of the history and fighting qualities of the American red men.

Would the Indians fight the Spaniards? They most certainly would. The American Indian has by no means forgotten how to fight. He is a natural-born fighter, and is just as anxious to go to war now as he ever was, and he would rather fight Spaniards than any other people on earth. Why? Because Spain sent the first white man to America. They hate Spain for having done that.

Most people who have had no experience with Indians will consider that a trivial thing for me to say. It is not. American Indians know about Columbus and who sent him here. I took a band of them to Barcelona, Spain, with me several years ago. I showed them the big statue of Columbus there. They gazed at it in silence and disgust for some time, and then I asked them what they thought about it.

"Bad medicine," repelled the leading man among them—the medicine man. If they consider a thing good they call it "good medicine," if bad it is "bad medicine." I asked for a further explanation and the medicine man said that they could never forgive Columbus for coming to rob their fathers of their beautiful land nor Spain for sending him. Trouble has been the Indian's lot, he said, ever since.

The American Indian has a natural appetite for war, and he is hungry to fight the nation that is responsible for his being disturbed in his Arcadian simplicity.

There are many great Indian chiefs still living, perhaps fifty chiefs and important sub-chiefs, who would make gallant and effective leaders in an Indian campaign in Cuba. There is American Horse, Sioux Chief, who, since the great Chief Red Cloud is totally blind, would be the great

Sioux leader. After him would come He Dog, Little Wound, Hump, Red Horn Bull, all Sioux chiefs, and Big Road, Kicking Bear and Short Bull, of the Ogallalla Sioux.

Red Horn Bull is with my show. He was in the battle of the Little Big Horn River in 1876, known as the Custer massacre, where Gen. Custer and his entire command were slain. Red Horn Bull carries the ugly mark of the last bullet from Custer's revolver. In the thick of the fight he came face to face with the gallant General, who, having lost his sword, drew his revolver, and as he did so the hammer fell and the 44-calibre bullet went through his jaw, carrying away part of the bone and knocking him down. He is very proud of Gen. Custer's bullet-hole.

An Indian with a record like that could be relied on to get the better of a good many Spaniards if he met them face to face. He said just a few days ago that he would like to fight Spain and would be glad to fight under the American flag. That, I believe, is the feeling among all Indians.

Then there is Chief Joseph, of the Nez Perces, one of the greatest Indian generals that this country ever produced and certainly the most humane of all Indian chiefs. He is in the prime of life, and so is his sub-chief, Ollicutt. Geronimo, the vicious chief of the Apaches, is at present a prisoner of war, but he is a great and wicked general and must be considered in any speculation like the present. These are only a few of the chiefs, still living, any one of whom is capable of leading his people to war against the Spaniards and to conduct a telling campaign.

Every one of the 30,000 or more Indian warriors is prepared for war. He could go on a moment's notice. Each owns his own war horse, many having numbers of them, and each is constantly equipped with arms and ammunition. All that would be necessary would be to load them, their horses and equipments on trains and ship them to the sea coast. Nothing would please the Indians more than an order to go to battle. Even their religion teaches them that it is good to fight. The better record an Indian has as a warrior on earth the better his chance of happiness in the hereafter, he is taught.

Ships could be provided for transporting the Indians from the United States sea coast to Cuba and I am assured by insurgents and others that a landing there could be effected even at so favorable a point as the open country about midway between Havana and Matanzas; not more than twenty miles from the capital, in fact.

If, as I have been told, there are bands of insurgents constantly camped within two or three miles of Havana, the Indians could be mobilized in the hills that surround the city. The conditions seem to be peculiarly favorable to Indian warfare. No people on earth can get the "lay" of a new country quicker than the American Indian. He is a natural astronomer and astrologer. He observes landmarks with unerring accuracy and has a wonderful faculty of determining direction. From the crest of some high hill one long sweep of the eyes would be enough to give each leader of the Indians the "lay of the land" and tell how best to employ his forces. The Indian is a great strategist.

If these 30,00 shouting Indian braves on horseback, resplendent in brilliant war paint, the eagle feathers on their war bonnets fluttering in the wind, should sweep down on Havana in a grand charge what a picture it would make! Taken unawares, hundreds of thousands of men could not withstand such an onslaught.

As to the rest of the island, it is just the kind of country in which Indians fight best. A ridge of mountains runs the whole length of the island about midway between the coasts, and the generally hilly nature of the rest of the island makes it adaptable to ambush fighting and sudden charges, the tactics employed most effectively by the Indians.

Of course all this is speculation. It perhaps can never come to pass; but it is interesting to reflect on what has been and what might still be accomplished by that noble but rapidly dying race, the American Indian.

WILLIAM F. CODY (Buffalo Bill)

1.7 *BUFFALO BILL'S WILD WEST AND CONGRESS OF ROUGH RIDERS OF THE WORLD* PROGRAM

Newburg, Thursday June 16, 1898

Just What It Is.

AT THE VERY OUTSET it is truthfully claimed and should be intelligently understood that BUFFALO BILL'S WILD WEST AND CONGRESS OF ROUGH RIDERS OF THE WORLD is, in its way, an absolutely distinct and original innovation in popular instruction and entertainment; an exact, complete and entirely genuine historical and equestrian revelation, many of the participants in which played brave and famous warrior parts in the dread and dangerous scenes of savage warfare, hazardous exploration and pioneer advancement which are so vividly, powerfully and accurately reproduced as to actually partake more of reality than of imitation. That, inasmuch as it either contains or commands all the personality and material indispensable to the complete and satisfactory formation of such an exhibition, it cannot be duplicated or even imitated above the level of petty and ludicrous travesty and imposition. That no similar enterprise was ever successfully projected, and none ever can be. That it is the only exhibition of any kind endorsed and contributed to by governments, armies and nations. That, as this season presented, it is destined to eclipse all its past memorable American and European triumphs. And, finally, that it is a grand and heroic object school, which the oftener it is seen the more highly it is appreciated, and every recurring visit to which affords additional instruction and novel and inspiring entertainment.

Cuba Libre.

A Mounted Detachment of Her Veteran Heroes.

Just as this beautiful publication goes to press we receive the most satisfactory and anxiously looked for information that prolonged negotiations have at last resulted in adding to the Cavalry forces of The Wild West a detachment of veterans from the Cuban Army of Independence, each and every member of which has seen service in the commands of either Maceo or Gomez and bears honorable wounds in proof of his devotion and valor. It is the first time that a genuine Cuban "Guerrilla," mounted and equipped exactly as if charging a Spanish squadron, was ever seen on American soil, and present conditions and future possibilities make him a warlike and patriotic figure of supreme popular interest. It seems almost superfluous to state that these "bravest of the brave" are men above the desire for notoriety, or mercenary considerations of any kind. Devoted to a cause far dearer to them than life itself, in their temporary enforced absence from the field, they are animated by but one honorable and unselfish purpose—the hope that by the association with American freemen afforded in the immense assemblages attracted to the Wild West exhibitions, they will be able to gain sympathy for themselves and their cause, by making it and themselves better understood. That is their mission, and it is one entitling them to the respect and favor of every one of Old Glory's sons.

1.8 *BUFFALO BILL'S WILD WEST AND CONGRESS OF ROUGH RIDERS OF THE WORLD* PROGRAM

New York, 1898

Congress of Rough Riders of the World.

Official Programme.

1—**OVERTURE**, "Star Spangled Banner,"—Cowboy Band, Wm. Sweeney, Leader.

2—**GRAND REVIEW**, introducing the Rough Riders of the World, Indians, Cowboys, Mexicans, Cossacks, Gauchos, Arabs, Scouts, Guides, Frontier Girls and Detachments of fully equipped Regular Soldiers of the Armies or America, England, Germany and Russia, and Color Guard of Cuban Veterans.

3—**RACE OF RACES**. Race between a Cowboy, a Cossack, a Mexican and Arab, a Gaucho and an Indian, on Spanish-Mexican, Bronco, Russian, Indian, and Arabian horses.

4—**U.S. ARTILLERY DRILL** by veterans from Capt. Thorpe's Battery D, Fifth Regiment, U.S. Artillery.

5—**ILLUSTRATING A PRAIRIE EMIGRANT TRAIN CROSSING THE PLAINS**. It is attacked by marauding Indians, who are in turn repulsed by "Buffalo Bill" and a number of Scouts and Cowboys. Quadrille on horseback.

6—**MISS ANNIE OAKLEY**, Celebrated Shot, who will illustrate her dexterity in the use of fire-arms.

7—**PONY EXPRESS** A former Pony Post-rider who will show how the letters and telegrams of the Republic were distributed across the immense continent previous to the building of railways and the telegraph.

8—**A GROUP OF RIFFIAN ARABIAN HORSEMEN** will illustrate their style of horsemanship, together with native sports and pastimes.

9—**BATTLE OF LITTLE BIG HORN**—or Custer's Last Rally, which took place on the Little Big Horn River, Montana, June 25th, 1876; preceding battle, the Indians will be seen in camp, reinforcements joining, War-dances, etc.

10—**A BEVY OF BEAUTIFUL RANCHERAS,** genuine and famous frontier girls in feats of daring equestrianism.

11—**JOHNNY BAKER,** Celebrated Young American Marksman.

12—**COSSACKS,** of the Caucasus of Russia, in feats of horsemanship, native dances, etc.

13—**ZOUAVE INFANTRY DRILL** by the celebrated Aurora Zouaves, ten years Interstate champions.

14—**A GROUP OF MEXICANS** from Old Mexico will illustrate the use of lasso and perform various feats of horsemanship.

15—**COWBOY FUN.** Picking objects from the ground, lassoing wild horses, riding the buckers, etc.

16—**COLOR GUARD OF THE CUBAN VETERANS,** on leave of absence in order to give their various wounds time to heal, all have fought for the flag of Cuba and will soon return to that country to act as scouts and guides, for which their familiarity with the topography of the island especially commends them.

17—**MILITARY MUSICAL DRILL** by a detachment from the Fifth Royal Irish Lancers and a detachment from the Garde Cuirassiers of His Majesty Kaiser William II.

18—**SIXTH U.S. CAVALRY.** Veterans from Col. Sumner's celebrated Regiment at Fort Myer, Va., in military exercises, and an exhibition of athletic sports and horsemanship.

NOTE.—The men will wear the Campaign Uniforms adopted by the U.S. Army on the frontier. The horses are Western Range Bronco Horses, used in this manner for the first time in history. The Army and National Guard use the "American" horse.

19—**ATTACK ON THE DEADWOOD MAIL COACH BY INDIANS.** Repulse of the Indians and rescue of the stage, passengers and mail by "Buffalo Bill" and his attendant Cowboys.

20—**RACING BETWEEN INDIAN BOYS ON BAREBACK HORSES.**

21—**THREE MINUTES WITH THE ROUGH RIDERS OF THE WORLD.**

22—**COL. W. F. CODY** ("Buffalo Bill") in his unique feats of sharpshooting at full speed.

23—**BUFFALO HUNT,** as it was in the Far West of North America—"Buffalo Bill" and Indians. The last of the only known Native Herd.

24—**ATTACK ON SETTLERS' CABINS** and rescue by "Buffalo Bill" and a band of Cowboys, Scouts and Frontiersmen.

25—**SALUTE.**

1.9 *BUFFALO BILL'S WILD WEST AND CONGRESS OF ROUGH RIDERS OF THE WORLD* PROGRAM

New York, 1899

Buffalo Bill's "Wild West"
AND CONGRESS OF ROUGH RIDERS OF THE WORLD.

OFFICIAL PROGRAMME.

(Note).—An exhibition, the intention of which is to educate the spectator, through the medium of animated pictures, in the picturesque life on the Western American Plains in the days just past, showing primitive horsemen who have attained fame; spiced with their counterparts of modern military horsemanship, all combined in an evening's entertainment, rendering reading books or viewing the work of the sculptors and artists on these subjects more easily comprehended and enjoyed in years to come. It is especially instructive to the untravelled and to the rising generation to see authenticated, genuine people of different nations and races in their characteristic costumes before they have passed away and are left as legacies to the future only through art and history. The principal incidents and episodes have additional interest from having been identified in the life of Col. W. F. Cody.

No. **1.** **Overtime**, "Star Spangled Banner." Cowboy Band. Wm. Sweeney, Director.

2. **Grand Review, introducing the Rough Riders of the World**, led by Col. W. F Cody, "Buffalo Bill."

3. **Exhibition of Seats in the Saddle**, by a Cowboy, a Cossack, a Mexican, an Arab, a Gaucho, and an Indian.

4. **Artillery Drill**, by Veterans of Battery D, Fifth Regiment, U.S. Artillery, showing the old-time muzzle-loading methods, in contradistinction to the more modern rapid-fire guns in the battle scene later.

5. **Illustrating a Prairie Emigrant Train Crossing the Plains**. The **Camp Fire**, the **Quadrille on Horseback**. Attack by Marauding Indians, who are in turn repulsed by Scouts and Cowboys.

6. **Col. W. F. Cody**, "Buffalo Bill," in unrivalled feats of shooting from horseback.

7. **Pony Express**. A Pony Post Rider will show how letters and telegrams of the Republic were distributed across the Continent previous to the building of the railways and telegraph.

8. **Life Savers**. A crew from the United States Life Saving Corps, with apparatus from the Government, giving an exhibition of the use of the mortar, throwing the life-line, and the use of the breeches buoy in rescuing the shipwrecked.

9. **Cossacks**, from the Caucasus of Russia, in feats of horsemanship.

10. **Johnnie Baker**, celebrated young American Marksman.

11. **Race**. Race between Western American Girls.

12. **A Group of Mexicans** from old Mexico will illustrate the use of the lasso.

13. **The Battle of San Juan Hill**. Introducing detachments from Roosevelt's Rough Riders, Twenty-fourth Infantry, Ninth and Tenth Cavalry, Grimes' Battery, Garcia's Cuban Scouts, Pack Train, etc., etc.

    SCENE 1.—BEFORE THE BATTLE. THE BIVOUAC.
    (Several hours are supposed to elapse before the opening of the second scene.)
    SCENE 2.—THE STORMING OF THE HILL

14. **A Group of Arab Horseman** will illustrate their style of horsemanship, together with native sports and pastimes.
15. **Cowboy Fun**. Picking objects from the ground, lassoing wild horses and riding the bucking broncho. This is the most severe test of horsemanship known in equestrianism, as the spectator must understand that the animals are untamed and the rider is contesting with an unknown quantity.
16. **Indians from the Sioux, Arrapahoe, Brule and Cheyenne Tribes** will illustrate an Indian skirmish and tribal war dances. This picture should be valued, as it is historically correct and participated in by some of the last of the Blanket Indians, and as one which will shortly be impossible to reproduce.
17. **Military Exercises by Veteran English Cavalrymen**, men from the firing line, who have seen service in all parts of the British Empire, and a detachment of the 10th United States Colored Cavalry.
18. **Veterans** from the Sixth U.S. Cavalry in Military Exercises and Practice Exhibition.

NOTE. The men wear the uniforms by the U.S. Army on the frontier. The horses are Western range horses, originally used for the first time by the Buffalo Bill Wild West, thus bringing their availability to the attention of the Military Market. Previosuly, the English and U.S. Army adhered to the English and American horse in distinction from the Spanish-American horse.

Origin of the Name "Rough Riders"

Colonel Theodre Roosevelt says: "Wood and I were speedily commissioned as Colonel and Lieutenant-Colonel of the First United States Volunteer Cavalry. This was the official title of the regiment, but for some reason or other the public promptly christened us the 'Rough Riders.' At first we fought against the use of the term, but to no purpose; and when finally, the Generals of division and Brigade began to write in formal communications about our regiment as the 'Rough Riders,' we adopted the term ourselves."

The name was one with which the public had become familiar, and in a way fascinated, through its adoption some years ago by Col. W. F. Cody—"Buffalo Bill"—to designate precisely the class of frontiersmen associated with his Wild West Exhibition, which, as Colonel Roosevelt himself remarks, "made up the bulk of the regiment and give it its peculiar character." The term was gradually widened to include the Cossack, Arabian, Mexican, South American, trooper and other free, fearless equestrians, now marshaled under the leadership of the greatest horseman of them all. Millions of people have grown to understand, fully appreciate, and unboundedly admire that title and what it stands for, and its transference to the first U.S. V. Cavalry was not only a deserved

Colonel Roosevelt and his Rough Riders at the top of the hill that they captured at the Battle for the San Juan Heights. After the war, many of these men would go on to perform that same military engagement at *Buffalo Bill's Wild West.*

compliment, but an honourable designation, whose admirable fitness was at once and universally recognized. Colonel Cody first introduced the name "Rough Riders," to the American public. The manner in which Colonal Roosevelt subsequently introduced it to the Spaniards has made it historically immortal. Col. Cody will now popularize it in a peaceful manner in Great Britain.

THE BATTLE OF SAN JUAN HILL

The Battle of San Juan Hill

A Realistic War Spectacle on Colossal Scale

Realistic reproduction of this battle which will for ever remain famous in the history of wars, will be one of the features of the programme of Buffalo Bill's Wild West and Congress of Rough Riders of the World.

The central figures of that battle were the now immortal regiment known as Roosevelt's Rough Riders, commanded by the present ruler of America and borrowing the name "Rough Riders" first coined by Col. Cody for his exhibition. It was officially known as the first regiment of volunteer cavalry. It was enlisted when the United States, in response to the call of humanity, determined that Cuba should be free from the growing thraldom of Spain.

The battle of San Juan Hill was the military companion piece to the naval battle of Santiago, and when it fell Spanish rule over the City of Santiago likewise fell. It was mainly made up of the class of scouts and trappers with which Buffalo Bill's Wild West has made the civilized world familiar; many of whom went from its arena to the larger one of the war in Cuba, and have again returned to it, bringing large accessions of their intrepid comrades and scores of their broncos, to give additional interest and verisimilitude to the introduction of a likewise, effective and vivid facsimile of the rowing and conclusive incident in where, to the utter amazement of the military world, and in valiant reversal of all accepted tactical authorities, a thin line of infantry, unsupported by artillery, charged upon and routed a superior force, strongly intrenched on a difficult eminence behind artillery protected breast-works and armed with the dreaded Mauser and smokeless powder. An important factor, too, in the successful presentation of this spectacle is the fact that both Colonel Cody and Mr. Nate Salsbury are war veterans, thoroughly familiar, through severe experience, with war in its sternest practical features, and fully competent to manage the large number of men required and utilized, to the plain untinselled reality of actual war.

1.10 *BUFFALO BILL'S WILD WEST AND CONGRESS OF ROUGH RIDERS OF THE WORLD* PROGRAM

New York, 1900

Resplendent Realism of Glorious War.

Stupendous Spectacular Reproduction of the Famous Battle of San Juan.

THE DECISIVE IMPORTANCE and far-reaching resultant effects of battles are not to be determined by the numbers engaged. That of Lexington blew the smoldering brands of rebellion into a flaming beacon of Freedom, whose light has illumined the darkness of the world. That of San Juan Hill, by completing the cordon of steel drawn grimly around doomed Santiago, gave the deathblow to Spanish dominion born of the discoveries of Columbus. In the latter engagement the regiment whose popular and famous title was borrowed from Colonel Cody's use and application of the term "Rough Riders," which was mainly composed of the physical qualities represented so splendidly in Buffalo Bill's Wild West, and which, moreover, included many volunteers from Colonel Cody's camp, so pre-eminently distinguished itself as to naturally suggest the idea of representing the terrific contest with the Spanish forces in the only arena spacious enough for such a production, and under the management of the only men controlling the requisite material. It was justly assumed that the realistic and commensurate re-enactment of such a fearless charge and desperate struggle, and the introduction of military incidents preceding it, upon the broadest and most accurate lines of army movements, discipline and life, *and by the very heroes and horses who were a part of what they portrayed*, was calculated to arouse public curiosity and enthusiasm to the white heat of patriotic fervor. Furthermore, that such a stupendous living battle lesson would form a fitting and triumphant climax to the Wild West's magnificent and unprecedented martial spectacles. Notwithstanding the fact that both Colonel Cody and Mr. Nate Salsbury are war veterans, as such, entirely familiar with war in its sternest practical features, and fully competent to command and manage the hundreds of men and horses required and utilized, the task confronting them was a huge and herculean one, involving not only an enormous expense, but infinite labor in investigation, procuring of genuine material, arrangement of detail, circumstance and scenery, and effective utilization of the space at command and indispensable to the manœuvers of so many troops, horses and guns. The results attained fully and faithfully harmonize with the heroic subject and the facts of history, presenting the events associated with the battle of San Juan in two scenes.

The first scene shows the bivouac of the troops on the road to San Juan the night before the battle. The invading American forces, composed of the artillery representing Grimes' Battery, the mule pack train carrying ammunition, the Colored Regulars, Roosevelt's Rough Riders, the Seventy-first Infantry, the Cuban scouts and guides, are seen at sunset, at the conclusion of a desperately hard day's march over rough and jungle-choked trails, under the blistering rays of a tropical sun, moving into an encampment selected for a resting place on the night preceding the morrow's grim work. The various commands take up the positions assigned them, and to the spectator the bivouac presents a most warlike and novel scene of disciplined bustle and preparation. The sentries are posted, the tired animals unloaded, unharnessed and picketed, the weary soldier boys gladly obey the order to stack arms, and, relieved of their haversacks and cumbersome accoutrements, loll and lie around in groups, while the camp fires are lighted and preparations for the evening meal quickly made. The hardtack and coffee disposed of and the stern hand of discipline temporarily relaxed, they indulge in an *al fresco* "smoker" and forget their toils and dangers in story, song and jest; the familiar songs and patriotic anthems of home, as chorused in melodies and stentorian tones from hundreds of throats, wafted toward doomed Santiago on the balmy wings of the night winds, and sounding singular and solemn on that vast natural stage, heretofore a stranger to the exultant notes of Freedom's sons. Night creeps on more stealthily than a Spanish guerrilla through the dense encircling foliage, until taps gives warning that the hour for sleep and silence has struck. Soon the entire command, with the exception of the watchful outposts, reclining on mother earth's broad bosom and canopied by the starry heavens, is wrapped in merciful oblivion or beguiled by dreams of distant loved ones. And, alas! many a noble fellow slumbering so peacefully there will, ere another sun has set, fall fighting into that sleep that knows no awakening, after recording in his own life-blood his name upon the scroll of his country's heroes.

The sharp rattle of the reveille arouses the camp to preparation for the onward march, and the scene closes with the advance of the army toward the stronghold of San Juan.

The Rough Riders' Immortal Charge.

The second scene reveals the regiments already named massed in the forks of the trail at the foot of San Juan Hill, a most exact and effective representation and reproduction of which is introduced, showing the blockhouse, the breastworks, the rifle pits, and the natural and apparently insurmountable difficulties our soldiers were obliged to encounter and overcome in their final and victorious assault. From the fancied impregnability of their position the superior Spanish force is seen pouring an incessant torrent of shrapnel and Mauser bullets into our exposed ranks, which choke up the narrow trail beyond the hope of extrication, and apparently beyond the possibility of escape. To add to the horrors of the situation, the infernal Spanish guerrillas, concealed in the treetops and using smokeless powder, which renders it impossible to locate them, make targets of our wounded and the surgeons and wearers of the sacred Red Cross. It is an hour of supreme trial and agony, in a veritable hell-pit and snare. The situation renders division and brigade commanders powerless and manœuvering impossible. Retreat they cannot; to remain is destruction, and to advance, according to all precedent and estimation, but speedier annihilation. But, casting theories, dictums and doubts to the winds, contemptuously fearless of conspicuous exposure, with splendid intrepidity, assuming and divining that what must be done can be done, a horseman, wearing the

"The Rough Riders" sheet music played during enacted battles, from *Wild West* program, 1900.

uniform of the Rough Riders, presses to the foot of the death-swept hill, and, calling upon the men to follow him, rides straight up and at the fortressed foe. There is a frantic yell of admiration and approval as the soldiers—*white, red and black*—spring from their cowering position of utter helplessness and follow Roosevelt and the flag. On and ever onward they leap, struggle and crawl, at first in small groups, but finally in a long thin line, which widens as it rushes, pants, wallows and creeps toward the flame-crowned summit inch by inch, and foot by foot, it mounts, with a tenacity of purpose, the moral effect of which carries, first, misconception; next, apprehension; and, finally, unreasoning fear into the enemy's works. The Spaniards cannot believe that so small a force would dare an assault so forlorn of all hope. They erroneously infer that an army is charging close behind it, and as it breathlessly comes closely on for a hand-to-hand death grapple, they pale, they flinch, and at last they turn and fly in panic. Their old and crimson emblem of ruthless oppression is torn from the ramparts, and Old Glory streams on the breeze, triumphant in its place. Their defences are turned against themselves, and Santiago is doomed.

Strange People From our New Possessions.

Families of Costa Ricans, Sandwich Islanders and Filipinos.

We have delayed the publication of this historical narrative until the last possible moment, in hopes—which as we go to press we are gratified to be able to announce have been fully realized—that our special agent sent to Porto Rico and the Sandwich and the Philippine Islands would be able to secure the finest representatives of the strange and interesting aboriginals of the West Indies and the intermediate and remote Pacific isles, now grouped by the fate of war, the hand of progress and the conquering march of civilization under Old Glory's protecting folds.

These insular and oceanic chiefs and warriors, with their dark-eyed wives and wildly cunning children, uniquely and fascinatingly complete the ethnological scope of the Congress of Rough Riders of the World, which thus adds the last and greatest of living novelties and racial object lessons to keep step with the marvelous, potential and gigantic expansion of the nation; the most stirring and romantic episodes in whose history it alone perpetuates, in both personality and heroic action. In semi-civilized and barbaric dress, ornaments and arms, these roamers of tropical jungles and surf-beaten volcanic shores will faithfully illustrate the martial, heathen and home peculiarities of their lives of intermingled feud, pastimes and superstitions; introducing extraordinary feats of strength and skill with primitive weapons, singular and sinuous dances, supple gymnastics, pagan ceremonies and peculiar sports, such as comparatively but few Christian eyes have ever seen.

Paradoxical, too, as it would naturally appear in connection with people born and raised under such insular conditions, there will be found among them horsemen fully meriting the high compliment of a place in COLONEL CODY'S Congress of Rough Riders of the World; equestrians full of nerve and dash and sure of seat, even if their accoutrements seem outlandish and their methods surprisingly grotesque to continental riders and audiences. Elsewhere they will receive and everywhere certainly secure, the wider recognition their fine physical characteristics and novel accomplishments so well deserve. Meantime, COL. CODY begs now to, for the first time, cordially introduce them to his and their future fellow-countrymen.

---

2. *Madame Butterfly*—David Belasco

Commentaries

Sources

Play

2.1 *MADAME BUTTERFLY*—WILLIAM WINTER

SOME LITTLE WHILE BEFORE THE PRODUCTION of "Naughty Anthony" Belasco had received from a stranger a letter in which he was urged to read a story, called "Madame Butterfly," by John Luther Long, with a view to making it into a play. When anxiously casting about for some means of providing required reinforcement for his farce he chanced to recollect that suggestion, procured a copy of Long's book containing his tragic tale, read it and was so much impressed by the possibilities which he perceived of basing on it a striking theatrical novelty that he entered into communication with Long and arranged with him for the use of his story. This proved, in several ways, a most fortunate occurrence: it led to a valued and lasting friendship and, ultimately, to the writing of two other memorable dramas,—"The Darling of the Gods" and "Adrea,"—as well as to the composition of a beautiful and extraordinarily popular opera, and it resulted, directly, in the making and production, by Belasco, of one of the most effective short plays of the last twenty-five years,—the success of which did much to sustain him under the disappointment of failure and the burden of heavy loss.

Belasco's tragedy of "Madame Butterfly" is comprised in one act, of two scenes, which, connected by a pictorial intercalation, are presented without a break, and it implicates eight persons, besides its heroine, all of whom are merely incidental to depiction of her tragic fate. The substance of its story is contained in Goldsmith's familiar lines about the sad consequences of lovely woman's genuflexion to folly. A man commits the worst and meanest of all acts, the wronging of an innocent girl, and then deserts her. The case has often been stated— but it is not less pathetic because it is familiar. In this instance the girl is a Japanese, and in Japan, and thus the image of her joy, sorrow, desolation, and death are investable with opulent color and quaint accessories. Her name is *Cho-Cho-San*, and, by her lover, she is called "*Madame Butterfly*." Her family is one of good position, but her father, a soldier of the emperor, having been defeated in battle, has killed himself, and her relatives, being poor, have induced *Cho-Cho-San*, in order that she may be able to provide maintenance for them, to enter into the relation of housekeeping prostitute with an officer of the United States Navy, *Lieutenant B. F. Pinkerton* by name, who is stationed for a few months at Higashi, Japan, and who feels himself to be in need of female companionship and that "comfort other than pecuniary" specified by Patrick Henry. According to the enlightened and advanced customs of Japan (which various English-speaking exponents of progress and free-everything, including free-"love," are laboring to establish in our benighted country) this relationship is not degrading and despicable but respectable and, in circumstances which are of frequent occurrence, to be desired. As *Butterfly* expresses it, though the naval officer is described by the Japanese as "a barbarian and a beast," "Aevery one say: 'yaes, take him—take him beas'—he's got moaneys,' so I say for jus' liddle while, perhaps I can stan'." *Pinkerton*, however, proves to be a delightful companion who wins the love of the Japanese girl and, with the crass cruelty common among viciously self-indulgent men, he assures that forlorn waif that her marriage to him is not merely a temporary arrangement of convenience, terminable, according to Japanese law, by the mere act of desertion, but is a binding, permanent one, according to American custom and law and that she is, in fact, *Mrs. B. F. Pinkerton*. Having led her to believe this, the amiable *Pinkerton* presently departs upon his ship, after making *Butterfly* a present of money, informing her that he has "had a very nice time" and assuring her that he will come back "when the robins nest again." The girl, confidently awaiting the return of her lover, whom she declares and believes to be her lawful husband, after a little time becomes a mother by him. Two years pass—during which she refuses many suitors—and the money given her by *Pinkerton* has been all but exhausted: *Butterfly* is confronted by the alternative of beggary or starvation, yet she contemptuously rejects all proffers of rich alliances, serenely trusting in the faith of *Pinkerton*. Then, at last, he comes back, and she is apprised that though for two weeks after leaving her he was "dotty in love with her" he recovered from his sublime passion and that he has married another woman (who magnanimously offers to take away her child and rear it!)—whereupon *Madame Butterfly* kills herself.

The play is a situation, and, though some of its detail is trivial, it reveals elemental extremes and contrasts of much human experience; in its essential passages it possesses the cardinal merits of simplicity and directness, and in representation its effect is tragic and afflictingly pathetic. One feature of its performance, devised by Belasco, was, in respect to execution, unique,—namely, the intercalation whereby the two scenes of the tragedy are connected. When, at evening, the forlorn *Butterfly*,—after *two* years "jus' waitin'—sometimes cryin'—sometimes watchin'—but always waitin'!"—sees the warship to which *Pinkerton* is attached entering the harbor of Higashi she believes that her "husband" will immediately repair to their abode and she becomes almost delirious with joy. She prepares for his reception, attiring herself and their little child in fine array and decking the house with flowers and lighted lanterns. Then, with the child and a servant maid, she takes station at a window, to give him welcome—and there she waits and watches through the night, until the morning breaks. The lapse of time was, in the performance, skilfully and impressively denoted,—the shades of evening darkening into night; stars becoming visible, then brilliant, then fading from view; the lighted lanterns one by one flickering out; the gray light of dawn revealing the servant and the child prone upon the floor sunk in slumber, with the deserted mother standing over them, pale and wan, still gazing fixedly down the vacant road, while the rosy glow of sunrise grew into the full light of day and the sweet sound of the waking songs of birds floated in from a flowering grove of cherry trees. In the representation this scene, during which no word was spoken and no motion made, occupied *fourteen minutes*—and surely no tribute to Belasco's resource and skill in stage management and stage mechanics could be more significant than the fact that during all that time never did the interest of his audiences waver nor their attention flag.

At the end, when *Butterfly* knows her lover faithless and her life ruined and desolate, she takes her father's sword,—on which is graven his dying monition, "To *die* with honor, when we can no longer *live* with honor,"—and with it deals herself a mortal stroke. This desperate deed is done out of the audience's sight and as, with ghastly face and a scarf wound round her throat to hide the wound, she staggers forward to clasp her child to her breast, *Pinkerton* enters the room and *Butterfly*, holding the child in her arms, sinks at his feet, turning on him a look of anguish as she murmurs "Too bad—those robin' —never nes'—again!"—and so dies.

"Madame Butterfly" was first presented at the Herald Square Theatre, March 5, 1900. The scenic habiliment in which Belasco attired that tragedy was one of great beauty and perfect taste and it had never been equalled by anything rightly comparable, excepting Augustin Daly's exquisite setting of "Heart of Ruby" (a play on a Japanese theme adapted by Justin Huntly McCarthy from Mme.

Judith Gautier's "La Marchande de Sourires"), produced at Daly's Theatre, January 15, 1895,—which was a complete failure: it cost Daly about $25,000 and it was withdrawn after seven performances. Belasco's Japanese venture, happily, was fortunate from the first, creating a profound impression and achieving instant success. A notably effective scenic innovation was the precedent use of "picture drops," delicately painted and very lovely pictures showing various aspects of Japan,—a rice field, a flower garden, a distant prospect of a snow-capped volcano in the light of the setting sun, and other views,— by way of creating a Japanese atmosphere before the scene of the drama was disclosed. Blanche Bates embodied the hapless *Butterfly* and animated the character with a winning show of woman's fidelity, with a lovely artlessness of manner and speech, and with occasional flashes of that vivid emotional fire which was her supreme attribute. Her personation at first caused laughter and at last touched the source of tears,—but the predominant figure in the history of this play, both at the first and now, was and is that of Belasco: more, perhaps, in respect to "Madame Butterfly" than of any other of his productions it may properly be said that his personality seemed to have permeated every detail of this performance and its environment. This was the original cast:

Cho-Cho-San (*Madame Butterfly*)	Blanche Bates.
Suzuki, her servant	Marie Bates.
Mr. Sharpless, American Consul	Claude Gillingwater.
Lieutenant B. F. Pinkerton	Frank Worthing.
Yamadori	Albert Bruning.
Nakodo	E. P. Wilks.
Kate, Mrs. Pinkerton	Katherine Black.
Trouble, the child	Kittie _______.
Attendant	William Lamp.
Attendant	Westropp Saunders.

2.2 EXTRACTS FROM *MADAME BUTTERFLY*: THE STORY—ARTHUR GROOS

TWO LITERARY REPRESENTATIONS OF JAPAN dominated the popular Western reception of oriental culture at the turn of the century: Pierre Loti's novel *Madame Chrysanthème* (1887),[1] and John Luther Long's short story (1898)[2] and ensuing play of 'Madame Butterfly' written with David Belasco (1900), which became the source for Puccini's opera. It is well established that Loti's novel is autobiographical and expanded from a diary,[3] but information about the origins of John Luther Long's story has been scanty and frequently garbled.[4] Although Long's text is often denigrated as an imitation of *Madame Chrysanthème*,[5] its origin is different: 'Madame Butterfly' is based on a real-life incident reported to Long by his sister, Sarah Jane (Jennie), a teacher and the wife of Irvin Correll, a Methodist Episcopal missionary in Japan.

In March and April 1931, two years before her death, Jennie Correll gave a series of talks and interviews in Japan and China; in September of that year she published a written version of these talks intended to reveal the 'long secret' of Madame Butterfly.[6] Implausible as it may seem, this reminiscence by the principal eyewitness to the tragedy celebrated in her brother's short story and play, and then in Puccini's opera, has escaped notice. To be sure, we will never have the 'real story' from first-person accounts by 'Chô-Chô-San' or 'Pinkerton' (accounts that would, one assumes, disagree radically). Nor will we ever grasp that 'story' except from a distance, through the words of others – words, moreover, that range from fact, to fiction based on fact, to reminiscences recorded long after the fact. But the attempt may prove interesting in its own right, revealing much about the event and its historical context as well as the forms of cultural discourse in which it is inscribed.

Jennie Correll's reminiscence exists in two versions: a transcription of a talk given to the Pan-Pacific Club in Tokyo on 13 March 1931, and a more polished revision printed six months later in *The Japan Magazine*. I will quote from the later text, adding the oral transcription in footnotes where the versions diverge. This is the setting of the story as recalled almost forty years later:

> We had a mission house beautifully situated on Higashi-yama, from which one had a wonderful view over what is perhaps the most beautiful harbour in the world . . . At night we were often disturbed in our sleep by the thunder of the ships paddling their way into port. As there were many foreign vessels in the harbour, and no proper place for the seamen to go in the evenings or in off-time, we often had them up to our bungalow; and the afternoons frequently saw our veranda full of wardroom officers having tea with us.[7]
>
> (May 1931, p. 13 (section 2, p. 1) and p. 20 col. 4; Mrs. Irvin H. Correl [sic], 'Madame Butterfly: Her Long Secret Revealed', The Japan Magazine, 21 (1931), 341–5, esp. 344f.)

The Corrells lived at No. 12, Higashi-yama or East Hill, also known as Missionary Hill, owing to its cluster of missions and missionary residences. The description of the mission house, a haven or 'proper place' for seamen to be entertained for afternoon tea (a not uncommon social activity), contrasts implicitly with a host of improper places, ranging from the bars and tea houses to the brothel district of Maruyama. These had given contemporary Nagasaki, a small city with a population of some 50,000 and several hundred foreign residents, a reputation among missionaries as 'a second Corinth'.[8]

It is difficult to imagine the rough, boom-town atmosphere following the opening of the treaty ports, which yielded little in rowdiness to the Wild West.[9] And although by the 1890s the Nagasaki foreign community no longer consisted of 'the disorderly elements of Californian adventurers, Portuguese desperadoes, runaway sailors, piratical outlaws and the moral refuse of European nations',[10] the situation still shocked the missionary community that formed a major part of its permanent American residents. A contemporary estimate places the number of bars catering to foreign sailors at about thirty-six, most of them crammed along the creek that ran through the narrow foreign settlement. Men drank 'not by the glass, but by the bottle'.[11] Apart from the bars, the only diversions for sailors were gambling dens and numerous places of licensed prostitution. A crew-member of the U.S.S. *Charleston*, seemingly one of the few seamen unhappy with this situation, confirms that:

> Nagasaki is the first city I have ever visited where I could not find a place to eat and sleep and rest when coming ashore without having to do so in a saloon, a gambling den, or a house of ill repute, and that is saying a great deal, for I have spent three years in travelling in foreign lands.[12]

The beginning trickle of tourists was less interested in the sailors' bars and gambling dens, but many found the heady atmosphere of the city's other enticement less resistible. One early visitor who apparently had done some comparison shopping thought the tea-house girls in Nagasaki ' the prettiest in Japan . . . simple, modest in their demeanor, and would, if they could, be honest and faithful'.[13] Kipling evokes the temptations of an 1889 encounter with a tea-house girl named O-Toyo as a utopian Eastern alternative to normal Western existence:

> My very respectable friends at all the clubs and messes, have you ever after a good tiffin lolled on cushions and smoked, with one pretty girl to fill your pipe and four to admire you in an unknown tongue? You do not know what life is. I looked round me at that faultless room, at the dwarf pines and creamy cherry blossoms without, at O-Toyo bubbling with laughter because I blew smoke through my nose, and at the ring of *Mikado* maidens over against the golden-brown bearskin rug. Here was colour, form, food, comfort and beauty enough for half a year's contemplation . . . I would be a Japanese – always with O-Toyo of course – in a cabinet-work house on a camphor-scented hillside.[14]

One of these Japanese tea-houses employed the original Chô-Chô-San, who lived near-by on the hill opposite the Methodist Episcopal mission in which Jennie Correll settled in March 1892. It is not clear whether Correll came to know the young woman as she explored the neighbourhood after arriving, or after beginning missionary work with women from the surrounding community – an activity for which Methodist Episcopal missionaries were much admired.[15] In any event, Jennie Correll's recollection invokes the experience of a group:

> On the hill opposite ours lived a little tea-house girl; her name was Chô-san, Miss Butterfly. She was so sweet and delicate that everyone was in love with her. In time we learned that she had a lover. That was not so strange, for all tea-house girls have lovers, if they can get and hold them. Chô-san's young man was quite nice, but very temperamental, of a moody, lonely disposition.
>
> One evening there was quite a sensation when it was learned that poor little Chô-san, and her baby, had been deserted. The man had promised to return at a certain time; had even arranged a signal so that Chô-san would know when his ship had come in; but the little girl-wife awaited that signal in vain. Many an hour and many a long night did she peer from her *shoji* over the lovely harbour, but to no purpose: he never returned.[16]

[. . .]

The reminiscence itself is surprisingly tolerant, expressing compassion for the moral conditions of Japanese life, and for the social and economic circumstances that forced many young women into tea houses and brothels. Although the account of Chô-san involves her lover only parenthetically, the brief aside also presents, compared with literary adaptations of the story, a sanguine image of the young man who subsequently became known as Lieutenant Benjamin Franklin Pinkerton. Most importantly, the denouement of the real-life drama differs from its literary and operatic representations: 'Pinkerton' did not return with his wife to claim the baby, and there is no mention of a suicide.[17]

[. . .]

In fact, John Luther Long's story of 'Madame Butterfly' reports that Chô-san had gone to the mission:

> she went secretly to the church of the missionary who served on the opposite hill . . . and learned, moreover, that she might adopt this new religion at any time she chose – even the eleventh hour.
>
> (p. 8)

Whether she was subsequently rescued 'at the eleventh hour' is equally uncertain; Long's story suggests that her attempted suicide represents a deliberate choice:

> She had not forgotten the missionary's religion; but on the dark road from death to Meido it seemed best to trust herself to the compassionate augustness.
>
> (p. 84)

[. . .]

Jennie Correll's reminiscence of the 'little girl-wife' Chô-san and her 'temperamental lover' almost certainly alludes to the widespread institution known as 'temporary' or 'Japanese' marriage. Desired by Western males living for extended periods in the Orient, and made possible by a conception of sexual relations different from that in the West, temporary marriages existed for centuries for Dutch and Chinese residents of Nagasaki, the only port to retain limited contact with the West after the closing of Japan. The practice spread rapidly after the opening of the treaty ports in 1858.[18] Clara Whitney, a young woman who moved to Japan with her family in 1875, observed succinctly:

> Young men here are wicked and depraved and insult the gentle Japanese as often as they can. Merchants – married men – keep native women in their houses as wives without marriage. Sailors are even worse still, and it is pitiful to see the poor little half-caste children running around uncared for, as the Japanese regard them as unclean and their fathers don't care.[19]

Located somewhere between prostitution and concubinage, the custom she alludes to might be called term marriage or 'marriage-by-the-month' – a liaison of specified or renewable duration entered into by contractual agreement of both parties. In Yokohama, this arrangement could be made with an official at the customs house; in Nagasaki it was done with the help of an intermediary. The interchangeability of both procedures is expressed by a series of etymological transformations: the *Gankiro* or prostitute quarter in Yokohama was known by a variety of

Western bowdlerisations, including the *Kangaroo*, which provided the name for Loti's matchmaker in Nagasaki, Mr. *Kangourou* (his real name was Sejiu), the model for Long's and then Puccini's *Goro*.[20]

The development of the institution, which was the focus of intense controversy, defended by believers in natural, prelapsarian Japanese virtue and condemned by Victorian moralists and missionaries,[21] can be illustrated by two descriptions written a quarter-century apart. In 1867, at the request of the British Foreign Office, Dr. William Willis made a detailed report on prostitution in Japan:

> At the open ports, especially Yokohama, a foreigner has to pay more than an ordinary Japanese. At one time the licence for keeping a prostitute as mistress at Yokohama reached 24 bu or about 32s. a month. This sum was paid to the brothel authorities of the place. The entire amount paid for a month's service by a foreigner at Yokohama amounted from twenty-five to thirty dollars a month. The established charge is higher at Yokohama than at Nagasaki. It is computed that there are about one thousand prostitutes at Yokohama, of which number between two and three hundred are employed as mistresses of foreigners, with an average wage, at the present time, of fifteen to twenty dollars a month each.[22]

While Dr. Willis attempted to distinguish between the socially acceptable custom among Japanese of keeping mistresses and the Western practice of hiring prostitutes from brothels, this distinction seems to have been partly obliterated within a few decades. The Japanese term '*rashamen*', which originally referred to a licensed prostitute hired out to foreigners, gradually came to include non-professionals as well, ranging from mistresses and concubines to live-in waitress-prostitutes or *shakufu*,[23] the most likely designation of Kipling's O-Toyo and the original Butterfly, Jennie Correll's 'little tea-house girl'. According to one English observer the practice was tolerated as a form of marriage by 1892, albeit one with the potential for tragedy:

> Every foreigner engaged in commercial pursuits is expected, if he has no family at home, to take a Japanese wife. I say 'wife' because, as in the State of New York, no religious ceremony is necessary to make the relation quite legal, according to Japanese law. But supposing the merchant retires from business? Then he 'divorces' his wife; provides for her future, and that of her children, if she has any; and sails away to European respectability. Sometimes he departs without making any provision for his offspring, and leaving their mother to poverty.[24]

As these comments make clear, the practice tended to resemble common-law marriage, although the term used by Loti, 'morganatic marriage', is more precise. The Japanese 'wife' remained without legal rights to alimony, property, inheritances or children.[25] As John Luther Long's Goro pointedly remarks to Chô-Chô-San, if Pinkerton 'returns he will probably take the child away with him – that is his right' (p. 35).

Participation in 'Japanese marriages' by naval officers resembles the development among merchants outlined above, though the relationship was necessarily made more tenuous by the extreme variability of a stay in port, which could range from a few days, weeks or months to several years in the case of officers stationed at the Russian naval base in Nagasaki. Liaisons between United

States Naval officers and *rashamen* will undoubtedly have been of shorter duration and less formal, owing to the greater uncertainty of postings. Samuel Pellman Boyer, a surgeon attached to the *Iroquois* in 1868–9, describes the practice in his diary shortly after arriving in Yokohama:

> Let us suppose a case. I am a young bachelor doing business in the place and wish a 'moosmie', as the young ladies are called. All I need do is call on the young lady and hand her $4, with which she buys a license from the Japanese customs house which entitles her to be my mistress for one month and a daily bath in the public bathhouse. I now have the right to have connection with the young lady. If she suits me, I tell her I will be her master. I then pay her from $15 to 25 per month and hire a room and servant for her, which costs $10 per month. Thus at an expense of $39 I can enjoy all the comforts of a married man. 'Will she be true to me?' some might say. As a general thing they are true as long as you treat them decently. 'Why don't they allow everyone that offers them money to have connections with them since they do it only for money in your case and not for love?' I hire her by the month. She is certain of $25 a month and a servant at her command, running no risk of becoming diseased so long as she is true. Thus ere long she can raise enough money to get married with.[26]

Although Boyer apparently did not try the custom that aroused his curiosity, he was familiar with it professionally, paying house calls on the 'moosmies' of fellow officers.[27]

[. . .]

The picture that emerges from such descriptions of 'Japanese marriage' does not diverge significantly from that in 'Madame Butterfly' and – by extension – Puccini's opera. The realisation of a wide-spread *fin-de-siècle* male fantasy, it is set in a beautiful retreat in an exotic landscape: Loti's '*maisonnette au milieu des fleurs*';[28] Kipling's 'cabinet-work house on a camphor-scented hillside'; Grand Duke Alexander's 'miniature houses, small gardens full of dwarf trees, tiny streams, cardboard bridges and Lilliputian flowers'; Long's 'little house on Higashi-yama' and Puccini's '*casetta*' in the '*fiorito asil*'. The pervasive diminutives not only convey a typical Western response to Japanese space, but also 'belittle' and thereby domesticate the exotic. In practice, this process extended to the relationship itself, which parodied and sometimes even approximated marriage, ranging from mock wedding ceremonies, which observers criticised decades before Sharpless warns Pinkerton of the '*pseudo sposalizio*' (pseudo-wedding),[29] to the designation of the *rashamen* as a 'little wife' and termination of the monthly relationship as 'divorce'. The real basis of this parodic marriage, however, was the rental contract for the house and servant, and the commercial sexual agreement they accommodated, which conflated a mercantile code of behaviour with the marital one. Western males often thought of their temporary 'wives' as involved only for financial gain, and – in a typical gesture of colonialist thinking – attributed their own lack of responsibility to the foreign custom of 'Japanese marriage'.

[. . .]

Given the extensive similarities between the late nineteenth-century practice of temporary 'marriages' and the operatic representation of Chô-Chô-San and Pinkerton, the reaction of Grand Duke Alexander, who both experienced a 'Japanese marriage' in Nagasaki and saw Puccini's opera, comes as something of a shock. Strangely enough, the Grand Duke, unfamiliar with the historical origins of *Madama Butterfly*, rejected the opera as laughably distant from reality:

> The heartbreak of Madame Butterfly brought a gale of laughter in the Empire of the Rising Sun because none of the wearers of the flowered kimonos were silly enough to expect to remain forever with their foreign 'husbands'. The usual 'marital contract' called for a period of from one to three years, depending on the length of the stay of a cruising man-of-war in the harbor of Nagasaki. At the end of that time another officer came along, or if the first one was sufficiently generous, the 'wife' saved enough money to obtain a place in the community.[30]

Far from characterising the actual reception of *Madama Butterfly* in Japan,[31] the 'gale of laughter' he imagines seems rather to be his own defence mechanism. The colonialist and chauvinist response to a 'silly wearer of a flowered kimono' may derive from a self-serving desire to defend his own behaviour in the identical situation with a clear-cut code of conduct and a belief in the Westerner's contribution to the 'wife's' well-being. Indeed, frequent references to providing for the financial future of the Japanese partner or to her eventual marriage suggest that escape from treaty-port servitude was at least possible, an escape emphasised in the Madame Butterfly story by the figure of Yamadori. Yet Grand Duke Alexander's outrage also hints at another facet of the story: the fact that, contrary to well-established norms of behaviour, the relationship between 'Pinkerton' and O-Chô did not run the smooth course expected of a temporary 'Japanese marriage'.

Indeed, the historical tragedy on which *Madama Butterfly* is based does not have to be attributed to the 'silliness' of the heroine, as the Grand Duke assumed, even though it may be impossible to decide between a number of possible scenarios. As far as the behaviour of 'Pinkerton' is concerned, the representations of Jennie Correll and John Luther Long differ markedly. The oral transcription and printed version of Jennie Correll's reminiscence present slight but significant variations. In the former, O-Chô's lover is 'a nice young fellow, but horribly lonely' – a basically good young person made vulnerable to a tragic relationship by circumstance. In the latter, he is 'quite nice, but very temperamental, of a moody, lonely disposition' – the 'quite' partly retracting the positive evaluation and shifting his unpredictable behaviour from the situation to his character ('lonely disposition'). In both versions, the abandonment of Butterfly remains unmotivated. The reminiscence matter-of-factly states that 'the man promised to return at a certain time, had even arranged a signal' but 'never returned' – a statement that could be interpreted in terms of deception ('the man' rather than 'the young man'), an uncertain commitment, or even circumstances beyond a junior officer's control.[32]

John Luther Long's short story generally seems to admit no such uncertainty, turning this ambiguous figure into a savage portrayal of colonialist and chauvinist self-interest. Pinkerton's manipulative 'joking' with the trusting Butterfly, which the consul straightforwardly calls 'deception', takes 'this dainty, vivid, eager, formless material, and molds it to his most wantonly whimsical wish' (p. 59), inexorably alienating her from her own culture and leaving her no choice but death: 'He had come, and substituted himself for everything; he had gone, and left her nothing' (p. 85). And yet, when Sharpless attempts to explain the motivations of the departed Pinkerton, his ruminations lead him to the possibility of an emotional commitment of sorts:

> Unless Pinkerton had changed, he had probably not thought of her again – except as the prompt wife of another man. He never explained anything. It was his theory that circumstances always did this for one; it was therefore a saving of energy to permit circumstances to do it. There was a saying in the navy that if any one could forget a played game or a spent bottle more quickly than Pinkerton, he had not yet been born. Providing her with a house and money meant nothing. . . . But, on the other hand, if she had been one of the sudden and insane fancies that occasionally visited him, the case was altogether different, and altogether like Pinkerton; for in case of an attractive woman the emotion might survive the absence in question. (p. 63)

It is difficult to say whether the consul's theory of Pinkerton's 'sudden and insane fancy' corresponds to Jennie Correll's 'very temperamental' and 'moody' officer.

More importantly, however, we know almost nothing about the original Butterfly, the 'little tea-house girl' named O-Chô, 'the little girl-wife' who peered in vain 'many an hour and many a long night from her *shoji* over the lovely harbour'. It seems nearly impossible to get beyond the well-meaning but colonial stereotype in Jennie Correll's characterisation ('so sweet and delicate that everyone was in love with her') and the racial one in John Luther Long's portrayal of laughing inscrutability. It is a sad fact that sources for women's history are so scanty, often extracted only between the lines of male history, and this is especially true for the exploitative system of Western male privilege that dominated the lives of Japanese women in the treaty ports.

[. . .]

If information does turn up, specialists in Japanese history might wish to see to what extent John Luther Long's 'true to the life' story elaborates the basic event related by Jennie Correll's reminiscence. Certainly the details of his narrative are plausible: according to it, Butterfly's father died in the Satsuma rebellion (1877), and she was seventeen the year after her 'marriage' – which yields a *terminus ante quem* of 1894. The names of those who died in the Satsuma rebellion are known and might be correlated with the craftsman who made her father's sword, 'Ikesada'. The upper-class, samurai background would also explain O-Chô's unfamiliarity with the rules of the game derided by Grand Duke Alexander, and perhaps even the 'silly' desire for a better relationship.

Beyond the story's scattered references to her occupations on the margins of poverty, dancing and singing, followed by a reluctant, economically necessitated and then overly trusting temporary marriage with an American naval officer, there hovers over us the question of O-Chô's fate. Jennie Correll's reminiscence merely says that the 'little girl-wife' waited 'many an hour and many a long night' to no avail; John Luther Long's story adds an unsuccessful suicide attempt. The often fugitive nature of early conversions makes it unlikely that O-Chô will appear among the few surviving Methodist Episcopal documents and photographs from Nagasaki, and one is reluctant to trust the several reports of her survival traceable to the notorious publicity-hound and soprano, Tamaki Miura.[33]

We may in fact never know any more about the historical O-Chô than what Jennie Correll tells us. To be sure, the real Madame Butterfly remains mute, like the imaginary 'sister' in *Twelfth Night*, about whose history Viola responds that it is 'A blank, my lord. She never told her love.' But Chô-san's history is not a blank, thanks to a missionary's sisterly commiseration. The tragic 'little sensation' recalled by Jennie Correll, elaborated by John Luther Long and popularised by Puccini, continues to move and puzzle us nearly a century later, exemplifying the difficulty of love between human beings of different cultures, races and nationalities, as well as the incalculable potential of a trusting heart.

Notes

1. Loti, Pierre, *Madame Chrysanthème* (Paris, 1895).
2. John Luther Long, 'Madame Butterfly'. *Century Illustrated Magazine* (1881–1906), January 1898, Vol. LV(3), p. 374.
3. Suetoshi Funaoka, *Le Journal du Japon de Loti – Sa vie étrange avec Madame Chrysanthème* (Yokohama: Yûrindô, 1979) [in Japanese]; Suetoshi Funaoka, *Pierre Loti et l'Extrême-Orient – Du Journal a l'œuvre* (Tokyo: Librarie-Editions France-Tosho, 1988).
4. The fact that Thomas Glover's mansion has survived has helped make it the 'Madame Butterfly House' of touristic and cinematographic fame. But the association between Glover (1838–1911) and Tsuru Yamamura (1851–99) is implausible (there is no naval officer, no desertion, and no attempted suicide – Tsuru died following surgery in Tokyo), a sham maintained by popular magazines and tourist brochures. See, for example, Duiti Miyasawa, 'The Original Cio-cio-san', *Opera News*, 17 (January 1953), 2–5; '*La vera Ciocio-san*', *Musica d'oggi*, NS 2 (1959), 2–3; Roderick Cameron, 'The Real Madame Butterfly', *Musical America*, 82 (November 1962), 10–11, 46. Edith Correll Spindle, a daughter of Jennie Correll, who had known the Glovers and studied the opera at the New England Conservatory of Music, was outraged over Miyasawa's speculation. *Opera News* did not print her letter of protest.
5. While Long does seem to have constructed a subversive, anticolonialist relationship with *Madame Chrysanthème*, the real use of Loti's novel begins with Puccini's librettists. See my 'Lieutenant F. B. Pinkerton: Problems in the Genesis of an Operatic Hero', *Italica*, 64 (1987), 654–75 (a revised and expanded version will appear in *The Puccini Companion*, ed. Simonetta Puccini and William Weaver); and 'Illica's *Butterfly*: The First Version of Act I', to appear in *I libretti di Puccini e la letteratura del suo tempo*, ed. Jürgen Maehder (Frankfurt: Peter Lang, 1992).
6. Mosco Carner, *Puccini: A Critical Biography*, 2nd ed. (London, 1974), 125, identifies her as Mrs Irwin Correl [*sic*]. On Irvin Correll, see the biographical sketch in *The Gospel in All Lands*, 23 (October 1897), 465–6, and the *New York Times* obituary, 18 June 1926, p. 23, col. 5; on Jennie Correll, see the *New York Times* obituary of 10 November 1933, p. 21, col. 3.
7. *The Japan Times*, 15 March 1931, gives a transcription of 'Mrs. Correll's talk in full' as delivered to the Pan-Pacific Club on p. 1, col. 6 and p. 8, col. 4; *The China Press*, 2.
8. Pan-Pacific Club transcription:

   > We lived in a big bungalow, but at a very small cost, so there was no missionary extravagance about it. It had a very wide veranda. Now in Nagasaki there were no places for men to go except the saloons, and you know what happens in saloons. There was one very nice hotel called Bellevue, nearly always crowded, and it was not a nice place to live at all, so we made it a point to invite the officers, the wardroom men and the junior messes to come up and enjoy our place, because there was a magnificent view of the bay and it was really charming. They did so, and whether we were there or not they came. Very often in the afternoon we would sit and have tea with them, very often when we came home we found the porch full. Of course, there were never the juniors and the seniors at the same time. But there were young ladies in the family, and that made up for what the juniors could not get during the day.

9. H. B. Johnson, 'Nagasaki and its Missions', *The Gospel in All Lands*, 23 (1897), 61.
10. See Harold S. Williams, 'Nagasaki Days', in *Tales of the Foreign Settlements in Japan* (Tokyo and Rutland, Vt., 1958), 27–36.
11. George Smith, Bishop of Victoria, *Ten Weeks in Japan* (London, 1861), 263.
12. Correspondence of Albertus Pieters to John H. Karsten, Western Theological Seminary Collection, Joint Archives of Holland, Holland, Mich., W88–060, letter of 20 November 1895, p. 4.
13. Earle D. Sims to 'a lady missionary here' (probably Elizabeth Russell), quoted in a letter of 12 January 1895 by Albertus Pieters to John H. Karsten, p. 14.
14. Rudyard Kipling, From Sea to Sea and Other Sketches: Letters of Travel, 2 vols. (London, 1900), I, 312–327, here p. 326f.
15. Henry Arthur Tilley, *Japan, the Amoor, and the Pacific* (London, 1861), 66f.
16. Rudyard Kipling, *From Sea to Sea and Other Sketches: Letters of Travel*, 2 vols. (London, 1900), I, 312–27, here p. 326f.

17. Pieters to Karsten (see n. 11), 12 January 1895, p. 9. On women's missionary work in Nagasaki, see the *Heathen Woman's Friend*, 13 (1881), 86f. and 134f.; 15 (1883), 25f. and 28f.; 18 (1887), 314f.
18. Pan-Pacific Club transcription (see n. 6):

    Now on the other hill was a dear little teahouse girl living, as pretty as a picture, and her name was Chô-san. No one ever [word missing] anything against her, and she was sweet and pretty and everyone liked her. But after a while we learned she had a lover. They all have lovers I guess if they can get them. The young man was a nice young fellow, but horribly lonely. . . . But one evening there was quite a little sensation. It was that Chô-san and her baby had been deserted. Poor little Chô-san. When he left her he made promises that he would return soon, and there was a signal to be given when his ship came, so she waited and broke her little shoji open to look out, but never a sign.

19. In an interview in the *fiji Shimpo* of 24 December 1935, Tamaki Miura reported that John Luther Long told her that the original Chô-Chô-San survived the suicide attempt, an assertion that is also consistent with the ending of his story 'Madame Butterfly'. The suicide seems to be a creation of the ensuing play and opera.
20. On prostitution in Nagasaki, see K. Motoyama, *Nagasaki Hanamachihen* (Tokyo, 1937). In a diary kept during the Perry Expedition, George H. Preble noted on 24 February 1854 that Japanese officials told the officers 'that when the Treaty was signed we could have plenty of Japanese wives'. *The Opening of Japan: A Diary of Discovery in the Far East 1853–56*, ed. Boleslaw Szczesniak (Norman, Ok., 1962), 123f.
21. *Clara's Diary: An American Girl in Meiji Japan*, eds M. William Steele and Tamiko Ichimata (Tokyo, New York, San Francisco, 1979), 38.
22. See Elinor Barnes and James A. Barnes, eds, *The Diary of Dr. Samuel Pellman Boyer. Naval Surgeon: Revolt in Japan* (Bloomington, Ind., 1963), 30; on Kangourou, see Funaoka, *Pierre Loti* (n. 2), 12.58
23. For a recent survey of early prelapsarian interpretations of Japan, see Toshio Yokoyama, *Japan in the Victorian Mind* (London, 1987); for moral outrage, e.g., Margaretha Weppner, *The North Star and the Southern Cross*, 3rd ed. (Albany, 1880), I, 192–5; Flora Best Harris, 'A Way to Help the Women of Japan', *Heathen Woman's Friend*, 18 (1887), 232–3. A general overview is provided by Jean-Pierre Lehmann, 'The Women of Japan – In Reality and Fantasy', in *The Image of Japan: From Feudal Isolation to World Power* (London, 1978), 68–96.
24. Hugh Cortazzi, *Dr Willis in Japan 1862–1874: British Medical Pioneer* (London, 1985), 55, 238f. The custom seems to have been widespread, except among missionaries or those who had brought families: a Japanese directory of foreign residents of Yokohama in 1861–2 documents the presence of a *musume* or young Japanese woman in 30 of 79 households. Harold S. Williams, 'Yokohama Musume', in *Foreigners in Mikado-land* (Tokyo and Rutland, Vt., 1963), 106–10.
25. Nakano Eizo, *Kuruwa no Seikatsu* [Life at the Licensed Quarters] (Tokyo: Yukaku-sha, 1972), 167f.; Nakayama Taro, *Baishô Sanzennen-Shi* [Three-Thousand-Year History of Prostitution] (Tokyo: Yôshundô, 1927), 625–7; Adachi Sunao, *Yûjo Fûzokusugata Saiken* [A Close Survey of the Customs and Manners of Prostitutes] (Tokyo: Tenbosha, 1976), 315.
26. Albert Tracy, *Rambles through Japan without a Guide* (London, 1892), 8–9.
27. Diplomatic dispatches of the period from the United States Consulate at Nagasaki discuss the wills of citizens who had died and left bequests to Japanese mistresses or common-law wives. In some cases, an attempt was made first to find relatives in the United States before carrying out the will.
28. *Madame Chrysanthème* (Paris, 1907), 262 (ch. 50).
29. C. Pemberton Hodgson, *A Residence at Nagasaki and Hakodate in 1859–1860* (London, 1860), 250f.
30. Alexander, Grand Duke of Russia, once a Grand Duke (New York, 1932).
31. See my 'Return of the Native: Japan in *Madama Butterfly* / *Madama Butterfly* in Japan', *Cambridge Opera Journal*, 1 (1989), 167–94.
32. Extensive institutional changes in the Navy may have prevented his return – the departure and retirement of outmoded ships from the Asiatic station, which were only gradually replaced by new steel vessels. Moreover, revolutions in Hawaii and then in Korea claimed the attention of the United States naval vessels still in the Pacific, leaving Japanese waters frequently unattended. See Robert Erwin Johnson, *Far China Station: The U.S. Navy in Asian Waters 1800–1898* (Annapolis, 1979), 240f.
33. See Homer L. Calkin, *Catalog of Methodist Archival and Manuscript Collections: II (Asia)* (World Methodist Historical Society, 1982), nos. JA–15 (the most likely source for a photograph of Chô-san), 30 and 153. On Tamaki Miura, see n. 17 and the news dispatch from Turin reported in the *Philadelphia Public Leger* (15 October 1923) reporting the discovery of Butterfly, feeble and impoverished, on the island of Kiousein.

2.3 MARKING TIME IN TOKIO—RICHARD HARDING DAVIS

TOKIO, *April 25, 1904*

WE PAID OUR FIRST VISIT to the tea house of the Hundred and One Steps even before we had registered at the hotel. We had been in Japan no longer than it takes the rikisha boy to run up the Bund from the Custom House to the Grand Hotel. On the steps the Sailor Man, Manila-bound to take over a battleship, ordered us back into the rikisha and set our course for the tea house. It was just before luncheon, and seemed a difficult moment for tea. But to be vouched for at that particular tea house by an officer of our navy was a piece of luck too obvious to be neglected. It was like being introduced to "Kid" McCoy by Lionel Barrymore.

Of all the tea houses in Japan, the one best known to foreigners is the tea house of the Hundred and One Steps, at Yokohama.

It is owned by O Kin San, the sister of Tenabe, who once used to manage it, and who now keeps the silk shop on the Honchi Dori. The uncle of these equally charming sisters was one of the minor officials who received Commodore Perry. Some say he was not an official, but the head man of the village, and that he owned the house in which Perry lived during his visits ashore. In any event, the uncle once "was with Perry," once talked to Perry, after the strange American etiquette Perry had shaken hands with him, and in Japan that is enough to give distinction to any man, even to his ancestors. It also was enough to make the tea house presided over by his nieces the favorite meeting-place of the officers of our navy. When they were midshipmen they climbed the hundred steps, now that they are admirals they still climb them. Their loyalty has never slackened, and their reward is that when they visit the tea house they again grow young. There is something about the place which makes people young. It has kept Tenabe and O Kin San young for forty years. It stands on what remains of the ancestral acres, a patch of garden clinging to the edge of a cliff. The cliff overlooks Yokohama, the generous harbor, the great bay, and, when the fogs allow, the Pacific Ocean. Flat against the face of the cliff, like a sea-ladder on the side of a ship, rise the hundred and one steps. After twenty days at sea their ascent made the climbing of Pike's Peak seem less of an effort than stepping into a cab.

It is a tradition of the house that O Kin San never forgets the face of a guest, his rank, or the name of his ship, but as six years had passed since the Sailor Man had touched at Yokohama, he was afraid O Kin San might not live up to her reputation. But she did not forget him. When we stooped to enter the low veranda, we found her kneeling prostrate before the Commander, clapping her hands softly and touching the floor with her forehead. Around her little nezans in dove-colored kimonos fluttered excitedly, rubbing their knees with their open palms, giggling and gurgling and uttering soft, cooing cries of welcome. When they saw the American ladies, they in turn dropped upon their knees, and beat the mats with their hands. Had the Commander been a long-lost son and we those who had returned him from a watery grave, we could not have been received with more apparent confusion and delight. They made it seem that that house had been kept open only in the hope that he might revisit it. We tied soft slippers over our heathen boots, slid across the slippery matting, and squatted upon cushions in a little cigar-box of a room. Our coming was as though some one had flung a handful of corn into a dovecote. From each corner of the tiny house the patter of feet echoed like the scamper of mice behind a wainscot, giggles sounded from kitchen to garden, and on every side the paper screens that formed the room slid apart in unexpected places, admitted a tottering, tripping nezan with a tray, and shut again into what looked like a solid wall. They brought us tea and sake, and tiny pipes in boxes of hot ashes, strange sweet cakes, and stranger salt fish, and they served us as though never before had such a service been rendered. It was a delicious, stupendous joke, in which we all were equally guilty. That we should light a pipe and puff at it was an act the humor and novelty of which threw them into an ecstasy of laughter, that we approved of the sake shook them with shivers of delight, that we drank the tea and asked for more set them violently rocking at our condescension. When they were not beseeching us to eat and drink and clapping their hands, they were passing on their knees from one to the other of the American women, exclaiming in apparent awe and wonder over the unusual beauty of their boots. It was a pretty comedy extremely well played, and while it deceived no one, it hurt no one. It reminded you of the acting at Paquin's, when the head woman, surrounded by a sympathetic chorus of vendeuses, tells Madame that the new gown is "charmant, ravissant" At such a time the mere man feels sorry for them. He hopes that when closing hour comes they will fold away the smiles with the frocks, cease flattering and exclaiming, and become as slovenly-looking and as cross and disagreeable as they please. And so it is with the nezans, you hope when your back is turned that O Kin San and the little waitresses get up off their knees and yaws and stretch their tiny bodies, and say, "Well, thank goodness, they've gone!" and sit down to a real meal. For you can not believe that they eat seaweed and live fish, and use chopsticks, and drink tea from thimbles and sit on the floor, for any other reason than that the tourist expects them to do so. You feel they are trying to live up to the idea of the Japanese tea house, which he has acquired from "The Geisha Girl" and "Madame Chrysanthème." I had the same feeling that it wasn't quite genuine when, in Edinburgh, I first saw a man in kilts. I was sure he wore them not because they were comfortable but because it was expected of him.

But no matter how much you may doubt its sincerity whenever you visit the tea house on the cliff you will receive the same fluttered, excited welcome. There will be the same chorus of "Please, please," the same delight when you approve, the same anxiety over your lack of appetite, and the same rare appreciation of your rare wit. Also, in time you will find that O Kin San will take the cue you give her. And if you prefer to sit overlooking the city "where the paper lanterns glow," and watch the lights along the Bund and the lamps of the ships at anchor on the berth, and talk of things Japanese, and not to joke and laugh, you will find O Kin San a simple, direct, and rarely intelligent hostess. She is a truly remarkable woman, a woman who speaks five languages, who can call off all the names in our navy register, relate the history of the Ronins, explain the complexities of the Shinto and Buddhist religions, or relate with true humor the story of the middy who climbed the steps on horseback.

Among the things they laid before us during our first hour in Japan were the cards of all the officers, of their sweethearts and wives, and of the tourists who had visited the tea house. They asked for our cards, and each of the nezans gave us one of hers. The one I received read "Miss O Yucha San." I tried to recollect where I had heard the name before, and then I remembered that at college there was a song of that title which we used to sing. It was set to the air of "Rosalie":

"I care not what others may say,
I'm in love with O Yucha San,
In Japan,
Ichiban,
I'm in love with O Yucha San."

The chorus brought back to me the June evenings when the glee club would sally forth to serenade the townspeople, and we freshmen abandoned our books and followed in its wake. And, instead of the tea house of the Hundred and One Steps and O Yucha San kneeling beside me, proffering a pair of chopsticks, I was conscious of the sleeping American town. The students grouped under the elms, the odor of their brier pipes, the beetles buzzing around the electric light globes in the street, and the black shadows across the professor's front lawn.

"When I was at college," I said, "I used to sing a song about a girl called O Yucha San."

The Commander looked up in hurt surprise, and O Yucha San bent low in embarrassment.

"But you know that this is the girl!" he said.

I protested that it could not be. I gallantly refrained from explaining why.

"Not at all," said the Commander. "F. M. Bostwick, who was a lieutenant then, wrote that song about O Yucha San when she was five years old. I remember her very well. She was just a little doll of a thing. She was only big enough to carry around the pipe boxes, and after she had filled the pipes she'd crawl into the lap of one of the officers and sleep curled up there until we went back to the ship. But now she's a young lady, and there is a book about her with her picture in colors on the cover."

So I told O Yucha San that over all the States young men were announcing to the world that they were in love only with her, and that in every college town the name and fame of O Yucha San was intimate and familiar.

O Yucha San covered her blushes with two small hands, and bowed her thanks to her admirers across the sea.

On other days we returned to the tea house, and one soon grew to understand why to the wandering naval officer and the globe trotter it becomes a house of call, a club, and a home. There are many tea houses in Japan more rich, larger, set in elaborate, beautiful gardens, with golden geishas to dance and jugglers to confuse, but in none will you find a more friendly welcome or a kindlier hostess. To sit at the feet of O Kin San is to learn wisdom and courtesy, and to look out from her tea house is to bring yourself in touch with all the world. For, when the paper screens are pushed aside you see on one hand the gardens and trees of the Foreign Settlement; on the other, below you, the tile-roofed city, with its temples, parks of cherry trees, distant hills of pine, and Fujiyama, the illusive, the mysterious, the beautiful, raising snow-white shoulders out of a robe of green; while at your feet lies the roadstead of Yokohama Harbor choked with ships of war, with great liners, monster tramps, gondola-like sanpans, and high-peaked square-sailed junks. The murmurs of a city float up to you mixed with all the noises of the sea; the impatient signals of the darting launches, the puffing donkey engines answering the boatswain's whistle with creak of winch, chains, and cordage; the songs of the coolies knee-deep in the lighters, the ships' bells ringing brokenly across the water, and the melancholy piping of the harbor gulls.

Against the curtain of blue you watch the steamers come and go, carrying your heart with them to Hongkong and Shanghai, Rangoon and Singapore, to Colombo and Bombay, to Sydney and Melbourne, around Cape Horn, through the islands of the South Pacific, or straight away to that Golden Gate that waits to welcome the wanderer Home.

2.4 THE BELLE OF JAPAN—F. M. BOSTWICK

ACCORDING TO THE CORRESPONDENT of the Rochester Express the tea-houses of the seaport towns of Japan are frequented by so many English-speaking people that some of the *musmees* [waiting maids] have learned English songs for their guests. Here is one of the latest, written by an American naval officer. Set to the air of "Rosalie" and sung by the pretty object it describes. Every stanza provokes the wildest merriment in the audience. O Yucha San is the very pretty daughter of Tanabe [owner of the Hundred and One Steps in Yokohama, the best known tea house to foreigners], and it was a pleasure to watch so charming a creature:

I call her the belle of Japan,
    Of Japan;
Her name it is O Yucha San,
    Yucha San;
Such tenderness lies
In her soft almond eyes
I tell you she's just Ichi ban. [first class]

[I care not what others may say.
I am in love with you O Yucha San,
Ichi ban in Japan,
I'm in love with O Yucha San]

Artistic, indeed, is her pose,
    Her pose,
And quaint is the style of her clothes,
    Her clothes,
From the ornaments rare
In her glossy black hair
To the clogs on her dear pigeon toes.

Perhaps she's too thick at the waist,
    The waist,
You see, she has never been laced,
    Been laced.
But her figure divine
Would a Venus outshine,
And she dresses in exquisite taste.

She looks so remarkably sweet,
    So sweet.
As she waddles along through the street,
    The street,
With fan and umbrella,
Alas! for the fellah
By chance she may happen to meet.

I call on this dear little miss,
    Little miss,
She welcomes me something like this,
    Like this,
Bows down to the floor,
As I enter the door,
Then draws in her breath with a kiss.

[I try to make love but in vain.
My language, I fear, is not plain.
Whenever I try,

She says, "Gomen nasai
Watieshki wakarimasen."]

She plays on the soft samisen,
Samisen,
She sings me a song now and then,
Now and then,
And smiling will say,
As I bid her "Good day,"
"Sayonara," and "Please come again."

You may call this a Japanese craze,
A craze;
You may say a weak mind it displays,
Displays.
But go to Japan
And see O Yucha San
And you'll have it the rest of your days.

Find all the dear girls of Japan,
Japan,
Go seek them wherever you can,
You can,
Yes, search the world over,
You'll never discover
The peer of sweet O Yucha San.

2.5 WHEN THE ROBINS NEST AGAIN—J. F. MARTINDALE

I will return, he said to me,
I will come back, my love, to thee;
When nature smiles on land and sea,
I will return again to thee.
When the robins nest again.
And the flowers are in bloom,
When the Spring-time's sunny smile
Seems to banish all sorrow and gloom;
Then my bonnie blue-eyed lad.
If my heart is true 'till then.
Has promised he'll return to me
When the robins nest again.
Life seems so bright when In thought I'm with thee,
Come, love, hasten-come back to me;
We'll build our nest with the robins in Spring-Ume,
Donald! return, love, to me.

Refrain.

When the robins nest again.
And the flowers are in bloom,
When the Spring-time's sunny smile
Seems to banish all sorrow and gloom;

Then my bonnie blue-eyed lad.
If my heart is true 'till then,
Has promised he'll return to me
When the robins nest again.

Last night, in a dream,
I saw his proud ship wreck'd at sea;
And I felt that my heart's dear love
Could never come back to me.
But the Spring-time and robins will come,
And with them the bravest of men:
For his last words were: Darling, I'll meet yon
When the robins nest again.

Refrain.

2.6 THE DEATH SCENE FROM *MADAME BUTTERFLY*

"Too bad—those robins—never nes'—again!" The Death Scene, from David Belasco's 1900 production of *Madame Butterfly*, which dramatizes the U.S. colonial mindset and projected image of the Asian "Other".

2.7 *MADAME BUTTERFLY*—DAVID BELASCO

The Original Cast of Characters

Herald Square Theatre, New York, March 5, 1900.

CHO-CHO-SAN (MADAME BUTTERFLY)	Miss Blanche Bates
SUZUKI, her servant	Miss Marie Bates
MR. SHARPLESS, the American Consul	Mr. Claude Gillingwater
LIEUTENANT B. F. PINKERTON, of the war ship *Connecticut*	Mr. Frank Worthing
YAMADORI, a citizen of New York	Mr. Albert Bruning
THE NAKODO, a marriage broker	Mr. E. P. Wilks
KATE, PINKERTON'S wife	Miss Katherine Black
"TROUBLE"	Little Kittie
ATTENDANT	Mr. William Lamp
ATTENDANT	Mr. Westropp Saunders

NOTE: During the scene in which MADAME BUTTERFLY waits at the shoji for her lover, a night is supposed to pass and the story is resumed on the morning of the following day.

Madame Butterfly

The play takes place in Japan in MADAME BUTTERFLY'S *little house at the foot of Higashi Hill, facing the harbor. Every-thing in the room is Javanese save the American locks and bolts on the doors and windows and an American flag fastened to a tobacco jar. Cherry blossoms are abloom outside, and inside. A sword rack, a shrine on which lie a sword and a pair of men's slippers, a chest of drawers on top of which is a tray containing two red poppies, rouge, powder and hair ornaments, a stand for the tobacco jar and tea, are the only pieces of furniture in the room. As the curtain rises,* MADAME BUTTERFLY *is spraying the growing flowers with a small watering pot. She snips off two little bunches, lays them on a plate of rice which she sets reverently on the shrine, then kneels, putting her hands on the floor, her forehead on them.*

MADAME BUTTERFLY. Oh, Shaka! Hail! Hail! Also perceive! Look down! I have brought a sacrifice of flowers and new rice. Also, I am quite clean. I am shivering with cleanness. Therefore grant that Lef-ten-ant B. F. Pik-ker-ton may come back soon.

(*She rises, clasps her hands, comes down to a floor cushion, and sits, fanning herself.*)

SUZUKI. (*Entering with a low bow.*) Madame Butterfly's wish?

MADAME BUTTERFLY. Suzuki, inform me, if it please you, how much more nearer beggary we are today than yesterday?

SUZUKI. Aye. (*She takes some coins from a small box in her sleeve, and lays them in three piles on her palm, touching them as she speaks.*) Rin, yen, sen. . . .

MADAME BUTTERFLY. (*Reprovingly.*) Suzuki, how many time I tellin' you—no one shall speak anythin' but those Unite' State' languages in these Lef-ten-ant Pik-ker-ton's house? (*She pronounces his name with much difficulty.*) Once more—an' I put you outside shoji! . . . That's one thin' aeverbody got recomlec' account it's 'Merican house—his wife, his maid.

SUZUKI. (*Mouthing to herself, making no sound, counting on her fingers.*) Two dollar.

(*She drops the money into the box, giving it to* MADAME BUTTERFLY.)

MADAME BUTTERFLY. O, how we waste my husban's be-autiful moaneys! Tha's shame! Mos' gone.

SUZUKI. This moaney hav' kep' us two year . . . Wha's happen to us now, if he don' come back?

MADAME BUTTERFLY. (*Scoffing, putting the money in her sleeve.*) O, if he don' come back! . . . Course he come, back! He's gone so long accoun' he's got business in those his large country. If he 's not come back to his house, why he sign Japanese lease for nine hundred and ninety nine year for me to live? Why he put 'Merican lock to bolt it door, to shut it window? Answer me those question.

SUZUKI (*Doubtfully.*) I dunno.

MADAME BUTTERFLY. Of course you dunno! You don' know whichaever. Wael I goin' tell you: to keep out those which are out, and in, those which are in. Tha's me.

(*She rises, goes to the window and looks out.*)

SUZUKI. But he don't writin' no ledder.

MADAME BUTTERFLY. 'Merican men don' naever write ledder—no time.

SUZUKI. (*Cynically.*) Aye . . . I don' naever know 'Merica navy man with Japanese wive come back.

MADAME BUTTERFLY. (*Impassively, her eyes narrowing.*) Speak concerning marriage once more, you die! (*She fans herself.* SUZUKI *salaams and backs quickly towards the door.* MADAME BUTTERFLY *claps her hands and* SUZUKI *pauses.*) Don' come back! Lef-ten-ant B. F. Pik-kerton don' come back! Ha! Me! I know w'en he comes back—he told me. W'en he goin' 'way, he say in tha's doors: "Madame Butterfly, I have had ver' nice times with my Japanese sweets heart, so now I goin' back to my own country and here's moaney—an' don' worry 'bout me—I come back w'en 'Robins nes' again!'" Ha-ha! Tha's w'en he come back—w'en robins nes' again.

(*She sways her head triumphantly from side to side, fanning herself.*)

SUZUKI. (*Not impressed.*) Yaes, I didn't like ways he said it—like those . . . (*She imitates a flippant gesture of farewell.*)

MADAME BUTTERFLY. (*Laughing.*) Aha, that's 'Merican way sayin' good-bye to girl. Yaes, he come back w'en robins nes' again. Shu'h! Shu'h! (*She claps her hands with delight.* SUZUKI, *with a look of unbelief starts to go.*) Sa-ey! Why no "shu'h" on you face for? Such a fools! (*Looking towards the window.*) O look! Suzuki—a robins. The firs' these Spring! Go, see if he's stay for nes'.

SUZUKI. (*Looking.*) It *is* a robins, O Cho—Cho-San!

MADAME BUTTERFLY. (*Running to the window.*) O! O!

SUZUKI. But he's fly away.

MADAME BUTTERFLY. O! How they are slow this year! Sa-ey, see if you don' fin' one tha's more in-dus-trial an' domestics.

SUZUKI. (*Looking out.*) There are none yet.

MADAME BUTTERFLY. But soon they nes' now. Suzuki, w'en we see that ship comin' in—sa-ey—then we goin' put flowers aevery where, an' if it's night, we goin' hang up mos' one thousan' lanterns—eh-ha?

SUZUKI. No got moaney for thousan'.

MADAME BUTTERFLY. Wael, twenty, mebby; an' sa-ey, w'en we see him comin' quick up path—(*imitates*) so—so—so— (*lifts her kimono and strides in a masculine fashion*) to look for liddle wive—me—me jus' goin' hide behind shoji (*making two holes with her wet finger in the low paper shoji and peeking through*) an' watch an' make believe me gone 'way; leave liddle note—sayin': "Goon-bye, sayonara, Butterfly." . . . Now he come in. . . . (*Hides.*) Ah! An' then he get angery! An' he say all kinds of 'Merican languages—debbils—hells! But before he get too angery, me run out an' flew aroun' his neck! (*She illustrates with* SUZUKI, *who is carried away and embraces her with fervor.*) Sa-ey! *You* no flew roun' his neck—jus' me. (*They laugh in each other's arms.*) Then he'll sit down an' sing tha's liddle 'Merican song—O, how he'll laugh. . . . (*She sings as though not understanding a word of it.*)

"*I* call her the belle of Japan—of Japan. Her name it is O Cho-Cho-San, Cho-Cho-San! Such tenderness lies in her soft almond eyes, I tell you, she 's just 'ichi ban.'"

(*Laughs.*) Then I'll dance like w'en I was Geisha girl.

(*She dances as* SHARPLESS, *the American consul, appears in the doorway, followed by the* NAKODO.)

NAKODO. This is the house, your Excellency.

SHARPLESS. (*Removing his clogs outside.*) You may wait. (NAKODO *bows and* SHARPLESS *enters.*) I beg pardon. . . .

(MADAME BUTTERFLY *still dancing, begins the song again.* SHARPLESS *goes to the door and knocks to attract her attention.*)

MADAME BUTTERFLY. Ah!

(SUZUKI, *bowing low, leaves the room.*)

SHARPLESS. This is Madame Cho-Cho-San?

MADAME BUTTERFLY. No, I am Mrs. Lef-ten-ant B. F. Pik-ker-ton.

SHARPLESS. I see. . . . Pardon my interruption. . . . I am Mr. Sharpless, the American consul.

MADAME BUTTERFLY. (*Once more salaaming to the ground, drawing in her breath between her teeth to express pleasure.*) O, your honorable excellency, goon night, —no, not night yaet: aexcuse me, I'm liddle raddle',—I mean goon mornin', goon evenin'. Welcome to 'Merican house, mos' welcome to 'Merican girl! (*Pointing to herself. They both bow.*) Be seat. (SHARPLESS *sits on a cushion on the floor, and* MADAME BUTTERFLY *sits at a little distance. There is a slight pause.*) How are those health? You sleepin' good? How are that honorable ancestors—are they well? And those paren's? That grandmother—how are she?

SHARPLESS. Thanks. They're all doing well, I hope.

MADAME BUTTERFLY. (*She claps her hands;* SUZUKI *enters and puts the little stand between them and leaves the room.*) Accep' pipe, your excellency. O, I forgettin'—I have still of those large American cigarette.

(MADAME BUTTERFLY *gestures towards* PINKERTON'S *tobacco jar decorated with the flag of his country.*)

SHARPLESS. (*Accepting a cigarette while she fills her pipe.*) Thanks. I'm on a little visit of inquiry, Madame Butterfly,—your name, I believe in our language. Lieutenant Pinkerton wrote to me to find out—

MADAME BUTTERFLY. (*Almost breathless.*) Ah, you have hear from him? He is well?

SHARPLESS. O, he's all right.

MADAME BUTTERFLY. (*Relieved.*) Ah! Tha's mak' me mos' bes' happy female woman in Japan—mebby in that whole worl'—w'at you thing?

SHARPLESS. Ha—ha! (*Puffing at the cigarette.*) Sawdust. Pinkerton must have left these!

MADAME BUTTERFLY. O! I so glad you came. . . . I goin' as' you a liddle question.

SHARPLESS. Well?

MADAME BUTTERFLY. You know 'bout birds in those your country?

SHARPLESS. Something.

MADAME BUTTERFLY. Tha's what I thing—you know aeverything. Tha's why your country sen' you here.

SHARPLESS. You flatter me.

MADAME BUTTERFLY. O, no, you got big head.

SHARPLESS. Pinkerton again—I can hear him!

MADAME BUTTERFLY. O, aexcuse me: I forgettin' my manners. I got liddle more raddle. (*She offers him her pipe which he gravely touches, returning it. She touches it again, then puts it down.*) Now, what you know 'bout jus' robins?

SHARPLESS. What?

MADAME BUTTERFLY. 'Bout when do they nes' again? Me, I thing it mus' be mor early in Japan as in America, accoun' they nestin' here now.

SHARPLESS. O, at the same time I fancy.

MADAME BUTTERFLY. (*Disappointed.*) Yaes? . . . then they's nestin' there. (*Then taking hope again.*) Sa-ey, I tell you—perhaps some time sooner, some time later, jus' how they feel like.

SHARPLESS. Possibly. Why do you ask?

MADAME BUTTERFLY. Because Lef-ten-ant B. F. Pik-ker-ton say he will come back to me w'en the robins nes' again.

SHARPLESS. (*To himself.*) Poor devil! One of his infernal jokes.

MADAME BUTTERFLY. (*Clapping her hands.*) Me, I thing it's time. . . . I've wait so long.

(SUZUKI *enters with a tea-pot.* MADAME BUTTERFLY *gives* SHARPLESS *a cup of tea.*)

NAKODO. (*Appearing at the door.*) Tea, most illustrious?

MADAME BUTTERFLY. Ah! Enter, Nakodo. Your presence lights up my entire house. (*She gives him a cup. Accepting it, he goes up to a cushion and sits.*) Tha's bad man. W'en my husban 's gone 'way, he try for get me marry again.

NAKODO. The rich Yamadori. Madame Cho-Cho-San is very poor.

MADAME BUTTERFLY. (*Bowing politely.*) O, liddle ol' *frlen'*; those are my business.

NAKODO. Rejected advice makes the heart sad.

MADAME BUTTERFLY. We-el, if those heart hurt you so much, you better not arrive here no more.

SHARPLESS. Madame Butterfly; may I ask—er—where are your people?

NAKODO. They have outcasted her!

MADAME BUTTERFLY. Sa-ey, tha's foanny! My people make me marry when I don' want; now I am marry, they don' want. Before I marry Lef-ten-ant B. F. Pik-ker-ton, my honorable Father—(*she bows low*—NAKODO *bows*—SHARPLESS *bows*) die—he's officer. These are his sword . . . (*pointing to an inscription*) 't is written. . . .

(*She holds out the sword that the inscription may be read.*)

NAKODO. (*Reading.*) "To die with honor, when one can no longer live with honor." (*He bows, then turns and bows towards the shrine and goes back to his cushion where he sits.*)

MADAME BUTTERFLY. He's kill' himself accoun' he soldier of Emporer an' defeat in battle. Then we get—O—ver' poor. Me? I go dance liddle. Also I thing if some rich man wish me, I gettin' marry for while, accoun' my grandmother, (*she bows respectfully*—NAKODO *bows*—SHARPLESS *politely nods*) don' got no food, no obi. Then ol' Nakodo, he say a (NAKODO *picks up his cushion and moves down to join in the conversation*) man's jus' as' him for nice wive for three monse. Nakodo tell him he don' know none more nizer as me.

NAKODO. (*Salaaming.*) Nizer as you.

MADAME BUTTERFLY. (*Salaaming.*) Nizer as me.

SHARPLESS. (*Looking from one to the other.*) Couldn't be nicer! . . .

(*He salaams profoundly—then all salaam.*)

MADAME BUTTERFLY. Then Nakodo say—

NAKODO. I say—I don' lig him account he 'Merica-jin.

MADAME BUTTERFLY. He also remark with me that he is barbarian an' beas'. But aeveryone say: "Yaes, take him—take him beas'—he's got moaneys." So I say for jus' liddle while, perhaps I can stan'. So Nakodo bring him. . . .

NAKODO. . . . For look-at meeting.

MADAME BUTTERFLY. (*Laughing.*) Me? Well, I thing that day Lef-ten-ant B. F. Pik-ker-ton is jus' a god! Gold button—lace on his unicorn. At firs', I frightened—he hol' my hans' so close—like—(*she illustrates by giving both hands to* SHARPLESS) and kizz. Japanese girl no lig' kizz; but when Lef-ten-ant B. F. Pik-ker-ton kizz me, I like vei' much. . . . What's use lie? It's not inside of me. (*Noticing that her hands' are still in* SHARPLESS'.) O, I beg your honorable pardon. (*She tucks her hands in her sleeves.*) So we's gettin' marry and then his ship order away an' me—I am jus' waitin'—sometimes cryin', sometimes watchin', but always waitin'.

NAKODO. (*In the doorway—bowing with servility.*) My client, the prosperous Yamadori, approaches for the third time today.

MADAME BUTTERFLY. Now I have my liddle joke again. You watch, he comes all time to make smash with me.

SHARPLESS. Pinkerton's slang.

(YAMADORI *enters attended by two servants.* SHARPLESS *rises and bows ceremoniously.* MADAME BUTTERFLY *does not rise, but bends her head and fans herself coquettishly. The two servants squat.*)

YAMADORI. Mr. Sharpless: always a pleasure to meet you here or in New York.

SHARPLESS. Thanks, Mr. Yamadori.

MADAME BUTTERFLY. (*Coquettishly.*) You have somethin' nize say to me again today?

YAMADORI. Perseverance shall be the religion of my life until the capricious Butterfly deigns to believe me.

MADAME BUTTERFLY. YOU goin' tell me 'gain you kill yourself I don' make kizz with you?

YAMADORI. (*Very much embarrassed—looking at consul.*) O!

MADAME BUTTERFLY. You can speak—consul know—I been tellin' him 'bout your liddle foolishness.

YAMADORI. Such treatment, Mr. Sharpless, is one of the penalties we incur when madly in love with a charming woman.

MADAME BUTTERFLY. Tha 's ver' nize. Ha-ha!

(*Winks behind her fan at* SHARPLESS.)

SHARPLESS. Heavens! Pinkerton's very wink.

(MADAME BUTTERFLY *gives a cup of tea to* YAMADORI *who drinks it and rolls a cigarette.*)

YAMADORI. (*To* SHARPLESS.) I am in Japan for two months—a pleasure trip. Do you blame me?

(*Pointing to* MADAME BUTTERFLY.)

MADAME BUTTERFLY. Aevery time he come home, get 'nother woman: must have mor'en eight now.

YAMADORI. But I *married* them all. . . .

MADAME BUTTERFLY. O *he!* He jus' marry whenaever he thing 'bout it.

YAMADORI. YOU shall be different. I will bury *you* with my ancestors. (*To* SHARPLESS.) I offered her a thousand servants.

NAKODO. (*Stunned.*) Thousan'!

MADAME BUTTERFLY. Ha! (*Fans.*)

YAMADORI. And a palace to live in.

(*The* NAKODO *is overcome by such generosity.*)

MADAME BUTTERFLY. He!

YAMADORI. Everything her heart can wish.

MADAME BUTTERFLY. Ha! Ha!

YAMADORI. Is that not enough? (*She shakes her head.*) Then in the presence of this statesman of integrity, I will give you a solemn writing. (SHARPLESS *gives, him a quizzical glance.*) Is *that* enough?

MADAME BUTTERFLY. Wha's good of that to married womans?

(*Pointing to herself.*)

YAMADORI. According to the laws of Japan, when a woman is deserted, she is divorced. (MADAME BUTTERFLY *stops fanning and listens.*) Though I have travelled much abroad, I know the laws of my own country.

MADAME BUTTERFLY. An' I know laws of my *husban's* country.

YAMADORI. (*To* SHARPLESS.) She still fancies herself married to the young officer. If your excellency would explain. . . .

MADAME BUTTERFLY. (*To* SHARPLESS.) Sa-ey, when some one gettin' married in America, don' he stay marry?

SHARPLESS. Usually—yes.

MADAME BUTTERFLY. Well, tha 's all right. I'm marry to Lef-ten-ant B. F. Pik-ker-ton.

YAMADORI. Yes, but a Japanese marriage!

SHARPLESS. Matrimony is a serious thing in America, not a temporary affair as it often is here.

MADAME BUTTERFLY. Yaes, an' you can't like 'Merican mans. Japanese got too many wive, eh?

SHARPLESS. (*Laughing.*) We are not allowed more than one at a time.

MADAME BUTTERFLY. Yaes, an' you can't divorce wive like here, by sayin': "walk it back to parent"—eh!?

SHARPLESS. O, no.

MADAME BUTTERFLY. Tha's right, aexactly. When I as' Lef-ten-ant B. F. Pik-ker-ton, he explain those law to me of gettin' divorce in those Unite' State'. He say no one can get aexcept he stan' up before Judge 2—3—4—7—year. Ver' tiresome. Firs' the man he got tell those Judge all he know 'bout womans; then womans, she got tell; then some lawyer quarrel with those Judge; the Judge get jury an' as' wha' they thing—an' if they don' know, they'll all get put in jails. Tha's all right! (*Folds hands.*)

YAMADORI. Your friend has told her everything she wanted him to tell her.

MADAME BUTTERFLY. (*Who has paid no attention.*) Tha's ver' nize, too, that 'Merican God.

SHARPLESS. I beg your pardon?

MADAME BUTTERFLY. Once times, Lef-ten-ant B. F. Pik-ker-ton—

YAMADORI. (*Aside to* SHARPLESS.) Pinkerton again!

MADAME BUTTERFLY. He's in great troubles, an' he said "God he'p me"; an' sunshine *came right out*—and God he did! Tha's ver' quick—Japanese gods take more time. Aeverything quick in America. Ha—me—sometime I thing I pray large American God to get him back soon; but no use,—he don' know me where *I* live. (*Attracted by a sound.*) Wha's that? . . . You hear?

SHARPLESS. No. (MADAME BUTTERFLY *runs to the window and listens; then takes up the glasses while* SHARPLESS *speaks in a low voice to* YAMADORI.) Lieutenant Pinkerton's ship was due yesterday. His young wife from America is waiting here to meet him. (*At the word "wife,"* YAMADORI *smiles—takes his fan from his sleeve and fans himself. The* NAKODO, *who is listening, is struck by an idea and departs in such haste that he tumbles over one of* YAMADORI'S *attendants who jabbers at him.*) I 'm devilish sorry for that girl.

YAMADORI. Then tell her the truth.

MADAME BUTTERFLY. Aexcuse me; but I always hearin' soun' like ship gun—ha—ha—tha 's naturels.

YAMADORI. (*Preparing to go.*) Good morning, Mr. Sharpless. (*Shaking hands. Turning to* MADAME BUTTER FLY.) I leave you today. Tomorrow the gods may prompt you to listen to me! (*He bows.*)

MADAME BUTTERFLY. (*Bowing.*) Mebby. (YAMADORI *and attendants go off, bowing. She turns to* SHARPLESS.) Mebby not. Sa-ey, somehow couldn't you let that Lef-ten-ant B. F. Pik-ker-ton know they's other all crazy 'bout me?

SHARPLESS. Madame Butterfly, sit down. (*While she, struck by his solemn manner, looks at him and obeys, he removes the tea-pot and sits on the stand, to the astonishment of* MADAME BUTTERFLY.) I am going to read you part of a letter I have received from Pinkerton.

(*He takes a letter from his pocket.*)

MADAME BUTTERFLY. O, jus' let me look at those ledder! (*She slips it under her kimono on her heart and with an indrawn breath, hands it back.*) Now read quick, you mos' bes' nize man in all the whole worl'.

SHARPLESS. (*Reads.*) "Find out about that little Jap girl. What has become of her? It might be awkward now. If little Butterfly still remembers me, perhaps you can help me out and make her understand. Let her down gently. You won't believe it, but for two weeks after I sailed, I was dotty in love with, her."

(SHARPLESS *is amazed to see* MADAME BUTTERFLY *convulsed with silent joy.*)

MADAME BUTTERFLY. Oh, all the gods how it was sweet!

SHARPLESS. Why really—

MADAME BUTTERFLY. Tha's what I'm afraid: that he loave' me so much he's goin' desert his country an' get in trouble with American eagle—what you thing? Oh, it's more bedder I wait than those!

SHARPLESS. (*Folding the letter.*) No use—you can't understand. Madame Butterfly, suppose this waiting should never end; what would become of you?

MADAME BUTTERFLY. Me? I could dance, mebby, or—die?

SHARPLESS. Don't be foolish. I advise you to consider the rich Yamadori's offer.

MADAME BUTTERFLY. (*Astonished.*) *You* say those? You, 'Merican consul?—when you know that me, I am marry?

SHARPLESS. You heard Yamadori: it is not binding.

MADAME BUTTERFLY. Yamadori lies!

SHARPLESS. His offer is an unusual opportunity for a girl who—for any Japanese girl in your circumstances.

MADAME BUTTERFLY. (*Enraged—she claps her hands.*) Suzuki! The excellent gentleman—(*bowing sarcastically*) who have done us the honor to call—he wish to go hurriedly. His shoes—hasten them!

(SUZUKI, *who has entered carrying a jar, gets* SHARPLESS' *clogs and gives them to him—then passes off with her jar.*)

SHARPLESS. (*Holding the clogs awkwardly.*) I'm really very sorry.

MADAME BUTTERFLY. No, no, don' be an-gery. But jus' now you tol' me—O, gods! You mean—(*Looks at him pitifully.*) I not Lef-ten-ant B. P. Pik-ker-ton's wive—Me?

SHARPLESS. Hardly.

MADAME BUTTERFLY. O, I—(*She sways slightly.* SHARPLESS *goes to her assistance, but she recovers and fans herself.*) Tha's all right. I got liddle heart illness. I can't . . . I can't some-ways give up thingin' he'll come back to me. You thing tha's all over? All finish? (*Dropping her fan.* SHARPLESS *nods assent.*) Oh, no! Loave don' forget some thin's or wha's use of loave? (*She claps her hands—beckoning off.*) Loave's got remember . . . (*pointing*) some thin's!

(*A child enters.*)

SHARPLESS. A child. . . . Pinkerton's? . . .

MADAME BUTTERFLY. (*Showing a picture of* PINKERTON'S.) Look! Look! (*Holding it up beside the child's face.*) Tha 's jus' his face, same hair, same blue eye. . . .

SHARPLESS. Does Lieutenant Pinkerton know?

MADAME BUTTERFLY. No, he come after he goe. (*Looking at the child with pride.*) You thing fath-er naever comes back—tha's what *you* thing? He do! You write him ledder; tell him 'bout one bes' mos' nize bebby aever seen. . . . Ha—ha! I bed all moaneys he goin' come mos' one million mile for see those chil'. Surely this is tie—bebby. Sa-ey, you did n' mean what you said 'bout me not bein' marry? You make liddle joke? (*Moved,* SHARPLESS *nods his head in assent, to the great relief of* MADAME BUTTERFLY.) Ha! (*She lays the baby's hand in* SHARPLESS'.) Shake hand consul 'Merican way.

SHARPLESS. (*Shaking hands with the child.*) Hm . . . hm . . . what's your name?

MADAME BUTTERFLY. Trouble. Japanese bebby always change it name. I was thinkin' some day w'en he come back, change it to Joy.

SHARPLESS. Yes . . . yes . . . I 'll let him know.

(*Glad to escape, he takes an abrupt departure.*)

SUZUKI. (*In the distance, wailing.*) Ay . . . ay . . . ay . . .

MADAME BUTTERFLY. Tha's wail . . .

SUZUKI. (*Nearer.*) O, Cho-Cho-San! (MADAME BUTTERFLY *goes to the door to meet* SUZUKI.) Cho-Cho-San!

MADAME BUTTERFLY. Speak!

SUZUKI. We are shamed through the town. The Nakodo—

NAKODO. (*Appearing.*) I but said the child—(*he points to the baby, whom* MADAME BUTTERFLY *instinctively shelters in her arms*) was a badge of shame to his father. In his country, there are homes for such unfortunates and they never rise above the stigma of their class. They are shunned and cursed from birth.

MADAME BUTTERFLY. (*Who has listened stolidly—now with a savage cry, pushing him away from her until he loses his balance and falls to the floor.*) You lie!

NAKODO. (*On the floor.*) But Yamadori—

MADAME BUTTERFLY. (*Touching her father's sword.*) Lies! Lies! Lies! Say again, I kill! Go . . . (*The* NAKODO *goes quickly.*) Bebby, he lies. . . . Yaes, it's lie. . . . When your fath-er knows how they speak, he will take us 'way from bad people to his own country. I am finish here. (*Taking the American flag from the tobacco jar and giving it to the child.*) Tha's your country—your flag. Now wave like fath-er say w'en excite—wave like "hell!" (*Waves the child's hand.*) Ha'rh! Ha'rh! (*A ship's gun is heard.*) Ah! (MADAME BUTTERFLY *and* SUZUKI *start for the balcony.* MADAME BUTTERFLY *runs back for the child as the gun is heard again; then returning to the shoji, looks through the glasses.*) Look! Look! Warship! Wait . . . can't see name. . . .

SUZUKI. Let me—

MADAME BUTTERFLY. No! Ah! Name is "Con-nec-ti-cut"! His ship! He 's come back! He's come back! (*Laughing, she embraces* SUZUKI—*then sinks to the floor.*) He's come back! Those robins nes' again an' we did n' know! O, bebby, bebby—your fath-er come back! Your fath-er's come back! O! O! (*Shaking a bough of cherry blossoms, which fall on them both.*) This is the bes' nize momen' since you was borned. Now your name's Joy! Suzuki; the Moon Goddess sent that bebby straight from Bridge of Heaven to make me courage to wait so long.

SUZUKI. Ah, ship's in. . . .

MADAME BUTTERFLY. (*Rising in great excitement.*) Hoarry, Suzuki, his room. (SUZUKI *pulls out a screen to form a little room.*) We mus' hoarry—(*Picking flowers from the pots and decorating the room*) like we got eagle's wings an' thousan' feete. His cigarettes. (*Setting the jar in the room.*) His slipper. (SUZUKI *gets them from the shrine.*) His chair, Suzuki—hustle! (SUZUKI *hastens off.* MADAME BUTTERFLY *shakes a cushion and drops it on the floor.*) His bed. (SUZUKI *enters with a steamer chair, which she places upside down.*) Now his room fixed! (SUZUKI *closes the shoji.* MADAME BUTTERFLY *adjusts the chair and sets the lanterns about the room.*) Bring me my wides' obi, kanzashi for my hair, poppies—mus' look vei' pretty!

SUZUKI. Rest is bes' beauty. He not come yet. Sleep liddle firs'. . . .

MADAME BUTTERFLY. No, no time. (*Taking up a small mirror and looking critically at herself.*) He mus' see me look mos' pretty ever. You thing I change since he went away—not so beauty? (SUZUKI *is silent.*) W'at? . . . I am! (*Brandishing the mirror.*) Say so!

SUZUKI. Perhaps you rest liddle, once more you get so pretty again.

MADAME BUTTERFLY. *Again?* . . .

SUZUKI. Trouble, tha's make change. . . .

MADAME BUTTERFLY. Moach change. (*Still looking in the glass.*) No, I am no more pretty—an' he come soon. (*On her knees in front of* SUZUKI*—resting her forehead on the maid's feet.*) Ah, Suzuki, be kin' with me—make me pretty . . . don' say you can't—you moas'. An' tomorrow, the gods will. Ah, yes! You can—you can—you got to! Bring powder, comb, rouge, henna, fix it hair like on wedding day. (SUZUKI *brings the toilet articles and they sit on the floor.* SUZUKI *puts the poppies and pins in* MADAME BUTTERFLY'S *hair, and she, in turn, dresses the baby, enveloping him in an obi, so wide that it almost covers the child.*) Now, bebby, when you cry, he 'll sing you those liddle 'Merican song he sing me when I cry—song all 'Merican sing for bebby. (*Sitting with the baby in front of her, swaying it by the arms, she sings.*)

"Rog' a bye bebby,
Off in Japan,
You jus' a picture,
Off of a fan."

(SUZUKI *has found it very difficult to finish the toilet, but at last she accomplishes it.* MADAME BUTTERFLY *lifts the baby up, gives it a doll, then touches it with rouge and adds a final dash of rouge to her own face.*) Now for watch for pa-pa!

(*Putting the flag in the child's hand, she takes it up to the window and makes three holes in the shoji, one low down for the baby. As the three look through the shoji, they form the picture she has already described.*)

(*During the vigil, the night comes on.* SUZUKI *lights the floor lamps, the stars come out, the dawn breaks, the floor lights flicker out one by one, the birds begin to sing, and the day discovers* SUZUKI *and the baby fast asleep on the floor; but* MADAME BUTTERFLY *is awake, still watching, her face white and strained. She reaches out her hands and rouses* SUZUKI.)

SUZUKI. (*Starting to her feet, surprised and looking about the room.*) He no come?

MADAME BUTTERFLY. No. . . .

SUZUKI. (*Pityingly.*) Oh!

MADAME BUTTERFLY. (*With an imperious gesture.*) No "Oh"! He will come. . . . Bring fresh flowers. (*She collects the lanterns as* SUZUKI *brings in fresh flowers.* MADAME BUTTERFLY *tears up the roses and throws their leaves in Pinkerton's room. Then pointing to the upper part of the house.*) Now I watch from liddle look out place. (*She picks up the child whose doll drops from its hand.* Have mos' bes' nize breakfas' ready w'en he come.

(*She leaves the room and* SUZUKI *goes to prepare the breakfast.*)

(*The stage is empty. Very faintly a strain of "I call her the Belle of Japan" is heard.* MADAME BUTTERFLY *is singing that she may not weep. A pause. Some one knocks on the door.* LIEUTENANT PINKERTON'S *voice calls outside the shoji.*)

LIEUTENANT PINKERTON. Madame Butterfly? Madame Butterfly? (*Coming into the room, he looks about.*) Butterfly?

SHARPLESS. (*Following him.*) They've seen the ship—these decorations were not here when I called.

MADAME BUTTERFLY. (*Singing to hush the baby.*)

"Rog'—a—bye, bebby,
Off in Japan,"

(LIEUTENANT PINKERTON *listens to the song coming from above.*)

"You jus' a picture,
Off of a fan."

LIEUTENANT PINKERTON. She is watching the ship. (*Noticing the screened off part of the room.*) My room . . . just as it used to look . . . my chair. (*Picking up the doll which the child has dropped.*) Poor kid! Poor little devil! . . . Sharpless, I thought when I left this house, the few tears, sobs, little polite regrets, would be over as I crossed the threshold. I started to come back for a minute, but I said to myself: "Don't do it; by this time she's ringing your gold pieces to make sure they're good." You know that class of Japanese girl and—

SHARPLESS. (*Seeing* NAKODO *who is at the shoji.*) Look here: I have something to settle with you! (NAKODO *comes in cautiously.*) Why did you seek out my friend's wife at the pier?

LIEUTENANT PINKERTON. Why did you tell her that story—the child and all? Answer me?

NAKODO. (*To* SHARPLESS.) Your Excellency, I but thought if trouble came between the two women, he would surely break with Cho-Cho-San, and then she would be glad to marry the rich Yamadori and I get big fee. (*Exit.*)

SHARPLESS. You'll never get it. (*To* PINKERTON.) She'll starve first.

LIEUTENANT PINKERTON. Sharpless, thank God, that's one thing I can do—money. (*He takes out an envelope containing some money.*)

SHARPLESS. What did your wife say, Pinkerton?

LIEUTENANT PINKERTON. Well, it was rather rough on her,—only married four months. Sharpless, my Kate's an angel, —she offered to take the child . . . made me promise I'd speak of it to Butterfly.

MADAME BUTTERFLY. (*Calling from above.*) Suzuki?

SHARPLESS. She's coming.

(PINKERTON *instinctively draws behind the screen.*)

MADAME BUTTERFLY. (*Coming down the stairs with the sleeping baby on her back, calling.*) Suzuki? Come for bebby. (*Kissing the child.*) Nize liddle eye, pick out of blue sky, all shut up.

LIEUTENANT PINKERTON. (*Aside to* SHARPLESS, *his eyes fixed on the* MOTHER *and child.*) I can't face it! I 'm going. Give her the money.

SUZUKI. (*Entering, and seeing* PINKERTON *as he passes out of the door.*) Ah! (SHARPLESS *gives her a warning gesture.*)

MADAME BUTTERFLY. (*Seeing* SUZUKI'S *astonished face.*) Wha'—? (*She puts the baby in* SUZUKI'S *arms.* SUZUKI *goes out quickly.* MADAME BUTTERFLY *sees the Consul.*) You! Oh! (*Joyously.*) You seen him?

SHARPLESS. Yes.

MADAME BUTTERFLY. An' you tole him?

SHARPLESS. Well . . .

MADAME BUTTERFLY. But you tole him . . . of bebby?

SHARPLESS. Yes.

MADAME BUTTERFLY. (*Wiping her dry lips.*) Yaes . . . tha's right. Tha's what I—as' you do . . . an'—an' what he *say?*

SHARPLESS. Well . . . (*Taking out the envelope, and giving her the money which she takes without looking at it.*) He said—er—he was crazy to see you and—(*Aside*) What the devil can I say! (*To her.*) You know he can't leave the ship just yet. (*Pointing to the package in her hand.*) That is in remembrance of the past. He wishes you to be always happy, to have the best of luck; he hopes to see you soon—and—

(*The lies die out on his lips.*)

MADAME BUTTERFLY. (*Bending and kissing his hand.*) All—all the gods in the heavens bless you!

(*Overcome, she staggers.* SHARPLESS *catches her, puts her into the chair—she leans against him—her face upraised, her eyes closed.*)

(KATE, *entering hurriedly.*)

KATE. Has Lieutenant Pinkerton gone? Has my husband been here?

(MADAME BUTTERFLY *hears and opens her eyes.*)

SHARPLESS. For God's sake—(*He looks at* MADAME BUTTERFLY *whose eyes are fixed on his with a look of despair.*) Come, we can overtake him.

KATE (*In a lower voice.*) Did he speak to her of the—

SHARPLESS. No.

KATE. Then I will ask. (*For the first time seeing* MADAME BUTTERFLY.) Is this—(SHARPLESS *nods and goes. There is a short pause, while the two women look at each other, then* MADAME BUTTERFLY, *still seated, slowly bows her head.*) Why, you poor little thing . . . who in the world could blame you or . . . call you responsible . . . you pretty little plaything.

(*Takes* MADAME BUTTERFLY *in her arms.*)

MADAME BUTTERFLY. (*Softly.*) No—playthin' . . . I am Mrs. Lef-ten-ant B. F.—No—no—now I am, only—Cho-Cho-San, but no playthin'. . . . (*She rises, then impassively.*) How long you been marry?

KATE. Four months. . . .

MADAME BUTTERFLY. (*Counting on her fingers.*) Oh . . . four.

KATE. Won't you let me do something for the child? Where is he? (MADAME BUTTERFLY *gestures toward the next room.* KATE, *seeing the child.*) Ah! The dear little thing! May I—

MADAME BUTTERFLY. No! Can look . . . no can touch. . . .

KATE. Let us think first of the child. For his own good . . . let me take him home to my country. . . . I will do all I would do for my own.

MADAME BUTTERFLY. (*Showing no emotion.*) He not know then—me—his mother?

KATE. It's hard, very hard, I know; but would it not be better?

MADAME BUTTERFLY. (*Taking the money box from her sleeve, and giving the coins to* KATE.) Tha's his . . . two dollar. All tha's lef' of his moaneys. . . . I shall need no more. . . . (*She hands* KATE *the envelope which* SHARPLESS *has just given.*) I lig if you also say I sawry—no—no—no—glad—*glad!* I wish him that same happiness lig he wish for me . . . an' tell him . . . I shall be happy . . . mebby. Thang him . . . Mister B. F. Pik-ker-ton for also that kindness he have been unto me . . . an' permit me to thang *you,* augustness, for that same. . . . You—you mos' bes' lucky girl in these whole worl'. . . . Goon-night—

(*She stands stolidly with her eyes closed.*)

KATE. (*Wiping her eyes.*) But the child?

MADAME BUTTERFLY. Come back fifteen minute. . . . (*With closed eyes, she bows politely.*) Sayonara. (KATE *reluctantly goes.*) God he'p me, but no sun kin shine. (SUZUKI, *who has listened, sinks at* MADAME BUTTERFLY'S *feet.*) Don' cry, Suzuki, liddle maiden . . . aecoun' I dizappoint, a liddle dizappoint' —don' cry. . . . (*Running her hand over* SUZUKI'S *head—as she kneels.*) Tha's short while ago you as' me res'—sleep. . . . (*Wearily.*) Well—go way an' I will res' now. . . . I *wish* res'—sleep . . . long sleep . . . an' when you see me again, I pray you look whether I be not beautiful again . . . as a bride.

SUZUKI. (*Understanding, sobbing.*) No—no—no.

MADAME BUTTERFLY. So that I suffer no more—goon bye, liddle maiden. (SUZUKI *does not go.* MADAME BUTTERFLY *claps her hands, and sobbing,* SUZUKI *leaves the room.* MADAME BUTTERFLY *bolts the shoji, and the door, lights fresh incense before the shrine, takes down her father's sword and reads the inscription:*) "To die with honor . . . when one can no longer live with honor." . . .

(*She draws her finger across the blade, to test the sharpness of the sword, then picks up the hand glass, puts on more rouge, re-arranges the pop-pies in her hair, bows to the shrine, and is about to press the blade of the sword against her neck, when the door is opened and the child is pushed into the room by* SUZUKI, *who keeps out of sight.* MADAME BUTTERFLY *drops the sword and takes the baby in her arms. A knocking is heard but she pays no heed. She sets the child on a mat, puts the American flag in its hand, and picking up the sword, goes be-hind the screen that the child may not see what she is about to do. A short pause—the sword is heard to drop.* MADAME BUTTERFLY *re-appears, her face deathly—a scarf about her neck to conceal the wound.* SUZUKI *opens the door, sees the face of her mistress—backs out of the room in horror.* MADAME BUTTERFLY *drops to her knees as she reaches the child, and clasps it to her. A hand is thrust through the shoji and the bolt is drawn.*)

(KATE *enters quickly urging the reluctant* PINKERTON *to follow her.*)

LIEUTENANT PINKERTON. (*Discerning what she has done.*) Oh! Cho-Cho-San! (*He draws her to him with the baby pressed to her heart. She waves the child's hand which holds the flag—saying faintly.*)

MADAME BUTTERFLY. Too bad those robins didn' nes' again. (*She dies.*)

3. The Pan-American Exposition (Guidebooks)

Commentary

Sources

Guidebooks

3.1 THE PAN-AMERICAN EXPOSITION, BUFFALO: "PAX 1901"—ROBERT RYDELL

> The Exposition must be at base philosophic, on the surface theatric. An understanding of the philosophy of the Pan-American is material for its fullest enjoyment.
>
> *Atlantic Monthly*, 1901

> Never in the history of expositions has there been a more carefully conceived and wrought-out fundamental plan than that of the Pan-American Exposition.
>
> John Milburn, in an address before the American Institute of Architects Convention at the Exposition, 1901

SHORTLY BEFORE THE PAN-AMERICAN EXPOSITION opened, the *Buffalo Evening News* reminisced about the Crystal Palace Exhibition fifty years earlier: "It was as if Darwin had pictured in panoramic view his 'Origin of Species' for the enlightenment of mankind." That simile, however, better suited the Buffalo fair. At the Pan-American Exposition evolutionary ideas about race and progress dictated the arrangement of buildings, the selection and placement of sculptural forms, and, above all, the color scheme that gave the exposition the name "Rainbow City" and inspired Richard Watson Gilder, editor of *Century Magazine,* to compose an ode to the "CITY OF LIGHT." On the exposition's midway, officially named the Pan, a show called the Evolution of Man, or the Connecting Link, joined the honky-tonk amusements, restaurants, and ethnological villages. As Eugene Richard Wright of the *Atlantic Monthly* observed, this was an exposition where "nothing was done fortuitously."

Through the Pan-American Exposition, America's ruling elites initiated Americans into the twentieth century with a utopian fantasy about peace and progress that forecast "the spiritual synthesis of the far future." According to one guidebook, the "dominant purpose" of the fair was to "illustrale progress during the century just closed and lay a strong and enduring foundation for international, commercial and social unity in the world." Exhibits of people, artifacts, and natural resources came primarily from the Western Hemisphere, but Secretary of State John Hay stressed the universal importance of the proceedings: "The benignant influences that shall emanate from this great festival of peace shall not be bounded by oceans nor by continents." Pax 1901, however, was interrupted by the assassination of President McKinley in the Temple of Music in early September.

The idea for holding an international exposition in Buffalo originated at the American Exhibitors Association banquet at the Atlanta Cotton States and International Exposition of 1895. On that occasion, a Buffalo railroad speculator, John M. Brinker, produced a map showing that forty million people lived within a twelve-hour train ride of the city he represented. That consideration, coupled with the presence of Niagara Falls as a major tourist attraction and electrical power source, persuaded the Exhibitors Association to sanction Brinker's plans to hold another fair to foster visions of Pan-American harmony. True to its origins, Buffalo's exposition emphasized access to new markets and resources in Latin America.

At century's turn, however, acquiring Latin American markets and resources meant overcoming heightened mistrust in these countries over the foreign policy objectives of the United States, in view of the explicit imperial consequences of the Spanish–American War. The exposition, its promoters hoped, would teach Latin Americans "that their gigantic northern neighbor is a comrade and friend, and not a potential tyrant or oppressor; and the inhabitant of the United Stales must learn that his nation's size and strength and wealth do not make unnecessary or unworthy the serious efforts of Latin and Teutonic communities to the south of us to build American institutions of their own." As evidence of their friendly intentions toward Mexico, Central America, and South America, the exposition directors decided to construct the exposition buildings in the style of the Spanish Renaissance. The *Nation* suggested that the architectural style atoned for America's commercial neglect of Latin America: "To-day our repentance assumes the form of architectural beauty at Buffalo." A United States naval representative to the exposition shed further light on the imperial subtleties that inspired the fair. As a result of the fair, Captain Richard Pearson Hobson explained, "the sister republics of the Western Hemisphere would come to know our flag better; and to know it would be to love it; to know that it represents all that is highest in human government and human civilization." The exposition directors underscored his point in promising that the twentieth century would be "an age of American dominance in international affairs."

From the outset of the undertaking there never was the slightest doubt that the goal of international hegemony would have its domestic corollary. "Expositions," a promotional publication asserted, represent "an efficient means of instruction for the people . . . and serve as a basis for study and consideration to the busy workers who have Contributed to make these expositions possible." The *Pan-American Herald*, official journal of the exposition, added that the fair would be "in the truest sense of the term, an exposition of the people, by the people and for the people," citing as proof that eleven thousand people, including "millionaires" and "laborers in the most humble positions in life," had subscribed to exposition stock. In actuality, however, this fair, like its predecessors, resembled a corporate autarchy. A railroad advertisement in *The World's Work* titled "How the Railroads Built the Exposition" contained more truth than fiction. Led by the Vanderbilt Lines, railroads had contributed substantial sums to the fair. Buffalo bank directors, moreover, collectively chose the board of directors for the exposition from among businessmen who subscribed to at least $300,000 worth of bonds. Among those selected were Charles W. Goodyear, lumberman and railroad magnate, John M. Brinker, who owned a coaling operation in addition to his railroad interests, George Urban, Jr., a banker, Herbert P. Bissel, lawyer and future Supreme Court justice, and Harry Hamlin, president of American Grape Sugar Company.

This group, which included other prominent bankers, lawyers, and industrialists, in turn selected as president John M. Milburn, an eminent attorney, trustee of Columbia and Barnard colleges, director of American Express Company, and a board member of Chase National Bank. To assist in overseeing the operations of the fair, the directors named William I. Buchanan as director-general. Buchanan possessed outstanding credentials. His success in the early 1890s with the Sioux City Corn Palace Exposition Company had led to his appointment as superintendent of agriculture at the World's Columbian Exposition. President Cleveland subsequently appointed him United Stales foreign minister to Argentina—a post that enabled him to assist Isaac W. Avery's efforts to generate Latin American interest in the Atlanta fair. Buchanan's considerable knowledge about Latin America and his exposition pedigree—testified to by Harlow N. Higinbotham's endorsement—perfectly suited the needs of the corporate interests sponsoring the Pan-American Exposition.

Buchanan, moreover, was only one of many former exposition makers to lend support to Buffalo's undertaking. When the directors deadlocked on selecting a site for the fair, they called in Daniel Burnham and Frederick Law Olmsted, Jr., to help resolve the issue. Other exposition specialists sped to Buffalo after the close of Omaha's two expositions. Luther Stieringer, the electrical engineer who had designed the lighting effects for the Trans-Mississippi Exposition, created electrical illumination for the Pan-American fair. Another figure from the Trans-Mississippi exposition, landscape architect Rudolph Ulrich, supervised the landscaping plans for the 1901 fair.

Buffalo's exposition promoters also selected Frederick W. Taylor, renowned horticulturist and head of the Horticultural Department al the 1898 fair, to take charge of the exhibits and concessions at Buffalo. Soon after assuming his position, Taylor stated that ethnology would be a central concern of the fair and proposed an Indian Congress for the midway—ideas that Edward Rosewater enthusiastically supported when he met with the managers of the Pan-American Exposition in late 1899 to share his insights about running an exposition. The knot linking earlier fairs and the Buffalo exposition tightened in the ensuing competition for the Indian Congress concession as Antonio Apache, one of Frederic Ward Putnam's assistants at Chicago, and Frederick Cummins, manager of the Indian Congress at the Greater America Exposition of 1899, emerged as front runners. When Cummins received the concession because of stronger financial backing, which he received from the Citizens Bank of Buffalo, the directors secured a proven show and another experienced showman for their fair.

Relying on experienced exposition hands offered clear advantages to the sponsors of the Pan-American Exposition. But in another sense the overflow effect from previous fairs—especially from the World's Columbian Exposition and its City Beautiful satellites—presented the problem of novelty. Too much continuity with preceding expositions threatened loss of public appeal. Could new forms be devised to convey the message of imperial progress without altering the fundamental purposes of the exposition?

The answer was affirmative and startling. Rainbow colors replaced the pervasive whiteness of earlier City Beautiful fairs in an all-encompassing evolutionary design of the world's progress. As they entered the fairgrounds, visitors to the Pan-American Exposition stepped into a carefully crafted allegory of America's rise to the apex of civilization. The color mosaic presented by the fair told the story of the nation's successful struggle with nature and forecast a future where racial fitness would determine prosperity. Inside the exposition, ethnological displays and midway attractions with ethnological attributes gave this historical and utopian narrative a basis in received scientific and pseudoscientific wisdom. But fairgoers first encountered the evolutionary message of the exposition in the mutually reinforcing effects of the architecture, the colors of the buildings, and the outdoor sculpture. This intermeshing visual panorama resulted from close collaboration among artists, architects, and the exposition management.

To design the exposition buildings, the directors selected architects R. S. Peabody, James Knox Taylor, George Cary, August Esenwein, Edward B. Green, George F. Sheply, John G. Howard, and Walter Cook and placed them under the supervision of John M. Carrère, who had submitted the winning plan for the fair in the architectural competition. Carrère's plan emphasized "formality picturesquely developed," with "a logical arrangement and significance in the groupings of the buildings." Carrère also drew up his plan with particular reference to the approaches to Delaware

Park, site of the fair. He virtually eliminated all secondary entrances to the exposition "so that the intended first impression, which is always the most lasting," would be commonly shared by the majority of fairgoers. "It was possible to paint this picture at Buffalo," he explained, "with a definite view point, placed at the Triumphal Bridge, and to make the principal approach through the park, so that the spectator, as he approaches the Exposition, will see it develop gradually until he reaches the Bridge, when the entire picture will appear before him and almost burst upon him." Across the bridge, Carrère placed the main exposition buildings in a progressive series along a broad north–south axis with several intersecting secondary axes. He devoted the first structural grouping to natural resources and to the United States Government Building, thereby planting the national identity firmly in the conquest of nature and the development of natural resources. The next cross-axis juxtaposed the Temple of Music to the Ethnology Building in an effort to mark a transitional point in the march from savagery to civilization. Buildings devoted to technology and to the "genius of man" found their home in the final secondary axis in Carrère's plan, which centered on the Court of Fountains—a courtyard highlighted by the heroically proportioned Fountain of Abundance and an enormous Electric Tower. To enhance the continuity of this general plan, the architects and directors agreed to "highly color the Exposition Buildings" and to style them in the fashion of the Spanish Renaissance.

In the spring of 1900 Carrère, as chairman of the Board of Architects, extended an invitation to the National Sculptors Society and the National Society of Mural Painters to nominate two individuals to supervise the sculptural work of the fair and to take charge of the coloring process. These organizations selected Karl Bitter and Charles Y. Turner. Neither arrived in Buffalo as a novice in the exposition business. Turner had worked as Frank Millet's assistant in painting the World's Columbian Exposition, and Bitter had modeled statuary groups for several buildings at the same fair. By the time they received their appointments, the architects and management had started working out the details of Carrère's plan. Exactly how color, sculpture, and architecture would relate to one another, however, remained unclear. Responsibility for the color scheme clearly lay in Turner's hands, but after an initial meeting with the Board of Architects he returned to his New York City studio uncertain how best to proceed. Meanwhile, as exposition president Milburn later described it, Bitter had "an inspiration."

At a meeting of the National Sculptors Society, Bitter proposed considering the sculpture for the fair "as a decorative feature forming a part of the entire artistic scheme of the composition." Rather than treating sculptural pieces as isolated works of art. Bitter stated his intention of having them designed with particular reference to the physical landscape of the fair, to the contents of the buildings, and to the overall purpose of the exposition. As Turner sat in the audience and listened to Bitter fill in the specifics, he concluded that Bitter's idea was "ingenious." Turner provided a full account of Bitter's proposal in a subsequent report to the exposition management:

> He proposed to treat the sculptural groups about the Government Building in such a manner as to suggest man in his primitive state, and the Horticultural group as the natural resources of the earth. Here the battle of life, which man has ever waged with elements, begins. We find as we progress up the grounds, the result of his labors in the Machinery and Transportation and Electricity Buildings shown on one side, and the Liberal Arts and Agricultural on the

> other suggesting the result of his struggles. The Restaurant and the entrances to the Midway and the Stadium should suggest amusements and games. The Electric Tower, the crowning achievement of man, could be dedicated to the great waterways and the power of Niagara which is utilized to generate the current which runs the Exposition.

Finding Bitter's proposal a "logical and proper treatment," Turner determined on "a similar course" to make the use of color part of the "general scheme which was indicated in the plan of the grounds, buildings and sculptural arrangement." Visitors crossing the Triumphal Bridge, Turner wrote, "would come upon the elementary conditions, that is, the earliest state of man suggested on one side and primitive nature on the other." Consequently, "the strongest primary colors should be applied here," while farther up, "the colors should be more refined and less contrasting, and the Tower which is to suggest the triumph of man's achievement, should be the lightest and most delicate in color." He could thus capture "the emerald green hue of the water as it curls over the crest of Niagara Falls," Turner claimed and he would "carry this color on some portion of every building," thereby giving a sense of continuity to the entire coloring plan.

The overall design so impressed the exposition directors that they rushed a descriptive pamphlet into print: "The whole group of buildings has been treated as one picture, and the colors made to harmonize, not only with one another, but with the foreground of green grass and water and the background blue of the sky." "Further," the pamphlet stressed, "an ethical significance is aimed at, in the chromatic arrangement as in the architectural plan; the whole symbolizing progression from a less civilized stage to a higher. Thus the strongest, crudest colors are nearest the entrances." Gradually, the colors evolved "from warm buff and ochre walls, with terra cotta roofs, through more refined and brilliant hues, to the Electric Tower at the head of the Court of Fountains, striking the highest and finest note of all in ivory white, delicate blue, green, and gold."

By all accounts, the visual impact of the fair overpowered visitors. "Such beautiful displays of man's thoughts are far more to the world than any form of dogmatic religion," wrote the correspondent for the *Arena*, "for they show in which way man is tending. And, believe me, it is always upward." The entire artistic production reminded George H. Daniels, general passenger agent for the New York Central Railroad, of "an immense oil painting" with an effect "somewhat like a sunrise." A local schoolteacher, Mabel E. Barnes, who pedaled her bicycle to the fair on thirty-two separate occasions and recorded her experience in a three-volume diary and scrapbook, stated: "As the sculpture symbolizes the progress of the race, the coloring represents in epitome the growth of the color sense." For future reference, she also copied down, almost verbatim, the official description of the artistic plan of the fair from the pamphlet first issued by the exposition directors. Other visitors applauded the "magic" quality of the fair and its "architectural somersaults." Claude Bragdon, in *American Architect and Building News*, complimented Turner for his "highly psychological and philosophic" coloring scheme and proclaimed the Electric Tower "the high C of the entire architectural symphony." For other spectators, the 375 foot tower possessed an alluring sexuality. "The shaft of the Electric Tower," Julian Hawthorne wrote, "at the further extremity of this interminable space, assumes a magical aspect, as if it had been summoned forth by the genius of our united people . . . and it makes a tender nuptial with the sky and seems to palpitate with beautiful life." Maurice F. Newton offered a similar perspective in the *American Architect and Building News*: "The Electric Tower is the climax. . . . It is the altar at the head of the aisle of increasing brilliance, spread with the cloth of white and illumined by golden candles—and that is the key." Amos K. Fiske, writing for *Harper's Weekly*, declared that the entire exposition culminated in the "cream and gold" of the tower top.

Despite the phallic implications of the Electric Tower, most journalistic discussion focused on the use of color. "If there is a touch of the fanciful in this endeavor to suggest the evolution of man by means of a scheme of color," Hamilton Wright Mabie confided to the *Outlook's* readers, "the general effect is rich and striking, and the eye which loves color finds delight in the warm tones modulated over great space with a harmonious sense of values." Writing in the *Architectural Record*, Herbert Croly, architectural critic and emerging spokesman for Progressi_ism, criticized the fair's excessive ornamentation, yet praised the designers for having successfully created "stimulating surroundings" that "embody something like the best ideals and training of American art." In contrast to Croly's modest praise for chromatic effects, a *New York Times* correspondent insisted that Turner had been too conservative. "But," the reporter conceded, "perhaps it is too much to expect from the staid white of North America that he should dare to be a Moor—someone might mistake him for a 'nigger' and that, bless his heart! would cut him to the quick." Like the artists and architects who had conceived the notion of color-coding the fair, this journalist linked perception of color to perceived racial qualities. "Color," the correspondent wrote, "is the most immediate speech that the outer world utters to our mind, for we see color before we detect term. . . . Color is in fact the primal language for the child as for the immature races."

At the Pan-American Exposition, rainbow colors linked to displays with ethnological messages produced an unforgettable image of American progress that helped structure those messages for the eight million people who visited the exposition. Outside the Government Building, Carrère placed a Fountain of Man adorned with statuary created under Bitter's guidance, illustrating the struggle of man against nature. Inside the building visitors found Smithsonian exhibits delineating grades of Indian cultures in North and South America as well as a large display of cultural artifacts and natural resources from the Philippine Islands. Art and ethnology intersected more dramatically in the Ethnology Building. Since Carrère had placed this building at the center of the exposition grounds, Turner arranged its exterior colors "halfway between crudity and artistic refinement." According to the Buffalo *Enquirer*, the colors also moved in an ascending pattern: "In accordance with the general color scheme, which placed the harsh, bright colors at the southern end of the grounds and in the lower part of the buildings, red will predominate near the base gradually merging toward the top with a pale yellow and then to bright ivory." The Ethnology Building housed artifacts arranged geographically together with oil paintings of various racial types set against a pyramidic backdrop of colors decorating the interior walls. "On the inside," the *Enquirer* commented, "the gradual change from an earthy red at the base to an ethereal blue at the top at once satisfies the artistic sense and prompts the analogy between it and the ascent of man from savagery to civilization." To ascend the spiral staircases to the galleries was thus presumably to follow the course of human development through evolutionary stages. A sign in the building told visitors that these lessons about racial progress continued on the midway, where ethnological villages formed "an integral part of the educational exhibits." Turner reinforced this link between the Pan and the overall design of the fair by treating the color of midway structures more liberally, thereby linking midway features with primitive passions and the lower orders of mankind.

Ethnological exhibits reinforced the artistic presentation of racial gradations. To organize the exposition's Ethnology Department, the directors selected A. L. Benedict, who held the "chair of physiology and digestive diseases" in the dental department at the University of Buffalo. An archaeologist by avocation, Benedict described his own role in the fair as "Editor of scientific work." In working out plans for the displays in his department, he solicited suggestions from "nearly every scientific anthropologist," including William Henry Holmes, Otis T. Mason, and W. J. McGee at the Smithsonian Institution and Frederic Ward Putnam at Harvard. With their aid, Benedict drafted plans to bring together "an exposition of the living natives of Pan America" encompassing "only the aboriginal races of the Western Continent and the islands geographically or politically associated with it."

Benedict's grand plan, however, ran headlong into several problems, which he discussed in some detail in his final report, First, he noted that the cost of the plan proved much too high. Additionally, Benedict worried about preserving "discipline and sanitation in a large population of uncivilized tribes, each possessing its own peculiarities and religious prejudices." Finally, he anticipated difficulties in finding "untainted native stocks [and] keeping the inmates of the proposed colony from acquiring rapidly the clothing and customs of their surroundings."

The net result of these problems was that when the exposition opened all that remained of Benedict's original plan was a "hexagonic stockade which enclosed Iroquois dwellings." Inside this enclosure he had hoped to have the Indians stage their religious celebrations, "but the execution of the plan was prevented by fear of competition with the Indian Congress on the Midway." Apparently Benedict accepted these setbacks philosophically and came to regard the ethnological villages along the Pan as offering the best solution to the problems he had encountered in trying to include live exhibits in his own department. On the midway, he observed, "the financial management and the discipline are adapted to the particular conditions, while criticism on the third point [the matter of representing 'untainted' racial stocks] is obviated by disclaiming all scientific responsibility on the part of the exposition." The midway area, in other words, permitted Benedict and the exposition directors to have their ethnological cake and eat it too by affirming or denying the scientific accuracy of the various ethnological villages to suit their needs. The beauty of the midway, once again, was that it made science and entertainment interchangeable.

With living specimens of nonwhites relegated to the Pan, Benedict contented himself with organizing artifacts depicting aboriginal modes of manufacture and warfare along geographical lines—exhibits that Turner enveloped with a panorama of colors depicting evolutionary development. Despite the absence of live aborigines, visitors poured into the Ethnology Building. Attendance figures showed that "on any average day about 75 percent of the visitors to the exposition were represented in the Ethnology Building." But from the vantage point of the exposition management, the presence of large crowds in the building underscored their feelings that the Ethnology Department's exhibits should have been better. Buchanan considered the results of the department "far from satisfactory," primarily "because no commercial motives exist on the part of anyone for making such an exhibit." In his opinion the Ethnology Department had wandered far from its original purpose and assumed a strong archaeological bent that had failed to convey the explicit commercial lessons that permeated the displays devoted to the Philippine Islands in the Government Building and the villages on the midway.

Early in the organization of the fair, the Philippine Islands emerged as the most important part of a planned exhibit depicting the newly acquired "outlying possessions." In the fall of 1899 exposition officials had written to the federal government's exposition board suggesting "the desirability of . . . a special governmental display of Exhibits from Cuba, Puerto Rico, Alaska, the Hawaiian and Philippine Islands, showing not only the products, resources and possibilities of these possessions, but also and particularly the ethnological features available." Such a display would satisfy the "intense interest felt by our people to learn all about the people and territories which have come under our charge and there has not been so good an opportunity as will present itself to reach the many million expected to visit us, as will be afforded al our exposition." In a second letter the exposition management promised that "[t]he exhibits would form the dominant feature of the Exposition," and emphasized that the government should "absolutely reproduce typical scenery . . . and [bring to] the Exposition grounds houses actually used in the respective countries." The plan included "bringing of 100, more or less, natives, housing and maintaining them during the Exposition period."

"This is the first and best opportunity we have had," Director-General Buchanan had written in December 1899 to J. H. Brigham, chairman of the government exposition board, "to justify, by means of the most available object lessons we can produce, the acquisition of new territory; to demonstrate, as I am sure can be done, that the results to be obtained promise to be for us all ample compensation for the sacrifice already made, and, for the burdens yet to be assumed." The colonial exhibit at the exposition, in short, would generate support in the United States for maintaining and extending America's colonial empire. The undertaking was crucial, Buchanan stressed, "because of the influence it can be made to exert upon interests reaching beyond the scope of the Exposition; it may be made of so much effectiveness that it will come to be beneficial as a guide for our people in their consideration of our Government policy in the Islands—the shaping of which will be more largely influenced by the Agricultural and Mineral wealth such an exhibit will show existing therein than by any other medium." Financing the display, Buchanan explained, could easily be arranged without additional government expense, since "surplus" revenues generated by the islands were "presumably to be expended for the betterment of the Islands and in their best interest." He concluded by repeating that "no more advisable or beneficial use could be made of such funds than the exhibit we talked over."

Buchanan's carefully articulated argument received a sympathetic hearing from the government board's Subcommittee on Outlying Possessions, headed by Frederick W. True of the Smithsonian Institution, but their hands were tied by the terms of the congressional appropriation for federal participation in the fair. Two days before Buchanan's last letter arrived attorneys for the Treasury Department, responding to the exposition directors' proposal about government funding for colonial villages, declared that the appropriation from Congress would not permit the use of federal funds for a display of "natives" from outlying possessions.

This legal opinion, coupled with reservations over the projected cost of establishing the villages, led the government board to restrict direct federal financial support for the colonial display to material artifacts and natural resources from the colonies. Nevertheless, this decision met the exposition management more than halfway: the board had guaranteed a federally funded colonial exhibit at the fair and left open the possibility for the management to finance villages along the midway—an option exposition officials exercised. The government board complied with the directors' request in yet another way by determining to focus the exhibit from America's imperial acquisitions on the Philippine Islands, giving relatively little attention to Hawaii, Guam, Cuba, and Puerto Rico. As a memorandum from the board explained, its members were "desirous of complying with the wishes of the Management, and in view of the fact that the Philippine Islands would furnish the most valuable collecting field, the Chairman was authorized to employ a suitable per[son] or persons to make as full a collection as possible from these Islands; the necessary funds for this purpose to be set aside."

In January 1900 the government board appointed Frank F. Hilder, employed as a translator by the Bureau of American Ethnology, to travel to the Philippines and gather material for the United States government exhibit at the Pan-American Exposition. Hilder's ethnological field research, along with his military and business background, amply fitted him for the job. Born in Hastings, England, in 1836, he had attended English military schools and served in the British army in lndia and Africa. After emigrating to America, he spent fifteen years as an international representative of Remington Arms Company, traveling around the world. Throughout his military and business careers, Hilder had actively pursued extensive ethnological, geographical, and archaeological research in Asia and the Americas. In the United States he became a popular public speaker on the "remote regions" of the earth and published many articles in the *Forum* and *National Geographic.* The BAE recognized his contributions to ethnology by appointing him to the position of ethnologic translator in 1898 and granted him leave to act as special agent for the government board to make the third and final trip of his career to the Philippine Islands.

The government board explained Hilder's mission in a directive sent to him shortly before he left for the Philippines in January 1900: "The object of sending a special agent to the Philippine Islands, is to obtain such articles and information as will illustrate the natural resources of the Islands, the characteristics and mode of life of the inhabitants, and the principal features and methods of government, past and present." Milder carried letters of introduction authorizing him "to collect by purchase, gift, or loan, articles of interest pertaining to each department of the Government, to be exhibited at the Pan-American Exposition."

Hilder also received explicit instructions from William Henry Holmes, curator of the Department of Anthropology in the United States National Museum, to keep the long-range interests of the United States National Museum in mind while gathering exhibits for the Buffalo fair: "It is the desire of the Anthropological Department of the National Museum to secure from the Philippines materials that will illustrate the peoples and culture in a permanent way in the Museum and that at the same time will afford means of preparing effective groups of exhibits for the Buffalo Exposition." Holmes went on to explain that what he had in mind were "a series of *Lay-figure groups* representing the native peoples, and the first object of the collector should be to secure data and collections for this purpose." The central aim, as Holmes put it, was "to give a complete idea of the character and culture of the people," adding that be preferred centering attention on "the more primitive peoples such as the Negritos, the Moros and the Igoroti [*sic*]."

Hilder did everything in his power to accommodate the heads of the various government departments composing the government board, despite the shortage of time and difficult conditions in the Philippines. Aided by United States military personnel, merchants, journalists, and Catholic clergy, Hilder succeeded in gathering, cataloging, and shipping more than five hundred cultural artifacts as well as "a series of photographs of representative groups of different tribes, also of individual pictures with all anthropological details, measurements, etc." He amassed "a number of statistical schedules of labor, wages, etc. for the Department of Labor" and information about Philippine currency for the Treasury Department. On his return to San Francisco after a month of intensive effort in the Philippines, he informed the *San Francisco Chronicle* that "the greatest and most profitable industry of the future in the Philippines will be connected with the marketing of the magnificent timber that covers the island." In his final report to the government board, Hilder rated his expedition to the Philippines "successful." But Hilder never saw the final fruit of his labors. Five months before the Buffalo exposition opened this unsung soldier–scientist and apostle of Anglo-Saxon imperialism died suddenly after a brief illness.

Rather than distributing the materials he had gathered to the separate departmental alcoves of the Government Building at the fair, the government board decided to keep the Hilder collection intact, to supplement it with commercial exhibits from the Philippines provided by importers in New York and Boston, and to give it a separate place in the north wing of the government structure. There, according to *World's Work*, the display "probably attracted more spectators than other parts of the federal exhibit," which included the War Department's display of Spanish–American War relics, newly invented dum-dum bullets and smokeless powder, and the display by Smithsonian ethnologists of twelve lay-figure groups of Pan-American aboriginal types "designed to show the status of various native races as regards culture." Even the Biograph motion pictures of military drills, shown by the Bureau of Education in the government's first public use of this new medium, drew smaller crowds than the "object lesson of the character and customs of the strange people" from the Philippines.

Minutes of the government board meetings matter-of-factly expressed satisfaction with the exhibit, noting that it evidenced "compliance with the desire of the Exposition Management that the Government present an exhibit from the Islands." F. W. Clarke, Interior Department representative on the board, applauded the efforts that went into the display: "Everything," he wrote, signified "the work of trained intelligence." "After all," another commentator pointed out, "the Government hasn't an equal in the show business."

The government, however, had stopped short of completely satsifying the exposition promoters. When the government board refused to fund the proposed village of Filipinos but left the door open for exposition backers to arrange one on their own, the management acted quickly. Knowing that all roads at the fair would eventually lead fairgoers to the midway, they relegated the Filipino Village to the Pan. Buffalo businessmen invested $40,000 in the projected show and guaranteed any additional money necessary to complete the display of what a contemporary newspaper termed America's "somewhat reluctant citizens." E. W. McConnell, an experienced showman, received the contract for the concession and added the Filipino Village to his Red Star Route of seven other features he managed along the Pan. McConnell designated "Pony" Moore as his agent to travel to the Philippines to gather material and people for the attraction. Moore, a Naval Academy graduate, Omaha newspaperman, and theatrical press agent who had formerly managed the short-lived Philippine Village at both Omaha expositions, returned to Buffalo with one hundred Filipinos.

The Filipino Village consisted of an eleven-acre enclosure loosely modeled after photographs of an actual village in the Philippines and embellished with many imperial touches added by McConnell. The village gateway somewhat resembled the fortifications at Manila Bay that had yielded to American assault and, as an added touch of realism, a detachment of United Stales soldiers was "on parade at the entrance at all times." Inside the compound, visitors found a colonial adventure awaiting them. Carts pulled by water buffalo provided free transportation among thatched huts, a lake complete with war canoes, a Catholic church, museum, and theater. It "is almost as good as a trip to the islands," the *New York Times* reported. The concession as a whole impressed anthropologist Frederick Starr from the University of Chicago as "really good." Like most other visitors, Starr was fascinated by the Filipino people and especially by "Buchanna," the Filipino girl who was born at the fair and christened after the director-general of the exposition. The theater Starr found especially noteworthy, for there "a sombre faced juggler did some tricks neatly and the [Filipino] band played the national anthem—*The Star Spangled Banner!*"

Assessing the nature of the Filipino people and the part they would play in the American empire became a popular pastime at the fair. An article in the *Pan-American Herald*, the journal produced by the exposition management, quoted a British report about the Philippines to make a point about "the natural indolence of the Filipino." "They have no idea of putting energy into any of their pursuits," the report staled, "and have no commercial instincts; they care little for money, loss or gain being to them apparently a matter of indifference." Like the Afro-Americans and Native Americans on display in other villages on the midway, Filipinos appeared to require American tutelage in managing their future—a future the exposition depicted as inexorably linked to the production of raw materials and consumption of finished American products. The task, as Richard Barry suggested in his popular sketch of the Pan, was not hopeless, because the Filipinos "have earnestness and they have modesty, and better than all else they are clean, wholesome and somewhat diffident."

The chief problem confronting American interests, the exposition management realized, involved teaching the Filipinos to be willing subjects. When Emilio Aguinaldo, leader of the Philippine resistance to the United States occupation, was captured in April 1901, the thought crossed several minds to put him on display in the Filipino Village, but the idea was dismissed as "not practical." The villagers already on display, however, seemed likely candidates for spreading the news of American power to other Filipinos upon their return to the Philippines. As they prepared to leave the Pan at the conclusion of the fair the Buffalo *Courier* commented: "the tidings of the goodness and greatness which [the Filipinos] will take back will be a great help in the furtherment of the United States Government's policy there." The next day the same newspaper noted approvingly that several Filipinos began crying as they left the midway. Yet their experience had not been altogether a positive one. Late in October, a twenty-five-year-old woman died in the hospital after contracting tuberculosis in the village.

Doubtless many Filipinos left without being persuaded of the benefits to be derived from being wards of the United Stales. To correct that situation the federal government, in cooperation with the management of the planned 1904 exposition for Saint Louis, began laying the groundwork for a larger and more spectacular Philippine colonial display. At the Pan-American Exposition, the various Philippine exhibits and additional ethnological villages along the Pan provided ample precedent to draw on.

"I tol ye wanst," Finley Peter Dunne's Mr. Dooley insisted, "that f'r wan man that goes to a wurruld's fair to see how boots is made, they'se twinty goes to see th' hootchy-kootchy an that's where th' wan lands fin'ally." The backers of the Pan-American Exposition never underestimated the magnetic power of the midway. Local capitalists, in conjunction with showmen who could finance their own ventures, invested between two and three million dollars in the midway shows for the Pan-American fair. For their money they expected the results to be instructive, entertaining, and profitable. According to the director of exhibits, Frederick W. Taylor: "The organization and bringing together of the features now known under the generic name 'Midway,' for the amusement, edification, and instruction of the public, has become so great a factor in Expositions that nowadays that department is considered one of the most important and requires many months of strenuous labor in order that satisfactory results may be worked out." The concessionaire played a critical role in making a given show a success. "He must be a social philosopher," explained Mary Bronson Hart in *World's Work*. "Nothing short of a close study of the people at play will teach him what will 'take.'" Rarely, however, did the management completely rely on the showman's perceptions of social reality, much less his philosophy. Especially in the case of the ethnological villages, the exposition sponsors carefully shaped the social theory that informed the attractions by specifying the content of the shows in the contracts awarded to the various showmen. As Taylor put it: "it is more than likely that no single phase of the Exposition in architecture, exhibits, or concessions will leave a more lasting impress than will the ethnological features of the various villages." With this thought in mind, the contracts for the ethnological villages emphasized exhibits of alleged racial characteristics as part of the overarching demonstration at the fair of the need for Anglo-Saxon domination of the non-white world. "Great effort has been made to have [the ethnological] features correct in every way," Taylor assured fairgoers.

After turning down one proposal to construct an African slave market on the Pan, Taylor awarded the concession for an African Village to French explorer–scientist Xavier Pené. This imperial entrepreneur had supplied African labor for the construction of the Pan-American Railroad in the 1880s and had managed the Dahomeyan Village at the World's Columbian Exposition. The contract he received for the African Village at the Pan-American Exposition stated that "the ground plan in a general way consists of groups of typical huts of at least twenty-five different races or tribes of Africa south of the Senegal River, the Desert of Sahara, and Egypt." The African people selected for display in the village, according to the contractual arrangement with the exposition directors, were expected "to present the racial peculiarities and customs . . . subject to the approval of the Director-General." Pené, with support from the Buffalo Society of Natural Sciences as well as from the geographical and anthropological societies of France, obtained permission of the various European powers controlling Africa to make the planned expedition. "The original purpose of the expedition," according to the souvenir guide to the village, "contemplated chiefly an ethnological and anthropological exhibit, to specially include those race types of African natives known to us hitherto only by the descriptions of Moffat, Livingston, DuChaillu, Stanley and others." Pené realized, however, "that an added popular interest would be given to the exhibit if the natives could be shown in their natural surroundings and living entirely in the native way."

Advertised as "REAL AFRICAN LIFE: IN A REAL AFRICAN VILLAGE" and as being "In the Midway but not of it," Pené's Darkest Africa included ninety-eight Africans living amid "the occasional chatter of the monkeys and the constant screaming of the flock of African parrots giving a final touch of local color to the scene." Above all, the show's promoters asserted, "the scientific features of the exhibit of Darkest Africa differentiate it altogether from the common Midway show." Visitors would he instructed and entertained by "those incidental features springing out of the peculiarity of native habits and customs, the childishness, humor and love of frolic inherent in the African race, and as strongly marked in the descendants of those who have enjoyed a century of civilization in America, as it is in these who represent the savage ancestry of our colored population." Even before she saw the show, Minnie J. Reynolds informed readers of the *New York Times*: "I felt sure that the darkest inhabitants came from somewhere south of Mason and Dixon's line." Another visitor observed: "[Africans] adopt customs rapidly, and the most rapid acquisition they have made has been the inborn attribute of the colored gentleman of the palace car, whose remote ancestors they suggest; they can solicit a tip on the slightest provocation."

Across the street from Darkest Africa, the Old Plantation cemented the impression of racial continuity. Elmer "Skip" Dundy, another emerging amusement industry magnate, had received the Old Plantation concession. In the contract he agreed to exhibit fifty "genuine negroes"—twenty men, twenty women, and ten children—who lived in the South. Richard Barry explained the importance of having southern blacks in the show: "It is easy to pick up the colored people of the North and draught them into the show business, but the darkies of the South do not take as kindly to the public rogue box." "They all love the beat of a bass drum and a limber-jointed abandon of a cake-walk," Barry continued, "but the Southern negro is a stay-at-home darkey, not so much through dislike for publicity as through the inherent laziness that will not run the risk of nomadic life." In addition to affording "more of the real ginger of genuine enjoyment," Barry wrote, a show consisting of southern blacks gives "more correctly a picture of real Southern life."

The picture, however, was slanted from the start, since many of the blacks selected for the show had first attended a performance school in Charleston run by Fred McClellan, another blossoming midway showman. What the Old Plantation correctly depicted was the ideology of racial reconciliation and subordination promulgated by the promoters of the New South. In the concession blacks appeared as "jocular, careless serfs, who in the South before the war gave slavery the deceptive hue of contented and oft-times happy dependence." Barry invited whites who visited the attraction to recall the "pitiful history" of blacks and to remember equally well that Afro-Americans had been graced with "cheerful" qualities that would enable them to endure hardship and survive despite their alleged racial limitations. Miniature cotton bales for sale as souvenirs served as a not-so-subtle reminder of how blacks would fit into the economic structure of the Pan-American utopia forecast by the exposition's directors. Equally telling was the offer made to Jim Parker, the black Atlanta waiter who aided Secret Service agents in subduing McKinley's assassin, to join in an unnamed midway attraction. Parker refused; but the attempt to caricature a black hero as mock-heroic stood, nevertheless, as a monument to an ideology that sharply delimited the social roles open to blacks.

As in the case of Africans, Afro-Americans, and Filipinos, the exposition also locked selected Latin Americans into villages with predetermined ideological contours. "In general," the contract for the Mexican Village concession read, "the 'Streets of Mexico' is to be a realistic reproduction of the architect of different cities and villages of Mexico, and the general entertainment is to be a display of the racial customs and characteristic street scenes of the Mexican people with the presentation of the Mexican sports and pastimes common to Mexican routine daily life." H. F. McGarvie, former director-general of the San Francisco Midwinter Exposition of 1894 and publicity director for the Trans-Mississippi fair, raised the capital for the show by forming a joint-stock company with several "responsible" Buffalo businessmen. Before he received the contract, however, the exposition management asked the Mexican government for its approval of the attraction. President Díaz gave his permission for the show on two conditions: "first—that the concession should not in any way bring ridicule upon Mexico, her inhabitants or buildings; and, second, that the concessionaire should guarantee to return to Mexico all Mexicans employed in the concession." Once assured that these provisions would be met, Díaz enhanced the semiofficial nature of the concession by agreeing to provide the show with a troop of *rurales*. In actuality, however, the location of the attraction on the Pan and the exposition management's insistence on a display of Mexican "racial customs" made compliance with Díaz's demand for respect a remote possibility at best. McGarvie's concession romanticized the Spanish influence in Mexico, emphasized the potential for American investment in the Mexican economy, and stressed the inferiority of the Mexican people.

The village, with its bullfights, dancers, archaeological and ethnological artifacts, and restaurants, alternately appealed to and repulsed visitors. "The laziness of the place is pleasing, and its rosiness attractive," Barry decided. "The life of Mexico is shown," he noted, and is complete with "the peons, the diminutive burros, and ever present bazaars, and the girls who dance with the abandon of the Midway and languor of Old Spain." Another fairgoer found the village utterly unbelievable, especially the symmetry of the architecture: "A Mexican has no such ingenuity. He is absolutely lacking in mechanical skill."

Other ethnological villages provided opportunities for comparison. Uncle Hank, the character in Thomas Fleming's novel about the Pan, for instance, commented favorably on the commercial possibilities evidenced in the Cuban Village and fully expected "Uncle Sam . . . [to] take [Cuba] to his heart and make her one of his beloved daughters by adoption." Apparently the only obstacle was the seemingly lackadaisical nature of the Cubans. "They need a little Yankee blood down thar," Uncle Hank observed. "Hustle ez a good word, a heap sight bettern Manany." Fairgoers came away from the Eskimo, Hawaiian, and Japanese villages convinced that the "slant-eyed" Eskimos living in papier-mâché igloos were basically harmless, that Hawaiians were "elemental," and that the Japanese were the "Yankees ov ther orient" who would soon "heve a Monroe doctrine ov ther own" and "give them Rooshins and Germans something to think about."

The same blend of affection and racial antipathy that characterized the popular response to the Streets of Mexico surfaced in the Indian Congress when Vice-President Theodore Roosevelt visited the concession and named a newborn Native American baby Pan-Anna. An official guidebook to the exposition underlined the didactic value of the Indian Congress: "No such lesson in history can be gleaned from books as is here shown by 'Native Americans'—long haired painted savages in all their barbaric splendor." A sketch in the Buffalo *Express* captured the image of Indians as presented by the show. According to the caption: "A wild Western Indian, at the Exposition, was observed absorbed in contemplation of a wolf. It was like meeting an old friend in the strange East. The wolfs howl, too, seemed to carry with it a note of recognition." With its sham battles and famous "living heroes," including Geronimo and a variety of United States military scouts, the Indian Congress left an indelible imprint on visitors, especially children. Mrs. William Jennings Bryan, for one, endorsed the attraction as "a school of instruction, a school-house of information, a happy, merry playground for little children." "Every man, every woman, every child in the Union should see it," she declared. A local kindergarten class apparently followed her advice. Two days after seeing the entire fair, the teacher asked the children to find illustrations of their favorite exhibits. Pictures of the Indian Congress outnumbered all others.

The ethnological villages on the Pan presented a variety of human types and cultures. One exhibit in particular, The Evolution of Man, linked the variety of human types to the greater evolutionary lessons about progress as presented by the exposition as a whole. This attraction, brainchild of Frank Bostock, manager of the Zoological Garden, presented visitors to the Wild Animal Show with the "missing link" to Darwin's evolutionary chain in the form of a well-trained chimpanzee. "Here the Darwinian theory of evolution is very completely illustrated," claimed the official exposition guidebook. "The successive stages of development by which the 'genus homo,' of the present day was evolved from its primaeval progenitors is shown by numerous well-selected examples, from the lowest type of Simian development to the 'missing link' or educated chimpanzee, Esau, who all but talks, and from the lowest savage to the polished gentlemen of today." Whether any human beings were actually displayed in the same show with Esau is uncertain, but the presence of the "missing link" in the larger setting of the midway only reinforced the lessons of racial hierarchy that saturated the artistic dimensions of the fair and the living ethnological shows.

If the midway colonies and related attractions reflected the imperial ambitions of the exposition promoters, the villages also evidenced an important concomitant to imperial expansion—disease. Tuberculosis hit the Filipino Village. Furthermore, the director of the exposition's medical department, Roswell Park, reported that eleven cases of measles appeared in the Eskimo Village and in several instances advanced to pneumonia. Park also recorded an outbreak of mumps in the Hawaiian Village and eight cases of tuberculosis in the Indian Congress. But despite quarantines imposed on several villages for varying lengths of time, visitors generally remained oblivious to these aspects of village life. Many fairgoers, like Uncle Hank, found the villagers "all rich in mirth-provoking possibilities."

As Americans stepped gingerly into the twentieth century, they found that the Pan offered an atmosphere of joy and gaiety where education and entertainment waltzed hand in hand. They discovered that all the world was a fair and found even the far reaches of the universe on display for their amusement and edification. Swaddled in the comfortable security of the exposition's utopian promises, many exposition visitors simply let themselves go when they hit the Pan. "Serious-minded clergymen cheer on the bloodless bull-fight," Mary Bronson Hart wrote about the midway, and "portly ex-senators run races on oriental donkeys several sizes too small for them, and timorous maiden ladies explore the awful mysteries of the Darkness and Dawn Under-World." This last concession initially horrified midway pleasure seekers with "seas of fire," the sudden "appearance of brown-suited young men wearing painted skeletons," and a confrontation with a likeness of Satan himself. Visitors, however, wrestled only briefly with the darker recesses of their psyches, for darkness soon gave way to the "Grotto of Dawn," a heavenly city of "soft lights," "flowing fountains," and "walls of jasper." At the conclusion, "the mist-like forms of floating angels" pointed the way back to the thoroughfare of the Pan. Once back on the midway, tourists alternated taking turns on the giant see-saw and rotating aero-cycle, which afforded sweeping panoramas of the Pan-American grounds. Another popular concession, Frederic W. Thompson's Trip to the Moon—with effects so realistic that many in the audience suffered from motion sickness—caused one journalist to exclaim: "There! you see, not satisfied with exhausting the earth, [showmen] have already begun upon the universe. Behold, the world is a sucked orange."

Throughout the summer visitors continued their revelry in the shadows of the displays devoted to American progress. As 5 September, President's Day, approached, the swell of self-congratulation grew. What the directors intended as the consummating moment of the fair, however, miscarried. The day after delivering one of the most memorable speeches of his career, while shaking hands with the crowd in the Temple of Music, President McKinley was shot by Leon Czolgosz, a reputed anarchist. The shooting triggered the arrests of anarchists and socialists across the country and, since Czolgosz was the son of recent Polish immigrants, escalated nationwide demands for immigration restrictions on European populations perceived as undesirable. McKinley's death—which occurred in the home of exposition president John Milburn eight days after the shooting—exposed the ethnic and class rifts in American society; it also underscored the fundamental importance of the exposition for maintaining a shared cultural faith in American progress at a time of acute political crisis.

In his President's Day address McKinley praised expositions as "timekeepers of progress," extolled industrial growth as the guarantor of progress, and charted the course to future utopia through the establishment of "reciprocal" commercial relations with Pan-American countries. Expositions played an important part in this process, McKinley explained, because "[t]hey record the world's advancement. They stimulate the energy, enterprise, and intellect of the people and quicken human genius. They go into the home. They broaden and brighten the daily life of the people." The force of McKinley's statement about the impact of expositions on everyday life received added weight in the aftermath of the shooting as souvenir prices on the grounds skyrocketed. "The demand for souvenirs with a picture of the Temple of Music or of the President was tremendous," the *Express* commented. "Little trays, ornamented with pictures of the Temple of Music, went like hotcakes." Such keepsakes would enliven memories of the assassination of McKinley and of the life of the fair.

"Do Not Neglect the Fair," the *Express* editorialized after McKinley's death. "The Exposition is recognized now as an enterprise of national importance to a greater extent than it ever was before." The same newspaper admonished its readers "to have faith in [the exposition], to admire it, to praise it to their friends." Between the first week of September and the first week of November, when the fair closed its gates, weekly attendance figures increased as nearly two million people visited the exposition. The experience of one elderly man was not untypical. As he and his wife entered the fairgrounds a local newspaper reporter observed that the old man burst into tears when he "spied an American flag flying on a tall flagpole" in the Esplanade. "Thank God, it's there yet!" the reporter heard him cry out. On Railroad Day, well over one hundred thousand people traveled to the fair, and many crammed the Temple of Music to hear Senator Chauncey Depew recite the accomplishments of American railroads and eulogize McKinley as "a Christian and a patriot." At the conclusion of the speech, the crowd sat motionless and silent. Then deafening applause broke out, the hand struck up the "Star-Spangled Banner," "and the audience arose, waving flags, [with] the Senator waving a flag and virtually leading the audience." Two days later the spirit of political authority infused the cultural sovereignty of the fair in yet another way as a likeness of McKinley mysteriously appeared on the floor of the Temple of Music near the spot where he was assassinated. No one ever discovered the origin of the design, but it had the same import as the remark by Governor Benjamin Odell on New York Day at the fair: "Our Government still lives, and as we turn from the bier of our martyred President let us resolve to be more earnest in our devotion." McKinley's death, in short, increased the stature of the exposition as a visible reminder of cultural and political continuity in a society wrenched by disturbing signs of class conflict.

As the Pan-American Exposition moved to conclusion, another effort to inspire patriotic devotion to imperial visions of progress through a world's fair was well under way in Saint Louis. Like the directors of the Buffalo exposition, the civic leaders sponsoring the celebration commemorating the one hundredth anniversary of the Louisiana Purchase understood that the "true function of an exposition is education" and that the "purpose and end of all its ministrations should be the development and ripening of each soul which comes within the scope of its influence." The directors of the Louisiana Purchase Exposition, however, did more than merely try to influence the souls of men. They sought to gain the world as well.

3.2 EXPOSITION AS AN EDUCATOR—MINNIE REYNOLDS

New York Times, October 6, 1901

UPON THE MIDWAY, the most interesting things are the villages; the Eskimo village, the Indian congress, Darkest Africa, the Philippine and Japanese inclosures. These are an integral part of the educational exhibits, as pointed out in a placard in the Ethnological Building; even though they are situated on the Midway and charge an extra admission fee. The Alaskan exhibit in its log cabin is of the same kind, although it is over near the State buildings. To the "fake" shows on the Midway people go once, and never again. But to the others they return.

Americans are a reading people. They are also a restless people, who travel whenever they have money in their purse, and long to do so when they have not. The many millioned masses of America cannot be globe trotters. They can never see the things they read about. And when they flock to expositions they want to have object lessons to explain and illuminate what they have read at home.

You find them at Buffalo lingering long in the Pan-American buildings; among the exhibits of Cuba, Chile, Mexico, Ecuador; around the magnificent exhibit of Philippine curios in the Government Building; around the different State exhibits in the Horticultural Buildings; among the curious and interesting things in the Ethnological Building; among the aquariums and kinetoscopes in the Government Fisheries Building; among the fragrant, clean smelling logs of the Forestry Building, and among the different villages.

[. . .]

At Buffalo the Alaska Building and the Eskimo village were especially interesting, because there were intelligent people there who explained everything in an interesting way. The "object lesson" is the salient feature of modern education, and grown-ups appreciate it just as much as children.

In the Alaska log cabin there is a saturnine and slangy young man who makes the round of the Crain collection of Alaskan curios, giving a running comment on each, and describing enough of the manners, customs, and history of the country to explain each. His tongue runs with the ease of perfect familiarity, and in a terse and vigorous vernacular that has a Kiplingesque touch. Under his treatment the carved ivories, the baskets, the mats, the bone dishes and cooking utensils, the big Hudson Bay "huskies" that rouse sleepily at his word, all glow with life and take on a warm, human interest. You see the land of the long Winter night and the long Summer day; the land of the "Black Wolf's Breed." Without his talk they would have been only a collection of musty old traps. But the slangy young man, who had learned his piece so well, transforms the whole collection with his eloquence. The lecture alone or the collection alone would not have been much to the casual observer, such as those who visit it. But put them together and they are of absorbing Interest. You see the Eskimo in his walrus skin kyak, tight and water-proof the skirt of his kamalinka or water-proof coat fastened over the hatch, dashing dry shod through the northern seas. You see the life of the women, making baskets of silken fineness and softness; carving ivory dolls for their children; making these bone needles like the cave women and the bone thimble, and the neat little ivory case to put them in; you see them making these coats of cedar bark, almost as soft as wool; and these robes and coats of fur, some with a thousand pieces in them. Curious that the beginnings of all art, in whatever race, were among the women.

If you remark on the kindly, pleasant disposition of the Eskimo, the man in charge, who has been on a polar expedition himself, will tell you that every polar expedition yet has owed more than it can tell to the kindness and hospitality of these little people of the north: that they are the most honest and moral of all people and that their first impulse on sight of a stranger is to offer him all the hospitality at their command. There is a lecture here, too, which is more than a running comment on the curios, and includes stereopticon illustrations of the homes and native scenes of the people in the village. The cute little girl solicits your stray nickels for pamphlets and you learn that though she is an Eskimo and wears the native costume, she has never seen Eskimo land. Sue was born eight years ago on the exposition grounds at Chicago, and named Columbia, and her small life has all been spent in shows of various kinds. Her mother, a full-blooded Eskimo, is a singularly attractive young woman, although decidedly blasé from her large experience of the great American public. She is the only woman of her race, it is said, who was ever made the heroine of a novel.

When I scanned the list of the Midway attractions, there was one which I decided not to patronize. It was "Darkest Africa," and I felt sure that the darkest inhabitants of it came from somewhere south of Mason and Dixon's line. One evening, though, I met two negroes strolling along the Midway. They were negroes, but I knew instantly that they were of a kind I had never seen before. It is hard to tell just why you know that they are not American negroes, but know it you do, instantly. I followed them into the village, and stumbled along an ill-lighted pathway, past low thatched huts, toward a lighted platform. Suddenly two great black figures, nude, except for a sort of fringe arrangement hanging from the waist line, sprang into view, dancing fiercely. The first sight of them was positively terrifying. I went to the seat that ran along the side of the great platform, and watched them dance the war dance; watched them an hour or more, in positive fascination. Nothing else I have ever seen conveys such an impression of wild savagery. Such ferocious sweeps of their great, curved weapons; such expressive motions of killing in every play of their magnificent muscles. One understands at last what the English met in the Zulu war, and the kind of man that killed the young Prince Napoleon. One understands at last what a really wild man is; the Indians are conventional citizens beside them. One understands also what a foe civilization is to the physical man; how the brain has been cultivated at the expense of the teeth, the muscles, and the physique. And yet, when some one in whom they have confidence speaks to them, the way their faces will light up is instructive. A woman who has had charge of the refreshment stand in the village this Summer went with me. She is of a very kind, sunny disposition, and had won their liking to a remarkable degree. Whenever she spoke to them they would smile, and a singularly childlike, trustful look would come over their faces. In fact, while they were wild men, and their war dances betrayed the ferocity of savages, they did not impress one as wicked or vicious any more than an animal is wicked or vicious.

In the Streets of Cairo, on the other hand, the natives impressed me as thoroughly bad people, in whom the low shrewdness of civilization has been cultivated, but the morale not at all. The man in charge of the African village has a coffee plantation somewhere down the Gold Coast and has lived among the natives for thirty years. He has taken a number of them out to every exposition in recent years, and he has never been able to take the same people twice, for in one season they take on too much civilization to ever serve the purpose successfully again.

Over in the Ethnological Building, . . . There is the great store of ethnological material from Samoa—the native materials, clothing, ornaments, utensils. There is the varied and magnificent collection of Aztec pottery from Mexico. There are all the things from the prehistoric village of Ohio; . . . Those skeletons, from the prehistoric graveyard in Ohio; why isn't there some one to explain them? And where is Baum, anyway? And how did they happen to discover all these highly interesting things? . . .

Ever since the last war collections of Filipino curios of greater or less extent have made their way to exhibits, museums, or the homes of returned soldiers. But nothing like the Government exhibit at Buffalo has been seen. And with the admirable explanatory cards affixed to each object, and taken in conjunction with a visit to the Filipino village, it is almost as good as a trip to the islands.

[. . .]

The exposition is a great advertising medium, and the best thing about it is that all the advertising educates.

3.3 AROUND THE "PAN" WITH UNCLE HANK: HIS TRIP THROUGH THE PAN-AMERICAN EXPOSITION—THOMAS FLEMING

WHILE HE WAS IN THE MIDWAY he bethought himself of the advisability of taking in some of the shows he had overlooked on his last visit. With this end in view he entered the "Old Southern Plantation," and in a short time was on familiar terms with the old darkies.

In front of the log cabin in which Lincoln was born stood an old, "befo'-the-wah" mammy industriously working an old-time spinning wheel. Her frowsy head was done up in a large bandanna, and periodically she emitted large whiffs of tobacco smoke from a long-stemmed corn-cob pipe which she firmly held between her thick lips. Surrounding her were several white "wooled" counterparts of Uncle Tom, and, to make the picture more complete, there were a half a dozen or so of little pickaninnies playing about.

The atmosphere was truly Southern and gave a very good idea of plantation life as it existed in *ante-bellum* days.

"'Pears ter me," he muttered to himself, "them darkies is good-natured and peaceful like; they don't look ez ef they needed Lynch Law keep 'em straight."

3.4 ATTEMPT TO KILL PRESIDENT MCKINLEY—ANON

Zion's Herald, September 11, 1901

WITHIN THE PAST WEEK the people of the United States have had their feelings stirred to the very depths by a dastardly attempt to assassinate President McKinley. The blow fell like a devastating bolt of lightning leaping from a cloudless sky. Seventy millions of people were smitten dumb with amazement that such a thing could be possible; then came a blaze of hot indignation against the assassin, followed quickly by most intense sympathy for the suffering President and his stricken wife. Every true American felt that a brother had been struck down. Messages came thick and fast from all quarters of the earth expressing the sympathy of rulers and statesmen with the American people in their sudden calamity. The attempt to kill the President was made while he was holding a public reception in the Temple of Music, at the Pan-American Exposition, Buffalo, last Friday afternoon. Thousands of people were crowding forward to shake hands with him. Leon Czolgosz, of Cleveland, O., a young anarchist, with a revolver concealed in a handkerchief wrapped about his right hand, approached in the throng, holding the bandaged hand as if it were injured. The President greeted him with his characteristic smile of good-will, and reached forward to take the left hand which Czolgosz was extending to him. At that instant the anarchist fired two shots in quick succession. Before he could fire a third he was struck in the face by a secret service agent, and knocked down by James Parker, a huge Negro, of New York city. Mr. McKinley was carried to a seat, and the assassin seized by the detectives and guards and taken to a place of safety from the mob. The President, still conscious but in pain, was conveyed to the Exposition Emergency Hospital. Fortunately, expert medical attendance was immediately available. One bullet had struck the breast bone and glanced off harmlessly. The second bullet entered the abdomen and perforated the stomach, passing through the front and rear walls. Proper attention was given to the wounds, but the second bullet could not be found. After the operation the President was carried to the home of President Milburn of the Exposition. Later in the day Mrs. McKinley, who was at the Milburn residence, was tactfully informed of the tragedy. She bore the shock bravely, and has since shown no sign of breaking down. The tender relationship existing between Mr. and Mrs. McKinley, and his care for her during her illness in San Francisco, have deeply impressed the whole world, and as the devoted wife watches by the bedside of the stricken husband, millions of hearts throb with inexpressible sympathy for her.

With his fine constitution and the best of medical attention the President is in a fair way to recover. The only danger now is from complications that may arise from blood-poisoning. Czolgosz has made a written confession, in which he states that he is an anarchist, and that he was influenced to deliberately attempt the life of the President by the teachings of Emma Goldman, anarchistic lecturer and agitator. The police are working on the theory that he is merely the tool of a band of conspirators. Vice President Roosevelt and the cabinet officers hurried promptly to Buffalo, where they are awaiting developments.

3.5 PHOTOS FROM THE PAN-AMERICAN EXPOSITION

"Despite the harmless child spieler outside, African Village inhabitants were portrayed as fascinating but dangerous: 'African warriors from Darkest Africa—Assegai Throwers, Zulus, Cannibals . . .' Sixty-two people supposedly representing 35 tribes were brought to Buffalo to demonstrate weapons, handicrafts, songs, dances, and it was said, witchcraft. Only one, John Tivie, had been outside Africa before, to Chicago in 1893, and they all remained secluded in their compound."
(Leary and Sholes 102)

Source: Image courtesy of The Buffalo History Museum

"Laughing Ben was the [Old] Plantation's image of 'good negroes,' the 'Uncles and Aunties' who were genial and compliant."
(Leary and Sholes 105)

Source: Image courtesy of The Buffalo History Museum

"The highlight of the [Indian] Congress was the daily 'sham battle.' They were touted as 'battles between the different tribes which at times will border more on the realistic than the sham, war dances, sun dances, and dances of different feasts and to their various Gods, in which the braves will appear in all the glory of war paint and feathers.' One Buffalo reporter estimated that 15,000 rounds of blank ammunition were expended each performance."
(Leary and Sholes 108)

Source: Image courtesy of The Buffalo History Museum

3.6 MAP OF THE PAN-AMERICAN EXPOSITION

Source: Courtesy of the University Archives, State University of New York at Buffalo

---

3.7 THE MIDWAY

From *The Official Catalogue and Guide to the Pan-American Exposition*

CHIEFLY FOR THE WANT OF A BETTER NAME, the amusement section of the Exposition has followed in the wake of Chicago, and been called "The Midway." The very large area lying in the northwestern end of the grounds has been allotted to the concessionaries whose business it is to amuse and at the same time instruct the visitors.

Here are found foreign villages with picturesque types of architecture and the curious and interesting evidences of civilization, so different from our own.

In modern expositions the Midway has come to be a fixture, and without it the Exposition would lose much of its charm. Visitors to all of the great National and International shows carry away with them the most pleasant recollections of scenes in the amusement section. This part of the Pan-American does not consist of mere fun-making exhibitions, but in addition to the legitimate amusement which is afforded visitors, there is much that is instructive and profitable.

Great care has been exercised by the Exposition management in making the concessions for these attractions, which, having passed through a period of evolution and development, have attained a degree of splendor quite impossible a few years ago.

Entering the Midway through the Plaza entrance, we give below a brief description of the attractions as they appear.

The Esquimau Village.

Genuine Arctic life, presented by representatives of three tribes of Esquimaux from Hudson Straits, with all their home belongings—dog teams, sledges, topeks, kayaks, weapons, etc. The Esquimaux are employed curing skins, carving ivory, manufacturing seal-skin clothing, etc. They present, in an ice-grotto, typical Esquimau dances, chants and athletic games, dog-races, also aquatic sports on the lake. The most instructive and entertaining ethnographic exhibit in the Midway. Special rates to schools and colleges.

The Moorish Palace (Pan-Opticon).

Is the first building on the left as one enters the Midway. Nothing at the Fair—certainly nothing on the Midway—is potent for more good in an educational sense than the Moorish Palace. It illustrates in a most vivid manner, scenes and events from the history of every country on the globe. Here may be found many pleasing features for those in search of amusement and for the lover of art a rare treat is in store.

Glass Factory.

A glass factory in full operation—illustrating the process employed in the manufacture of all kinds of glassware, from the raw materials to the finished products. Articles are made in the presence of the visitor and offered for sale.

McGarvie's Streets of Mexico.

This is one of the most pretentious and complete of the Midway exhibits. It includes a restaurant, market, dance hall, an old rural village, with the genuine adobe huts, a theater in which the native dances and songs are given and a bull-ring in which can be seen the famous Mexican bull fights by native toreadors and imported Mexican bulls. Every feature of Mexican life is here represented with strict fidelity to the original, while the amusements and general atmosphere are identical with those of the sister republic. A Mexican band plays the peculiar native instruments and free outdoor entertainments are given at regular intervals. Bull fights at 2, 3, 4, 8 and 10 P.M., daily. Theater, 2 to 11 P.M., hourly.

A Trip to the Moon.

Visitors are enabled to make a tour of the stars and planets, to really dart through space on a "Trip to the Moon." The tourist to the earth's satellite can recline upon his steamer chair and listen to sweet strains of music while soaring off into boundless space. Entering the atmosphere of the moon the ship drops slowly toward a sea of sunlit clouds and passing through it makes a landing on the moon. Guides meet each excursion party on the Landing Dock and show them to the wonderful underground city of the moon, with its palaces and shops, and hordes of queer people, and then on to the marvelous palace of the "Man in the moon," where all are welcomed by His Majesty, and are entertained with a revel of the "Maids of the Moon."

The Thompson Ærio-Cycle.

This attraction is the altitudinous novelty of the Midway. It resembles the "teeter" of boyhood days, constructed on a grand scale. It consists of two revolving wheels for carrying passengers, at the ends of a structural steel beam, and is so operated that when one wheel is down the other is at an altitude of 275 feet, affording a wonderful view of the Exposition.

Bonner—The Educated Horse.

This exhibit is of the celebrated horse Bonner, the wonderful talking–writing equine comedian, who is possessed of intelligence almost human, performing examples in addition, subtraction, multiplication and division in the same manner as a human being, and giving perfect imitations of a mustang buck, pitch, rear and kick.

Fall of Babylon.

Next to the building occupied by Darkness and Dawn, or really in a part of that structure, is the Fall of Babylon. The painting is by the famous French artist, George Rochgrosse, and represents a scene in Belshazzar's Temple. The army of Cyrus, the Persian, is seen entering the gates of the temple. Belshazzar's army, who spent the night in revelry, is surprised and Babylon taken.

The painting is extremely realistic and deserving of a generous patronage.

Darkness and Dawn.

A realistic representation of a departed spirit, whose life on earth has not been exemplary. The visitor witnesses the punishment meted out to scandal-mongers, umbrella borrowers and other offenders. After the seas of fire are passed, beautiful scenes to delight the eye appear, so that the visitor may become accustomed to the more familiar places above ground.

"Dawn" appears as a spectacular culmination of superb electrical and scenic effects.

Old Plantation.

Presenting a veritable Old Southern Plantation, representing the "South be'fo de Wah," introducing 150 Southern darkies in their plantation songs and dances. Old Uncles and Aunties, formerly slaves, living in the genuine cabins in which Abraham Lincoln and Jefferson Davis were born, also other historical cabins from the Old South. A Georgia cotton field with real growing cotton and a grand cake walk on the levee, participated in by the entire company.

African Village.

A collection of some thirty-five different African native tribes with their supremely ancient weapons, household gods and primitive handicraft. Native workmen show their skill in working of gold and silver. The enclosure contains sections of large villages in their primitive state, with a theatre in which are given at times free exhibitions of native dances and entertainment. The folk songs and tales of equatorial Africa are given, showing the derivation of our negro melodies, and witchcraft tales. A Boer exhibit with hospital and trek wagons, various curios illustrating the war in Africa, with the hammock carriers and means of transportation of the great African caravans.

Volcano of Kilauae.

A faithful reproduction of the Burning Mountain of the Sandwich Isles. The spectator stands within an extinct crater of this perpetual fire mountain, while its carmine hued fires belch forth and the streams of molten lava are forced from its cavernous depths. No lasting torment could be more horrible than the feeling which comes over you as you gaze into the depths of this Inferno of the world.

Hawaiian Village and Theater.

This attraction is especially interesting to visitors, since the life, customs, etc., of our new island possession are represented. In the village one can see the whole modus of sugar and coffee culture, gigantic palms, and the rites and ceremonies of the islanders. In the theater are given the native plays by native actors, introducing the famous Hulu-Hulu dancing girls, who dance this graceful measure as it is only danced to royalty. The hulu-pahu and the alaapa-apa dances are also given for the first time in this country. For good wholesome fun this concession affords one of the best Midway attractions.

Miniature World's Fair.

As its name implies, the World's Fair has been transported to the Pan-American Midway, and is here shown, though somewhat reduced in size, but still preserving its essential features. This attraction will prove of interest to those who did not attend the Chicago Fair, and will serve to refresh the memory of those who were more fortunate.

Roltair's House Upside Down.

(Palace of Illusions) This is the oddest attraction on the grounds and represents a real house standing on its roof and chimneys. The visitor enters through the roof and after passing through the various apartments (all appearing in topsy-turvy arrangement), reaches the grand palace of illusions, where twenty beautiful young women are shown in different living illusions, cleverly arranged with splendid settings. On the stage are shown four transformation illusions, one dissolving into the other and culminating with Roltair's masterpiece, "Niagara Falls."

Cleopatra's Temple.

The splendid building of Egyptian architecture, directly opposite the House Upside Down. Here are shown a series of grand paintings illustrating events in the life of the Egyptian Queen, culminating with Cooper's masterpiece, "Cleopatra," in which she is shown surrounded by her oriental splendor in a beautiful pose, and displaying her charms in order to captivate Antony. The paintings are extremely realistic, combining grace and beauty, and one almost believes the most beautiful woman in the world is there in flesh. The exhibit is owned by Alonzo Lincoln.

Around the World.

As its name implies, in this concession the visitor really enjoys a trip around the world. Native singing and dancing girls of the different countries render their peculiar songs and fascinating dances. By a very ingenious arrangement the surroundings are almost instantly changed, representing the different countries as illustrated.

Mutoscope.

Entrance to this attraction, being free, visitors may enter and satisfy themselves. Fully 150 moving picture or mutoscope machines, with an endless variety of subjects may be seen by dropping a "penny in the slot."

Colorado Gold Mine.

A faithful representation of a gold mine in working order, showing the manner employed in wresting the gold of commerce from the secret rock bound treasure troves of nature. On entering the mine competent guides explain the various drifts, veins and ledges.

This is not a model, but an actual reproduction of a Colorado mine.

Pabst's Pavilion.

In which the beer that made Milwaukee more famous, can be bought in quantities to quench the thirstiest thirst, while the strains of an excellent orchestra delight the ear. Solid refreshments are also provided.

Akoun's Beautiful Orient.

A dazzling, realistic display of the charms of the far east, reproducing the streets, villages and encampments of the principal countries. Some of the most noted buildings, mosques and minarets are reproduced and occupied by hundreds of natives, traders, fortune-tellers, etc., occupying booths, bazaars, theaters and coffee houses. Camel riding, donkey riding, elephant riding and the Oriental sports and pastimes furnish an endless amount of amusement to the visitor, while in the theater may be seen the congress of Oriental dancing girls, including La Belle Rosa, Fatma, Fatima, Carmen and many others in their peculiar native dances.

Dreamland.

At the west end of the Midway is the building occupied by Dreamland, or the Mirror Maze. Behind mirrors is a large amount of fun for those who attempt to explore its recesses. No illusion on the Midway is more confusing and amusing.

Cineograph.

In this building, located at the north end of the west Midway, are shown a collection of moving pictures of various scenes in life, faithfully reproducing motions, etc., so that the pictures appear extremely realistic. The pictures are entirely of scenes of interest, and are a highly creditable collection.

Mrs. McCready's Restaurant.

Here the visitor may procure foods of any description to satisfy "the inner man." A first-class restaurant in every particular and assured of a high-class patronage.

War Cyclorama.

Representing the Battles of Missionary Ridge and Lookout Mountain. The visitor has presented before him the scenes of this great battle of the Civil War. The proprietors could scarcely have selected a more interesting and instructive picture for the occasion.

The Cardiff Giant.

Here are exhibited the fossil remains of a prehistoric man. This curiosity was dug up near Cardiff, N.Y., in 1869, the remains being over ten feet in length and weighing nearly 3,000 pounds. The giant has caused considerable of a sensation and has been an object of interest to many of the most noted scientific men throughout the country.

Cora Beckwith.

Visitors to this concession will have the opportunity of seeing this noted lady swimmer. In a tank erected in the center of the building, continuous exhibitions are given in which Miss Beckwith performs the many aquatic feats of swimming, diving, etc., which have already made her famous.

Wild Water Sports.

Here a number of elks and other animals are exhibited. From platforms erected high above a lake constructed in the center of the building, living elks dive into the water below, and perform other equally daring feats for which they have been especially trained.

A feature of the exhibit is the "Wild Boar Chase," in which genuine Norwegian boars are seen pursued by hounds and mounted hunters through the mountain passes, the chase terminating by the boars, hounds and mounted hunters plunging into the lake.

Gypsy Camp.

In this exhibit the visitor is introduced to a genuine gypsy camp, with all its embellishments true to their manner of life. Fortunes are here told that cannot fail to come true, and the opportunity is afforded of purchasing the many various articles made by the gypsies and peculiar to their race.

In the theater is Princess Stellita with her troupe of Gypsy dancers, and Lola Cotton the phenomenal mind reader.

Bostock's Chariots.

Similar in operation to a merry-go-round, although possessing many new and distinct features, this concession cannot fail to do a rushing business. The amusement afforded is especially entertaining to people both old and young.

Johnstown Flood.

For this concession a large building has been constructed north of the Bazar building. In it is presented a graphic illustration of the storm leading up to the breaking of the artificial lake and the awful flood of the Conemaugh river which overwhelmed the city of Johnstown, Pa., in 1889. This exhibition will interest all lovers of the artistic and is indeed a phenomena of color effects. On the ground floor of the building, the management have provided parlors to be used as educational headquarters for teachers, etc.

Philippine Village.

This is the opportunity for all to learn just how a Filipino village looks. It contains representatives from all the races inhabiting the islands, ranging from cannibalism to the highest degree of civilization. The industries of the islands, cultivating with the water buffaloes, rope and cigaretos manufacturing, and the weaving of the beautiful pina silk are here seen. In the theater are given the native plays, and the great Bolo Sword dance, danced for the first time in this country.

Alt Nurnberg.

"Alt Nurnberg," the German Village of the Exposition, conveniently located at the corner of the Midway and the Mall, is one of the most picturesque spots to be found on the grounds. Its main features are the architectural reproductions of buildings in the famous old city of Nurnberg, and the idea is carried out in a most artistic manner. Among the many attractions to be found there are the Royal Bavarian Band of 48 pieces, under the direction of Herr Jacob Peuppus, Royal Bavarian Director of Music; Fraulein Antoine Stolle, with color reproductions of famous paintings; the Gebhard astronomical clock, the Koenigseer troupe of peasant singers and yodlers, and Luchow's famous German restaurant.

Infant Incubators.

This exhibit is housed in the brick structure which is the next east of the Service building. In it is a complete incubating plant where eleven prematurely born children are being reared. Many new and original devices are here illustrated, and not only in novelty but from an instructive point of view is the exhibit interesting.

Fair Japan.

Entering the Japanese village, through the gate of the Nikkil Temple, one can easily imagine himself to be in Fair Japan. Native girls in native costumes serve the tea, and geisha girls entertain you with dancing. The buildings and decorations are strictly Japanese. A reproduction of a royal dwelling is shown and in the numerous bazaars and shops all sorts of trinkets are exhibited and sold as souvenirs. A free outdoor performance is given at times and in the theater is given a strictly Japanese performance, by the native jugglers, dancers, etc.

Ideal Palace.

Opposite Venice in America is the Ideal Palace. This in reality is an artist's studio where are illustrated many of the famous art masterpieces. Living subjects are used entirely in illustrating the many pieces, the troupe consisting of some two dozen American and foreign models, selected from various studios. The different paintings are very faithfully reproduced and for lovers of art, and others as well, this is certainly a treat.

Scenic Railway and Aquarama.

Trains of cars glide up and down the Scenic Railway, upon which, the visitor may ride and enjoy a wonderful variety of landscape views. Electrically illuminated tunnels are passed which are filled with beautiful scenery. The sensation of the ride can be compared to that of coasting down hills in winter, without the element of danger to life and limb. The Aquarama consists of a canal over 1,100 feet long, winding through beautiful scenery, representing lakes, forests, etc., and terminating in the famous "Caves of Caprie." Securely built boats carry the visitor safely along, the beautiful electrical effects adding realism to the scenes.

The Zanzigs.

Here are seen the famous palmists, whose reputation in this art is almost universal. One can scarcely conceive the marvelous accuracy which this celebrated troupe displays in character and life-reading, as shown by the lines of the hands. Many are dissatisfied with their present vocations in life and this attraction affords them an opportunity of ascertaining their mistakes, and starting anew in their chosen calling.

Dawson City.

A series of skillfully worked-out transformation scenes, assisted with elaborate electric scenic effects, depicting a trip to Dawson City and terminating in the awful destruction of that city as it occurred in January, 1901. Starting his trip through Weber Canon, Utah, the visitor arrives at Seattle and departing by steamer encounters an ocean storm. After his arrival at Skagway, crossing the White Pass and shooting the White Horse Rapids, the traveler arrives at Dawson City in the land of the Midnight Sun. So vivid are the scenes representing the conflagration, that one can almost imagine himself an eye-witness of the catastrophe.

The Evolution of Man.

Here the Darwinian theory of evolution is very completely illustrated. The successive stages of development by which the "genus homo" of the present day was evolved from its primaeval progenitors is shown by numerous well-selected examples, from the lowest type of Simian development to the "missing link" or educated chimpanzee, Esau, who all but talks, and from the lowest savage to the polished gentlemen of today.

Bostock's Animal Arena.

Located just inside the Elmwood entrance, and west of the Horti-culture building. This is one of the greatest amusement features of the Midway. The exhibit presents one of the finest collections of trained wild animals ever before shown, more than 1,000 caged beasts appearing in the exhibit. Continuous performances are given in the cage erected in the center of the building, and the trained animals, birds and reptiles from every clime are made to do their trainers' bidding. The crowning feature is the challenge act of Capt. Bonavita, with 25 performing forest-bred lions.

Chiquita.

The next building south of the Animal Show is the home of Chiquita. This sprightly little midget was born on the Island of Cuba, a little over 31 years ago. Her height is but twenty-six inches, though she is proportionately developed and possesses a remarkably beautiful face. Her parlors, in which she receives visitors, are daintily furnished in keeping with the diminutive proportions of the mistress, who is a fluent conversationalist in seven different languages and, therefore, a most interesting hostess.

Venice in America.

This is a perfect replica of the living city, with real palaces, shops, bridges and canals, gondolas and gondoliers. Visitors can ride in the gondolas and be steered through the windings of the palace-lined waterways, while the ear is charmed with sweet songs and the music of the mandolin or guitar.

Ostrich Farm.

The ostrich farm consists of an enclosure of 2½ acres in which are shown about 75 ostriches, of all sizes from the chick to the full grown bird. The nests of the birds, with eggs and feathers in the unfinished conditions are shown, and the process of raising the birds, producing, curing and marketing the feathers is illustrated. From an instructive point of view the exhibit is assuredly interesting.

Jerusalem on the Day of the Crucifixion.

This consists of a cyclorama representing the scenes, conditions, &c., in and about Jerusalem on the day Christ was crucified. The fame of this production is quite well known throughout the country, and will be of special interest to those religiously inclined, and a lesson to others.

Miniature Railway.

This is indeed the smallest operating railroad in the world. Passengers have the same seating comforts as on first-class trains and are given a trip possessed of many novelties.

The Indian Congress.

Located at the south end of the Midway, west of the Horticulture building, and near the Elmwood avenue entrance. Here are congregated 700 Indians, representing 42 distinct tribes and living in their aboriginal and primitive state. Fifteen famous War Chiefs, Indian Rough Riders, Indian Dances, Sports and Pastimes, Indian Museum, Ceremonial House; Winona, the Sioux maiden and champion rifle shot of the world; Indian Blanket, Basket and Pottery makers; 500 Indians in great realistic sham battle. No such lesson in history can be gleaned from books as is here shown by "Native Americans"—long-haired painted savages in all their barbaric splendor.

The Captive Balloon.

To the left of the entrance to the Stadium is the space allotted for the exhibit of the Captive Balloon. The balloon is 100 feet in diameter, made of silk and carries a comfortable car for the seating of those who desire to make the trip upwards. It is operated by machinery and ascends to a height of 1,000 feet, remaining up 15 minutes, affording a magnificent view of the grounds and adjacent country.

3.8 EXTRACTS FROM *SNAPSHOTS ON THE MIDWAY OF THE PAN-AM EXPO*—RICHARD BARRY

Indian Dancers

INDIANS TAKE A CERTAIN RUDE, ecstatic enjoyment in their ceremonial dances, and all of them are of that character; but the glide and swelling ease that comes with a waltz in a modern ball room is as unknown to them as is the luxury of tailor made clothes. They dance as all primitive peoples do; as an outlet for their emotions. Excitement, not dilettanti desire, the intensity of momentary exaltation, not the puttering of energy, induces the elate, religious dances of the red man. The prospect of battle, the flush of victory, the lament for death, the joy for prosperous harvests, the chuckling in fierce triumph over fallen foes, the welcoming and speeding of guests, the anticipatory relish for the hunt, the terrifying, nameless ghost dance, all the great epochs in a savage life are heralded in expectation and commemorated in tireless rhythm.

On the Midway it is possible to give only sketches of a few of the great tribal dances. No audience will sit for more than twenty minutes in the elm bark ceremonial house in attendance even on the traditionary customs of the Sioux and the Apache. Nowhere else is the restlessness of an exposition crowd better illustrated. The continual surge and push and the ceaseless unrest of those who take the show as they do pills, so much in a dose, compel the change of the program three times every hour. That gives the Indians time enough to bob up and bob down again and time enough for the spectacular introduction of Geronimo, but with the feathers and war bonnets and the fresh bright pigment daubed in great gashes on naked flesh there is an effect of grim reality that brings a flood of history-bred recollection to many, and snickers of foolish laughter from the nondescript.

The defiance dance of the Iroquois is usually shown by two young warriors, who enter the small roped arena, one with a tom tom and the other with a war club and hunting knife. It is the dance that the Eastern braves give before starting on a war expedition, and is designed to show the war god the nature of the men who propose to contest for victory. The Indian buys his successes from his gods and he sometimes promises wondrous things. In this case he indicates what he will do in pursuit of the foe, and concludes with a demonstration of what will happen when he catches him. In about five minutes he succeeds in working himself into a frenzy, marked by all the symptoms of real temper, and secures from the audience little "Ahs" of suppressed fright and admiration. He throws the knife into the earth, seizes his war club and gesticulates about the weapon with the menace which he means to say to the god will be duplicated if he is permitted to meet his enemy.

The brave man dance is similar to the war dance of the Cape Lopez cannibals, in its embodiment of all the characteristic movements of a war party in action. It shows the attack and the retreat, the use of the war club and tomahawk and the fierce rhythm that controls each intricate step. The Omaha dance of the home guard, who like white militia have successfully repelled invasion or attack, generally concludes the performance. In it a full party of twenty braves, half of them naked except for a brief breech clout, tap the tan bark floor in tremulous, quick time to the incessant ki yi of the tom tom holders in the rear. Through it all is filtered the rank odor of common things and back of it all is the plaintive, patient, hardy faces of the men who have bade goodbye to actuality and are showing the sacred blood of an ancient race to strangers and dawdlers for a dollar.

Filipino Dances

That the Filipines are a people who have felt somewhat the influence of civilization is shown by the cut of the clothes they wear, by their methods of living, and surest of all by their dancing. It has been a beneficent civilization in their case at least, for the lurid and degenerate hue that has tinged the dances of other peoples has quite escaped them, as shown in the festive steps they display on the Midway. The asdero, or marriage dance, is as simple as a Virginia reel and as innocuous. It is so much so with its playful side step and half timid figure evolution that at first sight it appears as though improvised, as some of the other Midway dances are, for special Pan-American use. The dancers, three men and three women, accompanied by a tinkling guitar orchestra, in which further evidence of Filipino advancement is shown in the skillful playing of three violins, perform a delicate step which has the intricacy and reserve that all refined dancing has. Another of their quaint

Dancers of the Asdero at the Philippine Village.

performances is the esmeralda or star dance, showing another figure that would do credit to the designer of a cotillion, and indeed, it is said that many of the elaborate turns that are apparently improvised for fancy balls are merely excerpts from the native dances of such people as the Filipinos, the Mexicans and the Japanese. The bolo dancer is the only one of the company who shows the indigenous stock that derives its hardihood from the Malay race. He twirls a long bolo, or thick sword of good steel, and performs a series of significant evolutions, holding in his other hand a shield of stretched raw hide and hard wood, performing with high step and elaborate finish much of the glide that gives the fandango its subtle motion, and which may be seen in modified conventionality in the ball room waltz.

Oriental and Hawaiian Dances

There are many who come to the Midway to look for impropriety and who depart satisfied with the visit if they discover a rouged face or a bare leg. For these the Orient has its horrors, and the hula hula dancers are baneful, for they are the Midway's red lights that make the trip down the lane of laughter really worth while for a great number, just what per cent, no census can enumerate, but larger than would be revealed by responses to a category. The two dances are similar, but not alike. Both depend for their effects on the sinuous, gyratory movements of abdominal and body muscles. The gliding of feet is only an incident in either dance; the whole body moves in undulating pantomime that is also seen in the epithalamium or marriage festival of the blacks. Savage dancing is an instinct that civilization has not improved. American influence has affected the couchee couchee, while it has not yet had time to weaken the elemental dancing of the Hawaiian girls. One is the formless, free religious dance of the buoyant, open West, and the other the effeminate expression of a degenerate East, compared to which a stifling interior, rank with dank odors, would be mild and healthy. The hula hula is the genuine expression of real feeling, accompanied by no tuneful harp or glib piano or resinous violin, but filtered through all the monotonous fall of the soft, bare feet of the brown women on pine boards is the crescendic thump of two silent male crouchers, who pound with rhythmic regularity on hollow gourds. In the background stretches a desert waste of arid land, and its dull, tense, ever-repressed vitality shows in the vacant eyes and hollow stare of the women's faces, as they intermittently cry out in ejaculatory plaintiveness. It is the outward manifestation, which for ages has given relief to pent-up feeling. It recalls the wild, old Corybantian dance with the contestants wounding each other, the torture dance of the Soudan dervishes, the metrical shuffling of the feet of the Roman youth to the shrill sound of flageolets as he feverishly tossed his weapon on high.

There are many times in every life when outward expression is imperative. Sometimes it comes at night under the silent stars, sometimes at broad noon in the spray of laughing water, sometimes in feast and sometimes in sorrow. It must always have relief or it burns inwardly and consumes. Some men laugh, some women cry, the ancients danced seriously and soberly, compared to which the usual modern dilettanti shuffling is play and nonsense. The most used modern substitute is to take a drink. Saul and David and wise Solomon removed the stop cock by dancing in the sight of the Lord. The others of the world's annointed have painted pictures, or written books, or sung great songs, or acted superb dramas, but legs may substitute fancy and suppleness take the place of imagination. The Old Testament does not relate whether Israel's Kings tossed their belly buttons

(above) The Olupa Dancers from the royal Hula Hula House of Queen Lili' uokalani at the Hawaiian Village.

(left) Fatima "the Little Tempest," described as the "bewitching black-eyed couchee-couchee dancer at the Beautiful Orient."
(Barry 19)

under their legs or cut a figure eight with their collar bones or sedately twirled the minuet, but whatever their maneuvers, it was a holy sight.

There is nothing in the Midway's Oriental dances that recalls primitive emotion. The adepts in the art, for the couchee dance is an elaborate one, were not tutored in academic schools and the pleasing proficiency they assert is a polyglot of Eastern origin and east side corruption.

The Indian Congress

Enter the Indian Congress some evening. If you go at all early you will be in a hurry because of the shots that tell of coming activity within. There is sombre twilight, only. The boards of the arena are white and bare and in the dark corners are moving figures, like silent spectres in the grim dusk. A crowd slowly gathers, led by the same aniseed bait of exciting musketry that brought you in. The show begins in a little while, to the clear notes of the Indian band. The grand entrance comes; Indians in hundreds, the first on horseback, others follow on foot, slow-stepping feet and common features, sunken eyes, sprawling noses and ragged mouths, the fluid and friendly savage, brawny and quite harmless. Winona, the Sioux crack shot enters, her teeth the whitest on the Midway, her polished rifle barrel glinting in daredevil-coquetry in the last rays of the sinking sun. She raises her weapon and picks twenty glass balls in fifteen seconds from a moving board, the world's record. The races are announced, then the sham battle, the pitching of the wigwams, the skirmish, the retreat of the squaws, the rattle-clatter of musketry, the rosy flash amid the smoke, the shrill cries of daring and the groans of the wounded. Those wounded fall; the ground is strewn with dead. Savage conflict is hand to hand. Dirks glisten in the artificial light that throws over the scene a fitful pale gleam. The tumult dies away, the foes retreat, the victorious chant a diapason of joy.

Then the mimicry of it sinks home. The uncouth grandeur of the red man and his pitiful history are painful with these real specimens of a giant race so identified with painted scenery and gaudy tinsel. But behind artifice is candor, and in a circus ballyhoo are manly men, childlike in confidence and with the quick, receptive minds of children, and so tainted somewhat with the Midway's brass, but true in fibre and wise in observation. Their condition a mockery; their presence a rebuke; their exhibition a falsehood. Such is the conclusion, but listen to American Horse, the envoy extraordinary and minister plenipotentiary of the Sioux nation. President Schurman of Cornell University had expressed surprise that so noted and upright a chief should consent to degrade himself enough to join a Midway show.

"American Horse would be deeply grieved at the White Chief's slur were he not an Indian and so accustomed to the ways of the white man," wrote the chief. "Such a show as the White Chief will find here is not degrading to the Indian; it is an education to him. What would you have of the Indian? Would you have him wither away and die, forgotten. The white man knows the Indian. He studies him, knows his cunning, his bravery, his truth, his uprightness and his ignorance. Because the white man is not ignorant, while the Indian is, is why the white man has conquered him, owns him, is killing him. The Indian's heart fails him when he thinks of his people, so soon to be scattered and forgotten. The avarice of the white man shall prevail. But would the White Chief have the Indian remain as he is, ignorant and unknown? Would he have the Indian stay, rotting away through sloth as a farmer? Would he have him die with a hoe in his hands and know nothing

Group of "heroes" at the Indian Congress. Original caption reads: "First—Captain Hobson, Spanish War hero. Central figure—Geronimo, formerly wickedest of all red-skins, hero of many bloody frays upon the plains. Third—General Director Cummins, hero of many sanguinary sham battles in the Indian Congress." (Barry 65)

of the beauty and the wealth that the white man builds for himself? Would he have the white man remember him only through bad books and worse lies? No! Let the Indian see what there is in this civilization that has conquered him; let him crouch at the camp fires of the white man's wonderful electric lamp and learn from it something of that deep cunning, deeper than his own, that gives the plains and the world to him. There is no other way. The white man locks him up. He is stronger and he can do it, but by the grace of the white man's God this way remains. Let the Indian again bid the White Chief welcome and good bye."

There are moments, however, when regret departs and the Indian Congress furnishes a dashing spectacle. There is the entrance into the arena of Geronimo, mounted, lashing his horse with leather thongs, wearing the hereditary sign of Apache chieftainship, a yellow cap; straight as an arrow, 88 years old, with the face of Napoleon and the carriage of Grant, grim, preoccupied and inscrutable, the greatest war chief of his time, a figure fit for heroic commemoration. Waiting without, always waiting there, are United States regulars, for Geronimo is a prisoner of war and will remain so to the end of his time, for in his more palmy days he was the most vicious chief that that wild country of the West had known.

The Hawaiian Village

There are three exhibits in the Hawaiian village, the hula hula girls, the singers and Tobin. Tobin is in the bally-hoo, so that he is really to be enjoyed without the payment of an entrance fee, and, as Tobin will tell you, he is the whole show himself; it is hardly necessary to be entertained with the hula hula girls or the singers. Tobin is one of the best of the speilers, self styled "The King of the Midway," with all the assertive swing and ease of a real monarch. He has outgrown the necessity for loud bluster and buncombe, and has a delicious way of assuring a crowd that he is about the only man on the street who tells the truth, and he does tell the truth about everything except about himself, when he talks to the reporters. He possesses a huge scrap book filled with innumerable clippings, telling of his remarkable exploits in his travels about the world. He has associated much with royalty and cultivated persons and that may be the reason he has acquired the blandness he shows in his talks to the public, for he is a believer in the worthlessness of blatant assertion. He talks quietly and never makes an extravagant statement. He uses the inferential method of convincing, and he gets patronage enough to make the method popular.

"The rest will tell you they have the largest shows on the Midway, that they cost the most money, that they are the only features out here," calls Tobin, "but I tell you no such thing. This is not the greatest show that ever happened. It is not the most wonderful exhibition in the world, but I'll tell you what we have got. We've got the hulu hulu dancers, not 89 as they tell you at other places, but 23. Count 'em." Should you take Tobin's advice you would find 14, but that is another story.

Tobin is not as virtuous, though, as he would have it appear. One afternoon John Philip Sousa came down the Midway and bought a ticket for the Hawaiian village. He had been inside but a few moments when the place began to fill with an unusual crowd. At the close of the show it was packed and as he passed out he heard Tobin yelling: "Sousa is inside! Sousa! The superb Sousa, king of bandmasters! He is inside leading the Hawaiian orchestra. As he passes out he will give a souvenir to every lady. Sousa, the king, will give a souvenir to every lady. Inside! Inside!"

When Senator Depew came out from the same kind of a packed audience he discovered Tobin announcing to an eager crowd, almost fighting for a chance to get tickets: "Chauncey Depew is inside! Chauncey, the peach, is talking to them now. He is in there telling them about Hawaii as he found it. Depew will give a souvenir to every lady who attends the show. The souvenir will be a kiss. Chauncey will kiss every lady in the house. Inside!"

The performance which Tobin advertises would be attractive anyway, without the services of so prolific a spieler. The dancing girls form its most seductive enticement, but the tender melodies of the male singers get more applause. Probably the admiration for the muscular proficiency of the girls is a silent one, while the wholesome songs of the men bring spontaneous recognition.

The Filipino Village

The Filipino ballyhoo is about the oddest outdoor show ever offered American people. Of all the queer, unusual sights on the Midway it stands at the head. The blacks have perfect bodies; the Hawaiian girls, rush mats for dresses; the Esquimaux, suits of sealskin; the Orientals, swaths of limp linen; the Indians, feathers and war paint; the Mexicans, sombreros and gay dress, and they all have life and noise and grotesque nonsense, but the Filipinos have more. They have earnestness and

Interior of the Philippine Village. The 11-acre compound was based on the Philippine village of Binondo. There were one hundred Philippines living at the exhibit, presented as a colonial trophy from the Spanish-American War. They were guarded by U.S. soldiers to provide a military component to the scene.

they have modesty, and better than all else they are clean, wholesome and somewhat diffident. The ballyhoo shows all of this. In this outdoor show the bolo man is the principal figure, a grotesque combination of Oriental sword fighter, Japanese gaily-gowned priest and American circus clown. He wears the checkered clothes of the sword fighter, possesses the innate dignity of the priest and the rich broad humor of the clown. He stands there in solemn silence, a mere lay figure to attract attention, while the little brown Malays beside him furnish harmonious, sweet music on most peculiar wind instruments of wide bamboo and long reed stems.

The Filipinos and the Hawaiians have much in common, for they are both children of the Pacific seas, and the peace that Balboa thought he found in the waters of that great ocean seems to have permeated the root and fibre of the human dwellers by its shores. Most noticeable is the plaintive, sad-sweet music of the two, a rhythmic languid measure of simple melody, but musical in the highest degree. In the noise of the Midway's contemptuous bustle it is almost lost, but its persuasive inkling of an idyllic life floats intermittently through the village, and on the ballyhoo serves to make the show there genuine and pleasant.

Most of the peculiar things in the village are shown on the ballyhoo. The water buffalo, unwieldly with their great wide horned appendages, stand there in patience that is surprising after an observation of their somewhat ferocious appearance, but the water buffalo is a meek animal and a useful one. He serves as a producer of beef, for the use of tanners and shoemakers, for the dairy maid and chiefly as a beast of burden. Inside the gates he performs the service that the camels do in the Beautiful Orient; that the elephants do in Bostock's animal show, and that the funny little burros with weak knees and strong backs do in the Streets of Mexico. He gives visitors useless rides of no length and little excitement, and not even the danger that attends kissing the Blarney stone.

The houses of the Filipinos are shown to be not so very primitive, for they have cooking stoves and chairs and even door mats, and the people themselves, except for the two of the race of mountain wild men, are quiet and domestic and apparently industrious. The rope walk is the first one seen in America. It shows the laborious, but certain and safe way the natives have of twisting hemp fibre into serviceable lengths. There is a church in the village, a reproduction of a Catholic church in Manila, and on Sunday mornings, long before the Exposition's gates are open to the public, the Filipinos assemble there for worship.

Esquimau Village

The other places on the Midway use huge signs telling what General Miles or Chauncey Depew or Wu Ting Fang or William Jennings Bryan said about their wonders. It is all put in the language of the press agent, and its monotonous laudation is the same for a dance as it is for a spectacle. Before the Esquimau village the name of Benjamin Franklin is used, and Franklin himself probably authorized it about as much as Miles or Bryan did the hyperbolic quotations they are made to say. Franklin's aphorism proclaims to the public that an investment in knowledge pays the best interest. A good investment in knowledge that is difficult to be obtained can be gotten within, for the show is one that belongs to the instructive class. A lecture begins the entertainment, a staccato talk illumined by numerous stereopticon slides, that show the perils of an arctic voyage and the features of the principal arctic explorers from Franklin to Nansen. The ignus fatuis of the North pole is a fascinating study, and its impenetrable mystery is faintly conveyed in these stray sketches of its frigid terrors and phenomenal natural beauties.

In the village the ice stretches away in long, unbroken cliffs, greenly transparent and shimmering in the sun. It would take the capital and material of the ice trust to keep the real thing on hand, but the imitation that has been attained by the use of plaster and paint might worry the trust into thinking that ice of such material would supplant their ammonia product in the affections of the public. It is most wonderful ice, and the casual impression got from a trip to the village is that it is the real stuff. Below it are the topeks of the Esquimaux. A topek is a clean dwelling place, more so than the tepees of the Indians, at best a slovenly race. The Esquimaux are as cleanly as the Japanese, and these skin houses show it. There are also ice houses with windows of isinglass for the sunlight to struggle through, and pots of fat to give added warmth.

The Esquimaux do not need much artificial heat these days, and even if they did there would be enough exercise in the games they practice to furnish warmth with the mercury 50 degrees below zero. The games are simple, and modified by the exigencies of the snowy country they inhabit. One of them is the seal race, men racing for a penny on their bellies, their feet held up over their backs with their hands, while they grovel along with floundering slowness like the seals they imitate. It is very seldom that they finish a heat in the prescribed fashion. It is like a trotting race in which there are no judges; half-way down the course one breaks and the rest follow. Not the least of their skilled performances is the cracking of a cent from under two inches of earth at a distance of twenty paces with the single snap of a whip-lash.

Natives at the Esquimau Village.

Every curio in the village and every bit of substantial building is a direct transplantation from the North. Perhaps the most interesting is an igloo, or hut, made entirely of whalebone, a great rarity even in the North and never before seen in America. The Anthropological Society of France wants it, but it is to be presented to the Smithsonian Institute after the Exposition is over. It is one of the curious mementoes from the land of July blizzards and midnight suns.

The Old Plantation

There are two complete innovations in the exhibition of foreign life on the Midway, and both are quite essential to a Pan-American Exposition, for among all the curious peoples of the Western Hemisphere, aside from the Indians of the West, which were already more or less familiar through stage exploitation and printed fancy, these are the most interesting and offer the best inducements for spectacular presentment. They are the picturesque and sunnily ecstatic people of modern Mexico, and the remnants of the jocular, careless serfs, who in the South before the war gave slavery the deceptive hue of contented and oft-times happy dependence. The Streets of Mexico and the Old Plantation are the results of a choice from among the available children of these luminously transparent localities.

The Old Plantation has that which Mexico lacks, local interest, for school histories and the novels of a generation have given the American people a taste for more intimate knowledge of these transplanted blacks, whose pitiful history is a bitter memory, but whose cheerful life is a passing benediction. It is easy to pick up the colored people of the North and draught them into the show business, but the darkies of the South do not take as kindly to the public rouge box.

They all love the beat of a bass drum and the limber-jointed abandon of a cake-walk, but the Southern negro is a stay-at-home darkey, not so much through dislike for publicity as through the inherent laziness that will not run the risk of a nomadic life. And consequently he is a more valuable acquisition than the somewhat machine-made coon of the variety stage, has more of the real ginger of genuine enjoyment and gives more correctly a picture of real Southern life. Negroes of this kind are those that the Old Plantation has, and it has a lot of them, who go through a half-hour's desultory program of uttered melody, shakedown and variety sketch.

It is the exhibit of still life that is of more interest than the hilarious performances in the rustic theatre. The view from the entrance shows the vista of a southern cotton field, rich in white blooms and hazy with mellow air of a summer afternoon. A monstrous, unwieldy old cotton press and a half-dozen log cabins, built with real logs and real cement mortar, are but the introduction to what might be the most hallowed relic on the Exposition grounds, the log cabin in which Abraham Lincoln was born, weather beaten, and stanchioned in necessary places with modern stays. Its presence strongly recalls the predicament that Mark Twain found in going the rounds of the European cathedrals, each of which had a piece of the cross that held Christ through the crucifixion. He did not question the authenticity of the relics, for each plainly bore the announcement that it was a part of the real cross from Calvary, but Twain said that after a while he wondered a little how Christ was able to carry all those pieces in one cross through the streets of Jerusalem that morning. And so the Abraham Lincoln cabin cannot be questioned, for the sign plainly announces what it is; but the wonder is occasioned as to how it was located, when no one is just sure yet as to exactly which county in Kentucky it was that Lincoln's father lived in. Beside it is not the cabin in which Jefferson Davis was born, but one of the cabins from the plantation on which Jefferson Davis was born, for Davis, himself, first lived in a mansion that was palatial compared to the backwoods hovel of Tom Lincoln.

Farther beyond, in a plot of red iron filings, is the home of Laughing Ben, the oddest negro ever seen. Ben is a prodigious mountain of merriment. Poke your finger at him and he laughs, smile at him and he roars, laugh with him but gently and he doubles up in promiscuous peals of leviathan amusement that threaten to rupture the swelling black veins in his healthy neck. He laughs at nothing, at everything, and at all times, and the best part of the joke is that it is an uncontrollable, infectious glee that spreads and doubles back upon itself, giving visitors and Old Ben himself the hugest time for the least cause that is offered throughout the extent of the hilarious Midway.

4. *The Great Divide*—William Vaughn Moody

Commentary

Sources

Play

4.1 CIVILIZATION AND DISCONTENT IN WILLIAM VAUGHN MOODY'S *THE GREAT DIVIDE*—ALEX ROE

BY 1906, MOST OF THE LOWER 48 had joined the United States, but the Southwest still included a few, unadmitted "territories." So when William Vaughn Moody set his new play in southern Arizona, he was reaching as far into the "uncivilized" West as he could still go. Here he begins a tale that articulates and pursues a foundational American conflict: the spirited independence of the pioneer against the security of orderly, restrictive Society.

Nineteenth-century literature took up this opposition with relish: plays such as John Augustus Stone's *Metamora* (1825), or Anna Cora Mowatt's *Fashion* (1845), embrace it, while Cooper's Leatherstocking Tales, Twain's *Huckleberry Finn*, and Thoreau's *Walden* are other familiar incarnations. And whether it expresses itself as a rejection of European values, a fight between urban and rural interests, a yearning to go back to Nature, or a love for the outlaw, it is a primal and still current tension in American life.

Moody captured this tension at a watershed moment in the country's history, and he saw in it a spiritual dimension of profound import. In 1906, America had expanded across its own continent, and begun to reckon with the pressures of reaching the frontier's frontier. At the same time, with the annexation of Puerto Rico, Guam, and The Philippines, the populace woke to the new century as a colonial power, and the hegemonic assertion of Establishment values was a thorny issue as much in the popular consciousness as it is today.

The Great Divide figures this conflicted identity in a star-crossed couple. A combination of misfortune and plucky determination lead Ruth Jordan to stay the night alone in a desert cabin, with only the darkness for protection. A transplant from the East, she is enchanted by the "glorious unfulfilled" West, but it is not long before she is discovered—in a scene of striking brutality—by three drunken outlaws, who betray no qualms about taking her for their pleasure or one another's lives for their pains. But Ruth strikes a bargain with one, Stephen Ghent: she will give herself to him forever, if he will dispatch the other two.

Ruth and Ghent study one another and discover themselves over the course of their strained union. Struck by her offer as if by revelation, he sees in her a chance for redemption from the selfish life that led to their meeting, and he strives to be worthy of her unobtainable acceptance. But, ever conscious of having been bought, she cannot forgive him the transgression that brought them together, and labors doggedly and secretly to earn her freedom. It is only when she does return to the circumscribed comforts of New England, and he follows, that they can envision a life that nourishes their (in fact) deeply connected selves.

Originally entitled "The Sabine Woman," the play asks for a nuanced look at its premise: for all that the Sabines were abducted from their people by Romulus and his companions, they became the co-founders of a new and all-powerful civilization. In re-naming the play *The Great Divide* for its 1912 revival, Moody emphasized the deep and perhaps continentally enshrined divisions in American culture that the couple must overcome. Still, *The Great Divide* remains about the hope of creating a new relationship from such an inauspicious beginning. Ruth and Ghent's journey is across the gap between Eastern and Western sensibilities, between male and female inequalities, between life ruled by convention and life embracing serendipity, between salvation through penance and salvation by revelation, and finally between labors of duty and labors of love. Figured in an unlikely couple, the journey is not the romantic comedy's jaunt to the cute life deferred; it is a journey to a new vision of a moral life—neither Eastern nor Western, but American and hopeful.

The Lafayette (LA) *Advertiser* termed the play "the long awaited great American play," saying that "no other drama has so well reflected the manhood, the freedom, the honesty and the indomitable spirit characteristic of the people of our great Western country." Colloquial in its speech, and critical of both Eastern establishment and conventional mores, the play broke with the contemporary trend of drawing room dramas of the middle and upper class life, consciously indicting the very way of life they affirmed.

Moody anticipates O'Neill in these innovations and his exploration of psychological foible, writing a play that is defiant of its period's conventions in order to explore the larger assumptions of its time.

4.2 AN ODE IN TIME OF HESITATION—WILLIAM VAUGHN MOODY

(After seeing at Boston the statue of Robert Gould Shaw, killed while storming Fort Wagner, July 18, 1863, at the head of the first enlisted Negro regiment, the Fifty-fourth Massachusetts.)

I

BEFORE THE solemn bronze Saint Gaudens made
To thrill the heedless passer's heart with awe,
And set here in the city's talk and trade
To the good memory of Robert Shaw,
This bright March morn I stand,
And hear the distant spring come up the land;
Knowing that what I hear is not unheard
Of this boy soldier and his negro band,
For all their gaze is fixed so stern ahead,
For all the fatal rhythm of their tread.
The land they died to save from death and shame
Trembles and waits, hearing the spring's great name,
And by her pangs these resolute ghosts are stirred.

II

Through street and mall the tides of people go
Heedless; the trees upon the Common show
No hint of green; but to my listening heart
The still earth doth impart
Assurance of her jubilant emprise,
And it is clear to my long-searching eyes
That love at last has might upon the skies.
The ice is runneled on the little pond;
A telltale patter drips from off the trees;
The air is touched with southland spiceries,
As if but yesterday it tossed the frond
Of pendant mosses where the live-oaks grow
Beyond Virginia and the Carolines,
Or had its will among the fruits and vines
Of aromatic isles asleep beyond
Florida and the Gulf of Mexico.

III

Soon shall the Cape Ann children shout in glee,
Spying the arbutus, spring's dear recluse;
Hill lads at dawn shall hearken the wild goose
Go honking northward over Tennessee;
West from Oswego to Sault Sainte-Marie,
And on to where the Pictured Rocks are hung,
And yonder where, gigantic, wilful, young,
Chicago sitteth at the northwest gates,
With restless violent hands and casual tongue
Moulding her mighty fates,
The Lakes shall robe them in ethereal sheen;
And like a larger sea, the vital green
Of springing wheat shall vastly be out-flung
Over Dakota and the prairie states.
By desert people immemorial
On Arizonan mesas shall be done
Dim rites unto the thunder and the sun;
Nor shall the primal gods lack sacrifice
More splendid, when the white Sierras call
Unto the Rockies straightway to arise
And dance before the unveiled ark of the year,

Sounding their windy cedars as for shawms,
Unrolling rivers clear
For flutter of broad phylacteries;
While Shasta signals to Alaskan seas
That watch old sluggish glaciers downward creep
To fling their icebergs thundering from the steep,
And Mariposa through the purple calms
Gazes at far Hawaii crowned with palms
Where East and West are met, —
A rich seal on the ocean's bosom set
To say that East and West are twain,
With different loss and gain:
The Lord hath sundered them; let them be sundered yet.

IV

Alas! what sounds are these that come
Sullenly over the Pacific seas, —
Sounds of ignoble battle, striking dumb
The season's half-awakened ecstasies?
Must I be humble, then,
Now when my heart hath need of pride?
Wild love falls on me from these sculptured men;
By loving much the land for which they died
I would be justified.
My spirit was away on pinions wide
To soothe in praise of her its passionate mood
And ease it of its ache of gratitude.
Too sorely heavy is the debt they lay
On me and the companions of my day.
I would remember now
My country's goodliness, make sweet her name.
Alas! what shade art thou
Of sorrow or of blame
Liftest the lyric leafage from her brow,
And pointest a slow finger at her shame?

V

Lies! lies! It cannot be! The wars we wage
Are noble, and our battles still are won

By justice for us, ere we lift the gage.
We have not sold our loftiest heritage.
The proud republic hath not stooped to cheat
And scramble in the market-place of war;
Her forehead weareth yet its solemn star.
Here is her witness: this, her perfect son,
This delicate and proud New England soul
Who leads despised men, with just-unshackled feet,
Up the large ways where death and glory meet,
To show all peoples that our shame is done,
That once more we are clean and spirit-whole.

VI

Crouched in the sea fog on the moaning sand
All night he lay, speaking some simple word
From hour to hour to the slow minds that heard,
Holding each poor life gently in his hand
And breathing on the base rejected clay
Till each dark face shone mystical and grand
Against the breaking day;
And lo, the shard the potter cast away
Was grown a fiery chalice crystal-fine
Fulfilled of the divine
Great wine of battle wrath by God's ring-finger stirred.
Then upward, where the shadowy bastion loomed
Huge on the mountain in the wet sea light,
Whence now, and now, infernal flowerage bloomed,
Bloomed, burst, and scattered down its deadly seed, —
They swept, and died like freemen on the height,
Like freemen, and like men of noble breed;
And when the battle fell away at night
By hasty and contemptuous hands were thrust
Obscurely in a common grave with him
The fair-haired keeper of their love and trust.
Now limb doth mingle with dissolved limb
In nature's busy old democracy
To flush the mountain laurel when she blows
Sweet by the southern sea,
And heart with crumbled heart climbs in the rose: —
The untaught hearts with the high heart that knew

This mountain fortress for no earthly hold
Of temporal quarrel, but the bastion old
Of spiritual wrong,
Built by an unjust nation sheer and strong,
Expugnable but by a nation's rue
And bowing down before that equal shrine
By all men held divine,
Whereof his band and he were the most holy sign.

VII

O bitter, bitter shade!
Wilt thou not put the scorn
And instant tragic question from thine eye?
Do thy dark brows yet crave
That swift and angry stave —
Unmeet for this desirous morn —
That I have striven, striven to evade?
Gazing on him, must I not deem they err
Whose careless lips in street and shop aver
As common tidings, deeds to make his cheek
Flush from the bronze, and his dead throat to speak?
Surely some elder singer would arise,
Whose harp hath leave to threaten and to mourn
Above this people when they go astray.
Is Whitman, the strong spirit, overworn?
Has Whittier put his yearning wrath away?
I will not and I dare not yet believe!
Though furtively the sunlight seems to grieve,
And the spring-laden breeze
Out of the gladdening west is sinister
With sounds of nameless battle overseas;
Though when we turn and question in suspense
If these things be indeed after these ways,
And what things are to follow after these,
Our fluent men of place and consequence
Fumble and fill their mouths with hollow phrase,
Or for the end-all of deep arguments
Intone their dull commercial liturgies —
I dare not yet believe! My ears are shut!
I will not hear the thin satiric praise

And muffled laughter of our enemies,
Bidding us never sheathe our valiant sword
Till we have changed our birthright for a gourd
Of wild pulse stolen from a barbarian's hut;
Showing how wise it is to cast away
The symbols of our spiritual sway,
That so our hands with better ease
May wield the driver's whip and grasp the jailer's keys.

VIII

Was it for this our fathers kept the law?
This crown shall crown their struggle and their ruth?
Are we the eagle nation Milton saw
Mewing its mighty youth,
Soon to possess the mountain winds of truth,
And be a swift familiar of the sun
Where aye before God's face his trumpets run?
Or have we but the talons and the maw,
And for the abject likeness of our heart
Shall some less lordly bird be set apart? —
Some gross-billed wader where the swamps are fat?
Some gorger in the sun? Some prowler with the bat?

IX

Ah no!
We have not fallen so.
We are our fathers' sons: let those who lead us know!
'Twas only yesterday sick Cuba's cry
Came up the tropic wind, "Now help us, for we die!"
Then Alabama heard,
And rising, pale, to Maine and Idaho
Shouted a burning word.
Proud state with proud impassioned state conferred,
And at the lifting of a hand sprang forth,
East, west, and south, and north,
Beautiful armies. Oh, by the sweet blood and young
Shed on the awful hill slope at San Juan,
By the unforgotten names of eager boys
Who might have tasted girls' love and been stung

With the old mystic joys
And starry griefs, now the spring nights come on,
But that the heart of youth is generous, —
We charge you, ye who lead us,
Breathe on their chivalry no hint of stain!
Turn not their new-world victories to gain!
One least leaf plucked for chaffer from the bays
Of their dear praise,
One jot of their pure conquest put to hire,
The implacable republic will require;
With clamor, in the glare and gaze of noon,
Or subtly, coming as a thief at night,
But surely, very surely, slow or soon
That insult deep we deeply will requite.
Tempt not our weakness, our cupidity!
For save we let the island men go free,
Those baffled and dislaureled ghosts
Will curse us from the lamentable coasts
Where walk the frustrate dead.
The cup of trembling shall be drained quite,
Eaten the sour bread of astonishment,
With ashes of the hearth shall be made white
Our hair, and wailing shall be in the tent;
Then on your guiltier head
Shall our intolerable self-disdain
Wreak suddenly its anger and its pain;
For manifest in that disastrous light
We shall discern the right
And do it, tardily.—O ye who lead,
Take heed!
Blindness we may forgive, but baseness we will smite.

4.3 ON A SOLDIER FALLEN IN THE PHILIPPINES—WILLIAM VAUGHN MOODY

STREETS OF the roaring town,
Hush for him, hush, be still!
He comes, who was stricken down
Doing the word of our will.
Hush! Let him have his state,
Give him his soldier's crown.
The grists of trade can wait
Their grinding at the mill,
But he cannot wait for his honor, now the trumpet has been blown;
Wreathe pride now for his granite brow, lay love on his breast of stone.

Toll! Let the great bells toll
Till the clashing air is dim.
Did we wrong this parted soul?
We will make up it to him.
Toll! Let him never guess
What work we set him to.
Laurel, laurel, yes;
He did what we bade him do.
Praise, and never a whispered hint but the fight he fought was good;
Never a word that the blood on his sword was his country's own heart's-blood.

A flag for the soldier's bier
Who dies that his land may live;
O, banners, banners here,
That he doubt not nor misgive!
That he heed not from the tomb
The evil days draw near
When the nation, robed in gloom,
With its faithless past shall strive.
Let him never dream that his bullet's scream went wide of its island mark,
Home to the heart of his darling land where she stumbled and sinned in the dark.

4.4 GUESS I'LL KEEP 'EM—ANON

Illustration titled "Guess I'll Keep 'Em" of Uncle Sam peering with imperial interest at the Philippines, published in *Leslie's Weekly Newspaper* (1898).

4.5 PRODUCTION PHOTOS FROM *THE GREAT DIVIDE*—ANON

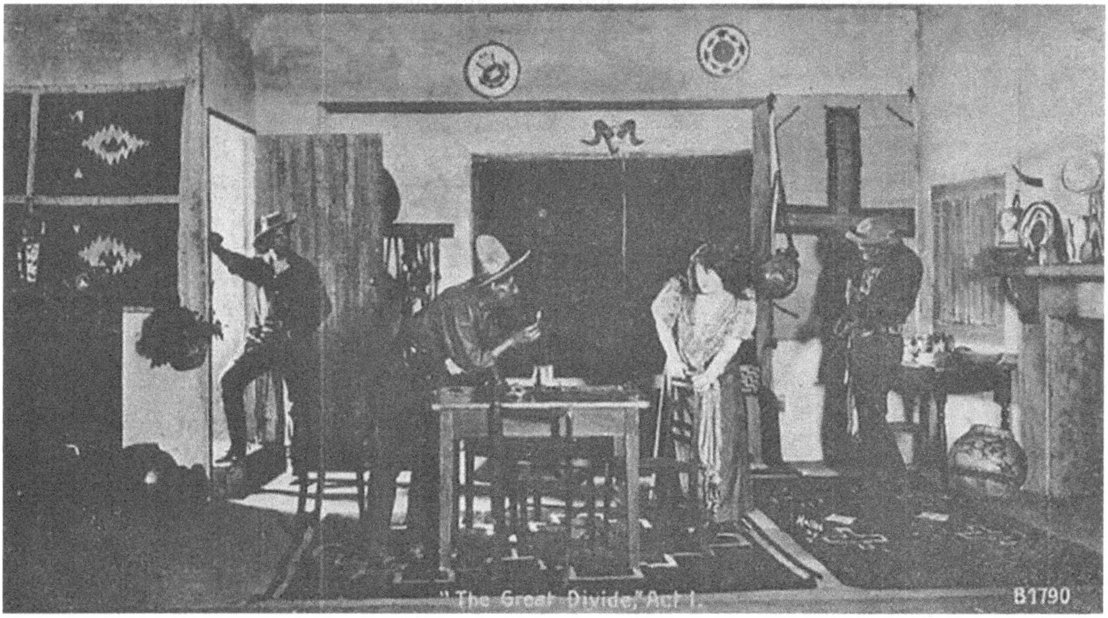

Act I scenes from the 1906 production of Richard Moody's *The Great Divide*. Moody, a prominent member of the Anti-Imperialist League, wrote several works criticizing U.S. imperial actions in Cuba, Puerto Rico and the Philippines.

4.6 *THE GREAT DIVIDE*—WILLIAM VAUGHN MOODY

Persons of the Play

PHILIP JORDAN
POLLY JORDAN, *Philip's wife*
MRS. JORDAN, *his mother*
RUTH JORDAN, *his sister*
WINTHROP NEWBURY
DR. NEWBURY, *Winthrop's father*
STEPHEN GHENT
DUTCH
SHORTY, A MEXICAN
LON ANDERSON
BURT WILLIAMS
A CONTRACTOR
AN ARCHITECT
A BOY

★

ACT I

Interior of Philip Jordan's cabin in southern Arizona, on a late afternoon in spring. A large room rudely built, adorned with blankets, pottery, weapons, and sacred images of the local Indian tribes, and hung with trophies of the chase, together with hunting-knives, saddles, bridles, nose-bags for horses, lariats, and other paraphernalia of frontier life. Through a long low window at the back the desert is seen, intensely colored, and covered with the uncouth shapes of giant cacti, dotted with bunches of gorgeous bloom. The entrance door is on the left (from the spectator's standpoint), in a projecting elbow of the room; farther to the left is a door leading to the sleeping-quarters. On the right is a cook-stove, a cupboard for dishes and household utensils, and a chimney-piece, over which hangs a bleached cow's-skull supporting a rifle.

At a rude table in the centre sits Philip Jordan, a man of thirty-four, mending a bridle. Polly, his wife, kneels before an open trunk, assisted in her packing by Winthrop Newbury, a recent graduate of an Eastern medical college. Ruth Jordan, Philip's sister, a girl of nineteen, stands at the window looking out.

WINTHROP.

As he hands the last articles to Polly.

What on earth possessed you to bring such a load of duds to Arizona?

POLLY.

They promised me a good time, meaning one small shindig—one—in the three months I've spent in this unholy place.

Philip makes an impatient movement with the bridle; speaks gruffly.

PHILIP.

You'd better hurry. It's getting late.

RUTH.

From the window.

It's getting cooler, which is more to the point. We can make the railroad easily by sunrise, with this delicious breeze blowing.

POLLY.

Gives the finishing touches to the trunk and locks the lid.

There, at last! Heaven help the contents.

PHILIP.

Gruffly, as he rises.

Give me a lift with the trunk, Win.

They carry the trunk outside. Polly, with the aid of a cracked mirror, puts on her travelling hat and cloak.

RUTH.

My, Pollikins! You'll be the talk of all the jack-rabbits and sage hens between here and the railroad.

POLLY.

Phil is furious at me for going, and it *is* rather mean to sneak off for a visit in a grand house in San Francisco, when you poor dears have to slave on here. But really, I can't endure this life a day longer.

RUTH.

It isn't in nature that you should. Fancy *that* (*she indicates Polly with a grandiose gesture*) nourishing itself on salt-pork, chickory beans, and airtight!

POLLY.

Do you really mean to say that apart from your pride in helping your brother, making the project go, and saving the family fortunes, you really *enjoy* yourself here?

RUTH.

Since Phil and I came out, one day has been more radiantly exciting than the other. I don't know what's the matter with me. I think I shall be punished for being so happy.

POLLY.

Punished for being happy! There's your simon-pure New-Englander.

RUTH.

True! I was discovered at the age of seven in the garret, perusing "The Twelve Pillars and Four Cornerstones of a Godly Life."

POLLY.

Pointing at Ruth's heart, speaks with mock solemnity.

If Massachusetts and Arizona ever get in a mixup in there, woe be!—Are you ever going to have that coffee done?

RUTH.

I hope soon, before you get me analyzed out of existence.

POLLY.

As Ruth busies herself at the stove.

The main point is this, my dear, and you'd better listen to what the old lady is a-tellin' of ye. Happiness is its own justification, and it's the sacreder the more unreasonable it is. It comes or it doesn't, that's all you can say about it. And when it comes, one has the sense to grasp it or one hasn't. There you have the Law and the Prophets.

Winthrop and Philip enter from outside. Ruth, who has set out the coffee and sandwiches on the table, bows elaborately, with napkin over arm.

RUTH.

Messieurs et Mesdames!

WINTHROP.

Coffee! Well, rather, with an all-night ride in the desert ahead of us.

They drink their coffee, Philip standing sullenly apart.

Where do we get our next feed?

RUTH.

With luck, at Cottonwood Wash.

WINTHROP.

And how far may Cottonwood Wash be?

RUTH.

Thirty miles.

WINTHROP.

Sarcastically.

Local measurement?

POLLY.

Poking Philip.

Phil, for Heaven's sake say something. You diffuse the gloom of the Pit.

PHILIP.

I've had my say out, and it makes absolutely no impression on you.

POLLY.

It's the impression on the public I'm anxious about.

PHILIP.

The public will have to excuse me.

POLLY.

I *am* horribly sorry for you two poor dears, left alone in this dreadful place. When Dr. Newbury goes, I don't see how you'll support life. I should like to know how long this sojourn in the wilderness is going to last, anyhow.

During the following, Ruth takes a candle from the shelf, lights it, and brings it to the table. The sunset glow has begun to fade.

RUTH.

Till Cactus Fibre makes our eternal fortune.

WINTHROP.

And how long will that be?

RUTH.

Counts on her fingers.

Two years to pay back the money we raised on mother's estate, two years of invested profits, two years of hard luck and marking time, two years of booming prosperity. Say eight years!

POLLY.

Shades of the tomb! How long do you expect to live?

RUTH.

Forever!

The sound of a galloping horse is heard, muffled by the sand.

WINTHROP.

Listen. What's that?

A boy of fifteen, panting from his rapid ride, appears at the open door.

PHILIP.

Rising and going toward the door.

What's the matter?

BOY.

I've come for the doctor.

PHILIP.

Who wants a doctor?

BOY.

Your man Sawyer, over to Lone Tree.—He's broke his leg.

RUTH.

Broken his leg! Sawyer? Our foreman?

PHILIP.

There's a nice piece of luck!—How did it happen?

BOY.

They was doin' some Navajo stunts on horseback, pullin' chickens out of the sand at a gallop and takin' a hurdle on the upswing. Sawyer's horse renigged, and lunged off agin a 'dobe wall. Smashed his leg all to thunder.

Winthrop looks vaguely about for his kit and travelling necessaries, while Polly gives the boy food, which he accepts shyly as he goes outside with Philip. Ruth has snatched saddle and bridle from their peg.

RUTH.

I'll have Buckskin saddled for you in a jiffy. How long will it take you to set the leg?

WINTHROP.

Perhaps an hour, perhaps three.

RUTH.

It's a big détour, but you can catch us at Cottonwood Wash by sunrise, allowing three hours for Sawyer. Buckskin has done it before. *She goes out.*

POLLY.

Pouting.

This will spoil all our fun! Why can't the creature wait till you get back?

WINTHROP.

Did you ever have a broken leg?

POLLY.

Well, no, not exactly a leg. But I've had a broken heart! In fact, I've got one now, if you're not going with us.

WINTHROP.

To tell you the truth, mine is broken too.

Pause.

Did you ever dream of climbing a long hill, and having to turn back before you saw what was on the other side?

Polly nods enthusiastically.

I feel as if I'd had my chance to-night to see what was over there, and lost it.

POLLY.

You'll excuse me if it sounds personal, Dr. Newbury, but did you expect to discern a—sort of central figure in the outrolled landscape?

WINTHROP.

Embarrassed repenting of his sentimental outburst.

No. That is—

POLLY.

With a sweep of her arm.

O, I see. Just scenery!

She laughs and goes into the inner room, left. Ruth reënters. The sky has partly faded and a great full moon begins to rise.

RUTH.

Buckskin is ready, and so is the moon. The boy knows the trails like an Indian. He will bring you through to Cottonwood by daylight.

WINTHROP.

Taking heart.

We shall have the ride back together, at any rate.

RUTH.

Yes.—I would go with you, and try to do something to make poor Sawyer comfortable, but we haven't another horse that can do the distance.

She holds out her hand. Good-bye.

WINTHROP.

Detaining her hand.

Won't you make it up to me?

He draws her toward him.

RUTH.

Gently but firmly.

No, Win. Please not.

WINTHROP.

Never?

RUTH.

Life is so good just as it is! Let us not change it.

He drops her hand, and goes out, without looking back. Polly reënters. The women wave Winthrop goodbye.

POLLY.

Takes Ruth by the shoulders and looks at her severely.

Conscience clear?

RUTH.

Humoring her.

Crystal!

POLLY.

Counts on her fingers.

Promising young physician, charming girl, lonely ranch, horseback excursions, spring of the year!

RUTH.

Not guilty.

POLLY.

Gracious! Then it's not play, it's earnest.

RUTH.

Neither the one nor the other. It's just your little blonde romantic noddle.

She takes Polly's head between her hands and shakes it as if to show its emptiness.

Do you think if I wanted to flirt, I would select a youth I've played hookey with, and seen his mother spank?

Suddenly sobered.

Poor dear Win! He's so good, so gentle and chivalrous. But—(*with a movement of lifted arms, as if for air*) ah me, he's—finished! I want one that isn't finished!

POLLY.

Are you out of your head, you poor thing?

RUTH.

You know what I mean well enough. Winthrop is all rounded off, a completed product. But the man I sometimes see in my dreams is—(*pausing for a simile*)—well, like this country out here, don't you know—?

She breaks off, searching for words, and makes a vague outline in the air, to indicate bigness and incompletion.

POLLY.

Drily.

Yes, thank you. I do know! Heaven send you joy of him!

RUTH.

Heaven won't, because, alas, he doesn't exist! I am talking of a sublime abstraction—of the glorious unfulfilled—of the West—the Desert.

POLLY.

Lifts Ruth's chin, severely.

We haven't by chance, some spring morning, riding over to the trading-station or elsewhere—just by the merest chance beheld a sublime abstraction—say in blue overalls and jumper?

Ruth shakes her head.

Honest?

More emphatic head-shaking. Polly drops Ruth's chin with a shrug of the shoulders. Philip enters.

RUTH.

Putting on her riding-hat.

Is Pinto saddled?

PHILIP.

Pinto is gone.

RUTH.

Astonished.

Gone where?

PHILIP.

To that Mexican blow-out over at Lone Tree. Every man-jack on the ranch has disappeared, without leave asked or notice given, except this paper which I just found nailed to the factory door.

Ruth takes the note and reads it anxiously. Then she slowly removes her hat and lays it away.

What are you up to now? We've no time to lose!

RUTH.

With quiet determination.

I am not going.

POLLY.

As Philip turns in surprise.

Not going?

RUTH.

I must stay and look after the ranch.

PHILIP.

O, come, that's out of the question!

RUTH.

We have put all mother's money into this venture. We can't take any risks.

PHILIP.

The men will be back to-morrow. It's not to be thought of—your staying here all alone.

POLLY.

Seats herself with decision.

One thing is certain: either Ruth goes or I stay.

PHILIP.

Takes off his hat and sets down the provision basket.

That suits me perfectly!

POLLY.

Hysterical.

But I can't stay! I won't stay! I shall go mad if I spend another night in this place.

RUTH.

No, you mustn't stay. You would never get us worked up to the point of letting you go, another time.

She lifts Polly, and with arm around her waist leads her to the door.

PHILIP.

I refuse to leave you here alone, just to satisfy a whim of Polly's. That's flat!

RUTH.

But, Phil, you forget the stores you're to fetch back. They will be dumped out there on the naked sand, and by to-morrow night—

She blows across her palm, as if scattering thistledown.

PHILIP.

Well, what of it? A few hundred dollars' worth of stuff!

RUTH.

A few hundred dollars means sink or swim with us just now.—Besides, there's poor Sawyer. He'll be brought back here to-morrow, and nobody to nurse him. Then inflammation, fever, and goodbye Sawyer.

Philip, with a gesture of accepting the inevitable, picks up the grain-sacks and basket.

POLLY.

At the door, embracing Ruth.

Good-bye, dear. Aren't you really afraid to stay?

RUTH.

I'm awfully sorry to miss the fun, but as for danger, the great Arizona Desert is safer than Beacon Hill.

POLLY.

You're sure?

RUTH.

If marauders prowl, I'll just fire the blunderbuss out the window, and they won't stop running this side of the Great Divide.

POLLY.

Kissing her.

Good-bye, dear.

RUTH.

Good-bye.

Polly goes out.

PHILIP.

Pausing beside Ruth, at the door.

Mind you put out the light early. It can be seen from the Goodwater trail. There's no telling what riff-raff will be straggling back that way after the dance.

RUTH.

Riff-raff! They're my sworn knights and brothers.

PHILIP.

In that case, what makes you uneasy about the property?

RUTH.

O, property! That's different.

PHILIP.

Well, you mind what I say and put out the light.

RUTH.

Yours for prudence!

She puts her arm around his waist and draws him to her, kissing him tenderly.

Good-bye, Phil.

He kisses her and starts to go. She still detains him. When she speaks again, her voice is softened and awed.

What a lovely night! Who would ever think to call this a desert, this moonlit ocean of flowers? What millions of cactus blooms have opened since yesterday!

PHILIP.

Looking at her dubiously.

What's the matter with you to-night?

RUTH.

Nothing. Everything. Life!—I don't know what's got into me of late. I'm just drunk with happiness the whole time.

PHILIP.

Well, you're a queer one.—Good-bye. I shall get back as soon as horseflesh will do it.

He goes out.

RUTH.

As the rumble of the wagon is heard.

Good-bye! Good-bye, Pollikins! Good-bye!

She takes the candle from the table and stands in the door for a time, then raises the light in one hand and waves her handkerchief with the other. She sets the candle again on the table, goes to the mantel-shelf, and takes down a photograph.

Dear Win! I forgot how disappointed *you* were going to be.

Pause, during which she still gazes at the picture.

Clear, kind heart!

After a moment she replaces it brusquely on the mantelshelf, and raises her arms above her head with a deep breath. She stands thus, with arms crossed behind her head, looking at the photograph. Her gaze becomes amused and mischievous; she points her finger at the picture and whispers mockingly.

Finished! Finished!

She begins to prepare for bed, taking down her hair, and re-coiling it loosely during the following. She hums a tune vaguely and in snatches, then with a stronger rhythm; at last she sings.

Heart, wild heart,
Brooding apart,
Why dost thou doubt, and why art thou sullen?
Flower and bird
Wait but thy word—

She breaks off, picks up a photograph from the table, and looks at it for a moment in silence.

Poor little mother! You look out at me with such patient, anxious eyes. There are better days coming for you, and it's troublesome me that's bringing them. Only you trust me!

A man's face appears at the edge of the window, gazing stealthily in. As Ruth turns, he disappears. She lays down the picture and sings again.

This is the hour,
And thine is the power.

Heart, high heart, be brave to begin it.
Dare you refuse?
Think what we lose!
Think what we gain—

The words grow indistinct as she takes up the candle and passes into the other room, from which her voice sounds from time to time in interrupted song. The man again appears, shading his face with a peaked Mexican hat so as to see into the darkened room. He turns and waves his hand as if signalling distant persons to approach, then enters through the open door. He looks cautiously about the room, tiptoes to the inner door and listens, then steals softly out, and is seen again at the window, beckoning. Ruth reënters, carrying the candle. She is shod in moccasins, and clad in a loose, dark sleeping-dress, belted at the waist, with wide, hanging sleeves and open throat. As she crosses to the table she sings.

Heart which the cold
Long did enfold—
Hark, from the dark eaves the night thaw drummeth!
Now as a god,
Speak to the sod,
Cry to the sky that the miracle cometh!

She passes her hand over a great bunch of wild flowers on the table.
Be still, you beauties! You'll drive me to distraction with your color and your odor. I'll take a hostage for your good behavior.
She selects a red flower, puts it in the dark mass of her hair, and looks out at the open door.
What a scandal the moon is making, out there in that great crazy world! Who but me could think of sleeping on such a night?
She sits down, folds the flowers in her arms, and buries her face in them. After a moment she starts up, listens, goes hurriedly to the door, and peers out. She then shuts and bolts the door, draws the curtains before the window, comes swiftly to the table, and blows out the light. The room is left in total darkness. There are muttering voices outside, the latch is tried, then a heavy lunge breaks the bolt. A man pushes in, but is hurled back by a taller man, with a snarling oath. A third figure advances to the table, and strikes a match. As soon as the match is lighted Ruth levels the gun, which she has taken from its rack above the mantel. There is heard the click of the hammer, as the gun misses fire. It is instantly struck from her hand by the first man (Dutch), who attempts to seize her. She evades him, and tries to wrest a pistol from a holster on the wall. She is met by the second man (Shorty), who frustrates the attempt, pocketing the weapon. While this has been going on the third man (Ghent) has been fumbling with the lamp, which he has at last succeeded in lighting. All three are dressed in rude frontier fashion; the one called Shorty is a Mexican half-breed, the others are Americans. Ghent is younger than Dutch, and taller, but less powerfully built. All are intoxicated, but not sufficiently so to incapacitate them from rapid action. The Mexican has seized Ruth and attempts to drag her toward the inner room. She breaks loose, and flies back again to the chimney-place, where she stands at bay. Ghent remains motionless and silent by the table, gazing at her.

DUTCH.

Uncorking a whiskey flask.
Plucky little catamount. I drink its health.
Drinks.

RUTH.

What do you want here?

DUTCH.

Laughs, with sinister relish.
Did you hear that, Steve?
He drinks again, and reaches out the flask to Ruth.
Take one, and pull in its purty little claws, eh? Jolly time. No more fuss and fury.
Ruth reaches for a knife, hidden behind the elbow of the chimney. Dutch wrests the knife from her and seizes her in his arms.
Peppery little devil!
With desperate strength she breaks from his clutch and reels from him in sickness of horror. Ghent remains gazing at her in a fascinated semi-stupor. Meanwhile, after closing the door, the Mexican has taken dice from his pocket, and, throwing them into a small vase on the table, shakes them and holds out the vase to Dutch. He takes it and turns to Ghent; the latter has moved a step or two toward Ruth, who in her retreat has reached the chimney-piece and stands at bay.

DUTCH.

Come, get into the game, curse you, Steve! This is going to be a free-for-all, by God!
As he rattles the dice, Ruth makes a supplicating gesture to Ghent.

RUTH.

Save me! Save me!
Her gesture is frozen by his advancing towards her. She looks wildly about, shrinking from him, then with sudden desperate resolution speaks.
Save me, and I will make it up to you!
Ghent again advances; she goes on pantingly, as she stands at bay.
Don't touch me! Listen! Save me from these others, and from yourself, and I will pay you—with my life.

GHENT.

With dull wonder.
With—your life?

RUTH.

With all that I am or can be.

GHENT.

What do you mean?—

Pause.

You mean you'll go along with me out of this? Stick to me—on the square?

RUTH.

In a tragic whisper.

Yes.

GHENT.

On the dead square?

RUTH.

Yes.

GHENT.

You won't peach, and spoil it?

RUTH.

No.

Pause, during which he looks at her fixedly.

GHENT.

Give me your hand on it!

She gives him her hand. The other men, at the table, have drawn their weapons, and hold them carelessly, but alert to the slightest suspicious movement on the part of Ghent.

DUTCH.

As Ghent turns to them.

Shorty and me's sittin' in this game, and interested, eh, Shorty?

The Mexican nods. Ghent comes slowly to the table, eyeing the two.

Dutch holds out the vase containing the dice.

Shake for her!

GHENT.

Shake how?

DUTCH.

Any damn way! Sole and exclusive rights. License to love and cherish on the premises!

Ghent takes the vase, shakes the due meditatively, is about to throw, then sets the vase down. He searches through his pockets and produces a few bills and a handful of silver, which he lays on the table.

GHENT.

There's all I've got in my clothes. Take it, and give me a free field, will you?

DUTCH.

Leaning over the table to Ghent, in plaintive remonstrance.

You don't mean me, Steve!

GHENT.

To the Mexican.

Well, you, then!

The Mexican spreads the money carelessly with his left hand to ascertain its amount, then thrusts it away with a disgusted grunt of refusal.

DUTCH.

Don't blame you, Shorty! A ornery buck of a dirt-eatin' Mojave 'd pay more 'n that for his squaw.

Ruth covers her face shudderingly. Ghent stands pondering, watching the two men under his brows, and slowly gathering up the money. As if on a sudden thought, he opens his shirt, and unwinds from his neck a string of gold nuggets in the rough, strung on a leather thread.

GHENT.

Well, it ain't much, that's sure. But there's a string of gold nuggets I guess is worth some money.

He throws it on the table, speaking to both men.

Take that, and clear out.

DUTCH.

Draws up angrily.

I've give you fair warning!

GHENT.

We'll keep everything friendly between me and you. A square stand-up shoot, and the best man takes her.

DUTCH.

Mollified.

Now you're comin' to!

GHENT.

To the Mexican.

Then it's up to you, and you'd better answer quick!

THE MEXICAN.

Eyeing Ghent and Ruth, points to the gun lying on the floor.

I take him, too.

GHENT.

No, you don't. You leave everything here the way you found it.

THE MEXICAN.

Alla right.

He pockets the chain and starts for the door.

GHENT.

Hold on a minute. You've got to promise to tie the man who falls, on his horse, and take him to Mesa Grande. Bargain?

The Mexican nods.

And mouth shut, mind you, or—

He makes a sign across his throat.

THE MEXICAN.

Nods.

Alla right.

He goes out.

GHENT.

Motioning toward the door.

Outside.

DUTCH.

Surprised.

What for?

GHENT.

Sternly.

Outside!

They move toward the door. Dutch stops and waves his hand to Ruth.

DUTCH.

Don't worry, my girl. Back soon.

GHENT.

Threateningly.

Cut that out!

DUTCH.

What's eatin' you? She ain't yours yet, and I guess she won't be, not till hell freezes over.

He taps his pistol and goes out. Ghent picks up the rifle which has previously missed fire; he unloads it, throws it on the window-seat, and follows Dutch. *Ruth stands beside the table, listening. Four shots are heard. After a short time Ghent appears and watches from the door the vanishing horses. He comes to the table opposite Ruth.*

RUTH.

In a low voice.

Is he dead?

GHENT.

No; but he'll stay in the coop for a while.

She sinks down in a chair. Ghent seats himself at the other side of the table, draws a whiskey flask from his pocket, and uncorks it awkwardly, using only his right hand.

RUTH.

As he is about to drink.

Don't!

GHENT.

Lowers the bottle and looks at her in a dazed way.

Is this on the square?

RUTH.

I gave you my promise.

Gazing at her, he lets the bottle sink slowly by his side; the liquor runs out, while he sits as if in a stupor. Ruth glances toward the door, and half starts from her seat, sinking back as he looks up.

GHENT.

Give me a drink of water.

She brings the water from a bucket in the corner. He sets the empty bottle on the table, drinks deeply of the water, takes a handkerchief from his neck, wets it, and mops his face.

GHENT.

Where are your folks?

RUTH.

My brother has gone out to the railroad.

GHENT.

Him and you ranching it here by yourselves?

RUTH.

Yes.

GHENT.

Write him a note.

He shoves paper, pen, and ink before her.

Fix it up anyway you like.

RUTH.

Tell me first what you mean to do with me.

GHENT.

Ponders awhile in silence.

Have you got a horse to ride?

RUTH.

Yes.

GHENT.

We can reach San Jacinto before sun-up. Then we're off for the Cordilleras. I've got a claim tucked away in them hills that'll buy you the city of Frisco some day, if you have a mind to it!

She shrinks and shudders.

What you shivering at?

Ruth does not answer, but begins to write. Ghent, still using only one hand, takes a pistol from his pocket, examines it, and lays it carelessly on the table, within Ruth's reach. He rises and goes to the fireplace, takes a cigarette from his pocket and lights it, and examines the objects on the mantel-shelf. Ruth stops writing, takes up the pistol, then lays it down, as he speaks without turning round.

Read what you've written.

Ruth, about to read, snatches up the pistol again, rises, and stands trembling and irresolute.

Why don't you shoot?

He turns round deliberately.

You promised on the square, but there's nothing square about this deal. You ought to shoot me like a rattlesnake!

RUTH.

I know that.

GHENT.

Then why don't you?

RUTH.

Slowly.

I don't know.

GHENT.

I guess you've got nerve enough, for that or anything.—Answer me; why not?

RUTH.

I don't—know.—You laid it there for me.—And—you have no right to die.

GHENT.

How's that?

RUTH.

You must live—to pay for having spoiled your life.

GHENT.

Do you think it is spoiled?

RUTH.

Yes.

GHENT.

And how about your life?

RUTH.

I tried to do it.

GHENT.

To do what?

RUTH.

To take my life. I ought to die. I have a right to die. But I cannot, I cannot! I love my life, I must live. In torment, in darkness—it doesn't matter. I want my life. I will have it!

She drops the weapon on the table, pushes it toward him, and covers her eyes.

Take it away! Don't let me see it. If you want me on these terms, take me, and may God forgive you for it; but if there is a soul in you to be judged, don't let me do myself violence.

She sinks down by the table, hiding her face in her hands.

O, God have pity on me!

Ghent puts the pistol back into his belt, goes slowly to the outer door, opens it, and stands for some moments gazing out. He then closes the door, and takes a step or two toward the table. As he speaks, Ruth's sobs cease, she raises her head and looks strangely at him.

GHENT.

I've lived hard and careless, and lately I've been going down hill pretty fast. But I haven't got so low yet but what I can tell one woman from another. If that was all of it, I'd be miles away from here by now, riding like hell for liquor to wash the taste of shame out of my mouth. But that ain't all. I've seen what I've been looking the world over for, and never knew it.—Say your promise holds, and I'll go away now.

RUTH.

O, yes, go, go! You will be merciful. You will not hold me to my cruel oath.

GHENT.

And when I come back?

Ruth does not answer. He takes a step nearer.

And when I come back?

RUTH.

You never—could—come back.

GHENT.

No, I guess I never could.

RUTH.

Eager, pleading.

You *will* go?

GHENT.

For good?

RUTH.

Yes.

GHENT.

Do you mean that?

RUTH.

Wildly.

Yes, yes, ten thousand times!

GHENT.

Is that your last word?

RUTH.

Yes.

Pause. She watches him with strained anxiety.

O, why did you come here to-night?

GHENT.

I come because I was blind-drunk and suncrazy, and looking for damnation the nearest way. That's why I come. But that's not why I'm staying. I'm talking to you in my right mind now. I want you to try and see this thing the way it is.

RUTH.

O, that is what I want you to do! You did yourself and me a hideous wrong by coming here. Don't do us both a more hideous wrong still! I was in panic fear. I snatched at the first thing I could. Think what our life would be, beginning as we have begun! O, for God's pity go away now, and never come back! Don't you see there can never be anything between us but hatred, and misery, and horror?

GHENT.

Hardening.

We'll see about that!—Are you ready to start?

Ruth, conscious for the first time of her undress condition, shrinks, and folds her gown closer about her neck.

Go, and be quick about it.

She starts toward her room; he detains her.

Where's your saddle?

She points at it and goes out. Ghent picks up the note she has written, reads it, and stands for a moment in reflection before laying it down. He gets more water from the bucket, drinks deeply, mops his face, and rolls up the sleeve of his left arm, which is soaked with blood. He tries awkwardly to stanch a wound in his forearm, gives it up in disgust, and rolls down his sleeve again. He reads the note once more, then takes Ruth's saddle and bridle from the wall and goes out. Ruth comes in; her face is white and haggard, but her manner determined and collected. She comes to the table, and sees the bloody handkerchief and basin of water. As Ghent enters, she turns to him anxiously.

RUTH.

You are hurt.

GHENT.

It's no matter.

RUTH.

Where?

He indicates his left arm. She throws off her hooded riding-cloak, and impulsively gathers together water, towels, liniment, and bandages; she approches him, quite lost in her task, flushed and eager.

Sit down.—Roll up your sleeve.

He obeys mechanically. She rapidly and deftly washes and binds the wound, speaking half to herself, between long pauses.

Can you lift your arm?—The bone is not touched.—It will be all right in a few days.—This balsam is a wonderful thing to heal.

GHENT.

Watching her dreamily, as she works.

What's your name?

RUTH.

Ruth—Ruth—Jordan.

Long pause.

There, gently.—It must be very painful.

He shakes his head slowly, with half-humorous protest.

GHENT.

It's not fair!

RUTH.

What isn't fair?

GHENT.

To treat me like this. It's not in the rules of the game.

RUTH.

As the sense of the situation again sweeps over her.

Binding your wound? I would do the same service for a dog.

GHENT.

Yes, I dare say. But the point is, I ain't a dog; I'm a human—the worst way!

She rises and puts away the liniment and bandages. He starts up, with an impulsive gesture.

Make this bad business over into something good for both of us! You'll never regret it! I'm a strong man!

He holds out his right arm, rigid.

I used to feel sometimes, before I went to the bad, that I could take the world like that and tilt her over. And I can do it, too, if you say the word! I'll put you where you can look down on the proudest. I'll give you the kingdoms of the world and all the glory of 'em.

She covers her face with her hands. He comes nearer.

Give me a chance, and I'll make good. By God, girl, I'll make good!—I'll make a queen of you. I'll put the world under your feet!

Ruth makes a passionate gesture, as if to stop her ears.

What makes you put your hands over your ears like that? Don't you like what I'm saying to you?

RUTH.

Taking the words with difficulty.

Do you remember what that man said just now?

GHENT.

What about?

RUTH.

About the Indian—and—his squaw.

GHENT.

Yes. There was something in it, too. I was a fool to offer him that mean little wad.

RUTH.

For—me!

GHENT.

Well, yes, for you, if you want to put it that way.

RUTH.

But—a chain of nuggets—that comes nearer being a fair price?

GHENT.

O, to buy off a greaser!

RUTH.

But to buy the soul of a woman—one must go higher. A mining-claim! The kingdoms of the world and all the glory of them!

Breaking down in sudden sobs.
O, be careful how you treat me! Be careful! I say it as much for your sake as mine. Be careful!

GHENT.
Turns from her, his bewilderment and discomfiture translating itself into gruffness.
Well, I guess we'll blunder through.—Come along! We've no time to lose.—Where are your things?
At her gesture, he picks up the saddle-pack which she has brought out of the bedroom with her, and starts toward the door.

RUTH.
Taking a hammer from the window-ledge and handing it to Ghent.
Fix the bolt. My brother must not know.
He drives in the staple of the bolt, while she throws the blood-stained water and handkerchief into the fire. He aids her in replacing the weapons on the walls, then takes the saddle-pack and stands at the door, waiting. She picks up her mother's picture, and thrusts it in her bosom. After standing a moment in hesitation, she takes the picture out, kisses it, lays it on the mantel, face down. She extinguishes the lamp, and goes out hastily. He follows, closing the door.

THE CURTAIN FALLS IN DARKNESS

★

ACT II

Stephen Ghent's home, in the Cordilleras. At the right, crowning a rude terrace, is an adobe cabin, stained a pale buff, mellowed to ivory by sun and dust. Over it clamber vines loaded with purple bloom. The front of the cabin is turned at an angle toward the spectator, the farther side running parallel with the brink of a cañon, of which the distant wall and upper reaches are crimsoned by the afternoon light. In the level space before the rocky terrace is a stone table and seats, made of natural rocks roughly worked with the chisel. The rude materials have manifestly been touched by a refined and artistic hand, bent on making the most of the glorious natural background. Against the rocks on the left stands a large hand-loom of the Navajo type, with weaving-stool, and a blanket half woven. On the table lies a half-finished Indian basket, and strips of colored weaving-materials lie in a heap on the ground. Cactus plants in blossom fill the niches of the rocks and lift their fantastic forms above the stones which wall the cañon brink. At one point this wall is broken, where a path descends into the cañon.

Lon Anderson, a venerable-looking miner, with gray hair and beard, sits smoking before the cabin. Burt Williams, a younger man, peeps up over the edge of the cañon, from the path.

BURT.
Hello, Lon. Is the missus inside?
Lon smokes on, without looking at the questioner.
Look here, I put a nickel in you, you blame rusty old slot-machine. Push out something!

LON.
Removes his pipe deliberately.
What you wantin' off 'n her now? A music lesson or a headache powder?

BURT.
Boss's waitin' down at the mine, with a couple o' human wonders he's brought back with him from wherever he's been this time. Something doin' on the quiet.

LON.
You can tell him his wife ain't nowheres about.

Burt produces an enormous bandana from his pocket, mounts the wall, and waves it. He sits on the wall and smokes for a moment in silence, looking down into the cañon, as if watching the approaching party. He points with his pipe at the cabin.

BURT.
Funny hitch-up—this here one—I think.

LON.
After a pause.
How much you gittin' a day now?

BURT.
Same little smilin' helpless three and six-bits.

LON.
Anything extry for thinkin'?

BURT.
Nope! Throwed in.

They smoke again. Burt glances down to reassure himself, then points at the loom and basket.
Queer business—this rug-weavin' and basket-makin', ain't it?—What d' ye s'pose she wants to sit, day in and day out, like a half-starved Navajo, slavin' over them fool things fur?—Boss ain't near, is he? Don't keep her short of ice-cream sodas and trolley-rides, does 'e?
Lon rises and approaches Burt, regarding him grimly.
Saw 'er totin' a lot o' that stuff burro-back over to the hotel week 'fore last.—An' Dod Ranger—you know what a disgustin' liar Dod is—he tells how he was makin' tests over in the cross-cañon, an' all of a sudden plump he comes on her talkin' to a sawed-off Mexican hobo, and when she sees Dod, she turns white's a sheet.

LON.

With suppressed ferocity.
You tell Dod Ranger to keep his mouth shet, and you keep yourn shet too—or by Jee-hosophat, I'll make the two of ye eat yer Adam's-apples and swaller the core!

BURT.

O, git down off'n yer hind legs, Lon! Nobody's intendin' any disrespect.

LON.

You boys keep yer blatherin' tongues off'n her! Or you'll get mixed up with Alonzo P. Anderson—*(he taps his breast)*—so's it'll take a coroner to untangle ye!

BURT.

Deprecatingly.
I guess I'd stick up fur 'er 's quick as you would, come to that.

LON.

Well, we don't need no stickin' up fur 'er. What we need is less tongue.
He leans down and speaks lower.
Especially when the boss is round. You tell the boys so.
Burt looks at him in surprise and is about to speak; Lon makes a warning signal, indicating the approach of the party below. Burt descends, saluting Ghent respectfully.

GHENT.

Peeping up over the edge of the cañon.
Coast clear, eh, Lon?

LON.

Yes, sir.

GHENT.

Where is she?

LON.

Points along the brink of the cañon.
Kind o' think she went out to Look-off Ledge.—
Guess she didn't expect you back to-day.

GHENT.

Speaking below.
Come up, gentlemen.
Ghent emerges from the cañon, followed by an architect, a dapper young Easterner; and a contractor, a bluff Western type. Ghent is neatly dressed in khaki, with riding-boots and broad felt hat. He has a prosperous and busy air, and is manifestly absorbed in the national game of making money.
Take a seat.

CONTRACTOR.

Seats himself by the table.
Don't care if I do. That new stage of yours just jumped stiff-legged from the go-off. And the trail up here from the mine is a good deal of a proposition for the seedentary.

ARCHITECT.

As he takes in the stupendous view.
What a wonderful place! Even better than you described it.

GHENT.

Yes. My wife picked it out.—Let's see your plans.
He removes basket from the table, where the architect unrolls several sheets of blue paper.

ARCHITECT.

I have followed your instructions to the letter. I understand that nothing is to be touched except the house.

GHENT.

Not a stone, sir; not a head of cactus. Even the vines you've got to keep, exactly as they are.

ARCHITECT.

Smiling.
That will be a little difficult.

GHENT.

You can put 'em on a temporary trellis.—A little pains will do it.

CONTRACTOR.

Maybe, with a man to shoo the masons off with a shotgun.

GHENT.

Over the plans.
Provide a dozen men, if necessary, with machine guns.

CONTRACTOR.

As you please, Mr. Ghent. The owner of the Verde mine has a right to his whims, I reckon.

ARCHITECT.

I have designed the whole house in the Spanish style, very broad and simple. This open space where we stand—

(*points to the plans*)—I have treated as a semi-enclosed *patio*, with arcaded porches.

GHENT.

Dubiously.

Good.

ARCHITECT.

This large room fronting the main arcade is the living-room.

GHENT.

I guess we'll have 'em all living-rooms. This place is to be lived in, from the word go.

ARCHITECT.

Humoring him.

To be sure, everything cheerful and open.—Here on the left of the inner court is the library and music-room.

GHENT.

I'm afraid we won't have much use for that. My wife don't go in much for frills. I used to play the concertina once, but it was a long while ago.

ARCHITECT.

It can be used for other purposes. For instance, as a nursery, though I had put that on the other side.

GHENT.

Embarrassed and delighted.

Um, yes, nursery.—Stamping-ground for the—?

The architect nods; the contractor follows suit, with emphasis. Lon nods solemnly over his pipe.

Good.

The architect bends over to make a note with his pencil. Ghent restrains him and says somewhat sheepishly in his ear.

You can leave it music-room on the map.

ARCHITECT.

Continuing his explanation.

This wing—

Ghent, interrupting him, holds the plan at arm's length, with head on one side and eyes squinted, as he looks from the drawings to the cabin and surroundings.

GHENT.

Looks a little—*sprawly* on paper. I had sort of imagined something more—more up in the air, like them swell tepees on the Hill in Frisco.

He makes a grandiose outline of high roofs and turrets in the air.

ARCHITECT.

I think this is more harmonious with the surroundings.

CONTRACTOR.

In answer to Ghent's inquiring look.

Won't look so showy from the new hotel across yonder.

He points to the left, down the curve of the cañon wall.

GHENT.

What's your estimate on this plan, now you've seen the location?

CONTRACTOR.

It's a long way to haul the stuff.—Say somewheres between twenty and twenty-five thousand. Twenty-five will be safe.

GHENT.

Slightly staggered.

That's a big lot of money, my friend!

CONTRACTOR.

With cold scorn.

I thought we was talkin' about a *house*! I can build you a good sheep-corral for a right smart less.

GHENT.

Well, I guess we don't want any sheep-corrals.

CONTRACTOR.

I should think not, with the Verde pumping money at you the way they tell she does.

GHENT.

Holds up the plans again and looks at them in perplexed silence.

I'll tell you, gentlemen, I'll have to consult my wife about this before I decide. The fact is, I've been working the thing out on the sly, up to now.

CONTRACTOR.

Expect to build it of an afternoon, while the lady was takin' her see-ester?

GHENT.

I thought I'd smuggle her off somewhere for a while.

He is silent a moment, pondering.

No! It's her house, and she must O.K. the plans before ground is broke.

He looks along the cañon rim.

Would you mind waiting a few minutes till I see if I can find her?

He starts irresolutely, then turns back.

Or better still, leave the plans, and I'll see you at the hotel to-morrow morning. I haven't been over there since it was opened. I'd like to know what they're making of it.

CONTRACTOR.

Astonished.

Hain't been over to the Buny Visty yet?

GHENT.

Too busy.

CONTRACTOR.

Well, you'll find it an up-to-date joint, and chock full of tourist swells and lungers.

GHENT.

Good-afternoon, gentlemen. You'll excuse me. You can find your way back all right? Take the left-hand path. It's better going.

The architect bows ceremoniously, the contractor nods. Ghent disappears along the cañon brink behind the cabin.

ARCHITECT.

Has been examining the work on the loom, and has then picked up the unfinished basket, admiringly.

What a beautiful pattern! I say, this is like those we saw at the hotel. (*To Lon.*) May I ask who is making this?

Lon smokes in silence; the architect raises his voice, slightly sharp.

May I ask who is making this?

LON.

Benignly.

You kin, my friend, you kin!

ARCHITECT.

Well, then, the question is put.

LON.

And very clear-put, too. You'd ought to be in the law business, young man.

He gets up deliberately.

Or some other business that'd take up all yer time.

ARCHITECT.

Between wrath and amusement.

Well, I'll be hanged!

He follows his companion down the cañon path, stopping a moment at the brink to look round with a professional air at the house and surroundings, then at Lon.

Tart old party!

He descends. Lon crosses to the table, looks over the plans, makes outlines in the air in imitation of Ghent, then shakes his head dubiously, as he rolls up the plans.

Ruth appears, emerging from the cañon path. She wears the same dress as at the close of Act I, with a dark scarf-like handkerchief thrown over her head. She is pale and exhausted. She sinks on the rocks at the edge of the cañon.

LON.

Approaching her, anxiously.

It's too much fer you, ma'am. You'd oughter let me go.

He brings her a glass of water from an Indian water-jar before the cabin.

RUTH.

Tasting the water.

O, I thought I should never get back!

She leans against a rock, with closed eyes, then rouses herself again.

Lon, take the glass, and see if you can make out any one down yonder, on the nearer trail. I—I thought some one was following me.

LON.

Speaks low.

Excuse me askin', Mis' Ghent, but is that dod-blamed Mexican a-botherin' you again?

RUTH.

No. He has gone away, for good. It's some one I saw at the hotel—some one I used to know.—Look if you can make out a man's figure, coming up.

LON.

Takes the glass from the niche in the rocks; and scans the cañon path.

Can't see nothin' but a stray burro, an' he ain't got no figger to speak of.—Might be t'other side o' Table Rock, down in the pinyon scrub.

Ruth gets up with an effort, takes the glass and looks through it, then lays it on the ledge.

Excuse me, ma'am, but—Mister Ghent come home this afternoon.

RUTH.

Startled.

Where is he?

LON.

Huntin' for you down Look-off Ledge way. I 'lowed you was there, not knowin' what else to say.

RUTH.

Thank you, Lon. You can go now.

He goes down the cañon path. Ruth looks once more through the glass, then crosses to the table, where she sits down and begins to finger the roll of plans. Ghent reënters. He approaches with soft tread and bends over Ruth. She starts up with a little cry, avoiding his embrace.

You frightened me.—When did you come back?

GHENT.

An hour ago.

RUTH.

Was your journey successful?

GHENT.

Yes. But my home-coming—that looks rather like a failure.

Pause.

I expected to find you out on the bluff.

RUTH.

Lon was mistaken. I had gone the other way.

As she stands at the table, she begins to unroll the plans.

What are these papers?

GHENT.

Haven't you one word of welcome for me, after five days?

Ruth remains silent, with averted head, absently unrolling the packet.

Not a look even?

He waits a moment, then sighs and seats himself moodily by the table.

I never can remember! After I've been away from you for twelve hours, I forget completely.

RUTH.

Forget what?

GHENT.

How it stands between us. It's childish, but for the life of me I can't help it.—After I've been away a few hours, this place gets all lit up with bright colors in my mind, like—(*searching for a simile*)—well, like a Christmas tree! I dare say a Christmas tree don't amount to much in real life, but I saw one once, in a play,—I was a little mining-camp roust-about, so high,—and ever since it has sort of stood to me for the gates o' glory.

RUTH.

With a hysterical laugh.

A Christmas tree!

She bows her head in her hands, and repeats the words, as if to herself, in a tone in which bitterness has given place to tragic melancholy.

A Christmas tree!

Ghent, watching her moodily, crumples up the plans and throws them upon the ground. He goes toward the cabin, hesitates, turns, and comes back to the table, where Ruth still sits with buried head. He draws from his pocket a jewel-case, which he opens and lays before her.

GHENT.

There is a little present I brought home for you. And here are some more trinkets.

He takes out several pieces of jewelry and tumbles them together on the table.

I know you don't care much for these things, but I had to buy something, the way I was feeling. And these papers—(*picks them up and spreads them out on the table*)—these mean that you're not to live much longer in a mud shanty, with pine boxes for furniture. These are the drawings for a new house that I want to talk over with you.

He points at the map and speaks glibly, trying to master his discomfiture at her lack of interest.

Spanish style, everything broad and simple! Large living-room opening on inner court. Library and music-room, bless your heart. Bedrooms; kitchen and thereunto pertaining. Wing where the proprietor retires to express his inmost feelings. General effect sprawly, but harmonious with the surroundings. Twenty thousand estimated, twenty-five limit. Is she ours?

RUTH.

In a dead, flat tone.

How much did you say the house is to cost?

GHENT.

Twenty-five thousand dollars at the outside.

RUTH.

And these—trinkets?

GHENT.

O, I don't know.—A few hundred.

RUTH.

Draws the plans toward her and pours the jewels in a heap upon them from her lifted hands.

Twenty-five thousand dollars and the odd hundreds!

She laughs suddenly and jarringly.

My price has risen! My price has risen!

She laughs again, as she rises from the table and looks down the cañon path.

Keep those displayed to show to our visitors! My honor is at stake.

She points down the path.

There is one coming now!

GHENT.

Visitors? What visitors?

RUTH.

Only an old school-friend of mine; a Mr. Winthrop Newbury.

GHENT.

What are you talking about? Are you crazy?

He joins her, where she stands looking down into the cañon.

This fellow, is he really what you say?

Ruth nods, with unnaturally bright eyes and mocking smile.

What does this mean?

RUTH.

It means that he caught sight of me, an hour ago, in the hotel.

GHENT.

In the hotel? What were you doing there?

RUTH.

With biting calm.

Nothing wicked—as yet. They don't pay twenty-five thousand dollars over there—at least not yet!

Ghent turns sharply, as if stung by a physical blow. She raises her hands to him, in a swift revulsion of feeling.

O, don't judge me! Don't listen to me! I am not in my right mind.

GHENT.

Sweeps the jewels together, and throws them over the cliff.

Do you want me to be here, while you see him?

She does not answer.

Won't you answer me?

RUTH.

Again cold.

Act as you think best.

GHENT.

It's a question of what will be easiest for you.

RUTH.

O, it's all easy for me!

Ghent stands irresolute, then raises his hand in a gesture of perplexity and despair, and goes into the house, closing the door. Winthrop Newbury appears at the top of the cañon path, looks curiously about, catches sight of Ruth's averted figure, and rushes toward her.

WINTHROP.

Ruth! Is it really you?

Ruth starts involuntarily toward him, stretching out her arms. As he advances, she masters herself, and speaks in a natural voice, with an attempt at gayety, as she takes his hand.

RUTH.

Well, of all things! Winthrop Newbury! How did you find your way to this eagle's nest?

WINTHROP.

I—we saw you—we caught a glimpse of you at the hotel, but we weren't sure. We followed you, but lost you in the cañon.

RUTH.

We? Who is we?

WINTHROP.

Your brother and his wife.

RUTH.

Turning the shock, which she has been unable to conceal, into conventional surprise.

Philip and Polly here!

WINTHROP.

They took the other turn, down there where the path forks. We didn't know which way you had gone.

RUTH.

Yes, but why on earth are they here at all?

WINTHROP.

They are on their way East. They stopped over to see me.

RUTH.

To see you? Are you—living here?

WINTHROP.

I have been here only a week.

He starts impulsively, trying to break through the conventional wall which she has raised between them.

Ruth—for God's sake—!

RUTH.

Interrupting him with exaggerated animation.

But tell me! I am all curiosity. How do you happen to be here—of all places?

WINTHROP.

What does it matter? I am here. We have found you, after all these miserable months of anxiety and searching. O Ruth—why—

RUTH.

I have acted badly, I know. But I wish not to talk of that. Not now. I will explain everything later. Tell me about yourself—about Philip and Polly—and mother. I am thirsty for news. What have you been doing all these months, since—our queer parting?

WINTHROP.

Solemnly.

Looking for you.

Pause.

O Ruth—how could you do it? How could you do it?

RUTH.

Touches him on the arm and looks at him with dumb entreaty, speaking low.

Winthrop!

WINTHROP.

In answer to her unspoken words.

As you will.

RUTH.

Resumes her hard, bright tone.

You haven't told me about mother. How is she?

WINTHROP.

Well. Or she will be, now. Ruth, you ought at least to have written to her. She has suffered cruelly.

RUTH.

Quickly, with a nervous uplift of her arms.

Yes, yes, I know that!—And you are—settled here? You mean to remain?

WINTHROP.

I am physician at the End-of-the-Rainbow mines, three miles below. At least I—I am making a trial of it.

Pause.

How pale and worn you are.—Don't turn away. Look at me.

She flinches, then summons her courage and looks him steadily in the face.
You are—you are ill—I fear you are desperately ill!

RUTH.

Moving away nervously.
Nonsense. I was never better in my life.
She goes toward the cañon brink.
You haven't praised our view. We are very proud of it.

WINTHROP.

Following her.
Yes, very fine. Magnificent.

RUTH.

But you're not looking at it at all! Do you see that bit of smoke far down yonder? That is the stamp mill of the Rio Verde mine.

WINTHROP.

Compelling himself to follow her lead.
Yes—the Rio Verde. One of the big strikes of the region. Dispute about the ownership, I believe.

RUTH.

None that I ever heard of, and I ought to know. For—(*she makes a sweeping bow*)—*we* are the Rio Verde, at your service.

WINTHROP.

You—your—husband is the owner of the Verde mine?

RUTH.

No less!

WINTHROP.

Embarrassed.
We found the record of your marriage at San Jacinto. The name was Ghent—Stephen Ghent.

RUTH.

Yes. He will be so glad to see some of my people.
Winthrop's eyes have fallen on the basket at the foot of the table. He picks it up, examines it curiously, and looks meaningly at Ruth, who snatches it from his hand and throws it over the cliff.
A toy I play with! You know I always have to keep my hands busy pottering at some rubbishy craft or other.

WINTHROP.

Is about to speak, but checks himself. He points at the loom.
And the blanket, too?

RUTH.

Yes, another fad of mine. It is really fascinating work. The Indian women who taught me think I am a wonder of cleverness.

WINTHROP.

So do—the women—over there.
He points across the cañon.

RUTH.

Flushing.
Ah, yes, you saw some of my stuff at the hotel. You know how vain I am. I had to show it.

WINTHROP.

Perhaps. But why should the wife of the man who owns the Verde mine *sell* her handiwork, and under such—such vulgar conditions?

RUTH.

Brilliantly explanatory.
To see if it will sell, of course! That is the test of its merit.
He looks at her in mute protest, then with a shake of the head, rises and puts on his hat.

WINTHROP.

Do you want to see the others?

RUTH.

Why, yes, to be sure I do. How should I not?

WINTHROP.

You haven't seemed very anxious—these last eight months.

RUTH.

True. I have been at fault. I so dread explanations. And Phil's tempests of rage! Poor boy, he must feel sadly ill-used.

WINTHROP.

He does.
Hesitates.
If there is any reason why you would rather he didn't see you, just now,—

RUTH.

There is no reason. At least, none valid.

WINTHROP.

Then I will bring them up.

RUTH.

By all means.
She holds out her hand, smiling.
Auf wiedersehen!
Winthrop releases her hand and goes toward the cañon path. He waves, and turns to Ruth.

WINTHROP.

They are just below.
As Ruth advances he takes her hand and looks searchingly into her eyes.
For old friendship's sake, won't you give me one human word before they come? At least answer me honestly one human question?

RUTH.

Keeping up her hard, bright gayety.

In the great lottery of a woman's answers there is always one such prize!

WINTHROP.

Dejectedly, as he drops her hand.

It's no use, if that is your mood.

RUTH.

My mood! Your old bugbear! I am as sober-serious as my stars ever let me be.

WINTHROP.

Did you, that night you bade me good-bye, know that—this was going to happen?

RUTH.

Cordially explanatory.

No. It was half accident, half wild impulse. Phil left me at the ranch alone. My lover came, impatient, importunate, and I—went with him.

WINTHROP.

And your—this man—to whom you are married—pardon me, you don't need to answer unless you wish—for how long had you known him?

RUTH.

Solemnly, as she looks him straight in the eyes.

All my life! And for æons before.

He looks at her for a moment, then goes toward the cañon path. Polly's voice is heard calling.

POLLY.

Not yet visible.

Win! Win!

WINTHROP.

Calls down the cañon.

Come up! Come up!

Ruth goes past him down the cañon path. In a moment she reappears, with Polly. They are laughing and talking as they come.

POLLY.

Ruth!

RUTH.

Dear old Polly!

POLLY.

You *naughty* girl!

RUTH.

If our sins must find us out, you are the kind of Nemesis I choose.

POLLY.

My! But you're a shady character. And sly!

Philip appears. Ruth hurries to embrace him, while Polly, fanning herself with her handkerchief, examines the house and surroundings with curiosity.

RUTH.

O Phil!—Dear old man!

She covers his face lightly with her hands.

No scolding, no frowns. This is the finding of the prodigal, and she expects a robe and a ring.

POLLY.

Seating herself on a rock.

Heavens, what a climb!—I'm a rag.

RUTH.

Motions to the men to be seated.

The cabin wouldn't hold us all, but there's one good thing about this place; there's plenty of outdoors.

WINTHROP.

Looking about.

I should say there was!

POLLY.

To think of our practical Ruth doing the one really theatrical thing known in the annals of Milford Corners, Mass.!—And what a setting! My dear, your stage arrangements are perfect.

RUTH.

In this case Providence deserves the credit. We may have come here to have our pictures taken, but we stayed to make a living.

Philip has drawn apart, gloomy and threatening. Polly keeps up her heroic efforts to give the situation a casual and humorous air.

POLLY.

With jaunty challenge.

Well, where is he?

RUTH.

Who?

POLLY.

He!

Ruth points at the cabin, smiling.

Well, produce him!

RUTH.

Following, with gratitude in her eyes, the key of lightness and raillery which Polly has struck.

You insist?

POLLY.

Absolutely.

RUTH.

O, very well!

She goes up the rocky incline, and enters the cabin, calling: "Steve! Steve!" Polly goes to Philip, and shakes him.

POLLY.

Now you behave!
Indicates Winthrop.
He's behaving.
Ruth reappears in the doorway, followed by Ghent.

RUTH.

With elaborate gayety, as they descend the rocks.
Well, Stephen, since they've run us to earth, I suppose we must put a good face on it, and acknowledge them.—This is Polly, of whom I've talked so much. Polly the irresistible. Beware of her!
Polly shakes his hand cordially.
And this is—my brother Philip.
Ghent extends his hand, which Philip pointedly ignores. Ruth goes on hastily, to cover the insult.
And this is my old school-friend, Winthrop Newbury.
They shake hands.

WINTHROP.

To Philip, formally explanatory.
Mr. Ghent is the owner of the famous Verde mine.

GHENT.

Part owner, sir. I hadn't the capital to develop with, so I had to dispose of a half-interest.

WINTHROP.

Isn't there some litigation under way?

RUTH.

Looking at Ghent, surprised.
Litigation?

GHENT.

Yes—a whole rigmarole.

POLLY.

Catching at a straw to make talk.
Heaven help you if you have got entangled in the law! I can conceive of nothing more horrible or ghostly than a court of law; unless (*she glances at Philip*) it is that other court of high justice, which people hold in private to judge their fellows, from hearsay and half-knowledge!

RUTH.

Keeping up the play desperately, as she blesses Polly with a look.
But there must be law, just the same, and penalties and rewards and all that. Else what's the use of being good?

POLLY.

Like you—for instance!

RUTH.

Well, yes, like me!

POLLY.

You are not good, you are merely magnificent. I want to be magnificent! I want to live on the roof of the world and own a gold mine! (*To Ghent.*) Show me where the sweet thing is.

GHENT.

We can get a better view of the plant from the ledge below. Will you go down?
Ghent, Polly, and Winthrop go down the cañon path. Ruth takes Philip by the arm, to lead him after.

PHILIP.

No. We must have a word together, before the gabble begins again. Winthrop has given me your explanation, which explains nothing.

RUTH.

Trying to keep up the light tone.
Hasn't that usually been the verdict on explanations of my conduct?

PHILIP.

Don't try to put me off! Tell me in two words how you came to run away with this fellow.

RUTH.

Hardening.
Remember to whom you are speaking, and about whom.

PHILIP.

I got your note, with its curt announcement of your resolve. Later, by mere accident, we found the record of your marriage at San Jacinto—if you call it a marriage, made hugger-mugger at midnight by a tipsy justice of the peace. I don't want to question its validity. I only pray that no one will. But I want to know how it came to be made, in such hurry and secrecy—how it came to be made at all, for that matter. How did you ever come to disgrace yourself and your family by clandestine meetings and a hedge-row marriage with a person of this class? And why, after the crazy leap was taken, did you see fit to hide yourself away without a word to me or your distracted mother? Though that perhaps is easier to understand!

RUTH.

The manner of your questions absolves me from the obligation to answer them.

PHILIP.

I refuse to be put off with any such patent subterfuge.

RUTH.

Subterfuge or not, it will have to suffice, until you remember that my right to choose my course in life is unimpeachable, and that the man whose destiny I elect to share cannot be insulted in my presence.

PHILIP.

Very well, I can wait. The truth will come out some day. Meanwhile, you can take comfort from the fact that your desertion at the critical moment of our enterprise has spelled ruin for me.

RUTH.

Overwhelmed.

Philip, you don't mean—!

PHILIP.

Absolute and irretrievable ruin.

RUTH.

Then you are going back East—for good?

PHILIP.

Yes.

RUTH.

But—mother's money! What will she do?

Philip shrugs his shoulders.

Is everything gone—everything?

PHILIP.

I shall get something from the sale. Perhaps enough to make a fresh start, somewhere, in some small way.

RUTH.

Comes to him, and lays her arms on his shoulders.

Phil, I am sorry, sorry!

He caresses her; she bursts into suppressed convulsive weeping and clings to him, hiding her face in his breast.

PHILIP.

Ruth, you are not happy! You have made a hideous mistake. Come home with me.

Ruth shakes her head.

At least for a time. You are not well. You look really ill. Come home with us, if only for a month.

RUTH.

No, no, dear Phil, dear brother!

She draws down his face and kisses him; then lifts her head, with an attempt at lightness.

There! I have had my cry, and feel better. The excitement of seeing you all again is a little too much for me.

PHILIP.

If there is anything that you want to tell me about all this, tell me now.

RUTH.

O, there will be plenty of time for explanations and all that! Let us just be happy now in our reunion.

PHILIP.

There will not be plenty of time. We leave tomorrow morning.

RUTH.

Then you will take me on trust—like a dear good brother. Perhaps I shall never explain! I like my air of mystery.

PHILIP.

Remember that if you ever have anything to complain of—in your life—it is my right to know it. The offender shall answer to me, and dearly, too.

RUTH.

Takes his head between her hands, and shakes it, as with recovered gayety.

Of course they will, you old fire-eater!

PHILIP.

Pointing to the blanket on the loom.

Ruth, at least tell me why—.

Ruth does not see his gesture, as she is looking at the others, who come up from below. The men linger in the background, Ghent pointing out objects in the landscape.

RUTH.

To Polly, who advances.

Well, what do you think of us, in a bird's-eye view?

POLLY.

In a bird's-eye view you are superb!

She draws Ruth to her, and speaks in a lower tone.

And looked at near, you are an enthralling puzzle.

RUTH.

Half to herself.

If you only knew how much!

POLLY.

Taking Ruth by the chin as in Act I.

So you had—just by chance—riding over to the trading-station or so—met the glorious unfulfilled—in blue overalls and a jumper! I thought so!

Ruth bows her head in a spasm of pain. Polly, who does not see her face, goes on teasingly.

I see now what you meant about wanting one that wasn't finished. This one certainly isn't finished. But when he is, he'll be grand!

Ruth moves away with averted head. Polly follows her, peeping round to view her face.

Don't sulk! I meant nothing disrespectful. On the contrary, I'm crazy about him.

In a louder tone.

And now that I've seen the outside of you, I must peep into that fascinating little house!

RUTH.

To Ghent, who has drawn nearer.

Polly wants to go inside the cabin. I can't let her until we have shown her what it's going to be.

With Ghent's aid she spreads out the plans, which Polly examines with curiosity.
These are the plans for our new house. You call us magnificent. We will show you that we are not. We are overwhelming!

WINTHROP.

Looking at his watch.
I am afraid we must be getting back. It grows dark very suddenly in the cañon.

RUTH.

To Polly.
Well, then you may come in, if you will promise to view the simple present in the light of the ornate future.
Polly goes in. Ruth, lingering at the door for an instant, looks back anxiously at the men.

PHILIP.

Curtly, to Ghent.
If you will permit me, I should like a word with you.

GHENT.

Certainly.
Winthrop effaces himself, making and lighting a cigarette, as he looks out over the cañon.

PHILIP.

In deference to my sister's wishes, I refrain from asking you for the explanation which is due me.
Ghent bows in silence.
But there is one thing which I think I am at liberty to question.

GHENT.

Do so.

PHILIP.

I hear of your interest in a valuable mine. I hear of plans for an elaborate house. Why, then, is my sister compelled to peddle her own handiwork in a public caravansery?

GHENT.

What do you mean? I don't understand you.

PHILIP.

Points at the loom.
Her rugs and baskets are on sale in the corridor of the hotel, fingered and discussed by the tourist mob.

GHENT.

Astonished.
This can't be true!

PHILIP.

It is, however.

GHENT.

I know nothing of it. I've had to be away a great deal. I knew she worked too hard over these things, but I took it for a mere pastime. Perhaps—No, I can't understand it at all!

PHILIP.

I advise you to make inquiries. She has taken pains to conceal her identity, but it is known nevertheless, and the subject of public curiosity. *Polly and Ruth come out from the cabin.*

POLLY.

To Philip.
Take me away quickly, or I shall never enjoy upholstery again!
To Ruth.
Please change your mind, dear, and come with us for the night.

RUTH.

No. I will see you in the morning.

WINTHROP.

We leave by the early stage.

RUTH.

Looking at him quickly.
You too?

WINTHROP.

Yes, I have decided so.

RUTH.

I will be there in good time, trust me.
She kisses Polly and Philip.
Good-bye, till morning.
Gives her hand to Winthrop.
Good-bye.
Philip ignores Ghent pointedly in the leave-takings. Polly bids him farewell with corresponding cordiality.

POLLY.

Good-bye, Mr. Ghent.
As they descend the cañon path, she is heard chatting enthusiastically.
O Phil, you ought to have seen the inside of that delightful little house!
Her voice is heard for some time, indistinctly. Ruth, at the top of the path, waves to them as they descend.

GHENT.

Looks long at her, with deep gratitude.
God bless you!
She sits down on the rocks of the cabin terrace. He walks up and down in anxious thought. Once or twice he makes as if to speak. At length he stops before her.

You must go in and lie down. You are worn out.

RUTH.

Rousing herself.

No, there is something I must tell you first.

GHENT.

Points at the rug.

It's about this—work you have been doing?

RUTH.

Slightly startled.

You know of that?

GHENT.

Your brother told me. I should have found it out tomorrow anyhow.

Pause.

Have you wanted money?

RUTH.

Yes.

GHENT.

I thought I—I thought you had enough. I have often begged you to take more.

RUTH.

I haven't spent what you gave me. It is in there.

She points toward the house.

GHENT.

Astonished.

You haven't spent—any of it?

RUTH.

A little. Nothing for myself.

GHENT.

But there has been no need to save, not after the first month or two. You surely knew that!

RUTH.

Yes, I knew it. It was not economy.

GHENT.

Slowly.

You haven't been willing to take money from me?

RUTH.

No. I know it was small of me, but I couldn't help it. I have paid for everything.—I have kept account of it—O, to the last dreadful penny! These clothes are the ones I wore from my brother's house that night. This shelter—you know I helped to raise that with my own hands. And—and some things I paid for secretly, from the little hoard I brought away with me. You were careless; you did not notice.

GHENT.

Sits down, dizzy from the shock of her words.

I must try to grasp this!

There is a silence, during which he sits perfectly motionless. At last he turns to her.

Why—why did you stand up so plucky, so splendid, just now? Put a good face on everything about our life? Call me by my first name and all that—before your own people?

RUTH.

We are man and wife. Beside that, my own people are as strangers.

GHENT.

Eagerly.

You say that? You can still say that?

RUTH.

Looks up, startled.

Can't you?

She awaits his answer tensely.

GHENT.

Desperately.

O, I don't know. I can't say or think anything, after what you have just told me!

RUTH.

Wails.

You can't say it! And it isn't true! It is we who are strangers.—Worse, a thousand times worse!

GHENT.

Rises and stands over her.

Don't let us dash ourselves to hell in one crazy minute!

He pauses and hesitates. When he speaks again it is with wistful tenderness.

Ruth, do you remember our journey here?

She lifts her head, looking at him with white, thirsty face.

I thought—it seemed to me you had—begun to care for me.

RUTH.

That night, when we rode away from the justice's office at San Jacinto, and the sky began to brighten over the desert—the ice that had gathered here—(*she touches her heart*)—began to melt in spite of me. And when the next night and the next day passed, and the next, and still you spared me and treated me with beautiful rough chivalry, I said to myself, "He has heard my prayer to him. He knows what a girl's heart is." As you rode before me down the arroyos, and up over the mesas, through the dazzling sunlight and the majestic silence, it seemed as if you were leading me out of a world of little codes and customs into a great new world.—So it was for those first days.—

And then—and then—I woke, and saw you standing in my tent-door in the starlight! I knew before you spoke that we were lost. You hadn't had the strength to save us!

GHENT.

Huskily.

Surely it hasn't all been—hateful to you? There have been times, since that.—The afternoon we climbed up here. The day we made the table; the day we planted the vines.

RUTH.

In a half whisper.

Yes!—Beautiful days!

She puts her hands suddenly before her face and sobs.

O, it was not my fault! I have struggled against it. You don't know how I' have struggled!

GHENT.

Against what? Struggled against what?

RUTH.

Against the hateful image you had raised up beside your own image.

GHENT.

What do you mean?

RUTH.

I mean that sometimes—often—when you stand there before my eyes, you fade away, and in your place I see—the Other One!

GHENT.

Speak plainly, for God's sake! I don't understand this talk.

RUTH.

Looking steadfastly, as at an invisible shape, speaks in a horrified whisper.

There he stands behind you now!—The human beast, that goes to its horrible pleasure as not even a wild animal will go—in pack, in pack!

Ghent, stung beyond endurance, rises and paces up and down. Ruth continues in a broken tone, spent by the violence of her own words.

I have tried—O, you don't know how I have tried to save myself from these thoughts.—While we were poor and struggling I thought I could do it.—Then—(*she points toward the cañon*)—then that hole down there began belching its stream of gold. You began to load me with gifts—to force easy ways upon me—

GHENT.

Well, what else did I care to make money for?

Ruth does not answer for a moment, then speaks slowly, taking the words with loathing upon her tongue.

RUTH.

Every time you give me anything, or talk about the mine and what it is going to do, there rings in my ears that dreadful sneer: "A dirt-eating Mojave would pay more than that for his squaw!"

She rises, lifting her arms.

I held myself so dear! And you bought me for a handful of gold, like a woman of the street! You drove me before you like an animal from the market!

Ghent has seated himself again, elbows on knees and face in his hands. Ruth takes slowly from her bosom the nugget chain and holds it crumpled up in her palm. Her tone is quiet, almost matter-of-fact.

I have got back the chain again.

GHENT.

Looks up.

Chain?—What chain?

RUTH.

In the same tone, as she holds it up, letting it unwind.

The one you bought me with.

GHENT.

Dumfounded.

Where the devil—? Has that fellow been around here?

RUTH.

It would have had no meaning for me except from his hand.

GHENT.

So that's what you've been doing with this rug-weaving and basket-making tomfoolery?

Ruth does not answer, but continues looking at the chain, running it through her fingers and weighing it in her hand.

How long has this been going on?

RUTH.

How long?—How long can one live without breathing? Two minutes? A few lifetimes? How long!

GHENT.

It was about a month after we came here that you began to potter with this work.

RUTH.

Draws her hand about her neck as if loosening something there; convulsively.

Since then this has been round my neck, around my limbs, a chain of eating fire. Link by link I have unwound it. You will never know what it has cost me, but I have paid it all. Take it and let me go free.

She tries to force it upon him, with wailing entreaty.

Take it, take it, I beseech you!

GHENT.

Holding himself under stern control.

You are killing yourself. You mustn't go on this way. Go and rest. We will talk of this to-morrow.

RUTH.

Rest! To-morrow! O, how little you have understood of all I have said! I know it is only a symbol—a make-believe. I know I am childish to ask it. Still, take it and tell me I am free.

Ghent takes the chain reluctantly, stands for a moment looking at it, then speaks with iron firmness.

GHENT.

As you say, your price has risen. This is not enough.

He throws the chain about her neck and draws her to him by it.

You are mine, mine, do you hear? Now and forever!

He starts toward the house. She holds out her hand blindly to detain him.

RUTH.

In a stifled voice.

Wait! There is—something else.

He returns to her, anxiously, and stands waiting. She goes on, touching the chain.

It isn't only for my sake I ask you to take this off me, nor only for your sake. There is—another life—to think of.

GHENT.

Leaning to look into her averted face.

Ruth!—Is it true?—Thank God!

RUTH.

Now will you take this off me?

GHENT.

Starts to do so, then draws back.

No. Now less than ever. For now, more than ever, you are mine.

RUTH.

But—*how* yours? O, remember, have pity! *How* yours?

Philip appears at the head of the cañon path. Hearing their voices, he waits, half concealed.

GHENT.

No matter how! Bought if you like, but mine! Mine by blind chance and the hell in a man's veins, if you like! Mine by almighty Nature whether you like it or not!

RUTH.

Nature! Almighty Nature!

She takes the chain slowly from her neck.

Not yours! By everything my people have held sacred!

She drops the chain.

Not yours! Not yours!

She turns slowly. Philip has come forward, and supports her as she sinks half fainting upon his neck.

PHILIP.

To Ghent.

I came back to get my sister for the night.—I don't know by what ugly spell you have held her, but I know, from her own lips, that it is broken.

To Ruth.

Come! I have horses below.

GHENT.

No!

PHILIP.

Measuring him.

Yes.

Pause.

GHENT.

Let her say!

RUTH.

Looks long at Ghent, then at the house and surroundings. At last she turns to her brother.

Take me—with you. Take me—home!

Philip, supporting her, leads her down the cañon path. Ghent stands gazing after them as they disappear below the rim. He picks up the chain and goes back, looking down after the descending figures. The sunset light has faded, and darkness has begun to settle over the mountain world.

CURTAIN

★

ACT III

Sitting-room of Mrs. Jordan's house at Milford Corners, Massachusetts. An old-fashioned New England interior, faded but showing signs of former distinction. The walls are hung with family portraits, several in clerical attire of the eighteenth century, one in the uniform of the Revolutionary War. Doors open right and left. At the back is a fireplace, flanked by windows, the curtains of which are drawn. On the left is a small table, with a lamp, books, and magazines; on the right, near the fireplace, a sewing-table, with lamp and sewing-basket. A bookcase and a writing-desk occupy opposite corners of the room, forward.

Winthrop and Philip stand near the desk, chatting. Polly is reading a newspaper at the table, left. Ruth sits before the grate, sewing; her face is turned away toward the fire.

PHILIP.
Offers Winthrop his cigar-case.
Have another cigar.

WINTHROP.
Well, as a celebration.
Takes one and lights it.

PHILIP.
Rather small business for the Jordan family, to be celebrating a bare escape from the poor-house.

WINTHROP.
Where did you scare up the benevolent uncle? I never heard of him before.

PHILIP.
Nor I, scarcely. He's always lived abroad.
Winthrops strolling about, peeps over Polly's shoulder.

WINTHROP.
To Philip, with a scandalized gesture.
Stock reports!

PHILIP.
Her latest craze.

WINTHROP.
Last week it was Japanese Samurai.

POLLY.
Crushingly.
And next week it will be—Smart Alecks.
The door on the left opens, and Mrs. Jordan enters, with Dr. Newbury. During the preceding conversation Ruth has sat sewing, paying no heed to the chatter. Mrs. Jordan and the doctor look at her as they come in, but she does not look up.

MRS. JORDAN.
Sit down, Doctor, at least for a moment.

DR. NEWBURY.
Seats himself, Mrs. Jordan near him.
I can never resist such an invitation, in this house.

MRS. JORDAN.
Dear Doctor, you've been a wonderful friend to me and mine all these years, since poor Josiah was taken.

DR. NEWBURY.
But just when you needed help most—

MRS. JORDAN.
I know how gladly you would have offered it, if you could.

DR. NEWBURY.
Your brother-in-law in England was able to redeem the property?

MRS. JORDAN.
Hastily.
Yes, yes.—But what we are to do for the future, with my little capital gone—
She speaks lower.
O, that dreadful West! If my children had only stayed where they were born and bred.
She glances at Ruth, who has let her sewing fall in her lap and sits staring into the fire.

DR. NEWBURY.
Sotto voce.
Poor child!
Polly looks up from the newspaper excitedly, holding her finger at a place on the sheet.

POLLY.
I say, Phil! Win! Look here.
Philip and Winthrop, who have been chatting and smoking apart, come to the table.

PHILIP.
What is it now?

POLLY.
Tapping on the paper.
Something about your Arizona scheme.

PHILIP.
Bending over her, reads:
"Alleghany pig-iron, 93¾, National Brick"—

POLLY.
Pointing.
No, there!

PHILIP.
Arizona Cactus Fibre, 84.
He picks up the paper, astounded.
Cactus Fibre listed! Selling at 84!
He tosses the paper to Winthrop.
This is the last straw!

MRS. JORDAN.

Who has been listening anxiously.
What does it mean, Phil?

PHILIP.

Only that the people who bought our plant and patents for a song, have made a fortune out of them.
Ruth has resumed her needle-work. Winthrop offers her the paper, with his finger at the line. She takes it, looks at it vaguely, and lays it on the table.

POLLY.

Leaning across.
Doesn't that interest you?

RUTH.

Tonelessly.
O, yes.
She rises, lays her work aside, and goes toward the door, left.

DR. NEWBURY.

As she passes him.
Won't you bid me good-night, my child?

RUTH.

Giving him her hand.
Good-night, Doctor.

DR. NEWBURY.

Shaking his finger.
Remember, no more moping! And from tomorrow, outdoors with you
Ruth looks at him vacantly, attempting to smile. She moves toward the door, which Winthrop opens for her.

WINTHROP.

Holding out his hand.
You must bid me good-night, too, and good-bye.

RUTH.

With a faint kindling of interest.
Are you going away?

WINTHROP.

Only back to Boston. Some time, when you are stronger, you will come down and see our new sailors' hospital.

RUTH.

Yes.—Good-bye.
She goes out, Winthrop closing the door.

WINTHROP.

To Dr. Newbury
I must be going along, father. Good-night, everybody!
Patting Philip's shoulder.
Hard luck, old man!
He goes out by the hall door on the right, Philip accompanying him.

DR. NEWBURY.

Looking after his son.
Brave boy! Brave boy! He keeps up a good show.

MRS. JORDAN.

You think he still grieves over her?

DR. NEWBURY.

Ah, poor chap! He's made of the right stuff, if he is mine.

MRS. JORDAN.

Let us not talk of it. It is too sad, too dreadful.
Philip reënters.

DR. NEWBURY.

About part of it we must talk.
He speaks so as to include Philip and Polly in the conversation.
Mrs. Jordan, I don't want to alarm you, but your daughter—I may as well put it bluntly—is in a dangerous state.

MRS. JORDAN.

Frightened.
Doctor! I thought she seemed so much stronger.

DR. NEWBURY.

She is, so far as her body is concerned.
Mrs. Jordan sits in an attitude of nervous attention, gazing at the doctor as if trying to formulate one of many questions pressing upon her. Philip comes forward and sits by the table, near them.

PHILIP.

Don't you think that the routine of life which she has taken up will soon restore her to a normal state of mind?

DR. NEWBURY.

Perhaps.—I hope so.—I would have good hope of it, if it were not for her attitude toward her child.

MRS. JORDAN.

Overwhelmed.
You have noticed that, too! I haven't spoken to you of it, because—I haven't been willing to see it myself.

PHILIP.

I can't see that there is anything particularly strange in her attitude. She takes care of the brat scrupulously enough.

POLLY.

Brat!

MRS. JORDAN.

Brat!
To Dr. Newbury, after a reproachful gaze at Philip.
With the most watchful, the minutest care, but—(*she speaks in a constrained voice, with a nervous glance at the door*)—exactly as if it were a piece of machinery!—Phil, do please

lay down that paper-knife before you break it! Your father brought that to me from India.

He obeys, but picks it up again absent-mindedly, after a few seconds.

Pardon me, Doctor. She goes about her daily business, and answers when she is spoken to, but as for her really being here—

She breaks out.

Doctor, what shall we do?

DR. NEWBURY.

She must be roused from this state, but how to do it, I don't know.

POLLY.

Rising with heightened color and nervous emphasis.

Well, I do!

MRS. JORDAN.

Looking at her with frightened interrogation.

Polly—?

POLLY.

What she needs is her husband, and I have sent for him!

PHILIP.

Inarticulate with surprise and anger.

You—!

POLLY.

Yes, I. He's been here a week. And he's an angel, isn't he, mother?

Philip snaps the paper-knife in two, flings the pieces to the floor, and rises, pale with rage.

MRS. JORDAN.

Gathering up the pieces with a wail.

O Phil! How could you! One of my most precious relics!

PHILIP.

To Mrs. Jordan.

Is this true, or is it another of her tedious jokes?

POLLY.

Protesting.

O, my dear, tedious!

MRS. JORDAN.

Wipes her eyes, after ruefully fitting the broken pieces of the knife together and laying them tenderly on the table.

You don't deserve to have me answer you, but it is true.

PHILIP.

Was this action taken with your knowledge?

MRS. JORDAN.

I do not expect to be spoken to in that tone. Polly telegraphed merely the facts. He came at his own instance.

PHILIP.

But you have consented to enter into relations with him?

MRS. JORDAN.

I have seen him several times.

POLLY.

Triumphantly.

And yesterday we showed him the baby! Such fun, wasn't it, mother?

MRS. JORDAN.

Wiping her eyes, sheepishly.

Yes, it was rather—enjoyable.

PHILIP.

He can't be in this town. I should have heard of it.

POLLY.

We've hid him safe.

PHILIP.

Where?

POLLY.

Never mind. He's on tap, and the sooner we turn on the spigot the better, is what I think. Doctor, what do you think?

DR. NEWBURY.

Let me ask you again to state your view of Ruth's case. I don't think I quite grasp your view.

POLLY.

Pluming herself, doctrinaire.

Well! Here on the one hand is the primitive, the barbaric woman, falling in love with a romantic stranger, who, like some old Viking on a harry, cuts her with his two-handed sword from the circle of her kinsmen, and bears her away on his dragon ship toward the midnight sun. Here on the other hand is the derived, the civilized woman, with a civilized nervous system, observing that the creature eats bacon with his bowie knife, knows not the manicure, has the conversation of a preoccupied walrus, the instincts of a jealous caribou, and the endearments of a dancing crab in the mating season.

MRS. JORDAN.

Polly! What ideas! What language!

DR. NEWBURY.

Don't be alarmed, Mrs. Jordan. The vocabulary has changed since our day, and—the point of view has shifted a little.

To Polly.

Well?

POLLY.

Well, Ruth is one of those people who can't live in a state of divided feeling. She sits staring at this cleavage in her life, like—like that man in Dante, don't you know, who is pierced by the serpent, and who stands there in hell staring at his wound, yawning like a sleepy man.

MRS. JORDAN.

O, Polly, do please try not to get our heads muddled up with literature!

POLLY.

All I mean is that when she married her man she married him for keeps. And he did the same by her.

Philip rises, with uncontrollable impatience, and goes back to the mantelpiece, against which he leans, nervously tearing a bit of paper to pieces.

DR. NEWBURY.

Don't you think that a mere difference of cultivation, polish—or—or something of that sort—is rather small to have led to a rupture, and so painful a one too?

POLLY.

A little nonplussed.

Well, yes, perhaps it does *look* small. But we don't know the particulars; and men *are* such *colossal* brutes, you know, dear Doctor!

DR. NEWBURY.

Judicially.

Yes, so they are, so they are!

POLLY.

And then her pride! You know when it comes to pride, Ruth would make Lucifer look like a charity-boy asking for more soup.

DR. NEWBURY.

I think perhaps the plan should be tried.

After a pause.

Yes, I think so decidedly.

PHILIP.

I call this a plot against her dignity and peace of mind!

DR. NEWBURY.

Rising.

Well, this conspirator must be going.

He shakes hands with Polly and Mrs. Jordan, takes his hat and stick. Philip remains plunged in angry reflection. Dr. Newbury taps Philip jestingly on the shoulder with the tip of his cane.

When you have lived as long as I have, my boy, you'll—you'll be just as old as I am!

He goes out, Polly accompanying him to the door.

Philip, disregarding his mother's conciliatory look and gesture as he passes her, goes out left. Polly stretches her arms and draws a deep breath as the door closes after him.

MRS. JORDAN.

Looking at her severely.

Pray what does that mean?

POLLY.

O, Phil is such a walking thunder-cloud, these days. It's a relief to get rid of him.

MRS. JORDAN.

Have you done what you could to make his life brighter?

POLLY.

I never had a chance. He has always been too much wrapped up in Ruth to think of me.

MRS. JORDAN.

How can you say such a thing? What do you suppose he married you for?

POLLY.

Heaven knows! What do they ever do it for? It is a most curious and savage propensity. But immensely interesting to watch.

MRS. JORDAN.

With a despairing gesture.

If you hold such heathenish views, why are you so bent on bringing those two together?

POLLY.

Soberly.

Because they represent—what Philip and I have missed.

MRS. JORDAN.

And pray what have "Philip and I" missed?

POLLY.

O, we're all right. But we're not like those two.

MRS. JORDAN.

I should hope not!

POLLY.

Even I believe that now and then a marriage is made in Heaven. This one was. They are predestined lovers!

MRS. JORDAN.

Mournfully, hypnotized by the evangelical note.

I pray it may be so.

She looks suspiciously at Polly.

You wretched girl! Predestined lovers and marriage made in Heaven, after all you've just been saying about how impossible he is.

POLLY.

He is quite impossible, but he's the kind we can't resist, any of us. He'd only have to crook his little finger at me.

MRS. JORDAN.

Lifting her hands in despair.

What are you young women coming to!
Pause.
He seems to me a good man.

POLLY.

Delighted.
O, he's *good!* So is a volcano between eruptions. And commonplace, too, until you happen to get a glimpse down one of the old volcanic rifts in his surface, and see—far below—underneath the cold lava-beds—fire, fire, the molten heart of a continent!

MRS. JORDAN.

I only hope you have some vague general notion of what you are talking about.

POLLY.

Amen.—And now let's consider when, where, and how we are to hale this dubious pair together.

MRS. JORDAN.

One thing is sure, it mustn't be here.

POLLY.

Why not?

MRS. JORDAN.

On Philip's account.

POLLY.

O, bother Philip!—Wasn't that the doorbell?

MRS. JORDAN.

Yes. You had better go.
Polly goes out. After a moment she reënters; excitedly.

POLLY.

It's Mr. Ghent!

MRS. JORDAN.

Amazed.
Mr. Ghent?
Polly nods enthusiastically. Ghent enters. He is conventionally dressed, a black string tie and the broad-brimmed hat which he carries being the only suggestions of Western costume remaining. Mrs. Jordan receives him in a flutter of excitement and alarm.
Mr. Ghent—! Surely at this hour—!

GHENT.

I beg your pardon. There was no other way. I am going West to-night.—Can I see you alone?

MRS. JORDAN.

Looks at Polly, who goes out, pouting.
Going West to-night?

GHENT.

Yes. Trouble at the mine.

MRS. JORDAN.

Isn't your business partner competent to attend to it?

GHENT.

He's competent to steal the whole outfit. In fact, is doing it, or has done it already.

MRS. JORDAN.

Vaguely alarmed.
And—my property here? Is that involved in the danger?

GHENT.

Certainly not.

MRS. JORDAN.

Relieved.
I have gone through such months of misery at the thought of losing the dear old place!—If Ruth only knew that we owe the very roof over our heads to you—

GHENT.

Well, she isn't to know, that's understood, isn't it? Besides, it's nothing to speak of. Glad if you think it a service. She wouldn't.

MRS. JORDAN.

You mean—?

GHENT.

I mean that if she knew about it, she wouldn't stay here overnight.

MRS. JORDAN.

Sit down.
She motions him to a seat at the table; she sits near him, speaking with nervous impulsiveness.
Tell me what is the trouble between you! It has all been a dreadful mystery from the beginning!

GHENT.

Is it a mystery that a woman like your daughter—?
He stops and sinks into gloomy thought.

MRS. JORDAN.

Should have chosen you?—Pardon me, I don't mean anything unkind—
He makes a gesture of brusque exoneration.
But having chosen—and broken faith with her brother to do it—

GHENT.

Nervously.
Let's drop that!
Pause.
Mrs. Jordan, you come of the old stock. Do you believe in the devil?

MRS. JORDAN.

Perhaps not in the sense you mean.

GHENT.

Tapping his breast.
I mean the devil inside of a man—the devil in the heart!

MRS. JORDAN.

O, yes. We are all forced by our lives to believe in that.

GHENT.

Our lives!
He looks slowly round the room.
How long have you lived here?

MRS. JORDAN.

For thirty years, in this house. Before I was married I lived in the old house down the road yonder, opposite the church.

GHENT.

To himself.
Think of it!

MRS. JORDAN.

What did you say?

GHENT.

Gathers himself together.
Mrs. Jordan, I want you to promise that what I put in your hands from time to time comes to your daughter as if from another source.

MRS. JORDAN.

You are going away for good?

GHENT.

Yes.

MRS. JORDAN.

You give her up?

GHENT.

A man can't give up what isn't his.

MRS. JORDAN.

What isn't his? She is your wife.

GHENT.

No. Never has been.

MRS. JORDAN.

Terrified.
O, pitiful heavens!

GHENT.

I beg your pardon.—I was only trying to say—I used to think that when a couple was married, there they were, man and wife, and that was the end of it. I used to think that when they had a child, well, sure enough it was their child, and all said.—And there's something in that, too.
He stares before him, smiting the table and speaking with low intensity.
Damn me if there ain't something eternal in it!
He sits for a moment more in gloomy thought.
Do you think she'll make up to the young one, after a bit?

MRS. JORDAN.

O, surely! To think otherwise would be too dreadful!

GHENT.

I'd give a good deal to know.—It's kind of lonesome for the little rooster, sitting out there all by himself on the world's doorstep!—I must see her for a minute before I go.—Do your best for me.

MRS. JORDAN.

I will do what I can.

GHENT.

You can put it as a matter of business. There is a matter of business I want to talk over with her, if I can get up the gumption.

MRS. JORDAN.

Hadn't you better tell me what it is?

GHENT.

Well, it's about your son Philip. That little scheme he started out in my country—the Cactus Fibre industry.

MRS. JORDAN.

Yes?

GHENT.

I believe he thinks his sister's going away when she did queered his game.

MRS. JORDAN.

It was a severe blow to him in every way. She was the life and soul of his enterprise.

GHENT.

I want her to give him back the Cactus Fibre outfit, worth something more than when he dropped it.

MRS. JORDAN.

Give it back to him? She?

GHENT.

Takes papers from his pocket.
Yes. I happened to hear it was knocking around for nothing in the market, and I bought it—for the house, really. Hated to see that go to the dogs. Then I looked over the plant, and got a hustler to boom it. I thought as a matter of transfer, to cancel her debt, or what she thinks her debt—
Pause.

MRS. JORDAN.

Fingering the paper with hesitation.
Mr. Ghent, we really can't accept such a thing. Your offer is quixotic.

GHENT.

Quix—what?

MRS. JORDAN.

Quixotic, it really is.

GHENT.

Doubtfully.

I guess you're right. It depends on the way you look at it. One way it looks like a pure business proposition—so much lost, so much made good. The other way it looks, as you say, quix—um—. Anyway, there are the papers! Do what you think best with them.

He lays the papers on the table, and picks up his hat.

MRS. JORDAN.

Wait in the parlor.

He opens the hall door.

The second door on the left.

With an awkward bow to Mrs. Jordan, he partly closes the door after him, when the inner door opens and Ruth appears. She goes to the sewing-table and picks up her sewing. Her mother, with a frightened glance at the half-open hall door, draws her back and kisses her. Ghent, unseen by Ruth, remains standing, with his hand on the door-knob.

MRS. JORDAN.

Ruth, you are a brave girl, and I will treat you like one.—Your husband is here.

RUTH.

Here?—Where?

Ghent pushes the door open, and closes it behind him. Ruth, sinking back against the opposite wall, stares at him blankly.

MRS. JORDAN.

He is leaving for the West again to-night. He has asked to see you before he goes.

Ruth covers her face with her hands, then fumbles blindly for the latch of the door. Her mother restrains her.

It is your duty to hear what he has to say. You owe that to the love you once bore him.

RUTH.

He killed my love before it was born!

MRS. JORDAN.

It is your duty to hear him, and part with him in a Christian spirit, for our sakes, if not for your own.

RUTH.

For whose sake?

MRS. JORDAN.

For mine, and your brother's.—We owe it to him, as a family.

GHENT.

Raises his hand restrainingly.

Mrs. Jordan—!

RUTH.

Owe?

MRS. JORDAN.

We owe it to him, for what he has done and wishes to do.

RUTH.

What he has done?—Wishes to do?

MRS. JORDAN.

Yes, don't echo me like a parrot! He has done a great deal for us, and is anxious to do more, if you will only let him.

RUTH.

What is this? Explain it to me quickly.

MRS. JORDAN.

With growing impatience.

Don't think to judge your mother!

RUTH.

I demand to hear what all this is! Tell me.

MRS. JORDAN.

Losing control of herself.

He has kept us from being turned into the street!

Ghent, who has tried dumbly to restrain her, turns away in stoic resignation to his fate.

He has given us the very roof over our heads!

RUTH.

You said that uncle—

MRS. JORDAN.

Well, it was not your uncle! I said so to shield you in your stubborn and cold-hearted pride.

RUTH.

Is there more of this?

MRS. JORDAN.

Yes, there *is* more. You wronged your brother to follow your own path of wilful love, and now you wrong him again by following your own path of wilful aversion. Here comes your husband, offering to make restitution—

RUTH.

What restitution?

MRS. JORDAN.

He has bought Philip's property out there, and wants you to give it back to him.

Ruth stands motionless for a moment, then looks vacantly about, speaking in a dull voice, as at first.

RUTH.

I must go away from this house.

MRS. JORDAN.

You don't understand. He claims nothing. He is going away himself immediately. Whatever this dreadful trouble is between you, you are his wife, and he has a right to help you and yours.

RUTH.

I am not his wife.

MRS. JORDAN.

Ruth, don't frighten me. He said those same words—

RUTH.

He said—what?

MRS. JORDAN.

That you were not his wife.

RUTH.

He said—that?

MRS. JORDAN.

Yes, but afterward he explained—

RUTH.

Flaming into white wrath.

Explained! Did he explain that when I was left alone that night at the ranch he came—with two others—and when gun and knife had failed me, and nothing stood between me and their drunken fury, I sold myself to the strongest of them, hiding my head behind the name of marriage? Did he explain that between him and the others money clinked—(*she raps on the table*)—my price in hard money on the table? And now that I have run away to the only refuge I have on earth, he comes to buy the very house where I have hidden, and every miserable being within it!

Long pause. She looks about blankly and sinks down by the table.

MRS. JORDAN.

Cold and rigid.

And you—married him—after that?

She turns away in horror-stricken judgment.

You ought to have—died—first!

Philip opens the door and enters; staring at Ghent with dislike and menace.

O Philip, she has told me!—You can't imagine what horrors!

Ruth rises, with fright in her face, and approaches her brother to restrain him.

PHILIP.

Horrors? What horrors?

MRS. JORDAN.

It was your fault! You ought never to have left her alone in that dreadful place! She—she married him—to save herself—from—O horrible!

Philip waits an instant, the truth penetrating his mind slowly. Then, with mortal rage in his face, he starts toward Ghent.

PHILIP.

You—dog!

Ruth throws herself in Philip's path.

RUTH.

No, no, no!

PHILIP.

Get out of my way. This is my business now.

RUTH.

No, it is mine. I tell you it is mine.

PHILIP.

We'll see whose it is. I said that if the truth ever came out, this man should answer to me, and now, by God, he shall answer!

With another access of rage he tries to thrust Ruth from his path. Mrs. Jordan, terrified at the storm she has raised, clings desperately to her son's arm.

RUTH.

I told him long ago it should be between us. Now it shall be between us.

MRS. JORDAN.

Philip! For my sake, for your father's sake! Don't, don't! You will only make it worse. In pity's name, leave them alone together. Leave them alone—together!

They force Philip back to the door, where he stands glaring at Ghent.

PHILIP.

To Ghent.

My time will come. Meanwhile, hide behind the skirts of the woman whose life you have ruined and whose heart you have broken. Hide behind her. It is the coward's privilege. Take it.

Philip, with Mrs. Jordan still clinging to his arm, goes out, Ruth closing the door after them. She and Ghent confront each other in silence for a moment, across the width of the room.

RUTH.

God forgive me! You never can.

GHENT.

It was a pity—but—you were in a corner. I drove you to it, by coming here.

RUTH.

It was base of me—base!

GHENT.

The way your mother took it showed me one thing.—I've never understood you, because—I don't understand your people.

RUTH.

You mean—her saying I ought to have died rather than accept life as I did?

GHENT.

Yes.

RUTH.

She spoke the truth. I have always seen it.

GHENT.

Ruth, it's a queer thing for me to be saying, but—it seems to me, you've never seen the truth between us.

RUTH.

What is the truth—between us?

GHENT.

The truth is—

He pauses, then continues with a disconsolate gesture.

Well, there's no use going into that.

He fumbles in his pocket, and takes from it the nugget chain, which he looks at in silence for a time, then speaks in quiet resignation.

I've got here the chain, that's come, one way and another, to have a meaning for us. For you it's a bitter meaning, but, all the same, I want you to keep it. Show it some day to the boy, and tell him—about me.

He lays it on the desk and goes toward the door.

RUTH.

What is the truth—between us?

GHENT.

I guess it was only of myself I was thinking.

RUTH.

What is it—about yourself?

GHENT.

After a pause.

I drifted into one of your meeting-houses last Sunday, not knowing where else to go, and I heard a young fellow preaching about what he called "The Second Birth." A year and a half ago I should have thought it was all hocus-pocus, but you can believe me or not, the way he went on he might have been behind the door that night in that little justice den at San Jacinto, saying to the Recording Angel: "Do you see that rascal? Take notice! There ain't an ounce of bone or a drop of blood in him but what's new man!"

RUTH.

You think it has been all my fault—the failure we've made of our life?

GHENT.

It's been no failure. However it is, it's been our life, and in my heart I think it's been—all—right!

RUTH.

All right! O, how can you say that?

She repeats the words with a touch of awe and wonder.

All right!

GHENT.

Some of it has been wrong, but as a whole it has been right—right! I know that doesn't happen often, but it has happened to us, because—(*he stops, unable to find words for his idea*) because—because the first time our eyes met, they burned away all that was bad in our meeting, and left only the fact that we *had* met—pure good—pure joy—a fortune of it—for both of us. Yes, for both of us! You'll see it yourself some day.

RUTH.

If you had only heard my cry to you, to wait, to cleanse yourself and me—by suffering and sacrifice—before we dared begin to live! But you wouldn't see the need!—O, if you could have felt for yourself what I felt for you! If you could have said, "The wages of sin is death!" and suffered the anguish of death, and risen again purified! But instead of that, what you had done fell off from you like any daily trifle.

GHENT.

Steps impulsively nearer her, sweeping his hand to indicate the portraits on the walls.

Ruth, it's these fellows are fooling you! It's they who keep your head set on the wages of sin, and all that rubbish. What have we got to do with suffering and sacrifice? That may be the law for some, and I've tried hard to see it as our law, and thought I had succeeded. But I haven't! Our law is joy, and selfishness; the curve of your shoulder and the light on your hair as you sit there says that as plain as preaching.—Does it gall you the way we came together? You asked me that night what brought me, and I told you whiskey, and sun, and the devil. Well, I tell you now I'm thankful on my knees for all three! Does it rankle in your mind that I took you when I could get you, by main strength and fraud? I guess most good women are taken that way, if they only knew it. Don't you want to be paid for? I guess every wife is paid for in some good coin or other. And as for you, I've paid for you not only with a trumpery chain, but with the heart in my breast, do you hear? That's one thing you can't throw back at me—the man you've made of me, the life and the meaning of life you've showed me the way to!

Ruth's face is hidden in her hands, her elbows on the table. He stands over her, flushed and waiting. Gradually the light fades from his face. When he speaks again, the ring of exultation which has been in his voice is replaced by a sober intensity.

If you can't see it my way, give me another chance to live it out in yours.

He waits, but she does not speak or look up. He takes a package of letters and papers from his pocket, and runs them over, in deep reflection.

During the six months I've been East—

RUTH.

Looking up.

Six months? Mother said a week!

GHENT.

Your sister-in-law's telegram was forwarded to me here. I let her think it brought me, but as a matter of fact, I came East in the next train after yours. It was rather a low-lived thing to do, I suppose, hanging about and bribing your servant for news—

Ruth lets her head sink in her hands. He pauses and continues ruefully.

I might have known how that would strike you! Well, it would have come out sooner or later.—That's not what I started to talk about.—You ask me to suffer for my wrong. Since you left me I *have* suffered—God knows! You ask me to make some sacrifice. Well—how would the mine do? Since I've been away they've as good as stolen it from me. I could get it back easy enough by fighting; but supposing I don't fight. Then we'll start all over again, just as we stand in our shoes, and make another fortune—for our boy.

Ruth utters a faint moan as her head sinks in her arms on the table. With trembling hands, Ghent caresses her hair lightly, and speaks between a laugh and a sob.

Little mother! Little mother! What does the past matter, when we've got the future—and him?

Ruth does not move. He remains bending over her for some moments, then straightens up, with a gesture of stoic despair.

I know what you're saying there to yourself, and I guess you're right. Wrong is wrong, from the moment it happens till the crack of doom, and all the angels in Heaven, working overtime, can't make it less or different by a hair. That seems to be the law. I've learned it hard, but I guess I've learned it. I've seen it written in mountain letters across the continent of this life.—Done is done, and lost is lost, and smashed to hell is smashed to hell. We fuss and potter and patch up. You might as well try to batter down the Rocky Mountains with a rabbit's heart-beat!

He goes to the door, where he turns.

You've fought hard for me, God bless you for it.—But it's been a losing game with you from the first!—You belong here, and I belong out yonder—beyond the Rockies, beyond—the Great Divide!

He opens the door and is about to pass out. Ruth looks up with streaming eyes.

RUTH.

Wait!

He closes the door and stands waiting for her to speak. Ruth masters herself and goes on, her eyes shining, her face exalted.

Tell me you know that if I could have followed you, and been your wife, without struggle and without bitterness, I would have done it.

GHENT.

Solemnly.

I believe you would.

RUTH.

Tell me you know that when I tore down with bleeding fingers the life you were trying to build for us, I did it only—because—I loved you!

GHENT.

Comes slowly to the table, looking at her with bewilderment.

How was that?

RUTH.

O, I don't wonder you ask! Another woman would have gone straight to her goal. You might have found such a one. But instead you found me, a woman in whose ears rang night and day the cry of an angry Heaven to us both—"Cleanse yourselves!" And I went about doing it in the only way I knew—(*she points at the portraits on the wall*)—the only way my fathers knew—by wretchedness, by self-torture, by trying blindly to pierce your careless heart with pain. And all the while you—O, as I lay there and listened to you, I realized it for the first time—you had risen, in one hour, to a wholly new existence, which flooded the present and the future with brightness, yes, and reached back into our past, and made of it—made of all of it—something to cherish!

She takes the chain, and comes closer.

You have taken the good of our life and grown strong. I have taken the evil and grown weak, weak unto death. Teach me to live as you do!

She puts the chain about her neck.

GHENT.

Puzzled, not yet realizing the full force of her words.

Teach you—to live—as I do?

RUTH.

And teach—*him!*

GHENT.

Unable to realize his fortune.

You'll let me help make a kind of a happy life for—the little rooster?

RUTH.

Holds out her arms, her face flooded with happiness.

And for us! For us!

CURTAIN

Part 2
Religion, Race and Ethnicity

MINSTRELS AND TOM SHOWS

ANTI-LYNCHING PLAYS

IMMIGRATION AND VAUDEVILLE

Part 2
Religion, Race and Ethnicity

5. *Uncle Tom's Cabin*—The Harmount Company Script

Commentary

Sources

Play

5.1 LONG LIVE UNCLE TOM! *UNCLE TOM'S CABIN* IN THE TWENTIETH CENTURY—JOHN FRICK

Uncle Tom in Ohio

In rural America, the twentieth century began much the way the nineteenth had ended: with a flourishing business on the road for traveling Tom shows in both the big cities and the tank towns. The majority of Uncle Tom productions in the big cities were, in fact, mounted by some of the larger traveling Tom shows (e.g., Martin's show in New York and Chicago; Jay Rial's *Uncle Tom's Cabin* in Chicago). And *everyone* was modernizing. At the beginning of the twentieth century, even the smaller traveling Tom shows were adopting modern devices and ideas, while still holding on to some past practices. Tom shows, like traveling circuses, even while still performing the same creaky old scripts under canvas, were abandoning or had already abandoned their time-tested wagons in favor of trucks or even trains. Thus, at the same time that Brady treated New York and Chicago audiences to an updated *Uncle Tom's Cabin*, Tom companies, which were likewise adopting modern techniques, were traversing the length and width of the country.

Although the exact number of Tom companies touring at the turn of the century will likely never be known for certain, one fact remains, and it was something that was evident to show business entrepreneurs as a new century began: there was still money to be made playing *Uncle Tom's Cabin* in America's hinterlands. In 1902, just 1 year after Brady's landmark production, while some pessimistic critics were already forecasting Uncle Tom's demise, more astute observers were predicting that thousands more patrons would attend one or more Tom show before the phenomenon would totally disappear. Thus, as older companies went out of existence, new ones were created, albeit at a slower rate than in the 1880s and 1890s. One of these "new" companies was the Harmount Uncle Tom's Cabin Company based in Williamsport, Ohio. Other than its being a family run operation, the Harmount Uncle Tom's Cabin Company was a "typical" small to medium size Tom company and is one of the best documented troupes in the history of tomming, with business letters, tour routes and schedules, photographs, reviews (recorded on the *Uncle Tom's Cabin & American Culture* website), and a doctoral dissertation on the show housed in the Jerome Lawrence and Robert E. Lee Theatre Research Institute at the Ohio State University. Closer study of this well-documented company affords valuable insights into the routine operation of a Tom troupe and thus a detailed description is provided here as an example of how a Tom show—both in the nineteenth and twentieth centuries—was organized and operated.

The Harmount Tom company was created in 1903 by former blacksmith and woodworker, Albert L. Harmount, an experienced and talented musician who organized local bands and personally taught music to his children. After witnessing a number of Tom shows, three of Harmount's sons joined the Long Brothers Uncle Tom company for the summer of 1902. Returning to Williamsport in the fall, the sons convinced their father to abandon his blacksmith trade and organize a Tom show. Thus, during the following winter, the Harmounts—the entire family—rehearsed *Uncle Tom's Cabin*, prepared horses and wagons for touring, and bought their first tent, which cost $210, a sum the Harmounts planned on paying off at $10 per week. The newly constituted

Tom company began its public life on May 15, 1903 in Williamsport and gave a second show the following night, grossing approximately $90 each night. The company on opening night included, in addition to Harmount himself, his 18-year-old daughter Anna, and sons Clarence (27), George (23), Dennis (20), and Charles (16). The fledgling company was "completed" by nonfamily members Charles Rector, Viola Allen, Lloyd Davis, and "a few others—about 12 people in all." For their initial season, Anna was cast as both Eliza and Aunt Ophelia, while Charles (Tad) played Topsy.

With the basic requirements for a tour (a cast, a script borrowed from the Longs, some horses and wagons (image 5.3), minimal scenery and props and two dogs in place), the Harmount show initiated its inaugural tour. During its first summer, the company played mainly in Ohio with just nine out-of-state performances in Indiana in August, 1903. The towns where they appeared ranged in population from 29 (Fairview, Ohio) to 2,690 in Raymond, Ohio, with shows in only five towns with a population of 1,000 or more. The majority of towns the Harmounts played had less than 400 citizens. The 1903 tour ended in Bloomingburg, Ohio, on October 12, a date that Al Harmount considered "early," but one necessitated by bad weather. Between the troupe's first road performance on May 18 and their final performance of the season on October 12, the Harmount company played in over 120 towns.

During the winter of 1903–4, the Harmount company, like all summer Tom shows, repaired and repainted their wagons and properties, while Al purchased a new tent for the troupe and son Clarence traveled to Cincinnati to arrange for new lithographs for the season. On May 9, 1904, the advance wagon set forth from Williamsport, followed on the sixteenth by the entire company. The 1904 summer tour that began on May 16 in Darbyville, Ohio, continued until October 10 and took the company into Indiana for a major portion of July and August, a total of 127 performances for the season and an increase of 7 over the 1903 tour. Like the 1903 tour, the 1904 Harmount tour consisted entirely of one-night stands, a practice that would continue until the 1917–18 season, when the company broke tradition and played two-night stands in Waterbury and Bridgeport, Connecticut; three-night stands in Paterson and Trenton, New Jersey; and full week runs in Philadelphia, Baltimore, and Washington, D.C. The practice of one-night stands, while geographically extending the troupe's reputation, was rough on the wagons, scenery and properties, and the company's tents.

Harmount's first tent was a modest affair with one central pole and a width of approximately 30 feet across the center. The capacity was never specified, but when filled, the gross proceeds never exceeded $90/week. Thus, the second tent (the one Al Harmount bought in 1904) which was described as being "similar to those of medium sized circuses" with a capacity of 3,000 spectators was an improvement, at least in terms of size. When it was set up, the central tent was surrounded by a series of service tents used for a dining room, a kitchen, a shelter for the horses, a storage tent for scenery and properties, and several smaller tents to house company members. Meals, described as the simplest and most staple of foods, were provided in the mess tent.

When the troupe arrived at a performance site, the wagons were unloaded and tents were the first to be set up, with the stage and seats for the spectators set up last. The stage, roughly 20 to 25 feet wide and 15 feet deep and approximately 5 feet high, was formed by a wagon that was set in place at one end of the show tent. The sides of the wagon were dropped down and were supported by jacks, and then a show curtain—a street scene—and a handful of drops described as being 9 feet by 12 feet and quite primitive were hung. There were no plantation or cabin or auction drops, the scenes being established by set props like bales of hay for the auction or a bed and a few chairs for Eva's death scene. The show tent dressing rooms were at the sides of the stage in a "three-cornered area" and the performers' trunks were deposited there once the tent had been erected.

During their later summer tours, the troupe, which averaged 20 performers per season with "extras" added as needed, offered both matinees and evening performances several days per week, frequently performing ten or more times each week. Throughout the existence of the company, it played over 90 stops per season, almost never returning to a town 2 years in a row and generally avoiding playing in large cities. A "typical" set of prices for an evening's performance ranged from ten to fifty cents, with tickets also available for twenty and thirty cents as well. The profit margin for the Harmount troupe was small with gross proceeds averaging $20/day. Daily expenses during the same time, however, were approximately $10.

Salaries for company members, even during the latter years, never exceeded $20.00/week and their contract specified that they also take part in the parade and "specialty" numbers. Anticipating problems, or perhaps reacting to existing problems, management also set forth a series of "conditions of employment" in actors' contracts. These included:

> No deviations from lines or business of the play, or "cutting" without permission from proper authority.
> No profane language allowed during performance or rehearsals.
> Acting people must dress all parts; faking of wardrobe and doubling will not be tolerated.

[In addition to these general rules, contracts established a set of "Special Fines":]

> For finding fault because another member of the Company receives a "reception bouquet" (sic!), round of applause, or other token of public approval . . . Five dollars ($5.00).
> For kicking because a certain part does not suit the person playing it . . . Five dollars ($5.00).
> For displaying annoyance or ill temper during a performance, either on stage, in the wings or in the dressing room Five dollars ($5.00).

Beginning with the first season (1903) and continuing for the next 8 years, the Harmount Uncle Tom's Cabin Company remained a summer touring troupe that pitched its tents for one night only and then moved on. During all of their summer touts, the company remained subject to the "usual" hazards that plagued all Tommers: storms that in some seasons caused the cancellation of as many as two shows/week; bad roads, especially in Illinois where the dirt roads were described as "primitive"; equipment breakdowns; and competition from other Tom shows. In transit, in order to ensure that no one got lost, the lead wagon left markers for those following, much as the circus has done during its entire existence. The preferred marker, left at the junction of two or more roads, was created by "stringing" grass from the roadside across the roads the company would *not* travel. The Harmounts "preferred the grass marking system because if they had made a marking in the dirt at the crossroads, "everybody else runnin' over it would obliterate it," but no one would bother with blades of grass.

Having started as a small summer endeavor in 1903, the Harmount Uncle Tom troupe continued to expand and to improve its show until, following the summer tour of 1911, the decision was made to continue to perform throughout the year. In part, the decision was predicated upon the realization that they could successfully compete with the larger traveling Tom shows and other forms of entertainment that played the theatres and opera houses in cities and larger towns. Thus, on November 15, 1911, billed as Jack Peters and Company, in a play titled *Jesse James*, the Harmount company began its winter touring at the town hall in their home town of Williamsport. The 1911 season also brought an expansion of the company's repertoire as *Ten Nights in a Bar-room* joined *Uncle Tom's Cabin* and *Jesse James* on the list of offerings. During the same season, the Harmounts added a bell ringer and a strongman to their company. How often the troupe played *Jesse James* and *Ten Nights* is not known, but it is reasonable to assume that when the Harmounts stayed in a town or city more than one night, more than one play was required. During the "teens," the Harmount Uncle Tom's Cabin Company continued to grow and become more polished, reaching its peak during the winter tour of 1917–18. By this time, truck (Image 5.4) and train transportation had replaced the show wagons of earlier days and, in some cities, the company even traveled by interurban street car. When the company ceased production in 1929, it could claim to having played in Ohio, Illinois, Indiana, New York, Connecticut, Pennsylvania, Michigan, Minnesota, Wisconsin, and Iowa.

Reviews for the company throughout its existence were generally positive. A typical critique stated that the Harmount company plays "'Uncle Tom' as well as it is ever seen save in the large theatres," with the featured performers regarded as the highlights of the company. In Sterling, Ohio, for example, the local newspaper reported that "everybody [at the Harmount show] was well pleased with the performers. The characters were well represented and there were plenty of good specialty" numbers. In addition to the actors, the Harmount band was consistently mentioned as one of the strongest features of the show, and the dogs (See Image 4.3, p. 124) garnered substantial praise. By 1911, the Harmount troupe was carrying five great danes and five American redbone bloodhounds, two of whom (Ben and Baker) were billed as being famous. Critics at the time described the Harmount canines as "without a doubt, the finest lot of dogs seen with any traveling organization." Throughout the troupe's existence, its popularity was further enhanced by the low prices they charged for their shows and a Harmount street parade that people described as being "grand, almost preposterous."

Although the Harmount script varied over the years, the basic text was the standard Samuel French version that was little more than the George Aiken *Uncle Tom's Cabin*, which had been widely adopted by the majority of Tommers. After initially using a script inherited from the Long Brothers for their first seasons, the Harmounts adapted their own version from the script purchased from the French catalog. In their "adaptation," entire scenes were deleted, as were the characters of Gumption Cute, Mr. Wilson, Deacon Perry, and Tom Loker, but programs indicate that at the same time the dogs, Prince and Keno, were added. After deletions, condensing of scenes, and general "paring down," the Harmount acting script consisted of four acts with fifteen scenes and one tableau, reduced from Aiken's six acts, thirty scenes and eight tableaux. Instead of beginning with Aiken's scene between Eliza and George Harris in which the latter declares that he is running away from his master, the Harmount text began with a short, spirited clash between George Harris and Haley when George catches the slave trader attempting to kiss his wife. In his 1967 dissertation, Blaine Quarnstrom notes that the first 17 speeches in the Harmount acting script were added by the company, since in both the novel and the Aiken play, Haley and George never meet face to face. The next scene in the Harmount script was set in Uncle Tom's cabin and dialog, albeit with extensive cutting, returned to the Aiken text. Quarnstrom also indicates that the Harmounts incorporated "vaudeville-type comedy," which was popular at the time, but does not define what that was.

In its own time, the Harmount *Uncle Tom's Cabin*—at least the later shows—would have been considered scenically and technologically sophisticated for a medium-sized company. While scenery and special effects for the early summer shows may have been "rustic," as the troupe grew and prospered, scenery and technology improved. As was common for Tom troupes on the road, the Harmounts carried and used its own scenery and special effects, even when playing well-equipped opera houses in the late teens and 1920s. Like other troupes, Harmount advertising claimed that it was "the largest and best" Tom company on the road and was equipped with $20,000 worth of scenery and effects.

According to Harmount Company records housed in the Lawrence and Lee Theatre Collection, the company acquired its scenery from M. Armbruster and Sons, Scenic Artists of Columbus, Ohio, one of the most respected scenic studios of the era. The studio had the reputation of being able to build scenery for classical as well as popular entertainments and was renowned for its excellence in executing detailed pattern work. During their 83 years of existence, Armbruster provided scenery for such stage luminaries as Tommaso Salvini, Sarah Bernhardt, James O'Neill, Robert Mantell, and Helena Modjeska. The studio also built and shipped scenery to theatres overseas. Armbruster drops used by the Harmount Company may be viewed on the *Uncle Tom's Cabin & American Culture* website (Performing the Play/Armbruster Scenic Drops).

Of the 15 scenes in the Harmount *Uncle Tom's Cabin*, Eliza's escape across the ice and the Grand Allegorical Transformation scene were generally considered essential to the success of the production—scenes that were expected by audiences everywhere and hence were indispensable. Given their significance, much attention was therefore devoted to the scenery and special effects for them. For the River Scene:

> The full stage was used for the River Crossing Scene. The backdrop . . . was generally hung in the 4th or 5th groove. In groove three, a four foot high batten which extended the full width of the stage was suspended a few inches from the stage floor by piano wire attached to the flies. The top of the batten was cut and painted to appear like jagged broken pieces of ice. Groove 2 contained a similarly constructed batten three feet high. Between these two battens the company's scenery trunks were spaced evenly across the stage. Directly in front *of* the three foot batten a ground row which was cut and painted in the same manner as the ice was placed on the stage floor. [A] winter leg . . . was hung in groove 1. There was nothing very complicated about the Harmount's method of achieving [the] effect of a river [with] moving ice blocks. Two stagehands from the wings simply swung the battens hanging in grooves 2 and 3 back and forth in opposite directions [as] Eliza jumped from scenery trunk *to* scenery trunk giving the illusion of her leaping from one ice block to the next.

In addition to the scenic scheme outlined above, the Harmount ice scene was provided with machines that created the illusion of ice and falling snow. According to Blaine Quarnstrom, the Harmounts traveled with two lights that created these effects. The snow machine was described as "a circular disk perforated with little holes . . . About 18 inches would be the size and it slipped on this machine. Then you had a key like [one that] winds a clock on the front. You'd wind it and [it] would start right away. The disc would turn and it gave the effect of snow falling on the ground. The snow machine was set on one side [of the stage] and the ice machine on the other, right in the proscenium, right inside the curtain line." Originally, the machine was equipped with a carbon lamp, but eventually it was rigged with an incandescent bulb. The realism of the ice scene, in Quarnstrom's opinion, was enhanced by the Harmounts' decision to not allow the dogs to chase Eliza across the ice. Instead, the four dogs used in the scene were trained to stop and lie down when they reached the ground row. There they whined and howled as though thwarted in their attempt to catch the runaway. According to spectators, the total effect of the Harmount ice scene was one of the best on the road at the time, even surpassing the same scene in the famed Stetson show.

Even more inherently dramatic and spiritually moving than the River Scene, the Grand Allegorical Transformation, which was furnished with the most beautiful and elaborate scenery owned by the company, was the spectacular conclusion to the Harmount show. The staging of the scene began with Uncle Tom's death at the end of the play. In the Harmount show, Tom died downstage in front of a woodland drop and he remained lying on the downstage floor until the final curtain. At Tom's death a "colored" quartet at the back of the stage was heard singing the hymn "Nearer My God to Thee," while a dark cloud drop fell into the 1st grooves. In lieu of the original six lines of stage directions for the scene in the French edition, the Harmounts substituted the following set of elaborate instructions which included the manipulation of the various drops used in the Transformation. For the Grand Allegorical Transformation scene, three separate drops were employed and stage directions state:

> The woods scene is in place until George Shelby leaves and then that's raised and you go into the heavens scene and that's your first scene of your Allegory. The first scene of the Allegory is the set of clouds with the Rock of Ages behind it, then the clouds are raised. . . . After Rock of Ages you've got two clouds that move. First is a cloud that covers the stage . . . then the second cloud is raised to reveal Eva standing in the small cloud circle with arms outstretched. You've got legs from the back to the front that are cloud-like and you keep movin' these clouds until you get clear back to [the] final one which lifts [to create] a cloud effect. . . . There's a whole curtain of clouds and you lift it up and that shows[Eva] standing there. That's the last one of the Allegory and then you drop the flag down right in front of Uncle Tom. That closes everything off and then you use your front curtain to close the show. . . . All the scenery for the allegory is scrim outside of the one piece that's right in front of Eva, so you can't see her until it's raised. It was a beautiful set of scenery, all colors.

The *Uncle Tom's Cabin & American Culture* website (Uncle Tom's Cabin on Stage/Performing the Play/Armbruster Scenic Drops/Flash Animation of the Transformation Scene) provides two conjectural animations showing the shifting of drops during the scene. While neither conforms exactly to the description above, they offer the reader an idea of the look of the drops and their movement in the final moments of the play. During the Grand Allegorical Transformation, there was no attempt to fly Tom into Heaven and he remained lying on the floor until Eva, encircled by angels, was revealed and a huge American flag was lowered to close the show. According to company records, closing the show with a flag was a Harmount tradition.

Advertising the most modern scenery and special effects of any of its competitors, the Harmount company continued to have success during both its summer and winter tours. With revenues and reputation constantly improving, in 1917 the Harmount management decided to split the company into two separate troupes, a practice that continued until the company's demise more than a decade later. The decision, however, eventually proved to be ill-advised, for in addition to the "horrendous" costs of starting a second company with its own tents, scenery, machinery, and animals, the troupe was no longer predominantly a "family" enterprise and ultimately outsiders brought disharmony. In the end, the Harmount Uncle Tom's Cabin Company was a victim of its own success as well as social and economic factors beyond their control (the Depression, impending war, higher taxes). Consequently in 1929, the company disbanded.

Uncle Tom Is Dead

Just 2 years later, Elizabeth Corbett, in an article titled "Uncle Tom is Dead" published in the *Theatre Guild Magazine*, proclaimed that "this year [1931], for the first time in more than three quarters of a century, there [is] no company playing *Uncle Tom's Cabin* in America." Ostensibly Uncle Tom was dead. Corbett's article was actually one of many in 1930–31 to make this claim for, as an anonymous writer in *The New York Times Magazine* on July 12, 1931 noted, the play, "a mainstay for decade after decade . . . has given way before modernity." In 1931, modernity took the form of automobiles, movies, and more luxurious, up-to-date theatres. With the creation of the narrative film by D. W. Griffith in 1915 and the advent of the "talkies" in 1927, film could do practically everything a stage production could do and do it better. And when the "new" films were projected in motion picture palaces, offering uniformed ushers and lavish facilities, the stage found it increasingly difficult to compete with movies. In fact, by the publication of Corbett's article, many theatres originally built for live theatre had been converted to film and all nine of the major American movie versions of *Uncle Tom's Cabin* had been made. The second modem invention—the automobile—enabled people in the early twentieth century to travel farther a field for their entertainment, giving them access to "bigger and better" shows in the big cities. With the increased travel, denizens of small town America were no longer forced to wait for shows to come to them; they could go to where the major entertainments were offered. In the process, as they were increasingly exposed to more professional and polished attractions, rural audience members became more sophisticated and less tolerant of crude, unpolished, small-town traveling Tom shows.

In addition to the increased competition from the automobile, the motion picture, and more modern theatres, the traveling Tom show was the victim of its own incompetence. Increasingly, during the latter decades of the nineteenth century, the Tom show became more famous for antiquated play texts, bad actors, poor production standards, and mismanagement than for its performing a stage classic. Thomas Gossett has found that as early as 1880, townspeople were growing tired of the moth-eaten Toms that annually visited their cities and villages. In 1880, no less than ten Uncle Toms visited Lancaster, Pennsylvania; the following year, in Cincinnati, someone predicted that "a long suffering public may arise in its might and extinguish the meekly prayerful Uncle Toms, the talkative Markses and the angelic Evas"; and in another unidentified town, when it was announced that yet another Uncle Tom company was coming, the citizens, claiming to be tortured by an invasion of Toms, "betook themselves to the woods."

Plagued by their own incompetence and suffering from the comparison to newer forms of entertainment, Tom companies both large and small, fell victim to economic forces beyond their control as well. Since their beginnings, every company had been forced to maintain its tents, vehicles, and equipment; but in the first decades of the twentieth century, they also faced ever-rising railroad fares and ballooning salaries for union actors and stage hands. To offset these costs, Tom troupes necessarily raised admission prices, rendering them even less competitive with the significantly cheaper ticket prices for movies. With the beginning of the Depression, the economic backs of the remaining Tom companies were broken.

And, finally, *Uncle Tom's Cabin* had lost its ideological relevance and by the 1930s was regarded as antiquated. Once the slaves had been freed and the injustice of slavery had been eradicated, the play no longer conveyed a sense of urgency—the very sense of urgency that provided the energy of Stowe's novel and Aiken's drama. Once the Tom show had transformed African Americans, whose nobility and humanity Stowe foregrounded in her narrative, into the caricatures of the minstrel show, the original moral lesson was muted. Nevertheless, since *Uncle Tom's Cabin* had originally gained a reputation as a moral reform drama, to the end of its days the Tom show retained a residue of moral righteousness and parents still brought their children to the Tom show to learn about Christian values and the evils of slavery, even though what they saw was more minstrel show than Stowe's religious narrative. Until the last tommers—likely the Harval Uncle Tom's Cabin Company which folded its tents in 1932—the title *Uncle Tom's Cabin* remained loosely associated in the minds of many Americans with the elimination of a social evil, even though by the 1930s, Uncle Tom had been reduced to mere entertainment, and poor entertainment at that.

5.2 PRODUCTION PHOTOS FROM *UNCLE TOM'S CABIN*

Uncle Tom's Cabin production photos entitled "The Harmount Company in Character" and "Legree and Tom" (1925). In 1852, Harriet Beecher Stowe wrote the novel version considered the most popular of its day. Abraham Lincoln credited Stowe's work as being a catalyst to the American Civil War: "So this is the little lady who started this great war." Far more people saw the adapted theatre performances than read the novel, and this phenomenon continued for several decades, carrying the stage traditions of blackface minstrelsy and all of its racial trappings well into the twentieth century.

Source: Images courtesy of the Ohio State University Libraries: Theatre Research Institute

5.3 ADVERTISEMENT FOR *UNCLE TOM'S CABIN*

1915 posters announcing the coming of Harmount's *Uncle Tom's Cabin* show.

Source: Image courtesy of the Ohio State University Libraries: Theatre Research Institute

5.4 SCHOOL CHILD TICKET FOR *UNCLE TOM'S CABIN*

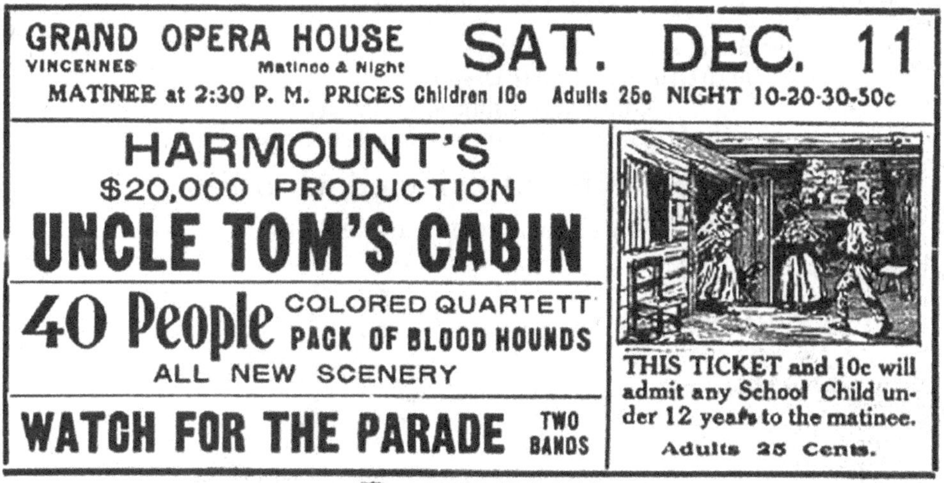

School child promotional ticket for matinee performance of Harmount's *Uncle Tom's Cabin*.

Source: Image courtesy of the Ohio State University Libraries: Theatre Research Institute

5.5 PUBLICITY KIT MATERIALS FOR *UNCLE TOM'S CABIN*

The auction scene, from Harmount *Uncle Tom's Cabin* Publicity Kit for 1914–15 and 1915–16.

Source: Image courtesy of the Ohio State University Libraries: Theatre Research Institute

5.6 *UNCLE TOM'S CABIN*—HARMOUNT COMPANY

Among the unpublished "Tom Show" scripts in the Jerome Lawrence and Robert E. Lee Theatre Research Institute at the Ohio State University [. . . is a script] used by The Harmount UTC Company. This was a small, family-run troupe from Williamsport, Ohio, that toured the Midwest from 1903 to 1929, playing under a tent during an annual Summer season, and in theaters in towns (never large cities) during the Winter season [. . .] The script itself was probably typed up in the early 1950s, but internal references to the death of Mark Hannah and to William Howard Taft suggest it was originally written in the first decade of the twentieth century. The typescript is full of errors [. . . For instance, in] Act 4 it jumps from Scene 3 to Scene 5, but there are no missing pages in the typescript. It also omits most of the stage directions, and accidentally leaves out at least one line of dialogue. According to Harmount's note, the company only used Act 1, Scene 1, during the Winter shows.

ACT ONE

Enter Eliza L. 3, Haley R. 2, Meet Center

HALEY: Hell, gal, who are you looking for?

ELIZA: I am looking for my master, sir.

HALEY: Who is your master?

ELIZA: Mr. Shelby is my master, sir.

HALEY: Well, you're a fine looking gal—how would you like to have me for a master?

ELIZA: Sir! I do not understand you. Let me pass.

HALEY: Not until you have given me a kiss. (grabs arms)

ELIZA: Help! Help! (George Harris enters R. 3 E. Throws Haley to right front, turns to Eliza.)

GEORGE: Are you hurt?

ELIZA: No, George.

GEORGE: What were you doing with my wife? (turns to Haley)

HALEY: Well, she's a slave, isn't she?

GEORGE: Yes, she's a slave, but she is my wife, and demands my protection. (embrace Eliza and Harris)

HALEY: Insolent slave, I'll—(attempts to strike George with whip; Harris grabs whip, throws it on floor)

GEORGE: Take care or the slave may have a chance to chastize its master. Your business is with Mr. Shelby, I believe. Yonder is his house, now go. (points off right)

HALEY: (picks up whip. George turns to Eliza. Haley draws knife, Eliza screams. George turns. Haley drops knife, makes exit backward.) Curse you, George Harris, you shall repent for this insult some day, and don't you forget it. (Exit R. 2 E)

GEORGE: Ha! Ha! threats are like chickens, they come home to roost. Well, Eliza, I have come to say Goodbye, for I am going away.

ELIZA: Going, George! Going where?

GEORGE: Going to try and find Canada.

ELIZA: Well, George, if you must, go. Go quietly and carefully and may heaven bless you.

GEORGE: Well, Eliza, Goodbye. (kiss, starts off R.)

ELIZA: But, George, our boy.

GEORGE: True, I had almost forgotten him; come, let's take one last fond look and then farewell forever. (Exit both R. 2)

HALEY: (backs on stage from Right 3, gets knife) Curse you, George Harris, little do you know I bought that brat of a kid of yours, and some day I'll buy you. And when I do you'll repent the day you ever insulted Tom Haley. (Exit L. 2)

ELIZA: (Enters R. 2 with Harry) Uncle Tom, Aunt Cloe.

CLOE: For the lands sake, who am that out thar?

ELIZA: Tis I, Eliza.

CLOE: Bustle up, old man, get on your panaloons, for I's gwine to open the door right away.

TOM: All right, Cloe. I'se a coming right along. (Enter Tom and Cloe L. 4) For the lands sake, if it hain't Eliza. Why, what's the matter child, has you done took sick or what has come over you?

ELIZA: I am running away, Uncle Tom. Carrying with me my child Harry; the master has sold him.

CLOE: Sold him!

ELIZA: Yes, sold him. I crept into Missus chamber last night and I heard master tell Missus that he had sold my child Harry and you, Uncle Tom, both to a slave trader, and the man is to take possession to-morrow.

CLOE: Now what's my old man done that Master wants to sell him?

ELIZA: He haint done anything, Aunt Cloe, it isn't for that that master wants to sell. I heard Missus plead and beg for us both, but he told that it was no use, that he was in this man's debt and if he did not sell then it would end in having to sell all the things on the place and move off.

CLOE: Now what are you going to cry for, old man, you want to break this poor old woman's heart? (cries)

ELIZA: I saw my husband this morning, I little knew then what was to come. He told me he was going to try and run away, if you see him you must give him my love and tell him if we never meet again on earth I trust we shall meet in heaven.

TOM: That's right, Eliza, put your trust in the good Lord, he is our best friend, our only comforter.

ELIZA: And you won't go with us, Uncle Tom?

TOM: No! No! Eliza child. Time was when I would but the good lord has given me work here among the poor people and I must bear my cross to the end.

CLOE: Now old man, you going to be toted down the river where they kill niggers by hard work and starvation. Come, I'll bustle up your clothes ready and you go with Eliza.

TOM: No! No! Cloe, I haint going. Let Eliza go if she wants to, it's her right and I wouldn't want to be the one to say No. But you heard what she said. And if I must be sold, why let me be sold. I expect I can bear my cross as well as any of them. Master always found me on the spot and he always will. I never broke my trust nor used my pass noaways contrary to his will and I never shall. It is best for me to go alone, Cloe, than for everything on the place to go to rack and ruin. Master haint to blame Cloe. And he'll take care of you and all the little ones when I am sold away.

CLOE: I expect you are right, old man, youse are always right.

ELIZA: Uncle Tom, you give us your blessing. (kneels)

TOM: May the good lord watch over you, guide and protect you on your journey. And that am my prayer, Eliza, that am my prayer.

ELIZA: Goodbye, Uncle Tom! Goodbye Aunt Cloe. Farewell my dear old home. Sweet dreams of the happy past farewell, farewell forever. (Exit R. 2)

CLOE: Take good care that child, Eliza, take good care that child. Now old man, what's going to become of the rest of us niggers I'd like to know.

TOM: Cloe, you know him who saved Daniel from the lion's den and saved the children from the fiery furnace, him who walked on the sea, he am still alive and I have faith to believe that he can and will deliver me. So come on into the cabin, Cloe, and have patience like old Job. (Exit cabin or E 4)

CLOE: Job! Job the debil, he never had no half dozen niggers hanging on his petticoat tails, now that's what come from those devilish nigger traders, if the devil don't catch those devilish devils what in the devil is the devil good for any way. (Exit C or 4)

Curtain—Street Scene

(Enter Phineas Fletcher right)

PHINEAS: Well, here I am and a devil of a hobble I've go myself into. I promised my gal Ruth I'd meet her on the adjacent bank of that pesky river, but how in the tarnation am I to do? It's all riled up like a cat and still rising, it's like a ice cream freezer in a tetotal state. Well, she'll be in my hair if I don't, so rile up there you old varmit and shake the dust off your back. (Exit L.; Enter Eliza R.)

ELIZA: Courage, my child, your mother will save you yet. Look, the river is one mass of floating ice. Oh Harry, my child, what shall we do, what shall we do? (kneels)

HARRY: Put your trust in God mama, that's what Uncle Tom says.

(Enter Phineas Fletcher L.)

PHINEAS: Why, hello gal, what seems to be the matter?

ELIZA: Oh, sir, is there any ferries or boats going across this evening?

PHINEAS: Well I reckon not gal, the boats have all stopped running.

ELIZA: Stopped running?

PHINEAS: Yes, but what's the matter, some one took sick and you want to get across?

ELIZA: Yes, I have a little child who is in great danger and I hadn't heard of it until last evening so I would like to get across.

PHINEAS: Well say, girl, there is an old friend of mine down the road here that is going over with a load of truck tonight, that is if he darst to, he'll stop at a little tavern down the road here, you come and go with me and I'll see if I cant get him to take you cross, so come right along gal.

Curtain up—Kitchen Scene

PHINEAS: Well gal, here's the tavern, but say, that a right smart looking chap you have there. I say youngster, what's your name?

HARRY: Harry Harris, sir.

PHINEAS: Harry Harris hey, well I say Harry, won't you have a chaw of tobacco.

HARRY: No thanks, I don't chew.

PHINEAS: Oh, you haven't come to that yet? Well, I have and don't feel none the worse for it neither. But what's the matter with the youngster, he looks kind of pale in the gills.

ELIZA: Yes, poor little fellow, he is not used to walking and I have hurried him so.

PHINEAS: Tuckered out hey? Well gal, there's a little room with a fire in it, you take the babe in there, warm his nose and toes, call for anything you want to eat or drink and I'll stand the damage.

ELIZA: Oh sir, how can I thank you for your kindness to a stranger?

PHINEAS: Well gal, if you don't know how, why just don't try, so come get vamoose. (Eliza goes into room) Well, there goes what I call a fine gal and a No. 1 sort of female, but I can't lay around here all night waiting for that ferry man. Never. (Exit)

(Enter Marks center door)

MARKS: Boo! boo! boo! just fell off a Xmas tree, cold! cold! devilish cold, what a good night for a bracer. (Phineas comes up from behind, taps Marks on shoulder) Don't shoot! don't shoot!

PHINEAS: Why, that aint a shooting iron, that's chewing tobacco. Wont you have a chaw?

MARKS: No thanks, I don't chew.

PHINEAS: You better chew.

MARKS: I don't choose to chew.

PHINEAS: Well I say chaw. (draws gun)

MARKS: Oh, I changed my mind right now. (chews, spits out)

PHINEAS: You don't seem to like my tobacco.

MARKS: No, I haven't come to it.

PHINEAS: Well, suppose we have a little gin.

MARKS: Now you're hitting me in a tender spot.

PHINEAS: Just squat yourself and we'll go for my ointment.

MARKS: If there is anything I like to do, it's squat.

PHINEAS: First tell me who you are, what you are, where did you come from and where are you going?

MARKS: I'm a lawyer, my name is Marks, I came from nowhere and I am going right back to the same place.

PHINEAS: A liar sir.

MARKS: A lawyer.

PHINEAS: Oh well, I don't think none the worse of you for it, for you see the law of unnecessary evils are like an old stump without fungus, so take a holt lawyer and fill up and I'll spin you a little toast.

MARKS: Well, if there is anything I love it's eggs on my toast.

PHINEAS: Well, here's hoping that the path of your true love shall never have an ice choked river to cross as mine has tonight.

MARKS: Well, here goes the ice choke, river and all.

PHINEAS: Let her flicker.

MARKS: So you wants to get across the river.

PHINEAS: Yes, the fact and the matter is that I have fell in love with the prettiest gal on the other side that ever wore a quaker bonnet. Sit down.

MARKS: I am sit.

PHINEAS: What'll you have?

MARKS: A little gin.

PHINEAS: Help yourself.

MARKS: I don't care if I do. (drinks) So you fell in love with a quaker bonnet.

PHINEAS: No, a pair or pretty black sparkling eyes beneath the bonnet.

MARKS: I suppose you gave them to her.

PHINEAS: No. You see the way of it was like this, I used to own a bunch of niggers and had them work on my plantation until my gal Ruth said she shouldnt have a thing to do with me as long as I owned a pesky nigger. Sit down.

MARKS: I am sit.

PHINEAS: What'll you have?

MARKS: A little gin.

PHINEAS: Help yourself.

MARKS: I dont care if I do. (drinks) Well, I suppose you sold them all.

PHINEAS: No, I gave them all their freedom and told them to skip skeedaddle and vamoose the ranch.

MARKS: I suppose this act of generosity on your part gained for you the lady's love.

PHINEAS: Wrong again.

MARKS: Always wrong.

PHINEAS: She said that she wouldnt have a thing to do with me unless I became a quaker, she told me to come over tonight and give my final word and I'll be totally chawed up if I haint made up my mind to do it, chawed up if I haint. Sit down.

MARKS: I am sit.

PHINEAS: What'll you have?

MARKS: A little gin.

PHINEAS: Help yourself.

MARKS: I don't care if I do.

PHINEAS: Now see here lawyer, if you don't quit your bobbing up and down when I am talking to you I'll knock you down.

MARKS: Yes you will! (jumps up)

PHINEAS: Yes I will! (jumps up)

MARKS: I said you would. (sits down) You seem sorta surprised.

PHINEAS: Well you see, I sorta surprised myself, for you see I am not the sort of stuff to make a quaker out of.

MARKS: No, I should say not, you would make a better horse thief.

PHINEAS: What's that?

MARKS: Oh that, a little joke on myself, that's all.

PHINEAS: Well, you had better be a little careful about your jokes, that's all, but there's the bottle, help yourself and when that's gone call for more. If you don't I rip you up for I am in a ruinationous state. (Exit R. 2.)

MARKS: So would I if he would rip me up. Well, his heart is in the right place. But his head is wrong. He said for me to drink all I wanted and he would stand the damages, here's looking at you, chaw-me-up. (Haley enters L. 2)

HALEY: Well here's luck, the very identical fellow I've been looking for. I say Marks, put that down. (slaps shoulder)

MARKS: Well, haint I putting it down.

HALEY: I guess you were about that time.

MARKS: Why, hello Haley old boy, what brought you up here from New Orleans?

HALEY: Well you see the fact and the matter is I bought a kid the other night from old man Shelby, the MOTHER gets wind of it and cuts her lucky, now I've tracked the fool gal to this very spot and I'm afraid she's took the kid and got across the river by this time so I want to get you to help catch them.

MARKS: So you want me to help catch the gal.

MARKS: No, hang the gal, it's the kid I want. Oh, I was a fool for ever buying the brat anyway.

MARKS: You're always a fool.

HALEY: What's that.

MARKS: I said that you always went to school.

HALEY: Well, that's different.

MARKS: Say Haley, I'll tell you a trick worth two of that.

HALEY: Let's hear.

MARKS: The baby belongs to you because you bought it, paid for it. The gal, we'll catch her, take her down to New Orleans, sell her for a cool thousand. And that will be $800 for me and $200 for you. What do you say to the bargain?

HALEY: That's a pretty fair bargain, say we take a drink of gin to wash the bargain down. (Phineas steps to table)

MARKS: Gin it is. (Phineas draws gun) No, I've quit drinking.

PHINEAS: Marks, whose your friend here? Introduce him to me.

MARKS: Mr. Haley, Mr. Chaw-me-up. Mr. Chaw-me-up, Mr Haley. Chaw him up, chaw everybody up. But for heaven's sake don't chaw me up.

PHINEAS: Hello, Mr. Scaley. (shakes)

HALEY: Haley, if you please (throws Phineas' hand, hits Marks in eye)

PHINEAS: Oh, Marks, I didn't see you there.

MARKS: Well, I cant see you there now.

PHINEAS: Well, what are you two fellows up to any way?

MARKS: Well, the fact and the matter is that Haley bought a baby from—

PHINEAS: Shut up.

MARKS: I am shut.

PHINEAS: Mr. Haley, you tell the story.

HALEY: The fact and the matter is I bought a baby from old man Shelby the other night and the MOTHER got wind of it and cuts her lucky, now I have tracked the fool gal to this very spot and I am afraid she's took the kid and got across the river by this time so I am going to get Marks here to help me catch them.

PHINEAS: Oh, so you are going to get Marks to help catch them.

MARKS: Yes, he is going to get me to help catch them.

PHINEAS: Don't you know that reminds me of a story.

MARKS: A good story?

PHINEAS: Something that happened along here about four years ago.

HALEY: let's hear it.

PHINEAS: Just squat yourself and I'll spin you the yarn.

MARKS: If there is anything I love, it is a good story.

PHINEAS: Well sir, about four years ago, a runaway gal with her babe was trying to make her escape from two of the meanest looking nigger catchers that was ever my misfortune to meet.

MARKS: Just like ours exactly.

PHINEAS: One of these fellows was a mean hang dog looking fellow, wore (describes dress) and say, Haley, he looked just like you.

HALEY: What's that? (draws whip)

PHINEAS: That was in the story four years ago.

MARKS: Ha! ha! what a good joke on Haley.

PHINEAS: Well, the other was a little red pedefogging lawyer chap (gives description) and say, Marks, he looked just like you.

MARKS: What's that?

PHINEAS: That was in the story four years ago.

MARKS: Well, that's different.

PHINEAS: When along happens an old trapper chap, something like me you know.

MARKS: A corn fed individual.

PHINEAS: He heard the gals story so resolved to help her out and so he placed her in a little side room about like that one over there. (points to room)

MARKS: Oh, she's in here, is she?

PHINEAS: No, that was in the story four years ago.

MARKS: Oh, yes. Don't get excited, Haley.

PHINEAS: So he took these two fellows down in one corner of the room and—

MARKS: Was it this corner over here? (starts left)

PHINEAS: No, I believe it was in this corner over here. Then he puts his arms around their necks in this manner, do you see the point?

MARKS: Yes, for heaven's sake, take it away.

PHINEAS: So he told these fellows a funny story. Told the gal to come out of her room, kneel down and offer up a prayer for the safety of herself and her child and made her escape while those pesky fools stood there in the corner and laughed, never knowing the difference.

MARKS: There she goes now.

PHINEAS: Down or I will fill you full of lead.

(2 Curtain drop Street Scene.)

(Eliza Making her Escape—Enter E.)

ELIZA: Look! They press upon our footsteps, they are close up on our trail, the river is full of floating ice! it rolls between us and our pursuers and we are safe may heaven have mercy up on us.

HALEY: Come on Marks, $200 for a boat.

PHINEAS: Make for the ice, gal! Make for the ice.

MARKS: Wait for me, Haley, wait for me.

PHINEAS: Here lawyer, which way are you going?

MARKS: I'm going this way.

PHINEAS: Well, you go that way. (Exit R.)

(Curtain up—Ice Scene)

PHINEAS: This way gal, this way.

HALEY: Come on, Marks.

PHINEAS: Ah, the dogs have turned on their masters. MARKS: Oh! Lord.

End Act One.

★

ACT TWO

Kitchen Scene

PHINEAS: Well, here I am again, I promised my gal Ruth that I'd find the husband of the gal who crossed the river the other night. But how in the tarnation am I to do it? He's not likely to be running around here with a full sized figure staring him in the face. Hello, what's this? $500 reward for the capture of the runaway George, said George was 5 feet 6 inches tall, branded on the left hand by the letter H. Signed by his master William Harris. Such papers as that are a disgrace to old Kentucky, you treat a man like a dog and you get a dog's pay every day in the week, them are my sentiments, and I don't give a tetotal damn who knows it. (Exit R. 1.)

(Enters C door.)

GEORGE: James, see to the trunks. At last I have escaped those human blood hounds, now to find my wife and child and away for Canada. Hello, what's this? (reads sign) and signed by my Master William Harris.

PHINEAS: Hello, George Harris.

GEORGE: What, you know me?

PHINEAS: Why don't get riled up George, I am no human bloodhound in disguise.

GEORGE: How did you discover me?

PHINEAS: By a tetotal smart guess, but say George, do you know I have been sent after you?

GEORGE: Who by, my master?

PHINEAS: No. By your wife.

GEORGE: My wife, where is she?

PHINEAS: With a quaker family over on the other side.

GEORGE: Then she's safe, is she?

PHINEAS: Tetotalamonsly.

GEORGE: Conduct me to her at once.

PHINEAS: Well, I will in a bracers shake, but I wouldn't advise you to do this.

GEORGE: I'll do it all on my own responsibility.

PHINEAS: Yes George, but you're breaking the laws of your country.

GEORGE: My country, sir! What country have I but the grave? and I wish to God I now laid there.

PHINEAS: I know George, but we must all submit to the indication of providence.

GEORGE: Indication of Providence! Phineas, suppose the indians were to capture you, take you away from your wife and children and set you to hoeing corn for them all your life. I suppose the first stray horse came your way you'd take it for an indication of providence, now shouldn't you?

PHINEAS: Well George, putting the matter somewhat peculiar like in that way I don't know but what I might, but what I might, but if you're taken it will be only the worse for you, beat you, half starve you and sell you off down the river.

GEORGE: Down that river I will never go, for if the worse comes to worse I can at least earn 6 feet of free soil, the first and last I shall ever own in old Kentuck.

PHINEAS: Why George, this state of mind is getting awful, it's getting really desperate. George, I'm concerned, going to set yourself in opposition to your country.

GEORGE: My country again! Sir, you have a country but what country have I or any one like me, born of slave mothers? I haven't any country anymore, any more than I have a father. But I am going to have one! I don't want anything of your country except to be let alone and to go peacefully out of it. But if any man tries to stop me, let him take care for I am desperate! I fight for my liberty until the last breath I breathe! You say your fathers did, if it is right for them it is right for me.

PHINEAS: Well George, I know you had a hard master and I will not defend him now. But here, you will need some money on your journey.

GEORGE: No, I have enough to see me safely through.

PHINEAS: You cant have much providing you came by it honestly. So take this.

GEORGE: I take it on one condition.

PHINEAS: And that is?

GEORGE: That you will allow me to repay it some day in the future.

PHINEAS: Oh, hang the future, we'll talk of the present now. But how far and how long are you going to travel on in this manner? It is a good game and well carried on, but best interests too bold.

GEORGE: I know that it is a bold game but they will never think of looking for me here. They will look farther on ahead and besides my disguise is so good, why you yourself hardly knew me.

PHINEAS: Yes George, but the mark on your hand?

GEORGE: Yes, the parting regards of Mr. Harris. It looks interesting, doesn't it?

PHINEAS: Put it away! George, it makes my very blood run cold when I think of your conditions and your risks.

GEORGE: Mine has run cold for a good many years but now it is up to the boiling point.

PHINEAS: Why George, what's come over you? you hold up your head and speak and act like another man.

GEORGE: I am a different man! I am a free man and I have said master the last time to any man. I am free!

PHINEAS: Don't be too sure, you may be retaken yet.

GEORGE: All men are free and equal in the grave. (Marks and Haley outside)

MARKS: Open the doors here or we'll bite the hinges off.

PHINEAS: Here they come, now let's conceal ourself.

GEORGE: Let's fight our way through them.

PHINEAS: No, you step in that little side room and let me parley with the varmints.

MARKS: Here's old chaw-me-up, we'll ask him all about it. We want to know—

PHINEAS: What?

MARKS: Nothing, nothing.

HALEY: Have you seen a man?

MARKS: Yes, have you seen a nigger?

PHINEAS: What's that?

MARKS: I said please don't pull the trigger.

PHINEAS: Well sir, I can look you two all over and say that I haven't seen a man all day.

MARKS: He looked right at me when he said it.

PHINEAS: It seems funny every time I see you two fellows, you're looking for a runaway nigger.

HALEY: Yes and every time we see you, you're protecting a runaway nigger.

PHINEAS: Bah!

MARKS: Yes, and every time I see you I see a nigger.

PHINEAS: What's that?

MARKS: That was in the story four years ago.

PHINEAS: Well, what sort of a fellow are you looking for anyway?

HALEY: He is a tall handsome fellow, very good looking—

PHINEAS: Oh, a right good looking fellow, hey?

MARKS: Yes, in fact the girls all say that he looked somewhat like me.

PHINEAS: He must have been a beauty.

MARKS: Oh he was a peach, but there are some bad peaches you know.

PHINEAS: You say he was a tall handsome fellow?

HALEY: Yes.

PHINEAS: Wore a stiff hat?

MARKS: Yes.

PHINEAS: Dark suit?

MARKS: Yes.

PHINEAS: Branded on the left hand by the letter H?

HALEY: Yes.

PHINEAS: And his name was George, George, George—?

MARKS: Harris. Where is he?

PHINEAS: Well gentlemen, I haven't seen a thing of him.

MARKS: Oh go to the devil, we'll search the house (Exit R.1. Marks and Haley)

PHINEAS: Come George, it's time to cut your hickory.

HALEY: Stand out of my way.

PHINEAS: Down, lawyer, and pray.

MARKS: I am a lawyer and lawyers never pray.

PHINEAS: Pray! I say Pray! Now I lay me down to sleep, &c. (Marks prays till curtain drops.)

Curtain—Street Scene

(Enter George with Eliza L. 1.)

GEORGE: Well Eliza, after many wanderings we are again united.

ELIZA: And may heaven bless us.

GEORGE: Yes, and not forgetting those generous quakers.

ELIZA: And one kind friend Phineas. It's indeed he who I owe much, him who helped me up that river's icy bank.

GEORGE: My brave girl, how did you get across the river? It was full of ice and heaving up and down.

ELIZA: I know it was. They were close behind me! I leaped upon the ice and how I got across I don't know. The first thing I knew some man was helping me up the bank and that man was Phineas.

GEORGE: My brave girl, you deserve your freedom, you have richly earned it.

ELIZA: Yes George, and when we get to Canada, I can get work and between us we can find something to live on.

GEORGE: Yes Eliza, as long as we have each other and our boy. Oh Eliza, if these people only knew what a blessing it is for a man to feel that his wife and child belong to him. I've often wondered to see men that could call their wives and children their own fretting and worrying about anything else. Why, I feel rich and strong though we have nothing but our bare hands. I feel as if I could scarcely ask god for any more yet. If they will only let me alone now I will be satisfied, yes, thankful.

ELIZA: But we are not quite out of danger, George. We are not yet in Canada.

GEORGE: True. But we are so near I can smell the fresh free air of freedom and it makes me strong again.

PHINEAS: Yea! Verily, verily, friend George and Eliza, how is it thee thou and thine?

GEORGE: Why Phineas. What means this strange metamorphis?

PHINEAS: It meaneth, friend George, that I have turned quaker.

GEORGE: What, you?

PHINEAS: Yea. Verily, friend George, I was driven to it by a powerful argument, that argument comprised a pair of bright sparkling eyes, rosy cheeks, and pouting lips. Those lips, friend George, are enough to make a man assassinate his own grandmother. Hold on quaker, you're getting off the track. Friend George, I have news of interest about thy party and it would be well that thee should hear it.

GEORGE: I pray thee Phineas, keep us not in suspense.

PHINEAS: Nay, I will not leave thee in suspense, friend George. After leaving thee along the road and being weary and tired from hard travels, I stopped at a little tavern, lay myself down on a pile of bags, pulled over me a buffalo robe and in a few minutes was fast asleep.

GEORGE: With one open ear.

PHINEAS: Nay, I slept with eyes ears and all closed for an hour or so, but presently I was awakened by a crowd of men drinking and talking of thee and thy party, friend George. They have a right smart notion of the road tonight and will be down upon us six or eight strong. Now, what's to be done?

ELIZA: Oh George, what shall we do?

GEORGE: I know what I shall do.

PHINEAS: Thou seest how it will be, sister Eliza, pistols, poppers, bing, bang, boom, some one is going to get shooted and I pray to God it is not I.

ELIZA: I see, Phineas, but I pray to heaven it come not to that.

GEORGE: Phineas, I do not wish to involve anyone with or for me but if you will lend me your vehicle and direct me I will drive to the next stand alone.

PHINEAS: Thee are quite welcome to my vehicle, also the grand magnificent quadruped attached thereto. But I knowest a thing or two about the road that thee does not. It would be well that I should accompany thee.

GEORGE: Yes Phineas, but I do not wish to involve thee.

PHINEAS: Involve me? why chaw-me-up-up-up, whoap quaker you're getting off the track again. When thou doest involve me, friend George, let me know it.

ELIZA: George, Phineas is a wise and skillful man and we would do well to abide by his judgment.

GEORGE: I know Eliza, but let any man dare take from me my wife and child and I will fight until the last breath. Phineas, can you blame me?

PHINEAS: Mortal man could not blame thee, friend George, flesh and blood could not do otherwise for whoa unto them who does offences and whoa unto them to whom the offence cometh and whoa unto the cannel light and whoa unto the Israelite whoa unto the mosquito bites and whoa—whoa—whoa—Emma, for is that not written in to scripture? Blessed be the man who sitteth down on a red hot stove.

GEORGE: And why so?

PHINEAS: For verily he shall rise again.

GEORGE: It is quite plain to be seen that Phineas was not cut out for a quaker, but don't you think we had better hasten on our flight?

PHINEAS: I don't know but what we had. Friend George, you take Sister Eliza and lead on and I will follow after thee. (Exit Phineas, George and Eliza)

PHINEAS: There goes friend George and sister Eliza, she am liken unto the lilly of the valley while I am like unto the poppy of the corn field or the dog fernell of the barn yard. So earth to earth and dust to dust, if the good Lord wont have us the devil must. (Exit R.)

Rocky Pass Scene

PHINEAS: Right up this way, it is an old hunting den of mine and they can't get us, and long as they come in single file and in full range of our guns, doest thou see?

GEORGE: I see, Phineas, but this is my affair, allow me to take all the risks and do all the fighting.

PHINEAS: Thou are quite welcome to do all the fighting, friend George, but will thou allow me one pleasure?

GEORGE: And that is?

PHINEAS: The pleasure of looking. (noise) Here they come, and now let's conceal ourselves.

HALEY: Come on, Marks, right up this way.

MARKS: Well, I can smell coon tracks agoing up this way.

HALEY: Come on, Marks, don't be afraid.

MARKS: Didn't you hear a noise?

HALEY: That was only superstition.

MARKS: Soup in the kitchen?

HALEY: No, superstition, but come right along now. Come on, Marks, and don't be a coward.

MARKS: I am no cow-yard but I can smell coon tracks going up here. (shot) There's your niggers and they are fairly treed.

HALEY: Yes, and I am for going up.

MARKS: Don't, Haley, them niggers might shoot and that would be bad you know.

HALEY: Oh hang it, Marks, you always was for saving your pesky skin.

MARKS: Well, why shouldn't I? It's the only one I ever had and them niggers do fight like the devil sometime.

GEORGE: Well gentlemen, who are you down there and what do you want?

MARKS: I'll tell you what we want.

GEORGE: What?

MARKS: Oh, I want to go home.

HALEY: We're after a party of runaway niggers. One George and Eliza Harris, now tell me, arent you George Harris that used to belong to William Harris of Shelbyville, Shelby Co., Kentucky?

GEORGE: Yes, I am George Harris.

MARKS: The very fellow, we've got him.

GEORGE: Mr. Harris did at one time claim me as his property but now I am in Ohio standing on Heaven's free soil! My wife and child I claim as my own! You can come up if you like but the first one that comes within range of my gun is a dead man.

MARKS: Oh, Lord, Haley, look at the gun.

HALEY: Oh hang it Marks, brace up.

MARKS: I cant, I busted my suspenders.

PHINEAS: Yes, and the first one of you two fellows that run up against them thar will think you've run up against the business end of a large size bumble bee. That means six months in a hospital, while this means sure and sudden death. Come up and take your choice.

MARKS: Go on up, Haley, and take your choice. I will stay here and wrestle with a hospital.

HALEY: I have no choice, see here Marks, you're a lawyer, go up there and give them a dose of law.

MARKS: And get a dose of lead.

HALEY: No, give them a few points of law.

MARKS: And get a punch off a bunch of bones. Oh, no! I stay right here.

HALEY: No, Marks, you don't understand. Go up and give them a dose of Blackstone.

MARKS: You mean expound Blackstone? Well, when it comes to expounding law I have got the world beat but first I must take a drink out of the black bottle. Now you watch them, Haley, while I drink.

HALEY: See here Marks, don't be a hog.

MARKS: Well, I don't like to see two hogs at the same time, now I'll sit this bottle right down here and you watch it while I go up. Now just watch it, I said, Haley—Say Haley, come here.

HALEY: Well, what is it?

MARKS: There's going to be a funeral here and I'll be in it.

HALEY: See here, Marks, you're a lawyer and I brought you here to talk.

MARKS: Yes, but you are trying to get me killed.

HALEY: Come Marks, go on up there. I'll be right here at your back.

MARKS: Yes, but I was in this late war and I would rather have a breast work.

HALEY: Go up, Marks, and tell them what you know, in fact tell them all you know.

MARKS: Might as well tell them what we both know, it wont take any longer.

HALEY: Go on up there now and talk to them.

MARKS: Look here, young man, put that down! It might go off and hurt someone and that would be bad. You know now we have come after you and we are going to have you! We have got the law and the power and the power and the law on our side. We have got the bloodhounds on the outside, we are on the inside and I've got the court house in my vest pocket so you might as well give yourself up first as last, for you have got to give up in the end, for I am a rut-em tut and cut and shoot and limb of the law from Arkansaw and don't you forget it! (shot) Oh Lord, the bottle—the bottle—higher—higher—

HALEY: Say Marks, are you shot?

MARKS: No, I am only half shot.

HALEY: Well, where did he hit you?

MARKS: He never touched me

GEORGE: I know you have the power and the law on your side, but by the great eternals you havent got us.

PHINEAS: No, and you are not going to get us either.

MARKS: We don't want you, Chaw-me-up, it's the other fellow we want.

PHINEAS: Well, we want you and we're going to get you, too.

MARKS: Not if I see you first.

PHINEAS: Say George, you see that scaley chap down there? Watch me take him in the eye with a chaw of tobacco.

HALEY: Well, Marks old boy, what is it?

MARKS: A chaw of tobacco.

HALEY: Well, throw it away.

MARKS: No, tobacco is too scarce now. I'll just eat this one.

PHINEAS: Say George, it wont do to waste two bullets on them fellows, you take the scaley chap and I'll take the one with the tall light hat on.

MARKS: All right, take him if you want him. Oh Lord, where is my sky piece?

HALEY: It's up there.

MARKS: Well, it can stay there. I'll never go up after it.

HALEY: See here, Marks, I was never afraid of a nigger in all my life, and I'm going up.

MARKS: Oh don't, Haley.

(Haley is shot by Harris and falls dead)

(Phineas grabs Marks, bends him over his knee and paddles him)

Curtain. End Act Two.

★

ACT THREE

Scene 1—Parlour

(Ophelia Enters Center Door.)

OPHELIA: Well, I just received a letter from St. Clair and according to this notice he should have been here a fortnight ago. (noise outside) Well, I guess the Wards have arrived at last

EVA: Oh, Auntie! Auntie! Auntie!

OPHELIA: Gracious Heavens, child, you make my headache.

ST. CLAIR: At last, cousin, the wards have arrived, and how do you like the appearance of our city?

OPHELIA: It's a pretty place, but it looks rather old and heathenish to me.

ST. CLAIR: Well Tom, my boy, this seems to suit you.

TOM: Yassa Massa, it seems to be about the right thing.

ST. CLAIR: See here, cousin, I've brought you a coachman to order. He's a regular hearse for blackness and sobriety and will drive you like a funeral if you like. Open your eyes now and look at him and don't say I never think of you when I'm gone.

OPHELIA: I know he'll get drunk.

ST. CLAIR: No, he's warranted a pious and sober article.

OPHELIA: Well, I hope that he will turn out well but it's more than I expect.

ST. CLAIR: But cousin, have you no curiosity as to how and where we picked up Tom?

EVA: Uncle Tom, Papa, that's his name.

ST. CLAIR: Right you are, my little sunbeam.

TOM: Please massa, that am no occasion to say nothing bout me.

ST. CLAIR: You're too modest, my modern Hannibal. You see cousin, we met Tom on board the steamer and Eva persuaded me to buy him.

OPHELIA: She's so odd.

ST. CLAIR: As the steamer approached the landing a sudden rush of passengers precipitated Eva into the river.

OPHELIA: Gracious Heavens!

ST. CLAIR: A man immediately sprang overboard and grasping her in his strong arms held her up until she could be drawn on board again.

OPHELIA: Merciful Heavens!

ST. CLAIR: Who was that man, Eva?

EVA: Uncle Tom! (kisses Tom)

TOM: The dear child.

OPHELIA: Oh St. Clair, how can you let her?

ST. CLAIR: Why, what my cousin?

OPHELIA: Well, I like to be good and kind to everything and don't like to see anything hurt but as for kissing—

ST. CLAIR: Niggers? that you're not up to, hey?

OPHELIA: Yes, that's just it.

ST. CLAIR: Oh, that's nothing when you get used to it.

OPHELIA: Used to it! Well, I could never get used to kissing a white man, let alone a nigger.

EVA: Come, Uncle Tom, let's go pick some flowers.

TOM: Please massa, may I go?

ST. CLAIR: Yes Tom, Eva is your new master and you are only supposed to obey her.

OPHELIA: Eva, my child.

EVA: Well, Auntie?

OPHELIA: Don't exert yourself.

EVA: No, Auntie. Come, Uncle Tom.

ST. CLAIR: Well cousin, what do you think of Tom?

OPHELIA: He's a perfect behemoth!

ST. CLAIR: Come, cousin, and say something pretty to a fellow.

OPHELIA: You've been gone a fortnight beyond the time.

ST. CLAIR: Yes, but I wrote you the reason why.

OPHELIA: Such a short cold letter.

ST. CLAIR: Dear me, the mail was just going and it had to be that or nothing.

OPHELIA: That's just the way always, something to make your journeys long and letters short.

ST. CLAIR: Oh hang the woman! Any way, come cousin, and let's take a stroll in the garden, and if you should step on any little nigger babies, well just let them mention it.

OPHELIA: Nigger babies under foot, how shiftless!

ST. CLAIR: Never mind, here come Tom and Eva now.

EVA: Uncle Tom, you look so funny.

TOM: I spect I do, little missie, but I begs the massa's pardon. You see the little missus would do it, she said that I am like the ox in the good book, all dressed up and ready for the sacrifice.

ST. CLAIR: I see you are, Tom, but Eva darling, which do you like best, to live as they do at your Uncle's in Vermont or to have a houseful of servants as they do here?

EVA: Oh, of course our way is the pleasantest.

ST. CLAIR: Why so?

EVA: Why, it makes so many more around you to love you, you know.

OPHELIA: Now that's just like Eva, one of her odd speeches.

EVA: Is it an odd speech, papa?

ST. CLAIR: Rather odd, as the world goes, but where has my little Eva been?

EVA: Oh, I've been up in Tom's room hearing him sing.

ST. CLAIR: Hearing Tom sing, hey?

EVA: Oh yes, he sings such beautiful things about the New Jerusalem and the bright angels and the lands of Canaan.

ST. CLAIR: I dare say it's better than the opera.

EVA: Yes, and he is going to teach them to me.

ST. CLAIR: Singing lessons! You are coming on.

EVA: Yes, he sings for me and I read to him out of my little Bible and he explains what it means you know. Come Uncle Tom, let's pick some more flowers.

TOM: All right little Missie, I'se coming right along.

ST. CLAIR: A Evangeline rightly named, for has not heaven made thee an Evangel to me?

OPHELIA: Well cousin St. Clair, how can you let her?

ST. CLAIR: Why not cousin?

OPHELIA: Why I don't know, it seems dreadful.

ST. CLAIR: You would think no harm in a child caressing a large dog, even if he was black, but a creature that can think, feel, reason and is immortal you shudder at. Confess it, cousin. I know the feeling of some of you Northerners well enough, not that there is a particle of virtue in our not having it, but custom with us does what christianity ought to do, obliterate personal prejudices. You loathe them as you would a snake or toad yet you are indignant at their wrongs. You would not have them abused but you don't want to have anything to do with them yourself. You would send them to Africa out of your sight and smell and then send a missionary or two to do all the self denial of elevating them consendiously. Isnt that it?

OPHELIA: Well cousin, there may be some truth in that.

ST. CLAIR: What would the poor and lonely do without children? Your little child is your only true democrat. Tom, now, is a hero to Eva, his stories are wonders in her eyes, his songs and methodist hymns are better than an Opera and the trape and little trinkets in his pockets a mine of jewels to her and he the most wonderful Tom that ever wore a black skin. This is one of the roses of Eden that the Lord has dropped down expressly for the poor and lonely who get few enough of any other kind.

OPHELIA: It's strange cousin, one might almost think you were a professor to hear you talk.

ST. CLAIR: A professor, cousin? Of what?

OPHELIA: Why, a professor of religion of course.

ST. CLAIR: Not at all, not a professor as you town folks call it, and what is more not a practicer either.

OPHELIA: Oh, what makes you talk so then?

ST. CLAIR: Nothing is easier than talking, while yours lies in doing. By the way, that reminds me that I have made a purchase for your department and here is the article now.

OPHELIA: Well, I do wonder what it is, something nice I suppose, a dog, a cat or a poll parrot.

ST. CLAIR: Here, Topsy, come up here.

TOPSY: Cant come now.

ST. CLAIR: Why not?

TOPSY: Cause the cooks done lost the lid to the cook stove and I done got to sit on the hole to hold the smoke in.

OPHELIA: Gracious Heavens!

ST. CLAIR: Never mind the smoke but come up here.

TOPSY: All right, I'se a coming.

OPHELIA: Gracious heavens! St. Clair, what did you bring that shiftless mortal up here for?

ST. CLAIR: For you to educate and bring up the way she should go.

OPHELIA: Well, I've had enough to do with her all ready, more than I care about. Gracious heavens! St. Clair, she's got on my new spring bonnet.

ST. CLAIR: Topsy, take off Miss Ophelia's bonnet.

TOPSY: Cant do it, massa

ST. CLAIR: Why not?

TOPSY: Because I got to go right down and take care of the little pickinininys.

ST. CLAIR: Never mind the little pickininies, but take off Miss Ophelia's bonnet.

OPHELIA: Oh St. Clair, my nice new spring bonnet.

TOPSY: By golly, I didn't feel no springs down there.

ST. CLAIR: Topsy, come over here! And now Topsy, this is your new mistress.

TOPSY: Golly, am that old woman new?

ST. CLAIR: No, I have given you to her.

TOPSY: Golly, I don't want her.

ST. CLAIR: You fail to understand me. Topsy, I am going to give you to her.

TOPSY: Oh, you give me to her?

ST. CLAIR: Certainly.

TOPSY: All right, Miss Ophelia. Here I is.

OPHELIA: Don't come close to me! Topsy, turn around, how dreadful dirty and so shiftless. How old are you?

TOPSY: Dunno missus.

OPHELIA: Don't know how old you are! didn't any one ever tell you? who was your mother?

TOPSY: Never had none

OPHELIA: Never had any mother! where were you born?

TOPSY: Never was born, I just growed on a blackberry bush and when I got ripe I dropped off and here I is.

OPHELIA: Now see here Topsy, I'm not playing with you.

TOPSY: No, and I'm not playing with you either.

OPHELIA: Now Topsy, tell me who your father and MOTHER were and where you were born.

TOPSY: Never was born, had no father or MOTHER or nothin, was raised by a speculator and Old Aunt Sue used to take care of us, didn't she massa?

ST. CLAIR: She speaks the truth cousin, speculators buy them up when small and raise them for the market.

OPHELIA: How long did you live with your late master and mistress?

TOPSY: Oh, about so long.

OPHELIA: Was it a year or more or less?

ST. CLAIR: She doesn't know the meaning of a year, cousin, and she doesn't even know her own age.

TOPSY: Golly, I never saw a woman that did.

OPHELIA: Well Topsy, what can you do?

TOPSY: I can stand on my head.

OPHELIA: Oh St. Clair!

ST. CLAIR: Wait Topsy, not here in the parlor.

OPHELIA: Oh cousin St. Clair!

ST. CLAIR: Why, what, cousin?

OPHELIA: Is she right side up yet?

ST. CLAIR: Right side up with care, cousin.

OPHELIA: Well Topsy, what did you do for your master and mistress?

TOPSY: Oh, I washed the dishes, fetched water, rubbed knives and forks, waited on the white folks and danced the breakdown.

OPHELIA: Cousin St. Clair, right on my favorite corn.

ST. CLAIR: You'll find plenty of virgin soil there cousin, put in your own ideas and you wont find many to pull up I dare say.

OPHELIA: Oh Cousin St. Clair, don't leave me with this shiftless mortal all alone. Topsy, take off my shawl.

TOPSY: Golly, am that thing a shawl?

OPHELIA: Certainly Topsy, what did you think it was?

TOPSY: I thought it was a bustle.

OPHELIA: Topsy, do you know anything about heaven?

TOPSY: Heaven, Heaven, is that something good to eat? have you got it there in that bag?

OPHELIA: No Topsy, heaven is a place of eternal bliss up there.

TOPSY: Well, if heaven is a place of eternal bliss up there, then down there must be a place of eternal blister.

OPHELIA: No Topsy, if you will only be a good girl when I go up home to Vermont I'll take you with me and send you to Sunday School.

TOPSY: With all them little white children?

OPHELIA: Yes Topsy.

TOPSY: And will they take hold of my little black hands?

OPHELIA: Why certainly, Topsy.

TOPSY: Golly, won't that be nice!

OPHELIA: But first you must be born again.

TOPSY: (cries)

OPHELIA: What's the matter, Topsy?

TOPSY: I don't want to be born again.

OPHELIA: Don't want to be born again, why not?

TOPSY: Because I am afraid they might make a mistake and born me a boy.

OPHELIA: No danger of that Topsy, but first I must teach you to say your prayers, so come on over here and kneel down. (Topsy sits down) No, on your knees.

TOPSY: Oh, you mean like they do in camp meetings?

OPHELIA: Certainly, now you put your hands up like this.

TOPSY: This way?

OPHELIA: No, like this. Now repeat slowly after me.

TOPSY: Slowly after me.

OPHELIA: No, I mean what I say and nothing else.

TOPSY: And nothing else. (Topsy steals gloves)

OPHELIA: Now I lay me down to sleep—

TOPSY: All curled up in a little heap.

OPHELIA: No, No. You shiftless mortal. If I should die before I wake—

TOPSY: Slap me in the mouth with a buckwheat cake.

OPHELIA: Well, I see that I cant make anything out of you so I'll take you up and let you make the attic beds, so come along.

TOPSY: All right Miss Feelie, I'se coming right along. (steals ribbon out of belt) Golly, what a long tail our old black cat has got. Now I'll just put this ribbon around my waist and go down to the nigger ball and them niggers will say Hello Tops. Where you get all that beautiful ribbon? I'll say go along, you nigger, don't know what a beautiful ribbon is.

OPHELIA: Topsy!

TOPSY: Golly, here come Miss Feelie, now I catch it sure pop this time.

OPHELIA: Topsy!

TOPSY: What? go! get up there, don't you know your business? (shoves ribbon up sleeve)

OPHELIA: Topsy, what are you doing there?

TOPSY: Nothing, only scratching my lower extremities.

OPHELIA: Topsy, did you see anything of my bow?

TOPSY: Golly, an old woman like her got a beau.

OPHELIA: No, I mean my sash.

TOPSY: Your mash? what color was he, black or white?

OPHELIA: No, I mean the ribbon that goes around my waist.

TOPSY: No. Indeed I didn't, Miss Feelie, what color was it, blue, green, white or orange?

OPHELIA: Now I have my suspicions. Topsy, come over here and show me your hand, no I mean the other—the other one—the other one.

TOPSY: Golly, Miss Feely, how many hand you suppose I got? I done show you three already.

OPHELIA: Topsy, you have been storying to me.

TOPSY: I hope I turn black in the face if I have, Miss Feely.

OPHELIA: I can see it sticking right out of your eyes.

TOPSY: Golly, I'd like to know how she can see it sticking out of my eyes when it's up my sleeve.

OPHELIA: There, what's that?

TOPSY: Well, I'se all raveling out! If there haint Miss Feelie ribbon! I wonder how that got cotched up my sleeve.

OPHELIA: Yes, there it is! Topsy, you know what I have a notion to do with you?

TOPSY: No, what, Miss Feelie?

OPHELIA: I have a notion to give you a good shaking. And there's my gloves too.

TOPSY: Well, I wonder where they come from.

OPHELIA: Topsy, hand me those gloves.

TOPSY: Am them your gloves, Miss Feelie?

OPHELIA: Certainly they are.

TOPSY: Then pick them up.

OPHELIA: Topsy, now hand me those gloves. Now Topsy, you have been stealing.

TOPSY: No, I hope to never see the back of my neck if I did.

OPHELIA: Topsy, I have a notion to give you a complete whipping, so there! there! and there!

TOPSY: Where? where? and where? Golly Miss Feelie, what do you call that?

OPHELIA: I call that a complete whipping.

TOPSY: Golly, that wouldn't kill a skeeter. You know what I got a notion to do to you?

OPHELIA: No, Topsy, what?

TOPSY: I've got a notion to butt you off the face of the earth, so look out, here I come! (business)

(Curtain 2nd Drop.)

Scene 2—Street Tom and St. Clair

Here, Tom, are the bills and the money to eliquidate them.

TOM: Yes, Massa.

ST. CLAIR: Why Tom, isnt all right there?

TOM: I'm afraid not, massa.

ST. CLAIR: Why, Tom, what's the matter, you look as solemn as a coffin.

TOM: I feel very bad. Massa, I always thought that massa would be very kind to everybody.

ST. CLAIR: Well Tom, havent I been, havent I always been kind to you?

TOM: Massa has always been good to me, I havent nothing to complain of, but there is one thing that Massa isnt good to.

ST. CLAIR: Why Tom, speak out, what do you mean?

TOM: Last night between one and two I lay and studied on the matter and I comes to find out that massa isnt good to himself.

ST. CLAIR: Oh, that all, is it?

TOM: All? oh! my dear young massa, I'm afraid it will be the loss of all, body and soul, and you know what the good book said, it biteth like a serpent and stingeth like an adder. Oh my dear kind massa!

ST. CLAIR: Oh, I see, Tom, you allude to the condition I came home in last night. Well, I admit that I had a little more champagne brand than I could comfortably carry, that's all.

TOM: All, my dear young kind massa, but I am afraid it will be the loss of all.

ST. CLAIR: Come now Tom, dry your eyes, I am not so wonderfully good that I am worth crying over. I have always despised it and myself for it. And I give you my promise that you shall never see me in that condition again.

TOM: Bless you, massa! Bless you.

ST. CLAIR: Never mind your blessings, Tom, but run along with your errands. There! I'll pledge my honor to you. Tom, you don't see me so again.

TOM: Bless you, bless you. (Exit R)

ST. CLAIR: There goes poor old Tom and I've given him my promise and I'll keep faith with him too. (Enter Ophelia & Topsy)

OPHELIA: Topsy, take your nose out of that cat's milk.

ST. CLAIR: There's that ink bottle in some more trouble.

TOPSY: Haint got my nose in that milk.

OPHELIA: Yes you have, come right along here, I am going to tell your master.

TOPSY: Let go my ear! let go my ear!

ST. CLAIR: Well, now what's the matter cousin?

OPHELIA: Well, what haint the matter? I took this child up to my room and gave her a hymn to learn with only 49 verses and what did she do but spy out where I kept my patches and cut them all up into doll pockets.

TOPSY: Well, my doll just had to have a jacket.

OPHELIA: What's that you're saying?

TOPSY: I'se just talking to this child of mine.

ST. CLAIR: Well cousin, what have you done?

OPHELIA: What havent I done? I just whipped and talked and talked.

TOPSY: That's the trouble with that old woman, she talks too much.

OPHELIA: What's that, Topsy?

TOPSY: Oh, I'se just talking to this baby. Shut up.

ST. CLAIR: Well cousin, I'll try my hand. Topsy, come over here. Now Tops, why cant you be good?

TOPSY: Don't know. Specs it's my wicked heart. Miss Feelie says so.

ST. CLAIR: Top, don't you love anybody?

TOPSY: Spose I am going to tell you?

ST. CLAIR: Why certainly Top, now I've been way up north for quite a while and evidently you have fallen in love with some one and I must know who it is.

TOPSY: Promise me you won't tell.

ST. CLAIR: Certainly.

TOPSY: Never tell that old woman over there.

ST. CLAIR: I'll never tell no one.

TOPSY: Then I love ———, but —— cut him out.

ST. CLAIR: Now Top, neither one of the boys care about you, and if you will be good, Miss Ophelia will love you.

TOPSY: Golly, that old woman love me!

ST. CLAIR: Certainly.

TOPSY: Golly, man, she'd rather have a toad touch her than me.

ST. CLAIR: Well, you just try her and see.

TOPSY: Miss Feelie.

OPHELIA: Well, Topsy?

TOPSY: Does you love me?

OPHELIA: Why certainly, Topsy, if you will only be a good girl.

TOPSY: Then if you loves your black baby, kiss her. (Exit L)

OPHELIA: Oh cousin St. Clair, you see how it is, every time my back is turned she is into mischief and I dare say she's into some thing this minute.

ST. CLAIR: Oh, no she isn't, cousin, give the child a chance.

OPHELIA: Well, you just call her up and see.

ST. CLAIR: Well, just to oblige you I will

OPHELIA: You'll find out.

ST. CLAIR: Topsy, come up here.

TOPSY: Yes, I'se a hurrying.

ST. CLAIR: Topsy, how dare you come to me with your back turned toward me. Turn around.

TOPSY: I don't want to.

ST. CLAIR: How many times have I told you not to do that? Turn around, I told you not to do that. What on earth have you been doing?

TOPSY: Powdering.

ST. CLAIR: Where on earth did you learn how to powder?

TOPSY: Miss Feely powders.

OPHELIA: Don't you believe her, St. Clair.

ST. CLAIR: Never mind cousin. But Topsy, how do you know Miss Ophelia powders?

TOPSY: I was going past her door the other day and I peeped through the keyhole.

ST. CLAIR: Peeped through the keyhole! Top, how often have I told you not to do that?

TOPSY: I only done it just this one time.

ST. CLAIR: Well, never let it happen again, but go ahead and tell me how you know Miss Ophelia powders.

TOPSY: I was going past her door and peeped through the keyhole.

OPHELIA: (Motions for Topsy to keep still)

TOPSY: I won't shut up.

ST. CLAIR: Cousin, can't you leave the child alone? Go ahead, Topsy.

TOPSY: I was going past the door and peeped through the keyhole and there stood Miss Feelie before the dressing glass going like this, like that, all over her face with a powderpuff.

ST. CLAIR: A powder puff, what on earth is that?

TOPSY: Golly, don't you know?

ST. CLAIR: I must confess I do not.

TOPSY: Well, I am astonished at you. I just explain a little. A powder puff is a little tip end of a jack rabbit's tail with the ——— rubbed off. Oh look!—look!

ST. CLAIR: What at, Topsy?

TOPSY: What is that just below your nose above your mouth?

ST. CLAIR: Oh that's my ————.

TOPSY: What kind of soup.

ST. CLAIR: No, my moustache.

TOPSY: Golly, I never had no stache, massa you nearly scared me to death

ST. CLAIR: How Topsy?

TOPSY: I thought you had swallowed a jassack and left the tail sticking out.

ST. CLAIR: Oh, get out of here.

OPHELIA: Oh, cousin St. Clair, what a good joke on you.

ST. CLAIR: What Cousin?

ST. CLAIR: Oh the [*blank space; a word may have been erased*] is all right, but how about the powder?

(Exit R., Ophelia follows.)

Scene 3—Garden Scene Tom & Eva

TOM: Read that passage again, Miss Eva.

EVA: And I saw a sea of glass mingled with fire. Uncle Tom, there it is.

TOM: Where, Miss Eva?

EVA: Don't you see, there—there's a sea of glass mingled with fire.

TOM: True enough, Miss Eva.

Oh had I the wings of the morning
I'd fly away to Canaan's shore;
Bright Angels would carry me home
To the new Jerusalem.

EVA: Where do you suppose new Jerusalem is, Uncle Tom?

TOM: Up in the clouds, Miss Eva.

EVA: Then I think I see it, look in those clouds. They look like great gates of pearl and you can see beyond them far far off. Uncle Tom, sing about the spirits bright.

TOM:

I see the band of spirits bright
That taste the glories there;
They are all robed in spotless white
And conquering palms they bear.

EVA: Uncle Tom, I've seen them.

TOM: To be sure you have and you're the brightest little spirit Uncle Tom has ever seen.

EVA: They come to me sometimes in my sleep, and those spirits—Uncle Tom, I'm a going there.

TOM: Where, Miss Eva?

EVA: I am going up there in the clouds to the spirits bright and I am going before long.

TOM: No use in talking, I've always said so, she am not born to live for the Lord's mark is on her forehead and there's something deep in her eye.

ST. CLAIR: There you are, my little darling, you are feeling better now a days, are you not?

EVA: Papa, I've had things I wanted to say to you for a long time and I want to say them to you now before I grow weaker.

ST. CLAIR: Before you grow weaker! Eva, that is only an idle fear of yours, you grow stronger every day.

EVA: Don't deceive yourself, papa, I am no better and I know it perfectly well and I am going before long. I am not low spirited, if it were not for you papa and my friends I should be perfectly happy. I want to go, I long to go.

ST. CLAIR: Eva my darling, what makes you so? what makes you so sad and what seems to be so dreadful to you?

EVA: I feel sad for our poor people, they love me dearly and they are all good and kind to me. I wish papa they were all free.

ST. CLAIR: Why, Eva child, don't you think they are well enough off now?

EVA: When I am dead, papa, you will do it and think for my sake.

ST. CLAIR: When you are dead, child? Oh Eva, don't talk so. You are all I have on earth.

EVA: Papa, the poor creatures love their children as much as you do me. Oh, do something for them.

ST. CLAIR: There, there, darling, only don't talk of dying and I will do anything you ask.

EVA: Then promise me, dear father, that Uncle Tom shall have his freedom as soon as I am gone. (Eva Song)

ST. CLAIR: Yes dear, I will do anything you ask me to. Here Tom, take Eva to her room, this night air is too chilly for her.

EVA: Papa, kiss me goodnight.

ST. CLAIR: Has there ever been a child like you, Eva? Yes there has been, but their names are always written on grave stone. When you see that deep spiritual light in the eye—when the little soul reveals itself in words sweeter and wiser than ordinary words of children, hope not to retain that child, for the seal of heaven is on it and the light of immortality looks out from its eyes. (Curtain 2nd)

Scene 4—Street Tom Kneeling

OPHELIA: (enters L E) Why Tom, when alive have you taken to sleeping anywhere and everywhere like a dog for? I thought that you was one of the orderly sort that liked to lie in bed in a christian way.

TOM: I do Miss Feely—but now—

OPHELIA: Well—what now?

TOM: Hush, Massa St. Clair wont hear of it. But Miss Feely, you know there must be somebody watching for the bridegroom.

OPHELIA: What do you mean, Tom?

TOM: You know it says in the scripture, at midnight there was a great cry made, Behold the bridegroom cometh. That's what I'm expecting now every night now, Miss Feely, and I couldn't sleep out of hearing of that blessed child now days.

OPHELIA: Why, Tom. Did Eva say she was worse this evening?

TOM: No, but she told me this morning that she was coming nearer, thar's them that tells it to the child, Miss Feely. It's the angels, it's the trumpet sound afore the break o day.

OPHELIA: Well Tom, I must be going now.

TOM: Miss Feely, may I go in and take one more look at that blessed child before she goes up thar?

OPHELIA: Yes Tom, you've been a good and faithful servant so come in.

TOM: Thank you, Miss Feely, thank you.

Scene 5—Parlor Death Bed

OPHELIA: Oh Cousin St. Clair, what is the matter?

ST. CLAIR: Hush, Cousin. Eva is dying.

OPHELIA: What, dying?

ST. CLAIR: Yes. Oh if she would only wake and speak to me once more. Eva! Darling, don't you know me?

EVA: Dear Papa.*

ST. CLAIR: Oh God, this is dreadful. Oh Tom my boy, it is killing me. Pray that this may be cut short, this wrings my heart.

TOM: Oh bless the Lord, it's all over! Dear massa, look at her, it's all over

ST. CLAIR: Oh Eva, tell us what it is you see.

EVA: I see the beautiful gates ajar and above them are written in letters of gold, suffer the little children who come unto me and forbid them not for such is the kingdom of heaven. Oh love—joy—peace.

ST. CLAIR: Farewell beloved child! The bright eternal doors have closed after thee, we shall see thy sweet face no more. Oh woe for them who watched thy entrance into heaven when they shall wake and find only the cold gray sky of daily life and thou, my Eva, gone forever! (Colored boys sing Eva's song. Slow Curtain Down.)

End Act Three

*

ACT FOUR

Opens Levee Scene. Colored Boys Singing and Dancing

SKEGGS: Hey! Hey! You niggers, cut that out! (Raps hammer on barrel) Well, you niggers want to look your best today, I am going to sell you all off.

MARKS: Here you niggers, hold up my hoss's head—hold up his tail then—Hello Skeggs, what's going on up here today?

SKEGGS: The sale of St. Clair niggers.

MARKS: St. Clair, what's the matter with him?

SKEGGS: Didn't you hear about it?

MARKS: No.

SKEGGS: He got killed a few weeks ago down here in a bar room fight by a man named Simon Legree. We're expecting him up here today and he's a bad man.

MARKS: So am I, let him come.

LEGREE: I say Jenks, if you don't pay that bill by tomorrow night you will have occasion to die with your boots on.

MARKS: I pity Jenks.

LEGREE: Hello Skeggs. I say, what's going on up here today?

SKEGGS: The sale of the St. Clair niggers.

LEGREE: The St. Clair—the devil! Who is your friend here? introduce him to me.

SKEGGS: This is Marks the lawyer—Mr. Legree, Marks, shake hands with Mr. Legree.

LEGREE: Hello Marks.

MARKS: Hold on! hold on!

LEGREE: Well, haint I holding on?

MARKS: I mean let go.

LEGREE: Why didn't you say so?

MARKS: Haint that a blame pretty looking thing, now? Say Simon, what do you call that?

LEGREE: I call that a hand

MARKS: Looks more like a ham to me.

LEGREE: What's that?

MARKS: Say Simon, that's an awful hard fist you've got.

LEGREE: Yes, do you know how I got that fist so hard?

MARKS: No, how did you get it so hard?

LEGREE: By knocking down niggers.

MARKS: Well, I am no nigger.

LEGREE: What's that?

MARKS: Yes I am.

SKEGGS: See here, there will be no fighting go on here today.

LEGREE: Well, who is to hinder, I like to know?

SKEGGS: Well, I will and if I can't the strong right arm of the law shall. Oh Marks, I didn't know you was there.

MARKS: Well, I knowed you was there all right.

SKEGGS: Well gentlemen, the first we have to put upon the stand today is a young mulatto boy answering by the name of Adoph, Adoph was Mr. St. Clair's valet. And a very handy boy about the house. Adolph, take the stand. Gentlemen, look him over.

MARKS: What do you call that?

Adolph: A head.

MARKS: That aint a head, that's only a pimple, it hasn't come to a head yet. Open your mouth, looks like a watermelon after a wagon had run over it. Throw out your chest, if you havent a chest throw out your stummick. Say Skeggs, there's something wrong with this nigger.

SKEGGS: No, there isnt.

MARKS: Yes, there is.

SKEGGS: Well, what is it?

MARKS: He's got the heaves

SKEGGS: No he's not, he's as sound as a doll. Well gentlemen, before we start I wish to state that the terms are cash or papers payable on the Bank of New Orleans.

MARKS: Oh, I always pay cash for what I buy.

SKEGGS: Well, gentlemen, what do I hear to start from?

LEGREE: I'll start him at $500.

MARKS: $75.

LEGREE: $600.

MARKS: $75.

LEGREE: $700.

MARKS: $75.

SKEGGS: 775. Gentlemen, are you all done? last and third call and sold to Mr. Marks at $775.

MARKS: Come over here, Adolph. Here, way off. Oh Adolph, I mean, now take my umbrella and run down to the office and dust off the dust &c.

SKEGGS: I beg your pardon but havent you forgotten something?

MARKS: What! a lawyer forget anything? let me see. Oh yes, my umbrella.

SKEGGS: No, I mean the muzuma.

MARKS: What's that?

SKEGGS: The long green.

MARKS: This is short green, they've cramped it all down.

SKEGGS: No, you fail to understand, you failed to pay for the boy.

MARKS: Oh yes, it's a thousand dollars neither here nor there with us?

SKEGGS: Why, certainly.

MARKS: It's sure not here. Adolph, have you got a dollar bill about you?

Adolph: Yes, massa.

MARKS: Here, give me 25 cents change.

SKEGGS: What, haven't you made a mistake?

MARKS: Is that a two?

SKEGGS: No, what did you bid for the boy?

MARKS: 75.

SKEGGS: 75 what?

MARKS: 75 cents.

SKEGGS: Do you suppose that I am standing up here and knocking down a full grown nigger for 75 cents?

MARKS: Well, I've been knocked down many times before.

SKEGGS: I expect you have, but you take that money and get, get.

MARKS: You bet.

SKEGGS: Well gentlemen, the next we have to place upon the stand is the young mulatto girl Emiline. Emiline was Mr. St. Clair's housemaid. And a very handy girl. Emiline, take the stand.

LEGREE: Pretty good looking gal, how old are you?

EMILINE: Don't you hurt me.

LEGREE: Well, I'll hurt you worse than that if I buy you. I'll start the girl at $500.

SKEGGS: $500 &c. &c.

MARKS: Oh! stop the sale, I lost something in here that was in the family for 100 years and I wouldn't take a $1000 for it.

SKEGGS: Well, what was it?

MARKS: I lost it right along in here.

SKEGGS: What was it?

MARKS: A collar button.

SKEGGS: Get out of here! I am offered 575 for the girl.

LEGREE: 600.

MARKS: Oh Skeggs, it's all over town.

SKEGGS: What, Marks?

MARKS: Mud.

SKEGGS: Get out of here! 675.

LEGREE: $700.

MARKS: Oh Skeggs, an awful acident just happened down the street.

SKEGGS: What was it, Marks?

MARKS: I am too full for utterance.

SKEGGS: Go on and tell me.

MARKS: A little boy went into a hardware store and got shot.

SKEGGS: Got shot, what did he get shot for?

MARKS: To go hunting with.

SKEGGS: Oh, get out of here. $775.

LEGREE: 800.

MARKS: 75, if I can win a gal I'll buy me.

SKEGGS: See here, didn't I tell you you could not bid here?

MARKS: Did you? I am awful forgetful.

SKEGGS: I stood on that very spot and told you that you could not bid.

MARKS: Oh, you're like a leopard, you change your spots.

SKEGGS: Well, I say that you cannot bid in here.

MARKS: I will bid.

SKEGGS: I say you wont bid.

MARKS: Skeggs, let me inform you that I am a free born American citizen, standing here under a blue canopy of heaven and I will bid.

SKEGGS: Well, what will you bid?

MARKS: I'll bid you goodnight.

SKEGGS: $875.

LEGREE: $900.

SKEGGS: $900, one, twice, thrice and last call, and are you all done? Sold to Simon Legree for $900.

LEGREE: Stand over there, gal.

SKEGGS: Gentlemen, the next we have to place upon the stand is a good old faithful darky called Uncle Tom. Tom was Mr. St. Clair's overseer, and if he had lived until today he wouldn't have taken his weight in gold for him. Tom, take the stand. Look him over.

MARKS: He has got a pedigree?

SKEGGS: Yessir, here it is.

LEGREE: He's a nigger with his boots blacked. Hold up your arm! Let's see how your teeth are. How old are you?

TOM: 60 years old, massa.

LEGREE: What did you do for your late master?

TOM: Had charge of massa plantation.

LEGREE: That's a likely tale, a nigger having charge of his master's plantation.

MARKS: He speaks the truth, it's down here in black and white.

LEGREE: Well, I'll give 800—900—$1000.

MARKS: I'll give $1100 for the old fellow.

LEGREE: You cant have that nigger, I give $1200, beat that if you dare.

MARKS: Mr. Simon, you might outbid me but you cant whip me.

LEGREE: What's that?

MARKS: Yes you can.

SKEGGS: $1200. Gentlemen, are you all done? Sold to S. Legree, $1200.

LEGREE: Now then, you two niggers belong to me.

TOM: And may the good lord have mercy on us both.

LEGREE: Bah!

SKEGGS: Gentlemen, that concludes the sale for today.

MARKS: And gentlemen, I must say that that old man was sold to the meanest man in New Orleans.

LEGREE: What's that?

MARKS: And there are the documents to prove it.

Curtain

Scene 2—Street, George Shelby and Marks

(George Shelby and Marks)

SHELBY: At last my mission of mercy has arrived and now to find the home of Mr. St. Clair, repurchase Uncle Tom and convey him back to his wife and children in Old Kentuck. Ah! a stranger approaches He might be able to give me some information. I'll just accost him—I beg your pardon but are you training for a race.

MARKS: No, I'm racing for a train.

SHELBY: Well, could you give me a little information?

MARKS: I'm a lawyer and lawyers never give anything

SHELBY: Perhaps you have no objections to selling it.

MARKS: Now you're talking business.

SHELBY: Well, what do you value it at?

MARKS: Oh, say a five.

SHELBY: I can give you that and never feel it.

MARKS: Well, make it ten and feel it.

SHELBY: No, I'll hold you at your original bargain, but could you tell me where Mr. St. Clair lives?

MARKS: In a place where you could not very handily find him.

SHELBY: What's that—not dead?

MARKS: He ought to be, he's been planted 6 weeks.

SHELBY: Did his death cause the sale of his negroes?

MARKS: It certainly did.

SHELBY: How was they sold, single or in lots?

MARKS: In the alley just back of the lots.

SHELBY: No, I mean did they go to one or two different bidders?

MARKS: Oh, they went here there and everywhere, I was one of the principle bidders myself.

SHELBY: You was! What did you bid?

MARKS: 75.

SHELBY: 75 what?

MARKS: 75 cents.

SHELBY: And what did you get?

MARKS: Kicked out.

SHELBY: That's what I thought, but while there did you see an old darkey answering the name of Uncle Tom?

MARKS: Uncle Tom.

SHELBY: The same.

MARKS: Yes, I bought that old negro myself but as I had more negroes than I cared for on my plantation I sold him to a man by the name of Legree.

SHELBY: Where could I find this man Legree?

MARKS: Well, in a little way out of the way place down by the Red River in a spot where you could not very handily find him without a very competent guide.

SHELBY: Where could I find such a guide?

MARKS: Well, let me see. As Mark Hanna is dead and Taft and I are on the best terms I might take the job myself providing you come down handsomely.

SHELBY: You direct me there and your reward shall be ample.

MARKS: Apples! what do you take me for—a cider mill?

SHELBY: No, you take me there and your reward shall be sufficient.

MARKS: Fish! I am not running a fish cart.

Shelby No, you fail to understand me. You direct me there and I shall pay you well.

MARKS: Oh well, I'll take the job providing you do.

SHELBY: Very well, meet me at the steamboat landing in one half hour for I am going to my hotel.

MARKS: Hotel, where have I heard that word before? What hotel are you stopping at?

SHELBY: Hotel Central.

MARKS: Well that's strange, I have been stopping there myself.

SHELBY: Well, I must say it is strange I have been stopping there for quite a while and I never saw you about.

MARKS: Perhaps you havent been down to the barn.

SHELBY: Perhaps not, but you be down to the steamboat landing in—

MARKS: By the way what is your name.

SHELBY: George U. Shelby

MARKS: Well, George, U. Shelby allowed to pay for my supper at the Hotel Central. By the way, do you smoke.

SHELBY: Certainly.

MARKS: Have a match.

Scene 3

TOM: I've come through the dark places, I've passed through the vale of the shadow, my heart sinks at times and feels like a chunk of lead, then it rises to my throat and chokes me until tears come down my cheeks, but when I take out that little lock of hair Miss Eva gave me it brings me peace and joy to my soul. I still has the bright silver dollar Master Geo. Shelby give me the day I was sold away. Massa George must have grown to be quite a young man by this time. I wonder if I shall ever see Cloe and the little ones again.

LEGREE: Hush up you niggers, I didn't buy you to howl, I bought you to work. Well gal, we're at home now, the jumping off place of all creation. Did you ever wear any ear rings?

EMILINE: No, Massa

LEGREE: Well, if you be a good gal I will buy you a pair. Tom, do you see those dogs out there in the shed?

TOM: Yes, Massa.

LEGREE: They are raised and trained to catch runaway niggers and just as leave chaw you up as eat their supper, so now you know what to expect if you try to get away.

TOM: Yes, Massa.

LEGREE: Well gal, come into the house, I'll make a lady out of you.

EMILINE: No, I'd rather work in the fields with the rest of the slaves.

LEGREE: Oh, you are going to be contrary. Well, I'll soon take that out of you.

EMILINE: Kill me if you like.

LEGREE: Here's a nigger willing to die. Tom, you know when I bought you I didn't buy you for a common field laborer.

TOM: Yes, Massa.

LEGREE: I am going to promote you.

TOM: Thank you, massa, thank you.

LEGREE: I am going to make a driver out of you.

TOM: Oh massa, not that, not that.

LEGREE: Yes, take that whip and give that girl a flogging within an inch of her life, you've seen enough of it in your time to know how, I reckon . . . stand over there, gal.

TOM: I begs the massa pardon but I hopes he wont set me to doing anything like that, it's something I never did do, cant do and wont do, no ways possible.

LEGREE: Well. You'll learn a right smart to do around this plantation before I'm through with you! Out there and up with hands. Out there, now and take that! and that! and that! now maybe you pretend it's wrong to flog the gal.

TOM: Yes massa, I think it's downright cruel.

LEGREE: Think! what right have you, you cursed black devil, got to do with thinking? I'll do all the thinking that is to be done on this plantation. You do the work, curse you! Maybe you think you're a gentleman, master Tom, to be telling me, your master, that's right and that's wrong. Now will you tell me you cant do it?

TOM: Yes massa, I am willing to work night and day and work while there's life and breath in this old body of mine but this thing I cant feel it right to do. I think, massa, it would be down right cruel and it's what I never will do. Massa, if you mean to kill me, kill me, but as to raising my hand agin on any one on this plantation and especially on women and that thar gal, it's something I shall never do.

LEGREE: What?

TOM: I'll die first.

LEGREE: Here's a pious dog let down among us sinners to tell us right from wrong, another nigger wants to die. Tom, didn't you ever read in that good book you are always talking about where it says Servant obey your master?

TOM: Yes, massa.

LEGREE: Well, haint I your Master?

TOM: You is my massa

LEGREE: Didn't I pay $1200 cash for all there is in that old black shell of yours? aint you mine mine, body and soul?

TOM: No massa, this poor old body may belong to you but my soul belongs to the one up above who has bought and paid for it. And you cant harm that, massa, you cant harm that.

LEGREE: Well, I cant, cant I! well, we'll find out! Here, Sambo, hold this old black beast while I beat him within an inch of his life.

EMILINE: Stop! Simon Legree, touch that old man at your peril.

Curtain

Scene 5 Act 4

LEGREE: Curses on them gals Cassy and Emiline, I'll be the death of them yet. Ever since I bought that Emiline, Cassy has had the very devil in her. I know what I'll do, I will call them gals up here and have them sing and dance for me and that will drive the blues away. Here Sambo, send them gals Cassy and Emiline up here at once.

Sambo: Cant do it massa, seen them going down the road about half an hour ago.

LEGREE: What! bolted, by the gods! saddle my horse! call the dogs! Hold, send that black beast of a Tom up here. He's at the bottom of this and I'll have it out of him or kill him, haint he mine? and whose he to hinder me, I'd like to know. See here Tom, do you know that I've made up my mind to kill you.

TOM: Very likely, massa, very likely.

LEGREE: Yes, I done just that very thing unless you out with what you know about them gals Emiline and Cassy, speak.

TOM: I haint got nothing to tell, massa.

LEGREE: Do you tell me you don't know? do you know anything?

TOM: I know, massa, but I cant tell. I will die first.

LEGREE: See here, Tom, do you think that because I have always been so good and kind to you and let you off before that I am going to do it again? But I am not going to. I have made up my mind, I have counted the costs well. You have always stood out against me, now I'll conquer you or kill you, one or tother. I'll count every drop of blood there is in you one by one and take them drop by drop until you give up. Speak!

TOM: Massa, if you was sick and in trouble and the taken every drop of blood in this poor old body would save you precious soul, I'd give them to you freely, but do your worse massa, my trouble will soon be over, but if you don't repent yours will never end.

LEGREE: Tom, what would you say if I bound you to a stake and built a slow fire at your feet and burned you to a crisp?

TOM: Massa, you burn me, you may beat me—

LEGREE: Beat you! why, damn you, I will kill you! How do you like that, you black beast?

TOM: Massa, you have done your worst but I forgive you with all my heart.

LEGREE: Oh! forgive the devil! here Sambo, take that old dog out and feed him to the hogs, here goes $1200 dollars to the devil! well, his black mouth is closed, that's one consolation.

Geo. SHELBY: I beg your pardon but is your name Legree, Sir?

LEGREE: Yes, my name is Legree and what of it?

SHELBY: At a recent sale did you purchase an old darkey called Uncle Tom?

LEGREE: Yes I did, and a devilish bad bargain I made of it too.

SHELBY: Where is he? could I see him?

LEGREE: Yes, you can see him out in the shed there, trying to die, you can go out and assist him if you like.

SHELBY: What! Tom trying to die? See here, Simon Legree, at one time he was my father's most faithful overseer and my loving companion through my childhood and if any harm has come to him through your cruel treatment, you shall answer to me.

LEGREE: What?

SHELBY: To me, with your life—not this evening. (Exit)

LEGREE: Well, I wonder who this young upart can be, some of Old Tom's friends I suppose. Well, I can keep an eagle eye on him. (Exit)

MARKS: So this is where Simon Legree lives. Now here is my little persusader, now you little son of a gun if you ever did stick to me stick now. I'll just take a stroll around the plantation and see if I can find him.

LEGREE: Here you niggers, get off that cotton down there.

MARKS: Is your name Legree, sir?

LEGREE: Yes, my name is Legree Sir.

MARKS: He says he's a greaser, he does look kind of slippery, that's a fact.

LEGREE: Who the devil are you?

MARKS: I don't know who the devil I am.

LEGREE: Well, what do you want?

MARKS: I want to go home.

LEGREE: Well go.

MARKS: Simon, I have got a warrant for your arrest.

LEGREE: A warrant for my arrest, what for?

MARKS: Murder.

LEGREE: Murder of who?

MARKS: Murder of St. Clair.

LEGREE: St. Clair, the devil.

MARKS: I've got him bluffed, I expect I had better go up and get him, I had better shoot him first and tell him what I want afterwards. Don't do that, Simon. I was raised a pet. Now Simon, I'll make you a proposition. You give me a $1000 and I'll tear up this warrant and never say a word about it.

LEGREE: I give you a thousand devils!

MARKS: No! No! Simon, wouldn't I be a pretty looking thing running around here with a thousand devils sticking in my pocket? now I have come after you and am going to have you.

LEGREE: What! you take me, why—

MARKS: Oh! No! Simon.

LEGREE: You little red petty foggin lawyer chap! I've whipped fifty better men than you are! I eat better men than you every morning for breakfast.

MARKS: Well Simon, if you have to eat me, you'll have more brains in your stomach than you have in your head.

LEGREE: What's that? (Shot, falls)

MARKS: You little son of a gun, you did do it. Lay still there or I'll pull the snapper on this, his palpatator has stopped palpin. Here Sambo, take this old beast out and slop him to the hogs, there goes 12 cents to the devil! (Curtain Street) Well, you little son of a gun, you did do it, well, I'm a lawyer, my name is Marks, don't you forget it.

Scene 6 Street Shelby and Tom

SHELBY: Stop, Uncle Tom, maybe you can regain your strength. Look up, don't you know me? See! it is I, your young master George Shelby

TOM: It is, bless the lord, now I can die in Peace.

SHELBY: You mustnt die, Uncle Tom. I've come to buy you and take you home to Old Kentuck

TOM: Oh Massa George, you came too late, the good Lord has bought me and is going to take me home with him.

SHELBY: Poor poor old fellow.

TOM: Don't call me a poor fellow. I was once a poor fellow but that's all past and gone. Now I am rich in the love of God, see the angels and the blessed Miss Eva beckoning me home, tell Cloe and the little ones to follow me to the other shore for I rest in peace.

SHELBY: Poor poor old fellow, his life has been a rough and rugged one but his body has rest beneath the blue grass of old Kentuck. Oh! witness eternal God! (Business, hands upright and off transformation scene slow curtain.)

The End

6. *Rachel*—Angelina Weld Grimké

Commentary

Sources

Play

6.1 "NEVER BORN": ANGELINA WELD GRIMKÉ'S *RACHEL* AS IRONIC RESPONSE TO TOPSY—ROBIN BERNSTEIN

THE TURN OF THE TWENTIETH CENTURY constituted, in the famous term of historian Rayford Logan, a "nadir" in the status and civil rights of African Americans;[1] the passage of Plessy *versus* Ferguson in 1896 institutionalized segregation; white southerners used violence and legal tricks to extirpate African American suffrage until the Fifteenth Amendment remained "in name only"; and anti-black race riots erupted in cities including Wilmington, North Carolina (1898), Atlanta, Georgia (1906), and Springfield, Illinois (1908).[2] Lynching terrorized African American communities throughout the United States, with one person lynched every fourth day between 1900 and 1909, and nine out of ten of these victims were African American.[3]

This physical and legal violence coupled with and depended on cultural violence, and sometimes the connection was direct; for example, a dramatization of Thomas Dixon's 1905 white supremacist novel, *The Clansman*, was staged in Atlanta immediately before the 1906 riot, and many scholars believe that the theatrical production fomented the violence.[4] However, such explicit connections were exceptional; more commonly, racist violence occurred alongside with and received justification from a rising mass culture—particularly advertising—that dehumanized African Americans and naturalized white supremacy.[5]

The African American poet Angelina Weld Grimké understood the connections between physical and cultural violence. An anti-lynching activist since her teens, Grimké wrote *Rachel*, a 1916 propagandistc drama that attacked both anti-black violence and racist imagery.[6] *Rachel* earns prominence in the history of American drama not merely because it was the first non-musical play that was written, professionally produced, and performed by African Americans, but more importantly because it deeply influenced African American theatre.[7] Errol G. Hill and James V. Hatch credit the play with "spark[ing]" the debate, most often associated with Alain Locke and W. E. B. Du Bois, on whether African American plays should aim to produce propaganda or "art for its own sake"; David Krasner reads the play in light of Walter Benjamin's work on mourning and allegory to argue that Grimké's drama "constructs the spiritual quest of redemption for those seeking answers to indescribable terror"; and Judith L. Stephens shows that *Rachel* inaugurated the genre of the anti-lynching drama, which was to include at least eleven extant plays written by African American women between 1916 and 1933.[8] Most recently, Koritha Mitchell argues persuasively that Grimké and her play inspired Du Bois to create the Drama Committee of the NAACP, and that Alain Locke and Montgomery Gregory constructed the influential theatre department of Howard University in reaction against Grimké's use of propaganda.[9] Mitchell's location of Grimké at the root of both Du Bois's and Locke's contrasting theatrical practices significantly revises scholarly understanding of both *Rachel* and the history of African American theatre. The case for *Rachel*'s influence as seminal—stimulating both congruent and oppositional drama—enables scholars to look for the play's strategies, ironies, and agonies echoing far beyond Grimké's period of productivity. Thus Mitchell shows that James V. Hatch was even more correct than he knew when he called Grimké the "Mother of African American Drama."[10]

Scholars largely agree that Grimké viewed physical and mass cultural violence as interdependent, and that *Rachel* constitutes a sophisticated and complex intervention in that intersection. Grimké acknowledged her intention to intervene in mass culture in a 1920 essay explaining why she wrote *Rachel*: "Whenever you say 'colored person' to a white man," she wrote, "he immediately, either through an ignorance that is deliberate or stupid, conjures up in his mind the picture of what he calls 'the darkey.'"[11] *Rachel* counteracted that tendency by presenting, as many scholars have noted, emphatically respectable, clean, hard-working, family-oriented African American characters who value their domestic life. Less commented upon, however, is Grimké's choice to counter mass cultural stereotypes specifically through her deployment of child characters. While many scholars have mentioned the plethora of child characters that appear in the play (enough children onstage to constitute a "director's nightmare"),[12] no one has considered the role these children played in Grimké's intervention in mass culture.[13] This essay shows that *Rachel* responds not only to physical racist violence, and not only, as Grimké acknowledged, to cultural violence perpetrated through the racist image of the "darkey," but also to the culturally violent figure of the "pickaninny." The pickaninny was a dehumanized black child who was typically depicted semi-naked, outdoors, eating watermelon, and merrily accepting (or even welcoming) comic violence.[14] As many scholars have noted, playwright George Aiken's dramatization of *Uncle Tom's Cabin* provided a central source for the popular cultural figure of the pickaninny. Grimké's *Rachel* contests the pickaninny image and re-writes elements of *Uncle Tom's Cabin*; however, her play's intervention does not end there. In *Rachel*, Grimké produces tender, fully-realized African American child characters who counter dehumanizing representations of black children, but then Grimké ironizes that humanization. *Rachel* ultimately suggests that a fully human, thinking, feeling, black child is ironically, in the face of racism, the greatest source of pain and vulnerability to African American families.

Angelina Weld Grimké was born in 1880, the daughter of a white mother and an African American father who was vice-president of the NAACP.[15] She was named for her great-aunt, the white abolitionist Angelina Grimké Weld, who died shortly before the playwright was born.[16] A well-educated writer of fiction and poetry with a long history of opposition to lynching, Grimké began writing *Rachel* by 1914.[17] Although the play's earliest draft preceded the premiere of D. W. Griffith's film, *Birth of a Nation*, in 1915, the completed *Rachel* is widely viewed as a response to that film.[18] Mitchell suggests that Grimké wrote her play in the context of not only Griffith's film, but also the 1906 tour of the dramatization of Thomas Dixon Jr.'s novel, *The Clansman*, upon which Griffith's film was based.[19] Grimké described her play as "the first attempt to use the stage for race propaganda in order to enlighten the American people relative to the lamentable condition of ten million of colored citizens in this free Republic."[20] Sally Burke notes that the play addressed this propaganda to "two audiences": both African American and white theatregoers.[21]

Rachel is a realistic drama with melodramatic elements. The plot centers on a teenaged girl named Rachel Loving who learns, in the course of the play, exactly how her father and brother died ten years earlier: what she learns is that they were lynched by a white mob. This discovery combines with a growing awareness of racism in daily life to convince Rachel that she must never bear children—although she desperately wants to be a mother. The play ends with Rachel turning away her suitor, John Strong, and sobbing as she resigns herself to a childless life.

The play debuted in a performance sponsored by the NAACP at the Myrtilla Miner Teachers College in Washington, D.C. on March 3–4, 1916.[22] Later performances were staged at the Neighborhood Playhouse in New York City in April 1917; in Cambridge, Massachusetts (where it was sponsored by St. Bartholomew's Church) in May 1917, and, in an adaptation, at Spelman College in March 1991.[23] While the productions were few in number, their influence on African American communities, and writers in particular, was vast. In 1920, the play was published in book form. It circulated and was reviewed widely; thus it continued and extended its influence.[24]

The play polarized not only Du Bois and Locke, but also critics and audience members. The African American sculptor Meta Vaux Warrick Fuller attended a performance in Cambridge, and she described a "mixed" and "sympathetic" audience that filled the house ("I think many people must have been turned away"). Although Fuller felt that the audience did not "ar[i]se to the high tention [sic] of the play in every instance," she called the play "beautiful—terribly beautiful. . . . [a] splendid drama."[25] Elizabeth C. Putnam, a white author, described *Rachel* as "interesting and very beautiful, self-restrained and convincing."[26]

About half the reviews were positive; the negative reviews, however, were vitriolic.[27] Grimké weathered attacks for her play's alleged over-emotionalism, its disturbing subject matter, and most of all, its apparent call to "race suicide." Grimké responded to this final charge in an essay in *Competitor.*

> Since it has been understood that "Rachel" preaches race suicide, I would emphasize that that was not my intention. To the contrary, the appeal is not primarily to the colored people, but to the whites.[28]

Within the category of white people, Grimké particularly addressed white women, and even more specifically, white mothers. Writing only eight months before the final ratification of the nineteenth amendment that granted American women the right to vote, Grimké criticized white women who "although they are beginning to awaken, form one of the most conservative elements of society." Such

> white women . . . are about the worst enemies with which the colored race has to contend. My belief was, then, that if a vulnerable point in their armor could be found, if their hearts could be active or passive enemies, they might become, at least, less inimical and possibly friendly. Did they have a vulnerable point and, if so, what was it? I believed it to be motherhood. Certainly all the noblest, finest, most sacred things in their lives converge about this. If anything can make all women sisters underneath their skins it is motherhood.[29]

Grimké's strategy to use motherhood to enable white women to empathize with black women—and thus to effect political change—partially echoes that of Harriet Beecher Stowe. Stowe's *Uncle Tom's Cabin* (1852) depicted slavery as a destroyer of families. Stowe aimed to recruit white women to the abolitionist cause by depicting, in heart-rending detail, scenes in which enslaved mothers and children are separated from each other. In *A Key to Uncle Tom's Cabin*, Stowe explicitly called for maternalism as a basis for cross-racial empathy:

> An incident which [Frederick] Douglass [whom Stowe claims as an inspiration for her character of George Harris] relates of his mother is touching; he states that it is customary at an early age to separate mothers from their children, for the purpose of blunting and deadening natural affection. When he was three years old his mother was sent to work on a plantation eight or ten miles distant, and after that he never saw her except in the night. After her day's toil she would occasionally walk over to her child, lie down with him in her arms, hush him to sleep in her bosom, then rise up and walk back again to be ready for her field-work by daylight. Now, we ask the highest-born lady in England or America, who is a mother, whether this does not show that this poor field-labourer had in her bosom, beneath her dirt and rags, a true mother's heart? . . . We are told, in fine phrase, by languid ladies of fashion, that it is not to be supposed that those creatures have the same feelings that we have, when, perhaps, the very speaker could not endure one tithe of the fatigue and suffering which the slave-mother often bears for her child. Every mother who has a mother's heart within her . . . should indignantly reject such a slander on all motherhood.[30]

While Grimké and Stowe both deployed maternalism in an effort to arouse white women's empathy for black women, Stowe did so with the straightforward sincerity prized in sentimental culture; Grimké, on the other hand, marbled the address to her audience with irony. Stowe appealed to white women, especially Northern white mothers, who regarded themselves as unimplicated in the system of slavery; she aimed to prick these women's consciences and thus to recruit them to the cause of abolition. Grimké, in contrast, addressed white women, and especially white mothers, not as passive colluders but as active enemies. Whereas Stowe wanted to implicate and recruit her well-intentioned readers to antislavery action, Grimké implicated her white audience members and demanded that they desist from their active viciousness.[31]

The simultaneously parallel and reversed connection between Stowe's and Grimké's strategies for arousing white women to action on behalf of African Americans ought not to surprise, because Grimké's drama responded indirectly to *Uncle Tom's Cabin*: Grimké completed *Rachel* in the context of, and in opposition to, both *Birth of a Nation* and Dixon's play and novels on which the film was based. The novels, *The Clansman* (1905) and *The Leopard's Spots* (1902), constituted Dixon's deliberate white supremacist responses to *Uncle Tom's Cabin*. Dixon attended a performance of *Uncle Tom's Cabin* in early 1901, and he "could hardly keep from jumping to his feet and denouncing the drama as false." When "the performance was over, he arose, vowed that he would tell the 'true story' of the South," and began drafting *The Leopard's Spots*.[32] The novel, which explicitly positioned itself as a sequel to Stowe's, included characters from *Uncle Tom's Cabin* such as Simon Legree and George Harris, Jr.[33] The trail of influence, then, reads thus: Stowe's novel was adapted for the stage by Aiken and others; these stage productions spurred Dixon to write his white supremacist riposte in the form of two novels and a play; Dixon's anti-Tom writing served as the kernel for Griffith's film; and Grimké completed *Rachel* in the context of, and in reaction to, Griffith's film and Dixon's work.

It is not surprising, then, that traces of *Uncle Tom's Cabin* should appear in *Rachel*. The most obvious of these traces appears in the character of Thomas, Rachel's brother: when Rachel adopts a neighborhood boy, Thomas becomes known as "Uncle Tom." This appellation, repeated and emphasized in many lines, cannot be accidental—particularly when one considers Grimké's decision to give characters blatantly meaningful names such as "Rachel Loving" and "John Strong."[34]

Even more significant than the echo in names and in the ironized strategy of demanding white mothers' empathy, however, is Grimké's contestation of the figure of Topsy as performed on stage. Grimké rewrites elements of *Uncle Tom's Cabin*, but she ultimately ironizes that rewriting. Whereas the theatrical Topsy, the titular pickaninny, dehumanized African American children, Grimké stages fully-realized black child characters who counter, blow by blow, racist libels. However, Grimké ironizes this humanization with the ultimate suggestion that racism renders a black child a source of pain and vulnerability to African American families.

Several scholars have traced the reach and influence of the character Topsy. Folklorist Patricia A. Turner calls Topsy "the first truly famous pickaninny," and performance scholar Tavia Nyong'o describes Topsy as "an inaugural figure in the genealogy of performing black children."[35] As Nyong'o correctly notes, it was Aiken's Topsy, not Harriet Beecher Stowe's, that became a staple of U.S. popular culture. The crucial difference between Aiken's and Stowe's Topsy was that Stowe's Topsy was a tragic figure, a human being damaged by violence, whereas Aiken's Topsy was comically impervious to pain.

For Stowe, the character of Topsy represents a set of problems with slavery: first, Stowe is unambiguous that Topsy's negative qualities—her lying and stealing, as well as her atheism—result directly from physical and emotional abuse. Furthermore, Stowe explicitly states that such abuse—and the damaged human beings that abuse creates—are widespread and inevitable within the system of slavery. Stowe delivers these points through the eyes of the white northerner, Aunt Ophelia St. Clare, who is disgusted with Topsy until Ophelia sees, "on the back and shoulders of the child, great welts and calloused spots, ineffaceable marks of the system under which she had grown up thus far." When Aunt Ophelia sees these signs of violence, Ophelia's "heart [becomes] pitiful within her."[36] The sentimental logic of Stowe's novel urges the reader's heart to follow suit and to feel for Topsy, whom Stowe calls a "neglected, abused child."[37]

Aiken crucially re-writes these points and thus reverses Stowe's antislavery politics. In Aiken's drama, Topsy arrives in the St. Clare household without welts and calluses, without any history of abuse legible on her body. In her first entrance, Topsy is described by Ophelia and St. Clare as an "object," a "thing," and a "funny specimen in the Jim Crow line."[38] Asked to sing and dance, Topsy belts out a catchy tune that highlights her signature lines, "I was never born," and "I's so wicked":

Oh! White-folks I was never born,
Aunt Sue, raise me on de corn,
Sends me errands night and morn,
Ching a ring a ring a ricked.

She used to knock me on de floor,
Den bang my head agin de door,
And tare my hair out by de core,
Oh! Cause I was so wicked.[39]

This song merrily, blithely reverses Stowe: violence is visited on Aiken's Topsy by a black caretaker, not by white slaveowners, and because Aiken's Topsy is "wicked," not because the system of slavery is evil. Whereas Stowe's Topsy believes herself to be "never born" because of ignorance and godlessness unnaturally imposed by the system of slavery, Aiken's Topsy transforms "never born" into a catchphrase, an automatic laugh line emptied of meaning. And finally, Aiken's Topsy responds to violence not by becoming physically and emotionally damaged, but by laughing and singing about her invulnerability. The contrast between Aiken's and Stowe's Topsies continues from this opening scene to the final actions of the characters: Aiken's Topsy exits her final scene after animalistically head-butting a corrupt lawyer, whereas the last that Stowe's reader learns of the novelist's Topsy, the character has grown up, become a Christian, and traveled to Africa as a missionary.

Grimké carefully counters the libels packed into the pickaninny image. Throughout the first act of *Rachel*, Grimké spotlights her African American child characters, showing them to be well-behaved, respectful, and respectable. The main such child character is Jimmy, an adorable three-year-old neighbor on whom the teenage Rachel dotes. While Rachel lavishes Jimmy with kisses, she makes clear that her love is not restricted to this individual child, nor is that love race-blind. "[T]he loveliest thing of all the lovely things in this world is . . . being a mother!" Rachel enthuses in the play's opening. "I love the little black and brown babies best of all" (143).[40] In Jimmy's first scene, Rachel leads the boy onstage "by the hand." The "little fellow is shy but smiling," the stage directions tell us. "This is my brown baby," Rachel announces proudly as she presents her little friend to her mother (144–45). The tenderness of this entrance rewrites the entrance of Topsy in Aiken's drama—an entrance spangled with words such as "object" and "thing." Over and over, Grimké presents Jimmy and other African American children as loving and lovable, needing and deserving protection. "There is something about [little black and brown babies] that—that—clutches at my heart," Rachel declares. "I don't understand [it]. More than the other babies, I feel that I must protect them. They're in danger, but from what? I don't know. I've tried so hard to understand, but I can't" (143).

This line strikes an early, ominous chord in Grimké's drama: Rachel, who does not yet know that her father and brother were lynched, wants to protect black and brown babies, but she cannot name the menace. Rachel's mother, however, knows that the menace is racism, as enacted through not only physical violence but also through a culture that imposes a thousand daily humiliations and griefs. Furthermore, Mrs. Loving knows a worse truth: adults cannot protect black children from racism. The central dramatic arc of the play consists of Rachel gradually apprehending both these facts, and then drawing the shocking conclusion that she must never bear children, despite her intense desire to be a mother.

Slowly, inexorably, the loving kisses that suffuse the first act link to this inability to protect black children from racism. Mrs. Loving laments, "When you [children] are little, we mothers can kiss away all the trouble, but when you're grown up—and go out—into the world—and get hurt—we are helpless" (151).[41] Thus the kisses—a chief means by which Grimké dramatizes the lovability of black children—become ironic. In Mrs. Loving's view, kisses provide temporary comforting, but they lose power when a child becomes an adult. But Grimké's play slowly proves Mrs. Loving wrong: kisses do not even provide temporary relief from racism's assaults.

Whereas loving kisses pervade the first act, impotent kisses dominate the second act. Act 2 opens four years after the close of act 1. Jimmy's parents have died of smallpox, and Rachel, now twenty-two, has adopted the child. Omnipresent racism has taken a toll on the Loving family. Rachel's suitor, John Strong, graduated from college, but while John's white classmates entered the professions, John could find work only as a waiter. He rose as high as possible, to head waiter, but racism prevents him from gaining employment that utilizes his education; he bitterly acknowledges that he will be head waiter for the rest of his life. Rachel's brother Tom trained as an electrical engineer, but he also cannot find work in his field. Tom investigated the individuals who lynched Tom and Rachel's father and brother, and discovered that the murderers and their children are prospering. Tom laments the disparity between the families' fates:

> Their children . . . are growing up around them; and they are having a square deal handed out to them—college, position, wealth, and best of all, freedom, without galling restrictions. . . . Look at us—and look at them. We are destined to failure—they, to success. Their children shall grow up in hope; ours, in despair. (153)

Systematic racism renders kisses useless, as Grimké dramatizes in one particularly moving episode. Immediately after her suitor delights Rachel with a tender kiss that leaves her dreamy, a "poorly dressed" black woman and child enter Rachel's apartment. The mother, Mrs. Lane, explains that she seeks information about the local elementary school. Rachel graciously receives the mother and daughter, and offers the girl, Ethel, a "big, red apple, cut into quarters" and served "with a fringed napkin" (158). Rachel says "very gently," "Here, dear, little girl, is a beautiful apple for you," but this tenderness has no effect on Ethel, who cowers. Mrs. Lane explains Ethel's strange behavior: until recently, the Lanes had been a happy family, but then Ethel began school. A racist teacher was cruel to her, and white students followed the teacher's lead. In only two weeks, Ethel transformed from a shy, slow child, to a terrified, self-loathing child. Now the family must move to place her in a new school. As Mrs. Lane tells her story, Ethel "makes no attempt to eat the apple" that Rachel lovingly prepared. Instead, Ethel "holds the plate in her lap with a care that is painful to watch" (158). Rachel describes the sight of Ethel as "heartbreaking." Thus Grimké reverses the move that George Aiken made when he adapted Topsy for the stage: whereas Stowe presented Topsy as a human tragically damaged by slavery, dramatic adaptations erased that damage and constructed Topsy as a pickaninny who was comically impervious to pain. Grimké, returning to Stowe's political strategy, emphasizes the damage done to an individual black child.

When Ethel and Mrs. Lane prepare to leave the apartment, Rachel tries to kiss Ethel goodbye. Unlike the many child characters who enjoyed Rachel's kisses throughout the play, Ethel refuses to be kissed. Rachel is dismayed: "Oh!—no child—ever did—that to me—before!" (160). Rachel is devastated to discover that her kisses cannot help the damaged child. Moments after the mother and daughter exit, six rosebuds are delivered to Rachel's door—a gift from her suitor John. The flowers comfort Rachel: "Dear little rosebuds—you—make me think—of sleeping, curled up, happy babies" (160). This pleasant moment is interrupted, however, by the entrance of her adopted Jimmy, who returns from school with the question, "Ma Rachel, what is a 'Nigger?'" (160).

The exchange that follows becomes the third of three linked moments in the drama. The first two moments seem benign, and it is only with this third event that Grimké's irony reaches full, devastating effect. Early in act 2, Jimmy comically describes the way in which he "runned lots of water in the tub" for his bath (149). Rachel gently corrects his grammar as she praises him for bathing himself. As many scholars have noted, Grimké's drama constantly emphasizes the Lovings' cleanliness as a sign of their respectability, and Jimmy's grammatical error—as well as Rachel's correction—seems only to highlight and ratify that respectability. Halfway through the second act, Jimmy again jubilantly reports his success at bathing: "I ranned, no[—]I runned, I think—the water . . . and got in it all by myself." The repetition of the bath, punctuated by the repeated grammatical error, underscores yet again the clean wholesomeness of the Loving family.

However, at the end of act 2, Jimmy asks Rachel what a nigger is, and Rachel "recoils as though she had been struck" (160). "Honey boy," she asks, "why do you ask that?" Jimmy replies,

> Some big boys called me that when I came out of school just now. They said, "Look at the little nigger!" And then they laughed. One of them *runned, no ranned*, after me and threw stones. (160, emphasis added)

In this third and final repetition of the grammatical error, "runned" refers not to cleansing water and attendant bourgeois respectability, but to Jimmy's attempt to escape racist violence. That attempt, we learn, failed: a mob of white boys chased Jimmy, hurling both racist epithets and stones. Jimmy reports, "One stone struck me hard in the back, and it hurt awful bad. . . . The stone hurts me there, Ma Rachel; but what they called me hurts and hurts here" (160–61). Jimmy, like Stowe's Topsy (and unlike theatrical Topsies), now has a bruised body and soul.

With this scene, Rachel finally confronts what her mother knew from the play's opening: she cannot save this or any other child from racism. She hugs and kisses Jimmy, but she knows that caresses are not enough. In an action that is pathetically inadequate, Rachel offers Jimmy cookies. After Jimmy exits with his treat, Rachel despairs: "First, it's little, black Ethel—and then it's Jimmy. Tomorrow, it will be some other little child. The blight—sooner or later—strikes all" (161). At that moment, Rachel makes the decision—which some black reviewers, in the parlance of the day, denounced as "race suicide"—never to have children. She has finally solved the play's central dilemma of how to protect black children from racism: the only way to keep black children safe is never to give birth to them. The solution devastates Rachel. "I am afraid—to go—to sleep," she explains in the final scene, "for every time I do—my children come—and beg me—weeping—not to—bring them here—to suffer" (172). And thus Grimké delivers her final ironic twist on the figure of Topsy: the only safe black child is the one who—like Topsy—was "never born."

In *Rachel*, Angelina Weld Grimké brilliantly counters not only D.W. Griffith's *Birth of a Nation*, but also the theatrical and novelistic iterations of *Uncle Tom's Cabin* on which the film was based. First, Grimké responds to the popular cultural figure of the pickaninny, the dehumanized black child who was invulnerable to pain, by creating fully-realized black child-characters who are painfully vulnerable to racist violence. Grimké goes far beyond a simple negation of a stereotype, however, when she reveals a terrible irony: *because* black children are thinking, feeling human beings, they cannot be fully protected from racism's physical or cultural violence. Aiken's *Uncle Tom's Cabin* and other elements of mass culture constructed black children as subhuman sources of comedy. Grimké's *Rachel* ironically countered: black children are fully human, but racism perverts that truth into tragedy.

Contributors

Robin Bernstein is an Assistant Professor of Women, Gender, and Sexuality and of History and Literature at Harvard University. The editor of *Cast Out: Queer Lives in Theater* (University of Michigan Press, 2006), she has published articles on Lorraine Hansberry and Anna Deavere Smith in *Modern Drama* and the *Journal of Dramatic Theory and Criticism*, respectively. She is currently writing a book that uses performance theory to argue that cultural constructions of childhood played a key role in U.S. racial formation from the mid-nineteenth through the early twentieth century.

Garrett Eisler is a Ph.D. candidate in Theatre at the Graduate Center of the City University of New York. He holds an M.A. in English from New York University, an M.F.A. in Directing from Boston University, and has served as a professional literary manager in regional theatre. He has published in *Studies in Musical Theatre* and is editing a forthcoming volume of the *Dictionary of Literary Biography* on Twentieth-Century American dramatists. His theatre and book reviews have appeared in *Theatre Journal* and *Theatre Survey*, as well as *The Village Voice* and *Time Out New York*. He also writes on contemporary theatre for his blog *The Playgoer* (http://play-goerblogspot.com).

Brian Hallstoos is a Ph.D. candidate in American Studies at the University of Iowa. His dissertation focuses on a passion play by Willa Saunders Jones—what it reveals about gender and racial politics in early twentieth-century Chicago and the links between black sacred music and drama. He has four biographical entries (including one on Jones) slated for publication in the forthcoming *African American National Biography* (Oxford University Press). He has an M.A. in Art History from Rutgers University.

Leigh Kennicott presently teaches at California State University, Northridge and the College of the Canyons in Santa Clarita, California. She received her Ph.D. in Theatre from the University of Colorado in 2002. Before returning to the university, she worked in film and television for many years, notably in Current Television at ABC and for Miller-Boyett Productions at Warner Brothers. She has written, directed, and produced two films: the short *Rubber Gloves* and the documentary *Streakin'*.

Notes

The author thanks Koritha Mitchell for her comments on this essay.

1. Rayford Logan, *Betrayal of the Negro: From Rutherford B. Hayes to Woodrow Wilson* (New York: Collier, 1965), 62. See also Logan, *The Negro in American Life and Thought: The Nadir, 1877–1901* (New York: Dial Press, 1954).
2. Nell Irvin Painter, *Standing at Armageddon: The United States, 1877–1919* (New York: W.W. Norton and Company, 1987), 167.
3. Joel Williamson, *The Crucible of Race: Black-White Relations in the American South Since Emancipation* (New York: Oxford University Press, 1984), 117–18. See also Jacqueline Denise Goldsby, *A Spectacular Secret: Lynching in American Life and Literature* (Chicago, IL: University of Chicago Press, 2006); Philip Dray, *At the Hands of Persons Unknown: The Lynching of Black America* (New York: Random House, 2002); and Michael J. Pfeifer, *Rough Justice: Lynching and American Society*, 1874–1947 (Urbana, IL: University of Illinois Press, 2004).
4. Painter, *Standing at Armageddon*, 219.
5. On the concomitant rise of advertising and of racist imagery, see Kenneth W. Goings, *Mammy and Uncle Mose: Black Collectibles and American Stereotyping* (Bloomington and Indianapolis, IN: Indiana University Press, 1994), 1.

6. At the age of nineteen, Grimké gathered signatures for a petition opposing lynching (Letter of Archibald H. Grimké to Angelina Weld Grimké, 16 November 1899, qtd in Gloria T. Hull, *Color, Sex, and Poetry: Three Women Writers of the Harlem Renaissance* [Bloomington and Indianapolis, IN: Indiana University Press, 1987], 131).
7. Kathy A. Perkins and Judith L. Stephens, Eds., *Strange Fruit: Plays on Lynching by American Women* (Bloomington, IN: Indiana University Press, 1998), 24.
8. Errol G. Hill and James V. Hatch, *A History of African American Theatre* (Cambridge, U.K.: Cambridge University Press, 2003), 220; David Krasner, *A Beautiful Pageant: African American Theatre, Drama, and Performance in the Harlem Renaissance*, 1910–1927 (New York: Palgrave MacMillan, 2002), 110–11; Judith L. Stephens, "Anti-Lynching Plays by African American Women; Race, Gender, and Social Protest in American Drama," *African American Review* 26, no. 2 (Summer 1992), 329–39. Koritha Mitchell counts fourteen known anti-lynching plays written between 1916 and 1935 (Koritha Mitchell, "Antilynching Plays: Angelina Weld Grimké, Alice Dunbar-Nelson, and the Evolution of African American Drama," chapt. in Barbara McCaskill and Caroline Gebhard, Eds., *Post-Bellum, Pre-Harlem: African American Literature and Culture, 1877–1919* [New York: New York University Press, 2006], 212).
9. Mitchell, "Antilynching Plays," 211–12.
10. Christina R. Gray, "Discovering and Recovering African American Women Playwrights Writing before 1930," chapt. in Brenda Murphy, Ed., *The Cambridge Companion to American Women Playwrights* (Cambridge, U.K.: Cambridge University Press, 1999), 245.
11. Angelina Weld Grimké, "'Rachel' The Play of the Month: The Reason and Synopsis by the Author," *Competitor* 1 (January 1920): 52.
12. James V. Hatch, Ed., *Black Theater USA: 45 Plays by Black Americans, 1847–1974* (New York: Macmillan, 1974), 138.
13. When Grimké placed children and childhood at the center of her anti-racist politics, she struck an early note in what would become a trope for Harlem Renaissance writers. As Katharine Capshaw Smith and Caroline F. Levander have recently shown, the figure of the child became central to the literary and political work of W. E. B. Du Bois and other African-American writers of the early twentieth century (see Smith, *Children's Literature of the Harlem Renaissance* [Bloomington, IN: Indiana University Press, 2004] and Levander, *Cradle of Liberty: Race, the Child, and National Belonging from Thomas Jefferson to W. E. B. Du Bois* [Durham, NC: Duke University Press, 2006]). Levander forcefully shows that in *The Souls of Black Folk* (1903), Du Bois figured the death of a black child as an "escape" from the "living death" of racism (Levander 157). Later, however, Du Bois changed his position. The juvenile magazine, *The Brownies Book*, which *The Crisis* (the official magazine of the NAACP) published and which Du Bois co-edited from 1920–1921, constructed black children as "culturally, politically, and aesthetically sophisticated" people capable of leading and uplifting the race (Smith, *Children's Literature*, 1). *Rachel*, which was first performed in 1916 and which ends with the protagonist deciding never to bear children, could be simplistically positioned a mediation between the 1903 and 1920–1921 extremes of viewing the death of black children as an "escape" and viewing black children as potential leaders or even saviors. Such a characterization would, however, elide the innovations unique to Grimké: her devastating use of irony, and her signification upon (rather than simple riposte to) the popular cultural figure of the pickaninny.
14. On the figure of the pickaninny, see Patricia A. Turner, *Ceramic Uncles and Celluloid Mammies: Black Images and their Influence on Culture* (New York: Anchor Books, 1994). A superb overview of the pickaninny image appears in The Jim Crow Museum of Racist Memorabilia at Ferris State University in Michigan www.ferris.edu/htmls/news/jimcrow/index.htm. See especially David Pilgrim's "The Picaninny Caricature" www.ferris.edu/htmls/news/jimcrow/picaninny/.
15. Hatch, *Black Theater USA*, 137.
16. Grimké's father, Archibald Grimké, was the son of Angelina Grimké Weld's brother Henry Grimké. See Sally Burke, *American Feminist Playwrights: A Critical History* (New York: Twayne Publishers, 1996), 86. See also Herron, "Introduction," *Selected Works of Angelina Weld Grimké*, 5 and Hull, 108.
17. Hull, *Color, Sex, and Poetry*, 118.
18. Hill and Hatch, *A History of African American Theatre*, 220.
19. Mitchell, "Antilynching Plays," 210.
20. Uncited program note quoted in Burke, *American Feminist Playwrights*, 87.
21. Burke, *American Feminist Playwrights*, 87.

22. Hill and Hatch, *A History of African American Theatre*, 220; Hull, *Color, Sex, and Poetry*, 119.
23. Hull, *Color, Sex, and Poetry*, 119; Addell Austin Anderson, "Review of Rachel by Angelina Weld Grimké," *Theatre Journal* 43, no. 3 (October 1991): 385–86.
24. Hull, *Color, Sex, and Poetry*, 121.
25. Meta Vaux Warrick Fuller to Angelina Weld Grimké, 25 May 1917, Angelina Weld Grimké Papers, Moorland-Spingarn Research Center, Howard University.
26 Elizabeth C. Putnam to Angelina Weld Grimké, 7 December 1918, Angelina Weld Grimké Papers.
27. Hull, *Color, Sex, and Poetry*, 121–22.
28. Grimké, *Competitor*, 51.
29. Ibid, 52.
30. Harriet Beecher Stowe, *A Key to Uncle Tom's Cabin: Presenting the Original Facts and Documents Upon Which the Story is Founded* (Boston, MA: John P. Jewett and Company, 1853), 16–17.
31. Attention to the subtleties and complexities of Grimké's address, combined with new understanding of *Rachel*'s widespread influence, prompts a fresh look at strategies employed throughout twentieth-century African American theatre. The Black Arts Movement of the 1960s and 70s, for example, is known for having centered African-American audiences and having declared non-black audiences irrelevant; Harlem's Black Arts Repertory Theatre/School (BART/S), founded by Amiri Baraka (then LeRoi Jones), barred white audience members. However, a *Rachel*-like irony in which racially diverse audiences are addressed, and white audiences are simultaneously engaged and attacked, emerges in the context of Baraka's Dutchman, which opened in 1964 not at BART/S, but instead for a "resolutely left-liberal, activist, but decidedly integrationist audience"(Mike Sell, "The Drama of the Black Arts Movement," chap, in David Krasner, Ed., *Companion to Twentieth-Century American Drama* [Malden, MA: Blackwell Publishers, 2005], 265; see also Hill and Hatch, *A History of African American Theatre*, 390). In the context of this audience, one sees the attack-within-engagement, the simultaneous invitation to white empathy and attack on white racism that is fundamental to Grimké's play.
32. Raymond Allen Cook, *Flint from the Fire: The Amazing Careers of Thomas Dixon* (Winston-Salem, NC: John F. Blair, 1968), 105.
33. For more on the connections between Uncle Tom's Cabin and Birth of a Nation, see Linda Williams, *Playing the Race Card: Melodramas of Black and White from Uncle Tom to O.J. Simpson* (Princeton, NJ: Princeton University Press, 2001) and Thomas F. Gossett, *Uncle Tom's Cabin and American Culture* (Dallas, TX: Southern Methodist University Press, 1985), 346–47.
34. Grimké's persistent attention to meaningful names caused her, at the last minute, to rename her protagonist from "Janet" to the Biblically resonant "Rachel" (Hull, *Color, Sex, and Poetry*, 118). Given Grimké's penchant for explicitly meaningful names, it is inconceivable that the "Uncle Tom" in *Rachel* bears no relationship to Stowe's hegemonic character of the same name.
35. Turner, *Ceramic Uncles and Celluloid Mammies* 13; Tavia Nyong'o, "Racial Kitsch and Black Performance," *The Yale Journal of Criticism* 15, no. 2 (2002): 376.
36. Harriet Beecher Stowe, *Uncle Tom's Cabin, Or, Life Among the Lowly* (1852; reprint, edited by Elizabeth Ammons, New York: W.W. Norton, 1994), 209.
37. Ibid.
38. George Aiken, "Uncle Tom's Cabin; or, Life Among the Lowly," 1852 in *Early American Drama*, Ed. Jeffrey H. Richards (New York: Penguin Books, 1997), 391.
39. George Howard, "'*Oh, I'se So Wicked*' As Sung by Mrs. G. C. Howard in Her Original Character of Topsy [in *Uncle Tom's Cabin*]" (New York: Horace Waters, 1854). The sheet music was "Respectfully Dedicated to G. L. Aiken, Esq." Although George Howard, the producer of the inaugural performance of *Uncle Tom's Cabin*, wrote the song, he did so for inclusion in Aiken's script. For the sake of simplicity, I refer to the iteration of Topsy who performs this song as "Aiken's Topsy." An audio clip of this song is available online as part of the University of Virginia's website, "*Uncle Tom's Cabin* in American Culture: A Multi-Media Archive" www.iath.virginia.edu/utc/songs/sowickedf.html.
40. Page numbers refer to the edition of *Rachel* included in Hatch, *Black Theater USA*.
41. Mrs. Loving refers here to hurts caused by racism, not to the inevitable knocks that assail all people.

6.2 ANGELINA WELD GRIMKÉ—ANON

Playwright Angelina Weld Grimké, whose drama *Rachel* was commissioned by the NAACP to counter D.W. Griffith's film *Birth of a Nation* and the rise of racism and lynching throughout the nation.

Source: Image courtesy of the Moorland-Spingarn Research Center at Howard University

---

6.3 TREES—ANGELINA WELD GRIMKÉ

God made them very beautiful, the trees:
He spoke and gnarled of bole or silken sleek
They grew; majestic bowed or very meek;
Huge-bodied, slim; sedate and full of glees.
And He had pleasure deep in all of these.
And to them soft and little tongues to speak
Of Him to us, He gave wherefore they seek
From dawn to dawn to bring unto our knees.
Yet here amid the wistful sounds of leaves,
A black-hued gruesome something swings and swings;
Laughter it knew and joy in little things
Till man's hate ended all. —And so man weaves.
And God, how slow, how very slow weaves He—
Was Christ Himself not nailed to a tree?

6.4 DULUTH LYNCHING—ANON

News Tribune photograph of the 1920 lynching of three black men accused of raping a young woman in Duluth, Minnesota. A large mob broke into the city jail, dragged out the accused men without any police obstruction, beat and then hanged them from a light pole.

6.5 *BIRTH OF A NATION* IMAGES

Theatrical release poster of D.W. Griffith's *Birth of a Nation*.

Birth of a Nation film still depicting the Ku Klux Klan capturing the "renegade Negro" Gus (played by white actor Walter Long in blackface).

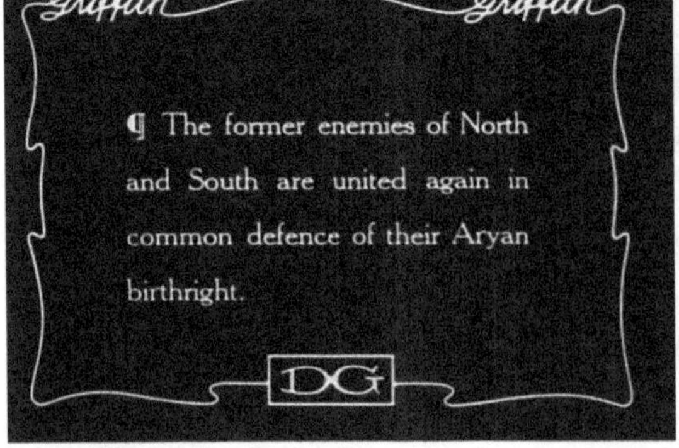

Birth of a Nation Intertitle.

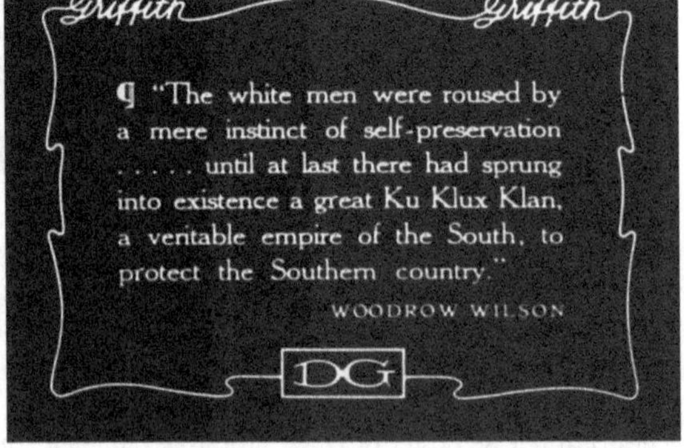

Birth of a Nation Intertitle.

6.6 *RACHEL*—ANGELINA WELD GRIMKÉ

Characters

MRS MARY LOVING, *a widow.*
RACHEL LOVING, *her daughter.*
THOMAS LOVING, *her son.*
JIMMY MASON, *a small boy.*
JOHN STRONG, *a friend of the family.*
MRS. LANE, *a caller.*
ETHEL LANE, *her daughter.*

MARY,
NANCY,
EDITH,
JENNY,
LOUISE,
MARTHA,
little friends of Rachel.

★

TIME: The first decade of the Twentieth Century.

ACT I. October 16th.
ACT II. October 16th, four years later.
ACT III. One week later.

PLACE: A northern city. The living room in the small apartment of Mrs. Loving.

All of the characters are colored.

★

RACHEL

ACT I.

The scene is a room scrupulously neat and clean and plainly furnished. The walls are painted green, the woodwork, white. In the rear at the left an open doorway leads into a hall. Its bare, green wall and white baseboard are all that can be seen of it. It leads into the other rooms of the flat. In the centre of the rear wall of the room is a window. It is shut. The white sash curtains are pushed to right and left as far as they will go. The green shade is rolled up to the top. Through the window can be seen the red bricks of a house wall, and the tops of a couple of trees moving now and then in the wind. Within the window, and just below the sill, is a shelf upon which are a few potted plants. Between the window and the door is a bookcase full of books and above it, hanging on the wall, a simply framed, inexpensive copy of Millet's "The Reapers." There is a run extending from the right center to just below the right upper entrance. It is the vestibule of the flat. Its open doorway faces the left wall. In the right wall near the front is another window. Here the sash curtains are drawn together and the green shade is partly lowered. The window is up from the bottom. Through it street noises can be heard. In front of this window is an open, threaded sewing-machine. Some frail, white fabric is lying upon it. There is a chair in front of the machine and at the machine's left a small table covered with a green cloth. In the rear of the left wall and directly opposite to the entrance to the flat is the doorway leading into the kitchenette, dishes on shelves can be seen behind glass doors.

In the center of the left wall is a fireplace with a grate in it for coals; over this is a wooden mantel painted white. In the center is a small clock. A pair of vases, green and white in coloring, one at each end, complete the ornaments. Over the mantel is a narrow mirror; and over this, hanging on the wall, Burne-Jones' "Golden Stairs," simply framed. Against the front end of the left wall is an upright piano with a stool in front of it. On top is music neatly piled. Hanging over the piano is Raphael's "Sistine Madonna." In the center of the floor is a green rug, and in the center of this, a rectangular dining-room table, the long side facing front. It is covered with a green table-cloth. Three dining-room chairs are at the table, one at either end and one at the rear facing front. Above the table is a chandelier with four gas jets enclosed by glass globes. At the right front center is a rather shabby arm-chair upholstered in green.

Left and right from the spectator's point of view.

Before the sewing-machine, Mrs. Loving is seated. She looks worried. She is sewing swiftly and deftly by hand upon a waist in her lap. It is a white, beautiful thing and she sews upon it delicately. It is about half-past four in the afternoon; and the light is failing. Mrs. Loving pauses in her sewing, rises and lets the window-shade near her go up to the top. She pushes the sash-curtains to either side, the corner of a red brick house wall being thus brought into view. She shivers slightly, then pushes the window down at the bottom and lowers it a trifle from the top. The street noises become less distinct. She takes off her thimble, rubs her hands gently, puts the thimble on again, and looks at the clock on the mantel. She then reseats herself, with her chair as close to the window as possible and begins to sew. Presently a key is heard, and the door opens and shuts noisily. Rachel comes in from the vestibule. In her left arm she carries four or five books strapped together; under her right, a roll of music. Her hat is twisted over her left ear and her hair is falling in tendrils about her face. She brings into the room with her the spirit of abounding life, health, joy, youth. Mrs. Loving pauses, needle in hand, as soon as she hears the turning key and the banging door. There is a smile on her face. For a second, mother and daughter smile at each other. Then Rachel throws her books upon the dining-room table, places the music there also, but with care, and rushing to her mother, gives her a bear hug and a kiss.

RACHEL: Ma dear! dear, old Ma dear!

MRS. LOVING: Look out for the needle, Rachel! The waist! Oh, Rachel!

RACHEL (*On her knees and shaking her finger directly under her mother's nose.*): You old, old fraud! You know you adore being hugged. I've a good mind . . .

MRS. LOVING: Now, Rachel, please! Besides, I know your tricks. You think you can make me forget you are late. What time is it?

RACHEL (*Looking at the clock and expressing surprise*): Jiminy Xmas! (*Whistles*) Why, it's five o'clock!

MRS. LOVING (*Severely*): Well!

RACHEL (*Plaintively*): Now, Ma dear, you're going to be horrid and cross.

MRS. LOVING (*Laughing*): Really, Rachel, that expression is not particularly affecting, when your hat is over your ear, and you look, with your hair over your eyes, exactly like some one's pet poodle. I wonder if you are ever going to grow up and be ladylike.

RACHEL: Oh! Ma dear, I hope not, not for the longest time, two long, long years at least. I just want to be silly and irresponsible, and have you to love and torment, and, of course, Tom, too.

MRS. LOVING (*Smiling down at Rachel*): You'll not make me forget, young lady. Why are you late, Rachel?

RACHEL: Well, Ma dear, I'm your pet poodle, and my hat is over my ear, and I'm late, for the loveliest reason.

MRS. LOVING: Don't be silly, Rachel.

RACHEL: That may sound silly, but it isn't. And please don't "Rachel" me so much. It was honestly one whole hour ago when I opened the front door down stairs. I know it was, because I heard the postman telling some one it was four o'clock. Well, I climbed the first flight, and was just starting up the second, when a little shrill voice said, "'Lo!" I raised my eyes, and there, half-way up the stairs, sitting in the middle of a step, was just the dearest, cutest, darlingest little brown baby boy you ever saw. "'Lo! yourself," I said. "What are you doing, and who are you anyway?" "I'm Jimmy; and I'm widing to New York on the choo-choo tars." As he looked entirely too young to be going such a distance by himself, I asked him if I might go too. For a minute or two he considered the question and me very seriously, and then he said, "'Es," and made room for me on the step beside him. We've been everywhere: New York, Chicago, Boston, London, Paris and Oshkosh. I wish you could have heard him say that last place. I suggested going there just to hear him. Now, Ma dear, is it any wonder I am late? See all the places we have been in just one "teeny, weeny" hour? We would have been traveling yet, but his horrid, little mother came out and called him in. They're in the flat below, the new people. But before he went, Ma dear, he said the "cunningest" thing. He said, "Will you turn out an' p'ay wif me aden in two minutes?" I nearly hugged him to death, and it's a wonder my hat is on my head at all. Hats are such unimportant nuisances anyway!

MRS. LOVING: Unimportant nuisances! What ridiculous language you do use, Rachel! Well, I'm no prophet, but I see very distinctly what is going to happen. This little brown baby will be living here night and day. You're not happy unless some child is trailing along in your rear.

RACHEL (*Mischievously*): Now, Ma dear, whose a hypocrite? What? I suppose you don't like children! I can tell you one thing, though, it won't be my fault if he isn't here night and day. Oh, I wish he were all mine, every bit of him! Ma dear, do you suppose that "she woman" he calls mother would let him come up here until it is time for him to go to bed? I'm going down there this minute. (*Rises impetuously*).

MRS. LOVING: Rachel, for Heaven's sake! No! I am entirely too busy and tired today without being bothered with a child romping around in here.

RACHEL (*Reluctantly and a trifle petulantly*): Very well, then. (*For several moments she watches her mother, who has begun to sew again. The displeasure vanishes from her face*). Ma dear!

MRS. LOVING: Well.

RACHEL: Is there anything wrong today?

MRS. LOVING: I'm just tired, chickabiddy, that's all.

RACHEL (*Moves over to the table. Mechanically takes off her hat and coat and carries them out into the entryway of the flat. She returns and goes to the looking glass over the fireplace and tucks in the tendrils of her hair in rather a preoccupied manner. The electric doorbell rings. She returns to the speaking tube in the vestibule. Her voice is heard answering*): Yes!—Yes!—No, I'm not Mrs. Loving. She's here, yes!—What? Oh! come right up! (*Appearing in the doorway*). Ma dear, it's some man, who is coming for Mrs. Strong's waist.

MRS. LOVING (*Pausing and looking at Rachel*): It is probably her son. She said she would send for it this afternoon. (*Rachel disappears. A door is heard opening and closing. There is the sound of a man's voice. Rachel ushers in Mr. John Strong.*)

STRONG (*Bowing pleasantly to Mrs. Loving*): Mrs. Loving? (*Mrs. Loving bows, puts down her sewing, rises and goes toward Strong*). My name is Strong. My mother asked me to come by and get her waist this afternoon. She hoped it would be finished.

MRS. LOVING: Yes, Mr. Strong, it is all ready. If you'll sit down a minute, I'll wrap it up for you. (*She goes into hallway leading to other rooms in flat*).

RACHEL (*Manifestly ill at ease at being left alone with a stranger; attempting, however, to be the polite hostess*): Do sit down, Mr. Strong. (*They both sit*).

RACHEL (*Nervously after a pause*): It's a very pleasant day, isn't it, Mr. Strong?

STRONG: Yes, very. (*He leans back composedly, his hat on his knee, the faintest expression of amusement in his eyes*).

RACHEL (*After a pause*): It's quite a climb up to our flat, don't you think?

STRONG: Why, no! It didn't strike me so. I'm not old enough yet to mind stairs.

RACHEL (*Nervously*): Oh! I didn't mean that you are old! Anyone can see you are quite young, that is, of course, not too young, but,—(*Strong laughs quietly*). There! I don't blame you for laughing. I'm always clumsy just like that.

MRS. LOVING (*Calling from the other room*): Rachel, bring me a needle and the sixty cotton, please.

RACHEL: All right, Ma dear! (*Rummages for the cotton in the machine drawer, and upsets several spools upon the floor. To Strong*): You see! I can't even get a spool of cotton without spilling things all over the floor. (*Strong smiles, Rachel picks up the spools and finally gets the cotton and needle*). Excuse me! (*Goes out door leading to other rooms. Strong left to himself, looks around casually. The "Golden Stairs" interests him and the "Sistine Madonna"*)

RACHEL (*Reenters, evidently continuing her function of hostess*): We were talking about the climb to our flat, weren't we? You see, when you're poor, you have to live in a top flat. There is always a compensation, though; we have bully—I mean nice air, better light, a lovely view, and nobody "thud-thudding" up and down over our heads night and day. The people below have our "thud-thudding," and it must be something *awful*, especially when Tom and I play "Ivanhoe" and have a tournament up here. We're entirely too old, but we still play. Ma dear rather dreads the climb up three flights, so Tom and I do all the errands. We don't mind climbing the stairs, particularly when we go up two or three at a time,—that is—Tom still does. I can't, Ma dear stopped me. (*Sighs*). I've got to grow up it seems.

STRONG (*Evidently amused*): It is rather hard being a girl, isn't it?

RACHEL: Oh, no! It's not hard at all. That's the trouble; they won't let me be a girl. I'd love to be.

MRS. LOVING (*Reentering with parcel. She smiles*): My chatterbox, I see, is entertaining you, Mr. Strong. I'm sorry to have kept you waiting, but I forgot, I found, to sew the ruching in the neck. I hope everything is satisfactory. If it isn't, I'll be glad to make any changes.

STRONG (*Who has risen upon her entrance*): Thank you, Mrs. Loving, I'm sure everything is all right. (*He takes the package and bows to her and Rachel. He moves towards the vestibule, Mrs. Loving following him. She passes through the doorway first. Before leaving, Strong turns for a second and looks back quietly at Rachel. He goes out too. Rachel returns to the mirror, looks at her face for a second, and then begins to touch and pat her hair lightly and delicately here and there. Mrs. Loving returns*).

RACHEL (*Still at the glass*): He *was* rather nice, wasn't he, Ma dear?—for a man? (*Laughs*). I guess my reason's a vain one,—he let me do all the talking. (*Pauses*). Strong? Strong? Ma dear, is his mother the little woman with the sad, black eyes?

MRS. LOVING (*Resuming her sewing; sitting before the machine*): Yes. I was rather curious, I confess, to see this son of hers. The whole time I'm fitting her she talks of nothing else. She worships him. (*Pauses*). It's rather a sad case, I believe. She is a widow. Her husband was a doctor and left her a little money. She came up from the South to educate this boy. Both of them worked hard and the boy got through college. Three months he hunted for work that a college man might expect to get. You see he had the tremendous handicap of being colored. As the two of them had to live, one day, without her knowing it, he hired himself out as a waiter. He has been one now for two years. He is evidently goodness itself to his mother.

RACHEL (*Slowly and thoughtfully*): Just because he is *colored!* (*Pauses*). We sing a song at school, I believe, about "The land of the free and the home of the brave." What an amusing nation it is.

MRS. LOVING (*Watching Rachel anxiously*): Come, Rachel, you haven't time for "amusing nations." Remember, you haven't practised any this afternoon. And put your books away; don't leave them on the table. You didn't practise any this morning either, did you?

RACHEL: No, Ma dear,—didn't wake up in time. (*Goes to the table and in an abstracted manner puts books on the bookcase; returns to the table; picks up the roll of sheet music she has brought home with her; brightens; impulsively*) Ma dear, just listen to this lullaby. It's the sweetest thing. I was so "daffy" over it, one of the girls at school lent it to me. (*She rushes to the piano with the music and plays the accompaniment through softly and then sings, still softly and with great expression, Jessie Gaynor's "Slumber Boat"*)—

Baby's boat's the silver moon;
Sailing in the sky,
Sailing o'er the sea of sleep,
While the clouds float by.

Sail, baby, sail,
Out upon that sea,
Only don't forget to sail
Back again to me.

Baby's fishing for a dream,
Fishing near and far,
His line a silver moonbeam is,
His bait a silver star.

Sail, baby, sail, etc.

Listen, Ma dear, right here. Isn't it lovely? (*Plays and sings very softly and slowly*):

"Only don't forget to sail
Back again to me."

(*Pauses; in hushed tones*) Ma dear, it's so beautiful—it—it hurts.

MRS. LOVING (*Quietly*): Yes, dear, it is pretty.

RACHEL (*For several minutes watches her mother's profile from the piano stool. Her expression is rather wistful*): Ma dear!

MRS. LOVING: Yes, Rachel.

RACHEL: What's the matter?

MRS. LOVING (*Without turning*): Matter! What do you mean?

RACHEL: I don't know. I just *feel* something is not quite right with you.

MRS. LOVING: I'm only tired—that's all.

RACHEL: Perhaps. But—(*Watches her mother a moment or two longer; shakes her head; turns back to the piano. She is thoughtful; looks at her hands in her lap*). Ma dear, wouldn't it be nice if we could keep all the babies in the world—always little babies? Then they'd be always little, and cunning, and lovable; and they could never grow up, then, and—and—be bad. I'm so sorry for mothers, whose little babies—grow up—and—and—are bad.

MRS. LOVING (*Startled; controlling herself, looks at Rachel anxiously, perplexedly. Rachel's eyes are still on her hands. Attempting a light tone*): Come, Rachel, what experience have you had with mothers whose babies have grown up to be bad? You—you talk like an old, old woman.

RACHEL (*Without raising her eyes, quietly*): I *know* I'm not old; but, just the same I know that is true. (*Softly*) And I'm so sorry for the mothers.

MRS. LOVING (*With a forced laugh*): Well, Miss Methuselah, how do you happen to know all this? Mothers whose babies grow up to be bad don't, as a rule, parade their faults before the world.

RACHEL: That's just it—that's *how* you know. They don't talk at all.

MRS. LOVING (*Involuntarily*): Oh! (*Ceases to sew; looks at Rachel sharply; she is plainly worried. There is a long silence. Presently Rachel raises her eyes to Raphael's "Madonna" over the piano. Her expression becomes rapt; then, very softly, her eyes still on the picture, she plays and sings Nevin's "Mighty Lak A Rose"*)—

Sweetest li'l feller,
Ev'rybody knows;
Dunno what to call him,
But he mighty lak' a rose!
Lookin' at his Mammy
Wid eyes so shiny blue,
Mek' you think that heav'n
Is comin' clost ter you!

W'en his dar a sleepin'
In his li'l place
Think I see de angels
Lookin' thro' de lace.
W'en de dark is fallin',
W'en de shadders creep,
Den dey comes on tip-toe,
Ter kiss him in his sleep.

Sweetest li'l feller, etc.

(*With head still raised, after she has finished, she closes her eyes. Half to herself and slowly*) I think the loveliest thing of all the lovely things in this world is just (*almost in a whisper*) being a mother!

MRS. LOVING (*Turns and laughs*): Well, of all the startling children, Rachel! I am getting to feel, when you're around, as though I'm shut up with dynamite. What next? (*Rachel rises, goes slowly to her mother, and kneels down beside her. She does not touch her mother*). Why so serious, chickabiddy?

RACHEL (*Slowly and quietly*): It is not kind to laugh at sacred things. When you laughed, it was as though you laughed—at God!

MRS. LOVING (*Startled*): Rachel !

RACHEL (*Still quietly*): It's true. It was the best in me that said that—it was God! (*Pauses*). And, Ma dear, if I believed that I should grow up and not be a mother, I'd pray to die now. I've thought about it a lot, Ma dear, and once I dreamed, and a voice said to me—oh! it was so real—"Rachel, you are to be a mother to little children." Wasn't that beautiful? Ever since I have known how Mary felt at the "Annunciation." (*Almost in a whisper*) God spoke to me through some one, and I believe. And it has explained so much to me. I know now why I just can't resist any child. I have to love it—it calls me—it—draws me. I want to take care of it, wash it, dress it, live for it. I want the feel of its little warm body against me, its breath on my neck, its hands against my face.

(*Pauses thoughtfully for a few moments*). Ma dear, here's something I don't understand: I love the little black and brown babies best of all. There is something about them that—that—clutches at my heart. Why—why—should they be—oh!—pathetic? I don't understand. It's dim. More than the other babies, I feel that I must protect them. They're in danger, but from what? I don't know. I've tried so hard to understand, but I can't. (*Her face radiant and beautiful*). Ma dear, I think their white teeth and the clear whites of their big black eyes and their dimples everywhere—are—are (*Breaks off*). And, Ma dear, because I love them best, I pray God every night to give me, when I grow up, little black and brown babies—to protect and guard. (*Wistfully*). Now, Ma dear, don't you see why you must never laugh at me again? Dear, dear, Ma dear? (*Buries her head in her mother's lap and sobs*).

MRS. LOVING (*For a few seconds, sits as though dazed, and then instinctively begins to caress the head in her lap. To herself*) And I suppose my experience is every mother's. Sooner or later—of a sudden she finds her own child a stranger to her. (*To Rachel, very tenderly*) Poor little girl! Poor little chickabiddy!

RACHEL (*Raising her head*): Why do you say, "Poor little girl," like that? I don't understand. Why, Ma dear, I never saw tears in your eyes before. Is it—is it—because you know the things I do not understand? Oh! it *is* that.

MRS. LOVING (*Simply*): Yes, Rachel, and I cannot save you.

RACHEL: Ma dear, you frighten me. Save me from *what?*

MRS. LOVING: Just life, my little chickabiddy!

RACHEL: Is life so terrible? I had found it mostly beautiful. How can life be terrible, when the world is full of little children?

MRS. LOVING (*Very sadly*): Oh, Rachel! Rachel!

RACHEL: Ma dear, what have I said?

MRS. LOVING (*Forcing a smile*): Why, the truth, of course, Rachel. Life is not terrible when there are little children—and you—and Tom—and a roof over our heads—and work—and food—and clothes—and sleep at night. (*Pauses*). Rachel, I am not myself today. I'm tired. Forget what I've said. Come, chickabiddy, wipe your eyes and smile. That's only an imitation smile, but it's better than none. Jump up now, and light the lamp for me, will you? Tom's late, isn't he? I shall want you to go, too, for the rolls and pie for supper.

RACHEL (*Rises rather wearily and goes into the kitchenette. While she is out of the room Mrs. Loving does not move. She sits staring in front of her. The room for some time has been growing dark. Mrs. Loving can just be seen when Rachel reenters with the lamp. She places it on the small table near her mother, adjusts it, so the light falls on her mother's work, and then lowers the window shades at the windows. She still droops. Mrs. Loving, while Rachel is in the room, is industrious. Rachel puts on her hat and coat listlessly. She does not look in the glass*): Where is the money, Ma dear? I'm ready.

MRS. LOVING: Before you go, Rachel, just give a look at the meat and see if it is cooking all right, will you, dearie?

RACHEL (*Goes out into the kitchenette and presently returns*): It's all right, Ma dear.

MRS. LOVING (*While Rachel is out of the room, she takes her pocket-book out of the machine-drawer, opens it, takes out money and gives it to Rachel upon her return*): A dozen brown rolls, Rachel. Be sure they're brown! And, I guess,—an apple pie. As you and Tom never seem to get enough apple pie, get the largest she has. And here is a quarter. Get some candy—any kind *you* like, chickabiddy. Let's have a party tonight, I feel extravagant. Why, Rachel! why are you crying?

RACHEL: Nothing, dear Ma dear. I'll be all right when I get in the air. Goodbye! (*Rushes out of the flat. Mrs. Loving sits idle. Presently the outer door of the flat opens and shuts with a bang, and Tom appears. Mrs. Loving begins to work as soon as she hears the banging door*).

TOM: 'Lo, Ma! Where's Sis,—out? The door's off the latch. (*Kisses his mother and hangs hat in entryway*)

MRS. LOVING (*Greeting him with the same beautiful smile with which she greeted Rachel*): Rachel just went after the rolls and pie. She'll be back in a few minutes. You're late, Tommy.

TOM: No, Ma—you forget—it's pay day. (*With decided shyness and awkwardness he hands her his wages*). Here, Ma!

MRS. LOVING (*Proudly counting it*): But, Tommy, this is every bit of it. You'll need some.

TOM: Not yet! (*Constrainedly*) I only wish—. Say, Ma, I hate to see you work so hard. (*Fiercely*) Some day—some day—. (*Breaks off*).

MRS. LOVING: Son, I'm as proud as though you had given me a million dollars.

TOM (*Emphatically*): I may some day,—you see. (*Abruptly changing the subject*): Gee! Ma, I'm hungry. What's for dinner? Smell's good.

MRS. LOVING: Lamb and dumplings and rice.

TOM: Gee! I'm glad I'm living—and a pie too?

MRS. LOVING: Apple pie, Tommy.

TOM: Say, Ma, don't wake me up. And shall "muzzer's" own little boy set the table?

MRS. LOVING: Thank you, Son.

TOM (*Folds the green cloth, hangs it over the back of the armchair, gets white table-cloth from kitchenette and sets the table. The whole time he is whistling blithely a popular air. He lights one of the gas jets over the table*): Ma!

MRS. LOVING: Yes, Son.

TOM: I made "squad" today,—I'm quarterback. Five other fellows tried to make it. We'll all have to buy new hats, now.

MRS. LOVING (*With surprise*): Buy new hats! Why?

TOM (*Makes a ridiculous gesture to show that his head and hers are both swelling*): Honest, Ma, I had to carry my hat in my hand tonight,—couldn't even get it to perch aloft.

MRS. LOVING (*Smiling*): Well, I for one, Son, am not going to say anything to make you more conceited.

TOM: You don't *have* to say anything. Why, Ma, ever since I told you, you can almost look down your own back your head is so high. What? (*Mrs. Loving laughs. The outer door of the flat opens and shuts. Rachel's voice is heard*)

RACHEL (*Without*): My! that was a "dreffful" climb, wasn't it? Ma, I've got something here for you. (*Appears in the doorway carrying packages and leading a little boy by the hand. The little fellow is shy but smiling*). Hello, Tommy! Here, take these things for me. This is Jimmy. Isn't he a dear? Come, Jimmy. (*Tom carries the packages into the kitchenette. Rachel leads Jimmy to Mrs. Loving*). Ma dear, this is my brown baby. I'm going to take him right down stairs again. His mother is as sweet as can be, and let me bring him up just to see you. Jimmy, this is Ma dear. (*Mrs. Loving turns expectantly to see the child. Standing before her, he raises his face to hers with an engaging smile. Suddenly, without word or warning, her body stiffens; her hands grip her sewing convulsively; her eyes stare. She makes no sound*).

RACHEL (*Frightened*): Ma dear! What is the matter? Tom! Quick! (*Tom reenters and goes to them*).

MRS. LOVING (*Controlling herself with an effort and breathing hard*): Nothing, dears, nothing. I must be—I am—nervous tonight. (*With a forced smile*) How do-you-do, Jimmy? Now, Rachel—perhaps—don't you think—you had better take him back to his mother? Good-night, Jimmy! (*Eyes the child in a fascinated way the whole time he is in the room. Rachel, very much perturbed, takes the child out*). Tom, open that window, please! There! That's better! (*Still breathing deeply*). What a fool I am!

TOM (*Patting his mother awkwardly on the back*): You're all pegged out, that's the trouble—working entirely too hard. Can't you stop for the night and go to bed right after supper?

MRS. LOVING: I'll see, Tommy dear. Now, I must look after the supper.

TOM: Huh! Well, I guess not. How old do you think Rachel and I are anyway? I see; you think we'll break some of this be-au-tiful Hav-i-land china, we bought at the "Five and Ten Cent Store." (*To Rachel who has just reentered wearing a puzzled and worried expression. She is without hat and coat*). Say, Rachel, do you think you're old enough?

RACHEL: Old enough for what, Tommy?

TOM: To dish up the supper for Ma.

RACHEL (*With attempted sprightliness*): Ma dear thinks nothing can go on in this little flat unless she does it. Let's show her a thing or two. (*They bring in the dinner. Mrs. Loving with trembling hands tries to sew. Tom and Rachel watch her covertly. Presently she gets up.*)

MRS. LOVING: I'll be back in a minute, children. (*Goes out the door that leads to the other rooms of the flat. Tom and Rachel look at each other*).

RACHEL (*In a low voice keeping her eyes on the door*): Why do you suppose she acted so strangely about Jimmy?

TOM: Don't know—nervous, I guess,—worn out. I wish—(*Breaks off*).

RACHEL (*Slowly*): It may be that; but she hasn't been herself this afternoon. I wonder—. Look out! Here she comes!

TOM (*In a whisper*): Liven her up. (*Rachel nods. Mrs. Loving reenters. Both rush to her and lead her to her place at the right end of the table. She smiles and tries to appear cheerful. They sit down, Tom opposite Mrs. Loving and Rachel at the side facing front. Mrs Loving asks grace. Her voice trembles. She helps the children bountifully, herself sparingly. Every once in a while she stops eating and stares blankly into her plate; then, remembering where she is suddenly, looks around with a start and goes on eating. Tom and Rachel appear not to notice her*).

TOM: Ma's "some" cook, isn't she?

RACHEL: Is she! Delmonico's isn't in it.

TOM (*Presently*): Say, Rachel, do you remember that Reynolds boy in the fourth year?

RACHEL: Yes. You mean the one who is flat-nosed, freckled, and who squints and sneers?

TOM (*Looking at Rachel admiringly*): The same.

RACHEL (*Vehemently*): I hate him!

MRS. LOVING: Rachel, you do use such violent language. Why hate him?

RACHEL: I do—that's all.

TOM: Ma, if you saw him just once, you'd understand. No one likes him. But, then, what can you expect? His father's in "quod" doing time for something, I don't know just what. One of the fellows says he has a real decent mother, though. She never mentions him in any way, shape or form, he says. Hard on her, isn't it? Bet I'd keep my head shut too;—you'd never get a yap out of me. (*Rachel looks up quickly at her mother; Mrs. Loving stiffens perceptibly, but keeps her eyes on her plate. Rachel catches Tom's eye; silently draws his attention to their mother; and shakes her head warningly at him*).

TOM (*Continuing hastily and clumsily*): Well, anyway, he called me "Nigger" today. If his face isn't black, his eye is.

RACHEL: Good! Oh! Why did you let the other one go?

TOM (*Grinning*): I knew he said things behind my back; but today he was hopping mad, because I made quarterback. He didn't!

RACHEL: Oh, Tommy! How lovely! Ma dear, did you hear that? (*Chants*) Our Tommy's on the team! Our Tommy's on the team!

TOM (*Trying not to appear pleased*): Ma dear, what did I say about er—er "capital" enlargements?

MRS. LOVING (*Smiling*): You're right, Son.

TOM: I hope you got that "capital," Rachel. How's that for Latin knowledge? Eh?

RACHEL: I don't think much of your knowledge, Tommy dear; but (*continuing to chant*) Our Tommy's on the team! Our Tommy's on the team! Our—(*Breaks off*). I've a good mind to kiss you.

TOM (*Threateningly*): Don't you dare.

RACHEL (*Rising and going toward him*): I will! I will! I will!

TOM (*Rising, too, and dodging her*): No, you don't, young lady. (*A tremendous tussle and scuffle ensues*).

MRS. LOVING (*Laughing*): For Heaven's sake! children, do stop playing and eat your supper. (*They nod brightly at each other behind her back and return smiling to the table*).

RACHEL (*Sticking out her tongue at Tom*): I will!

TOM (*Mimicking her*): You won't!

MRS. LOVING: Children! (*They eat for a time in silence*).

RACHEL: Ma dear, have you noticed Mary Shaw doesn't come here much these days?

MRS. LOVING: Why, that's so, she doesn't. Have you two quarreled?

RACHEL: No, Ma dear. (*Uncomfortably*). I—think I know the reason—but I don't like to say, unless I'm certain.

TOM: Well, I know. I've seen her lately with those two girls who have just come from the South. Twice she bowed stiffly, and the last time made believe she didn't see me.

RACHEL: Then you think—? Oh! I was afraid it was that.

TOM (*Bitterly*): Yes—we're "niggers"—that's why.

MRS. LOVING (*Slowly and sadly*): Rachel, that's one of the things I can't save you from. I worried considerably about Mary, at first—you do take your friendships so seriously. I knew exactly how it would end. (*Pauses*). And then I saw that if Mary Shaw didn't teach you the lesson—some one else would. They don't want you, dearies, when you and they grow up. You may have everything in your favor—but they don't *dare* to like you.

RACHEL: I know all that is generally true—but I had hoped that Mary—(*Breaks off*).

TOM: Well, I guess we can still go on living even if people don't speak to us. I'll never bow to *her* again—that's certain.

MRS. LOVING: But, Son, that wouldn't be polite, if she bowed to you first.

TOM: Can't help it. I guess I can be blind, too.

MRS. LOVING (*Wearily*): Well—perhaps you are right—I don't know. It's the way I feel about it too—but—but I wish my son always to be a *gentleman.*

TOM: If being a *gentleman* means not being a *man*—I don't wish to be one.

RACHEL: Oh! well, perhaps we're wrong about Mary—I hope we are. (*Sighs*). Anyway, let's forget it. Tommy guess what I've got. (*Rises, goes out into entryway swiftly, and returns holding up a small bag*). Ma dear treated. Guess!

TOM: Ma, you're a thoroughbred. Well, let's see—it's—a dozen dill pickles?

RACHEL: Oh! stop fooling.

TOM: I'm not. Tripe?

RACHEL: Silly!

TOM: Hog's jowl?

RACHEL: Ugh! Give it up—quarter-back.

TOM: Pig's feet?

RACHEL (*In pretended disgust*): Oh! Ma dear—send him from the table. It's CANDY!

TOM: Candy? Funny, I never thought of that! And I was just about to say some nice, delicious chitlings. Candy! Well! Well! (*Rachel disdainfully carries the candy to her mother, returns to her own seat with the bag and helps herself. She ignores Tom*).

TOM (*In an aggrieved voice*): You see, Ma, how she treats me. (*In affected tones*) I have a good mind, young lady to punish you, er—er corporeally speaking. Tut! Tut! I have a mind to master thee—I mean—you. Methinks that if I should advance upon you, apply, perchance, two or three digits to your glossy locks and extract—aha!—say, a strand—you would no more defy me. (*He starts to rise*).

MRS. LOVING (*Quickly and sharply*): Rachel! give Tom the candy and stop playing. (*Rachel obeys. They eat in silence. The old depression returns. When the candy is all gone, Rachel pushes her chair back, and is just about to rise, when her mother, who is very evidently nerving herself for something, stops her*). Just a moment, Rachel. (*Pauses, continuing slowly and very seriously*). Tom and Rachel! I have been trying to make up my mind for some time whether a certain thing is my duty or not. Today—I have decided it is. You are old enough, now,—and I see you ought to be told. Do you know what day this is? (*Both Tom and Rachel have been watching their mother intently*). It's the sixteenth of October. Does that mean anything to either of you?

TOM and RACHEL (*Wonderingly*): No.

MRS. LOVING (*Looking at both of them thoughtfully, half to herself*): No—I don't know why it should. (*Slowly*) Ten years ago—today—your father and your half-brother died.

TOM: I do remember, now, that you told us it was in October.

RACHEL (*With a sigh*): That explains—today.

MRS. LOVING: Yes, Rachel. (*Pauses*). Do you know—how they—died?

TOM and RACHEL: Why, no.

MRS. LOVING: Did it ever strike you as strange—that they—died—the same day?

TOM: Well, yes.

RACHEL: We often wondered, Tom and I; but—but somehow we never quite dared to ask you. You—you—always refused to talk about them, you know, Ma dear.

MRS. LOVING: Did you think—that—perhaps—the reason—I—I—wouldn't talk about them—was—because, because—I was ashamed—of them? (*Tom and Rachel look uncomfortable*).

RACHEL: Well, Ma dear—we—we—did—wonder.

MRS. LOVING (*Questioningly*): And you thought?

RACHEL (*Haltingly*): W-e-l-l—

MRS. LOVING (*Sharply*): Yes?

TOM: Oh! come, now, Rachel, you know we haven't bothered about it at all. Why should we? We've been happy.

MRS. LOVING: But when you have thought—you've been ashamed? (*Intensely*) Have you?

TOM: Now, Ma, aren't you making a lot out of nothing?

MRS. LOVING (*Slowly*): No. (*Half to herself*) You evade—both—of you. You *have* been ashamed. And I never dreamed until today you *could* take it this way. How blind—how almost criminally blind, I have been.

RACHEL (*Tremulously*): Oh! Ma dear, don't! (*Tom and Rachel watch their mother anxiously and uncomfortably. Mrs. Loving is very evidently nerving herself for something*).

MRS. LOVING (*Very slowly, with restrained emotion*): Tom—and Rachel!

TOM: Ma!

RACHEL: Ma dear! (*A tense, breathless pause*).

MRS. LOVING (*Bracing herself*): They—they—were lynched!!

TOM and RACHEL (*In a whisper*): Lynched!

MRS. LOVING (*Slowly, laboring under strong but restrained emotion*): Yes—by Christian people—in a Christian land. We found out afterwards they were all church members in good standing—the best people. (*A silence*). Your father was a man among men. He was a fanatic. He was a Saint!

TOM (*Breathing with difficulty*): Ma—can you—will you—tell us—about it?

MRS. LOVING: I believe it to be my duty. (*A silence*). When I married your father I was a widow. My little George was seven years old. From the very beginning he worshiped your father. He followed him around—just like a little dog. All children were like that with him. I myself have never seen anybody like him. "Big" seems to fit him better than any other word. He was big-bodied—big-souled. His loves were big and his hates. You can imagine, then, how the wrongs of the Negro—ate into his soul. (*Pauses*). He was utterly fearless. (*A silence*). He edited and owned, for several years, a small negro paper. In it he said a great many daring things. I used to plead with him to be more careful. I was always afraid for him. For a long time, nothing happened—he was too important to the community. And then—one night—ten years ago—a mob made up of the respectable people in the town lynched an innocent black man—and what was worse—they knew him to be innocent. A white man was guilty. I never saw your father so wrought up over anything: he couldn't eat; he couldn't sleep; he brooded night and day over it. And then—realizing fully the great risk he was running, although I begged him not to—and all his friends also—he deliberately and calmly went to work and published a most terrific denunciation of that mob. The old prophets in the Bible were not more terrible than he. A day or two later, he received an anonymous letter, very evidently from an educated man, calling upon him to retract his words in the next issue. If he refused his life was threatened. The next week's issue contained an arraignment as frightful, if not more so, than the previous one. Each word was white-hot, searing. That night, some dozen masked men came to our house.

RACHEL (*Moaning*): Oh, Ma dear! Ma dear!

MRS. LOVING (*Too absorbed to hear*): We were not asleep—your father and I. They broke down the front door and made their way to our bedroom. Your father kissed me—and took up his revolver. It was always loaded. They broke down the door. (*A silence. She continues slowly and quietly*) I tried to shut my eyes—I could not. Four masked men fell—they did not move any more—after a little. (*Pauses*). Your father was finally overpowered and dragged out. In the hall—my little seventeen-year-old George tried to rescue him. Your father begged him not to interfere. He paid no attention. It ended in their dragging them both out. (*Pauses*). My little George—was—a man! (*Controls herself with an effort*). He never made an outcry. His last words to me were: "Ma, I am glad to go with Father." I could only nod to him. (*Pauses*). While they were dragging them down the steps, I crept into the room where you were. You were both asleep. Rachel, I remember, was smiling. I knelt down by you—and covered my ears with my hands—and waited. I could not pray—I couldn't for a long time—afterwards. (*A silence*). It was very still when I finally uncovered my ears. The only sounds were the faint rustle of leaves and the "tap-tapping of the twig of a tree" against the window. I hear it still—sometimes in my dreams. *It was the tree—where they were.* (*A silence*). While I had knelt there waiting—I had made up my mind what to do. I dressed myself and then I woke you both up and dressed you. (*Pauses*). We set forth. It was a black, still night. Alternately dragging you along and carrying you—I walked five miles to the house of some friends. They took us in, and we remained there until I had seen my dead laid comfortably at rest. They lent me money to come North—I couldn't bring you up—in the South. (*A silence*). Always remember this: There never lived anywhere—or at any time—any two whiter or more beautiful souls. God gave me one for a husband and one for a son and I am proud. (*Brokenly*) You—must—be—proud—too. (*A long silence. Mrs. Loving bows her head in her hands. Tom controls himself with an effort. Rachel creeps softly to her mother, kneels beside her and lifts the hem of her dress to her lips. She does not dare touch her. She adores her with her eyes*).

MRS. LOVING (*Presently raising her head and glancing at the clock*): Tom, it's time, now, for you to go to work. Rachel and I will finish up here.

TOM (*Still laboring under great emotion goes out into the entryway and comes back and stands in the doorway with his *cap. He twirls it around and around nervously*): I want you to know, Ma, before I go—how—how proud I am. Why, I didn't believe two people could be like that—and live. And then to find out that one—was your own father—and one—your own brother.—It's wonderful! I'm—not much yet, Ma, but—I've—I've just got to be something now. (*Breaks off*). (*His face becomes distorted with passion and hatred*). When I think—when I think—of those devils with white skins—living somewhere today—living and happy—I—see—red! I—I—goodbye! (*Rushes out, the door bangs*).

MRS. LOVING (*Half to herself*): I was afraid—of just that. I wonder—if I did the wise thing—after all.

RACHEL (*With a gesture infinitely tender, puts her arms around her mother*): Yes, Ma dear, you did. And, hereafter, Tom and I share and share alike with you. To think, Ma dear, of ten years of this—all alone. It's wicked! (*A short silence*).

MRS. LOVING: And, Rachel, about that dear, little boy, Jimmy.

RACHEL: Now, Ma dear, tell me tomorrow. You've stood enough for one day.

MRS. LOVING: No, it's better over and done with—all at once. If I had seen that dear child suddenly any other day than this—I might have borne it better. When he lifted his little face to me—and smiled—for a moment—I thought it was the end—of all things. Rachel, he is the image of my boy—my George!

RACHEL: Ma dear!

MRS. LOVING: And, Rachel—it will hurt—to see him again.

RACHEL: I understand, Ma dear. (*A silence. Suddenly*) Ma dear, I am beginning to see—to understand—so much. (*Slowly and thoughtfully*) Ten years ago, all things being equal, Jimmy might have been—George? Isn't that so?

MRS. LOVING: Why—yes, if I understand you.

RACHEL: I guess that doesn't sound very clear. It's only getting clear to me, little by little. Do you mind my thinking out loud to you?

MRS. LOVING: No, chickabiddy.

RACHEL: If Jimmy went South now—and grew up—he might be—a George?

MRS. LOVING: Yes.

RACHEL: Then, the South is full of tens, hundreds, thousands of little boys, who, one day may be—and some of them with certainty—Georges?

MRS. LOVING: Yes, Rachel.

RACHEL: And the little babies, the dear, little, helpless babies, being born today—now—and those who will be, tomorrow, and all the tomorrows to come—have *that* sooner or later to look forward to? They will laugh and play and sing and be happy and grow up, perhaps, and be ambitious—just for *that?*

MRS. LOVING: Yes, Rachel.

RACHEL: Then, everywhere, everywhere, throughout the South, there are hundreds of dark mothers who live in fear, terrible, suffocating fear, whose rest by night is broken, and whose joy by day in their babies on their hearts is three parts—pain. Oh, I know this is true—for this is the way I should feel, if I were little Jimmy's *mother.* How horrible! Why—it would be more merciful—to strangle the little things at birth. And so this nation—this white Christian nation—has deliberately set its curse upon the most beautiful—the most holy thing in life—motherhood! Why—it—makes—you doubt—God!

MRS. LOVING: Oh, hush! little girl. Hush!

RACHEL (*Suddenly with a great cry*): Why, Ma dear, *you know. You* were a *mother, George's mother.* So, this is what it means. Oh, Ma dear! Ma dear! (*Faints in her mother's arms*).

★

ACT II.

TIME: *October sixteenth, four years later; seven o'clock in the morning.*

PLACE: *The same room. There have been very evident improvements made. The room is not so bare; it is cosier. On the shelf, before each window, are potted red geraniums. At the windows are green denim drapery curtains covering fresh white dotted Swiss inner curtains. At each doorway are green denim portieres. On the wall between the kitchenette and the entrance to the outer rooms of the flat, a new picture is hanging, Millet's "The Man with the Hoe." Hanging against the side of the run that faces front is Watts's "Hope." There is another easy-chair at the left front. The table in the center is covered with a white table-cloth. A small asparagus fern is in the middle of this. When the curtain rises there is the clatter of dishes in the kitchenette.*

Presently Rachel enters with dishes and silver in her hands. She is clad in a bungalow apron. She is noticeably all of four years older. She frowns as she sets the table. There is a set expression about the mouth. A child's voice is heard from the rooms within.

JIMMY (*Still unseen*): Ma Rachel!

RACHEL (*Pauses and smiles*): What is it, Jimmy boy?

JIMMY (*Appearing in rear doorway, half-dressed, breathless, and tremendously excited over something. Rushes toward Rachel*): Three guesses! Three guesses! Ma Rachel!

RACHEL (*Her whole face softening*): Well, let's see—maybe there is a circus in town.

JIMMY: No siree! (*In a sing-song*) You're not right! You're not right!

RACHEL: Well, maybe Ma Loving's going to take you somewhere.

JIMMY: No! (*Vigorously shaking his head*) It's—

RACHEL (*Interrupting quickly*): You said I could have three guesses, honey. I've only had two.

JIMMY: I thought you had three. How many are three?

RACHEL (*Counting on her fingers*): One! Two! Three! I've only had one! two!—See? Perhaps Uncle Tom is going to give you some candy.

JIMMY (*Dancing up and down*): No! No! No! (*Catches his breath*) I leaned over the bath-tub, way over, and got hold of the chain with the button on the end, and dropped it into the little round place in the bottom. And then I runned lots and lots of water in the tub and climbed over and fell in splash! just like a big stone; (*Loudly*) and took a bath all by myself alone.

RACHEL (*Laughing and hugging him*): All by yourself, honey? You ran the water, too, boy, not "runned" it. What I want to know is, where was Ma Loving all this time?

JIMMY: I stole in "creepy-creep" and looked at Ma Loving and she was awful fast asleep. (*Proudly*) Ma Rachel, I'm a "nawful," big boy now, aren't I? I are almost a man, aren't I?

RACHEL: Oh! Boy, I'm getting tired of correcting you—"I am almost a man, am I not?" Jimmy, boy, what will Ma Rachel do, if you grow up? Why, I won't have a little boy any more! Honey, you mustn't grow up, do you hear? You mustn't.

JIMMY: Oh, yes, I must; and you'll have me just the same, Ma Rachel. I'm going to be a policeman and make lots of money for you and Ma Loving and Uncle Tom, and I'm going to buy you some trains and fire-engines, and little, cunning ponies, and some rabbits, and some great 'normous banks full of money—lots of it. And then, we are going to live in a great, big castle and eat lots of ice cream, all the time, and drink lots and lots of nice pink lemonade.

RACHEL: What a generous Jimmy boy! (*Hugs him*). Before I give you "morning kiss," I must see how clean my boy is. (*Inspects teeth, ears and neck*). Jimmy, you're sweet and clean enough to eat. (*Kisses him; he tries to strangle her with hugs*). Now the hands. Oh! Jimmy, look at those nails! Oh! Jimmy! (*Jimmy wriggles and tries to get his hands away*). Honey, get my file off of my bureau and go to Ma Loving; she must be awake by this time. Why, honey, what's the matter with your feet?

JIMMY: I don't know. I thought they looked kind of queer, myself. What's the matter with them?

RACHEL (*Laughing*): You have your shoes on the wrong feet.

JIMMY (*Bursts out laughing*): Isn't that most 'normously funny? I'm a case, aren't I—(*pauses thoughtfully*) I mean—am I not, Ma Rachel?

RACHEL: Yes, honey, a great big case of molasses. Come, you must hurry now, and get dressed. You don't want to be late for school, you know.

JIMMY: Ma Rachel! (*Shyly*) I—I have been making something for you all the morning—ever since I waked up. It's awful nice. It's—stoop down, Ma Rachel, please—a great, big (*puts both arms about her neck and gives her a noisy kiss. Rachel kisses him in return, then pushes his head back. For a long moment they look at each other; and, then, laughing joyously, he makes believe he is a horse, and goes prancing out of the room. Rachel, with a softer, gentler expression, continues setting the table. Presently, Mrs. Loving, bent and worn-looking, appears in the doorway in the rear. She limps a trifle.*)

MRS. LOVING: Good morning, dearie. How's my little girl, this morning? (*Looks around the room*). Why, where's Tom? I was certain I heard him running the water in the tub, sometime ago. (*Limps into the room*).

RACHEL (*Laughing*): Tom isn't up yet. Have you seen Jimmy?

MRS. LOVING: Jimmy? No. I didn't know he was awake, even.

RACHEL (*Going to her mother and kissing her*): Well! What do you think of that! I sent the young gentleman to you, a few minutes ago, for help with his nails. He is very much grown up this morning, so I suppose that explains why he didn't come to you. Yesterday, all day, you know, he was a puppy. No one knows what he will be by tomorrow. All of this, Ma dear, is preliminary to telling you that Jimmy boy has stolen a march on you, this morning.

MRS. LOVING: Stolen a march! How?

RACHEL: It appears that he took his bath all by himself and, as a result, he is so conceited, peacocks aren't in it with him.

MRS. LOVING: I heard the water running and thought, of course, it was Tom. Why, the little rascal! I must go and see how he has left things. I was just about to wake him up.

RACHEL: Rheumatism's not much better this morning, Ma dear. (*Confronting her mother*) Tell me the truth, now, did you or did you not try that liniment I bought you yesterday?

MRS. LOVING (*Guiltily*): Well, Rachel, you see—it was this way, I was—I was so tired, last night,—I—I really forgot it.

RACHEL: I thought as much. Shame on you!

MRS. LOVING: As soon as I walk around a bit it will be all right. It always is. It's bad, when I first get up—that's all. I'll be spry enough in a few minutes. (*Limps to the door; pauses*) Rachel, I don't know why the thought should strike me, but how very strangely things turn out. If any one had told me four years ago that Jimmy would be living with us, I should have laughed at him. Then it hurt to see him; now it would hurt not to. (*Softly*) Rachel, sometimes—I wonder—if, perhaps, God—hasn't relented a little—and given me back my boy,—my George.

RACHEL: The whole thing was strange, wasn't it?

MRS. LOVING: Yes, God's ways are strange and often very beautiful; perhaps all would be beautiful—if we only understood.

RACHEL: God's ways are certainly very mysterious. Why, of all the people in this apartment-house, should Jimmy's father and mother be the only two to take the smallpox, and the only two to die. It's queer!

MRS. LOVING: It doesn't seem like two years ago, does it?

RACHEL: Two years, Ma dear! Why it's three the third of January.

MRS. LOVING: Are you sure, Rachel?

RACHEL (*Gently*): I don't believe I could ever forget that, Ma dear.

MRS. LOVING: No, I suppose not. That is one of the differences between youth and old age—youth attaches tremendous importance to dates,—old age does not.

RACHEL (*Quickly*): Ma dear, don't talk like that. You're not old.

MRS. LOVING: Oh! yes, I am, dearie. It's sixty long years since I was born; and I am much older than that, much older.

RACHEL: Please, Ma dear, please!

MRS. LOVING (*Smiling*): Very well, dearie, I won't say it any more. (*A pause*). By the way,—how—does Tom strike you, these days?

RACHEL (*Avoiding her mother's eye*): The same old, bantering, cheerful Tom. Why?

MRS. LOVING: I know he's all that, dearie, but it isn't possible for him to be really cheerful. (*Pauses; goes on wistfully*) When you are little, we mothers can kiss away all the trouble, but when you grow up—and go out—into the world—and get hurt—we are helpless. There is nothing we can do.

RACHEL: Don't worry about Tom, Ma dear, he's game. He doesn't show the white feather.

MRS. LOVING: Did you see him, when he came in, last night?

RACHEL: Yes.

MRS. LOVING: Had he had—any luck?

RACHEL: No. (*Firmly*) Ma dear, we may as well face it—it's hopeless, I'm afraid.

MRS. LOVING: I'm afraid—you are right. (*Shakes her head sadly*) Well, I'll go and see how Jimmy has left things and wake up Tom, if he isn't awake yet. It's the waking up in the mornings that's hard. (*Goes limping out rear door. Rachel frowns as she continues going back and forth between the kitchenette and the table. Presently Tom appears in the door at the rear. He watches Rachel several moments before he speaks or enters. Rachel looks grim enough*).

TOM (*Entering and smiling*): Good-morning, "Merry Sunshine"! Have you, perhaps, been taking a—er—prolonged draught of that very delightful beverage—vinegar? (*Rachel, with a knife in her hand, looks up unsmiling. In pretended fright*) I take it all back, I'm sure. May I request, humbly, that before I press my chaste, morning salute upon your forbidding lips, that you—that you—that you—er—in some way rid yourself of that—er—knife? (*Bows as Rachel puts it down*). I thank you. (*He comes to her and tips her head back; gently*) What's the matter with my little Sis?

RACHEL (*Her face softening*): Tommy dear, don't mind me. I'm getting wicked, I guess. At present I feel just like—like curdled milk. Once upon a time, I used to have quite a nice disposition, didn't I, Tommy?

TOM (*Smiling*): Did you, indeed! I'm not going to flatter you. Well, brace yourself, old lady. Ready, One! Two! Three! Go! (*Kisses her, then puts his hands on either side of her face, and raising it, looks down into it*). You're a pretty, decent little sister, Sis, that's what T. Loving thinks about it; and he knows a thing or two. (*Abruptly looking around*) Has the paper come yet?

RACHEL: I haven't looked, it must have, though, by this time. (*Tom, hands in his pockets, goes into the vestibule. He whistles. The outer door opens and closes, and presently he saunters back, newspaper in hand. He lounges carelessly in the arm-chair and looks at Rachel*).

TOM: May T. Loving be of any service to you?

RACHEL: Service! How?

TOM: May he run, say, any errands, set the table, cook the breakfast? Anything?

RACHEL (*Watching the lazy figure*): You look like working.

TOM (*Grinning*): It's at least—polite—to offer.

RACHEL: You can't do anything; I don't trust you to do it right. You may just sit there, and read your paper—and try to behave yourself.

TOM (*In affectedly meek tones*): Thank you, ma'am. (*Opens the paper, but does not read. Jimmy presently enters riding around the table on a cane. Rachel peeps in from the kitchenette and smiles. Tom puts down his paper*). 'Lo! Big Fellow, what's this?

JIMMY (*Disgustedly*): How can I hear? I'm miles and miles away yet. (*Prances around and around the room; presently stops near Tom, attempting a gruff voice*) Good-morning!

TOM (*Lowering his paper again*): Bless my stars! Who's this? Well, if it isn't Mr. Mason! How-do-you-do, Mr. Mason? That's a beautiful horse you have there. He limps a trifle in his left, hind, front foot, though.

JIMMY: He doesn't!

TOM: He does!

JIMMY (*Fiercely*): He doesn't!

TOM (*As fiercely*): I say he does!

MRS. LOVING (*Appearing in the doorway in the rear*): For Heaven's sake! What is this? Good-morning, Tommy.

TOM (*Rising and going toward his mother, Jimmy following astride of the cane in his rear*): Good-morning, Ma. (*Kisses her; lays his head on her shoulder and makes believe he is crying; in a high falsetto*) Ma! Jimmy says his horse doesn't limp in his hind, front right leg, and I say he does.

JIMMY (*Throws his cane aside, rolls on the floor and kicks up his heels. He roars with laughter*): I think Uncle Tom is funnier than any clown in the "Kickus."

TOM (*Raising his head and looking down at Jimmy; Rachel stands in the kitchenette doorway*): In the *what*, Jimmy?

JIMMY: In the "kickus," of course.

TOM: "Kickus"! "Kickus"! Oh, Lordy! (*Tom and Rachel shriek with laughter; Mrs. Loving looks amused; Jimmy, very much affronted, gets upon his feet again. Tom leans over and swings Jimmy high in the air*). Boy, you'll be the death of me yet. Circus, son! Circus!

JIMMY (*From on high, soberly and with injured dignity*): Well, I thinks "Kickus" and circus are very much alike. Please put me down.

RACHEL (*From the doorway*): We laugh, honey, because we love you so much.

JIMMY (*Somewhat mollified, to Tom*): Is that so, Uncle Tom?

TOM: Surest thing in the world! (*Severely*) Come, get down, young man. Don't you know you'll wear my arms out? Besides, there is something in my lower vest pocket, that's just dying to come to you. Get down, I say.

JIMMY (*Laughing*): How can I get down? (*Wriggles around*).

TOM: How should I know? Just get down, of course. (*Very suddenly puts Jimmy down on his feet. Jimmy tries to climb up over him*).

JIMMY: Please sit down, Uncle Tom?

TOM (*In feigned surprise*): Sit down! What for?

JIMMY (*Pummeling him with his little fists, loudly*): Why, you said there was something for me in your pocket.

TOM (*Sitting down*): So I did. How forgetful I am!

JIMMY (*Finding a bright, shiny penny, shrieks*): Oh! Oh! Oh! (*Climbs up and kisses Tom noisily*).

TOM: Why, Jimmy! You embarrass me. My! My!

JIMMY: What is 'barrass?

TOM: You make me blush.

JIMMY: What's that?

MRS. LOVING: Come, come, children! Rachel has the breakfast on the table. (*Tom sits in Jimmy's place and Jimmy tries to drag him out*).

TOM: What's the matter, now?

JIMMY: You're in *my* place.

TOM: Well, can't you sit in mine?

JIMMY (*Wistfully*): I wants to sit by my Ma Rachel.

TOM: Well, so do I.

RACHEL: Tom, stop teasing Jimmy. Honey, don't you let him bother you; ask him please prettily.

JIMMY: Please prettily, Uncle Tom.

TOM: Oh! well then. (*Gets up and takes his own place. They sit as they did in Act I. only Jimmy sits between Tom, at the end, and Rachel*).

JIMMY (*Loudly*): Oh, goody! goody! goody! We've got sau-sa-ges.

MRS. LOVING: Sh! Jimmy (*Silenced for a few moments; Rachel ties a big napkin around his neck, and prepares his breakfast. He breaks forth again suddenly and excitedly*): Uncle Tom!

TOM: Sir?

JIMMY: I took a bath this morning, all by myself alone, in the bath-tub, and I ranned, no (*Doubtfully*) I runned, I think—the water all in it, and got in it all by myself; and Ma Loving thought it was you; but it was *me*.

TOM (*In feignedly severe tones*): See here, young man, this won't do. Don't you know I'm the only one who is allowed to do that here? It's a perfect waste of water—that's what it is.

JIMMY (*Undaunted*): Oh! no, you're not the only one, 'cause Ma Loving and Ma Rachel and me—alls takes baths every single morning. So, there!

TOM: You 'barrass me. (*Jimmy opens his mouth to ask a question; Tom quickly*) Young gentleman, your mouth is open. Close it, sir; close it.

MRS. LOVING: Tom, you're as big a child exactly as Jimmy.

TOM (*Bowing to right and left*): You compliment me. I thank you, I am sure. (*They finish in silence.*)

JIMMY (*Sighing with contentment*): I'm through, Ma Rachel.

MRS. LOVING: Jimmy, you're a big boy, now, aren't you? (*Jimmy nods his head vigorously and looks proud.*) I wonder if you're big enough to wash your own hands, this morning?

JIMMY (*Shrilly*): Yes, ma'am.

MRS. LOVING: Well, if they're beautifully clean, I'll give you another penny.

JIMMY (*Excitedly to Rachel*): Please untie my napkin, Ma Rachel! (*Rachel does so.*) "Excoose" me, please.

MRS. LOVING AND RACHEL: Certainly. (*Jimmy climbs down and rushes out at the rear doorway.*)

MRS. LOVING (*Solemnly and slowly; breaking the silence*): Rachel, do you know what day this is?

RACHEL (*Looking at her plate; slowly*): Yes, Ma dear.

MRS. LOVING: Tom.

TOM (*Grimly and slowly*): Yes, Ma. (*A silence.*)

MRS. LOVING (*Impressively*): We must never—as long—as we live—forget this day.

RACHEL: No, Ma dear.

TOM: No, Ma.

(*Another silence*)

TOM (*Slowly; as though thinking aloud*): I hear people talk about God's justice—and I wonder. There, are you, Ma. There isn't a sacrifice—that you haven't made. You're still working your fingers to the bone—sewing—just so all of us may keep on living. Rachel is a graduate in Domestic Science; she was high in her class; most of the girls below her in rank have positions in the schools. I'm an electrical engineer—and I've tried steadily for several months—to practice my profession. It seems our educations aren't of much use to us: we aren't allowed to make good—because our skins are dark. (*Pauses*) And, in the South today, there are white men—(*Controls himself*). They have everything; they're well-dressed, well-fed, well-housed; they're prosperous in business; they're important politically; they're pillars in the church. I know all this is true—I've inquired. Their children (our ages, some of them) are growing up around them; and they are having a square deal handed out to them—college, position, wealth, and best of all, freedom, without galling restrictions, to work out their own salvations. With ability, they may become—anything; and all this will be true of their children's children after them. (*A pause*). Look at us—and look at them. We are destined to failure—they, to success. Their children shall grow up in hope; ours, in despair. Our hands are clean;—theirs are red with blood—red with the blood of a noble man—and a boy. They're nothing but low, cowardly, bestial murderers. The scum of the earth shall succeed.—God's justice, I suppose.

MRS. LOVING (*Rising and going to Tom; brokenly*): Tom, promise me—one thing.

TOM (*Rises gently*): What is it, Ma?

MRS. LOVING: That—you'll try—not to lose faith—in God. I've been where you are now—and it's black. Tom, we don't understand God's ways. My son, I know, now—He is beautiful. Tom, won't you try to believe, again?

TOM (*Slowly, but not convincingly*): I'll try, Ma.

MRS. LOVING (*Sighs*): Each one, I suppose, has to work out his own salvation. (*After a pause*) Rachel, if you'll get Jimmy ready, I'll take him to school. I've got to go down town shopping for a customer, this morning. (*Rachel rises and goes out the rear doorway; Mrs. Loving, limping very slightly now, follows. She turns and looks back yearningly at Tom, who has seated himself again, and is staring unseeingly at his plate. She goes out. Tom sits without moving until he hears* MRS. LOVING*'s voice within and Rachel's faintly; then he gets the paper, sits in the arm-chair and pretends to read*).

MRS. LOVING (*From within*): A yard, you say, Rachel? You're sure that will be enough. Oh! you've measured it. Anything else?—What?—Oh! all right. I'll be back by one o'clock, anyway. Good-bye. (*Enters with Jimmy. Both are dressed for the street. Tom looks up brightly at Jimmy*).

TOM: Hello! Big Fellow, where are you taking *my* mother, I'd like to know? This is a pretty kettle of fish.

JIMMY (*Laughing*): Aren't you funny, Uncle Tom! Why, I'm not taking her anywhere. She's taking me. (*Importantly*) I'm going to school.

TOM: Big Fellow, come here. (*Jimmy comes with a rush*). Now, where's that penny I gave you? No, I don't want to see it. All right. Did Ma Loving give you another? (*Vigorous noddings of the head from Jimmy*). I wish you to promise me solemnly—Now, listen! Here, don't wriggle so! not to buy—Listen! too many pints of icecream with my penny. Understand?

JIMMY (*Very seriously*): Yes, Uncle Tom, cross my "tummy"! I promise.

TOM: Well, then, you may go. I guess that will be all for the present. (*Jimmy loiters around looking up wistfully into his face*). Well?

JIMMY: Haven't you—aren't you—isn't you—forgetting something?

TOM (*Grabbing at his pockets*): Bless my stars! what now?

JIMMY: If you could kind of lean over this way. (*Tom leans forward*). No, not that way. (*Tom leans toward the side away from Jimmy*). No, this way, this way! (*Laughs and pummels him with his little fists*). This way!

TOM (*Leaning toward Jimmy*): Well, why didn't you say so, at first?

JIMMY (*Puts his arms around Tom's neck and kisses him*): Good-bye, dear old Uncle Tom. (*Tom catches him and hugs him hard*). I likes to be hugged like that—I can taste—sau-sa-ges.

TOM: You 'barrass me, son. Here, Ma, take your boy. Now remember all I told you, Jimmy.

JIMMY: I 'members.

MRS. LOVING: God bless you, Tom. Good luck.

JIMMY (*To Tom*): God bless you, Uncle Tom. Good luck!

TOM (*Much affected, but with restraint, rising*): Thank you—Good-bye. (*Mrs. Loving and Jimmy go out through the vestibule. Tom lights a cigarette and tries to read the paper. He soon sinks into a brown study. Presently Rachel enters humming. Tom relights his cigarette; and Rachel proceeds to clear the table. In the midst of this, the bell rings three distinct times*).

RACHEL and TOM: John!

TOM: I wonder what's up—It's rather early for him.—I'll go. (*Rises leisurely and goes out into the vestibule. The outer door opens and shuts. Men's voices are heard. Tom and John Strong enter. During the ensuing conversation Rachel finishes clearing the table, takes the fern off, puts on the green table-cloth, places a doily carefully in the centre, and replaces the fern. She apparently pays no attention to the conversation between her brother and Strong. After she has finished, she goes to the kitchenette. The rattle of dishes can be heard now and then*).

RACHEL (*Brightly*): Well, stranger, how does it happen you're out so early in the morning?

STRONG: I hadn't seen any of you for a week, and I thought I'd come by, on my way to work, and find out how things are going. There is no need of asking how you are, Rachel. And the mother and the boy?

RACHEL: Ma dear's rheumatism still holds on.—Jimmy's fine.

STRONG: I'm sorry to hear that your mother is not well. There isn't a remedy going that my mother doesn't know about. I'll get her advice and let you know. (*Turning to Tom*) Well, Tom, how goes it? (*Strong and Tom sit*).

TOM (*Smiling grimly*): There's plenty of "go," but no "git there." (*There is a pause*).

STRONG: I was hoping for better news.

TOM: If I remember rightly, not so many years ago, you tried—and failed. Then, a colored man had hardly a ghost of a show;—now he hasn't even the ghost of a ghost. (*Rachel has finished and goes into the kitchenette*).

STRONG: That's true enough. (*A pause*). What are you going to do?

TOM (*Slowly*): I'll do this little "going act" of mine the rest of the week; (*pauses*) and then, I'll do anything I can get to do. If necessary, I suppose, I can be a "White-wing."

STRONG: Tom, I came—(*Breaks off; continuing slowly*) Six years ago, I found I was up against a stone wall—your experience, you see, to the letter. I couldn't let my mother starve, so I became a waiter. (*Pauses*). I studied waiting; I made a science of it, an art. In a comparatively short time, I'm a head-waiter and I'm up against another stonewall. I've reached my limit. I'm thirty-two now, and I'll die a head-waiter. (*A pause*). College friends, so-called, and acquaintances used to come into the restaurant. One or two at first—attempted to commiserate with me. They didn't do it again. I waited upon them—I did my best. Many of them tipped me. (*Pauses and smiles grimly*). I can remember my first tip, still. They come in yet; many of them are already powers, not only in this city, but in the country. Some of them make a personal request that I wait upon them. I am an artist, now, in my proper sphere. They tip me well, extremely well—the larger the tip, the more pleased they are with me. Because of me, in their own eyes, they're philanthropists. Amusing, isn't it? I can stand their attitude now. My philosophy—learned hard—is to make the best of everything you can, and go on. At best, life isn't so very long. You're wondering why I'm telling you all this. I wish you to see things exactly as they are. There are many disadvantages and some advantages in being a waiter. My mother can live comfortably; I am able, even, to see that she gets some of the luxuries. Tom, it's this way—I can always get you a job as a waiter; I'll teach you the art. If you care to begin the end of the week—all right. And remember this, as long as I keep my job—this offer holds good.

TOM: I—I—(*Breaks off*) Thank you. (*A pause; then smiling wryly*) I guess it's safe enough to say, you'll see me at the end of the week. John you're—(*Breaking off again. A silence interrupted presently by the sound of much vigorous rapping on the outer door of the flat. Rachel appears and crosses over to the vestibule*). Hear the racket! My kiddies gently begging for admittance. It's about twenty minutes of nine, isn't it? (*Tom nods*). I thought so. (*Goes into the entryway; presently reappears with a group of six little girls ranging in age from five to about nine. All are fighting to be close to her; and all are talking at once. There is one exception: the smallest tot is self-possessed and self-sufficient. She carries a red geranium in her hand and gives it her full attention).*

LITTLE MARY: It's my turn to get "Morning kiss" first, this morning, Miss Rachel. You kissed Louise first yesterday. You said you'd kiss us "alphebettically." (*Ending in a shriek*). You promised! (*Rachel kisses Mary, who subsides*).

LITTLE NANCY (*Imperiously*): Now, me. (*Rachel kisses her, and then amid shrieks, recriminations, pulling of hair, jostling, etc., she kisses the rest. The small tot is still oblivious to everything that is going on*).

RACHEL (*Laughing*): You children will pull me limb from limb; and then I'll be all dead; and you'll be sorry—see, if you aren't. (*They fall back immediately. Tom and John watch in amused silence. Rachel loses all self-consciousness, and seems to bloom in the children's midst*). Edith! come here this minute, and let me tie your hair-ribbon again. Nancy, I'm ashamed of you, I saw you trying to pull it off. (*Nancy looks abashed but mischievous*). Louise, you look as sweet as sweet, this morning; and Jenny, where did you get the pretty, pretty dress?

LITTLE JENNY (*Snuffling, but proud*): My mother made it. (*Pauses with more snuffles*). My mother says I have a very bad cold. (*There is a brief silence interruped by the small tot with the geranium*).

LITTLE MARTHA (*In a sweet, little voice*): I—have—a—pitty—'ittle flower.

RACHEL: Honey, it's beautiful. Don't you want "Morning kiss" too?

LITTLE MARTHA: Yes, I do.

RACHEL: Come, honey. (*Rachel kisses her*). Are you going to give the pretty flower to Jenny's teacher? (*Vigorous shakings of the head in denial*). Is it for—mother? (*More shakings of the head*). Is it for—let's see—Daddy? (*More shakings of the head*). I give up. To whom are you going to give the pretty flower, honey?

LITTLE MARTHA (*Shyly*): "Oo."

RACHEL: You, darling!

LITTLE MARTHA: Muzzer and I picked it—for "oo." Here 't is. (*Puts her finger in her mouth, and gives it shyly*).

RACHEL: Well, I'm going to pay you with three big kisses. One! Two! Three!

LITTLE MARTHA: I can count, One! Two! Free! Tan't I? I am going to school soon; and I wants to put the flower in your hair.

RACHEL (*Kneels*): All right, baby. (*Little Martha fumbles and Rachel helps her*).

LITTLE MARTHA (*Dreamily*): Miss Rachel, the 'ittle flower loves you. It told me so. It said it wanted to lie in your hair. It is going to tell you a pitty 'ittle secret. You listen awful hard—and you'll hear. I wish I were a fairy and had a little wand, I'd turn everything into flowers. Wouldn't that be nice, Miss Rachel?

RACHEL: Lovely, honey!

LITTLE JENNY (*Snuffling loudly*): If I were a fairy and had a wand, I'd turn you, Miss Rachel, into a queen—and then I'd always be near you and see that you were happy.

RACHEL: Honey, how beautiful!

LITTLE LOUISE: I'd make my mother happy—if I were a fairy. She cries all the time. My father can't get anything to do.

LITTLE NANCY: If I were a fairy, I'd turn a boy in my school into a spider. I hate him.

RACHEL: Honey, why?

LITTLE NANCY: I'll tell you sometime—I hate him.

LITTLE EDITH: Where's Jimmy, Miss Rachel?

RACHEL: He went long ago; and chickies, you'll have to clear out, all of you, now, or you'll be late. Shoo! Shoo! (*She drives them out prettily before her. They laugh merrily. They all go into the vestibule*).

TOM (*Slowly*): Does it ever strike you—how pathetic and tragic a thing—a little colored child is?

STRONG: Yes.

TOM: Today, we colored men and women, everywhere—are up against it. Every year, we are having a harder time of it. In the South, they make it as impossible as they can for us to get an education. We're hemmed in on all sides. Our one safeguard—the ballot—in most states, is taken away already, or is being taken away. Economically, in a few lines, we have a slight show—but at what a cost! In the North, they make a pretence of liberality: they give us the ballot and a good education, and then—snuff us out. Each year, the problem just to live, gets more difficult to solve. How about these children—if we're fools enough to have any? (*Rachel reenters. Her face is drawn and pale. She returns to the kitchenette.*)

STRONG (*Slowly, with emphasis*): That part—is damnable! (*A silence.*)

TOM (*Suddenly looking at the clock*): It's later than I thought. I'll have to be pulling out of here now, if you don't mind. (*Raising his voice*) Rachel! (*Rachel still drawn and pale, appears in the doorway of the kitchenette. She is without her apron*). I've got to go now, Sis. I leave John in your hands.

STRONG: I've got to go, myself, in a few minutes.

TOM: Nonsense, man! Sit still. I'll begin to think, in a minute, you're afraid of the ladies.

STRONG: I am.

TOM: What! And not ashamed to acknowledge it?

STRONG: No.

TOM: You're lots wiser than I dreamed. So long! (*Gets hat out in the entry-way and returns; smiles wryly.*) "Morituri Salutamus." (*They nod at him—Rachel wistfully. He goes out. There is the sound of an opening and closing door. Rachel sits down. A rather uncomfortable silence, on the part of Rachel, ensues. Strong is imperturbable.*)

RACHEL (*Nervously*): John!

STRONG: Well?

RACHEL: I—I listened.

STRONG: Listened! To what?

RACHEL: To you and Tom.

STRONG: Well,—what of it?

RACHEL: I didn't think it was quite fair not to tell you. It—it seemed, well, like eavesdropping.

STRONG: Don't worry about it. Nonsense!

RACHEL: I'm glad—I want to thank you for what you did for Tom. He needs you, and will need you. You'll help him?

STRONG (*Thoughtfully*): Rachel, each one—has his own little battles. I'll do what I can. After all, an outsider doesn't help much.

RACHEL: But friendship—just friendship—helps.

STRONG: Yes. (*A silence*). Rachel, do you hear anything encouraging from the schools? Any hope for you yet?

RACHEL: No, nor ever will be. I know that now. There's no more chance for me than there is for Tom,—or than there was for you—or for any of us with dark skins. It's lucky for me that I love to keep house, and cook, and sew. I'll never get anything else. Ma dear's sewing, the little work Tom has been able to get, and the little sewing I sometimes get to do—keep us from the poorhouse. We live. According to your philosophy, I suppose, make the best of it—it might be worse.

STRONG (*Quietly*): You don't want to get morbid over these things, you know.

RACHEL (*Scornfully*): That's it. If you see things as they are, you're either pessimistic or morbid.

STRONG: In the long run, do you believe, that attitude of mind—will be—beneficial to you? I'm ten years older than you. I tried your way. I know. Mine is the only sane one. (*Goes over to her slowly; deliberately puts his hands on her hair, and tips her head back. He looks down into her face quietly without saying anything*).

RACHEL (*Nervous and startled*): Why, John, don't! (*He pays no attention, but continues to look down into her face*).

STRONG (*Half to himself*): Perhaps—if you had—a little more fun in your life, your point of view would be—more normal. I'll arrange it so I can take you to some theatre, one night, this week.

RACHEL (*Irritably*): You talk as though I were a—a jellyfish. You'll take me, how do you know I'll go?

STRONG: You will.

RACHEL (*Sarcastically*): Indeed! (*Strong makes no reply*). I wonder if you know how—how—maddening you are. Why, you talk as though my will counts for nothing. It's as if you're trying to master me. I think a domineering man is detestable.

STRONG (*Softly*): If he's, perhaps, the man?

RACHEL (*Hurriedly, as though she had not heard*): Besides, some of these theatres put you off by yourself as though you had leprosy. I'm not going.

STRONG (*Smiling at her*): You know I wouldn't ask you to go, under those circumstances. (*A silence*). Well, I must be going now. (*He takes her hand, and looks at it reverently. Rachel, at first resists; but he refuses to let go. When she finds it useless, she ceases to resist. He turns his head and smiles down into her face*). Rachel, I am coming back to see you, this evening.

RACHEL: I'm sure we'll all be very glad to see you.

STRONG (*Looking at her calmly*): I said—you. (*Very deliberately, he turns her hand palm upwards, leans over and kisses it; then he puts it back into her lap. He touches her cheek lightly*). Good-bye—little Rachel. (*Turns in the vestibule door and looks back, smiling*). Until tonight. (*He goes out. Rachel sits for some time without moving. She is lost in a beautiful day-dream. Presently she sighs happily, and after looking furtively around the room, lifts the palm John has kissed to her lips. She laughs shyly and jumping up, begins to hum. She opens the window at the rear of the room and then commences to thread the sewing-machine. She hums happily the whole time. A light rapping is heard at the outer door. Rachel listens. It stops, and begins again. There is something insistent, and yet hopeless in the sound. Rachel looking puzzled, goes out into the vestibule . . . The door closes. Rachel, a black woman, poorly dressed, and a little ugly, black child come in. There is the stoniness of despair in the woman's face. The child is thin, nervous, suspicious, frightened*).

MRS. LANE (*In a sharp, but toneless voice*): May I sit down? I'm tired.

RACHEL (*Puzzled, but gracious; draws up a chair for her*): Why, certainly.

MRS. LANE: No, you don't know me—never even heard of me—nor I of you. I was looking at the vacant flat on this floor—and saw your name—on your door,—"Loving!" It's a strange name to come across—in this world.—I thought, perhaps, you might give me some information. (*The child hides behind her mother and looks around at Rachel in a frightened way*).

RACHEL (*Smiling at the woman and child in a kindly manner*): I'll be glad to tell you anything, I am able Mrs.—

MRS. LANE: Lane. What I want to know is, how do they treat the colored children in the school I noticed around the corner? (*The child clutches at her mother's dress*).

RACHEL (*Perplexed*): Very well—I'm sure.

MRS. LANE (*Bluntly*): What reason have you for being sure?

RACHEL: Why, the little boy I've adopted goes there; and he's very happy. All the children in this apartment-house go there too; and I know they're happy.

MRS. LANE: Do you know how many colored children there are in the school?

RACHEL: Why, I should guess around thirty.

MRS. LANE: I see. (*Pauses*). What color is this little adopted boy of yours?

RACHEL (*Gently*): Why—he's brown.

MRS. LANE: Any black children there?

RACHEL (*Nervously*): Why—yes.

MRS. LANE: Do you mind if I send Ethel over by the piano to sit?

RACHEL: N—no, certainly not. (*Places a chair by the piano and goes to the little girl holding out her hand. She smiles beautifully. The child gets farther behind her mother*).

MRS. LANE: She won't go to you—she's afraid of everybody now but her father and me. Come Ethel. (*Mrs. Lane takes the little girl by the hand and leads her to the chair. In a gentler voice*) Sit down, Ethel. (*Ethel obeys. When her mother starts back again toward Rachel, she holds out her hands pitifully. She makes no sound*). I'm not going to leave you, Ethel. I'll be right over here. You can see me. (*The look of agony on the child's face, as her mother leaves her, makes Rachel shudder*). Do you mind if we sit over here by the sewing-machine? Thank you. (*They move their chairs*).

RACHEL (*Looking at the little, pitiful figure watching its mother almost unblinkingly*): Does Ethel like apples, Mrs. Lane?

MRS. LANE: Yes.

RACHEL: Do you mind if I give her one?

MRS. LANE: No. Thank you, very much.

RACHEL (*Goes into the kitchenette and returns with a fringed napkin, a plate, and a big, red apple, cut into quarters. She goes to the little girl, who cowers away from her; very gently*). Here, dear, little girl, is a beautiful apple for you. (*The gentle tones have no appeal for the trembling child before her*).

MRS. LANE (*Coming forward*): I'm sorry, but I'm afraid she won't take it from you. Ethel, the kind lady has given you an apple. Thank her nicely. Here! I'll spread the napkin for you, and put the plate in your lap. Thank the lady like a good little girl.

ETHEL (*Very low*): Thank you. (*They return to their seats. Ethel with difficulty holds the plate in her lap. During the rest of the interview between Rachel and her mother, she divides her attention between the apple on the plate and her mother's face. She makes no attempt to eat the apple, but holds the plate in her lap with a care that is painful to watch. Often, too, she looks over her shoulder fearfully. The conversation between Rachel and her mother is carried on in low tones*).

MRS. LANE: I've got to move—it's Ethel.

RACHEL: What is the matter with that child? It's—it's heartbreaking to see her.

MRS. LANE: I understand how you feel,—I don't feel anything, myself, any more. (*A pause*). My husband and I are poor, and we're ugly and we're black. Ethel looks like her father more than she does like me. We live in 55th Street—near the railroad. It's a poor neighborhood, but the rent's cheap. My husband is a porter in a store; and, to help out, I'm a caretaker. (*Pauses*). I don't know why I'm telling you all this. We had a nice little home—and the three of us were happy. Now we've got to move.

RACHEL: Move! Why?

MRS. LANE: It's Ethel. I put her in school this September. She stayed two weeks. (*Pointing to Ethel*) That's the result.

RACHEL (*In horror*): You mean—that just two weeks—in school—did that?

MRS. LANE: Yes. Ethel never had a sick day in her life—before. (*A brief pause*). I took her to the doctor at the end of the two weeks. He says she's a nervous wreck.

RACHEL: But what could they have done to her?

MRS. LANE (*Laughs grimly and mirthlessly*): I'll tell you what they did the first day. Ethel is naturally sensitive and backward. She's not assertive. The teacher saw that, and, after I had left, told her to sit in a seat in the rear of the class. She was alone there—in a corner. The children, immediately feeling there was something wrong with Ethel because of the teacher's attitude, turned and stared at her. When the teacher's back was turned they whispered about her, pointed their fingers at her and tittered. The teacher divided the class into two parts, divisions, I believe, they are called. She forgot all about Ethel, of course, until the last minute, and then, looking back, said sharply: "That little girl there may join this division," meaning the group of pupils standing around her. Ethel naturally moved slowly. The teacher called her sulky and told her to lose a part of her recess. When Ethel came up—the children drew away from her in every direction. She was left standing alone. The teacher then proceeded to give a lesson about kindness to animals. Funny, isn't it, kindness to animals? The children forgot Ethel in the excitement of talking about their pets. Presently, the teacher turned to Ethel and said disagreeably: "Have you a pet?" Ethel said, "Yes," very low. "Come, speak up, you sulky child, what is it?" Ethel said: "A blind puppy." They all laughed, the teacher and all. Strange, isn't it, but Ethel loves that puppy. She spoke up: "It's mean to laugh at a little blind puppy. I'm glad he's blind." This remark brought forth more laughter. "Why are you glad," the teacher asked curiously. Ethel refused to say. (*Pauses*). When I asked her why, do you know what she told me? "If he saw me, he might not love me any more." (*A pause*). Did I tell you that Ethel is only seven years old?

RACHEL (*Drawing her breath sharply*): Oh! I didn't believe any one could be as cruel as that—to a little child.

MRS. LANE: It isn't very pleasant, is it? When the teacher found out that Ethel wouldn't answer, she said severely: "Take your seat!" At recess, all the children went out. Ethel could hear them playing and laughing and shrieking. Even the teacher went too. She was made to sit there all alone—in that big room—because God made her ugly—and black. (*Pauses*). When the recess was half over the teacher came back. "You may go now," she said coldly. Ethel didn't stir. "Did you hear me?" "Yes'm." "Why don't you obey?" "I don't want to go out, please." "You don't, don't you, you stubborn child! Go immediately!" Ethel went. She stood by the school steps. No one spoke to her. The children near her moved away in every direction. They stopped playing, many of them, and watched her. They stared as only children can stare. Some began whispering about her. Presently one child came up and ran her hand roughly over Ethel's face. She looked at her hand and Ethel's face and ran screaming back to the others, "It won't come off! See!" Other children followed the first child's example. Then one boy spoke up loudly: "I know what she is, she's a nigger!" Many took up the cry. God or the devil interfered—the bell rang. The children filed in. One boy boldly called her "Nigger!" before the teacher. She said, "That isn't nice,"—but she smiled at the boy. Things went on about the same for the rest of the day. At the end of school, Ethel put on her hat and coat—the teacher made her hang them at a distance from the other pupils' wraps; and started for home. Quite a crowd escorted her. They called her "Nigger!" all the way. I made Ethel go the next day. I complained to the authorities. They treated me lightly. I was determined not to let them force my child out of school. At the end of two weeks—I had to take her out.

RACHEL (*Brokenly*): Why,—I never—in all my life—heard anything—so—pitiful.

MRS. LANE: Did you ever go to school here?

RACHEL: Yes. I was made to feel my color—but I never had an experience like that.

MRS. LANE: How many years ago were you in the graded schools?

RACHEL: Oh!—around ten.

MRS. LANE (*Laughs grimly*): Ten years! Every year things are getting worse. Last year wasn't as bad as this. (*Pauses.*) So they treat the children all right in this school?

RACHEL: Yes! Yes! I know that.

MRS. LANE: I can't afford to take this flat here, but I'll take it. I'm going to have Ethel educated. Although, when you think of it,—it's all rather useless—this education! What are our children going to do with it, when they get it? We strive and save and sacrifice to educate them—and the whole time—down underneath, we know—they'll have no chance.

RACHEL (*Sadly*): Yes, that's true, all right.—God seems to have forgotten us.

MRS. LANE: God! It's all a lie about God. I know.—This fall I sent Ethel to a white Sunday-school near us. She received the same treatment there she did in the day school. Her being there, nearly broke up the school. At the end, the superintendent called her to him and asked her if she didn't know of some nice colored Sunday-school. He told her she must feel out of place, and uncomfortable there. That's your Church of God!

RACHEL: Oh! how unspeakably brutal. (*Controls herself with an effort; after a pause*) Have you any other children?

MRS. LANE (*Dryly*): Hardly! If I had another—I'd kill it. It's kinder. (*Rising presently*) Well, I must go, now. Thank you, for your information—and for listening. (*Suddenly*) You aren't married, are you?

RACHEL: No.

MRS. LANE: Don't marry—that's my advice. Come, Ethel. (*Ethel gets up and puts down the things in her lap, carefully upon her chair. She goes in a hurried, timid way to her mother and clutches her hand*). Say good-bye to the lady.

ETHEL (*Faintly*): Good-bye.

RACHEL (*Kneeling by the little girl—a beautiful smile on her face*) Dear little girl, won't you let me kiss you good-bye? I love little girls. (*The child hides behind her mother; continuing brokenly*) Oh!—no child—ever did—that to me—before!

MRS. LANE (*In a gentler voice*): Perhaps, when we move in here, the first of the month, things may be better. Thank you, again. Good-morning! You don't belie your name. (*All three go into the vestibule. The outside door opens and closes. Rachel as though dazed and stricken returns. She sits in a chair, leans forward, and clasping her hands loosely between her knees, stares at the chair with the apple on it where Ethel Lane has sat. She does not move for some time. Then she gets up and goes to the window in the rear center and sits there. She breathes in the air deeply and then goes to the sewing-machine and begins to sew on something she is making. Presently her feet slow down on the pedals; she stops; and begins brooding again. After a short pause, she gets up and begins to pace up and down slowly, mechanically, her head bent forward. The sharp ringing of the electric bell breaks in upon this. Rachel starts and goes slowly into the vestibule. She is heard speaking dully through the tube*).

RACHEL: Yes!—All right! Bring it up! (*Presently she returns with a long flower box. She opens it listlessly at the table. Within are six, beautiful crimson rosebuds with long stems. Rachel looks at the name on the card. She sinks down slowly on her knees and leans her head against the table. She sighs wearily*) Oh! John! John!—What are we to do?—I'm—I'm—afraid! Everywhere—it is the same thing. My mother! My little brother! Little, black, crushed Ethel! (*In a whisper*) Oh! God! You who I have been taught to believe are so good, so beautiful how could—You permit—these—things? (*Pauses, raises her head and sees the rosebuds. Her face softens and grows beautiful, very sweetly*). Dear little rosebuds—you—make me think—of sleeping, curled up, happy babies. Dear beautiful, little rosebuds! (*Pauses; goes on thoughtfully to the rosebuds*) When—I look—at you—I believe—God is beautiful. He who can make a little exquisite thing like this, and this can't be cruel. Oh! He can't mean me—to give up—love—and the hope of little children. (*There is the sound of a small hand knocking at the outer door. Rachel smiles*). My Jimmy! It must be twelve o'clock. (*Rises*). I didn't dream it was so late. (*Starts for the vestibule*). Oh! the world can't be so bad. I don't believe it. I won't. I must forget that little girl. My little Jimmy is happy—and today John—sent me beautiful rosebuds. Oh, there are lovely things, yet. (*Goes into the vestibule. A child's eager cry is heard; and Rachel carrying Jimmy in her arms comes in. He has both arms about her neck and is hugging her. With him in her arms, she sits down in the armchair at the right front*).

RACHEL: Well, honey, how was school today?

JIMMY (*Sobering a trifle*): All right, Ma Rachel. (*Suddenly sees the roses*) Oh! look at the pretty flowers. Why, Ma Rachel, you forgot to put them in water. They'll die.

RACHEL: Well, so they will. Hop down this minute, and I'll put them in right away. (*Gathers up box and flowers and goes into the kitchenette. Jimmy climbs back into the chair. He looks thoughtful and serious. Rachel comes back with the buds in a tall, glass vase. She puts the fern on top of the piano, and places the vase in the centre of the table*). There, honey, that's better, isn't it? Aren't they lovely?

JIMMY: Yes, that's lots better. Now they won't die, will they? Rosebuds are just like little "chilyun," aren't they, Ma Rachel? If you are good to them, they'll grow up into lovely roses, won't they? And if you hurt them, they'll die. Ma Rachel do you think all peoples are kind to little rosebuds?

RACHEL (*Watching Jimmy shortly*): Why, of course. Who could hurt little children? Who would have the heart to do such a thing?

JIMMY: If you hurt them, it would be lots kinder, wouldn't it, to kill them all at once, and not a little bit and a little bit?

RACHEL (*Sharply*): Why, honey boy, why are you talking like this?

JIMMY: Ma Rachel, what is a "Nigger"?

(*Rachel recoils as though she had been struck*).

RACHEL: Honey boy, why—why do you ask that?

JIMMY: Some big boys called me that when I came out of school just now. They said: "Look at the little nigger!" And they laughed. One of them runned, no ranned, after me and threw stones; and they all kept calling "Nigger! Nigger! Nigger!" One stone struck me hard in the back, and it hurt awful bad; but I didn't cry, Ma Rachel. I wouldn't let them make me cry. The stone hurts me there, Ma Rachel; but what they called me hurts and hurts here. What is a "Nigger," Ma Rachel?

RACHEL (*Controlling herself with a tremendous effort. At last she sweeps down upon him and hugs and kisses him*): Why, honey boy, those boys didn't mean anything. Silly, little, honey boy! They're rough, that's all. How could they mean anything?

JIMMY: You're only saying that, Ma Rachel, so I won't be hurt. I know. It wouldn't ache here like it does—if they didn't mean something.

RACHEL (*Abruptly*): Where's Mary, honey?

JIMMY: She's in her flat. She came in just after I did.

RACHEL: Well, honey, I'm going to give you two big cookies and two to take to Mary; and you may stay in there and play with her, till I get your lunch ready. Won't that be jolly?

JIMMY (*Brightening a little*): Why, you never give me but one at a time. You'll give me two?—One? Two? (*Rachel gets the cookies and brings them to him. Jimmy climbs down from the chair*). Shoo! now, little honey boy. See how many laughs you can make for me, before I come after you. Hear? Have a good time, now. (*Jimmy starts for the door quickly; but he begins to slow down. His face gets long and serious again. Rachel watches him*).

RACHEL (*Jumping at him*): Shoo! Shoo! Get out of here quickly, little chicken. (*She follows him out. The outer door opens and shuts. Presently she returns. She looks old and worn and grey; calmly. Pauses*). First, it's little, black Ethel—and then's it's Jimmy. Tomorrow, it will be some other little child. The blight—sooner or later—strikes all. My little Jimmy, only seven years old, poisoned! (*Through the open window comes the laughter of little children at play. Rachel, shuddering, covers her ears*). And once I said, centuries ago, it must have been: "How can life be so terrible, when there are little children in the world?" Terrible! Terrible! (*In a whisper, slowly*) That's the reason it is so terrible. (*The laughter reaches her again; this time she listens*). And, suddenly, some day, from out of the black, the blight shall descend, and shall still forever—the laughter on those little lips, and in those little hearts. (*Pauses thoughtfully*). And the loveliest thing—almost, that ever happened to me, that beautiful voice, in my dream, those beautiful words: "Rachel, you are to be the mother to little children." (*Pauses, then slowly and with dawning surprise*). Why, God, you were making a mock of me; you were laughing at me. I didn't belive God could laugh at our sufferings, but He can. We are accursed, accursed! We have nothing, absolutely nothing. (*Strong's rosebuds attract her attention. She goes over to them, puts her hand out as if to touch them, and then shakes her head, very sweetly*) No, little rosebuds, I may not touch you. Dear, little, baby rosebuds,—I am accursed. (*Gradually her whole form stiffens, she breathes deeply; at last slowly*). You God!—You terrible, laughing God! Listen! I swear—and may my soul be damned to all eternity, if I do break this oath—I swear—that no child of mine shall ever lie upon my breast, for I will not have it rise up, in the terrible days that are to be—and call me cursed. (*A pause, very wistfully; questioningly*). Never to know the loveliest thing in all the world—the feel of a little head, the touch of little hands, the beautiful utter dependence—of a little child? (*With sudden frenzy*) You can laugh, Oh God! Well, so can I. (*Bursts into terrible, racking laughter*) But I can be kinder than You. (*Fiercely she snatches the rosebuds from the vase, grasps them roughly, tears each head from the stem, and grinds it under her feet. The vase goes over with a crash; the water drips unheeded over the table-cloth and floor*). If I kill, You Mighty God, I kill at once—I do not torture. (*Falls face downward on the floor. The laughter of the children shrills loudly through the window*).

★

ACT III.

TIME: *Seven o'clock in the evening, one week later.*

PLACE: *The same room. There is a coal fire in the grate. The curtains are drawn. A lighted oil lamp with a dark green porcelain shade is in the center of the table. Mrs. Loving and Tom are sitting by the table, Mrs. Loving sewing, Tom reading. There is the sound of much laughter and the shrill screaming of a child from the bedrooms. Presently Jimmy clad in a flannelet sleeping suit, covering all of him but his head and hands, chases a pillow, which has come flying through the doorway at the rear. He struggles with it, finally gets it in his arms, and rushes as fast as he can through the doorway again. Rachel jumps at him with a cry. He drops the pillow and shrieks. There is a tussle for possession of it, and they disappear. The noise grows louder and merrier. Tom puts down his paper and grins. He looks at his mother.*

TOM: Well, who's the giddy one in this family now?

MRS. LOVING (*Shaking her head in a troubled manner*): I don't like it. It worries me. Rachel—(*Breaks off*).

TOM: Have you found out, yet—

MRS. LOVING (*Turning and looking toward the rear doorway, quickly interrupting him*): Sh! (*Rachel, laughing, her hair tumbling over her shoulders, comes rushing into the room. Jimmy is in close pursuit. He tries to catch her, but she dodges him. They are both breathless*).

MRS. LOVING (*Deprecatingly*): Really, Rachel, Jimmy will be so excited he won't be able to sleep. It's after his bedtime, now. Don't you think you had better stop?

RACHEL: All right, Ma dear. Come on, Jimmy; let's play "Old Folks" and sit by the fire. (*She begins to push the big armchair over to the fire. Tom jumps up, moves her aside, and pushes it himself. Jimmy renders assistance.*)

TOM: Thanks, Big Fellow, you are "sure some" strong. I'll remember you when these people around here come for me to move pianos and such things around. Shake! (*They shake hands*).

JIMMY (*Proudly*): I am awful strong, am I not?

TOM: You "sure" are a Hercules. (*Hurriedly, as Jimmy's mouth and eyes open wide*). And see here! don't ask me tonight who that was. I'll tell you the first thing tomorrow morning. Hear? (*Returns to his chair and paper*).

RACHEL (*Sitting down*): Come on, honey boy, and sit in my lap.

JIMMY (*Doubtfully*): I thought we were going to play "Old Folks."

RACHEL: We are.

JIMMY: Do old folks sit in each other's laps?

RACHEL: Old folks do anything. Come on.

JIMMY (*Hesitatingly climbs into her lap, but presently snuggles down and sighs audibly from sheer content; Rachel starts to bind up her hair*): Ma Rachel, don't please! I like your hair like that. You're—you're pretty. I like to feel of it; and it smells like—like—oh!—like a barn.

RACHEL: My! how complimentary! I like that. Like a barn, indeed!

JIMMY: What's "complimentry"?

RACHEL: Oh! saying nice things about me. (*Pinching his cheek and laughing*) That my hair is like a barn, for instance.

JIMMY (*Stoutly*): Well, that is "complimentary." It smells like hay—like the hay in the barn you took me to, one day, last summer. 'Member?

RACHEL: Yes honey.

JIMMY (*After a brief pause*): Ma Rachel!

RACHEL: Well?

JIMMY: Tell me a story, please. It's "story-time," now, isn't it?

RACHEL: Well, let's see. (*They both look into the fire for a space; beginning softly*) Once upon a time, there were two, dear, little boys, and they were all alone in the world. They lived with a cruel, old man and woman, who made them work hard, very hard—all day, and beat them when they did not move fast enough, and always, every night, before they went to bed. They slept in an attic on a rickety, narrow bed, that went screech! screech! whenever they moved. And, in summer, they nearly died with the heat up there, and in winter, with the cold. One wintry night, when they were both weeping very bitterly after a particularly hard beating, they suddenly heard a pleasant voice saying: "Why are you crying, little boys?" They looked up, and there, in the moonlight, by their bed, was the dearest, little old lady. She was dressed all in gray, from the peak of her little pointed hat to her little, buckled shoes. She held a black cane much taller than her little self. Her hair fell about her ears in tiny, grey corkscrew curls, and they bobbed about as she moved. Her eyes were black and bright—as bright as—well, as that lovely, white light there. No, there! And her cheeks were as red as the apple I gave you yesterday. Do you remember?

JIMMY (*Dreamily*): Yes.

RACHEL: "Why are you crying, little boys?" she asked again, in a lovely, low, little voice. "Because we are tired and sore and hungry and cold; and we are all alone in the world; and we don't know how to laugh any more. We should so like to laugh again." "Why, that's easy," she said, "it's just like this." And she laughed a little, joyous, musical laugh. "Try!" she commanded. They tried, but their laughing boxes were very rusty, and they made horrid sounds. "Well," she said, "I advise you to pack up, and go away, as soon as you can, to the Land of Laughter. You'll soon learn there, I can tell you." "Is there such a land?" they asked doubtfully. "To be sure there is," she answered the least bit sharply. "We never heard of it," they said. "Well, I'm sure there must be plenty of things you never heard about," she said just the "leastest" bit more sharply. "In a moment you'll be telling me flowers don't talk together, and the birds." "We never heard of such a thing," they said in surprise, their eyes like saucers. "There!" she said, bobbing her little curls. "What did I tell you? You have much to learn." "How do you get to the Land of Laughter?" they asked. "You go out of the eastern gate of the town, just as the sun is rising; and you take the highway there, and follow it; and if you go with it long enough, it will bring you to the very gates of the Land of Laughter. It's a long, long way from here; and it will take you many days." The words had scarcely left her mouth, when, lo! the little lady disappeared, and where she had stood was the white square of moonlight—nothing else. And without more ado these two little boys put their arms around each other and fell fast asleep. And in the grey, just before daybreak, they awoke and dressed; and, putting on their ragged caps and mittens, for it was a wintry day, they stole out of the house and made for the eastern gate. And just as they reached it, and passed through, the whole east leapt into fire. All day they walked, and many days thereafter, and kindly people, by the way, took them in and gave them food and drink and sometimes a bed at night. Often they slept by the roadside, but they didn't mind that for the climate was delightful—not too hot, and not too cold. They soon threw away their ragged little mittens. They walked for many days, and there was no Land of Laughter. Once they met an old man, richly dressed, with shining jewels on his fingers, and he stopped them and asked: "Where are you going so fast, little boys?" "We are going to the Land of Laughter," they said together gravely. "That," said the old man, "is a very foolish thing to do. Come with me, and I will take you to the Land of Riches. I will cover you with garments of beauty, and give you jewels and a castle to live in and servants and horses and many things besides." And they said to him: "No, we wish to learn how to laugh again; we have forgotten how, and we are going to the Land of Laughter." "You will regret not going with me. See, if you don't," he said; and he left them in quite a huff. And they walked again, many days, and again they met an old man. He was tall and imposing-looking and very dignified. And he said: "Where are you going so fast, little boys?" "We are going to the Land of Laughter," they said together very seriously. "What!" he said, "that is an extremely foolish thing to do. Come with me, and I will give you power. I will make you great men: generals, kings, emperors, Whatever you desire to accomplish will be permitted you." And they smiled politely: "Thank you very much, but we have forgotten how to laugh, and we are going there to learn how." He looked upon them haughtily, without speaking, and disappeared. And they walked and walked more days; and they met another old man. And he was clad in rags, and his face was thin, and his eyes were unhappy. And he whispered to them: "Where are you going so fast, little boys?" "We are going to the Land of Laughter," they answered, without a smile. "Laughter! Laughter! that is useless. Come with me and I will show you the beauty of life through sacrifice, suffering for others. That is the only life. I come from the Land of Sacrifice." And they thanked him kindly, but said: "We have suffered long enough. We have forgotten how to laugh. We would learn again." And they went on; and he looked after them very wistfully. They walked more days, and at last they came to the Land of Laughter. And how do you suppose they knew this? Because they could hear, over the wall, the sound of joyous laughter,—the laughter of men, women, and children. And one sat guarding the gate, and they went to her. "We have come a long, long distance; and we would enter the Land of Laughter." "Let me see you smile, first," she said gently. "I sit at the gate; and no one who does not know how to smile may enter the Land of Laughter." And they tried to smile, but could not. "Go away and practice," she said kindly, "and come back tomorrow." And they went away, and practiced all night how to smile; and in the morning they returned, and the gentle lady at the gate said: "Dear little boys, have you learned how to smile?" And they said: "We have tried. How is this?" "Better," she said, "much better. Practice some more, and come back tomorrow." And they went away obediently and practiced. And they came the third day. And she said: "Now try again." And tears of delight came into her lovely eyes. "Those were very beautiful smiles," she said. "Now, you may enter." And she unlocked the gate, and kissed them both, and they entered the Land—the beautiful Land of Laughter. Never had they seen such blue skies, such green trees and grass; never had they heard such birds songs. And people, men, women and children, laughing softly, came to meet them, and took them in, and made them as home; and soon, very soon, they learned to sleep. And they grew up here, and married, and had laughing, happy children. And sometimes they thought of the Land of Riches, and said: "Ah! well!" and sometimes of the Land of Power, and sighed a little; and sometimes of the Land of Sacrifice—and their eyes were wistful. But they soon forgot, and laughed again. And they grew old, laughing. And then when they died—a laugh was on their lips. Thus are things in the beautiful Land of Laughter. (*There is a long pause*).

JIMMY: I like that story, Ma Rachel. It's nice to laugh, isn't is? Is there such a land?

RACHEL (*Softly*): What do you think, honey?

JIMMY: I thinks it would be awful nice if there was. Don't you?

RACHEL (*Wistfully*): If there only were! If there only were!

JIMMY: Ma Rachel.

RACHEL: Well?

JIMMY: It makes you think—kind of—doesn't it—of sunshine medicine?

RACHEL: Yes, honey,—but it isn't medicine there. It's always there—just like—well—like our air here. It's *always* sunshine there.

JIMMY: Always sunshine? Never any dark?

RACHEL: No, honey.

JIMMY: You'd—never—be—afraid there, then, would you? Never afraid of nothing?

RACHEL: No, honey.

JIMMY (*With a big sigh*): Oh!—Oh! I *wisht* it was here—not there. (*Puts his hand up to Rachel's face; suddenly sits up and looks at her*). Why, Ma Rachel dear, you're crying. Your face is all wet. Why! Don't cry! Don't cry!

RACHEL (*Gently*): Do you remember that I told you the lady at the gate had tears of joy in her eyes, when the two, dear, little boys smiled that beautiful smile?

JIMMY: Yes.

RACHEL: Well, these are tears of joy, honey, that's all—tears of joy.

JIMMY: It must be awful queer to have tears of joy, 'cause you're happy. I never did. (*With a sigh*). But, if you say they are, dear Ma Rachel, they must be. You knows everything, don't you?

RACHEL (*Sadly*): Some things, honey, some things. (*A silence*).

JIMMY (*Sighing happily*): This is the beautiful-est night I ever knew. If you would do just one more thing, it would be lots more beautiful. Will you, Ma Rachel?

RACHEL: Well, what, honey?

JIMMY: Will you sing—at the piano, I mean, it's lots prettier that way—the little song you used to rock me to sleep by? You know, the one about the "Slumber Boat"?

RACHEL: Oh! honey, not tonight. You're too tired. It's bedtime now.

JIMMY (*Patting her face with his little hand; wheedlingly*): Please! Ma Rachel, please! pretty please!

RACHEL: Well, honey boy, this once, then. Tonight, you shall have the little song—I used to sing you to sleep by (*half to herself*) perhaps, for the last time.

JIMMY: Why, Ma Rachel, why the last time?

RACHEL (*Shaking her head sadly, goes to the piano; in a whisper*): The last time. (*She twists up her hair into a knot at the back of her head and looks at the keys for a few moments; then she plays the accompaniment of the "Slumber Boat" through softly, and, after a moment, sings. Her voice is full of pent-up longing, and heartbreak, and hopelessness. She ends in a little sob, but attempts to cover it by singing, lightly and daintily, the chorus of "The Owl and the Moon." Then softly and with infinite tenderness, almost against her will, she plays and sings again the refrain of the "Slumber Boat"*):

"Sail, baby, sail
Out from that sea,
Only don't forget to sail
Back again to me."

(*Presently she rises and goes to Jimmy, who is lolling back happily in the big chair. During the singing, Tom and Mrs. Loving apparently do not listen; when she sobs, however, Tom's hand on his paper tightens; Mrs. Loving's needle poises for a moment in mid-air. Neither looks at Rachel. Jimmy evidently has not noticed the sob*).

RACHEL (*Kneeling by Jimmy*): Well, honey, how did you like it?

JIMMY (*Proceeding to pull down her hair from the twist*): It was lovely, Ma Rachel. (*Yawns audibly*). Now, Ma Rachel, I'm just beautifully sleepy. (*Dreamily*) I think that p'r'aps I'll go to the Land of Laughter tonight in my dreams. I'll go in the "Slumber Boat" and come back in the morning and tell you all about it. Shall I?

RACHEL: Yes, honey. (*Whispers*) "Only don't forget to sail Back again to me."

TOM (*Suddenly*): Rachel! (*Rachel starts slightly*). I nearly forgot. John is coming here tonight to see how you are. He told me to tell you so.

RACHEL (*Stiffens perceptibly, then in different tones*): Very well. Thank you. (*Suddenly with a little cry she puts her arms around Jimmy*) Jimmy! honey! don't go tonight. Don't go without Ma Rachel. Wait for me, honey. I do so wish to go, too, to the Land of Laughter. Think of it, Jimmy; nothing but birds always singing, and flowers always blooming, and skies always blue—and people, all of them, always laughing, laughing. You'll wait for Ma Rachel, won't you, honey?

JIMMY: Is there really and truly, Ma Rachel, a Land of Laughter?

RACHEL: Oh! Jimmy, let's hope so; let's pray so.

JIMMY (*Frowns*): I've been thinking—(*Pauses*). You have to smile at the gate, don't you, to get in?

RACHEL: Yes, honey.

JIMMY: Well, I guess I couldn't smile if my Ma Rachel wasn't somewhere close to me. So I couldn't get in after all, could I? Tonight, I'll go somewhere else, and tell you all about it. And then, some day, we'll go together, won't we?

RACHEL (*Sadly*): Yes, honey, some day—some day. (*A short silence*). Well, this isn't going to "sleepy-sleep," is it? Go, now, and say good-night to Ma Loving and Uncle Tom.

JIMMY (*Gets down obediently, and goes first to Mrs. Loving. She leans over, and he puts his little arms around her neck. They kiss; very sweetly*): Sweet dreams! God keep you all the night!

MRS. LOVING: The sweetest of sweet dreams to you, dear little boy! Good-night! (*Rachel watches, unwatched, the scene. Her eyes are full of yearning*).

JIMMY (*Going to Tom, who makes believe he does not see him*): Uncle Tom!

TOM (*Jumps as though tremendously startled; Jimmy laughs*): My! how you frightened me. You'll put my gizzard out of commission, if you do that often. Well, sir, what can I do for you?

JIMMY: I came to say good-night.

TOM (*Gathering Jimmy up in his arms and kissing him; gently and with emotion*): Good-night, dear little Big Fellow! Good-night!

JIMMY: Sweet dreams! God keep you all the night! (*Goes sedately to Rachel, and holds out his little hand*). I'm ready, Ma Rachel. (*Yawns*) I'm so nice and sleepy.

RACHEL (*With Jimmy's hand in hers, she hesitates a moment, and then approaches Tom slowly. For a short time she stands looking down at him; suddenly leaning over him*): Why, Tom, what a pretty tie! Is it new?

TOM: Well, no, not exactly. I've had it about a month. It is rather a beauty, isn't it?

RACHEL: Why, I never remember seeing it.

TOM (*Laughing*): I guess not. I saw to that.

RACHEL: Stingy!

TOM: Well, I am—where my ties are concerned. I've had experience.

RACHEL (*Tentatively*): Tom!

TOM: Well?

RACHEL (*Nervously and wistfully*): Are you—will you—I mean, won't you be home this evening?

TOM: You've got a long memory, Sis. I've that engagement, you know. Why?

RACHEL (*Slowly*): I forgot; so you have.

TOM: Why?

RACHEL (*Hastily*): Oh! nothing—nothing. Come on, Jimmy boy, you can hardly keep those little peepers open, can you? Come on, honey. (*Rachel and Jimmy go out the rear doorway. There is a silence*).

MRS. LOVING (*Slowly, as though thinking aloud*): I try to make out what could have happened; but it's no use—I can't. Those four days, she lay in bed hardly moving, scarcely speaking. Only her eyes seemed alive. I never saw such a wide, tragic look in my life. It was as though her soul had been mortally wounded. But how? how? What could have happened?

TOM (*Quietly*): I don't know. She generally tells me everything; but she avoids me now. If we are alone in a room—she gets out. I don't know what it means.

MRS. LOVING: She will hardly let Jimmy out of her sight. While he's at school, she's nervous and excited. She seems always to be listening, but for what? When he returns, she nearly devours him. And she always asks him in a frightened sort of way, her face as pale and tense as can be: "Well, honey boy, how was school today?" And he always answers, "Fine, Ma Rachel, fine! I learned—"; and then he goes on to tell her everything that has happened. And when he has finished, she says in an uneasy sort of way: "Is—is that all?" And when he says "Yes," she relaxes and becomes limp. After a little while she becomes feverishly happy. She plays with Jimmy and the children more than ever she did—and she played a good deal, as you know. They're here, or she's with them. Yesterday, I said in remonstrance, when she came in, her face pale and haggard and black hollows under her eyes: "Rachel, remember you're just out of a sickbed. You're not well enough to go on like this." "I know," was all she would say, "but I've got to. I can't help myself. This part of their little lives must be happy—it just must be." (*Pauses*). The last couple of nights, Jimmy has awakened and cried most pitifully. She wouldn't let me go to him; said I had enough trouble, and she could quiet him. She never will let me know why he cries; but she stays with him, and soothes him until, at last, he falls asleep again. Every time she has come out like a rag; and her face is like a dead woman's. Strange isn't it, this is the first time we have ever been able to talk it over? Tom, what could have happened?

TOM: I don't know, Ma, but I feel, as you do; something terrible and sudden has hurt her soul; and, poor little thing, she's trying bravely to readjust herself to life again. (*Pauses, looks at his watch and then rises, and goes to her. He pats her back awkwardly*). Well, Ma, I'm going now. Don't worry too much. Youth, you, know, gets over things finally. It takes them hard, that's all—. At least, that's what the older heads tell us. (*Gets his hat and stands in the vestibule doorway*). Ma, you know, I begin with John tomorrow. (*With emotion*) I don't believe we'll ever forget John. Good-night! (*Exit. Mrs. Loving continues to sew. Rachel, her hair arranged, reenters through the rear doorway. She is humming*).

RACHEL: He's sleeping like a top. Aren't little children, Ma dear, the sweetest things, when they're all helpless and asleep? One little hand is under his cheek; and he's smiling. (*Stops suddenly, biting her lips. A pause*) Where's Tom?

MRS. LOVING: He went out a few minutes ago.

RACHEL (*Sitting in Tom's chair and picking up his paper. She is exceedingly nervous. She looks the paper over rapidly; presently trying to make her tone casual*): Ma,—you—you—aren't going anywhere tonight, are you?

MRS. LOVING: I've got to go out for a short time about half-past eight. Mrs. Jordan, you know. I'll not be gone very long, though. Why?

RACHEL: Oh! nothing particular. I just thought it would be cosy if we could sit here together the rest of the evening. Can't you—can't you go tomorrow?

MRS. LOVING: Why, I don't see how I can. I've made the engagement. It's about a new reception gown; and she's exceedingly exacting, as you know. I can't afford to lose her.

RACHEL: No, I suppose not. All right, Ma dear. (*Presently, paper in hand, she laughs, but not quite naturally*). Look! Ma dear! How is that for fashion, anyway? Isn't it the "limit"? (*Rises and shows her mother a picture in the paper. As she is in the act, the bell rings. With a startled cry*). Oh! (*Drops the paper, and grips her mother's hand*).

MRS. LOVING (*Anxiously*): Rachel, your nerves are right on edge; and your hand feels like fire. I'll have to see a doctor about you; and that's all there is to it.

RACHEL (*Laughing nervously, and moving toward the vestibule*): Nonsense, Ma dear! Just because I let out a whoop now and then, and have nice warm hands?

(*Goes out, is heard talking through the tube*) Yes! (*Her voice emitting tremendous relief*). Oh! bring it right up! (*Appearing in the doorway*) Ma dear, did you buy anything at Goddard's today?

MRS. LOVING: Yes; and I've been wondering why they were so late in delivering it. I bought it early this morning. (*Rachel goes out again. A door opens and shuts. She reappears with a bundle*).

MRS. LOVING: Put it on my bed, Rachel, please. (*Exit Rachel rear doorway; presently returns empty-handed; sits down again at the table with the paper between herself and mother; sinks in a deep revery. Suddenly there is the sound of many loud knocks made by numerous small fists. Rachel drops the paper, and comes to a sitting posture, tense again. Her mother looks at her, but says nothing. Almost immediately Rachel relaxes*).

RACHEL: My kiddies! They're late, this evening. (*Goes out into the vestibule. A door opens and shuts. There is the shrill, excited sound of childish voices. Rachel comes in surrounded by the children, all trying to say something to her at once. Rachel puts her finger on her lip and points toward the doorway in the rear. They all quiet down. She sits on the floor in the front of the stage, and the children all cluster around her. Their conversation takes place in a half-whisper. As they enter they nod brightly at Mrs. Loving, who smiles in return*). Why so late, kiddies? It's long past "sleepy-time."

LITTLE NANCY: We've been playing "Hide and Seek," and having the mostest fun. We promised, all of us, that if we could play until half-past seven tonight we wouldn't make any fuss about going to bed at seven o'clock the rest of the week. It's awful hard to go. I *hate* to go to bed!

LITTLE MARY, LOUISE AND EDITH: So do I! So do I! So do I!

LITTLE MARTHA: I don't. I love bed. My bed, after my muzzer tucks me all in, is like a nice warm bag. I just stick my nose out. When I lifts my head up I can see the light from the dining-room come in the door. I can hear my muzzer and fazzer talking nice and low; and then, before I know it, I'm fast asleep, and I dream pretty things, and in about a minute it's morning again. I love my little bed, and I love to dream.

LITTLE MARY (*Aggressively*): Well, I guess I love to dream too. I wish I could dream, though, without going to bed.

LITTLE NANCY: When I grow up, I'm never going to bed at night! (*Darkly*) You see.

LITTLE LOUISE: "Grown-ups" just love to poke their heads out of windows and cry, "Child'run, it's time for bed now; and you'd better hurry, too, I can tell you." They "sure" are queer, for sometimes when I wake up, it must be about twelve o'clock, I can hear by big sister giggling and talking to some silly man. If it's good for me to go to bed early—I should think—

RACHEL (*Interrupting suddenly*): Why, where is my little Jenny? Excuse me, Louise dear.

LITTLE MARTHA: Her cold is awful bad. She coughs like this (*giving a distressing imitation*) and snuffles all the time. She can't talk out loud, and she can't go to sleep. Muzzer says she's fev'rish—I thinks that's what she says. Jenny says she knows she could go to sleep, if you would come and sit with her a little while.

RACHEL: I certainly will. I'll go when you do, honey.

LITTLE MARTHA (*Softly stroking Rachel's arm*): You're the very nicest "grown-up," (*loyally*) except my muzzer, of course, I ever knew. You knows all about little chil'-run and you can be one, although you're all grown up. I think you would make a lovely muzzer. (*To the rest of the children*) Don't you?

ALL (*In excited whispers*): Yes, I do.

RACHEL (*Winces, then says gently*): Come, kiddies, you must go now, or your mothers will blame me for keeping you. (*Rises, as do the rest. Little Martha puts her hand into Rachel's*). Ma dear, I'm going down to sit a little while with Jenny. I'll be back before you go, though. Come, kiddies, say good-night to my mother.

ALL (*Gravely*): Good-night! Sweet dreams! God keep you all the night.

MRS. LOVING: Good-night dears! Sweet dreams, all! (*Exeunt Rachel and the children. Mrs. Loving continues to sew. The bell presently rings three distinct times. In a few moments, Mrs. Loving gets up and goes out into the vestibule. A door opens and closes. Mrs. Loving and John Strong come in. He is a trifle pale but his imperturbable self. Mrs. Loving, somewhat nervous, takes her seat and resumes her sewing. She motions Strong to a chair. He returns to the vestibule, leaves his hat, returns, and sits down*).

STRONG: Well, how is everything?

MRS. LOVING: Oh! about the same, I guess. Tom's out. John, we'll never forget you—and your kindness.

STRONG: That was nothing. And Rachel?

MRS. LOVING: She'll be back presently. She went to sit with a sick child for a little while.

STRONG: And how is she?

MRS. LOVING: She's not herself yet, but I think she is better.

STRONG (*After a short pause*): Well, what *did* happen—exactly?

MRS. LOVING: That's just what I don't know.

STRONG: When you came home—you couldn't get in—was that it?

MRS. LOVING: Yes. (*Pauses*). It was just a week ago today. I was down town all the morning. It was about one o'clock when I got back. I had forgotten my key. I rapped on the door and then called. There was no answer. A window was open, and I could feel the air under the door, and I could hear it as the draught sucked it through. There was no other sound. Presently I made such a noise the people began to come out into the hall. Jimmy was in one of the flats playing with a little girl named Mary. He told me he had left Rachel here a short time before. She had given him four cookies, two for him and two for Mary, and had told him he could play with her until she came to tell him his lunch was ready. I saw he was getting frightened, so I got the little girl and her mother to keep him in their flat. Then, as no man was at home, I sent out for help. Three men broke the door down. (*Pauses*). We found Rachel unconscious, lying on her face. For a few minutes I thought she was dead. (*Pauses*). A vase had fallen over on the table and the water had dripped through the cloth and onto the floor. There had been flowers in it. When I left, there were no flowers here. What she could have done to them, I can't say. The long stems were lying everywhere, and the flowers had been ground into the floor. I could tell that they must have been roses from the stems. After we had put her to bed and called the doctor, and she had finally regained consciousness, I very naturally asked her what had happened. All she would say was, "Ma dear, I'm too—tired—please." For four days she lay in bed scarcely moving, speaking only when spoken to. That first day, when Jimmy came in to see her, she shrank away from him. We had to take him out, and comfort him as best we could. We kept him away, almost by force, until she got up. And, then, she was utterly miserable when he was out of her sight. What happened, I don't know. She avoids Tom, and she won't tell me. (*Pauses*). Tom and I both believe her soul has been hurt. The trouble isn't with her body. You'll find her highly nervous. Sometimes she is very much depressed; again she is feverishly gay—almost reckless. What do you think about it, John?

STRONG (*Who has listened quietly*): Had anybody been here, do you know?

MRS. LOVING: No, I don't. I don't like to ask Rachel; and I can't ask the neighbors.

STRONG: No, of course not. (*Pauses*). You say there were some flowers?

MRS. LOVING: Yes.

STRONG: And the flowers were ground into the carpet?

MRS. LOVING: Yes.

STRONG: Did you happen to notice the box? They must have come in a box, don't you think?

MRS. LOVING: Yes, there was a box in the kitchenette. It was from "Marcy's." I saw no card.

STRONG (*Slowly*): It is rather strange. (*A long silence, during which the outer door opens and shuts. Rachel is heard singing. She stops abruptly. In a second or two she appears in the door. There is an air of suppressed excitement about her*).

RACHEL: Hello! John. (*Strong rises, nods at her, and brings forward for her the big arm-chair near the fire*). I thought that was your hat in the hall. It's brand new, I know—but it looks—"Johnlike." How are you? Ma! Jenny went to sleep like a little lamb. I don't like her breathing, though. (*Looks from one to the other; flippantly*) Who's dead? (*Nods her thanks to Strong for the chair and sits down*).

MRS. LOVING: Dead, Rachel?

RACHEL: Yes. The atmosphere here is so funereal,—it's positively "crapey."

STRONG: I don't know why it should be—I was just asking how you are.

RACHEL: Heavens! Does the mere inquiry into my health precipitate such an atmosphere? Your two faces were as long, as long—(*Breaks off*). Kind sir, let me assure you, I am in the very best of health. And how are you, John?

STRONG: Oh! I'm always well. (*Sits down*).

MRS. LOVING: Rachel, I'll have to get ready to go now. John, don't hurry. I'll be back shortly, probably in three-quarters of an hour—maybe less.

RACHEL: And maybe more, if I remember Mrs. Jordan. However, Ma dear, I'll do the best I can—while you are away. I'll try to be a credit to your training. (*Mrs. Loving smiles and goes out the rear doorway*). Now, let's see—in the books of etiquette, I believe, the properly reared young lady, always asks the young gentleman caller—you're young enough, aren't you, to be classed still as a "young gentleman caller?" (*No answer*). Well, anyway, she always asks the young gentleman caller sweetly something about the weather. (*Primly*) This has been an exceedingly beautiful day, hasn't it, Mr. Strong? (*No answer from Strong, who, with his head resting against the back of the chair, and his knees crossed is watching her in an amused, quizzical manner*). Well, really, every properly brought up young gentleman, I'm sure, ought to know, that it's exceedingly rude not to answer a civil question.

STRONG (*Lazily*): Tell me what to answer, Rachel.

RACHEL: Say, "Yes, very"; and look interested and pleased when you say it.

STRONG (*With a half-smile*): Yes, very.

RACHEL: Well, I certainly wouldn't characterize that as a particularly animated remark. Besides, when you look at me through half-closed lids like that—and kind of smile—what are you thinking? (*No answer*) John Strong, are you deaf or—just plain stupid?

STRONG: Plain stupid, I guess.

RACHEL (*In wheedling tones*): What were you thinking, John?

STRONG (*Slowly*): I was thinking—(*Breaks off*)

RACHEL (*Irritably*): Well?

STRONG: I've changed my mind.

RACHEL: You're not going to tell me?

STRONG: No.

(*Mrs. Loving dressed for the street comes in*)

MRS. LOVING: Goodbye, children. Rachel, don't quarrel so much with John. Let me see—if I have my key. (*Feels in her bag*) Yes, I have it. I'll be back shortly. Goodbye. (*Strong and Rachel rise. He bows*).

RACHEL: Good-bye, Ma dear. Hurry back as soon as you can, won't you? (*Exit Mrs. Loving through the vestibule. Strong leans back again in his chair, and watches Rachel through half-closed eyes. Rachel sits in her chair nervously*).

STRONG: Do you mind, if I smoke?

RACHEL: You know I don't.

STRONG: I am trying to behave like—Reginald—"the properly reared young gentleman caller." (*Lights a cigar; goes over to the fire, and throws his match away. Rachel goes into the kitchenette, and brings him a saucer for his ashes. She places it on the table near him*). Thank you. (*They both sit again, Strong very evidently enjoying his cigar and Rachel*). Now this is what I call cosy.

RACHEL: Cosy! Why?

STRONG: A nice warm room—shut in—curtains drawn—a cheerful fire crackling at my back—a lamp, not an electric or gas one, but one of your plain, old-fashioned kerosene ones—

RACHEL (*Interupting*): Ma dear would like to catch you, I am sure, talking about *her* lamp like that. "Old-fashioned! plain!"—You have nerve.

STRONG (*Continuing as though he had not been interrupted*): A comfortable chair—a good cigar—and not very far away, a little lady, who is looking charming, so near, that if I reached over, I could touch her. You there—and I here.—It's living.

RACHEL: Well! of all things! A compliment—and from *you*! How did it slip out, pray? (*No answer*). I suppose that you realize that a conversation between two persons is absolutely impossible, if one has to do her share all alone. Soon my ingenuity for introducing interesting subjects will be exhausted; and then will follow what, I believe, the story books call, "an uncomfortable silence."

STRONG (*Slowly*): Silence—between friends—isn't such a bad thing.

RACHEL: Thanks awfully. (*Leans back; cups her cheek in her hand, and makes no pretense at further conversation. The old look of introspection returns to her eyes. She does not move*).

STRONG (*Quietly*): Rachel! (*Rachel starts perceptibly*) You must remember I'm here. I don't like looking into your soul—when you forget you're not alone.

RACHEL: I hadn't forgotten.

STRONG: Wouldn't it be easier for you, little girl, if you could tell—some one?

RACHEL: No. (*A silence*)

STRONG: Rachel,—you're fond of flowers,—aren't you?

RACHEL: Yes.

STRONG: Rosebuds—red rosebuds—particularly?

RACHEL (*Nervously*): Yes.

STRONG: Did you—dislike—the giver?

RACHEL (*More nervously; bracing herself*): No, of course not.

STRONG: Rachel,—why—why—did you—kill the roses—then?

RACHEL (*Twisting her hands*): Oh, John! I'm so sorry, Ma dear told you that. She didn't know, you sent them.

STRONG: So I gathered. (*Pauses and then leans forward; quietly*). Rachel, little girl, why—did you kill them?

RACHEL (*Breathing quickly*): Don't you believe—it—a—a—kindness—sometimes—to kill?

STRONG (*After a pause*): You—considered—it—a—kindness—to kill them?

RACHEL: Yes. (*Another pause*)

STRONG: Do you mean—just—the roses?

RACHEL (*Breathing more quickly*): John!—Oh! must I say?

STRONG: Yes, little Rachel.

RACHEL (*In a whisper*): No. (*There is a long pause. Rachel leans back limply, and closes her eyes. Presently Strong rises, and moves his chair very close to hers. She does not stir. He puts his cigar on the saucer*).

STRONG (*Leaning forward; very gently*): Little girl, little girl, can't you tell me why?

RACHEL (*Wearily*): I can't.—It hurts—too much—to talk about it yet,—please.

STRONG (*Takes her hand; looks at it a few minutes and then at her quietly*): You—don't—care, then? (*She winces*) Rachel!—Look at me, little girl! (*As if against her will, she looks at him. Her eyes are fearful, hunted. She tries to look away, to draw away her hand; but he holds her gaze and her hand steadily*). Do you?

RACHEL (*Almost sobbing*): John! John! don't ask me. You are drawing my very soul out of my body with your eyes. You must not talk this way. You mustn't look—John, don't! (*Tries to shield her eyes*).

STRONG (*Quietly takes both of her hands, and kisses the backs and the palms slowly. A look of horror creeps into her face. He deliberately raises his eyes and looks at her mouth. She recoils as though she expected him to strike her. He resumes slowly*) If—you—do—care, and I know now—that you do—nothing else, *nothing* should count.

RACHEL (*Wrenching herself from his grasp and rising. She covers her ears; she breathes rapidly*): No! No! No!—You *must* stop. (*Laughs nervously; continues feverishly*) I'm not behaving very well as a hostess, am I? Let's see. What shall I do? I'll play you something, John. How will that do? Or I'll sing to you. You used to like to hear me sing; you said my voice, I remember, was sympathetic, didn't you? (*Moves quickly to the piano*). I'll sing you a pretty little song. I think it's beautiful. You've never heard it, I know. I've never sung it to you before. It's Nevin's "At Twilight." (*Pauses, looks down, before she begins, then turns toward him and says quietly and sweetly*) Sometimes—in the coming years—I want—you to remember—I sang you this little song.—Will you?—I think it will make it easier for me—when I—when I—(*Breaks off and begins the first chords. Strong goes slowly to the piano. He leans there watching intently. Rachel sings*):

"The roses of yester-year
Were all of the white and red;
It fills my heart with silent fear
To find all their beauty fled.
The roses of white are sere,
All faded the roses red,
And one who loves me is not here
And one that I love is dead."

(*A long pause. Then Strong goes to her and lifts her from the piano-stool. He puts one arm around her very tenderly and pushes her head back so he can look into her eyes. She shuts them, but is passive*).

STRONG (*Gently*): Little girl, little girl, don't you know that suggestions—suggestions—like those you are sending yourself constantly—are wicked things? You, who are so gentle, so loving, so warm—(*Breaks off and crushes her to him. He kisses her many times. She does not resist, but in the midst of his caresses she breaks suddenly into convulsive laughter. He tries to hush the terrible sound with his mouth; then brokenly*) Little girl—don't laugh—like that.

RACHEL (*Interrupted throughout by her laughter*): I have to.—God is laughing.—We're his puppets.—He pulls the wires,—and we're so funny to Him.—I'm laughing too—because I can hear—my little children—weeping. They come to me generally while I'm asleep,—but I can hear them now.—They've begged me—do you understand?—begged me—not to bring them here;—and I've promised them—not to.—I've promised. I can't stand the sound of their crying.—I have to laugh—Oh! John! laugh!—laugh too!—I can't drown their weeping. (*Strong picks her up bodily and carries her to the armchair*).

STRONG (*Harshly*): Now, stop that!

RACHEL (*In sheer surprise*): W-h-a-t?

STRONG (*Still harshly*): Stop that!—You've lost your self-control.—Find yourself again!

(*He leaves her and goes over to the fireplace, and stands looking down into it for some little time. Rachel, little by little, becomes calmer. Strong returns and sits beside her again. She doesn't move. He smoothes her hair back gently, and kisses her forehead—and then, slowly, her mouth. She does not resist; simply sits there, with shut eyes, inert, limp*).

STRONG: Rachel!—(*Pauses*). There is a little flat on 43rd Street. It faces south and overlooks a little park. Do you remember it?—it's on the top floor?—Once I remember your saying—you liked it. That was over a year ago. That same day—I rented it. I've never lived there. No one knows about it—not even my mother. It's completely furnished now—and waiting—do you know for whom? Every single thing in it, I've bought myself—even to the pins on the little bird's-eye maple dresser. It has been the happiest year I have ever known. I furnished it—one room at a time. It's the prettiest, the most homelike little flat I've ever seen. (*Very low*) Everything there—breathes love. Do you know for whom it is waiting? On the sitting-room floor is a beautiful, Turkish rug—red, and blue and gold. It's soft—and rich—and do you know for whose little feet it is waiting? There are delicate curtains at the windows and a bookcase full of friendly, eager, little books.—Do you know for whom they are waiting? There are comfortable leather chairs, just the right size, and a beautiful piano—that I leave open—sometimes, and lovely pictures of Madonnas. Do you know for whom they are waiting? There is an open fireplace with logs of wood, all carefully piled on gleaming andirons—and waiting. There is a bellows and a pair of shining tongs—waiting. And in the kitchenette painted blue and white, and smelling sweet with paint is everything: bright pots and pans and kettles, and blue and white enamel-ware, and all kinds of knives and forks and spoons—and on the door—a roller-towel. Little girl, do you know for whom they are all waiting? And somewhere—there's a big, strong man—with broad shoulders. And he's willing and anxious to do anything—everything, and he's waiting very patiently. Little girl, is it to be—yes or no?

RACHEL (*During Strong's speech life has come flooding back to her. Her eyes are shining; her face, eager. For a moment she is beautifully happy*). Oh! you're too good to me and mine, John. I—didn't dream any one—could be—so good. (*Leans forward and puts his big hand against her cheek and kisses it shyly*).

STRONG (*Quietly*): Is it—yes—or no, little girl?

RACHEL (*Feverishly, gripping his hands*): Oh, yes! yes! yes! and take me quickly, John. Take me before I can think any more. You mustn't let me think, John. And you'll be good to me, won't you? Every second of every minute, of every hour, of every day, you'll have me in your thoughts, won't you? And you'll be with me every minute that you can? And, John, John!—you'll keep away the weeping of my little children. You won't let me hear it, will you? You'll make me forget everything everything—won't you?—Life is so short, John. (*Shivers and then fearfully and slowly*) And eternity so—long. (*Feverishly again*) And, John, after I am dead—promise me, promise me you'll love me more. (*Shivers again*). I'll need love then. Oh! I'll need it. (*Suddenly there comes to their ears the sound of a child's weeping. It is monotonous, hopeless, terribly afraid, Rachel recoils*). Oh! John!—Listen!—It's my boy, again.—I—John—I'll be back in a little while. (*Goes swiftly to the door in the rear, pauses and looks back. The weeping continues. Her eyes are tragic. Slowly she kisses her hand to him and disappears. John stands where she has left him looking down. The weeping stops. Presently Rachel appears in the doorway. She is haggard, and grey. She does not enter the room. She speaks as one dead might speak—tonelessly, slowly*).

RACHEL: Do you wish to know why Jimmy is crying?

STRONG: Yes.

RACHEL: I am twenty-two—and I'm old; you're thirty-two—and you're old; Tom's twenty-three—and he is old. Ma dear's sixty—and she said once she is much older than that. She is. We are all blighted; we are all accursed—all of us—, everywhere, we whose skins are dark—our lives blasted by the white man's prejudice. (*Pauses*) And my little Jimmy—seven years old, that's all—is blighted too. In a year or two, at best, he will be made old by suffering. (*Pauses*). One week ago, today, some white boys, older and larger than my little Jimmy, as he was leaving the school—called him "Nigger"! They chased him through the streets calling him, "Nigger! Nigger! Nigger!" One boy threw stones at him. There is still a bruise on his little back where one struck him. That will get well; but they bruised his soul—and that—will never—get well. He asked me what "Nigger" meant. I made light of the whole thing, laughed it off. He went to his little playmates, and very naturally asked them. The oldest of them is nine!—and they knew, poor little things—and they told him. (*Pauses*). For the last couple of nights he has been dreaming—about these boys. And he always awakes—in the dark—afraid—afraid—of the now—and the future—I have seen that look of deadly fear—in the eyes—of other little children. I know what it is myself.—I was twelve—when some big boys chased me and called me names.—I never left the house afterwards—without being afraid. I was afraid, in the streets—in the school—in the church, everywhere, always, afraid of being hurt. And I—was not—afraid in vain. (*The weeping begins again*). He's only a baby—and he's blighted. (*To Jimmy*) Honey, I'm right here. I'm coming in just a minute. Don't cry. (*To Strong*) If it nearly kills me to hear my Jimmy's crying, do you think I could stand it, when my own child, flesh of my flesh, blood of my blood—learned the same reason for weeping? Do you? (*Pauses*). Ever since I fell here—a week ago—I am afraid—to go—to sleep, for every time I do—my children come—and beg me—weeping—not to—bring them here—to suffer. Tonight, they came—when I was awake. (*Pauses*). I have promised them again, now—by Jimmy's bed. (*In a whisper*) I have damned—my soul to all eternity—if I do. (*To Jimmy*) Honey, don't! I'm coming. (*To Strong*) And John,—dear John—you see—it can never be—all the beautiful, beautiful things—you have—told me about. (*Wistfully*) No—they—can never be—now. (*Strong comes toward her*) No,—John dear,—you—must not—touch me—any more. (*Pauses*). Dear, this—is—"Good-bye."

STRONG (*Quietly*): It's not fair—to you, Rachel, to take you—at your word—tonight. You're sick; you've brooded so long, so continuously,—you've lost—your perspective. Don't answer, yet. Think it over for another week and I'll come back.

RACHEL (*Wearily*): No,—I can't think—any more.

STRONG: You realize—fully—you're sending me—for always?

RACHEL: Yes.

STRONG: And you care?

RACHEL: Yes.

STRONG: It's settled, then for all time—"Good-bye!"

RACHEL (*After a pause*): Yes.

STRONG (*Stands looking at her steadily a long time, and then moves to the door and turns, facing her; with infinite tenderness*): Good-bye, dear, little Rachel—God bless you.

RACHEL: Good-bye, John! (*Strong goes out. A door opens and shuts. There is finality in the sound. The weeping continues. Suddenly; with a great cry*) John! John! (*Runs out into the vestibule. She presently returns. She is calm again. Slowly*) No! No! John. Not for us. (*A pause; with infinite yearning*) Oh! John,—if it only—if it only—(*Breaks off, controls herself. Slowly again; thoughtfully*) No—No sunshine—no laughter—always, always—darkness. That is it. Even our little flat—(*In a whisper*) John's and mine—the little flat—that calls, calls us—through darkness. It shall wait—and wait—in vain—in darkness. Oh, John! (*Pauses*). And my little children!

my little children! (*The weeping ceases; pauses*). I shall never—see—you—now. Your little, brown, beautiful bodies—I shall never see.—Your dimples—everywhere—your laughter—your tears—the beautiful, lovely feel of you here. (*Puts her hands against her heart*). Never—never—to be. (*A pause, fiercely*) But you are somewhere—and wherever you are you are mine! You are mine! All of you! Every bit of you! Even God can't take you away. (*A pause; very sweetly; pathetically*) Little children!—My little children!—No more need you come to me—weeping—weeping. You may be happy now—you are safe. Little weeping, voices, hush! hush! (*The weeping begins again. To Jimmy, her whole soul in her voice*) Jimmy! My little Jimmy! Honey! I'm coming.—Ma Rachel loves you so. (*Sobs and goes blindly, unsteadily to the rear doorway; she leans her head there one second against the door; and then stumbles through and disappears. The light in the lamp flickers and goes out . . . It is black. The terrible, heart-breaking weeping continues*).

The End

7. *Vaudeville Humor: The Collected Jokes, Routines, and Skits of Ed Lowry*—Ed Lowry

Commentaries

Sources

Play

7.1 HUMOR AND ETHNIC STEREOTYPES IN VAUDEVILLE AND BURLESQUE—LAWRENCE E. MINTZ

THE HALCYON DAYS of the American vaudeville and burlesque theater, roughly from 1890 through 1910, compose the period in which ethnic humor on stage was most manifest. These decades were also years in which American humor changes significantly, moving away from the familiar literary and journalistic pseudo-folklore, the Yankee and Southwestern wise fools, commonsense philosophers, tricksters and con men, to the more universal "little man" of the twenties and the modernist and post-modernist comedy which would develop after the "golden age" (roughly from the end of the first World War to the early 1930s) (see McLean, Jr., chapter 3, Pinsker). The period was also one in which two other genres, film comedy and comic strips, as well as the popular theater, emerged to compete with the published word and to a lesser extent the platform lecture, as the forum for American humor.

While it is easy to see the differences in the humor of the nineteenth century with the emerging "modern" forms, it is important to note similarities and continuities as well and to be reminded that cultural changes take place neither suddenly nor absolutely. All of the familiar characters of earlier American humor can be located throughout twentieth century sources, in all genres, and many important motifs recur as well. In his recent book, *American Laughter: Immigrants, Ethnicity, and 1930's Film Comedy*, Mark Winokur presents the interesting argument that American literary comedy was always, in a sense, "ethnic," in its contrasting of immigrants to the new land with Europeans and immigrants to the western frontier with more established easterners (23–73, for reference to vaudeville, see esp. 63–73). Ethnic humor in the popular theater has a lot in common with the dialect humor of nineteenth century writers, and it reaches forward as well as backward in the literary humor of writers such as Roth, Heller, Malamud, Bellow and Reed, among others, though not always overtly.

Ethnic humor itself is not a uniquely American phenomenon of a specific historical period or particular form of popular entertainment. There are examples from the classical theater and folk theater worldwide which would be included under any reasonable definition of ethnic humor, and in our own theatrical tradition ethnic humor is to be found in the pre-Civil War minstrel theater, the rural tent theater circuit, the urban popular theater, and other popular stage entertainment vehicles from the late eighteenth century. Ethnic humor is present from the earliest days of the variety theater (I use the term "variety theater" here generically to embrace minstrel theater, vaudeville, burlesque and the revues), for instance in the "Double Irish" acts of McNulty and Murray in 1865 or of the Russell Brothers, John and James, as early as 1876.

Though stage expression of ethnic humor faded by the end of the 20s, along with the decline of vaudeville and burlesque, it did not die out entirely, surviving if not thriving in the Broadway revues such as George White's "Scandals," Earl Carroll's "Vanities," and Florenz Ziegfeld's "Follies," in the standup comedy of resorts and nightclubs, and in the mass media of film and television situation comedy. It is also manifested in American popular literature and journalism, appearing in the voice of Finley Peter Dunne's Mr. Dooley, Leo Rosten's Hyman Kaplan, Langston

Hughes's memorable Jesse B. Semple aka "Simple," in Milt Gross's "Nize Baby" pieces, and elsewhere in America's newspaper columns, magazine features and popular books.

The ethnic humor of the variety theater is easy to describe. It consists of comic monologues, two-acts, and comic sketches. The core of the humor is the construction of caricatures based on familiar ethnic stereotypes and linguistic humor—puns, malapropisms, double entendres, and accent-play, including broad exaggeration and misunderstandings which result from faulty pronunciation. The two-acts and the sketches provided, as we will see, a bit more thematic content and complexity, but for the most part, the ethnic humor was formulaic—pretty basic stuff.

The monologues and two-acts provided the structure, such as it was, for the construction of the caricatures and for the language play. Virtually all of the ethnic characters in the variety theater were flat representations of familiar stereotypes. A few of the better performers added their own twists and stylistic signatures, but even these were glosses and aesthetic adventures rather than deviations from the expectations of type. The Irish characters are drunk, belligerent, and dumb (dumb was the term commonly used in the comedy—it meant stupid or unintelligent, but it also meant culturally naive, "green" or bewildered, "unhip" as well). The Italians are happy rascals, promiscuous, prolificate, and irresponsible, comically hyper-emotional—and dumb; the Germans, usually called "Dutch" in vaudeville from the same corruption of Deutch which gave us the Pennsylvania Dutch, are lazy, stodgily conservative, and of course, also dumb. Blacks are lazy, dishonest, promiscuous, prolificate, irresponsible and—guess what—dumb. Jews are usually "canny" to use the term provided by the basic classification system established in Christie Davies's important study, *Ethnic Humor Around the World*, that is, they are smart in the sense of too clever, manipulative, dishonest—but they are also portrayed, perhaps surprisingly, as dumb, especially as lacking in "street smarts," and potential suckers. Jewish men are also particularly weak, cowardly, the victims of bullies (including Jewish women). Some of the traits are more specific and particular than the generic categories described by Davies. For instance, blacks are associated with an insatiable desire for watermelon, chicken, or pork chops; Italian immigrants are associated with crime and huge families, "Dutchmen" with sauerkraut and beer, and so forth. Some of the jokes deal specifically with the issues and dynamics of immigrant assimilation, as in the case of Cohen, who thanked his gentile friend for providing him with a nice salmon dinner the previous night. When his host corrects him by noting that the dinner was actually ham, Cohen replies indignantly, "So who asked you?" Here Cohen is the target of the joke, perhaps, for his hypocrisy and for his glib willingness to manipulate the truth, but he is also triumphant, that is he can eat his ham and have it be salmon too. Another latent but not unimportant theme encoded in this simple bit is the social mingling of Jews and gentiles, the gentile's willingness to host the Jew, and the price the Jew must pay, in terms of fidelity to religious law and custom, to accept the invitation.

Collectively the immigrant caricatures sketch men who fit many of the basic categories in Christie Davies's classification scheme, which outlines several oppositional pairs, stupid versus canny, lazy versus relentlessly acquisitive and competitive, cowardly or militaristic and aggressive, cheap or recklessly spendthrift. Alcohol abuse, a trait associated most prominently with the Irish in vaudeville humor, but also ascribed to Dutch, Black, and Italian ethnics, is another important theme. These ethnic men often have problems with women. They are straddled with nagging and demanding wives and/or with jealous girlfriends, or they are the victims of attractive flirts who control, torment, or disorient them. Needless to say, the women are often the victims of the men's infidelities, broken promises, fiscal irresponsibility and so forth. Indeed most of the male versus female humor clearly is much more sexist than it is ethnic. For instance a song like "The Widow Rosenbalm" in which a soldier's widow lives high off of his pension, neglects her children, and toys with her many suitors, might be seen as an anti-Semitic theme, but it is actually an adaptation of "The Widow Dunn," a misogynist Irish song, and it could easily surface as well in any other ethnic costume. Another central element of the ethnic humor in the variety theater are the jokes and routines which deal with the immigrant's problems with money, the lack of which, the need for which, and the quest for which are omnipresent. Characters are always trying to get money from each other, help each other solve pressing financial dilemmas, and in other ways familiar to the working class audience, get ahead in the new world of opportunity or, perhaps more characteristically, scramble for survival on streets which are not exactly paved with gold.

Language humor provides much of the actual laughter in stage ethnic comedy. The Italian character thinks that the mayor is a horse (mare), he confuses the pallbearer with a polar bear, and he asserts with confidence that the student who went to college to get a diploma could have saved a lot of time, money, and effort simply by looking in the telephone book under Pipes, Repair. Ikey Blatt was invited to an affair in which evening dress was requested. Naturally he came in his pajamas. A famous Bert Lahr song, "Ach, Gott How that Voman Could Cook, Jawohl," offers such lines as: "Her Zoop had a flavor / Like bitches and cream / her pancakes—ah—vot a bootiful dreaaaaaaaaam / And her oysters and fishes—were simply—*malicious.* / Ach Gott how dot vornan could cook, jahwohl" (56). Such linguistic humor is often derided as simplistic and juvenile, and indeed it is, as its popularity with young children attests. But it is also a reference to problems of language acquisition, a serious matter for immigrants, who realize constantly that understanding and misunderstanding vocabulary and pronunciation can be crucially important, even literally a matter of life and death!

The ethnic two-acts, called Double Dutch, Double Hebe, Double Wop, Minstrel (for Blackface, borrowing from the dialogues of the End Men, Tambo and Bones, in the minstrel theater), and the sketches or skits offer opportunities for the development of somewhat more complex themes and images. The opposition of a dumb or culturally naive character with a smarter, more hip, possibly "street wise," or even a con man, compatriot allows for the adaptation of very familiar American comic structures and character types to the specific contexts of the immigrant experience. The stupid character can play the various roles of the fool, from the negative bumpkin to the naif to the commonsense philosopher, exposing folly accidentally through fortuitous, ironic misunderstanding or through innocent honesty. Or he can employ simple folk wisdom in opposition to more sophisticated error. His foil can be a trickster-con man, a slick rascal who uses his wit to survive in a hostile environment. As that prominent observer of American culture from Southwestern humor, Simon Suggs, liked to put it, "its good to be shifty in a new country." The smart/dumb opposition recalls the Yankee humor of Hosea Biglow, the southwestern humor of Sut Lovingood and Simon Suggs, the literary comedians from Artemus Ward to the above-mentioned Mr. Dooley, Hyman Kaplan and "Simple."

The two-act also allows for other oppositional examinations, such as those described by Davies. Norms of honesty versus dishonesty, of generosity versus thriftiness, of sobriety versus conviviality—

in short just about all moral, ethical and social belief and behavior can be defined and described. The brief sketches allowed for even further development of humor revolving around the everyday lifestyle common to just about all of the immigrants. In one Dutch sketch, for instance, "Dot Quied Lotchings," the laughter is provided by the usual language gags and stereotypes. The stock Irishman grouses about the Dutchman's taste for lager, "Divil burn me if I can understand people drinkin' lager beer when they can get drunk so much quicker an' better on whiskey." But the sketch also provides a humorous glimpse at the business of taking in boarders, a common practice in urban, immigrant America. It shows how hard it is to get a landlord to rent you a room unless you are the "perfect tenant" (i.e., no kids, pets, bad habits, domestic needs), and how having boarders disrupts the serenity of the landlord forced by financial exigency to open his or her home (McNamara 129–31).

Accounting for the prevalence of ethnic humor in the popular variety theater of the late nineteenth and early twentieth centuries and exploring its various motives and functions is not nearly as easy as describing it. Beyond the small, mostly descriptive set of histories of American humor, Hill and Blair, Bier, and others, there is a sizable shelf of pertinent theoretical literature, both dealing with the motives and functions of humor generally and tackling the questions of ethnic humor specifically. In several conference papers, I have made my own modest contribution—a continuum description of the motives and functions of racial, ethnic and gender humor—and others including Lawrence LaFave, Marvin Koller, William Martineau, and the above mentioned Christie Davies have tackled the issue directly. John Lowe's 1986 article in *American Quarterly*, "Theories of Ethnic Humor: How to Enter, Laughing," is an indispensable introduction to the topic.

The most immediate and obvious explanation for ethnic and racial joking is that it allows for expression of hostility and superiority. This observation still leaves open the question of whether such expression tends to lead to or to justify actual acts of hostility, or whether it might neutralize or soften anger by providing alternative channels of expression for it or perhaps by providing some sort of "safety valve" for letting off the steam generated by people of different cultural backgrounds, often also historical enemies, who are living in very close quarters in the American urban environment. It has been argued that even aggressive, hostile humor is a mock attack, rather than an actual blow. Perhaps the most persuasive modern scholar taking a more jaundiced view of the effects of ethnic humor is Joseph Boskin, whose important essays in *Humor and Social Change in the Twentieth Century* are, fortunately, scheduled to be reprinted in a new, more accessible edition. Boskin points out that humor allows, that is licenses, cruel, hostile, negative sentiments which both directly and indirectly sanction and frame oppression, social control. According to Boskin, "Humor is one of the most effective and vicious weapons in the repertory of the human mind" (28).

A theoretical position which supports this view is the argument advanced by Hugh Dalziel Duncan, among others, that humor can have a conservative function, ridiculing that which is different from the norm, from the status quo, and "bringing it into line." Umberto Eco echoes this line, arguing in "The Comic and the Rule" that the liberating effects of comedy's licensing of deviation—Bakhtin's spirit of carnival—is offset, at least, by the realization that, after the comedy, there is a return to order; the sanctioned norms prevail (275).

Some, but not most, of the texts support the argument that the ethnic humor of the variety theater was hostile and aggressive. For one instance, an Irish character, informed of an accident in which forty Italians and one Irishman are killed responds: "the poor man." Certainly many of the ethnic stereotypes are at least derisive, more characteristically offensive, unpleasant, at least to our contemporary tastes. There are plenty of examples of ethnic humor which might justify holding a member of the targeted group in contempt, and that would obviously support Boskin's point that it then further justifies oppression. In this sense, theatrical humor in the decades before and after the turn of the twentieth century can be understood as a means by which the public expressed resentment against the waves of new immigrants and also allowed for conflict and hostility between ethnic groups to be expressed in a displaced, but not necessarily, socially benign manner.

Other approaches, however, suggest more positive motives and functions. The portrait painted by many of the participants—performers and audiences—perhaps fueled by nostalgia and selective memory, is that ethnic humor was harmless fun, light amusement, pleasant banter, enjoyed by all. Joe Laurie, Jr. argues that ethnic humor was generally accepted as gentle fun, because it was a familiar staple in every day discourse; it had not yet acquired the assigned designation of improper or insulting (81). Albert McLean, Jr. claims that while the "new humor" of the popular stage was more aggressive and confrontational than earlier humor had been, its effects were more to create harmony than to exacerbate discord. According to McLean, in *American Vaudeville as Ritual*, ". . . vaudeville as a ritual of a New folk, was one of the means by which Americans came to terms with a crisis in culture" (3). Constance Rourke, the dean of American humor historians, contends, in *American Humor: A Study of the National Character*, that "Its [humor's] objective—the unconscious objective of a disunited people—has seemed to be that of creating fresh bonds, a new unity, the semblance of a society, and the rounded completion of an American type."

A related, but more sophisticated case for positive functions of ethnic humor is that of Charles Winick, who states that "a joke reflects social attitudes and provides a vehicle through which people can voice feelings for which there is no socially acceptable or easily accessible outlet" (125). Similarly, Mary Douglas, among others, emphasizes the liberating qualities of humor, allowing sentiments which are repressed or blocked in the "official culture" to surface and to be processed, often with positive benefits for social change. Bakhtin is also cited, very frequently, supporting this position in his account of the motives and functions of carnival and of Rabelaisian deviations from polite social norms.

Christie Davies's theories about ethnic humor also provide potent arguments for less negative assessment. Davies maintains that the oppositional pairs which frame most ethnic jokes allow a society to establish boundaries of approved and scorned behavior. This is not entirely in opposition to Boskin, of course, but it sees the social control as operating within the society, rather than imposed on it from outside or above. Davies also sees the social and cultural control functions of ethnic humor as subordinate to their cognitive value, that is, to the ways in which they contribute to cultural awareness, to the process of acculturation. "The assertion and maintenance of ethnic identity are themselves values, and each individual is expected to strike a reasonably happy mean between the anomie and paralysis that would result from total cultural relativism and the crass ethnocentrism that automatically negates the cultural values of others" (309).

Characteristically, alas, my own answer is (d)—all of the above! The theories described above are correct, and there are still a few more ways to account for the many varied motives and functions of ethnic humor in the popular theater. The uses and gratifications of any humor depend upon a number of variables: *who says what to whom under what contextual circumstances*. The same joke, image, or caricature can have hostile intent and aggressive function, it can enhance group moral, it can be an aesthetic comedy-creating exercise, or it can be employed ironically as a sign of friendship and acceptance that is so strong, so transcendent that otherwise taboo utterances are acceptable. The audience might react entirely differently to texts according to how they are presented, to the mood or spirit created by the artist, but the experience also varies according to the composition of the audience; homogeneous audiences react to comedy entirely differently than do heterogeneous ones. The members of any audience do not have uniform reactions to humorous stimuli. It depends on your sense of humor. You had to be there. Smile when you say that. This approach to ethnic humor as polysemic is not intended to suggest that the responses are so infinite that they defy any intelligent hypotheses about the role of such humor in the popular theater of the late nineteenth and early twentieth century. As I have maintained in this essay, there are useful explanations which make some sense of it all. The significance of ethnic humor in the variety theater has to be mapped, however, rather than nailed down in one spot.

It remains for us to consider, briefly, why ethnic humor faded by the teens and died by the end of the twenties. One view is that the audience outgrew it and began to reject it. Supporting the idea that the audience voted, democratically, by its expression of approval or disapproval, Joe DiMeglio claims that "if no group was dismayed, an ethnic joke was in order. If a group objected, the particular ethnic joke was removed" (6). Paul Antoine Distler traces the decline in the popularity of ethnic humor to the assimilation of the ethnic population and a corresponding disinterest in the themes and images of immigrant life, but the dates just do not work to support his thesis. Ethnic humor had been banished, essentially, from the variety stage long before it would have been foreign to its audience" (40). James Dorman describes an audience which became too sophisticated for crass, vulgar ethnic humor, as do Abel Green and Joe Laurie, Jr., who notes that the ethnic humor reigned until the audience "achieved a new economic and social dignity" (7).

However, there is more compelling evidence that ethnic humor on the variety stage suffered a more violent, untimely death, as opposed to having simply withered away. As has been reported thoroughly by the historians of the popular theater, a conscious and concerted effort was made to "clean up" the variety entertainments, particularly vaudeville, but burlesque and the revues as well. B. F. Keith played a leading role, from within the profession, in this particular form of ethnic cleansing (along with his expurgation of "dirty" language and suggestive sexuality), but it was also spurred from outside, from pressure groups, usually organized ethnic societies, which attacked humor deemed offensive to the group's image, often with boycotts, demonstrations, disruptions, and other activist techniques. Geraldine Mascio reports that the Russell Brothers, for instance, were brought down not by audience boredom or neglect, but by an organized protest movement orchestrated by the United Irish Societies, a group composed of ninety-one Irish societies. As Maschio informs us, a special committee called the "Society for the Prevention of Ridiculous and Perversive Misrepresentation of the Irish Character" pretty much single-handedly accounted for the Russell Brothers' humor suddenly becoming politically incorrect (85).

In his essay "On Vaudeville," William Dean Howells imagines a dialogue between the editor and his visitor. "Then what you wish, the editor suggested, is to elevate vaudeville. The visitor got himself out of his easy chair with a groan and a growl. You mean, to kill it" (77). As we know from our own contemporary experience, ethnic humor did not die. It was merely buried alive, forced underground into popular, vernacular, serendipitous joke telling rather than more formal theatrical and media forums. And now, of course, efforts are being made that it be exhumed . . . so that a stake might be driven through its heart.

Works Cited

Bakhtin, M.M. *The Dialogic Imagination.* Austin, TX: University of Texas Press, 1981.

——. *Rabelais and His World.* Bloominton: Indiana UP, 1968.

Boskin, Joseph. *Humor and Social Change in 20th Century America.* Boston, MA: Boston Public Library, 1979.

Boskin, Joseph, and Joseph Dorinson. "Ethnic Humor: Subversion and Survival." *American Humor.* Ed. Arthur P. Dudden. New York: Oxford UP, 1987. 97–117.

Cohen, Sandy. "Racial and Ethnic Humor in the United States." *Amerika Studien* 30:2 (1985): 203–11.

Davies, Christie. *Ethnic Humor Around the World: A Comparative Analysis.* Bloomington, IN: Indiana University Press, 1990.

DiMeglio, Joe. *Vaudeville, USA.* Bowling Green: Popular, 1973.

Distler, Paul Antoine, "Ethnic Comedy in Vaudeville and Burlesque." *American Popular Entertainment.* Ed. Myron Matlaw. Westport, CT: Greenwood, 1979.

Dorinson, Joseph and Joseph Boskin, "Racial and Ethnic Humor." *Humor in America.* Ed. Lawrence E. Mintz. Westport, CT: Greenwood, 1988. 163–93.

Dorman, James. "Ethnic Cultures of the Mind: The Harrington-Hart Mosaic." *American Studies* 33:2 (Fall 1992): 21–40.

Douglas, Mary. *Implicit Meanings: Essays in Anthropology.* Boston, MA: Routledge, 1975.

Duncan, Hugh Dalziel. *Communication and Social Order.* New York: Oxford University Press, 1962.

Eco, Umberto. *Travels in Hyperreality.* New York: Harcourt, 1986.

Gilbert, Douglas. *American Vaudeville: Its Life and Times.* New York: Dover, 1963.

Goldstein, Jeffrey, and Paul McGhee. *The Psychology of Humor.* New York: Academic, 1977.

Green, Abel, and Joe Laurie. *Show Biz: From Vaude to Video.* New York: Holt, 1951.

Howells, William Dean. "On Vaudeville." *American Vaudeville as Seen by its Contemporaries.* Ed. Charles W. Stein. New York: DaCapo, 1984.

Lahr, John. *Notes on a Cowardly Lion.* New York: Ballantine, 1969.

Laurie, Jr. Joe. *Vaudeville: From the Honky-Tonks to the Palace.* New York: Holt, 1953.

Lowe, John. "Theories of Ethnic Humor: How to Enter, Laughing." *American Quarterly* 38:3 (1986): 439–59.

McLean, Jr., Albert. *American Vaudeville as Ritual.* Lexington, MA: University of Kentucky Press, 1965.

McNamara, Brooks. *American Popular Entertainments: Jokes, Monologues, Bits and Sketches.* New York: Performing Arts Journal, 1993.

Maschio, Geraldine. "Ethnic Humor and the Demise of the Russell Brothers." *Journal of Popular Culture* 26:1 (Summer 1992): 81–92.

Mintz, Lawrence E. "A Continuum Description of the Motives and Functions of Racial, Ethnic and Sexist Humor." *The Study of Humor.* Ed. Harvey Mindess and Joy Turek. Los Angeles, CA: Antioch University Press, 1980. 53–54.

——. "Ethnic Humor: A Discussion." *Its a Funny Thing, Humour.* Ed. Antony Chapman and Hugh Foot. London: Pergamon, 1976.

——. "Humor and Popular Culture." *Handbook of Humor Research.* Ed. Paul E. McGhee and Jeffrey H. Goldstein. Volume 2. New York: Springer, 1983. 2 vols. 129–42.

Pinsker, Sanford. "On or About December 1910: When Human Character—and American Humor—Changed." *Critical Essays on American Humor.* Ed. William Bedford Clark and W. Craig Turner. Boston, MA: Hall, 184–89.

Rourke, Constance. *American Humor: A Study of the National Character.* New York: Doubleday, 1953.

Winick, Charles. "The Social Contexts of Humor." *Journal of Communication* 26:3 (Summer 1976): 124–28.

Winokur, Mark. *American Laughter: Immigrants, Ethnicity, and 1930s Film Comedy.* New York: St. Martin's, 1996.

7.2 THE COMPETITION OF RACES—MADISON GRANT

WHERE TWO RACES OCCUPY a country side by side, it is not correct to speak of one type as changing into the other. Even if present in equal numbers one of the two contrasted types will have some small advantage or capacity which the other lacks toward a perfect adjustment to surroundings. Those possessing these favorable variations will flourish at the expense of their rivals and their offspring will not only be more numerous, but will also tend to inherit such variations. In this way one type gradually breeds the other out. In this sense, and in this sense only, do races change.

Man continuously undergoes selection through the operation of the forces of social environment. Among native Americans of the Colonial period a large family was an asset and social pressure and economic advantage counselled both early marriage and numerous children. Two hundred years of continuous political expansion and material prosperity changed these conditions and children, instead of being an asset to till the fields and guard the cattle, became an expensive liability. They now require support, education and endowment from their parents and a large family is regarded by some as a serious handicap in the social struggle.

These conditions do not obtain at first among immigrants, and large families among the newly arrived population are still the rule, precisely as they were in Colonial America and are to-day in French Canada where backwoods conditions still prevail.

The result is that one class or type in a population expands more rapidly than another and ultimately replaces it. This process of replacement of one type by another does not mean that the race changes or is transformed into another. It is a replacement pure and simple and not a transformation.

The lowering of the birth rate among the most valuable classes, while the birth rate of the lower classes remains unaffected, is a frequent phenomenon of prosperity. Such a change becomes extremely injurious to the race if unchecked, unless nature is allowed to maintain by her own cruel devices the relative numbers of the different classes in their due proportions. To attack race suicide by encouraging indiscriminate reproduction is not only futile but is dangerous if it leads to an increase in the undesirable elements. What is needed in the community most of all is an increase in the desirable classes, which are of superior type physically, intellectually and morally and not merely an increase in the absolute numbers of the population.

The value and efficiency of a population are not numbered by what the newspapers call souls, but by the proportion of men of physical and intellectual vigor. The small Colonial population of America was, on an average and man for man, far superior to the present inhabitants, although the latter are twenty-five times more numerous. The ideal in eugenics toward which statesmanship should be directed is, of course, improvement in quality rather than quantity. This, however, is at present a counsel of perfection and we must face conditions as they are.

The small birth rate in the upper classes is to some extent offset by the care received by such children as are born and the better chance they have to become adult and breed in their turn. The large birth rate of the lower classes is under normal conditions offset by a heavy infant mortality, which eliminates the weaker children.

Where altruism, philanthropy or sentimentalism intervene with the noblest purpose and forbid nature to penalize the unfortunate victims of reckless breeding, the multiplication of inferior types is encouraged and fostered. Indiscriminate efforts to preserve babies among the lower classes often result in serious injury to the race. At the existing stage of civilization, the legalizing of birth control would probably be of benefit by reducing the number of offspring in the undesirable classes. Regulation of the number of children is, for good or evil, in full operation among the better classes and its recognition by the state would result in no further harm among them.

Mistaken regard for what are believed to be divine laws and a sentimental belief in the sanctity of human life tend to prevent both the elimination of defective infants and the sterilization of such adults as are themselves of no value to the community. The laws of nature require the obliteration of the unfit and human life is valuable only when it is of use to the community or race.

It is highly unjust that a minute minority should be called upon to supply brains for the unthinking mass of the community, but it is even worse to burden the responsible and larger but still overworked elements in the community with an ever increasing number of moral perverts, mental defectives and hereditary cripples. As the percentage of incompetents increases, the burden of their support will become ever more onerous until, at no distant date, society will in self-defense put a stop to the supply of feebleminded and criminal children of weaklings.

The church assumes a serious responsibility toward the future of the race whenever it steps in and preserves a defective strain. The marriage of deaf mutes was hailed a generation ago as a triumph of humanity. Now it is recognized as an absolute crime against the race. A great injury is done to the community by the perpetuation of worthless types. These strains are apt to be meek and lowly and as such make a strong appeal to the sympathies of the successful. Before eugenics were understood much could be said from a Christian and humane viewpoint in favor of indiscriminate charity for the benefit of the individual. The societies for charity, altruism or extension of rights, should have in these days, however, in their management some small modicum of brains, otherwise they may continue to do, as they have sometimes done in the past, more injury to the race than black death or smallpox.

As long as such charitable organizations confine themselves to the relief of suffering individuals, no matter how criminal or diseased they may be, no harm is done except to our own generation and if modern society recognizes a duty to the humblest malefactors or imbeciles that duty can be harmlessly performed in full, provided they be deprived of the capacity to procreate their defective strain.

Those who read these pages will feel that there is little hope for humanity, but the remedy has been found, and can be quickly and mercifully applied. A rigid system of selection through the elimination of those who are weak or unfit—in other words, social failures—would solve the whole question in a century, as well as enable us to get rid of the undesirables who crowd our jails, hospitals and insane asylums. The individual himself can be nourished, educated and protected by the community during his lifetime, but the state through sterilization must see to it that his line stops with him or else future generations will be cursed with an ever increasing load of victims of misguided sentimentalism. This is a practical, merciful and inevitable solution of the whole problem and can be applied to an ever widening circle of social discards, beginning always with the criminal, the diseased and the insane and extending gradually to types which may be called weaklings rather than defectives and perhaps ultimately to worthless race types.

Efforts to increase the birth rate of the genius producing classes of the community, while most desirable, encounter great difficulties. In such efforts we encounter social conditions over which we have as yet no control. It was tried two thousand years ago by Augustus and his efforts to avert race suicide and the extinction of the old Roman stock were singularly prophetic of what some far seeing men are attempting in order to preserve the race of native Americans of Colonial descent.

Man has the choice of two methods of race improvement. He can breed from the best or he can eliminate the worst by segregation or sterilization. The first method was adopted by the Spartans, who had for their national ideals military efficiency and the virtues of self-control, and along these lines the results were completely successful. Under modern social conditions it would be extremely difficult in the first instance to determine which were the most desirable types, except in the most general way and even if a satisfactory selection were finally made, it would be in a democracy a virtual impossibility to limit by law the right to breed to a privileged and chosen few.

Interesting efforts to improve the quality as well as the quantity of the population, however, will probably be made in more than one country after the war has ended.

Experiments in limiting reproduction to the undesirable classes were unconsciously made in mediaeval Europe under the guidance of the church. After the fall of Rome social conditions were such that all those who loved a studious and quiet life were compelled to seek refuge from the violence of the times in monastic institutions and upon such the church imposed the obligation of celibacy and thus deprived the world of offspring from these desirable classes.

In the Middle Ages, through persecution resulting in actual death, life imprisonment and banishment, the free thinking, progressive and intellectual elements were persistently eliminated over large areas, leaving the perpetuation of the race to be carried on by the brutal, the servile and the stupid. It is now impossible to say to what extent the Roman Church by these methods has impaired the brain capacity of Europe, but in Spain alone, for a period of over three centuries from the years 1471 to 1781, the Inquisition condemned to the stake or imprisonment an average of 1,000 persons annually. During these three centuries no less than 32,000 were burned alive and 291,000 were condemned to various terms of imprisonment and other penalties and 17,000 persons were burned in effigy, representing men who had died in prison or had fled the country.

No better method of eliminating the genius producing strains of a nation could be devised and if such were its purpose the result was eminently satisfactory, as is demonstrated by the superstitious and unintelligent Spaniard of to-day. A similar elimination of brains and ability took place in northern Italy, in France and in the Low Countries, where hundreds of thousands of Huguenots were murdered or driven into exile.

Under existing conditions the most practical and hopeful method of race improvement is through the elimination of the least desirable elements in the nation by depriving them of the power to contribute to future generations. It is well known to stock breeders that the color of a herd of cattle can be modified by continuous destruction of worthless shades and of course this is true of other characters. Black sheep, for instance, have been practically obliterated by cutting out generation after generation all animals that show this color phase, until in carefully maintained flocks a black individual only appears as a rare sport.

In mankind it would not be a matter of great difficulty to secure a general consensus of public opinion as to the least desirable, let us say, ten per cent of the community. When this unemployed and unemployable human residuum has been eliminated together with the great mass of crime, poverty, alcoholism and feeblemindedness associated therewith it would be easy to consider the advisability of further restricting the perpetuation of the then remaining least valuable types. By this method mankind might ultimately become sufficiently intelligent to choose deliberately the most vital and intellectual strains to carry on the race.

In addition to selection by climatic environment man is now, and has been for ages, undergoing selection through disease. He has been decimated throughout the centuries by pestilences such as the black death and bubonic plague. In our fathers' days yellow fever and smallpox cursed humanity. These plagues are now under control, but similar diseases now regarded as mere nuisances to childhood, such as measles, mumps and scarlatina, are terrible scourges to native populations without previous experience with them. Add to these smallpox and other white men's diseases and one has the great empire builders of yesterday. It was not the swords in the hands of Columbus and his followers that decimated the American Indians, it was the germs that his men and their successors brought over, implanting the white man's maladies in the red man's world. Long before the arrival of the Puritans in New England, smallpox had flickered up and down the coast until the natives were but a broken remnant of their former numbers.

At the present time the Nordic race is undergoing selection through alcoholism, a peculiarly Nordic vice, and through consumption. Both these dread scourges unfortunately attack those members of the race that are otherwise most desirable, differing in this respect from filth diseases like typhus, typhoid or smallpox. One has only to look among the more desirable classes for the victims of rum and tubercule to realize that death or mental and physical impairment through these two causes have cost the race many of its most brilliant and attractive members.

7.3 BERT WILLIAMS

The black vaudevillian Bert Williams. Silent screen star W. C. Fields called Williams "the funniest man I ever saw and the saddest." Williams performed in blackface makeup, as expected in vaudeville, but replaced comedy that ridiculed black culture with comedy based on more universal situations.

Source: Photo © Bettmann/Corbis

7.4 JOE WEBER AND LEW FIELDS AS "DUTCH" CHARACTERS

Joe Weber and Lew Fields performing as "Dutch" (German) characters. Notorious vaudevillians Weber and Fields used make-up, costumes, accents, mispronunciations and physical comedy to create exaggerated German stereotypes.

7.5 PAT ROONEY AS AN "IRISHMAN"

Vaudevillian Pat Rooney, Sr., in character as a stereotyped Irishman.

7.6 THE RUSSELL BROTHERS AS "IRISH MAIDS"

John and James Russell in character as Irish maids. The Russell brothers developed female characters with embellished Irish accents to satirize the new Irish immigrants and their awkward assimilation into the United States.

Source: Image courtesy of the New York Public Library

7.7 FRANK BUSH AND FANNY PRICE AS "STAGE JEWS"

Gentile comedian Frank Bush created and perpetuated ethnic stereotypes for his famous "stage Jew", which set the pattern for subsequent representations of Jews in U.S. popular entertainment.

Ziegfeld actress Fanny Brice. Composer Irving Berlin insisted that this Jewish comedian perform with a Yiddish accent, even though she did not know any Yiddish. It quickly became her trademark dialect.

Source: Photo © Bettmann/Corbis

7.8 EXCERPTS FROM *VAUDEVILLE HUMOR*—ED LOWRY

Ireland and the Irish

There's a great inventor . . . that Irishman whose name you see on everything: Pat Pending.

Two Irishmen were walking down the street, when Pat said to Mike, "Have you ever heard the story about the feet?" Mike said "No." Pat said, "Be jabbers, you have two."

—So your name is Murphy, is it? Are you any relation to John Murphy?
—Well, distantly. You see he was the first child and I was the fifteenth.

MULHERN: Which would yez rather be in, Mike, an explosion or a collision?
MURPHY: Why, in a collision, Pat. Because in a collision there yez are, but in an explosion, where are yez?

I went to the zoo today. There was an Irish nurse there with some children. They were looking at the kangaroos. She asked the keeper what they were. He said, "They're kangaroos, a native of Australia." The nurse said, "Good heavens, my sister married one of them."

A Jew and an Irishman were on board a ship bound for Ireland.
IRISHMAN (*catching sight of his homeland*): Hurrah for Ireland.
JEW (*riled*): Hurrah, hell.
IRISHMAN : That's right. Every man for his own country.

O'Brien was reading a letter for his friend Murphy, who was standing behind him with hands over O'Brien's ears. When Murphy was asked why, he explained, "I just got a letter from my girl and I can't read. So O'Brien's reading it for me; but I'm stopping his ears so that he can't hear what she's written me."

An Irishman was killed while working. His mates engaged in a lengthy discussion about who should break the news to Mrs. Clancy—and how. Fitzpatrick was elected. He went to the Clancy home and timidly rang the bell. When Mrs. Clancy opened the door, he asked, "Are you the widow Clancy?" She said, "I'm Mrs. Clancy, but I'm not a widow." He said, "No, what'll ya bet?"

An Irishman called O'Brien went out seeking a job. He saw a long line of men standing at the construction site waiting to be hired. So he got in line. Finally, he reached the point where the foreman was doing the hiring. The man in front of O'Brien was asked his trade and replied, "Mason and bricklayer." Next came O'Brien. When he was asked his trade he said, "Knights of Columbus and builder."

A fellow with two wooden legs entered a speakeasy and got very drunk. The barman, wishing to be rid of him, threw him into a telephone booth. About half an hour later, an Irishman who had had a few drinks decided to call his wife and tell her that he was working late. He opened the door of the telephone booth, stepped in, and yelled. "That's a foine place to put a wheelbarrow."

Before the plane took off, the pilot advised everyone to take his parachute. One big burly Irishman refused. The pilot told him, "You'd better have one, flying's not so good today." He still refused. So they started up. After about fifty miles, the plane went into a spin and the pilot gave orders for everyone to jump. All the passengers did, including the Irishman, who jumped last of all. As he went down, he passed the pilot and said, "You're just a sissy."

Two Irishmen were standing outside the Catholic church and saw the good priest come out carrying an umbrella. It was just starting to rain, so the good man loosened the strap on the umbrella, which was one of those newfangled kind that opens with the press of a button. He pressed the button, the umbrella flew open, and he walked away. One of the Irishmen slapped the other and said, "What a pity such a wonderful thing to happen and not a Protestant around to see it."

An Irishman, stewed to the gills, began to feel remorseful and went to confession. The priest surveyed his condition and said, "Go home like a good man. You haven't killed anyone, have you?" "Certainly not," mumbled the Irishman and staggered out. Just outside the church, he saw his friend heading in. He went over to him and said, "Shay, it's no use going in there. The good Father's only hearing murder cases today."

Pat had been drinking to excess for months. One day he was met by the priest. "Why don't you stop drinking," scolded the holy man, "and support your family as you should?" "I'll take the pledge right now, Father," Pat promised. "That's fine," smiled the priest. "But remember, Pat, if I ever see you drunk again. I'll have you excommunicated." Pal heeded the warning and kept sober for six months. Then he fell off the wagon. Staggering up the street, he saw the priest approaching. Just as he met him, Pat shouted at the top of his voice: "Make way for a Protestant!"

Billy O'Sullivan went to confession and told the priest that he had swiped a jug of "Minnesota thirteen" likker from old man Smith, and hid it in the culvert near the school house. Billy was given penance to do, and as soon as darkness fell the priest removed the jug and returned it to Smith. Well, Billy went looking for his jug, and when he found it gone he suspected Father O'Leary. The next Sunday, Billy had another sin to confess. He told the priest he had been out for a buggy ride with a widow. "What's her name?" asked Father O'Leary. "Never you mind, Father. Remember that I told you where the jug was," said Billy.

Italy and Italians

He used to run a laundry in Italy until they started wearing black shirts.

An American tourist drowned while touring Italy. He got drunk in Venice and tried to sleep in the gutter.

—Were you ever in Venice?
—Yeah
—Did you like it?
—No, the darn place was flooded.

Jews

Goof, the smartest man in college, can speak Yiddish with one hand.

A Jewish fellow wanted to enter a synagogue to look for his brother. The doorman resisted, but finally let him in with the warning, "All right, you can go in, but don't let me catch you praying."

Ginsberg: What's the difference between a shilling and pence?
Goldberg: You can walk down the street without a shilling [but not without pants].

—I swallered a pan only yesterday und it hoits sometings turrible.
—Vat kind of a pan—a dishpan maybe or a frying pan perhaps?
—No, no. A fountain pan.

—Mulligan, Mulligan, Levy and Mulligan
—What's Levy doing in there?
—That's what the Mulligans want to know.

—Will the person who wins the schnozola contest be able to smoke a cigar under a shower?
—He ought to be able to. Sam Bloomenbaum smokes a cigarette under one now.

Two Jewish fellows with a heavy dialect. One of them is trying to think of a word in the middle of a sentence. As he is struggling and waving his arms, the other says the word: catastrophe. The other says. "That's it! You took the words right out of my hands."

An old Jewish man boarded a streetcar with his son and refused to pay the fare for the boy. The conductor said, "That kid is fourteen if he's a day. In fact, that kid looks at least fifteen years old." The old man said, "Can I help it if he worries?"

A New York theatrical agent heard of an all-Indian jazz band playing in a small town and he went there to book them. "Are all of you really Indians?" he asked. "If you are. I'm sine I can put you over big on Broadway." "Vat vould be the use of kiddin' mid you?" replied the chief, "Ve are all fool blodt."

An Irishman and a Jewish fellow are moved next to each other in ceremony of laying "t'fillin." The Irishman says, "You can't beat these Jewish people. Look, he's here only two days and already he's taking his own blood pressure." [T'fillin: phylacteries; black straps that Orthodox Jews wrap around one arm for purposes of prayer]

In a forty-four story building, four Jewish guys were walking upstairs because the elevator was out of order. One of them said, "Okay, we each walk eleven floors and tell a story. That way we won't notice how bad it is." When they climbed the last eleven flights and reached the top, the fourth man said, "Oy, fellows, have I got a sad story for you. I forgot the key."

Two little boys, Jewish and Irish, always played together. One day the Irish boy's mother told him she didn't want him to play with little Abie. He asked her why and she told him. A few days later, the Irish boy was playing alone. The Jewish boy came up to him and said, "Come on, let's play together." The Irish boy said, "No, I can't play with you." The other said, "Aw, come on." But the other persisted, "No, I can't." The Jewish boy asked him why he wouldn't play, and the Irish kid said, "Mamma says I'm not to play with Jewish boys." Little Abie replied, "Aw, come on, we won't play for money."

A priest came upon some youths playing in the street, and thought he'd test them by offering a quarter to anyone who could tell him who was the best known patron saint. The kids began to think. One of them said, "St. Louis." The priest said, "Very good, but that's not the one I'm thinking of." Then he turned to a little Hebrew boy. "What do you say?" He replied, "St. Patrick." The priest said, "Excellent! You win the quarter. But tell me: why did you say St. Patrick? Surely you would think of Moses first." The kid replied, "Well, I did think of Moses first, but business is business."

A little Hebrew was on his way to the coast. A big burly cowboy got on the train out west and offered the Hebrew a ham sandwich. "What kind of sandvitch?" asked the Hebrew. "Ham," said the cowboy. "Pork?" "Yeah." "No thanks." The cowboy offered him a cigar. "Sorry, I never could smoke." After a few more miles, the cowboy offered him a drink. The Little guy said. "No thanks, I never drink." The cowboy knocked back a few drinks and offered the bottle again. The little guy refused, so the cowboy pulled a gun and said. "Here, take a drink of this or I'll give you a dose of lead." The little guy said, "Vell, if it's a holdup, I'll take the sandwich too."

An orthodox Jew was walking down the street on the Sabbath, a day on which Jews are not supposed to handle any money until sunset. He saw a twenty dollar bill lying in the road, walked past it a few times, then around it, and finally he stepped on it. After a while a cop appeared and started to question him. "I've noticed you've been standing here for three hours. What's it all about?" The Jewish man said, "Am I hurting anybody? I'm not causing a disturbance, am I?" The cop replied, "Yes, you're causing a disturbance with me. I want to know why you're standing here, and if you don't tell me quick I'll hit you over the head with my billy club." The man wouldn't speak or move, so the cop hit him with the club. Then the Jewish man said, "Gee, it's dark, it must be night," and picked up the note.

A little Hebrew looking through the art gallery with a friend for a guide came to the picture of the Holy Family. He puzzled about it. He asked about each person in the picture.

—This is Joseph.
—But he has no shoes.
—Of course not, he was only a poor carpenter.
—And this one dressed in rags?
—Mary, the mother.
—And the child sitting on the bare floor with a crust of bread?
—Jesus.
—Huh, no rugs on the floor, only a crust of bread in the house, but they can have their pictures took!

Scotland and Scots

A Scotsman was found dead in a pay-as-you-leave car.

Scotch Chicken: a frankfurter with a feather in it.

He's as happy as a Scotsman at a free-for-all fight.

A Scotsman phoned the poorhouse and reversed the charges.

A Scotsman found a bottle of iodine, so he cut his finger.

A taxi was smashed in Scotland. Eighteen people were killed.

I just heard there is a terrible epidemic of grippe in Scotland.

One good thing about a Scotsman: he never gives his friends away.

A Scotsman went next door and turned on the gas to commit suicide.

A Scotsman gave his wife a new spring outfit—a pair of rubber heels.

I telephoned a Scotsman for a donation and he sent me his best wishes.

A Scotsman's friend asked for a stiff drink, so he put starch in it.

A Scotsman shot his wife for washing out his lather (*shaving*) brush.

You know what a clutching movement on a song is called? Scotch palsy.

A Scotsman married the half-witted girl because she was fifty percent off.

A Scotsman married a rosy-cheeked girl so he wouldn't have to buy rouge.

I have a request here written in shorthand. I guess it's from a Scotsman.

Did you hear about the Scottish athlete who hated to loosen up his muscles?

Then there was the Scotsman who bought the car because the clutch was thrown in.

The good old Scottish remedy for seasickness: hold a sixpence between your teeth.

A man was selling sandwiches in the street and two Scotsmen took a bite at him.

A Scotsman used a straightjacket for a nightgown, so he'd be sure to sleep tight.

I know a Scotsman who carries a fiddle around so he won't have to have his hair cut.

A Scotsman went on his honeymoon alone because his wife had seen Niagara Falls.

I just saw a terrible accident at the baseball game. A Scotsman fell out of a tree.

It will be a Scotsman who will find a way to condense shampoo suds back into soap.

Then there's the Scottish sheik who gave his sweetie moth balls to put in her hope chest.

A kid swallowed a penny so his parents let him keep it for Christmas. (*Or:* his birthday)

A Scotsman walked twelve miles to see the ballgame and was too tired to climb the fence.

A Scotsman got a present of a box of corn pads, so he went out and bought tight shoes.

A fellow asked a Scotsman for something for a cup of coffee. He gave him a lump of sugar.

—What is your idea of rigid economy?
—A dead Scotsman.

He: For two cents I'd kiss you.
She: Migawd, a Scotch gigolo!

—What started the Grand Canyon?
—A Scotsman lost a penny in a ditch.

A Scotsman put green glasses on his horse and fed him straw to make him believe it was grass.

Our Scottish landlady is so stingy that she heats our knives so we can't use so much butter.

A Scotsman bought a car and expected to run it cheaper because his wife had gas on the stomach.

A Scotsman went to the Grand Hotel because he thought he could get away with a couple of towels.

A Scotsman started biting his fingernails when his doctor told him he needed more iron in his system.

Then there is the Scotsman who moved next door to the church because he was so fond of rice pudding.

I know a Scotsman who wanted to smoke monogrammed cigarettes. So he changed his name to Chesterfield.

A Scotsman bought a car with free wheeling and took it back when he found out he had to buy gas and oil.

A Scots murderer upon entering the death chamber complained to the warden that he was being overcharged.

A Scotsman went outside at Christmas, fired a shot, came in, and told the kids that Santa had committed suicide.

A Scotsman's wife was running a fever of 105, so he had her moved into the basement and used her to heat the house.

Once there was a Scotsman who was so tight that he put boric acid in his grapefruit in order to get a free eyewash.

CLERK: And you get an extra pair of pants with this suit.
SCOTSMAN: Throw in an extra coat and I'll take it.

A Scotsman was invited out to tea. He was asked how many lumps of sugar with his tea. He said, "How many do ye give?"

A Scotsman hoped it would be a damp night Christmas eve, so he could have a rattle in his chest to take home to the kiddies.

Have you heard of the lady who asked a Scottish tenor to sing as he'd never sung before? She asked him to sing for charity.

A Scotsman was celebrating his golden wedding so he took along his friend Goldberg; and Goldberg brought along a goldfish.

A terrible thing just happened in Scotland. A little boy killed his father and mother so he could go to the orphans' picnic.

WEDDING GUEST: Isn't this your fourth daughter getting married?
CANNY SCOT: Aye, and our rice is getting a wee bit dirty.

A Scottish wife almost fainted when her aviator husband did a loop. She remembered she'd left some loose change in his pocket.

A Scot took his little boy to church one Sunday morning and told him to take bigger strides to save the new shoes he was wearing.

And then there was the Scotsman who died on the way to the electric chair. He happened to think that he was paying for his crime.

A Scotsman came to America. He came on one boat and his baggage on the next boat, so that if one sank he wouldn't lose everything.

A Scotsman wouldn't let his daughter go to school because she had to pay attention and didn't receive any interest from the principal.

Another theory has been advanced as to why George Washington stood up in the boat. He was Scottish and had just had his pants pressed.

Then there was the Scotsman who, when asked what he had clenched in his fist, answered: "My wife's false teeth. She's been eating between meals."

DRIVER OF OVERTURNED TAXI (*to Scottish passenger*): Are you hurt, sir?
SCOT: Don't be a bothering about my being hurt, man. Stop that wee clock of yours.

A Scotswoman bought her son a pair of glasses because he was shortsighted and told him to take them off when he wasn't looking at anything.

A Scot bought two tickets for a raffle. With the first he won a thousand dollars; then he cried because he'd wasted his money on the second.

A Scot went to the doctor to have an examination and was told he had too much sugar in his system. The next morning he cried into his grapefruit.

A Scotsman wanted to go into the pictures for half price because he had only one eye. The Scottish manager asked him double price saying it would take him twice as long to see the show.

A Scotsman visiting New York said, "It's wonderful here. Free parks. Free museums. Free picture galleries. And the restaurant I go to always has a quarter under the plate for a surprise."

A Scotsman, sending his wife to a theatre to see an illusionist, advised her, "Listen Maggie, when he comes to that trick where he makes twenty omelettes with one egg, watch verra close."

—Hear about the Scotsman who wanted his money back?
—No, what was the matter?
—He bought a score card at the game, and the team scored.

—Why, said McPherson, this car has such swell brakes I can stop her on a dime.
—Yeah, and you probably would, if you saw one!

GLORIA: I'm going downtown and exchange the present Sandy gave me for Christmas.
GLADYS: I've got to go to the five-and-ten, too.

A Scotsman living on the outskirts of Chicago became engaged to a girl who got so fat that he wanted to break off the engagement. But the girl couldn't gel the ring off, so he had to marry her.

A Scotsman took his girl to the free city art exhibit, told her to walk quickly, and then pointed out that by so doing they got the effect of watching moving pictures.

A Scots boy asked his girl in a picture theatre the other day if she would care for some chewing gum. She answered, "Indeed I would, Jock." "All right," said he, "feel under your seat."

A young man in a Scots family swallowed a fountain pen. His father was telling someone about it, and the party asked, "Whatever did you do about it?" The father said, "Well, we have had to use a pencil."

A big-hearted Scotsman waited at the stage entrance of a theatre where the Siamese Twins were playing. When they came out, he whispered to one of them, "If you can get away, I'll treat you to a drink."

A Scottish traveling salesman, held up in the Orkney Islands by a bad storm, telegraphed to his firm in Aberdeen: MAROONED HERE BY STORM WIRE INSTRUCTIONS. The reply came: START SUMMER VACATION AS FROM YESTERDAY.

Coming over on the boat, we took a collection and on counting up we found ten dollars and three cents on the plate. I said, "It looks like we have a Scotsman here among us." A voice from the back said, "You're wrong, there's three of us."

It is rumored that on Lindbergh's recent flight across the Atlantic he experienced much trouble. His engine tore loose, the nuts and bolts began to fall, and the wings flopped. Then he crossed Scotland and everything tightened up.

—It will be just too bad if I Herb ever gets sick, because his folks have a Scottish doctor.
—What has being Scottish got to do with it?
—He is so tight that he will never treat a patient.

(*Variation*)
You know why Scotsmen are not good doctors? They won't treat their patients.

—Ye wouldna buy your sweetie a ring at the five-and-ten, would ye, Sandy?
— Na, mon, it's better to gang to the twenty-five cent store and get her a guid one.

A Scotsman, an Irishman, a German, and a Jew were eating dinner together. When the meal was finished and the waiter came with the bill the Scotsman promptly said that he would take it. The next day a Jewish ventriloquist was found murdered.

"Your wife needs a change." said the doctor. "Salt air will cure her." The next time the physician called, he found the Scotsman sitting by the bedside fanning his wife with a herring.

SCOTSMAN (*at football stadium gate*): What are the prices of your seats?
GATE KEEPER: Students, fifty cents, all others, seventy-five cents; and programs, ten cents.
SCOTSMAN: I'll sit on a program, please.

Two old Scotsmen sat by the road puffing solemnly at their pipes, "There's no' much pleasure in smoking, Donald," said Sandy. "Hoo dae ye mak' that oot?" questioned Donald. "Weel, if ye're smoking ye ain bacca, ye're thinking o' the awful expense, and if ye're smoking some ither body's y'r pipe's rammed saw ticht it winna draw."

SCOTSMAN: My lad, are you to be my caddie?
CADDIE: Yes, sir.
SCOTSMAN: And how are you at finding lost balls?
CADDIE: Very good, sir.
SCOTSMAN: Well, look around and find one and we'll start the game.

A man boarded a cross-country train, gave the pullman porter half of a five-dollar bill, and told him if the service was good he'd give him the other half when they reached their destination. He went into the drawing room and discovered his friend, a Scotsman, biting a nickel in two.

Sandy McGregor gazed at the sign on the hat cleaner's doorway, gazed until he was purple in the face. "Two dollars and a quarter for cleanin' a little hat! Oh, the robbers!" So he went along and finally came to a Turkish Bath. The sign said, "Turkish Bath, $1.50." Inside went Sandy and paid his money. "Take off your clothes," said the attendant. "Sure," said Sandy. "But I'm wearin' ma hat!"

A couple went into a restaurant in Glasgow and ordered a sandwich. The waiter brought the sandwich and put it on the table. The husband proceeded to cut it in half, putting one half on his plate and giving the other half to his wife. The husband began to eat and the wife watched him. The waiter, seeing that the woman wasn't eating, went to her and asked her if there was anything wrong with her half. She told him, "No, it's all right. I'm waiting until my husband gets through with the teeth."

McPherson's condition was critical and his wife was much anguished at having to leave him to go to the neighbors to call a doctor. As she looked down at his shrunken form, her hard face softened, and tears spilled over her cheeks. Pulling herself together with an effort, she put on her old bonnet, dabbed at her eyes with the back of her hand, and went over to say goodbye to her husband. "Now remember, Angus, no extravagance. If you feel yourself going, blow out the light."

Germans

I asked a little German girl how she came by the name Alice. I explained that Alice was a very unusual name for a German girl. She said: "You see it happens like this. Ven I was born, before me in the family there were eight odder kids. I must haf been sick at the time because I vuz in bed vit Momma. Pappa, he comes home, he looks at me, und den he looks at der odder eight kids playing on the floor, und den again at me unt say, 'Momma, das iss alles!'"

A pair of portly Teutons met on the street one day and began talking about their sons. "Ach. hullo, Fritz," said the first. "Und wie geht's, wie geht's? And how iss it by your son Otto?" "Ach ja, my son Otto is simply fine. He goes along very good in his new chob." "His new chob, eh? Vat kind off a position has he?" "He iss a butler." "A butler, eh? T'ink of leetle Otto a butler. Dot is very good. Iss he mit a chvell family?" "Family? V'y no. He's not mit any family." "Not mit any family? V'y I t'ought you said he iss a butler." "Sure he's a butler," answered Fritz proudly. "He's mit a ginger ale buttling company."

Greeks

—What's Greek for boiled water?
—Soup.

African Americans

He's so black that lightning bugs follow him around in the daytime.

DOCTOR: Why, man, you are color blind.
PATIENT: Heavens, Doc, I got married last week, too.

—Rastus, I'll give you a pint of Scotch if you'll hurry over to my house and get my grip. Hurry now . . . what! Haven't you gone yet?
—Gone? Boss, I's back!

—Say, Mose, whafor youall name youah baby "Electricity"?
—Well mah wife's name's Dinah and mine's Mose and by golly, if Dinahmose don't make "Electricity," ah don't know what does.

A Negro preacher discovered two men playing cards on Sunday and for money. "Rastus," said the preacher, "don't you know it's wrong to play cards on de Sabbath?" "Yes, pahson," answered Rastus ruefully, "but believe me, ah's payin' foh ma sins."

—Whuffo you rubberin' at me lak 'at foah, black boy?
—Ah's jus' a lookin' you over foah a grand slam, pardner.
—Well, jus' don't try any of you' tricks, bub, 'cause I'll club you down, trump all ovah yo' daid body, spade you under, an' bury you wid simple honors.

Two colored men were standing on the corner discussing family trees.
—Yes suh, man, I can trace my relations back to a family tree.
—Chase 'em back to a family tree?
—Naw man, trace 'em, trace 'em. Get me?
—Well, they ain't but two kind of things dat live in trees. Birds and monkeys and you sho' ain't got no feathers on you.

The other day in a courtroom, Judge White was reproving a colored man for deserting his wife, and dwelt at great length on the injustice he was doing. "Wife desertion is something, Rastus, that I just deal with severely. I'm afraid I feel very strongly on the subject." "But Judge," said Rastus, "you don't know that woman. I ain't no deserter, I'se a refugee."

A man stopped a small colored boy on the street and asked him his name. The little boy answered, "Abraham Lincoln Jackson Smith." The man said, "What a wonderful thing to be named after such important people," and asked the boy, "Do you know who Abraham Lincoln is?" The little boy said that he didn't. The man was surprised and said, "Do you know who George Washington is?" The colored kid's face brightened and said, "Sure! That's my brother."

RUFUS: What's matter with yo' head, man?

RASTUS: Arithmetical bugs.

RUFUS: What?

RASTUS: Cooties.

RUFUS: Why arithmetical bugs?

RASTUS: Well, dey add to my misery, subtract from my pleasure, divide my attention, and multiply like the dickens.

8. *I'm Going to Mexico*—Netty and Jesús Rodríguez

Commentaries

Sources

Play

8.1 BRIEF HISTORY OF HISPANIC THEATRE IN THE UNITED STATES—NICOLÁS KANELLOS

IN THE 1920s AND 1930s, Hispanic playwrights in the United States addressed the needs of their audiences for reliving their history on both sides of the border and for reviving the glories of their own language and cultural tradition with the decorum and professionalism befitting the type of family entertainment that the community leaders believed served the purposes of reinforcing Hispanic culture and morality while resisting assimilation to Anglo-American culture. But with the rise of vaudeville and the greater access of working class people to theatrical entertainment, vaudeville-type revues and variety shows became more and more popular and gradually displaced more serious theater. But Mexican vaudeville and musical comedy did not avoid the themes that were so solemnly treated in three-act dramas. Rather, the Mexican stage had developed its own type of revue: the *revista*. *Revistas* were musical revues that had developed in Mexico under the influence of the Spanish *zarzuela* and the French *revue* and vaudeville, but had taken on their own character in Mexico as a format for piquant political commentary and social satire. Also, like the *zarzuela*, which celebrated Spanish regional customs, music and folklore, the Mexican *revista* also created and highlighted the character, music, dialects and folklore of the various Mexican regions. Under the democratizing influence of the Mexican Revolution, the *revista* highlighted the life and culture of the working classes. During the Revolution, the *revista política* in particular rose to prominence on Mexico City stages, but later all *revista* forms degenerated into a loose vehicle for musical and comedic performance in which typical regional and underdog characters, such as the *pelado* (literally, skinned or penniless), often improvised a substantial part of the action.

Many critics and historians of Mexican theater see in the *revista* the birth of a truly Mexican theater. In the words of Miguel Covarrubias, "These rebellious Mexican *commedias dell'arte* have produced not only a new national theater, the only one worthy of the name, but a fine corps of actors and comedians whose style and careers have been strongly influenced by the dominant politics of the time."[1]

The Los Angeles stages hosted many of the writers and stars of *revistas* that had been active during the time of formation of the genre in Mexico, including Leopoldo Beristáin and Guz Aguila. In the theaters of Los Angeles and the Southwest were staged most of the *revistas* that were popular in Mexico and that were of historical importance for the development of the genre. Such works as *El Tenorio maderista* (Pro-Madero Don Juan), *El país de los cartones* (The Country Made of Boxes) and *La ciudad de los volcanes* (The City of Volcanoes) and numerous others were continuously repeated from Los Angeles to Laredo. Such innovators of the genre as Guz Aguila were for a time a perennial attraction at the Los Angeles theaters. Even important composers of scores for the *revistas*, such as Lauro D. Uranga, graced the Los Angeles Hispanic stages. With their low humor and popular music scores, the *revistas* in Los Angeles articulated grievances and poked fun at both the U.S. and Mexican governments. The Mexican Revolution was satirically reconsidered over and over again in Los Angeles from the perspective of the expatriates, and Mexican American culture was contrasted with the "purer" Mexican version. This social and political commentary was carried out despite the fact that both audiences and performers were mostly immigrants and thus liable to deportation or repatriation. The Los Angeles writers and composers were serving a public that was hungry to see itself reflected on stage, an audience whose interest was piqued by *revistas* relating to current events, politics and the conflict of cultures that was produced while living in the Anglo-dominated environment. The *revistas* kept the social and political criticism leveled at the authorities, be they Mexican or American, within the light context of music and humor in such pieces as Guz Aguila's *México para los mexicanos* (Mexico for the Mexicans) and *Los Angeles vacilador* (Swinging Los Angeles), Gabriel Navarro's *La ciudad de irás y no volverás* (The City of You Go There Never to Return) and Don Catarino's *Los efectos de la crisis* (The Effects of the Depression), *Regreso a mi tierra* (The Return to My Country), *Los repatriados* (The Repatriated), *Whiskey, morfina y marihuana* and *El desterrado* (The Exile).

It is in the *revista* that we find a great deal of humor based on the culture shock typically derived from following the misadventures of naive, recent immigrants from Mexico who have difficulty in getting accustomed to life in the big Anglo-American metropolis. Later on in the 1920s, and when the Depression and Repatriation take hold, the theme of culture shock is converted to one of outright cultural conflict. At that point Mexican nationalism becomes more intensified as anti-Mexican sentiments become more openly expressed in the Anglo-American press as a basis for taking Mexicans off the welfare rolls and deporting them. In the *revista*, the Americanized, or *agringado* and *renegado*, become even more satirized and the barbs aimed at American culture become even sharper. It is also in the *revista* that the raggedly dressed underdog, the *pelado*, comes to the fore with his low-class dialect and acerbic satire. A forerunner of characters like Cantinflas, the *pelado* really originates in the humble tent theaters that evolved in Mexico and existed in the Southwest of the United States until the 1950s. With roots in the circus clown tradition, and a costume and dialect that embody poverty and marginality, the *pelado* was free to improvise and exchange witticisms with his audiences that often embodied working class distrust of societal institutions and the upper classes. Although the *pelado* or *peladito*, as he was affectionately called, was often criticized for his low humor and scandalous language, theater critics today consider the character to be a genuine and original Mexican contribution to the history of theater.

Note

1. Miguel Covarrubias, "Slapstick and Venom," Theatre Arts Monthly 22/8 (August 1938): 588.

8.2 INTRODUCTION TO *I'M GOING TO AMERICA*—NICOLÁS KANELLOS

JESÚS AND NETTY RODRÍGUEZ WERE A HUSBAND-AND-WIFE song, dance, and stand-up comedy act that was popular on Hispanic vaudeville circuits throughout the Southwest during the 1920s and in New York during the Depression and into the early 1950s. The star attraction of the act was Netty, who often received solo billing on fliers and marquees as La Bella Netty, for he beauty, her lovely voice, and her quick-witted comic repartee. Through their humorous dialogs,

Jesús and Netty dramatized the culture conflict felt by both native Mexican Americans and Mexican immigrants. They often chose the Anglified *agringado* or *pocho* as the butt for their jokes and often reflected the tensions felt by men and women because of conflicting social and gender roles among Mexicans in the United States. As in the comic sketch below, which ends quite conventionally so as not to scandalize working-class audiences, the character Netty pushes, stretches, and attempts to broaden her woman's rights as she challenges male prerogatives. Throughout the skit the complete set of double references to Mexican and Anglo cultures is glossed on and explored, as in much of immigrant literature; but it was precisely through these types of cultural explorations—and in the Spanish original, language explorations—that a Mexican American cultural sensibility arose (as opposed to a Mexican immigrant stance).

8.3 THE IMMIGRANTS (*LOS ENGANCHADADOS*—"THE HOOKED ONES")—MANUEL GAMIO

On the 28th day of February,
That important day
When we left El Paso,
They took us out as contract labor.

We arrived on the first day
And on the second began to work.
With our picks in our hands
We set out tramping.

Some unloaded rails
And others unloaded ties,
And others of my companions
Threw out thousands of curses.

Those who knew the work
Went repairing the jack
With sledge hammers and shovels
Throwing earth up the track.

Said Jesús, "El Coyote,"
As if he wanted to weep
"It would be better to be in Juárez
Even if we were without work."

These verses were composed
by a poor Mexican
To spread the word about
The American system.

8.4 NETTY AND JESÚS RODRÍGUEZ

Netty Egdell de Rodgríguez and her husband Jesús Rodríguez, performing at the Teatro Nacional in San Antonia, Texas, 1938. The Rodríguezes were a popular song, dance, and stand-up comedy act in Hispanic vaudeville circuits throughout the Southwest and New York. Their routines often involved societal tensions from Mexican culture. They articulated grievances and poked fun at both the U.S. and Mexican governments, commenting on current events, politics and the conflicts between Mexican and Anglo cultures.

Source: Photo © San Antonio Express-News/ZUMA Press/(Image courtesy of UTSA Special Collections)

8.5 *I'M GOING TO MEXICO*—NETTY AND JESÚS RODRÍGUEZ

NETTY: When are we leaving, Panchito?

JESÚS: Well, who knows, honey?

NETTY: What we did was real bad, and the thing is, I won't be leaving.

JESÚS: Be a little patient.

NETTY: Patience! I've had enough.

JESÚS: You're so impatient! It's worth it to keep on. We shouldn't back down about seeing our homeland.

NETTY: I'm not hesitating anymore. I'm staying here and looking for work. You can go if you want, 'cause no matter what, honey, I'm out of it.

JESÚS: What's the matter, sweety? What's wrong? Shut your smart little mouth! You can't stay, your husband's leaving!

NETTY: Well, go ahead, if you want, leave. Because I'm fine right here. And you don't give me orders, got it? I'm not going!

JESÚS: Look at you getting all worked up! The man gives the orders, you hear?

NETTY: I'm not your errand girl. Here, the man orders, and . . . doesn't.

JESÚS: And doesn't give the orders? That's what you think.

NETTY: I don't just think it, I know it.

JESÚS: You learned that pretty fast! And what I taught you, how soon you forgot it. A man is a man anywhere, and he should always be respected by his woman. When you snared me back in Celaya with your romantic illusions, I wore the pants and you wore the skirt. And because you've heard talk that here the law is a tyrant, you want me to turn everything upside down. Well, this ungrateful woman is mistaken! If she squawks because she's here, I'll break her leg, just to remind her of me.

NETTY: Ah, aren't you the tough guy! Get out of here with your threats! If you call a cop, you'll see if he pays attention to me!

JESÚS: I'll show you!

NETTY: Go ahead! Hit me!

JESÚS: Why should I hit you? Back home Mexico in there are plenty women who'll want me!

NETTY: Boy, aren't you exaggerating, Pancho! But I don't care, *compadre*, I've got the road wide open to go wherever I want.

JESÚS: Well, I hope you're happy, baby. If you don't want to come, go ahead and stay. It won't kill me. Down there there's lots of women who'll love me. When I get to Manzanillo, I'll hook up with somebody else. And down there I won't be so stupid, I'll look for a real woman who doesn't give up, and who knows how to be grateful for her husband's hard work. A completely Mexican woman who doesn't change her mind and doesn't give up tortillas for hot cakes and ham.

NETTY: Now you've gone too far.

JESÚS: Why did you give up, you sad woman?

NETTY: What are you talking about, loud mouth! Shut up!

JESÚS: Why should I shut up? When did I not love you enough to make you want to stay here? Didn't I work nice and hard to buy you those tennis shoes?

NETTY: Sure.

JESÚS: Didn't your good man take you for a good time at Venice Beach?

NETTY: Uh huh.

JESÚS: Didn't I work like a dog for you for a whole year without a break? And you just havin' a good time learnin' to make yourself up? You are so ungrateful! You've given me such a hard time! My woman treats me so bad! She's even forgotten her homeland!

NETTY: That's it, don't you say that to me.

JESÚS: Then why don't you come with me?

NETTY: How can you ask me to go with you if you don't have any more land down there?

JESÚS: She's really laying it on heavy. She has no shame at all. Man, has she picked up the customs up here. I'm getting a divorce!

NETTY: All right, very well, all right!

JESÚS: Lady, speak gibberish to me. I know how to speak that language, but talk to me like you know how, and don't get me all tangled up.

NETTY: Don't tell me I tangle you up, nothing could be clearer! If you leave, I'm staying. Goodbye, Panchito! Bye bye, toodeloo!

JESÚS: Why does your love rule me like some kind of tyrant, even if I know that money makes you love me? And if your love is unhealthy and impure, it dishonors me. Because Mexico is in my heart, I'm going back, you'll see. Our love dies right here. Love down there will be even better. In my beloved Mexico to be in love is an honor. The only price for love there is love in return.

NETTY: Oh, Panchito baby, I can't stand it anymore. My homeland has won out. I want to go, too.

JESÚS: At last, she's coming with me.

NETTY: I hope you'll forgive me, I'll follow you anywhere.

JESÚS: To Mexico, baby, to Mexico.

9. Te Ata (Performance Material)

Commentary

Sources

Play

9.1 INTRODUCTION FROM *TE ATA: CHICKASAW STORYTELLER*—RICHARD GREEN

AT THE WHITE HOUSE on April 22, 1933, President Franklin D. Roosevelt and his wife Eleanor, hosted the first official State Dinner of his administration. Some sixty-two guests filed into the Blue Room to honor the visiting prime minister of Great Britain, the honorable Ramsey MacDonald. In accordance with the usual pomp and protocol, many toasts were made to Anglo-American friendship and a splendid banquet was served on the official White House dinner service. Afterward, in the East Room, Eleanor Roosevelt introduced the evening's entertainment.

She told the audience that the featured performer, Te Ata, was a member of the Chickasaw tribe and a longtime friend. Te Ata, she announced, would be presenting a "delightful" program of Indian folklore. But as the audience would soon realize, these were not mere recitations but artistic presentations, imbued with drama, rhythm, pathos, and occasional humor. This blending of authentic folklore with artistry is what made Te Ata's performance unique. Like her, many other Indian entertainers crisscrossed the American landscape for portions of the period from the 1920s to the postwar years. Bit players were killed off daily in Wild West shows; relatively anonymous singers, dancers, and actors performed for the masses in burlesque theaters; very few actors (most notably Will Rogers, one-fourth Cherokee) starred in successful movies but not as Indians; a number of accomplished musicians performed in concert halls but normally playing show tunes or opera; a few others made small circuits presenting Indian folklore—but none had Te Ata's appeal and artistry.

Te Ata's stunning appearance captured the East Room audience's attention before she uttered a word. Wearing an elegant white buckskin Sioux dress, Te Ata, at age 37, was five feet seven, slender, and beautiful. Her voice was strong, full, and somewhat deep for a woman. At times she accompanied herself by shaking a gourd rattle or beating a drum. Throughout her performance, she moved sparingly but always with grace and fluidity. Without a change of dress, she assumed widely disparate roles as she moved through her program. From a bumptious young brave to an old woman at the end of her trail, Te Ata modulated her voice and gesture to be in character and complement the stories and songs.

Performance art Anna Deveare Smith

As with all great performers, the seeming effortlessness of her performance was illusory. She learned her first Indian stories from her father, a Chickasaw tribal official before Oklahoma became a state in 1907. Her college drama teacher refined her talent and contributed to the poise and judgement she needed to launch her career in the 1920s. Apart from her talent as a dramatist, she needed vision, commitment, and grit to control her shyness and to break through the social mores holding that a woman's proper place was in the home. . . .

Te Ata's career took her all over America in venues of all kinds, from great stages to school auditoriums to Indian reservations. But no matter the quality of the facility or the degree of education or sophistication of the audience or that she was sometimes exhausted or ill, Te Ata's performance was never less than inspired. She never compromised her integrity or her material. Her mission was to entertain and educate, to enlighten and inspire, and she gladly accepted this honor and responsibility during the decades when the dominant white society was not nearly as receptive to minorities as it is today. During the first thirty years of her career, the great majority of Americans scarcely knew or cared that Indians still existed. Moreover, many of the tribes and their traditional cultures had been weakened, some to the point of extinction, by federal programs designed to abolish tribal governments and force members to blend into the American melting pot.

When a grassroots movement to revitalize her own tribal government was building in the mid-1950s, she appeared as the star of the tribe's constitutional centennial celebration in 1955 in her home-town, Tishomingo. She said this honor rivaled that of being invited to entertain at the White House or at Stratford-on-Avon. Two years later she was inducted into the Oklahoma Hall of Fame and later was the third inductee into the Chickasaw Hall of Fame.

Te Ata continued to tour for another twenty years—into the modern era of tribal self-determination. She helped bring this era about . . . by presenting the beauty and wisdom of tribal folklore to thousand[s] of Americans, many of whom never forgot her.

9.2 TE ATA

Te Ata performing at Bear Mountain. Mary Frances Thompson or "Te Ata" was a Chickasaw Nation performer who countered derogatory representations of Native Americans by dancing and telling stories that exhibited the beauty and wisdom of her culture.

Source: Courtesy of the Chickasaw Cultural Centre and the Susan Ledford collection at the Chickasaw Council House Museum.

Te Ata performing in Hyde Park for King George VI and Queen Elizabeth, June 12, 1939.

Source: Courtesy of the Franklin D. Roosevelt Presidential Library and Museum, Hyde Park, New York

9.3 TE ATA PROGRAM (UNDATED)

Te Ata

Program

of

American Indian Folk Lore

The Last Song
God's Drum
Cities of White Men
When We Dance All Together
Hartley Alexander

NATIVE LEGENDS
Iroquois Creation Legend
Seneca Romance Legend
Why Folks Die
Sign Story

NATIVE SONGS
Lullaby
Love Song
Sunset Song

The Grass on the Mountain - - - - Paiute
Song of the New Born - - - - Grande Pueblo
Song of a Woman Abandoned - - - Shoshone
Song of Greatness - - - - - Sioux
Translated by Mary Austin

The Blue Duck - - - - - Lew Sarett
Corn Planting Ceremony
Music by Thurlow Lieurance

Tenney Management
Steinway Hall
113 West 57th Street
New York City

Undated Te Ata program of American Indian Folk Lore.

Source: Image courtesy of the Chickasaw Cultural Centre and the Susan Ledford collection at the Chickasaw Council House Museum.

9.4 VIVIAN SHIRLEY LEARNS CULTURE OF INDIANS—VIVIAN SHIRLEY

Vivian Shirley Learns Culture of Indians from Talk With Princess on Dramatic Tour
Recites Story of Old Romance to Cite Idea of Life in Days Before White Man Came to America

MANY, many moons ago, before the small, white children skated to school on wide, cement pavements, before there were any cement pavements, before there were any white children in America, little Indian children sat around the camp fire and listened to the story of the singing maiden who went in search of a husband.

Once upon a time, said the story, a singing maiden came into the great woods.

"Who wants me for a wife?" she sang, and her song echoed back from the green branches.

"I'd like a wife," said a deep voice.

"What would you feed me if I should be your wife?" said the little singer.

"I would feed you the leaves from the trees and the soft, green shrubs," he answered, because he was a big elk.

"No, no, no!" said the singer. "I do not like green leaves and shrubs to eat." And she went on her way singing.

Then the Deer Answered

"WHO wants me for a wife, or where shall I find a husband?"

"I'd like a wife," said and antlered deer when he heard her voice.

"What would you feed your wife?" she asked.

"Nice, soft moss," said the deer, "and tender grass."

"No, no, no!" answered the little singer. "I don't like to eat tender grass." On she went singing her little song. Just then a red-breasted robin came along.

"I would like a wife." he said.

"What would you feed her on?" asked the little singer.

"I would give her nice, juicy seed kernels," he answered.

"Then I will be your wife," said the little singer. "For there is nothing that I like better than nice, juicy seed kernels."

And together they flew away through the treetops into the sunset.

Indian Has Much to Give

THE soft voice of the slender Indian Princess died a away for a moment.

"That is what I mean," she began again, "by a typical romance story of the Indians. The Indian, the real native American, has so much to offer in folklore and in tribal art. 'Pity the poor Indian,' say some of the white men. But they do not realize that the real Indian, too, has much about him to be envied."

Princess Te Ata is a daughter of a chief of the Chickasaw. From her native Oklahoma she has traveled far portraying the Indian ritual and old legend in quaint dances, and rhythmic folklore.

"As a small child," said Princess Te Ata, "I went to a tribal school on the reservation. I was shy and yet at the little programs we gave I found myself forgetting my shyness entirely.

Family Became Poor

"LIKE most Indian families, mine was rich no longer, and when the time came for me to go to college I found out that I would have to put myself through. I had enough money for a year, no more.

"Imagine my surprise then, when one of my teachers suggested that the little folk tales I told the girls were the stuff of which drama was made. Since then I have been trying to express some of the loveliness, the beauty and the pride to which the Indians rightfully were entitled.

"There is such a wide difference between the Indians as they are and the ordinary person's idea of an Indian. What my people need is education, not the cheap, spurious kind, which takes them from all the background they have known, and forces them into a totally different environment for which they are not prepared, but an education which will give them the knowledge to live more richly and more sensibly, and education which will make them proud of the old, beautiful things which they have, and at the same time, show them how to build on those old things for a wider future.

Indians Are Individualists

"THE Indian is always an individualist and that is why long ago the tribes rarely united. There was no such thing as a national Indian Government and this individualism is their strength and their weakness. It could be utilized to help them.

"The Government takes some of the children from the tribal schools and sends them up to strange schools, where they have the most mediocre teaching, with teachers who in many cases, would not even be allowed to teach in white schools. Even the books which they study, instead of building on something which they know, like teepees and sagebrush, begin with brick houses and roses. The small Indian child does not know what a brick house or a rose is, and he is so deeply overwhelmed with a sense of the own inferiority that it is hardly to be expected he will go back to his tribe as a leader. That's the point!

Te Ata Poem "My Feet Are Dancing" (1932)

"Over in Europe they say of Americans that we are raw, uncultured, but it would not be so if we would only utilize our Indian heritage of culture, which is thousands of years old. The Indian has instinctively good breeding and poise and calmness."

Indian Has Poise

"HE DOES not go about talking in a loud, raucous voice, nor show rude curiosity when he sees something that interests him, in such a way as I have unfortunately seen some of our own tourists do abroad.

"'Oh I know Indians!' a woman who had traveled in the West said to me once. 'I have seen lots of them standing by railroad stations. They don't look as if they could learn much.'

"It was so easy to say to her that I have seen many white people, too gawking at trains in small villages, or selling knickknacks from pushcarts who also did not appear to be very bright.

"But what is the use of that? What we want most of all for the Indian is understanding and appreciation of the very beautiful things which he has done in tribal art.

"That is why I am so glad," Princess Te Ata concluded, "that the Art Alliance is holding its exhibition of various specimens of art from the different tribes. It gives persons who are interested an opportunity to see what the Indian can do in the way of beauty."

9.5 EXCERPT FROM *TE ATA: CHICKASAW STORYTELLER*—RICHARD GREEN

First Indian Folklore Performance (1919)

When the curtains parted, Te Ata, wearing the Kiowa dress, entered the stage, doing an interpretive dance to the well-known song "From the Land of the Sky Blue Water." She spoke rather than sang the words:

From the Land of the Sky Blue Water
They brought a captive maid,
And her eyes they are lit with lightnings,
And her heart is unafraid.
But I steal to her lodge at dawning,
I woo her with my flute,
She is sick for the Sky Blue Water—
The captive maid is mute!

After she changed into her Chickasaw calico dress, she told four short legends dealing with the creation of the world, romance, war, and death. She introduced the legends with lines from Longfellow's "Hiawatha":

Should you ask me when these stories,
When these legends and tradition
With the odor of the forest
With the dew and damp of meadows,
With the rushing of great rivers . . .
I should answer, I should tell you
In the birds' nests of the forest
In the lodges of the beaver
In the hoofprints of the bison
In the aerie of the eagle!
Listen to these Indian legends.

Later she dramatized four native songs, the kind she was prohibited from singing in Chickasaw or Choctaw when she was at Bloomfield. She did not sing the songs because she did not like her singing voice; her singing, she believed, detracted from the words and drama, but her increasingly powerful speaking voice heightened the drama and enhanced the words. She performed other short legends before closing with "The Moon Drops Low," by Cadman. It tells of the Indians' desperate attempts to avoid the forces that were destroying their way of life. Her backdrop was a sky blue screen with a painted sun setting over the trees. In front of the screen was a large spider web made of heavy twine, suspended from above and anchored snugly on both sides. As she neared the end of this last piece, the climax looming, she recited:

The moon drops low
That once soared high
As an eagle soars
In the morning sky
And the deep dark lies
Like a death-web spun
'Twixt the setting moon
And the rising sun.
Our glory sinks
Like the sinking moon
The Red Man's race
Shall Perish soon.
Our feet shall trip
Where the web is spun
For no dawn shall be ours
And no rising sun—
No dawn for us and no rising sun!

The music crescendoed as Te Ata danced ever more frantically about the stage, seeking to escape the forces of destruction. But she became enmeshed in the spider's web, the white man's way of life, and as the curtain rang down Te Ata was still trying piteously to claw free.

Navajo Chant (1929)

You see, I am alive.
You see, I stand in good relation to the earth.
You see, I stand in good relation to the gods.
You see, I stand in good relation to all that is beautiful.
You see, I stand in good relation to you.
You see, I am alive. I am alive!

Performance at the Folk Festival of the Homelands (1932)

The prestigious Folk Festival of the Homelands at the Guild Theater in New York. . . . The festival was presented by the Folk Festival Council of New York, and groups representing eleven nations performed traditional songs and dances. It was a major cultural event in the city and received wide publicity; of all the performers, Te Ata's picture was chosen by the sponsor to appear in newspapers. Representing American Indians, Te Ata performed the mask and provided the evening's prologue, reciting the long-ago vision of the Cheyenne chief Hiamovi, a prophecy of racial and ethnic harmony, which was so attuned to her belief and mission that it became a permanent part of her repertoire.

> It was meant by the Great Mystery that the Indian should give to all peoples. But the white man has never known the Indian. It is thus: there are two roads, the white man's road and the Indian's road. Neither traveler knows the road of the other. Thus ever has it been, from the long ago, even unto today. . . . But I know that it is the mind of the Great Mystery that the white men and the Indians who fought together should now be one people.
>
> There are birds of many colors . . . yet it is all one bird. There are horses of many colors . . . yet it is all one horse. So all living things—animals, flowers, trees. So men: white, black, yellow, red, yet all one people. That this should come to pass was in the heart of the Great Mystery. It is right thus. And everywhere there shall be peace.

In her journal Te Ata wrote that the festival had gone very well and that the newspaper accounts had singled her out for praise. Earlier that month she had revealed to the public another side of herself, an opinionated side. In a newspaper interview, Te Ata noted a gulf between actual Indian life and the way white people perceive it. This misconception had serious ramifications. Indians need the type of education "which will give them the knowledge to live more richly and more sensibly, an education to make them proud of the old, beautiful things they have, and at the same time, show them how to build on those old things for a wider future." What is happening now, she said, is destructive. In a misguided effort to produce leaders, the government puts Indian students "into schools that are strange to them, with insensitive, inferior teachers and incomprehensible books." The Indian student is "so overwhelmed with his own sense of inferiority that it is hardly to be expected he will go back to his tribe as a leader."

Te Ata Poem "My Feet Are Dancing" (1932)

Down the gone-away trail
My heart walks with him.
His strength is mine now
His gifts are mine
His Dancing spirit now a part of me.
I am strong now!
Now my spirit feet are dancing
Now my spirit feet invade the hills
Now my spirit feet have touched the mountains
There in the blue they dance
Upon the corners of the winds.

Part 3
Gender and Sexuality

FEMINISM AND FEMINIST THEATRE

THE SEXUAL REVOLUTION AND BROADWAY

10. *Trifles*— Susan Glaspell

Commentary

Sources

Play

10.1 "MURDER, SHE WROTE": THE GENESIS OF SUSAN GLASPELL'S *TRIFLES*—LINDA BEN-ZVI

I

IN THE PREFACE TO HER BOOK *Women Who Kill*, Ann Jones explains that her massive study of women murderers began with a quip. After working through a reading list which included *The Awakening*, *The House of Mirth*, and *The Bell Jar*, a student asked her: "Isn't there anything a woman can do but kill herself?" Jones responded, "She can always kill somebody else."[1]

Women killing somebody else, especially when that somebody is male, has fascinated criminologists, lawyers, psychologists, and writers. Fascinated and frightened them. Fear is the subtext of Jones's book: "the fears of men who, even as they shape society, are desperately afraid of women, and so have fashioned a world in which women come and go only in certain rooms; and . . . the fears of those women who, finding the rooms too narrow and the door still locked, lie in wait or set the place afire."[2] Or kill.

Women who kill evoke fear because they challenge societal constructs of femininity—passivity, restraint, and nurture; thus the rush to isolate and label the female offender, to cauterize the act. Her behavior *must* be aberrant, or crazed, if it is to be explicable. And explicable it must be; her crime cannot be seen as societally-driven if the cultural stereotypes are to remain unchallenged.[3]

Theatre loves a good murder story: violence, passion, and purpose. The stuff of tragedy is the stuff of the whodunit; *Oedipus* is, among other things, the Ur-detective story. Therefore, it is not surprising that contemporary dramatists should turn to murder—to murder by women—as sources for plays. And, following the thesis of Jones's book, it is also not surprising that the most powerful of the dramas, those that are more than exempla, docudramas, or hysterogenic flights, should be written by women who share with Jones an awareness that often the murderer, like the feminist, in her own way "tests society's established boundaries."[4]

Three plays of this century, based on murder cases and written by American women are Sophie Treadwell's *Machinal*, Wendy Kesselman's *My Sister in This House*, and Susan Glaspell's *Trifles*. All do more than rework a tale of murder; they reveal in the telling the lineaments of the society that spawned the crime. *Machinal*, written in 1928 and successfully revived in New York in 1990, is loosely based on one of the most sensational murder cases of the 1920s: Ruth Snyder and Judd Gray's killing of Snyder's husband. Diverting attention from that other case of 1927—Sacco and Vanzetti—articles blazed, "If Ruth Snyder is a woman then, by God! you must find some other name for my mother, wife or sister."[5] Treadwell turns this tabloid hysteria on its head. Her Ruth is neither aberrant nor insane; she is ordinary, unexceptional, exactly someone's mother, wife, or sister, worn down by the societal machine of the title.

More disturbing because less easily domesticated is the equally famous 1933 murder case, from Le Mans, France, in which two maids, the sisters Christine and Lea Papin, bludgeoned, stabbed, and mutilated the bodies of their employer and her daughter: Mme. and Mlle. Lancelin. The crime was directed against women; however, the two plays that have sprung from the murder—Jean Genet's *The Maids* and Kesselman's *My Sister in This House*—focus on repressed sexuality and its relation to power, victimization, and enforced gender roles, Kesselman's version moving beyond the acts of horror to implicate "the rage of all women condensed to the point of explosion."[6]

While Treadwell and Kesselman reconstitute celebrated murder cases and alter the historicity to shape their readings of female experience, Glaspell's *Trifles* takes its leave from a previously unknown source; therefore, it has been impossible until now to determine what contextual material Glaspell employs and how she reworks it in order to create her one-act masterpiece and its fictional offshoot, "A Jury of her Peers."[7]

In *The Road to the Temple*, her biography of her husband George Cram Cook, Glaspell offers a brief comment on the genesis of the play, and on the conditions under which it was written. In the summer of 1916, she, Cook, and other transplanted Greenwich Village writers, artists, and political activists were summering in Provincetown, Massachusetts, and, for the second season, were amusing themselves by staging their own plays on a fishing wharf, converted at night to a makeshift theatre. At the end of July, Glaspell had brought Eugene O'Neill to the group, and they had staged his play, *Bound East for Cardiff*. Now they needed a play for their third bill. As Glaspell tells the story, Cook urged her to supply one:

> I protested. I did not know how to write a play. I had never "studied it."
>
> "Nonsense," said Jig. "You've got a stage, haven't you?"
>
> So I went out on the wharf, sat alone on one of our wooden benches without a back, and looked a long time at that bare little stage. After a time the stage became a kitchen—a kitchen there all by itself. . . . Then the door at the back opened, and people all bundled up came in—two or three men, I wasn't sure which, but sure enough about the two women, who hung back, reluctant to enter that kitchen.[8]

Whenever she became stuck at a certain point in the writing, Glaspell would walk across the narrow street that separated the wharf from her home, and sit once more in the theatre until she could visualize the scene; after structuring it on paper she would test it in the actual space where it would be played. And so *Trifles* was written under conditions many playwrights would envy.[9]

As for its genesis, she claimed it was based on an actual murder case: "When I was a newspaper reporter out in Iowa, I was sent down-state to do a murder trial, and I never forgot going into the kitchen of a woman locked up in town." In numerous interviews throughout her life, she offered variations on this memory; but she never provided the name of the murderer or the details of the trial.[10]

In the process of completing research for a biography of Susan Glaspell, I discovered the historical source upon which *Trifles* and "Jury" are based: the murder of a sixty-year-old farmer named John Hossack on December 2, 1900, in Indianola, Iowa. Glaspell covered the case and the subsequent trial when she was a reporter for the *Des Moines Daily News*, a position she began full-time the day after she graduated from Drake University in June 1900, a twenty-four-year-old woman with a Ph.B. in philosophy and several years of newspaper work in Davenport and Des Moines behind her.[11] Although her general beat was the Iowa statehouse, and she would later say that the experiences there provided her with sufficient material to quit her job a year later and turn to fiction, it was the Hossack murder case that was the central story of her brief journalistic career.

Although not as sensational as the Snyder or as horrific as the Papin case, the Hossack killing also focuses on a woman accused of murder. The investigation and subsequent trial offer one more example of what Jones so graphically details in her book: the process by which juridical attitudes toward, and prosecution of, women are shaped by societal concepts of female behavior, the same concepts that may have motivated the act of murder. However, the position of the author in relation to the material differs among the plays. While Treadwell probably attended the Snyder trial, she was not an active participant in the situations she recasts. Glaspell was. And while Kesselman could make a thorough, dispassionate investigation of the commentary and reactions that surrounded the history of the Papin case, Glaspell was actually a primary contributor to the shaping of public opinion about the woman being tried. The news accounts Glaspell filed, therefore, offer more than an important contextual basis for approaching the fictional texts. They also provide important biographical information about the author and her own personal and artistic evolution, and document the cultural shifts which took place between 1900 when the murder took place and 1916 when Glaspell wrote her play.

II

The case at first glance seemed simple. Some time after midnight on December 2, 1900, John Hossack, a well-to-do farmer, was struck twice on the head with an axe, while he slept in bed. Margaret Hossack, his wife of thirty-three years—who was sleeping beside him—reported that a strange sound, "like two pieces of wood striking," wakened her; she jumped out of bed, went into the adjoining sitting room, saw a light shining on a wall, and heard the door to the front porch slowly closing. Only then did she hear her husband's groans. Assembling the five of her nine children who still lived at home, she lit a lamp, reentered the bedroom, and discovered Hossack bleeding profusely, the walls and bedsheets spattered, brain matter oozing from a five inch gash, his head crushed. One of his sons claimed that the mortally injured man was still able to speak. When he said to his father, "Well, pa, you are badly hurt," Hossack replied, "No, I'm not hurt, but I'm not feeling well."[12]

It was assumed that prowlers must have committed the crime; but when a search of the farmhouse failed to reveal any missing items, a coroner's inquest was called. Its findings were inconclusive. However, after discovering the presumed murder weapon smeared with blood under the family corn crib, and listening to reports and innuendos from neighbors, who hinted at a history of marital and family trouble, the Sheriff arrested Mrs. Hossack, "as a matter of precaution" (5 December) while the funeral was still in progress or, as Glaspell would more vividly report, "just as the sexton was throwing the last clods on the grave of her murdered husband" (14 January).

There was really nothing unique about such a murder in the Iowa of 1900 which if no more violent than it is today was certainly no less so. Sandwiched between ubiquitous advertisements for "Female Nerve Cures" and romantic accounts of the courtships of Vanderbilts and Rockefellers are a whole range of lurid tales that would keep a contemporary tabloid busy—and happy: reports of a woman being set on fire, a farm hand murdering another man with a neck yoke, a young man attempting to kill his parents, and a garden-variety assortment of rural knifings, insanity, and violence.[13] What makes the Hossack case stand out are the extended length of the coverage and the vivid style of the reporter. Her paper seems to have charged Glaspell with two tasks: rousing the readership and insuring that the story stay on the first page. She accomplishes both.

Employing the techniques of Gonzo journalism sixty years before Hunter Thompson, Glaspell filed twenty-six stories on the Hossack case, from the fifteen-line item on page three, dated December

3, 1900 that summarily described the event of the murder, to the page one, full-column story on 11 April 1901 that reported the jury's decision at the trial. Most are indistinguishable from her own unsigned "Newsgirl" features running in the paper at the time. They make ready use of hyperbole, invention, and supposition, all filtered through one of Glaspell's common devices in her column: a lively, often opinionated persona. Whether labeled "your correspondent," "a representative from the *News*," or "a member of the press," she is a constructed presence who invites the reader to share some privileged information, intriguing rumor, and running assessment of the case and of the guilt or innocence of the accused.

In her first extended coverage of the crime, under the headline, "Coroner's Jury Returns its Verdict this Morning—Mrs. Hossack Thought to be Crazy," Glaspell announces the imminent arrest of the woman, a fact "secretly revealed to your correspondent." She also provides the first of many rumors that become increasingly prominent in her coverage, although never attributed to specific sources: "Friends of Mrs. Hossack are beginning to suggest that she is insane, and that she has been *in* this condition for a year and a half, under the constant surveillance of members of the family," and "the members of the Hossack family were not on pleasant relations with each other," information which comes as "a complete surprise, as Hossack was not supposed to have an enemy in the world." She concludes by citing the most damaging evidence used against the accused woman throughout her trial: Mrs. Hossack's claim that she lay asleep beside her husband and was not awakened while the murder was taking place (5 December).

Glaspell continues to mix fact, rumor, and commentary, with a superfluity of rousing language and imagery, opening her next report with the reminder that Mrs. Hossack has been arrested for the death of her husband, "on charge of having beaten out his brains with an axe," that the accused woman has employed the legal services of Mr. Henderson and State Senator Berry, that when arrested she showed no emotion and absolutely declined to make any statement concerning her guilt or innocence, and that while her family supported her "the public sentiment is overwhelming against her." How she gleaned this information or arrived at these conclusions, Glaspell does not say. She does, however, provide her first description of the accused woman: "Though past 50 years of age, she is tall and powerful and looks like she would be dangerous if aroused to a point of hatred." She again repeats the rumors of domestic tensions, and quotes a neighbor, named Haines—a witness at the inquest—who implies that Mrs. Hossack had years before asked him to get her husband "out of the way" (6 December).

"Public sentiment is still very much against the prisoner," the 8 December news story begins, reiterating the claim that Mrs. Hossack wanted "to get rid of her husband" and adding that she was willing to pay liberally for the services of anyone undertaking the task—a story "the public generally accepts" and will, therefore, "sympathize with the county attorney in his efforts to convict the woman." In an added development, Glaspell reports that Mrs. Hossack had left home a year before but had been persuaded to return "with the idea of securing a division of the property, but this division had never been made." Although the sheriff had refused all requests to see photographs of the murdered man, Glaspell announces, "a representative of the *News* was accorded this privilege though it must be confessed there is little satisfaction in it" (8 December).

Waiving a preliminary hearing, Mrs. Hossack's attorneys decided to take the case directly to the grand jury which bound her over for trial in April. In the interim the defendant requested and was given bail. The story Glaspell filed immediately prior to the release contains a new element. The reporter, who only days before had described Mrs. Hassock as cold, calm, and menacing, now described her as "worn and emaciated" as she was led from her cell, with "red and swollen eyelids indicating that she had been weeping" (11 December). Since Mrs. Hossack was immediately released after this date and remained in her home until the trial, it is likely that what caused Glaspell to alter her description was her own visit to the Hossack farm, the event she uses as the basis for *Trifles*. From this point on in her reporting, Glaspell's references to the accused woman become more benign, the "powerful" murderer becoming with each story older, frailer, and more maternal.[14]

Glaspell was probably at the farmhouse gathering material for the front page, double-column feature that appeared on 12 December, the most extensive coverage of the pre-trial events. It began with the headline, "Mrs Hossack may yet be proven innocent," followed by the subheadings, "Tide of sentiment turns slightly in her favor—Notified today that she will soon be released—First photographs bearing on the tragedy." The photographs turn out to be three simple pencil drawings: Mrs. Hossack, sitting in a rocking chair, her head bent down, her eyes closed (Plate I); her dead husband with the two gashes to his head (Plate II); and the axe, complete with four dots of blood. Captions indicate that the first is "sketched from life," the second "from flashlight photograph of the dead man" that "others tried to obtain access to . . . but failed." In more detail, Glaspell describes her revisionary image of Mrs. Hossack: "the aged prisoner . . . looked up into the officer's face, smiled and remarked that she would be glad to get home again with her children but did not manifest any great degree of joy at the news." Bail, the reader is told, will not be excessive because the accused "is an aged woman and one who would not try in any manner to escape."

As much as she may have altered her own perceptions of Mrs. Hossack and may have tried to influence her readers, Glaspell still had the job of keeping them interested in the case. Borrowing devices from popular detective fiction of the time,[15] she dangles tantalizing questions: the test on the murder weapon may now be known, but the readers will have to wait until the trial to learn the results; the same for the blood stains on Mrs. Hossack's clothing. Glaspell does hint that the results substantiate the claim that the blood on the axe comes from slaughtered fowl, and continues, "if that is true one of the strongest links in the chain of circumstantial evidence is broken. If the blood is human, it will look bad for the accused." If still not intrigued, the reader is given a gruesome detail—a "substance resembling brains" has also been found on the axe—and a rumor that the defense will enter a plea of insanity if their efforts on behalf of their client fail. She must be crazy or innocent "the best people of Indianola" surmise, since visits to the home in the past few months did not indicate problems, but only a wife attentive to her husband's needs, seeing "that he lacked for nothing." Of Mrs. Hossack's character, these unnamed sources reveal, "She is said to be a woman who is quick tempered, high strung, like all Scotch women, but of a deeply religious turn of mind" (12 December).

In the months before the trial, Glaspell filed only three small articles about the case, each one using the opportunity of a new piece of news to summarize the details of the murder, the grisly events becoming more grisly with the retelling. On 23 March she reports that new evidence has emerged "and that in all probability it would result in Mrs. Hossack's acquittal at an early date." She does not say what the evidence is but she offers an important turn in the case. Mr. Haines, the primary source of information about trouble in the Hossack home and the party to whom, it is believed, Mrs. Hossack turned to get rid of her husband, "had gone insane brooding over the tragedy, and was yesterday sentenced to the insane asylum."

Although there had been talk of moving the venue of the trial because of the strong feelings against Margaret Hossack and the fear that an impartial jury could not be found (14 January), the trial finally began in the Polk County Courthouse on 1 April 1901 and was held every day except Sundays for the next ten days. Glaspell had apparently been successful in stirring public interest because she reports that on the first day over 1,200 people attended, far more than the tiny rural court could accommodate and that on the day the jury returned its verdict more than 2,000 were present. Noting the composition of the observers, she says that the "conspicuous feature so far is the large attendance of women in court. Over half of the spectators present today belong to the gentler sex. The bright array of Easter hats lent a novelty to the scene, giving it much the appearance of some social function" (2 April).[16]

The seventy-eight witnesses, fifty-three for the prosecution and twenty-five for the defense, focused on seven specific questions during the trial: (1) Would it have been possible, as his son testified, for John Hossack, who had sustained two traumatic blows—one made with the axe head, the second with the blunt handle—to talk and call for his wife and children; (2) Was the blood found on the axe and the hairs later discovered nearby human, or were they, as claimed by the family, the residue of the turkey killed two days earlier for Thanksgiving; (3) How had the axe, which the youngest son said he placed inside the corn crib after killing the turkey, come to be found under it, in its usual place; (4) Had the axe and Mrs. Hossack's night clothes been washed to remove incriminating stains of blood; (5) Was the dog, who always barked when strangers appeared, drugged on the night of the crime, as family members testified; (6) Had earlier domestic troubles in the Hossack house been resolved and all dissension ceased for over a year before the murder, as the family stated; and (7) Would it have been possible for an intruder or intruders to enter the house through the bedroom window, stand at the foot of the bed and reach up to strike the fatal blows without rousing the woman who slept by her husband's side? An eighth question—what prompted Mrs. Hossack to leave home and wish her husband "out of the way"—only entered the testimony twice. One neighbor, the wife of Mr. Haines, stated that she and her husband had come to aid Mrs. Hossack, who thought her husband would kill the family (3 April). Another neighbor testified that he had to act as protector when Mrs. Hossack returned to her home "in case her husband again maltreated her as she had reason for believing" (2 April).

Glaspell's reports do not suggest that the prosecution or the defense pursued the possibility of violence in the home, and she does not broach the subject herself. Instead her stories of the trial tend to be summaries of testimony by experts and lay people who describe the structure of the brain, the disposition of the body in the bed, and the configuration of the blood spots on the walls. She does pause to describe the shock caused when the Hossack bed was brought into the courtroom complete with bloodstained bedding, and when two vials of hairs were displayed: one found near the axe, the other obtained by exhuming John Hossack.

Interspersed between these accounts are her descriptions of the accused and of those attending the trial. During day one, for example, Glaspell describes Mrs. Hossack's reaction to the recital of counts against her: "Her eyes frequently filled with tears and her frame shook with emotion" (2 April). On the next day, when the murder scene was again invoked, she notes that Mrs. Hossack, who occupied a seat by the Sheriff's wife, surrounded by three of the Hossack daughters and all but one of the sons, broke down and wept bitterly: "Grief was not confined to her alone, it spread until the weeping group embraced the family and the sympathetic wife of Sheriff Hodson who frequently applied her handkerchief to her eyes" (3 April).

Since there were no witnesses to the crime, the prosecution's case was based entirely on circumstantial evidence, and Glaspell often stops in her narration of the testimony to weigh the success of the unsubstantiated arguments, and to prod her readers to keep following the case. After one lengthy argument about how well Mrs. Hossack was able to wield an axe, Glaspell comments: "It must be admitted, however, that the prosecution has not thus far furnished any direct evidence and it is extremely doubtful if the chain of circumstantial evidence thus far offered will be sufficient to eliminate all doubt of the defendant's guilt from the minds of the jurors . . . on the other hand it is claimed by the prosecution attorney that the best evidence is yet to come" (4 April). When Mrs. Hossack took the stand in her own defense and repeated the story she had held since the inquest, describing how she and her husband had spent a typical evening together the night of the crime—"He sat in the kitchen reading . . . later played with his whip . . . [while] I was patching and darning"—Glaspell observes, "When she left the stand, there seemed to be the impression on the audience that she had told the truth" (8 April). Earlier questions of Mrs. Hossack's sanity apparently were dispelled by her composed appearance in court.

Like the novelist she would soon become, Glaspell saves her most impassioned descriptions for the climax of the trial: the summations by the lawyers. Of State Senator Berry, the defense counsel, she writes:

> It is said to be the master effort of his life . . . at times the jury without exception was moved to tears. Strong men who had not shed a tear in years sat in their seats mopping their eyes and compressing their lips in a vain effort to suppress the emotion caused by the Senator's eloquent pleas.
>
> [9 April]

This lachrymose display, she says, even extended to the prosecution attorneys who were "seen to turn their heads fearful lest the anguish of the family would unman them and the jury would have an impression which they could not afterward remove." The spectators were also moved. When the court was adjourned at noon, she writes, "fully two thousand people went out in the sunshine, their faces stained by the tears which had coursed down their cheeks."

Aside from tears, Berry's chief strategy was to charge that Mr. Haines, "the insane man," was the real murderer. When he had been asked by the Hossack children to come to the house on the night of the murder, he had refused, saying that there were tramps about. It was he who had first implicated Mrs. Hossack by suggesting that she had wanted her husband dead and had sought his aid. And it was Mrs. Haines who had provided some of the most damning evidence about dissension in the Hossack home.

As successful as Berry may have been in concluding for the defense, Glaspell warns her readers that "it is certain that when attorney McNeal closes the argument for the prosecution the effect of Senator Berry's eloquence will have been lost and the verdict, if any at all is reached, can hardly be acquittal" (9 April). Why, she does not say.

On the last day of the trial, County Attorney Clammer and Mr. McNeal summarized for the prosecution; and, as Glaspell predicted, McNeal was able to rouse the audience with his indictment—"She did it, gentlemen, and I ask you to return her in kind . . . she has forfeited her right to live and she should be as John Hossack, who lies rotting beneath the ground." He too had his own bombshell: Margaret Hossack had been pregnant and given birth to a child before their marriage. This, McNeal claimed, was the dark secret often referred to in the trial, the story Hossack said he would take to his grave, and the reason for the unhappiness in the Hossack home. Just how a pregnancy thirty-three years earlier could have been the sole cause of trouble in the marriage and how it proved Mrs. Hossack's guilt in the murder of her husband was not clear; but, as Glaspell reports, it provided the jury with the impression that she was a woman who could not be trusted. It was with this revelation that the trial ended (10 April).

The case went to the jury on 10 April, the judge presenting the following charge:

> when evidence consists of a chain of well authenticated circumstances, it is often more convincing and satisfactory and gives a stronger ground of assurance of the defendant's guilt than the direct testimony of witnesses unconfirmed by circumstances.
>
> [11 April]

In less than twenty-four hours the jury returned its verdict. Margaret Hossack was found guilty as charged and was sentenced to life imprisonment at hard labor. Glaspell reported the outcome, but made no comment on the finding.

It was the last story she filed in the case; it was also the last story she filed as a reporter for the *Des Moines Daily News*. Immediately after the trial, she resigned and returned home to Davenport to begin writing fiction, and by the summer of 1901 she had moved to Chicago and enrolled in the graduate English program at the University of Chicago. Therefore, she may never have learned the final disposition of the Hossack case, for the story was not yet over. In April 1901 lawyers Henderson and Berry lost an appeal with a lower court, but in April 1902 the Supreme Court of the State of Iowa agreed to hear the case. Citing several instances where the trial judge had ruled incorrectly on the evidence, the higher court overturned the original conviction and requested a new trial.[17] A second trial took place in Madison County, in February 1903. This time the jury, after twenty-seven hours of deliberation, was unable to reach a verdict: nine voted for conviction and three for acquittal.[18] In papers filed in April 1903, the prosecutor stated that since no further information had surfaced, it would be a waste of taxpayers' money to ask a third jury to hear the case.[19] Mrs. Hossack, then near sixty and in failing health, was ordered released, and was allowed to return to her home, her guilt or innocence still in question.

Eight years earlier, a court in Fall River, Massachusetts had freed Lizzie Borden because they could not imagine that a refined, New England "Maiden" who wore demure silk, carried flowers, and wept copiously in court could wield the axe that slew her family. So strong were the prevailing views about femininity, that even the prosecuting attorney found it hard "to *conceive*" of the guilt of "one of that sex that all high-minded men revere, that all generous men love, that all wise men acknowledge their indebtedness to."[20]

What is striking in the Hossack case is how ready the community was to assume the guilt of "one of that sex." Unlike Lizzie, who quickly read the signs of the time and played the part that was demanded of her—she learned to cry in court—Margaret Hossack, for all her tears and Glaspell's mid-course correction and subsequent, embellished descriptions of "the frail mother of nine," did not win over the jury. The jury may not have been convinced that she was guilty of murder, but she certainly was guilty of questionable female behavior. She had left her husband, discussed her marital troubles with neighbors, and—most damaging—had been pregnant before marriage. To have found such a woman innocent or to have explored the question of justifiable homicide would have been unthinkable in the Iowa court of 1901. Such a direction in the trial would have necessitated an investigation of the family, the power wielded by the husband, his physical abuse over a long period, and the circumscribed lives of the wife and children; both the prosecution and, tellingly, the defense seemed loath to pursue such investigations. Instead, as Glaspell's accounts indicate, their cases were each discourses in evasion, argued on small, tangential points, few of which addressed the central issue of motive. Even the Supreme Court ruling, which acknowledged John Hossack's repeated beatings of his wife—with his hands and with a stove lid—couched its findings:

> The family life of the Hossacks had not been pleasant perhaps [sic] the husband was most to blame. He seems to have been somewhat narrow minded and quite stern in his determination to control all family matters.[21]

However, absent from the seven points on which the Supreme Court reversed the lower court decision was abuse. In fact the court argued that prior relations in the family should not have been introduced in the original trial since harmony had been established for over a year. Domestic life, thus, remained untarnished.

Why such juridical sidestepping? Because John Hossack was a pillar of the society, he had been nominated "for some of the highest offices in Warren County" (12 December), and "the twelve good men" Glaspell describes sitting in judgment of Mrs. Hossack were all men who knew him well and who had a vested interest in protecting his name if they could no longer protect his person. The women attending the trial in their Easter finery—perhaps even the sympathetic Sheriff's wife—might have been able to offer a different reading of the case, but they were not accorded the opportunity in the court or in the newspaper accounts Glaspell filed. Sixteen years later, in her play Glaspell offers them the opportunity to be heard.

III

Trifles begins at home. A murder has been committed, a man strangled while he slept; his wife—who claimed to be sleeping beside him at the time—has been accused of the crime and taken to jail to await trial. Those prosecuting the case, County Attorney Henderson and Sheriff Peters, have returned to the scene to search for clues that will provide "a motive; something to show anger, or—sudden feeling," and explain "the funny way" the man was murdered, "rigging it all up like that."[22] Accompanying them are Mr. Hale, who found the body; Mrs. Peters, the Sheriff's wife, charged with bringing the accused woman some of her things; and Mrs. Hale, who keeps her company in the kitchen below while the men move around the upstairs bedroom and perimeter of the farmhouse searching for clues.

In the absence of the wife, the women, like quilters, patch together the scenario of her life and her guilt. As they imagine her, Minnie Foster is a lonely, childless woman, married to a taciturn husband, isolated from neighbors because of the rigors of farm life. When they discover a bird cage with its door ripped off and a canary with its neck wrung, they have no trouble making the connection. The husband has killed the bird, the wife's only comfort, as he has killed the bird-like spirit of the woman. The motive and method of murder become clear to them as the signs of sudden anger they infer from the half-wiped kitchen table, and Minnie's erratic quilt stitching. Based on such circumstantial evidence, the women try the case, find the accused guilty, but dismiss the charge, recognizing the exigencies that led her to the act. In the process of judging, they become compeers: Mrs. Peters recognizes her own disenfranchisement under the law and her own potential for violence, and Mrs. Hale recognizes her failure to sustain her neighbor and thus her culpability in driving the desperate woman to kill.

This brief summary indicates how few specific details remain in Glaspell's re-visioning of the Hossack case. There is mention of "that man who went crazy" (4), but he is not named or connected to the events.[23] Of the names of the participants, only Henderson is used, assigned to the country attorney rather than the defense lawyer. Margaret Hossack has been renamed Minnie Foster Wright, the pun on the surname marking her lack of "rights," and implying her "right" to free herself against the societally sanctioned "right" of her husband to control the family, a right implicit in the Hossack case.[24]

Glaspell's most striking alterations are her excision of Minnie and the change of venue. The accused woman has been taken away to jail before *Trifles* begins, her place signified by the empty rocking chair that remains in her kitchen. By not bringing Minnie physically on to the stage, the playwright focuses on issues that move beyond the guilt or innocence of one person. Since the audience never actually sees Minnie, it is not swayed by her person, but by her condition, a condition shared by other women who can be imagined in the empty subject position. And by situating her play in the kitchen, not at the court, in the private space where Minnie lived rather than the public space where she will be tried, Glaspell offers the audience a composite picture of the life of Minnie Wright, Margaret Hossack, and the countless women whose experiences were not represented in court because their lives were not deemed relevant to the adjudication of their cases. Most important, by shifting venue, Glaspell brings the central questions never asked in the original Hossack case into focus: the motives for murder, what goes on in the home, and why women kill.

Motives are writ large in *Trifles*. The mise-en-scène suggests the harshness of Minnie's life. The house is isolated, "down in a hollow and you don't see the road" (21)—dark, foreboding, a rural, gothic scene. The interior of the kitchen replicates this barrenness and the commensurate disjunctions in the family, as the woman experienced them. Things are broken, cold, imprisoning; they are also violent. "Preserves" explode from lack of heat, a punning reminder of the causal relationship between isolation and violence. The mutilated cage and bird signify Wright's brutal nature and the physical abuse his wife has borne. Employing expressionistic techniques, Glaspell externalizes Minnie's desperation and the conditions that caused it.[25] She also finds the dramatic correlative for revenge. Rather than use an axe, this abused wife strangles her husband: a punishment to fit his crime. So powerfully does Glaspell marshall the evidence of Minnie's strangled life, that the jury on the stage and the jury who observe them from the audience presume the wife's "right" to take violent action in the face of the violence done to her. They see what might cause women to kill.

When Glaspell turns to the characters in her play, she again reworks the figures from the Hossack case, offering a revisionary reading of their roles in the original trial. The lawmen in *Trifles* bear traces of the original investigators: the County Attorney and the Sheriff. Mr. Hale, however, is Glaspell's invention, a composite of the Indianola farmers who testified at the Hossack trial, his name possibly derived from Mr. Haines. By introducing a man not directly charged with prosecution of the case, Glaspell is able to show patriarchal power and privilege, the united front that judged Margaret Hossack. She also illustrates the process through which an individual joins the ranks. In "A Jury of her Peers," she goes to great lengths to indicate Mr. Hale's awkwardness at the beginning of the story, as he relates the details of the case, and how easily he is intimidated by the County Attorney. However, when he is allowed–by virtue of his gender—to go upstairs with the men of law, it is Hale, not they, who directly taunts the women: "But would the women know a clue if they did come upon it."[26] Glaspell ironically describes Hale as speaking "with good natured superiority" when he declares, "women are used to worrying over trifles" (44). Gender transcends class here, as it did in the original trial, where the farmers, jurors, and lawyers had a common connection: they were male and as such they were in control of the court and the direction of the testimony.

However, Glaspell also indicates that the privileged club does have a pecking order. Mr. Hale is recently admitted—or more likely, only temporarily admitted—and, therefore, more likely to chide those below him in order to gain favor with those above. A similar desire to ingratiate themselves with the law and to establish a camaraderie that temporarily suspended class was clearly apparent among the farmers of Indianola, eager to play a part in convicting Mrs. Hossack, some so ready that their zeal in intruding themselves into the investigation was cited in the Supreme Court reversal.

Constructing her category of men across class lines, establishing their connectedness based on legal empowerment and rights, Glaspell summarily dismisses them to roam about on the periphery of the tale, their presence theatrically marked by shuffling sounds above the heads of the women, and occasional appearances as they scurry out to the barn. With her deft parody, Glaspell undercuts the authority the men wielded in the original case, and throws into question their sanctioned preserve of power. They physically crisscross the stage as they verbally crisscross the details of the crime, both actions leading nowhere, staged to show ineffectuality and incompetence.

In her version of the Hossack case, the women, also drawn across class lines, occupy the men's place, standing in stage center and functioning as the composite shaping consciousness that structures the play.[27] Glaspell carefully chooses the two women who will usurp legal agency. Mrs. Peters is the wife of the Sheriff, patterned after Sheriff Hodson's wife, whose acts of kindness to Margaret Hossack seem to have stayed in Glaspell's memory. At first, Mrs. Peters parrots the masculinist view and voice of her husband, defending the search of the home as the men's "duty." However, she gradually comes to recognize that marital designation—wife of the Sheriff—

offers her no more freedom than it does Minnie; in fact, it completely effaces her as an individual. Glaspell illustrates this condition by having the women identified only by their surnames, while, at the same time, they seek to particularize Minnie, referring to her by both her first and her maiden name.[28]

To the men, however, Minnie is John Wright's wife, just as Mrs. Peters is the Sheriff's wife: "married to the law" (*Trifles*, 29), "one of us" ("Jury," 37), she "doesn't need supervising" (*Trifles*, 29). Even Mrs. Hale at the beginning of "Jury" assumes that Mrs. Peters will be an extension of her husband and will share his views of murder. However, as Mrs. Peters slowly ferrets out the facts of Minnie's life—the childlessness, the isolation—and conflates the experience with her own early married days, she begins to identify with Minnie. It is when she comes upon the bird cage and the dead canary that she makes the most important connection: an understanding of female helplessness in front of male brutality: "When I was a girl—my kitten—there was a boy took a hatchet, and before my eyes—and before I could get there—[covers her face an instant] If they hadn't held me back I would have—[Catches herself, looks upstairs where steps are heard, falters weakly]—hurt him" (*Trifles*, 25).

It is significant that Glaspell attributes to Mrs. Peters, the Sheriff's wife, the memory of a murder with an axe, the murder weapon in the Hossack case, and offers as sign of brutality the dismemberment of an animal, a trace, perhaps, of the turkey in the original case. In the reversal of roles that Glaspell stages—in having Mrs. Peters act in lieu of her husband, dispensing her verdict based on her reading of the case and the motives for murder—she destroys the notion that a woman is her husband. She also stages what a woman may become when given legal power: a subject acting under her own volition, her decisions not necessarily coinciding with her husband's or with the male hegemony. She becomes self-deputized.

If Mrs. Peters is taken from life, so too is Mrs. Hale, a possible surrogate for the young reporter Susan Glaspell.[29] Just as Mrs. Peters recognizes her own potential for murder in the face of powerlessness, and this recognition motivates her to act and to seize the juridical position, so Mrs. Hale comes to her own awareness in the course of the play. What she discovers in the kitchen of the Wright home is her own complicity in Minnie's situation, because of her withheld aid. "We live close together and we live far apart. We all go through the same things—it's just a different kind of the same thing," she says, summarizing her insight about "how it is for women" (27). In light of the Hossack case and Glaspell's role in sensationalizing the proceedings and in shaping public opinion, the lines appear to be confessional; so to her question, "Who's going to punish that?" (27), Mrs. Hale's words seem to indicate Glaspell's awareness in 1916 of her omissions and commissions in 1901: her failure to act in Margaret Hossack's behalf, and her failure to recognize the implications of the trial for her own life.

Given this awareness, it may seem strange that when Glaspell has the opportunity to retry Margaret Hossack and change the outcome of the case, she does not acquit the woman, or, as KayAnn Short argues, give her "her day in court" to prove her innocence.[30] Instead she has Mrs. Peters and Mrs. Hale assume Minnie's guilt and—as in the original trial—base their findings on circumstantial evidence instead of incontrovertible proof. However, when approaching *Trifles* in relation to the Hossack case, it becomes clear that acquittal is not Glaspell's intention, not why she wrote the play. Whether Margaret Hossack or Minnie Wright committed murder is moot; what is incontrovertible is the brutality of their lives, the lack of options they had to redress grievances or to escape abusive husbands, and the complete disregard of their plight by the courts and by society. Instead of arguing their innocence, Glaspell concretizes the conditions under which these women live and the circumstances that might cause them to kill. She thus presents the subtext that was excised from the original trial and that undergirds so many of the cases cited in Ann Jones's study: men's fears of women who might kill, and women's fears of the murder they might be forced to commit. In so doing, she stages one of the first modern arguments for justifiable homicide.[31] By having Mrs. Peters and Mrs. Hale unequivocally assume Minnie's guilt and also assume justification for her part, Glaspell presents her audience/jury with a defense that forces it to confront the central issues of female powerlessness and disenfranchisement and the need for laws to address such issues.[32]

However, Glaspell does not actually present the victimization of women or the violent acts such treatment may engender; instead she stages the potential for female action and the usurpation of power.[33] By having the women assume the central positions and conduct the investigation and the trial, she actualizes an empowerment that suggests that there are options short of murder that can be imagined for women. Mrs. Peters and Mrs. Hale may seem to conduct their trial sub rosa, because they do not actively confront the men; but in Mrs. Hale's final words, "We call it—knot it, Mr. Henderson" (30), ostensibly referring to a form of quilting but clearly addressed to the actions the women have taken, they become both actors and namers. Even if the men do not understand the pun—either through ignorance or, as Judith Fetterley suggests, through self-preservation—the audience certainly does.[34] It recognizes that the women have achieved an important political victory: they have wrested control of language, a first step in political ascendancy; and they have wrested control of the case and of the stage. Not waiting to be given the vote or the right to serve on juries, Glaspell's women have taken the right for themselves. Her audience in 1916 would get the point. It would have understood that Glaspell is deconstructing the very assumption of the law's incontrovertibility, its absolutist position.[35] Mrs. Peters and Mrs. Hale, by suturing into their deliberations their own experiences and fears—just as the men in the Hossack case had done—illustrate the subjective nature of the reading of evidence, and, by implication, of all essentialist readings.

In 1916 it would have been clearer than it often is to contemporary audiences that Glaspell is more concerned with legal and social empowerment than with replacing one hierarchy with another; that women's surreptitious action may comment less on women's natures than on the political systems that breed such behavior; that women do not speak "in a different voice," but speak in a manner deriving from their different position under the law, that is, from their common erasure. Glaspell's depiction of the conditions of her women is close to what Catherine MacKinnon describes in *Feminism Unmodified*: women's actions—their voices—deriving not from some innate nature but from the ways they have been forced to speak and to act. MacKinnon suggests that if legal and social changes could occur, it would then be time to decide how a woman "talks."[36] When women are powerless, she argues, they "don't just speak differently. A lot, [they] don't speak." Speech is "not differently articulated, it is silenced."[37] In *Trifles* Glaspell, like MacKinnon, posits gender as a production of the inequality of power under law, "a social status based on who is permitted to do what to whom."[38]

IV

That Susan Glaspell was able to reshape the events of the Hossack case in order to focus on contemporary issues in 1916 can be attributed to at least two causes. The first is biographical. Glaspell herself had changed in the sixteen years that separated the trial from the composition of the play. When she covered the Hossack case, she was twenty-four, right out of college; when she wrote *Trifles*, she had just turned forty, and had already published three well-received novels, thirty-one short stories, and a collection of short fiction, all focusing on the lives of women. She had also spent a year in Paris, and had lived in Chicago, Greenwich Village, and Provincetown, before her marriage at the age of thirty-seven to fellow Davenport native George Cram Cook.[39]

It is a mistake to claim that Glaspell was a slumbering midwestern woman until Cook brought her to life and political awareness when they married. Before her marriage, and even before her coverage of the Hossack case, she was already something of an iconoclast, aware of the imposition of cultural restriction on women, at least as they had an impact on her own life and the lives of the women she observed as Susie Glaspell, the eighteen-year-old Society Editor of a local Davenport newspaper. However, her nascent feminism was based on the class structure of the city. She was poor in a town that valued wealth; she worked in a society where women were expected to find others to work for them.

What she seems to have experienced for the first time in her coverage of the Hossack case was a legal rather than social powerlessness that cut across class lines: the testimony of Mrs. Hossack, the ladies in their Easter finery attending the trial, and even the Sheriff's wife were equally silenced. While Glaspell may have felt sympathy, if not empathy, for Mrs. Hossack when she entered her kitchen in 1901, and while she may have been aware of the skewed nature of the trial, she was not able to translate this experience or insight into her writing, certainly not into her newspaper reports. As Ann Jones shows in her description of the coverage of a variety of murder trials of women during the period, the news accounts offer what the society will bear. The possibility of exploring the implications of the Hossack trial in terms of gender roles or of pursuing the question of justifiable homicide would have been unthinkable in Iowa in 1901, even if Glaspell had consciously been moved to do so.

In 1916, it was not. If Glaspell had changed, so had society. Although the general public might still resist such positions, the people for whom Glaspell fashioned her theatre, if not her fiction, would certainly see the Hossack trial in light of their own agitation for the nineteenth amendment, women's rights, socialism, and the dismantling of absolutist thought in all areas.[40]

At the time she wrote *Trifles*, Glaspell was living in a community passionately concerned with socialism and feminism; she herself was a founding member of Heterodoxy, the New York-based group of women whose numbers included activists Maria Jenny Howe, Crystal Eastman, Elizabeth Irwin, Mary Heaton Vorse, and—for a time—Charlotte Perkins Gilman.[41] The audience for the Provincetown Players was already a body of the committed, who in 1916 agitated for suffrage and for social reform that would redress class distinctions in America, and who for the most part were opposed to Wilson and the war. Unlike many suffragists, their arguments were usually posited on a materialist rather than an essentialist reading of gender, concerned either with class struggles of which gender limitations were part or with enlightenment ideals of individualism applicable to both women and men. They did not romanticize femininity; most debunked the "cult of the home." Their major concern was in insuring "that women shall have the same right as man to be different, to be individuals not merely a social unit," and that this individualism would manifest itself in legal and social freedom.[42] It was for this audience and at this time that Glaspell returned to the Hossack case.

Trifles, therefore, is grounded in a double-focused historical context: the Iowa of 1901 and the Provincetown of 1916, the two periods leaving traces and providing many of the tensions and fissures that produce the contemporary feel of Glaspell's best works. Thus posited, her writing acts as a palimpsest for the shifting roles of women in the early twentieth century, and for her own shifting attitudes toward the possibilities for women and for herself. It is either a testament to the skill with which Glaspell constructed *Trifles* and "A Jury of her Peers," or proof of how little women's lives have changed since 1916 that contemporary feminist critics still use the play and story as palimpsests for their own readings of contemporary feminist issues, readings that still point to some of the dilemmas which faced Glaspell and her personae in 1901 and in 1916: how to free women from the stereotypical roles into which they have been cast, how to articulate their lives and their rights without reinscribing them in the very roles against which they inveigh, how to represent female power not victimization, in short how to represent Margaret Hossack. However, in reading the works through a contemporary grid, critics should be careful of turning them into contemporary tracts, assuming that just because Glaspell offers a picture of two women who bond she is arguing for a higher moral ground for women, romanticizing femininity and home, arguing sexual difference, or the categorization of women under a fixed moral genus.[43] Given her own interests and concerns at the time, and her own relation to the Hossack case, it is more likely that her play and story are illustrating the need to provide both male and female voices in court—and in art—if human experience is not to be forever subsumed under the male pronoun and if women's voices are to be heard not as difference but as equally registered.

Notes

1. Ann Jones, *Women Who Kill* (New York: Holt, Rinehart and Winston, 1980), xv.
2. Ibid, xvi.
3. At the turn of the century, the father of modern criminology, Cesare Lombroso, offered a checklist of physical qualities that would identify women who might kill: they "approximate more to males . . . than to normal women, especially in the superciliary arches in the seam of sutures, in the lower jaw-bones, and in peculiarities of the occipital region" (Jones, *Women Who Kill*, 6).
4. Jones, *Women Who Kill*, 13.
5. Ibid, 257.
6. As qtd. in Lynda Hart, "They Don't Even Look Like Maids Anymore: Wendy Kesselman's *My Sister in This House*," in *Making a Spectacle*, Ed. Lynda Hart (Ann Arbor, MI: University of Michigan Press, 1989), 145.
7. Unless otherwise specified, when I mention *Trifles*, I am also assuming "A Jury of her Peers."
8. Susan Glaspell, *The Road to the Temple* (New York: Frederick Stokes, 1927), 255–56. Glaspell's comments in *The Road to the Temple* are often misleading. The book is hagiography, and just as she constructed other scenes to make them more dramatic—and to dramatize the role of Cook—she may be doing so here. That she should want to portray his role in her shift to drama as that of a mentor encouraging his tutor is, however, revealing. It may be attributed to Cook's recent death in Greece, her return alone to Provincetown, and her immediate love affair with Norman Matson. See Kathleen Carroll, "Centering Women Onstage: Susan Glaspell's Dialogic Strategy of Resistance," Diss. University of Maryland, 1990; and Ann Larabee, "Death in Delphi: Susan Glaspell and the Companionate Marriage," *Mid-Western Review* (1987): 93–106 for other explanations. Glaspell offers

variations on this scene in notes for the book. In one version, she writes, "I began writing plays because my hisband [sic] George Cram Cook made me [crossed out and replaced with 'forced me to']. 'I have announced a play of yours for the next bill,' he told me, soon after we started the Provincetown Players. I didn't want my marriage to break up so I wrote *Trifles* . . ." (Notes from Berg Collection, New York Public Library).

9. Judith Barlow, in an unpublished essay entitled "Susan's Sisters: The 'Other' Women Writers of the Provincetown Players," suggests that Glaspell may have also been influenced by her friend Neith Boyce's play *White Nights*, a work produced by the group the year before, that has as its theme a troubled marriage and a wife who wishes independence. See Barlow, *Susan Glaspell: A Collection of Critical Essays*, Ed. Linda Ben-Zvi (unpublished). *White Nights*, first published in 1928, is reprinted in Rachel France, Ed., *A Century of Plays by American Women* (New York: Richards Rosen, 1979).
10. Glaspell, *The Road to the Temple*, 256.
11. Glaspell first started writing for newspapers after she graduated from high school in Davenport, Iowa, in 1894. She covered local news and social events for the *Trident*, the *Davenport Morning Republican*, and the *Weekly Observer*, which listed her as Society editor, under the name Susie Glaspell.
12. Susan Glaspell, "The Hossack Case," *Des Moines Daily News*, 4 December 1900. Glaspell reported the story from 2 December 1900 to 13 April 1901; references to Glaspell's *Des Moines Daily News* stories will appear in the text.
13. Glaspell may have covered the story about murder by a neck yoke, or at least read of it, because she appropriates the method for use in *Trifles*.
14. It is possible that Glaspell was actually accompanied to the Hossack house by the Sheriff and the County Attorney, who made several trips there during this period to gain evidence. One of the points cited by the Supreme Court of Iowa in its opinion on the trial was the possible impropriety of having the same County Attorney who would conduct the trial gather the evidence. There is no indication, however, that the Sheriff's wife also traveled to the Hossack farm, although the possibility exists that she did.
15. See Jones, *Women Who Kill*, 111–16.
16. The Hossack case was not unique in the number of women in attendance. Jones offers examples of irate ministers commenting on the large number of women who attended celebrated murder trials around the same period. In one case, a minister comments that, "It is a strange thing that women, under no compulsion whatever, are found in large numbers in every notorious trial everywhere, and the dirtier the trial the more women usually will be found in attendance" (*Women Who Kill*, 139). He does not conjecture about this phenomenon.
17. See State vs. Hossack, Supreme Court of Iowa, 9 April 1902, *Northwestern Reporter*: 1077–81. There were seven procedural points upon which the Supreme Court of Iowa based its reversal, the most significant of which were the following: that the hairs found under the corn crib were not proven to be from the murder weapon and had been taken by the County Attorney and given to the Sheriff and could not, therefore, be introduced as evidence; that the dissension in the Hossack house had abated at least a year prior to the murder, and could not, therefore, be introduced in the case.
18. See Polk County Transcripts of Court Records, Case #805, 2 April 1901–3 March 1903.
19. Warren County Court Records, Hossack Trial, April 1903. I thank the Warren and Polk County Court Recorders' Offices for their help in securing these files.20
20. Jones, *Women Who Kill*, 231.
21. *Northwest Reporter*, 9 April 1902.
22. Susan Glaspell, *Trifles*, in *Plays* (Boston, MA: Small, Maynard, and Co., 1920), 15. All further page references appear in the text.
23. See Elaine Hedges, "Small Things Reconsidered: Susan Glaspell's 'A Jury of her Peers,'" in *Women Studies* 12 (1986), 89–110. Rpt. in *Susan Glaspell: A Collection of Critical Essays*, Ed. Linda Ben-Zvi. Hedges discusses insanity in rural American life and also the practice of women on the plains having canaries to provide them company.
24. For other associations connected with the name, see Karen Alkalay-Gut, "Murder and Marriage: another Look at *Trifles*," in *Susan Glaspell: A Collection of Critical Essays*, Ed. Linda Ben-Zvi.
25. Glaspell often employed expressionistic techniques in her plays. See Yvonne Shafer, "Susan Glaspell and American Expressionism," in *Susan Glaspell: A Collection of Critical Essays*, Ed. Linda Ben-Zvi. Shafer discusses expressionism in the one-act plays *The People* and *Woman's Honor*, and in the full-length play *The Verge*. Also see Linda Ben-Zvi, "Susan Glaspell and Eugene O'Neill," *The Eugene O'Neill Newsletter* 6 (1982): 22–29, and Linda Ben-Zvi, "Susan Glaspell, Eugene O'Neill, and the Imagery of Gender," *Eugene O'Neill Newsletter* 10 (1986): 22–28 for further discussions of expressionism in Glaspell's plays.

26. Susan Glaspell, "A Jury of her Peers," in *Everyman*, 5 March 1917, 42. All further page references appear in the text.
27. Mrs. Peters and Mrs. Hale are of different classes, a fact visually captured by the filmmaker Sally Heckel, in her version of "A Jury of her Peers" (Texture Films). Mrs. Hale wears a plain, cloth coat and head scarf; Mrs. Peters has a fur tippet and large, feathered hat. Their language also bears signs of their classes—a technique Glaspell often repeats. In *Trifles*, Mrs. Hale makes grammatical errors, has unfinished sentences, drops letters. Mrs. Peters speaks in a grammatically correct manner befitting the Sheriff's wife. For example, Mrs. Hale's, "I wonder if she was goin' to quilt it or just knot it?" becomes Mrs. Peters's, "We think she was going to—knot it," the omitted *g* being Glaspell's way of marking different education and position. What joins the women is the men's categorization of them, predicated on gender, erasing difference, dismissing individuality.
28. At the time Glaspell was writing the play, the question of women taking their husband's names was a political issue. One of Glaspell's friends, Ruth Hale, launched a movement called the Lucy Stone League which supported married women who chose to keep their maiden names . See Judith Schwarz, *Radical Feminists of Heterodoxy: Greenwich Village 1912–1940* (Lebanon, NH: New Victorian Publishers, 1982), 14, 58, 83. Also see Liza Maeve Nelligan, "'The Haunting Beauty of the Life We've Left': A Contextual Reading of Susan Glaspell's *Trifles* and *The Verge*," in *Susan Glaspell: A Collection of Critical Essays*, Ed. Linda Ben-Zvi. Glaspell, like her fellow writers Neith Boyce, Mary Heaton Vorse, and others never assumed her husband's name.
29. When the Provincetown Players staged the play, Glaspell chose to play Mrs. Hale and had her husband, George Cram Cook, play Hale.
30. Kay Ann Short, "A Different Kind of the Same Thing: The Erasure of Difference in 'A Jury of her Peers,'" *Susan Glaspell: A Collection of Critical Essays*, Ed. Linda Ben-Zvi.
31. One could argue that the precedent for staging a case of justifiable homicide for women was established in *The Oresteia*, where the motives leading to Clytemnestra's murder of Agamemnon are delineated, or would be if one affixed to the work the murder of Iphigenia, as Ariane Mnouchkine recently has done in a production of Aeschylus' trilogy at the Theatre du Soleil that is prefaced by Euripides' *Iphigenia in Aulis* (see *New York Times*, 27 March 1991: B-3, for a description of this performance). For a discussion of contemporary wife battering cases and the plea of justifiable homicide, see Jones, *Women Who Kill*, Chapter 6.
32. In most of Glaspell's plays, there is a political component that is directly connected to particular events of her period, which would be immediately evident to her audience, but which is often lost in contemporary discussions of her works. In *Suppressed Desires*, for instance, she takes on a noted anti-feminist of the period, one Professor Sedwick, who had said, "All women were hens" (reported in the *New York Times*, 18 February 1914). In the play, Glaspell and Cook play on the name Stephen, parodying both Freudianism and Cook's childhood pronunciation of the word (*Road*, 25). However, they also are answering Sedwick, a reference her audience would immediately have understood. Even more overtly, *Inheritors* challenges contemporary issues such as the Alien and Sedition laws, and the Red Scare, and *Chains of Dew* argues for birth control. For the relation between events of her period and Glaspell's plays, see Barbara Ozieblo, "Suppression and Society," in *Susan Glaspell: A Collection of Critical Essays*, Ed. Linda Ben-Zvi, and J. Ellen Gainor, "*Chains of Dew* and the Drama of Birth Control," in *Susan Glaspell: A Collection of Critical Essays*, Ed. Linda Ben-Zvi.
33. See Judith Butler, "Performing Acts and Gender Constitution: An Essay in Phenomenology and Feminist Theory," in *Performing Feminisms: Feminist Critical Theory and Theatre*, Ed. Sue-Ellen Case (Baltimore, MD: Johns Hopkins University Press, 1990), 270–82, on the problems of staging victimization and thus representing the very condition the writer may wish to dismantle.
34. See Judith Fetterley, "Reading about Reading: 'A Jury of Her Peers,' 'The Murder in the Rue Morgue,' and 'The Yellow Wallpaper,'" in *Gender and Reading: Essays on Readers, Texts, and Contexts*, Eds. Elizabeth A. Flynn and Patrocinio P. Schweickart (Baltimore, MD: Johns Hopkins University Press, 1986).
35. Questions concerning the binding nature of law were hotly debated in 1916—a time of war and protest against that war—in issues of *The Masses* and other periodicals with which Glaspell was connected.
36. Catherine MacKinnon, *Feminism Unmodified: Discourses on Life and Law* (Cambridge: Harvard University Press, 1987). While acknowledging the work of such writers as Carol Gilligan, MacKinnon argues that Gilligan "achieves for moral reasoning what the special protection rule achieves in law: the affirmative rather than the negative valuation of that which has accurately distinguished women from men, by making it seem as though those attributes, with their consequences, really are somehow ours, rather than what male supremacy has attributed to us for its own use. For women to affirm difference, when difference means dominance, as it does with

gender, means to affirm the qualities and characteristics of powerlessness" (38–39). What is relevant about MacKinnon's argument in relation to *Trifles* and "Jury" is her emphasis on law and enfranchisement. Reading Glaspell through MacKinnon allows the critic to move beyond the questions of "different voice" that were the critical bulwarks of the first moment of Glaspell criticism. For example, see Linda Ben-Zvi, "Susan Glaspell and Eugene O'Neill," "Susan Glaspell, Eugene O'Neill, and the Imagery of Gender," and "Susan Glaspell's Contributions to Contemporary Women Playwrights," *Feminine Focus: The New Women Playwrights*, Ed. Enoch Brater (New York: Oxford University Press, 1988), 147–66; Karen Stein, "The Women's World of Glaspell's *Trifles*," *Women in American Theatre*, Eds. Helen Krinch Chinoy and Linda Walsh Jenkins (New York: Theatre Communications Group, 1987), 253–56; Karen Alkalay-Gut, "'A Jury of her Peers': The Importance of Trifles," *Studies in Short Fiction* 21 (1984): 3–11; and Karen Malpede, "Introduction," *Women in Theatre* (New York: Limelight, 1983). See also the more recent materialist readings: Judith Stephens, "Gender Ideology and Dramatic Convention in Progressive Era Plays, 1890–1920," in *Performing Feminisms: Feminist Critical Theory and Theatre*, Ed. Sue-Ellen Case (Baltimore, MD: Johns Hopkins University Press, 1990), 283–93; Kay Ann Short, "A Different Kind of the Same Thing: The Erasure of Difference in 'A Jury of Her Peers,'" in *Susan Glaspell: A Collection of Critical Essays*; Liza Maeve Nelligan, "The Haunting Beauty from the Life We've Left: A Contextual Reading of Susan Glaspell's *Trifles* and *The Verge*," in *Susan Glaspell: A Collection of Critical Essays*; Kathleen Carroll, "Centering Women Onstage: Susan Glaspell's Dialogic Strategy of Resistance," Diss., University of Maryland, 1990; and Linda Williams, "'A Jury of her Peers': Marlene Gorris's 'A Question of Silence,'" *Postmodernism and Its Discontents: Theories and Practices*, Ed. E. Ann Kaplan (London: Verso, 1988), 107–15. However, it should be noted that as much as MacKinnon's ideas, as used here, may provide one way of approaching *Trifles*, it is hard to imagine that Glaspell would have supported MacKinnon's stance on censorship as a way of alleviating pornography. Repeatedly in her writing, Glaspell objected to any form of censorship, for any reason. She was involved in several anti-censorship cases, one involving the attempted banning of a book by the Davenport Public Library in 1910, and in later controversies surrounding celebrated censorship cases.

37. MacKinnon, *Feminism Unmodified*, 39.
38. Ibid, 8.
39. Glaspell's marriage parallels almost exactly the paradigm Caroline Heilbrun presents in *Writing A Woman's Life* (New York: W. W. Norton, 1988), a marriage near middle age that is scandal-ridden and that both forces the woman out of society and allows her a freedom such societal marginalization provides.
40. It is important to note that *Trifles* and "A Jury of her Peers" were written for different audiences. The fiction, appearing in the popular magazine, *Everyweek*, 5 March 1917, stresses identification between the reader and Mrs. Hale, a familiar farm housewife, and leads to a reading that seems to romanticize housework and traditional feminine roles far more than *Trifles* does. For example, in the story version, Glaspell has Mrs. Hale say, "The Law is the law and a bad stove is a bad stove. How'd you like to cook on this?," an image and a question with which her readers could identify, just as they could identify with Mrs. Hale's sudden call from her own kitchen to travel to the kitchen of Minnie Wright. One of the anomalies in the criticism of the two works is the failure of most critics to note that there are two versions of the same basic story and to take into consideration the differences in accordance with the nature of the audience and the differences implicit in the genre. Two of the most influential essays on these works use "Jury" and make no reference to the more subtle and radical *Trifles*. See Annette Kolodny, "A Map for Re-Reading: Or Gender and the Interpretation of Literary Texts," in *The New Feminist Criticism*, Ed. Elaine Showalter (New York: Pantheon, 1985), 93–106, and Judith Fetterley, "Reading about Reading: 'A Jury of her Peers,' 'The Murder in the Rue Morgue,' and 'The Yellow Wallpaper.'" When Linda Williams compares the Dutch film "A Question of Silence" to Glaspell's work, she also uses "Jury" not *Trifles*. See Williams, "'A Jury of her Peers.'"
41. See Judith Schwarz's description of Heterodoxy in *Radical Feminists of Heterodoxy*, in which she lists Glaspell as a founding member; also see Nancy Cott, *The Grounding of Modern Feminism* (New Haven, CI: Yale University Press, 1987), for a detailed study of the feminist movement in New York in the years 1910–1920; and June Sochen, *The New Woman in Greenwich Village, 1910–1920* (New York: Quadrangle, 1972), for a description of the period and of Glaspell's relation to feminists in Greenwich Village. In her *Women and American Socialism, 1870–1902* (Champaign: University of Illinois Press, 1981), Mari Jo Buhle discusses how Glaspell "created female characters as working-class women with capacities to feel intensely, to understand injustice rather than internalizing oppression, and when conditions allowed to strike back at their oppressors" (203).

42. These quotations are taken from the *New York Times* (18 February 1914) report concerning a meeting organized by Heterodoxy president Marie Jenny Howe at Cooper Union, billed as "the first feminist meeting ever convened." At the time Glaspell was in Davenport, after suffering a miscarriage, but many of her friends were there, and she would most likely have been in the audience, if not on the dais. For other references to articles on feminism written between 1913–1916, see Cott, *The Grounding of Modern Feminism*. I thank Liza Maeve Nelligan for calling my attention to the Rally, and for sharing her research on heterodoxy and the feminist movements of the period with me.
43. Five years later Glaspell would write *The Verge*, her most powerful and most feminist play. Her persona, Claire Archer, would demand a life not circumscribed by the traditional roles assigned to women—mother, caregiver, hostess—and would stand in juxtaposition to her daughter and her sister, who represent conventional women whose gender does not provide them with an insight into Claire's life or her aspiration. In *The Verge* Glaspell also pursues feminism as a "transvaluation of values" on a Nietzschean model. See Cott, *The Grounding of Modern Feminism*, 296, in relation to Dora Marsden and a similar position. Also see Nelligan, "The Haunting Beauty of the Life We've Left," and Carroll "Centering Women Onstage."

10.2 SUSAN GLASPELL'S REPORTAGE ON THE HOSSACK MURDER CASE

The Des Moines Daily News

PROMINENT FARMER ROBBED AND KILLED.

Supposed the Burglars Assaulted Farmer Hossack—Coroner Holding an Investigation Today.

INDIANOLA, Dec. 3.—(Special.)—A foul murder was committed Saturday night near Medford, fifteen miles southwest of Indianola. A farmer named Hossack was struck over the head and killed by unknown parties, at his home a few miles out from Medford.

The assault was probably committed by burglars, though of this the officers are not yet sure. Sheriff Lew Hodson and Dr. Harry Dale, coroner, went to the place Sunday, and subpoenaed a jury which was called to meet this morning for an inquest. Mr. Hossack was an early settler, a prominent farmer, highly respected. He was about 60 years of age and leaves a wife and large family.

SURROUNDED BY MYSTERY: MURDER OF JOHN HOSSACK WAS NOT FOR MONEY.

Some One Held Grudge Against Him—Said to Have Been Chicken Blood on Ax.

INDIANOLA, Dec. 4.—(Special)—Persons who went to the home of John Hossack Monday and saw the murdered man in his bed, and heard portions of the testimony before the coroner's jury, are all at sea as to who killed Hossack or for what reason. There is no evidence of burglary. The murderer came through a porch and front room to the bed room where Mr. and Mrs. Hossack slept. He evidently reached across the bed with an ax and struck two blows. One crushed in the skull and the other made a deep cut, yet Hossack lived from Saturday night until 10 a.m. Sunday, though he did not regain consciousness, and no one has yet been found who can give a clue to the murder. The ax was found under a shed about fifty feet from the house. Mrs. Hossack swore before the jury that she was awakened about midnight by the slamming of a door, saw a flash of light and then all was dark. She called to her husband but as he did not respond, she got up and lighted a lamp. Then she discovered him on the bed, with blood all over the clothing. She said she did not hear the blows nor see any one. The officers are investigating.

It is rumored that trouble had arisen in the Hossack household and that possibly some relative committed the murder.

The funeral of Mr. Hossack was set for Wednesday at 1 p.m. from the First M.E. church at New Virginia. The family consisted of wife, and four children, who were at home.

Burt Osborn and Harry Hartman of Indianola went to the Hossack home Sunday afternoon and took flashlight photographs of the remains of Hossack as they lay on the bed. The left temple is crushed in, probably by the butt end of the ax; while the upper part of the head is deeply gashed.

The ax, which was found under a shed and covered with blood, has been sent to a chemist, who is to report whether or not the blood is human or from chickens, as stated by some members of the family.

The report that Hossack did not regain consciousness, is contradicted. One of his sons testified before the coroner's jury that he said to his father, "Well, pa, you are badly hurt," and that he replied:

"No, I'm not hurt, but I'm not feeling well."

It is said that Hossack did not make any statement as to whom he suspected of the crime.

SHERIFF AFTER MRS. HOSSACK.

SENSATIONAL TURN TAKEN AT INDIANOLA.

Coroner's Jury Returns Its Verdict This Morning—Mrs. Hossack Thought to Be Crazy.

INDIANOLA, Dec. 5.—(Special)—The Hossack murder case took a sensational turn today when the sheriff went to Medora for the avowed purpose of arresting Mrs. Hossack, wife of the murdered man. The departure of the sheriff was kept a profound secret for a time, but eventually some of the county officials were induced to reveal to your correspondent that the object of the trip was the arrest of Mrs. Hossack.

The evidence is by no means conclusive of Mrs. Hossack's guilt, but the testimony before the coroner's jury was such as to raise a suspicion of guilt and her arrest was decided upon as a matter of precaution.

Members of the Hossack family are understood to have testified before the coroner's jury that the blood on the ax found under the corn crib was caused by chopping off the head of a turkey the day before the murder. It is now reported that a child admitted on cross-examination that he himself placed the ax in the corn crib the evening before the murder and that at that time there was no blood on it.

Friends of Mrs. Hossack are beginning to suggest that she is insane and that she has been in this condition for a year and a half under the constant surveillance of members of the family.

The robbery theory has been wholly abandoned, as absolutely nothing was taken and no suspicious characters were seen in the neighborhood prior or subsequent to the murder.

The most suspicious circumstance in connection with the crime is the testimony of Mrs. Hossack that she lay in bed by the side of her husband while his skull was crushed in two places, and was not awakened in time to see anyone leave the house.

The developments since the murder that the members of the Hossack family were not on pleasant relations with each other is a complete surprise, as Hossack was not supposed to have an enemy in the world.

The verdict of the coroner's jury found this morning was as follows:

"We do find said deceased came to his death by two blows upon the head; one with a sharp instrument and one with a blunt instrument. (Signed) C.D. Johnson, Fred Johnston, T.W. Passwater."

SHE PREPARES TO FIGHT.

MRS. HOSSACK WILL RESIST CHARGE OF MURDER.

Was Locked Up In Indianola Jail Last Night—Public Against Her.

INDIANOLA, Dec. 6.—The wife of John Hossack, arrested on the charge of having beaten out his brains with an ax, has employed Henderson and Berry as her attorneys and is preparing to fight the case to the end.

She was locked up in the county jail here last night at 8:30. She manifested no emotion, took her arrest calmly and absolutely declined to make any statement concerning her guilt or innocence.

Members of the Hossack family are standing by her solidly, but public sentiment is overwhelmingly against her.

Though past 50 years of age, she is tall and powerful and looks like she would be dangerous if aroused to a point of hatred. It is claimed by the prosecution that she and her husband quarreled violently over their second son, John Hossack, Jr., because the father was unwilling to overlook his son's shortcomings.

An effort was made at the coroner's inquest to bring out that Mrs. Hossack had threatened her husband's life and had intimated to William Haines that she would like to get her husband out of the way. Haines only partially corroborated this story.

Hossack owned 300 acres of fine land and was considered well-off. It is claimed now, however, that the farm was in his wife's name and that possession of it could have furnished no incentive to the crime. Deceased, however, carried $2,000 in life insurance, made payable to his wife.

10.3 IMAGES AND CAPTIONS OF THE HOSSACK MURDER

Original caption: "THE MURDERED MAN—Sketched from flashlight photograph of the dead man now in possession of the county attorney. The sharp edge of the instrument laid the skull open. The mark near the eye was caused by blunt portion. Other newspapers tried to obtain access to this photograph but failed."

Original caption: "Mrs Hossack, sketched from life by G.A. Proctor as Mrs Hossack sat at the preliminary trial. She kept her eyes almost continuously on the floor."

Original caption: "The ax which is supposed to have been used in murdering John Hossack. The cut shows the blood spots on the handle."

Source: Images used by kind permission of the Susan Glaspell Estate

10.4 PRODUCTION PHOTO FROM *TRIFLES*

Performance of *Trifles* at The Theatre, Jan. 1917. *Trifles* was derived from the Margaret Hossack murder trial (1900–01), which was attended by the playwright Susan Glaspell. The trial was a highly theatrical and well-watched public spectacle, which garnered countless front-page headlines with sensational accounts of the hearings, considered the most dramatic of their day for the Iowa community. This show trial and its corresponding play—written before the 1920 enactment of the Nineteenth Amendment—illuminate the long struggle of accused women in the United States to be juried by their peers, and the severe effects of a gendered law and concept of justice.

Source: Image courtesy of the New York Public Library

10.5 *TRIFLES*—SUSAN GLASPELL

ORIGINAL CAST

- GEORGE HENDERSON, *County Attorney* . . . ROBERT ROGERS
- HENRY PETERS, *Sheriff* . . . ROBERT CONVILLE
- LEWIS HALE, *A Neighboring Farmer* . . . GEORGE CRAM COOK
- MRS. PETERS . . . ALICE HALL
- MRS. HALE . . . SUSAN GLASPELL

TRIFLES

[*SCENE: The kitchen in the now abandoned farmhouse of JOHN WRIGHT, a gloomy kitchen, and left without having been put in order—unwashed pans under the sink, a loaf of bread outside the bread-box, a dish-towel on the table—other signs of incompleted work. At the rear the outer door opens and the SHERIFF comes in followed by the COUNTY ATTORNEY and HALE. The SHERIFF and HALE are men in middle life, the COUNTY ATTORNEY is a young man; all are much bundled up and go at once to the stove. They are followed by the two women—the SHERIFF's wife first; she is a slight wiry woman, a thin nervous face. MRS. HALE is larger and would ordinarily be called more comfortable looking, but she is disturbed now and looks fearfully about as she enters. The women have come in slowly, and stand close together near the door.*]

COUNTY ATTORNEY

[*Rubbing his hands.*]

This feels good. Come up to the fire, ladies.

MRS. PETERS

[*After taking a step forward.*]

I'm not—cold.

SHERIFF

[*Unbuttoning his overcoat and stepping away from the stove as if to mark the beginning of official business.*]

Now, Mr. Hale, before we move things about, you explain to Mr. Henderson just what you saw when you came here yesterday morning.

COUNTY ATTORNEY

By the way, has anything been moved? Are things just as you left them yesterday?

SHERIFF

[*Looking about.*]

It's just the same. When it dropped below zero last night I thought I'd better send Frank out this morning to make a fire for us—no use getting pneumonia with a big case on, but I told him not to touch anything except the stove—and you know Frank.

COUNTY ATTORNEY

Somebody should have been left here yesterday.

SHERIFF

Oh—yesterday. When I had to send Frank to Morris Center for that man who went crazy—I want you to know I had my hands full yesterday. I knew you could get back from Omaha by today and as long as I went over everything here myself —

COUNTY ATTORNEY

Well, Mr. Hale, tell just what happened when you came here yesterday morning.

HALE

Harry and I had started to town with a load of potatoes. We came along the road from my place and as I got here I said, "I'm going to see if I can't get John Wright to go in with me on a party telephone." I spoke to Wright about it once before and he put me off, saying folks talked too much anyway, and all he asked was peace and quiet—I guess you know about how much he talked himself; but I thought maybe if I went to the house and talked about it before his wife, though I said to Harry that I didn't know as what his wife wanted made much difference to John—

COUNTY ATTORNEY

Let's talk about that later, Mr. Hale. I do want to talk about that, but tell now just what happened when you got to the house.

HALE

I didn't hear or see anything; I knocked at the door, and still it was all quiet inside. I knew they must be up, it was past eight o'clock. So I knocked again, and I thought I heard somebody say, "Come in." I wasn't sure, I'm not sure yet, but I opened the door—this door [*indicating the door by which the two women are still standing*] and there in that rocker—[*pointing to it*] sat Mrs. Wright. [*They all look at the rocker.*]

COUNTY ATTORNEY

What—was she doing?

HALE

She was rockin' back and forth. She had her apron in her hand and was kind of—pleating it.

COUNTY ATTORNEY

And how did she—look?

HALE

Well, she looked queer.

COUNTY ATTORNEY

How do you mean—queer?

HALE

Well, as if she didn't know what she was going to do next. And kind of done up.

COUNTY ATTORNEY

How did she seem to feel about your coming?

HALE

Why, I don't think she minded—one way or other. She didn't pay much attention. I said, "How do, Mrs. Wright, it's cold, ain't it?" And she said, "Is it?"—and went on kind of pleating at her apron. Well, I was surprised; she didn't ask me to come up to the stove, or to set down, but just sat there, not even looking at me, so I said, "I want to see John." And then she—laughed. I guess you would call it a laugh. I thought of Harry and the team outside, so I said a little sharp: "Can't I see John?" "No," she says, kind o' dull like. "Ain't he home?" says I. "Yes," says she, "he's home." "Then why can't I see him?" I asked her, out of patience. "'Cause he's dead," says she. "Dead?" says I. She just nodded her head, not getting a bit excited, but rockin' back and forth. "Why—where is he?" says I, not knowing what to say. She just pointed upstairs—like that [*himself pointing to the room above*]. I got up, with the idea of going up there. I walked from there to here—then I says, "Why, what did he die of?" "He died of a rope round his neck," says she, and just went on pleatin' at her apron. Well, I went out and called Harry. I thought I might—need help. We went upstairs and there he was lyin'—

COUNTY ATTORNEY

I think I'd rather have you go into that upstairs, where you can point it all out. Just go on now with the rest of the story.

HALE

Well, my first thought was to get that rope off. It looked . . . [*Stops, his face twitches*] . . . but Harry, he went up to him, and he said, "No, he's dead all right, and we'd better not touch anything." So we went back down stairs. She was still sitting that same way. "Has anybody been notified?" I asked. "No," says she, unconcerned. "Who did this, Mrs. Wright?" said Harry. He said it business-like—and she stopped pleatin' of her apron. "I don't know," she says. "You don't *know?*" says Harry. "No," says she. "Weren't you sleepin' in the bed with him?" says Harry. "Yes," says she, "but I was on the inside." "Somebody slipped a rope round his neck and strangled him and you didn't wake up?" says Harry. "I didn't wake up," she said after him. We must 'a looked as if we didn't see how that could be, for after a minute she said, "I sleep sound." Harry was going to ask her more questions but I said maybe we ought to let her tell her story first to the coroner, or the sheriff, so Harry went fast as he could to Rivers' place, where there's a telephone.

COUNTY ATTORNEY

And what did Mrs. Wright do when she knew that you had gone for the coroner?

HALE

She moved from that chair to this one over here [*Pointing to a small chair in the corner*] and just sat there with her hands held together and looking down. I got a feeling that I ought to make some conversation, so I said I had come in to see if John wanted to put in a telephone, and at that she started to laugh, and then she stopped and looked at me—scared. [*The* COUNTY ATTORNEY, *who has had his notebook out, makes a note.*]

I dunno, maybe it wasn't scared. I wouldn't like to say it was. Soon Harry got back, and then Dr. Lloyd came, and you, Mr. Peters, and so I guess that's all I know that you don't.

COUNTY ATTORNEY

[*Looking around.*]

I guess we'll go upstairs first—and then out to the barn and around there. [*To the* SHERIFF.] You're convinced that there was nothing important here—nothing that would point to any motive.

SHERIFF

Nothing here but kitchen things. [*The* COUNTY ATTORNEY, *after again looking around the kitchen, opens the door of a cupboard closet. He gets up on a chair and looks on a shelf. Pulls his hand away, sticky.*]

COUNTY ATTORNEY

Here's a nice mess. [*The women draw nearer.*]

MRS. PETERS

[*To the other woman.*]

Oh, her fruit; it did freeze. [*To the* LAWYER.]

She worried about that when it turned so cold. She said the fire'd go out and her jars would break.

SHERIFF

Well, can you beat the women! Held for murder and worryin' about her preserves.

COUNTY ATTORNEY

I guess before we're through she may have something more serious than preserves to worry about.

HALE

Well, women are used to worrying over trifles. [*The two women move a little closer together.*]

COUNTY ATTORNEY

[*With the gallantry of a young politician.*]

And yet, for all their worries, what would we do without the ladies? [*The women do not unbend. He goes to the sink, takes a dipperful of water from the pail and pouring it into a basin, washes his hands. Starts to wipe them on the roller-towel, turns it for a cleaner place.*]

Dirty towels! [*Kicks his foot against the pans under the sink.*]

Not much of a housekeeper, would you say, ladies?

MRS. HALE

[*Stiffly.*]

There's a great deal of work to be done on a farm.

COUNTY ATTORNEY

To be sure. And yet [*With a little bow to her*] I know there are some Dickson county farmhouses which do not have such roller towels. [*He gives it a pull to expose its full length again.*]

MRS. HALE

Those towels get dirty awful quick. Men's hands aren't always as clean as they might be.

COUNTY ATTORNEY

Ah, loyal to your sex, I see. But you and Mrs. Wright were neighbors. I suppose you were friends, too.

MRS. HALE

[*Shaking her head.*]

I've not seen much of her of late years. I've not been in this house—it's more than a year.

COUNTY ATTORNEY

And why was that? You didn't like her?

MRS. HALE

I liked her well enough. Farmers' wives have their hands full, Mr. Henderson. And then —

COUNTY ATTORNEY

Yes —?

MRS. HALE

[*Looking about.*]

It never seemed a very cheerful place.

COUNTY ATTORNEY

No—it's not cheerful. I shouldn't say she had the homemaking instinct.

MRS. HALE

Well, I don't know as Wright had, either.

COUNTY ATTORNEY

You mean that they didn't get on very well?

MRS. HALE

No, I don't mean anything. But I don't think a place'd be any cheerfuller for John Wright's being in it.

COUNTY ATTORNEY

I'd like to talk more of that a little later. I want to get the lay of things upstairs now. [*He goes to the left, where three steps lead to a stair door.*]

SHERIFF

I suppose anything Mrs. Peters does'll be all right. She was to take in some clothes for her, you know, and a few little things. We left in such a hurry yesterday.

COUNTY ATTORNEY

Yes, but I would like to see what you take, Mrs. Peters, and keep an eye out for anything that might be of use to us.

MRS. PETERS

Yes, Mr. Henderson. [*The women listen to the men's steps on the stairs, then look about the kitchen.*]

MRS. HALE

I'd hate to have men coming into my kitchen, snooping around and criticising. [*She arranges the pans under sink which the* LAWYER *had shoved out of place.*]

MRS. PETERS

Of course it's no more than their duty.

MRS. HALE

Duty's all right, but I guess that deputy sheriff that came out to make the fire might have got a little of this on. [*Gives the roller towel a pull.*]

Wish I'd thought of that sooner. Seems mean to talk about her for not having things slicked up when she had to come away in such a hurry.

MRS. PETERS

[*Who has gone to a small table in the left rear corner of the room, and lifted one end of a towel that covers a pan.*]

She had bread set. [*Stands still.*]

MRS. HALE

[*Eyes fixed on a loaf of bread beside the bread-box, which is on a low shelf at the other side of the room. Moves slowly toward it.*]

She was going to put this in there. [*Picks up loaf, then abruptly drops it. In a manner of returning to familiar things.*]

It's a shame about her fruit. I wonder if it's all gone. [*Gets up on the chair and looks.*]

I think there's some here that's all right, Mrs. Peters. Yes—here; [*Holding it toward the window*] this is cherries, too. [*Looking again.*]

I declare I believe that's the only one. [*Gets down, bottle in her hand. Goes to the sink and wipes it off on the outside.*]

She'll feel awful bad after all her hard work in the hot weather. I remember the afternoon I put up my cherries last summer. [*She puts the bottle on the big kitchen table, center of the room. With a sigh, is about to sit down in the rocking-chair. Before she is seated realizes what chair it is; with a slow look at it, steps back. The chair which she has touched rocks back and forth.*]

MRS. PETERS

Well, I must get those things from the front room closet. [*She goes to the door at the right, but after looking into the other room, steps back.*]

You coming with me, Mrs. Hale? You could help me carry them. [*They go in the other room; reappear,* MRS. PETERS *carrying a dress and skirt,* MRS. HALE *following with a pair of shoes.*]

MRS. PETERS

My, it's cold in there. [*She puts the clothes on the big table, and hurries to the stove.*]

MRS. HALE

[*Examining the skirt.*]

Wright was close. I think maybe that's why she kept so much to herself. She didn't even belong to the Ladies Aid. I suppose she felt she couldn't do her part, and then you don't enjoy things when you feel shabby. She used to wear pretty clothes and be lively, when she was Minnie Foster, one of the town girls singing in the choir. But that—oh, that was thirty years ago. This all you was to take in?

MRS. PETERS

She said she wanted an apron. Funny thing to want, for there isn't much to get you dirty in jail, goodness knows. But I suppose just to make her feel more natural. She said they was in the top drawer in this cupboard. Yes, here. And then her little shawl that always hung behind the door. [*Opens stair door and looks.*]

Yes, here it is. [*Quickly shuts door leading upstairs.*]

MRS. HALE

[*Abruptly moving toward her.*]

Mrs. Peters?

MRS. PETERS

Yes, Mrs. Hale?

MRS. HALE

Do you think she did it?

MRS. PETERS

[*In a frightened voice.*]

Oh, I don't know.

MRS. HALE

Well, I don't think she did. Asking for an apron and her little shawl. Worrying about her fruit.

MRS. PETERS

[*Starts to speak, glances up, where footsteps are heard in the room above. In a low voice.*]

Mr. Peters says it looks bad for her. Mr. Henderson is awful sarcastic in a speech and he'll make fun of her sayin' she didn't wake up.

MRS. HALE

Well, I guess John Wright didn't wake when they was slipping that rope under his neck.

MRS. PETERS

No, it's strange. It must have been done awful crafty and still. They say it was such a—funny way to kill a man, rigging it all up like that.

MRS. HALE

That's just what Mr. Hale said. There was a gun in the house. He says that's what he can't understand.

MRS. PETERS

Mr. Henderson said coming out that what was needed for the case was a motive; something to show anger, or—sudden feeling.

MRS. HALE

[*Who is standing by the table.*]

Well, I don't see any signs of anger around here. [*She puts her hand on the dish towel which lies on the table, stands looking down at table, one half of which is clean, the other half messy.*]

It's wiped to here. [*Makes a move as if to finish work, then turns and looks at loaf of bread outside the breadbox. Drops towel. In that voice of coming back to familiar things.*]

Wonder how they are finding things upstairs. I hope she had it a little more red-up up there. You know, it seems kind of *sneaking*. Locking her up in town and then coming out here and trying to get her own house to turn against her!

MRS. PETERS

But Mrs. Hale, the law is the law.

MRS. HALE

I s'pose 'tis. [*Unbuttoning her coat.*]

Better loosen up your things, Mrs. Peters. You won't feel them when you go out. [MRS. PETERS *takes off her fur tippet, goes to hang it on hook at back of room, stands looking at the under part of the small corner table.*]

MRS. PETERS

She was piecing a quilt. [*She brings the large sewing basket and they look at the bright pieces.*]

MRS. HALE

It's her log cabin pattern. Pretty, isn't it? I wonder if she was goin' to quilt it or just knot it? [*Footsteps have been heard coming down the stairs. The* SHERIFF *enters followed by* HALE *and the* COUNTY ATTORNEY.]

SHERIFF

They wonder if she was going to quilt it or just knot it! [*The men laugh, the women look abashed.*]

COUNTY ATTORNEY

[*Rubbing his hands over the stove.*]

Frank's fire didn't do much up there, did it? Well, let's go out to the barn and get that cleared up. [*The men go outside.*]

MRS. HALE

[*Resentfully.*]

I don't know as there's anything so strange, our takin' up our time with little things while we're waiting for them to get the evidence. [*She sits down at the big table smoothing out a block with decision.*]

I don't see as it's anything to laugh about.

MRS. PETERS

[*Apologetically.*]

Of course they've got awful important things on their minds. [*Pulls up a chair and joins* MRS. HALE *at the table.*]

MRS. HALE

[*Examining another block.*]

Mrs. Peters, look at this one. Here, this is the one she was working on, and look at the sewing! All the rest of it has been so nice and even. And look at this! It's all over the place! Why, it looks as if she didn't know what she was about! [*After she has said this they look at each other, then start to glance back at the door. After an instant* MRS. HALE *has pulled at a knot and ripped the sewing.*]

MRS. PETERS

Oh, what are you doing, Mrs. Hale?

MRS. HALE

[*Mildly.*]

Just pulling out a stitch or two that's not sewed very good. [*Threading a needle.*]

Bad sewing always made me fidgety.

MRS. PETERS

[*Nervously.*]

I don't think we ought to touch things.

MRS. HALE

I'll just finish up this end. [*Suddenly stopping and leaning forward.*]

Mrs. Peters?

MRS. PETERS

Yes, Mrs. Hale?

MRS. HALE

What do you suppose she was so nervous about?

MRS. PETERS

Oh—I don't know. I don't know as she was nervous. I sometimes sew awful queer when I'm just tired. [MRS. HALE *starts to say something, looks at* MRS. PETERS, *then goes on sewing.*]

Well I must get these things wrapped up. They may be through sooner than we think. [*Putting apron and other things together.*]

I wonder where I can find a piece of paper, and string.

MRS. HALE

In that cupboard, maybe.

MRS. PETERS

[*Looking in cupboard.*]

Why, here's a bird-cage. [*Holds it up.*]

Did she have a bird, Mrs. Hale?

MRS. HALE

Why, I don't know whether she did or not—I've not been here for so long. There was a man around last year selling canaries cheap, but I don't know as she took one; maybe she did. She used to sing real pretty herself.

MRS. PETERS

[*Glancing around.*]

Seems funny to think of a bird here. But she must have had one, or why would she have a cage? I wonder what happened to it.

MRS. HALE

I s'pose maybe the cat got it.

MRS. PETERS

No, she didn't have a cat. She's got that feeling some people have about cats—being afraid of them. My cat got in her room and she was real upset and asked me to take it out.

MRS. HALE

My sister Bessie was like that. Queer, ain't it?

MRS. PETERS

[*Examining the cage.*]

Why, look at this door. It's broke. One hinge is pulled apart.

MRS. HALE

[*Looking too.*]

Looks as if someone must have been rough with it.

MRS. PETERS

Why, yes. [*She brings the cage forward and puts it on the table.*]

MRS. HALE

I wish if they're going to find any evidence they'd be about it. I don't like this place.

MRS. PETERS

But I'm awful glad you came with me, Mrs. Hale. It would be lonesome for me sitting here alone.

MRS. HALE

It would, wouldn't it? [*Dropping her sewing.*]

But I tell you what I do wish, Mrs. Peters. I wish

I had come over sometimes when *she* was here. I—[*Looking around the room*]—wish I had.

MRS. PETERS

But of course you were awful busy, Mrs. Hale—your house and your children.

MRS. HALE

I could've come. I stayed away because it weren't cheerful—and that's why I ought to have come. I—I've never liked this place. Maybe because it's down in a hollow and you don't see the road. I dunno what it is, but it's a lonesome place and always was. I wish I had come over to see Minnie Foster sometimes. I can see now—[*Shakes her head.*]

MRS. PETERS

Well, you mustn't reproach yourself, Mrs. Hale. Somehow we just don't see how it is with other folks until—something comes up.

MRS. HALE

Not having children makes less work—but it makes a quiet house, and Wright out to work all day, and no company when he did come in. Did you know John Wright, Mrs. Peters?

MRS. PETERS

Not to know him; I've seen him in town. They say he was a good man.

MRS. HALE

Yes—good; he didn't drink, and kept his word as well as most, I guess, and paid his debts. But he was a hard man, Mrs. Peters. Just to pass the time of day with him—[*Shivers.*]

Like a raw wind that gets to the bone. [*Pauses, her eye falling on the cage.*]

I should think she would 'a wanted a bird. But what do you suppose went with it?

MRS. PETERS

I don't know, unless it got sick and died. [*She reaches over and swings the broken door, swings it again, both women watch it.*]

MRS. HALE

You weren't raised round here, were you? [MRS. PETERS *shakes her head.*]

You didn't know—her?

MRS. PETERS

Not till they brought her yesterday.

MRS. HALE

She—come to think of it, she was kind of like a bird herself—real sweet and pretty, but kind of timid and—fluttery. How—she—did—change. [*Silence; then as if struck by a happy thought and relieved to get back to every day things.*]

Tell you what, Mrs. Peters, why don't you take the quilt in with you? It might take up her mind.

MRS. PETERS

Why, I think that's a real nice idea, Mrs. Hale. There couldn't possibly be any objection to it, could there? Now, just what would I take? I wonder if her patches are in here—and her things. [*They look in the sewing basket.*]

MRS. HALE

Here's some red. I expect this has got sewing things in it. [*Brings out a fancy box.*]

What a pretty box. Looks like something somebody would give you. Maybe her scissors are in here.

[*Opens box. Suddenly puts her hand to her nose.*]

Why—[MRS. PETERS *bends nearer, then turns her face away.*]

There's something wrapped up in this piece of silk.

MRS. PETERS

Why, this isn't her scissors.

MRS. HALE

[*Lifting the silk.*]

Oh, Mrs. Peters—its—[MRS. PETERS *bends closer.*]

MRS. PETERS

It's the bird.

MRS. HALE

[*Jumping up.*]

But, Mrs. Peters—look at it! It's neck! Look at its neck! It's all—other side *to.*

MRS. PETERS

Somebody—wrung—its—neck. [*Their eyes meet. A look of growing comprehension, of horror. Steps are heard outside.* MRS. HALE *slips box under quilt pieces, and sinks into her chair. Enter* SHERIFF *and* COUNTY ATTORNEY. MRS. PETERS *rises.*]

COUNTY ATTORNEY

[*As one turning from serious things to little pleasantries.*]

Well, ladies, have you decided whether she was going to quilt it or knot it?

MRS. PETERS

We think she was going to—knot it.

COUNTY ATTORNEY

Well, that's interesting, I'm sure. [*Seeing the birdcage.*]

Has the bird flown?

MRS. HALE

[*Putting more quilt pieces over the box.*]

We think the—cat got it.

COUNTY ATTORNEY

[*Preoccupied.*]

Is there a cat? [MRS. HALE *glances in a quick covert way at* MRS. PETERS.]

MRS. PETERS

Well, not now. They're superstitious, you know. They leave.

COUNTY ATTORNEY

[*To* SHERIFF PETERS, *continuing an interrupted conversation.*]

No sign at all of anyone having come from the outside. Their own rope. Now let's go up again and go over it piece by piece. [*They start upstairs.*]

It would have to have been someone who knew just the—[MRS. PETERS *sits down. The two women sit there not looking at one another, but as if peering into something and at the same time holding back. When they talk now it is in the manner of feeling their way over strange ground, as if afraid of what they are saying, but as if they can not help saying it.*]

MRS. HALE

She liked the bird. She was going to bury it in that pretty box.

MRS. PETERS

[In a whisper.]

When I was a girl—my kitten—there was a boy took a hatchet, and before my eyes—and before I could get there—*[Covers her face an instant.]*

If they hadn't held me back I would have—*[Catches herself, looks upstairs where steps are heard, falters weakly]*

— hurt him.

MRS. HALE

[With a slow look around her.]

I wonder how it would seem never to have had any children around. *[Pause.]*

No, Wright wouldn't like the bird—a thing that sang. She used to sing. He killed that, too.

MRS. PETERS

[Moving uneasily.]

We don't know who killed the bird.

MRS. HALE

I knew John Wright.

MRS. PETERS

It was an awful thing was done in this house that night, Mrs. Hale. Killing a man while he slept, slipping a rope around his neck that choked the life out of him.

MRS. HALE

His neck. Choked the life out of him. *[Her hand goes out and rests on the bird-cage.]*

MRS. PETERS

[With rising voice.]

We don't know who killed him. We don't know.

MRS. HALE

[Her own feeling not interrupted.]

If there'd been years and years of nothing, then a bird to sing to you, it would be awful—still, after the bird was still.

MRS. PETERS

[Something within her speaking.]

I know what stillness is. When we homesteaded in Dakota, and my first baby died—after he was two years old, and me with no other then—

MRS. HALE

[Moving.]

How soon do you suppose they'll be through, looking for the evidence?

MRS. PETERS

I know what stillness is. *[Pulling herself back.]*

The law has got to punish crime, Mrs. Hale.

MRS. HALE

[Not as if answering that.]

I wish you'd seen Minnie Foster when she wore a white dress with blue ribbons and stood up there in the choir and sang. *[A look around the room.]*

Oh, I wish I'd come over here once in a while! That was a crime! That was a crime! Who's going to punish that?

MRS. PETERS

[Looking upstairs.]

We mustn't—take on.

MRS. HALE

I might have known she needed help! I know how things can be—for women. I tell you, it's queer, Mrs. Peters. We live close together and we live far apart. We all go through the same things—it's all just a different kind of the same thing. *[Brushes her eyes, noticing the bottle of fruit, reaches out for it.]*

If I was you I wouldn't tell her her fruit was gone. Tell her it ain't. Tell her it's all right. Take this in to prove it to her. She—she may never know whether it was broke or not.

MRS. PETERS

[Takes the bottle, looks about for something to wrap it in; takes petticoat from the clothes brought from the other room, very nervously begins winding this around the bottle. In a false voice.]

My, it's a good thing the men couldn't hear us. Wouldn't they just laugh! Getting all stirred up over a little thing like a—dead canary. As if that could have anything to do with—with—wouldn't they laugh! *[The men are heard coming down stairs.]*

MRS. HALE

[Under her breath.]

Maybe they would—maybe they wouldn't.

COUNTY ATTORNEY

No, Peters, it's all perfectly clear except a reason for doing it. But you know juries when it comes to women. If there was some definite thing. Something to show—something to make a story about—a thing that would connect up with this strange way of doing it—*[The women's eyes meet for an instant. Enter* HALE *from outer door.]*

HALE

Well, I've got the team around. Pretty cold out there.

COUNTY ATTORNEY

I'm going to stay here a while by myself. [*To the* SHERIFF.]

You can send Frank out for me, can't you? I want to go over everything. I'm not satisfied that we can't do better.

SHERIFF

Do you want to see what Mrs. Peters is going to take in? [*The* LAWYER *goes to the table, picks up the apron, laughs.*]

COUNTY ATTORNEY

Oh, I guess they're not very dangerous things the ladies have picked out. [*Moves a few things about, disturbing the quilt pieces which cover the box. Steps back.*]

No, Mrs. Peters doesn't need supervising. For that matter, a sheriff's wife is married to the law. Ever think of it that way, Mrs. Peters?

MRS. PETERS

Not—just that way.

SHERIFF

[*Chuckling.*]

Married to the law. [*Moves toward the other room.*]

I just want you to come in here a minute, George. We ought to take a look at these windows.

COUNTY ATTORNEY

[*Scoffingly.*]

Oh, windows!

SHERIFF

We'll be right out, Mr. Hale. [HALE *goes outside. The* SHERIFF *follows the* COUNTY ATTORNEY *into the other room. Then* MRS. HALE *rises, hands tight together, looking intensely at* MRS. PETERS, *whose eyes make a slow turn, finally meeting* MRS. HALE*'s. A moment* MRS. HALE *holds her, then her own eyes point the way to where the box is concealed. Suddenly* MRS. PETERS *throws back quilt pieces and tries to put the box in the bag she is wearing. It is too big. She opens box, starts to take bird out, cannot touch it, goes to pieces, stands there helpless. Sound of a knob turning in the other room.* MRS. HALE *snatches the box and puts it in the pocket of her big coat. Enter* COUNTY ATTORNEY *and* SHERIFF.]

COUNTY ATTORNEY

[*Facetiously.*]

Well, Henry, at least we found out that she was not going to quilt it. She was going to—what is it you call it, ladies?

MRS. HALE

[*Her hand against her pocket.*]

We call it—knot it, Mr. Henderson.

[(CURTAIN)]

11. *How Poor Women Prostitute Themselves*—Luisa Capetillo

Commentary

Sources

Play

11.1 INTRODUCTION TO *HOW POOR WOMEN PROSTITUTE THEMSELVES*—SARAH TOWNSEND

THE PUERTO RICAN WRITER AND LABOR AGITATOR Luisa Capetillo (1879–1922) is more famous for her offstage activities than her dramatic works. Most likely, this would not have disappointed her. A radical feminist and anarchist, Capetillo believed in the power of words to change people's ideas, but she also believed that true change only happens when people put ideas into action. She was a proponent of free love who denounced marriage as legalized prostitution, and she had her three children out of wedlock. She wrote propaganda arguing that workers should have the right to determine the conditions of their labor, and then she followed it up by organizing farmhands in the fields and leading strikes. She thought dresses were unhygienic and impractical, so she became the first woman in Puerto Rico to wear pants in public.

Capetillo's life exemplifies the global circulation of people and ideas that fostered the emergence of working-class movements at the turn of the century. Born in the town of Arecibo, she was the daughter of a French (possibly French Caribbean) laundress and a Spanish immigrant who worked a variety of odd jobs. Both of her parents were well versed in the radical ideas of their day, and although Capetillo completed no more than two years of formal schooling, she received a broad education at home. One of her first jobs was as a *lectora* (reader) in a tobacco factory. At the time, workers throughout the Caribbean and United States commonly pooled their resources and hired someone to read aloud as they rolled cigars; consequently, even though many were unable to read or write, cigar workers often knew the ins and outs of novels by writers such as Zola, Dostoyevsky, and the Colombian anarchist José María Vargas Vilar and engaged the ideas of political philosophers in debates. They were also among the most militant workers, and it was here that Capetillo got her start in the labor movement. Her debut as an organizer came in 1905 during a farmworkers' strike, and she soon became a prominent leader of the Federación Libre de Trabajadores (Free Federation of Workers), traveling all over the island giving speeches and selling the union newspaper along with a publication of her own called *La mujer* (Woman). In the face of considerable resistance, she pushed the union to prioritize women's workplace issues and challenged male workers to embrace the fight for gender equality as central to their own struggle.

Capetillo's travels were not limited to the country of her birth. In 1912, she made the first of many trips to New York City, where she wrote articles for the local Spanish press and established a guesthouse. Later she lived and worked as a reader at a tobacco factory in the Cuban/Italian/African American community of Ybor City, Florida. And it was in Havana, in 1915, that she was arrested for dressing as a man—a provocative, highly theatrical act that landed her a picture in the newspaper and a public platform at the trial.

What we might now identify as "performance" was an important part of the vibrant working-class culture that arose throughout Latin America during this time period. Effective public orators such as Capetillo were praised for their ability to mobilize people to action, strikers improvised songs and chants on the picket line, and mass demonstrations incorporated music, comedy, and occasional skits. Given the high level of illiteracy and the focus on collective action, it is no surprise that theater also played an important role. Workers commonly contributed a portion of their salaries to cultural societies that sponsored festivals and evenings of entertainment combining instrumental and choral music, politico-philosophical dialogues, speeches, poetry (usually recited by children), theatrical pieces (in which women were particularly active), and, frequently, a final dance. The early works of Florencio Sanchez, who later went on to become one of Latin America's foremost playwrights, were written to be performed in anarchist cultural centers in Uruguay. Workers in the salt mines of northern Chile formed a collective called Arte y Revolución that presented plays such as Luis Emilio Recabarren's *Desdicha obrera* (Workers' Misfortune) and the *First of May* by Pietro Gori, the notorious Italian anarchist who lived for several years in Argentina and the United States. In São Paulo, Brazil, where nearly a third of the city's population was made up of Italian immigrants, a 1902 performance of Gori's drama was interrupted by police, who made several unwarranted arrests and harassed the audience of men, women, and children.

The culture that took shape on these stages was in many ways more "international" than the elite theater of its day. In countries where immigrants made up a large percentage of laborers, an evening's program frequently brought together multiple languages and divergent intellectual and performative traditions. No single style prevailed, though there were heated debates about the proper nature of "proletarian art"—anarchists in Cuba and Argentina, for example, condemned traditions such as Carnival for perpetuating unequal power relations and providing another opportunity for the bourgeois to make money off the masses. Yet in many cases what are now accepted as self-evident distinctions between "high" and "low" were routinely ignored and "education" and "entertainment" were not viewed as mutually exclusive. In Puerto Rico, the few surviving programs from these sorts of events list *zarzuelas* (operettas), *milongas* (Argentine music related to the tango), dialogues by the Mexican revolutionary Ricardo Flores Magón, arias from Verdi operas, rousing choral renditions of the "La Marseillaise," and the ever-popular allegorical drama *La emancipación del obrero* (The Emancipation of the Worker), written by the Puerto Rican typesetter Ramón Romero Rosa.

Although there is no direct evidence that Capetillo's works were performed—the physical archive of these theaters is slim—her widespread fame presumably would have made them obvious choices. In many of her plays, however, she also has another audience in mind: middle- and upper-class feminist readers. Capetillo never joined forces with suffragists like the writer and educator Ana Roqué, who founded the Puerto Rican Feminist League in 1917; most suffragists took issue with Capetillo's belief in free love and the general strike, and she saw little reason to support a movement that was fighting for voting rights on behalf of "educated," "literate" women. Yet through her own writings Capetillo engaged with their ideas, arguing that women's liberation and workers' freedom were inextricably linked. In 1911, she published *My Opinion about Woman's Liberties, Rights, and Duties*, now commonly cited as the first feminist treatise by a Puerto Rican author. In this heterodox collection of texts, she defends women's right to experience sexual pleasure, explains her unusual interest in spiritism, and reiterates her call for solidarity across all cultures, races, and borders. Such resolute internationalism was a bone of contention in Puerto Rico, where nationalist ideology was gaining strength as a defense against the United States, which had taken over from Spain as the imperial power in 1898. Capetillo pulled no punches in responding to those who dismissed her ideas as utopian: "[T]hey call themselves patriots and fathers of the homeland. What idea of the homeland can they have? One that is egotistical, which begins and ends with them."

Capetillo's fictional work appears in *The Influence of Modern Ideas* (1916), most of which was written during her time in New York and Florida. A multi-generic book of short fiction, letters, first-person narratives, informal "notes," and drama, it invokes various literary paradigms while remaining on the margins of the "literary." The author critiques Schopenhauer, quotes Diderot, and waxes poetic on the beauty of nature and the "agony of love"; yet she also discusses breast-feeding and the importance of physical exercise, a reflection of her belief that the body is an integral part of the person and worthy of respect. Her writing highlights the class-based assumptions underlying Romantic and modernist aesthetics, and it tests the universality of humanism's ideals of love and liberation by holding them to the letter of their own law and showing where they fall short in the context of women's daily lives. Capetillo does not dismiss literature, nor is her writing a straightforward parody; rather, in keeping with anarchist discourse, she insists that "true art," like free love, can lead to political change.

Nowhere is this more evident than in her theatrical pieces. The title play in *The Influence of Modern Ideas* is a three-act drama about an upper-class woman who, through her readings of Tolstoy and her romantic relationship with a young proletarian, comes to support the striking workers in her father's factory. Most of the other pieces are brief, no more than a few pages long. A group of sketches called *The Corruption of the Rich and the Poor*, for example, draws attention to the ways in which women, regardless of class, become objects of exchange. In *How Rich Women Are Prostituted*, an affluent woman escapes being married off to a Spanish nobleman by stealing her inheritance and running away with her lover; its companion piece, *How Poor Women Are Prostituted*, has no such happy ending since the protagonist's only alternative to literal prostitution is to go work in an unsanitary factory for a starving wage. Very few of the plays give any indication of their geographical location; although Capetillo's language is informal, she avoids colloquial terms or references that would place the characters or setting. Rather, her plays seem as though they were written to be transported, easily adapted, and understood by any Spanish-speaking audience.

[. . .]

In *How Poor Women Are Prostituted*, when a client enjoins the protagonist to take a job as a wage slave rather than ruin her virtue, she asks him, "If they buried two girls of the same size and age, one an immaculate virgin, the other corrupted by poverty and vice, would the earth respect one more than the other? Would the virgin be saved from the worms?" Capetillo had seen women's bodies destroyed by hard labor and consumed by diseases contracted in overcrowded factories; she, too, would die of tuberculosis at the age of forty-two. *How Poor Women Prostitute Themselves* is a reminder that none of us will be saved from the worms and that it is here, in *this* life, that we must act.

—Sarah J. Townsend

11.2 LUISA CAPETILLO IN HAVANA

Luisa Capetillo in 1915 wearing male clothing to challenge the period's social mores, which would result in her being sent to jail. Capetillo was one of Puerto Rico's most famous working-class labor activists and women's rights advocates during the country's transition, after the Spanish–American War, from Spanish rule to U.S. control.

Source: Image supplied by Arté Publico Press

11.3 PREFACE TO *A NATION OF WOMEN*—LUISA CAPETILLO

IT'S BEEN SOME TIME NOW that I have wanted to express my opinions on the life of woman in all its manifestations. After some light study, I found myself confronted with an arduous and difficult task, as I was faced with a social system so contrary to my ideals. Light study, I said. Yes, due to the fact that most of my study has been through my own experience. It is collected from events, incidents, and mistakes that for some years now I have observed in my own life. It is relatively short, to demonstrate in all its detail. But I will be able to offer a more complete picture later in another study.

For the moment, you must acknowledge these concepts that I have developed in the few years of scant freedom of women. It is a result of the analysis and study I have undertaken.

Woman, as an important factor in human civilization, is worthy to obtain complete liberty.

If we were to provide a detailed history of the powerful influence of women since the antiquity of primitive times, the list would be endless, and that is not my objective. These important details have been published in Emilio Castelar's *Mujeres Célebres* (Famous Women), in which he lays out in minute detail the general history of the slavery, sovereignty, and intellectual and emotional activity of women, from primitive times to the present.

Need we repeat or plagiarize him? No, read the work.

The only thing we want to put forth is that women must acquire greater freedom and rights.

The current social system, with all its errors, is sustained by the ignorance and slavery of women.

We will begin by narrating the slavery of woman in marriage, the inconveniences resulting from her lack of education, and the manner in which the consequences of her misfortune are reflected in her children.

Then we examine how women should understand education so that they may explain it to their children. Because woman must enlighten herself in order to free herself from a slavery that ruins her as a woman and a mother.

We also examine what method she should adopt to educate her children and her husband.

11.4 *HOW POOR WOMEN PROSTITUTE THEMSELVES*—LUISA CAPETILLO

A One Act Play

SCENE: A simple living room

WOMAN: (*Enters scene in a house dress, followed by a well-dressed man who gives her money.*)

YOUNG MAN: Are you happy with this life?

WOMAN: No, but what choice do I have?

YOUNG MAN: Work at a factory.

WOMAN: I don't know a trade, and besides, how much would I make?

YOUNG MAN: Enough to feed yourself.

WOMAN: You're telling me to go earn a miserable wage, to breathe bad air, and to listen to the impertinences of some vulgar foreman. That won't fix the harm done: we women will always be sacrificed in this infinite holocaust to a hypocritical social lie. It's all the same, for me or for someone else: it's human flesh that is humiliated or despised, that is sold and that atrophies, that is outraged, that is used and trampled on in the name of Christian morality. (*with energy*) What could you say to me that any other woman doesn't deserve to hear? It's all the same: treat me the same. We can only vindicate ourselves as a whole, or not at all—I'm no better than any other woman.

YOUNG MAN: That's true, one person alone is powerless. All women have the right to be happy, to be respected.

WOMAN: Along with stupid courtesies, social respect is a farce. If it can't prevent a poor tubercular girl from getting sick, why should she give a damn? Would respect give her the means to live comfortably? Because of the rich people's virtue and decorum they'll give her an apology when her soul has been left twisted and her body in the factory; why doesn't respect guarantee health and get rid of deprivation? Useless words!

YOUNG MAN: You're selfishness incarnate in an ignorant lady.

WOMAN: Why isn't that virtue inaccessible to the poor people in the grave? Why doesn't it take the stench out of the fermentation in the ditch? If you buried two girls of equal size and age, one an immaculate virgin, the other surrounded by vice and misery, would the dirt respect one more than the other? Would the dirt free the virgin from the worms?

YOUNG MAN: No, Mother Nature doesn't make those choices. For her, the virgin is the same as the prostitute. She is the equalizer, the lever par excellence.

WOMAN: Then, friend, what's the sense of living one way or the other? It's all the same; social hypocrasies don't bother my soul or disturb my mind.

YOUNG MAN: I understand. But if those things don't matter to you, I should remind you that you're exposed to thousands of diseases, and you practice vices that pleasure the mob of degenerates that use you and then treat you with scorn.

WOMAN: All that is very splendid to say, but if you were in my circumstances you would surely accept it one way or the other. One day a drunk came, and my opinions meant nothing to him. I was disgusted to go near him. He usually comes every Friday; he'll surely come this evening. What can I do about it?

YOUNG MAN: Well, I need to go. Please excuse my questions. Until another day. (*He salutes her courteously with his hat.*)

WOMAN: (*Alone*) An excellent young man. But it is already very late—what can I do?—and besides, it's the same to do it with only one as to do it with many. Aren't they all brothers, like in the Bible and all other religions? All that mess of uselessness seems ridiculous and stupid to me. If everything is for sale, why worry so much because we charge a fee? If she who joins herself with a man—through civil marriage or through some religion—also sells herself, doesn't the husband have to cover all the costs? Very few of them go to the factories, but isn't that a kind of sale? They don't want to call it that, but it's a sale just like ours.

DRUNK MAN: Good evening!

WOMAN: Come in.

THE MAN: May I? Very good then, let's hurry, I have to go. (*Shaking*)

WOMAN: Then enter, so you can go . . .

MAN: No, you go first. You want to do it, right? Look—you thieves—not even paying you makes you listen. Let's go, or I'll whip you! (*Pushing her*)

WOMAN: I'm going, pig, what do you think! . . . I'd be better off killing myself. . . .

MAN: For what you're worth, you may as well have already done it. (*They enter the house, he pushing her forward.*)

12. *Sex*—Mae West

Commentary

Sources

Play

12.1 MAE WEST LIVE: *SEX, THE DRAG*, AND 1920S BROADWAY—MARYBETH HAMILTON

MAE WEST. THE NAME BRINGS familiar images immediately to mind: the platinum hair, the swaying hourglass figure, the ironically murmured invitation to "come up and see me." Few movie voices are as instantly recognizable; few performance styles as widely, and amusingly, imitated. From a movie career that spanned only ten films, West made herself into an enduring cinema legend—a performer who continues to fascinate a decade after her death.

Over the past five years, in the course of researching West's early stage and film career, I've been struck not only by the strength of that fascination but by its social and political breadth. Throughout her long career onstage and in films, West drew a remarkably diverse range of fans, many of whom held widely varying interpretations of her ironic humor. To feminists (from French novelist Colette to film critic Molly Haskell), West's tongue-in-cheek swagger signaled her disdainful rejection of traditional modest femininity. To gay men, in contrast, it was the essence of camp, a playful enactment of the theatricality and artificiality that sustain *all* sex roles. And, although West became famous for battles with censors, she exerted an appeal to some social conservatives, who viewed her humor as an agent of moral enlightenment, a gentle satire of and corrective to Hollywood's overemphasis on passion.

In short, Mae West's fans were united in their adoration for her but blatantly disagreed about her comedy's real meaning. That wealth of disparate, even contradictory, interpretations points to precisely what made West such a unique and powerful figure. Mae West could inspire such a breadth of reaction from such a wide range of fans because she was no ordinary sex symbol. What made her screen performances unique was not so much her sexuality as the aura in which she clothed it: a hint of good-humored self-mockery, a touch of irony, a suggestion that she was not simply playing a sex symbol but parodying one too. If her fans still disagree about the "real" Mae West, the reason lies in that enigmatic style: the suggestion, embedded within her screen performances, that more is going on than lies on the surface, a vague something that is left up to the viewer to interpret. West's performances seem to be infused with some sort of a joke—but it is up to the viewer to supply her own punch line.

That such an open-ended style should form the basis of West's appeal would not surprise many analysts of mass culture. Historian Peter Bailey, for example, in his study of the British comic strip "Ally Sloper's Half-Holiday," has argued that 20th-century mass culture works by taking intriguing but socially divisive entities—class, sexuality—and investing their treatment with a deliberate ambiguity, an open-ended quality that allows a diverse public to read its meaning in a variety of ways (Bailey 1983).

In West's case her own enigmatic persona developed out of the social and sexual tensions of New York City in the 1920s—and, more specifically, out of the need to negotiate the sizable and varied middle-class public flocking to the Broadway stage. In 1928 West created a Broadway hit with her self-scripted play *Diamond Lil* (brought to the screen in 1933 as *She Done Him Wrong*). West played Diamond Lil, a scarlet woman on the turn-of-the-century Bowery, and in doing so introduced the persona on which she built her career—a wry and humorous dance-hall madam, devastatingly sexy to all the men around but seemingly amused by her own allure. That play brought West critical raves and a broad spectrum of fans—by all accounts spanning divisions of gender, class, and generation, from the morally conservative to the sexually adventurous.

This essay explores the roots of West's performance style and the resonances it carried to its Broadway audience. To make those resonances clear, we must look, not at *Diamond Lil*, but at the two years that immediately preceded it. *Diamond Lil* brought Mae West a mass public for the first time, but it did not rocket her from obscurity to stardom. West had been a household name in New York since 1926, a full two years before *Diamond Lil*, but she was famous, or rather notorious, with a very different type of renown. From 1926 to 1928, West was known throughout New York as a pornographer, infamous for her association with two sensational (and, according to many, obscene) productions.

In 1926 Mae West was an ambitious actress who had failed to find legitimate work. At age 32 she was a 25-year veteran of the popular theatre but her name was virtually unknown. The last few years had been particularly dispiriting. After repeated failures in vaudeville and musical comedy, West seems to have become a featured player on the Mutual Burlesque Wheel (or Circuit) between 1922 and 1925 (Tuska 1973:30–31).

That she did so indicates just how far her career had plummeted. Burlesque in general was avoided by all ambitious legitimate performers, and the Mutual Wheel carried the greatest stigma of all. Founded in July 1922, it gained instant notoriety through cheap, sensational revues flaunting no-holds-barred lewdness—in the words of one chronicler, "such feverish shimmying and shaking," "cooching and undressing," as had never been envisioned in burlesque theatres before (Zeidman 1967:92–98).

Having sunk so low in the popular theatre, in April 1926, West embarked on a last-ditch effort to gain mainstream Broadway success and, in so doing, began an adventure that would make her one of New York's most infamous celebrities. On the strength of financial backing put together by rather dubious means, West rented a theatre, hired a director, and with what little money remained, staged a play she had written especially for herself, a tale of a Montreal prostitute to which she gave the provocative title *SEX*.

The play was unanimously panned by New York's theatre critics, all of whom predicted its immediate failure and some of whom called for police intervention. Yet despite this condemnation —or rather, no doubt, in part because of it—*SEX* became one of the major hits of the 1926 season, playing to mostly full houses until forced to close in March 1927.

West's production of *SEX* was sufficiently sensational in itself to have guaranteed its creator citywide notoriety. But West topped her reputation in early 1927, writing and staging a play in which she herself did not appear, but which she proudly advertised as her own work. She billed the play as a "homosexual comedy-drama," and called it *The Drag*. Throughout January 1927, *The Drag* played a series of widely publicized preview performances in Connecticut and New Jersey; by early February, against the united opposition of theatrical producers, antivice reformers, and public officials, it stood poised on the New York City limits, making loud preparations for a Broadway run. But the premiere was prevented by the police.

On 9 February 1927, New York's vice squad raided *SEX* and two other Broadway productions, charging all three with public obscenity. Under pressure of an impending trial, West had little choice but to abandon *The Drag*. This did not, however, improve her fate in court. As *SEX*'s author, coproducer, and star, West was found guilty of writing and staging an obscene production. In April she entered the Women's Reformatory on Roosevelt Island to serve a ten-day sentence (Eells and Musgrove 1982:73).

To any diehard Mae West fan these events are well known. Over the course of her long career, West turned her Broadway arrest into part of her public mythology, portraying her jailers as she would always describe her Hollywood censors—as puritanical killjoys who could not see the humor of her good-natured, ironic mockery of sex. But the facts themselves tell another story. In 1926 Mae West was a very different performer than she would become only a few years later. As we shall see, when West created *SEX* and *The Drag*, ironic self-mockery could not have been further from her mind.

SEX starred West as Margy Lamont, a tough, bitter, imperious prostitute who presides over the roughest brothel in all of Montreal. Over the course of three acts, the play follows Margy from Montreal to Trinidad to the plush suburbs of New York, where she travels in pursuit of money, adventure, and sex. The plot is relatively convoluted—an absurd and at times incoherent blend of comedy and melodrama—and I need not attempt to describe its intricacies in full. For my purposes, the crucial moments of the play are those on which, above all others, its notoriety rested—Acts I and II, when we see Margy in her element, the reigning whore in a cheap Montreal brothel and the presiding entertainer in a sleazy Trinidad nightclub. In these largely comic scenes, Margy herself is always the focus, bantering suggestively with her sponging pimp, enflaming the lust of her male customers, and dismissing unwanted admirers with derisive comments on their sexual prowess.

It is almost impossible to exaggerate the amount of condemnation that critics heaped upon *SEX*. These were not simply negative reviews, dismissing the play in the vocabulary of dramatic criticism, in terms of structure, technique, and execution. *SEX*'s critics all but abandoned that vocabulary and used terminology that made clear their fundamental revulsion at what they had seen onstage. One typical example came in the *New York Daily Mirror*, on 30 April 1926 under the headline "*SEX* an Offensive Play. Monstrosity Plucked From Garbage Can, Destined to Sewer." The reviewer continued: "This production is not for the police. It comes rather in the province of our Health Department. It is a sore spot in the midst of our fair city that needs disinfecting."

The *Daily Mirror* was a tabloid, and thus habitually given to hyperbole. Yet in making their case against *SEX* even the more restrained papers employed a vocabulary of infection, disease, and filth. The script, wrote the *New Yorker*, on 8 May 1926 was composed of "street sweepings"; the play, argued another critic, left the viewer afflicted with "that 'dark brown' taste which results from proximity to anything indescribably filthy." The reviewer for the *New York Herald Tribune* was somewhat more subdued, but he too came to essentially the same point. "*SEX*," he wrote on 27 April 1926, was

> an ostensible reflection of the underworld as it is supposed to exist in Montreal and Trinidad. A world of ruthless, evil-minded, foulmouthed crooks, harlots, procurers and other degenerate members of that particular zone of society. Never in a long experience of theatergoing have

> we met with a set of characters so depraved. [. . .] All the barriers of conventional word and act that the last few seasons of the theatre have shown us were swept away and we were shown not sex but lust—stark, naked lust.

SEX, in short, created a furor, but one that Mae West in subsequent years was never at a loss to explain. *SEX*, she argued, had appeared at a time when Broadway shied away from all mention of physical passion. The legitimate theatre in 1926 did not present sexual subject matter, West asserted—it did not, for that matter, even employ the word. Before she used "sex" as a play title, it had never appeared in the mass media, at least not to indicate physical acts. (Its only usages, West claimed, had been in medical journals, or as a synonym for gender—"the fair sex," "the gentler sex.") No city newspaper, she asserted, would advertise her play under its real title; instead, they ran notices for "Mae West in That Certain Play" (Eells and Musgrove 1982:62).

The truth, however, as one might guess, is more complex than West paints it. She did not introduce sex to Broadway. By 1926, Broadway abounded in plays dealing with sexual relations, including prostitution: the 1925/26 theatre season, for example, featured such hits as *The Shanghai Gesture*, the story of China's most successful madam; and *Lulu Belle*, the tale of a mean, merciless, unrepentant mulatto hooker seducing black and white lovers from Harlem to Paris. Advertisements for *SEX*, with the title appearing in large, boldfaced capitals, did appear in every New York City newspaper; moreover, they did so alongside ads that more than outshone them in garish suggestiveness.

This was, it must be noted, a relatively new state of affairs, and one that was provoking no end of criticism from New York's clerics and civic reformers. Ever since the mid-19th century, when the "legitimate theatre" first marked itself off as a discrete genre of public entertainment, distinct from variety theatre and melodrama, it had geared itself specifically toward a middle-class public. Not only had its ticket prices catered to such patrons (discouraging poorer ones), but its content had as well. Until the early years of the 20th century, the legitimate theatre specialized in decorous, sentimental, desensualized productions tailored for a Victorian middle class that found any staged representation of sexuality to be dangerous and degrading.

But by World War I, a new generation of middle-class patrons began to fill Broadway theatres—a generation that harbored much less suspicion of sexual expressiveness. By the 1920s, the old genteel productions had by no means disappeared, but far more producers catered to the younger crowd by offering distinctly racier fare. Indeed, though productions like *The Shanghai Gesture* and *Lulu Belle* aroused comment (and vigorous protest from social reformers), they were common enough to be perceived as part of an established Broadway genre, the "sex play."

With those facts in mind, we must interpret critics' response to *SEX* in a different light than that suggested by West. Broadway critics in the 1920s were, no less than audiences, a product of this generational change: they were accustomed to sexually expressive plays, in many cases praising them; and they prided themselves on their urbane sophistication, their bemused tolerance for even inept producers' infatuation with sex. Their response to bad sex-plays was typically ridicule, not condemnation. Moreover, they were capable of responding to these productions as theatre, of analyzing them in the terms of dramatic criticism, with attention to structure, technique, and execution.

But *SEX*, clearly, was different. With *SEX*, critics' carefully wrought tone of urbanity disintegrated, replaced by one that sputtered with talk of disease, infection, and filth. Something more complex than "prudery" was at work here. Reviewers did not simply hate West's play; they were incapable of responding to it in terms of their trade, incapable of responding to it as theatre. Indeed, that it was not theatre was precisely the point. Remember the distinction that the *Herald Tribune* reviewer had drawn: that West's play presented "not sex but lust—stark, naked lust." Critics' words continually implied that *SEX* was no theatrical representation of a brothel, but that it uncomfortably resembled a real one; that it was not merely about sex, but was somehow a literal presentation of it, a "sore" that fell in the province of the Health Department or vice squad. It did not belong on Broadway, wrote the theatre journal *Variety* on 28 April 1926; rather, it suited another neighborhood, another class. It was, the journal argued, "a nasty red-light district show."

Critics labeled *SEX* as offensively "realistic," a word whose meaning is always hard to pin down. We can more readily penetrate the controversy if we depart from their vocabulary—if we investigate not its "realism," but its style of representation, and the meanings and resonances that theatrical style carried. *SEX* shocked critics because it presented sexuality in a style that "legitimate theatre" scorned. It created its brothel by drawing on "illegitimate" sources that, in the context of Broadway, made it unusual and distinctly unnerving.

In part, *SEX* took its unsettlingly "authentic" tone from its humor. The play did not really have much of a plot. The first act was particularly loose in construction. Set in a Montreal brothel, it gained what coherence it had not by any development of character or situation but by a series of comic sketches: rapid-fire exchanges between Margy Lamont and her pimp, her fellow prostitutes, and her male customers—exchanges laden with leering double-entendres and punctuated with unmistakably graphic gestures. In one of *SEX*'s most notorious scenes, a customer named Lt. Gregg loomed provocatively over Margy while explaining what it was that he had waited three months to give her.

> GREGG: Oh, I've got something for you, wait until you see this, wait until you see this.
> MARGY: Well, come on and let's see it.
> GREGG: You'll get it, you'll get it. I don't mind telling you I had an awful time saving it for you. Why, all the women were fighting for it.
> MARGY: It better be good.
> GREGG: It's good alright. It's the best you could get, but you've got to be very careful not to bend it.
>
> (West 1926: I, 15)

In speaking the final line, Lt. Gregg accompanied it by what one critic described as "a Rabelaisian gesture to indicate a certain anatomical virtuosity" (Nathan 1972 [1928]:90). After completing the "Rabelaisian gesture," Lt. Gregg reached into his pocket and pulled out Margy's gift—an ostrich feather.

This style of humor, marked by rapid-fire comic banter, transparently sexual double meanings, and graphic physical movements, characterized one type of theatre above all: the burlesque show. Nearly all of the critics who condemned *SEX* mentioned just that resemblance. To understand how damning such a comparison was, it is necessary to turn to burlesque history, to see the kind of seamy associations it held for anyone who knew even a little about theatrical performance.

By the 1910s and '20s, burlesque had firmly established itself as the outcast of popular theatre—insofar as it was regarded as theatre at all. It had taken root in urban areas of the United States in the late 19th century, a mishmash of suggestive songs, dances, and comedy sketches that became a fixture of working-class, male-oriented entertainment districts like New York's Bowery, alongside concert saloons and variety theatres. But unlike variety, which under the flashier name of vaudeville was able to tone down its performers, move to central shopping and theatre districts, and broaden its appeal to a middle-class public, burlesque never managed to "class itself up."

Indeed, if anything, burlesque sank in social status in the early 20th century, drawing an audience that middle-class observers regarded as the most dissolute and degraded of the male working class. In the 1910s and '20s, burlesque in New York largely remained outside the Broadway mainstream, concentrated instead in lower-class areas associated with an underworld of drugs and prostitution. Because they prided themselves on their ostentatious wickedness, on showing what was unshowable in respectable entertainments, burlesque theatres from the 1910s on were periodically investigated by the Committee of Fourteen, a group of New York social reformers intent on combating the spread of commercialized vice. To many observers in the 1920s, burlesque theatres seemed little removed from brothels, and burlesque actresses themselves were widely assumed to be prostitutes (Zeidman 1967; Sobel 1931; Hartt 1909:7; Edwards 1915:46).

Burlesque humor and the associations it carried were part of what gave *SEX* its offensive appearance of "realism," but an even more important factor was Mae West herself. Critics were riveted by West's performance—riveted, however, not with pleasure, but with a kind of horrified fascination. Over and over in the words they used to describe her—"raw," "crude," "unvarnished" —one senses critics' discomfort at finding themselves faced, not with a conventional theatrical portrait of a prostitute, but with something that came uncomfortably close to the real thing.

West gave this unsettling depiction in part by her plainspoken definition of prostitution as an economic, and specifically working-class, activity. Margy Lamont was clearly, unmistakably a working prostitute, explicitly linked, as all real-life prostitutes were, to the cash nexus fueling the urban vice economy. She took money for sex, and West's play made no attempt to gloss over that fact. To the contrary. Much of its "repellent" humor turned on just that circumstance, dwelling on it with a kind of gleeful relish. Take, for example, the following moment, when Margy responds to a rival prostitute's accusation that she has stolen one of her customers, Sailor Dan from Kansas.

> MARGY (*flipping through her customer book*): Sailor Dan from Kansas, Sailor Dan from Kansas—oh Sailor Dan from Kansas. Yeh Sailor Dan from Kansas, flat feet, asthma, check came back, o, baby, I'll make you a present of that bird, he's yours.
>
> (West 1926:I, 12)

Jokes like this made glaringly clear the fundamental reality of prostitution: a meeting of bodies and an exchange of cash, and often (as the bounced check reminds us) very little cash at that. It was a jarring truth, at least in a theatrical context. For while prostitutes had long been depicted on the legitimate stage, they had assumed a relatively romanticized form that had obscured the reality of what they did, its place at the bottom of the economic order, and its nature as paid labor.

Margy, in contrast, was explicitly a sexual commodity, an ill-paid sex worker who traded her body on the streets. West made that fact unmistakable. As West embodied her, Margy was palpably from the lower orders: she spoke in working-class argot (assailing a female adversary as a "dirty charity"—"charity" being street slang for a woman who bartered sexual favors, not for cash, but for a "good time"); and she voiced a violent hatred of "decent folk"—of the supposedly "respectable" who sin on the side and who exhort the poor to uplift themselves while denying them the means to do so.

Margy is bitterly conscious of herself as a member of an oppressed class, and the grimness and harshness of her manner are reflected in the world she inhabits. Her Montreal red-light district is a mean and unglamorous place, untouched by sentiment, charm, or romance. Rife with class antagonisms, it's the kind of place a middle-class person would feel distinctly uncomfortable upon entering. As a critic from the *New York Herald Tribune* noted on 23 January 1927, "It may be said of [Mae West] and *SEX* that they do not make sin attractive. The hell they picture is uninviting, a horrible place whose principal lady-viper has a tough hiss, an awkward strut and an overplump figure."

That last statement leads me to what is really the most crucial element in West's "unsettling" portrait of Margy Lamont. Her depiction of Margy's lower-class status would not have been nearly so disturbing had it not been reinforced by her peculiarly vivid handling of sexuality. By the time she took the stage in *SEX*, and probably even as far back as her vaudeville years, Mae West had developed a distinctive manner of moving and speaking on the stage. Entering a scene, she did not so much walk as ooze—moving with a controlled, deliberate slouch, her full hips swaying in a languid rhythm. She delivered her lines in nasal yet resonant tones that spilled from the corner of her mouth, lending every word an insinuating sexual toughness.

To anyone who has ever seen Mae West onscreen, all that might sound familiar, but in *SEX* there was a crucial difference: there was not the least hint of an ironic joke. There was no amiable self-mockery in *SEX*, no suggestion, either in the script or in West's performance, that she was parodying a sexy woman as well as playing one. Remembering this is crucial to understanding the startling impact of West's physicality; as contemporary reaction makes clear, West's sexual style, unmediated by self-mockery, evoked a lower-class world with nearly palpable, tangible force.

To understand how it did so, one has to look at the broader context of female sexual expressiveness on the Broadway stage. As I suggested earlier, Broadway did not shy away from such presentations. But its representation of female sexuality reflected the fashions and styles of a middle-class public, a public that was not nearly as comfortable with women's sexuality as it often liked to pretend, a public that prided itself on its sexual sophistication while remaining uneasy with eroticism's overt manifestations.

High fashion in the 1920s, for example, brought sexual expressiveness to the wardrobes of respectable women more directly than ever before, but conveyed it in restrained or teasing fashion—through bound breasts, a straight silhouette, and a slender, boyish body that evoked aloof sophistication or sporty independence rather than full-fleshed eroticism.

Middle-class entertainment, like middle-class fashion, reflected this unease. The Ziegfeld Girls from Flo Ziegfeld's *Follies* took the stage with their breasts bared, but they did so with an aloof, near-motionless elegance—a style that gave them a detached, aristocratic allure (Toll 1976:317–19).

Lulu Belle, in contrast, put its prostitute heroine emphatically in motion. But as portrayed by actress Leonore Ulrich she was a stylishly slim, buoyant, kinetically charged woman whose sexiness, through jazzy physical exuberance, emerged flapper-style.

What Mae West displayed in *SEX* was indeed, as critics charged, raw and unvarnished by comparison: eroticism conveyed through an insolent nasal hiss; an awkward, deliberate slouch; and the graphic undulations of her thick-set body. The heaviness of that body, clad in short and flimsy modern attire, was particularly crucial. In the 1920s, while a boyish silhouette defined respectable sexuality, a thick-set body like West's brought seamy and distinctly lower-class associations to mind: burlesque actresses, for one, who were widely equated with prostitutes and whose famously overblown figures signaled their supposedly aggressive embrace of sensual passion.

Like a burlesque chorus girl, Mae West as Margy Lamont manipulated her full figure to convey a wide ranging sexual appetite, freely indulged and unabashedly savored. So convincing was she, and so unsettling, that most critics could not see it as a performance. While none accused West of being a prostitute herself, a few implied that she received actual sexual pleasure onstage—in their minds the most offensive "realism" of all. One disgusted *New York Daily Mirror* reviewer assessed West's performance, writing on 31 December 1926: "[She] cavorts her own sex about the stage in one of the most reviling exhibits allowed public display. She undresses before the public, and appears to enjoy doing so."

If in *SEX* West brought the urban underworld alive with an unsettling realism, she accomplished the same, by different means, in her "homosexual comedy-drama," *The Drag*.

West was not the first to bring homosexuality to the legitimate stage. In September 1926, four months before her play's out-of-town premiere, Broadway saw the debut of *The Captive*, an American adaptation of Edouard Bourdet's *La Prisonniere*. Emphasizing the psychic turmoil engendered by same-sex passion, Bourdet's drama was restrained in the extreme. It focused attention on the anguish of the "captive," a young woman tempted by lesbian desire. But the woman is never seen to act on that desire; moreover, her "captor," her lesbian seductress, never appears onstage.

Bourdet's drama quickly became one of the big hits of the 1926/27 season. Critics lauded its intellectual rigor and intense dramatic power, and spectators jammed the Empire Theatre. For her part, West composed *The Drag*, which she advertised as "A Male 'Captive'" in an unabashed effort to capitalize on *The Captive*'s spectacular success. But, perhaps unsurprisingly, *The Drag* carried a very different focus from *The Captive*. Observing the crowds lined up for Bourdet's drama, West surmised that they were interested not in intellectual rigor but in something far more sensational.

The Drag ostensibly told the story of Rolly Kingsbury, the son of a wealthy, respectable New York City judge married to the daughter of a Park Avenue doctor. Their marriage, the audience learns in the first scene, has problems, and by the end of the first act the audience learns why: Rolly is homosexual, involved with a set of flamboyant male friends. He married simply to hide his true nature from his family. For the remainder of the drama, the audience watches the consequences of Rolly's deception: the unhappiness of his wife, the confusion of his heterosexual friends, and finally the death of Rolly himself, shot by a despondent young man named David Caldwell, Rolly's former lover.

West prefaced the play with what might be called an "educational" prolog: two brief scenes involving an enlightened physician who argues that homosexuals are not criminals but victims of a disease, deserving compassion and pity. Under cover of that preface, West posed *The Drag* as a vehicle of sex education. Through the story of Rolly Kingsbury and David Caldwell, she ostensibly illustrated the tragic consequences of society's cruel censure of what was in reality a curable sickness.

Having described that, I must stop and acknowledge what is probably no surprise: this ostensible message was pure pretense, having nothing to do with what *The Drag* was actually up to. West dispatched her "educational" scenes so hastily that her audience could barely have had a chance to absorb what was said. With the exit of Dr. Richmond a scant five minutes into the play, the "pity versus censure" debate disappears, to be resurrected only briefly at the play's conclusion when the anguished David Caldwell returns to explain his murder of Rolly. The scenes centering on Rolly Kingsbury consumed perhaps half, if not less, of *The Drag*'s actual running time. These "educational" scenes provided a convenient pretense, but they were not at all what West knew her audience had come for.

The scenes that formed *The Drag*'s real focus showcased a large supporting cast of flamboyantly expressive homosexual men recruited from New York's burgeoning gay underworld. This part of *The Drag*'s history never managed to make it into Mae West's reminiscences. According to a writer for *Studio* magazine, in 1926 West and manager James Timony paid a late night visit to

> a dimly lit Village hangout for chorus girls and boys. [. . .] Word got out that she was casting a play about homosexuals [. . .] and those kids really turned it on. [. . .] She did not stay long and before she left borrowed an order book from the waiter and personally wrote passes for everyone present, telling them to see her show [*SEX*] the following night and then stay for a regular tryout.
>
> (in Eells and Musgrove 1982:65)

From the tryout West and her director, Edward Elsner, assembled 60 male players for the supporting company and began afternoon rehearsals at Daly's 63rd Street Theatre. At that point West was probably working with only a fragmentary script. To judge by reports that began to surface in *Variety*, such as the following from the 12 January 1927 edition, much of what audiences eventually saw in *The Drag* originated in the raunchy ad libs of her very uninhibited cast.

> "THE DRAG" REHEARSING WITH SIXTY "VILLAGERS"
>
> [. . .] Rehearsals are being held daily at the 63rd Street, with the chances that a good pre-gross might be rolled up if admission could be charged to watch the Villagers practicing.
>
> [. . .] At rehearsals Elsner permits the "our sex" members to cavort and carry on as they like. Results are more natural and spontaneous.

Out of West's "natural and spontaneous" rehearsals grew two lengthy scenes that formed *The Drag*'s highpoints. The first, lasting for most of the second act, presents a visit to Rolly Kingsbury's apartment by four male friends—Clem, Rosco, Winnie, and "the Duchess"—in which the group discusses a party they are to attend the following night. Assuming (so the stage directions inform us) "artistic" poses, shrieking and giggling, and flourishing powder puffs, the men gather around the piano for a few musical numbers and needle each other with bawdy jibes delivered in affected, effeminate slang.

DUCHESS: Oh, my goodness. I've got the most gorgeous new drag. Black satin very tight, with a long train of rhinestones.

CLEM: Wait until you see the creation I'm wearing dearie. Virginal white, no back, with oceans of this and oceans of that, trimmed with excitement in front. You know I'm more the flapper type, not so much like a canal boat.

DUCHESS: Creation—ha! That old thing. I knew that three years ago. Oh, Annie.

CLEM (*very angry*): For Chris' sake sit. This big bitch thinks nobody has anything or looks like anything but her.

DUCHESS: Oh, shut up.

ROLLY: Say, how about a little drink?

CLEM: Yes! How about a little drink?

DUCHESS: I don't mind a little drink once in a while.

CLEM: Why you big Swede. You'd take it through a funnel if anybody would give it to you.

WINNIE: Funnel? That's nothing. I take it through a hose. Whoops!

(West 1927:II, 4)

The real high point of the play, however, came in Act III, with the scene from which the play took its title. For a full 30 minutes, West showcased Rolly Kingsbury's "drag ball," an elaborate get-together for his uninhibited male friends. While a jazz orchestra played "hot" music in the background, the male supporting cast capered onstage, some dressed in women's gowns and some in tuxedos, and all, according to 2 February 1927's *Variety*, "rouged, lip-sticked and liquid-whited to the last degree." Between the group numbers came "specialty" songs ("How Come You Do Me Like You Do," "Goody-Goody-Good") performed by individual cast members, including one man "dressed as an Oriental dancer, bare legs and wearing only what amounts to a brassiere above the waist," who accompanied his singing with a suggestive "muscle dance." At moments, the musical numbers halted for snappy, burlesque-style comic bits—insults, jibes, and double-entendres on the subject of police raids and male lovers.

WINNIE: My but you're getting thin.

KATE: I am not. I can at least cling to a man without wearing him out. You're terribly fat.

WINNIE: Fat! I should say not. I'm the type that men prefer. I can at least go through the navy yard without having the flags drop to half mast.

KATE: Listen, dearie—pull in your aerial, you're full of static. I'm just the type that men crave. The type that burns 'em up. Why, when I walk up Tenth Avenue, you can smell the meat sizzling in Hell's Kitchen.

(West 1927:III, 2–3)

To appreciate what West was up to, it is important to see that her supporting cast was not a group of otherwise isolated oddities. They were part of a New York City subculture that, while relatively well established, was still new enough to seem shadowy and mysterious to most heterosexual New Yorkers.

When the character Kate spoke of strolling through Hell's Kitchen, he referred to only one among many New York City neighborhoods—including Harlem, Greenwich Village, and the Tenderloin south of Times Square—that since the end of the 19th century housed a network of gay bars, bathhouses, and other meeting places. New York was not the only American city to see the rise of a gay underworld during those years. As newspaper accounts, medical case histories, and personal correspondences testify, gay life took root in major centers across the nation, as gay men and women staked out urban spaces and established institutions in Washington, Chicago, St. Louis, and San Francisco (Chauncey 1986; D'Emilio 1983; Katz 1976).

Why the sudden growth of what was a distinctly new type of community? Certainly, it was not that homosexual desire had never before existed. Even looking at American history alone, one finds numerous prosecutions for homosexual behavior, of both women and men, as early as the Colonial period.

But, as historian John D'Emilio points out, homosexual behavior is not the same as homosexual identity. It was not until the late 19th century that a complex set of social changes enabled individuals to turn homosexual desire into a personal identity, a way of life they sought out with others like themselves. Those years saw the creation of an ideological climate in which sexual desire was separated from procreation and "personal life" distinguished from work life, with "personal life" identified as the site of the authentic self. In that climate, men and women with homosexual desires saw those desires as defining who they were. In the relative anonymity offered by cities, they constructed a homosexual identity and a distinctive social life. By the early 20th century, New York's homosexual population was more than a group of disparate individuals who happened to be drawn to members of their own sex. It was, in the words of a correspondent of British sexologist Havelock Ellis, "a community distinctly organized—[with] words, customs, traditions of its own" (in Katz 1976:52).

The Drag showcased those "words, customs, traditions," exploiting them to intrigue and titillate mainstream theatre audiences. West's characters laced their raucous banter with geographically specific references to their community's distinctive pastimes. The Duchess spoke of "cruising" Central Park and Riverside Drive; Clem described sashaying around Times Square; and others made reference to summer excursions to particular New York coastal resorts.

Specific words and phrases were also part of the novelty the play offered. Addressing each other as "molls," "queers," and "queens" and describing themselves as "gay," West's characters brought spectators in contact with a large and colorful in-group vocabulary organized around gender reversal and rife with specific sexual overtones. When, for example, Clem pursued a burly and presumably straight Brooklyn taxi driver, another character leered knowingly, "Rough trade, dearie"—from which the audience could infer that "rough trade" designated a heterosexual, working-class male who, for a price, indulged in homosexual sex. Much of this slang has entered the mainstream in the past decades—so much so, in fact, that we must make an effort to sense its foreignness to 1920s ears. So odd did the jargon sound to many that several reporters covering *The Drag*'s out-of-town tryouts felt obliged to act as translators—particularly when it came to the play's "mysterious" title.

Finally, West spotlighted the novelty and outrageousness of gay life by encouraging her cast to "play up" and exaggerate what was already a distinctive in-group style. Characters like Clem, Winnie, and the Duchess were markedly, flamboyantly effeminate. They minced when they walked, postured suggestively when they stood, and assumed "artistic" poses when they seated themselves in chairs. Many of the male characters had feminine names; others referred to themselves as "women" and "girls" and addressed their fellows with feminine pronouns. Not only did their slang evoke "womanish" images—so too did the tone in which it was delivered: shrill, giddy, and affected, punctuated with bitchy insults and hysterical shrieks.

> WINNIE: Oh, you look gorgeous. What a lovely robe. I have one just like it. Oh.
> CLEM: Sit down and shut up.
> WINNIE: Oh, for goodness sake.
> CLEM: I want you to meet the Duchess.
> ROLLY: Oh, the Duchess, yes. I think we have met before. I just can't remember where.
> DUCHESS: It must have been my apartment on Riverside Drive.
> CLEM: Your apartment on Riverside Drive? What are you doing? Trying to make us think you're a kept woman?
> WINNIE: Oh, Oh (*screams*).
>
> (West 1927:II, 3)

For anyone encountering it 60 years after its premiere, this aspect of *The Drag* can be hard to stomach. And, indeed, no one would deny that the play, with its shrill and preening homosexuals and mincing drag queens, painted a one-dimensional portrait of New York City gay life. Depth of characterization was not what West was interested in; nor, for that matter, was she concerned with the dignity of those she presented. She was, without question, exploiting them, using them for the fascination she believed they held for the public.

But it is important to see that West sought to do so by drawing out behavior that did play an important part in 1920s gay reality. As historians are just beginning to document, that early gay community had moments of public visibility in the 1920s. And while the "drag queen" may not have represented the whole of gay culture, he did set the pace for gay public life in the 1920s, far more than he does today.

The drag queen and his effete, flamboyant though conventionally attired brother, exemplified what historian George Chauncey has called "the culture of effeminancy," the distinctive style of behavior and mannerism that dominated gay public interaction since that community's beginnings in the late 19th century. Chauncey's investigation of New York's early gay community suggests that, far more commonly than in later years, gay men found in affected and "womanish" banter, even feminine pronouns, the clearest means of participating in a gay social world. He writes:

> More gay men in the 1920s than today *did* adopt effeminate mannerisms: they provided one of the few sure means of announcing one's sexuality. But acting like a "fairy" was more than just a code; it was the dominant role model available to men forming a gay identity, and one against which every gay man had to measure himself.
>
> (1986:29–30)

For some, effeminacy became a way of life, a persona both public and private by which they announced their sexual tastes; for others, it was a style adopted to fit the occasion, set aside for work but put on after hours for New York's vital homosexual nightlife. At night, effeminate style set the tone, particularly at what became New York's largest gay social event in the 1920s—its series of drag balls, held six or seven times each year at Harlem's Rockland Palace, the old Madison Square Garden, and the Astor Hotel, and often attended by thousands (Chauncey 1986:29–30).

Mae West, for her part, put those drag balls under the Broadway spotlight. Though she presented her play as an exercise in sex education, in reality she highlighted not a conventional story that aimed to illuminate, but a jumbled mishmash that aimed to intrigue—a random assortment of songs, dances, and racy one-liners bearing little connection to the play's supposed plot and focusing instead on her players' "real life" practices: their distinctive slang, their habitual customs, and their characteristic style.

This may not sound like conventional theatre—and, indeed, most of West's Broadway colleagues refused to dignify it by that name. But in fact there was commercial precedent, however lowly, for the kind of entertainment West offered in *The Drag*. Since the turn of the century, sensational and suggestive gay performers had been a staple of certain New York nightlife districts, as entertainer Jimmy Durante could attest. Durante got his first job as a pianist in a gay bar on New York's Bowery; after the club was raided in 1905, he went to work at Diamond Tony's, a rundown saloon on Coney Island. As he remembered in 1930, Diamond Tony's drew its public with entertainment not too dissimilar to that offered in *The Drag*.

> At our place and Jack's [the club across the street], the entertainers were all boys who danced together and lisped. They called themselves Edna May and Leslie Carter and Big Tess and things like that. You know. Just like the first joint I worked in. When they had sung their numbers, they sat at the tables the way hostesses do today, "spinning their web," as they called it. Some of them were six feet tall and built like Dempsey, so it was never very healthy to make nasty cracks.
>
> Outside of the queer entertainers, our place was no different from most of the others. The usual number of girls hung out there, and the customers were mostly on the level; that is to say, they were not interested in our entertainers any more than they would have been in the freaks that filled the Surf Avenue sidewalks.
>
> It was a tough enough joint, but it didn't bother me, even if I was only fifteen. The Bowery, where I was brought up, isn't any sort of Sunday-school picnic, and I had seen enough to get acclimated to almost anything.
>
> (Durante and Kofoed 1931:54–55)

Since the turn of the century, concert saloons on the Bowery and Coney Island had brought members of New York's gay underworld onstage as a standard part of their entertainment fare. And they were not alone—Bowery burlesque houses did the same. In burlesque, the effeminate and suggestive "nance" (as gay men were termed in underground slang) became a fixture of each evening's entertainment, offering patrons ribald amusement in company with cootch dancers and raunchy comedians. By 1910, if not before, "nance humor" of much the sort that Mae West's play would offer had become, in *Variety*'s words, in the 2 February 1927 edition, "a staple of low comedy."

But an important distinction separated West's endeavor from burlesque and the concert saloon. The latter had been concentrated in the Bowery and Coney Island, which were distinctly stigmatized areas of the city—neighborhoods regarded by the middle class as debased, corrupting territory, where social interaction revolved around alcohol, drugs, and male and female prostitution. Bowery saloons and burlesque halls offered underworld entertainment to underworld audiences—shows where entertainer and audience shared membership in a world the "respectable" strictly avoided. This underworld entertainment, in short, drew a very limited patronage: working-class men, a few slumming gentlemen, and virtually no women who were not prostitutes.

Mae West was up to something different: she was attempting to showcase that same sexual underworld for a mainstream public in the heart of New York's most celebrated theatrical district. She explained her project, if rather obliquely, in January 1927, attempting in the midst of a citywide furor to legitimate her unusual theatrical style. She was quoted in the 1 February 1927 edition of the *New York Morning Telegraph*:

> There is one play which we never grow weary of seeing. That is the great show of life as it flows along. *The Drag* is the second of what I am calling "comedy-dramas of life." The first is *SEX*, which is playing in New York.

The Drag and *SEX*, West claimed, were "comedy-dramas of life." She may well have invented that label on the spur of the moment, but nonetheless it pinpoints the factor that made her style of theatre stand out. What distinguished both plays was their appearance of staging "real life," of bringing the sexual underworld onstage. *The Drag* did this in an obvious fashion, offering its audience not actors depicting homosexuals but homosexuals themselves. As for *SEX*, West was not a "real-life" prostitute, but she did all she could through her characterization and performance style to replicate a real woman of the streets. Moreover, the style of humor of both plays clearly followed the lead of burlesque. As audiences knew from vice investigations, burlesque's provocative actresses were often prostitutes; its suggestive, effeminate comics were often gay men. Burlesque did not so much represent the underworld as it was itself an underworld product, drawing no clear line between the stage and the street, between sexy performances and sexual acts, between the theatre and the disorderly house.

The Drag and *SEX* followed in that burlesque tradition, staging, West wrote, "the great show of life as it flows along." By "life," she meant sensational nightlife: racy, flamboyant urban experience of the type whose intrinsic drama was being accentuated in the 1920s by vice investigations and by photographic coverage in the newly flourishing tabloid press. Her "comedy-dramas of life," again like burlesque, offered intimate, seemingly candid glimpses of the urban underworld, bringing their audience face-to-face with the shadowy terrain of crime, drugs, and offbeat sexual practice.

West created *SEX* and *The Drag* by drawing directly on the rawest elements of working-class culture: its "men-only" theatre, its underworld streetlife, its class resentments, and its sexual styles. This was not an intentionally political act—West was, from all accounts, colossally uninterested in politics. It was performed with an eye fixed squarely on the box office. The sensational success of *The Shanghai Gesture* and *Lulu Belle* revealed an eager middle-class market for racy tales of prostitution; *The Captive*, in turn, had proved that fascination extended to homosexuality. *SEX* and *The Drag* were products of that cultural moment: shrewd pieces of exploitation by a would-be celebrity capitalizing on theatrical trends—convinced that if audiences flocked to the ersatz realism of *Lulu Belle* they would come in droves to the real thing. As West allegedly told one of *SEX*'s backers when he expressed hesitation about the play's rawness, Broadway audiences *wanted* "dirt"—and, she added emphatically, quoted in the *New York World* on 31 March 1927, "I'll give it to them!"

Mae West was in a position to "give it to them" more authentically than most Broadway performers. Not only was she an urban working-class product, abundantly experienced and interested in sex, more important, she had firsthand knowledge of the pornographic stage. Her experience on the Mutual Burlesque Wheel taught her how to craft Margy Lamont in unnervingly lewd fashion. Whether real prostitutes acted like Margy was irrelevant—the point was that burlesque depicted them that way, and burlesque was itself a part of the sexual underworld, a medium in which "reality" was hard to distinguish from "theatre."

West's strategy paid off, despite the critics. When *SEX* opened, few critics doubted its immediate failure: no audience paying $3.00 per ticket, they asserted, would be interested in smut. But within days of the play's premiere, newspapers reported that fans were storming the box office—fans, moreover, of a very different social stratum from the usual burlesque crowd. Robert Benchley, writing in *Life Magazine* on 20 May 1926, noted:

> The sudden rush to see *SEX* is not confined to the canaille. The agencies are hot after tickets, and each night soft purring limousines roll up with theatre parties of gentry, out "just for a lark."

SEX's fans came from the respectable, even elite, end of the social spectrum. And they included well-groomed, upper—middle class women no less than upper—middle class men—three times more women than men, according to one police report. Their patronage turned the play into a genuine phenomenon. By their enthusiasm, they made *SEX* into a craze, a Broadway fad, an arena for middle-class theatregoers to parade their adventurousness and daring. Critic Stark Young, writing in the *New Republic* in 27 June 1928, recalled the months after its premiere: "Who does not know how frequent or chic [. . .] it was to say that this show was fine, grand, swell, the best in town, I take everybody, etc.?" (1928:145, 146).

So *SEX* had its public and a larger one than any critic anticipated. Yet despite that fact, the play was never a mass success. *SEX* became what we would term a cult hit, drawing a young, affected, self-consciously jaded crowd—*Variety* called its members the "Broadway weisenheimers"—people bemused by the novelty of real dirt on Broadway. That kind of appeal could only last so long; and, indeed, *Variety*'s records indicate that attendance had begun to flag by early 1927, before the police raid in February sent it skyrocketing once more.

It's no surprise, I think, that *SEX* should have drawn a limited public. Both *SEX* and *The Drag* were raw and unvarnishedly staged plays by a working-class actress fresh out of burlesque. For Broadway's largely middle-class public, West's plays were the theatrical equivalent of a slumming excursion; and while that indisputably recommended them to some, many less adventurous theatregoers shied away—just as they would have balked at venturing into the back alleys of Harlem to seek out rough, frank blues alongside a black clientele. But those same theatregoers might have gone to Harlem's Cotton Club, where risque lyrics were somewhat more circumspect and where black patrons were banned. Or they might have gone to one of Texas Guinan's nightclubs, lavishly decorated places that, with their dim lighting, velvet-canopied ceilings, and fourteen-year-old chorus girls, unmistakably suggested brothels, but that tempered those associations with crazy circus-style antics: encouraging patrons to play leapfrog, for example, and dressing the orchestra in clown suits.

In short, while many of New York's nightlife patrons would not have gone to the real thing, they might have gone to its glamorized or caricatured imitation, where they could let loose among their own kind in a safer, less threatening setting that glossed over discomforting matters of sexuality and class. That commercial strategy—presenting a romanticized underworld, a sanitized slumming excursion—lay at the heart of 1920s New York's most successful nightlife amusements. They retained a tantalizing air of wickedness that still lured the adventurous, but they contained elements to reassure the more reticent as well.

This is the context that encouraged the creation of the self-mocking Mae West of *Diamond Lil.* That persona and that play put this commercial strategy into practice. In *Diamond Lil* West again played a prostitute, queen of a sensational urban underworld marked by white slavery, drug dealing, political corruption, and murder. But this time the milieu had a very different feel, a glamorous and sentimentalized turn-of-the-century red-light district, a lighthearted underworld completely free from class antagonisms. Lil herself was far more likable than Margy; she was also no longer recognizably working class; and, as West played her, she teetered on the verge of parody, thus giving spectators the chance, if they so chose, to dismiss the sex and sensationalism as a good-natured joke.

In *Diamond Lil* West capitalized on her newfound notoriety and encouraged her audience to think she had been kidding all along. It is no accident that, in so doing, she created her first mass Broadway success and the persona on which she would build her career. With the faintly tongue-in-cheek Diamond Lil, West gave the public a very different figure than the woman who had created *The Drag* and *SEX.* Lil was provocative, yet enigmatic; sexual, but somehow not serious; or, in West's own words, "a little bit spicy, but not too raw."

Note

References for many of the quotes from reviews that I cite in this article are incomplete. All reviews not listed in the references were found in the *SEX* clipping file at the Billy Rose Theatre Collection of the Performing Arts Research Center, New York Public Library.

References

Bailey, Peter
1983 "Ally Sloper's Half-Holiday: Comic Art in the 1880s." *History Workshop* 16 (Autumn):4–31.
Chauncey, George
1986 "The Way We Were: Gay Male Society in the Jazz Age." *Village Voice*, July 1:29–30, 34.
D'Emilio, John
1983 *Sexual Politics, Sexual Communities: The Making of a Homosexual Minority in the U.S., 1940–1970.* Chicago, IL: University of Chicago Press.
Durante, Jimmy, and Kofoed, Jack
1931 *Nightclubs.* New York: Alfred A. Knopf.

Edwards, Richard H.
1915 *Popular Amusements*. New York.

Eells, George, and Musgrove, Stanley
1982 *Mae West: A Biography*. New York: William Morrow & Co, Inc.

Hartt, Rollin L.
1909 *The People at Play*. Boston, MA: Houghton Mifflin.

Katz, Jonathan
1976 *Gay American History: Lesbians and Gay Men in the USA*. New York: Thomas Y. Crowell.

Nathan, George Jean
1972 [1928] *Art of the Night*. Rutherford, NJ: Farleigh Dickinson Press.

Sobel, Bernard
1931 *Burleycue: An Underground History of Burlesque Days*. New York: Farrar & Rinehart.

Toll, Robert
1976 *On With The Show*. New York: Oxford University Press.

Tuska, Jon
1973 *The Films of Mae West*. Secaucus, NJ: The Citadel Press.

West, Mae
1926 *SEX*. Unpublished manuscript held in the Mae West Collection, Manuscripts Division, Library of Congress, Washington, DC.
1927 *The Drag*. Unpublished manuscript held in the Mae West Collection, Manuscripts Division, Library of Congress, Washington, DC.

Zeidman, Irving
1967 *The American Burlesque Show*. New York: Hawthorn Books.

12.2 EXTRACTS FROM *CRIMINAL LAW AND PRACTICE OF THE STATE OF NEW YORK*—FRANK GILBERT

§ 1140a. Immoral plays and exhibitions and the use and leasing of real property therefor.

Any person who as owner, manager, director or agent or in any other capacity prepares, advertises, gives, presents or participates in, any obscene, indecent, immoral or impure drama, play, exhibition, show or entertainment, which would tend to the corruption of the morals of youth or others, and every person aiding or abetting such act, and every owner or lessee or manager of any garden, building, room, place or structure, who lessee or lets the same or permits the same to be used for the purposes of any such drama, play, exhibition, show or entertainment, knowingly, or who assents to the use of the same for any such purpose, shall be guilty of a misdemeanor.

§ 1530. Public nuisance defined.

A "public nuisance" is a crime against the order and economy of the state, and consists in unlawfully doing an act, or omitting to perform a duty, which act or omission:

1. Annoys, injures or endangers the comfort, repose, health or safety of any considerable number of persons; or,

2. Offends public decency; or,
3. Unlawfully interferes with, obstructs, or tends to obstruct, or renders dangerous for passage, a lake, or a navigable river, bay, stream, canal or basin, or a stream, creek or other body of water which has been dredged or cleared at public expense, or a public park, square, street or highway: or,
4. In any way renders a considerable number of persons insecure in life, or the use of property.

Subd. 2, Offends public decency.

A pantomime, symbolical of the retiring of a husband and wife, upon their wedding night, although unattended by improper language or actual exposure of the person, may be indictable as a public nuisance where it suggests indecency, excites impure imaginations and is calculated to corrupt public morals.

12.3 LEGAL PAPERS ON THE *SEX* TRIAL

Sex *opened at Daly's 63rd Street Theatre on April 26, 1926, and was raided on February 21, 1927, after 385 performances. The District Attorney argued that* Sex *was obscene and endangered the morals of youth. A jury found West and the other principals guilty. West was fined $500 and sentenced to ten days on Welfare Island. She had herself driven to jail in an open car carrying armloads of white roses, she claimed the warden let her keep her silk underwear, and she gave $1000 to the Mae West Memorial Library in the Women's House of Detention "Considering what* Sex *got me," she said, "a few days in the pen 'in' a $500 fine ain't too bad a deal."*

1, Case #168495, Grand Jury Indictment of Mae West, William Morganstern, James Timony, John Cort, The Moral Producing Company and the Cast of Actors.

LIST OF WITNESSES:

Patrick D. Kenneally, 3rd Division
Frank Keeney
John J. Byrnes
Adeline Leidzbach
Harry Cohen
Irving M. Feurelicht
Edward F. Cullebon
Ralph Pape

Filed, 2nd day of March, 1927. Pleads not guilty.

THE PEOPLE

vs.

Clarence William Morganstern
John Cort
James A. Timony
Mae West
Barry O'Neill
Eeda Von Beulow
Lyons Wickland
Pacie Ripple
Gordon Burby
David Hughes
Daniel J. Hamilton
Constance Morganstern
Ann Reader
Warren Sterling
Thomas V. Morrison
Alfred L. Rigali
John Coleman
Mary Morrisey
Ida Mantell
Conde Brewer
Ivan Jordan
Florence Doherty
Pete Segreto
Edward Elsner
63rd St. Theatres Limited Inc. and Moral Productions Corporation
Defendants

Joan H. Banton District Attorney

COURT OF GENERAL SESSIONS OF THE COUNTY OF NEW YORK.

THE GRAND JURY OF THE COUNTY OF NEW YORK, by this indictment, accuse THE SAID DEFENDANTS of the Crime of UNLAWFULLY PREPARING, ADVERTISING, GIVING, PRESENTING AND PARTICIPATING IN AN OBSCENE, INDECENT, IMMORAL AND IMPURE DRAMA, PLAY, EXHIBITION, SHOW AND ENTERTAINMENT, committed as follows:

The said defendants, on the fifth day of February, nineteen hundred twenty-seven, and for a long time prior thereto, and thence continuously to the date of the finding of this indictment, at a certain building and theatre in said county situate and known as Daly's Theatre, unlawfully did prepare, advertise, give, present and participate in an obscene, indecent, immoral and impure drama, play, exhibition, show and entertainment then and there called "SEX," a more particular description of which said drama, play, exhibition, show and entertainment would be offensive to this Court and improper to be spread upon the records thereof, wherefore such description is not here given, which said drama, play, exhibition, show and entertainment at all times herein mentioned would and did tend to the corruption of the morals of youth and others, and in such act and acts unlawfully [alone and with] each other the said defendants did then aid and abet; against the form of the statute in such case made and provided, and against the peace of the People of the State of New York and their dignity.

SECOND COUNT.

AND THE GRAND JURY AFORESAID, by this indictment, further accuse THE SAID DEFENDANTS of the Crime of MAINTAINING A PUBLIC NUISANCE, committed as follows:

The said defendants, at the time aforesaid, in the county aforesaid, contriving and wickedly intending, so far as in them lay, to debauch and corrupt the morals of youth and of other persons and to raise and create in their minds inordinate and lustful desires, unlawfully, wickedly and scandalously did keep and maintain a certain theatre and play house there commonly known as Daly's Theatre, for the purpose of exhibiting and exposing to the sight of any persons willing to see and desirous of seeing the same and of paying for admission into the said theatre, a certain wicked, lewd, scandalous, bawdy, obscene, indecent, infamous, immoral and impure exhibition, show and entertainment, being the same exhibition, show and entertainment described in the first count of this indictment, to which reference is hereby made, and in the said theatre, at the time aforesaid, did unlawfully, wickedly and scandalously, for lucre and gain, produce, present, exhibit and display the said exhibition, show and entertainment to the sight and view of divers and many people, all to the great offense of public decency, against the order and economy of the state and to the common nuisance of all the people; against the form of the statue in such case made and provided, and against the peace of the People of the State of New York and their dignity.

THIRD COUNT.

AND THE GRAND JURY AFORESAID, by this indictment, further accuse THE SAID DEFENDANTS of the Crime of UNLAWFULLY PERMITTING A PLACE TO BE USED FOR AN IMMORAL PLAY, committed as follows:

The said defendant, 63rd St. Theatres Ltd., Inc., at the time aforesaid, in the county aforesaid, was a corporation and the owner and manager of the building, place and theatre commonly known as Daly's Theatre, mentioned and described in the first count of this indictment, to which reference is hereby made; and then and there unlawfully, as such owner and manager, the said defendant corporation unlawfully and knowingly did lease, let, permit and assent to the said building, place and theatre unlawfully to be used for the purpose of the said wicked, lewd, scandalous, bawdy, obscene, indecent, infamous, immoral and impure exhibition, show and entertainment called *Sex*, being the same exhibition, show and entertainment mentioned and described in the first count of this indictment;

And all the other said defendants were then and there unlawfully concerned in the commission of the said unlawfully permitting a place to be used for an immoral play, and crime by the said defendant, 63rd St. Theatres Ltd., Inc., in the manner and form aforesaid, and did then and there unlawfully aid and abet the said defendant, 63rd St. Theatres Ltd., Inc., in the commission of the same in the manner and form aforesaid, and did then and there unlawfully counsel, command, induce and procure the said defendant, 63rd St. Theatres Ltd., Inc., the said unlawfully permitting a place to be used for an immoral play, and crime, in the manner and form aforesaid then and there to do and commit; against the form of the statute in such case made and provided, and against the peace of the People of the State of New York and their dignity.

JOAB H. BANTON,
District Attorney.

[Norman Schloss, Mae West's attorney, attempted to have the charges dismissed and then to have the case moved. Both efforts failed, and then he filed to have the case heard by a jury rather than by a three judge panel. The court agreed and the case was heard by a special jury in general sessions. With a flair for theatricality and comedy equal to Mae West's, Schloss defended *Sex* as a work of art comparable to *A Tale of Two Cities*, *Hamlet* and the *Bible*. —LS.]

4. The People vs. William Morganstern, Mae West, et al., #168495, City Magistrate's Court, 10th District, 2/15/27. Descriptions of the Scenes, Actions and Dialogue of the Play Provided the Basis for Its Prosecution.

The People vs. Wm. Morganstern

CITY MAGISTRATE'S COURT
BOROUGH OF MANHATTAN

THE PEOPLE OF THE STATE OF NEW YORK

on complaint of James S. Bolan,

against—

C. WILLIAM MORGANSTERN, EDWARD ELSNER, MAE WEST, BARRY O'NEILL, EEDA VON BEULOW, LYONS WICKLAND, PACIE RIPPLE, GORDON BURBY, DAVID HUGHES, D.J. HAMILTON, CONSTANCE MORGANSTERN, ANN READER, WARREN STERLING, THOMAS V. MORRISON, ALFRED L. RIGALI, FRANK R. WOOD, MARY MORRISEY, IDA MANTWELL, CONDE BREWER, FRED LE QUORNE, FLORENCE DOHERTY, AND PETE SEGRETO. DEFENDANTS

STATE OF NEW YORK

CITY AND COUNTY OF
NEW YORK

JAMES S. BOLAN, being duly sworn, deposes and says, I am a Deputy Inspector of the Police Department of the City of New York, On Saturday, February 5th, 1927, in the City and County of New York, and for a long time prior thereto, the defendants above unlawfully advertised, gave, presented and participated in, an obscene, indecent, immoral and impure drama, play, exhibition, show and entertainment which then and there tend to the corruption of the morals of youth and others, and committed unlawfully an act which then and there offended against public decency in that on the said date at a certain theatre and playhouse known as Daly's Theatre, situated there 24 West 63rd Street, the above named defendants unlawfully advertised, gave, presented and participated in a play then and there known as "Sex"; that said play then and there consisted of three certain "acts" and six "episodes," two "episodes" taking place in each act. "Episode" 1, as appears from the annexed programme, called Exhibit A, which deponent received at the time of his visit to said theatre, takes place in the living room of Margie LaMont in Montreal. The "episode" takes place in a room that purports to be for the encouragement of lewdness, fornication and unlawful sexual intercourses, and the defendant, Mae West, who appears in the character of Margie LaMont throughout said scene, portrays the character of a prostitute engaged in plying her trade at that place. In such scene or "episode" the defendant, Warren Sterling, who portrays the character of Rocky Waldron, takes the part of a pimp and procurer engaged in collecting moneys from such prostitutes who appear in the "episode," and the defendant, Gordon Burby, portrays character of one Dawson who, as a corrupt policeman, seeks to obtain "protection" money from the said pimp and prostitute. In the said "episode" the defendant Ann Reader portrays the character of Agnes Scott, another prostitute engaged in plying her trade in these premises thus exhibited. In the same "episode" the defendant D. J. Hamilton portraying the character of Ensign Jones, and Barry O'Neill portraying the character of Lieutenant Gregg, appear as patrons of this disorderly resort and the prostitutes aforesaid and endeavor to enter into arrangements with the said Mae West, in the character of Margie LaMont, to commit an act of prostitution with them.

The second "episode" takes place four hours later in the same disorderly resort. In it appears the same prostitute, Margie LaMont, portrayed by the defendant Mae West, the same Lieutenant Gregg, portrayed by defendant Barry O'Neill, the same Dawson, portrayed by defendant Gordon Burby, the same pimp, portrayed by Warren Sterling, and a new character who has not heretofore appeared, known as Clara Smith by the defendant Eeda Von Beulow. Clara Smith proves to be the wife of a wealthy man in Connecticut who is traveling without her husband and who informs the pimp, Rocky Waldron, in this "episode" that she is in Montreal looking for a thrill, and he solicits her to take him home with her. This married woman away from her husband then becomes friendly with the pimp, Rocky Waldron, and kisses him. He drugs and robs her; and it is at this point that the drunken prostitute, Margie LaMont, comes into the room with the drunken Lieutenant Gregg who, in "episode" 1 some four hours ago, had solicited her to have sexual intercourse with him. They had a conversation in which she invites him to stay for the evening, and he turns over to her a roll of money in bill form. She kisses him and sits on his lap. He then describes to her a trip that the fleet to which he is attached is to make to Trinidad and solicits this prostitute to accompany him on that trip. She thereupon dances before him in a way that causes him to grab her and say "You'd make a savage out of any man." Their attention is attracted to the character Clara Smith. The character Dawson enters and enquires as to the identity of the said Clara Smith, and upon the said Clara Smith informing the character, Dawson, that she was there as a result of what Margie LaMont had done, Margie LaMont threatens to get even with said Clara Smith and the act thereupon terminates.

Act II "episode" 1 takes place in the cafe in Hotel Port au Prince, Trinidad, to which place the prostitute, Margie LaMont, following out the request of Lieutenant Gregg, in "episode" 2, has come with Lieutenant Gregg. In this "episode" the prostitute dances before the sailors of the fleet and the officers in a way that causes Ensign Jones, the same character in which "episode" 1 had solicited Margie LaMont to commit an act of prostitution with him, to say "You'd make a bulldog break its chain," the said dance having been performed by the defendant Mae West by moving her buttocks and other parts of her body in such a way as to suggest an act of sexual intercourse. In this scene defendant Lyons Wickland, portraying the character of Jimmy Stanton, makes his appearance, He is introduced to the prostitute with whom he falls in love. The second "episode" in the same act takes place after an interval of one week and is at the same scene as "episode" 1 of that act. In these scene the same prostitute, Agnes Scott, portrayed by defendant Ann Reader, again appears and announces to the prostitute Margie LaMont that she had heard that Margie LaMont was following the fleet and doing well, and for that reason she had come along. Jimmy Stanton asked the prostitute Margie LaMont to marry him and it is arranged that Jimmy Stanton and Margie LaMont shall leave for the United States the following morning.

The first "episode" of Act III takes place in Robert Stanton's home in Westchester, Robert Stanton being the father of Jimmy Stanton. It is then discovered that the character, Clara Smith, who in "episode" 2 of Act 1 was the married woman away from her husband, brought into the disorderly house in Montreal by the pimp, Rocky Waldron, is the mother of Jimmy Stanton who is in love with the prostitute Margie LaMont. Mutual recriminations take place between the prostitute and the character of Clara Stanton, alias Clara Smith, in which after Clara Smith has called the prostitute a woman of the street, the prostitute, after announcing that hers was a profession followed to earn a living, tells the mother of the man whom she expects to marry that such mother was a prostitute except that the mother gave her virtue away without pay. At another point all the characters have left the scene except Jimmy Stanton and the prostitute Margie LaMont. Jimmy embraces Margie LaMont and goes through with her the business of making love to her by lying on top of her on a couch, each embracing the other. When this is terminated and Jimmy Stanton offers to call a maid to show the prostitute to her room, Margie LaMont answers "Can't you show me to my room?" The character Jimmy Stanton takes her to her room. On the threshold, after kissing and embracing, they step into that room and the scene ends.

Prior to the termination of the act, and at the same time of the talk referred to between the character Clara Stanton and Margie LaMont, Margie LaMont tells Clara Stanton that inasmuch as Clara Stanton had used the home of Margie LaMont in Montreal, she, Margie LaMont, intended to use Clara Stanton's home to have sexual intercourse with Jimmy Stanton and test out whether or not he really was in love with her. The language they used does not contain the words "sexual intercourse" but the purport and tenor of the business and language is to that effect.

"Episode" 2 of Act III takes place the following morning in the same scene and is opened by Jimmy Stanton stealing out of the prostitute's room into which he had gone as indicated at the end of the last act, after kissing and embracing her. In this last "episode" the pimp, Rocky Waldron, again appears, but the forgiving prostitute, Margie LaMont, upon his threatening to kill her, does not turn him over to the police but gives him another chance, so the pimp escapes justice. Margie LaMont confesses to Jimmy Stanton that she is a prostitute but indicates that she has reformed and is going to marry Lieutenant Gregg, the navy lieutenant who, in "episode" 1 and 2, solicited her to commit an act of prostitution with him.

The foregoing is a public performance at which the general public was admitted upon the payment of a price for tickets. At the time of my observing the said play, several hundred other persons were present of both sexes as part of the public audience watching the play. I was accompanied by Sergeant Patrick D. Keneally and Patrolman James T. Powers, both attached to the Third Division of the Municipal Police Department of the City of New York.

There is annexed hereto and made a part of this affidavit as Exhibit B a more detailed summary of what occurred during the play at the time of my visit and observation of the same with verbatim excerpts from and reports of dialogues that occurred in the course of the exhibition and play. The audience was not only of both sexes but was chiefly made up of young persons whose ages appeared to me to be between 17 and 20 years.

As appears from the said exhibit and hereto annexed, and from Exhibit C hereto annexed, the defendant C. William Morganstern advertises and presents, and the defendant Edward Elsner directs and at all times herein mentioned did advertise, present and direct the said play, exhibition and show. Exhibit C was at the time purchased in the lobby of the said theatre from persons who purported to be employees of the said theatre, by Sergeant Patrick D. Keneally, and Exhibit A was received from one of the ushers in the theatre as the programme of the play, after the tickets of admission had been presented to the person in charge of the gate and entrance obtained as a result thereof.

The corroborative affidavit of Sergeant Patrick D. Keneally and Patrolman James T. Powers, both of whom accompanied me at the time, are hereto annexed and made a part of this affidavit.

As to the other persons named as defendants and for whom warrants are sought, they each aided and abetted in that they played parts in the presentation of said play, exhibition and show, as appears from the exhibit marked "People's Exhibit A."

WHEREFORE deponent asks that warrants be issued for the arrest of the above named persons and that they may be dealt with according to law.

James S. Bolan
Subscribed and sworn to
before me this 9th
day of February 1927
William McAdoo
Chief City Magistrate

12.4 MAE WEST IN COURT

Mae West and Barry O'Neill, her co-star in *Sex*, on trial for obscenity at Jefferson Market Courthouse in 1927.

Source: Photo © Bettmann/Corbis

12.5 PRODUCTION PHOTO OF MAE WEST IN *SEX*

Mae West as Margy Lamont in *Sex*.

Source: Photo © Bettmann/Corbis

12.6 *SEX*—MAE WEST

THE CAST

Margy LaMont, a prostitute
Rocky Waldron, a pimp
Manly, a thug
Curley, a pimp
Dawson, an officer of the law
Agnes, a prostitute
Red, a prostitute
Flossie, a prostitute
Jones, a client
Lieutenant Gregg, an English naval officer
Captain Carter, an officer
Condez, host of the Cafe Port au Prince
Clara Stanton, a wealthy woman
Jimmy Stanton, her son
Robert Stanton, her husband
Marie, the Stantons' French maid
Jenkins, the Stantons' butler
Policeman
First Man, Second Man, Waiter

★

The action takes place in Montreal's red light district; a cafe in Trinidad; and in a wealthy home outside New York City. The role of Margy LaMont was played by Mae West.

★

Act One.	Scene One.	An "apartment" on Caidoux Street in Montreal.
	Scene Two.	The same.
Act Two.	Scene One.	Trinidad, the Cafe Port au Prince.
	Scene Two.	One week later.
Act Three.	Scene One.	The Stanton residence.
	Scene Two.	The same, the next day.

★

The copyright script of *Sex* is dated July 24, 1926, three months after the play opened at Daly's 63rd Street Theatre on April 26th. The cover page shows Mae West as author, but the play was originally attributed to Jane Mast, a pseudonym that was a combination of Matilda West's middle name and the first two letters of Mae West's given and surnames. The script was hastily typed—it contains a profusion of errors and inaccuracies.

The script offers no description of the set. In several places stage directions have been added where none appear.

SEX

ACT ONE

Scene One

An "apartment" MARGY *shares with the blackmailer* ROCKY *on Caidoux Street, in Montreal's notorious red light district. Night. The curtain rises in the middle of a conversation between* ROCKY *and* MANLY, *with* CURLEY *off to the side.*

ROCKY: You ought to be lousy with coin. You ain't depending on any particular lady friend for your jack. What's the matter, ain't the police giving you fifty-fifty on the graft you collect?

MANLY: Aw.

ROCKY: Don't try to tell me—

MANLY: Keep your shirt on—take a tip, old man, and watch your step.

ROCKY: What the—

MANLY: Who's the swell dame you been running around with the last week? Some class to you, picking up a jane at the Ritz—the police have got you spotted.

ROCKY: What do you know?

MANLY: The last one you picked up, she's the kind'll squeal.

ROCKY: I'll take the chance.

MANLY: Yeah? What's the lay?

ROCKY: What's it to you?

MANLY: That's enough.

ROCKY: Are you trying to shake me down?

MANLY: I'm giving you a tip straight.

ROCKY: You'll not get any of my money.

MANLY: Your money? (*Laughs.*)

ROCKY: Yes mine. And you stop butting into my affairs.

MANLY: Your affairs? Say you're none too safe here yourself—get that and get it straight.

ROCKY: Well, it'll take more than a low down graft collector like you to tell it to me.

MANLY: Yeah? Alright. If I can't collect I'll send someone in who will.

(*Exit* MANLY.)

ROCKY: Can you tie that, Curley?

CURLEY: Let him squawk. He's looking for a meal.

ROCKY: Come on, snap into it. Get some duds on and come up to the Ritz with me.

CURLEY: Not tonight, Rocky I'm broke.

ROCKY: With the British Fleet in the harbor—what's wrong? Agnes holding out on you—you should worry—Montreal is full of janes glad to supply the bank roll for a pretty kid like you.

CURLEY: I'm kinder used to Agnes, I'd hate to change now.

ROCKY: Ain't you the kind-hearted dearie.

CURLEY: Well I got no kick coming, I've got it pretty soft, Agnes don't hold out on me.

(*Enter* AGNES.)

ROCKY: Hello, Agnes.

AGNES: Oh, there you are Curley, I thought I'd find you here.

CURLEY: Alright dear, I'll be right with you.

AGNES: Where's Margy?

ROCKY: In her room, I guess she's awake.

(*Exit* AGNES.)

CURLEY: I'll see you later Rocky. (*Opens door.*) Here comes Dawson.

(*Enter* DAWSON.)

DAWSON: (*Enters*): Hello.

(*Enter* AGNES.)

ROCKY: Hello Dawson.

CURLEY: Hello Dawson.

AGNES: Hello Dawson.

CURLEY: I'll be around tomorrow Rocky. Goodnight.

(*Exit* CURLEY *and* AGNES.)

DAWSON: Business must be good the way you got this dump all dolled up.

ROCKY: Don't call this joint a dump.

DAWSON: I met Manly outside and he said you were a pretty tough customer.

ROCKY: Yeah?

DAWSON: If you think you can run this joint without giving [it] up, you've got another think coming.

ROCKY: Look here, Dawson, I'm a pretty good sort of scout, but I don't like being hounded by a guy like Manly.

DAWSON: Cut the argument and pay up.

ROCKY: Pay up? Hey Margy! Margy!

MARGY: What do you want?

ROCKY: Come out here. Pay up.

MARGY (*Enters*): Well, what's all the noise?

ROCKY: Dawson wants [his] commission.

MARGY: Commission? Is that all he wants? Let him try and get it.

DAWSON: Now look here—You listen to me.

MARGY: Just a minute, I don't want any unnecessary noise around here. I had a pretty busy night last night and my nerves need quiet. (*She lights a cigarette.*)

DAWSON: What do you think this is? An ash can? Don't try to pull that wise stuff on me. You been getting away with murder.

MARGY: I don't see why I should pay for the privilege of working. You got about all you're going to get out of me.

DAWSON: Well, if that's the way you feel about it, we'll see how far you get.

MARGY: Don't slam the door on the way out.

(*Exit* DAWSON. *Door slams.*) He did.

ROCKY: Looks like he's going to start something.

MARGY: Well, he can start it and I'll finish it. How many times have I told you to keep him out of here?

ROCKY: Well, I didn't ask him to come up. Where are my collars? (*Exits. Calls from offstage:*) Hey Marge, where are my collars? Marge, come on and find them for me.

MARGY: Find them yourself, they're your collars.

ROCKY: Why don't you leave things where I put them? (*Enters.*) You didn't even put buttons on my shirt.

MARGY: What do you think I am, your wife? The trouble with you, you've been spoiled. Too many janes been waiting on you. Here's one jane don't fall for that stuff.

ROCKY: Is that so?

MARGY: If there's any waiting on around here, I'm the one that's going to get it. I'm a jane that craves service.

ROCKY: Ain't you funny.

MARGY: Don't wise crack at me, because I'm about ready to give you the air.

ROCKY: Give me the air? Give me the air? You can't get away with that so easy.

MARGY: No?

ROCKY: Not after what I've done for you.

MARGY: What did you ever do for me?

ROCKY: Say, who meets the guys and steers them down here to you? Me. Who's the business head of this here dump? Me. Who raised your price? Me. And you want to know what I did? I started you didn't I? Yes, and I didn't only start you, I made you, get me I made you.

MARGY: You made me what I am today, I hope you're satisfied. I'll admit you're a great guy and all that.

ROCKY: You do admit I'm a great guy.

MARGY: Oh, without question. But just the same, I'm getting tired of you and this dump.

ROCKY: Not good enough for you, eh?

MARGY: Oh, I'm going somewhere where I can play around with the heavy sugar daddies and see life and get something for it, instead of sitting around here night after night waiting for your cheap bunch.

ROCKY: Gee, getting high brow. Want to play rich. You're alright where you are.

MARGY: Think so?

ROCKY: Getting some fool ideas about bein' decent, eh?

MARGY: Suppose I am.

ROCKY: Baby, you'll never be anything but what you are. So that's that.

MARGY: If a jane like Nan Chalmers can do it, I certainly can.

ROCKY: You mean that gal that used to live next door?

MARGY: Yes. She had a guy she thought she was in love with and thought she needed and then she got wise. Now she's married to an old guy, and she's got a mansion up near Boston and a limousine and diamonds and everything she wants.

ROCKY: And wait until the old gink finds out what she is. Watch him unload her.

MARGY: How's he going to find out?

ROCKY: Easy kid, easy. Plenty of nice people ready to spill the good news.

MARGY: But suppose he really loves her?

ROCKY: Don't make me laugh. It can't be done. Anyway, his friends and family won't stand for it. Listen, you lose this idea about being decent. Stick to your trade, kid, you were made for it. Rocky wouldn't steer you wrong.

MARGY: No, Rocky wouldn't steer me wrong. Rocky's just a wise guy, at least he thinks he is. Anyway my mind's made up and that's that. What's the idea of dolling up? You look like you have a heavy date. Meetin' the society dame Manly was talking about? The one you picked up at the opera?

ROCKY: You can't tell, maybe yes, maybe no.

MARGY: Well good luck to you—you'll need it.

ROCKY: She knows a nifty guy when she sees one. I'm class, babe. Just look at that figure.

MARGY: Take it to her and let her look at it. I'm tired of looking at it.

ROCKY: There's plenty of dames ready to take me in.

MARGY: White ones? Just take the tooth brush and park the body some place else.

ROCKY: Where are you going tonight?

MARGY: I don't know.

ROCKY: What time are you coming back?

MARGY: I don't know. Maybe I won't come back at all.

ROCKY: Now don't pull that stuff on me, because you aren't going to get away from me so easy. You're mine and you belong to me. You try to get away from me and I'll plant you under the daisies.

MARGY: What are you trying to do? Scare someone? Just because you croaked a guy and got away with it don't think I'm afraid of you. You know if I start talking, I can put a rope around that lily white neck of yours.

ROCKY: You wouldn't dare squawk on a fellow for that. Besides, I know you too well. You haven't the heart to turn anyone up. If I thought you had, I'd finish you now. I won't get any more for killing two than I will for killing one.

MARGY: Don't be too sure about that. Now I'm going to give you a little inside information—I'm going to leave you the first chance I get.

ROCKY: What are we doing, telling jokes to each other? Get that idea out of your head about leaving me, because if you did, I'd go get you. Lose this idea about being decent. You're just what you are and that's all you ever will be. There's only one thing about you to hold a guy, and outside of that you're merely nothing. Want to give Rocky a little kiss before he goes, you beautiful thing you?

MARGY: Go kiss your society dame.

(*Enter AGNES.*)

ROCKY: Thanks. (*Exits.*)

MARGY: Hello kid.

AGNES: Margy, I just wanted to give you some more money to keep for me. There's five there.

MARGY: Alright, I'll put it with the rest.

AGNES: I don't know what I'd do if it wasn't for you. You can't trust anyone.

MARGY: Good motto, Agnes. Trust no one and you'll never be gyped.

AGNES: I wonder what Curley would do if he ever found out?

MARGY: What, that you are putting little away for yourself? Don't suppose I hand over the day's receipts to Rocky.

AGNES: No, it ain't only that. I'm planning to go away as soon as I have enough.

MARGY: Going where?

AGNES: Back home.

MARGY: Home? Do you think you can get away with it?

AGNES: Why not? They think I'm working for a living.

MARGY: Well ain't you?

AGNES: I manage to send them a few dollars once in a while.

MARGY: Listen Agnes. They'll find out and then it will be worse than this for you.

AGNES: Home. It seems like years since I've been there.

MARGY: You've spilled the tale about the old folks and the little white cottage so often, kid, I can almost see the place. What's the use of breaking their hearts as well as your own?

AGNES: But I can't go on. I—Oh, Margy, I wasn't meant for this sort of thing.

MARGY: If I was as dissatisfied as you are I'd join the Salvation Army.

FIRST MAN: (*Knocks. MARGY opens the door*): Hello Margy.

MARGY: I'm sorry, but I'm not entertaining tonight.

FIRST MAN: I come down extra to see you. Can't you help a fellow out?

MARGY: I'm sorry.

FIRST MAN: But listen girlie—

MARGY: Good night.

FIRST MAN: Jees. (*Closes door.*)

(*Church bells. AGNES cries.*)

MARGY: Well, what's the matter?

AGNES: Those bells, every time they ring it seems as if—Oh I—can't stand it Margy, I can't stand it. Back home the little old church—

MARGY: Don't give me that church business again. You'll have me going back to the old homestead.

AGNES: Oh, Margy, if you'd only understand.

MARGY: I understand that you got to get a grip on yourself or you'll never get anywhere.

AGNES: Anywhere in this life?

MARGY: Why not? There's a chance of rising to the top of every profession.

AGNES: Profession? You call this—Oh Gawd.

MARGY: Yes, I said rising to the top of my profes-sion. Why not? Others do it, why can't I? Why can't you? When I think of the dames riding around in swell limousines, buying imported gowns, living at the swellest hotels, terrible looking janes, too. You know if I have to I can put on the ritz, too. Course I don't pull that stuff around here, not at these prices. And there's nothing the matter with you. You're a pretty refined kid. Come from good folks, at least you say you do. It's all a question of getting some guy to pay for the certain business, that's all.

AGNES: Oh, that's what you mean to do?

MARGY: That's what I'm going to do. I'm sick of this town and everything in it.

AGNES: Yeah, and how are you going to find the rich man?

MARGY: Advertise for him in the daily papers. Tack a sign up around the town for him. Say, either you're so wise we can't catch up with you or you're the original Dumb Dora.

AGNES: Oh, I see what you mean.

MARGY: Oh, you do.

AGNES: I'm sorry I made you angry, Margy. You've been pretty good to me and when I get back home—

MARGY: When you get back home, old girl, you'll be buying a through ticket back here, mark my words. They won't let you go straight. They'll hold you up as an example. I tried it. I know.

AGNES: You're wrong, Margy, and maybe some day—

MARGY: Yeah, and until that some day comes, I'm satisfied to be wrong. Going out tonight?

AGNES: No I'm staying in with Curley. I feel I'm kinder doing him wrong, leaving him like this, and that's what's holding me back.

MARGY: Curley?

AGNES: Yes, he'd be lost without me.

MARGY: The lost and found department will take care of him alright.

AGNES: I loved him Margy in the beginning and—

MARGY: Loved him in the beginning, and you thought you couldn't live without him, and then you found out you couldn't live with him. That's the trouble with women like us. They have a tag on them. Go it alone Agnes, there's more chance of getting ahead.

AGNES: I'll leave Curley enough money—

MARGY: Let the big bum go to work.

AGNES: But he ain't very strong, Marge.

MARGY: Would be tough on that guy if he had to get a job for himself. Well you run along to your Curley, I've got to fix this dress up.

AGNES: Alright, goodnight Marge.

MARGY: Good night.

(*RED and FLOSSIE knock.*)

MARGY: Open up that door and let's see what this is. (*AGNES opens door.*) (*Enter RED and FLOSSIE.*)

AGNES: My goodness, it's fighting Red.

RED: Say, I want to talk to you!

MARGY: Well, shoot, what is it?

RED: I want you to lay off my man.

MARGY: Which one?

RED: Sailor Dan from Kansas.

MARGY: Sailor Dan from Kansas? Never heard of him.

RED: Oh, yes you have.

MARGY: I'll tell you whether I have or not. Hey Aggie, over on that table you'll find a little book.

AGNES: No, it ain't here.

MARGY: Red, you look in the second drawer, and Flossie give us a cigarette. (*AGNES takes things out of the drawer.*) Hey, just the book, just the book. Sailor Dan from Kansas . . . oh, sailor Dan from Kansas. Yeah Sailor Dan from Kansas, flat feet, asthma, check came back, oh, baby, I'll make you a present of that bird. He's yours.

RED: Well, you better.

MARGY: Now, don't be a girl like that.

MARGY: Say Floss, do you still go around with Oklahoma Jack?

FLOSSIE: Oh, he got married.

MARGY: Yes, but you didn't answer my question.

RED AND FLOSSIE: Well, the nerve of her—(*Ad lib and exit.*)

AGNES: Good night, Marge.

MARGY: Good night. (*Exit AGNES.*)

(*A knock.*):

MARGY: Come in.

JONES (*Enters*): Well, well, if it isn't the beautiful blonde mamma they're all raving about. I always did like blondes. I don't care how they get that way, just so long as they're blondes.

MARGY: Sorry, but you'll have to go.

JONES: You don't mean to tell me you're going to give me the gate? Oh, mamma, you don't know what you're missing.

MARGY: You wouldn't fool me?

JONES: If I go now, can I come back later?

MARGY: Yeah, you can come back.

JONES: In one hour I'll be back to the girl I left behind me. Oh, baby, I've got something you want.

MARGY: You wouldn't fool me?

JONES: Listen kid, Jones is my moniker, clean underwear and everything. Over the river. (*Exits.*)

(*Phone rings.*)

MARGY: Hello, hello. Oh hello there, kid, how are you? Great, great. Where are you? Where? Oh the Tremaine Cafe. Who's with you? Who? Oh, and how! Yeah. Oh, in about fifteen minutes. Well, say, I've got to get dressed. Yeah, alright. Goodbye kid.

GREGG (*Knocks and enters*): Hello, Marge. How are you?

MARGY: When did you get in?

GREGG: Oh, I got into port this morning. Couldn't think of spending my shore leave with anyone but you, old gal. Warm in here. Mind if I take my jacket off?

MARGY: Sorry, but I'm not entertaining company tonight, Gregg.

GREGG: Oh, don't consider me company. Just treat me as one of the family. I'm back with three months pay and aching for a good time. You and I'll have plenty of sport.

MARGY: I'm in no mood for sport, Gregg.

GREGG: Oh, you're out of sorts. Anything on your mind?

MARGY: You wouldn't understand.

GREGG: I'd hate to say you're not telling the truth, but you are out of sorts. I'll just play a tune on the jolly old music box, that'll cheer you up a bit.

MARGY: Gregg, if you want to do me a favor, you'll get out of here as quick as you can.
GREGG: Now, you don't mean that.
MARGY: Do I look as if I were kidding?
GREGG: What's the matter? Some of the neighbors' kids been stealing your marbles?
MARGY: What is that supposed to be—one of your English wisecracks?
GREGG: No, no. It's rather clever though. Don't be angry with me, old dear. I didn't mean any harm, just couldn't resist the temptation of a bright remark. Oh, I've got something for you, wait until you see this, wait until you see this.
MARGY: Well, come on and let's see it.
GREGG: You'll get it, you'll get it. I don't mind telling you I had an awful time saving it for you. Why all the women were fighting for it.
MARGY: It better be good.
GREGG: It's good alright. It's the best you could get, but you've got to be very careful not to bend it.

(*Produces the feather of a bird of paradise.*)

MARGY: What a bird, what a bird! How did you know I wanted one?
GREGG: Oh, I know your little weaknesses.
MARGY: You know too much. Where did you get it, honey?
GREGG: Away down south.
MARGY: Won't I burn the janes up when I wear this!
GREGG: Now you're happy, suppose you spill the trouble.
MARGY: Oh, you wouldn't understand.
GREGG: Never can tell, old gal.
MARGY: I'm sick of this town and everything that goes with it. Damn him.
GREGG: Oh the gentleman friend, eh?
MARGY: Gentleman—hell. You're the first one to ever call him that!
GREGG: Well of course, I never met him. Why don't you chuck the bugger? Leave him and travel around a bit. You'd soon forget him. Good lord, gal, I've forgotten a hell of a lot in the same way. I'm serious about this travelling around. It would be good for you. But maybe you don't care for travelling.
MARGY: The way I feel now I'd take a trip to hell if I could get a return ticket.
GREGG: Oh well, I don't expect to go as far as that at present. But seriously speaking, you could make a lot of money travelling around with me. All the gals who are following the fleet are getting rich, and besides they see the world and its ceilings.
MARGY: Sounds good. I'll think it over.
GREGG: Oh it's a sweet existence. I wish I were a gal. You know I'd love to meet up with you in every port I go into. And I could help you a lot by dropping a word here and there among the boys.
MARGY: Sort of an agent.
GREGG: Oh, I wouldn't put it like that. But maybe you and I could hit it up together, eh?
MARGY: What are you trying to do, set yourself in for a home?
GREGG: No, no.
MARGY: Never mind. You wouldn't be the first.

(*Knock.* MARGY *opens the door.*)

SECOND MAN: Hello dearie, don't you remember me?
MARGY: No, I don't remember you.
SECOND MAN: What, you mean to say you don't remember me?
MARGY: No, you yellow-bellied piece of cheese, I don't remember you!
SECOND MAN: Yellow-bellied? I thought you said you didn't remember me?

(GREGG *shuts the door hard.*)

MARGY (*to* GREGG): What are you doing?
GREGG: Locking up.
MARGY: What's the idea?
GREGG: These interruptions are damned annoying. We don't want to be disturbed. I expect to be here for a long time.
MARGY: Well, you're out of luck.
GREGG: Just exactly what do you mean?
MARGY: I'm going out.
GREGG: I'd hate to be disappointed. I put myself out a lot to come and see you, I don't mind telling you.
MARGY: That's your hard luck. Here's your jacket.
GREGG: Oh, I say.
MARGY: Come on. Put it on.
GREGG: You can't really mean that, you know.
MARGY: No, I'm just exercising my lungs.
GREGG: Well, of course, if you insist. Just to show you I'm not a bad sort, I'll take you down to the Black Cat Cafe and spend the money I was going to spend here.
MARGY: Alright, only I'll let you take me to the Tremaine instead.
GREGG: Anywhere you say, old dear.
MARGY: Take that key out of the door. Put it on the outside.
GREGG: But I say old dear, it's a hell of a trick to lay on a fellow.

(MARGY *takes his arm and they exit together.*)

CURTAIN

Scene Two

Later that evening. The same room. Lights dim. ROCKY *leads* CLARA*, his "society dame," into the apartment. He looks around suspiciously.*

ROCKY (*Enters*): Oho—Oho. Alright, come right in. I thought maybe some of my friends were parked around here. I'm good natured and they take advantage of it.

(*CLARA enters.*)

CLARA: It's rather dark in here.

ROCKY: Just a minute and I'll light up. (*Lights come up.*) There we are.

CLARA: What an interesting place you have.

ROCKY: Oh, the diggings ain't so bad. Sit down and make yourself comfortable. You're going to be right at home here, you know.

CLARA: I feel very much at home already.

ROCKY: Let me take your wraps.

CLARA: Thank you.

ROCKY: Sit down and make yourself comfortable. Nothin' swell about this joint, but you can do as you please, and there's no one to put a damper on the works.

CLARA: It's so wonderful here in Montreal, I'd like to stay here forever.

ROCKY: Is this your first visit to the town?

CLARA: Yes.

ROCKY: Well I'm going to fix it so you won't forget it as long as you live. Where is your home?

CLARA: My home is in Connecticut.

ROCKY: You're fibbing to me, but it's alright. I can stand for almost anything from a woman as beautiful as you are.

CLARA: You do say the nicest things.

ROCKY: Thanks. When are you going to tell me your real name?

CLARA: I have told you. Clara Smith is my real name.

ROCKY: A two-year-old would know that was phoney.

CLARA: What's in a name? I'm here with you.

ROCKY: That ought to be enough for any man.

CLARA: You have the most persuasive ways.

ROCKY: So you won't tell me what your real name is?

CLARA: You must not ask me so many questions. I'm here to enjoy myself.

ROCKY: And believe me, you're going to have the time of your young life. We'll start off with a little drink, that's always a good start for any party. How about it, Clara dear?

CLARA: Clara dear?

ROCKY: You must get used to me getting familiar like.

CLARA: You do say the cutest things.

ROCKY: Thanks. How about that drink?

CLARA: Yes. I believe I would enjoy a drink.

ROCKY: You'll enjoy this alright, pure Canadian Club, and it's got a kick like a mule. Drink.

CLARA: This is so thrilling. I love it because it's so . . . unconventional.

ROCKY: It's worse than that. There's nothing like sneaking away and stealing a march once in a while, is there?

CLARA: It's wonderful!

ROCKY: I knew you'd love a thrill so I'm going to give you one. Do you know what street this house is on?

CLARA: No.

ROCKY: It's on Caidoux Street. You've heard of Caidoux Street, haven't you?

CLARA: I don't believe I have.

ROCKY: Well Caidoux Street is most notorious street in Montreal. It's in the heart of the red light district.

CLARA: How perfectly thrilling.

ROCKY: I knew that would strike you right.

CLARA: It's such a departure from the usual course of life! So daring!

ROCKY: Anything for a thrill, dear. A new sensation, eh? I bet you get plenty of them on these little trips, eh?

CLARA: Anything to get away from the dull, monotonous routine in my daily existence. Always doing the same thing in the same way. Seeing the same people day in and day out almost drives me insane. Yes, I do enjoy a little fling once in a while. It sort breaks the monotony.

ROCKY: I'm sure lucky to have met you, and it's me that knows it.

CLARA: You say the most wonderful things.

ROCKY: Not half as wonderful as I'd like to say to you. But I suppose after you leave Montreal I'll never see you again. What a beautiful soft hand you have. Gee, this is funny. Here I am falling in love with a married woman, and when you get back home and meet your husband, I fade right out of the picture. You'll forget you ever met me, and I'll be here in Montreal just pining away.

CLARA: Don't be foolish. You're certainly not falling in love with a woman almost old enough to be—well, anyway, you know, is much older than you.

ROCKY: What's age got to do with it? You're wonderful. You need someone like me, someone to cheer you up and say nice things to you. Someone who understands you. Someone who would really appreciate y ou.

CLARA: Yes, I know I do. I'm neglected too much. You see, I'm married to a tired businessman who gives all his time to making money, and who's years my senior.

I have everything that money can buy, every luxury, but the one thing I need most of all—love. Of course you understand.

ROCKY: Let's have another drink. I know just how you feel, dear.

CLARA: Dear? Oh don't make it quite so strong. I'm not used to being petted in that way, my dear boy. You think we are quite safe here?

ROCKY: Why, honey, what do you mean?

CLARA: I mean safe from intrusion. You know, in such a notorious district I'm afraid the police may come in.

ROCKY: Don't worry about that, honey. After you drink this next drink you won't give a rap if the whole Montreal police force comes in.

CLARA: But suppose they did come and there was a scandal? Think of my poor husband.

ROCKY: What's a husband or two among friends? Wrap yourself around this. Atta girl. A few minutes from now and you won't care for a whole flock of husbands.

CLARA: Wasn't that drink terribly strong?

ROCKY: Of course not. Come on over here, babe, and let's get together. Now, I'd like to be around you all the time. Can't you take me back home with you?

CLARA: Why, you silly boy, how could I? My husband would find out.

ROCKY: Couldn't I play chauffeur to you or some other excuse to be around you? I'll promise you a new thrill every day, babe.

CLARA: You say the sweetest things.

(*They kiss.*)

ROCKY: Come on, let's have another drink.

CLARA: No, I think I've had too much already. I'm not used to drinking so fast—I feel sick.

ROCKY: Right over there babe. Help yourself.

(*Exit* CLARA *to bathroom. After a pause she reenters.*)

CLARA: Oh dear, I'm sick, I feel terrible.

ROCKY: Come here, dear. Is my baby feeling sick? Sit down and I'll give you something that will fix you fine. Just this one drink is what you need.

CLARA: No, no, I don't want any more.

ROCKY: But dear, you must take this one, it's just what you need. It'll fix you proper. I'll take good care of you, babe.

CLARA: You say the nicest things.

ROCKY: That's the way—you'll be perfect in a moment.

CLARA: I hope so.

ROCKY: I know so.

CLARA: I'm getting so dizzy—everything is just blank—I feel like I'm in space.

ROCKY: Feel like you're passing out?

CLARA: Oh dear—I—I—

(CLARA *faints.* ROCKY *leads her staggering off toward the bedroom.*)

AGNES (*Outside*): Margy Margy. (*She enters.*)

MARGY (*Enters with* GREGG *in conversation*): Oh hello, kid.

AGNES: I thought I heard someone in here, Margy.

MARGY: Wait till I light up. Maybe Rocky's back.

GREGG: Then maybe I'd better go.

MARGY: I'm paying the freight on this joint, and what I say goes. Come on and have a drink with us Agnes. Agnes lives across the hall. Her idea of a good time is listening to the church bells ring and having a good cry. She's all right when you know her. Sit down.

GREGG: Anything you say. You're the boss.

MARGY: You bet your sweet life I am. Anything I say around here goes. Ain't that right, Agnes?

AGNES: Yes.

MARGY: Take off your jacket and stay.

GREGG: On the level? Here take this. (*Gives her money.*)

MARGY: What's this for?

GREGG: Saves you the trouble of taking it while I'm asleep.

MARGY: You're thoughtful, anyway.

GREGG: I always go the easiest way about everything.

MARGY: What a man, what a man . . . (*They kiss.*) Pardon me, pardon me while I go down to the English Channel. (*They kiss again.*) Now to show you I'm a good sport, I'll have a drink.

GREGG: That's a jolly good idea.

MARGY: That is, if the boy friend hasn't made love to it.

GREGG: This boy friend seems to be sort of a necessity.

MARGY: Not a necessity. A luxury. Where are you going?

AGNES: I'm afraid that Curley might miss me.

MARGY: Do him good.

AGNES: If you don't mind I'd rather—

MARGY: Goin to crab the party?

AGNES: I'd like to. Good night, Margy.

MARGY: I told you her idea of a good time, didn't I?

GREGG: I think she's jolly considerate three's always a crowd.

MARGY: So long as you're satisfied I don't care. (*They drink.*)

GREGG: Cheerio! You know, Margy, we go on quite a trip from here. Panama, Cuba and Trinidad, and I was thinking how wonderful it would be if I could meet you there. You know, what we were talking about, following the fleet. I wish you'd do that.

MARGY: Trinidad? What kind of a jungle is it?

GREGG: It's an island just north of South America.

MARGY: Oh, where the parrots and the monkeys come from?

GREGG: It's a place where you can live cheap. Why down there you can get a room and bath, a wife and a bottle of liquor for two dollars.

MARGY: It must be bum liquor.

GREGG: It's a place where a girl like you would make a fortune. Say, think it over. All the girls down there are half breeds or a bit off-color. It's the place for a girl like you. You'd coin money.

MARGY: I'll think it over, old dear. I promise you I will, on my word.

GREGG: I wish you would, you don't know how much I want you. Damn you, you don't know how much I want to be with you. You know every time I go to Montreal I spend my shore leave with you, and I could do the same thing any place we go to. (*They kiss.*) Where are you going?

MARGY: I'm goin' to put on a good hot tune and have a little dance.

GREGG: By Jove, you're certainly showing me a good time!

MARGY: Baby, you're goin' to write this night down in your diary in red ink. (*They dance.*)

GREGG: I'm good on swimming, but short on stepping.

MARGY: Have another drink.

GREGG: God girl, you're beautiful, you've got the kind of beauty that makes a savage out of man. Make feel as though he'd like to take you in his arms and tear and crush you.

(*CLARA groans offstage.*)

GREGG: What's that?

MARGY: What's what?

GREGG: I thought I heard someone groan.

MARGY: Oh, you're the greatest guy for hearing things. (*CLARA groans again. MARGY opens door of bedroom and looks inside.*) Well I'll be damned.

GREGG: What's up?

MARGY: He's pulled something. (*GREGG follows MARGY to bedroom door.*)

GREGG: Who is she? One of your lady-friends?

MARGY: I'll bet it's that society jane.

GREGG: This is hardly the place for a society woman. Is she drunk?

MARGY: He's given her the works.

GREGG: He's what?

MARGY: Given her the works.

GREGG: He's given her what?

MARGY: He's doped her. Don't you understand English?

GREGG: Doped her. This is awkward.

MARGY: A fine mess the dirty rat left on my hands. He's given her enough stuff to kill a mule.

GREGG: You don't mean to tell me there's a possibility of the woman dying?

MARGY: Sure there is. That's why he made a quick getaway. Quick, get her off the floor.

(*GREGG carries CLARA to the chaise lounge. MARGY exits to bathroom.*)

GREGG: Don't let her die, old thing, she's a fine looking woman.

MARGY (*Enters with bottle*): If this don't bring her round, it's lillies for her.

GREGG: That gentleman friend of yours must be a nice playmate.

MARGY: Don't talk. Rub her hand and rub it good.

GREGG: He was a generous dog, he gave her plenty of the stuff while he was about it. How could he do this? He gave her enough to kill her.

MARGY: Because he's a rat and always will be. Hold her head back while I . . .

GREGG: I think she's coming to.

MARGY: Get some cold water and bathe her face. (*GREGG exits. To CLARA.*) Come on and take this. (*GREGG enters with glass of water. To GREGG.*) Don't spill it all over her.

GREGG: She's bloomin' lucky to be among those present.

CLARA: Where am I? Where am I?

MARGY: You know damn well where you are.

CLARA (*Coming to*): Oh, I'm so sick.

MARGY: That's what you get for fooling around like this. You came here for a thrill. You got one, but not the kind you expected. Serves you right.

GREGG: I say, old dear, don't you think you're rather rough on the poor thing?

MARGY: Rough on her? She ain't getting half what she deserves. She's one of those respectable society dames who poses as decent, and is looking for the first chance to cheat without being found out.

GREGG: Well, old dear, you can't blame her. All of us are looking for a little party at times.

DAWSON (*Enters*): Hello, Marge.

MARGY: Oh, hello.

GREGG: Pardon me, old thing, I think you're intruding.

MARGY: Lay off you fool, he's a cop.

GREGG: Oh, a Bobby.

DAWSON: Officer of the law. It sounds better. What's coming off here? Manly said he saw Rocky coming out of here with a grip in his hand.

MARGY: That ain't a crime, is it?

DAWSON: He said Rocky was in a pretty big hurry, so I thought I'd come up and see what all the haste was about.

MARGY: Had a date, perhaps.

DAWSON: Yeah? Who's the dame?

MARGY: A lady friend of mine.

DAWSON: A lady friend of yours? Don't look much like the sort of company you keep. That looks more like your speed over there.

GREGG: Thanks for the compliment, old thing.

DAWSON: Save your comedy till you get back to the fleet. You have a variety of friends, haven't you? This one looks like she was all in. What's wrong with her? Is she sick?

MARGY: She's not feeling well.

DAWSON: Too bad, poor thing. Stop stalling. Come clean. What's the game?

MARGY: No game that I know of.

DAWSON: What's this woman doing in your place?

MARGY: Paying me a visit.

DAWSON: Don't look much like she's enjoying her visit. Well, if you won't tell me what the play is, maybe she will. Hey you—what are you doing with this pair of crooks?

GREGG: Pardon me, old thing, we may be a bit loose, but we're not crooks.

DAWSON: That's enough from you. Well, out with it now. What's the idea? What are you doing here? Do you know what kind of house you're in?

CLARA: Why—I—I—

DAWSON: The truth, lady. It's the best way out.

CLARA: Why, sir, I was lured here.

DAWSON: By whom?

CLARA (*Pointing to MARGY*): By that woman there. She brought me here. She told me a pitiful tale, then she gave me something to drink. After that I don't remember. My jewels—they are gone!

MARGY: She's a dirty liar!

DAWSON: You shut up.

MARGY: No I won't shut up! She's lying to you do you hear? She's trying to make me the goat. But she can't do it! She's ashamed to tell you why she came here, but I will. She came here with Rocky. She came here with him so that he could make her!

DAWSON: Wait—you needn't tell me what she came here for. I know.

GREGG: Pardon me—

DAWSON: You stay where you are. We're going on a little sightseeing tour and you're going to be one of the party. Now you women get your wraps.

CLARA: You're not going to arrest me, are you?

DAWSON: I'm going to take you to headquarters for further investigation.

CLARA: No, no, don't do that please! The publicity would ruin me! Isn't there some way I could fix this with you?

DAWSON: Well, perhaps.

CLARA: I understand. (*She hands money to DAWSON.*)

MARGY: No you don't. This dame is going to take her medicine even if I have to go to jail.

DAWSON: You mind your own business or *you will* go to jail. I'm on to this game; Rocky's been up to his old tricks again. If I take you two, it means I get Rocky. You won't want him in jail, because you know what he'd do to you when he got out. Come on Miss, I'll see you safely out of the district. And as for you, you better take a little tip and blow. Montreal is getting a little hot for you. That's just a hint, and you'd better take it.

MARGY: Just a minute (*She faces CLARA.*) You were almost dead when I found you in this room. I brought you back to life, and you try to frame me to save yourself. I don't count, I suppose, because I'm what I am, but I'll tell you something. I'll remember this night as long as I live. And if I ever get a chance, I'll get even with you, you dirty charity, I'll get even.

CURTAIN

ACT TWO

Scene One

The Cafe Port au Prince in Trinidad. The scene begins with musical numbers. The company sings "Sailor's Sweetheart," followed by solo choruses and specialty dances. The entire company dances the finale. Onstage, CONDEZ, sailors.

JONES (*Entering*): Oh señor Condez.

CONDEZ: Cómo está usted señor?

JONES: I thought this affair was going to be over at the Casino.

CONDEZ: No, no, no, no, señor, I told you the Cafe Port au Prince. You like it?

JONES: And who is giving the affair?

CONDEZ: We are giving this in honor of the boys of the fleet.

JONES: Some fellow to give an affair like this. I think I'll stay a while.

CONDEZ: Sí, sí. There is a table some place.

JONES: Thank you, I'll sit over here.

(*Musical numbers "Bells of the Sea," "I'm Sorry, Dear." Soprano and baritone solos; "Castles in Spain," tango by sailor and one of the fleet women.*)

(*Enter GREGG and MARGY, who are greeted by JONES.*)

JONES: Hello there, lieutenant. Sit down and have a drink. I've been looking for you. Say, isn't that the baby from Montreal? (*MARGY turns.*) Well, well, if it isn't the beautiful blonde mamma from Montreal.

MARGY: Well, if it isn't the loud-speaking papa. Who is your friend, Gregg?

GREGG: Name is Jones.

MARGY: Jones?

JONES: Yes, you remember me, baby.

MARGY: Now could I ever forget you?

JONES: That was some wait you gave me that night in Montreal. If the milkman hadn't spilled the milk on me I'd have been waiting there yet. Now baby, when I got back I rapped on the door . . . (*GREGG stops him.*) Say what are you trying to do, high hat me? (*Turns to MARGY.*) Now listen baby, give us a kiss and we'll call it quits.

GREGG (*Stopping him again*): Now take it easy.

JONES: What is she, private property?

GREGG: No, but don't get personal.

JONES: Yes, but I'm your friend. Gee, if I were only a lieutenant I might stand some chance with her. (*Turns to* MARGY.) Now listen, kid, I'm different and I work fast.

MARGY: Now don't give me that business.

(*Song, "Myilenberg Joys," and dancing. Applause.*)

(*MARGY sings "My Sweet Man." Much applause.*)

(*MARGY sings and dances to "Shake That Thing." Applause.*)

CONDEZ: Ladies and Gentlemen, there will be dancing in the main ball room. There we will have señorita Carmentina and señor Bollontino, entertainment extraordinaire. (*Applause and ensemble exits.*)

JONES (*Starting for ballroom*): Baby, you'd make a bull dog break his chain. (*Sees Captain Carter. Drunk sailors exit.*) Oh, here comes the Captain.

CAPTAIN CARTER: Ensign—Lieutenant. How do you do, Miss Lamont. Having a good time?

MARGY: Yes, indeed.

CONDEZ: Capitan, Cómo está usted?

CAPTAIN CARTER: Hello, Condez.

CONDEZ: Siéntese aquí Capitan y Usted teniente aquí.

CAPTAIN CARTER: Thank you. Thank you.

JONES: Fix up something for the Captain.

CONDEZ: Sí, sí, oh waiter, clear the table, and give the Captain the best in the house.

(*Enter JIMMY STANTON.*)

Stanton! Usted conoce a el Capitán, verdad?

JIMMY: Hello captain, how are you?

CAPTAIN CARTER: Oh Stanton, come and sit down.

CONDEZ (*Rushing to MARGY*): Señorita, that is the young millionaire señor Stanton! He is son of the Stanton U.S.A. He is—what you call him—inspector for his father's plantation. He is a very fine gentleman and he is very wealthy. Ah—sí, sí, tiene mucho dinero, y ojálá tenga la oportunidad de conocerle señorita. Perdone, regreso después.

CAPTAIN CARTER (*Crossing to MARGY*): Miss Lamont, may I present Mr. Stanton.

MARGY: Yes, you may.

CAPTAIN CARTER: Mr. Stanton, Miss Lamont. Mr. Stanton, Lieutenant Gregg.

JIMMY: How do you do?

(*Exit CONDEZ and JONES.*)

CAPTAIN CARTER: Pardon me lieutenant, just a moment.

(*Exit CAPTAIN CARTER and GREGG.*)

JIMMY: Now don't think me foolish, but I don't suppose you remember going up the gangplank on the ship leaving Cuba for Trinidad?

MARGY: Cuba for Trinidad? Oh yes, yes.

JIMMY: You were talking to a young naval officer.

MARGY: Naval officer? Yes, yes.

JIMMY: Oh, I shall never forget it. I just stood in the middle of that gangplank like a big sap, and forgot they were waiting to pull it up—and you glanced at me. There was a certain look in your eyes.

MARGY: Certain look? What kind of a certain look?

JIMMY: I don't know, but I only hope you don't look at any other man that way.

MARGY: You silly boy.

JIMMY: And just now I asked the Captain here who you were. I told him I thought I'd met you in New York. He said that your name was Miss LaMont, and that he didn't know very much about you except that you were beautiful, and he expected that every man on the ship would want to dance with you. Then I told him that here was one man who did want to dance with you—and then we were introduced.

MARGY: Oh, I see.

JIMMY: I had to get acquainted with you some way, didn't I?

MARGY: And just what was it about me that attracted you.

(*Music. "Always."*)

JIMMY: Oh, I—I don't know, just everything. Your eyes, they're so marvelous—they're heavenly and yet again—I'm afraid of them. And your hair—and the way you smile. You know, you are just perfect to me. (*He gets up to dance*) May I? (*Asking for the dance and a kiss.* GREGG *enters rear on parapet, smoking. He watches them silently.*)

MARGY: You may.

(*They kiss and waltz off toward ballroom. GREGG shrugs and saunters off. Music swells.*)

CURTAIN

Scene Two

(*One week later. Lobby of hotel where* JIMMY *is staying. Musicians playing "Stars and Stripes." Curtain up on second chorus.*)

(*Enter* JONES *and* GREGG.)

JONES: What is the idea of running away from the fun, Gregg?

GREGG: Oh, you don't have to follow me, old fellow.

JONES: What, leave you alone on your last night in Trinidad? I should say not.

GREGG: You'd do me a great favor if you'd slip along and let me have a word with her alone.

JONES: What, is she stopping here? Some class to her. So that's the kind she is, hey? Never mind, old fellow, we'll find a way to show her up.

GREGG: Has it ever occufred to you that a girl may be wanting to go straight?

JONES: Straight? Don't make me laugh.

GREGG: Anyway, she's off the game and she's off me since she met this Stanton.

JONES: He's that rich guy, isn't he? She'll get enough out of him to lay off and live comfortable ever after. Come on, Gregg, I'm going over to the Casino.

JIMMY (*Entering from hotel left*): Hello! Well, well, where have you been keeping yourself? I haven't seen you in the last few days.

GREGG: I've been around here. I've been rather busy.

JIMMY: Getting ready to leave? What is your next port?

GREGG: We leave for the States in the morning. It's my last trip as a naval officer.

JIMMY: You don't mean to say—

GREGG: Yes, my last trip. I've sent in my resignation.

JIMMY: Well, good luck, old man.

GREGG: Thanks awfully.

JIMMY: I'm leaving for the States myself in the morning. While you're there, I'm just a short way out and I'd be very glad to have you spend a weekend with me. I'll show you the finest golf course in Westchester.

GREGG: Golf—that's very interesting. I used to be considered quite a golfer myself.

JIMMY: Is that so? What do you go around in?

GREGG: About 80.

JIMMY: That's too good for me. Won't you join me in a little walk?

GREGG: In a few minutes. (*JIMMY exits rear. GREGG turns to WAITER.*) Oh, Waiter, let me have a pencil.

WAITER: Yes, sir.

GREGG (*Writing on card*): Give this card to Miss LaMont, please.

WAITER: Yes, sir.

GREGG: Remember. (*Exit.*)

(*A waltz plays softly offstage. Enter MARGY. Waiter gives her card and exits.*)

JIMMY (*Entering from rear*): Here I am.

MARGY: Why, dear, I thought you were down at the ball at the flagship?

JIMMY: You wouldn't go, and I wouldn't go without you.

MARGY: I wasn't feeling well.

JIMMY: If it's alright now, can't we still go?

MARGY: I'd rather not.

JIMMY: Dear, I'm going to leave for the States in the morning. When are you going to promise to marry me?

MARGY: Why, we've only known each other a week. You don't know anything about me, who I am, or what I am.

JIMMY: You're the sweetest girl in the world, and that's all I want to know.

MARGY: You're just a big boy out of college, and you don't know what you're talking about.

JIMMY: I do know what I'm talking about. But it's funny.

MARGY: What's funny?

JIMMY: When Dad sent me down here to see how his plantation was running, I didn't want to come. I didn't have any idea I was going to bring back the most wonderful wife in the world. (*MARGY turns her head away.*) Why, dear, you're not married already?

MARGY: Oh no, dear, no.

JIMMY: Then it's all settled.

MARGY: Nothing's settled, only that you go back home, and you'll promise to think of me sometimes, won't you?

JIMMY: I don't want to rush you honey, but I'm leaving tomorrow and you'll say yes—? I always get what I want, and I want you. (*Taps bell.*)

MARGY: Why, what are you doing?

(*Enter WAITER.*)

JIMMY: Celebrating our engagement.

WAITER: Yes, Sir.

JIMMY: Bring us a bottle of Pol Roger.

WAITER: Yes, sir. (*Exits.*)

JIMMY: Just think of it. Tomorrow we'll be on our way home. Home, isn't it glorious?

MARGY: What would your folks say?

JIMMY: They'd love you because I do.

MARGY: I'm not so sure about that.

JIMMY: Yes they would. You're adorable and I love you so much.

WAITER (*Enters with champagne*): Yes, sir.

JIMMY: Thanks, waiter. I'll pour it myself.

WAITER: Yes, Sir. (*Exits.*)

JIMMY (*Lifting glass*): Here's to the future and the dearest girl in the world. I'm crazy about you Margy. There's not another girl like you.

MARGY: Let's be serious.

JIMMY (*He drinks*): Alright now, we're very serious. (*JIMMY drinks several drinks more.*)

MARGY: Not so fast, dear, take it slow. (*She starts to drink.*)

JIMMY: You little darling, what do you know about drinking?

MARGY (*Chokes*): Here in the tropics, wine goes to your head, and I want you to know what you're doing.

JIMMY: Alright, now we are serious.

MARGY: Suppose you found you'd made a mistake in me?

JIMMY: I'm not making a mistake.

MARGY: Suppose I'm not all you think I am?

JIMMY: Are you trying to frighten me? You can't do it. All I know is that I love you and you're going to be mine. Are you satisfied?

MARGY: Yes I am.

JIMMY: Then it's yes?

MARGY: Yes.

JIMMY: Hurrah, I'm the happiest man in Trinidad!

MARGY: Honey, not so loud. (*They kiss.*) You do love me don't you dear? Tell me, I want to hear you say it again.

JIMMY: I love you more than anything in the world—I love you—love you. (*MARGY pushes him away. JIMMY is smashed.*) Why dear, I'm sorry, you were right. Wine does go to your head in the tropics, I didn't realize. But say you love me and we leave tomorrow?

MARGY: Yes, dear, I'll go. (*He kisses her hand.*)

JIMMY: I'm off to arrange for the staterooms and I'll take care of everything.

(*Exits.*)

MARGY (*Starting after him*) Dear, dear . . . Damn it.

AGNES (*Enters*): Margy, Margy.

MARGY: Agnes, Agnes—You poor kid, I thought you went home.

AGNES: I did, but you were right. They wouldn't let me come back.

MARGY: What? Your folks?

AGNES: When I got back home, Mother was dead. If she had lived it might have been different. But the others—

MARGY: They forgive you but they won't let you forget—Oh what's the difference? (*Pats AGNES on the back.*)

AGNES: And when I got back to Montreal, Curley was—

MARGY: What, another jane?

AGNES: No, an overdose of morphine.

MARGY: You poor kid. But what brought you here?

AGNES: I heard you were following the fleet and doing well—And I thought travelling around would help me to forget.

MARGY: But you didn't—

AGNES: No, it's all too much—My—Mother—(*Cough. AGNES is crying.*)

MARGY: You poor kid—Come on over here and have a drink. Pull yourself together. (*Offers her a drink.*)

AGNES: Thanks. (*Drinks.*) I been trying to get a chance to talk to you, but the gobs said you were ritzing it.

MARGY: So that's what they think?

AGNES: I wanted to tell you that I saw Rocky before I left and I'm afraid that he—

MARGY: I don't want to hear anything about that rat.

AGNES: Gee, you must have caught that rich guy you were talking about in Montreal!

MARGY: Kid, I could have caught a dozen had I been so inclined.

AGNES: And you didn't?

MARGY: No, I did not. I guess I've been saved up to try and forget.

AGNES: Margy, you're in love with someone.

MARGY: How did you guess?

AGNES: Who?

MARGY: A clean boy, Agnes, and he loves me and wants me to marry him. A boy that believes I'm straight.

AGNES: My Gawd, that's wonderful. What are you going to do?

MARGY: I'm sending him back to his folks. Sometimes I feel that I should tell him the truth.

AGNES: Don't do that—don't do that—What he don't know won't hurt him.

MARGY: You mean I should marry this boy and pretend—No, I can't. That's what's worrying me.

AGNES: Margy, this is your chance! Suppose you tell him, what good would it do? If he really loves you it won't matter to him what you've been, but for God's sake get out of this life—just look at me—I'm a wreck—my health is all gone—and I'm nothing—(*She coughs.*)

MARGY: Come on, pull yourself together, you're all to pieces.

AGNES: Sometimes I wish I were out of it all.

MARGY: Come, Aggie, brace up, I've never seen you as bad as this before.

AGNES: Marge, promise me you'll do it, promise me you'll marry him, you must! God, if I had your chance nothing in the world would keep me from it. Don't be a fool, it don't matter what you were—it's the kind of a wife you make that counts.

MARGY: Maybe you're right.

AGNES: I *am* right! (*Coughs.*)

MARGY: Come on, I can't let you get away like this. Let me get you a room and some clothes, and get these rags off of you.

AGNES: No Marge, what would they think of you if they saw me here—

MARGY: The whole hotel is down at the ball on the flagship.

AGNES: No Marge, I got to go—I got to walk—I got to think—I may see you later—But I got to go—I got to go—(*Exits sobbing.*)

GREGG (*Enters right*): Hello, Marge, I knew they'd all be down at the ball on the flagship, and I thought this would be a good chance to have a word with you alone. You look pretty well set here.

MARGY: Yes, he thinks I'm a tourist. It's a lot different when they don't know. You've something to say to me, Gregg.

GREGG: Yes, that's why I'm here.

MARGY: I know it wasn't just the right thing to do leaving you like this.

GREGG: It's a bit beyond me old dear, but there's something else I wanted to talk to you about—The fleet's leaving port in the morning, and it's my last trip as a naval officer, then I'm going out to Australia.

MARGY: Australia, that's pretty far, isn't it?

GREGG: Yes, but it's a place where a fellow and a girl can start a new life out there.

MARGY: I see.

GREGG: You see what I mean? We could hit it off together.

MARGY: No Gregg, I'm through.

GREGG: You don't understand. I mean we'll get married.

MARGY: Thanks, Gregg.

GREGG: I'm not so bad, Marge.

MARGY: Why you're the best old scout I ever run into. Sometimes I wonder why you're where you are.

GREGG: It's a long story, the same old tale, though. Decent folks over in old England, father's a clergyman, I'm the black sheep—it's not only girls that drop out of the City Directory, old dear. What do you say to my little idea?

MARGY: No Gregg, I couldn't do it.

GREGG: Why I've got plenty to live on, a beautiful little white cottage, a garden, and a church—

MARGY: My God, you sound like Agnes—I'm sorry Gregg. Two weeks ago I'd have thought that over, but now—I can't.

GREGG: I guess I know.

MARGY: What do you mean?

GREGG: That youngster I see you walking around with every night since you struck Trinidad. Young Stanton, isn't he?

MARGY: It's just been kind of a dream, Gregg.

GREGG: I thought so. You've changed since you met him.

MARGY: You don't understand, Gregg.

GREGG: Oh, I'm no fool. Only don't singe your wings, old dear.

MARGY: Singe my wings? Don't make me laugh.

GREGG: Marge, the body doesn't mean a thing—but when it's the heart, it hurts.

MARGY: What do I know about a heart? To me every man is just an asset.

GREGG: Yes, and for this one chap you're giving up everything—and you say you know nothing about a heart? Why, Marge, ever since Montreal you've been mine, and I've been yours, all of me, every bit of me. There was a time I could share you with other men, but not now. Why, the thought of it drives me mad, almost. Tell me, do you really want this other fellow? Do you really love him?

MARGY: I guess I do.

GREGG: So that's it. And all the time I thought you were only making a play for his money.

MARGY: No Gregg, I couldn't roll him, of all men. From the moment I met him I knew.

GREGG: What do you mean?

MARGY: I'm beginning to see things different, Gregg, since I met that boy. He made me feel ashamed. He asked me to marry him.

GREGG: Haven't I asked you the same thing? Hasn't every officer in the fleet offered you the ring? And a dozen rich traders asked you to the altar?

MARGY: Yes, but he was the first one who asked me while he was sober.

GREGG: And you said yes?

MARGY: I'm beginning to see things different, Gregg. Why ever since I've been enough to know Sex I've looked at men as hunters. They're filled with Sex. In the past few years I've been a chattel to that Sex. All the bad that's in me has been put there by men. I began to hate every one of them, hated them, used them for what I could get out of them, and laughed at them, and then he came.

GREGG: But what about when you said you loved me? When you held me in your soft arms and kissed me and told me you loved me? Do you think you can get away from me as easy as this. To walk into another man's life and tell him the same things. Then all the beautiful things you told me you didn't mean?

MARGY: You don't understand, Gregg. When I held you in my arms and kissed you, when I felt your strong, warm body close to mine I wanted you, I needed you, I loved you more than any man I'd ever known. Don't you understand Gregg? I loved you in that one way. But this is different. It's a clean, wonderful love I have for this boy. I'm sorry, but I can't help it. God, it's good to be in love this way even if I have to pay for it with tears.

GREGG: All I can say is, don't be looking for heartaches. If this fellow really loves you, I suppose that's all there is to it. But remember if ever you want me, I'm yours, all yours.

MARGY: Don't talk to me that way Gregg. I suppose I shouldn't be doing what I am to you—but I can't help it.

GREGG: But you know your positions are pretty far apart. Why, that boy's folks are real folks. They're aristocrats. Tell me, are you sure that it's really love that's drawing him to you?

MARGY: I'm sure.

GREGG: Oh well, whenever you want me you'll know where a word reaches me. What I said about Australia goes. It's a long way and far between, but it's a place where a fellow and a girl can start a new life.

MARGY: Gregg, don't leave me like this. You've given me the chance. I'm not ungrateful, but it's . . . things just happen, that's all, that we can't explain.

GREGG: It's alright Marge, we all have to float with the tide.

(The "Meditation from Thaïs" is heard playing softly on the flagship in the bay. JIMMY enters and goes to MARGY.)

JIMMY: I've arranged everything, we leave tomorrow.

(Noise offstage of suppressed shouts and murmurs as though a town wer e awakening to a catastrophe. The only distinguishable word is "Overboard!")

MARGY: What's that?

JIMMY: They're crowding down al the docks. Let's go see!

MARGY: No, no, wait.

JIMMY: Don't be nervous, you're all upset.

MARGY: Go, see what it is.

JIMMY: I'll find out. *(Calls offstage.)* What's going on down there?

OFFSTAGE VOICE: One of those fleet women jumped into the bay! *(Music and voices swell and fade. MARGY nearly faints.)*

JIMMY: Nothing to worry us, dear. Just one of those poor wretches that follow the fleet.

(Music and voices swell to a crescendo.)

CURTAIN

ACT THREE

Scene One

(The Stanton residence. A richly appointed room. Onstage, ROBERT STANTON and JENKINS, the butler.)

MARIE *(Enters with a vase of flowers)*: I'm taking these to the young lady's room, sir.

STANTON: Yes, yes, go ahead Marie. See that everything is ready Marie.

MARIE *(Exits)*: Yes sir.

STANTON: They ought to be along any minute. *(Exits.)*

MARIE *(Enters)*: If he would only keep his watch in his pocket. It hasn't left his hand since Mr. Jimmy went to the station to meet the train.

JENKINS: Well, any man would be anxious to meet his future daughter-in-law.

MARIE: Yes, when he don't know very much about her.

JENKINS: She's evidently very wealthy. Mr. Jimmy met her while she was touring the world.

MARIE: Yes. She travel all alone, no chaperone.

JENKINS: Oh, the days of chaperones are past. Wealthy orphan, no doubt. Marguerite LaMont is her name.

MARIE: Marguerite LaMont. That sounds like a French name.

JENKINS: Mr. Jimmy calls her Margy.

MARIE: Short for Marguerite. French descent, no doubt. All Mr. Stanton he worry about is what church she belong to.

JENKINS: I haven't any idea.

STANTON *(Enters)*: When they arrive, Jenkins, call me. I'll be in the library.

JENKINS: Yes, Sir.

STANTON: I'm going to lose a couple of hours sleep as it is—I have to get up early to be at business. *(Exits.)*

MARIE: If he were not at his desk at nine A.M. to the minute, the world would come to an end.

(*An auto horn is heard.*)

JENKINS: System, my dear, that's what makes a man successful. (*Exits.*)

JIMMY (*Enters with MARGY*): Home at last, darling. By Jove, it was hard work to get you to come out here. Take this to Miss LaMont's room, Marie, and wait just a minute. Well, darling, how do you like it?

MARGY: This is the first case of cold feet I ever had.

JIMMY: Why, darling? Mother and Dad are just a pair of peaches. You'll love them, you can't help it.

MARGY: That part's alright. I know I couldn't help loving your dad and your mother, but the question is, how about me? Am I the kind of a girl they've pictured for their only son? You know, parents are funny.

JIMMY: Mother and Dad are just crazy to meet you. I've talked to them about you ever since I came back from Trinidad. Let me take your wraps. (*To MARIE and JENKINS*) Take these also. Marie and Jenkins you may go. (*Exit MARIE and JENKINS. Enter CLARA.*)

JIMMY: Oh, there you are, Mother. I've been looking for you. Mother, this is Margy. (*CLARA and MARGY recognize each other—and pause.*)

CLARA: How do you do.

JIMMY: I hope you'll like each other.

MARGY: Well, we'll understand each other anyway.

(*Enter STANTON.*)

JIMMY: Oh, Dad!

STANTON: Well, son?

JIMMY: Margy, this is Dad.

STANTON: Well, well, so this is the young lady that Jimmy's been raving about ever since he came back from Trinidad! Why he's been going around with his heart in his fist.

JIMMY: Oh, Dad. You're telling tales now.

STANTON: I'm going to show you right up! Margy—of course I'll call you Margy?—you've certainly worked a great change in my boy. He used to read nothing but the sporting news but now, he reads the furniture ads, isn't that right, Clara?

CLARA: Yes.

STANTON: I hope you're going to like it out here, Margy.

MARGY: I'm sure I will.

STANTON: You've never been to our little town before?

MARGY: This is one place I've missed.

STANTON: Enjoy travelling, don't you? Jimmy says you are a regular globe trotter. Well, you'll find everything here. We've got everything they've got in the big cities, parks, YMCA buildings, churches—er—which one do you attend?

MARGY: One's as good as another to me.

CLARA: Naturally, I presume—travelling so much.

MARGY: Yes, naturally, when in Rome do as Rome does, or again when in Trinidad follow Trinidad's customs, or Montreal—

CLARA: I've visited Montreal myself, Miss LaMont.

MARGY: Why, you don't say—we can compare notes.

STANTON: You two girls'll have a lot to talk about. Jimmy I'll bet Mother's just dying to get acquainted, and here's your old talkative Dad not giving her a chance.

CLARA: I would like a few minutes alone with Miss LaMont.

STANTON: Come on Jimmy—we'll let the ladies talk, and we'll drink to their health.

JIMMY: Alright, Dad.

STANTON: Then we'll let you ladies take a drink to our health. (*Exit JIMMY and STANTON.*)

MARGY: What's your idea?

CLARA: You certainly don't intend to marry my son.

MARGY: That's your idea.

CLARA: I'll not let him make such a mistake. I'll tell him what you are.

MARGY: Suppose he should ask you how you know what I am?

CLARA: I'll tell him everything. Everything that happened during my visit to Montreal.

MARGY: No, you won't. You haven't the nerve. If you did, I'd have a better opinion of you. You wouldn't sacrifice yourself for anyone. Your pride's what you're thinking of.

CLARA: I'm thinking of my boy's welfare. He certainly is deserving of a better fate.

MARGY: I know my past is nothing to rave about. I'll admit he deserves a better life, yes, and he deserves a better mother, too.

CLARA: How dare you speak like that?

MARGY: How dare I speak like that? Who are *you?*

CLARA: I'll not permit a woman of the streets to talk to me like that.

MARGY: Say, you've got a nerve putting yourself on a pedestal above me. The things I've done, I had to do for a living. I know it was wrong. I'm not trying to alibi myself. But you've done those same things for other reasons.

CLARA: Stop—

MARGY: No, I won't stop. I'm going to dig under the veneer of your supposed respectability and show you what you are.

CLARA: I'll not listen.

MARGY: Oh, yes you will. You've got the kind of stuff in you in makes women of my type. If our positions were changed—you in my place, and I in yours—I'd be willing to bet that I'd make a better wife and Mother than you are. Yeah, and I'll bet without this beautiful home, without money, and without any restrictions, you'd be worse than I have ever been.

CLARA: No, no—.

MARGY: Yes, you would. You'd do it and like it.

CLARA: For God's sake stop it, I can't endure any more—

MARGY: Now you're down off your pedestal. You're down where you can see—it's just a matter of circumstances. The only difference between us is that you could afford to give it away.

CLARA: I'm not considering my feelings. It's the welfare of my boy.

MARGY: I've thought of his welfare, perhaps more than you have. I didn't want to come here. I told him from the start that I wasn't the woman for him, but he wouldn't listen.

CLARA: But you have no right to expect him to marry you.

MARGY: I don't know. He could do worse by marrying some little tart who'd wear my colors after she was married to him, some jane who would take a little trip to Montreal. I've had my share of men. They all look alike to me except one—him.

CLARA: I can understand your viewpoint, but even if this marriage was to take place, you could never live down the sins of the past. People would talk.

MARGY: They'd talk anyway.

CLARA: Yes, but we are governed to a great extent by what they say and think.

MARGY: Let them talk. We love each other and that's all that matters.

CLARA: Don't say he loves you. It's ridiculous—he is a boy, scarcely out of his teens. You are perhaps the first woman he has ever come into close contact with. It's only natural that you should attract him with the physical attraction that a woman has for a boy so young.

MARGY: All I've been is a physical attraction to men. I'm sick and tired of being that sort of thing. Now I want a man whose love goes beyond that.

CLARA: If you should get married, you'd find out just how far it goes.

MARGY: Well, I'll find out before. Here.

CLARA: What do you mean?

MARGY: You know what I mean. You're a pretty wise gal yourself.

CLARA: You don't mean that you'd use my home—

MARGY: Well, you used mine.

CLARA: But—

MARGY: We'll at least know where we stand.

(*Enter* JIMMY *and* STANTON.)

JIMMY: Dad and I think you've had enough time to get acquainted. Mother, don't you just love her?

MARGY: She's just crazy about me.

CLARA: Yes, son, she's very interesting.

STANTON: And trying to keep her all to yourself. Now that's a shame. But you wait until after business hours tomorrow. I'll take charge of Margy. You'll have to tell me all about your travels and your experiences. I'll warrant you had a lot of them, didn't you?

MARGY: I'll say I did.

STANTON: Well, we'll have a lot of time to talk that over. I must be going.

JIMMY: Dad, you're not leaving us?

STANTON: Well, son, you know I get up early, and it's pretty late for me. Margy'll excuse me, I know.

MARGY: Of course I will.

STANTON: I'm so glad you're here, child. You'll be such good company for Mrs. Stanton. Won't she, dear?

CLARA: Yes—yes—indeed.

MARGY: That's so sweet of you, Mrs. Stanton. You don't know how I appreciate your feelings toward me.

CLARA: Thank you. I presume you've a great deal to say to each other. I'd only be intruding. When you are ready to retire Miss LaMont just ring for the maid. She'll show you to your room.

MARGY: Thanks.

STANTON: My goodness. It's past my hour for retiring.

JIMMY: Dad always goes to bed early. He hasn't been up as late as this in six months.

STANTON: I'm the first one up in this house. Have to catch an early morning train to get to the city. You'll forgive me, I'm sure. Besides you and Jimmy have a lot to say to each other.

JIMMY: Well, now Dad . . .

STANTON: Don't make any excuses. I was a youngster once myself. And say Jimmy, if Margy should feel like a bite, you'll find a little spread all ready on the dining room table.

JIMMY: Thanks Dad. I—I never did think of asking Margy—

STANTON: Jimmy, even Cupid has to have his dinner. Make yourself at home, child. Get acquainted. If there's anything you want and you don't see it, just ask for it.

MARGY: You're awfully good, Mr. Stanton.

STANTON: I want you to like Jimmy's folks, child.

MARGY: Thanks—why I'm sure—

STANTON: I'm sure that you will, and I'm going to see that you do.

MARGY: Good night, Mr. Stanton.

JIMMY: 'Night, Dad.

(*Exit* STANTON.)

MARGY: Your dad is a prince.

CLARA: You'll pardon me, I'm sure.

MARGY: Surely.

CLARA: When you are ready to retire, Miss LaMont, Jimmy will ring for the maid. She'll show you to your room. Good night.

JIMMY: Good night, mother.

MARGY: Good night, Mrs. Stanton.

(*Exit* CLARA.)

JIMMY: You'll have to learn to call her "Mother," you know.

MARGY: Say Jimmy, that'll be the hardest job I ever tackled.

JIMMY: Why—don't you like Mother?

MARGY: There's no question to it.

JIMMY: I'm so glad. It's wonderful to have you here with me, dear.

MARGY: Yes Jimmy, it's been a wonderful night.

JIMMY: I was afraid you didn't mean what you promised in Trinidad—I had such a hard time getting you here. You didn't know what sleepless nights I've had thinking of you and being afraid—

MARGY: Afraid of what?

JIMMY: That maybe you—you found out that you didn't love me after all, and perhaps met some other fellow and—oh, hang it, Margy, a man thinks up all kinds of things when he's in love with a girl.

MARGY: You weren't sure of me?

JIMMY: How could I be, with you so far away, but now tonight, you're in my own home—I'm content for the first time in months. You do love me, don't you?

MARGY: Love you? Jimmy, I never knew what it was all about until I met you.

JIMMY: And we'll be married soon, won't we?

MARGY: Do you really want to marry me?

JIMMY: Why, of course—what do you expect?

MARGY: You see, I've been kind of worried too, I thought maybe some other girl—

JIMMY: There's no other girl in the world for me, save you.

MARGY: And why just me?

JIMMY: I love you.

MARGY: Why do you love me, Jimmy?

JIMMY: I love you because you're different, you fascinate me, you draw me to you, you're wonderful and I adore you.

MARGY: Come on over here, dear.

JIMMY: I've been telling you what I like about you. Now you tell me what you like about me. Tell—

MARGY: There's so many things about you that I like—but I never did like bright lights.

JIMMY: I'll turn them down. (*He dims the lights.*) There, is that better? Now, tell me what you like about me!

MARGY: I like your ears.

JIMMY: You like my ears? (*MARGY strokes his face.*) Who do you think came into the office today?

MARGY: Who, dear?

JIMMY: Lieutenant Gregg.

MARGY: What did he want?

JIMMY: When I left him in Trinidad I told him where I lived and asked him if he ever came to New York to spend the weekend with me, so of course when he came to the office I asked him out.

MARGY (*Undoing his necktie*): Take that thing off.

(*JIMMY removes tie. MARGY examines it, and lets it fall.*)

MARGY: Very pretty, what size collar do you wear?

JIMMY: Fifteen and a half. (*They kiss.*) God, I've never kissed anyone like that before—

MARGY: You have.

JIMMY: I swear I haven't.

MARGY: You have. (*They kiss again.*)

JIMMY: I'll ring for the maid.

MARGY: Can't you show me to my room?

JIMMY: Yes, dear—Good night, dear.

CURTAIN

Scene Two

(*The next morning. JIMMY runs out, picks up necktie and returns to bedroom. His father enters, dressed for the day's business. He fills his flask. JIMMY reenters, fully dressed, but very nervous.*)

STANTON: Hello, Son, I didn't know you were up. Why didn't you breakfast with me?

JIMMY: Why—I don't know—I—

STANTON: I suppose you're so happy that you can't even sleep in peace.

JIMMY: Dad, you like her, don't you?

STANTON: Of course I like her. Any man would have to like her. She's a fine girl. You're just like your old Dad, a good picker.

JIMMY: I'm so glad.

STANTON: Yes, but I can't let your happiness make me late for business. I'll take the train and you can come down later in the car.

JIMMY: Must I go into the city today?

STANTON: Yes, Son, I need you about the Hoyden affair. Sorry to take you away from Margy, but you can leave as soon as we settle with Hoyden.

JIMMY: But can't you let that go till later? That deal is practically closed. He'll be in today, you really don't need me. Besides that Lieutenant Gregg is coming in.

STANTON: Lieutenant Gregg? Who's he?

JIMMY: He's that English officer that came into the office yesterday. He's coming in on the next train.

STANTON: Well, alright, Son, perhaps I can let you stay. Say good morning to Margy and tell her that I hope she slept well.

JIMMY: I will, thanks.

(*STANTON exits.*)

MARIE (*Entering from right. She sees JIMMY*): Good morning, monsieur.

JIMMY: Oh Marie, have you seen Mother?

MARIE: Oui monsieur, she's not feeling very well, sir. She's having her breakfast in her room.

JIMMY: What's the matter with Mother?

MARIE: A bad headache, I think sir. (*Exits left.*)

(*JIMMY exits right, JENKINS enters from left as MARGY comes on from back room.*)

MARGY: Good morning, Jenkins.

JENKINS: Good morning, Madam. (*Crossing over.*) Does Madam wish anything?

MARGY: No, if I want something I'll ring.

JENKINS: Very well, Madam. (*Exits right.*)

MARGY: I don't like this Madam business.

JIMMY (*Entering from right*): Margie.

(*He goes over to her on the divan with a worried look and kisses her.*)

MARGY: What's the matter, you look worried?

JIMMY: Mother's not feeling very well this morning.

MARGY: That's too bad. What's the matter with her?

JIMMY: Oh, I guess it's her nerves again.

MARGY: Is there anything I can do? Er—has she been saying anything about last night?

JIMMY: No, but she seems upset. I imagine it's about last night—I wonder if she—I wonder if she knows about last night—you and I. Oh dear, why did you let me go to your room. It's the thing I've been lighting against ever since I met you.

MARGY: Perhaps I'd better not stay here?

JIMMY: What do you mean—what do you mean?

MARGY: Well, your Mother isn't feeling well—and you're all upset—

JIMMY: Why—Margy—

MARGY: You want me to stay?

JIMMY: Want you? I want you always, always. Oh, don't you understand I love you, love you. I realize it now more than ever. To lose you would be to lose every bit of happiness out of my life—I couldn't live without you.

MARGY: Jimmy, you're mad.

JIMMY: Yes, mad about you dear. We'll get married at once—

MARGY: Married!

JIMMY: Margy—of course—there was never any other thought in my mind. You hold everything in the world for me. We'll be happy together, you and I. (*Holds her in his arms and kisses her.*) Why dear, I couldn't leave you out of my sight long enough to join Dad at the office today.

MARGY: You should have attended to business and—and—

JIMMY: And what?

MARGY: You've got me so nervous, Jimmy, I don't know what I did want to say.

JIMMY: There, I forgot about Lieutenant Gregg again. I've got to go meet him at once. I can't think of anything but you, you see?

MARGY: But why did you invite him here?

JIMMY: I think he's a fine fellow. He seemed very much interested in you. He asked how you were feeling.

MARGY: Oh, he's a wonderful man and all that, but I wanted to be alone with you, dear.

JENKINS (*Entering from left*): The car is waiting, Mr. Stanton.

JIMMY: Very well, Jenkins.

(*Exit JENKINS.*)

(*JIMMY rises and kisses MARGY.*)

I won't be long, sweetheart.

MARGY: Hurry back, dear.

(*JIMMY exits.*)

(*MARGY rises and after looking off at JIMMY leaving, makes several ludicrous attempts to rearrange the furnishings of the room. The result is a garish display of taste.*)

CLARA (*Entering from right*): Good morning, Miss LaMont.

MARGY: Oh, good morning—I—was just making a few changes here to kind of suit myself.

CLARA: So I see.

MARGY: I thought that thing would look better over here and this thing would look better over here. (*She is wiping her hands on a brocade.*)

CLARA: Well—well—hmm—

MARGY (*Holding up the brocade*): Oh, what's this thing supposed to be?

CLARA: Oh goodness! That "thing" is supposed to be a brocade from Marie Antoinette, Queen of France.

MARGY: Oh, is that what that thing is supposed to be?

CLARA: And this thing is supposed to have been worn by Madame DuBarry when she used her wiles on King Louis XV.

MARGY: What a break that jane got! I remember reading about that boy.

CLARA: Oh, my nerves, my nerves.

MARGY: Jimmy said you weren't feeling very well, and I was going in to see how you were, but I thought I had better not after the argument last night.

CLARA: Yes, I forgive you for taking the attitude you did. I realize I was quite harsh with you, but you didn't understand my feelings in the matter.

MARGY: No, and I guess you didn't understand mine.

CLARA: At first I thought you came here in a spirit of revenge.

MARGY: Say, I didn't have any idea I was going to meet you here. I should say not! But that was a pretty mean trick you pulled on me that night in Montreal. After the story you told, I could have done time.

CLARA: I'm sorry, but I have a clearer understanding of your problem now.

MARGY: I'm glad you have. Of course we all make mistakes.

CLARA: Yes, I've made mistakes, too. I only caught myself in time. You don't know the agony, the mental suffering I've endured on account of that Montreal affair.

MARGY: I don't know how you ever fell for that guy. Of course with me it was more business than anything else.

CLARA: It was my first and last experience of anything like that. I swear to you from that night to this I've given all of my love, every one of my thoughts to my husband and boy. God, what a lesson it was to me, my nerves go to pieces at the very thought of it.

MARGY: Don't worry about the past. That's my motto. Always think of what you're going to do tomorrow.

CLARA: And what are you going to do tomorrow? You hold my boy's future in your hands. Some day he'll find out—and then, don't you see what it'll be?

MARGY: He loves me and it won't matter.

CLARA: Oh, yes it will matter. He'll never forgive you for deceiving him. He'll hate you and you'll both be miserable.

MARGY: I—I—don't believe it.

CLARA: Those things can never remain a secret—Some day they will come to life, and even though he did love you well enough to forgive, what would it be for him, dreading the very meeting of every man he sees thinking that perhaps his wife—Oh, don't you understand it would be enough to madden him, and you, how would you feel? You would never know a moment of peace.

MARGY: You're certainly not drawing a pretty picture.

CLARA: Yes, but I'm drawing a true picture. Tell me you'll give him up, please. (*MARGY turns her head away MARIE enters dressed for the street.*) Oh Marie, are you going out?

MARIE: Madame said I could—the others have all gone on ahead.

CLARA: Oh yes, yes, I'd forgotten, our neighbor's cook—you're all invited to her wedding. My nerves are in such a state, I don't remember.

MARIE: If Madame wish me to remain—

CLARA: No, you go, but call up the druggist, and tell him to send over the nerve prescription Dr. Gordon left for me.

MARIE: Oui, Madame.

CLARA: Has Jenkins returned from the station?

MARIE: I think not, madame. (*Auto horn offstage.*) I think it is the car now. (*MARIE exits and returns later followed by JIMMY and GREGG dressed in civilian clothes. MARIE exits again.*)

JIMMY: Come right in, lieutenant.

GREGG: Thanks, awfully.

JIMMY: Mother, this is Lieutenant Gregg.

CLARA: How do you do Lieutenant Gregg. (*CLARA and GREGG recognize each other, but before GREGG gets a chance to admit it, MARGY jabs him. JIMMY notices nothing. GREGG and CLARA falter in their greetings.*)

MARGY (*To Jimmy*): Oh dear—

CLARA: You'll pardon me, Lieutenant Gregg, but I'm not feeling well. I'll see you later.

GREGG: I'm sorry to hear you're indisposed. It's quite alright, I quite understand.

JIMMY: Mother isn't quite herself today.

MARGY: No, she's not feeling well.

JIMMY: Now, dear, that the lieutenant is here I'd like to show him around the place. Won't you join us?

MARGY: Honey, I don't feel that I'd care to go out today. You go.

JENKINS (*Entering from right*): Your Mother would like to see you, Mr. Stanton.

JIMMY: Pardon me, I'll be right back. (*Exit JIMMY and JENKINS.*)

GREGG: Isn't that the woman from Montreal?

MARGY: Of course it is. Who did you think it was?

GREGG: I wasn't quite sure. I was just going to ask her when you started all this sort of business. (*He indicates the jabs she had given him.*)

MARGY: That's all I need around here, just one bright remark from you.

GREGG: But doesn't he know?

MARGY (*Going over to the piano*): No, he doesn't know.

GREGG: Aren't you going to tell him?

MARGY: No I'm going to let you tell him. (*She plays "Home Sweet Home." GREGG watches her, smoking silently.*)

GREGG (*At end of piece*): That doesn't sound a bit like you, Marge.

MARGY: It's not supposed to be me. (*Starts to play blues number, stopping just long enough to answer him.*)

GREGG: That's more like you, Marge, You're looking beautiful, Marge, more beautiful than ever.

MARGY: Yeah?

GREGG: You're not saying how I look?

MARGY: You're looking alright.

GREGG: There was a time I looked rather good to you.

MARGY: You look the same to me now.

GREGG: But how do you like me in civilian clothes?

MARGY: They look alright. But I think I like the uniform better.

GREGG: Why?

MARGY: I don't know, I guess it's because I'm so patriotic.

JIMMY (*Entering*): What is my little sweetheart doing? Entertaining?

MARGY: Not tonight, dear.

JIMMY: Won't you change your mind and join us, dear.

MARGY: No, you two run along and hurry back, dear.

JIMMY: Alright. Come along lieutenant, we'll go.

GREGG: You don't care to come, too?

MARGY: No, I don't care to come too.

GREGG: Will you be here when I get back?

MARGY: I'll be here when you get back.

(*Exit JIMMY and GREGG. Enter JENKINS.*)

JENKINS (*Sees CLARA entering*): Have I permission to go to the wedding?

CLARA: Yes, you may go.

JENKINS: Thank you, madam.

(*Door bell rings. JENKINS exits and returns with a card on a salver.*)

CLARA (*Looking at card*): Show the gentleman in. (*JENKINS exits and returns ushering in ROCKY WALDRON. JENKINS exits.*) And you have the impudence to come back here!

ROCKY: Your little boy friend is broke again.

CLARA: I refuse to give you any more money.

ROCKY: Then I park the body here until you do.

CLARA: I can't let you stay here.

ROCKY: I'd be a handy man to have around the house. That husband of yours is an old gink. A young chap like me isn't to be found everywhere.

CLARA: You must leave.

ROCKY: Be reasonable. You don't want to lose a home like this and a husband with plenty of jack.

CLARA (*Rising*): But I can't let you have any more money.

ROCKY: You can't bluff me, Clara. You play a bum poker hand.

CLARA: I can't let you stay here. You must go. My husband, my boy. Oh for God's sake, please go, go.

ROCKY: I don't mind taking a little jewelry with me. What a nice new collection you have. That husband of yours does like to drape you in gems. By the way, what did you tell him you did with the others?

CLARA: I told him they were stolen.

ROCKY: Well, tell him the same thing about these.

(*CLARA is standing by the door to MARGY's room. ROCKY makes a grab for her, and CLARA picks up a gun from a table. She is about to shoot him, but MARGY enters and takes her gun, hiding it behind her own back. ROCKY is astonished by MARGY's entrance.*)

ROCKY (*To MARGY*): You? What are you pulling here?

CLARA: He threatened to tell my husband about Montreal unless I gave him money.

MARGY: Don't my little pet know that blackmail is against the law?

ROCKY: It's none of your business.

MARGY: Yes, but I'm going to make it my business. You know you're not in Montreal now, dearie. No, to be exact you're just three hundred fifty-four miles from there. You're in the States now, get out your little map. Rocky Waldron, alias Gentleman Jack, wanted for several things including murder.

ROCKY (*To MARGY*): So that's what you're pulling! If you think I'd let you get away with it . . . You're mine, you belong to me! (*He starts at her. MARGY drives a chair between him and herself.*)

ROCKY (*To CLARA*): You stopped my allowance in Montreal but it's going to start again here. You're going to come across with that jack. We're going to blow this town right now.

(*MARGY goes to telephone.*)

ROCKY (*Back to MARGY*): What are you going to do?

MARGY: Make a reservation, dear. Now, just where would my little pet care to spend his next twenty or thirty years? I know a beautiful place down South dear, called Atlanta, where I know they're waiting to welcome you with open arms.

ROCKY: You think so?

MARGY: Or maybe you don't care for the warm climate? I could very easily arrange a beautiful trip up the Hudson. Where you get free tonsorial visits. In other words the closest haircut you ever had. And Baby, the classiest suit of clothes, you know, sort of zebra effect. I can just see it draped on that perfect figure of yours.

ROCKY: Who do you think you're kidding? You trying to waste my time around here—why I'd—

(*MARGY brings the gun out on him. He recoils in fear. She takes receiver off phone.*)

MARGY (*Calmly*): Hello, police headquarters, yes please hurry. (*To Rocky*): Mmmm—I can just see it draped on that perfect figure of yours. Hello, police headquarters? This is the Robert Stanton residence, Boulevard Road, yes, will you kindly send someone here immediately, yes, to take a desperate character. Yes, please hurry, thank you.

ROCKY: So you'd turn me up after all I've done for you?

MARGY: After all you've done for me? A fine thing you did when you left this woman on my hands. If she hadn't come to, I'd be in jail yet.

ROCKY: I'd have come back, I'd have got you out.

MARGY: Yes you would. Yes you would.

ROCKY: Come on Marge, you're not going to turn me up. Why they're on my trail now. That's why I came here. I just wanted more jack to make a get away. Please don't turn me up.

MARGY: Alright rat. I'll give you a chance. Escaped convict 3844. I've got a pretty good memory, haven't I? Why, if I didn't have a certain amount of refinement, I'd kick your teeth all over this floor. Now blow bum, blow. Not that way, you ought to know better than that. Come on, come on. (*ROCKY exits hastily.*) (*To CLARA:*) Where do you keep this thing? (*She indicates the revolver.*)

CLARA: Just put it on the table.

MARGY (*She writes on a pad on the table and hands CLARA a piece of paper*): Now any time your little boyfriend should forget his promise and come back, a little phone call will put him right where he belongs.

CLARA: Thank you very much. When he threatened to tell my husband about Montreal I thought about my boy and everything. I picked up that gun and I would have shot him.

MARGY: You must never do that. You must never shoot anyone.

CLARA: Oh, why did I do it? I went mad. (*Door bell rings.*) Oh, the police are here. What are you going to tell them?

MARGY: Now don't worry, I know how to handle those babies. (*Exits to door.*)

POLICEMAN (*Off stage*): Alright Mike, you stay outside.

VOICE (*Off stage*): Look out Al, he's desperate.

POLICEMAN (*Entering with MARGY*): What's the trouble, lady?

MARGY: I'm very sorry, officer. But there has been a slight mistake on our part.

POLICEMAN: Why, the report at headquarters was to come and get a desperate character.

MARGY: Yes, he was desperate, in the beginning, very desperate, wasn't he, Mrs. Stanton?

CLARA: Yes, he was very desperate. You see, we ladies were all alone. The servants have gone to a wedding.

MARGY: Yes, the butler and the maid, they had a friend, a cook. And she just got back from her honeymoon and is going to be married tonight.

CLARA: Why, she hasn't had her honeymoon yet—

MARGY: Oh, I don't know how it is, but I will make those mistakes. Yes, she's going to be married tonight and tomorrow night she's going to have her honeymoon. I will do those things. And you see, we ladies were here alone. And this man, he came in, and he wanted money, he wanted carfare, he was going some place. And of course we ladies, we felt that we didn't dare to give it to him. And then he became very annoyed, oh very angry. But after a while he cooled off and he began to see things our way, and he left. I don't think he'll be back, in fact I'm sure he won't. (*She starts to flirt with officer in her attempt to make him believe her.*) So you see, officer, a slight mistake and very sorry to have troubled you, really.

POLICEMAN (*Starting to exit*): It's alright lady, no harm done. (*Stops. Comes to MARGY.*) I beg your pardon. Haven't I seen you some place before?

MARGY: I beg pardon?

POLICEMAN: Haven't I seen you some place before?

MARGY: Well, I've been some place.

POLICEMAN: Don't you remember me?

MARGY: I can't say that I do.

POLICEMAN: Sailor Gordon?

MARGY: Do you mind stepping out here for just a minute? (*Starts to exit.*)

POLICEMAN: Coitenly.

(*They exit together. CLARA stands and looks out after them thoughtfully. After a few moments, MARGY returns. She cannot look CLARA in the face, and goes to her room in silence. JIMMY and GREGG enter.*)

JIMMY: Mother, has there been any trouble here?

CLARA: Why no, Son, Why?

JIMMY: I saw Warren and he said he saw some officers coming in here.

CLARA: Yes, they were here but they had the wrong place, darling.

JIMMY: I'm so glad. We certainly did hurry to get here, didn't we Lieutenant?

GREGG: We whizzed, what?

JIMMY: Mother, where's Margy?

CLARA: Up in her room.

JIMMY: Mother, you haven't been saying anything to offend her have you?

CLARA: Of course not, Son.

(*MARGY enters dressed to go away and carrying a bag. They all turn and stare at her.*)

JIMMY: Why, dear, what's the matter?

MARGY: I'm leaving, dear.

JIMMY: You're leaving? Why?

MARGY: Do you remember that last night in Trinidad?

JIMMY: How could I ever forget it?

MARGY: Do you remember the woman that threw herself into the bay?

JIMMY: Why yes, of course. But what has that got to do with us?

MARGY: I was no better than she.

JIMMY: What are you saying?

MARGY: I was one of those women.

JIMMY: You? Why that's not true!

MARGY: Ask Gregg.

(*GREGG turns away, too ashamed to look at him.*)

JIMMY: I can't believe . . . (*He sits down, heartbroken, and puts head in hands.*)

MARGY: Mrs. Stanton, I'm giving back your boy. I'm sure you'll teach him to forget me.

CLARA: But you are not going back to that life?

(*GREGG appeals to her mutely to remember his feeling for her. She looks at him and smiles.*)

MARGY: No, I'm going straight—to Australia. (*Holds out hand to GREGG.*)

FINAL CURTAIN

13. *Machinal*— Sophie Treadwell

Commentaries

Sources

Play

13.1 EXTRACT FROM *WOMEN WHO KILL*—ANN JONES

BY FAR THE MOST DIRECT AND DRAMATIC public punishments of this century, however, were reserved for women who exercised their "erotic rights" in their own behalf; for the so-called sexual emancipation of woman had never been intended to set women free but merely to enlist their sexuality in the service of men. In fact, one of the most distinctive features of the new sexuality—just like the old sexuality—was its exclusivity. The good woman was to be sexually emancipated only in the master bedroom. The Finnish anthropologist Edward Westermarck announced in 1891 his scientific discovery that the traditional Western family—patriarchal, monogamous—was a primeval human institution; and luckily enough the new sexology fit right in. All the experts agreed that while woman was surprisingly sexual, her ardor was a "slumbering" thing. Waking this sleeping giant was a long process. A woman might not be aroused until after she had given birth to at least one child; in any given case, it might take years. And since woman's sexuality was so intimately connected with "love" it could be elicited, in most cases, only by one man—her husband. So, the naturally active man must go on practicing the art of love on his naturally passive wife, and perhaps after a few years her dormant desires would spring to life and fix themselves gratefully, permanently, on him. For her part, the woman who had waited for marriage had only to continue to wait for orgasm. Waiting and praying, as religion counseled, was her lot in life; she scarcely needed science to tell her it was also her "nature." So passivity engendered passivity—and perhaps children. And maybe after the next child or the one after that she would experience the "new womanhood." If not, she had only herself to blame for her failure to make an adequate sex adjustment.

Instead of sexually freeing woman, as it pretended to do, the new sexology bound her to one man and to a life of watching for orgasm as earlier generations of women had watched for signs of their own salvation. To woman's traditional duties as wife and mother, sexology added the duty of "developing" passion. Later sex experts encouraged the woman who did not experience orgasm to fake it for the sake of her husband's ego; but the early sexologists required her to develop the genuine article.

An American doctor wrote to Havelock Ellis about the case of a "fine womanly young woman with splendid figure" who, try as she might, simply could not "develop desire and passion" for her husband. The doctor was afraid that "the man will someday appear who will be able to develop the latent feelings," but Ellis passed over that subversive possibility. Although men, throughout the twenties, belatedly discovered their pretty "spiritual affinities" only after contracting wives, woman's desire had to be constant or slumber on. Every woman, said Margaret Sanger, is a Cinderella at heart; she could be transformed, presumably, only by the fit of the right shoe.

The social fathers, profoundly uneasy about this tricky business of female sexual "liberation" from the outset, understood that a promiscuous Cinderella mocked the whole patriarchal fairy tale. They were fully prepared to make a bad example of the princess if she dared to run off with the coachman. And, thanks to the growth of news media, they had the means to do it. Radio was a new craze; and newspapers, which had proliferated and added pages of plentiful wartime news, now searched for any new sensation to fill space and keep up circulation. But the Hall-Mills case that sustained more than one paper for half a decade was ultimately disappointing; for the guilty princess was already dead, her paunchy Prince Charming beside her. And if she had been killed by her husband, or her lover's wife and family, or the Klan, so much the better. However serviceable it might be as moral exemplum, as public spectacle a corpse was not very gratifying. But almost before the ink had dried on the last of the Hall-Mills stories, another Cinderella named Ruth Snyder took up with a salesman—a corset and brassiere salesman to be exact—and together they murdered her husband in his bed. In its own way her crime was as subversive of American domesticity as the anarchism of Nicola Sacco and Bartolomeo Vanzetti was of the American political and economic order. Like Sacco and Vanzetti, Ruth Snyder died in the electric chair while the whole country watched the clock. The limits of acceptable American behavior in the twenties were drawn by these highly publicized punishments: the electrocution of two "Bolsheviks" and a "flapper"—two immigrant workingmen and a suburban Long Island housewife. But while the execution of political wrongdoers Sacco and Vanzetti prompted outraged demonstrations, the execution of sexual transgressor Snyder gratified the public. Almost everyone agreed that Ruth Snyder had to die.

2.

Ruth Brown was born on 125th Street in Manhattan in 1895, the daughter of a working-class Scandinavian family. She left school after the eighth grade and got a job with the telephone company; at night she took business classes in shorthand and typing. She was a hard worker and determined to get ahead, but like most young women of her time, she said that she "thought more of marriage than [of] a business career." So when at nineteen she landed a secretarial job with *Motor Boating* magazine and handsome thirty-two-year-old Albert Snyder, an art editor, took an interest in her, she didn't discourage him. Albert Snyder was Ruth Brown's first real "gentleman friend" and after keeping company with him for a few months, she married him in 1915.

The couple lived first in Brooklyn; after their daughter, Lorraine, was born in 1918 they moved to a larger apartment in the Bronx. And as Albert advanced with the magazine, he moved his family to an eight-room house in Queens Village on Long Island. For Albert the move to Queens was a mark of success. For Ruth it was a lonely step into the isolation of suburban life, but she worked hard at housekeeping, sewing curtains and slipcovers and clothing for herself and Lorraine. By 1925 Ruth Brown Snyder had achieved "everything that most women wish for." The newspapers, telling her story after she came to public attention, reported that "she had a house of her own, an automobile, a radio, good furniture, money in the bank, protection and an athlete for a husband." Albert Snyder was not actually an "athlete" but he kept a motorboat for weekend outings and often had a tan. He was also, according to the papers, "a good man, a faithful husband. He took pride in his wife, his child and his home. Made little things to ornament the house. Was thrifty. Worked hard and late. Bought a home, an automobile, a radio and turned in most of his money at home. A model husband."

Unfortunately, he was also gloomy and evil-tempered. His mother-in-law, Josephine Brown, who moved into the Queens Village house with the Snyders when she was widowed, told reporters that while Ruth was gay and fun-loving, Albert was almost always "glum." Ruth liked people and parties; her friends nicknamed her "Tommy" because she was such a good sport—like one of the boys. Albert liked to stay at home. Ruth enjoyed restaurants, the theater, bridge. Albert's hobbies were tinkering with his car and puttering in his garden. Ruth loved animals and would have filled the house with them; Albert grimly tolerated a lone canary and filled the house instead with inanimate "artistic knickknacks" of his own devising. Ruth loved children and was devoted to her daughter, Lorraine. Albert, who hadn't wanted children at all, was doubly disappointed at being stuck with a girl. On the whole, Albert found Ruth too young and giddy for him; he often told her about his previous, more "serious" fiancée Jessie Guischard, who had died before the wedding. It was a pity, he said, that Ruth couldn't be more like her. The unfortunate Snyder alliance probably was no more badly mismatched than any of hundreds of others behind the drawn curtains of Queens communities, but it was unhappy enough that Josephine Brown advised her daughter to seek a divorce, and that Ruth Snyder found a lover, and that little Lorraine Snyder mentioned to a policeman, after her father had been found dead in bed, that her mama and daddy fought all the time.

That remark coupled with the peculiarly amateurish look of the burglary of the Snyder house and the ferocity of Albert's murder kept the police questioning Ruth Snyder long after she first told them of the swarthy intruder—"a tall man with a dark mustache"—who struck her on the head and left her bound hand and foot. They questioned her through the day and night while they searched the Snyder home and found her "stolen" jewelry under the mattress, the five-pound sash-weight—with which Albert had been struck three times—in the basement, and her address book listing the names of twenty-eight men. On the floor in the bedroom where Albert had been clubbed, chloroformed, and finally strangled with picture wire, the police found a small pin bearing the initials *J.G.* for Jessie Guischard. Albert Snyder had carried it as a memento of his former sweetheart, but the police, thinking it might have been dropped by the murderer, matched the initials to a name in Ruth Snyder's address book and asked her: "What about Judd Gray?" Exhausted and surprised, Ruth asked, "Has he confessed?" The police said he had. Then it was only a matter of hours before Henry Judd Gray, Ruth's lover, was arrested at his hotel in Syracuse and returned to New York to confess his part in the killing. Both Snyder and Gray admitted they had conspired together, but each blamed the other for the murder.

Albert Snyder was murdered shortly after he returned from a party at 2:00 Sunday morning and went to bed. By Tuesday morning, all the daily papers carried photographs of the illicit lovers and the text of their confessions of murder. The papers were delighted to have another big case to replace the Hall-Mills affair in their columns. The tabloid *Daily Mirror*, which had dug up so much of the evidence in the New Jersey case, immediately reassigned its top reporters to the Snyder story and began recruiting celebrities to write about the upcoming trial. Even Charlotte Mills, who made her name reporting on the murder of her own mother, was reassigned to the Snyder case. But what was to be said of it? Unlike the Hall-Mills case, there was no mystery, no element of the whodunit about the Snyder story. The murderers had confessed their conspiracy, and the question of which one twisted the lethal wire around Albert Snyder's neck seemed inconsequential. Certainly the people involved in the Snyder affair were, if anything, even more drearily ordinary than those associated with the Hall-Mills case. But there, according to the popular magazine *Outlook*, was the real mystery of the Snyder case. For if Ruth Snyder and Judd Gray were no different from their neighbors, what was to deter those neighbors from committing similar adulteries and murders?

The question was not an idle one. Certainly infidelity and murder of the sort made notorious by the Hall-Mills case seemed epidemic. Only the year before, in 1926, Fanny Soper was convicted of killing her husband, Harry, a deputy sheriff in Blauvelt, New York, and very narrowly escaped the death penalty. In 1924 the notorious Risteen-Plummer triangle and in 1921 the Hemming-Eberhardt affair left husbands murdered in both cases. In 1922, right beside the lurid Hall-Mills letters, newspapers reported the intimate correspondence between Harold GaNun and Ivy Giberson, whose husband, William, supposedly was murdered, like Albert Snyder, by intruders. Mrs. Giberson was sentenced to life. As prosecutors prepared for the Snyder trial, Sadie Raser confessed that she and her lover Frank Van Sickle had murdered her husband, Edward, in Newton, New Jersey, two years before. And during the Snyder trial, Ruth Snyder sometimes shared headlines with Lucy Baxter Earley, on trial in Newburgh, New York, for allegedly murdering her husband with the help of her lover William Wegley. Overworked medical experts dashed between Newburgh and Queens, testifying in both trials at once. The adulterous mate-slaying was certainly nothing new, and whether it occurred any more often during the twenties than it had in the past is impossible to say. But there is no doubt that mate-slaying, like the extramarital relations that led to it, *seemed* to be increasing dramatically. The New York *Post* noted alarmingly that "if even a small percentage of irregular love affairs should lead to killings, the streets of our great cities would resemble the battle of Gettysburg." There was good reason then to ask, as the *Outlook* did of Ruth Snyder and Judd Gray, "If these two could commit such a murder, why not any of countless thousands of others?"

It was more than just a question of deterring murder, for these killings seemed, to contemporary commentators, to reflect a profound social malaise; the New York *Herald Tribune* called it "a social cancer" or "psychopathia suburbis." Murder was only the last act in a long, sordid history of family obligations betrayed and common decencies violated. In the Snyder case, the rather commonplace, shabby affair between the two lovers had been going on for a year and a half—months of lies and coded notes and bribed postmen and clandestine afternoon sex at the Waldorf, while Lorraine entertained herself by riding the elevators. And there was an even more mundane motive in three insurance policies which Albert Snyder did not know he held; they would have paid his widow, who secretly met the premiums, about $100,000. The Snyder murder, like so many others at the time, seemed to have been prompted by "the pettiest, the most ignoble, kind of self-indulgence." And that self-indulgence was thought to be the besetting sin of a society that had lost track altogether of the boundaries of right conduct.

The newspapers, then, in cooperation with the court, took up the task of excising that social cancer, of reestablishing old standards, of ensuring, as the *Herald Tribune* put it, that the "slightly pale yellow dawn of a new decadence, which rose after the lurid sunsets of the war," would deepen "into the clear blue of another, an almost Victorian earnestness." The more respectable dailies tended to serious reflections upon the case while the tabloids went in for sensational, and often wholly fictitious, sidelights. Among them all, they turned the Snyder case into one of the top media events of the decade—and its most important morality play, designed like medieval moral drama to point the way to heaven. By the time it was over, all of the papers had written volumes and, incidentally, sold more newspapers than ever before.

The hundreds of thousands of words written about the case at the time repeatedly sounded two refrains. In the first place, as one reporter coolly noted, everyone is interested in things that are "sexy" and "vile." The tabloids increased their circulation by reporting every little kink in the Snyder-Gray love affair, so that every reader could indulge vicariously in the forbidden; it was a heyday for voyeurs, at least until Gray was called upon to enumerate from the stand every drink he had ever drunk at every lunch he had ever eaten with Ruth Snyder—and the thrilling affair became so tedious that bored spectators left the courtroom. But this exposure of every detail of the adulterers' conduct appealed to the readers' prurient interest and also served to define precisely what conduct was bad and what was permissible. Before it was all over, avid readers knew that respectable women did not smoke, drink, dye their hair, cross their legs, lunch out with strange men, or feel ingratitude toward their husbands. Still, despite the obvious lessons of the Snyder case, the notion of slipping off to the Waldorf for an afternoon of clandestine sex did have a certain sinister appeal to bored wives and husbands; so the newspapers carefully stressed that Snyder and Gray were *not* ordinary folks. They might *appear* ordinary to reflective publications like the *Outlook*, given to raising ponderous questions better left alone; but at heart they were very different. Gray was not truly a man, and Snyder was certainly no woman. As the trial went on, more and more reporters noticed that Snyder didn't even *look* like a woman anymore. Luckily, the reassurance that Snyder and Gray were not, after all, ordinary people made it easier for newspaper readers to indulge vicariously in their crimes without fear of falling into such sin. And the inescapable conclusion, by the end of the trial, that Ruth Snyder was scarcely human at all made it that much easier to send her to the electric chair.

These two themes of the trial coverage—establishing the standards of right conduct and setting apart the evildoers from the great mass of upstanding citizens who supposedly followed those standards—came together in the public presentation of Ruth Snyder: a bad woman, a bad wife, a bad mother, and at the same time an utterly cold, inhuman vampire completely unlike those good, warm, self-sacrificing wives and mothers who represented the best of American womanhood.

In the first reports of the Snyder murder, Ruth Snyder was described as the "beautiful wife" of the slain art director; but the newspapers quickly realized their mistake. After her confession the *Mirror* made one attempt to point up the contrast between Ruth's lovely appearance and hideous crimes; on March 24, just after she confessed, the paper ran a full-page studio portrait with instructions to "study this face, pretty, soft, smiling, with curling hair and delicate features. One of a loving wife and a devoted mother, you would say. Yet it is that of Mrs. Ruth Brown Snyder. . . ." But that line was quickly abandoned. Ruth Snyder became instead the "Fiend Wife," the "faithless wife," the "blonde fiend," the "marble woman" encased from head to toe in a "mask of marble," "flaming Ruth," a "vampire," and "Ruthless Ruth, the Viking Ice Matron of Queens Village." The more sober New York *Post* found her to be a "hard-faced woman," probably "oversexed" and certainly overly interested in "power and authority."

Physically, the *Post* said, she was "heavy and coarse." The New York *Herald Tribune*, apparently casting about for the right approach to the story, called her a "woman of steel" and then criticized her for having rough skin, straight hair, and a wrinkled dress, concluding its report of the first press interview given by the confessed conspirator in murder with the apparently damning judgment: "She is not well groomed."

But it was to the tabloid *Mirror* that readers turned for murder news, and in its pages Ruth Snyder was compared to Lucretia Borgia, Messalina, and Lady Macbeth. The paper hired Dr. Edgar C. Beall, a well-known phrenologist, to study three photographs of Snyder and prepare an analysis that guided the subsequent observations of many celebrity reporters. Dr. Beall noted that Snyder had "flattened" eyelids, "especially on the left side," a configuration "very pronounced in Brigham Young" and clearly indicating a "polygamous disposition." Her other distinctive feature—which everyone was to notice—was her mouth: "as cold, hard, and unsympathetic as a crack in a dried lemon." Although some reporters commented on her square "masculine" jaw, Dr. Beall thought that her chin tapered "like the lower face of a cat," suggesting her "treachery" and "ingratitude." All in all, Dr. Beall judged that it was easy to see in her face "the character of a shallow-brained pleasure seeker, accustomed to unlimited self-indulgence, which at last ends in an orgie [*sic*] of murderous passion and lust, seemingly without a parallel in the criminal history of modern times." Thanks to such pseudoscientific clues, celebrity-reporter Natacha Rambova, second wife of Rudolph Valentino, was able to conclude after watching Ruth Snyder for one hour in the courtroom: "There is lacking in her character that real thing, selflessness. She apparently doesn't possess it and never will. Her fault is that she has no heart." By the time novelist Thyra Samter Winslow visited the courtroom on May 6, there was little left to say, but she mentioned all the telltale features. Snyder, she said, has "cold, mean eyes, and her slit of a mouth is even crueler than I had been led to suppose. Her determined jaw is all that the papers have said it is." "If Ruth Snyder is a woman," thundered playwright Willard Mack in a highly acclaimed article, "then, by God! you must find some other name for my mother, wife or sister. . . ."

On the other hand, Henry Judd Gray, Snyder's lover and co-defendant, was thought to be an awfully nice fellow. Even the detective who arrested him commented, "He's as nice appearing a gentleman as you'd want to meet." Married for eleven years to his childhood sweetheart and, like Snyder, the parent of a nine-year-old daughter, he was regarded in his community—East Orange, New Jersey—as a "model" citizen. As the *Herald Tribune* reported, "He was a Red Cross worker in the World War, was an assiduous worker for the Sunday school of the First Methodist Church, was quiet mannered in the home and a local country club man. He golfed and bridged and motored. He was a member of the Orange Lodge of Elks." In short, a regular fellow. But he also seemed to be a murderer. How could that be explained?

His defense team first followed up the suggestion of Gray's shocked wife: "He must be insane!" Four "alienists" tapped Gray's spinal fluid, X-rayed his head, and interviewed him for days; but they could not find him insane. In fact, he seemed to Dr. Sylvester Lahey, spokesman for the group, a "fine cultured fellow" and "very affable." So the alienists reverted to a theory first advanced by the police on the very day that Gray confessed. As the *Herald Tribune* reported at the time: "All facts now adduced point to a love-mad man completely in the sway of the woman whose will was steel, and brain active and intelligent. She dominated him, police said, and forced her will upon him, even when he desired to back out on some of her proposals." The alienists took up the notion and repeated it to the press before the trial began: "A strange charm of Mrs. Snyder made him do it. . . . Her personality dominated him—he was helpless." At 5 feet 5 inches and 120 pounds, Gray suited the part of the cringing weakling. So by the time attorney William J. Millard summed up the case for the defense of Henry Judd Gray the theory had become gospel.

"That woman," he said to the jury and the ranks of reporters who copied down every word, "like a poisonous snake, drew Judd Gray into her glistening coils, and there was no escape. It was a peculiarly alluring seduction. Just as a piece of steel jumps and clings to the powerful magnet, so Judd Gray came within the powerful, compelling, attractive force of that woman. She held him fast. This woman, this peculiar venomous species of humanity, was abnormal, possessed of an all-consuming, all-absorbing passion, an animal lust, which seemingly was never satiated." In the updated Eden of attorney Millard's imagination, Ruth Snyder became the temptress Eve and the serpent too; while poor Judd Gray, like Adam, unwisely but helplessly succumbed. Judd Gray became a pathetic figure, a "putty man" malleable to the will of the Viking woman of steel, as much her victim as was poor deceived Albert Snyder. Fortunately, the very weakness that made Gray a creature to be pitied also distinguished him from ordinary men, for the true *manly* man retained the power to dominate and control women.

It was the detectives—all men—who first found Gray such a likable fellow and passed on to the public as fact his story that he had been bewitched and dominated. As it happened, in their initial confessions both Snyder and Gray lied and with increasingly bitter recriminations each blamed the other for the actual killing, but the police believed Gray; and even when he later changed his story, neither he nor they gave up the theory that he had been the woman's puppet. The male alienists, too, accepted Gray's interpretation of himself as victim and never interviewed Snyder at all. In court the jurors were still by law in New York all men, all at mid-life, married, with children—men very much like the dead Albert Snyder, or Judd Gray. Women, for their part, judged Ruth Snyder no more generously; she repeatedly appealed for the sympathy of wives and mothers, and apparently received none. Women journalists unanimously found her "unfeminine" and unsympathetic, and the wife of one of the jurors publicly expressed her hope that her husband could not be swayed by such a "brazen woman." Snyder thought that women jurors would see her "side of the case better than a crowd of men" because they would "know the complications and cross-currents of domestic life," but an informal press jury made up of six female and six male reporters condemned her to death. Women, like men, accepted the officially sanctioned version of the case.

That version was firmly grounded in the old double sexual standard, which had not, after all, been "ironed flat." Snyder and Gray had to be judged differently because they were not weighed in the same scales of justice. Ruth Snyder was marked as a "bad woman" from the moment she first met Judd Gray. It was bad to send him a note, bad to visit his office for a "corset fitting," bad to have sex with him. And as the *Post* noted, when Snyder took the stand to face the prosecutor she seemed to be on trial "for adultery instead of murder."

Judd Gray, on the other hand, until he participated in killing Albert Snyder, had done nothing wrong. Officially adultery was frowned upon for both sexes, and Cornelius Vanderbilt, Jr., touted a single sexual standard—including marital fidelity for all—in an editorial for the *Mirror*, but off the record, men knew better. As Havelock Ellis put it: "Promiscuous women, who were not professional prostitutes, or feeble-minded, or insane, have always been rare, while many men who seem practically promiscuous have cut a figure in the world." That is why playwright and *Post* columnist W. E. Woodward could approve Gray's assessment of himself—"I have always been a gentleman and I have always been on the level with everybody"—although "everybody" obviously did not include Gray's wife.

Gray had established his alibi for the murder with the help of an old friend, Haddon Gray (no relation), who posted two letters to Judd's wife, rumpled his bed in the hotel, and hung out a Do Not Disturb sign to make it appear that Judd was still in Syracuse when in fact, so far as Haddon knew, he was really visiting a girl friend. Haddon even lied to the police, maintaining his friend's alibi, until he learned that Judd had confessed to murder. When Haddon Gray took the stand at the trial to tell the truth, he was described in the press as a loyal friend and a true gentleman who had bravely done what any man would do for a good pal: lie so the man could visit his girl friend without his wife's knowledge. To some commentators even Judd Gray's elaborate plans for the murder seemed a harmless amusement. Columnist Woodward speculated in the *Post* that "this mild corset salesman" probably was entertained on "his lonely trips" by the thought "of crushing a rival, of being a strong, brutal caveman." And just before the murder Gray had wrapped the sashweight in paper so it wouldn't hurt Snyder quite so much—a "humane" gesture which showed that Gray was a "kindhearted man at bottom." Playwright Willard Mack echoed in the *Mirror* that Gray had "never been a murderer in his heart." He was simply, to one courtroom observer, the admirable "kind of fellow who'd do anything in the world for somebody he liked." Because of the double sexual standard that still persisted after the so-called sexual revolution, Snyder and Gray, who had sinned together, could not be judged alike. If they had stopped short of murder, Ruth Snyder would still have been a "bad" woman while Judd Gray would have been merely a regular fellow. As it was Gray seemed to be no worse than what the papers called him: a poor boob, a weakling, a puppet, a sap. He was simply "a bunch of dough that somebody forgot to knead," a man who couldn't "put up a croquet set without help."

The Snyder case as media event—the great morality play of the decade—was meant almost exclusively for the edification of women. Gray's sister, Margaret Logan, touched upon the need for the lesson in her prepared statement to the press during the trial: "I never before realized how much tragedy is concealed in houses all around us. This is created by evil women. Most of their depredations upon happy domestic life don't become public. Few come to such a dreadful pass as the catastrophe in our own family." With woman cast as the source of evil, as Eve in league with Satan, all the old-fashioned notions of chivalry were turned inside out. Ruth Snyder became a fiend "unworthy of the chivalry, protection and consideration which right thinking men have always accorded decent womanhood." So when one of Snyder's attorneys, summing up her case, made a misguided plea for chivalry, he was answered by titters from the audience. As the *Post* reporter described it: "He was a knight fighting a battle of terrific odds for a golden damozel disguised as a blonde, fattish and ice-hard housewife."

True femininity in this case was represented by the loyal, grieving mothers of the defendants, Josephine Brown and Margaret Gray. Judd's mother, in particular, was a woman so dignified in her relations with the press that rumors she had made Judd a mamma's boy quickly were squelched. She was not blamed for his crime but left to wonder aloud, "Wherein did I fail?" Little was said during the trial about Gray's wife, Isabel, who had gone into seclusion, but when she visited the prison after his conviction to forgive him, she was praised for displaying the loyalty of a "good little wife." The daughters, Lorraine Snyder and Jane Gray, were greatly pitied because both had been deprived of a father's love.

If there was to be a hero of the drama, amid this chorus of weeping women, it could only be Judd Gray; and curiously enough, with the old chivalric code upended, he was able to fill that role not by protecting his ladylove but by ratting on her. In the final days of the trial, Gray took the stand to redeem his manliness by telling "the truth": Ruth Snyder committed the murder. Judd was there, of course. He never denied that. But, he said, he had tried to talk her out of it, tried lo leave the house; he was powerless against her. So, incited by Ruth and a bottle of whiskey, he struck the first blow with the sashweight only to have Albert wake up and fight back. Unable to carry on, Gray called out "Help me, Momsie." And Momsie finished the job. At the end of his testimony Gray broke into tears that swept all skepticism away. As the *Mirror* put it, Gray "emerged from the mire into which he slipped wearing a crown that few achieve—the crown of truth." Even the district attorney, summing up the state's case against Snyder and Gray, called Gray "a decent, red-blooded, upstanding American citizen."

Ruth had her own story to tell, but no one wanted to hear it. In court the attorneys and the judge kept telling her to answer yes or no and stop trying to explain. The papers said she "lied like a dog to save her own cheap hide." There were things she never got a chance to say, so later, on death row, she wrote out her story for the *Mirror*—an erratic jumble of painful remembering, rage, religious platitudes, and grief. She had been a respectable and faithful wife, she said, until she met Gray, a sweet-talking commercial traveler accustomed to "selling" women. She fell in love with him, though she knew he saw other women: Alice in Rochester and someone called "Snooks." But he started asking her for money—ninety dollars here, a hundred dollars there—and suggesting that he might have to speak to Albert if she didn't come up with it. She did as he asked—even though she wanted to break off the affair—for fear that in a showdown with Albert, she would lose her daughter. The insurance policies and the murder, she claimed, were Gray's idea; he talked about it whenever he was "liquor-logged" as he was almost all the time, but Ruth thought she could talk him out of it as she had done before. On the night of the murder she set out the bottle of bootleg whiskey he demanded, but Gray, instead of taking the bottle and leaving, as she expected him to do, drank it and stayed. He was still there hiding when she and Albert came home from the party. After Albert went to sleep, she tried to persuade Judd to leave; and just when she thought she had succeeded, he went upstairs while she was in the bathroom and murdered Albert. And ever since, the "lying, cringing jackal" had been hiding behind her skirts.

On the face of it, Ruth Snyder's story was no less plausible than Judd Gray's. And while witnesses established that Gray had bought the murder weapons and set up an alibi well in advance, the only evidence that Ruth Snyder had participated in the murder was the testimony of Gray himself. Still, no one believed any part of her story. Even when she converted to Catholicism in jail, most New Yorkers who spoke to the *Mirror*'s inquiring reporter about it thought she had converted only in hopes of winning a commutation from Catholic Governor Al Smith. Writing her final story, Ruth Snyder asked, "Don't the 'outside' believe ANYTHING I tell?" But she already knew the answer.

The newspaper-reading public, which doubted Ruth Snyder and condemned her, eagerly supported her right to die in the electric chair. Even before the trial began, a female social worker argued in the *Mirror*, "Any woman who commits a man's crime should be given a man's punishment." And State Senator William Lathrop Love of Brooklyn urged "equal 'rights' for Women

Criminals. . . . Women should suffer the same penalties that are meted out to men for the crimes they commit," he maintained. "If a woman enters the competition with men she has a chance to gain the same ends, and I see no reason why she should not suffer the same penalties." While the verdict was being awaited in the Snyder case, several papers published accounts of the death in 1899 of Martha Place, the last woman to die in the electric chair in New York; and the *Mirror* quoted approvingly from then Governor Theodore Roosevelt's decision denying clemency: "In the commission of a crime, a woman is deserving of the same blame as a man in a similar case. I would deal with the woman as with the man—no whit differently." On January 10, 1928, while Snyder and Gray waited on death row at Sing Sing, Governor Al Smith issued a similar statement denying their application for executive clemency. "The execution of this judgment on a woman is so distressing," he said, "that I had hoped that the appeal to me for executive clemency would disclose some fact which would justify my interference with the processes of the law. But this did not happen." It was widely predicted that Smith's firm stand would do him good in his campaign for the presidency; certainly Roosevelt's firmness in the Place appeal had not harmed his political future. Pleased with Smith's decision, *The New York Times* said in an editorial: "Equal suffrage has put women in a new position. If they are equal with men before the law, they must pay the same penalties as men for transgressing it."

Feminists could scarcely quarrel with the argument for equal rights, yet in this case it smacked unmistakably of expediency rather than justice. No one could claim that Snyder and Gray had been treated "no whit differently" in the courtroom where Snyder had been tried for adultery and murder, Gray for murder alone. And as a spokeswoman for the American Association of Labor Legislation pointed out in another context: "Equal treatment of unequals is the greatest inequality." But Ruth Snyder had claimed for herself sexual prerogatives that belonged only to men; through her execution the full implications of "equality" could be brought home to feminists and flappers alike. Arguing that both Gray and Snyder should be executed, Willard Mack gave away the vindictiveness behind the equal rights argument. Ruth Snyder had wanted "ONE BED" with her lover, Mack said. Let her have "ONE CHAIR."

In the last act of the drama, both Snyder and Gray did go to the chair on the night of January 12, 1928. And even then Snyder got a bad press. When the sentence was passed on May 9, 1927, the "stone woman" became hysterical, and afterward in her cell she suffered from "nervous paralysis" and "epileptic spasms" that the papers called "the forerunners of insanity." Gray, on the other hand, received the sentence "with calmness and prayer." "Gray finds enough of traditional manhood in him to take his medicine without whining," reported the *Mirror*. But "Ruth Snyder—woman—turns to the immemorial device of her sex to wring pity from male hearts. Already she is ill and suffering. Expect her to grow worse and worse as the hour of her atonement nears." No change in their behavior could change the opinion the press had already formed of Snyder and Gray; and by the night set for execution Ruth Snyder had indeed grown worse. In keeping with a Sing Sing tradition of executing the more distraught prisoner first, she went first to the electric chair. She was "a disheveled wreck" in a drab prison shirtwaist and smock; her blonde hair had gone almost gray. She entered the death chamber murmuring prayers, but she cried out and collapsed when she saw the electric chair and had to be lifted into it by the two matrons who accompanied her. Quickly the executioners strapped her in; the matrons retired; Warden Lewis Lawes, who opposed capital punishment, turned away; and while the priest intoned prayers and Snyder, sobbing, cried out "Father, forgive them for they know not what they do," chief executioner Robert Elliott threw the switch. An imaginative reporter for the New York *World* wrote that as the current passed through her body "her left hand twisted back and upward as if trying to escape the imprisoning strap and the index finger of this hand stiffened in a pointed accusation at herself." And an imaginative photographer from the Chicago *Tribune*, smuggled in by the New York *Daily News* in a last attempt to one-up its competitor, the *Mirror*, raised his trouser leg and snapped her picture with a miniature camera strapped to his ankle. She died under the eyes of thirty reporters, doctors, and prison officials—all men—wearing a regulation football helmet wired to 2,000 volts.

A few minutes later Judd Gray, wearing a well-pressed dark gray suit "with invisible stripe," entered the room with the prison chaplain. "Here was a man," said the New York *Sun*, "who was going to his death with a controlled spirit. He crossed the threshold without the need of a supporting hand. His step was firm and assured. He walked upright, with shoulders thrown back slightly. There was no weakening of the knees, no trembling of hands or lips." The chaplain recited the beatitudes, and until the switch was thrown, Gray followed them inaudibly: "Blessed are the poor in spirit; for theirs is the kingdom of Heaven."

Then it was all over. Judd Gray had repeatedly urged young men to stay away from bad liquor and bad women; and in the end he had died like a man. On the front page of the *Mirror* Ruth Snyder's portrait was replaced by the smiling face of Charles Lindbergh. The show-business celebrities who had haunted the trial went back to Hollywood and the Great White Way: D. W. Griffiths to the movies, Evelyn Law to the Ziegfeld Follies, and David Belasco—who had attended the trial to gather material for a new play—went back to Broadway, where lesser shows had folded while thousands were turned away from the Queens courthouse. *The New York Times* hoped the execution of a husband-slayer—the first such execution in New York in forty years—would have a much-needed deterrent effect, while the *Mirror* congratulated itself that the "impressive lesson of the Snyder case—more effective than a thousand sermons"—would save countless people from their own "follies." The morality play was over. After the executions, which the *Post* termed the "Finale of Queens Pageant," columnist Nunnally Johnson summed up the "drama of violence": "That was the end. It was a grand show. It never failed once. It had no surprises, no Theatre Guild stuff, no modernisms. It was the good old stuff done well and fiercely. It was grim and grand. It moved slowly and inevitably like Dreiser. And it came at last, last night, to the magnificent, the tremendous, the incomparable curtain that the audience was counting on. Everybody walked out with a satisfied feeling. It was regular."

And well might everyone feel satisfied, for the moral could not have been more clear. The final lesson of the Snyder–Gray drama was the lesson that had been taught to Ruth Snyder herself. In her last interview and in her final story for the *Mirror* she, in turn, restated the lesson for the public. "If I were to live over again," she said, "I would be what I want my child to be—a good girl, really making the fear of God a guide to a straight life." Again she wrote: "I said before 'Go Straight' and I mean it more than ever. And I wish a lot of women who may be sinning could come here and see what I have done for myself through sinning and maybe they would do some of the thinking I have done for months and they would be satisfied with their homes and would stop wishing for things they should try to get along without when they can't have them.

"Maybe there are women who have nice homes (and husbands who do the best they can for them) even if they don't like their husbands and they could bear it if they would only make up their minds everything can't be just perfect.

"Some husbands don't make enough money to get their wives the things they wish they had and if the wives have any brains they will just take what they can get and try to make the best of it."

And again she wrote: "OH, GOD, HOW A LOT OF WOMEN WOULD CHANGE IF THEY COULD COME HERE AND SEE MY PUNISHMENT."

13.2 TREADWELL'S NEOLOGISM: *MACHINAL*—GINGER STRAND

In 1923, Elmer Rice's Expressionist drama *The Adding Machine* opened in New York. In 1927, Ruth Snyder was tried for conspiring with her lover Judd Gray to murder her husband, becoming the first woman to be executed by the electric chair in the state of New York. Both the Expressionist and the real-life drama caught the attention of a young Californian journalist. Sophie Treadwell worked fast: her play *Machinal*—revived in New York in 1990 to remarkable acclaim—premiered in 1928. The play was understood to be based on the previous year's spectacular Snyder–Gray trial. But as its title suggests, *Machinal* can also be read as a feminist revision of *The Adding Machine*, both plays being Expressionist attempts to contextualize an isolated act of murder. Treadwell rewrites a man's plot—that of Rice's Mr. Zero—with a woman as the subject.

To do so is to worry the abstract mode of Expressionism itself. Writing a type of play meant to highlight the universality of a subject's experience, Treadwell begins by suggesting her subject's specificity—as a woman, and as a woman based on one individual woman. It is the protagonist's relationship to Ruth Snyder—a woman constructed by newspapers—which is crucial here. I want to argue that Treadwell's appropriation of news is the locus of her play's meaning. *Machinal* re-creates the proliferation of news narratives surrounding Ruth Snyder's trial, using the relationships between event, news story, and play to stage the process through which event becomes representation, and a woman's experience is obscured, as legal and journalistic forces transform it to narrative.

Roland Barthes has asserted that "Language is legislation, speech is its code."[1] *Machinal*, ostensibly a play about civil law, reveals itself to be a play about the law of language: the hand of narrative ultimately sentences the protagonist not only to death, but to silence. But in portraying the lethal languages which surround and stifle her heroine, Treadwell diminishes their very capacity to do so. This is, after all, the aim of theatre. Barthes reminds us:

> We must, therefore, not be surprised if on the impossible horizon of linguistic anarchy—at the point where language attempts to escape its own power, its own servility—we find something which relates to theater . . . We might say that literature's third force, its strictly semiotic force, is to *act* signs rather than to destroy them—to feed them into a machinery of

> language whose safety catches and emergency brakes have exploded; in short, to institute, at the very heart of servile language, a veritable heteronomy of things.
>
> [10]

Barthes, like Treadwell, sees language as a machine—subject and henchman of its own unchangeable logic. But the machine can be turned against itself. Treadwell coined a new word as the title of her play. She is, as Barthes would say, both persisting and shifting ground. In the very act of describing from within the oppressive nature of discourse, she moves a step beyond it.

Treadwell outlines her protagonist's successive alienation from each role imposed upon her by a patriarchal discourse: daughter, wife, mother, defendant, Christian. In her desperation, Helen Jones turns to tabloid news as a model for her own experience: "Woman finds husband dead" she reads aloud in a domestic scene with her husband. George Jones chastises her for reading tabloid journalism, and forces her to listen instead to a pompous editorial about the rights of man. Even the facts of a woman's existence are destined to be upstaged by a masculine abstract philosophy. But the news towards which Helen turns is no refuge; it is the place where finally even the sad truth of her own story is occluded. Ruth Snyder's murder trial, in court and in the newspapers, was the perfect example of how a woman's narrative becomes obscured in the operation of these discourses.

Even before Treadwell began to write, journalists had acknowledged their inability to represent the real story of Ruth Snyder, although none associated this difficulty with gender. Several papers editorialized about the inadequacy of the trial in determining the "truth" of the murder. One magazine asked

> What broke down the moral character of these two people? What creates this insensate desire for material satisfaction as the end of being? And if these two could commit such a murder, why not any of countless thousands of others?
>
> This is the real Snyder mystery and its challenge to the standards of American life.[2]

The *New York Evening Post* columnist W. E. Woodward found a similar lack of explanation in the legal process:

> How then does Mrs. Snyder differ from those other dissatisfied wives with heavily insured husbands? Or from other subtle women who meet men without their husbands' knowledge? We do not know the answers to these questions, and will perhaps never know them. The law does not try to find out; it deals only with events and the superficial motives leading to them. So here is the real mystery in the Snyder case. It is the profound mystery of personality, the mystery of impulses that arise from obscure physical or mental changes.
>
> ["Law Does Not Try to Find Real Impulses For Snyder Killing," 3 May 1927]

The vast desire to understand combined with the superficial nature of legal conclusions probably accounts for the fascination such media events hold. Approximately 1,500,000 words about the Snyder story were filed on press wires by May 5, 1927 according to the *Evening Post* of that day. Albert Snyder's murder, and the subsequent trial of his wife and her lover was one of the most sensational media events of the 1920s. The *New York Times* ran a piece of the story, usually on the front page, every day from March 27, 1927, the day after Albert Snyder was killed, until May 5. After that, up through the executions on January 13, 1928, there were very few days when the paper did not run a story on the Snyder–Gray trial. Other New York papers were equally if not more thorough in their coverage of the case. Newspapers published the testimony in full, reported everything that the defendants said, did, or ate in their cells, and commented constantly on Mrs. Snyder's dress and appearance. They reprinted the remarks of preachers who discussed the trial in their sermons, and periodically editorialized on it themselves. The Snyder story spawned more stories, as when one Alice Johnson shot her husband in a quarrel over the case. It was copy as hot as the recent Chambers–Levin trial or the murder of Lisa Steinberg, and it was more brazenly, if not any more cruelly, exploited.

Treadwell borrowed much of *Machinal*'s language from the media coverage of Ruth Snyder. Even the title alluding to Rice's play suggests the language used by the press about Mrs. Snyder. The *New York Herald Tribune* began an article with the same image:

> The clank of the court machinery that police had expected would place Mrs. Ruth Snyder and Henry Judd Gray, East Orange corset salesman, in the electric chair for the murder of Mrs. Snyder's husband . . . broke the calm of the accused pair yesterday and caused them to recant their confessions.
>
> ["Gray Swears Mrs. Snyder Led in Killing Her Husband," 23 March 1927]

Ruth Snyder was generally assumed to have murdered her husband for similar reasons Treadwell's Young Woman does: she was having an affair with another man, hated her older husband (whom she also met when he was her boss), and was isolated and lonely in her unsatisfying life. The *New York Times* explains:

> Mrs. Snyder regarded her home merely as a lodging and had practically nothing to do with the people about her. . . . The lack of neighborhood interest to act as a restraint on her is a factor in explaining the violent effort of this woman to escape from her life and environment after more than a decade of submission to her lot.
>
> ["Wife Betrays Paramour as Murderer of Snyder, and He Then Confesses," 22 March 1927]

The *New York Times*'s pontification is echoed tragically in the Young Woman's desperate cry: "I won't submit." It is clear from Ruth Snyder's example that the news to which Helen turns to find examples for actions is not only destined to fail her when it comes to describing her own, but will itself figure the process by which the woman will be forced to submit.

At times, as in the *Times* story above, the news coverage of Ruth Snyder's trial and conviction seemed almost sympathetic. Certainly coverage of her execution tempered its morbid fascination with broad gestures towards pity, and even some anti-capital punishment sentiment. But sympathy never equates with understanding, and the sympathy shown Mrs. Snyder could only sustain itself by relegating her to the realm of the theatrical. Interestingly, the *New York Times* notes that during her testimony, "the one real murmur of sympathy which she got from the audience was when she said that only once in her married life had her husband taken her to the theatre" ("Mrs. Snyder Weeps on the Witness Stand but Tells Her Story Quietly," 30 April 1927).

For the most part, however, the media accorded little sympathy of even the superficial sort to Ruth Snyder. She was assumed to be guilty from the first. Because she had admitted to an ongoing extra-marital affair, the defense attorney's exclamations about her well-kept home and her own pious assertions of love for her family sounded ludicrous. The defense's only hope was to paint her as completely without agency. "Woman is just as God intended her to be," declared her lawyer,

> were it not for some man, and we will prove to you that Mrs. Ruth Snyder is just as God intended her to be were it not for her incompatible husband, [and] the deceiver Gray.
>
> ["Crowd Fights to Hear Story of Mrs. Snyder," *New York Herald Tribune*, 30 April 1927]

In return, the defense for Gray, which received much more press space, argued that Ruth Snyder was the brains behind the brawn, an evil woman who had "hypnotized" the average man into helping her murder her husband.

> The theory of the defense, as it was outlined by one of Gray's many legal advisors, is that Gray was kept under a sort of hypnotic domination by Mrs. Snyder; that she planned the details of the murder, summoned him on the hurried trip from Syracuse and coerced him into executing it. . . . According to this account of Gray's defense, Mrs. Snyder was a powerful-minded and imperious woman who reduced the East Orange corset salesman to a state of mental slavery, transforming him in a few months from a man of good standing and good record to a cold-blooded assassin.
>
> ["Police Endeavor to Find Out Which One Bought Poison," *New York Times*, 28 March 1927]

Mrs. Snyder was characterized as a "human fiend, a human serpent," and her character was defamed at every possible juncture. In a moment eerily similar to the trial of Robert Chambers for the murder of Jennifer Levin, detectives produced a "memorandum book" containing "the names, addresses and telephone numbers of twenty-eight men" ("Mrs. Snyder To Ask For Separate Trial," *New York Times*, 9 April 1927).

Thus, the case was constructed along the classic virgin/whore opposition: if Ruth Snyder was guilty, she was an evil temptress; if she was not guilty, she was a tragic victim with no will of her own. The press coverage divided roughly into these categories. Alternately sensational and moralistic, the press presented her accordingly as either evil subject or helpless object.

The defense for Gray necessarily assaulted Mrs. Snyder's character, but the duality was carried out in news analysis as well as in the defendants' opposing stories. W. E. Woodward, columnist for the *New York Evening Post*, observed

> I don't know, but I suspect that he [Gray] was under the spell of Circe. It was she who turned the companies of Ulysses into swine, and there have been Circes of every age.
>
> ["Law Does Not Try to Find Real Impulses for Snyder Killing," 3 May 1927]

Three days later, he decides in favor of a more contemporary myth:

> My impression is that he was dominated by Mrs. Snyder because she stood for the time being in the place of his mother. . . . As this case unrolls, inch by inch, it seems to me that it embodies, in some faint undefined way, a picture of the Oedipus complex.
>
> ["Law Veils Gray, Woodward Finds," 6 May 1927]

No matter which myth predominates, the depiction of Ruth Snyder as the crime's mastermind always appears as submission to a narrative imperative: when she is considered in this light she is inevitably compared to fictional characters—she is Circe, or Lady Macbeth.

Undoubtedly, the relentless narratization of Mrs. Snyder contributed to Treadwell's focus on the repressive nature of narrative. Her courtroom scene becomes a study of the process by which stories are constructed, contrasting sharply with Elmer Rice's treatment in his *Adding Machine* trial scene. For Rice, the trial and media coverage are simply the channels through which Mr. Zero's story emerges. Rice's courtroom scene is simply a monologue: Mr. Zero sits on the stand and his story pours forth uninterrupted and uncontested. At the end, the jury rises and pronounces "Guilty!" For Mr. Zero and his jury, what is at issue is not the story itself, but the State's judgment upon it: was the act legal or illegal, and what should the punishment be? The truth about the event is simply presumed to reside in the subject's narrative.

Treadwell's courtroom scene is not based, as Rice's is, on the presumption that facts are an easily accessible commodity. *Machinal*'s courtroom scene, having learned from the real trial upon which it is based, demonstrates vividly how stories are created, and how women's stories are transformed into that different thing we know as narrative. Treadwell outlines the process by which the reality of Ruth Snyder's story was transformed into narrative—the process by which any woman's story is reconfigured, retold, and absorbed into an ideology not her own.

As Helen Jones takes the stand, the first and second reporters begin narrating the scene. Immediately, her simple actions are transmuted into two conflicting stories as the two reporters narrate entirely different interpretations of her mental state. She is sworn in, and the defense begins the examination:

> LAWYER FOR DEFENSE: Mrs. Jones, you are the widow of the late George H. Jones, are you not?
>
> YOUNG WOMAN: Yes.
>
> LAWYER FOR DEFENSE: How long were you married to the late George H. Jones before his demise?
>
> YOUNG WOMAN: Six years.
>
> LAWYER FOR DEFENSE: Six years! And it was a happy marriage, was it not? (YOUNG WOMAN hesitates.) Did you quarrel?
>
> YOUNG WOMAN: No, sir.
>
> LAWYER FOR DEFENSE: Then it was a happy marriage, wasn't it?
>
> YOUNG WOMAN: Yes, sir.[3]

The defense strategy seeks to place the Young Woman within the context of her feminine roles, beginning by constructing her as a "good wife." The concurrent construction of her marriage as a "happy" one is revealing: judged by the law's narrow definition of a "happy" marriage—one in which there are no quarrels—the Jones marriage was indeed happy. Already the truth of the woman's experience is obscured by a restrictive legal logic.

Ruth Snyder had similar exchanges with her questioners, in which the "truth" a word held for her conflicted with the meaning accepted by the court. The *New York Times*, printing the text of her testimony, explained that

> Mr. Froessel [the prosecutor] quarreled with the witness at some length over the exact meaning of "plastered up." She contended that one person might use it to mean "thoroughly intoxicated" and another might use it to mean merely "having a good time."
>
> ["Widow Is Hammered Hard by the State on Secrecy Over Husband's Insurance," 3 May 1927]

Regardless of the accused woman's drinking habits, this quarrel begins to suggest why it is that Ruth Snyder, when told that her jury would be entirely composed of men, said

> I'm sorry. I believe that women would understand this case better than men, and then women have a better sense of justice.
>
> ["Gray to Seek Trial Outside of Queens," *New York Times*, 26 March 1927]

The justice meted out by men in both the real and the fictional trials is a justice based entirely on the ability to assign simple definitions to words and actions. The relational qualities of women's languages are subordinated to a monologic language, in which a word has a single meaning at all times and for all people, and in which an action is always right or always wrong, according to formalized rules of behavior.

In the introduction to *Doing What Comes Naturally*, Stanley Fish sums up the gendering of law by quoting from the introduction to another book, *Women's Way of Knowing*. He notes that such gendering relies upon an epistemology which posits "a distinction between a male reliance 'on abstract laws and universal principles to adjudicate disputes' and a female preference 'for an understanding of the context for . . . choice,' for 'dialogue and exchange of views' rather than an impersonal procedure."[4] Fish is among those by whom it has been argued lately that the law is not the foundationalist structure it appears to be: that "the law" is as constructed an entity as any other culturally produced discourse, hence equally subject to interpretation. The constructedness of law, Fish suggests, invalidates any epistemology which posits a difference between men's and women's ways of knowing:

> It would be my contention that this distinction will not hold up from either end: abstract laws are never abstract or universal but are always reflections of some (albeit unacknowledged) context; and an understanding of context will never be simply inductive, but will always be produced by principles (themselves contingent and transformable) already in place.
>
> [22]

Without disagreeing with Fish's assertions, it is possible to think that he is here, to use one of his own favorite metaphors, putting the cart before the horse. Regardless of whether or not one believes law to be a universal and objective principle, it is difficult to deny that it has been treated and accepted as one at specific historical moments, most notably by the very subjects who were constructing and enforcing it. To argue that the law is not universal does not negate a long history in which the very *thinking* of law as a universal principle has led to the exclusion and silencing of contextual modes of understanding, whether those modes were themselves contingent on abstract principles or not. The point is not that either epistemology is the right or wrong one, or even that discrediting both collapses the difference between them. A very real struggle has taken place again and again, in which the most common outcome has been the silencing of a mode of thought and articulation most otten identified with femininity. This is the struggle which Treadwell stages in her courtroom scene.

Carol Gilligan has taken an empirical rather than an essential approach to theorizing the difference between predominantly masculine morality based on concepts of "rights," and a predominantly feminine one based on "responsibilities":

> The psychology of women that has consistently been described as distinctive in its greater orientation toward relationships and interdependence implies a more contextual mode of judgment and a different moral understanding.[5]

Ruth Snyder's fear of an all-male jury, and her belief that "women have a better sense of justice" exemplifies the conflict between the two systems described by Gilligan:

> Thus it becomes clear why a morality of rights and noninterference may appear frightening to women in its potential justification of indifference and unconcern. At the same time, it becomes clear why, from a male perspective, a morality of responsibility appears inconclusive and diffuse, given its insistent contextual relativism.
>
> [22]

Ruth Snyder was justified in fearing her jury on the grounds of moral incompatibility. It was of course, composed of men, all but one of whom were married. They were "a group of average, small-town businessmen, merchants, and clerks . . . likely to take their duties seriously and not let sentiment or forceful oratory interfere with their conception of right and wrong" ("Analyst Finds Snyder Jury Cold to Lawyers' Oratory," *New York Evening Post*, 4 May 1927). So concluded Dr. Thaddeus Bolton, hired by the *Post* to give an individual psychological profile for each juror after closely examining their photographs. The *New York Times* concurred with his opinion, noting that when Mrs. Snyder wept, the jury "avoided gazing at her. Instead, they looked about the court room" ("Mrs. Snyder Weeps on the Witness Stand," 30 April 1927).

Ignoring the actual relational qualities of the Young Woman's experience, the defense in *Machinal* seeks only to locate her within the matrix of traditional roles assigned to women, in order to exercise a deductive logic: she is a normal woman; normal women don't kill their husbands, *ergo*, she didn't kill her husband. "A devoted daughter, gentlemen of the jury!" the defense lawyer proclaims; "As well as a devoted wife and a devoted mother!" (521).

The defense then asks her to tell her story "in her own words." The lawyer interjects constantly, however, adjusting her words to fit the portrait he is attempting to paint:

LAWYER FOR DEFENSE: And then what happened?

YOUNG WOMAN: The man struck him again and he fell back.

LAWYER FOR DEFENSE: I see. What did the men do then? The big dark looking men.

YOUNG WOMAN: They turned and ran out of the room.

LAWYER FOR DEFENSE: I see. What did you do then, Mrs. Jones?

YOUNG WOMAN: I saw Mr. Jones was bleeding from the temple. I got towels and tried to stop it, and then I realized he had—passed away—

LAWYER FOR DEFENSE: I see. What did you do then?

YOUNG WOMAN: I didn't know what to do. But I thought I'd better call the police. So I went to the telephone and called the police.

LAWYER FOR DEFENSE: What happened then.

YOUNG WOMAN: Nothing. Nothing happened.

LAWYER FOR DEFENSE: The police came, didn't they?

YOUNG WOMAN: Yes—they came.

[522]

Even while collaborating in the construction of an obviously pre-planned story, the Young Woman seems unable to prevent what seems to be the real story from breaking through. The narrative falters whenever the Young Woman does not know what to say, or responds negatively: "Nothing. Nothing happened." It is here that we feel the emptiness of Helen's experience making itself known. In the gaps between the defense lawyer's story and her mechanical repetition of it, we sense the real story of the Young Woman's alienation lurking.

The lawyer answers many of the Young Woman's statements with "I see," as if the facts are straightforward enough to present irrefutable visual evidence. But it is his vision, not the Young Woman's, which predominates. Just as Mr. Jones constantly insists on his wife verbalizing whatever she is reading or seeing—"You must be reading something"—the lawyer does not accept "Nothing" as an answer to his question "What happened then." "Nothing" may be the answer truest to the Young Woman's experience, but the law must have a confirmable fact in order to judge the situation.

The reporters intervene before the cross-examination, again demonstrating how the trial is being manipulated into narrative to serve the agendas of individual newspapers:

1ST REPORTER (WRITING): The accused woman told a straightforward story of—

2ND REPORTER: The accused woman told a rambling, disconnected story of—

[522]

The mark of Treadwell's skill is that neither report sounds more nor less true.

The second round of questioning begins by casting into doubt the Young Woman's capacity for vision:

LAWYER FOR PROSECUTION: Ah! You saw Mr. Jones was hurt! You saw this—how did you see it?

YOUNG WOMAN: I just saw it.

LAWYER FOR PROSECUTION: Then there was a light in the room?

YOUNG WOMAN: A sort of light.

LAWYER FOR PROSECUTION: What do you mean—a sort of light? A bed light?
YOUNG WOMAN: No. No, there was no light on.
LAWYER FOR PROSECUTION: Then where did it come from—this sort of light?
YOUNG WOMAN: I don't know.

[522]

In contrast to the defense lawyer's insistent vision, the Young Woman's ability to see is made to seem a figment of her imagination. Casting doubt upon her capacities as subject, the prosecuting lawyer then produces the murder weapon in order to begin telling the Young Woman stories about herself. He introduces rubber gloves, a nightgown, and the vase given to her by her lover (all, incidentally, objects introduced as evidence against Mrs. Snyder as well). Finally, he produces an affidavit from her lover, from which he reads to the court Richard Roe's narrative of their affair. In order to stop the agonizing display, the Young Woman breaks down and confesses:

YOUNG WOMAN: Don't read any more! No more!
LAWYER FOR PROSECUTION: Why not?
YOUNG WOMAN: I did it! I did it! I did it!
LAWYER FOR PROSECUTION: You confess?
YOUNG WOMAN: Yes—I did it!
LAWYER FOR DEFENSE: I object, your Honor.
JUDGE: You confess you killed your husband?
YOUNG WOMAN: I put him out of the way—yes.
JUDGE: Why?
YOUNG WOMAN: To be free.
JUDGE: To be free? Is that the only reason?
YOUNG WOMAN: Yes.

[526]

Ruth Snyder confessed the first time she was questioned at length. In her case, it was the mention of her lover which brought about the breakdown and confession. The *New York Times* describes how the woman accused of battering her husband to death with a window-weight was brought to confess when her lover's "name was used on her like a battering-ram" ("Wife Betrays Paramour as Murderer of Snyder," 22 March 1927). The prosecution in her case was also described as "hammering" her: "Her Story Hammered" (*New York Evening Post*, 2 May 1927); "Widow is Hammered Hard by the State" (*New York Times*, 3 May 1927).

Whether the press's metaphorical payback was intended or not, the impulse to take the woman's own action and use it against her parallels the process in both *Machinal* and Ruth Snyder's trial—a process whereby the accused's story is taken away from her, rewritten, and forced back upon her. Helen's collaboration with the defense lawyer's story gives way to her unavoidable collaboration with the prosecutor's story. Neither story, it is clear, represents her own experience or intentions. With her confession, her own story begins to come forth. But it is a story so inconceivable to the courtroom and the law that it only completes the process of her conversion from subject to object. Confronted with her inscrutable subjectivity, the courtroom transforms her to total voicelessness: she becomes a spectacle.

The prosecutor asks the Young Woman why, if she wanted to be free, she didn't simply divorce her husband:

> YOUNG WOMAN: Oh I couldn't do that!! I couldn't hurt him like that!
> *(Burst of laughter from ALL in the court. The* YOUNG WOMAN *stares out at them, and then seems to go rigid.)*
> JUDGE: Silence!
> BAILIFF: Silence!
> *(There is gradual silence.)*
> JUDGE: Mrs. Jones, why—(YOUNG WOMAN begins to moan—suddenly—as though the realization of her enormity and her isolation had just come upon her. It is a sound of desolation, of agony, of human woe. It continues until the end of the scene.) Why—?
> *(*YOUNG WOMAN *cannot speak.)*
>
> [526]

When she tells the fundamental truth of her own story—that she had not been striking out against her little, human husband, but rather against the entire repressive system—Helen receives not understanding but laughter.

Like the courtroom crowd at Ruth Snyder's trial, which was constantly compared to a Broadway audience and often rebuked for its unruliness, the spectators in *Machinal*'s courtroom have made the leap from empathy to seeing the Young Woman as a tragicomic figure, an unreal character whose "lines" can provide amusement. In fact, the courtroom crowd at Ruth Snyder's trial had a very similar outburst:

> Mr. Froessel asked her if she had ever given her husband any cause for dissatisfaction. She said "No." The courtroom laughed and Justice Scudder threatened to clear it. That was the last laugh.
>
> [*New York Times*, 3 May 1927]

The last laugh indeed. At the courtroom's hilarity, Treadwell's Young Woman realizes the complete powerlessness of her situation and "goes rigid," reacting with hysteria's most common symptom: aphasic revolt. In the face of the State's overwhelming power to retell her story with her as object, rather than subject, Helen Jones responds with the language of silence—"Silence!" orders the judge—that has always been the final refuge of women denied the right to speak their own words.

As language fails the Young Woman, the court adjourns, and the reporters—now three—file their sensational headlines:

> 1ST REPORTER: Murderess confesses.
> 2ND REPORTER: Paramour brings confession.
> 3RD REPORTER: I did it! Woman cries!
>
> [526]

These three short statements encapsulate in brief the entire process which has just constructed a narrative on the wreckage of the Young Woman's experience. The first labels her according to the court's judgment, the second places her in relation to the leading male character in the trial, and the third simply repeats her words as spectacle.

When the State has successfully obliterated the Young Woman's sentence, it can hand down to her its own. The courtroom scene demonstrates how narrative is typically constructed on the suppression of female experience. As Hélène Cixous explains:

> The philosophical constructs itself starting with the abasement of woman. Subordination of the feminine to the masculine order which appears to be the condition for the functioning of the machine.[6]

Writing almost fifty years later, Hélène Cixous finds the same metaphor Treadwell used apt to describe a system of abstractions which engulfs and destroys the stories of women. Treadwell's final episode, "A Machine," completes this process for her tragic protagonist.

Perhaps the most potent symbol of patriarchy's monolithic narrative, a priest, dominates the final episode of the Young Woman's life. As the priest intones programmatic prayers in English and then in Latin, the Young Woman articulates directly her frustration with an abstract system that doesn't speak to her at all. Listening instead to the spiritual sung by a black fellow prisoner, she asserts "I understand him" (527). Forced to submit to the final indignity of having her hair cut, her calm breaks and she raves "Submit! Submit! Is nothing mine? The hair on my head! The very hair on my head—" (527).

In another parallel with Ruth Snyder's story, the Young Woman's concern for her hair is one of the play's final images. "Did you see that?" a reporter cries out. "She fixed her hair under the cap—pulled her hair out under the cap" (529). The *New York Evening Post* was hardly less moving in its description of Ruth Snyder's execution. The story ended:

> [The Reverend George P. Murphy] quoted Mrs. Snyder. She said she had better die than live the life she had lived before the murder, he said. He called her "spiritually strong."
>
> Ruth made a woman's gesture, too, in her last hours. For some reason—a reason that went unexplained—she chose that time to wash her hair. That is why it hung so limply in the execution chamber.
>
> ["Snyder and Gray Brought Here After Chair Avenges Murder," 13 January 1928]

Both Ruth Snyder and Treadwell's Young Woman go to their deaths still more in touch with the feminine experience of fixing their hair than with an abstract and distant God, whose hair "doesn't matter," as Helen says earlier in the play in answer to her own question "What kind of hair has God?" The wordless "woman's gesture" of fixing her hair represents, more than the prayers of either the real or the fictional priest, the woman's experience of spirituality.

Michel Foucault has suggested that the aim of the public execution is to "deploy before all eyes an invincible force," in order

> not so much to re-establish a balance as to bring into play, as its extreme point, the dissymmetry between the subject who has dared to violate its law and the all-powerful sovereign who displays his strength.[7]

The presence of reporters at the scene makes clear that even though it is not directly witnessed by the populace, this execution, like Ruth Snyder's, is destined to be experienced by great numbers of people through press mediation. In his memoirs, Edmund Wilson recalls the festive and public nature of the execution:

> Gathered outside the prison, an enthusiastic crowd made holiday, as if for a medieval burning or a breaking on the wheel.[8]

In the 1990 Public Theater production, the lights dimmed during the execution, and then went down completely. There was a single camera flash: the death of the Young Woman becoming a representation. This representation, printed on posters for the production, encapsulates what the play demonstrates for us: the Young Woman being destroyed by the machine of the State.

When the *Daily News* published an alleged photograph of Ruth Snyder's execution, "respectable" newspapers responded with outrage. Warden Lewis E. Lawes (his real name!), who had presided, reportedly declared that execution chamber henceforth off-limits to all but one reporter, "and he'll be a man I know" ("Statement by Warden Lawes," *New York Times*, 14 January 1928). The role of the press in disseminating the execution as narrative is not really at stake: it is the multiplicity of narratives which must be contained. A photograph directs attention to the individual body of the criminal rather than to the State's awesome symbol. The scathing *New York Times* editorial, "The End of the Show," bemoaned the "paresis" of the photographer and the "glorification of criminals" in one angry breath (14 January 1928), even while its title acknowledged the spectacular function of the execution.

To return to Foucault's definition: the State's desire to limit—but not restrict—access to the execution proves the point that by 1928 the function of the public execution had changed. No longer meant to demonstrate asymmetry between subject and State, execution is intended to create a false unity: the subject wholly absorbed into the State. The tradition of *amende honorable* and the immortalization of a criminal's last speech is replaced by the subordination of the subject's voice to the State's master narrative. Even while printing the photo of Ruth Snyder on the cover of its 13 January 1928 extra edition, the *Daily News* emphasizes the silencing aspect of the execution, titling one section of the story "Ruth Snyder Whines as Strap Stops Voice Forever."

But Treadwell demonstrates that the Young Woman's execution is only the final step in the long process of silencing her voice. "Her lips are moving—what is she saying?" a reporter asks as she is taken to the chamber. "Nothing," replies the other. "Nothing," the unsatisfactory answer for all of the woman's questioners, is finally the correct word when imposed from without. The Young Woman's words no longer matter—her story has been completed by others. Her last words, calling "Somebody! Somebod—" end with the stage direction "Her voice is cut off" (p. 529). It is no longer necessary to dismember the body, as Foucault points out. In *Machinal* the body is dismembered in language, the last y cut off from the word itself, leaving the unanswered "Why" still hanging in the air. For, as crime narratives proved, cutting off the head did not always cut off the voice.

Nor is it obvious that cutting off the voice is any more effective. Foucault uses *Machinal*'s central metaphor to explain that the subordination of the individual voice to the master narrative is not only non-democratic, it is non-theatrical:

> Our society is not one of spectacle, but of surveillance . . . We are neither in the amphitheatre, nor on the stage, but in the panoptic machine, invested by its effects of power, which we bring to ourselves since we are part of its mechanism.
>
> [217]

Dramatization itself subverts the machine, giving voice to the voiceless. In the case of Ruth Snyder, the *New York Times*'s dour prediction was proven true by Treadwell's play:

> Doubtless these two martyrs of Sing Sing will appear posthumously in the pages of their fautors until their legend is exhausted.
>
> ["The End of the Show," 14 January 1928]

As the Public Theater's 1990 revival proved, the legend is far from being exhausted. With this in mind, the first reporter's question, "Suppose the machine shouldn't work!" (529), is as absurd as it is unsavory: like the electric chair, the machine of the State will always have enough power to suppress its victims. Thus the second reporter's reply—"It'll work!—It always works!"—is the play's final stroke of genius. It has the ring of truth, having just been demonstrated by the fate of the play's protagonist. But it is also a perfect example of the restrictive master narrative which Sophie Treadwell has managed to subvert. Her play, like the neologism that names it, is the first step in the long and arduous task of telling the stories of women's experiences. And as our own recent Supreme Court nomination hearings prove, the end of the struggle is a long way off. In the spectacular machinery of our legal system, women's stories are still falling upon decidedly deaf ears.

Notes

1. "Lecture in Inauguration of the Chair of Literary Semiology, Collège de France, January 7, 1977," trans. Richard Howard, *October* 8 (Spring 1979): 5. Page references are to this edition.
2. "The Snyder Murder Mystery," *The Outlook*, 18 May 1927: 146–47. References to journalistic sources which covered the Snyder trial are hereafter incorporated in the text.
3. Sophie Treadwell, *Machinal*, in *Twenty-Five Best Plays of the Modern American Theatre*, Ed. John Gassner (New York: Crown, 1949), 520. Page references are to this edition.
4. Stanley Fish, *Doing What Comes Naturally* (Durham, NC and London: Duke University Press, 1989), 2. Page references are to this edition.
5. Carol Gilligan, *In a Different Voice* (Cambridge, MA.: Harvard University Press, 1982), 22. Page references are to this edition.
6. Hélène Cixous, "Sorties," in *The Newly Born Woman*, by Hélène Cixous and Catherine Clément, trans. Betsy Wing (Minneapolis, MN: University of Minnesota Press, 1986), 65.
7. Michel Foucault, *Discipline and Punish*, trans. Alan Sheridan (New York: Vintage Books, 1979), 49. Page references are to this edition.
8. Edmund Wilson, *The American Earthquake: A Documentary of the Twenties and Thirties* (Garden City, NY: Doubleday, 1958), 161–62.

13.3 MODERN GIRLS FACE CERTAIN DISASTER: "FLAPPERS" CALLED SADDEST TYPE OF ALL

El Paso Herald, May 20th 1920

London, Eng., May 1.—"Girls with no aim in life but to walk up and down the streets, satisfied if they can get enough money to take them to picture palaces and keep them supplied with high heeled shoes."

This was the indictment delivered by Miss N. de Silva against the modern girl of the middle class. Miss de Silva is the wife of Martin Harvey, the actor, and she herself is high in the play world.

She was speaking on the subject of "Women's Work" at a meeting in Brandford of the People's League and Housewives' union when she so strongly arraigned the modern young girl. Other points she mad were . . .

Share in Public Life.

"Now women are taking a larger share in public life they must take care that they do not lose in their emancipation and the knowledge that they could organize, the very thing which in the past had been the backbone of England—their love of home.

"These little girls, the type of womanhood known as the 'flapper,' become almost a type for this generation alone. It is one of the saddest types this country has ever known. They do nothing and are of no use: on the contrary, they do incalculable harm. They do not qualify for mothers or for wives and there is nothing before them but disaster.

The streets of our towns are crowded with these little girls, fifteen and sixteen years of age, with no aim at all. For the most part they do typing or serve in shops and they just endure these few hours of work in order to be able to dress up and walk about in the evenings.

No Love For Home.

"In the wealthy classes we have found exactly the same thing—there is no love for home and very little respect for the parents Their idea of life is teas and lunches in hotels and smoking cigarettes. What does it end in? Misery and nothing else. Smoking itself is not a harmful thing, but when acquired as a female habit it is a sign of general looseness.

"Why should a girl smoke? I have never been able to find out. I have had a pretty long experience and I can count on my fingers the women who smoke because they really like it.

"I recognize that youth must have enough recreation and pleasure," said Mrs. Harris; in conclusion, "but it is the deeper things that matter—mothers, fathers, home life and work."

13.4 BROOKLYN PARENTS' BLUE LAWS FOR FLAPPERS

The New York Times, June 1st 1922

Members of the Parents' League of Brooklyn have decided to take a hand in the social life of school boys and girls between the ages of 15 and 18 years by promulgating certain edicts calculated to counteract the flapper invasion into the life of young girls. League members will see that the following "blue laws" for the young are enforced in their own families, and will also try to extend the movement to other Brooklyn homes.

Here are the rules for flappers:

1. Hours for evening parties are limited from 8:30 to 12. It's curfew after midnight.
2. Parties are to be held only on Friday and Saturday nights.
3. Simple, refined clothes are to be worn at all times.
4. Chaperones must be present at all parties.
5. Chaperones will accompany the girls home.
6. Censorship over the plays and movies to be attended.
7. Improper dancing forbidden.
8. No refreshments served after dances.
9. Not more than one party to be attended on the same evening.

Here are the rules which both boys and girls in Brooklyn must observe:

1. Entertain in small groups.
2. Serve very simple refreshments at parties.
3. All games must be supervised.
4. Use simple favors and no prizes.
5. Parties must end at 8:30 P.M.
6. Simple afternoon dress is to be worn on all occasions.
7. No movies or theatres, except those recommended by the school or investigated and approved by parents.

"We can do nothing with the older boys and girls, whose customs have become more or less established," said Mrs. Otto Affeld of 113 Willow Street, Brooklyn, yesterday. Mrs. Affeld is president of the league. Girls over 18 years of age are left to whatever rules their parents prescribe.

13.5 TYPICAL FLAPPER

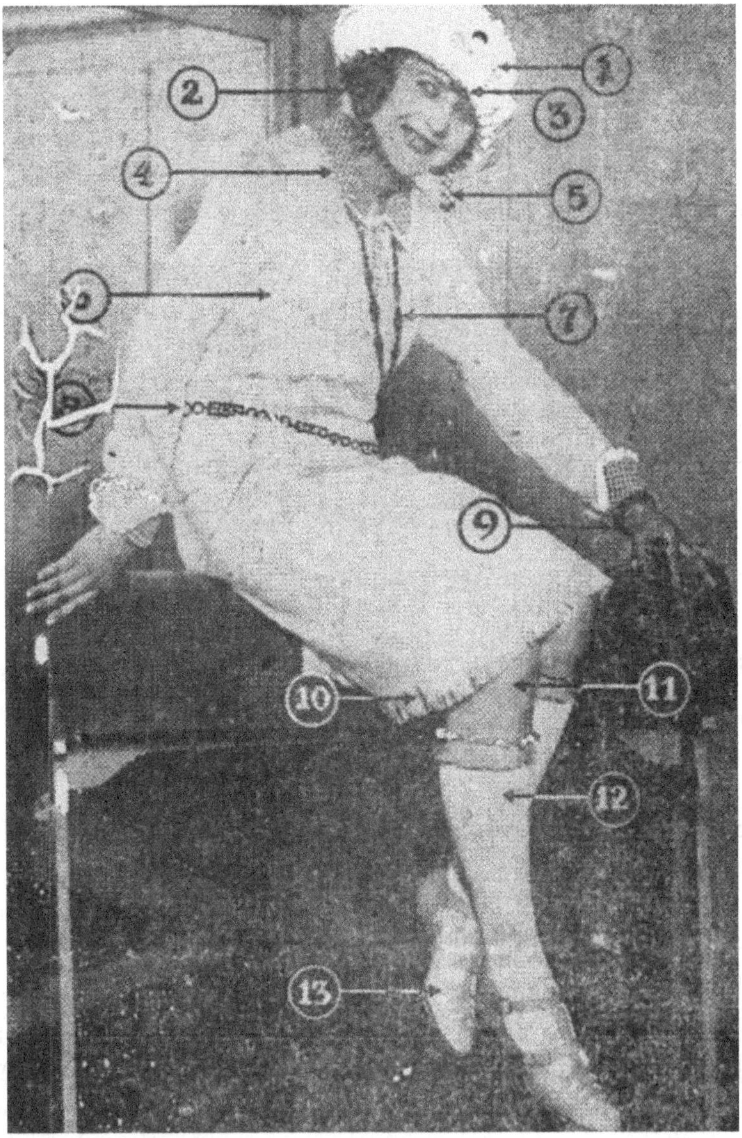

Weekly Journal Miner, August 2nd 1922

Original caption: "Typical Flappers. You've often heard 'em called that, but did you ever really understand what it meant? This will straighten you out. It's a picture of a flapper, 100 per cent, from head to foot. Thirteen qualifications. Count 'em: No. 1, hat of soft silk or felt; No. 2, bobbed hair; No. 3, flapper curl on forehead; No. 4, flapper collar; No. 5, flapper earrings; No. 6, slip-over sweater; No. 7, flapper beads; No. 8, metallic belt; No. 9, bracelet of strung jet; No. 10, knee-length fringed skirt; No. 11, exposed, bare knees; No. 12, rolled hose with fancy garter; No. 13, flat-heeled little girl sandals."

13.6 RUTH SNYDER IN THE ELECTRIC CHAIR

Ruth Snyder strapped to the electric chair.

Source: Photo by Tom Howard/NY Daily News Archive via Getty Images

13.7 TEXT OF MRS. SNYDER'S CONFESSION

New York Times, April 27th 1927

Text of Confession Mrs. Snyder Made

Statement Given After Murder Details Marital Quarrels and Plans for Crime.

Avows Her Love for Gray

Says Husband Twice Threatened to "Blow Her Brains Out"—Tells of Meetings With Paramour.

The confession of Ruth Snyder, which was made part of the evidence yesterday at the trial of Mrs. Snyder and Henry Judd Gray for the murder of Albert Snyder, follows:

"My name is Ruth May Snyder, and I want to make a full and truthful statement about the death of my husband, Albert Snyder, and I understand that anything I may say may be used against me.

"I reside at 9,327 Twenty-second Street, Queens Village, and I will be 32 years of age on Sunday, March 27, 1927. I was born at Morningside Avenue and 125th Street, New York City. My father's same was Harry Brown and my mother's name Josephine Brown. My mother was born in Sweden and my father in Norway. I am a graduate of a public school and of Wadleigh High School, New York City, and after my graduation I worked for the telephone company for a year and a half and then took a secretarial course in Bird's Business school. The last permanent position I had before I was married was with M. Russling Wood Company, Beaver Street. New York City, where I was employed as a stenographer.

19 When She Met Husband.

"I met my husband, Albert Snyder, while I was employed with the Cosmopolitan Magazine, which was the position I held before the one with M. Russling Wood. I was about 19 when I first met him and he was 32 then and was working for a motor magazine as an artist. I was married on July 24, 1915, in the Bronx by a minister whose name I remember as Pastor Young. We first lived at 651 Fifty-first Street, Brooklyn, for about three years, and there's where I was living when my daughter Lorraine was born on Nov. 15, 1917. I then moved to 1,120 Woodycrest Avenue, Bronx, where I lived for about a year, and then we moved to 31 Canterbury Road, Jamaica, where we lived for about three years. We then moved to my present address and purchased the house in which we live, in the name of myself and my husband, for $11,500, with a $4,000 mortgage.

"I began having difficulty with my husband almost immediately after our marriage. I was apparently too giddy and young for his years; while he was only 33 at the time, he was like a man of 50 to me. He was not companionable to me at all. He took care of me and my daughter all right from a financial standpoint. We quarreled quite frequently about accounting for the money which he gave me.

"He had a position which he was holding on Saturday for about fifteen years and earned about $115 a week in addition to some sketching he did occasionally. He maintained a Buick seven-passenger car for us and clothed myself and daughter well. He never took me out, and that is why I had to seek the company of others.

Introduced to Gray.

"I had girl friends and about two years ago I met Henry Judd Gray in the office of the Bien Jolie Corset Company at Thirty-fourth Street and Fifth Avenue. I was introduced to him by Mr. Folsom, whom I knew was connected with the stocking business, and I met Mr. Gray quite frequently. He was employed by the Bien Jolie Corset Company as a salesman and traveled quite a little. I think he had the territory of the best part of Pennsylvania and parts of New York, Utica, Buffalo and Syracuse. When he would make a trip he would correspond with me and I would correspond with him. Of course my husband knew nothing of my relations with Mr. Gray. Mr. Gray is a slight built man about 135 or 140 pounds, fair complexion, brown curly hair, clean shaven, wears glasses with the rims over the ears. He is American born. He lives at 37 Wayne Avenue, East Orange, N.J., and he is married and has a daughter of about 10 or 11.

"On a number of occasions we got a room as Mr. and Mrs. Henry Judd Gray. The first time that I occupied a room with him as Mrs. Gray, was at the Imperial Hotel in New York City, which was some time during the month of July, 1925. We went to the Imperial a few times, we did not like that, so then went to the Waldorf-Astoria. The first time we were at the Waldorf-Astoria was during the month of September, 1925, and from that time on, on numerous occasions Mr. Gray got a room at the Waldorf-Astoria. We always registered under the name of Mr. and Mrs. Gray.

Visited Her Home.

"He has been to my home at Queens Village a number of times. My mother lives with me at Queens Village and my daughter and my mother both knew Mr. Gray. Whenever we registered at the hotel, I had a tan suit case which I have seen at the District Attorney's office today. He came to my house when my husband would be away.

"I was constantly being belittled by my husband. My husband and I had quarreled frequently and things became worse since we moved to Queens Village. He was constantly picking and nagging at me and I had gotten at that stage where I would take any means to get out of it all. I could not divorce him. Mr. Gray was the only one who would listen to my troubles. During the time that I have known Mr. Gray I have told him more and more of the trouble with my husband.

"Things became unbearable and I was looking for a way out, and in talking with Mr. Gray a method was proposed whereby we were talking about getting rid of him, and finally things came to a climax, about two or three weeks ago when I had an other argument with my husband when my husband said he was going to blow my brains out and I wrote this to Mr. Gray. I wrote back to Mr. Gray after he had asked me in the letter whether I thought my husband would do it or not, that I certainly thought he would do anything in a fit of temper because he had an awful temper. Then Mr. Gray wrote back to me in a code which only we two understand, that it was better for Mr. Gray and I to get him (my husband) before he got me.

Obtained Window Weight.

"We discussed various ways of getting rid of my husband. We had talked about chloroform, but Mr. Gray said he didn't know if that would be sufficient alone, and I met him on March 5, 1927, and he told me to take home a window weight; in case we were going to do anything, that was the way we were going to do it. I took home this window weight which I have seen at the District Attorney's office today, attached to which is a tag, on which tag I have signed my name.

"Since the 5th of March, Mr. Gray came to my house one evening. I am not clear on the dates and I don't remember exactly, but it was on a Monday night at about 11 o'clock. I think it was hailing. He came to Queens Village after he had given me this window weight, and he came out with the purpose of getting rid of my husband. It was understood between Mr. Gray and myself on that night that he was to hit my husband on the head with this window weight and stun him after he had gotten to sleep and then administer chloroform to him, but Mr. Gray and I both got cold feet that night and the two of us cried like babies and I said to him, 'Go on home, you're not going to do it.' Mr. Gray went home. The next day I got a letter from Mr. Gray from Buffalo, saying he was glad I sent him home.

"On Saturday, March the 12th, 1927, I had a quarrel with my husband, in which he told me that I could either get to hell out or he would blow my brains out, and I wrote this in a letter to Mr. Gray. Mr. Gray then wrote back and asked me if I thought he would do it, and I said he would do anything in a fit of temper.

"Going to Deliver Goods."

"Mr. Gray wrote a letter to me stating that we were going to deliver goods Saturday, which I knew from my understanding with Mr. Gray to mean that we were going to do the job of getting rid of my husband on Saturday, March the 19th. I received this letter sometime during the week of March the 14th, probably three or four days before the 19th, exactly when I don't remember, and I received another letter on Saturday morning, March the 19th, which was a very formal letter from Mr. Gray, stating that he would be at my house on Saturday, March the 19th, about 11:30 P.M. for the purpose of getting rid of my husband, by going through with what we had planned, on Saturday, March 19th.

"Myself and my husband and daughter went to a friend's house, named Fidgeon. I made it my business to see that the cellar door and the kitchen door would be unlocked. At the party at Fidgeon's I was careful so that I wouldn't drink too much intoxicating liquor and on one occasion suggested that they give my drink to my husband. We had been drinking ginger ale high balls at Fidgeon's.

"My husband and daughter and I arrived home about 2 A.M. on Sunday morning, the 20th. My husband left my daughter and I out on the sidewalk. We entered by the front door. As you enter our house through the front door you enter into a foyer. On one side of the building, on the first floor, is a living room and sun parlor; on the other side of the foyer is a dining room and kitchen and the stairway leading upstairs brings you into a hall. The bathroom is in the southeast corner of the building in the rear, and the baby's room is in the southwest corner. Mother's room faces west, and my room runs the whole length of the building, facing northeast and west.

"I took the baby to her room and she undressed and I put her to bed. Before this, as I was passing to the baby's room, I saw Mr. Gray in my mother's room and I said: 'I'll see you in a little while.' My mother was not home since Tuesday, March 15, and Mr. Gray knew this before he came to the house, and we had arranged in our correspondence that he was to go into my mother's room and wait for me there.

Waited Until Husband Slept.

"After putting the baby to bed I went into my own room, in which we have twin beds, and I got undressed and went to bed. After I had been in bed for about ten minutes my husband got undressed and went to bed. After about a half hour, when I was sure he was asleep I got up and went into my mother's room and told Mr. Gray my husband was asleep. When I went into my mother's room Mr. Gray had the window weight which I had shown in the District Attorney's office. I had brought the window weight up from the cellar that afternoon of March 19, 1927, to have it all ready for Mr. Gray. These details were all arranged during the week in the correspondence between myself and Mr. Gray. We had arranged in the correspondence for Mr. Gray to get a bottle of chloroform and when he went into my mother's room he had the bottle of chloroform.

"He had a regular 8-ounce medicine bottle with one and a half ounces of chloroform in it. He also had a piece of cheese cloth and cotton waste with him. In addition to that he had a blue cotton handkerchief and he put the waste in the cotton handkerchief and then poured the chloroform on the waste and cotton handkerchief. The original paper that was on the weight when I first received it from Mr. Gray was on it Saturday night. I left a quart of liquor for him on Saturday night.

"I told him it was either my husband going or my going and after we had all the details arranged he kissed me and walked into my husband's room. There were no lights in the house. He walked from me where I was standing in my mother's bedroom into my own bedroom and I followed him into the hall. I stood in the hall between my mother's door and our door and my mother's door is only three feet from my room and my husband's bed is at the door.

Saw Gray Raise Weight.

"In the darkness I could see Mr. Gray raise his arm, holding what I believed to be the weight in his hand and in the darkness the white paper around the weight stood out. I saw this weight in Mr. Gray's hand start to travel and immediately heard a thud and my husband groaned twice after I heard the thud. I saw Mr. Gray tie my husband's hands behind his back. I was able to see in the dark because there is a street arc light on the opposite side of the street from our house which at all times during the night lights up my room so that you can see objects in it.

"When Mr. Gray struck my husband he was lying on his left side. He tied his hands behind his back and put the blue handkerchief and the waste with the chloroform on it on the pillow and then turned my husband face down on the pillow so that the waste and blue handkerchief with the chloroform on it would cover his nose and mouth. He then covered his head with the blankets to make sure of suffocation. He then tied his feet. I'm quite sure that Mr. Gray then came out of the room and said to me, 'I guess that's it.'

"He and I then went downstairs. Before he went downstairs he took off a pair of rubber gloves which he had purchased to use to avoid any fingerprints and he washed his hands in the bathroom. While in the bathroom he discovered that he had quite a few blood stains on his shirt and I went back to my husband's room and took one of my husband's new blue shirts; it had a silk stripe in it and he changed it in my mother's room. We then went downstairs and took the weight and the shirt and the bloodstained paper down to the cellar and burned the shirt and the paper with the bloodstains on it in the furnace. We then put the window weight, sprinkled with ashes, into the tool box, and then we came upstairs to the living room and sat there.

Bound Wire Around Neck.

"While we were sitting there he thought of binding his neck with the wire to make sure of everything. He took this piece of wire from his pocket. He had two pieces of wire when he came in; one was intended, I think, for the hands and the other for the feet. In the shuffle one piece of wire had gotten lost, so he took the piece that he had left and went upstairs and I went with him, and he put it around his throat to make sure of everything. He tightened it up with his fingers.

"While Mr. Gray and I were in my mother's room before he went into my husband's room, we had planned that in order to avoid detection, to upset the house and throw the stuff in the house around, so that it would look like a burglary or robbery, and we planned that I was to tell the police that it was a robbery.

"After we had disposed of the shirt and the paper around the weight, we then went back upstairs and emptied out all the drawers in all the rooms except my daughter's room. After upsetting everything upstairs we then came downstairs and upset everything and then I took the wallet out of my husband's pocket, which I had been shown at the District Attorney's office and which I have marked with the initials R._._. on his identification card. I gave Mr. Gray the contents of this wallet. I didn't count how much it was.

He Left at Daybreak.

"We sat in the living room and waited until almost daybreak, at which time he left and took a train for Syracuse. Before he left he tied my feet and my hands and I laid down on my mother's bed, where I remained until about 3 o'clock, when I rolled out of the bed and crawled to my daughter's door and awoke her and told her to get Mrs. Mulhauser. Mrs. Mulhauser came over first. Then the baby called Mr. Mullhauser and he came over and the police were notified for the second time.

"I told Mrs. Mulhauser and the police that I was attacked by a man coming out of my mother's room and fainted with fright. This was not the truth. I was asked about an Italian newspaper. That was part of the plan so as to make it appear that they were Italians who had come in and killed my husband and had bound and gagged me.

"The pistol that was found on the floor belonged to my husband. It was put there by us as part of our plan to make it appear more like a robbery.

"I was in love with Mr. Gray and Mr. Gray loved me, and if my husband hadn't said that he would take my life we would not have thought of taking his life. But after talking it over a number of times with Mr. Gray we decided that the only way out of our difficulties was to take his life.

"I make this statement of my own free will, without any fear or threat or promise, and knowing that anything I say may be used against me.

"March 21, 1927."

13.8 PHRENOLOGICAL ANALYSIS OF MRS RUTH SNYDER—DR EDGAR C. BEALL

Daily Mirror, March 26th 1927

Metamorphosis of Woman Charged with Murder

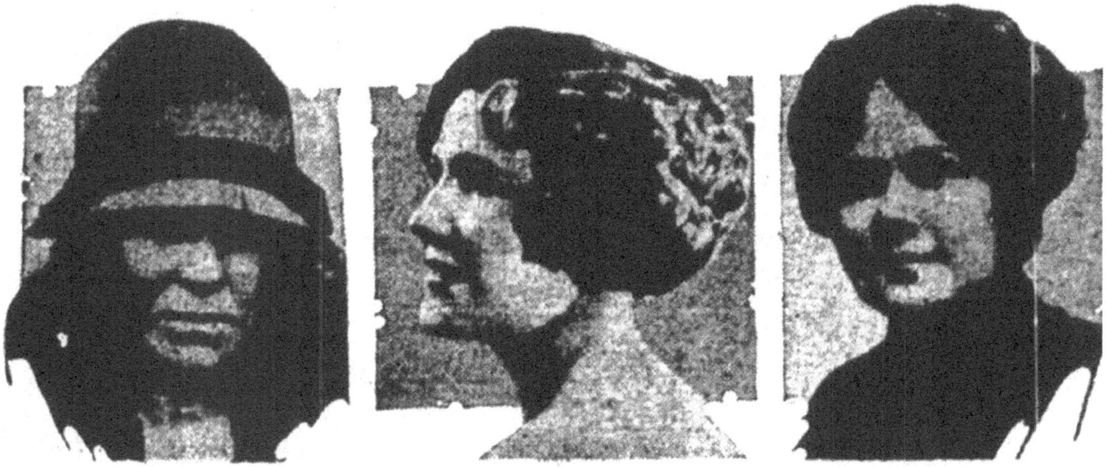

Original caption: THREE STUDIES OF MRS. SNYDER, whose character Dr. Beall analyzes for the Mirror, are shown here. At the left is her picture since the murder charge was made against her. In the centre she is shown as she looked about three years ago. And photo at right shows her at the time of her marriage.

HERE is "one more unfortunate, rashly unfortunate," woman who has taken a fatal plunge. But unlike the despairing creature in Hood's poem who finds peace in the river, this victim leaps into a quenchless blaze of disgrace and shame far worse than death. What was the urge, the impulse, the reptilian lure that cajoled or wheedled this comfortably situated wife and mother into such a fearful blunder?

Peculiar Eyes.

In several of the portraits, but especially in the earliest, which shows her at the time of her marriage, we can trace a very definite answer. It is truly said that "the eyes are the windows of the soul." And as we look into these laughing orbs, or rather at the curtains that almost hide them, we notice a striking and rare peculiarity. It consists in a compressed or flattened appearance of the lids, especially on the left side. This formation, which was very pronounced in Brigham Young and other famous characters who shared his views, has long been known as a sign of a polygamous disposition.

Voluptuous nature.

The contrary indication, or perfectly arched form of the eyelids, is also very obvious in birds that are true to their mates. There can be no question about the validity of this mark, and the reader may easily verify it by a study of historical portraits or by observing the people of his own acquaintance. In the present subject, therefore, it is clear that the element of conjugal fidelity was practically non-[text missing here]

At the same time, the woman was endowed with an exceptionally voluptuous nature, the demands of which were ceaseless, imperious, and utterly beyond control. In this combination we must also include the effects of ignorance, and the absence of all dignity and sense of justice. Benevolence is also entirely wanting.

Cold, Hard Mouth.

In two or three of the later pictures the mouth is as cold, hard, and unsympathetic as a crack in a dried lemon. In at least one portrait the chin tapers downward like the lower face of a cat. This accords perfectly with her treachery and ingratitude. Finally, the cat-like width of the cheek bones reveals the two qualities of thievishness and cruelty. In the sum of these most legible traits we may thus readily perceive the character of a shallow-brained pleasure seeker, accustomed to unlimited self-indulgence, which at last ends in an orgie of murderous passion and lust, seemingly without a parallel in the criminal history of modern times.

13.9 REVIEW OF MACHINAL—J. BROOKS ATKINSON

New York Times, September 8th 1928

A Tragedy of Submission.

MACHINAL, a play in two acts and ten "episodes," by Sophie Treadwell. Settings by Robert Edmond Jones; Incidental music by Frank Harlins; staged and produced by Arthur Hopkins. At the Plymouth Theatre.

A Young Woman	Zita Johann
A Telephone Girl	Millicent Green
A Stenographer	Grace Atwell
A Filing Clerk	Leopold Badia
An Adding Clerk	Conway Washburn
A Mother	Jean Adair
A Husband	George Stillwell
A Bellboy	Otto Frederick
A Nurse	Nancy Allan
A Doctor	Monroe Childs
A Young Man	Hal K. Dawson
A Girl	Zenaide Ziegfeld
A Man	Jess Sidney
A Boy	Clyde Stork

A Man	Clark Gable
Another Man	Hugh M. Hite
A Waiter	John Hanloy
A Judge	John Waters
A Lawyer for Defense	John Connery
A Lawyer for Prosecution	James MacDonald
A Court Reporter	Otto Frederick
A Bailiff	John Hanloy
A Reporter	Conway Washburn
Second Reporter	Hugh M. Hite
Third Reporter	Hal K. Dawson
A Jailer	John Hanley
A Matron	Mrs. Charles Willard
A Priest	Charles Kennedy

From the sordid mess of a brutal murder the author, actors and producer of "Machinal," which was staged at the Plymouth last evening, have with great skill managed to retrieve a frail and sombre beauty of character. In superficial details the story resembles the Snyder and Gray murder case. But Sophie Treadwell, who is Mrs. W. O. McGeehan in private life, has in no sense capitalized a sensational murder trial in her strangely-moving, shadowy drama. Rather has she written a tragedy of submission; she has held an individual character against the hard surface of a mechanical age. And Zita Johann acts the leading part with a bewildered droop and a wistfulness that quite redeem the chief character from the commonness of the environment. Subdued, monotonous, episodic, occasionally eccentric in its style, "Machinal" is fraught with a beauty unfamiliar to the stage.

Throughout the rather common-place story Miss Treadwell has kept the young woman pathetically individual. The first scene, treated expressionistically, discloses her in a business office, fumbling about her work, unhappy and afraid. She marries her giggling, complacement employer as the easiest way out of her private muddle. Successive episodes chronicle her career through marriage and motherhood. Once, vaguely pursuing some ideal, she falls in with an engaging adventurer; and now happy for the first time she takes him for her lover. In the last half of the play she is on trial for the murder of her husband. In conclusion, one scene shows her in prison on the eve of electrocution, and the last, played in darkness, reports bits of descriptive conversation and her frightened scream from the electric chair.

It is difficult by description to communicate the precise quality that distinguishes "Machinal" and that casts a subtly moving spell on the audience. Mr. Hopkins, as the producer and director, quite as much as Miss Treadwell, has isolated a fineness of spirit in the midst of shoddy externals. The husband's endless giggles and obese platitudes about success, the doctor's hurried, perfunctory observations in the sick room, the deadly average of the love scene, the impersonal hurry on all sides—all in contrast with the uncertainty of a human character, tell more of "Machinal" than its story. It is the tragedy of one who lacks strength; she is not adaptable; she submits. Events, people, circumstances stream by her, glib and optimistic, but they never relieve her loneliness. It is too much for her always. Wherever life touches her, it swamps her in mediocrity. Being the exposition of a character, stark and austere in style, "Machinal" makes no excuses for the tragedy it unfolds.

As the director Mr. Hopkins has kept it in a shade of monotone that does not produce the exhilaration we like in the theatre but that expresses the central character well. Personally and artistically Miss Johann represents the young woman in a studied, lucid performance. Without sentimentalizing the character, she conveys its frailty in the midst of a heedless world. As the husband, George Stillwell is amazingly true—simple and effortless in his fat, mirthful smugness. And Clark Gable likewise plays the casually good-humored lover without a hackneyed gesture.

Excellent settings by Robert Edmond Jones, a warm, compelling light effect by George Schaff as the concluding scene, contribute to the distinction of Mr. Hopkins's production. Yet still the precise quality of "Machinal" escapes definition in this ambiguous review.

13.10 PRODUCTION PHOTO FROM *MACHINAL*

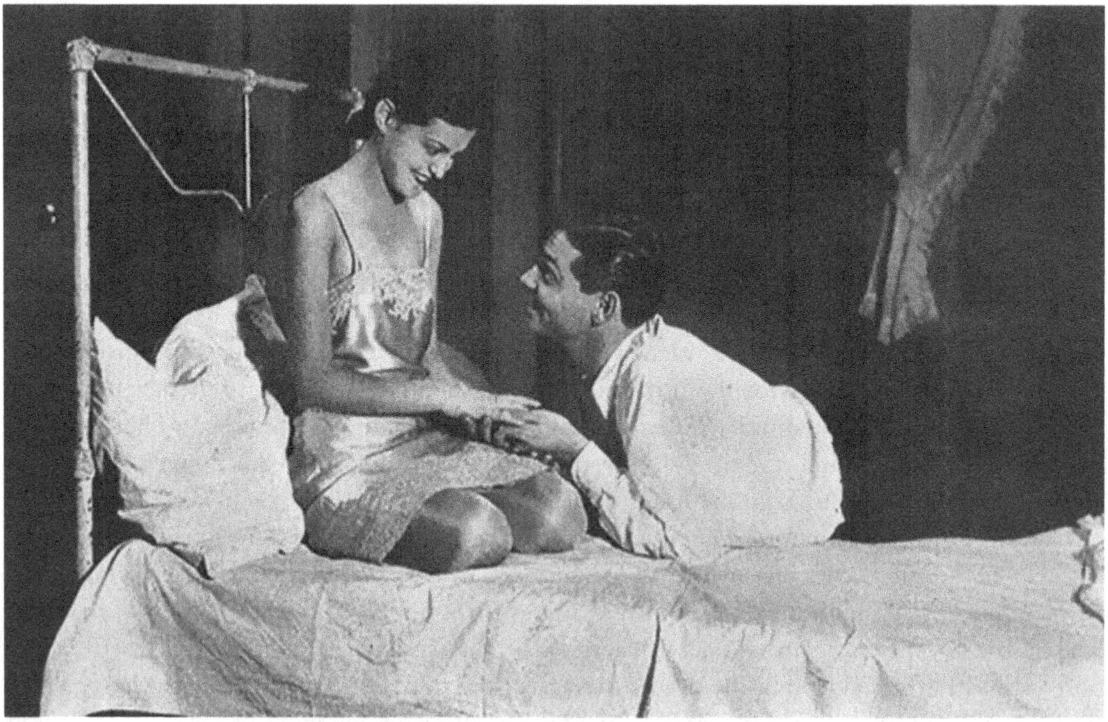

1928 production photo of Sophie Treadwell's *Machinal*. Treadwell's play dramatizes the societal tensions of the Jazz Age flapper, who smoked, drank, and spurned marriage, as well as the image of women from the previous era—the Gibson Girl, the feminine ideal of beauty that safeguarded the home and morality.

13.11 *MACHINAL*—SOPHIE TREADWELL

By Sophie Treadwell

Characters

YOUNG WOMAN
TELEPHONE GIRL
STENOGRAPHER
FILING CLERK
ADDING CLERK
MOTHER
HUSBAND
BELLBOY
NURSE
DOCTOR
YOUNG MAN
GIRL
MAN
BOY
MAN
ANOTHER MAN
WAITER
JUDGE
LAWYER FOR DEFENSE
LAWYER FOR PROSECUTION
COURT REPORTER
BAILIFF
REPORTER
SECOND REPORTER
THIRD REPORTER
JAILER
MATRON
PRIEST

★

EPISODE 1, *To Business*
EPISODE 2, *At Home*
EPISODE 3, *Honeymoon*
EPISODE 4, *Maternal*
EPISODE 5, *Prohibited*
EPISODE 6, *Intimate*
EPISODE 7, *Domestic*
EPISODE 8, *The Law*
EPISODE 9, *A Machine*

★

***The Plot**: The story of a woman who murders her husband—an ordinary young woman, any woman.*
***The Plan**: To tell this story by showing the different phases of life that the woman comes in contact with, and in none of which she finds any place, any peace. The woman is essentially soft, tender, and the life around her is essentially hard, mechanized. Business, home, marriage, having a child, seeking pleasure—all are difficult for her—mechanical, nerve nagging. Only in an illicit love does she find anything with life in it for her, and when she loses this, the desperate effort to win free to it again is her undoing*

The story is told in nine scenes. In the dialogue of these scenes there is the attempt to catch the rhythm of our common city speech, its brassy sound, its trick of repetition, etc.

Then there is, also, the use of many different sounds chosen primarily for their inherent emotional effect (steel riveting, a priest chanting, a Negro singing, jazz band, etc.), but contributing also to the creation of a background, an atmosphere.

***The Hope**: To create a stage production that will have 'style', and at the same time, by the story's own innate drama, by the directness of its telling, by the variety and quick changingness of its scenes, and the excitement of its sounds, to create an interesting play.*

***Scenically**: This play is planned to be handled in two basic sets (or in one set with two backs).*

The first division—the first Four Episodes—needs an entrance at one side, and a back having a door and a large window. The door gives, in

Episode 1—to Vice President's office.
Episode 2—to hall.
Episode 3—to bathroom.
Episode 4—to corridor.

And the window shows, in

Episode 1—An opposite office.
Episode 2—An inner apartment court.
Episode 3—Window of a dance casino opposite.
Episode 4—Steel girders. (Of these, only the casino window is important. Sky could be used for the others.)

The second division—the last Five Episodes—has the same side entrance, but the back has only one opening—for a small window (barred).

Episode 5—window is masked by electric piano.
Episode 6—window is disclosed (sidewalk outside).
Episode 7—window is curtained.
Episode 8—window is masked by Judge's bench.
Episode 9—window is disclosed (sky outside).

There is a change of furniture, and props for each episode—only essential things, full of character. For Episode 9, the room is closed in from the sides, and there is a place with bars and a door in it, put straight across stage down front (back far enough to leave a clear passageway in front of it).

Lighting concentrated and intense.—Light and shadow—bright light and darkness.—This darkness, already in the scene, grows and blacks out the light for dark stage when the scene changes are made.

***Offstage Voices** (Characters in the Background Heard, but Unseen):*

A Janitor
A Baby
A Boy and a Girl
A Husband and Wife
A Husband and Wife
A Radio Announcer
A Negro Singer

Mechanical Offstage Sounds:

A small jazz band
A hand organ
Steel riveting
Telegraph insruments
Aeroplane engine

Mechanical Onstage Sounds:

Office Machines (typewriters, telephones, etc.)
Electric piano.

Characters in the Background Seen, Not Heard *(seen off the main set, i.e., through a window or door):*

Couples of men and women dancing
A Woman in a bathrobe
A Woman in a wheel chair
A Nurse with a covered basin
A Nurse with a tray
The feet of men and women passing in the street

★

Episode 1

TO BUSINESS

SCENE: *An office: a switchboard, filing cabinet, adding machine, typewriter and table, manifold machine.*

SOUNDS: *Office machines: typewriters, adding machine, manifold, telephone bells, buzzers.*

CHARACTERS AND THEIR MACHINES: *A Young Woman (typewriter); A Stenographer (typewriter); A Filing Clerk (filing cabinet and manifold); An Adding Clerk (adding machine); Telephone Operator (switchboard); Jones*

BEFORE THE CURTAIN: *Sounds of machines going. They continue throughout the scene, and accompany the* YOUNG WOMAN'*s thoughts after the scene is blacked out.*

AT THE RISE OF THE CURTAIN: *All the machines are disclosed, and all the characters with the exception of the Young Woman.*

Of these characters, the Young Woman, going any day to any business. Ordinary. The confusion of her own inner thoughts, emotions, desires, dreams cuts her off from any actual adjustment to the routine of work. She gets through this routine with a very small surface of her consciousness. She is not homely and she is not pretty. She is preoccupied with herself—with her person. She has well kept hands, and a trick of constantly arranging her hair over her ears.
The Stenographer is the faded, efficient woman office worker. Drying, dried.

The Adding Clerk is her male counterpart.
The Filing Clerk is a boy not grown, callow adolescence.
The Telephone Girl, young, cheap and amorous.

Lights come up on office scene. Two desks right and left.

Telephone booth back right center. Filing cabinet back of center. Adding machine back left center.

ADDING CLERK (*in the monotonous voice of his monotonous thoughts; at his adding machine*). 2490, 28, 76, 123, 36842, 1, 1/4, 37, 804, 23 1/2, 982.

FILING CLERK (*in the same way—at his filing desk*). Accounts—A. Bonds—B. Contracts—C Data—D. Earnings—E.

STENOGRAPHER (*in the same way—left*). Dear Sir—in re—your letter—recent date—will state—

TELEPHONE GIRL. Hello—Hello—George H. Jones Company good morning—hello hello—George H. Jones Company good morning—hello.

FILING CLERK. Market—M. Notes—N. Output—O. Profits—P.—! (*Suddenly*) What's the matter with Q?

TELEPHONE GIRL. Matter with it—Mr. J.—Mr. K. wants you—What you mean matter? Matter with what?

FILING CLERK. Matter with Q.

TELEPHONE GIRL. Well—what is? Spring 1726?

FILING CLERK. I'm asking yuh—

TELEPHONE GIRL. Well?

FILING CLERK. Nothing filed with it—

TELEPHONE GIRL. Well?

FILING CLERK. Look at A. Look at B. What's the matter with Q?

TELEPHONE GIRL. Ain't popular. Hello—Hello—George H. Jones Company.

FILING CLERK. Hot dog! Why ain't it?

ADDING CLERK. Has it personality?

STENOGRAPHER. Has it Halitosis?

TELEPHONE GIRL. Has it got it?

FILING CLERK. Hot dog!

TELEPHONE GIRL. What number do you want? (*Recognizing but not pleased.*) Oh—hello—sure I know who it is—tonight? Uh, uh—(*Negative, but each with a different inflection.*) You heard me—No!

FILING CLERK. Don't you like him?

STENOGRAPHER. She likes 'em all.

TELEPHONE GIRL. I do not!

STENOGRAPHER. Well—pretty near all!

TELEPHONE GIRL. What number do you want? Wrong number. Hello—hello—George H. Jones Company. Hello, hello—

STENOGRAPHER. Memorandum—attention Mr. Smith —at a conference of—

ADDING CLERK. 125—83 3/4—22—908—34—1/4—28593.

FILING CLERK. Report—R, Sales—S, Trade—_

TELEPHONE GIRL. Shh—! Yes, Mr. J.—? No—Miss A. ain't in yet—I'll tell her, Mr. J.—just the minute she gets in.

STENOGRAPHER. She's late again, huh?

TELEPHONE GIRL. Out with her sweetie last night, huh?

FILING CLERK. Hot dog.

ADDING CLERK. She ain't got a sweetie.

STENOGRAPHER. How do you know?

ADDING CLERK. I know.

FILING CLERK. Hot dog.

ADDING CLERK. She lives alone with her mother.

TELEPHONE GIRL. Spring 1876? Hello—Spring 1876. Spring! Hello, Spring 1876? 1876! Wrong number! Hello! Hello!

STENOGRAPHER. Director's meeting semi-annual report card.

FILING CLERK. Shipments—Sales—Schedules—S.

ADDING CLERK. She doesn't belong in an office.

TELEPHONE GIRL. Who does?

STENOGRAPHER. I do!

ADDING CLERK. You said it!

FILING CLERK. Hot dog!

TELEPHONE GIRL. Hello—hello—George H. Jones Company—hello—hello—

STENOGRAPHER. I'm efficient. She's inefficient.

FILING CLERK. She's inefficient.

TELEPHONE GIRL. She's got J. going.

STENOGRAPHER. Going?

TELEPHONE GIRL. Going and coming.

FILING CLERK. Hot dog.

Enter JONES.

JONES. Good morning, everybody.

TELEPHONE GIRL. Good morning.

FILING CLERK. Good morning.

ADDING CLERK. Good morning.

STENOGRAPHER. Good morning, Mr. J.

JONES. Miss A. isn't in yet?

TELEPHONE GIRL. Not yet, Mr. J.

FILING CLERK. Not yet.

ADDING CLERK. Not yet.

STENOGRAPHER. She's late.
JONES. I just wanted her to take a letter.
STENOGRAPHER. I'll take the letter.
JONES. One thing at a time and that done well.
ADDING CLERK (*yessing*). Done well.
STENOGRAPHER. I'll finish it later.
JONES. Hew to the line.
ADDING CLERK. Hew to the line.
STENOGRAPHER. Then I'll hurry.
JONES. Haste makes waste.
ADDING CLERK. Waste.
STENOGRAPHER. But if you're in a hurry.
JONES. I'm never in a hurry—That's how I get ahead! (*Laughs. They all laugh.*) First know you're right—then go ahead.
ADDING CLERK. Ahead.
JONES (*to Telephone Girl*). When Miss A. comes in tell her I want her to take a letter. (*Turns to go in—then.*) It's important.
TELEPHONE GIRL (*making a note*). Miss A.—important.
JONES (*starts up—then*) And I don't want to be disturbed.
TELEPHONE GIRL. You're in conference?
JONES. I'm in conference. (*Turns—then.*) Unless it's A.B.—of course.
TELEPHONE GIRL. Of course—A.B.
JONES (*starts—turns again; attempts to be facetious*). Tell Miss A. the early bird catches the worm.

Exit JONES.

TELEPHONE GIRL. The early worm gets caught.
ADDING CLERK. He's caught.
TELEPHONE GIRL. Hooked.
ADDING CLERK. In the pan.
FILING CLERK. Hot dog.
STENOGRAPHER. We beg leave to announce—

Enter YOUNG WOMAN. *Goes behind telephone booth to desk right.*

STENOGRAPHER. You're late!
FILING CLERK. You're late.
ADDING CLERK. You're late.
STENOGRAPHER. And yesterday!
FILING CLERK. The day before.
ADDING CLERK. And the day before.
STENOGRAPHER. You'll lose your job.
YOUNG WOMAN. No!
STENOGRAPHER. No?

Workers exchange glances.

YOUNG WOMAN. I can't!
STENOGRAPHER. Can't?

Same business.

FILING CLERK. Rent—bills—installments—miscellaneous.
ADDING CLERK. A dollar ten—ninety-five—3.40—35—12.60.
STENOGRAPHER. Then why are you late?
YOUNG WOMAN. Why?
STENOGRAPHER. Excuse!
ADDING CLERK. Excuse!
FILING CLERK. Excuse.
TELEPHONE GIRL. Excuse it, please.
STENOGRAPHER. Why?
YOUNG WOMAN. The subway?
TELEPHONE GIRL. Long distance?
FILING CLERK. Old stuff!
ADDING CLERK. That stall!
STENOGRAPHER. Stalled?
YOUNG WOMAN. No—
STENOGRAPHER. What?
YOUNG WOMAN. I had to get out!
ADDING CLERK. Out!
FILING CLERK. Out?
STENOGRAPHER. Out where?
YOUNG WOMAN. In the air!
STENOGRAPHER. Air?
YOUNG WOMAN. All those bodies pressing.
FILING CLERK. Hot dog!
YOUNG WOMAN. I thought I would faint! I had to get out in the air!
FILING CLERK. Give her the air.
ADDING CLERK. Free air—
STENOGRAPHER. Hot air.
YOUNG WOMAN. Like I'm dying.
STENOGRAPHER. Same thing yesterday. (*Pause*). And the day before.
YOUNG WOMAN. Yes—what am I going to do?
ADDING CLERK. Take a taxi! (*They laugh*).
FILING CLERK. Call a cop!
TELEPHONE GIRL. Mr. J. wants you.
YOUNG WOMAN. Me?
TELEPHONE GIRL. You!
YOUNG WOMAN (*rises*). Mr. J.!
STENOGRAPHER. Mr. J.
TELEPHONE GIRL. He's bellowing for you!

YOUNG WOMAN *gives last pat to her hair—goes off into door—back.*

STENOGRAPHER (*after her*). Get it just right.
FILING CLERK. She's always doing that to her hair.
TELEPHONE GIRL. It gives a line—it gives a line—
FILING CLERK. Hot dog.
ADDING CLERK. She's artistic.
STENOGRAPHER. She's inefficient.
FILING CLERK. She's inefficient.

STENOGRAPHER. Mr. J. knows she's inefficient.
ADDING CLERK. 46—23—84—2—2—2—1,492—678.
TELEPHONE GIRL. Hello—hello—George H. Jones Company—hello—Mr. Jones? He's in conference.
STENOGRAPHER (*sarcastic*). Conference!
ADDING CLERK. Conference.
FILING CLERK. Hot dog!
TELEPHONE GIRL. Do you think he'll marry her?
ADDING CLERK. If she'll have him.
STENOGRAPHER. If she'll have him!
FILING CLERK. Do you think she'll have him?
TELEPHONE GIRL. How much does he get?
ADDING CLERK. Plenty—5,000—10,000—15,000—20,000—25,000.
STENOGRAPHER. And plenty put away.
ADDING CLERK. Gas Preferred—4's—steel—5's—oil—6's.
FILING CLERK. Hot dog.
STENOGRAPHER. Will she have him? Will she have him? This agreement entered into—party of the first part—party of the second part—will he have her?
TELEPHONE GIRL. Well, I'd hate to get into bed with him. (*Familiar melting voice.*) Hello—humhum—hum—hum—hold the line a minute—will you—hum hum. (*Professional voice.*) Hell, hello—A.B., just a minute. Mr. A.B.—Mr. J.? Mr. A.B.—go ahead, Mr. A.B. (*Melting voice.*) We were interrupted—huh—huh—huh—huh-huh—hum—hum.

Enter YOUNG WOMAN*—she goes to her chair, sits with folded hands.*

FILING CLERK. That's all you ever say to a guy—
STENOGRAPHER. Hum—hum—or uh huh—(*Negative.*)
TELEPHONE GIRL. That's all you have to. (*To phone.*) Hum—hum—hum hum—hum hum.
STENOGRAPHER. Mostly hum hum.
ADDING CLERK. You've said it!
FILING CLERK. Hot dog.
TELEPHONE GIRL. Hum hum huh hum humhumhum—tonight? She's got a date—she told me last night—humhumhuh—hum—all right. (*Disconnects*) Too bad—my boy friend's got a friend—but my girl friend's got a date.
YOUNG WOMAN. You have a good time.
TELEPHONE GIRL. Big time.
STENOGRAPHER. Small time.
ADDING CLERK. A big time on the small time.
TELEPHONE GIRL. I'd ask you, kid, but you'd be up to your neck!
STENOGRAPHER. Neckers!
ADDING CLERK. Petters!
FILING CLERK. Sweet papas.
TELEPHONE GIRL. Want to come?
YOUNG WOMAN. Can't.
TELEPHONE GIRL. Date?
YOUNG WOMAN. My mother.
STENOGRAPHER. Worries?
TELEPHONE GIRL. Nags—hello—George H. Jones Company—Oh hello—

YOUNG WOMAN *sits before her machine—hands in lap, looking at them*

STENOGRAPHER. Why don't you get to work?
YOUNG WOMAN (*dreaming*). What?
ADDING CLERK. Work!
YOUNG WOMAN. Can't.
STENOGRAPHER. Can't?
YOUNG WOMAN. My machine's out of order.
STENOGRAPHER. Well, fix it!
YOUNG WOMAN. I can't—got to get somebody.
STENOGRAPHER. Somebody! Somebody! Always somebody! Here, sort the mail, then!
YOUNG WOMAN (*rises*). All right.
STENOGRAPHER. And hurry! You're late.
YOUNG WOMAN (*sorting letters*). George H. Jones and Company—George H. Jones Inc. George H. Jones—
STENOGRAPHER. You're always late.
ADDING CLERK. You'll lose your job.
YOUNG WOMAN (*hurrying*). George H. Jones—George H. Jones Personal—
TELEPHONE GIRL. Don't let 'em get your goat, kid—tell 'em where to get off.
YOUNG WOMAN. What?
TELEPHONE GIRL. Ain't it all set?
YOUNG WOMAN. What?
TELEPHONE GIRL. You and Mr. J.
STENOGRAPHER. You and the boss.
FILING CLERK. You and the big chief.
ADDING CLERK. You and the big cheese.
YOUNG WOMAN. Did he tell you?
TELEPHONE GIRL. I told you!
ADDING CLERK. I told you!
STENOGRAPHER. I don't believe it.
ADDING CLERK. 5,000—10,000—15,000.
FILING CLERK. Hot dog.
YOUNG WOMAN. No—it isn't so.
STENOGRAPHER. Isn't it?
YOUNG WOMAN. No.
TELEPHONE GIRL. Not yet.
ADDING CLERK. But soon.
FILING CLERK. Hot dog.

Enter JONES.

TELEPHONE GIRL (*busy*). George H. Jones Company—Hello—Hello.

STENOGRAPHER. Awaiting your answer—

ADDING CLERK. 5,000—10,000—15,000—

JONES (*crossing to* YOUNG WOMAN—*puts hand on her shoulder, all stop and stare*). That letter done?

YOUNG WOMAN. No. (*She pulls away.*)

JONES. What's the matter?

STENOGRAPHER. She hasn't started.

JONES. O.K.—want to make some changes.

YOUNG WOMAN. My machine's out of order.

JONES. O.K.—use the one in my room.

YOUNG WOMAN. I'm sorting the mail.

STENOGRAPHER (*sarcastic*). One thing at a time!

JONES (*retreating—goes back center*). O.K. (*To* YOUNG WOMAN.) When you're finished. (*Starts back to his room.*)

STENOGRAPHER. Haste makes waste.

JONES (*at door*). O.K.—don't hurry.

Exits.

STENOGRAPHER. Hew to the line!

TELEPHONE GIRL. He's hewing.

FILING CLERK. Hot dog.

TELEPHONE GIRL. Why did you flinch, kid?

YOUNG WOMAN. Flinch?

TELEPHONE GIRL. Did he pinch?

YOUNG WOMAN. No.

TELEPHONE GIRL. Then what?

YOUNG WOMAN. Nothing!—Just his hand.

TELEPHONE GIRL. Oh—just his hand—(*Shakes her head thoughtfully.*) Uhhuh. (*Negative.*) Uhhuh. (*Decisively.*) No! Tell him no.

STENOGRAPHER. If she does she'll lose her job.

ADDING CLERK. Fired.

FILING CLERK. The sack!

TELEPHONE GIRL (*on the defensive*). And if she doesn't?

ADDING CLERK. She'll come to work in a taxi!

TELEPHONE GIRL. Work?

FILING CLERK. No work.

STENOGRAPHER. No worry.

ADDING CLERK. Breakfast in bed.

STENOGRAPHER (*sarcastic*). Did Madame ring?

FILING CLERK. Lunch in bed!

TELEPHONE GIRL. A double bed! (*In phone.*) Yes, Mr. J. (*To* YOUNG WOMAN.) J. wants you.

YOUNG WOMAN (*starts to get to her feet—but doesn't*). I can't—I'm not ready—in a minute. (*Sits staring ahead of her.*)

ADDING CLERK. 5,000—10,000—15,000—

FILING CLERK. Profits—plans—purchase—

STENOGRAPHER. Call your attention our prices are fixed.

TELEPHONE GIRL. Hello—hello—George H. Jones Company—hello—hello—

YOUNG WOMAN (*thinking her thoughts aloud—to the subdued accompaniment of the office sounds and voices*). Marry me—wants to marry me—George H. Jones—George H. Jones and Company—Mrs. George H. Jones—Mrs. George H. Jones. Dear Madame—marry—do you take this man to be your wedded husband—I do—to love, honor and to love—kisses—no—I can't—George H. Jones—How would you like to marry me—What do you say—Why Mr. Jones I—let me look at your little hands—you have such pretty little hands—let me hold your pretty little hands—George H. Jones—Fat hands—flabby hands—don't touch me—please—fat hands are never weary—phase don't—married—all girls—most girls—married—babies—a baby—curls—little curls all over its head—George H. Jones—straight—thin—bald—don't touch me—please—no—can't—must—somebody—something—no rest—must rest—no rest—must rest—no rest—late today—yesterday—before—late—subway—air—pressing—bodies pressing—bodies—trembling—air—stop—air—late—job—no job—fired—late—alarm clock—alarm clock—alarm clock—hurry—job—ma—nag—nag—nag—ma—hurry—job—no job—no money—installments due—no money—money—George H. Jones—money—Mrs. George H. Jones—money—no work—no worry—free!—rest—sleep till nine—sleep till ten—sleep till noon—now you take a good rest this morning—don't get up till you want to—thank you—oh thank you—oh don't!—please don't touch me—I want to rest—no rest—earn—got to earn—married—earn—no—yes—earn—all girls—most girls—ma—pa—ma—all women—most women—I can't—must—maybe—must—somebody—something—ma—pa—ma—can I, ma? Tell me, ma—something—somebody.

The scene blacks out. The sounds of the office machines continue until the scene lights into Episode 2—and the office sounds become the sound of a radio, offstage.

★

Episode 2

AT HOME

SCENE: *A kitchen: table, chairs, plates and food, garbage can, a pair of rubber gloves. The door at the back now opens on a hall—the window, on an apartment house court.*

SOUNDS: *Buzzer, radio (voice of announcer; music and singer).*

CHARACTERS: *Young Woman; Mother*

OUTSIDE VOICES: *Characters heard, but not seen: A Janitor; A Baby; A Mother and a Small Boy; A Young Boy and Young Girl; A Husband and a Wife; Another Husband and a Wife*

AT RISE: *Young Woman and Mother eating—radio offstage—radio stops.*

YOUNG WOMAN. Ma—I want to talk to you.
MOTHER. Aren't you eating a potato?
YOUNG WOMAN. No.
MOTHER. Why not?
YOUNG WOMAN. I don't want one.
MOTHER. That's no reason. Here! Take one.
YOUNG WOMAN. I don't want it.
MOTHER. Potatoes go with stew—here!
YOUNG WOMAN. Ma, I don't want it!
MOTHER. Want it! Take it!
YOUNG WOMAN. But I—oh, all right. (*Takes it—then.*) Ma, I want to ask you something.
MOTHER. Eat your potato.
YOUNG WOMAN (*takes a bite—then*). Ma, there's something I want to ask you—something important.
MOTHER. Is it mealy?
YOUNG WOMAN. S'all right. Ma—tell me.
MOTHER. Three pounds for a quarter.
YOUNG WOMAN. Ma—tell me (*Buzzer.*)
MOTHER (*her dull voice brightening*). There's the garbage. (*Goes to door—or dumbwaiter—opens it. Stop radio.*)
JANITOR'S VOICE (*offstage*). Garbage.
MOTHER (*pleased—busy*). All right. (*Gets garbage can—puts it out.* YOUNG WOMAN *walks up and down.*) What's the matter now?
YOUNG WOMAN. Nothing.
MOTHER. That jumping up from the table every night the garbage is collected! You act like you're crazy.
YOUNG WOMAN. Ma, do all women—
MOTHER. I suppose you think you're too nice for anything so common! Well, let me tell you, my lady, that it's a very important part of life.
YOUNG WOMAN. Oh, Ma!
MOTHER. Well, are you?
YOUNG WOMAN. Am I what?
MOTHER. Glad! Grateful.
YOUNG WOMAN. Yes!
MOTHER. You don't act like it!
YOUNG WOMAN. Oh, Ma, don't talk!
MOTHER. You just said you wanted to talk.
YOUNG WOMAN. Well now—I want to think. I got to think.
MOTHER. Aren't you going to finish your potato?
YOUNG WOMAN. Oh, Ma!
MOTHER. Is there anything the matter with it?
YOUNG WOMAN. No—
MOTHER. Then why don't you finish it?
YOUNG WOMAN. Because I don't want it.
MOTHER. Why don't you?
YOUNG WOMAN. Oh, Ma! Let me alone!
MOTHER. Well, you've got to eat! If you don't eat—
YOUNG WOMAN. Ma! Don't nag!
MOTHER. Nag! Just because I try to look out for you—nag! Just because I try to care for you—nag! Why, you haven't sense enought to eat! What should become of you I'd like to know—if I didn't nag!

Offstage—a sound of window opening—all these offstage sounds come in through the court window at the back.

WOMAN'S VOICE. Johnny—Johnny—come in now!
A SMALL BOY'S VOICE. Oh, Ma!
WOMAN'S VOICE. It's getting cold.
A SMALL BOY'S VOICE. Oh, Ma!
WOMAN'S VOICE. You heard me! (*Sound of window slamming.*)
YOUNG WOMAN. I'm grown up, Ma.
MOTHER. Grown up! What do you mean by that?
YOUNG WOMAN. Nothing much—I guess. (*Offstage sound of baby crying.* MOTHER *rises, clatters dishes.*) Let's not do the dishes right away, Ma. Let's talk—I gotta.
MOTHER. Well, I can't talk with dirty dishes around—you may be able to but—(*Clattering—clattering.*)

YOUNG WOMAN. Ma! Listen! Listen!—There's a man wants to marry me.
MOTHER (*stops clattering—sits*). What man?
YOUNG WOMAN. He says he fell in love with my hands.
MOTHER. In love! Is that beginning again! I thought you were over that!

Offstage BOY'S VOICE—*whistles*—GIRL'S VOICE *answers.*

BOY'S VOICE. Come on out.
GIRL'S VOICE. Can't.
BOY'S VOICE. Nobody'll see you.
GIRL'S VOICE. I can't.
BOY'S VOICE. It's dark now—come on.
GIRL'S VOICE. Well—just for a minute.
BOY'S VOICE. Meet you round the corner.
YOUNG WOMAN. I got to get married, Ma.
MOTHER. What do you mean?
YOUNG WOMAN. I gotta.
MOTHER. You haven't got in trouble, have you?
YOUNG WOMAN. Don't talk like that!
MOTHER. Well, you say you got to get married—what do you mean?
YOUNG WOMAN. Nothing.
MOTHER. Answer me!
YOUNG WOMAN. All women get married, don't they?
MOTHER. Nonsense!
YOUNG WOMAN. You got married, didn't you?
MOTHER. Yes, I did!

Offstage voices.

WOMAN'S VOICE. Where you going?
MAN'S VOICE. Out.
WOMAN'S VOICE. You were out last night.
MAN'S VOICE. Was I?
WOMAN'S VOICE. You're always going out.
MAN'S VOICE. Am I?
WOMAN'S VOICE. Where you going?
MAN'S VOICE. Out.

End of offstage voices.

MOTHER. Who is he? Where did you come to know him?
YOUNG WOMAN. In the office.
MOTHER. In the office!
YOUNG WOMAN. It's Mr. J.
MOTHER. Mr. J.?
YOUNG WOMAN. The Vice-President.
MOTHER. Vice-President! His income must be—Does he know you're got a mother to support?
YOUNG WOMAN. Yes.
MOTHER. What does he say?
YOUNG WOMAN. All right.
MOTHER. How soon you going to marry him?
YOUNG WOMAN. I'm not going to.
MOTHER. Not going to!
YOUNG WOMAN. No! I'm not going to.
MOTHER. But you just said—
YOUNG WOMAN. I'm not going to.
MOTHER. Are you crazy?
YOUNG WOMAN. I can't, Ma! I can't!
MOTHER. Why can't you?
YOUNG WOMAN. I don't love him.
MOTHER. Love!—what does that amount to! Will it clothe you? Will it feed you? Will it pay the bills?
YOUNG WOMAN. No! But it's real just the same!
MOTHER. Real!
YOUNG WOMAN. If it isn't—what can you count on in life?
MOTHER. I'll tell you what you can count on! You can count that you've got to eat and sleep and get up and put clothes on your back and take 'em off again—that you got to get old—and that you got to die. That's what you can count on! All the rest is in your head!
YOUNG WOMAN. But Ma—didn't you love Pa?
MOTHER. I suppose I did—I don't know—I've forgotten—what difference does it make—now?
YOUNG WOMAN. But then!—oh Ma, tell me!
MOTHER. Tell you what?
YOUNG WOMAN. About all that—love!

Offstage voices.

WIFE'S VOICE. Don't.
HUSBAND'S VOICE. What's the matter—don't you want me to kiss you?
WIFE'S VOICE. Not like that.
HUSBAND'S VOICE. Like what?
WIFE'S VOICE. That silly kiss!
HUSBAND'S VOICE. Silly kiss?
WIFE'S VOICE. You look so silly—oh I know what's coming when you look like that—and kiss me like that—don't—go away—

End of offstage voices.

MOTHER. He's a decent man, isn't he?
YOUNG WOMAN. I don't know. How should I know—yet.
MOTHER. He's a Vice-President—of course he's decent.
YOUNG WOMAN. I don't care whether he's decent or not. I won't marry him.
MOTHER. But you just said you wanted to marry—
YOUNG WOMAN. Not him.
MOTHER. Who?
YOUNG WOMAN. I don't know—I don't know—I haven't found him yet!
MOTHER. You talk like you're crazy!
YOUNG WOMAN. Oh, Ma—tell me!

MOTHER. Tell you what?

YOUNG WOMAN. Tell me—(*Words suddenly pouring out.*) Your skin oughtn't to curl—ought it—when he just comes near you—ought it? That's wrong, ain't it? You don't get over that, do you—ever, do you or do you? How is it, Ma—do you?

MOTHER. Do you what?

YOUNG WOMAN. DO you get used to, it—so after a while it doesn't matter? Or don't you? Does it always matter? You ought to be in love, oughtn't you, Ma? You must be in love, mustn't you, Ma? That changes everything, doesn't it—or does it? Maybe if you just like a person it's all right—is it? When he puts a hand on me, my blood turns cold. But your blood oughtn't to run cold, ought it? His hands are—his hands are fat, Ma—don't you see—his hands are fat—and they sort of press—and they're fat—don't you see?—Don't you see?

MOTHER (*stares at her bewildered*). See what?

YOUNG WOMAN (*rushing on*). I've always thought I'd find somebody—somebody young—and—and attractive —with wavy hair—wavy hair—I always think of children with curls—little curls all over their head—somebody young—and attractive—that I'd like—that I'd love—But I haven't found anybody like that yet—I haven't found anybody—I've hardly known anybody—you'd never let me go with anybody and—

MOTHER. Are you throwing it up to me that—

YOUNG WOMAN. No—let me finish, Ma! No—let me finish! I just mean I've never found anybody—anybody—nobody's ever asked me—till now—he's the only man that's ever asked me—And I suppose I got to marry somebody—all girls do—

MOTHER. Nonsense.

YOUNG WOMAN. But, I can't go on like this, Ma—I don't know why—but I can't—it's like I'm all tight inside—sometimes I feel like I'm stifling!—You don't know—stifling. (*Walks up and down.*) I can't go on like this much longer—going to work—coming home—going to work—coming home—I can't—Sometimes in the subway I think I'm going to die—sometimes even in the office if something don't happen—I got to do something—I don't know—it's like I'm all tight inside.

MOTHER. You're crazy.

YOUNG WOMAN. Oh, Ma!

MOTHER. You're crazy.

YOUNG WOMAN. Ma—if you tell me that again I'll kill you! I'll kill you!

MOTHER. If that isn't crazy!

YOUNG WOMAN. I'll kill you—Maybe I am crazy—I don't know. Sometimes I think I am—the thoughts that go on in my mind—sometimes I think I am—I can't help it if I am—I do the best I can—I do the best I can and I'm nearly crazy! (MOTHER *rises and sits.*) Go away! Go away! You don't know anything about anything! And you haven't got any pity—no pity—you just take it for granted that I go to work every day—and come home every night and bring my money every week—and just take it for granted—you'd let me go on forever—and never feel any pity—

Offstage radio—a voice singing a sentimental MOTHER *song or popular home song.* MOTHER *begins to cry—crosses to chair left—sits.*

Oh Ma—forgive me! Forgive me!

MOTHER. My own child! To be spoken to like that by my own child!

YOUNG WOMAN. I didn't mean it, Ma—I didn't mean it! (*She goes to her mother—crosses to left.*)

MOTHER (*clinging to her hand*). You're all I've got in the world—and you don't want me—you want to kill me.

YOUNG WOMAN. No—no, I don't, Ma! I just said that!

MOTHER. I've worked for you and slaved for you!

YOUNG WOMAN. I know, Ma.

MOTHER. I brought you into the world.

YOUNG WOMAN. I know, Ma.

MOTHER. You're flesh of my flesh and—

YOUNG WOMAN. I know, Ma, I know.

MOTHER. And—

YOUNG WOMAN. You rest now, Ma—you rest—

MOTHER (*struggling*). I got to do the dishes.

YOUNG WOMAN. I'll do the dishes—You listen to the music, Ma—I'll do the dishes.

Ma sits. YOUNG WOMAN *crosses to behind screen. Takes a pair of rubber gloves and begins to put them on. The* MOTHER *sees them—they irritate her—there is a return of her characteristic mood.*

MOTHER. Those gloves! I've been washing dishes for forty years and I never wore gloves! But my lady's hands! My lady's hands!

YOUNG WOMAN. Sometimes you talk to me like you're jealous, Ma.

MOTHER. Jealous?

YOUNG WOMAN. It's my hands got me a husband.

MOTHER. A husband? So you're going to marry him now?

YOUNG WOMAN. I suppose so.

MOTHER. If you ain't the craziest—

The scene blacks out. In the darkness, the mother song goes into jazz—very faint—as the scene lights into

★

Episode 3

HONEYMOON

SCENE: *Hotel bedroom: bed, chair, mirror. The door at the back now opens on a bathroom; the window, on a dancing casino opposie.*

SOUNDS: *A small jazz band (violin, piano, saxophone—very dim, at first, then louder).*

CHARACTERS: *Young Woman; Husband; Bellboy*

OFFSTAGE: *Seen not heard, Men and Women dancing in couples.*

AT RISE: *Set dark. Bellboy, Husband,* and *Young Woman enter. Bellboy carries luggage. He switches on light by door. Stop music.*

HUSBAND. Well, here we are. (*Throws hat on bed;* BELLBOY *puts luggage down, crosses to window; raises shade three inches. Opens window three inches. Sounds of jazz music louder. Offstage.*)

BELLBOY (*comes to man for tip*). Anything else, Sir? (*Receives tip. Exits.*)

HUSBAND. Well, here we are.

YOUNG WOMAN. Yes, here we are.

HUSBAND. Aren't you going to take your hat off—stay a while? (YOUNG WOMAN *looks around as though looking for a way out, then takes off her hat, pulls the hair automatically around her ears.*) This is all right, isn't it? Huh? Huh?

YOUNG WOMAN. It's very nice.

HUSBAND. Twelve bucks a day! They know how to soak you in these pleasure resorts. Twelve bucks! (*Music.*) Well—we'll get our money's worth out of it all right. (*Goes toward bathroom.*) I'm going to wash up. (*Stops at door.*) Don't you want to wash up?

(YOUNG WOMAN *shakes head 'No'*)

HUSBAND. I do! It was a long trip! I want to wash up!

Goes off—closes door; sings in bathroom. YOUNG WOMAN *goes to window—raises shade—sees the dancers going round and round in couples. Music is louder. Re-enter* HUSBAND.

Say, pull that blind down! They can see in!

YOUNG WOMAN. I thought you said there'd be a view of the ocean!

HUSBAND. Sure there is.

YOUNG WOMAN. I just see people—dancing.

HUSBAND. The ocean's beyond.

YOUNG WOMAN (*desperately*). I was counting on seeing it!

HUSBAND. You'll see it tomorrow—what's eating you? We'll take in the boardwalk—Don't you want to wash up?

YOUNG WOMAN. No!

HUSBAND. It was a long trip. Sure you don't? (YOUNG WOMAN *shakes her head 'No'. Husband takes off his coat—puts it over chair.*) Better make yourself at home. I'm going to. (*She stares at him—moves away from the window.*) Say, pull down that blind! (*Crosses to chair down left—sits.*)

YOUNG WOMAN. It's close—don't you think it's close?

HUSBAND. Well—you don't want people looking in, do you? (*Laughs.*) Huh—Huh?

YOUNG WOMAN. No.

HUSBAND (*laughs*). I guess not. Huh? (*Takes off shoes.* YOUNG *WOMAN leaves the window, and crosses down to the bed.*) Say—you look a little white around the gills! What's the matter?

YOUNG WOMAN. Nothing.

HUSBAND. You look like you're scared.

YOUNG WOMAN. No.

HUSBAND. Nothing to be scared of. You're with your husband, you know. (*Takes her to chair, left.*)

YOUNG WOMAN. I know.

HUSBAND. Happy?

YOUNG WOMAN. Yes.

HUSBAND (*sitting*). Then come here and give us a kiss. (*He puts her on his knee.*) That's the girlie. (*He bends her head down, and kisses her along the back of her neck.*) Like that? (*She tries to get to her feet.*) Say—stay there! What you moving for?—You know—you got to learn to relax, little girl—(*Dancers go off. Dim lights. Pinches her above knee.*) Say, what you got under there?

YOUNG WOMAN. Nothing.

HUSBAND. Nothing! (*Laughs.*) That's a good one! Nothing, huh? Huh? That reminds me of the story of the pullman porter and the—what's the matter—did I tell you that one? (*Music dims off and out.*)

YOUNG WOMAN. I don't know.
HUSBAND. The pullman porter and the tart?
YOUNG WOMAN. No.
HUSBAND. It's a good one—well—the train was just pulling out and the tart—
YOUNG WOMAN. You did tell that one!
HUSBAND. About the—
YOUNG WOMAN. Yes! Yes! I remember now!
HUSBAND. About the—
YOUNG WOMAN. Yes!
HUSBAND. All right—if I did. You're sure it was the one about the—
YOUNG WOMAN. I'm sure.
HUSBAND. When he asked her what she had underneath her seat and she said—
YOUNG WOMAN. Yes! Yes! That one!
HUSBAND. All right—But I don't believe I did. (*She tries to get up again, and he holds her.*) You know you have got something under there—what is it?
YOUNG WOMAN. Nothing—just—just my garter.
HUSBAND. Your garter! Your garter! Say did I tell you the one about—
YOUNG WOMAN. Yes! Yes!
HUSBAND (*with dignity*). How do you know which one I mean?
YOUNG WOMAN. You told me them all!
HUSBAND (*pulling her back to his knee*). No, I didn't! Not by a jugful! I got a lot of 'em up my sleeve yet—that's part of what I owe my success to—my ability to spring a good story—You know—you got to learn to relax, little girl—haven't you?
YOUNG WOMAN. Yes.
HUSBAND. That's one of the biggest things to learn in life. That's part of what I owe my success to. Now you go and get those heavy things off—and relax.
YOUNG WOMAN. They're not heavy.
HUSBAND. You haven't got much on—have you? But you'll feel better with 'em off. (*Gets up.*) Want me to help you?
YOUNG WOMAN. No.
HUSBAND. I'm your husband, you know.
YOUNG WOMAN. I know.
HUSBAND. You aren't afraid of your husband, are you?
YOUNG WOMAN. No—of course not—but I thought maybe—can't we go out for a little while?
HUSBAND. Out? What for?
YOUNG WOMAN. Fresh air—walk—talk.
HUSBAND. We can talk here—I'll tell you all about myself. Go along now. (YOUNG WOMAN *goes toward bathroom door. Gets bag.*) Where are you going?
YOUNG WOMAN. In here.
HUSBAND. I thought you'd want to wash up.
YOUNG WOMAN. I just want to—get ready.
HUSBAND. You don't have to go in there to take your clothes off!
YOUNG WOMAN. I want to.
HUSBAND. What for?
YOUNG WOMAN. I always do.
HUSBAND. What?
YOUNG WOMAN. Undress by myself.
HUSBAND. You've never been married till now—have you? (*Laughs.*) Or have you been pulling something over on me?
YOUNG WOMAN. No.
HUSBAND. I understand—kind of modest—huh? Huh?
YOUNG WOMAN. Yes.
HUSBAND. I understand women—(*Indulgently.*) Go along.

She goes off—starts to close door. YOUNG WOMAN *exits.*

Don't close the door—thought you wanted to talk.

He looks around the room with satisfaction—after a pause—rises—takes off his cottar.

You're awful quiet—what are you doing in there?
YOUNG WOMAN. Just—getting ready—
HUSBAND (*still in his mood of satisfaction*). I'm going to enjoy life from now on—I haven't had such an easy time of it. I got where I am by hard work and self denial—now I'm going to enjoy life—I'm going to make up for all I missed—aren't you about ready?
YOUNG WOMAN. Not yet.
HUSBAND. Next year maybe we'll go to Paris. You can buy a lot of that French underwear—and Switzerland—all my life I've wanted a Swiss watch—that I bought right there—I coulda' got a Swiss watch here, but I always wanted one that I bought right there—Isn't that funny—huh? Isn't it? Huh? Huh?
YOUNG WOMAN. Yes.
HUSBAND. All my life I've wanted a Swiss watch that I bought right there. All my life I've counted on having that some day—more than anything—except one thing—you know what?
YOUNG WOMAN. No.
HUSBAND. Guess.
YOUNG WOMAN. I can't.
HUSBAND. Then I'm coming in and tell you.
YOUNG WOMAN. No! Please! Please don't.
HUSBAND. Well hurry up then! I thought you women didn't wear much of anything these days—huh? Huh? I'm coming in!
YOUNG WOMAN. No—no! Just a minute!
HUSBAND. All right. Just a minute. (YOUNG WOMAN *is silent.* HUSBAND *laughs and takes out watch.*) 13—14—I'm counting the seconds on you—that's what you

said, didn't you—just a minute!—49—50—51—52—53—

Enter Young Woman.

YOUNG WOMAN (at the door). Here I am. (She wears a little white gown that hangs very straight. She is very still, but her eyes are wide with a curious, helpless, animal terror.)

HUSBAND (*starts toward her—stops. The room is in shadow except for one dim light by the bed. Sound of girl weeping*). You crying? (*Sound of weeping.*) What are you crying for? (*Crosses to her.*)

YOUNG WOMAN (*crying out*). Ma! Ma! I want my mother!

HUSBAND. I thought you were glad to get away from her.

YOUNG WOMAN. I want her now—I want somebody.

HUSBAND. You got me, haven't you?

YOUNG WOMAN. Somebody—somebody—

HUSBAND. There's nothing to cry about. There's nothing to cry about.

The scene blacks out. The music continues until the lights go up for Episode 4. Rhythm of the music is gradually replaced by the sound of steel riveting for Episode 4.

★

Episode 4

MATERNAL

SCENE: *A room in a hospital: bed, chair. The door in the back now opens on a corridor; the window on a tall building going up.*

SOUNDS: *Outside window—riveting.*

CHARACTERS IN THE SCENE: *Young Woman; Doctors; Nurses; Husband*

CHARACTERS SEEN BUT NOT HEARD: *Woman in Wheel Chair; Woman in Bathrobe; Stretcher Wagon; Nurse with Tray; Nurse with Covered Basin*

AT RISE: *Young Woman lies still in bed. The door is open. In the corridor, a stretcher wagon goes by. Enter Nurse.*

NURSE. How are you feeling today? (*No response from* YOUNG WOMAN.) Better? (*No response.*) No pain? (*No response. Nurse takes her watch in one hand,* YOUNG WOMAN'*s wrist in the other—stands, then goes to chart at foot of bed—writes.*) You're getting along fine. (*No response.*) Such a sweet baby you have, too. (*No response.*) Aren't you glad it's a girl? (YOUNG WOMAN *makes sign with her head 'No'.*) You're not! Oh, my! That's no way to talk! Men want boys—woman ought to want girls. (*No response.*) Maybe you didn't want either, eh? (YOUNG WOMAN *signs 'No'. Riveting machine.*) You'll feel different when it begins to nurse. You'll just love it then. Your milk hasn't come yet—has it? (*Sign—'No'.*) It will! (*Sign—'No'.*) Oh, you don't know Doctor! (*Goes to door—turns.*) Anything else you want? (YOUNG WOMAN *points to window.*) Draft? (*Sign—'No'.*) The noise? (YOUNG WOMAN *signs 'Yes'.*) Oh, that can't be helped. Hospital's got to have a new wing. We've the biggest Maternity Hospital in the world. I'll close the window, though. (YOUNG WOMAN *signs 'No'.*) No?

YOUNG WOMAN (*whispers*). I smell everything then.

NURSE (*starting out the door—riveting machine*). Here's your man!

Enter HUSBAND *with large bouquet. Crosses to bed.*

HUSBAND. Well, how are we today? (YOUNG WOMAN—*no response.*)

NURSE. She's getting stronger!

HUSBAND. Of course she is!

NURSE (*taking flowers*). See what your husband brought you.

HUSBAND. Better put 'em in water right away. (*Exit nurse.*) Everything O.K.? (YOUNG WOMAN *signs 'No'.*) Now see here, my dear, you've got to brace up, you know! And—and face things! Everybody's got to brace up and face things! That's what makes the world go round. I know all you've been through but— (YOUNG WOMAN *signs 'No'.*) Oh, yes I do! I know all about it! I was right outside all the time! (YOUNG WOMAN *makes violent gestures of 'No'. Ignoring.*) Oh yes! But you've got to brace up now! Make an effort! Pull yourself together! Start the up-hill climb! Oh I've been down—but I haven't stayed down. I've been licked but I haven't stayed licked! I've pulled myself up by my own bootstraps, and that's what you've got to do! Will power! That's what conquers! Look at me! Now you've got to brace up! Face the music! Stand the gaff! Take life by the horns! Look it in the face!—Having a baby's natural! Perfectly natural thing—why should—

(YOUNG WOMAN *chokes—points wildly to door. Enter* NURSE *with flowers in a vase.)*

NURSE. What's the matter?

HUSBAND. She's got that gagging again—like she had the last time I was here.

YOUNG WOMAN *gestures him out.*

NURSE. Better go, sir.

HUSBAND (*at door*). I'll be back.

YOUNG WOMAN *gasping and gesturing.*

NURSE. She needs rest.

HUSBAND. Tomorrow then. I'll be back tomorrow—tomorrow and every day—goodbye. (*Exits*)

NURSE. You got a mighty nice husband, I guess you know that? (*Writes on chart.*) Gagging.

*Corridor life—*WOMAN *in a Bathrobe passes door. Enter* DOCTOR, YOUNG DOCTOR, NURSE, *wheeling surgeon's wagon with bottles, instruments, etc.*

DOCTOR. How's the little lady today? (*Crosses to bed.*)

NURSE. She's better, Doctor.

DOCTOR. Of course she's better! She's all right—aren't you? (YOUNG WOMAN *does not respond.*) What's the matter? Can't you talk? (*Drops her hand. Takes chart.*)

NURSE. She's a little weak yet, Doctor.

DOCTOR (*at chart*). Milk hasn't come yet?

NURSE. No, Doctor.

DOCTOR. Put the child to breast. (YOUNG WOMAN—'*No—no'!—Riveting machine.*) No? Don't you want to nurse your baby? (YOUNG WOMAN *signs 'No'.*) Why not? (*No response.*) These modern neurotic women, eh, Doctor? What are we going to do with 'em? (YOUNG DOCTOR *laughs,* NURSE *smiles.*) Bring the baby!

YOUNG WOMAN. No!

DOCTOR. Well—that's strong enough. I thought you were too weak to talk—that's better. You don't want your baby?

YOUNG WOMAN. No.

DOCTOR. What do you want?

YOUNG WOMAN. Let alone—let alone.

DOCTOR. Bring the baby.

NURSE. Yes, Doctor—she's behaved very badly every time, Doctor—very upset—maybe we better not.

DOCTOR. I decide what we better and better not here, Nurse!

NURSE. Yes, doctor.

DOCTOR. Bring the baby.

NURSE. Yes, Doctor.

DOCTOR (*with chart*). Gagging—you mean nausea.

NURSE. Yes, Doctor, but—

DOCTOR. No buts, nurse.

NURSE. Yes, Doctor.

DOCTOR. Nausea!—Change the diet!—What is her diet?

NURSE. Liquids.

DOCTOR. Give her solids.

NURSE. Yes, Doctor. She says she can't swallow solids.

DOCTOR. Give her solids.

NURSE. Yes, Doctor. (*Starts to go—riveting machine.*)

DOCTOR. Wait—I'll change her medicine. (*Takes pad and writes prescription in Latin. Hands it to* NURSE.) After meals. (*To door.*) Bring her baby.

Exit DOCTOR, *followed by* YOUNG DOCTOR *and* NURSE *with surgeon's wagon.*

NURSE. Yes, Doctor.

Exits.

YOUNG WOMAN (*alone*). Let me alone—let me alone—let me alone—I've submitted to enough—I won't submit to any more—crawl off—crawl off in the dark—Vixen crawled under the bed—way back in the corner under the bed—they were all drowned—puppies don't go to heaven—heaven—golden stairs—long stairs—long—too long—long golden stairs—climb those golden stairs—stairs—stairs—climb—tired—too tired—dead—no matter—nothing matters—dead—stairs—long stairs—all the dead going up—going up—to be in heaven—heaven—golden stairs—all the children coming down—coming down to be born—dead going up—children coming down—going up—coming down—going up—coming down—going up—coming down—going up—stop—stop—no—no traffic cop—no—no traffic cop in heaven—traffic cop—traffic cop—can't you give us a smile—tired—too tired—no matter—it doesn't matter—St. Peter—St. Peter at the gate—you can't come in—no matter—it doesn't matter—I'll rest—I'll lie down—down—all written down—down in a big book—no matter—it doesn't matter—

I'll lie down—it weighs me—it's over me—it weighs—weighs—it's heavy—it's a heavy book—no matter—lie still—don't move—can't move—rest—forget—they say you forget—a girl—aren't you glad it's a girl—a little girl—with no hair—none—little curls all over his head—a little bald girl—curls—curls all over his head—what kind of hair had God? No matter—it doesn't matter—everybody loves God—they've got to—got to—got to love God—God is love—even if he's bad they got to love him—if he's got fat hands—fat hands—no no—he wouldn't be God—His hands make you well—He lays on his hands—well—and happy—no matter—doesn't matter—far—too far—tired—too tired Vixen crawled off under bed—eight—there were eight—a woman crawled off under the bed—a woman has one—two three four—one two three four—one two three four—two plus two is four—two times two is four—two times four is eight—Vixen had eight—one two three four five six seven eight—eight—Puffie had eight—all drowned—drowned—drowned in blood—blood—Oh God! God—God never had one—Mary had one—in a manger—the lowly manger—God's on a high throne—far—too far—no matter—it doesn't matter—God Mary Mary God Mary—Virgin Mary—Mary had one—the Holy Ghost—the Holy Ghost—George H. Jones—oh don't—please don't! Let me rest—now I can rest—the weight is gone—inside the weight is gone—it's only outside—outside—all around—weight—I'm under it—Vixen crawled under the bed—there were eight—I'll not submit any more—I'll not submit—I'll not submit—

The scene blacks out. The sound of riveting continues until it goes into the sound of an electric piano and the scene lights up for Episode 5.

★

Episode 5

PROHIBITED

SCENE: *Bar: bottles, tables, chairs, electric piano.*

SOUND: *Electric piano.*

CHARACTERS: *Man behind the bar; Policeman at bar; Waiter; At Table 1: a Man and a Woman; at Table 2: a Man and a Boy; at Table 3: Two Men waiting for Two Girls, who are; Telephone Girl of Episode 1 and Young Woman.*

AT RISE: *Everyone except the Girls on. Of the characters, the Man and Woman at Table 1 are an ordinary and woman. The man at Table 2 is a middle-aged fairy; the Boy is young, untouched. At Table 3, First Man is pleasing, common, vigorous. He has coarse wavy hair. Second Man is an ordinary salesman type.*

At Table 3.

FIRST MAN. I'm going to beat it.

SECOND MAN. Oh, for the love of Mike.

FIRST MAN. They ain't going to show.

SECOND MAN. Sure they'll show.

FIRST MAN. How do you know they'll show?

SECOND MAN. I tell you can't keep that baby away from me—just got to—(*Snaps fingers.*)—She comes running.

FIRST MAN. Looks like it.

SECOND MAN (*to* WAITER *makes sign '2' with his fingers*). The same. (WAITER *goes to the bar.*)

At Table 2.

MAN. Oh, I'm sorry I brought you here.

BOY. Why?

MAN. This Purgatory of noise! I brought you here to give you pleasure—let you taste pleasure. This sherry they have here is bottled—heaven. Wait till you taste it.

BOY. I don't drink.

MAN. Drink! This isn't drink! Real amontillado is sunshine and orange groves—it's the Mediterranean and blue moonlight and—love? Have you ever been in love?

BOY. No.
MAN. Never in love with—a woman?
BOY. No—not really.
MAN. What do you mean really?
BOY. Just—that.
MAN. Ah! (*Makes sign to* WAITER.) To—you know what I want—Two. (WAITER *goes to the bar.*)

At Table 1.

MAN. Well, are you going through with it, or ain't you?
WOMAN. That's what I want to do—go through with it.
MAN. But you can't.
WOMAN. Why can't I?
MAN. How can yuh? (*Silence.*) It's nothing—most women don't think anything about it—they just—Bert told me a doctor to go to—gave me the address—
WOMAN. Don't talk about it!
MAN. Got to talk about it—you got to get out of this. (*Silence*—MAN *makes sign to* WAITER.) What you having?
WOMAN. Nothing—I don't want anything. I had enough.
MAN. Do you good. The same?
WOMAN. I suppose so.
MAN (*makes sign '2' to* WAITER). The same. (WAITER *goes to the bar.*)

At Table 3.

FIRST MAN. I'm going to beat it.
SECOND MAN. Oh say, listen! I'm counting on you to take the other one off my hands.
FIRST MAN. I'm going to beat it.
SECOND MAN. For the love of Mike have a heart! Listen—as a favor to me—I got to be home by six—I promised my wife—sure. That don't leave me no time at all if we got to hang around—entertain some dame. You got to take her off my hands.
FIRST MAN. Maybe she won't fall for me.
SECOND MAN. Sure she'll fall for you! They all fall for you—even my wife likes you—tries to kid herself it's your brave exploits, but I know what it is—sure she'll fall for you.

Enter two girls—TELEPHONE GIRL *and* YOUNG WOMAN.

GIRL (*coming to table*). Hello—
SECOND MAN (*grouch*). Good night.
GIRL. Good night? What's eatin' yuh?
SECOND MAN (*same*). Nothin's eatin' me—thought somethin' musta swallowed you.
GIRL. Why?
SECOND MAN. You're late!
GIRL (*unimpressed*). Oh—(*Brushing it aside.*) Mrs. Jones—Mr. Smith.
SECOND MAN. Meet my friend, Mr. Roe. (*They all sit. To the* WAITER.) The same and two more. (WAITER *goes.*)
GIRL. So we kept you waiting, did we?
SECOND MAN. Only about an hour.
YOUNG WOMAN. Was it that long?
SECOND MAN. We been here that long—ain't we Dick?
FIRST MAN. Just about, Harry.
SECOND MAN. For the love of God what delayed yuh?
GIRL. Tell Helen that one.
SECOND MAN (*to* YOUNG WOMAN). The old Irish woman that went to her first race? Bet on the skate that came in last—she went up to the jockey and asked him, 'For the love of God, what delayed yuh'.
All laugh.
YOUNG WOMAN. Why, that's kinda funny!
SECOND MAN. Kinda!—What do you mean kinda?
YOUNG WOMAN. I just mean there are not many of 'em that are funny at all.
SECOND MAN. Not if you haven't heard the funny ones.
YOUNG WOMAN. Oh I've heard 'em all.
FIRST MAN. Not a laugh in a carload, eh?
GIRL. Got a cigarette?
SECOND MAN (*with package*). One of these?
GIRL (*taking one*). Uhhuh.

He offers the package to YOUNG WOMAN.

YOUNG WOMAN (*taking one*). Uhhuh.
SECOND MAN (*to First Man*). One of these?
FIRST MAN (*showing his own package*). Thanks—I like these.

He lights YOUNG WOMAN's *cigarette.*

SECOND MAN (*lighting* GIRL's *cigarette*). Well—baby—how they comin', huh?
GIRL. Couldn't be better.
SECOND MAN. How's every little thing?
GIRL. Just great.
SECOND MAN. Miss me?
GIRL. I'll say so—when did you get in?
SECOND MAN. Just a coupla hours ago.
GIRL. Miss me?
SECOND MAN. Did I? You don't know the half of it.
YOUNG WOMAN (*interrupting restlessly*). Can we dance here?
SECOND MAN. Not here.
YOUNG WOMAN. Where do we go from here?
SECOND MAN. Where do we go from here! You just got here!
FIRST MAN. What's the hurry?
SECOND MAN. What's the rush?
YOUNG WOMAN. I don't know.
GIRL. Helen wants to dance.
YOUNG WOMAN. I just want to keep moving.

FIRST MAN (*smiling*). You want to keep moving, huh?

SECOND MAN. You must be one of those restless babies! Where do we go from here!

YOUNG WOMAN. It's only some days—I want to keep moving.

FIRST MAN. You want to keep moving, huh? (*He is staring at her smilingly.*)

YOUNG WOMAN (*nods*) Uhhuh.

FIRST MAN (*quietly*). Stick around a while.

SECOND MAN. Where do we go from here! Say, what kind of a crowd do you run with, anyway?

GIRL. Helen don't run with any crowd—do you, Helen?

YOUNG WOMAN (*embarrassed*). No.

FIRST MAN. Well, I'm not a crowd—run with me.

SECOND MAN (*gratified*). All set, huh?—Dick was about ready to beat it.

FIRST MAN. That's before I met the little lady.

Waiter serves drinks.

FIRST MAN. Here's how.

SECOND MAN. Here's to you.

GIRL. Here's looking at you.

YOUNG WOMAN. Here's—happy days.

They all drink.

FIRST MAN. That's good stuff!

SECOND MAN. Off a boat.

FIRST MAN. Off a boat?

SECOND MAN. They get all their stuff here—off a boat.

GIRL. That's what *they* say.

SECOND MAN. No! Sure! Sure they do! Sure!

GIRL. It's all right with me.

SECOND MAN. But they do! Sure!

GIRL. I believe you, darling!

SECOND MAN. Did you miss me?

GIRL. Uhhuh. (*Affirmative.*)

SECOND MAN. Any other daddies?

GIRL. Uhhuh. (*Negative.*)

SECOND MAN. Love any daddy but daddy?

GIRL. Uhhuh. (*Negative.*)

SECOND MAN. Let's beat it!

GIRL (*a little self-conscious before* YOUNG WOMAN). We just got here.

SECOND MAN. Don't I know it—Come on!

GIRL. But—(*indicates* YOUNG WOMAN).

SECOND MAN (*not understanding*). They're all set—aren't you?

FIRST MAN (*to* YOUNG WOMAN). Are we? (*She doesn't answer.*)

SECOND MAN. I got to be out to the house by six—come on—(*Rising—to* GIRL.) Come on, kid—let's us beat it! (GIRL *indicates* YOUNG WOMAN. *Now understanding —very elaborate.*) Business is business, you know! I got a lot to do yet this afternoon—thought you might go along with me—help me out—how about it?

GIRL (*rising, her dignity preserved.*) Sure—I'll go along with you—help you out. (*Both rise.*)

SECOND MAN. All right with you folks?

FIRST MAN. All right with me.

SECOND MAN. All right with you? (*To* YOUNG WOMAN.)

YOUNG WOMAN. All right with me.

SECOND MAN. Come on, kid. (*They rise.*) Where's the damage?

FIRST MAN. Go on!

SECOND MAN. No!

FIRST MAN. Go on!

SECOND MAN. I'll match you.

YOUNG WOMAN. Heads win!

GIRL. Heads I win—tails you lose.

SECOND MAN (*impatiently*). He's matching me.

FIRST MAN. Am I matching you or are you matching me?

SECOND MAN. I'm matching you. (*They match.*) You're stung!

FIRST MAN (*contentedly*). Not so you can notice it. (*Smiles at* YOUNG WOMAN.)

GIRL. That's for you, Helen.

SECOND MAN. She ain't dumb! Come on.

GIRL (*to FIRST MAN*). You be nice to her now. She's very fastidious.—Goodbye.

Exit SECOND MAN *and* GIRL.

YOUNG WOMAN. I know what business is like.

FIRST MAN. You do—do yuh?

YOUNG WOMAN. I used to be a business girl myself before—

FIRST MAN. Before what?

YOUNG WOMAN. Before I quit.

FIRST MAN. What did you quit for?

YOUNG WOMAN. I just quit.

FIRST MAN. You're married, huh?

YOUNG WOMAN. Yes—I am.

FIRST MAN. All right with me.

YOUNG WOMAN. Some men don't seem to like a woman after she's married—

Waiter comes to the table.

FIRST MAN. What's the difference?

YOUNG WOMAN. Depends on the man, I guess.

FIRST MAN. Depends on the woman, I guess. (*To* WAITER, *makes sign of '2'.*) The same. (WAITER *goes to the bar.*)

At Table 1.

MAN. It don't amount to nothing. God! Most women just—

WOMAN. I know—I know—I know.

MAN. They don't think nothing of it. They just—

WOMAN. I know—I know—I know.

Re-enter SECOND MAN *and* GIRL. *They go to Table 3.*

SECOND MAN. Say, I forgot—I want you to do something for me, will yuh?

FIRST MAN. Sure—what is it?

SECOND MAN. I want you to telephone me out home tomorrow—and ask me to come into town—will yuh?

FIRST MAN. Sure—why not?

SECOND MAN. You know—business—get me?

FIRST MAN. I get you.

SECOND MAN. I've worked the telegraph gag to death—and my wife likes you.

FIRST MAN. What's your number?

SECOND MAN. I'll write it down for you. (*Writes.*)

FIRST MAN. How is your wife?

SECOND MAN. She's fine.

FIRST MAN. And the kid?

SECOND MAN. Great. (*Hands him the card. To* GIRL.) Come on, kid. (*Turns back to* YOUNG WOMAN.) Get this bird to tell you about himself.

GIRL. Keep him from it.

SECOND MAN. Get him to tell you how he killed a couple of spig down in Mexico.

GIRL. You been in Mexico?

SECOND MAN. He just came up from there.

GIRL. Can you teach us the tango?

YOUNG WOMAN. You killed a man?

SECOND MAN. Two of 'em! With a bottle! Get him to tell you—with a bottle. Come on, kid. Goodbye.

Exit SECOND MAN *and* GIRL.

YOUNG WOMAN. Why did you?

FIRST MAN. What?

YOUNG WOMAN. Kill 'em?

FIRST MAN. To get free.

YOUNG WOMAN. Oh.

At Table 2.

MAN. You really must taste this—just taste it. It's a real amontillado, you know.

BOY. Where do they get it here?

MAN. It's always down the side streets one finds the real pleasures, don't you think?

BOY. I don't know.

MAN. Learn. Come, taste this! Amontillado! Or don't you like amontillado?

BOY. I don't know. I never had any before.

MAN. Your first taste! How I envy you! Come, taste it! Taste it! And die.

BOY *tastes wine—finds it disappointing.*

MAN (*gliding it*) Poe was a lover of amontillado. He returns to it continually, you remember—or are you a lover of Poe?

BOY. I've read a lot of him.

MAN. But are you a lover?

At Table 3.

FIRST MAN. There were a bunch of bandidos—bandits, you know, took me into the hills—holding me there—what was I to do? got the two birds that guarded me drunk one night, and then I filled the empty bottle with small stones—and let 'em have it!

YOUNG WOMAN. Oh!

FIRST MAN. I had to get free, didn't I? I let 'em have it—

YOUNG WOMAN. Oh—then what did you do?

FIRST MAN. Then I beat it.

YOUNG WOMAN. Where to—?

FIRST MAN. Right here. (*Pause.*) Glad?

YOUNG WOMAN (*nods*). Yes.

FIRST MAN (*makes sign to* WAITER *of '2'*). The same. (WAITER *goes to the bar.*)

At Table 1.

MAN. You're just scared because this is the first time and—

WOMAN. I'm not scared.

MAN. Then what are you for Christ's sake?

WOMAN. I'm not scared. I want it—I want to have it—that ain't being scared, is it?

MAN. It's being goofy.

WOMAN. I don't care.

MAN. What about your folks?

WOMAN. I don't care.

MAN. What about your job? (*Silence.*) You got to keep your job, haven't you? (*Silence.*) Haven't you?

WOMAN. I suppose so.

MAN. Well—there you are!

WOMAN (*silence—then*). All right—let's go now—You got the address?

MAN. Now you're coming to.

They get up and go off. Exit MAN *and* WOMAN.

At Table 3.

YOUNG WOMAN. A bottle like that? (*She picks it up.*)

FIRST MAN. Yeah—filled with pebbles.

YOUNG WOMAN. What kind of pebbles?

FIRST MAN. Pebbles! Off the ground.

YOUNG WOMAN. Oh.

FIRST MAN. Necessity, you know, mother of invention. (*As* YOUNG WOMAN *handles the bottle.*) Ain't a bad weapon—first you got a sledge hammer—then you got a knife.

YOUNG WOMAN. Oh. (*Puts bottle down.*)

FIRST MAN. Women don't like knives, do they? (*Pours drink.*)

YOUNG WOMAN. No.

FIRST MAN. Don't mind a hammer so much, though, do they?

YOUNG WOMAN. No—

FIRST MAN. I didn't like it myself—any of it—but I had to get free, didn't I? Sure I had to get free, didn't I? (*Drinks.*) Now I'm damn glad I did.

YOUNG WOMAN. Why?

FIRST MAN. You know why. (*He puts his hand over hers.*)

At Table 2.

MAN. Let's go to my rooms—and I'll show them to you—I have a first edition of Verlaine that will simply make your mouth water. (*They stand up.*) Here—there's just a sip at the bottom of my glass—

BOY *takes it.*

That last sip's the sweetest—Wasn't it?

BOY (*laughs*). And I always thought that was dregs. (*Exit* MAN *followed by* BOY.)

At Table 3.

The MAN *is holding her hand across the table.*

YOUNG WOMAN. When you put your hand over mine! When you just touch me!

FIRST MAN. Yeah? (*Pause.*) Come on, kid, let's go!

YOUNG WOMAN. Where?

FIRST MAN. You haven't been around much, have you, kid?

YOUNG WOMAN. No.

FIRST MAN. I could tell that just to look at you.

YOUNG WOMAN. You could?

FIRST MAN. Sure I could. What are you running around with a girl like that other one for?

YOUNG WOMAN. I don't know. She seems to have a good time.

FIRST MAN. So that's it?

YOUNG WOMAN. Don't she?

FIRST MAN. Don't you?

YOUNG WOMAN. No.

FIRST MAN. Never?

YOUNG WOMAN. Never.

FIRST MAN. What's the matter?

YOUNG WOMAN. Nothing—just me, I guess.

FIRST MAN. You're all right.

YOUNG WOMAN. Am I?

FIRST MAN. Sure. You just haven't met the right guy—that's all—girl like you—you got to meet the right guy·

YOUNG WOMAN. I know.

FIRST MAN. You're different from girls like that other one—any guy'll do her. You're different.

YOUNG WOMAN. I guess I am.

FIRST MAN. You didn't fall for that business gag—did you—when they went off?

YOUNG WOMAN. Well, I thought they wanted to be alone probably, but—

FIRST MAN. And how!

YOUNG WOMAN. Oh—so that's it.

FIRST MAN. That's it. Come along—let's go—

YOUNG WOMAN. Oh, I couldn't! Like this?

FIRST MAN. Don't you like me?

YOUNG WOMAN. Yes

FIRST MAN. Then what's the matter?

YOUNG WOMAN. Do—you—like me?

FIRST MAN. Like yuh? You don't know the half of it—listen—you know what you seem like to me?

YOUNG WOMAN. What?

FIRST MAN. An angel. Just like an angel.

YOUNG WOMAN. I do?

FIRST MAN. That's what I said! Let's go!

YOUNG WOMAN. Where?

FIRST MAN. Where do you live?

YOUNG WOMAN. Oh, we can't go to my place.

FIRST MAN. Then come to my place.

YOUNG WOMAN. Oh I couldn't—is it far?

FIRST MAN. Just a step—come on—

YOUNG WOMAN. Oh I couldn't—what is it—a room?

FIRST MAN. No—an apartment—a one room apartment.

YOUNG WOMAN. That's different.

FIRST MAN. On the ground floor—no one will see you—coming or going.

YOUNG WOMAN (*getting up*). I couldn't.

FIRST MAN (*rises*). Wait a minute—I got to pay the damage—and I'll get a bottle of something to take along.

YOUNG WOMAN. No—don't.

FIRST MAN. Why not?

YOUNG WOMAN. Well—don't bring any pebbles.

FIRST MAN. Say—forget that! Will you?

YOUNG WOMAN. I just meant I don't think I'll need anything to drink.

FIRST MAN (*leaning to her eagerly*). You like me—don't you, kid?

YOUNG WOMAN. Do you me?

FIRST MAN. Wait!

He goes to the bar. She remains, her hands outstretched on the table, staring ahead. Enter a MAN *and a* GIRL. *They go to one of the empty tables. The* WAITER *goes to them.*

MAN (*to* GIRL). What do you want?

GIRL. Same old thing.

MAN (*to the* WAITER). The usual. (*Makes a sign '2'.*)

The First Man crosses to Young Woman with a wrapped bottle under his arm. She rises and starts out with him. As they pass the piano, he stops and puts in a nickel—the music starts as they exit. The scene blacks out.

The music of the electric piano continues until the lights go up for Episode 6, and the music has become the music of a hand organ, very faint.

★

Episode 6

INTIMATE

SCENE: *A dark room.*

SOUNDS. *A hand organ; footbeats, of passing feet.*

CHARACTERS: *Man; Young Woman*

AT RISE: *Darkness. Nothing can be discerned. From the outside comes the sound of a hand organ, very faint, and the irregular rhythm of passing feet. The hand organ is playing Cielito Lindo, that Spanish song that has been on every hand organ lately.*

MAN. You're awful still, honey. What you thinking about?

WOMAN. About sea shells. (*The sound of her voice is beautiful.*)

MAN. Sheshells? Gee! I can't say it!

WOMAN. When I was little my grandmother used to have a big pink sea shell on the mantle behind the stove. When we'd go to visit her they'd let me hold it, and listen. That's what I was thinking about now.

MAN. Yeah?

WOMAN. You can hear the sea in 'em, you know.

MAN. Yeah, I know.

WOMAN. I wonder why that is?

MAN. Search me. (*Pause.*)

WOMAN. You going? (*He has moved.*)

MAN. No. I just want a cigarette.

WOMAN (*glad, relieved*), Oh.

MAN. Want one?

WOMAN. No. (*Taking the match.*) Let me light it for you.

MAN. You got mighty pretty hands, honey. (*The match is out.*) This little pig went to market. This little pig stayed home. This little pig went—

WOMAN (*laughs*). Diddle diddle dee. (*Laughs again.*)

MAN. You got awful pretty hands.

WOMAN. I used to have. But I haven't taken much care of them lately. I will now—(*Pause. The music gets clearer.*) What's that?

MAN. What?

WOMAN. That music?

MAN. A dago hand organ. I gave him two bits the first day I got here—so he comes every day.

WOMAN. I mean—what's that he's playing?

MAN. *Cielito Lindo.*

WOMAN. What does that mean?

MAN. Little Heaven.

WOMAN. Little Heaven?

MAN. That's what lovers call each other in Spain.

WOMAN. Spain's where all the castles are, ain't it?

MAN. Yeah.

WOMAN. Little Heaven—sing it!

MAN (*singing to the music of the hand organ*). Da la sierra morena viene, bajando viene, bajando; un par de ojitos negros—cielito lindo—da contrabando.

WOMAN. What does it mean?

MAN. From the high dark mountains.

WOMAN. From the high dark mountains—?

MAN. Oh it doesn't mean anything. It doesn't make sense. It's love. (*Taking up the song.*) Ay-ay-ay-ay.

WOMAN. I know what that means.

MAN. What?

WOMAN. Ay-ay-ay-ay. (*They laugh.*)

MAN (*talking up the song*). Canta non llores—Sing don't cry—

WOMAN (*taking up the song*). La-la-la-la-la-la-la-la-la-la—Little Heaven!

MAN. You got a nice voice, honey.

WOMAN. Have I? (*Laughs—tickles him.*)

MAN. You bet you have—hey!

WOMAN (*laughing*). You ticklish?

MAN. Sure I am! Hey! (*They laugh.*) Go on, honey, sing something.

WOMAN. I couldn't.

MAN. Go on—you got a fine voice.

WOMAN (*laughs and sings*). Hey, diddle, diddle, the cat and the fiddle, The cow jumped over the moon, The little dog laughed to see the sport, And the dish ran away with the spoon—

Both laugh.

I never thought that had any sense before—now I get it.

MAN. You got me beat.

WOMAN. It's you and me—La-lalalalalala—lalalalalalala—Little Heaven. You're the dish and I'm the spoon.

MAN. You're a little spoon all right.

WOMAN. And I guess I'm the little cow that jumped over the moon. (*A pause.*) Do you believe in sorta guardian angels?

MAN. What?

WOMAN. Guardian angels?

MAN. I don't know. Maybe.

WOMAN. I do. (*Taking up the song again.*) Lalalalala—lalalalala—lalalala—Little Heaven. (*Talking.*) There must be something that looks out for you and brings you your happiness, at last—look at us! How did we both happen to go to that place today if there wasn't something!

MAN. Maybe you're right.

WOMAN. Look at us!

MAN. Everything's us to you, kid—ain't it?

WOMAN. Ain't it?

MAN. All right with me.

WOMAN. We belong together! We belong together! And we're going to stick together, ain't we?

MAN. Sing something else.

WOMAN. I tell you I can't sing!

MAN. Sure you can!

WOMAN. I tell you I hadn't thought of singing since I was a little bit of a girl.

MAN. Well sing anyway.

WOMAN (*singing*). And every little wavelet had its night cap on—its night cap on—its night cap on—and every little wave had its night cap on—so very early in the morning. (*Talking.*) Did you used to sing that when you were a little kid?

MAN. Nope.

WOMAN. Didn't you? We used to—in the first grade—little kids—we used to go round and round in a ring—and flop our hands up and down—supposed to be the waves. I remember it used to confuse me—because we did just the same thing to be little angels.

MAN. Yeah?

WOMAN. You know why I came here?

MAN. I can make a good guess.

WOMAN. Because you told me I looked like an angel to you! That's why I came.

MAN. Jeez, honey, all women look like angels to me—all white women. I ain't been seeing nothing but Indians, you know for the last couple a years. Gee, when I got off the boat here the other day—and saw all the women—gee I pretty near went crazy—talk about looking like angels—why—

WOMAN. You've had a lot of women, haven't you?

MAN. Not so many—real ones.

WOMAN. Did you—like any of 'em—better than me?

MAN. Nope—there wasn't one of 'em any sweeter than you, honey—not as sweet—no—not as sweet.

WOMAN. I like to hear you say it. Say it again—

MAN (*protesting good humoredly*). Oh—

WOMAN. Go on—tell me again!

MAN. Here! (*Kisses her.*) Does that tell you?

WOMAN. Yes. (*Pause.*) We're going to stick together—always—aren't we?

MAN (*honestly*). I'll have to be moving on, kid—some day, you know.

WOMAN. Where?

MAN. Quien sabe?

WOMAN. What does that mean?

MAN. Quien sabe? You got to learn that, kid, if you're figuring on coming with me. It's the answer to everything—below the Rio Grande.

WOMAN. What does it mean?

MAN. It means—who knows?

WOMAN. Keen sabe?

MAN. Yep—don't forget it now.

WOMAN. I'll never forget it!

MAN. Quien sabe.

WOMAN. And I'll never get used to it.

MAN. Quien sabe.

WOMAN. I'll never get—below the Rio Grande—I'll never get out of here.

MAN. Quien sabe.

WOMAN (*change of mood*). That's right! Keen sabe? Who knows?

MAN. That's the stuff.

WOMAN. You must like it down there.

MAN. I can't live anywhere else—for long.

WOMAN. Why not?

MAN. Oh—you're free down there! You're free!

A street light is lit outside. The outlines of a window take form against this light. There are bars across it, and from outside it, the sidewalk cuts across almost at the top. It is a basement room. The constant going and coming of passing feet, mostly feet of couples, can be dimly seen. Inside, on the ledge, there is a lily blooming in a bowl of rocks and water.

WOMAN. What's that?
MAN. Just the street light going on.
WOMAN. Is it as late as that?
MAN. Late as what?
WOMAN. Dark.
MAN. It's been dark for hours—didn't you know that?
WOMAN. No!—I must go! (*Rises.*)
MAN. Wait—the moon will be up in a little while—full moon.
WOMAN. It isn't that! I'm late! I must go!

She comes into the light. She wears a white chemise that might be the tunic of a dancer, and as she comes into the light she fastens about her waist a little skirt. She really wears almost exactly the clothes that women wear now, but the finesse of their cut, and the grace and ease with which she puts them on, must turn this episode of her dressing into a personification, an idealization of a woman clothing herself. All her gestures must be unconscious, innocent, relaxed, sure and full of natural grace. As she sits facing the window pulling on a stocking.

What's that?
MAN. What?
WOMAN. On the window ledge.
MAN. A flower.
WOMAN. Who gave it to you?
MAN. Nobody gave it to me. I bought it.
WOMAN. For yourself?
MAN. Yeah—Why not!
WOMAN. I don't know.
MAN. In Chinatown—made me think of Frisco where I was a kid—so I bought it.
WOMAN. Is that where you were born—Frisco?
MAN. Yep. Twin Peaks.
WOMAN. What's that?
MAN. A couple of hills—together.
WOMAN. One for you and one for me.
MAN. I bet you'd like Frisco.
WOMAN. I knew a woman went out there once!
MAN. The bay and the hills! Jeez, that's the life! Every Saturday we used to cross the Bay—get a couple nags and just ride—over the hills. One would have a blanket on the saddle—the other, the grub. At night, we'd make a little fire and eat–and then roll up in the old blanket and—
WOMAN. Who? Who was with you?
MAN (*indifferently*). Anybody. (*Enthusiastically.*) Jeez, that dry old grass out there smells good at night—full of tar weed—you know—
WOMAN. Is that a good smell?
MAN. Tar weed? Didn't you ever smell it? (*She shakes her head 'No'.*) Sure it's a good smell! The Bay and the hills.

She goes to the mirror of the dresser, to finish dressing. She has only a dress to put on that is in one piece—with one fastening on the side. Before slipping it on, she stands before the mirror and stretches. Appreciatively but indifferently.

You look in good shape, kid. A couple of months riding over the mountains with me, you'd be great.
WOMAN. Can I?
MAN. What?
WOMAN. Some day—ride mountains with you?
MAN. Ride mountains? Ride donkeys!
WOMAN. It's the same thing!—with you!—Can I—some day? The high dark mountains?
MAN. Who knows?
WOMAN. It must be great!
MAN. You ever been off like that, kid?—high up? On top of the world?
WOMAN. Yes.
MAN. When?
WOMAN. Today.
MAN. You're pretty sweet.
WOMAN. I never knew anything like this way! I never knew that I could feel like this! So,—so purified! Don't laugh at me!
MAN. I ain't laughing, honey.
WOMAN. Purified.
MAN. It's a hell of a word—but I know what you mean. That's the way it is—sometimes.
WOMAN (*she puts on a little hat, then turns to him*). Well—goodbye.
MAN. Aren't you forgetting something? (*Rises.*)

She looks toward him, then throws her head slowly back, lifts her right arm—this gesture that is in so many statues of women—Volupte. He comes out of the shadow, puts his arm around her, kisses her. Her head and arm go further back—then she brings her arm around with a wide encircling gesture, her hand closes over his head, her fingers spread. Her fingers are protective, clutching. When he releases her, her eyes are shining with tears. She turns away. She looks back at him—and the room—and her eyes fasten on the lily.

WOMAN. Can I have that?
MAN. Sure—why not?

She takes it—goes. As she opens the door, the music is louder. The scene blacks out.

WOMAN. Goodbye. And—(*Hesitates.*) And—thank you.

Curtain

The music continues until the curtain goes up for Episode 7. It goes up on silence.

★

Episode 7

DOMESTIC

SCENE: *A sitting room: a divan, a telephone, a window.*

CHARACTERS: *Husband; Young Woman*

They are seated on opposite ends of the divan. They are both reading papers—to themselves.

HUSBAND. Record production.
YOUNG WOMAN. Girl turns on gas.
HUSBAND. Sale hits a millions—
YOUNG WOMAN. WOMAN leaves all for love—
HUSBAND. Market trend steady—
YOUNG WOMAN. Young wife disappears—
HUSBAND. Owns a life interest—

Phone rings. YOUNG WOMAN *looks toward it.*

That's for me. (*In phone.*) Hello—oh hello, A.B. It's all settled?—Everything signed? Good. Good! Tell R.A. to call me up. (*Hangs up phone—to* YOUNG WOMAN.) Well, it's all settled. They signed!—aren't you interested? Aren't you going to ask me?
YOUNG WOMAN (*by rote*). Did you put it over?
HUSBAND. Sure I put it over.
YOUNG WOMAN. Did you swing it?
HUSBAND. Sure I swung it.
YOUNG WOMAN. Did they come through?
HUSBAND. Sure they came through.
YOUNG WOMAN. Did they sign?
HUSBAND. I'll say they signed.
YOUNG WOMAN. On the dotted line?
HUSBAND. On the dotted line.
YOUNG WOMAN. The property's yours?
HUSBAND. The property's mine. I'll put a first mortgage. I'll put a second mortage and the property's mine. Happy?
YOUNG WOMAN (*by rote*). Happy.
HUSBAND (*going to her*). The property's mine! It's not all that's mine! (*Pinching her cheek—happy and playful.*) I got a first mortgage on her—I got a second mortgage on her—and she's mine!

YOUNG WOMAN *pulls away swiftly.*

What's the matter?
YOUNG WOMAN. Nothing—what?
HUSBAND. You flinched when I touched you.
YOUNG WOMAN. No.
HUSBAND. You haven't done that in a long time.
YOUNG WOMAN. Haven't I?
HUSBAND. You used to do it every time I touched you.
YOUNG WOMAN. Did I?
HUSBAND. Didn't know that, did you?
YOUNG WOMAN (*unexpectedly*). Yes. Yes, I know it.
HUSBAND. Just purity.
YOUNG WOMAN. No.
HUSBAND. Oh, I liked it. Purity.
YOUNG WOMAN. No.
HUSBAND. You're one of the purest women that ever lived.
YOUNG WOMAN. I'm just like anybody else only—(*Stops.*)
HUSBAND. Only what?
YOUNG WOMAN (*pause*). Nothing.
HUSBAND. It must be something.

Phone rings. She gets up and goes to window.

HUSBAND (*in phone*). Hello—hello, R.A.—well, I put it over—yeah, I swung it—sure they came through—did they sign? On the dotted line! The property's mine. I made the proposition. I sold them the idea. Now watch me. Tell D.D. to call me up. (*Hangs up.*) That was R.A. What are you looking at?
YOUNG WOMAN. Nothing.
HUSBAND. You must be looking at something.
YOUNG WOMAN. Nothing—the moon.
HUSBAND. The moon's something, isn't it?
YOUNG WOMAN. Yes.
HUSBAND. What's it doing?
YOUNG WOMAN. Nothing.
HUSBAND. It must be doing something.

YOUNG WOMAN. It's moving—moving—(*She comes down restlessly.*)

HUSBAND. Pull down the shade, my dear.

YOUNG WOMAN. Why?

HUSBAND. People can look in.

Phone rings.

Hello—hello D.D.—Yes—I put it over—they came across—I put it over on them—yep—yep—yep—I'll say I am—yep—on the dotted line—Now you watch me—yep. Yep yep. Tell B.M. to phone me. (*Hangs up.*) That was D.D. (*To* YOUNG WOMAN *who has come down to davenport and picked up a paper.*) Aren't you listening?

YOUNG WOMAN. I'm reading.

HUSBAND. What you reading?

YOUNG WOMAN. Nothing.

HUSBAND. Must be something. (*He sits and picks up his paper.*)

YOUNG WOMAN (*reading*). Prisoner escapes—lifer breaks jail—shoots way to freedom—

HUSBAND. Don't read that stuff—listen—here's a first rate editorial. I agree with this. I agree absolutely. Are you listening?

YOUNG WOMAN. I'm listening.

HUSBAND (*importantly*). All men are born free and entitled to the-pursuit of happiness. (YOUNG WOMAN *gets up.*) My, you're nervous tonight.

YOUNG WOMAN. I try not to be.

HUSBAND. You inherit that from your mother. She was in the office today.

YOUNG WOMAN. Was she?

HUSBAND. To get her allowance.

YOUNG WOMAN. Oh—

HUSBAND. Don't you know it's the *first*.

YOUNG WOMAN. Poor Ma.

HUSBAND. What would she do without me?

YOUNG WOMAN. I know. You're very good.

HUSBAND. One thing—she's grateful.

YOUNG WOMAN. Poor Ma—poor Ma.

HUSBAND. She's got to have care.

YOUNG WOMAN. Yes. She's got to have care.

HUSBAND. A mother's a very precious thing—a good mother.

YOUNG WOMAN (*excitedly*). I try to be a good mother.

HUSBAND. Of course you're a good mother.

YOUNG WOMAN. I try! I try!

HUSBAND. A mother's a very precious thing—(*Resuming his paper.*) And a child's a very precious thing. Precious jewels.

YOUNG WOMAN (*reading*). Sale of jewels and precious stones.

YOUNG WOMAN *puts her hand to throat.*

HUSBAND. What's the matter?

YOUNG WOMAN. I feel as though I were drowning.

HUSBAND. Drowning?

YOUNG WOMAN. With stones around my neck.

HUSBAND. You just imagine that.

YOUNG WOMAN. Stifling.

HUSBAND. You don't breathe deep enough—breathe now—look at me. (*He breathes.*) Breath is life. Life is breath.

YOUNG WOMAN (*suddenly*). And what is death?

HUSBAND (*smartly*). Just—no breath!

YOUNG WOMAN (*to herself*). Just no breath.

Takes up paper.

HUSBAND. All right?

YOUNG WOMAN. All right.

HUSBAND (*reads as she stares at her paper. Looks up after a pause.*) I feel cold air, my dear.

YOUNG WOMAN. Cold air?

HUSBAND. Close the window, will you?

YOUNG WOMAN. It isn't open.

HUSBAND. Don't you feel cold air?

YOUNG WOMAN. No—you just imagine it.

HUSBAND. I never imagine anything. (YOUNG WOMAN *is staring at the paper.*) What are you reading?

YOUNG WOMAN. Nothing.

HUSBAND. You must be reading something.

YOUNG WOMAN. Woman finds husband dead.

HUSBAND (*uninterested*). Oh. (*Interested.*) Here's a man says 'I owe my success to a yeast cake a day—my digestion is good—I sleep very well—and—' (*His wife gets up, goes toward door.*) Where you going?

YOUNG WOMAN. No place.

HUSBAND. You must be going some place.

YOUNG WOMAN. Just—to bed.

HUSBAND. It isn't even eleven yet. Wait.

YOUNG WOMAN. Wait?

HUSBAND. It's only ten-forty-six—wait! (*Holds out his arms to her.*) Come here!

YOUNG WOMAN (*takes a step toward him—recoils*). Oh—I want to go away!

HUSBAND. Away? Where?

YOUNG WOMAN. Anywhere—away.

HUSBAND. Why, what's the matter?

YOUNG WOMAN. I'm scared.

HUSBAND. What of?

YOUNG WOMAN. I can't sleep—I haven't slept.

HUSBAND. That's nothing.

YOUNG WOMAN. And the moon—when it's full moon.

HUSBAND. That's nothing.

YOUNG WOMAN. I can't sleep.

HUSBAND. Of course not. It's the light.

YOUNG WOMAN. I don't see it! I feel it! I'm afraid.

HUSBAND (*kindly*). Nonsense—come here.
YOUNG WOMAN. I want to go away.
HUSBAND. But I can't get away now.
YOUNG WOMAN. Alone!
HUSBAND. You've never been away alone.
YOUNG WOMAN. I know.
HUSBAND. What would you do?
YOUNG WOMAN. Maybe I'd sleep.
HUSBAND. Now you wait.
YOUNG WOMAN (*desperately*). Wait?
HUSBAND. We'll take a trip—we'll go to Europe—I'll get my watch—I'll get my Swiss watch—I've always wanted a Swiss watch that I bought right there—isn't that funny? Wait—wait. (YOUNG WOMAN *comes down to davenport—sits.* HUSBAND *resumes his paper.*) Another revolution below the Rio Grande.
YOUNG WOMAN. Below the Rio Grande?
HUSBAND. Yes—another—
YOUNG WOMAN. Anyone—hurt?
HUSBAND. No.
YOUNG WOMAN. Any prisoners?
HUSBAND. No.
YOUNG WOMAN. All free?
HUSBAND. All free.

He resumes his paper. YOUNG WOMAN *sits, staring ahead of her. The music of the hand organ sounds off very dimly, playing Cielito Lindo. Voices begin to sing it—'Ay-ay-ay-ay'—and then the words—the music and voices get louder.*

THE VOICE OF HER LOVER. They were a bunch of bandidos—bandits you know—holding me there—what was I to do—I had to get free—didn't I? I had to get free—
VOICES. Free—free—free—
LOVER. I filled an empty bottle with small stones—
VOICES. Stones—stones—precious stones—millstones—stones—stones—millstones—
LOVER. Just a bottle with small stones.
VOICES. Stones—stones—small stones—
VOICE OF A HUCKSTER. Stones for sale—stones—stones—small stones—precious stones—
VOICES. Stones—stones—precious stones—
LOVER. Had to get free, didn't I? Free?
VOICES. Free? Free?
LOVER. Quien sabe? Who knows? Who knows?
VOICES. Who'd know? Who'd know? Who'd know?
HUCKSTER. Stones—stones—small stones—big stones—millstones—cold stones—head stones—
VOICES. Head stones—head stones—head stones.

The music—the voices—mingle—increase—the YOUNG WOMAN *flies from her chair and cries out in terror.*

YOUNG WOMAN. Oh! Oh!

The scene blacks out—the music and the dim voices, 'Stones—stones—stones,' continue until the scene lights for Episode 8.

★

Episode 8

THE LAW

SCENE: *Courtroom*

SOUNDS: *Clicking of telegraph instruments offstage.*

CHARACTERS: *Judge; Jury; Lawyers; Spectators; Reporters; Messenger Boys; Law Clerks; Bailiff; Court Reporter; Young Woman*

The words and movements of all these people except the Young Woman are routine—mechanical. Each is going through the motions of his own game.

AT RISE: *All assembled, except Judge.*

Enter JUDGE

BAILIFF (*mumbling*). Hear ye—hear ye—! (*All rise. Judge sits. All sit. Lawyer for Defense gets to his feet—He is the verbose, 'eloquent' typical criminal defense lawyer. Judge signs to him to wait—turns to Law Clerks, grouped at foot of the bench.*)
FIRST CLERK (*handing up a paper—routine voice*). State versus Kling—stay of execution.

JUDGE. Denied.

FIRST CLERK *goes.*

SECOND CLERK. Bing vs. Ding—demurrer.

JUDGE *signs.* SECOND CLERK *goes.*

THIRD CLERK. Case of John King—habeas corpus.

JUDGE *signs.* THIRD CLERK *goes.* JUDGE *signs to* BAILIFF.

BAILIFF (*mumbling*). People of the State of _______ versus Helen Jones.

JUDGE (*to* LAYER FOR DEFENSE). Defense ready to proceed?

LAWYER FOR DEFENSE. We're ready, your Honor.

JUDGE. Proceed.

LAWYER FOR DEFENSE. Helen Jones.

BAILIFF. Helen Jones!

YOUNG WOMAN *rises.*

LAWYER FOR DEFENSE. Mrs. Jones, will you take the stand?

YOUNG WOMAN *goes to witness stand.*

FIRST REPORTER (*writing rapidly*). The defense sprang a surprise at the opening of court this morning by putting the accused woman on the stand. The prosecution was swept off its feet by this daring defense strategy and—(*Instruments get louder.*)

SECOND REPORTER. Trembling and scarcely able to stand, Helen Jones, accused murderess, had to be almost carried to the witness stand this morning when her lawyer—

BAILIFF (*mumbling—with Bible*). Do you swear to tell the truth, the whole truth and nothing but the truth—so help you God?

YOUNG WOMAN. I do.

JUDGE. You may sit.

She sits in witness chair.

COURT REPORTER. What is your name?

YOUNG WOMAN. Helen Jones.

COURT REPORTER. Your age?

YOUNG WOMAN (*hesitates—then*). Twenty-nine.

COURT REPORTER. Where do you live?

YOUNG WOMAN. In prison.

LAWYER FOR DEFENSE. This is my client's legal address.

Hands a scrap of paper.

LAWYER FOR PROSECUTION (*jumping to his feet*). I object to this insinuation on the part of counsel of any illegality in the holding of this defendant in jail when the law—

LAWYER FOR DEFENSE. I made no such insinuation.

LAWYER FOR PROSECUTION. You implied it—

LAWYER FOR DEFENSE. I did not!

LAWYER FOR PROSECUTION. You're a—

JUDGE. Order!

BAILIFF. Order!

LAWYER FOR DEFENSE. Your Honor, I object to counsel's constant attempt to—

LAWYER FOR PROSECUTION. I protest—I—

JUDGE. Order!

BAILIFF. Order!

JUDGE. Proceed with the witness

LAWYER FOR DEFENSE. Mrs. Jones, you are the widow of the late George H. Jones, are you not?

YOUNG WOMAN. Yes.

LAWYER FOR DEFENSE. How long were you married to the late George H. Jones before his demise?

YOUNG WOMAN. Six years.

LAWYER FOR DEFENSE. Six years! And it was a happy marriage, was it not? (YOUNG WOMAN *hesitates.*) Did you quarrel?

YOUNG WOMAN. No sir.

LAWYER FOR DEFENSE. Then it was a happy marriage, wasn't it?

YOUNG WOMAN. Yes, sir.

LAWYER FOR DEFENSE. In those six years of married life with your late husband, the late George H. Jones, did you EVER have a quarrel?

YOUNG WOMAN. No, sir.

LAWYER FOR DEFENSE. Never one quarrel?

LAWYER FOR PROSECUTION. The witness has said—

LAWYER FOR DEFENSE. Six years without one quarrel! Six years! Gentlemen of the jury, I ask you to consider this fact! Six years of married life without a quarrel. (*The* JURY *grins.*) I ask you to consider it seriously! Very seriously! Who of us—and this is not intended as any reflection on the sacred institution of marriage—no—but!

JUDGE. Proceed with your witness

LAWYER FOR DEFENSE. You have one child—have you not Mrs. Jones?

YOUNG WOMAN. Yes, sir.

LAWYER FOR DEFENSE. A little girl, is it not?

YOUNG WOMAN. Yes, sir.

LAWYER FOR DEFENSE. How old is she?

YOUNG WOMAN. She's five—past five.

LAWYER FOR DEFENSE. A little girl of past five. Since the demise of the late Mr. Jones you are the only parent she has living, are you not?

YOUNG WOMAN. Yes, sir.

LAWYER FOR DEFENSE. Before your marriage to the late Mr. Jones, you worked and supported your mother, did you not?

LAWYER FOR PROSECUTION. I object, your honor! Irrelevant—immaterial—and—

JUDGE. Objection sustained!

LAWYER FOR DEFENSE. In order to support your mother and yourself as a girl, you worked, did you not?

YOUNG WOMAN. Yes, sir.

LAWYER FOR DEFENSE. What did you do?

YOUNG WOMAN. I was a stenographer.

LAWYER FOR DEFENSE. And since your marriage you have continued as her sole support, have you not?

YOUNG WOMAN. Yes, sir.

LAWYER FOR DEFENSE. A devoted daughter, gentlemen of the jury! As well as a devoted wife and a devoted mother!

LAWYER FOR PROSECUTION. Your Honor!

LAWYER FOR DEFENSE (*quickly*). And now, Mrs. Jones, I will ask you—the law expects me to ask you—it demands that I ask you—did you—or did you not—on the night of June 2nd last or the morning of June 3rd last—kill your husand, the late George H. Jones—did you, or did you not?

YOUNG WOMAN. I did not.

LAWYER FOR DEFENSE. You did not?

YOUNG WOMAN. I did not.

LAWYER FOR DEFENSE. Now, Mrs. Jones, you have heard the witnesses for the State—They were not many—and they did not have much to say—

LAWYER FOR PROSECUTION. I object.

JUDGE. Sustained.

LAWYER FOR DEFENSE. You have heard some police and you have heard some doctors. None of whom was present! The prosecution could not furnish any witness to the crime—not one witness!

LAWYER FOR PROSECUTION. Your Honor!

LAWYER FOR DEFENSE. Nor one motive.

LAWYER FOR PROSECUTION. Your Honor—I protest! I—

JUDGE. Sustained.

LAWYER FOR DEFENSE. But such as these witnesses were, you have heard them try to accuse you of deliberately murdering your own husband, this husband with whom, by your own statement, you had never had a quarrel—not one quarrel in six years of married life, murdering him, I say, or rather—they say, while he slept, by brutally hitting him over the head with a bottle—a bottle filled with small stones—Did you, I repeat this, or did you not?

YOUNG WOMAN. I did not.

LAWYER FOR DEFENSE. You did not! Of course you did not! (*Quickly.*) Now, Mrs. Jones, will you tell the jury in your own words exactly what happened on the night of June 2nd or the morning of June 3rd last, at the time your husband was killed.

YOUNG WOMAN. I was awakened by hearing somebody —something—in the room, and I saw two men standing by my husband's bed.

LAWYER FOR DEFENSE. Your husband's bed—that was also your bed, was it not, Mrs. Jones?

YOUNG WOMAN. Yes.

LAWYER FOR DEFENSE. You hadn't the modern idea of separate beds, had you, Mrs. Jones?

YOUNG WOMAN. Mr. Jones objected.

LAWYER FOR DEFENSE. I mean you slept in the same bed, did you not?

YOUNG WOMAN. Yes.

LAWYER FOR DEFENSE. Then explain just what you mean by saying 'my husband's bed'.

YOUNG WOMAN. Well—I—

LAWYER FOR DEFENSE. You meant his side of the bed, didn't you?

YOUNG WOMAN. Yes, His side.

LAWYER FOR DEFENSE. That is what I thought, but I wanted the jury to be clear on that point. (*To the* JURY.) Mr. and Mrs. Jones slept in the same bed. (*To her.*) Go on, Mrs. Jones. (*As she is silent.*) You heard a noise and—

YOUNG WOMAN. I heard a noise and I awoke and saw two men standing beside my husband's side of the bed.

LAWYER FOR DEFENSE. Two men?

YOUNG WOMAN. Yes.

LAWYER FOR DEFENSE. Can you describe them?

YOUNG WOMAN. Not very well—I couldn't see them very well.

LAWYER FOR DEFENSE. Could you say whether they were big or small—light or dark, thin or—

YOUNG WOMAN. They were big dark looking men.

LAWYER FOR DEFENSE. Big dark looking men?

YOUNG WOMAN. Yes.

LAWYER FOR DEFENSE. And what did you do, Mrs. Jones, when you suddenly awoke and saw two big dark looking men standing beside your bed?

YOUNG WOMAN. I didn't do anything!

LAWYER FOR DEFENSE. You didn't have time to do anything—did you?

YOUNG WOMAN. No. Before I could do anything—one of them raised—something in his hand and struck Mr. Jones over the head with it.

LAWYER FOR DEFENSE. And what did Mr. Jones do?

Spectators laugh.

JUDGE. Silence.

BAILIFF. Silence.

LAWYER FOR DEFENSE. What did Mr. Jones do, Mrs. Jones?

YOUNG WOMAN. He gave a sort of groan and tried to raise up.

LAWYER FOR DEFENSE. Tried to raise up!

YOUNG WOMAN. Yes!

LAWYER FOR DEFENSE. And then what happened?

YOUNG WOMAN. The man struck him again and he fell back.

LAWYER FOR DEFENSE. I see. What did the men do then? The big dark looking men.

YOUNG WOMAN. They turned and ran out of the room.

LAWYER FOR DEFENSE. I see. What did you do then, Mrs. Jones?

YOUNG WOMAN. I saw Mr. Jones was bleeding from the temple. I got towels and tried to stop it, and then I realized he had—passed away.

LAWYER FOR DEFENSE. I see. What did you do then?

YOUNG WOMAN. I didn't know what to do. But I thought I'd better call the police. So I went to the telephone and called the police.

LAWYER FOR DEFENSE. What happened then?

YOUNG WOMAN. Nothing. Nothing happened.

LAWYER FOR DEFENSE. The police came, didn't they?

YOUNG WOMAN. Yes—they came.

LAWYER FOR DEFENSE (*quickly*). And that is all you know concerning the death of your husband in the late hours of June 2nd or the early hours of June 3rd last, isn't it?

YOUNG WOMAN. Yes sir.

LAWYER FOR DEFENSE. All?

YOUNG WOMAN. Yes sir.

LAWYER FOR DEFENSE (*to* LAWYER FOR PROSECUTION). Take the witness.

FIRST REPORTER (*writing*). The accused woman told a straightforward story of—

SECOND REPORTER. The accused woman told a rambling, disconnected story of—

LAWYER FOR PROSECUTION. You made no effort to cry out, Mrs. Jones, did you, when you saw those two big dark men standing over your helpless husband, did you?

YOUNG WOMAN. No sir. I didn't. I—

LAWYER FOR PROSECUTION. And when they turned and ran out of the room, you made no effort to follow them or cry out after them, did you?

YOUNG WOMAN. No sir.

LAWYER FOR PROSECUTION. Why didn't you?

YOUNG WOMAN. I saw Mr. Jones was hurt.

LAWYER FOR PROSECUTION. Ah! You saw Mr. Jones was hurt! You saw this—how did you see it?

YOUNG WOMAN. I just saw it.

LAWYER FOR PROSECUTION. Then there was a light in the room?

YOUNG WOMAN. A sort of light.

LAWYER FOR PROSECUTION. What do you mean—a sort of light? A bed light?

YOUNG WOMAN. No. No, there was no light on.

LAWYER FOR PROSECUTION. They where did it come from—this sort of light?

YOUNG WOMAN. I don't know.

LAWYER FOR PROSECUTION. Perhaps—from the window.

YOUNG WOMAN. Yes—from the window.

LAWYER FOR PROSECUTION. Oh, the shade was up!

YOUNG WOMAN. No—no, the shade was down.

LAWYER FOR PROSECUTION. You're sure of that?

YOUNG WOMAN. Yes. Mr. Jones always wanted the shade down.

LAWYER FOR PROSECUTION. The shade was down—there was no light in the room—but the room was light—how do you explain this?

YOUNG WOMAN. I don't know.

LAWYER FOR PROSECUTION. You don't know!

YOUNG WOMAN. I think where the window was open—under the shade—light came in.

LAWYER FOR PROSECUTION. There is a street light there?

YOUNG WOMAN. No—there's no street light.

LAWYER FOR PROSECUTION. Then where did this light come from—that came in under the shade?

YOUNG WOMAN (*desperately*). From the moon!

LAWYER FOR PROSECUTION. The moon!

YOUNG WOMAN. Yes! It was a bright moon!

LAWYER FOR PROSECUTION. It was a bright moon—you are sure of that!

YOUNG WOMAN. Yes.

LAWYER FOR PROSECUTION. How are you sure?

YOUNG WOMAN. I couldn't sleep—I never can sleep in the bright moon. I never can.

LAWYER FOR PROSECUTION. It was bright moon. Yet you could not see two big dark looking men—but you could see your husband bleeding from the temple.

YOUNG WOMAN. Yes sir.

LAWYER FOR PROSECUTION. And did you call a doctor?

YOUNG WOMAN. No.

LAWYER FOR PROSECUTION. Why didn't you?

YOUNG WOMAN. The police did.

LAWYER FOR PROSECUTION. But you didn't?

YOUNG WOMAN. No.

LAWYER FOR PROSECUTION. Why didn't you? (*No answer.*) Why didn't you?

YOUNG WOMAN (*whispers*). I saw it was—useless.

LAWYER FOR PROSECUTION. Ah! You saw that! You saw that—very clearly.

YOUNG WOMAN. Yes.

LAWYER FOR PROSECUTION. And you didn't call a doctor.

YOUNG WOMAN. It was—useless.

LAWYER FOR PROSECUTION. What did you do?

YOUNG WOMAN. It was useless—there was no use of anything.

LAWYER FOR PROSECUTION. I asked you what you did?

YOUNG WOMAN. Nothing.

LAWYER FOR PROSECUTION. Nothing!

YOUNG WOMAN. I just sat there.

LAWYER FOR PROSECUTION. You sat there! A long while, didn't you?

YOUNG WOMAN. I don't know.

LAWYER FOR PROSECUTION. You don't know? (*Showing her the neck of a broken bottle.*) Mrs. Jones, did you ever see this before?

YOUNG WOMAN. I think so.

LAWYER FOR PROSECUTION. You think so.

YOUNG WOMAN. Yes.

LAWYER FOR PROSECUTION. What do you think it is?

YOUNG WOMAN. I think it's the bottle that was used against Mr. Jones.

LAWYER FOR PROSECUTION. Used against him—yes—that's right. You've guessed right. This neck and these broken pieces and these pebbles were found on the floor and scattered over the bed. There were no fingerprints, Mrs. Jones, on this bottle. None at all. Doesn't that seem strange to you?

YOUNG WOMAN. No.

LAWYER FOR PROSECUTION. It doesn't seem strange to you that this bottle held in the big dark hand of one of those big dark men left no mark! No print! That doesn't seem strange to you?

YOUNG WOMAN. No.

LAWYER FOR PROSECUTION. You are in the habit of wearing rubber gloves at night, Mrs. Jones—are you not? To protect—to soften your hands—are you not?

YOUNG WOMAN. I used to.

LAWYER FOR PROSECUTION. Used to—when was that?

YOUNG WOMAN. Before I was married.

LAWYER FOR PROSECUTION. And after your marriage you gave it up?

YOUNG WOMAN. Yes.

LAWYER FOR PROSECUTION. Why?

YOUNG WOMAN. Mr. Jones did not like the feeling of them.

LAWYER FOR PROSECUTION. You always did everything Mr. Jones wanted?

YOUNG WOMAN. I tried to—Anyway I didn't care any more—so much—about my hands.

LAWYER FOR PROSECUTION. I see—so after your marriage you never wore gloves at night any more?

YOUNG WOMAN. No.

LAWYER FOR PROSECUTION. Mrs. Jones, isn't it true that you began wearing your rubber gloves again—in spite of your husband's expressed dislike—about a year ago—a year ago this spring?

YOUNG WOMAN. No.

LAWYER FOR PROSECUTION. You did not suddenly begin to care particularly for your hands again—about a year ago this spring?

YOUNG WOMAN. No.

LAWYER FOR PROSECUTION. You're quite sure of that?

YOUNG WOMAN. Yes.

LAWYER FOR PROSECUTION. Quite sure?

YOUNG WOMAN. Yes.

LAWYER FOR PROSECUTION. Then you did not have in your possession, on the night of June 2nd last, a pair of rubber gloves?

YOUNG WOMAN (*shakes her head*). No.

LAWYER FOR PROSECUTION (*to judge*). I'd like to introduce these gloves as evidence at this time, your Honor.

JUDGE. Exhibit 24.

LAWYER FOR PROSECUTION. I'll return to them later—now, Mrs. Jones—this nightgown—you recognize it, don't you?

YOUNG WOMAN. Yes.

LAWYER FOR PROSECUTION. Yours, is it not?

YOUNG WOMAN. Yes.

LAWYER FOR PROSECUTION. The one you were wearing the night your husband was murdered, isn't it?

YOUNG WOMAN. The night he died—yes.

LAWYER FOR PROSECUTION. Not the one you wore under your peignoir—I believe that it's what you call it, isn't it? A peignoir? When you received the police—but the one you wore before that—isn't it?

YOUNG WOMAN. Yes.

LAWYER FOR PROSECUTION. This was found—not where the gloves were found—no—but at the bottom of the soiled clothes hamper in the bathroom—rolled up and wet—why was it wet, Mrs. Jones?

YOUNG WOMAN. I had tried to wash it.

LAWYER FOR PROSECUTION. Wash it? I thought you had just sat?

YOUNG WOMAN. First—I tried to make things clean.

LAWYER FOR PROSECUTION. Why did you want to make this—clean—as you say?

YOUNG WOMAN. There was blood on it.

LAWYER FOR PROSECUTION. Spattered on it?

YOUNG WOMAN. Yes.

LAWYER FOR PROSECUTION. How did that happen?

YOUNG WOMAN. The bottle broke—and the sharp edge cut.

LAWYER FOR PROSECUTION. Oh, the bottle broke and the sharp edge cut!

YOUNG WOMAN. Yes. That's what they told me afterwards.

LAWYER FOR PROSECUTION. Who told you?

YOUNG WOMAN. The police—that's what they say happened.

LAWYER FOR PROSECUTION. Mrs. Jones, why did you try so deperately to wash that blood away—before you called the police?

LAWYER FOR DEFENSE. I object!

JUDGE. Objection overruled.

LAWYER FOR PROSECUTION. Why, Mrs. Jones?

YOUNG WOMAN. I don't know. It's what anyone would have done, wouldn't they?

LAWYER FOR PROSECUTION. That depends, doesn't it? (*Suddenly taking up bottle.*) Mrs. Jones—when did you first see this?

YOUNG WOMAN. The night my husband was—done away with.

LAWYER FOR PROSECUTION. Done away with! You mean killed?

YOUNG WOMAN. Yes.

LAWYER FOR PROSECUTION. Why don't you say killed?

YOUNG WOMAN. It sounds so brutal.

LAWYER FOR PROSECUTION. And you never saw this before then?

YOUNG WOMAN. No sir.

LAWYER FOR PROSECUTION. You're quite sure of that?

YOUNG WOMAN. Yes.

LAWYER FOR PROSECUTION. And these stones—when did you first see them?

YOUNG WOMAN. The night my husband was done away with.

LAWYER FOR PROSECUTION. Before that night your husband was murdered—you never saw them? Never before then?

YOUNG WOMAN. No sir.

LAWYER FOR PROSECUTION. You are quite sure of that!

YOUNG WOMAN. Yes.

LAWYER FOR PROSECUTION. Mrs. Jones, do you remember about a year ago, a year ago this spring, bringing home to your house—a lily, a Chinese water lily?

YOUNG WOMAN. No—I don't think so.

LAWYER FOR PROSECUTION. You don't think you remember bringing home a water lily growing in a bowl filled with small stones?

YOUNG WOMAN. No—no I don't.

LAWYER FOR PROSECUTION. I'll show you this bowl, Mrs. JONES. Does that refresh your memory?

YOUNG WOMAN. I remember the bowl—but I don't remember—the lily.

LAWYER FOR PROSECUTION. You recognize the bowl then?

YOUNG WOMAN. Yes.

LAWYER FOR PROSECUTION. It is yours, isn't it?

YOUNG WOMAN. It was in my house—yes.

LAWYER FOR PROSECUTION. How did it come there?

YOUNG WOMAN. How did it come there?

LAWYER FOR PROSECUTION. Yes—where did you get it?

YOUNG WOMAN. I don't remember.

LAWYER FOR PROSECUTION. You don't remember?

YOUNG WOMAN. No.

LAWYER FOR PROSECUTION. You don't remember about a year ago bringing this bowl into your bedroom filled with small stones and some water and a lily? You don't remember tending very carefully that lily till it died? And when it died you don't remember hiding the bowl full of little stones away on the top shelf of your closet—and keeping it there until—you don't remember?

YOUNG WOMAN. No, I don't remember.

LAWYER FOR PROSECUTION. You may have done so?

YOUNG WOMAN. No—no—I didn't! I didn't! I don't know anything about all that.

LAWYER FOR PROSECUTION. But you do remember the bowl?

YOUNG WOMAN. Yes. It was in my house—you found it in my house.

LAWYER FOR PROSECUTION. But you don't remember the lily or the stones?

YOUNG WOMAN. No—No I don't!

(LAWYER FOR PROSECUTION *turns to look among his papers in a brief case.*)

FIRST REPORTER (*writing*). Under the heavy artillery fire of the State's attorney's brilliant cross-questioning, the accused woman's defense was badly riddled. Pale and trembling she—

SECOND REPORTER (*writing*). Undaunted by the Prosecution's machine-gun attack, the defendant was able to maintain her position of innocence in the face of rapid-fire questioning that threatened, but never seriously menaced her defense. Flushed but calm she—

LAWYER FOR PROSECUTION (*producing paper*). Your Honor, I'd like to introduce this paper in evidence at this time.

JUDGE. What is it?

LAWYER FOR PROSECUTION. It is an affidavit taken in the State of Guanajato, Mexico.

LAWYER FOR DEFENSE. Mexico? Your Honor, I protest. A Mexican affidavit! Is this the United States of America or isn't it?

LAWYER FOR PROSECUTION. It's properly executed—sworn to before a notary—and certified by an American Consul.

LAWYER FOR DEFENSE. Your Honor! I protest! In the name of this great United States of America—I protest—are we to permit our sacred institutions to be thus—

JUDGE. What is the purpose of this document—who signed it?

LAWYER FOR PROSECUTION. It is signed by one Richard Roe, and its purpose is to refresh the memory of the witness on the point at issue—and incidentally supply a motive for this murder—this brutal and cold-blooded murder of a sleeping man by—

LAWYER FOR DEFENSE. I protest, your Honor! I object!

JUDGE. Objection sustained. Let me see the document. (*Takes paper which is handed to him—looks at it.*) Perfectly regular. Do you offer this affidavit as evidence at this time for the purpose of refreshing the memory of the witness at this time?

LAWYER FOR PROSECUTION. Yes, your Honor.

JUDGE. You may introduce the evidence.

LAWYER FOR DEFENSE. I object! I object to the introduction of this evidence at this time as irrelevant, immaterial, illegal, biased, prejudicial, and—

JUDGE. Objection overruled.

LAWYER FOR DEFENSE. Exception.

JUDGE. Exception noted. Proceed.

LAWYER FOR PROSECUTION. I wish to read the evidence to the jury at this time.

JUDGE. Proceed.

LAWYER FOR DEFENSE. I object.

JUDGE. Objection overruled.

LAWYER FOR DEFENSE. Exception.

JUDGE. Noted.

LAWYER FOR DEFENSE. Why is this witness himself not brought into court—so he can be cross-questioned?

LAWYER FOR PROSECUTION. The witness is a resident of the Republic of Mexico and as such not subject to subpoena as a witness to this court.

LAWYER FOR DEFENSE. If he was out of the jurisdiction of this court how did you get this affidavit out of him?

LAWYER FOR PROSECUTION. This affidavit was made voluntarily by the deponent in the furtherance of justice.

LAWYER FOR DEFENSE. I suppose you didn't threaten him with extradition on some other trumped-up charge so that—

JUDGE. Order!

BAILIFF. Order!

JUDGE. Proceed with the evidence.

LAWYER FOR PROSECUTION (*reading*). In the matter of the State of ———— vs. Helen Jones, I Richard Roe, being of sound mind, do herein depose and state that I know the accused, Helen Jones, and have known her for a period of over one year immediately preceding the date of the signature on this affidavit. That I first met the said Helen Jones in a so-called speakeasy somewhere in the West 40s in New York City. That on the day I met her, she went with me to my room, also somewhere in the West 40s in New York City, where we had intimate relations—

YOUNG WOMAN (*moans*). Oh!

LAWYER FOR PROSECUTION (*continues reading*).—and where I gave her a bowl filled with pebbles, also containing a flowering lily. That from the first day we met until I departed for Mexico in the Fall, the said Helen Jones was an almost daily visitor to my room where we continued to—

YOUNG WOMAN. No! No! (*Moans.*)

LAWYER FOR PROSECUTION. What is it, Mrs. Jones—what is it?

YOUNG WOMAN. Don't read any more! No more!

LAWYER FOR PROSECUTION. Why not?

YOUNG WOMAN. I did it! I did it! I did it!

LAWYER FOR PROSECUTION. You confess?

YOUNG WOMAN. Yes—I did it!

LAWYER FOR DEFENSE. I object, your Honor.

JUDGE. You confess you killed your husband?

YOUNG WOMAN. I put him out of the way—yes.

JUDGE. Why?

YOUNG WOMAN. To be free.

JUDGE. To be free? Is that the only reason?

YOUNG WOMAN. Yes.

JUDGE. If you just wanted to be free—why didn't you divorce him?

YOUNG WOMAN. Oh I couldn't do that!! I couldn't hurt him like that!

Burst of laughter from all in the court. The YOUNG WOMAN *stares out at them, and then seems to go rigid.*

JUDGE. Silence!

BAILIFF. Silence!

(*There is a gradual silence.*)

JUDGE. Mrs. Jones, why—

YOUNG WOMAN *begins to moan—suddenly—as though the realization of the enormity of her isolation had just come upon her. It is a sound of desolation, of agony, of human woe. It continues until the end of the scene.*

Why—?

(YOUNG WOMAN *cannot speak.*)

LAWYER FOR DEFENSE. Your Honor, I ask a recess to—

JUDGE. Court's adjourned.

Spectators begin to file out. The YOUNG WOMAN *continues in the witness box, unseeing, unheeding.*

FIRST REPORTER. Murderess confesses.

SECOND REPORTER. Paramour brings confession.

THIRD REPORTER. I did it! Woman cries!

There is a great burst of speed from the telegraphic instruments. They keep up a constant accompaniment to the Woman's moans. The scene blacks out as the courtroom empties, and two policemen go to stand by the woman. The sound of the telegraph instruments continues until the scene lights into Episode 9—and the prayers of the Priest.

★

Episode 9

A MACHINE

SCENE: *A prison room. The front bars face the audience. They are set back far enough to permit a clear passageway across the stage.*

SOUNDS: *The voice of a Negro singing; the whir of an aeroplane flying.*

CHARACTERS: *Young Woman; A Priest; A Jailer; Two Barbers; A Matron; Mother; Two Guards*

AT RISE: *In front of the bars, at one side, sits a Man; at the opposite side, a Woman—the Jailer and the Matron. Inside the bars, a Man and a Woman—the Young Woman and a Priest. The Young Woman sits still with folded hands. The Priest is praying.*

PRIEST. Hear, oh Lord, my prayer; and let my cry come to Thee. Turn not away Thy face from me; in the day when I am in trouble, incline thy ear to me. In what day soever I shall call upon Thee, hear me speedily. For my days are vanished like smoke; and my bones are grown dry, like fuel for the fire. I am smitten as grass, and my heart is withered; because I forgot to eat my bread. Through the voice of my groaning, my bone hath cleaved to my flesh. I am become like to a pelican of the wilderness. I am like a night raven in the house. I have watched and become as a sparrow all alone on the housetop. All the day long my enemies reproach me; and they that praised me did swear against me. My days have declined like a shadow, and I am withered like grass. But Thou, oh Lord, end rest forever. Thou shalt arise and have mercy, for it is time to have mercy. The time is come.

Voice of NEGRO *offstage—begins to sing a Negro spiritual.*

PRIEST. The Lord hath looked upon the earth, that He might hear the groans of them that are in fetters, that He might release the children of—

Voice of NEGRO *grown louder*

JAILER. Stop that nigger yelling.

YOUNG WOMAN. No, let him sing. He helps me.

MATRON. You can't hear the Father.

YOUNG WOMAN. He helps me.

PRIEST. Don't I help you, daughter?

YOUNG WOMAN. I understand him. He is condemned. I understand him,

The voice of the NEGRO *goes on louder, drowning out the voice of the* PRIEST.

PRIEST (*chanting in Latin*). Gratiam tuum, quaesumus, Domine, metibus nostris infunde, ut qui, angelo nuntiante, Christifilii tui incarnationem cognovimus, per passionem eius et crucem ad ressurectionis gloriam perducamus. Per eudem Christum Dominum nostrum.

Enter TWO BARBERS. *There is a rattling of keys.*

FIRST BARBER. How is she?

MATRON. Calm.

JAILER. Quiet.

YOUNG WOMAN (*rising*). I am ready.

FIRST BARBER. Then sit down.

YOUNG WOMAN (*in a steady voice*). Aren't you the death guard come to take me?

FIRST BARBER. No, we ain't the death guard. We're the barbers.

YOUNG WOMAN. The barbers.

MATRON. Your hair must be cut.

JAILER. Must be shaved.

BARBER. Just a patch.

The BARBERS *draw near her.*

YOUNG WOMAN. No!

PRIEST. Daughter, you're ready. You know you are ready.

YOUNG WOMAN (*crying out*). Not for this! Not for this!

MATRON. The rule.

JAILER. Regulations.

BARBER. Routine.

The BARBERS *take her by the arms.*

YOUNG WOMAN. No! No! Don't touch me—touch me!

(*They take her and put her down in the chair, cut a patch from her hair.*)

I will not be submitted—this indignity! No! I will not be submitted!—Leave me alone! Oh my God am I never to be let alone! Always to have to submit—to submit! No more—not now—I'm going to die—I won't submit! Not now!

BARBER (*finishing cutting a patch from her hair*). You'll submit, my lady. Right to the end, you'll submit! There, and a neat job too.

JAILER. Very neat.

MATRON. Very neat.

Exit BARBERS.

YOUNG WOMAN (*her calm shattered*). Father, Father! Why was I born?

PRIEST. I came forth from the Father and have come into the world—I leave the world and go onto the Father.

YOUNG WOMAN (*weeping*). Submit! Submit! Is nothing mine? The hair on my head! The very hair on my head—

PRIEST. Praise God.

YOUNG WOMAN. Am I never to be let alone! Never to have peace! When I'm dead, won't I have peace?

PRIEST. Ye shall indeed drink of my cup.

YOUNG WOMAN. Won't I have peace tomorrow?

PRIEST. I shall raise Him up at the last day.

YOUNG WOMAN. Tomorrow! Father! Where shall I be tomorrow?

PRIEST. Behold the hour cometh. Yea, is now come. Ye shall be scattered every man to his own.

YOUNG WOMAN. In Hell! Father! Will I be in Hell!

PRIEST. I am the Resurrection and the Life.

YOUNG WOMAN. Life has been hell to me, Father!

PRIEST. Life has been hell to you, daughter, because you never knew God! Gloria in excelsis Deo.

YOUNG WOMAN. How could I know Him, Father? He never was around me.

PRIEST. You didn't seek Him, daughter. Seek and ye shall find.

YOUNG WOMAN. I sought something—I was always seeking something.

PRIEST. What? What were you seeking?

YOUNG WOMAN. Peace. Rest and peace. Will I find it tonight, Father? Will I find it?

PRIEST. Trust in God.

A shadow falls across the passage in the front of the stage—and there is a whirring sound.

YOUNG WOMAN. What is that? Father! Jailer! What is that?

JAILER. An aeroplane.

MATRON. Aeroplane.

PRIEST. God in his Heaven.

YOUNG WOMAN. Look, Father! A man flying! He has wings! But he is not an angel!

JAILER. Hear his engine.

MATRON. Hear the engine.

YOUNG WOMAN. He has wings—but he isn't free! I've been free, Father! For one moment—down here on earth—I have been free! When I did what I did I was free! Free and not afraid! How is that, Father? How can that be? A great sin—a mortal sin—for which I must die and go to hell—but it made me free! One moment I was free! How is that, Father? Tell me that?

PRIEST. Your sins are forgiven.

YOUNG WOMAN. And that other sin—the other sin—that sin of love—That's all I ever knew of Heaven—heaven on earth! How is that, Father? How can that be—a sin—a mortal sin—all I know of heaven?

PRIEST. Confess to Almighty God.

YOUNG WOMAN. Oh, Father, pray for me—a prayer—that I can understand!

PRIEST. I will pray for you, daughter, the prayer of desire. Behind the King of Heaven, behold thy Redeemer and God, Who is even now coming; prepare thyself to receive Him with love, invite him with the ardor of thy desire; come, oh my Jesus, come to thy soul which desires Thee! Before Thou givest Thyself to me, I desire to give Thee my miserable heart. Do Thou accept it, and come quickly to take possession of it! Come my God, hasten! Delay no longer! My only and Infinite Good, my Treasure, my Life, my Paradise, my Love, my all, my wish is to receive thee with the love with which—

Enter the MOTHER. *She comes along the passageway and stops before the bars.*

YOUNG WOMAN (*recoiling*). Who's that woman?

JAILER. Your Mother

MATRON. Your Mother.

YOUNG WOMAN. She's a stranger—take her away—she's a stranger.

JAILER. She's come to say goodbye to you—

MATRON. To say goodbye.

YOUNG WOMAN. But she's never known me—never known me—ever—(*To the* MOTHER.) Go away! You're a stranger! Stranger! Stranger! (MOTHER *turns and starts away. Reaching out her hands to her.*) Oh Mother! Mother! (*They embrace through the bars.*)

Enter TWO GUARDS.

PRIEST. Come, daughter.

FIRST GUARD. It's time.

SECOND GUARD. Time

YOUNG WOMAN. Wait! Mother, my child; my little strange child! I never knew her! She'll never know me! Let her live, Mother. Let her live! Live! Tell her—

PRIEST. Come, daughter.

YOUNG WOMAN. Wait! Wait! Tell her—

The JAILER *takes the* MOTHER *away.*

GUARD. It's time.

YOUNG WOMAN. Wait! Wait! Tell her! Wait! Just a minute more! There's so much I want to tell her—Wait—

The JAILER *takes the* MOTHER *off. The* TWO GUARDS *take the* YOUNG WOMAN *by the arms, and start through the door in the bars and down the passage, across stage and off: the* PRIEST *follows; the* MATRON *follows the* PRIEST; *the* PRIEST *is praying. The scene blacks out. The voice of the* PRIEST *gets dimmer and dimmer.*

PRIEST. Lord have mercy—Christ have mercy—Lord have mercy—Christ hear us! God the Father of Heaven! God the Son, Redeemer of the World, God the Holy Ghost—Holy Trinity one God—Holy Mary—Holy Mother of God—Holy Virgin of Virgins—St. Michael—St. Gabriel—St. Raphael—

His voice dies out. Out of the darkness come the voices of REPORTERS.

FIRST REPORTER. What time is it now?

SECOND REPORTER. Time now.

THIRD REPORTER. Hush.

FIRST REPORTER. Here they come.

THIRD REPORTER. Hush.

PRIEST (*his voice sounds dimly—gets louder—continues until the end*). St. Peter pray for us—St. Paul pray for us—St. James pray for us—St. John pray for us—all ye holy Angels and Archangels—all ye blessed orders of holy spirits—St. Joseph—St. John the Baptist—St. Thomas—

FIRST REPORTER. Here they are!

SECOND REPORTER. How little she looks! She's gotten smaller.

THIRD REPORTER. Hush.

PRIEST. St. Phillip pray for us. All you Holy Patriarchs and prophets—St. Phillip—St. Matthew—St. Simon—St. Thaddeus—All ye holy apostles—all ye holy disciples—all ye holy innocents·—Pray for us—Pray for us—Pray for us—

FIRST REPORTER. Suppose the machine shouldn't work!

SECOND REPORTER. It'll work!—It always works!

THIRD REPORTER. Hush!

PRIEST. Saints of God make intercession for us—Be merciful—Spare us, oh Lord—be merciful—

FIRST REPORTER. Her lips are moving—what is she saying?

SECOND REPORTER. Nothing.

THIRD REPORTER. Hush!

PRIEST. Oh Lord deliver us from all evil—from all sin—from Thy wrath—from the snares of the devil—from anger and hatred and every evil will—from—

FIRST REPORTER. Did you see that? She fixed her hair under the cap—pulled her hair out under the cap.

THIRD REPORTER. Hush!

PRIEST.—Beseech Thee—hear us—that Thou would'st spare us—that Thou would'st pardon us—Holy Mary—pray for us—

SECOND REPORTER. There—

YOUNG WOMAN (*calling out*). Somebody! Somebod—

Her voice is cut off.

PRIEST. Christ have mercy—Lord have mercy—Christ have mercy—

Curtain

Part 4
Economic Structure

THE GREAT DEPRESSION AND THE WORKERS' THEATRE MOVEMENT

THE NEW DEAL AND THE FEDERAL THEATRE PROJECT

14. *Scottsboro, Limited*—Langston Hughes

Commentary

Sources

Play

14.1 HUGHES' MOVE TO THE LEFT: *SCOTTSBORO, LIMITED*—SUSAN DUFFY

Langston Hughes' embrace of the political Left in the early 1930s coincides with two events, one personal, the other public. First was his very traumatic personal split with Charlotte Mason, his wealthy New York patron, who had supported his writing efforts through a kind of perverse philanthropic bondage. Mason, a prominent New York socialite, took it upon herself to financially support and encourage promising black writers. In return, she assumed the role of artistic mentor and literary agent. In reading accounts of Mason's control of young artists, one is struck by an unsavory, even unhealthy, quality in these professional relationships. Mason's support came with conditions. Hughes was one of the few who sought personal independence in his writing schedule and choice of topics. It cost him dearly both financially and emotionally.

The second event that caused Hughes' embrace of leftist politics and personalities was, according to Arnold Rampersad, "certainly the Scottsboro Controversy." The incarceration of nine black youths charged with raping two white women in a railway car ignited a national outcry. Many artists immortalized the "Scottsboro Boys" in the 1930s. But Hughes' embrace of the political Left was more complex and self-serving than would appear at first glance. Attributing Hughes' political rebirth solely to the Scottsboro incident might move one precariously close to the sort of post hoc fallacy historians and critics are careful to avoid.

The early 1930s, the depression years, were a period in which Hughes needed to find financial as well as artistic moorings. Thrown out of "Godmother" Mason's white bourgeois environment that had served as a safe, even affluent, haven during the first two years of the Great Depression, Hughes sought solace and redirection in a trip to Cuba. The Scottsboro incident occurred prior to Hughes' departure. In the intervening months before his return to the United States, the legal defense for the Scottsboro defendants was supplied by the American Communist Party, which raised the case to national prominence in order to attract new members. Scottsboro became a vehicle to advance leftist political and labor issues. The Scottsboro case allowed the International Labor Defense (ILD), the legal branch of the American Communist Party, to garner national favor with political liberals and minority workers. Rampersad saw this as a direct campaign to enact Stalin's goals to increase "black participation in the party" and to establish "self-determination for Afro-Americans as a commitment of the communist effort in the United States."

Hughes' return to New York came in the midst of the Scottsboro appeal. Feeling the need to reestablish himself professionally, he sought new, independent literary associations. Hughes gravitated towards individuals among the political Left, particularly writers and editors. Fortuitously, the radical writers who formed the membership of the John Reed Club in New York offered friendship as well as literary connections and publication outlets for Hughes. His poems and translations of poems by Federico García Lorca soon appeared in the pages of *New Masses*. The camaraderie extended by the JRC and the adoption of the Scottsboro case as the American Communist Party's cause celebre resulted in Hughes immersion in leftist politics and art. Whether this commitment was part of a newfound political activism or a part of a psychological distancing from the controlling wealth of Charlotte Mason is not clear. Nonetheless, Hughes was drawn to the dramatic racial controversy marked by white injustice towards young black men. Consequently he became actively involved not only in the John Reed Club but also in the American Negro Labor Congress and other groups with leftist leanings.

The whirlwind of labor causes in the early part of the 1930s touched all aspects of society. An artistic development that grew out of leftist activities and the American labor movement was political theater. It emerged strongly in New York and was evident in the South as well. Plays used by leftist and labor groups as political ends for agitation and propaganda surfaced in a variety of forms, ranging from documentaries to strident proselytizing scripts. The style and content of these plays was revolutionary and politically topical. They generated a great deal of attention in the press and attracted theatrical artists such as playwrights Paul Peters, Elia Kazan, Clifford Odets, George Sklar, and John Wexley. Production companies that evolved out of this revolutionary movement include Labor Stage, the Group Theatre, and the Federal Theater Project.

The theater offered a potentially lucrative means to reach a broader audience and brought with it, if not fortune, some fame. Though Hughes' initial foray into commercial theatrical writing with Zora Neale Hurston had been unsatisfactory because of the controversy over authorship, throughout his life he continually eyed the theater and film industry as a potential outlet for his own dramatic writings. His failed collaboration with Hurston colored all of his subsequent cooperative efforts, which were undertaken in a shadow of suspicion. Initially he embarked on the script for *Scottsboro, Limited* with Wallace Thurman, but when Thurman withdrew, Hughes had him attest in writing that the idea had been Hughes'.

Scottsboro, Limited

Scottsboro, Limited offers a unique example of Hughes' verse coupled with leftist agit-prop techniques. The mention of "agit-prop" and other forms of didactic drama usually call up images of Bertolt Brecht for most American readers. Yet there was an indigenous political theater in the United States that took root in the late 1920s and early 1930s employing the same techniques as its European counterpart. Traditionally, agitation-propaganda plays were loosely structured presentational plays whose intent was the movement of the audience to some kind of discernible action. This might be an immediate action characterized by audience participation in shouting slogans or calling for strikes. Many of the early agit-prop plays relied on performers planted in the audience to encourage and prod the audience to participate. The action may have been less immediate but equally profound, asking audience members to join unions or demonstrate for worker rights. There was a general call for the audience to recognize that strength in numbers comes through solidarity, whether it is ethnic solidarity or the solidarity of labor. The agit-prop scripts and productions of the 1930s were rallying vehicles produced for union meetings or mounted near factory gates. Because they sought to move the audience to action, they were often bellicose and reactionary and used the productions as a means to shock and affront their audience. In 1930, the Communist Party in the United States established theatrical companies in New York for the sole purpose of producing agit-prop plays: the Proletbuehne, a German speaking troupe; the Workers' Laboratory Theater; and the Theater Collective. Some speculate that the Communist Party began using agit-props as part of their campaign strategy in the elections of the early 1930s. The structure of agit-props influenced the Living Newspaper productions of the Federal Theater Project in the middle of the decade.

Scottsboro, Limited employs all of the traditional early agit-prop techniques to great effect. It has audience plants designated in the text as "Mob Voices," who unexpectedly shout out from the audience in support of a racist white character. These voices are eventually overpowered by "Red Voices," who also rise from the audience. Eventually they join the Scottsboro defendants on stage, clasping hands in a biracial show of support against the injustices of the American system. One of the hallmarks of this kind of agit-prop theater is a conclusion that prompts the audience to rise en masse, shouting slogans or singing songs. Hughes' script does both. *Scottsboro, Limited* ends with stirring intensity as characters inveigh against the color line, hands joined onstage and in the audience, shouting "Fight, Fight, Fight, Fight!" As they sing "The Internationale," a red flag descends above the heads of the workers. The audience is manipulated to respond to the event both physically and emotionally. The group participation strategically called for in these plays imbued the audience with a fervor, enmity, even rivalry, the intensity of which might be compared to that provoked by frenetic sporting events. What might ordinarily be perceived as a mob response becomes transformed and sanctified by song, chants, and participatory zeal. Workers onstage and in the audience raise their voices in a collective hymn against capitalism. The song, the group choral response, and the injustices exposed galvanize a righteous indignation and moral imperative within the audience to "Fight!"

The agit-prop techniques used in *Scottsboro, Limited* reveal unquestioningly that Hughes was familiar with the form. He consciously set about to use all of the propaganda techniques he saw already being staged in New York. In *Scottsboro, Limited*, eight black men are employed to represent the collective protagonist of the Scottsboro Boys. One white actor assumes multiple roles of antagonists: racist audience member, Sheriff, Judge, Prison Guard, and Preacher. Hughes employs this rhetorical tactic masterfully. He maintains the individuality of the Scottsboro defendants with lines revealing their individual ethos. The white actor, on the other hand, comes to represent the entire white race in the United States. Each social and professional persona he assumes in the script espouses a racist and discriminatory position. Hughes' decision to have the white antagonist rise unexpectedly from the audience presses the antagonist's association with them. His emergence from them as an unchosen spokesman poses a dilemma and creates extraordinary tension. The audience must find ways to disembarrass themselves and to show that he does not represent them as a group. This is made more difficult as other audience plants shout racial slurs and seemingly corroborate the racist activity of the trial. As the "Red Voices" bravely assert themselves from the audience toward the end of the play, the "real" audience members readily side with them against the atrocities that they have seen enacted and to which they have been tacitly accused. Hughes employs social psychology so aptly in the script that everyone, actors and audience, will be on their feet shouting, "Fight!" and singing the Communist anthem.

In *Scottsboro, Limited*, as in subsequent scripts, Hughes takes pains to establish the musicality of the lines and to provide indication of how they should be delivered. While some playwrights write with a specific look, feel, or attitude in mind, Hughes consistently wrote with a specific sound for his plays and included musical directions. Essentially, he scored his scripts for the reader so that it would be clear that the tension in certain scenes resided in rhythmic, almost orchestral, builds. An example in this play is found in the stage directions for the court scene. Hughes writes, "The trial is conducted in jazz tempo: the white voices staccato, high and shrill; the black voices deep as the rumble of drums." This scene builds as the two girls sit at the downstage corners with the judge alternately pointing from one girl to the other accusing the defendants, "You raped that girl!" and being answered with a resounding "No!" eight times. This is repeated with the repetition of "You had a gun," again met with negative responses. The rhythm and tension builds until the mob voices in the audience erupt with "Kill the niggers!" Hughes has the defendants rise and circle the judge's chair, dance-like, echoing the slurs of the mob. His juxtaposition of scene and rhythmic shifts is masterful. Reading the script, one feels the tensions build and recede only to flare up again in heated exchanges that culminate in the burning resolve to fight.

The fight to which the audience should commit itself seems purposely ambiguous. The group call for "Fight!" in the closing moments of the play would find some audience members crying to fight racism, while others would be convinced that they were fighting capitalism. The first half of the play stands as a chronicle of racism. The trial scene offers a climactic moment not only in terms of dramatic structure but also in terms of political propaganda. As the defendants await execution, they talk of the Communist lawyer sent to appeal the sentence. The racial issue becomes subordinated to an economic labor issue. The Scottsboro defendants defiantly assert that they will speak for themselves, ultimately conceding to the Red Voices who assure them that "the Red flag, too, will talk for you." The Scottsboro Boys are transformed from maligned individuals suffering the atrocities of a racist society to workers who, like the audience, suffer under a capitalist system. In this script, the identification forged between the Scottsboro Boys and the audience is more economic than racial.

When finally the Red Voices rise as a group, it is in response to mob calls to kill the Scottsboro defendants in the electric chair. They rise from the audience as the eight Scottsboro victims proclaim that "[t]he new Red Negro will come: / That's me!" Their unified front announces, "NO DEATH IN THE CHAIR!" A litany of pain and despair chronicles the suffering of workers, white and black. The promise is held out to the characters and the audience that "the red world" will bring about change. Hughes' characters boldly assert party propaganda in statements about the "Red Negro" and in lines intoning "The voice of the red world *is* you! . . . The hands of the red world *are* you!" Finally, the singing of "The Internationale" and the unfurling of the red flag leave little doubt where the political sentiments of the play and its author rested.

Although Hughes would not renounce his leftist activities until a decade later, he realized that such associations jeopardized his literary career. His business venture with Prentiss Taylor and Carl Van Vecten that resulted in the founding of the Golden Stair Press may have been an attempt to ensure that someone would publish his works. Hughes and Taylor decided that the 1932 publication for their new press would be a small volume of works on the Scottsboro theme incorporating Hughes' *Scottsboro, Limited*, four related poems, and four lithographs of Scottsboro by Taylor. Hughes, however, capitulated, wondering whether the play was "too red to be included."

Despite this instance of private reservation, Hughes remained publicly dedicated to the Scottsboro case through the mid-1930s. He was an active participant in the National Committee for the Defense of Political Prisoners (northern California branch), and his name appears on its letterhead along with other prominent leftist artists and writers. In November 1933, Hughes participated in a letter-writing campaign to American authors soliciting their financial support and statements for publication protesting the incarceration of the Scottsboro Boys. A month later, Noel Sullivan, Hughes' patron in Carmel where he was staying, sent a telegram to the National Committee for the Defense of Political Prisoners in New York. In this correspondence, he requested advice or permission for "a small delegation from [the] national committee here to go now to Decatur. . . . If we could be guaranteed admission to court room during trial . . . or would Scottsboro Committee prefer to receive money we would expend for journey for continuation of defense." Presumably, Hughes planned to participate in this delegation, since he stayed with Sullivan throughout December 1933.

The two organized an auction in January 1934 to raise money for the legal defense fund of the Scottsboro defendants. Their efforts were met with positive responses from several literary figures who sent signed manuscripts and memorabilia to be auctioned. Elmer Rice sent a draft of *Street Scene*, a version of which Hughes would work on years later with Rice and Kurt Weill. While the auction enhanced Hughes' reputation and commitment with the members of the literary Left, it would become a personal and political liability to him and to many of its participants. It haunted actor James Cagney, who served as the auctioneer for the event and who would later need to disassociate himself from all previous leftist affiliations to save his career. Allegations of Communist affiliations surfaced ominously against Hughes in the coming years, and he too would find renunciation of past political associations a personal necessity.

Neither *Scottsboro, Limited* nor the other plays examined in this study nearly ended Hughes' literary career in the late 1930s. However, his political poems written after the plays came back to haunt him. In the 1930s and 1940s, the general public was unaware of Hughes' leftist plays calling for the rise of the "Red Negro." Only years later would Hughes gain public notice as a dramatist. His entrée into the ranks of recognized playwrights came because of his dramatic and humorous treatment of social themes rather than political ones. His early political plays of this study went unnoticed in the controversy concerning his Communist associations that came to a head in 1941. Rampersad explains Hughes' dismissal of the inflammatory poem "Goodbye Christ," written after *Scottsboro, Limited* and his renunciation of his leftist associations, as "a regrettable error of his immature youth, an error that he would not repeat." After 1941, this political shift extended to Hughes' writing dramatic works as well. Though all his plays have a political edge, only scripts in this volume vehemently express the radical political ideology associated with the American Communist Party.

Hughes was not alone in treating the Scottsboro theme dramatically, but unfortunately his script failed to be produced in New York. The most notable New York productions came in the mid-1930s when the Workers' Laboratory Theater presented a production of the play *Scottsboro*, directed by Alfred Saxe in 1934. On 21 February of that same year, John Wexley's *They Shall Not Die*, a Theater Guild production treating the Scottsboro trial, opened. Wexley's production, though it used fictitious names of characters and organizations, incorporated dialogue from the actual court transcript, giving it a documentary element not contained in the other scripts.

The production of Hughes' script in New York may well have been hindered by his departure from the city to embark on a western tour. Hughes left New York in March 1932, arriving in Los Angeles in April where he visited Loren Miller, a black lawyer, active in the local John Reed Club. Hughes' script preceded him. When he arrived in the city, the Los Angeles police had banned the local John Reed Club's production of *Scottsboro, Limited.* The political atmosphere in which Hughes found himself led him to write a poem supporting and lionizing Tom Mooney, a political radical convicted in a 1916 terrorist bombing in San Francisco. Lydia Filatova maintains that Hughes wrote the poem "after an interview with Tom Mooney in St. [sic] Quentin prison."

Mooney's conviction earned him martyr status with some elements of the political Left. Hughes' poem, intended as a participatory chant, was performed Sunday, 8 May 1932, and accompanied a production of *Scottsboro, Limited* that finally escaped police censorship. Though relatively short, the poem retains the elements of agitprop structure in its encouragement of audience participation through unified chanting:

A Chant for Tom Mooney

Tom Mooney!
Tom Mooney!
Tom Mooney!
A man with the title of governor has spoken:
And you do not go free.

A man with the title of governor has spoken:
And the steel bars surround you,
And the prison walls wrap you about,
And you do not go free.
But the man with the title of governor
Does not know
That all over the earth today
The workers speak the name:
Tom Mooney!
Tom Mooney!
Tom Mooney!
And the sound vibrates in waves
From Africa to China,
India to Germany,
Russia to the Argentine,
Shaking the bars,
Shaking the walls,
Shaking the earth
Until the whole world falls into the hands of
The workers.

Of course, the man with the title of governor
Will be forgotten then
On the scrap heap of time—
He won't matter at all.
But remembered forever will be the name:
TOM MOONEY.
Schools will be named:
TOM MOONEY.
Farms will be named:
TOM MOONEY.
Dams will be named:
TOM MOONEY.
Ships will be named:
TOM MOONEY.
Factories will be named:
TOM MOONEY.
And all over the world—
Banner of force and labor, strength and union,
Life forever through the workers' power—
will be the name:
TOM MOONEY.

For Hughes, the political Left of the early 1930s served as a boon to his career rather than the bane it would become years later. As his capital increased with leftist activists, so did the pressure to continue writing in a radical vein. Eugene Gordon singled out Hughes for political praise in his 1933 article "Negro Novelists and the Negro Masses." Noting that Negro writers such as Wallace Thurman, Countee Cullen, Rudolph Fisher, and Langston Hughes all dealt with Negro workers in fiction, "none of them except Hughes has evidently heard of the class struggle." In reference to *Not Without Laughter*, Gordon maintained, "Hughes . . . has written the only novel in which the Negro worker is pictured as seeing the way out through the class struggle." For Gordon, Hughes' subsequent political leanings to the Left "indicated a fulfillment of the promise it contained."

Hughes' political stock was high, and subsequently he received an invitation to address the first American Writers Congress, a gathering of liberal and leftist literati to promote the political efficacy of literature as a means to unite the masses. His address led a series of speakers who chastised the audience for indifference and lack of political involvement. Hughes' speech entitled "To Negro Writers" was a call to action. He exhorted other American Negro writers

> to reveal to the Negro masses . . . our potential power to transform the now ugly face of the southland into a region of peace and plenty . . . reveal to the white masses those Negro qualities which go beyond the mere ability to laugh and sing and dance and make music and which are a part of the useful heritage that we place at the disposal of a future free America . . . expose . . . the sicksweet smile of organized religion—which lies about what it doesn't

> know and what it does know . . . expose . . . the false leadership that besets the Negro people—bought and paid for leadership, owned by capital, afraid to open its mouth except in the old conciliatory way so advantageous to the exploiters . . . [and] write about the irony and pathos of the *colored* American Legion.

The conclusion of the speech uses language reminiscent of the final scene *of Scottsboro, Limited.* Clearly Hughes intended a rousing finale to his speech: "We want an America that will be ours, a world that will be ours—we Negro workers and white workers! Black writers and white! We'll make that world!"

Fortuitously for Hughes, Eugene Gordon, who had publicly praised Hughes' political activism, spoke directly after Hughes. Gordon's speech, "Social and Political Problems of the Negro Writer," expressed disappointment with "Negro writers from the middle class." Gordon saw the "Negro writer . . . along with the Negro preacher" as his people's chief propagandist. "It is the writer," he maintained, "more than any other articulate agent of the Negro people, who interprets and pleads for them to the white ruling class." Eugene Clay, who in turn followed Gordon, claimed in his address that "most Negro intellectuals have remained indifferent to the increasing leftward movement in American thought." His address continued as a diatribe against Negro intellectuals who participated in the white discovery and exploitation of the "Harlem tradition." Surprisingly, Hughes, who has come to be known as a leading figure in the Harlem Renaissance, is spared Clay's invective. Clay asserted: "The most notable example of one who has made the decisive step to the Left is Langston Hughes . . . Hughes has not followed in the retrogressive paths of his 'new Negro' renaissance colleagues. His works from 1926–1931 were links in his evolution, with only occasional retrogressions . . . There began to appear in his work an antibourgeois intelligentsia outlook . . . As long as Hughes' technique and purpose seem to be in an ascending scale, we can hope to see his work progress."

This pressure placed on Hughes to carry the party banner as its leading black proponent is discernible throughout the 1930s. The relationship was symbiotic. The Communist Party, hoping to attract more black members, often encouraged and solicited Hughes to speak at John Reed Club meetings on both coasts. Hughes, in turn, found himself "hobnobbing" with some of the most successful leftist writers of the period, who provided him entree into prominent homes and publishing houses. Mrs. Mason, the domineering patron who had controlled his writing, became a distant memory. He found a willing patron in Noel Sullivan, a liberal San Francisco millionaire who offered Hughes the use of his Carmel retreat. In Carmel, Hughes socialized with muckraking journalist Lincoln Steffens and his wife, Ella Winter, a founder of the John Reed Club in what was then a rural artistic conclave. There, he became involved, at least by association, in yet more leftist activities as Winter and Sullivan visited labor camps and organized meetings. Hughes willingly lent his name to labor causes and rallies, the result of which would be a script done in collaboration with Ella Winter about California's most notorious labor strike.

The International Workers Order chose Hughes as "its first author in a series of literary pamphlets for the people." In 1938, the International Workers Order published a volume of Hughes' poetry entitled *A New Song.* Claiming that "American labor [had] at last entered the field of culture," Michael Gold in his introduction noted that the IWO published ten thousand copies of the first edition of the work, "a rare and startling figure in the American poetry world." Even at fifteen cents per copy, the price listed on the cover of the book, Hughes stood to do well on royalty receipts as well as to increase awareness of his works.

Scottsboro, Limited punctuated a radical period in Hughes' literary endeavors. Coming at the beginning of the decade of the 1930s, it is a part of Hughes' initiation into American leftist politics. Clearly, he wrote it as a signal that he, too, could work and write with the best of the leftist literati. The significance of the leftist political scripts in the body of Hughes' works is equal to his Simple essays, his poems, or even his later plays of social satire, which achieved greater commercial success. The political proselytizing that marks his plays of the 1930s and his commitment to leftwing causes provide evidence that the labor movement in the United States achieved the support of minority writers. His political plays of this decade have not received the attention they merit possibly because they reveal Hughes' very close working relationships with Communist groups and individuals deemed subversive by agencies of the United States government.

Though Rampersad supports Hughes' contention that he was never an actual member of the Communist Party, Hughes' protestation belies the truth. Whether Hughes' activities on behalf of the American Communist Party were those of a member or of an interested nonmember does not matter today. Such political associations do not carry with them the damning exile from American letters they once did. Bringing to light the leftist plays of Langston Hughes will not cause a fall from literary grace or remove him as a figure studied in American schools. It does, however, reveal a new avenue of inquiry in American cultural history, that of the activities and support of black artists for the political Left in the 1930s. The whole idea of the "Red Negro" and "the black masses," as Hughes calls them, a labor group seeking a political franchise within the American system as a political force, is a fascinating area not fully examined by historians or literary critics. Whether Hughes used the party or the party used Hughes is not as significant as the political works written because of that relationship. *Scottsboro, Limited* marks the beginning of Hughes' sojourn into radical politics, a journey he would wish later he had not taken. Bringing these plays to light helps to understand the man as well as the leanings of disenfranchised labor groups in the United States who rejected New Deal altruism in favor of political revolt.

14.2 A THEATRE IS BORN—HALLIE FLANAGAN

A THEATRE IS BEING BORN in America. Its songs are being sung and its plays acted in far places—in Seattle along the docks where ships anchor, in Chicago down a dark huddle of streets far removed from the cubistic palaces in which the World's Fair plans to house 'modern drama', in Detroit against the roar and tumult of machines, in New York from Union Square and Harlem to the Bronx.

At a time when Broadway is offering alibis for a disastrous season, during a period when art and community theatres are closing in many cities, when managers are frantically debating how to revive stock, when dramatic schools are considering the problem of what to do with theatre students who go out to an already surfeited market—at this confused time, a new theatre, unknown in spite of the fact that it has been smouldering for ten years, leaps into life.

The theatre being born in America today is a theatre of workers. Its object is to create a national culture by and for the working class of America. Admittedly a weapon in the class struggle, this theatre is being forged in the factories and the mines. Its mouthpiece is the *Workers' Theatre*, a magazine mimeographed monthly by the Workers' Laboratory Theatre of New York. The first issue, published in April, 1931, analyzes in its foreword the present economic situation in the United States, and declares that the only hope for the worker lies in the reorganization of society. In this reorganization, the theatre can play a part; for while the press, the radio, the movies, the schools, and the churches, are all closed, in their present form, to the worker who wishes to reach his own class, but has no money with which to do so, the theatre is his weapon if he is strong enough to make it over for his own purpose.

Strong he must be, however, for the theatre, if it is to be of use to the worker, must be divorced from the non-essentials which have become synonymous with it—divorced from expensive buildings, stage equipment, painted sets, elaborate costumes and properties, made up plays; above all, divorced from actors who want to show off or make money. If the theatre can throw all these things into the discard it may perhaps become, as it has been at certain great moments of its history, a place where an idea is so ardently enacted that it becomes the belief of actors and audiences alike.

Where are these theatres to exist? According to the pamphlet I am quoting, everywhere:

"If you are a worker in a shop, a factory, or a mine, where struggle for existence makes one day as dark as the next; if you are oppressed by capitalism and want to cry out in protest—organize a dramatic group. . . . Start dramatic groups in unions, in fraternal organizations, in social clubs, in company unions, in Y.M.C.A.'s. Start dramatic groups in the north, south, east and west. Let dramatic groups dot the land from coast to coast. Don't expect profit in money. These theatres exist to awaken the workers."

More than a prophecy, however, these words, for theatres of workers exist in America today. On June 13, 1931, I attended in New York a conference of workers' cultural societies, the object of which was to organize these groups as a base for the federation in the near future of all the workers' theatres in the United States. At this meeting, delegates from 224 workers' cultural groups in New York and vicinity were present and reports were read from scores of other theatres throughout the country. The John Reed Club, which, together with the *New Masses*, sponsored this initial meeting, states that there are in the United States today, some 2000 cultural organizations of workers.

The international aspect of the meeting was evident, not only from the many messages read from foreign theatre groups—but from the nationality of the speakers and actors themselves—Germans, Finns, Hungarians, Russians, Negroes, and Chinese.

The red banner, *Workers of the World Unite*, across the wall back of the platform, and the many messages from theatres in the U.S.S.R., suggested that these workers' theatres were to be modelled entirely upon those of the Russian Soviets; but as the meeting progressed, a number of speakers emphasized the fact that the problems of America are not the problems of the U.S.S.R., and consequently that, although workers here must study the proletarian theatre of other countries, they must work out their own ideas and their own style. It was pointed out that they must avoid, on the one hand, the inborn distrust of culture which is the heritage of the native born American; they must avoid, on the other hand, too great emphasis on the folklore which is transplanted from any other land.

"Our workers' theatres must create their own culture out of the conditions they will themselves create," declared Michael Gold at this conference. Urging the workers to beware of fondling the old themes dear to the bourgeois stage, themes of personal love and hate, Michael Gold told these young writers, directors and actors to go deep into the life of the worker, and to learn to portray that life on the stage in such a way that its problems will be clear to all.

The only example of workers' drama given at the conference was a skit which seemed a combination of American vaudeville and Russian Blue Blouse technique. A score of workers marched up the aisle singing, and argued with another worker whose silk topper and over-refined accent proclaimed him to be a capitalist. Their conflict was over the purpose of drama, the capitalist insisting that art was an expression of man's craving for beauty, while the workers insisted that art was a weapon in man's struggle for justice; to the apparent delight of the audience, the workers overcame the capitalist, argumentatively and physically.

In view of the rather childish nature of this performance, Michael Gold's warning against an enthusiasm which might blind the workers to mediocre performance, seemed particularly apropos.

"We must have not only ideas, but fitting stage forms for those ideas," he said. "A worker will not come to a workers' theatre where the production is poor when he can go to a bourgeois theatre where the production is good. It is not enough that we are doing a new thing. We must do it in a new way and we must do it well."

How are they to be trained, these workers, unused to the simplest technique of the stage, men and women who work by day in shops, factories, or mines, and come together at night to make a theatre? They will not be trained in the art of illusion, for their object is to remain themselves—workers—expressing workers' problems. Their object is to attack those evils from which they themselves are suffering: wage cuts, unemployment, deportation, lynching, race prejudice, legal discrimination, war, and all oppression and injustice. Being craftsmen, however, they are not oblivious to the fact that the dramatic medium is a new craft to them. They will learn this craft from the only theatre at hand, the theatre of the class they are attacking.

So great is the scorn of the workers' theatre for the bourgeois stage which it defines variously as a soporific, making the worker forget his injustices, as a weapon of capitalism used in glorification of that system, and as an entertainment catering to man's lust, greed, and prejudice, that one might expect a romantic attitude on the part of the workers toward the despised upper-class stage. That is, one might expect them to ignore or attempt to negate the existence of the bourgeois theatre, or at least to denounce it fiercely, together with all its ways. Instead, the attitude of the workers toward the bourgeois stage is entirely realistic, a coldly critical questioning with the resolve to adopt its good points and profit by its mistakes. In the first issue of the *Workers' Theatre* the editor writes:

> "Every worker aspiring to become a director in a workers' theatre should become acquainted with the arts as well as the history of the stage. We recommend the following books on these subjects: Mantzius—*History of the Theatre*; Sheldon Cheney—*History of the Theatre*; Havemeyer—*Drama of Primitive People*; Huntly Carter—*The New Spirit in the European Theatre*; Huntly Carter—*The Theatre and Cinema of Soviet Russia*; Haigh—*The Attic Theatre*.
>
> "These books should be read for what they are, books by critics and theatre workers who do not understand (with the exception of Havemeyer and Carter) or do not care to show that the form of the theatre at a given time is determined by social and economic conditions and is a reflection of contemporary society. These books are dry enumerations of names, dates, and the like, but the reader must attempt to get behind them and envision the social and utilitarian causes that gave rise to each particular form. The primitive theatre is very interesting and instructive. Books on anthropology will also help."

The same fierce scrutiny is directed upon the work of designers here and abroad. What can we learn from Adolphe Appia, from Max Reinhardt, from Robert Edmond Jones? In Detroit I was amazed to hear a worker say, "The man who is going to be most help to workers' theatres is Gordon Craig." Remembering the vast distances, the lofty, towering heights of Craig's designs, remembering also that these designs have recently been attacked as impracticable and untheatric by one of our leading American designers, Lee Simonson, I demanded, "Why Craig?" The worker said, "Because he sees the stage in simple, practical terms. He doesn't call for a lot of paint and a lot of scenery. We can get Craig's enormous shadows, silhouettes and effects of distance, all by a spot light focussed on a screen—and the screen and the light we can carry with us."

Not only theory of the bourgeois theatre is under fire by the workers; the plays, those dealing with any problem of social justice, are studied in a form of dramatic criticism bold and unmistakable in its point of view.

When we read the usual dramatic criticism published in our press or in our theatre journals, we do not know the base of the criticism. Sometimes the critic is frank and tells us that the play was terrible because he had had a poor dinner; George Jean Nathan was once honest enough to declare that in his then state of mind a pretty actress was a good actress and no nonsense about it. Oftener, however, the critic merely denounces or acclaims in a Jovian manner, which, while it reveals charming glimpses of Olympus, leaves us quite in the dark as to why the thunderbolt or garland fell upon a particular play.

In the *Workers' Theatre*, criticism is on grounds of utilitarianism only. Does the play purporting to be on some theme of social justice state its problem clearly, develop it fearlessly, and send the audience out ready to do something about that problem? For example, A. Prentiss, reviewing what he calls *The Mess at Verdun*, gives several pages, not of vituperation, but of lucid and often witty analysis of why an idea, excellent though trite—that the war dead died in vain—was muddled by lack of logical thinking and lack of fundamental sympathy with the concept, on the part of writer and director. He shows how their desire to build dramatic climaxes, or to develop individual characters (both remnants of the old dramaturgy) together with their ambition to create a sensation, or a success, ruined the stern simplicity of the original idea.

> "The 'direction' has been thorough," he writes. "Aside from the satire on militaristic speeches that even the *Nation* could print, not a word of protest appeared in this play, every situation of which is pregnant with protest. As the director has to hold on to his job, nothing harmful to our ethics was said during the entire play. The picture as the dead soldiers marched around the hill was very, very pretty . . . which proves again what money can do. . . . The customer is satisfied, the directors get checks—art they calls it. Everyone is happy. As for conveying social ideas—bother them—they give you headaches, better leave them alone. Your turn next, John—will you use a mashie or a niblick?"

In the same way, *Precedent* is adversely criticised on three grounds: first, as to play, because the writer does not show the Mooney-Billings case truly in that he conceals the treacherous role played by the American Federation of Labor; second, as to production, because the heavy realism, expensive sets and slick acting necessitate a greater expenditure than workers can afford to make; and third, as to social implication, because people go away vaguely indignant at our legal system, but not clear as to the fact that this legal system is a natural result of the capitalistic system.

In accordance with the workers' theatres' principles of self criticism, the attack is launched most heavily against so-called proletarian theatres or propaganda plays. A. Saks, writing of the Artef Theatre, is biting in his comment that if the Artef is trying to compete with the Yiddish Art Theatre, it is a success, but that if the Artef calls itself a working class theatre, then that success is negligible. Of *Jim Copperhead* he says:

> "It is amazing to see how badly proletarian actors can handle a scene in Communist headquarters. . . . Carry home a blank except perhaps the flash at the opening and closing."

Saks gives credit where credit is due, however, and of *The Whirl of the Machines*, he writes:

> "The Artef finally lands with both feet squarely on this continent. Here is a play that with all its faults (sloppy construction, lack of unity in direction, bad handling of masses) is part and parcel of a worker's life."

The new theatres plan, of course, to write their own plays. The first issue of their magazine says:

> "Do not be discouraged if you have never written before—playwriting can be learned just like any other trade. Plays written for the commercial theatre are written with the aim of entertaining people for money. They are cock and bull stories written to amuse the bourgeoisie for two hours after dinner; they deal with situations with which the audience is familiar—love affairs, bootleggers, racketeers, etc.; and they end in a pleasant manner so as not to upset the stomachs of the audience.

"But you are not writing to entertain or to make money. Don't expect to make a living by writing plays. You can't. The bourgeois theatre won't use your plays, the workers' theatre can't pay for them. Write to liberate the working class, including yourself. That's enough compensation."

How does this philosophy, that playwriting is a trade which can be learned like any other trade, actually work? Rapidly, at least, for the next three issues of the magazine carry a play each: *Unemployment; Lynch Law*, a play about the Scottsboro case; and *It's as Funny as Hell*, a satire on various suggestions to relieve unemployment. Crude, biased, and violent, these dramas, but nevertheless exciting and moving. Unlike most plays by untrained writers, they are not merely exercises in dramatic technique, but bold attacks on an idea. They are simple to the point of bareness, unsubtle, unadorned.

Unemployment starts in this way:

(*The stage is empty. One worker walks slowly across. His head is bowed. After a moment another worker follows him. One after another the whole group of workers comes out and walks to and fro on the stage.*)

1 WORKER: I am hungry.
2 WORKER: My family is hungry.
3 WORKER: I want to work.
4 WORKER: I want a job.
5 WORKER: Won't somebody give me a job?
1 WORKER: I am hungry, why can't I have food? I see lots of food in restaurants. I am cold, why can't I have a coat? I see many coats in clothing stores.

(*Capitalist comes in, sits in chair, takes up phone, listens, laughs.*)

CAPITALIST: There isn't anyone can have a better yacht than I. I've got to have the best little yacht in the world. I want special attention paid to the bar . . . what's that damn noise out there?
SERVANT: Master, it is the unemployed complaining—etc.

Perhaps because they are unconcerned with style, these worker-writers achieve the beginning of a distinct style. One sees in such plays as *What Price Goal, It's as Funny as Hell, Men of Steel, The Great Money Trick, Mr. God Is Not In*, a direct, terse, hard hitting phraseology, a machine gun repetition, a sharp, type analysis with no individual characterization, and a climax often ending in a mass demonstration. Take, for example, the end of *Lynch Law*: You have seen in the earlier part of the play the frame up of innocent negroes for a crime they did not commit; the judge, after he has convicted them of murder and sentenced them to die, sits in his office and receives congratulations:

BUSINESS MAN (*rushing in, shaking judge's hand*): Congratulations! You won't let the negroes get away?
JUDGE: There is no court in Alabama that will let them get away.

MASS CHORUS OFF STAGE: Workers, unite to smash the Scottsboro frame up!

D.A.R.: (*rushes in*) Congratulations, Judge! You will always uphold southern traditions of justice.

JUDGE: Niggers must be taught to respect southern justice.

MASS CHORUS OFF STAGE: Southern justice is boss class justice! Workers, negro and white, unite to smash the Scottsboro frame up!

KU KLUX KLAN: Congratulations! Congratulations! You will teach the nigger to know his place.

JUDGE: Niggers must be taught to respect law and order.

MASS CHORUS OFF STAGE: Fight for the rights of the oppressed negro worker! Smash the Scottsboro frame up!

VISITOR: Congratulations! You have set a dignified example for the rest of America.

JUDGE: Niggers must be taught to know their place. Our institutions must uphold the supremacy of the white man.

(*Tableau of Judge and his lackeys on stage.*)

MASS CHORUS OFF STAGE: United Front to smash the Scottsboro frame up!
Organize! Unite and fight!
Smash the Scottsboro frame up!
Smash the Scottsboro frame up!
Smash the Scottsboro frame up!

So far I have found no indication in the plays I have read or seen or heard described by workers, of any aspect of workers' life except that of revolt; there is not, as in Russia, a glorification of the splendor of work or of the strength of the worker. Occasionally there is slapstick humor, as in *The Big Stiff*, in which you see Uncle Sam in bed with a swollen stomach, which Dr. Hoover, without much success, tries to relieve. The treatment of economic and industrial themes, aside from some burlesque of the upper classes, is deadly serious, perhaps because people who are hungry are not apt to be humorous about the situation.

The power of these theatres springing up everywhere throughout the country lies in the fact that they know what they want. Their purpose—restricted, some will call it, though it is open to question whether any theatre which attempts to create a class culture can be called restricted—is clear. This is important because there are only two theatres in the country today that are clear as to aim: one is the commercial theatre which wants to make money; the other is the workers' theatre which wants to make a new social order.

The workers' theatres are neither infirm nor divided in purpose. Unlike any art form existing in America today, the workers' theatres intend to shape the life of this country, socially, politically, and industrially. They intend to remake a social structure without the help of money—and this ambition alone invests their undertaking with a certain Marlowesque madness.

When we see, as we probably shall during the next year, their street plays and pageants, their performances on trucks and on street corners, we shall doubtless find them crude, violent, childish, and repetitious. Yet we must admit that here is a theatre which can afford to be supremely unconcerned with what we think of it. It does not ask our advice, our interest, our advertising, or our money. We need not deplore the lack of art in the workers' theatre for we shall not be invited to witness its performances. It is only in the event of the success of its herculean aim—the reorganization of our social order—that we shall become involuntary audience.

14.3 SCOTTSBORO POEMS—LANGSTON HUGHES

Justice

That Justice is a blind goddess
Is a thing to which we black are wise.
Her bandage hides two festering sores
That once perhaps were eyes.

The Town of Scottsboro

Scottsboro's just a little place:
No shame is writ across its face—
Its courts too weak to stand against a mob,
Its people's heart, too small to hold a sob.

14.4 COVER OF *SCOTTSBORO, LIMITED*—PRENTISS TAYLOR

Cover of Langston Hughes' *Scottsboro Limited, Four Poems and a Play in Verse*. Hughes, sympathetic to the plight of the Scottsboro Boys, visited Kilby Prison in Montgomery where eight of the nine defendants were held in 1932. Hughes advocated with his pen for the young men, as did the American Communist Party with their legal team. In *Scottsboro*, Hughes, using communist ideology, connected racial and class lines by comparing the struggles of the Scottsboro Boys to the white oppressed underclass, and called for class solidarity.

Source: © The estate of Prentiss Taylor, used with permission

14.5 *SCOTTSBORO, LIMITED*—LANGSTON HUGHES

HUGHES BEGAN HIS INVOLVEMENT with the Left in the 1920s, when he started to publish in such Leftist journals as *New Masses* and to associate with various radical causes taken up by both black and white writers of the period, most notably that of convicted murderers Nicola Sacco and Bartolomeo Vanzetti. By 1931, Hughes's work was appearing with great frequency in *New Masses*, as well as in other publications connected with the American Communist Party (CPUSA).

The subject of this play is the Scottsboro case, which involved nine black youths in Alabama who, in the spring of 1931, were convicted of rape on flimsy evidence; eight were sentenced to execution and one to life imprisonment. Later a cause célèbre, the Scottsboro case profoundly concerned Hughes from the beginning, and his commitment to the Left deepened when the International Labor Defense, the legal arm of the CPUSA, took up the defense after the NAACP failed to do so. Written during the fall of 1931, *Scottsboro, Limited* is classic agitprop: its concise analysis of its subject, rhythmic language and choreographed movement, audience involvement, and final call for action are all typical of the form.

Scottsboro, Limited was first performed in Los Angeles on May 8, 1932, an earlier production having been prevented by the police. It was also produced in Paris and in Moscow and translated into Russian during Hughes's Moscow visit later that year. The version given here is the one that appeared in *New Masses* in October 1931.

Characters

EIGHT BLACK BOYS
A WHITE MAN
TWO WHITE WOMEN
EIGHT WHITE WORKERS
VOICES IN THE AUDIENCE

SETTING: *One chair on a raised platform. No curtains or other effects needed.*

THE PLAY OPENS: *The eight* BLACK BOYS, *chained by the right foot, one to the other, walk slowly down the center aisle from the back of the auditorium. As they approach the middle of the house, there is a loud commotion, and the* WHITE MAN *rises in the audience.*

MAN: (*To* BOYS) What are you doing here? (*The* BLACK BOYS *continue marching without turning their heads. The* MAN *shouts louder, and more sternly.*) What are you-all doing in here? (*As the* BOYS *mount the stage, the* MAN *rushes up to them threateningly.*) What the hell are you doing in here, I said?

1ST BOY: (*Turning simply*)
We come in our chains
To show our pain.

MAN: (*Sneeringly*) Your pain! Stop talking poetry and talk sense.

8TH BOY: (*As they line up on the stage*)
All right, we will—
That sense of injustice
That death can't kill.

MAN: Injustice? What d'yuh mean? Talking about injustice, you coon?

2ND BOY: (*Pointing to his comrades*)

Look at us then:
Poor, black, and ignorant,
Can't read or write—
But we come here tonight.

MAN: (*Sitting down jauntily on the edge of stage*) Not supposed to read or write. You work better without it.

1ST BOY: (*Shrugging his shoulders*)
O.K. Chief,
We won't argue with you.
Tonight there's
Too much else to do.

MAN: Now that you got the public eye, you want to show off, heh?

2ND BOY: (*Seriously*) Not show off—die!

5TH BOY: (*Earnestly*)
So the people can see
What it means to be
A poor black workman
In this land of the free.

2ND BOY: (*Harshly*)
Where every star in the flag
Is stained with a lie!

MAN: Do you want to get arrested for treason?

8TH BOY:
We're already in jail.
Have you got a darker cell
Any worse
Than this-here Southern Hell?

7TH BOY: Can a man die twice?

MAN: You-all ain't dead.

8TH BOY: (*Defiantly*)
No, but we will be dead
If we stay quiet here.
That's why we come tonight
To lift our troubles high.
Like a flag against the sky.

2ND BOY:
To show that we're living—
Even though we die.

3RD BOY:
To let the world see
That even in chains
We will be free!

4TH BOY: Watch this play for our misery:

(*The chains break away, and the* BOYS *find themselves on a moving freight train. They sit down in a haphazard line on the stage, as though they were seated on the top of boxcars, rocking back and forth as the train moves.*)

6TH BOY: (*Happily*)
Man this train sho is speedin'!
Look a-yonder at de Sunny South.

4TH BOY:
I wish I had some sugar cane in ma mouth.
I'se hongry!

7TH BOY:
Well it's sho too bad
How when you ain't got no job
Things get sad.

5TH BOY:
I ain't got no job.

1ST BOY: Neither is I, but I wish I had.

2ND BOY: Looks like white folks is taking all de work.

5TH BOY: Is niggers got *exclusive* rights on work?

3RD BOY: Shut up, boy!

4TH BOY: He ain't joking, Perk.

2ND BOY:
All them little town jobs we used to do,
Looks like white folks is doin' 'em now, too.

1ST BOY: Just goes to prove there ain't no pure nigger work.

6TH BOY: (*In wonder*)
Look a-yonder you-all, at dem fields
Burstin' wid de crops they yields.
Who gets it all?

3RD BOY: White folks.

8TH BOY: You means de rich white folks.

2ND BOY:
Yes, 'cause de rich ones owns de land.
And they don't care nothin' 'bout de po' white man.

3RD BOY:
You's right. Crackers is just like me—
Po' whites and niggers, ain't neither one free.

8TH BOY: Have to work like a fool to live and then you starve dead.

4TH BOY: Man, this country is sho too bad! (*The train stops and the rocking motion of the* BOYS *ceases. One or two of them get up and stretch.*)

3RD BOY: Uh-O! This train done stopped. Where is this?

7TH BOY: Well, wherever it is, I'm gonna take a—. (*Turning his back.*)

5TH BOY: No, you ain't. Can't you see this is a town?

MAN: (*As* SHERIFF, *at foot of stage, with a police star and a club*) Come on, you niggers, and get down.

6TH BOY: Uh-ooooo! Yonder stands the sheriff.

2ND BOY: Ha-ha-ha! Uh!

3RD BOY: Fool, this ain't no time to laugh.

SHERIFF: Come on and get down off that train!

6TH BOY: Yes, sir, Mister Boss Man!

4TH BOY: Soon's we can. (*The* BOYS *climb down.*)

SHERIFF: (*To* BOYS *who line up before him*) What you-all doin' on that train?

BOYS:
Just tryin' to bum our way on through
To Memphis where maybe there's work to do.

SHERIFF: (*Yelling up the line*) Get everybody off this train, deputy. (*To* BOYS) Stand over there, boys. (*Shouting to deputy*) What you say? Some girls getting off dressed in overalls? White girls? (*To himself*) Whee-oooo! (*To the* BOYS) What you-all doin' on the same train with them white women there?

BOYS: (*In wonder*) Where?

SHERIFF: There!

BOYS: Where?

SHERIFF: (*Fiercely*) You'll see where! Get back and let these white ladies by.

(*While the succeeding action goes on the* BOYS *get behind the chair, four on each side in a line—convicts already.*)

MOB VOICES IN AUDIENCE: (*Murmuring and muttering*) Damned niggers . . . white girls and niggers riding together . . . nerve of them niggers . . . had no business in there . . . etc.

SHERIFF: (*As the two white* GIRLS *enter left, powdered and painted, but dressed in overalls.*) What you doin', girls? Out for a ride?

1ST GIRL: Yes sir.

SHERIFF: Where to?

1ST GIRL: Goin' home, I reckon.

SHERIFF: Where?

2ND GIRL: Huntsville.

SHERIFF: And these niggers on the train with you!

1ST GIRL: Ain't seen 'em before.

SHERIFF: Ain't these black brutes been botherin' you?

GIRLS: No, they ain't been near.

SHERIFF: Is that true? (*Sternly*) Ain't they had their hands on you?

GIRLS: (*Wavering*) Well, they . . . er . . .

SHERIFF: (*Positively*) I knew it! Which one of these black apes touched you?

GIRLS: Why . . . er . . .

SHERIFF: We'll have a trial and burn 'em up. And you'll get paid for testifying, and your pictures in the paper. Which ones?

1ST GIRL: That two there.

SHERIFF: Two? You sho it wasn't more?

2ND GIRL: No, we ain't sure.

1ST GIRL: It might-a been all right.

SHERIFF: All right? A trial's too good for black bastards like that. (*Pompously*) But we owe it to the state.

(*He parades sternly up to the raised chair. He is the judge now and, as he mounts the legal bench, he puts on a black gown that has been lying there. The* GIRLS *slip off their overalls, displaying cheap loud dresses underneath, and powder their faces tittering. It is the court room, and the black prisoners come forward before the judge. The trial is conducted in jazz tempo: the white voices staccato, high and shrill; the black voices deep as the rumble of drums.*)

MOB VOICES: (*Murmuring*) Imagine a trial for niggers . . . a trial for niggers . . . a trial for niggers . . . etc.

JUDGE: (*From the chair*) The State of Alabama versus Andy Butler, Willie Johnson, Clarence Bates, Olen Jones, Ozie Jenkins, Roy Perkins, Ted Lucas, and Haywood Lane. (*The* GIRLS *sit, one on either side of the stage, grinning and pleased*) You raped that girl? (*Pointing at each boy in turn.*)

1ST BOY: No.

JUDGE: You raped that girl? (*Pointing from one girl to the other in rotation.*)

2ND BOY: No.

JUDGE: You raped that girl?

3RD BOY: No.

JUDGE: You raped that girl?

4TH BOY: No.

JUDGE: You raped that girl?

5TH BOY: No.

JUDGE: You raped that girl?

6TH BOY: No.

JUDGE: You raped that girl?

7TH BOY: No.

JUDGE: You raped that girl?

8TH BOY: No.

JUDGE: (*To* GIRLS) How about it girls?

1ST GIRL: They lie!

2ND GIRL: They raped us in a box car underneath the sky.

JUDGE: You niggers lie.

BOYS: We lie . . . White man always says we lie. . . . Makes us work and says we lie . . . Takes our money and says we lie.

JUDGE: Shut up. No talking back in the court. (*Pointing at each one in turn*) You had a gun.

1ST BOY: No.

JUDGE: You had a gun.

2ND BOY: No, sir.

JUDGE: You had a gun.

3RD BOY: (*Shaking head*) Not one.

JUDGE: You had a gun.

4TH BOY: Not nary one.

JUDGE: You had a gun.

5TH BOY: We didn't have none.

JUDGE: You had a gun.

6TH BOY: No gun.

JUDGE: You had a gun!

7TH BOY: No, sir, none.

JUDGE: You had a gun.

8TH BOY: No gun.

JUDGE: How about it, girls?

1ST GIRL: They lie.

2ND GIRL: They all had guns.

JUDGE: (*To BOYS*) You all had guns. (*To GIRLS*) And they raped you, one by one. (*GIRLS nod heads*) How long did it take? How long was it?

1ST GIRL: Why they didn't even let us up to spit!

2ND GIRL: It was rough!

JUDGE: To spit what?

GIRLS: Snuff!

JUDGE: You hear that, Jury? This court is done.

1ST GIRL: Convict these brutes. (*Smiling at audience.*)

2ND GIRL: Every black one. (*Also smiling*)

MOB VOICES: Convict 'em! Ever damn black one!

JUDGE: Don't worry, folks, 'tis done.

MOB VOICES: Kill the niggers! Keep 'em in their places! Make an example of 'm for all the black races . . . etc.

BOYS: (*Rising and circling round and round the chair echoing the angry mob*) Kill the niggers! Keep them in their places! Make an example of 'em for all the black races, for all the black races, for all the black races.

JUDGE: (*Descending from the bench, to audience*) Don't worry folks, the law will take its course. They'll burn, and soon at that.

(*He and the GIRLS exit, talking and smiling*)

MOB VOICES: (*Applauding and shouting*) Make it soon. Kill the niggers. Let 'em die.

BOYS: (*Echoing the Voices*) Make it soon. Let us die. Make it soon. Soon. Soon.

6TH BOY: (*Breaking away from the dumb circle*) No, no, no! What do they want to kill us for?

3RD BOY: I'll break free!

(*The BOYS divide up into groups of two's now, in a row across the stage, in the cells of the death house, some of them sitting down, some of them weeping, some of them pushing against the bars with their hands.*)

2ND BOY:
How you gonna git out o' here
With these iron bars and this stone wall
And the guards outside and the
Guns and all?

8TH BOY:
There ain't no way for a nigger to break free,
They got us beaten, and that's how we gonna be
Unless we learn to understand—
We gotta fight our way out like a man.

5TH BOY: Not out o' here.

4TH BOY:
No, not out o' here,
Unless the ones on the outside
Fight for us, too,
We'll die—and then we'll be through.

MOB VOICES:
You oughta be through—
Oughta be through.
In this white man's land
There's no place for you.

MURMUR OF RED VOICES: (*In audience*)
We'll fight for you, boys. We'll fight for you.
The Reds will fight for you.

6TH BOY:
We'll die, and then we'll all be through—
Through livin', through lovin', through lookin' at the sky.
I don't wanta die.

8TH BOY:
Who does want to die?
That's why all the free black men
Have got to fight,
Or else we'll all die in poverty's night.

3RD BOY: You're right.

RED VOICES:
We'll fight! The Communists will fight for you.
Not just black—but black and white.

3RD BOY: Then we'll trust in you.

MAN: (*Become the PRISON KEEPER now, marching across the front of the cell-row with a long stick in his hand.*)
Shut up in there, with your plots and plans.
Don't you niggers know yet this is a white man's land?
And I'm the keeper, understand.

8TH BOY:
We ain't half as low as you!
Paid to kill people, that's what you do.
Not just niggers—but your white brothers too.

RED VOICES: (*Stronger now*)
That's true! True!

PRISON KEEPER: (*Striking boy*) Shut up!

8TH BOY:
I won't shut up.
I've nobody to talk for me,
So I'll talk for myself, see.

RED VOICES: And the red flag, too, will talk for you.

1ST BOY:
Listen, boys! That's true—they've sent a lawyer to talk for me and you.

6TH BOY: But they told us not to bother with a communist.

8TH BOY: But who else is there will help us out o' this?

3RD BOY:
And not just us, but help all the black South
Hungry for freedom, and bread, and new words in their mouth.

MAN: (*Entering this time as a PREACHER, sanctified, with a Bible in his hand.*)
Ashes to ashes and dust to dust—

If the law don't kill you then the lynchers must.
(*Piously*) I've come to say a little prayer
Before you go away from here.

3RD BOY: (*Questioning*)
A prayer to a white God in a white sky?
We don't want that kind of prayer to die.

6TH BOY:
I want a prayer!

(*The Death Bell rings*)

Oh, Lord, I want a prayer.

8TH BOY:
No prayer! No prayer!
Lemme out o' here.
Take me on to the chair
With no God damn prayer.

(*To the* PREACHER)

May they choke in your mouth,
Every praying white lie!

PREACHER: (*In horror, hurrying out*) Let the niggers die!

MOB VOICES: Let 'em die!

8TH BOY: (*Starting on the march to the chair, walking straight across the stage to the center, then turning, straight back to the Electric Chair where he seats himself, unafraid, slipping his hands into the cords that bind him to the arms of the chair.*)
Because I talked out loud, you kill me first:
Death in the flesh is the fighters curse.

MOB VOICES: Yes, you must die! Let the nigger die! Let all of 'em die!

8TH BOY:
Let all of us die:
That's what the mobs cry.
All I've ever known:
Let the niggers die!
All my life long:
Let the niggers die!

BOYS: (*Helplessly crouching back at the foot of chair.*)
Let us die! Let us die!

MOB VOICES:
Let 'em die!
Beat 'em! Shoot 'em!
Hang 'em with a rope,
Burn 'em in the chair.
Let 'em choke.

BOYS:
Burn us in the chair!
The chair! The Chair!
Burn us in the chair!

8TH BOY:
Burn *me* in the chair?
NO!

(*He breaks his bonds and rises, tall and strong.*)

NO! For me not so!
Let the meek and humble turn the other cheek—
I am not humble!
I am not meek!
From the mouth of the death house
Hear me speak!

RED VOICES: Hear him speak! Hear him speak!

MOB VOICES: Shut up, you God-damn nigger!

RED VOICES: Hear him speak!

BOYS: Hear us speak!

8TH BOY:
All the world, listen!
Beneath the wide sky
In all the black lands
Will echo this cry:
I will not die!

BOYS: We will NOT DIE!

MOB VOICES: (*Snarling*)
Quick! Quick! Death there!
The chair! The electric chair!

8TH BOY:
No chair!
Too long have my hands been idle
Too long have my brains been dumb.
Now out of the darkness
The new Red Negro will come:
That's me!
No death in the chair!

BOYS: (*Rising*) No death in the chair!

RED VOICES: (*Rising in audience*) NO DEATH IN THE CHAIR!

BOYS: NO DEATH IN THE CHAIR! (*They circle platform and lifting the electric chair up, they smash it on the stage.*) NO DEATH IN THE CHAIR!

MOB VOICES: (*Roaring helplessly*) Aw-w-w-w-ooo-aw!

RED VOICES:
No death in the chair.
Together, we'll make the world clean and fair.

8TH BOY:
Too long have we stood
For the whip and the rope.

RED VOICES: Too long! Too long!

8TH BOY:
Too long have we labored
Poor, without hope.

BOYS: Too long!

RED VOICES: Too long!

8TH BOY:
Too long have we suffered
Alone.

BOYS: Alone!

8TH BOY: But not now!
RED VOICES: No, not now.
8TH BOY:
The voice of the red world
Is our voice, too.
RED VOICES: The voice of the red world *is* you!
8TH BOY:
The hands of the red world
Are our hands, too.
RED VOICES: The hands of the red world *are* you!
8TH BOY:
With all of the workers,
Black or white,
We'll go forward
Out of the night.
BOYS: Out of the night.
8TH BOY
Breaking down bars,
Together.
BOYS: Together.
RED VOICES: Together. (*The* RED VOICES *of the white workers come forward toward the stage.*)
BOYS: (*Breaking their bars and coming forward toward the front of the stage to meet their white comrades*) Seeking the stars!
RED VOICES: Seeking the stars of hope and life.
8TH BOY: Not afraid of the struggle.
BOYS: Not afraid of the strife.
RED VOICES: Not afraid to fight:
8TH BOY: For new life!
BOYS: New life!
RED VOICES: New life!

(*The white workers and black workers meet on the stage*)

BOYS: Comrades!
RED VOICES: Comrades!

(*They clasp hands and line up in a row of alternating blacks and whites.*)

BOYS: Joining hands to build the right.
RED VOICES: White and black!
BOYS: Black and white!
8TH BOY: To live, not die!
ALL: To fight! To fight!
8TH BOY:
In the heart of a fighter, death is a lie:
O, my black people, you need not die!
RED VOICES: All the down trodden—you need not die!
AUDIENCE: We need not die! We need not die!
8TH BOY:
Black and white together
Will fight the great fight
To put greed and pain
And the color line's blight
Out of the world
Into time's old night.
BOYS AND REDS: All hands together will furnish the might.
AUDIENCE: All hands together will furnish the might.
RED VOICES: Rise from the dead, workers, and fight!
BOYS:
All together, black and white,
Up from the darkness into the light.
ALL: Rise, workers, and fight!
AUDIENCE: Fight! Fight! Fight! Fight!

★

(*Here the* Internationale *may be sung and the red flag raised above the heads of the black and white workers together.*)

THE END

ADDENDUM:

The Internationale

Arise ye workers from your slumbers
Arise ye prisoners of want
For reason in revolt now thunders
And at last ends the age of cant.
Away with all your superstitions
Servile masses arise, arise
We'll change henceforth the old tradition
And spurn the dust to win the prize.

Refrain:
So comrades, come rally
And the last fight let us face
The Internationale unites the human race.

No more deluded by reaction
On tyrants only we'll make war
The soldiers too will take strike action
They'll break ranks and fight no more
And if those cannibals keep trying
To sacrifice us to their pride
They soon shall hear the bullets flying
We'll shoot the generals on our own side.

No saviour from on high delivers
No faith have we in prince or peer
Our own right hand the chains must shiver
Chains of hatred, greed and fear
E'er the thieves will out with their booty
And give to all a happier lot.
Each at the forge must do their duty
And we'll strike while the iron is hot.

15. *Waiting for Lefty*—Clifford Odets

Commentary

Sources

Play

15.1 EXCERPTS FROM *THE FERVENT YEARS: THE STORY OF THE GROUP THEATRE AND THE THIRTIES*—HAROLD CLURMAN

THERE WERE ONLY NINE MEMBERS of the Group company in Clifford Odet's *Awake and Sing*. Most of the others were busy with rehearsals of *Waiting for Lefty* under the direction of Sanford Maiser and Clifford Odets. It was to be given at a benefit for the *New Theatre Magazine*, unofficial organ of the new insurgent movement in the theatre.

Sunday night, January 5, 1935, at the old Civic Repertory Theatre on Fourteenth Street, an event took place to be noted in the annals of the American theatre. The evening had opened with a mildly amusing one-act play by Paul Green. The audience, though attracted by the guest appearance of a good part of the Group company, had no idea of what was to follow.

The first scene of *Lefty* had not played two minutes when a shock of delighted recognition struck the audience like a tidal wave. Deep laughter, hot assent, a kind of joyous fervor seemed to sweep the audience toward the stage. The actors no longer performed; they were being carried along as if by an exultancy of communication such as I had never witnessed in the theatre before. Audience and actors had become one. Line after line brought applause, whistles, bravos, and heartfelt shouts of kinship.

The taxi strike of February 1934 had been a minor incident in the labor crisis of this period. There were very few taxi-drivers in that first audience, I am sure; very few indeed who had ever been directly connected with such an event as the union meeting that provided the play its pivotal situation. When the audience at the end of the play responded to the militant question from the stage: "Well, what's the answer?" with a spontaneous roar of "Strike! Strike!" it was something more than a tribute to the play's effectiveness, more even than a testimony of the audience's hunger for constructive social action. It was the birth cry of the thirties. Our youth had found its voice. It was a call to join the good fight for a greater measure of life in a world free of economic fear, falsehood, and craven servitude to stupidity and greed. "Strike!" was *Lefty*'s lyric message, not alone for a few extra pennies of wages or for shorter hours of work, strike for greater dignity, strike for a bolder humanity, strike for the full stature of man.

The audience, I say, was delirious. It stormed the stage, which I persuaded the stunned author to mount. People went from the theatre dazed and happy: a new awareness and confidence had entered their lives.

A series of *Lefty* performances was given every Sunday thereafter at the Civic Repertory Theatre—all of them benefits. Finally on February 10 the press was invited to see *Lefty*, given together with the Group's experimental sketches.

The reviewers liked *Lefty* very much. At this time, after the Theatre Union had done three productions, and the Jewish workers' group known as Artef had won a degree of esoteric fame, one or two commentators noted that "the progress of the revolutionary drama in New York City during the last two seasons is the most recent development in the theatre."

[. . .]

Odets became the central figure of the so-called Left movement in the theatre. But the relation of his work to Marxism or Communism was of a special sort not to be understood in terms of glib political commentary. The Marxist drift of the thirties no more "caused" *Lefty* or *Awake and Sing* in January and February of 1935 than *Lefty* and *Awake and Sing* caused the organization of the CIO in November of that year. All these phenomena, including also the NRA and the later acts of the New Deal (the National Labor Act and so on), were an outgrowth of and a response to a common dislocation that convulsed our whole society. They were all undoubtedly related, but they are by no means comprehensible if they are lumped together mechanically as if they were identical.

Odets's work from the beginning contained "a protest that is also prophecy." There was in it a fervor that derived from the hope and expectation of change and the desire for it. But there was rarely any expression of political consciousness in it, no deep commitment to a coherent philosophy of life, no pleading for a panacea. "A tendril of revolt" runs through all of Odets's work, but that is not the same thing as a consistent revolutionary conviction. Odets's work is not even proletarian in the sense that Gorky's work is. Rather is it profoundly of the lower middle class with all its vacillation, dual allegiance, fears, groping, self-distrust, dejection, spurts of energy, hosannas, vows of conversion, and prayers for release. The "enlightenment" of the thirties, its effort to come to a clearer understanding of and control over the anarchy of our society, brought Odets a new mental perspective, but it is his emotional experience, not his thought, that gives his plays their special expressiveness and significance. His thought, the product chiefly of his four years with the Group and the new channels they led to, furnished Odets with the more conscious bits of his vocabulary, with an occasional epithet or slogan that were never fully integrated in his work. The feel of middle-class (and perhaps universal) disquiet in Odets's plays is sharp and specific; the ideas are general and hortatory. The Left movement provided Odets with a platform and a loud-speaker; the music that came through was that of a vast population of restive souls, unaware of its own mind, seeking help. To this Odets added the determination of youth. The quality of his plays is young, lyrical, yearning—as of someone on the threshold of life.

It was nonsense for the New York *Sun*'s reviewer, in order to challenge the validity of *Lefty*, to check with a taxidriver on his average earnings. *Lefty* was not basically about the hackman's low wages, but about every impediment to that full life for which youth hungers. Hence the play's wide appeal.

Perhaps Odets privately harbored the belief that socialism offers the only solution for our social-economic problems. Perhaps his desire to share a comradely closeness to his fellowmen might attract him to those who hoped to bring about a socialist society, but he must also have suspected that temperamentally he might prove a trial to any well-knit party. Instead of being an adherent of a fixed program, a disciplined devotee of a set strategy or system, Odets possessed a talent that always had an ambiguous character. If because of all this the regular press was misled into chatter about his "Marxism" while the Left press was frankly perplexed and troubled by him, it may also be guessed that Odets too was pretty much in the dark on this score.

On the one hand, Odets felt himself very close to the people—the great majority of Americans—even in his bent for the "good old theatre"; on the other hand, his heart was always with the rebels. But who precisely were the rebels, and what did they demand of him? Those he knew were a small minority, and they marked out a line for him that he could not altogether accept. After the first flurry of Odets's success had passed, everyone discovered a "change" in him. The conventional reviewers were glad; the Left was disconcerted. But, in the sense they had in mind, both were wrong—Odets had not changed.

Perhaps the truth is that the vast majority, to which Odets felt he belonged as much as to any rebellious few, had not yet created for itself a cultural clarity or form, not to speak of other kinds of clarity or form—had not, for example, yet made for itself a theatre in which he could function freely. Perhaps the "few" who often criticized him more harshly than anyone else did not know how much they had in common with those they professed to scorn.

Whatever later wisdom might declare, Odets in the spring of 1935 was the man of the hour. Theatrically speaking, the climax of the Odets vogue came with the production of *Lefty* as a regular show on Broadway.

Since *Lefty* was only an hour long, we had to have a companion piece to go with it. Odets himself supplied this by dramatizing a short story purporting to be a letter from Nazi Germany he had read in the *New Masses*. The play, written to order, was finished in less than a week. Cheryl Crawford directed it, and the setting was designed by an unofficial Group apprentice, Paul Morison, who had performed similar services for us at Green Mansions.

This twin bill opened at the Longacre Theatre on March 26, 1935 at a price range from fifty cents to a dollar and a half—something of an innovation on Broadway.

In order not to disturb disturb the casting of *Awake and Sing*, all the actors not engaged in that play took over the production of *Lefty* and *Till the Day I Die*, which, incidentally, was one of the first serious anti-Nazi plays to reach the New York stage.

Odets himself played Dr. Benjamin in *Lefty* (originally played by Luther Adler), and on opening night his appearance was greeted by an ovation. This was the last acting assignment of his career. Lee Strasberg under an assumed name played a small part in the anti-Nazi play. In the new *Lefty* cast Elia Kazan, replacing Bromberg, was thunderously effective. Everyone was sure we had picked him off a taxi to play the part—our "discovery" from Constantinople, Williams College, and Yale!

New theatre societies were being formed all over the country to give the three Odets plays. Group Theatres shot up like mushrooms: in Chicago, Hollywood, New Orleans, San Francisco. A Negro People's Theatre was set up in Harlem to give *Lefty* under the direction of our own Bill Challee. All in all, *Lefty* was being done in some 60 towns, which had never before witnessed a theatrical performance. Thirty-two cities were seeing the twin bill of *Lefty* and *Till the Day I Die* at the same time.

Even suppressions, bans, arrests on the grounds of "unlawful assembly" or "profanity," served to increase the play's prestige. These occurred in Philadelphia, Boston, New Haven, Newark, Dorchester, Chelsea, and Roxbury.

15.2 REVIEW OF *WAITING FOR LEFTY*—STANLEY BURNSHAW

New Masses, January 29th 1935

ON JAN. 5, WHEN THE CURTAIN RANG DOWN on the first performance of Clifford Odets' *Waiting for Lefty* the audience cheered, whistled and screamed with applause. One week later when the same actors had repeated their performance, the Fifth Avenue Theatre, packed to capacity with hundreds of standees, fairly burst with a thunder of hand-claps and shouting. A valuable new play had been written into the history of the American revolutionary theatre, a dramatic work with roots coiled about an actual event in the life of the New York proletariat. (It was Joe Gilbert, Secretary of the Taxi Drivers' Union, who emerged from the wings to say that just such a meeting as Odets presents took place last March when members of the Union met in the Bronx and overwhelmingly voted to strike.)

And yet the audience went away not altogether sure that it was a play that had electrified them to the marrow. Some of them referred to it as an unforgettable experience but a disjointed, structurally arbitrary piece of playwriting, in which the union meeting was a convenient device for tying together dramatically unintegrated scenes. The actors felt no such flaw. Intoxicated by the tension of the rapid, compact episodes, they forgot to pull their punches during the tussles. The spectator, however, may feel uncertain that the play is a dramatic entity. But a second seeing provides sufficient perspective for discerning in the juxtaposition of scenes a clear logic binding them into a solid, dramatic whole.

The first of the eight scenes opens on the union meeting. At once the audience is tied into the action as members of the strike meeting shout from the floor to the speakers on the stage who address not one another, but the entire house. A slick union misleader tries to pour oily words on the rebellious rank and file who challenge him from the floor and riddle his pussyfooting periods with pungent, hard-boiled guffaws. Confident that they can carry the decision to strike, they are marking time, awaiting the arrival of their spokesman, Lefty. But Lefty is still absent. One of them, Joe Mitchell, demands the floor. He wants to tell what happened to him. And as he begins to talk the setting blends into a new scene where his story is acted.

It is brief, turbulent, final. Bringing home his miserable earnings and expecting sympathy from his wife, he receives her icy scorn instead. She is through with her wretched existence, and through with a man too yellow to do anything about it. Faced with losing his wife or fighting for a decent life for her and his children, he is momentarily lost before these iron alternatives. In a scene packed with intensity and knife-like dialogue, he rises to the one decision and runs off to join his comrades in the call for strike.

Suddenly the audience discovers a chemistry worker in the office of his employer. He is given a raise. Learning that his researches are used for war chemistry he is racked by the memory of his brother murdered by the last war. Yet needing the money, he accepts. When he is told his job includes spying on a fellow worker, the hate that has been rising during the interview seizes upon him. He lashes his employer with insinuations which glance off the latter who shrugs and retorts with suave cynicism. Finally, no longer able to bridle his fury, he drives his fist into his enemy's face. This young worker, facing alternatives essentially analogous to those which confronted Joe Mitchell in the previous scene, struggles to reach a decision—and arrives at exactly the same conclusion that Mitchell reached in the previous scene. So far the playwright has shown a typical segment of taxi-workers in their evolution toward militancy and he has emphasized its emotional and ideological significance by extending this situation to another locale of the class-struggle. The dramatic parenthesis which Scene III affords is far more than a flash-back: it is a broadening of the scope of the play by an authentic and original departure in dramatic form.

In the scenes that follow the same method may be discerned. A young hackie at his sweetheart's home. Three years of waiting and working (she is a sales-clerk) but no better off today! He has finally determined to give her up rather than marry her into a starvation existence. To cover up his suffering he tries to dance, wisecrack, buffoon—but both of them break down. In a frantic attempt to make out why they are being sacrificed, they grope with pathetic generalizations. This masterly scene compresses into a few minutes of dialogue and action the pain inflicted on millions of American workers who are unaware of the pitiless logic of their positions in a system responsible for their tragedies. The parenthesis to this episode follows as Scene V: the office of a casting director living islanded in decadence. An actor as much at sea about the world as the hackie of the previous scene tries to get a job and fails. But the parallel between these two situations is made dynamic. Before turning from the office in bewildered despair, the young actor runs into a fusillade of words from the secretary, a class-conscious worker who tries to telescope her whole revolutionary philosophy into a half-dozen speedy sentences.

Ordinarily her sloganizing would seem mechanical and flat, but coming after a previous scene whose power was built with nuances of action and understatement, the oversimplified speech manages to carry. From the viewpoint of structure it ties into the next scene: the strike meeting which is still waiting for Lefty. The audience long identified as witnesses at the meeting where it has heard individual stories of the rank and file, now watches the union's misleader pull out his trump card. He brings on Clancy, who's going to tell from his own experience in Philadelphia just why strikes don't work. But before Clancy lets drop many lies, one of the rank and file leaps up from the audience and runs to the platform to accuse him of being a paid company agent with a long strike-breaking record. The ensuing physical clash that threatens the meeting is dramatically resolved in one taut moment: the accuser reveals that he has been exposing his own brother.

During this scene the rank and file workers emerge from under the smooth lies of their opponents whom they begin to recognize as such. They are fiercely determined on straightforward action. And in the parenthetical scene that follows, the same progression is traced. An interne, whose patient has been killed by an incompetent colleague with "influence," demands an explanation. His elderly chief, who has watched corruption strangle scientific work throughout his career, tells him more than he bargained for, among others things that he is fired—retrenchment closes the charity ward first! With studied moderation he manages to channel the interne's sputtering rebelliousness into the direction of organized militancy.

By the opening of the final scene, therefore, the clear revolutionary path has been exposed; now it is up to the union membership to take it. Through a brief scene of rapid-fire action the rank and file rises in an uncompromising body, to demand "Where is Lefty?" When one of their number rushes in with the news that Lefty has been found murdered they don't wait to ask who ordered the job, or if it was a cold-blooded effort to abort the strike. Flaunting the doublecrossers, who no longer try to protest, a rank and filer immediately assumes the role left vacant for Lefty. In an electric appeal to the meeting he demands that it vote to strike, and the play ends with the whole house—actors and audience—yelling "Strike, strike, strike!"

The terrific emotional drive of the play as a unit is more than the total effectiveness of the eight scenes. Here the whole is decidedly more than the sum of its parts. In fact some of the weaker scenes derive added power from their position in the thematic development. This does not mean that they could not be profitably strengthened. The encounter between the casting director's secretary and the semi-stunned actor is elliptical; that the audience accepts it as it now stands cannot condone its weak drama. To a lesser degree the same criticism can be made of the final scene. Its effect now depends on hair-trigger timing and sheer dynamics of acting which J. Edward Bromberg manages with effect. But a fuller writing of the close would take the burden off histrionics and give the finale the firmness it requires.

One basic reason for the impressiveness of *Waiting for Lefty* is the idiom used throughout. The phrases are pungent, fresh, simple, mobile, the ringing speech of flesh and blood proletarians. This all too rare ingredient keeps the play racing at a robust tempo but occasionally it intoxicates the author. The result is almost a cancellation of the necessary effect; a tense moment vitiated by a wisecrack. When the young hackie reiterates "He don't know from nothin', that dumb basketball player," he all but undermines the poignancy of the scene. When the worker who exposes his brother in Scene VI adds, "The Clancy family tree is bearing nuts," the audience, until that point held tight by the clash of forces, is let down into a laugh by a dramatically unfortunate pun.

These flaws of oversimplification and gratuitous humor (which may easily be remedied in future performances) are minor matters when considering the play as a whole. The actors (the cast of *Gold Eagle Guy*) have given magnificent performances, Kazan and Carnovsky in particular. And the simplicity of the production is extraordinarily successful. Its author, actors and producers deserve every congratulation on an impressive contribution to the revolutionary theatre.

15.3 PRODUCTION PHOTO FROM *WAITING FOR LEFTY*—ANON

Scene from *Waiting for Lefty* by Clifford Odets, 1935. *Lefty*, a powerful dramatization of a taxi drivers' strike against labor racketeering and capitalism, was, as Harold Clurman saw it, "the birth cry of the thirties. Our youth had found its voice. It was a call to join the good fight for a greater measure of life in a world free of economic fear, falsehood, and craven servitude and greed. 'Strike!' was *Lefty*'s lyric message, not alone for a few extra pennies of wages or for shorter hours of work, strike for greater dignity, strike for a bolder humanity, strike for the full stature of man" (*Fervent Years* 147–48).

15.4 *WAITING FOR LEFTY*—CLIFFORD ODETS

This play was first presented by the Group Theatre at the Longacre Theatre on the evening of March 26th, 1935.

INTRODUCTION

By Alan Wald

Waiting for Lefty and the Radical Theater Tradition

Ever since its first production in 1934, critics have pondered the qualities, aesthetic and political, of *Waiting for Lefty*. The play has been excoriated as a simplistic exercise in "agit-prop" techniques (referring to the Soviet promotion of political propaganda through art), and defended as "transcendent" of those very conventions.[1] Less in debate are the recollections of those who viewed the first performance; their unrestrained acclamation, such as that of Harold Clurman's description of it as "the birth cry of the thirties," are regularly quoted in scholarship about Odets.[2]

Even more remarkable is the extraordinary international impact of the play. Margaret Brenman-Gibson observes that *"Waiting for Lefty* would be more frequently produced and more frequently banned all over the world—from Union Square to Moscow, from Tokyo to Johannesburg—than any other play in all of theater history."[3] One explanation for this appeal is *Waiting For Lefty*'s intimate connection with the workers theater tradition. While the tradition unfolded with certain unique features in the United States in the 1920s and 1930s, it was part of a worldwide left-wing cultural effort, with the aim of creating entertainment to which members of the non-elite classes might respond—to provide pleasure with a content that might open their eyes to the possibilities of a future and better world. Subsequently, the tradition lived on through various enterprises, usually with names such as "People's Theater," as well as specific projects such as the American Negro Theater Company, followed by various kinds of political theater in the 1960s in tandem with the New Left, Feminism, and Black Power and Chicano Power movements.

Odets's *Waiting for Lefty* appeared at the moment of orthodox "Third Period" Communism, when President Roosevelt was viewed as a fascist, the leadership of the labor movement as working at the behest of the bosses, and an all-out struggle for power was believed to be the order of the day. Odets was fully caught up in this dream of "a better world" modeled on some egregiously idealized vision of the Soviet Union; without that dream his play—and, indeed, his whole career—might have been still-born.

Waiting for Lefty, although borrowing episodes from a recent taxi cab strike in New York City, was also intended to dramatize a call to arms in just one of the many coordinated battles necessary to produce the "final conflict" that will lead to a truly human society. Nevertheless, the play achieved a unique rapport with its audience due to Odets's capacity to reinvigorate familiar tropes from radical culture that were in the air in 1934, along with a narrative that brought briefly to life a range of people in paradigmatic situations.

★

CHARACTERS

FATT	AGATE KELLER
JOE	HENCHMAN
EDNA	SECRETARY
MILLER	ACTOR
FAYETTE	REILLY
IRV	DR. BARNES
FLORRIE	DR. BENJAMIN
SID	AMAN
CLAYTON	VOICES

As the curtain goes up we see a bare stage. On it are sitting six or seven men in a semi-circle. Lolling against the proscenium down left is a young man chewing a toothpick: a gunman. A fat man of porcine appearance is talking directly to the audience. In other words he is the head of a union and the men ranged behind him are a committee of workers. They are now seated in interesting different attitudes and present a wide diversity of type, as we shall soon see. The fat man is hot and heavy under the collar, near the end of a long talk, but not too hot: he is well fed and confident. His name is HARRY FATT.

FATT: You're so wrong I ain't laughing. Any guy with eyes to read knows it. Look at the textile strike—out like lions and in like lambs. Take the San Francisco tie-up—starvation and broken heads. The steel boys wanted to walk out too, but they changed their minds. It's the trend of the times, that's what it is. All we workers got a good man behind us now. He's top man of the country—looking out for our interests—the man in the White House is the one I'm referrin' to. That's why the times ain't ripe for a strike. He's working day and night—

VOICE FROM THE AUDIENCE: For who?

The GUNMAN *stirs himself.*

FATT: For you! The records prove it. If this was the Hoover regime, would I say don't go out, boys? Not on your tintype! But things is different now. You read the papers as well as me. You know it. And that's why I'm against the strike. Because we gotta stand behind the man who's standin' behind us! The whole country—

ANOTHER VOICE: Is on the blink!

The GUNMAN *looks grave.*

FATT: Stand up and show yourself, you damn red! Be a man, let's see what you look like! [*Waits in vain.*] Yellow from the word go! Red and yellow makes a dirty color, boys. I got my eyes on four or five of them in the union here. What the hell'll they do for you? Pull you out and run away when trouble starts. Give those birds a chance and they'll have your sisters and wives in the whore houses, like they done in Russia. They'll tear Christ off his bleeding cross. They'll wreck your homes and throw your babies in the river. You think that's bunk? Read the papers! Now listen, we can't stay here all night. I gave you the facts in the case. You boys got hot suppers to go to and—

ANOTHER VOICE: Says you!

GUNMAN: Sit down, Punk!

ANOTHER VOICE: Where's Lefty?

[*Now this question is taken up by the others in unison.* FATT *pounds with gavel.*]

FATT: That's what I wanna know. Where's your pal, Lefty? You elected him chairman—where the hell did he disappear?

VOICES: We want Lefty! Lefty! Lefty!

FATT: [*Pounding.*] What the hell is this—a circus? You got the committee here. This bunch of cowboys you elected. [*Pointing to man on extreme right end.*]

MAN: Benjamin.

FATT: Yeah, Doc Benjamin. [*Pointing to other men in circle in seated order.*] Benjamin, Miller, Stein, Mitchell, Phillips, Keller. It ain't my fault Lefty took a run-out powder. If you guys—

A GOOD VOICE: What's the committee say?

OTHERS: The committee! Let's hear from the committee!

[FATT *tries to quiet the crowd, but one of the seated men suddenly comes to the front. The* GUNMAN *moves over to center stage, but* FATT *says:*

FATT: Sure, let him talk. Let's hear what the red boys gotta say!

[*Various shouts are coming from the audience.* FATT *insolently goes back to his seat in the middle of the circle. He sits on his raised platform and relights his cigar. The* GUNMAN *goes back to his post.* JOE, *the new speaker, raises his band for quiet. Gets it quickly. He is sore.*]

JOE: You boys know me. I ain't a red boy one bit! Here I'm carryin' a shrapnel that big I picked up in the war. And maybe I don't know it when it rains! Don't tell me red! You know what we are? The black and blue buys! We been kicked around so long we're black and blue from head to toes. But I guess anyone who says straight out he don't like it, he's a red boy to the leaders of the union. What's this crap about goin' home to hot suppers? I'm asking to your faces how many's got hot suppers to go home to? Anyone who's sure of his next meal, raise your hand! A certain gent sitting behind me can raise them both. But not in front here! And that's why we're talking strike—to get a living wage!

VOICE: Where's Lefty?

JOE: I honest to God don't know, but he didn't take no run-out powder. That Wop's got more guts than a slaughter house. Maybe a traffic jam got him, but he'll be here. But don't let this red stuff scare you. Unless fighting for a living scares you. We gotta make up our minds. My wife made up my mind last week, if you want the truth. It's plain as the nose on Sol Feinberg's face we need a strike. There's us comin' home every night—eight, ten hours on the cab. "God," the wife says, "eighty cents ain't money—don't buy beans almost. You're workin' for the company," she says to me, "Joe! You ain't workin' for me or the family no more!" She says to me, "If you don't start . . ."

★

I Joe and Edna

The lights fade out and a white spot picks out the playing space within the space of seated men. The seated men are very dimly visible in the outer dark, but more prominent is FATT *smoking his cigar and often blowing the smoke in the lighted circle.*

A tired but attractive woman of thirty comes into the room, drying her hands on an apron. She stands there sullenly as JOE *comes in from the other side, home from work. For a moment they stand and look at each other in silence.*

JOE: Where's all the furniture, honey?

EDNA: They took it away. No installments paid.

JOE: When?

EDNA: Three o'clock.

JOE: They can't do that.

EDNA: Can't? They did it.

JOE: Why, the palookas, we paid three-quarters.

EDNA: The man said read the contract.

JOE: We must have signed a phoney . . .

EDNA: It's a regular contract and you signed it.

JOE: Don't be so sour, Edna. [*Tries to embrace her.*]

EDNA: Do it in the movies, Joe—they pay Clark Gable big money for it.

JOE: This is a helluva house to come home to. Take my word!

EDNA: Take MY word! Whose fault is it?

JOE: Must you start that stuff again?

EDNA: Maybe you'd like to talk about books?

JOE: I'd like to slap you in the mouth!

EDNA: No you won't.

JOE: [*Sheepish.*] Jeez, Edna, you get me sore some time . . .

EDNA: But just look at me—I'm laughing all over!

JOE: Don't insult me. Can I help it if times are bad? What the hell do you want me to do, jump off a bridge or something?

EDNA: Don't yell. I just put the kids to bed so they won't know they missed a meal. If I don't have Emmy's shoes soled tomorrow, she can't go to school. In the meantime let her sleep.

JOE: Honey, I rode the wheels off the chariot today. I cruised around five hours without a call. It's conditions.

EDNA: Tell it to the A & P!

JOE: I booked two-twenty on the clock. A lady with a dog was lit . . . she gave me a quarter tip by mistake. If you'd only listen to me—we're rolling in wealth.

EDNA: Yeah? How much?

JOE: I had "coffee and—" in a beanery. [*Hands her silver coins.*] A buck four.

EDNA: The second month's rent is due tomorrow.

JOE: Don't look at me that way, Edna.

EDNA: I'm looking through you, not at you. . . . Everything was gonna be so ducky! A cottage by the waterfall, roses in Picardy. You're a four-star-bust! If you think I'm standing for it much longer, you're crazy as a bedbug.

JOE: I'd get another job if I could. There's no work—you know it.

EDNA: I only know we're at the bottom of the ocean.

JOE: What can I do?

EDNA: Who's the man in the family, you or me?

JOE: That's no answer. Get down to brass tacks. Christ, gimme a break, too! A coffee cake and java all day. I'm hungry, too, Babe. I'd work my fingers to the bone if—

EDNA: I'll open a can of salmon.

JOE: Not now. Tell me what to do!

EDNA: I'm not God!

JOE: Jeez, I wish I was a kid again and didn't have to think about the next minute.

EDNA: But you're not a kid and you do have to think about the next minute. You got two blondie kids sleeping in the next room. They need food and clothes. I'm not mentioning anything else—But we're stalled like a flivver in the snow. For five years I laid awake at night listening to my heart pound. For God's sake, do something, Joe, get wise. Maybe get your buddies together, maybe go on strike for better money. Poppa did it during the war and they won out. I'm turning into a sour old nag.

JOE: [*Defending himself.*] Strikes don't work!

EDNA: Who told you?

JOE: Besides that means not a nickel a week while we're out. Then when it's over they don't take you back.

EDNA: Suppose they don't! What's to lose?

JOE: Well, we're averaging six-seven dollars a week now.

EDNA: That just pays for the rent.

JOE: That is something, Edna.

EDNA: It isn't. They'll push you down to three and four a week before you know it. Then you'll say, "That's somethin'," too!

JOE: There's too many cabs on the street, that's the whole damn trouble.

EDNA: Let the company worry about that, you big fool! If their cabs didn't make a profit, they'd take them off the streets. Or maybe you think they're in business just to pay Joe Mitchell's rent!

JOE: You don't know a-b-c Edna.

EDNA: I know this—your boss is making suckers outa you boys every minute. Yes, and suckers out of all the wives and the poor innocent kids who'll grow up with crooked spines and sick bones. Sure, I see it in the papers, how good orange juice is for kids. But dammit our kids get colds one on top of the other. They look like little ghosts. Betty never saw a grapefruit. I took her to the store last week and she pointed to a stack of grapefruits. "What's that!" she said. My God, Joe—the world is supposed to be for all of us.

JOE: You'll wake them up.

EDNA: I don't care, as long as I can maybe wake you up.

JOE: Don't insult me. One man can't make a strike.

EDNA: Who says one? You got hundreds in your rotten union!

JOE: The Union ain't rotten.

EDNA: No? Then what are they doing? Collecting dues and patting your back?

JOE: They're making plans.

EDNA: What kind?

JOE: They don't tell us.

EDNA: It's too damn bad about you. They don't tell little Joey what's happening in his bitsie witsie union. What do you think it is—a ping pong game?

JOE: You know they're racketeers. The guys at the top would shoot you for a nickel.

EDNA: Why do you stand for that stuff?

JOE: Don't you wanna see me alive?

EDNA: [*After a deep pause.*] No . . . I don't think I do, Joe. Not if you can lift a finger to do something about it, and don't. No, I don't care.

JOE: Honey, you don't understand what—

EDNA: And any other hackie that won't fight . . . let them all be ground to hamburger!

JOE: It's one thing to—

EDNA: Take your hand away! Only they don't grind me to little pieces! I got different plans. [*Starts to take off her apron.*]

JOE: Where are you going?

EDNA: None of your business.

JOE: What's up your sleeve?

EDNA: My arm'd be up my sleeve, darling, if I had a sleeve to wear. [*Puts neatly folded apron on back of chair.*]

JOE: Tell me!

EDNA: Tell you what?

JOE: Where are you going?

EDNA: Don't you remember my old boy friend?

JOE: Who?

EDNA: Bud Haas. He still has my picture in his watch. He earns a living.

JOE: What the hell are you talking about?

EDNA: I heard worse than I'm talking about.

JOE: Have you seen Bud since we got married?

EDNA: Maybe.

JOE: If I thought . . . [*He stands looking at her.*]

EDNA: See much? Listen, boy friend, if you think I won't do this it just means you can't see straight.

JOE: Stop talking bull!

EDNA: This isn't five years ago, Joe.

JOE: You mean you'd leave me and the kids?

EDNA: I'd leave you like a shot!

JOE: No . . .

EDNA: Yes!

[JOE *turns away, sitting in a chair with his back to her. Outside the lighted circle of the playing stage we hear the other seated members of the strike committee. "She will . . . she will . . . it happens that way," etc. This group should be used throughout for various comments, political, emotional and as general chorus. Whispering. . . . The fat boss now blows a heavy cloud of smoke into the scene.*]

JOE: [*Finally.*] Well, I guess I ain't got a leg to stand on.

EDNA: No?

JOE: [*Suddenly mad.*] No, you lousy tart, no! Get the hell out of here. Go pick up that bull-thrower on the corner and stop at some cushy hotel downtown. He's probably been coming here every morning and laying you while I hacked my guts out!

EDNA: You're crawling like a worm!

JOE: You'll be crawling in a minute.

EDNA: You don't scare me that much! [*Indicates a half inch on her finger.*]

JOE: This is what I slaved for!

EDNA: Tell it to your boss!

JOE: He don't give a damn for you or me!

EDNA: That's what I say.

JOE: Don't change the subject!

EDNA: This is the subject, the EXACT SUBJECT! Your boss makes this subject. I never saw him in my life, but he's putting ideas in my head a mile a minute. He's giving your kids that fancy disease called the rickets. He's making a jellyfish outa you and putting wrinkles in my face. This is the subject every inch of the way! He's throwing me into Bud Haas's lap. When in hell will you get wise—

JOE: I'm not so dumb as you think! But you are talking like a Red.

EDNA: I don't know what that means. But when a man knocks you down you get up and kiss his fist! You gutless piece of boloney.

JOE: One man can't—

EDNA: [*With great joy.*] I don't say one man! I say a hundred, a thousand, a whole million, I say. But start in your own union. Get those hack boys together! Sweep out those racketeers like a pile of dirt! Stand up like men and fight for the crying kids and wives. Goddammit! I'm tired of slavery and sleepless nights.

JOE: [*With her.*] Sure, sure! . . .

EDNA: Yes. Get brass toes on your shoes and know where to kick!

JOE: [*Suddenly jumping up and kissing his wife full on the mouth.*] Listen, Edna. I'm goin' down to 174th Street to look up Lefty Costello. Lefty was saying the other day . . .[*He suddenly stops.*] How about this Haas guy?

EDNA: Get out of here!

JOE: I'll be back! [*Runs out.*]

[*For a moment* EDNA *stands triumphant. There is a blackout and when the regular lights come up,* JOE MITCHELL *is concluding what he has been saying:*]

JOE: You guys know this stuff better than me. We gotta walk out! [*Abruptly he turns and goes back to his seat and blackout.*]

Blackout

★

II Lab Assistant Episode

Discovered: MILLER *a lab assistant, looking around; and* FAYETTE, *an industrialist.*

FAY: Like it?

MILLER: Very much. I've never seen an office like this outside the movies.

FAY: Yes, I often wonder if interior decorators and bathroom fixture people don't get all their ideas from Hollywood. Our country's extraordinary that way. Soap, cosmetics, electric refrigerators—just let Mrs. Consumer know they're used by the Crawfords and Garbos—more volume of sale than one plant can handle!

MILL: I'm afraid it isn't that easy, Mr. Fayette.

FAY: No, you're right—gross exaggeration on my part. Competition is cut-throat today. Markets up flush against a stone wall. The astronomers had better hurry—open Mars to trade expansion.

MILL: Or it will be just too bad!

FAY: Cigar?

MILL: Thank you, don't smoke.

FAY: Drink?

MILL: Ditto, Mr. Fayette.

FAY: I like sobriety in my workers . . . the trained ones, I mean. The Pollacks and niggers, they're better drunk—keeps them out of mischief. Wondering why I had you come over?

MILL: If you don't mind my saying—very much.

FAY: [*Patting him on the knee.*] I like your work.

MILL: Thanks.

FAY: No reason why a talented young man like yourself shouldn't string along with us—a growing concern. Loyalty is well repaid in our organization. Did you see Siegfried this morning?

MILL: He hasn't been in the laboratory all day.

FAY: I told him yesterday to raise you twenty dollars a month. Starts this week.

MILL: You don't know how happy my wife'll be.

FAY: Oh, I can appreciate it. [*He laughs.*]

MILL: Was that all, Mr. Fayette?

FAY: Yes, except that we're switching you to laboratory A tomorrow. Siegfried knows about it. That's why I had you in. The new work is very important. Siegfried recommended you very highly as a man to trust. You'll work directly under Dr. Brenner. Make you happy?

MILL: Very. He's an important chemist!

FAY: [*Leaning over seriously.*] We think so, Miller. We think so to the extent of asking you to stay within the building throughout the time you work with him.

MILL: You mean sleep and eat in?

FAY: Yes . . .

MILL: It can be arranged

FAY: Fine. You'll go far, Miller.

MILL: May I ask the nature of the new work?

FAY: [*Looking around first.*] Poison gas . . .

MILL: Poison!

FAY: Orders from above. I don't have to tell you from where. New type poison gas for modern warfare.

MILL: I see.

FAY: You didn't know a new war was that close, did you?

MILL: I guess I didn't.

FAY: I don't have to stress the importance of absolute secrecy.

MILL: I understand!

FAY: The world is an armed camp today. One match sets the whole world blazing in forty-eight hours. Uncle Sam won't be caught napping!

MILL: [*Addressing his pencil.*] They say 12 million men were killed in that last one and 20 million more wounded or missing.

FAY: That's not our worry. If big business went sentimental over human life there wouldn't be big business of any sort!

MILL: My brother and two cousins went in the last one.

FAY: They died in a good cause.

MILL: My mother says "no!"

FAY: She won't worry about you this time. You're too valuable behind the front.

MILL: That's right.

FAY: All right, Miller. See Siegfried for further orders.

MILL: You should have seen my brother—he could ride a bike without hands . . .

FAY: You'd better move some clothes and shaving tools in tomorrow. Remember what I said—you're with a growing organization.

MILL: He could run the hundred yards in 9:8 flat . . .

FAY: Who?

MILL: My brother. He's in the Meuse-Argonne Cemetery. Momma went there in 1926 . . .

FAY: Yes, those things stick. How's your handwriting, Miller, fairly legible?

MILL: Fairly so.

FAY: Once a week I'd like a little report from you.

MILL: What sort of report?

FAY: Just a few hundred words once a week on Dr. Brenner's progress.

MILL: Don't you think it might be better coming from the Doctor?

FAY: I didn't ask you that.

MILL: Sorry.

FAY: I want to know what progress he's making, the reports to be purely confidential—between you and me.

MILL: You mean I'm to watch him?

FAY: Yes!

MILL: I guess I can't do that . . .

FAY: Thirty a month raise . . .

MILL: You said twenty . . .

FAY: Thirty!

MILL: Guess I'm not built that way.

FAY: Forty . . .

MILL: Spying's not in my line, Mr. Fayette!

FAY: You use ugly words, Mr. Miller!

MILL: For ugly activity? Yes!

FAY: Think about it, Miller. Your chances are excellent . . .

MILL: No.

FAY: You're doing something for your country. Assuring the United States that when those goddam Japs start a ruckus we'll have offensive weapons to back us up! Don't you read your newspapers, Miller?

MILL: Nothing but Andy Gump.

FAY: If you were on the inside you'd know I'm talking cold sober truth! Now, I'm not asking you to make up your mind on the spot. Think about it over your lunch period.

MILL: No . . .
FAY: Made up your mind already?
MILL: Afraid so.
FAY: You understand the consequences?
MILL: I lose my raise
MILL: And my job!}
FAY: And your job!} *Simultaneously*
MILL: You misunderstand—
MILL: Rather dig ditches first!
FAY: That's a big job for foreigners.
MILL: But sneaking—and making poison gas—that's for Americans?
FAY: It's up to you.
MILL: My mind's made up.
FAY: No hard feelings?
MILL: Sure hard feelings! I'm not the civilized type, Mr. Fayette. Nothing suave or sophisticated about me. Plenty of hard feelings! Enough to want to bust you and all your kind square in the mouth!

[*Does exactly that.*]

Blackout

★

III The Young Hack and his Girl

Opens with girl and brother. FLORENCE *waiting for* SID *to take her to a dance.*

FLOR: I gotta right to have something out of life. I don't smoke, I don't drink. So if Sid wants to take me to a dance, I'll go. Maybe if you was in love you wouldn't talk so hard.
IRV: I'm saying it for your good.
FLOR: Don't be so good to me.
IRV: Mom's sick in bed and you'll be worryin' her to the grave. She don't want that boy hanging around the house and she don't want you meeting him in Crotona Park.
FLOR: I'll meet him anytime I like!
IRV: If you do, yours truly'll take care of it in his own way. With just one hand, too!
FLOR: Why are you all so set against him?
IRV: Mom told you ten times—it ain't him. It's that he ain't got nothing. Sure, we know he's serious, that he's stuck on you. But that don't cut no ice.
FLOR: Taxi drivers used to make good money.
IRV: Today they're makin' five and six dollars a week. Maybe you wanta raise a family on that. Then you'll be back here living with us again and I'll be supporting two families in one. Well . . . over my dead body.
FLOR: Irv, I don't care—I love him!
IRV: You're a little kid with half-baked ideas!
FLOR: I stand there behind the counter the whole day. I think about him—
IRV: If you thought more about Mom it would be better.
FLOR: Don't I take care of her every night when I come home? Don't I cook supper and iron your shirts and . . . you give me a pain in the neck, too. Don't try to shut me up! I bring a few dollars in the house, too. Don't you see I want something else out of life. Sure, I want romance, love, babies. I want everything in life I can get.
IRV: You take care of Mom and watch your step!
FLOR: And if I don't?
IRV: Yours truly'll watch it for you!
FLOR: You can talk that way to a girl . . .
IRV: I'll talk that way to your boy friend, too, and it won't be with words! Florrie, if you had a pair of eyes you'd see it's for your own good we're talking. This ain't no time to get married. Maybe later—
FLOR: "Maybe later" never comes for me, though. Why don't we send Mom to a hospital? She can die in peace there instead of looking at the clock on the mantelpiece all day.
IRV: That needs money. Which we don't have!
FLOR: Money, Money, Money!
IRV: Don't change the subject.
FLOR: This is the subject!
IRV: You gonna stop seeing him? [*She turns away.*] Jesus, kiddie, I remember when you were a baby with curls down your back. Now I gotta stand here yellin' at you like this.
FLOR: I'll talk to him, Irv.
IRV: When?
FLOR: I asked him to come here tonight. We'll talk it over.
IRV: Don't get soft with him. Nowadays is no time to be soft. You gotta be hard as a rock or go under.
FLOR: I found that out. There's the bell. Take the egg off the stove I boiled for Mom. Leave us alone, Irv.

[SID *comes in—the two men look at each other for a second.* IRV *exits.*]

SID: [*Enters*] Hello, Florrie.
FLOR: Hello, Honey. You're looking tired.
SID: Naw, I just need a shave.

FLOR: Well, draw your chair up to the fire and I'll ring for brandy and soda . . . like in the movies.

SID: If this was the movies I'd bring a big bunch of roses.

FLOR: How big?

SID: Fifty or sixty dozen—the kind with long, long stems—big as that . . .

FLOR: You dope . . .

SID: Your Paris gown is beautiful.

FLOR: [*Acting grandly.*] Yes, Percy, velvet panels are coming back again. Madame La Farge told me today that Queen Marie herself designed it.

SID: Gee . . .!

FLOR: Every princess in the Balkans is wearing one like this. [*Poses grandly.*]

SID: Hold it. [*Does a nose camera—thumbing nose and imitating grinding of camera with other hand. Suddenly she falls out of the posture and swiftly goes to him, to embrace him, to kiss him with love. Finally*]

SID: You look tired, Florrie.

FLOR: Naw, I just need a shave. [*She laughs tremorously.*]

SID: You worried about your mother?

FLOR: No.

SID: What's on your mind?

FLOR: The French and Indian War.

SID: What's on your mind?

FLOR: I got us on my mind, Sid. Night and day, Sid!

SID: I smacked a beer truck today. Did I get hell! I was driving along thinking of US, too. You don't have to say it—I know what's on your mind. I'm rat poison around here.

FLOR: Not to me . . .

SID: I know to who . . . and I know why. I don't blame them. We're engaged now for three years . . .

FLOR: That's a long time . . .

SID: My brother Sam joined the navy this morning—get a break that way. They'll send him down to Cuba with the hootchy-kootchy girls. He don't know from nothing, that dumb basketball player!

FLOR: Don't you do that.

SID: Don't you worry, I'm not the kind who runs away. But I'm so tired of being a dog, Baby, I could choke. I don't even have to ask what's going on in your mind. I know from the word go, 'cause I'm thinking the same things, too.

FLOR: It's yes or no—nothing in between.

SID: The answer is no—a big electric sign looking down on Broadway!

FLOR: We wanted to have kids . . .

SID: But that sort of life ain't for the dogs which is us. Christ, Baby! I get like thunder in my chest when we're together. If we went off together I could maybe look the world straight in the face, spit in its eye like a man should do. Goddamit, it's trying to be a man on the earth. Two in life together.

FLOR: But something wants us to be lonely like that—crawling alone in the dark. Or they want us trapped.

SID: Sure, the big shot money men want us like that.

FLOR: Highly insulting us—

SID: Keeping us in the dark about what is wrong with us in the money sense. They got the power and mean to be damn sure they keep it. They know if they give in just an inch, all the dogs like us will be down on them together—an ocean knocking them to hell and back and each singing cuckoo with stars coming from their nose and ears. I'm not raving, Florrie—

FLOR: I know you're not, I know.

SID: I don't have the words to tell you what I feel. I never finished school . . .

FLOR: I know . . .

SID: But it's relative, like the professors say. We worked like hell to send him to college—my kid brother Sam, I mean—and look what he done—joined the navy! The damn fool don't see the cards is stacked for all of us. The money man dealing himself a hot royal flush. Then giving you and me a phoney hand like a pair of tens or something. Then keep on losing the pots 'cause the cards is stacked against you. Then he says, what's the matter you can't win—no stuff on the ball, he says to you. And kids like my brother believe it 'cause they don't know better. For all their education, they don't know from nothing.

But wait a minute! Don't he come around and say to you—this millionaire with a jazz band—listen Sam or Sid or what's-your-name, you're no good, but here's a chance. The whole world'll know who you are. Yes sir, he says, get up on that ship and fight those bastards who's making the world a lousy place to live in. The Japs, the Turks, the Greeks. Take this gun—kill the slobs like a real hero, he says, a real American. Be a hero!

And the guy you're poking at? A real louse, just like you 'cause they don't let him catch more than a pair of tens, too. On that foreign soil he's a guy like me and Sam, a guy who wants his baby like you and hot sun on his face! They'll teach Sam to point the guns the wrong way, that dumb basketball player!

FLOR: I got a lump in my throat, Honey.

SID: You and me—we never even had a room to sit in somewhere.

FLOR: The park was nice . . .

SID: In Winter? The hallways . . . I'm glad we never got together. This way we don't know what we missed.

FLOR: [*In a burst.*] Sid, I'll go with you—we'll get a room somewhere.

SID: Naw . . . they're right. If we can't climb higher than this together—we better stay apart.

FLOR: I swear to God I wouldn't care.

SID: You would, you would—in a year, two years, you'd curse the day. I seen it happen.

FLOR: Oh, Sid . . .

SID: Sure, I know. We got the blues, Babe—the 1935 blues. I'm talkin' this way 'cause I love you. If I didn't, I wouldn't care . . .

FLOR: We'll work together, we'll—

SID: How about the backwash? Your family needs your nine bucks. My family—

FLOR: I don't care for them!

SID: You're making it up, Florrie. Little Florrie Canary in a cage.

FLOR: Don't make fun of me.

SID: I'm not, Baby.

FLOR: Yes, you're laughing at me.

SID: I'm not.

[They stand looking at each other, unable to speak. Finally, he turns to a small portable phonograph and plays a cheap, sad, dance tune. He makes a motion with his hand; she comes to him. They begin to dance slowly. They hold each other tightly, almost as though they would merge into each other. The music stops, but the scratching record continues to the end of the scene. They stop dancing. He finally unlooses her clutch and seats her on the couch, where she sits, tense and expectant.]

SID: Hello, Babe.

FLOR: Hello.

[For a brief time they stand as though in a dream.]

SID: [*Finally.*] Good-by, Babe.

[He waits for an answer, but she is silent. They look at each other.]

SID: Did you ever see my Pat Rooney imitation? [*He whistles Rosy O'Grady and soft shoes to it. Stops. He asks.*]

SID: Don't you like it?

FLOR: [*Finally*] No. [*Buries her face in her hands.*]

[Suddenly he falls on his knees and buries his face in her lap.]

Blackout

★

IV Labor Spy Episode

FATT: You don't know how we work for you. Shooting off your mouth won't help. Hell, don't you guys ever look at the records like me? Look in your own industry. See what happened when the hacks walked out in Philly three months ago! Where's Philly? A thousand miles away? An hour's ride on the train.

VOICE: Two hours!!

FATT: Two hours . . . what the hell's the difference. Let's hear from someone who's got the practical experience to back him up. Fellers, there's a man here who's seen the whole parade in Philly, walked out with his pals, got knocked down like the rest—and blacklisted after they went back. That's why he's here. He's got a mighty interestin' word to say. [*Announces.*] TOM CLAYTON!

[As CLAYTON *starts up from the audience,* FATT *gives him a hand which is sparsely followed in the audience.* CLAYTON *comes forward.]*

Fellers, this is a man with practical strike experience—Tom Clayton from little ole Philly.

FATT: [*A thin, modest individual.*] Fellers, I don't mind your booing. If I thought it would help us hacks get better living conditions I'd let you walk all over me, cut me up to little pieces. I'm one of you myself. But what I wanna say is that Harry Fatt's right. I only been working here in the big town five weeks, but I know conditions just like the rest of you. You know how it is—don't take long to feel the sore spots, no matter where you park.

CLEAR VOICE: [*From audience.*] Sit down!

CLAYTON: But Fatt's right. Our officers is right. The time ain't ripe. Like a fruit don't fall off the tree until it's ripe.

CLEAR VOICE: Sit down, you fruit!

FATT: [*On his feet.*] Take care of him, boys.

VOICE: [*in audience, struggling.*] No one takes care of me.

[Struggle in house and finally the owner of the voice runs up on stage, says to speaker:]

SAME VOICE: Where the hell did you pick up that name! Clayton! This rat's name is Clancy, from the old Clancys, way back! Fruit! I almost wet myself listening to that one!

FATT: [*Gunman with him.*] This ain't a barn! What the hell do you think you're doing here!

SAME VOICE: Exposing a rat!

FATT: You can't get away with this. Throw him the hell outa here.

VOICE: [*Preparing to stand his ground.*] Try it yourself . . . When this bozo throws that slop around. You know who he is? That's a company spy.

FATT: Who the hell are you to make—

VOICE: I paid dues in this union for four years, that's who's me! I gotta right and this pussy-footed rat ain't coming in here with ideals like that. You know his record. Lemme say it out—

FATT: You'll prove all this or I'll bust you in every hack outfit in town!

VOICE: I gotta right. I gotta right. Looka *him,* he don't say boo!

CLAYTON: You're a liar and I never seen you before in my life!

VOICE: Boys, he spent two years in the coal fields breaking up any organization he touched. Fifty guys he put in jail. He's ranged up and down the east coast—shipping, textiles, steel—he's been in everything you can name. Right now—

CLAYTON: That's a lie!

VOICE: Right now he's working for that Bergman outfit on Columbus Circle who furnishes rats for any outfit in the country before, during, and after strikes.

[*The man who is the hero of the next episode goes down to his side with other committee men.*]

CLAYTON: He's trying to break up the meeting, fellers!

VOICE: We won't search you for credentials . . .

CLAYTON: I got nothing to hide. Your own secretary knows I'm straight.

VOICE: Sure. Boys, you know who this sonovabitch is?

CLAYTON: I never seen you before in my life!!

VOICE: Boys, I slept with him in the same bed sixteen years. MY OWN LOUSY BROTHER!!

FATT: [*After pause.*] Is this true?

No answer from CLAYTON.

VOICE to CLAYTON: Scram, before I break your neck!

[CLAYTON *scrams down center aisle.* VOICE *says, watching him:*]

Remember his map—he can't change that—Clancy!

[*Standing in his place says:*]

Too bad you didn't know about this, Fatt! [*After a pause.*] The Clancy family tree is bearing nuts!

[*Standing isolated clear on the stage is the hero of the next episode.*]

Blackout

★

V The Young Actor

A New York theatrical producer's office. Present are a STENOGRAPHER *and a young actor. She is busy typing; he, waiting with card in hand.*

STEN: He's taking a hot bath . . . says you should wait.

PHILIPS: [*The actor.*] A bath did you say? Where?

STEN: See that door? Right through there—leads to his apartment.

PHIL: Through there?

STEN: Mister, he's laying there in a hot perfumed bath. Don't say I said it.

PHIL: You don't say!

STEN: An oriental den he's got. Can you just see this big Irishman burning Chinese punk in the bedroom? And a big old rose canopy over his casting couch . . .

PHIL: What's that—casting couch?

STEN: What's that? You from the sticks?

PHIL: I beg your pardon?

STEN: [*Rolls up her sleeves, makes elaborate deaf and dumb signs.*] No from side walkies of New Yorkie . . . savvy?

PHIL: Oh, you're right. Two years of dramatic stock out of town. One in Chicago.

STEN: Don't tell him, Baby Face. He wouldn't know a good actor if he fell over him in the dark. Say you had two years with the Group, two with the Guild.

PHIL: I'd like to get with the Guild. They say—

STEN: He won't know the difference. Don't say I said it!

PHIL: I really did play with Watson Findlay in "Early Birds."

STEN: [*Withering him.*] Don't tell him!

PHIL: He's a big producer, Mr. Grady. I wish I had his money. Don't you?

STEN: Say, I got a clean heart, Mister. I love my fellow man! [*About to exit with typed letters.*] Stick around—Mr. Philips. You might be the type. If you were a woman—

PHIL: Please. Just a minute . . . please . . . I need the job.

STEN: Look at him!

PHIL: I mean . . . I don't know what buttons to push, and you do. What my father used to say—we had a gas station in Cleveland before the crash—"Know what buttons to push," Dad used to say, "and you'll go far."

STEN: You can't push me, Mister! I don't ring right these last few years!

PHIL: We don't know where the next meal's coming from. We—

STEN: Maybe . . . I'll lend you a dollar?

PHIL: Thanks very much: it won't help.

STEN: One of the old families of Virginia? Proud?

PHIL: Oh, not that. You see, I have a wife. We'll have our first baby next month . . . so . . . a dollar isn't much help.

STEN: Roped in?

PHIL: I love my wife!

STEN: Okay, you love her! Excuse me! You married her. Can't support her. No . . . not blaming you. But you're fools, all you actors. Old and young! Watch you parade in and out all day. You still got apples in your cheeks and pins for buttons. But in six months you'll be like them—putting on an act: Phoney strutting "pishers"—that's French for dead codfish! It's not their fault. Here you get like that or go under. What kind of job is this for an adult man!

PHIL: When you have to make a living—

STEN: I know, but—

PHIL: Nothing else to do. If I could get something else—

STEN: You'd take it!

PHIL: Anything!

STEN: Telling me! With two brothers in my hair!

[MR. GRADY *now enters; played by* FATT.]

Mr. Brown sent this young man over.

GRADY: Call the hospital: see how Boris is. [*She assents and exits.*]

PHIL: Good morning, Mr. Grady . . .

GRADY: The morning is lousy!

PHIL: Mr. Brown sent me. [*Hands over card.*]

GRADY: I heard that once already.

PHIL: Excuse me . . .

GRADY: What experience?

PHIL: Oh, yes . . .

GRADY: Where?

PHIL: Two years in stock, sir. A year with the Goodman Theatre in Chicago . . .

GRADY: That all?

PHIL: [*Abashed.*] Why no . . . with the Theatre Guild . . . I was there . . .

GRADY: Never saw you in a Guild show!

PHIL: On the road, I mean . . . understudying Mr. Lunt . . .

GRADY: What part?

[PHILIPS *can not answer.*]

You're a lousy liar, son.

PHIL: I did . . .

GRADY: You don't look like what I want. Can't understand that Brown. Need a big man to play a soldier. Not a lousy soldier left on Broadway! All in pictures, and we get the nances! [*Turns to on desk.*]

PHIL: [*Immediately playing the soldier.*] I was in the ROTC in college . . . Reserve Officers' Training Corps. We trained twice a week . . .

GRADY: Won't help.

PHIL: With real rifles. [*Waits.*] Mr. Grady, I weigh a hundred and fifty-five!

GRADY: How many years back? Been eating regular since you left college?

PHIL: [*Very earnestly.*] Mr. Grady, I could act this soldier part. I could build it up and act it. Make it up—

GRADY: Think I run a lousy acting school around here?

PHIL: Honest to God I could! I need the job—that's why I could do it! I'm strong. I know my business! you'll get an A-l performance! 'cause I need this job! My wife's having a baby in a few weeks. We need the money. Give me a chance!

GRADY: What do I care if you can act it! I'm sorry about your baby. Use your head, son. Tank Town stock is different. Here we got investments to be protected. When I sink fifteen thousand in a show I don't take chances on some youngster. We cast to type!

PHIL: I'm an artist! I can—

GRADY: That's your headache. Nobody interested in artists here. Get a big bunch for a nickel on any corner. Two flops in a row on this lousy street nobody loves you—only God, and He don't count. We protect investments: we cast to type. Your face and height we want, not your soul, son. And Jesus Christ himself couldn't play a soldier in this show . . . with all his talent. [*Crosses himself in quick repentance for this remark.*]

PHIL: Anything . . . a bit, a walk-on?

GRADY: Sorry: small cast. [*Looking at papers on his desk.*] You try Russia, son. I hear it's hot stuff over there.

PHIL: Stage manager? Assistant?

GRADY: All filled, sonny. [*Stands up; crumples several papers from the desk.*] Better luck next time.

PHIL: Thanks . . .

GRADY: Drop in from time to time. [*Crosses and about to exit.*] You never know when something—

[*The* STENOGRAPHER *enters with papers to put on desk.*]

What did the hospital say?

STEN: He's much better, Mr. Grady.

GRADY: Resting easy?

STEN: Dr. Martel said Boris is doing even better than he expected.

GRADY: A damn lousy operation!

STEN: Yes . . .

GRADY: [*Belching.*] Tell the nigger boy to send up a bromo seltzer.

STEN: Yes, Mr. Grady. [*He exits.*] Boris wanted lady friends.

PHIL: What?

STEN: So they operated . . . poor dog!

PHIL: A dog?

STEN: His Russian Wolf Hound! They do the same to you, but you don't know it! [*Suddenly.*] Want advice? In the next office, don't let them see you down in the mouth. They don't like it—makes them shiver.

PHIL: You treat me like a human being. Thanks . . .

STEN: You're human!

PHIL: I used to think so.

STEN: He wants a bromo for his hangover. [*Goes to door*] Want that dollar?

PHIL: It won't help much.

STEN: One dollar buys ten loaves of bread, Mister. Or one dollar buys nine loaves of bread and one copy of The Communist Manifesto. Learn while you eat. Read while you run . . .

PHIL: Manifesto? What's that? [*Takes dollar.*] What is that, what you said . . . Manifesto?

STEN: Stop off on your way out—I'll give you a copy. From Genesis to Revelation, Comrade Philips! "And I saw a new earth and a new heaven; for the first earth and the first heaven were passed away; and there was no more sea."

PHIL: I don't understand that . . .

STEN: I'm saying the meek shall not inherit the earth!

PHIL: No?

STEN: The MILITANT! Come out in the light, Comrade.

Blackout

★

VI Interne Episode

DR. BARNES, *an elderly distinguished man, is speaking on the telephone. He wears a white coat.*

DR. BARNES: No, I gave you my opinion twice. You outvoted me. You did this to Dr. Benjamin yourself. That is why you can tell him yourself.

[*Hangs up phone, angrily. As he is about to pour himself a drink from a bottle on the table, a knock is heard.*]

BARNES: Who is it?

BENJAMIN: [*Without.*] Can I see you a minute, please?

BARNES: [*Hiding the bottle.*] Come in, Dr. Benjamin, come in.

BENJ: It's important—excuse me—they've got Leeds up there in my place—He's operating on Mrs. Lewis—the historectomy—it's my job. I washed up, prepared . . . they told me at the last minute. I don't mind being replaced, Doctor, but Leeds is a damn fool! He shouldn't be permitted

BARNES: [*Dryly.*] Leeds is the nephew of Senator Leeds.

BENJ: He's incompetent as hell.

BARNES: [*Obviously changing subject, picks up lab jar.*] They're doing splendid work in brain surgery these days. This is a very fine specimen . . .

BENJ: I'm sorry, I thought you might be interested.

BARNES: [*Still examining jar.*] Well, I am, young man, I am! Only remember it's a charity case!

BENJ: Of course. They wouldn't allow it for a second, otherwise.

BARNES: Her life is in danger?

BENJ: Of course! You know how serious the case is!

BARNES: Turn your gimlet eyes elsewhere, Doctor. Jigging around like a cricket on a hot grill won't help. Doctors don't run these hospitals. He's the Senator's nephew and there he stays.

BENJ: It's too bad.

BARNES: I'm not calling you down either. [*Plopping down jar suddenly.*] Goddammit, do you think it's my fault?

BENJ: [*About to leave.*] I know . . . I'm sorry.

BARNES: Just a minute. Sit down.

BENJ: Sorry, I can't sit.

BARNES: Stand then!

BENJ: [*Sits.*] Understand, Dr. Barnes, I don't mind being replaced at the last minute this way, but . . . well, this flagrant bit of class distinction—because she's poor—

BARNES: Be careful of words like that—"class distinction." Don't belong here. Lots of energy, you brilliant young men, but idiots. Discretion! Ever hear that word?

BENJ: Too radical?

BARNES: Precisely. And some day like in Germany, it might cost you your head.

BENJ: Not to mention my job.

BARNES: So they told you?

BENJ: Told me what?

BARNES: They're closing Ward C next month. I don't have to tell you the hospital isn't self supporting. Until last year that board of trustees met deficits . . . You can guess the rest. At a board meeting Tuesday, our fine feathered friends discovered they couldn't meet the last quarter's deficit—a neat little sum well over $100,000. If the hospital is to continue at all, its damn—

BENJ: Necessary to close another charity ward!

BARNES: So they say . . . [*A wait.*]

BENJ: But that's not all?

BARNES: [*Ashamed.*] Have to cut down on staff too . . .

BENJ: That's too bad. Does it touch me?

BARNES: Afraid it does.

BENJ: But after all I'm top man here. I don't mean I'm better than others, but I've worked harder.

BARNES: And shown more promise . . .

BENJ: I always supposed they'd cut from the bottom first.

BARNES: Usually.

BENJ: But in this case?

BARNES: Complications.

BENJ: For instance?

[BARNES *hesitant.*]

BARNES: I like you, Benjamin. It's one ripping shame.

BENJ: I'm no sensitive plant—what's the answer?

BARNES: An old disease, malignant tumescent. We need an anti-toxin for it.

BENJ: I see.

BARNES: What?

BENJ: I met that disease before—at Harvard first.

BARNES: You have seniority here, Benjamin.

BENJ: But I'm a Jew!

[BARNES *nods his head in agreement.* BENJ *stands there a moment and blows his nose.*]

BARNES: [*Blows his nose.*] Microbes!

BENJ: Pressure from above?

BARNES: Don't think Kennedy and I didn't fight for you!

BENJ: Such discrimination, with all those wealthy brother Jews on the board?

BARNES: I've remarked before—doesn't seem to be much difference between wealthy Jews and rich Gentiles. Cut from the same piece!

BENJ: For myself I don't feel sorry. My parents gave up an awful lot to get me this far. They ran a little dry goods shop in the Bronx until their pitiful savings went in the crash last year. Poppa's peddling neckties . . . Saul Ezra Benjamin—a man who's read Spinoza all his life.

BARNES: Doctors don't run medicine in this country. The men who know their jobs don't run anything here, except the motormen on trolley cars. I've seen medicine change—plenty—anesthesia, sterilization—but not because of rich men—in *spite* of them! In a rich man's country your true self's buried deep. Microbes! Less . . . Vermin! See this ankle, this delicate sensitive hand? Four hundred years to breed that. Out of a revolutionary background! Spirit of '76! Ancestors froze at Valley Forge! What's it all mean! Slops! The honest workers were sold out then, in '76. The Constitution's for rich men then and now. Slops!

[*The phone rings.*]

BARNES: [*Angrily.*] Dr. Barnes. [*Listens a moment, looks at* BENJAMIN.] I see. [*Hangs up, turns slowly to the younger* DOCTOR.] They lost your patient.

[BENJ *stands solid with the shock of this news but finally hurls his operation gloves to the floor.*]

BARNES: That's right . . . that's right. Young, hot, go and do it! I'm very ancient, fossil, but life's ahead of you, Dr. Benjamin, and when you fire the first shot say, "This one's for old Doc Barnes!" Too much dignity—bullets. Don't shoot vermin! Step on them! If I didn't have an invalid daughter—[*Goes back to his seat, blows his nose in silence.*] I have said my piece, Benjamin.

BENJ: Lots of things I wasn't certain of. Many things these radicals say . . . you don't believe theories until they happen to you.

BARNES: You lost a lot today, but you won a great point.

BENJ: Yes, to know I'm right? To really begin believing in something? Not to say, "What a world!," but to say, "Change the world!" I wanted to go to Russia. Last week I was thinking about it—the wonderful opportunity to do good work in their socialized medicine—

BARNES: Beautiful, beautiful!

BENJ: To be able to work—

BARNES: Why don't you go? I might be able—

BENJ: Nothing's nearer what I'd like to do!

BARNES: Do it!

BENJ: No! Our work's here—America! I'm scared . . . What future's ahead, I don't know. Get some job to keep alive—maybe drive a cab—and study and work and learn my place—

BARNES: And step down hard!

BENJ: Fight! Maybe get killed, but goddam! We'll go ahead! [BENJAMIN *stands with clenched fist raised high.*]

Blackout

★

AGATE: LADIES AND GENTLEMEN, and don't let anyone tell you we ain't got some ladies in this sea of upturned faces! Only they're wearin' pants. Well, maybe I don't know a thing; maybe I fell outa the cradle when I was a kid and ain't been right since–you can't tell!

VOICE: Sit down, cockeye!

AGATE: Who's paying you for those remarks, Buddy?—Moscow Gold? Maybe, I got a *glass eye*, but it come from working in a factory at the age of eleven. They hooked it out because they didn't have a shield on the works. But I wear it like a medal 'cause it tells the world where I belong—deep down in the working class! We had delegates in the union there—all kinds of secretaries and treasurers . . . walkin' delegates, but not with blisters on their feet! Oh no! On their fat little ass from sitting on cushions and raking in mazuma.

[SECRETARY *and* GUNMAN *remonstrate in words and actions here.*]

Sit down, boys. I'm just sayin' that about unions in general. I know it ain't true here! Why no, our officers is all aces. Why, I seen our own secretary Fatt walk outa his way not to step on a cockroach. No boys, don't think—

FATT: [*Breaking in.*] You're out of order!

AGATE: [*To audience.*] Am I outa order?

ALL: No, no. Speak. Go on, etc.

AGATE: Yes, our officers is all aces. But I'm a member here—and no experience in Philly either! Today I couldn't wear my union button. The damnest thing happened. When I take the old coat off the wall, I see she's smoking. I'm a sonovagun if the old union button isn't on fire! Yep, the old celluloid was makin' the most god-awful stink: the landlady come up and give me hell! You know what happened?—that old union button just blushed itself to death! Ashamed! Can you beat it?

FATT: Sit down, Keller! Nobody's interested!

AGATE: Yes they are!

GUNMAN: Sit down like he tells you!

AGATE: [*Continuing to audience.*] And when I finish—

[*His speech is broken by* FATT *and* GUNMAN *who physically handle him. He breaks away and gets to other side of stage. The two are about to make for him when some of the committee men come forward and get in between the struggling parties.* AGATE*'s shirt has been torn.*]

AGATE: [*To audience.*] What's the answer, boys? The answer is, if we're reds because we wanna strike, then we take over their salute too! Know how they do it? [*Makes Communist salute.*] What is it? An uppercut! The good old uppercut to the chin! Hell, some of us boys ain't even got a shirt to our backs. What's the boss class tryin' to do—make a nudist colony outa us?

[*The audience laughs and suddenly agate comes to the middle of the stage so that the other cabmen back him up in a strong clump.*]

AGATE: Don't laugh! Nothing's funny! This is your life and mine! It's skull and bones every incha the road! Christ, we're dyin' by inches! For what? For the debutant-ees to have their sweet comin' out parties in the Ritz! Poppa's got a daughter she's gotta get her picture in the papers. Christ, they make 'em with our blood. Joe said it. Slow death or fight. It's war!

[*Throughout this whole speech* AGATE *is backed up by the other six workers, so that from their activity it is plain that the whole group of them are saying these things. Several of them may take alternate lines out of this long last speech.*]

You Edna, God love your mouth! Sid and Florrie, the other boys, old Doc Barnes—fight with us for right! It's war! Working class, unite and fight! Tear down the slaughter house of our old lives! Let freedom really ring.

These slick slobs stand here telling us about bogeymen. That's a new one for the kids—the reds is bogeymen! But the man who got me food in 1932, he called me Comrade! The one who picked me up where I bled—he called me Comrade too! What are we waiting for . . . Don't wait for Lefty! He might never come. Every minute—

[*This is broken into by a man who has dashed up the center aisle from the back of the house. He runs up on stage, says:*]

MAN: Boys, they just found Lefty!
OTHERS: What? What? What?
SOME: Shhh . . . Shhh . . .
MAN: They found Lefty . . .
AGATE: Where?
MAN: Behind the car barns with a bullet in his head!
AGATE: [*Crying.*] Hear it, boys, hear it? Hell, listen to me! Coast to coast! HELLO AMERICA! HELLO. WE'RE STORMBIRDS OF THE WORKING-CLASS. WORKERS OF THE WORLD . . . OUR BONES AND BLOOD! And when we die they'll know what we did to make a new world! Christ, cut us up to little pieces. We'll die for what is right! Put fruit trees where our ashes are! [*To audience.*] Well, what's the answer?
ALL: STRIKE!
AGATE: LOUDER!
ALL: STRIKE!

AGATE *and* OTHERS *on stage*: AGAIN!

ALL: STRIKE, STRIKE, STRIKE!!!

CURTAIN

Notes

1. Gabriel Miller, *Clifford Odets* (New York: Continuum, 1989). Pp. 166–167.
2. See Harold Clurman, *The Fervent Years* (New York: Hill and Wang, 1961).
3. Margaret Brenman-Gibson, *Clifford Odets: American Playwright. The Years from 1906–1940.*

16. *The Revolt of the Beavers*—Oscar Saul and Lou Lantz

Commentaries

Sources

Play

16.1 THE *REVOLT OF THE BEAVERS* CONTROVERSY—LOWELL SWORTZELL

TERMED A "FANTASTIC COMEDY" by its authors, Oscar Saul and Louis Lantz, *The Revolt of the Beavers* opened at New York's Adelphi Theatre in May 1937 and after twelve performances was withdrawn by FTP officials who were under attack by theatre critics and city officials alike. Even then the uproar refused to abate and the *Beavers* controversy continued to pursue [Hallie] Flanagan for the next two years. When she appeared in August 1938 before the Dies Congressional Committee, which was investigating un-American activities within the Project, her brief devoted thirteen pages of defense to this play, insisting it was a simple fable for children. Yet, however skillfully she argued, her testimony convinced few who remembered Brooks Atkinson's admonition in his original review in *The New York Times* that the story was "Mother Goose Marx," espousing the theme, "Beavers of the World Unite." "This newest adventure of the WPA theatre," he cynically suggested, "ought to improve our diplomatic relations with Soviet Russia."

Actually, after Flanagan had first read *Beavers*, she confided to her husband that it was "class conscious." The central action of the plot depicts the step-by-step preparation and carrying out of a revolution in which oppressed beavers defeat their leader who has held them in bondage to work on the "busy, busy wheel," a device for converting bark into commodities. The Chief had made the workers sad and hungry, closed their schools, imposed curfews, and outlawed their spokesman. And when he threatens to "hit" them and worse ("I'm gonna teach them the biggest lesson there is . . . I'm gonna kill them tomorrow lunch time."), the cause of the revolution is clear and fully justified: The Barkless Beavers will "wanna do something big against the Chief."

The play repeatedly advocates the importance of a scheme or strategy to achieve the workers' desires which is to be carried out through the formation of a club. By dividing the beavers into the workers and those forbidden to work, the plot stresses the importance of the right to work, along with the potential political power of the labor force. Among the working beavers the fear is so real that their workless brothers, once admitted to Beaverland, will take over their jobs, that the Chief gains yet another weapon with which to strengthen his position. He is defeated only when the scheme results in a battle scene that contains the most visual elements of stage warfare known from Shakespeare to Hollywood.

Beavers exhibits imagination in combining traditional ingredients of children's fiction such as fantasy, anthropomorphism, and the dreamed odyssey (Charlotte Chorpenning also uses these devices in *A Letter to Santa Claus*), and in placing them in a modern setting involving a boy skeptical of fairy tales in contrast to his sister, a true believer. Mary's teacher has told her that "some real stories are so full of lies that they're fairy tales and some fairy tales are so full of truth that they're just like real stories." It is this possibility the play explores and from which it receives much of its vitality. No sooner are Paul and Mary delivered to Beaverland by the Wind than they learn that "trouble" abounds there and they are in the middle of it. Once a beaver asks, "What good is lunch time; we ain't got no lunch," the "trouble" is defined as well as the goal of the plot: to gain food and the happiness that accompanies it. At first fiercely loyal to the working beavers, Paul soon shifts his sympathies when confronted with the plight of the sad barkless beavers. Audiences watching the action through his eyes, of course, concur, and thereby prove the play is innately political in its purpose.

Certainly, Brooks Atkinson, otherwise one of FTP's foremost allies, thought so: "Many children now unschooled in the techniques of revolution now have an opportunity, at government expense, to improve their tender minds. Mother Goose is no longer a rhymed escapist. She has been studying Marx; Jack and Jill lead the class revolution." And the overjoyed critic for the *Daily Worker*, proclaiming that *Beavers*' rich social significance "made history in the children's theatre in America," applauded its lesson, "That a club of all the beavers together can make sad beavers happy by throwing out the chief." Ending with the slogan, the "WPA must go on," the review promised underprivileged children a fuller enjoyment of life if they saw this play. But when a Deputy Police Commissioner refused 1,400 free tickets on the grounds that members of the Police Athletic League would be persuaded towards Marxism as Atkinson predicted, the City made it clear that it wanted no part in teaching revolution to its youth. Shortly after the Deputy called for action "to suppress or at least censor" the production, *Beavers* closed abruptly with the controversy reported fully in the press and to members of Congress.

In her testimony, Flanagan told the Dies Committee she regretted that Atkinson and the Deputy had been disturbed, "But we did not write the play for drama critics or policemen. We wrote it for children." She contended that in every fairy tale a poor child is abused by a selfish stepmother or bad giant, only to triumph over them in the end. So she argued that in an up-to-date story about beavers, the poor should also prosper by driving out their leader. Among those who agreed with her were educators, child welfare experts, social workers, religious leaders, and child psychologists whose names and credentials were submitted. Together they declared that children saw no social implications in the play but viewed it as if taking sides in a game, that it was no more Communistic than Christian, and that the moral was simply that entrenched greed and cruelty are not desirable. Reactions of children were also cited, "What I really liked best is when the Chief ate the ice cream and when the beaver put his hands in the Chief's ice cream . . ."

The results of a survey conducted by a Professor of Psychology at New York University who asked questions of "hundreds of children who had seen the play" revealed that audiences found no similarity to present-day conditions, did not come away with a unified idea of the action, nor discover social implications beyond "Don't be selfish." In Class 3A in Public School #65 in New York City, sixty-five children were asked to give the "main idea" they received from the play; most were impressed by aspects of the performance but a few expressed themes such as "It is better to be good than bad"; "If you are unkind you will always regret it"; and "It doesn't pay to be mean." The strongest impression among this group focused on the play's comic notion that the world would be a better place if everyone in it were nine years old, an idea that appealed to ten of the respondents, each aged around nine.

Members of the original company recalling almost forty years later their impressions of the furor over the production still expressed surprise, several claiming that the word "Revolt" had been the real reason for concern and suspicion, not the text itself. "It was just a children's story. That's all it was," said one. "It was an interesting script and it was an attempt to do a different kind of children's play. It was really marvelous. The kids loved it . . ." Audiences, they remembered, cheered the good beavers, booed the bad, and after performances, "There'd be a gang of kids at the stage door waiting for the Chief" in order to pummel or beat him up. FTP officials suggested no changes in the script, even after Atkinson's review appeared, and audience response remained the same, total enthusiasm. "It was so imaginative, so different from any children's theatre at that time," another actor recalled, "It still to this day would be considered an extraordinary work . . . inventive and beautifully directed and acted . . ."

But the harm had been done. *Beavers* gave critics of FTP a new weapon with which to threaten its existence. Cries that this was propaganda, Communistic, subversive, and un-American in intent were sounded at the time the Project's funding was up for Congressional renewal and as the Dies Committee was gathering evidence. True, the controversy had its lighter moments, especially when spoofed by Earl Wilson in the *New York Post* who headlined his column "Beavers Fairy-Tale Too Much for City's Finest," and claimed that inasmuch as the play would instill in policemen doctrines directly opposed to the democratic principles upon which this country is founded the Boy Scouts of America should launch an immediate investigation to protect their own. Too few found Wilson's jibes funny enough to change the prevailing impression that the play was dangerous.

Fortunately, with the emergence of a brilliant young director in California, the children's theatre unit secured the means to overshadow the controversy with the best work in its brief history.

16.2 THE RESPONSE TO *REVOLT OF THE BEAVERS*—LOU LANTZ

THE RESPONSE TO THE BEAVERS was an almost hysterical one. No child in his right mind, and most children are in their right minds, could possibly have been influenced by this play in any way, because essentially it was in all of its important aspects a real classic kind of Robin Hood—good guy versus bad guy—story, in the most primitive and obvious sense. But because of a particular philosophical orientation, there were kinds of specific spikes, almost guidelines, that were set in that gave it a particular flavor and made it recognizable to some people. I remember that Brooks Atkinson became furious about it: This had been written by people who had been reading Marx. But it was not really in any important aspects Marxist. It was a primitive and basic story of good and bad—good guy, bad guy, the suffering poor, the oppressive rich—which is classic. It's all through history. There was some very authentic poor boy background, in terms of some of the images, story patterns, and thrusts, but the essence of it was very old and very familiar. There really wasn't anything new about it.

16.3 "THE YEAST WHICH MAKES THE BREAD RISE": HALLIE FLANAGAN ON DRAMA AS POLITICS—HALLIE FLANAGAN

"THE THEATER MUST GROW UP," declared Hallie Flanagan, director of the New Deal-era Federal Theatre Project (FTP), which provided employment for actors, directors, and technicians during the Depression. By the 1930s, theater was rapidly losing its audiences to movies, and Flanagan sought to win audiences back by revitalizing drama with the excitement and conflict of contemporary life and politics. Her energy and sense of urgency came through in this talk on theater as social action, entitled "First Federal Summer Theatre: A Report." She borrowed the rhetoric of the militant labor movement as she summarized the work of a 1937 summer project that gathered FTP workers from around the country.

"Our Federal Theatre, born of an economic need, built by and for people who have faced terrific privation, cannot content itself with easy, pretty or insignificant plays. We are not being given millions of dollars to repeat, however expertly, the type of plays which landed 10,000 theatre people on relief rolls. By a stroke of fortune unprecedented in dramatic history, we have been given a chance to help change America at a time when twenty million unemployed Americans proved it needed changing. And the theatre, when it is any good, can change things.

"The theatre can quicken, start things, make things happen. Don't be afraid when people tell you this is a play of protest. Of course it's protest, protest against dirt, disease, human misery. If, in giving great plays of the past as greatly as we can give them, and if, in making people laugh, which we certainly want to do, we can't also protest—as Harry Hopkins is protesting and as President Roosevelt is protesting—against some of the evils of this country of ours, then we do not deserve the chance put into our hands. . . .

"Here is one necessity for our theatre—that it help reshape our American life.

"Nor do we work, hereafter, alone. We work not in isolated centers, but in a nationwide Federal Theatre. From that union we should gain tremendous strength. The greatest thing that this conference has given to me, personally, is the sense that in its endeavor we do not work alone in isolated units.

"We should, as we go out from here, forget all personal differences, all inevitable clashes or personality. We should remember the strong, the clear, the positive line, the line which expresses pride in having a part in Federal Theatre, the line which expresses our determination to make the best possible use of the talents of our workers, of the federal funds at our disposal, and of the theatre medium in which we work.

"There will be other such meetings, other such summer theatres, but to you, the pioneers, will always go the credit of having been the first to take the risks, first to encounter the difficulties in this new reaching out toward a stronger theatre.

"From it we shall all learn. Through it we shall mutually create a theatre which need not be just the frosting on the cake. It may be the yeast which makes the bread rise."

16.4 REVIEW OF *THE REVOLT OF THE BEAVERS*—J. BROOKS ATKINSON

New York Times, May 21st 1937

'The Revolt of the Beavers,' or Mother Goose Marx, Under WPA Auspices

THE REVOLT OF THE BEAVERS, a play in three acts, by Oscar Saul and Lou Lantz, with music by Oscar Waller. Staged by Lewis Leverett and Peter Hyun under the supervision at Jack Rennick; settings and costumes by Samuel Leve; director of dance mime, Sylvia Manning; lighting by Ira Silberstein; presented by the Children's Theatre unit of the Federal Theatre Project. At the Adelphi Theatre.

Paul	Sam Bonnell	Choppy	Nat Loesberg
Mary	Kathleen Hoyt	Chuck	Robert Livingston
Skeeball	Carl Lerner	First General	William E. Triplett
Sally	Paula Joh	Second General	Al Lipton
Pinky	Hilda Reis	Huff	Perry Bruskin
Skating Beaver	Perry Bruskin	Guppie	Hilda Reis
Windy	Charles Willett	Beanpole	Anna Zolna
Ruff	Allen Frank	Birch	Robert Miller
Tuff	Mortimer Lippman	Goldenrod	Isabel Keightley
Gruff	Elena Karam	Flunkey	Sally Raye
B. Professor	Joseph Dixon	The Chief	Ben Ross
Oakleaf	Jules Dassin	The Hoot-Owl	Ed Moore
Porky	Hilda Minter	Barkless	Adele Albert
Patty Wack	Lucy Kaye		

The Barkless Beavers—George Cohan, Gertrude Wasinsky, Rebecca Rosenberg, Estelle Howe, Sara Segal, Al Rosenblum, Estelle Weiss, Elizabeth Baker, Mildred Albert, Marie Sabadin, Virginia Daly.

The Working Beavers—Dorothy Gammon, Paula Joh, Edith Edison, Elizabeth Evans, Carl Goldman, Frances Hayes, Joe Curtis.

By BROOKS ATKINSON

Believing that plays for children should have a moral significance, the Federal Theatre has conscientiously produced a revolutionary bed-time story, "The Revolt of the Beavers," which was acted at the Adelphi yesterday afternoon. In the form of Mother Goose fantasy it is a primer lesson in the class struggle, written by Oscar Saul and Lou Lantz with an ideological score by Oscar Waller. To the kiddies of New York the battle of the laboring classes against the sleek and obese chieftains of property may be a little too remote; unformed minds accustomed to innocent play in the streets may not grasp the Marxian dialectic. But the colorful little fable which the WPA has produced for their entertainment and education portrays the struggle playfully in terms of oppressed beavers. "Beavers of the world, unite!" is the unspoken sense of the drama. By uniting and shooting down the chief's company police with revolvers and machine-guns concealed in their lunch-boxes, the hungry beavers joyfully overthrow their industrial oppressors. The newest adventure of the WPA theatre ought to improve our diplomatic relations with Soviet Russia.

"The Revolt of the Beavers" begins in a vacant lot in the outskirts of the city, where children of the proletariat are gathering firewood and wishing that they could be as "free as the wind." By a stroke of good fortune, Old Man Wind himself comes and befriends them. Summoned by telephone to the North Pole to supply a cold wind to the sweating polar bears, he takes them with him and drops them in the woods close by the kingdom of the beavers. They are enchanted at first. But under the tutelage of a learned beaver professor they enter beaverland, where they discover that the lean beavers are being exploited by their rich chief, who is entrenched behind beaver police and soldiers.

Already the laboring beavers are groaning over the speed of their working rhythm and the lack of food to sustain them. But the professor is on their side, as well as Oakleaf, the beaver organizer, who has been banished from beaverland under penalty of death. A strike of the working beavers is on the point of failure when the chief sends for the "barkless beavers," who apparently are unusually dispirited animals. But Oakleaf manages covertly to persuade them to join the beaver union. United, armed and ably guided, the workers of beaverland overthrow their oppressors in a gay pitched battle. Finally the terrified chief and his satellites are exuberantly punished and driven away. The class struggle bursts the thongs that have been binding beavers.

This first lesson in labor warfare is staged against some whimsical settings and in imaginative costumes designed by Samuel Leve and to an abstract score of music played by a WPA orchestra. It is acted with any number of capricious capers by a competent cast of child entertainers. The style is playful; the mood is gravely gay and simple-minded. Many children now unschooled in the technique of revolution now have an opportunity, at government expense, to improve their tender minds. Mother Goose is no longer a rhymed escapist. She has been studying Marx; Jack and Jill lead the class revolution.

16.5 PRODUCTION PHOTO FROM *THE REVOLT OF THE BEAVERS*

The Beavers gather under Oakleaf's flag to discuss overthrowing the Chief, from the 1937 production of *The Revolt of the Beavers*. Oscar Saul and Louis Lantz's play was one of most controversial productions to come out of The Federal Theatre Project (FTP). Congress saw the play as promoting Communist ideals, as did *New York Times* critic Brooks Atkinson: "Mother Goose is no longer a rhymed escapist. She has been studying Marx; Jack and Jill lead the class revolution" (Atkinson, 19).

16.6 HUAC TESTIMONY OF HALLIE FLANAGAN, NATIONAL DIRECTOR, FEDERAL THEATRE PROJECT

Mr. THOMAS. I have a few questions.

You heard the testimony yesterday relative to Byrnes McDonald's letter to you in connection with the Revolt of the Beavers?

Mrs. FLANAGAN. I did. In fact, I have a complete copy of that in my brief.

Mr. THOMAS. Do you have the answer there that you sent to Byrnes McDonald?

Mrs. FLANAGAN. No. I have not. That is, I think, a great oversight on our part. We would like definitely to have that letter written into the record.

It was a letter in which I simply said that I was sorry that the police commissioner had been disturbed; but all I could say about it was that the play was for children, and that the children had found it pleasant and entertaining.

And may I speak to that point now, because it took up so much of the testimony yesterday, and I really would like to say something about the Revolt of the Beavers.

I was very sorry that Mr. Brooks Atkinson, whose skill as a critic and whose learning are valued very greatly, was disturbed by this play, and that the police commissioner was disturbed; but we did not write this play for dramatic critics, nor did we write it for policemen. We wrote it for children; and I wish to write into the record what the children thought about the play.

Mr. STARNES. Of course, you know they were not criticizing it because they thought that it was not an amusing play for policemen?

Mrs. FLANAGAN. They were criticizing it because they said that they thought that it was poisoning the minds of youth.

Mr. STARNES. That is correct.

Mrs. FLANAGAN. Now, I wish to write into the record a survey on the Revolt of the Beavers which was conducted under the supervision of Dr. Francis Holder of the department of psychology of New York University, together with 14 honor students of the college, on the reactions of the children.

They made many tests covering a number of public schools; and I would like to read you the questions which they asked, not only about this play, but about every play which we do, because one function of the committee, as you mentioned yesterday, is to be sure that the plays that we do are good for children.

Mr. STARNES. They asked those questions of whom?

Mrs. FLANAGAN. Of 50 children in the public schools. And I have the answers of each one of the 50 briefed for you. I don't propose to read the whole thing, but I do propose to read the questions and a number of the answers. It is very short and I think it will interest you, because I know, and I want you to know, that I would not wish to poison the minds of children.

These are the questions :

Could the child see and hear everything in the play clearly?

You understand that these are not just on the Revolt of the Beavers. This has to do with every play that we do.

The CHAIRMAN. But this questionnaire was sent out in connection with the Revolt of the Beavers?

Mrs. FLANAGAN. Yes. But the answers that I will read have to do only with that. You couldn't understand the answers unless I first read the questions in here.

2. Was the story or idea of the play thoroughly understood by the child?

3. Was any part of the play unclear to the child?

4. If possible, get the child to express an opinion or preference on the acting and scenery, lighting, music, dancing, and the meaning of the play; what characters were liked or disliked by the child, and why; whether anything in the play has left the child upset or afraid. Would he like to see and hear more plays of this type, or would not the child like to see them?

Now, I have all fifty answers and they are all quite simple. I won't read all of them, but I would like to sketch through them.

The first answer was:

The play teaches us never to be selfish; never to be selfish because you don't get anything out of it.

The acting—how to get around on the stage. That is what I like, the acting big people do as small children, and how good they acted as beavers on roller skates.

I thought that the grown people acted their parts as children very well, especially on roller skates.

That it is better to be good than bad. That beavers have manners just like children. To teach that if you are unkind any time in your life, you will always regret it. Never to be selfish.

To show you the ways of beavers in Beaverland. The way that big people act to make them look just like children and beavers, and the way they act, and the way they work.

How the children would want the whole world to be 9 years old and happy.

To get the beavers to be like children 9 years old, thinking it would be more fun if everyone was 9 years old and a land of talking beavers on roller skates.

How the beavers live in Beaverland. How a boy and girl can make beavers be happy.

I could read all of this, but it would eventually be repetition. But I want to put special stress on the fact of how wonderful it would be to be 9 years old, and they wanted everybody to be 9 years old and kind and happy and unselfish.

Just a minute. I don't want you to understand that we only did that with the Revolt of the Beavers. We do that with all the plays that we send out.

Mr. THOMAS. I think their reaction is very interesting, but at the same time what was the reaction of Mr. Atkinson?

Mrs. FLANAGAN. Oh, I thought you were barring out critics.

Mr. THOMAS. And the reaction of the police commissioner in New York City. What attention did you pay to their reaction?

Mrs. FLANAGAN. Let us divide that into two parts. What attention did we pay to Mr. Brooks Atkinson? We value his critical opinion on the subject, as any play producer must.

Mr. THOMAS. Did you, in regard to this particular play?

Mrs. FLANAGAN. As to this particular play we found that the children, the audience for which it was planned, enjoyed it and found, as I have told you, nothing subversive in it; and we went right on giving it.

To the best of my knowledge the police commissioner did not say in his letter that he had seen the play. He was alleged to have seen it.

16.7 *THE REVOLT OF THE BEAVERS*—OSCAR SAUL AND LOU LANTZ

"THE REVOLT OF THE BEAVERS"

ACT 1—SCENE 1

CHARACTERS

PAUL	SAMUEL BONNELL
MARY	KATHLEEN HOYT
SKEEBALL	CARL LERNER
SALLY	PAULA JOH
PINKIE	HILDA REIS
SKATING BEAVER	PERRY BRUSHKIN
WINDY	CHARLES WILLETT
BACKWOODS	JOE CURTIS

ACT 1—SCENE 1

RIGHT:

1 Box off stage (with wood)
1 Pr. Skates—Size 7
Skate Key
1 Telephone Buzzer
1 Telephone on extension
2 Wind Sirens
1 Bird whistle (with water)

CENTER:

Stones (on stage)

LEFT:

1 Baby carriage
1/2 Door
Bushel basket with wood

ACT 1—SCENE 2

RIGHT:
Berry
4 Knapsacks

CENTER:
Comb
Atomizer
Quill
Large Pencil
Book
Inkwell
Eyeglasses
Umbrella
Large Handkerchief
Clothes

LEFT:
Four Bundles

ACT 1—SCENE 3

RIGHT:

CENTER:
1 Pair Skates—Size 9
Chair
Table
Table Cloth
Knife
Fork
Napkin
Medals

LEFT:
1 Police Whistle
4 Rifles
1 Tray—Turkey
1 Tray—Ice Cream
Professor's Book

ACT 2—SCENE 1

RIGHT:
Wood fire
10 Clubs

CENTER:
1 Club in foots
3 Clubs behind ramp

LEFT:
Whistle for B.B.
4 Rifles

ACT 2—SCENE 2

RIGHT:
Chalk
Potzie
Rope
Oakleaf's flag

CENTER:
Sign—"No Talkin No Walkin"
Fire-fly Lamp

ACT 3

RIGHT:
Stake
Machine-guns (in front of Busy-Busy)

CENTER:
Bango-gun (Loaded)
5 Machine guns
Trumphet

LEFT:
Piece of Ice
Oakleaf's flag
Pea Shooter
Lunch Boxes with guns inside
3 Pair Skates—Sizes 6–7–8

★

ACT 1—SCENE 1

STAGE RIGHT:
PAUL
MARY
SKATING BEAVER
WINDY

STAGE LEFT:
SKEEBALL
SALLY
PINKIE
BACKWOODS

(Enter PAUL R., kicking box onstage. Throws wood into box)

PAUL

I DON'T CARE IF HE IS A TEACHER. I DON'T BELIEVE IT.

(Picks up wood, throws it into box. X's cylinder, climbs over it, down again on upstage side.)

(Enter MARY, R.)

MARY

MY FATHER SAYS HE'S SMART ENOUGH TO BE A PROFESSOR, AND YOU GOTTA BE VERY SMART TO BE A PROFESSOR.

PAUL

(Steps down onstage)

YEAH!

HE THINKS JUST BECAUSE WE'RE NINE YEARS OLD HE CAN TELL US FAIRY TALES.

(X's C.)

WELL? I DON'T LIKE 'EM AND I DON'T BELIEVE 'EM.

(X's D.L. to auto seat, picks up piece of wood, goes on knee, aims wood at imaginary enemy.)

I LIKE REAL STORIES—ABOUT COPS AND ROBBERS AND COWBOYS AND INDIANS—WHERE THEY GO BANG! BANG! BANG!

MARY

(Runs to Paul, L.)

YOU JUST WAIT TILL WE GET IN THE WOODS. THEN WE'LL FIND A BEAVER AND WE'LL TALK TO HIM AND YOU'LL SEE THE TEACHER'S STORY IS REAL!

PAUL

AW! ANIMALS CAN'T TALK, MARY. COME ON, PICK SOME MORE WOOD.

(MARY X's to R.)

(PAUL L. behind auto seat)

IF THEY COULD, THEY'D BE JUST AS SMART AS HUMAN BEINGS—AND THEN WE COULDN'T LOCK THEM IN A ZOO. DID YOU EVER SEE A LION OR A CAMEL OR EVEN A BEAVER SAY "HELLO"?

MARY

(near cylinder R.)

JUST THE SAME—I BET YOU WISH YOU HAD A WISHING STONE AND COULD HAVE THREE WISHES.

PAUL

(X's slowly from behind auto seat to C. Suddenly bends down, picks up stone)

AW! THERE AIN'T NO WISHING STONES. HERE, LOOK!

(MARY X's to Paul, stands next to him R.)

IT'S A NICE STONE, AIN'T IT? I RUB IT.

(does so)

IBBIDY, BIBBIDY, BIBBIDY, BAKE, I WISH I HAD A PIECE OF CAKE!

(Their eyes are closed. PAUL opens eyes, looks at empty palm. Nudges MARY.)

THERE, YOU SEE, NO CAKE!

(Outstretched arm is under MARY's nose. Nudges her. Her eyes open, looks. HE throws stone off, L.)

MARY

WELL,

(Steps toward C.)

IF IT WERE A REAL WISHING STONE—

PAUL

(X's to L.)

AW, MARY—PICK SOME MORE WOOD, WILL YOU?

MARY

(X's behind cylinder, picking wood)

WELL IF I HAD A REAL WISHING STONE, I WOULD NEVER BE SAD—'CAUSE FIRST I WOULD WISH FOR A BIG PIECE OF CHOCOLATE—AND THEN I WOULD WISH MY FATHER GOT A JOB—

PAUL

(X's from L. to R.)

YOU KNOW WHAT I WOULD WISH FOR?

(climbing up cylinder)

A BLUE SWEATER AND A PAIR OF SKATES!

(sits on cylinder)

AND THAT EVERYBODY IN THE WHOLE WORLD WAS NINE YEARS OLD.

(Mary X's over, sits below cylinder, L. side)

THEN I'D NEVER BE SAD, 'CAUSE THEN I COULD GO TO THE CANDY STORE AND JUST IMAGINE—MR. BERGER WOULD BE NINE YEARS OLD, TOO,—AND I WOULD SAY, "MR. BERGER, I HAVEN'T GOT A PENNY—GIMME A PIECE OF CANDY, WILL, YA?"

(turns to her)

AND HE'D GIVE IT TO ME! AND THEN I WOULD WISH TO BE AS FREE AS THE WIND! SO I COULD DO WHATEVER I WANT—FLY AWAY AND HAVE A GOOD TIME.

(Pause)

MARY, YOU THINK THE PRINCIPAL WOULD CATCH ME IF I WAS FREE AS THE WIND?

MARY

IF SHE HAD A MAGIC STONE—

PAUL

(Climbs down from cylinder upstage; X's to R.)

AW! MAGIC STONES! I DON'T BELIEVE IT! I WAS JUST FOOLIN'! C'MON—WE GOTTA GO HOME.

(moves to Exit, R.)

WE GOT ENOUGH WOOD.

MARY

NO!

(Rises, X's to C.)

DON'T YOU REMEMBER WHAT THE TEACHER SAID? THAT IT WAS A REAL FAIRY TALE—AND YOU SAID WE WERE GONNA FIND THE BEAVERS.

PAUL

AW, MARY! WHAT'S THE MATTER WITH YOU? HOW CAN A FAIRY TALE BE REAL? C'MON! IT'S GETTING DARK.

MARY

(X's to auto seat L.) (Stretches, yawns, pretending tiredness, sits.)

AHHHH! WAIT A MINUTE! LET'S SIT DOWN—I'M AWFULLY TIRED, JUST FOR A LITTLE WHILE.

PAUL

AWW! ALL RIGHT!

(X'S to auto seat L.)

MARY

(Stretches out)

MAYBE A BEAVER'LL COME OUT OF THE WOODS WHILE WE'RE RESTING.

PAUL

AW! NO BEAVER'LL COME OUT!

(Enter SKEEBALL & SALLY, pushing a baby carriage loaded with wood; followed by PINKIE, carrying box top.)

(SKEEBALL and SALLY run on; PINKEE follows, behind.)

SKEEBALL

(At C.)

WHOA!

(Stops, let go carriage; PINKIE bumps into HIM, dropping box top, thrown back a few steps. Gets on line behind SALLY, watching PAUL & MARY)

HULLO, PAUL. HULLO, MARY.

MARY

HELLO.

PAUL

HELLO, SKEEBALL. HELLO, SALLY.

SKEEBALL

WHAT ARE Y' DOIN?

MARY

LOOKIN' FOR WOOD.

PAUL

YEAH—WHAT ARE YOU DOIN'?

SKEEBALL

SAME THING, WE GOT SOME EGG BOXES.

SALLY

AND BUSHEL BASKETS, TOO.

SKEEBALL

(Turns, picks up handle of carriage)

COME ON, GANG!

PAUL

WHY DON'T YOU HANG AROUND, SKEEBALL?

SKEEBALL

(breaks hold, turns to Paul.)

I CAN'T. MY MOTHER'S IN A HURRY FOR THE WOOD. SO LONG!

(SKEEBALL and SALLY take hold of carriage; exit R. PINKIE tries to pick up box too. Cannot. PAUL sets PINKIE'S arms, picks up top, sets it on PINKIE, who turns to Exit.)

PAUL

SO LONG, PINKIE!

PINKIE

(Turns completely around, to see PAUL)

SO LONG!

(Exits R.)

PAUL

GEE! I FEEL SORRY FOR SKEEBALL—HE NEVER HAS TIME TO PLAY.

MARY

YEAH. THEY MAKE ME FEEL AWFULLY SAD.

[[END DIALOGUE]]

(PULLS legs up on auto seat, stretches out, goes to sleep.)

★

ACT 1—SCENE 2

CHARACTERS

PAUL	SAM BONELL
MARY	KATHLEEN HOYT
WINTERSTAR	REBECCA ROSENBERG
GOLDENLEAF	ESTELLE WEISS
GREEN BUD	GEORGE COHAN
SILVER BARK	MARIE SABADIN
BROKEN TOOTH	AL ROSENBLUM
FALLEN LEAF	SARA SEGAL
CHIPPY CHIRP	ESTELLE HOWE
SHOELESS	VIRGINIA DALY
WHISTLING CLUBS	
BUFF	ALLAN FRANK
TUFF	M. LIPPMAN
GRUFF	ELENA KARAM
PROFESSOR	JOSEPH DIXON
OAKLEAF	JULES DASSIN

(CURTAIN)

(PAUL & MARY on stage, calling out to WINDY. PROFESSOR asleep up on pedestal, C.)

PAUL

SO LONG, WINDY!

MARY

DON'T FORGET TO COME BACK AND GET US!

PAUL

YEAH, DON'T FORGET!

WINDY

(Offstage L.)

I WON'T! GOOD-BYE!

PAUL AND MARY

GOOD BYE! GOOD BYE!

(Enter WINTERSTAR R., walks slowly to C., see KIDS; is frightened, throws hands in air, turns, *runs off, R.*)

(MUSIC)

(Enter BARKLESS BEAVERS from all points, humming sad tune. In bent over position, they seem to be searching for something on ground. MARY and PAUL do the same thing, and are still doing so as last of BEAVERS disappears.)

1. GOLDEN LEAF
2. SILVER BARK
3. GREEN BUD
4. BROKEN TOOTH
5. FALLEN LEAF
6. CHIPPY CHIRP
7. SHOELESS

PAUL

(On ramp)

HEH, MARY, WHAT ARE THEY LOOKING FOR?

MARY

(L. below ramp)

I DON'T KNOW.

(PROFESSOR'S loud snore scares KIDS)

PAUL

WOW; LOOK, MARY.

MARY

(X's L.)

A REAL, LIVE BEAVER—*SLEEPING*!

(Whistling Clubs cross from R. to L.)

(*WHISTLE*)

MARY

I WONDER WHAT THE WHISTLING IS ABOUT!

PAUL

(L on ramp)

I BET SOMETHING IS HAPPENING!

(*WHISTLING STOPS*)

I THINK WE OUGHT TO WAKE HIM UP—

JUST TO WARN HIM.

(X's to pedestal)

HEY, BEAVER—WAKE UP! HEY, BEAVER—WAKE UP, WILL YA? WAKE UP! WAKE UP!

(Mary X R of Professor on ramp)

PROFESSOR

(Stirs drowsily, lifts head)

DON'T YOU KNOW I'M THE BEAVER WHO LOVES PEACE AND QUIET!

PAUL

BUT I THINK SOMETHING IS HAPPENING!

PROFESSOR

SOMETHING IS ALWAYS HAPPENING.

MARY

(On knees, nudges Paul)

TELL HIM YOU WANNA ASK HIM SOMETHING.

PAUL

HEY, HOW CAN WE HAVE A GOOD TIME?

PROFESSOR

(Lifts head, speaks sharply)

NO MORE GOOD TIMES!

PAUL

LISTEN! WINDY SAID HE HAD TO GO TO THE NORTH POLE AND HE COULDN'T TAKE US ALL THE WAY—

PROFESSOR

(Interrupts, in a temper)

I DON'T CARE EVEN IF WINDY DID SAY IT! STOP BOTHERING ME!

(Kids frightened, step back)

(Awake, on elbow)

LISTEN! IF YOU'LL BE A GOOD BEAVER AND GO AWAY, I'LL SING YOU A SONG.

(Kids Jump off ramp, stand C.)

PAUL

(Whispers to MARY)

HEY, MARY, HE THINKS WE'RE A BEAVER!

MARY

MAYBE HE'S UNDER A MAGIC SPELL! DON'T SAY ANYTHING—LET HIM SING.

PAUL

ALL RIGHT.

(To Professor)

BING A BONG.

(Professor on knees—scratches his chest—slowly rises)

MUSIC, Introduction:

PROFESSOR

(Rises, takes comb and hand mirror, and combs hair, clears throat)

ONCE UPON A TIME—

(Atomizer business)

ONCE UPON A TIME—

(Atomizer business)

(Stands, facing audience with hands folded in front)

MY FAVORITE INSTRUMENT IS THE FIFE, BUT I'M ALSO FOND OF THE FIDDLE. I SIT ON THE LEFT AND I SIT ON THE RIGHT BUT MY FAVORITE SPOT IS THE MIDDLE.

(Takes out handkerchief, blows nose)

I LIKE TO GET UP IN THE EARLY DAWN,

I'M FOND OF THE MORNING LIGHT,

THERE'S NOTHING I LIKE AS MUCH AS THE MORN,

BUT THE BEAUTIFUL, BEAUTIFUL NIGHT—THE NIGHT.

(Song continued)

(KIDS sit on floor near ramp— MARY L. PAUL R.)

(PROFESSOR in lively mood sways body with music)

OH, I WAS OUT IN THE WOODS ONE DAY,

AND THE SIGHTS WERE FAIR TO SEE;

ON EITHER SIDE WAS A GAY ARRAY

OF SIGHTS CALLING ME.

(KIDS on knees watching PROFESSOR)

OH, THE SIGHT ON THE RIGHT WAS A GORGEOUS VIEW AND THERE I WOULD HAVE SPED

(Stands on one leg—arises outstretched)

(PAUL climbs ramp, sits watching PROFESSOR)

BUT THE CLEFT ON THE LEFT WAS LOVELY, TOO SO I SAY ON THE RIGHT, INSTEAD.

HERE I SIT,

(Points downward)

HERE I SIT?

WITH A HEART AS HEAVY AS LEAD.

(Kneels)

I COULD ONLY SEE ONE

SO I DIDN'T SEE NONE

GIVE ME EYES IN THE BACK OF MY HEAD.

(Song continued)

(Rises, places both hands back of head)

IT'S A PITY

IT'S A PITY

IT'S A TERRIBLE, TERRIBLE SHAME.

IT'S A PITY

IT'S A PITY,

AND I DON'T KNOW WHOM TO BLAME.

(KIDS applaud; PROFESSOR bows, low)

(MARY up ramp to pedestal)

PROFESSOR

(Relaxes again)

WELL, I SANG YOU A SONG, DIDN'T I?

PAUL

(Jumps on ramp)

AND IT WAS A NICE SONG, TOO. DID YOU MAKE IT UP YOURSELF?

(MARY on ramp)

PROFESSOR

(Raises head)

DON'T YOU KNOW I'M PROFESSOR?

(Turns around, facing L.)

PAUL

(Jumps off ramp X R to Mary)

HEY, MARY, HOW CAN HE BE A PROFESSOR? HE'S ONLY A BEAVER! RIGHT, MARY?

(KIDS watch PROFESSOR closely C. stage)

MARY

SHHHH! HE MUST BE A BEAVER PROFESSOR!

PROFESSOR

(Slowly, suspiciously)

SAY!! THAT DOESN'T SOUND LIKE A BEAVER. WAIT A MINUTE!

(Sits up—then slowly rises, takes out glasses, puts them on) (Looks at PAUL and MARY—Yowls in surprise)

WOW! HUMAN BEINGS!!

(Jumps up on pedestal)

MARY

(Jumping up on ramp—R.)

DON'T BE AFRAID! WE'RE NOT GOING TO TAKE YOU TO THE ZOO!

PAUL

(Jumps on ramp L.)

YEAH, DON'T BE SCARED!

PROFESSOR

(Jumping around)

WOW! HUMAN BEINGS! WOW! HUMAN BEINGS! IN BEAVERLAND! HOW'D YOU GET HERE?

MARY

WINDY BLEW US HERE.

PROFESSOR

GET OUT OF BEAVERLAND! YOU'D BETTER GET OUT, RIGHT AWAY!

PAUL

WHY?

PROFESSOR

BECAUSE—

(MARY faces front as PROFESSOR puts on trousers)

BECAUSE THERE'S A LOT OF TROUBLE IN BEAVERLAND, AND YOU MIGHT GET RIGHT IN THE MIDDLE OF THE TROUBLE!

PAUL

I'M NOT SCARED, ARE WE, MARY?

MARY

(Faces PROFESSOR again)

NO! WE CAME TO HAVE A GOOD TIME, MR. BEAVER.

PROFESSOR

GOOD TIME! IT'S EASY TO SEE YOU DON'T KNOW WHAT'S HAPPENING IN BEAVERLAND. I'M TELLING YOU FOR YOUR OWN GOOD—YOU'D BETTER GET OUT!

PAUL

WE AIN'T GOT NO PLACE TO GO. WE GOTTA HANG ABOUND, TILL WINDY COMES.

PROFESSOR

THEN IT'S YOUR OWN HARD LUCK!

(MARY turns, looks at PROFESSOR, who adjusts his glasses, looks at kids.)

HOW OLD ARE YOU?

MARY

NINE YEARS OLD.

PAUL

WE'RE BOTH NINE YEARS OLD.

PROFESSOR

(Takes good look at PAUL and MARY)

THAT'S VERY GOOD! BECAUSE EVERYBODY IN BEAVERLAND IS NINE YEARS OLD—EXCEPT THE BABIES—BUT THEY GROW UP VERY, VERY FAST.

(WARNING)

(Picks up notebooks, pencil)

(BERRIES)

WELL, IF YOU'RE REALLY GOING TO STAY, TELL ME YOUR NAMES, SO I CAN PUT THEM IN THE BOOK.

PAUL

(Both watch PROFESSOR closely)

MY NAME IS PAUL—AND HER NAME IS MARY. WHAT'S YOUR NAME?

PROFESSOR

(Steps down, takes handkerchief, polishes plate; X's D.R. front)

CAN'T YOU READ?

(MARY follows PROFESSOR)

PAUL

IS THAT YOUR NAME—B. PROFESSOR?

BERRIES

(Xing R. on ramp to Stage R. near footlight, squeezes berries into bottle)

PROFESSOR

THAT'S RIGHT.

PAUL

(X's R. on ramp)

HOW CAN YOU BE A PROFESSER, IF YOU'RE ONLY NINE YEARS OLD?

PROFESSOR

BECAUSE I'M SMART!

PAUL

YEAH!

(Steps off ramp)

WARN:
3 Sharp Blasts
Whistling

PROFESSOR

(Xing C.)

YEAH! I'M THE BIGGEST PROFESSOR IN BEAVERLAND. THE BEST STORY TELLER, TOO.

(Writes in air; steps up on ramp; puts ink, pencil, book, away.)

BESIDES, I'M SMARTER THAN A TEACHER, THAT MAKES ME A PROFESSOR, RIGHT, MARY?

MARY

(On ramp)

THAT'S RIGHT!

PAUL

(X's on stage to ramp, C.)

IF YOU'RE A REAL PROFESSOR, YOU WOULDN'T BE SLEEPING RIGHT NOW. WHAT ARE YOU DOIN' HERE?

PROFESSOR

(X's R.)

THE CHIEF OF THE BEAVERS DON'T LIKE STORIES, AND HE HATES SONGS. HE SAID I WAS ALWAYS BOTHERING THE BEAVERS WITH MY STORIES, SO HE TOLD ME TO KEEP OUT OF BEAVERLAND.

PAUL

SO WHAT'S THE USE IF YOU'RE A PROFESSOR—AND YOU'RE SMART?

PROFESSOR

(Steps off ramp, sits near tree. MARY L. of PROFESSOR)

NO USE! I MIGHT JUST AS WELL BE DUMB! AND THAT'S WHY I'M VERY SAD.

(Sits. MARY sits)

PAUL

(X R. Stage)

Y' SEE MARY? IT LOOKS LIKE EVERYBODY IN THE WORLD IS SAD.

(Sits. All sigh)

AND Y'KNOW, PROFESSOR, JUST BEFORE, WE SAW A BUNCH OF ANIMALS MARCHING AROUND, SINGING A VERY SAD SONG, RIGHT, MARY?

MARY

YEAH, THAT'S RIGHT.

PROFESSOR

THOSE WERE THE BARKLESS BEAVERS.

MARY

THE BARK "LESS" BEAVERS?

PAUL

DID THE CHIEF MAKE THEM SAD?

PROFESSOR

SURE—THEY ATE UP SOME OF HIS BARK, SO HE BENT DEM OVER AND CHASED THEM OUT OF BEAVERLAND. THEY HAVE TO STAY IN THE COLD WOODSALL THE TIME.

THEY HAVE NOTHING TO EAT, NOTHING TO WEAR, NO PLACE TO GO—AND THEY'RE ALWAYS CRYING.—

Whistling continues.

(PROFESSOR on ramp L. to R.)

(PAUL and MARY Jump up)

Whistle

MARY

WHAT'S THAT NOISE, PROFESSOR?

PROFESSOR

THE WHISTLING CLUBS! THEY'RE AFTER SOMEBODY.

MARY

MAYBE WE'D BETTER GET OUT OF BEAVERLAND. PAUL.

PAUL

(Looks around C., then X to R)

NO! C'MON, MARY, LET'S SEE WHAT IT'S ALL ABOUT!

PROFESSOR

(As KIDS X R.)

WHAT! YOU'LL, GET HURT IN THOSE WOODS! MARY!

GET OFF THE RABBIT'S HOUSE!

MARY

I'M NOT STANDING ON ANYBODY'S HOUSE!

PROFESSOR

C'MON, MOVE AWAY! SUPPOSE SOMEONE WANTS TO COME OUT?

KNOCK

(PAUL & MARY jump towards C. Stg.)

MUSIC ta-ra-ta-ta

THERE! YOU SEE? SOMEONE WANTS TO COME OUT.

RIGHT NOW!

MUSIC

(OAKLEAF entrance)

(OAKLEAF comes out of RABBIT's house—R. stg. rear,—in crouched position; he looks about, looks off R. stg.) slowly turning X to C.—standing directly in front of PAUL & MARY—slowly lifts body and looks at KIDS for a second)

OAKLEAF

WOW! HUMAN BEINGS!

MUSIC ta-ra-ta-ta

PROFESSOR

OAKLEAF!

(To KIDS)

GEE WHIZ! YOU SCARED THE BRAVEST BEAVER IN BEAVERLAND!

(X's to door, knocks)

HEY, OAKLEAF, C'MON OUT! DON'T BE AFRAID, THEY WON'T HURT YOU—THEY'RE ONLY NINE YEARS OLD.

(MARY R. PROF. C., PAUL L. of door)

MARY

DON'T BE FRIGHTENED, BEAVER—WE'RE GOOD HUMAN BEINGS.

PAUL

HEY, PROFESSOR, TELL HIM WE WANT TO SHAKE HANDS WITH HIM.

PROFESSOR

DO YOU HEAR THAT, OAKLEAF?

MUSIC ta-ra-ta-ta

(OAKLEAF'S hand comes out, MARY SHAKES IT; OAKLEAF COMES OUT, turns to PAUL, shakes his hand. OAKLEAF X's L. below ramp, Jumps up on ramp. ALL FOLLOW.)

OAKLEAF

(X L on ramp)

ANY WHISTLING CLUBS AROUND?

PROFESSOR

YEAH! WATCH OUT.

(OAKLEAF X's L. ALL follow him)

WHO'S CHASING YOU?

OAKLEAF

THE WHISTLING CLUBS.

(To PAUL)

THAT'S THE CHIEF'S GANG. THEY'RE CHASING ME OFF OF BEAVERLAND.

PROFESSOR

THEY'RE THE TOUGHEST BEAVERS IN THE WOODS!

OAKLEAF

THEY'RE RIGHT BEHIND ME.

PAUL

(Xing to tree)

DO THEY WANNA HIT YOU?

OAKLEAF

(X's near tree, ALL follow)

SURE! THREE AGAINST ONE!

PAUL

YEAH! I'M SORRY I LEFT MY ZOPPO GUN HOME.

OAKLEAF

WHAT? A ZIPPO GUN! WHAT D'Y'WANNA DO? START A *REGULAR WAR*? LISTEN, I'LL TELL YOU—

WHISTLE

3 BLASTS (1–2–3) (1–2–3)

(OAKLEAF X'S L., Jumps up on ramp, ALL follow. OAKLEAF disappears in back, reappears R.)

C'MON! THE WHISTLING CLUBS! EVERYBODY DOWN THE RABBIT'S HOUSE, COME ON!

(Opens door)

PROFESSOR!

(PROFESSOR exits)

COME ON MARY!

(MARY exits)

GO AHEAD, PAUL!

(PAUL exits, immediately reappears)

PAUL

HEY, OAKLEAF, NO MORE ROOM!

OAKLEAF

WOW! AND THE WHISTLING CLUBS ARE RIGHT BEHIND ME!

PAUL

WHAT ARE YOU GONNA DO?

OAKLEAF

DON'T WORRY!

(X'S C., hides in toadstool near ramp)

(PAUL disappears)

(Behind ramp)

MUSIC

[INTRODUCTION.

RUFF (appears) (R)

TUFF (Appears) (L.)

(Gruff C)

YES, WE'RE RUFF	AND TUFF	AND GRUFF
(Up ramp)	(Up ramp)	(Up ramp)

RUFF

TUFF

(All X on ramp—L.)

YES, WE'RE RUFF AND TUFF AND GRUFF

WE'RE ALWAYS IN A TERRIBLE HUFF

(Back to C.)

WHENEVER WE'RE OUT TO DO OUR STUFF

(All Jump from ramp to stg.)

Ruf-uh-uh-uh-uhfff!

Ruf-uh-uh-uh-uhfff!

RUFF AND TUFF AND GRUFF!

(All C. stg. near footlights)

(TUFF—L)

(RUFF—R)

(GRUFF—C)

THE HILLS BEGIN TO SHIVER

(Face front)

AND THE MOUNTAINS START TO SHAKE

AND THE FISHES IN THE RIVER

RUN FOR SHELTER IN THE LAKE

WHEN WE SAY RUFF—TUFF

(S to L.)

YES WE ARE RUFF AND TUFF AND GRUFF.

(Face front)

THE WHALE TURNS INTO A HERRING

THE LION BECOMES A MOUSE

AND THE TIGER IS SO TIMID

YOU CAN KEEP HIM IN THE HOUSE.

(ALL X to L. stg. (business)

(GRUFF & TUFF to toadstool—sniff around)

(GRUFF up ramp—TUFF somersaults D.L.)

(RUFF X R stg., walk around XL, pick up GRUFF and X R and back to L.)

(Here RUFF leaves TUFF alone X R stg. GRUFF Jumps to floor)

(TUFF stretches out on floor L. GRUFF kicks RUFF, he X R stg., looks off stage R—turns)

TUFF

Whistles

(X L)

RUFF

(R stg·)

D'YA SEE HIM?

TUFF

(L stg.)

NO!

GRUFF

(C stg.)

LOOKS LIKE HE GIVE US THE SLIP!

RUFF

YEAH!

OAKLEAF

LET'S GO HOME.

RUFF

(X's up on ramp) (R.)

OKAY.

TUFF

(Starts up ramp R. stg.)

WHERE YOU GOING?

RUFF

DIDN'T YOU SAY "LET'S GO HOME"?

TUFF

NO!

RUFF

DID YOU SAY IT?

GRUFF

NO!

RUFF

WHISTLE

(Start smelling around and look about.)

DAT'S FUNNY!

SOMEBODY SAID IT!

(Notice toadstool)

(ALL close in on toadstool)

HEY, Y'KNOW, THAT'S A FUNNY LOOKIN' TOADSTOOL.

I NEVER SAW IT AROUND HERE BEFORE.

TUFF

AW! THEY GROW UP OVERNIGHT!

GRUFF

(Turns ardund facing audience TUFF R. of toadstool RUFF L. of toadstool)

WHAT ARE WE GONNA DO?

OAKLEAF

LET'S SEARCH IN DA CANAL!

GRUFF

O. K.!

(X's up on ramp, C.)

DA CANAL!

MUSIC

RUFF

(Up ramp)

TUFF

(Up ramp)

YES, WE'RE RUFF AND TUFF AND GRUFF.

(ALL X L then back to C)

WE'RE ALWAYS IN A TERRIBLE HUFF

WHENEVER WE'RE OUT TO DO OUR STUFF

(ALL Jump off ramp)

RUFF

(Disappears)

AND TUFF

(Disappears)

AND GRUFF

(Disappears)

(OAKLEAF hops out, X'S to door, opens door)

OAKLEAF

(Out of toadstool)

OKAY! THE COAST'S CLEAR.

(THEY all clamber out) X to C

PAUL

WHAT'S THE MATTER, OAKLEAF?

OAKLEAF

(PAUL & PROFESSOR at his R., MARY L. PAUL sits next to OAKLEAF)

ONE NIGHT I BORROWED THE CHIEF'S SKATES—BUT I FORGOT TO TELL HIM ABOUT IT. WHEN HE FOUND OUT, HE GOT VERY MAD AND CALLED ME "A SKATE-STEALER." AND HE SAID, "WHY DIDN'T YOU ASK ME?" SO I ASKED HIM.

PAUL

WHAT DID HE SAY!

OAKLEAF

"NO!" YOU KNOW, PAUL, ALL THE BEAVERS ARE SAD, VERY SAD—AND ME, TOO—SO I GOT MAD AND SAID,

"WHY DON'T WE MAKE A CLUB FOR SAD BEAVERS TO GET GLAD?" SO ALL THE BEAVERS SAID, "YAAAAAAAAY!!"

BUT WHEN THE CHIEF HEARD ABOUT IT, HE SAID, "OAKLEAF, YOU'RE TRYING TO BUST UP BEAVERLAND—GET OUT AND NEVER COME BACK! NOT EVEN IN A MILLION YEARS!" AND YOU KNOW WHAT HE TOLD THE WHISTLING CLUBS? "IF YOU CATCH HIM, HIT HIM TILL HE CRIES!" AND WHY? WHY? JUST BECAUSE I DIDN'T WANT THE BEAVERS TO BE SAD.

PROFESSOR

OAKLEAF, I TOLD YOU A MILLION TIMES NOT TO DO ANYTHING THAT'LL MAKE THE CHIEF MAD! IF YOU'LL LEAVE HIM ALONE AND JUST ACT NICE, HE'LL BECOME A GOOD CHIEF.

OAKLEAF

(Off ramp, X to PROFESSOR)

PROFESSOR, ARE YOU A BAD BEAVER?

PROFESSOR

(Rises)

WHO SAID I WAS A BAD BEAVER?

OAKLEAF

THEN WHY DID THE CHIEF MAKE YOU SAD?

(To KIDS)

NO MATTER HOW GOOD THE BEAVERS ARE, HE MAKES THEM SADDER AND SADDER EVERY SINGLE DAY.

(PROFESSOR steps up on ramp)

PAUL

YOU KNOW WHAT YOU OUGHTTA DO, OAKLEAF? YOU OUGHTTA GIVE THAT CHIEF A PUNCH IN THE NOSE!

PROFESSOR

Y' CAN'T, HE'S GOT A BIG GANG!

PAUL

(Up Ramp)

AW! WHO'S SCARED OF HIS GANG? THEY'RE ALL NINE YEARS OLD, AIN'T THEY? C'MON, OAKLEAF, I'LL GO WITH YOU.

(Jumps down, X's L.)

WE'LL GO RIGHT INTO BEAVERLAND AND SHOW THAT CHIEF!

OAKLEAF

(X'S to PAUL, D.L.)

YOU'RE A BRAVE FIGHTER, PAUL—BUT YOU CAN'T PUNCH THE CHIEF ON THE NOSE! THE PROFESSOR IS RIGHT!

PROFESSOR

(On ramp)

SURE! I'M RIGHT!

OAKLEAF

(To PROFESSOR)

THE CHIEF HAS A BIG GANG, BUT DON'T YOU WORRY, PROFESSOR! SOME DAY THE BEAVERS'LL GET SORE! THEY'LL WANNA DO

SOMETHING VERY BIG AGAINST THE CHIEF—AND THEN THEY'LL CALL ME BACK—BECAUSE I'M ON THEIR SIDE—AND I GOT A LOT OF SCHEMES!

(ALL get in huddle)

(MARY & PROFESSOR on ramp, OAKLEAF & PAUL below)

OAKLEAF

I'M GOING TO OWL LAND—AND IF THE BEAVERS WANT ME BACK—YOU GOTTA TELL THEM TO SEND A HOOT OWL!

PAUL

DON'T WORRY, OAKLEAF, I'LL TELL THE BEAVERS, CAUSE WE'RE SAD, TOO.

MARY

AND WE'RE FOR THE BEAVERS BECAUSE THE BEAVERS *ARE SAD!*

(PAUL and MARY STAND C. stg. near ramp)

MUSIC

OAKLEAF

YOU WOULDN'T BELIEVE HOW SAD THEY ARE. Y'KNOW, NOT A SINGLE BEAVER HAS GOT A BLUE SWEATER AND A PAIR OF SKATES—EXCEPT THE CHIEF AND HIS GANG. I GOTTA GO NOW.

(S towards footlights C.—returns to KIDS)

MARY

OUT OF BEAVERLAND?

OAKLEAF

SO LONG, PROFESSOR.

PROFESSOR

GOOD-BYE, OAKLEAF.

MARY

SO LONG.

OAKLEAF

(S's to PAUL)

PAUL, DON'_ FORGET, I'LL BE IN *OWL LAND.*

(X's R., Exits)

ALL wave to OAKLEAF as MUSIC stops)

MUSIC

ta-ra-ta-ta

(PAUL & MARY XR)

(Wave farewell)

(PAUL & MARY C to ramp)

PROFESSOR

(On ramp)

POOR OAKLEAF! ONE OF THE BEST BEAVERS IN BEAVERLAND—CHASED OUT, FOREVER!

PAUL

(On ramp)

Y'KNOW, MARY, THAT CHIEF MAKES ME MAD! I'M GOING RIGHT INTO BEAVERLAND MYSELF AND PUNCH HIM RIGHT ON THE NOSE! AND HIS WHOLE GANG, TOO!

(X's C.)

PROFESSOR

(Stopping PAUL)

I TOLD YOU, YOU CAN'T DO THAT!

PAUL

NO? I'M THE BEST FIGHTER IN MY SCHOOL! RIGHT, MARY?

MARY

SURE! THEY ALWAYS SEND HIM DOWN TO THE PRINCIPAL!

PAUL

(Off Ramp C.)

C'MON, PROFESSOR, YOU WANNA. GO WITH ME AND GET EVEN WITH THAT CHIEF?

PROFESSOR

AW! I CAN'T GO TO BEAVERLAND—THE CHIEF IS MAD AT ME.

PAUL

ALL RIGHT, IF YOU'RE SCARED—I'LL GO MYSELF, WITH MARY.

(X to L to PAUL)

PROFESSOR

(On ramp)

I'M NOT SCARED!

PAUL

THEN WHY DON'T YOU COME TO BEAVERLAND AND HELP THE BEAVERS?

PROFESSOR

I LIKE TO STAY HERE, IT'S SO PEACEFUL AND QUIET.

PAUL

(BOTH walk up and down L. stage, watching Professor)

C'MON MARY, WE'LL GO OURSELVES.

PROFESSOR

(As KIDS exit D.L.)

GOOD BYE, HUMAN BEINGS.

MARY

GOOD-BYE.

(Exit L. stage)

(PROFESSOR X R on ramp—sheepishly looks around)

PAUL & MARY

(Sticking heads on stage)

YOUR LAST CHANCE, PROFESSOR, TO HELP YOUR OWN FRIENDS, THE BEAVERS!

(PROFESSOR X to R Stg. on ramp, stops sheepishly, looks around towards KIDS)

MARY

ARE YOU COMING, PROFESSOR?

PROFESSOR

ALL RIGHT!

(X's D.L. Jumps off ramp, passing KIDS, who dash up beyond him, ALL meet D.L.)

BUT NO FIGHTS! LET ME DO SOMETHING! I'LL TELL THE CHIEF A STORY—NOT A PLAIN STORY,—BUT A STORY WITH A MORAL, TO SHOW HIM. HOW MEAN HE IS—AND THEN HE'LL TURN INTO A GOOD CHIEF, AND HE'LL MAKE THE BEAVERS GLAD AND LET OAKLEAF COME BACK TO BEAVERLAND.

PAUL

ALL RIGHT! YOU TELL HIM A STORY WITH A MORAL—BUT, JUST LET HIM GET SMART!

MARY

YOU BETTER WATCH OUT FOR HIS GANG!

PAUL

AW! WHO'S SCARED!

PROFESSOR

ALL RIGHT!—*LET'S GO!*

MUSIC

(ALL march up ramp R., across ramp, Exit L. PROFESSOR, then MARY, followed by PAUL)

CURTAIN

★

ACT 1—SCENE 3

CHARACTERS

SCALY BROTHERS:

PORKY	HILDA MINTER
PATTYWACK	LUCY KAYE
CHOPPY	NAT LOESBERG
CHUCK	BOB HOROWITZ
1ST GENERAL	WM. TRIPLETT
2ND GENERAL	ALBERT LIPTON
RUFF	PERRY BRUSKIN

WORKING BEAVERS:

BEANPOLE	ANNA ZOLNA
BLUBBER	FRANCIS HAYES
BACKWOODS	JOE CURTIS
GOLDENROD	ISABELLE KEIGHTLEY
DEWDROP	DOROTHY GOLDBERG
YELLOW LEAF	PAULA JOH
BIRCH	ROBERT MILLER
SUNRAY	EDITH ANSLEY
PINE CONE	ELIZABETH GERARD
MOSS ROCK	CARL GOLDMAN
FLUNKEY	SALLY RAYE
THE CHIEF	BEN ROSS

PROFESSOR	JOSEPH DIXON
MARY	KATHLEEN HOYT
PAUL	SAMUEL BONNELL

WHISTLING CLUBS:

RUFF	ALLAN FRANK
TUFF	M. LIPPMAN
GRUFF	ELENA KARAM

STRIPPERS:	*CLIPPERS:*	*STACKERS:*	*PACKERS:*
ISABELLE KEIGHTLEY	FRANCES HAYES	CARL GOLDMAN	PAULA JOH
DOROTHY GOLDBERG	CARL LERNER	ELIZABETH GERARD	ROBERT MILLER
ANNE ZOLNA	EDITH ANSLEY		

1ST GROUP: (Choppers)	*2ND GROUP: (Choppers)*
FRANCES HAYES	CARL GOLDMAN
BOB MILLER	PAULA JOH
ELIZABETH GERARD	EDITH ANSLEY

(CURTAIN opens on Industrial Center of Beaverland. Beavers at work on "Busy Busy")

MUSIC

ALL

BUSY, BUSY, BUSY, BUSY,
STRIP, STRIP, STRIP, STRIP,
BUSY, BUSY, BUSY, BUSY,
CLIP, CLIP, CLIP, CLIP.
BUSY, BUSY, BUSY, BUSY,
STACK, STACK, STACK, STACK,
BUSY, BUSY, BUSY, BUSY,
PACK, PACK, PACK, PACK.

(1st GROUP run to front, chop few times X L.)

BUSY, BUSY BEAVERS,
LIKE BUSY, BUSY BEES,
WITH SHARP AND SHINY CLEAVERS,
WE ARE CHOPPING UP THE TREES.

(2nd GROUP runs front L. chop)

BUSY, BUSY BEAVERS
LIKE BUSY, BUSY BEES
WITH SHARP AND SHINY CLEAVERS,
WE ARE CHOPPING UP THE TREES.

(1st & 2nd GROUPS X back to original positions)

AND WE STRIP, STRIP, STRIP,
AND WE CLIP, CLIP, CLIP,
AND WE STACK, STACK, STACK,
AND WE BACK, PACK, PACK.

STRIPPERS

AND WE STRIP IT

CLIPPERS

AND WE CLIP IT

STACKERS

AND WE STACK IT

PACKERS

AND WE PACK IT.

ALL

(Stop work)

AND WE WORK, WORK, WORK ALL DAY.

ALL

AND WE STRIP IT
AND WE CLIP IT
AND WS STACK IT
AND WE PACK IT
AND WE WORK, WORK, WORK ALL DAY.

(Stop working)

WORK, WORK, WORK,
WORK, NO PLAY,
WORK, WORK, WORK,
WORK ALL DAY,
WORK! WORK!

BIRCH

(Steps down to foots, C.)

IF YOU ASK US WHY WE'RE GIVING
OUR ATTENTION TO THE BARK,
THAT'S HOW BEAVERS MAKE THEIR LIVING,
SINCE THE DAY THEY LEFT THE ARK.

PINE CONE

(Steps to foots C.)

WHEN THE BEAVERS BUILD THEIR HOUSES IT'S THE BARK THEY'VE GOT TO USE AND THE SAME APPLIES TO TROUSERS DITTO, DITTO, FOR THE SHOES.

ALL

So, WE STRIP, STRIP, STRIP,
AND WE CLIP, CLIP, CLIP
AND WE STACK, STACK, STACK,
AND WE PACK, PACK, PACK.

(STRIPPERS)

AND WE STRIP IT

(CLIPPERS)

AND WE CLIP IT

(STACKERS)

AND WE STACK IT

(PACKERS)

AND WE PACK IT.

ALL

(Walk about, hands behind backs)

AND WE WORK, WORK, WORK, WORK,
WORK, WORK, WORK,
WORK, NO PLAY,
WORK, WORK, WORK,
WORK ALL DAY,
WORK! WORK!

PINE CONE

(Steps to foots C.)

BUT THE CHIEF OF ALL THE BEAVERS,
HE GETS ALL THE BARK WE MAKE
ALL HE DOES IS PULL THE LEVERS
WHILE WE WORK UNTIL WE ACHE.

ALL

(Put hands on backs, indicating aches)

WHILE WE WORK UNTIL WE ACHE!

BIRCH

(Steps to foots, C.)

SO, WE'RE POOR, UNHAPPY BEAVERS,
WORKING BUSY AS THE BEES,
WHILE HE SITS AND PULLS THE LEVERS
AND GETS FATTER, IF YOU PLEASE!

ALL

(Show to stomachs)

AND—GETS FATTER—IF—YOU—PLEASE!

(Have stopped working; start again, while singing)

AND WE STRIP, STRIP, STRIP,
AND WE CLIP, CLIP, CLIP,
AND WE STACK, STACK, STACK,
AND WE PACK, PACK, PACK.

(STRIPPERS)

AND TO STRIP IT

(CLIPPERS)

AND WE CLIP IT.

(STACKERS)

AND WE STACK IT

(PACKERS)

AND WE PACK IT·

ALL

(Walk about, hands behind backs)

AND WE WORK, WORK, WORK, WORK,
WORK, WORK, WORK,
WORK, NO PLAY,
WORK, WORK, WORK,
WORK ALL DAY!
WORK! WORK!

PINE CONE

(Steps to foots, C.)

BUT THE CHIEF OF ALL THE BEAVERS
HE GETS ALL THE BARK WE MAKE,
ALL HE DOES IS PULL THE LEVERS,
WHILE WE WORK UNTIL WE ACHE!

ALL

(Hands on back, indicating aches)

WHILE WE WORK UNTIL WE ACHE!

BIRCH

(Steps to foots, C., as PINE CONE returns to position U.C.)

SO WE'RE POOR, UNHAPPY BEAVERS,
WORKING BUSY AS THE BEES,

WHILE HE SITS AND PULLS THE LEVERS

AND GETS FATTER IF YOU PLEASE!

ALL

(Hands at stomachs)

AND GETS FATTER IF YOU PLEASE

AND WE STRIP, STRIP, STRIP,

AND WE CLIP, CLIP, CLIP,

AND WE STACK, STACK, STACK,

AND WE PACK, PACK. PACK

(STRIPPERS)

AND WE STRIP IT

(CLIPPERS)

AND WE CLIP IT

(STACKERS)

AND WE STACK IT

(PACKERS)

AND WE PACK IT.

ALL

(Stop work, unbend, face front)

AND WE WORK, WORK, WORK ALL DAY,

(Return to work)

AND WE STRIP IT, AND WE CLIP IT,

AND WE STACK IT AND WE PACK IT,

AND WE WORK, WORK, WORK, WORK.

BIRCH:	PINE CONE:	ALL:
WORK WORK	WORK	STRIP
WORK WORK	WORK	CLIP
WORK WORK	WORK	STACK
WORK WORK	WORK	PACK

(Repeated 4 times)

ALL

WORK! WORK! WORK!

1st WHISTLE: (HUFF: Off L)

MUSIC STOPS

(As HUFF blows whistle, BEAVERS stop, turn L., throw hands in air, rush to 1st position at wheel, in fright, begin Busy, Busy)

2nd Whistle; (HUFF: Off L)

Music

(Enter: HUFF, thru gate down steps; sniffing from D.L. to foots C., turns H., X's to BEAVERS, sniffs around, winds up standing onstage to R. of CHIEF'S platform)

(3rd WHISTLE: by HUFF: Enter: GENERALS, thru gate, down steps, X R front of BEAVERS, turn few steps to L., stop face L.)

(4th WHISTLE: by HUFF: Enter: SCALY BROS., thru gate, down steps, march around at fence L., turn facing R.)

MUSIC

(Enter: THE CHIEF: C. down steps X's C. near platform, to HUFF)

CHIEF

GOOD MORNING, HUFF.

(GENERALS and SCALY BROS, snap to attention and salute)

HUFF

GOOD MORNING, CHIEF.

CHIEF

(X'ing to GENERALS)

GOOD MORNING, GENERALS.

GENERALS

GOOD MORNING, CHIEF.

CHIEF

(Turns to HUFF)

HOW'S THE BUSY BUSY TODAY?

HUFF

OKAY.

CHIEF

HEY, HUFF? YOU DIDN'T SEE ANY WILD ANIMALS OF THE FOREST HANGING AROUND, DID YA?

HUFF

I'LL CHECK UP!

(Steps C., facing front)

SCALY BROTHERS! BUFF!

(They snap to attention)

PORKY!

PORKY

(Executes triangular X to CHIEF, faces him, Salutes)

HUFF

ANY WILD ANIMALS OF THE FOREST AROUND?

PORKY

NOT EVEN ONE, CHIEF!

CHIEF

(Pins medal on PORKY)

THAT'S GOOD.

(PORKY salutes, returns)

HUFF

(X's to SCALY BROS)

OKAY! KEEP YOUR EYES OPEN!

CHIEF

HEY, HUFF!

HUFF

(X'ing to CHIEF, C.)

COMIN' UP, CHIEF!

CHIEF

LISTEN, HUFF. I SMELL TROUBLE IN THE AIR.

(HUFF DASHES BEHIND CHIEF, thru BEAVERS, GENERALS back into position. GENERALS & SCALY BROS. sniff about heads down body forward; wind up, upright into position)

ANY BEAVER BEEN ACTING WISE SINCE I CHASED OAKLEAF OUT OF BEAVERLAND!

HUFF

DEY'RE A LITTLE WILD BUT I GOT 'EM ALL TAMED!

CHIEF

IN CASE YOU HEAR ANY BEAVERS TALKIN' ABOUT OAKLEAF OR HIS SAD BEAVER CLUB—GIVE HIM A SOCK RIGHT AWAY!

HUFF

DON'T WORRY CHIEF! YOU KNOW ME! JUST

SAY THE WORD AND I'LL BEAT THE FUR OFF DEM!

CHIEF

(Restraining HUFF)

SAVE IT FOR LATER. IT'S TIME FOR LUNCH NOW.

(X's R. to BEAVERS)

OKAY, BEAVERS! YOU CAN STOP THE BUSY BUSY! IT'S TIME FOR LUNCH NOW.

STOP WHEEL

(Turns, facing L. arm extended)

[MUSIC

(BEAVERS relax, rest sit)

(As music starts. HUFF X's, takes CHIEF'S ARM, ESCORTS HIM slowly up steps on platform; GENERALS and SCALY BROS. KEEP step thru music.)

(BEAVERS have begun playing games)

(FLUNKEY enters: after GENERALS and SCALY BROS, hade X'd into position near fence. HUFF

1st GENERAL

2nd GENERAL

CHUCK

CHOPPY

PATTYWACK

PORKY.

(FLUNKEY brings in table, places it before CHIEF, exits; re-enters with FORK and KNIFE and NAPKIN, hands same to CHIEF, arranges NAPKIN. Steps down, runs off L)

BEANPOLE

WHAT GOOD IS LUNCH TIME IF WE HAVE NO LUNCH?

CHIEF

AHHH! DON'T GET WISE, EAT YOUR LUNCH.

BIRCH

WHAT LUNCH!

MUSIC

(FLUNKEY re-enters with tray of turkey: CHIEF'S GANG watches closely, raise arms aloft as FLUNKEY passes, X'ing up to platform. THE CHIEF pulls off leg of turkey. BEAVERS watch intently. CHIEF satisfied, nods to FLUNKEY, nod is passed down the line.

(HUFF is playing marbles with BIRCH, BEANPOLE, DEW DROP) (Argument develops)

HUFF

YOU'RE INCHIN'! YOU'RE INCHIN'!

BIRCH

I AM NOT! GO ON, I WAS NOT!

CHIEF

(Disturbed by commotion)

GEE WHIZ, YOU BEAVERS, CAN'T YOU KEEP QUIET WHEN EVERBODY IS EATING?

(Commotion doesn't die down)

HEY, HUFF!

HUFF

(Reluctantly leaving argument)

YOU WERE INCHIN'!

(Takes position on line)

(FLUNKEY removes tray on order of CHIEF, hands it down line, as each snags a bite after passing tray on. PORKY takes tray off, as FLUNKEY exits. RE-enter PORKY)

MUSIC

(FLUNKEY enters with tray of ice cream. GANG'S hands go up again higher. Is set before CHIEF, who tastes, approves. BEANPOLE and BLUBBER sneak over to platform. BOTH try to reach a lick of ice cream.)

MUSIC

CHIEF

(Almost in tears)

DIDN'T I TELL YA A MILLION TIMES NOT TO STICK YOUR FINGERS INTO MY ICE CREAM?

BLUBBER

GEE, IT LOOKED SO GOOD, CHIEF.

CHIEF

ALL RIGHT! SO WHY DON'T YOU ASK ME?

(BEANPOLE and BLUBBER snap to attention, stand facing CHIEF.)

BOTH

CAN WE HAVE SOME ICE CREAM, CHIEF!

CHIEF

NO!!

(Continues eating, attended by FLUNKEY)

BEANPOLE

(Disgusted, as both turn back)

GEE WHIZ! WHAT A LUNCH TIME! THERE AIN'T A SINGLE FAT BEAVER LEFT.

(Kneels, D.R.)

NOT EVEN BLUBBER.

(BLUBBER sits, disconsolate, UR.)

BIRCH

YEAH, TAKE A LOOK AT THE CHIEF!

SUN RAY

LOOK AT HIM, EATIN' A MILE A MINUTE! NO WONDER HE'S SO FAT!

BLUBBER

(Rises, X's D.R.)

YEAH, LOOK AT ME!

(Indicates)

LUNCH TIME IS TERRIBLE. I EVEN MADE UP A POEM ABOUT IT.

ALL

(Ad Lib.)

HOW DOES IT GO? RECITE IT! GO AHEAD, BLUBBER!

BLUBBER

(X's D.R., facing L.)

(Recites)

I USED TO LOVE MY LUNCHTIME
I USED TO SIT AND MUNCH
A PIECE OF BARK AT LUNCH TIME
I'D CRUNCH AND CRUNCH AND CRUNCH.
BUT NOW—

(Leans indicating CHIEF)

I DON'T LIKE LUNCHTIME
I HAVE NO BARK TO CRUNCH
AND WHAT'S THE GOOD OF LUNCHTIME
IF YOU HAVEN'T GOT NO LUNCH!

(CHIEF laughs, followed by GANG)

BEANPOLE

IT'S A VERY GOOD POEM!

SUN RAY

VERY TRUE!

PROFESSOR

KNOCK KNOCK! (Off 1)

(As PROFESSOR knocks, HUFF Jumps to steps L.C. GENERALS X C. SCALY BROTHERS wheel up L., facing gate.)

PORKEY

WHO GOES THERE? BEAVER OR WILD ANIMAL OF THE FOREST!

PROFESSOR

(Off L with PAUL & MARK)

IT'S ME! THE BIGGEST PROFESSOR IN BEAVER-LAND!

BEAVERS

(ALL rise, happy to hear PROFESSOR is back; ad lib. among selves)

THE PROFESSOR! HE WOKE UP! MAYBE HE'LL HELP US! WOW! THE PROFESSOR! OH, BOY!

PROFESSOR

(Still off L. with KIDS)

LET ME IN! I GOTTA SEE THE CHIEF RIGHT AWAY! VERY IMPORTANT!

PORKY

WHO'S THAT WITH YOU?

PROFESSOR

TWO HUMAN BEINGS.

(CHIEF Jumps behind chair, crouches. FLUNKEY disappears behind pedestal; BEAVERS all in huddle ad. lib.)

CHIEF

HEY, YOU BEAVERS, KEEP QUIET!

(Calls off L.)

ARE THEY BIG OR ARE THEY LITTLE?

PROFESSOR

THEY'RE NINE YEARS OLD!

CHIEF

(Relieved, comes out from behind chair)

OKAY, LET THEM IN!

(Site down, waits)

1ST GENERAL

HUPP!!

(SCALY BROS. wheel back into position, watch for entrance)

(Enter PROFESSOR, followed by PAUL and MARY, thru gate, down Steps. As PROF. passes C. sheepishly exchanges glances looks with CHIEF, X's to BEAVERS D.R.)

(PAUL & MARY stop C. facing CHIEF)

(PROFESSOR exchanges greetings with BEAVERS, CALLS TO PAUL & MARY)

PROFESSOR

BEAVERS, I WANT YOU TO MEET THE HUMAN BEINGS, PAUL AND MARY. PAUL AND MARY, COME! I WANT YOU TO MEET THE BEAVERS.

(PAUL & MARY X to BEAVERS)

BEAVERS

HELLO! HOW DO YOU DO! HELLO!

KIDS

HELLO!

BIRCH

WHAT ARE YOU DOING IN BEAVERLAND, PROFESSOR?

PROFESSOR

I CAN'T TELL YOU NOW. JUST CHEER UP A LITTLE BIT!

PAUL

THAT'S RIGHT, BEAVERS. DON'T WORRY!

CHIEF

HEY, PROFESSOR! HOW ABOUT TELLING ME SOMETHING ABOUT THIS? I'M THE CHIEF, AIN'T I?

PROFESSOR

COMIN' RIGHT up, CHIEF!

(X's to ramp, followed by KIDS, who stand R. of platform, watching CHIEF)

THIS IS THE CHIEF OF THE BEAVERS. THIS IS PAUL AND MARY. LISTEN, CHIEF, I WANT TO TALK TO YOU.

CHIEF

I WANNA TALK TO THE HUMAN BEINGS FIRST. COME ON UP. COME ON UP!

(PAUL & MARY step on platform. PROFESSOR X's to steps C. HUFF bars his path; stands nose to nose; PROFESSOR gives ground, returns to platform U R., mortified)

THESE ARE THE FIRST HUMAN BEINGS I EVER SAW. GO AHEAD, HUMAN BEINGS. TALK TO ME. ASK ME QUESTIONS. DO YOU KNOW WHO I AM? I'M THE CHIEF—THE CHIEF OF THE BEAVERS.

(Picks up skates, shows them)

HOW DO YOU LIKE MY SKATES?

(As KIDS turn wheels)

BALL BEARYUN!

(Opens neck, exposes sweater)

HOW DO YOU LIKE THIS?

(Rises, turns, flips tail, sits)

Y'WANNA SEE SOMETHING ELSE? HEY, GENERALS! MAKE THE SCALY BROTHERS MARCH AROUND AND DO SOME *EXERCISES*!

(GENERALS change position, 1st G. D.L. 2nd G. U.L.)

MUSIC

1ST GENERAL

HUPP!!

(SCALY BROS, snap to attention, march to C. on cue line up. Go into drill)

(On cue)

GENERAL

ATTENTION!

(SCALY BROTHERS scramble about, snap to attention, facing front)

1ST GENERAL

AT EAST!

(SCALY BROS. throw guns to floor, break ranks)

1ST GENERAL

ATTENTION!

(SCALY BROS. pick up rifles, scramble to attention)

(GENERALS X to position, front of SC.B.)

HUPP!

(THEY ALL return to former positions at fence, salute as CHIEF and HUFF applaud)

CHIEF

DIDJA SEE THAT! THAT'S IN CASE ANYBODY GETS WISE!

(Exposes sweater slowly, leans back)

(PAUL and MARY overwhelmed)

HOW D'Y'LIKE MY SWEATER? Y'KNOW, I'M THE FANCIEST BEAVER IN BEAVERLAND, THE SMARTEST, TOO. RIGHT, PROFESSOR?

(PROFESSOR turns away, nose in air)

AHHH! Y'WISE PROFESSOR, YOU THINK YOU'RE SMARTER THAN EVERYBODY ELSE. I'LL SHOW YA! GO AHEAD, HUMAN BEINGS, ASK ME ANY QUESTION Y'WANNA!

MARY

(Indicates wheel)

WHAT DO THE BEAVERS MAKE ON THE WHEEL, CHIEF?

CHIEF

(Delighted)

THEY MAKE BARK. A BEAVER CAN'T LIVE WITHOUT BARK. HE EATS IT—

(Indicates on fingers)

HE MAKES PANTS OUT OF IT, AND COATS,—AND —

(Stuck)

EVERYTHING!

PAUL

WHY DON'T THEY TAKE THE BARK OFF THE TREES OUT IN THE WOODS?

CHIEF

(Delighted to show smartness)

WHAT D'Y'THINK THIS IS THE OLDEN TIMES? WE'RE NOT OLDEN TIME BEAVERS. WE CAN'T EAT RAW BARK. WE GOTTA FIX IT UP ON THE WHEEL.

(In excellent humor)

GO AHEAD, HUMAN BEINGS, ASK ME MORE QUESTIONS.

PAUL

ALL RIGHT, I'LL ASK YOU. WHAT'S THE IDEA OF MAKING ALL THE BEAVERS SO SAD?

CHIEF

WHAT D'YA MEAN, I MAKE THEM SAD?

PAUL

WELL, THEY LOOK SAD. YOU DON'T GIVE THEM ENOUGH BARK.

CHIEF

(Aggrieved)

THAT HAS NOTHING TO DO WITH YOU. YOU JUST ASK ME QUESTIONS ABOUT—

(Stuck)

BEAVERLAND.

MARY

IS IT HARD TO PULL THE LEVERS?

CHIEF

(In good humor again, indicates)

NO. IT'S EASY.

MARY

THEN, WHY DON'T THE BEAVERS PULL THE LEVERS AND KEEP THE BARK THEMSELVES?

(CHIEF laughs) (Picked up by GANG)

(CHIEF stops, as HUFF shakes head in negative. GANG stops, too)

CHIEF

(To KIDS, annoyed and puzzled)

WHAT D'Y'MEAN "WHY DON'T THEY PULL THE LEVERS AND KEEP THE BARK?"

THEN THEY'D OWN THE WHEEL AND THE BARK! AND IT'S MY WHEEL AND MY BARK! WHAT D'Y'MEAN ASKING ME THAT? I'M GETTING SORE! Y'BETTER ASK ME SOMETHING ELSE!

PAUL

(His dander is up)

ALL RIGHT! WHY IS IT YOU HAVE SUCH A BIG FAT BELLY AND ALL THE BEAVERS ARE SO SKINNY?

(Beavers enjoy the situation, giggling, hiding their smiles, etc.)

CHIEF

(Explains, naturally)

MY WHOLE FAMILY HAS FAT BELLIES.

(Puzzled)

DON'T Y'LIKE IT?

PAUL

NO! IT LOOKS STUFFED UP! 'CAUSE YOU CAN EAT LUNCH WHENEVER Y'WANNA, AND THE

BEAVERS CAN'T EVEN EAT LUNCH LUNCH-TIME, THAT'S WHY!

CHIEF

(Infuriated)

LISTEN, HUMAN BEINGS, I'M GETTING SORE! I'M GETTING VERY SORE! I'LL GIVE YOU ONE MORE CHANCE TO ASK ME A QUESTION, AND IF I DON'T LIKE IT, I'LL CHASE YOU OUT OF BEAVERLAND.

(PAUL is about to give an angry retort, when MARY and PROFESSOR intervene)

MARY

WAIT A MINUTE!

(MARY pulls PAUL to PROFESSOR. ALL whisper animatedly, rise, face CHIEF again, plan all set)

PAUL

GO AHEAD, MARY, ASK HIM AN EASY QUESTION.

MARY

DO YOU LIKE STORIES, CHIEF?

CHIEF

(Suspicious, eyes PROFESSOR)

STORIES? YEAH, I LIKE 'EM.

MARY

PROFESSOR, TELL HIM A STORY.

(PROFESSOR X'S to C., bows to BEAVERS, who applaud, bows to GANG, who applaud, and standing at ease)

CHIEF

(Looks at them sternly, yells)

HEY!!!

(THEY snap back to attention)

PROFESSOR

(Turns to CHIEF, swift nod is answered by CHIEF, gingerly)

THANKS TO YOU, I'M OUT OF PRACTICE, BUT I'LL DO MY BEST!

CHIEF

DON'T GET SMART!—JUST TELL THE STORY!

KNOCK! KNOCK! Off L.

WHISTLING CLUBS

(GENERALS X TO C., SCALY BROTHERS wheel, facing gate)

PORKY

WHO GOES THERE, BEAVER OR WILD ANIMAL OF THE FOREST?

WHISTLING CLUBS

(From off L.)

RUFF! TUFF! AND GRUFF!

(PROFESSOR, in terror, hides behind platform U.R.)

CHIEF

(Relieved)

LET 'EM IN!

1ST GENERAL

MUSIC

HUPP!!

(SCALY BROS, and GENERALS return to original positions, fence L.)

(Enter: in order, RUFF, TUFF, GRUFF, thru gate, down steps in single file, face front, stop, awaiting command from CHIEF, WHO STEPS DOWN)

CHIEF

HUPP!!

(RTG about face, facing R.)

HUPP!!

(RTG march R., halt in echelon)

HUPP!!

(RTG about face, facing R.)

YOH!!

(GRUFF X'S to CHIEF)

DID Y'CHASE HIM OUT?

MUSIC STOPS

(CHIEF gives out medals)

GRUFF

YEAH! HE MUST BE A MILLION MILES AWAY!

TUFF

BOY, DID WE CHASE HIM! OVER THE MOUNTAINS—

GRUFF

THRU THE WOODS—

TUFF

IN DA CANAL—

GRUFF

YEAH! UP A TREE!

CHIEF

(In supreme joy)

DID YA HIT HIM TILL HE CRIED?

GRUFF

NAHH! HE GIVE US DA SLIP.

CHIEF

HE DID, HUH?

(Snatches back the medals)

TUFF

(Has X'd to CHIEF, C)

MAYBE, IF YOU'D GIVE US SKATES LIKE YOU PROM—

CHIEF

(Accusing finger almost in TUFF's eye)

SKATES, HUH!!! ALL RIGHT! HUPP!!!

(WHISTLING CLUBS Jump D.R. in one leap) (CHIEF X's back up on platform, in high dudgeon; yells to hiding PROFESSOR)

HEY, PROFESS—HEY PROFESSOR, ALL RIGHT, START TELLING YOUR STORY.

PROFESSOR

(Comes out of hiding, X's C. bows as before, only BEAVERS applaud)

ONCE UPON A TIME THERE WAS A GOOD BEAVER. HE WAS VERY BRAVE AND VERY SMART. BUT HE WAS CHASED OUT OF HIS BEAVERLAND, AND HIS NAME WAS—

CHIEF

(Having anticipated this)

OAKLEAF, HUH!! SO YOU'RE TAKING OAKLEAF'S PART!!

PROFESSOR

(Scared, but gives no ground)

YEAH! HE'S A GOOD BEAVER!

CHIEF

I BET YOU'RE EVEN A MEMBER OF HIS CLUB!

PROFESSOR

(Slams book shut)

I'M NOT! I CAME TO TALK TO YOU BECAUSE I'M A PROFESSOR AND I'M SMART!

CHIEF

(Body bent, hands on hips)

IF YOU'RE SO SMART, YOU BETTER STOP TRYING TO BUST UP BEAVERLAND!

PROFESSOR

(Imitating CHIEF)

YOU'RE THE ONE WHO'S TRYING TO BUST IT UP!

CHIEF

(Almost in tears)

SO NOW I'M THE ONE TRYING TO BUST UP BEAVERLAND. GET OUT OF HERE, RIGHT AWAY, JUST AS FAST AS YOU CAN GO! GO AHEAD!

PROFESSOR

ALL RIGHT, I'LL GO.

(X's D.L., stops, wheels back to CHIEF)

BUT I'M TELLING YOU THE BEAVERS GOTTA HAVE MORE BARK. MAYBE IF YOU GAVE THEM MORE BARK, INSTEAD OF BEING GREEDY, YOU WOULDN'T HAVE TO CHASE OAKLEAF OUT OF BEAVERLAND!

CHIEF

(Almost the last straw)

THAT'S ENOUGH—THAT'S TOO MUCH! GET OUT!

PROFESSOR

I'M GOING!

(X's to go D.L. wheels again to CHIEF)

BUT REMEMBER I'M A STORY TELLER, AND A GOOD ONE, TOO! AND I'M GONNA TELL STORIES ABOUT YOU, SO THE WHOLE WOODS WILL KNOW YOU FOR WHAT YOU ARE—AND THEN YOU'LL BE SORRY!

CHIEF

(This is the last straw; explodes)

AND JUST FOR THAT YOU CAN GET OUT OF BEAVERLAND FOREVER! WHISTLING CLUBS! START CHASING HIM!

(PROFESSOR looks on as WHISTLING CLUBS prepare chase, leap forward, PROFESSOR back; on second Jump PROFESSOR at steps; 3rd jump PROFESSOR runs up steps, disappears behind platform; chased by TUFF; CHIEF notions to GRUFF and RUFF, to catch PROFESSOR as he emerges; PROFESSOR runs into RUFF'S arms and is taken U.L., as PAUL Jumps down from platform, takes D.L. in front of HUFF)

PAUL

WAIT A MINUTE! I AIN'T GONNA LET YOU CHASE THE PROFESSOR OUT OF BEAVERLAND! YOU LET HIM STAY HERE, YA GET ME?

CHIEF

SUP-POSIN' I DON'T WANNA?

PAUL

THEN I'LL PUNCH YOU ON THE NOSE!

(Squares off, fists flailing the air)

C'MON! Y'FAT CHIEF, YA!

(ALL are motionless, gasp in surprise at PAUL'S daring)

CHIEF

(Stepping down, followed by MARY)

WHO? ME???? THE CHIEF OF THE BEAVERS????

(Whistles to HUFF, who imprisons PAUL'S arms, wheels him across to L.C., as MARY yells warning)

MARY

LOOK OUT, PAUL!

(Is held firmly by RUFF)

CHIEF

(X's to PAUL, clenched fist poised to sock)

SO Y'THINK YOU'RE GONNA PUNCH THE CHIEF OF THE BEAVERS ON THE NOSE, HUH? I'LL SHOW YA.'

(Punches PAUL on nose)

HOW DO YOU LIKE THAT?

(Punches PAUL several times, time to WHISTLING CLUBS)

GO AHEAD, SCALY BROTHERS, MAKE THEM DANCE!

(SCALY BROS. lower guns, advance, give five volleys, making them dance. CHIEF stamps on PROFESSOR'S foot, who hods and jumps about)

WARNING CAW-CAW

CHIEF

GO AHEAD, WHISTLING CLUBS, START THROWING THEM OUT. AND HIT 'EM ALL, EVEN THE GIRL!

(WHISTLING CLUBS chase KIDS and PROFESSOR up ramp, steps thru gate)

PAUL

(On exit)

I'LL GET EVEN WITH YOU, Y'FAT CHIEF!

MARY

(On exit)

YOU'LL BE SORRY FOR HITTING A GIRL!

CHIEF

(X's up to platform, yells after them)

THAT'LL TEACH YOU A BIG LESSON NOT TO START UP WITH ME.

(Turns on BEAVERS)

C'MON, YOU BEAVERS, GET BACK ON THE BUSY BUSY.

BIRCH

(Breaks thru, X's to CHIEF)

LISTEN, CHIEF, YOU'RE GOING TOO FAR! THE BEAVERS ARE SORE! I'M WARNING YA, WE'RE GETTING VERY SORE!

CHIEF

SO NOW YOU'RE SORE, HUH! HOW WOULD YOU LIKE IT IF THE BARKLESS BEAVERS WORKED ON THE WHEEL INSTEAD OF YOU—AND YOU WERE THE BARKLESS BEAVERS, WALKING AROUND ALL BENT OVER IN THE COLD WOODS?

(Whistles signal to PORKY, who dashes up behind BIRCH, to knees on floor. CHIEF points in air, BIRCH looks up, CHIEF pulls BIRCH'S hat over eyes, pushes him over PORKY, BIRCH falls down, caught by TUFF, U.R.)

HEY, CAW-CAW BIRDS! GO TELL THE BARKLESS BEAVERS TO COME TO BEAVERLAND. RIGHT AWAY!

CAW-CAW

CAW-CAW BIRDS

(Off L.)

CAW! CAW! CAW! CAW! BARKLESS BEAVERS COME BACK TO BEAVERLAND! BARKLESS BEAVERS COME BACK TO BEAVERLAND!

BIRCH

Y'CANT DO THAT CHIEF! YOU CAN'T MAKE US THE BARKLESS BEAVERS!

CHIEF

NO????? WHO WANTS TO BE THE FIRST BARKLESS BEAVER? WHO WANTS TO GET BENT OVER? WHERE IS HE? LET HIM SAY SOMETHING! GO AHEAD! WHO WANTS TO GET WISE, GO AHEAD!

(BEAVERS, realize they are helpless, return slowly to positions at wheel, ready for BUSY BUSY)

ALL RIGHT! THAT'S BETTER! NOW WE CAN START MAKING BARK AGAIN.

(To the stragglers)

COME ON! GET BACK ON THE BUSY BUSY

(X's to platform)

BUSY BUSY BUSY BUSY ONE TWO THREE FOUR WHOOOOAAAAAA!

WHEEL STARTS

MUSIC

BEAVERS

(At work)

BUSY BUSY BUSY BUSY

STRIP STRIP STRIP STRIP

BUSY BUSY BUSY BUSY

CLIP CLIP CLIP CLIP.

CURTAIN

★

ACT 2—SCENE 1

CURTAIN

(AT RISE, PAUL and MARY are seated R. near foots, near fire)

PAUL

GEE WHIZ! THAT PROFESSOR MAKES ME FEEL SAD. BUT WE AIN'T GOING TO RUN AWAY LIKE THE PROFESSOR. I'M GONNA GET EVEN WITH THAT CHIEF FOR PUNCHIN' ME ON THE NOSE AND HITTING YOU!

MARY

PAUL! WHY DON'T WE SEND FOR OAKLEAF? HE'LL HELP US!

PAUL

THAT'S RIGHT, MARY! LET' S CALL A HOOT OWL!

(BOTH KIDS rise, walk about R.)

(Calling:

HOOT! HOOT! HOOT! HOOT! HOOT!

SOUND

HOOT OWL

(Enter: HOOT OWL)

AHOOT! AHOOT! AHHOOOOOOOT OWL!

PAUL

LISTEN, MARY! YOU HEAR SOMETHING?

MARY

YEAH!

(KIDS look L. and see HOOT OWL, on ramp L.)

(KIDS step toward C.)

HOOT OWL

WHAT DO YOU WANT?

PAUL

CAN YOU FLY FAST?

HOOT OWL

A MILLION MILES A MINUTE!

PAUL

IT AIN'T EVEN A MILLION MILES—HOW FAST CAN YOU REALLY FLY?

HOOT OWL

I'M THE FASTEST FLYER IN THE WOODS. I'LL FLY AWAY SO FAST—YOU WON'T EVEN SEE ME FLY—I'LL JUST DISAPPEAR!

PAUL

CAN YOU REMEMBER A MESSAGE?

HOOT OWL

(annoyed by question)

WHO'S THE SMARTEST ANIMAL IN THE HUMAN BEING'S BOOKS?

MARY

THE OWL!

HOOT OWL

RIGHT, MARY! WHAT'S THE MESSAGE?

PAUL

I WANT YOU TO TELL OAKLEAF I HAD A BIG FIGHT WITH THE CHIEF, AND HE PUNCHED ME ON THE NOSE, AND HE HIT MARY! AND HE CHASED US OUT OF BEAVERLAND—AND THE PROFESSOR, TOO. AND TELL HIM—THE CHIEF SENT FOR THE BARKLESS BEAVERS—AND THEY'RE MARCHING INTO BEAVERLAND, RIGHT NOW!

MARY

AND TELL HIM IT'S NIGHTTIME, AND WE'RE ALL ALONE IN THE WOODS—AND WILL HE PLEASE HURRY!

PAUL

NOW LET ME SEE HOW FAST YOU CAN REALLY FLY!

HOOT OWL

O.K. JUST WATCH ME DISAPPEAR!

AHOOT! AHOOT! AHOOOOOOOOT!

(Turns, flaps wings, exit L.)

PAUL

WOW! WHAT A FAST FLYER!

MARY

GEE, I HOPE OAKLEAF COMES IN A *HURRY*!

(KIDS X L to investigate noise)

(KIDS back away, toward fire D.R.)

NOISE—Off L

NOISE—Louder

PAUL

HEY, MARY, Y'SCARED?

MARY

I AIN'T SCARED, ARE YOU!

PAUL

NO.

(KIDS huddle together, scared)

NOISE—LOUDER

HEY, MARY! D'Y'HEAR SOMETHING FUNNY?

MARY

YEAH!

PAUL

DON'T WORRY! YOU KNOW I'M A GOOD FIGHTER!

(Picks up stick)

AND I GOT A BIG FAT STICK, AND I'LL HIT ANYBODY THAT COMES NEAR THE FIRE!

MARY

MAYBE IT'S THE CHIEF, PAUL?

(Enter—BEAVERS, on ramp L.)

PAUL

WHAT SHOULD WE DO, HIDE?

MARY

YEAH, LET'S HIDE!

(KIDS run U.R., hide behind tree! as BEAVERS walk down ramp to fire)

BIRCH

HEY, BEAVERS, HERE'S THE FIRE!

BEANPOLE

BUT WHERE'S THE HUMAN BEINGS?

BIRCH

THEY MUST HAVE RUN AWAY!

(KIDS come out from hiding, X'ing down to BEAVERS, who surround them, rejoicing.)

PAUL & MARY

HERE WE ARE!

MARY

WE THOUGHT IT WAS THE CHIEF!

GOLDENROD

WHERE'S THE PROFESSOR?

PAUL

(Xing towards first)

HE RAN AWAY! A MILLION MILES AWAY! AND HE SAID HE'S NEVER COMING BACK!

BIRCH

DID YOU SEE THE BARKLESS BEAVERS?

PAUL

NO.

BIRCH

NO? THAT MEANS THEY DIDN'T PASS YET!

BEANPOLE

IF THEY TRY TO GET INTO BEAVERLAND—THERE'LL BE A FIGHT!

NOISE: Professor off L

(BIRCH steps toward C followed by BEAVERS, looking off L)

BIRCH

GET STICKS, EVERYBODY!

(BEAVERS pick up stick, so does MARY)

GET READY, BEAVERS. HERE THEY COME!

(THEY stand together, arms aloft, D. R. near fire)

BEAN POLE

THEY AIN'T GONNA GET INTO BEAVERLAND!

(Enter: PROFESSOR, RUNNING on from D.L., straight to BEAVERS)

BEAVERS

WOW! THE PROFESSOR! HE AIN'T OUT OF BEAVERLAND!

PROFESSOR

(All exhausted)

HEY, BEAVERS! BEAVERS! I HAD TO COME BACK TO WARN YOU! THE BARKLESS BEAVERS ARE COMING RIGHT NOW!

MUSIC

BIRCH

C'MON, BEAVERS! MAKE A BIG, FAT LINE!

BEANPOLE

THEY AIN'T GONNA GET INTO BEAVERLAND!

GOLDENROD

WE'LL SHOW THEM!

BIRCH

JUST STAND STILL!

PAUL

D'Y'HEAR THAT, MARY? THAT'S SOME SAD SONG!

MARY

YEAH. IT'S THE SAME SONG WE HEARD WHEN WE FIRST CAME TO BEAVERLAND.

BEANPOLE

DON'T FORGET, BEAVERS—SOCK 'EM HARD!

MARY

(Steps out, facing group)

Y'CAN'T HIT THEM. THEY LOOK TOO SAD.

PAUL

(Steps out, X's to MARY)

MARY, DIDN'T WE PROMISE OAKLEAF WE'D HELP HIM? HEY, BEAVERS, THAT'S RIGHT! Y'CAN'T HIT 'EM.

GOLDENROD

(Steps out, facing KIDS)

WHAT'S THE HATTER, HUMAN BEINGS, AIN'T WE SAD?

BIRCH

IF WE LET THEM INTO BEAVERLAND—THEN WE'LL BE THE BARKLESS BEAVERS, WALKING AROUND BENT OVER. ALWAYS CRYING.

(Enter: BARKLESS BEAVERS, FROM D.L.) (ALL bent over, arms hanging, X to C)

BEANPOLE

HEY, BIRCH! HERE THEY COME!

BIRCH

(X's to Stop BARKLESS)

WHERE DO YOU THINK YOU'RE GOING, BARKLESS BEAVERS?

BARKLESS

INTO BEAVERLAND.

BIRCH

(Pushing B)

Y'CAN'T GET IN!

BARKLESS

(Pushing BIRCH)

WHO'S GONNA STOP US?

BEAVERS

WE ARE!

BARKLESS

(Pushing BIRCH)

WAIT TILL I TELL THE CHIEF—HE'S WAITING FOR US!

BIRCH

(Pushing B)

I'M WARNING YOU, BARKLESS BEAVERS!

BARKLESS

YEAH!

(Turns to BARKLESS BEAVERS)

C'MON, MARCH RIGHT THRU THEM!

(WEDGE & LOCOMOTIVE FORMATION)

(BARKLESS BEAVERS move in wedge formation, toward BEAVERS, R.)

(BEAVERS in interlock formation are pushed back)

1–2–3 BACK

1–2–3 FORWARD

1–2–3 BACK

1–2–3 FORWARD

BIRCH

ALL RIGHT, BEAVERS—START HITTING THEM!

HOOT! Off L

(OAKLEAF enters)

HOOT OWL

(Off L)

A HOOT! AHOOT! AHOOOOOOOOT!

A HOOT! AHOOT! AHOOOOOOOOT!

MARY

(Breaks thru)

HEY, BEAVERS! STOP FIGHTING! THE HOOT OWL IS HERE! STOP FIGHTING!

BLUBBER

WHAT'S THAT?

BEAVERS

WHAT IS IT? WHAT?

PAUL

THE HOOT OWL! THE HOOT OWL!

(OAKLEAF Jumps, appears ramp L)

Glissando

BEANPOLE

WOW! WHAT'S THAT?

GOLDENROD

WHAT IS IT?

BLUBBER

A WALKING TOADSTOOL!

Stops

OAKLEAF

(X's down ramp thru BEAVERS, X's L.—goes thru BARKLESS winds up C., after ALL have scattered in fright)

(Throws off disguise)

IT'S ME, OAKLEAF! HELLO, BEAVERS!

TA-RA-TA-TA! Stops

(ALL in Joyous surprise, surround OAKLEAF, except BARKLESS BEAVERS D. L.)

BEAVERS

HELLO! GEE, IT'S OAKLEAF! HURRAY! WOW!

OAKLEAF

(After greeting BEAVERS, notices BARKLESS D. L.)

WHAT'S THE MATTER, PAUL?

PAUL

TELL HIM, BIRCH.

BIRCH

THE CHIEF SENT FOR THEM. WE WERE GOING TO CHASE THEM OUT OF BEAVERLAND—AND WE WERE HAVING A FIGHT BECAUSE WE DON'T WANT TO BE TURNED INTO BARKLESS BEAVERS.

BARKLESS

YEAH, THEY WERE HITTING US! WE DON'T WANT TO BE THE BARKLESS BEAVERS, EITHER. YOU THINK WE WANT TO BE SAD ALL THE TIME?

PAUL

WHAT ARE THEY GOING TO DO?

OAKLEAF

I GOT A SCHEME! THEY DESERVE TO BE IN OUR CLUB FOR SAD BEAVERS TO GET GLAD.

(Turns to BEAVERS)

RIGHT?

BEAVERS

(After a second's hesitation)

RIGHT!!!

OAKLEAF

(X's D.L. to BARKLESS)

BARKLESS BEAVERS, DO YOU WANT TO JOIN OUR CLUB?

BARKLESS

WHAT DO WE HAVE TO DO?

OAKLEAF

Y'GOTTA TELL THE CHIEF YOU AIN'T GONNA WORK ON THE WHEEL, UNLESS ALL OF US WORK ON IT, TOO.

BIRCH

WOW! THAT'S A WONDERFUL SCHEME!

OAKLEAF

THEN HE'LL HAVE TO LET ALL THE BEAVERS INTO BEAVERLAND—OTHERWISE HE WON'T HAVE ANY BARK.

BEANPOLE

THEN WE'LL HAVE PLENTY OF TIME TO PLAY POTZIE—

BLUBBER

THEN WE'LL HAVE LOTS MORE BARK—

BEANPOLE

AND WE WON'T HAVE TO WORK SO HARD ON THE BUSY BUSY!

BIRCH

AND Y'KNOW WHAT ELSE, BEAVERS? THE CHIEF HAS TO LET OAKLEAF COMEBACK TO BEAVERLAND.

BEAVERS

YEA!!!

PROFESSOR

HEY, BEAVERS! WHAT ABOUT ME?

OAKLEAF

THE PROFESSOR, TOO! AND PAUL AND MARY! EVERYBODY!!!

BEAVERS

YAAAAAAAAAAY!!!

OAKLEAF

(X's to BARKLESS)

WHAT DO YOU SAY, BARKLESS BEAVERS? DO YOU WANT TO BE IN OUR CLUB?

BARKLESS

(Turns, smells noses, turns again back to OAKLEAF)

OKAY!

(OAKLEAF and BARKLESS shake hands, BARKLESS BEAVERS RISE, ARE SENT over to BEAVERS by OAKLEAF, ALL greet, make friends)

MUSIC

(CHIEF'S BANG, off L., begin tum-tum-ta-ram-tum-tum. Continues, thru entrance.)

(ALL, bewildered, look off L. off R., all over)

SUNRAY

THE WHISTLING CLUBS! 3

BEANPOLE & BIRCH

THE SCALY BROTHERS! 1

BLUBBER & BACKWOODS

THE GENERALS! 2

GOLDENROD & BIRCH

THE CHIEF! 4

WHISTLE: Off L (Huff)

(OAKLEAF runs behind BEAVERS, X's from C to D R, disappears behind ramp R. appears on ramp C. looks off L.)

(BARKLESS BEAVERS, in fear, X D L BEAVERS, huddle R.)

OAKLEAF

(TRYING TO HALT B.B.)

STAY WHERE YOU ARE, BARKLESS BEAVERS! DON'T MOVE!

BIRCH

(Steps forward)

WHAT ARE WE GONNA DO, OAKLEAF?

OAKLEAF

DON'T BE SCARED, BEAVERS! I GOTTA HIDE, BUT I'LL TRY TO HELP YOU!

(Disappears behind ramp, C., with toadstool)

MARY

IT'S THE CHIEF, PAUL! WE GOTTA HIDE, TOO!

PAUL

YEAH, MARY—C'MON, PROFESSOR!

(KIDS and PROFESSOR X D R; run into TUFF, MARY screams. THEY turn, X up C to scale ramp, met by GRUFF. MARY screams, XDL., run into RUFF)

(WHISTLING CLUBS close in on KIDS, who are backed D.R.)

WHISTLE: Off L (Huff)

(Enter: HUFF, running down ramp, Jumps off C., sniffs thru BEAVERS, X's to L, sniffs toward BARKLESS winds up at ramp L.C. Whistles)

(Enter GENERALS; X down ramp, take position, below HUFF. HUFF whistles)

(Enter: SCALY BROTHERS; march down ramp, X to fence L, take position, face R., GENERALS then X to L front of SCALY BROTHERS, face R.)

MUSIC: Stops segue

MUSIC:

(Enter: THE CHIEF, down ramp, X's D. R.—Stops C.)

MUSIC: Stops

(OAKLEAF appears from behind ramp C in toadstool. X's D.C. Stops behind CHIEF; faces upstage, on knees)

CHIEF

D.R. (X'ing/to KIDS)

HELLO, HUMAN BEINGS! HELLO, PROFESSOR! STILL HANGING AROUND BEAVERLAND? HEY, WHISTLING CLUBS, WATCH 'EM!

(THEY do so. CHIEF sits on OAKLEAF)

HUFF

(X's toward CHIEF)

HEY CHIEF! THAT'S A VERY FAMILIAR TOAD-STOOL YOU'RE SITTING ON.

CHIEF

CHOP IT DOWN!

(HUFF X'S to do so)

LATER, NOT NOW, Y'DUMB RUFF! DON'T Y'SEE THE BARKLESS BEAVERS ARE WAITING FOR ME?

(Turns to BARKLESS)

HELLO, BARKLESS BEAVERS.

BARKLESS

HELLO!

CHIEF

YOU LOOK VERY SAD.

BARKLESS

WE ARE.

CHIEF

(Rises from OAKLEAF, X's to B.B.)

Y'KNOW, I WAS THINKING ABOUT YOU. AND THIS MORNING I SAID, THE BARKLESS BEAVERS AIN'T GONNA BE SAD ANY MORE.

PAUL

DON'T YOU BELIEVE HIM, BARKLESS BEAVERS!

CHIEF

(Turns to PAUL)

WHAT ARE YOU BUTTING IN FOR, ARE YOU A BEAVER?

BIRCH

(Breaks thru to CHIEF)

HOW ABOUT US, CHIEF?

CHIEF

YOU WISE BEAVERS ARE GONNA BE THE BARKLESS BEAVERS FROM NOW ON. AND THE BARKLESS BEAVERS ARE GONNA BE THE GOOD BEAVERS!

AND I'M GONNA GIVE EVERY GOOD BEAVER A BLUE SWEATER, JUST LIKE MINE. NOT EXACTLY, BUT SOMETHING LIKE IT,—MAYBE!

PAUL

REMEMBER WHAT YOU PROMISED, BARKLESS BEAVERS!

CHIEF

(Turns to PAUL)

DIDN'T I GIVE YOU A WARNING NOT TO BUTT IN?

COME ON BARKLESS BEAVERS! LET'S MARCH INTO BFAVERLAND. HUFF!

1ST GENERAL

FORWARD MARCH! HUFF!

(CHIEF, D.C. Heads procession up ramp, R. SCALY BROTHERS, then GENERALS, then HUFF—OAKLEAF moves U.R.)

CHIEF

(AT C. on ramp, discovering B.B. have not marched)

HALT!! WHAT'S THE MATTER? BARKLESS BEAVERS, WHY AIN'T Y' MARCHING INTO BEAVERLAND?

BARKLESS

WE DON'T WANNA!

PAUL

THAT'S RIGHT, BARKLESS BEAVERS!

CHIEF

BACKWARDS, MARCH!!!

(CHIEF'S GANG backs down ramp back to original position)

CHIEF

(Whips on PAUL)

YOU BUTTIN' IN AGAIN?

PAUL

YEAH! THEY'RE ALL MEMBERS OF OUR CLUB.

CHIEF

(Stumped, X's slowly to B.B.)

WHAT! YOU GOT A CLUB? WHAT KIND OF A CLUB?

OAKLEAF

WHADD'YA THINK, A POTZIE CLUB!!

CHIEF

(Whips on BEAVERS, looking for speaker)

WHO SAID THAT? WHO'S THE WISE BEAVER WHO SAID THAT?

(Turns to PAUL)

SO IT AIN'T A POTZIE CLUB, HUH?

PAUL

NO, IT'S OAKLEAF'S CLUB! A CLUB FOR SAD BEAVERS TO GET GLAD!

CHIEF

I'LL TAKE CARE OF YUH, LATER, Y'HUMAN BEINGS, YUH!

(Backing up toward C to sit)

I'M GIVING Y' FAIR WARNING, BEAVERS! IF Y'DOU'T STOP MAKING ME MAD, I'LL—

(discovers OAKLEAF has moved)

HEY, RUFF! WHY DID Y'CHOP DOWN THE TOADSTOOL?

RUFF

(Puzzled)

I DIDN'T, CHIEF!

(Sees it)

THERE IT IS, CHIEF!

CHIEF

HEY, HUFF! WHAT'S THE IDEA OF TAKING MY SEAT AWAY?

HUFF

I DIDN'T TAKE IT AWAY, CHIEF!

CHIEF

NO? SO WHAT'S IT DOING, STANDING RIGHT IN FRONT OF YOU? WHAT ARE YOU TRYING TO DO, GET ME MIXED UP? AIN'T EVERYTHING UPSIDE DOWN, ALREADY? BOY, AM I GOING TO GET EVEN?

(SLAMS hat down on OAKLEAF, who takes hat and hides it.)

BIRCH

LISTEN, CHIEF! Y'GOTTA LET THE BARKLESS BEAVERS BACK ON THE WHEEL SO WE CAN HAVE MORE TIME TO PLAY POTZIE!

YELLOW LEAF

AND Y'GOTTA GIVE US MORE BARK!

CHIEF

AND WHAT ELSE?

PAUL

Y'GOTTA LET OAKLEAF BACK INTO BEAVERLAND. 'CAUSE HE'S PRESIDENT OF OUR CLUB!

CHIEF

(On knees, crawls step to PAUL)

OAKLEAF, HUH! I DOUBLE-TRIPLE DARE THAT WISE BEAVER, THAT SKATE-STEALER, TO COME NEAR BEAVERLAND!

PAUL

(Crawls step forward)

YEAH, Y'BETTER LET HIM IN!

CHIEF

(Way forward, on knees)

I BET Y'SENT THE HOOT OWL FOR HIM, ALREADY!

PAUL

YEAH!

CHIEF

(Rises, X's to GENERALS, C.)

GENERALS! AS SOON AS YOU SEE OAKLEAF AND HIS FRIEND, THE HOOT OWL, KILL THEM.

(Turns to BEAVERS)

YOU BEAVERS ARE GETTING TOO WISE! AND I'M SORE! I WAS NEVER SO SORE IN MY LIFE! BOY! AM I GONNA START GETTING EVEN!

OAKLEAF

Y'GONNA LET HIM DO THAT, BEAVERS?

CHIEF

(Whips on B.B. X's to them)

SO YOU BARKLESS BEAVERS ARE GETTING BRAVE, TOO? TALKING BEHIND MY BACK.

BARKLESS

YEAH! WE AIN'T BENT OVER NO MORE! WE'RE GOING TO STICK TOGETHER WITH THE BEAVERS IN OUR CLUB!

CHIEF

GENERALS! CHASE THEM OUT OF BEAVERLAND, AND LET THEM BE THE BARKLESS BEAVERS FOR A BILLION YEARS. NO! FOREVER!

1ST GENERAL

HUPP!!

(SCALY BROTHERS come to attention. LOWER guns, march to B.B.., force B.B. off L In three charges, GENERALS in position, swords raised.)

(BARKLESS BEAVERS call for help. BEAVERS BEAVERS, realizing danger to B.B., X to C on way to help)

(THE CHIEF, notices advance, calls to WHISTLING CLUBS, then to GENERALS, who respond, force BEAVERS back D.R.)

(SCALY BROTHERS remain on guard, guns poised, facing off L.)

CHIEF

ALL RIGHT, GENERALS! GET THOSE TWO HUMAN BEINGS AND THE PROFESSOR

(GENERALS X D R)

AND THE REST OF YOU BEAVERS, GET INTO BEAVERLAND. AND FROM NOW ON, A NEW RULE! ANY BEAVER THAT GETS WISE, I'M GONNA LOCK HIM IN A CAVE FOR A LONG TIME—MAYBE FOREVER!

(Turns to SCALY BROTHERS)

O. K., SCALY BROTHERS!

GENERAL

HUPP!!

(SCALY BROTHERS SNAP TO ATTENTION, march across U.R. to BEAVERS, herd then off up ramp to exit L., followed by GENERALS. BIRCH exits R.)

CHIEF

(Turns to KIDS)

(RUFF holds PROFESSOR, U.R.)

(TUFF holds PAUL R.C.)

(GRUFF holds MARY, D.R.)

CHIEF

AND YOU HUMAN BEINGS AND PROFESSOR, I'M GONNA TEACH YOU THE BIGGEST LESSON THERE IS! AND THE LESSON IS—STARTING TOMORROW—LUNCHTIME—EVERY DAY FOR A HUNDRED YEARS—YOU'RE GONNA GET KILLED!

MARY

I DON'T WANNA BE KILLED! I CAME TO BE BEAVERLAND TO HAVE A GOOD TIME!

PROFESSOR

I TOLD YOU HE'D DO SOMETHING VERY BAD!

CHIEF

HUPP!! FORWARD MARCH!!

(WHISTLING CLUBS herd KIDS & PROFESSOR up ramp. RUFF, after pushing PROFESSOR on ramp, notices toadstool, Remains. GRUFF and TUFF continue herding them off)

PAUL

(On way out)

Y'WISE CHIEF! YOU'LL BE SORRY SOME DAY!

MARY

(On way out)

IF I HAD A MAGIC STONE, I'D TURN YOU INTO A FROG!

(Exit L.)

CHIEF

(C—suddenly misses hat)

WHERE'S MY HAT?

(OAKLEAF's arm brings out hat, which the CHIEF takes, puts on, continues up on ramp, followed by RUFF)

CHIEF

THANKS.

(RUFF amazed, sees hat business, collect wits, calls to CHIEF)

RUFF

HEY, CHIEF! SHALL I CHOP IT DOWN NOW?

CHIEF

(Stopping HUFF)

DON'T WASTE ANY MORE TIME, Y'DUMB RUFF! C'HERE! I GOT A SPECIAL JOB FOR YOU TO DO. THAT OAKLEAF IS GONNA SNEAK INTO BEAVER-LAND ANY MINUTE. WHILE HE'S SNEAKING IN—YOU CATCH HIM! WHEN Y'CATCH HIM—KILL HIM, RIGHT AWAY! HUPP!!

MUSIC

(RUFF X's R., runs up ramp, follows HUFF and CHIEF, who march off L.)

(as OAKLEAF comes out of toadstool)—

CURTAIN.

★

ACT 2—SCENE 2

CURTAIN

(At Curtain rise, we see RUFF, L. Stg., on guard, walking up and down, L to C., C to L. BIRCH, GOLDENROD and BEANPOLE are in a huddle R.—at potzie game. BIRCH stands watching BEANPOLE jump)

GOLDENROD

O.K. BEANPOLE, YOU GO.

(Beanpole throws potzie and jumps, goes to about middle of potzie field, turns, jumps back, throws again and jumps—steps on line)

BIRCH & GOLDENROD

YOU STEPPED ON LINE.

BEANPOLE

AH—

(Throws potzie to floor, X's towards R, sits on floor and keeps score)

BEANPOLE

GO AHEAD, BIRCH, YOU GO.

BIRCH

OKAY.

(Throws potzie—jumps to number and back)

GOLDENROD

OKAY.

RUFF

(X's towards C to potzie game)

WHO'S WINNING?

BIRCH

MIND YOUR BUSINESS, WHISTLING CLUB.

RUFF

(X's towards L. STG.)

YOU BET I'LL MIND MY BUSINESS. THERE'S ONE BEAVER THAT AIN'T GETTING INTO BEAVER-LAND AND THAT'S OAKLEAF.

(BIRCH motions to BEANPOLE and GOLDEN-ROD. THEY quickly go into huddle)

BIRCH

WE'VE GOT TO DO SOMETHING VERY FAST. OAKLEAF AND THE HOOT-OWL WILL BE HERE ANY MINUTE.

GOLDENROD

WHAT ARE WE GONNA DO?

BIRCH

KEEP PLAYING POTZIE . . .

(HUFF turns quickly L. stg. and X's to C. stage.)

RUFF

HOW ABOUT GIVING ME A GAME OF POTZIE, HUH?

BIRCH

GO PLAY WITH THE CHIEF. . . . YOU'RE ON HIS GANG ANYWAYS. . . .

BEANPOLE

I WOULDN'T PLAY WITH A WHISTLING CLUB.

RUFF

YEAH! BETTER HURRY UP AND FINISH YOUR GAME BECAUSE THERE'S A NEW RULE . . . SEE IT!

(Steps toward C. ramp, and points to sign C Stg., near ramp)

NO WALKIN'! NO TALKIN'! NO NOTHIN'! NINE O'CLOCK IN DA HOUSE!

BIRCH

IT ISN'T NINE O'CLOCK YET!

RUFF

I'M JUST GIVING YOU FAIR WARNING.

(X's to L Stg. and looks off L. as if looking out for something. Then walks up and down stg. L.)

(ALL three quickly in huddle as they notice RUFF interested in something else.

GOLDENROD

DID YOU FIGURE OUT A SCHEME, BIRCH? IF OAKLEAF IS CAUGHT WE'LL NEVER BE ABLE TO SAVE THE PROFESSOR AND THE HUMAN BEINGS.

GOLDENROD

WE GOTTA GET RUFF OUT OF THE WAY.

BIRCH

SHHHHHHHH!!!

I GOT A SCHEME. IS LITTLE GUPPIE IN THE HOUSE?

GOLDENROD

YEAH, BUT SHE CAN'T DO ANYTHING . . . SHE'S A BABY!

BIRCH

WE GOTTA TAKE A CHANCE.

(ALL THREE exit R Stg. front)

(RUFF X's from L. to R.)

(RUFF X's from L to C stg. Then walks over to R stg., quickly turning he goes to potzie field, and Jumps)

RUFF

I HOPE THAT HOOT-OWL HURRIES UP SO I CAN CATCH HIM. DAT WISE OAKLEAF TRYIN' TO BUST UP BEAVERLAND. I'LL SHOW HIM.

(GUPPIE enters from R. front. X's to L stg., watches RUFF—jumps about him, trying to get his attention. He just glances at Her, and walks to R. stg. GUPPIE quickly runs after him. Again she does tricks in front of RUFF. RUFF turns, X's to C stg., GUPPIE follows, does a turn over in front of RUFF)

RUFF

(Notices GUPPIE)

HELLO, GUPPIE! . . . C'MON, GET BACK IN DA HOUSE.

GUPPIE

(Jumps on potzie field)

AW, I WANNA PLAY . . . C'MON, LET'S PLAY A GAME OF POTZIE, RUFF.

RUFF

AW, WHAT'S DA USE PLAYIN' YOU! I CAN BEAT YOU EASY. IMAGINE DOSE WISE BEAVERS. WOULDN'T GIVE ME A GAME OF POTZIE. I DON'T CARE. I CAN PLAY WIT DA CHIEF IF I WANNA. I CAN EVEN LEND HIS SKATES.

GUPPIE

(Jumps potzie field) (Talking to RUFF)

I GOT A GOOD GAME.

RUFF

(Turns—for first time interested)

YEAH? WHAT KIND OF A GAME?

GUPPIE

BLIND BEAVER!

RUFF

(X's L. stg.)

DAT'S A VERY GOOD GAME! . . . BUT I CAN'T PLAY, I GOTTA WATCH FOR OAKLEAF AND THE HOOT-OWL.

GUPPIE

(Runs over L to RUFF, pleading)

JUST A LITTLE GAME, RUFF. I'LL EVEN BE BLIND BEAVER FIRST.

RUFF

OKAY, GUPPIE. COME ON.

(RUFF ties handkerchief around GUPPIE, turns her around several times, then releases her.)

RUFF

OKAY, CATCH ME.

GUPPIE IS A BLIND BEAVER!

(Touches GUPPIE with club)

GUPPIE IS A BLIND BEAVER!

(Tickles GUPPIE! Jumps around)

GUPPIE IS A BLIND BEAVER!

(RUFF runs around—X's to R Stg.)

(GUPPIE pulls handkerchief from one eye. Sees RUFF stand R. stg, with back to her,—she runs over and touches him.)

GUPPIE

YOU'RE BLIND BEAVER—

RUFF

GEE WHIZ!

GUPPIE

I'M GONNA TIE YOU TIGHT SO YOU CAN'T LOOK.

RUFF

BUT IN CASE YOU SEE SOMEONE COMING, TELL ME RIGHTAWAY.

GUPPIE

SURE, I'LL TELL YOU.

(GUPPIE ties handkerchief around RUFF'S eyes—turns him around and pushes him—He falls about C stg. GUPPIE rushes off stg. R. to call the others)

RUFF

(Slowly rising, gropes around on knees first, then rises, calling)

HEY, GUPPIE, WHERE ARE YA? GUPPIE, WHERE ARE YOU? HOW CAN I CATCH YOU IF YOU DON'T TALK? . . .

GUPPIE

(Coming back, runs toward RUFF)

HERE I AM, HERE I AM.

I DARE YOU CATCH ME . . .

RUFF

I JUST GOTTA COUNT THREE AND I'LL CATCH YOU. . . . ONE. . . . TWO. . . .

(After trying twice, GUPPIE succeeds in getting whistle away from RUFF)

THREE!

SOUND OFF L. HOOT—HOOT HOOT

OWL

HOOT. . . . HOOT. . . . HOOT. . . . HOOT. . . . (ETC.)

HOOT HOOT HOOT HOOT HOOT

RUFF

WOW! THE HOOT OWL! OAKLEAF IS IN BEAVER-LAND.

WHERE'S MY WHISTLE? HEY, GUPPIE, HELP ME GET THIS OFF.

(He tries vainly to remove handkerchief)

I GOTTA GET DAT BEAVER. . . .

(BIRCH, BEANPOLE and GOLDENROD rush over to RUFF)

HELP! HELP! HELP!

(BIRCH hits him over head with club)

(HE collapses)

BIRCH

TIE HIM UP AND PUT HIM IN THE HOLLOW TREE.

(They tie him up)

BEANPOLE

UPSIDE DOWN?

BIRCH

NO. . . . JUST STRAIGHT. . . .

(They drag him out L. stg.)

(They return, stand C., ready to signal)

SOUND

OWL

HOOT. . . . HOOT. . . . HOOT. . . . HOOT. . . . (ETC.)

BIRCH

OAKLEAF . . . COME ON!!!

MUSIC

(All run to L. stg.)

BEANPOLE

WOW!! WHAT'S THAT, BIRCH?

GOLDENROD

A POLAR BEAR. . . . FROM THE NORTH POLE.

BIRCH

WHERE'S OAKLEAF?

(Enter POLAR BEAR from R. to C. Goes to ramp, sits, lifts legs up in the air, X's legs and looks at group L—THEY are all frightened, and all turn to R. front)

GOLDENROD

I BET HE ATE HIM UP!

(POLAR BEAR X's to group. Grabs BEANPOLE by arm. All yell, frightened, and pull against him)

BIRCH

KEEP AWAY, POLAR BEAR. . . . KEEP AWAY. . . .

(OAKLEAF, (Polar Bear) X's to C. Stg. They stand, watching him closely. Takes off disguise.)

MUSIC TARATA TA

(ALL run over to him) (Happy to see him back)

BEAR

I SCARED YOU HUH? YOU THOUGHT I WAS A POLAR BEAR . . . IT'S ME . . . OAKLEAF. SOME DISGUISE, HUH?

THE CHIEF'LL NEVER RECOGNIZE ME.

BIRCH

OAKLEAF! WOW! GEE WHIZ, I THOUGHT HE ATE YOU UP!

OAKLEAF

WHO?

BEANPOLE

THE POLAR BEAR.

OAKLEAF

WHAT'S THE MATTER WITH YOU? POLAR BEARS DON'T EAT BEAVERS. ONLY FISH.

BIRCH

GEE WHIZ! OAKLEAF . . . I'M GLAD WE SNEAKED YOU IN.

OAKLEAF

I GOT A SCHEME TO DO SOMETHING VERY BIG AGAINST THE CHIEF. BUT I CAN'T TELL YOU NOW! IT'S VERY BIG. WE GOTTA GET ALL THE BEAVERS TOGETHER FIRST.

BIRCH

THEY'RE SCARED. IF THEY DO SOMETHING WRONG, THEY MIGHT GET PUT IN THE CAVE!

OAKLEAF

YOU GOT A SIGNAL!

BEANPOLE

YEAH!

OAKLEAF

(Undressing)

THEN GIVE THE SIGNAL. IF THEY COME, WE'LL DO SOMETHING BIG. IF NOT, BEAVERLAND IS LOST. GIVE THE SIGNAL.

WAVE A FLAG, GUPPIE.

FLAG

BEANPOLE

(JUMPS on ramp, as does GUPPIE. Gives signal.)

(1–2–3 L.)

(1–2–3 R.)

(1–2–3 L.)

(1–2–3 L.)

(BEAVERS enter from R. C. & L. Stg.)

1. L. Stg.—BLUBBER
2. C. Stg.—behind ramp—MOSS ROCK
3. R. Stg.—WINTERSTAR.

(Then, from all sides BEAVERS and BARKLESS BEAVERS.)

(THEY ALL gather around OAKLEAF)

OAKLEAF

BEAVERS—TOMORROW MORNING WHEN YOU ARE WORKING ON THE WHEEL.—

CURTAIN.

★

ACT 3

CURTAIN

(MARY, PAUL & PROFESSOR tied to stake, D. R.—RUFF sleeping in CHIEF'S chair.—SCALY BROTHERS asleep on ramp L. FLUNKEY near gate ramp L. 1st GENERAL on step ramp L.—2nd GENERAL on the step of CHIEF'S platform)

MUSIC

MARY

GEE, I WISH I HAD SOME BERRIES. I NEVER KNEW I COULD BE SO HUNGRY!

PROFESSOR

I'M SO HUNGRY I COULD EAT A WHOLE TREE.

PAUL

(Looks about, admiring bright new day)

WOW, WHAT A NICE DAY! YOU THINK HE'D KILL US ON A NICE DAY LIKE THIS?

PROFESSOR

HE DOESN'T CARE ABOUT NICE DAYS!

MARY

I DON'T WANNA BE KILLED LUNCH TIME. I DON'T WANNA BE KILLED AT ALL.

(In tears)

I WANNA GO HOME.

PAUL

DON'T CRY, MARY.

PROFESSOR

SURE. DON'T BE SAD, MARY. YOU GOTTA KEEP UP YOUR HOPE.

MUSIC STOP

PAUL

MAYBE OAKLEAF GOT INTO BEAVERLAND LAST NIGHT.

PROFESSOR

I HOPE HE DID. GEE, HE'S A SMART BEAVER. I'M JUST GETTING TO BE SMART, AND NOW I'M GONNA BE KILLED.

(CHIEF whistles, enters C. Stg. R. THE CHIEF skates in, flanked by GRUFF and TUFF)

CHIEF

HEY YOU DUMB WHISTLING CLUBS THAT'S NO EXCUSE—NO EXCUSE—

(He skates from R. to L. and keeps on skating in large circles, while conversation keeps up)

(TUFF & GRUFF talking on run behind him)

TUFF

GEE, CHIEF, HE MIGHT BE IN THE CANAL. . . .

CHIEF

(To RUFF & TUFF)

WHAT DO YA MEAN, HE MIGHT BE IN THE CANAL. . . .

PAUL

C'HERE, YOU FAT CHIEF! I DARE YOU COME NEAR ME.

CHIEF

SHUT UP, OR I'LL KILL YOU BEFORE LUNCH-TIME.

GRUFF

(To CHIEF)

HE MIGHT HAVE TRIPPED AND FALLEN IN.

CHIEF

WHY DON'TCHA LOOK FOR HIM INSTEAD OF TELLIN' ME HE MIGHT BE THERE. . . .

TUFF

WE WUZ LOOKIN' AROUND, CHIEF. AND YOU OUGHTA SEE DEM BEAVERS. . . .

GRUFF

THEY'RE ACTIN' LIKE THEY'RE UP TO SOME-THING. . . . THEY'RE TOO QUIET, CHIEF. . . .

CHIEF

THEY SAW MY NEW RULES. JUST LET 'EM START SOMETHING. DID YOU LOOK ALL OVER?

TUFF

ALL OVER BEAVERLAND.

CHIEF

AND YOU COULDN'T FIND OAKLEAF OR RUFF, HUH?

GRUFF

(Yelling)

(CHIEF stunned—sits on floor—GRUFF & TUFF lift him, drop him again, then finally help him to hie feet.)

CHIEF

IT LOOKS VERY BAD. I THINK THAT WISE BEAVER, OAKLEAF, SNEAKED INTO BEAVER-LAND.

NOW MAKE SURE, YOU WHISTLING CLUBS, DON'T DISAPPEAR LIKE THAT DUMB RUFF. HANG AROUND AND WATCH EVERYTHING. I SMELL A LOT OF TROUBLE IN THE AIR.

TUFF

OKAY, CHIEF!

(TUFF and GRUFF X to Wheel)

(GENERALS X down to CHIEF, salute)

CHIEF

GOOD MORNING, GENERALS.

GENERALS

GOOD MORNING, CHIEF.

CHIEF

DO YOU SMELL THE TROUBLE IN THE AIR?

GENERALS

(Tremble)

YEAH, ALL AROUND BEAVERLAND.

CHIEF

OAKLEAF MUST HAVE SNEAKED IN LAST NIGHT.

YOU BETTER WATCH OUT.

HEY, HUFF! SEND THEM WHISTLING CLUBS OVER TO WATCH THE HUMAN BEINGS—AND DON'T DISAPPEAR!! GO DOWN AND WATCH THE HUMAN BEINGS ... AND DON'T DISAPPEAR!

WARNING

(GRUFF & TUFF X D. R. to stand watch; Factory whistle, off C. by FLUNKEY, who enters, takes off CHIEF skates)

BUSY BUSY

CHIEF

(Sitting on steps)

IT'S TIME FOR THE BUSY-BUSY.

(Whistles)

ALL RIGHT, YOU BEAVERS,—COME ON IN!

TUFF

HERE DEY COME.

(CHIEF'S GANG forms triangle, protecting CHIEF)

(Enter the BEAVERS—from L, X R, with lunch boxes, to their places at wheel)

GRUFF

HEY CHIEF, LOOK DOSE LUNCH BOXES ... DEY AIN'T GOT SO MUCH BARK. DERE UP TO SOMETHING', I TELL YA.

CHIEF

WHAT ARE YOU WORRYING ABOUT? JUST LET 'EM START SOMETHIN'....

(BEAVERS stand ready for work)

CHIEF

NOW LISTEN, YOU BEAVERS. I'M GLAD TO SEE YOU ALL BROUGHT YOUR LUNCH BOXES, BECAUSE I WANT EVERYBODY TO BE HERE LUNCH TIME TO SEE THE BIG LESSON. ALL RIGHT.... GET READY.

BUSY-BUSY

BUSY, BUSY, BUSY, BUSY....

ONE, TWO ... THREE, FOUR, WHHHHHHHHOO-OOOOOOOOOOO MUSIC

BEAVERS

(Picking up chant and beginning to work)

BUSY, BUSY, BUSY, BUSY,

STRIP, STRIP, STRIP, STRIP,

BUSY, BUSY, BUSY, BUSY,

CUP, CLIP, CLIP, CLIP,

(ETC. ETC. ETC. ETC.)

CHIEF

(X down on stage, D R to BEAVERS)

(Shouting above the chant)

COME ON YOU BEAVERS ... KEEP IT UP ... KEEP IT UP....

COME ON, THERE, A LITTLE FASTER....

(WHISTLING CLUBS parade up and down)

WHISTLING CLUBS KEEP YOUR EYES ON 'EM ... AND YOU GENERALS, YOU BETTER WATCH THEM BEAVERS, TOO.... THEY LOOK TOO QUIET.

CHIEF

(GENERALS are about to X)

(GENERALS and SCALY BROS. WHEEL into position.)

(They face gate)

KNOCK

PATTY WACK

WHO GOES THERE? BEAVER OR WILD ANIMAL OF THE FOREST?

OAKLEAF

(Offstage L.)

A POLAR BEAR!

(BEAVERS react)

CHIEF

A POLAR BEAR....

(Pause)

FRIEND OR FOE?

OAKLEAF

FRIEND!

CHIEF

NORTH POLE OR SOUTH POLE?

OAKLEAF

SOUTH POLE!

CHIEF

WHAT DO YOU WANT?

OAKLEAF

LET ME IN. I WANT TO TALK TO YOU.

CHIEF

YEAH? TELL ME WHAT YOU WANT, FIRST.

OAKLEAF

THE PRESIDENT OF THE POLAR BEARS SENT ME DOWN TO COPY YOUR WHEEL. HE WANTS TO MAKE ONE JUST LIKE IT FOR THE SOUTH POLE.

CHIEF

I AIN'T PROMISING TO LET YOU COPY MY WHEEL . . . BUT COME ON IN . . . I WANNA TALK TO YOU SOME MORE . . .

(To GENERALS)

LET HIM IN.

(BEAVERS go back to work)

GENERAL

HUPP!!

(SCALY BROS. return to old position)

(Enter OAKLEAF, steps down, growls, scaring CHIEF'S GANG, who jump back)

OAKLEAF

HELLO, CHIEF OF BEAVERLAND.

CHIEF

HELLO, POLAR BEAR. . . . WHAT DOES THE PRESIDENT WANNA MAKE ON THE WHEEL?

OAKLEAF

ICE CREAM BRICKS.

(BEAVERS all stop working, interested)

. . . AND HE'LL SEND YOU A STACK EVERY WEEK.

CHIEF

AHH . . . I DON'T KNOW IF I SHOULD LET YOU COPY MY WHEEL. . . . WHAT FLAVORS IS HE GONNA MAKE?

OAKLEAF

STRAWBERRY . . . CHERRY . . . PINEAPPLE . . . AND VANILLA.

CHIEF

HOW ABOUT CHOCOLATE?

OAKLEAF

AND CHOCOLATE, TOO!

CHIEF

GO AHEAD . . . COPY THE WHEEL.

OAKLEAF

OKAY! THANKS, CHIEF.

(MUSIC.)

(Dances to C. bows, dances D.L. to BEAVERS, whispers to them, while pretending to copy wheel.)

(HUFF X to L of platform)

TUFF

(X to the CHIEF)

HEY, CHIEF, HE'S A VERY FUNNY LOOKIN' POLAR BEAR, VERY SAGGY.

CHIEF

AHHH, Y'DUMB TUFF, IT'S VERY HOT FOR A POLAR BEAR IN BEAVERLAND. THEY LOSE WEIGHT! THIS AIN'T THE SOUTH POLE, IS IT?

TUFF

NO. HEY, CHIEF, IF IT WAS, WE'D BE POLAR BEARS, TOO, HUH, CHIEF!

CHIEF

SURE, THAT'S RIGHT. AWWW, GO AHEAD AND WATCH THE BEAVERS!

(TUFF X'S D.R.) (TO HUFF)

ANYWAYS, HE'S A VERY SAGGY POLAR BEAR.

(CHIEF AND FLUNKEY exit into house)

(HUFF X'S down C., sniffs, notices something wrong, as BEANPOLE stands waving flag. HUFF runs to platform, yelling)

BUSY-BUSY STOPS

HUFF

HEY, CHIEF! HEY, CHIEF! THEY'RE DOING SOMETHING FUNNY ON THE WHELL!

CHIEF

(Rushes in, on platform)

WHAT'S THE MATTER?

(Sees flag being waved)

BEANPOLE! WHAT ARE YOU WAVING FOR?

BEANPOLE

O. K. POLAR BEAR!

OAKLEAF

O. K., BEAVERS, LINE UP!

(BEAVERS fall into formation,

on knees, first lines:

crouching, 2nd line:

BIRCH, DEWDROP, BEANPOLE, BLUBBER, BACKWOODS, YELLOWLEAF, MOSSROCK, GOLDENROD, PINE CONE & SUN RAY.

CHIEF

HEY, POLAR BEAR! WHAT ARE YOU BUTTING IN FOR?

OAKLEAF

(Throwing off disguise)

IT'S ME, OAKLEAF!

CHIEF

OAKLEAF! BACK IN BEAVERLAND! HOW'D YOU GET IN? I STILL CAN'T FIND MY SKATE KEY. HOW DID YOU GET IN?

OAKLEAF

BY THE MAIN ENTRANCE.

CHIEF

I KNEW IT. A POLAR BEAR, HUH? I'LL MAKE YOU SORRY YOU EVER CAME BACK. TO BEAVERLAND. YOU'LL WISH YOU WERE REALLY A POLAR BEAR IN THE SOUTH POLE.

OAKLEAF

LISTEN, CHIEF. YOU'VE BEEN A WISE CHIEF LONG ENOUGH, AND WE'RE GOING TO GET EVEN WITH YOU. WE'RE GOING TO BEND YOU OVER. WHAT D'Y'SAY, BEAVERS?

BEAVERS

RIGHT!

OAKLEAF

AND WE'RE GONNA SAVE THE HUMAN BEINGS.

KIDS

WE'RE SAVED! WE'RE SAVED.

OAKLEAF

GO AHEAD, BEAVERS, SAVE THEM.

(BEANPOLE and BACKWOODS do so)

WARNING BANGO GUN.

CHIEF

JUST A MINUTE, YOU WISE BEAVERS! DON'T THINK YOU'RE GONNA BE SAVED SO EASY. WHISTLING CLUBS, GO DOWN THERE AND KEEP THEM AWAY FROM THOSE THREE. I'LL SHOW YOU WHO'S CHIEF OF BEAVERLAND!

GRUFF

O. K. C'MON, LET'S GIVE THEM THE WORKS.

(TUFF & GRUFF X. D. R.)

STAY WHERE YOU ARE, WHISTLING CLUBS, I'M WARNING YA!

(TUFF & GRUFF advance, BIRCH fires shot. WHISTLING CLUBS retreat to steps at ramp. HUFF and GENERALS hide behind SCALY BROS.)

(BEAVERS take out Zippo guns, sling shots, bean shooters, etc.)

CHIEF

ZIPPO GUNS! THEY STOLE SOME OF MY ZIPPO GUNS!

GO AHEAD, WHISTLING CLUBS! I DARE THEM SHOOT!

RUFF

(Retreating)

HEY CHIEF, THEY GOT ZIPPO GUNS!

(Hides at foot of platform)

CHIEF

AW SHUT UP, I CAN SEE! I'LL SHOW THEM WHO'S CHIEF! WAIT A MINUTE, YOU BEAVERS. DON'T THINK YOU'RE SO SMART. I'LL SHOW YOU SOMETHING. HEY, HUFF!

(HUFF runs to house, brings out bango gun)

PAUL

WOW! A BANGO GUN!

ALL

WOW!

(HUFF trips, firing the bango gun, terrific crash. ALL duck, crouch, fall flat, stay down)

(Pause)

BANGO GUN

CHIEF

(Looks about)

GEE WHIZ! IT WENT OFF BY ACCIDENT. HEY, HUFF, TAKE IT AWAY. IT'S DANGEROUS. Y'WANT SOMEONE TO GET HURT?

(HUFF removes bango gun into house, C. returns)

HEY, WHAT'S THE MATTER, YOU BEAVERS? Y'ALL KILLED?

GUPPIE

(Rises)

YEAH!

CHIEF

AHHH, Y'WISE GUPPIE, YA. ANYWAYS, MY WHOLE GANG IS HERE, Y'WISE BEAVERS!

(To SCALY BROS.)

GO AHEAD, SCALY BROTHERS, MAKE SOME NOISE!

(They do so, charge, march about, growl like mad dogs.)

ALL RIGHT, ALL RIGHT, THAT'S ENOUGH.

(To BEAVERS)

NOW D'Y'THINK YOU'RE WISE?

PROFESSOR

GIVE ME A PEA SHOOTER, I'LL SHOW HIM!

(Takes pea shooter, shoots CHIEF in eye)

CHIEF

(Hit, dances about, rubbing face, in tears)

WAIT TILL I GET HOLD YOU, Y'WISE PROFESSOR! I'M SORRY I DIDN'T START KILLING YOU YESTERDAY!

PROFESSOR

FIRST THING, MAKE PAUL GENERAL! HE'S THE BEST FIGURER IN HIS SCHOOL!

OAKLEAF

PAUL, YOU BE GENERAL. GIVE HIM THE GENERAL'S HAT, BEAVERS.

(YELLOWLEAF gives PAUL hat)

PAUL

O.K. BEAVERS! TAKE IT EASY!

(Putting on hat)

CHIEF

AHH, YOU'RE SCARED ALREADY. C'MON, GET BACK ON THE BUSY BUSY. READY? BUSY BUSY BUSY BUSY, ONE, TWO, THREE, FOUR, WHOOAAA!

BEAVERS

(Derisively)

WHOOAAA!!!

PAUL

NOBODY'S SCARED OF YOU, Y'FAT CHIEF!

CHIEF

NO! I'LL SHOW YOU!

ROLL OF DRUMS

TARATATATATA!

(Blows bugle)

GENERAL

SCALY BROTHERS, GET READY!

(SCALY BROS. go thru exercises.

MUSIC: Drums

2 forward

2 back

2 forward

GENERALS stand behind them)

PAUL

TARATATATATA!

BEAVERS, GET READY!

(BEAVERS get into position. Execute march)

OAKLEAF

YOUR LAST CHANCE, CHIEF. GIVE UP AND Y'WONT GET BENT OVER.

CHIEF

BEFORE YOU CAN BEND ME OVER, YOU'LL HAVE TO FIGHT ME AND MY WHOLE GANG. AND YOU CAN NEVER DO THAT.

OAKLEAF

WE'RE GONNA DO IT RIGHT NOW.

CHIEF

GENERALS, YOU READY?

HEY, BEAVERS, ARE YOU READY?

GO AHEAD, SCALY BROTHERS.

TARATATATATA!

THE BATTLE IS ON!

MUSIC: ROLL OF DRUMS.

PAUL

BEAVERS, GET READY! TARATATATA! THE BATTLE IS ON!

(EVERYBODY is Shooting)

(OAKLEAF sneaks up on platform, behind CHIEF. Gives Indian war whoop)

OAKLEAF

WHEEEE WHOOOOOO WHEEE WKOOOO.

COME ON, BARKLESS BEAVERS, OVER THE TOP!

(BARKLESS BEAVERS answer call, come over the top, from U.L., L.C.)

(CHIEF is stranded on platform, as GANG is surrounded by BEAVERS and herded D.R., hands aloft in surrender)

(OAKLEAF, PROFESSOR on platform)

CHIEF

(On Platform)

WOW! SURROUNDED! C'MON, GANG, DON'_ LET 'EM SCARE YUH!

OAKLEAF

THE BATTLE IS OVER. THEY GAVE UP. WE ARE GOING TO BEND THEM OVER.

CHIEF

YEAH? I DON'T GIVE UP.

OAKLEAF

I'LL TAKE YOU HAND TO HAND, FAIR AND SQUARE.

CHIEF

(To HUFF)

FAIR AND SQUARE?

HUFF

THAT'S RIGHT, CHIEF. FAIR IS FAIR!

OAKLEAF

C'MON, EVERYBODY! MAKE ROOM!

(Open space is made, C)

(The Duel)

(End of Duel; CHIEF overcome, by OAKLEAF,—stands on platform, hands in air)

BEAVERS

YAAAAAAAAAY!

OAKLEAF

C'MON, BEAVERS, BEND THEM OVER AND KICK THEM OUT.

(GANG is pushed along formed line, bent over by PAUL, kicked out U.C.)

(CHIEF hides D.R.)

(PROFESSOR on platform, checks on names. Notices CHIEF is missing.)

PROFESSOR

THE CHIEF, THE CHIEF'S NEXT. WHERE'S THE CHIEF? WHERE'S THE CHIEF?

(ALL begin search for CHIEF)

(PROFESSOR discovers CHIEF D.R. at foots)

PROFESSOR

WOW! THE CHIEF!

(ALL rush towards CHIEF. OAKLEAF gets there first.)

OAKLEAF

C'MON, BEND HIM OVER. HEY, PAUL, BEND HIM OVER AND KICK HIM OUT.

(ALL rejoice, cheer, as CHIEF is bent over and thrown out, U. L.)

(SKATERS FROM L to R.)

(BACKWOODS somersaults from L to R)

(ALL move about, low, whistling, milling)

CRASH

(Enter WINDY from House C. PAUL and MARY run to him, embrace him, as ALL yell greeting)

MUSIC

PAUL AND MARY

HEY, WINDY!

WINDY

DID YOU HAVE A GOOD TIME?

PAUL

WE JUST CHASED THE CHIEF AND HIS WHOLE GANG RIGHT OUT OF BEAVERLAND.

WINDY

THAT'S GOOD! I NEVER DID LIKE THAT CHIEF! HE WAS VERY MEAN. C'MON NOW, I GOT TO TAKE YOU HOME!

MARY

WE WANT TO HAVE SOME FUN FIRST, WINDY!

WINDY

O. K. LET'S HAVE A GOOD TIME FIRST. THEN I'LL BLOW UP A BIG MEDIUM HURRICANE, AND BLOW YOU HOME.

MUSIC.

(PINE CONE begins VICTORY SONG

PINE CONE

O, SING THE BEAVERS' HAPPY SONG!

ALL

THE BEAVERS SING IT ALL DAY LONG TO ALL THE BEAVERS NOW BELONG ALL OF BEAVER-LAND.

1ST LINE

(On Knees)

SO SING THE BEAVERS' HAPPY SONG,
WE'LL STRIP AND CLIP AND STACK AND PACK
WE'LL STRIP AND CLIP AND STACK AND PACK
WE'LL

2ND LINE

(Bend on knees)

EVERY DAY WE'LL WORK AND PLAY
WORK AND PLAY, WORK AND PLAY
STRIP AND CLIP AND STACK AND PACK
WE'LL

STRIP AND STRIP AND STRIP AWAY
STRIP AND CLIP AND STACK AND PACK
BARK FOR BEAVERLAND.

SO SING THE BEAVERS' HAPPY SONG
SO SING THE BEAVERS' HAPPY SONG

THERE'S BARK FOR EVERY BEAVER
WHO SWINGS A CLEAVER

(WINDY faces R., steps front of 1st line, begins parade, followed by double line, PROFESSOR and MARY, PAUL and OAKLEAF, etc.)

OR PULLS A LEVER

THERE'S NOT A BARKLESS BEAVER
IN ALL OF BEAVER BEAVERLAND
IN ALL OF BEAVERLAND.
(U. L. line reform, as before)
SO HEAR OUR VOICES SINGING
WITH JOY THEY'RE RINGING
(ALL move forward with dignity to front)
THIS MESSAGE BRINGING
TO ALL THE WORLD WE'RE SINGING
ABOUT OUR BEAVERS' BEAVERLAND
ABOUT OUR BEAVERLAND
ABOUT OUR BEAVERLAND.

CURTAIN

17. *One-Third of a Nation*— Arthur Arent

Commentary

Sources

Play

17.1 STATES UNITED: *ONE-THIRD OF A NATION*—HALLIE FLANAGAN

ON THE EVENING OF JUNE 19, 1937, a meeting took place in the drawing room of Josselyn Hall on the Vassar campus. Forty director, actors, designers, and technicians from Federal Theatres throughout the United States gathered for a six weeks' course in theatre training under the joint auspices of Vassar College, the Rockefeller Foundation, and the government of the United States.

They were welcomed by President MacCracken, who threw open to them the resources of the Experimental Theatre, the residence halls, library, gymnasium, and the campus in general.

The Rockefeller Foundation had collaborated on this unique experiment by a grant of money, administered by Vassar College, sufficient to meet such costs as could not be met from federal funds—that is, transportation, board, lodging, and material costs; and the Works Progress Administration paid regular wages for the prescribed number of hours on production or teaching.

Here were men and women selected by their own regional directors on the basis of professional qualifications and accomplishments in such varied theatre fields as drama, vaudeville, and musical comedy, who now brought to a common enterprise their talents and their knowledge of Federal Theatre conditions, needs, and audiences in Louisiana, Iowa, Florida, Connecticut, Oregon, Washington, Massachusetts, Illinois, Michigan, Ohio, Colorado, New Jersey, Georgia, California, Indiana, and New York.

The plan for this meeting had been developing since January, when I first discussed it with Mr. Hopkins and found him greatly interested. On February 17, I wrote Dr. David Stevens, Director of Humanities of the Rockefeller Foundation:

> One of our greatest needs is the retraining of gifted professionals on our project who, due to the economic situation, have not been able to practice their profession for a number of years. A second need lies in a closer relationship between the theatre and education. With this in mind, we wish to set up our first retraining center on a national scale, bringing together some forty of our most gifted designers, directors, and playwrights.

On that first evening, as I met these highly individualized people, strangers to each other, who had worked in the past under diverse methods and forms of theatre experience, I wondered whether in the space of six weeks they could come to know each other, to say nothing of being able to produce a play together. For that was the intent of the summer theatre. These people had not been brought here to go to school. It was the theory on which I had always worked that theatre practice could not be taught academically, but that it might be learned by a group of people working together on something which became for a time, more important than any one of them. If we chose a play together, planned its direction and design, costumed, staged, and acted it, in the meantime focusing all our courses in music, movement, and allied theatre fields on that one mutual problem, I believed that we could not only produce a play, but in the process learn something basically necessary to each project in the country—that is, how to weld a group thrown together from every conceivable background into a creative producing theatre.

If you want to know what it was like to tell this group that there wouldn't be an acting company because they were all going to act, and that there wouldn't be a stage force because, under the guidance of two of our New York stagehands, Pat Patterson and Willy Carbone, they would build and paint scenery and properties, if you want to know whether this took unmitigated nerve, not to say foolhardiness, get the *Report on the Federal Summer Theatre*[1] and look at the faces of the people. Look at Manuel Aparicio from Tampa with his relaxed avoirdupois and his leisurely cheroot, look at Eddie Michaels and William Sully, illustrating with flying arcs in air all anyone could say about movement. You can tell just by looking at Herbert Ashton, Lorin Raker, and John Cameron that they are actor-managers and have toured their own companies all over the country. Look at Abe Feder, who knows more about light than anyone has a right to know and who uses more cable to express it than anyone has a right to unroll. Look at Clair Leonard, who can play a fugue with his fingernail; Tamiris, whose temper is as electric as her hair and her dancing; Arthur Arent, scowling his way through his last act; Howard Bay, Scott McLean, Rainey Bennett, and Bill Perkins, darkly designing each in his own way. And if you don't believe they turned these energies in new directions, turn the pages of the *Report* and see these same directors, designers, managers, musicians, acrobats, and dancers building scenery, painting stereopticon screens, running sewing machines, going to acting laboratory under Madalyn O'Shea, going through gymnastic gyrations under Tamiris' eagle scrutiny, and finally acting in the première production of *One-Third of a Nation*.

I don't want to convey the idea that this all came about in the space of a thunderclap or a revelation from heaven. There were mutterings in corners and fights in the open. There was a geographic feud between the East and the West, there was an occasional re-fighting of the Civil War between the North and the South, and there was a stirring exchange of hostilities on the subject of realism versus non-realism in stage design. Every time I got back from New York or Washington—and it was unfortunately necessary that I spend some time in each of these places because we were engaged in the ghastly business of cutting the project 30 per cent—I would find frantic messages from various members of the staff that the theatre was getting out of hand. Well, I wouldn't give anything for a theatre that wouldn't get out of hand. It was up to us to use all this energy—and once we got under way we certainly used it, as the chart below will show.

What the chart doesn't show is the growing excitement of working with this group from all over the country on a script which had a definite bearing on the life of people all over the country. From research[2] by the living newspaper unit in New York, Arthur Arent had written part one of a living newspaper on housing. Pierre de Rohan suggested the title, *One-Third of a Nation*, from the President's statement in the Second Inaugural, "I see one-third of a nation ill-housed, ill-clad, ill-nourished."

Great economic, social, and educational forces interpenetrated our theatre, even to the circumstances of our meeting here, and our theatre to be worth its creation by the government must at times concern itself with the aim of our government—a better life for more people.

A play about people living in slums, about the historic development of slums and about their tragic effect on human lives, also afforded an exciting problem in design: a small stage, a small budget—and a script calling for a multiplicity of scenes showing city streets, tenements, and many interiors of these tenements.

	9–10:30	10:30–12:45	2:00–4:00	4:15–5:15	7:30–10:30
Monday	Theatre Production lecture	Rehearsal	Stage Crew Scene-building	Dance and Movement	Crew
Tuesday	Acting Technique	Stage Crew Scene-building	Design Lecture	Music	Rehearsal
Wednesday	Theatre Production lecture	Rehearsal	Stage Crew Scene-building	Dance and Movement	Lighting Lecture and Demonstration
Thursday	Acting Technique	Stage Crew Scene-building	Costume Design Lecture	Music Class	Rehearsal
Friday	Theatre Production discussion	Rehearsal	Stage Crew Scene-building	Dance and Movement	Crew
Saturday	Acting Technique	Stage Crew Scene-building	Design Round-table	Free	Free
Sunday	Free	Free	Crew-Lights	Lighting Lecture and Demonstration	

Various ingenious models, notably one by Samuel Leve, were designed along the line of the vast construction later used in New York, and those in favor of such a setting held that in a play about slum conditions it was necessary to show actual slum details. Directors from small projects, however, argued that they could not afford to build expensive sets and they wanted to know how to suggest this scene, or any scene, effectively without much money.

It was possible, because the essence of slum life is not the building itself. Anyone who has walked through the slum district of any city knows that its most ghastly aspect is not the exterior, nor do people who live under such conditions talk about their houses. They talk about the leaky faucets, the saggy beds, the crumbling walls, the broken stair-rail, the roach-infested sinks, the fire-escapes down which no one could escape. Howard Bay therefore conceived the idea of a setting in which the audience would see people living under the shadow of these horrible objects. As you entered the theatre you would see on the uncurtained stage no tenement and no rooms but, suspended in space, strange phantasmagoria of actual objects so gigantic and awesome that it would be difficult to say whether it was real or the materialization of a nightmare. As the play progressed you would gradually, through changing light, be conscious of these objects not as a visual pattern but as actual elements of the disease, misery, and crime bred in the slums—for example, the contagion spreading from the gigantic, leprous faucet down to the head of the child in the cholera scene, or the leap of fire, as the siren sounded, from one rickety object to another, each playing its part in the entombment of its victims.

Obviously, in such a treatment much would depend upon the actors, upon their ability to create through movement the life in the street and in the squalid tenement. Harold Bolton, chosen to direct the play, Tamiris, working on its movement, and Clair Leonard, composing the score, as well as the designer of scenery and costume, worked closely with the author on this problem, and here they were helped by the various courses, technical and practical. Clair Leonard, at the piano, demonstrating musical progress, also discussed and illustrated theatre uses of integrated scores, incidental and background music, pointing all this up with his own expressive score for the play—a score which suggested the surge of city noises, the shriek of the fire siren, the bell of the ambulance, at the same time that it established the varying moods of indignation, despair, and hope in the audience. Madalyn O'Shea's acting laboratory worked through improvisations, connections between characters, group and mass reactions, all of which were useful in the play; and Tamiris confined her courses on the gym floor to basic exercises developing rhythm reactions of the actor to music and the percussive beat, to space, to other actors, and to places and objects. As an example of the way this work often bore specifically on the script in hand, I remember an hour in which Tamiris took a scene from the play in which a fire commissioner questioned four witnesses. Through the expedient of having the commissioner pace around in circles as he questioned the witnesses she conveyed through movement the confusion of his attempt to fix responsibility for the fire.

Howard Bay conducted his design classes as round tables, and in the course of the session we heard from various designers the theories of realism and impressionism. Howard Bay's idea, vividly illustrated in the set he designed for this production, was that a designer can often arouse emotion in an audience so conditioned by the ultra-realism of the films that stage realism seems tepid, by using everyday objects in ways and for purposes different from the customary significance of such objects. Thus, while the elements he planned to use in *One-Third of a Nation* were the subjective psychological materials of a surrealist painter and would make the same assault on the senses, at the same time these objects were factual material recognizable to everyone, enlarged or distorted only as life in slum conditions distorts such objects.

The costume project for *One-Third of a Nation* was somewhat staggering, for thirty actors were called upon to make ninety-three costume changes in seventy minutes of stage action—action ranging from realistic contemporary opening and closing scenes to stylized episodes covering the entire period of New York City's housing history. Mary Merrill's course in costuming consisted of a demonstration as to how, with merely one simple basic costume and the addition of such details as exaggerated period cuffs, coats, or head-dresses, these changes could be effected simply, speedily, and inexpensively.

The most violent course was that given by Feder, who, encoiled like the Laocoön group in his own cable, gave a weekly demonstration of his basic twelve-lamp hook-up and how it could be adapted to interiors, exteriors, musical shows, vaudeville, and drama, as well as to this specific living newspaper. Feder was heckled by directors of small projects who complained that he used too many lights, but he refused to yield. "Don't buy flats, don't buy paint, don't buy costumes, and don't buy make-up! Buy lights!" he thundered. His insistence resulted in a loan system by which we later sent lights, cable, and switchboards from New York to the field.

While the main stream of work was directed toward our own production we saw other performances. We drove over to Bennington to see a highly stylized and provocative showing of *Electra*; the *How Long Brethren?* company came from New York to repeat the performance which had won the Dance Award of the year. There were visits from Washington officials,

Mrs. Woodward and Mr. Morris, and from many theatre people on and off the project. Every week there were discussions for those especially interested in playwriting, children's theatre, vaudeville. During long conferences I learned of the problems of each project in the field; valuable suggestions made by field directors were drawn up in a report by a planning committee.

Six weeks from the night of our first meeting I stood in the back of a crowded theatre. Out of darkness I saw those incredible objects emerge; and out of the confusion, the differing points of view, I saw a group emerge, working with crisp co-ordination. I saw people who had been headliners playing bits, I saw all playing not themselves, but the play. Together they were, through the power of the material and their immersion in it, more than the sum total of their individual selves; together they created luminous scenes in which play, light, acting, music, and movement became one thing transcending any of these elements—in other words, theatre.

At the request of Mr. Barber, who was later to direct the play in New York, New York critics were not invited. *Variety*, however, sent a reporter and reviewed the production at length in the August 4 issue, saying in part:

> *One-Third of a Nation* ranks easily with such efforts as *Injunction Granted* and *Power* and, in forcefulness and compression, is perhaps even better. . . . It is all frankly non-realistic and tremendously effective . . .
>
> Federal Summer Theatre, which has produced this play, is a professional company composed of directors, actors, and designers from Federal Theatre units throughout the United States, meeting for a six weeks' session of study and experimentation at Vassar. Thus very few of the performers in *One-Third of a Nation* have appeared in previous living newspaper productions on Broadway but the general level of acting is up to the usual standard and there are many individual stand-outs—too many for mention in a review.
>
> Show has been mounted with maximum effectiveness. Howard Buy's setting adroitly lighted by Feder is an A-1 piece of suggestion. A huge garbage can, cracked toilet seat, a rusty water tap, an old-law fire escape—all the objects one associates with the slums—dangle from the flies and set the mood of the entire presentation. Harold Bolton, assisted by Tamiris as choreographer, has directed with pace and rhythm. Original music for piano and organ by Clair Leonard provides an apt running commentary.

This particular play, done under these particular conditions, was, in its ever-widening circle of influence, like a pebble thrown into a pool.

The effect on the people is in itself a chronicle of significance in any future planning for any kind of an American theatre and the necessary academy which would accompany such a theatre. Such effect, of course, was not in every case immediate, nor was it universal. A report[3] made two years later shows that the majority of people from the summer session returned to their various projects to do work of such caliber that they either were picked up for jobs in private industry (production manager for Columbia Broadcasting in Seattle, mural painter sent by the Standard Oil to Venezuela, announcer for radio station WDAE) or else they won recognition such as Arthur Arent's Guggenheim Fellowship and Shirley Graham's fellowship from the Rosenwald Foundation enabling her to study at Yale, and Howard Bay's Guggenheim Fellowship; or else they became leaders in Federal Theatre activity. Shirley Graham is an important example, since it is her intention to devote her talents to the development of the Negro theatre in this country. Before Miss Graham was sent by the Chicago project to Poughkeepsie, her experience had been confined to opera performance. At the summer session she plunged into every type of work, on stage and backstage. She set lights, dyed and made costumes, composed music. Returning to Chicago she started classes in acting, movement and speech, to such effect that her production for Federal Theatre of *Little Black Sambo*, for which she designed, composed, and directed, won her praise from the critics and a fellowship at Yale. As a thesis for her doctorate she plans to write the history of the Negro in the Federal Theatre—a record which she believes suggests what the Negro race might, given an opportunity, accomplish in the theatre of our country.

A letter from Michael Slane, director of the Denver Federal Theatre, is typical of many from all over the country :

> The Federal Summer Theatre gave me a much broader view of the theatre than I had had before: it impressed me with the need for music and dance in the theatre and I have used both in production ever since. . . . I now understand and can use light as a basic element of production . . . on my own time I am having classes for our actors and playwriting classes at the Denver Art Museum.[4]

According to information received from the directors, the summer theatre was responsible for such productions in the classical field as Eliot Duvey's *Macbeth* and *Dr. Faustus* in Boston; such inventive uses of vaudeville technique as the Los Angeles *Ready! Aim! Fire!* and *Two-A-Day*, written by Eugene Stone and Jack Robinson, and directed by Lorin Raker; such outstanding work in design as Scott McLean's for the West Coast productions of *Run, Little Chillun* and *Prologue to Glory*, and as William Perkins' for the New Orleans *If Ye Break Faith*; such contributions to children's plays as Bess Whitcomb's Oregon *Alice in Wonderland* and Michael Slane's *The Dragon's Wishbone* in Denver; and in general for a fresher approach and higher production standard.

One-Third of a Nation was revised to meet local conditions and put on in many cities under the auspices of civic and educational groups. New York City saw it, and Detroit, Cincinnati, Portland (Oregon), Philadelphia, Hartford, New Orleans, and Seattle. In each city it was adapted to the specific housing problem of that locality. It was still running in San Francisco two years later when the project ended.

The press throughout the country considered *One-Third of a Nation* the most important contribution to date.

Edward Carberry in the *Cincinnati Post* reviewed the play as "one of those very rare things in the theatre: a play which makes an important subject tremendously exciting."

Philadelphia was rather cool to the play, the *Public Ledger* commenting acidly on the number of people employed in the cast, "makes Goldwyn with his huge aggregation of players look like a piker." This reviewer, seeming to forget the fact that the pressing job of the Federal Theatre was to employ people, nevertheless admitted that *One Third* "frequently smacks you between the eyes with its dramatic force. If you're interested in stagecraft or housing, it's an experiment worth your money."

Detroit afforded such large audiences that the play was held over for four weeks. Ralph Holmes in the *Detroit Times* said:

> The worst thing about *One-Third of a Nation* is that it is true . . . unforgettable vividness and compelling power . . . thrilling beyond description . . . a rare experience in the theatre—not to be missed by anyone.

The history of this play, from its première at Vassar, is an amazing story. It became one of the greatest successes in New York City Federal Theatre, playing at the Adelphi from January 17, 1938, to October 22, 1938, and being seen by over 217,458 persons in that city alone.

Again designed by Howard Bay, it affords testimony to his versatility, since it used for the metropolitan production a real tenement, a huge and horrifying cross-section of a slum which filled the vast stage of the Adelphi and which was burned nightly in an effective moment of stage necromancy. Although the method of production differed from the earlier one, the emphasis on integration of music, movement, and theme remained; and the six weeks of experimentation at the summer session made this play the most mature living newspaper we had done.

This opinion was expressed by the New York critics. Burns Mantle pronounced it "the most interesting of the living newspaper series . . . as fine a setting as any stage in this town has ever shown." Sidney Whipple said: "vividly and artistically presents a human document . . . told in a setting which for stark realism has never been surpassed . . . an important piece of work." Richard Watts, calling the play "invariably forceful, striking and remarkably skillful" declared that "the Federal Theatre has another hit on its hands." Arthur Pollock in the *Brooklyn Eagle* struck a patriotic note: "This government of ours is just about as fine a producer of plays, judging by *One-Third of a Nation*, as we have in the country." Walter Winchell in "This is New York," called the play "Uncle Sam's first big footlight smash," and John Anderson in the *New York Journal and American* said: "A play that any play-goer with a heart and a roof to shelter it owes it to himself to see."

On June 22, 1938, Harold Orlob purchased the movie rights to *One-Third of a Nation*, later releasing it under the same title through Paramount Pictures. The proceeds of the sale, $5,000, were given in escrow to the Guild Committee for Federal Writers' Publications, a non-profit-making organization composed of Heywood Broun, Franklin P. Adams, Lewis Mumford, and others. Random House issued it as one of six Federal Theatre plays chosen for publication in 1938.

Perhaps the most unusual circumstances under which *One-Third of a Nation* was performed, circumstances which, incidentally, testify to the dramatic nature of the script with or without scenery, involved debate in the United States Senate, where on Washington's Birthday, 1938,[5] Senator Bailey of North Carolina discussed the play at length and read a part of it into the *Record*. He commented acidly upon the extensive bibliography of source material for the play contained in the program, upon the number of books read by the author in preparation for writing the play, upon the fact that as a part of this research the author interviewed many people and visited libraries. "He was a very industrious young man, and I must say he did a great deal of reading for the money. I should hate to have done it. If the government is going to pay people to sit up and read this stuff, I do not know how many will do this sort of thing."

Senator Bailey read Act II, Scene 4, interspersing it with comments of his own which drew laughter from the Senate, such as his comment on the stage direction which placed Senator Borah "left of center." "That is a new description of Senator Borah, but I judge it is right." He read into the *Congressional Record* words which he apparently did not know were taken from the *Congressional Record*:[6]

MR. BORAH: Is the Senator going to discuss the question of causes of slums? Why do we have these awful degraded conditions?

LOUDSPEAKER: *Senator Robert F. Wagner, of New York.*

MR. WAGNER: I think it is a very simple matter. It is because of low incomes received by the individuals who live in the slums. That is the fundamental difficulty. If overnight we could increase their incomes by a more fair distribution of the wealth of the country, we would not have any slums.

LOUDSPEAKER: *Senator C. O. Andrews, of Florida.*

MR. ANDREWS: Mr. President, I should like to ask the Senator from New York where the people who live in slums come from?

MR. WAGNER: A great many of them have been here a long time. What does the Senator mean by, "Where do they come from"? Whether they come from some other country?

MR. ANDREWS: I think we ought not to offer any inducement to people to come in from our country or foreign countries or anywhere else and take advantage of our government in supplying them with homes. For instance, if we examine the birth records in New York, we will find that most of the people there in the slums were not born in New York, but the bright lights have attracted them from everywhere and that is one reason why there are so many millions in New York without homes.[7]

After reading several more pages of the play, Senator Bailey interrupted himself with extended comments:

> Senators, I think this activity is a fine thing for us. After all, our little brief authority here will not go very far. We shall soon be forgotten; but it is a great thing to know that we have this great activity for which we may appropriate money, and which will make us all actors on the stage forever.
>
> The play to which I have referred probably will be reproduced longer than *Hamlet*, and people will be talking about the Senator from New York instead of the Prince of Denmark. . . . When most of us die we are forgotten almost before the resolution to pay for our burial is passed; but with the national service theatre we may rest assured that down yonder at the W.P.A. there are playwrights who are putting us down in books, and that we may become a part of the permanent literature of the ages.
>
> Men will walk the stage a thousand, two thousand, three thousand years from now, representing us in our proper persons and our dignity. It is the first time, I think, that the Senate ever won immortality.

One-Third of a Nation, like any powerful play on a controversial subject, made enemies as well as friends. There is nothing new about this situation. Aristophanes was accused of treason because *The Babylonians*, paid for out of government money, criticized Athens' foreign policy; as late as 1937, the Greek government censored *Antigone* because in it Sophocles argued for the freedom of the individual conscience against the State; *Coriolanus* caused riots in the streets of Paris in 1934.

"Big money is going to fight this play," the owner of a theatre which we leased told me. He was complaining, though with some amusement, that the money he made on rent from Federal

Theatre was not enough to pay for the repairs he was being forced to make, because of the public interest aroused by the play in his various slum properties. He stated the position frankly, "Big-monied people like landlords don't want people thinking about slum conditions."

Works Progress Administration officials, so far as I was informed at the time, were enthusiastic about the production, except for Mr. Aubrey Williams who called me into his office on February 15 and asked me what the project meant by "insulting Senators." I explained that the project was doing a serious historical treatment of slum conditions in America and in so doing quoted verbatim and in context from material which I understood was in the public domain—the *Congressional Record*. Surely we couldn't quote only people who favored improvement in housing. The opposing side must also be quoted. "If Senators and Congressmen oppose an increase in appropriations for housing and say so in Congress why should they object to being quoted on the subject?"

I asked Mr. Williams whether he would not satisfy himself that there was no caricature of any sort in the play; and shortly afterward he saw the New York production and was so enthusiastic that he went backstage and spoke to the cast. Fervor carried him to the point where he asked the actors what wages they were receiving and was understood by them to say something to the effect that they deserved more. Thereafter I received a number of delegations protesting that Mr. Aubrey Williams had "promised" them higher wages and why didn't I do something about it.

Enemies made by the living newspaper were, I believe, powerful enemies, instrumental in the final closing of the project. I think of this fact at times and wonder whether it would have been better for the people on our project to have remained aloof from all subjects in any way controversial. Then I realize that this would have barred from our stages, judging by the plays which involved us in censorship, Aristophanes, Shakespeare, Ben Jonson, Maxwell Anderson, Elmer Rice, Eugene O'Neill, Paul Green, and many other important dramatists both classical and modern.

Perhaps we must balance against the criticism the play received, oilier values. On the night of the first production of *One-Third of a Nation* at Poughkeepsie, Langdon Post, at that time Tenement House Commissioner for New York City, in speaking to the cast after the show said that he had often been impressed with the fact that when he talked about tenements and threw picture on the screen, no one was impressed. "The houses look large, and in America size means comfort." Consequently he said that the sight of people moving, as one-third of a nation actually does move, under the pressure of garbage cans and filthy walls and broken fire-escapes gave a truer sense of reality than any number of tenements erected on the stage. "This play, performed as it was tonight, can do more to convert people to proper housing than all the shouting I have done in the past three years."

Paul Green, Herman Shumlin, Kurt Weill, President MacCracken, and many other guests discussed the play with us in much the same vein, and among them was Mrs. Roosevelt. She spoke of another kind of immortality than that discussed on the floor of Congress, of the immortality a play may sometimes achieve. She believed that *One-Third of a Nation* achieved "something for which we will be grateful for many years to come, something which will mean a tremendous amount in the future, socially, and in the education and growing-up of America . . . far more than any amount of speeches which Langdon Post or I—or even the President—might make."

Notes

1. *Report on the Federal Summer Theatre*, June, July, 1937 (W.P.A. Federal Theatre Records, Washington, DC).
2. Bibliography of *One-Third of a Nation, Living Newspaper Magazine*, Vol. 5, No. 19 (W.P.A. Federal Theatre Records, Washington, DC).
3. *Report on the Results of the First Federal Summer Theatre*, by Pierre de Rohan, May 8, 1938 (W.P.A. Federal Theatre Records, Washington, DC).
4. *Report on the Results of the First Federal Summer Theatre*, by Pierre de Rohan, May 8, 1938 (W.P.A. Federal Theatre Records, Washington, DC).
5. *Congressional Record*, February 22, 1938. Senate. Vol. 83, Part 2, pp. 2304–2308.
6. *Congressional Record*, Senate, August 2, 1937, pp. 7967–77–78.
7. *One-Third of a Nation* goes on to say, through the Loudspeaker, that despite his position during the debate, Senator Andrews voted for and supported the Wagner-Steagall Housing Bill in its final form. (*Congressional Record*, Senate, August 6, 1937, p. 8373.)

17.2 HUAC TESTIMONY OF HALLIE FLANAGAN, NATIONAL DIRECTOR, FEDERAL THEATRE PROJECT

The CHAIRMAN. Now, will you just tell us briefly the duties of your position?

Mrs. FLANAGAN. Yes, Congressman Dies. Since August 29, 1935, I have been concerned with combating un-American inactivity.

The CHAIRMAN. No. We will get to that in a minute.

Mrs. FLANAGAN. Please listen. I said I am combating un-American inactivity.

The CHAIRMAN. Inactivity?

Mrs. FLANAGAN. I refer to the inactivity of professional men and women; people who, at that time when I took office, were on the relief rolls; and it was my job to expend the appropriation laid aside by congressional vote for the relief of the unemployed as it related to the field of the theater, and to set up projects wherever in any city 25 or more of such professionals were found on the relief rolls.

Mr. THOMAS. Mr. Chairman, I think before her statement is made, we should find out something about Mrs. Flanagan's history. I think it is of great importance that we know something about her history, and that that go in the record—where she went to college, and so forth.

The CHAIRMAN. We are going to get to that, but I wanted to give her an opportunity.

I think that you said you are the director of all these activities?

Mrs. FLANAGAN. Yes; thank you. May I add to that fact that the project is national in scope; and that we have projects in Washington, Oregon, California, in Colorado and Michigan, in Ohio and Illinois, in Oklahoma and North Carolina, in Maine and New Hampshire, in New York State and Massachusetts, and New Jersey and Delaware; in other words, in any place where there were a sufficient number of qualified relief applicants. I wanted to say that, gentlemen, as a background for the project.

The CHAIRMAN. I think we have that all right.

Mr. STARNES. When was the Federal Theater Project set up, Mrs. Flanagan?

Mrs. FLANAGAN. It was set up on August 29, 1935.

Mr. STARNES. What was the primary purpose of setting up this Federal Theater Project?

Mrs. FLANAGAN. The primary purpose was to put back to work the unemployed professional people; to put them back to work and rehabilitate them and conserve their skills. That was then and always has been the prime purpose of the theater project.

Now, if I may say so, the fact that we have returned to private industry some 2,000 people would seem to me to prove that we are considering that always as our major objective.

[. . .]

Mr. STARNES. Now, there is another statement you have made here, that some of the plays that were put out by the Federal Theater Project are propagandistic or that they breed class consciousness—is that true or untrue?

Mrs. FLANAGAN. When we remember—

Mr. STARNES. Not all of them, because the testimony is that 924 plays have been produced, and only 26, as I recall, were in question. Let us confine ourselves to those that are in question.

Mrs. FLANAGAN. I do want to go into the matter of the 26 plays as much as this committee will allow me to do. But before I go into that I would like to say that I could not say that we never did a propaganda play. But I should like to go to the actual definition of "propaganda."

Propaganda, after all, is education. It is education focused on certain things.

For example, some of you gentlemen have doubtless seen *One-third of the Nation*; and I certainly would not sit here and say that that was not a propaganda play.

I think in the discussion yesterday the word "propaganda" was used in this connotation only—that any play which was propaganda was necessarily propaganda for communism.

I should like to say very truthfully that to the best of my knowledge we have never done a play which was propaganda for communism, but we have done plays which were propaganda for democracy, propaganda for better housing.

Mr. THOMAS. I think you ought to develop that point right there. You said that some plays were propaganda for democracy. What do you mean by that? Propaganda for what forms of democracy and what particular things? Like housing, as you just mentioned?

Mrs. FLANAGAN. Yes.

Mr. THOMAS. What others?

Mrs. FLANAGAN. I would say—shall we go into a discussion of democracy?

Mr. THOMAS. No. Just name some of the things that the Federal Theater Project has put out propaganda plays for.

Mrs. FLANAGAN. Yes. Well, let us say first, *One-third of the Nation*. In that the definite propaganda was for better housing for American citizens.

Mr. THOMAS. What others?

Mrs. FLANAGAN. I would say that in general, Mr. Thomas, *The Living Newspaper* would be propaganda for——

Mr. THOMAS. But you are not answering the question. You mentioned housing?

Mrs. FLANAGAN. Yes.

Mr. THOMAS. How about Power?

Mrs. FLANAGAN. Yes. I would say that Power was propaganda for a better understanding of the derivation and the scientific meaning of power and for its wide use.

Mr. THOMAS. Was it for public ownership of power?

Mrs. FLANAGAN. That portrayed as effectively as possible both sides of that controversy, and quoted both sides.

[. . .]

The CHAIRMAN. You recently made a report of your activities and you gave the number of people you estimated you have played to since the establishment of the project. How many people do you figure you had as audiences in the United States for these plays?

Mrs. FLANAGAN. The recorded figure, Congressman Dies, was something like 25,000,000 people.

The CHAIRMAN. In other words, you have reached approximately 25 percent of our population with your plays?

Mrs. FLANAGAN. Something like that.

One of the great problems, if you will permit me to speak for just a minute——

The CHAIRMAN. Yes, ma'am.

Mrs. FLANAGAN. One of the great problems is that, while in the other art projects it is possible to establish them in every State in the Union, which we would also like to do here, it is not possible with us, because, while an artist can paint or a musician play or a writer write if there is no audience or only one or two people involved, we cannot set up theaters except in States where there are 25 or more people of satisfactory type on the relief rolls.

So that one of our problems is this centralization of the theater industry. Our big centers are New York, Los Angeles, and Chicago; and we, as much as possible, want to tour people out from those regions and want to set up small projects in the country.

However, it is very difficult to tour, because, as you know, it is very expensive business. We are touring a great deal out of the regional centers, covering the rural areas in Michigan and Illinois and so on. But we have not gone as extensively into touring as we would like to do.

May I go on for just a minute?

The CHAIRMAN. Where have your audiences been? What localities have you played mostly?

Mrs. FLANAGAN. We have played to, I think I am safe in saying, the widest variety of American audiences that any theater has ever played before.

The CHAIRMAN. In what localities, Mrs. Flanagan?

Mrs. FLANAGAN. The chief localities are, first, New York City, and next Los Angeles and Chicago, because that is where the greatest unemployment exists. They are the three largest centers. But if you are speaking now of the audiences themselves—I want to pick up that point, if you don't mind——

The CHAIRMAN. It is quite all right, but I merely want to know the places where you have played. But if you want to discuss audiences, it is all right.

Mrs. FLANAGAN. I do want to discuss them.

The CHAIRMAN. That is all right.

Mrs. FLANAGAN. Because that allegation was made here by one of your witnesses, which I would not like to remain in the minds of any of you around this table, because my impression is that you are trying to get at all the facts.

The CHAIRMAN. That is correct. And if this statement is untrue, we want you to refute it.

Mrs. FLANAGAN. I want to quote from her allegation. Miss Huffman says: "They couldn't get any audiences for anything except communistic plays."

Now, gentlemen, I absolutely deny that allegation, and I have here the proof that that is an absolutely false statement.

We have, as sponsoring bodies for the Federal Theater, lists of organizations covering 20 pages of this brief, which I intend to write into the record; and I will summarize them for you, if you like.

Two hundred and sixty-three social clubs and organizations, 264 welfare and civic organiaztions, 271 educational organizations, 95 religious organizations, 91 organizations from business industries, 16 mass organizations, 66 trade-unions, 62 professional unions, 17 consumers unions, 25 fraternal unions, and 15 political organizations.

Note, gentlemen, that every religious shade is covered and every political affiliation and every type of educational and civic body in the support of our theater. It is the widest and most American base that any theater has ever built upon; and I do request you not only to write that into the record, but to read the list of public schools and universities and churches and the civic and social groups that are supporting this Federal Theater.

[. . .]

Mr. STARNES. The statement has been made in the testimony that you are in sympathy with communistic doctrines.

Mrs. FLANAGAN. Congressman Starnes, I am an American, and I believe in American democracy. I believe the Works Progress Administration is one great bulwark of that democracy. I believe the Federal Theater, which is one small part of that large pattern, is honestly trying in every possible way to interpret the best interests of the people of this democracy. I am not in sympathy with any other form of government in this country.

Mr. STARNES. That is your statement. You are absolutely not in sympathy with communism. Now, have you, as Director of this National Art Project, produced productions for the purpose of promoting class hatred, we will say?

Mrs. FLANAGAN. I have not.

Mr. STARNES. Do you recognize only the Workers' Alliance as the bargaining agency among employees on your project?

Mrs. FLANAGAN. Certainly not. We have something like 24 theatrical unions that we are dealing with constantly on this project. It is one of the most complicated ramifications which I will go into if you wish.

Mr. STARNES. No, I am trying to make this thing specific because specific statements were made.

Mrs. FLANAGAN. I realize that. I have specific answers if you want to go into them.

Mr. STARNES. The question was raised as to whether or not there are Communists on your project. We understand, and we know, that no restrictions have been placed on your employing people who might believe in a communistic form of government. We understand that. And unquestionably you have, according to the testimony, Communists working on the job, but the thing the committee is interested in is the question of communistic activity on the project.

Do you know of your own knowledge, personal knowledge, of any communistic activities that are being carried on there, in other words, the promulgation of communistic doctrines and theory, the recruiting of soldiers for Loyalist Spain, the dissemination of communistic literature, or the collection of funds for the Workers' Alliance and for the Communist Party on project time?

Mrs. FLANAGAN. Congressman Starnes, those are opposed to the administrative restrictions, copies of which are in this brief.

Mr. STARNES. You are opposed to it, and you know nothing of it personally, but you can't deny, of course, of your own personal knowledge, such is the case, but if it is the case, it is without your knowledge and consent?

Mrs. FLANAGAN. Right.

The CHAIRMAN. Mrs Flanagan, I want to ask you one or two questions. What, in your opinion, as the director of the Federal Theaters is the primary purpose to be kept in mind in the production of plays? Is it amusement? I am not talking about the relief angle now.

Mrs. FLANAGAN. Yes, sir.

The CHAIRMAN. I am talking about the selection of material in the production of plays. What principal objective do you keep in mind, amusement, or, on the other hand, the teaching of a particular idea or the presentation of facts or material in a way to leave a definite impression?

Mrs. FLANAGAN. I am glad you asked that question, because it is an important one. The basis of the choice of plays is that we have always believed on the Federal Theater Project that any theater supported by the Federal funds should do no plays of a subversive, or cheap, or shoddy, or vulgar, or outworn, or imitative nature, but only such plays as the Government could stand behind in a program which is national in scope and regional in emphasis and democratic in American attitude.

Mr. THOMAS. Democratic!

Mrs. FLANAGAN. Not democratic in the narrow sense.

The CHAIRMAN. Then in a sense primarily it is for amusement; isn't that true?

Mrs. FLANAGAN. The second objective, if I may go on, is wide diversity. I think we should do plays of as great diversity as the geographic range and the varieties of our people. I can't say just entertainment or education, Congressman Dies.

The CHAIRMAN. You are not in a position to say whether the primary purpose should be to entertain the audience or instruct the audience?

Mrs. FLANAGAN. A good play must always entertain the audience.

THE CHAIRMAN. That is the primary purpose of it?

Mrs. FLANAGAN. The primary purpose of a good play is to entertain, isn't it?

The CHAIRMAN. Entertain?

Mrs. FLANAGAN. It must also and can also often teach. It can inculcate religious principles. It can entertain simply if it is a musical comedy. Think of the varieties of things that it can do to train people in the great field of the classics.

The CHAIRMAN. It can be used as a vehicle, in other words, to impart to an audience certain ideas either along moral lines or along social lines or economic lines; isn't that a fact?

Mrs. FLANAGAN. Yes.

The CHAIRMAN. And in the production of these plays, while you have kept in mind primarily the objective of entertainment, you have considered it your duty likewise to convey such, we will say, instruction or to impart ideas along social and economic lines; isn't that true?

Mrs. FLANAGAN. I would like to answer that rather fully, because it is an important point. The list of the plays that we have done is open to you, and the proof of the types of plays that we do can be found there. Over 500 of the 924 plays are plays by tested American authors which have had previous successes on Broadway. They are plays of the great body of American—

The CHAIRMAN. Am I not right?

Mrs. FLANAGAN. I really would like to go on – I know the bell rang or something, but I really would like to get this in. That is the major field, and then there are also musical comedies, because they use great numbers of people, you see. There are also children's plays which we have built up as a great speciality, chiefly fairy tales, not with the connotation mentioned, and then we have also done dance dramas, and we have placed great emphasis on the classics. We have done plays by Euripides, Plautus, Marlowe, Shakespeare, Beaumont, and Fletcher, Lope de Vega, Molière, Sheridan, Labiche, Ibsen, Wilde, Shaw, and O'Neill, and I have written into the record a list of the very distinguished dramatists whose plays we have produced. Therefore I would say that a wide variety is one of the guiding principles.

If you are not too bored, I would like to say that another guiding principle is to stress American material. The board of choice that decides upon plays is made up of the regional representatives who know their regions, and each one brings in the plan of the productions that he wants to do. He wants to do something classic, the children's theater, a musical comedy, and he wants to develop from his own region something about that region. For example, in Portland we are doing the great Paul Bunyan festival, and in North Carolina we are doing the history of America in the Lost Colony. So that the stressing of American plays has been one of our great desires from the first of the project.

The CHAIRMAN. But one of the most important functions of the theater, as you recognize it – I am just asking you to get your opinion – is to promote an idea either along social, economic, or, we will say, political lines; is that true? Is that a legitimate function of the theater as you understand it?

Mrs. FLANAGAN. I defined propaganda very clearly, or tried to, in the early stages of this.

The CHAIRMAN. I know, but is that a legitimate function of the stage?

Mrs. FLANAGAN. It is one legitimate function.

The CHAIRMAN. It is one legitimate function?

Mrs. FLANAGAN. Yes.

[. . .]

The CHAIRMAN. Do you think that the Federal Theater should be used for the purpose, for one purpose of conveying ideas along social, economic or political lines?

Mrs. FLANAGAN. I would hesitate on the political. So far as I know we have never stressed—

The CHAIRMAN. Eliminate political, upon social and economic lines.

Mrs. FLANAGAN. I think it is one logical, reasonable, and I might say imperative thing for our theater to do.

The CHAIRMAN. And for educational purposes; is that right?

Mrs. FLANAGAN. Yes.

The CHAIRMAN. In other words, you believe it is correct to use the Federal Theater to educate people, audiences, along social or economic lines; is that correct?

Mrs. FLANAGAN. Among other things; yes. I have pointed out to the committee that only 10 percent of the plays that we do——

The CHAIRMAN. I understand.

Mrs. FLANAGAN. But that is important, and I am not sure all of these people do understand it, and I want them to. The definite proof is we do and have only done 10 percent of the plays in that category.

The CHAIRMAN. I am not questioning that fact. You have plays and dances that have nothing to do with economics.

Mrs. FLANAGAN. Right. Among others we have plays that have to do with ideas.

The CHAIRMAN. Plays that have nothing to do with social or economic ideas, but you do believe that it is proper in the Federal Theater that some of the plays produced by the Federal Theaters should be used for that purpose?

Mrs. FLANAGAN. I do, Congressman Dies.

[. . .]

The CHAIRMAN. Then this Federal Theater is a very powerful vehicle of expression, isn't it, and of propaganda, because, as you say, it reaches 25,000,000 people. It therefore can be used or abused.

Mrs. FLANAGAN. Yes.

The CHAIRMAN. With serious consequences, can it not?

Mrs. FLANAGAN. Yes, sir.

The CHAIRMAN. And do you know of any way in which it could be more seriously abused than it would be to portray, as I said a few moments ago, one class, putting them at an advantage over another class?

Mrs. FLANAGAN. I have been giving a long list of illustrations of the fact that we do not so do.

The CHAIRMAN. I am not asking you that. I say, isn't that a fact?

Mrs. FLANAGAN. I am asking you for illustrations where we have done that. I claim you are stating a hypothetical case, Congressman Dies.

The CHAIRMAN. Then, will you say that you have not produced a play in which throughout the play one class of workers is not portrayed in an advantageous roll?

Mrs. FLANAGAN. No; you have stated your question definitely. First you asked me if I could give you a single play in which we have not done that.

The CHAIRMAN. You gave that.

Mrs. FLANAGAN. I say I can show you a myriad, so I would not take the position you have said, that is too strong a position.

[. . .]

The CHAIRMAN. We heard considerable testimony which forms an important part of this, that numerous people working on the project were Communists. We got that from one or two who are members of the Communist Party themselves. We got it from their own signatures, and statements that they were Communists, and received testimony that Communist literature was disseminated through the premises during project time, that they were printed on the bulletin board until this investigation began and it stopped, that meetings of the Communists units were held on project time in the premises, and other testimony.

I am just citing you some of the highlights. Now, that is the material fact involved here, as to whether that was done.

Mrs. FLANAGAN. May I ask is that all in the record which I have studied, or are you referring to other records?

The CHAIRMAN. I do not know what record you have studied, but that is in the record of the hearing, in all of the records.

Mrs. FLANAGAN. I think you must be confusing some of our testimony, because I have read it very carefully, because I have not found a single witness brought up before us that said he was a Communist.

The CHAIRMAN. Before us?

Mrs. FLANAGAN. Before you.

The CHAIRMAN. Well, Mr. DeSolo said he was a Communist.

Mrs. FLANAGAN. But he is not on the Federal Theater Project.

The CHAIRMAN. He is on the Writers Project.

Mrs. FLANAGAN. Yes; but not our project.

The CHAIRMAN. You are dealing with the Federal Theater Project.

Mrs. FLANAGAN. Because that is what I have jurisdiction over.

17.3 PRODUCTION PHOTOS FROM *ONE-THIRD OF A NATION*

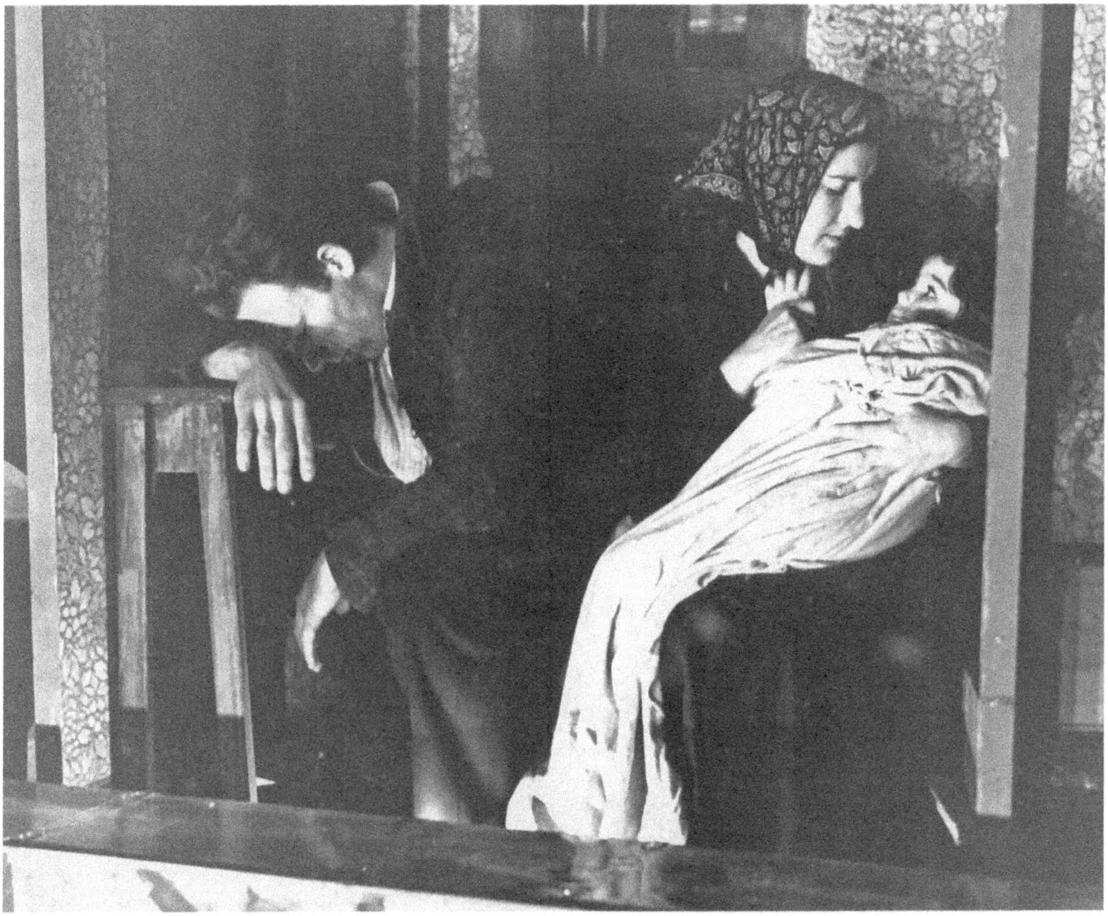

Scene depicting the sufferings of the lower class, from the Federal Theatre Project (FTP) production of *One-Third of a Nation*, Seattle, 1938 (courtesy University of Washington Libraries, Special Collections Division). The FTP was the most ambitious and well-organized government subsidized theatre project in the history of the United States. In the brief four seasons of its existence, the Federal Theatre produced over 1,200 individual productions and employed over 13,000 people in 35 states, in an impoverished country wracked by the Great Depression. Though director Hallie Flanagan produced a variety of different types of productions, there was a strong leftist sentiment in parts of the FTP, as seen in *One-Third of a Nation*. This was, no doubt, the influence of Flanagan's ties to left-wing theatre prior to the FTP.

Source: Photo © University of Washington Libraries, Special Collections, UW36504

Scene portraying class inequity from the Seattle production of *One-Third of a Nation*.

Source: Photo © University of Washington Libraries, Special Collections, UW36505

Intricate scene showing, as Franklin Roosevelt described them, the "ill-housed, ill-clad, ill-nourished," from the Seattle production of *One-Third of a Nation*, Seattle.

Source: Photo © University of Washington Libraries, Special Collections, UW36506

17.4 *ONE-THIRD OF A NATION*—ARTHUR ARENT

CAST OF CHARACTERS

ACT I

VOICE OF LIVING NEWSPAPER	CHARLES DILL

Scene 1—Fire

MAN IN CELLAR	JAMES WILLIAMS
BOYS	ROY LeMAY NAT LOESBERG
FATHER	CHARLES DEIGHAN
MOTHER	MAY RITCHIE
DAUGHTER	JENNIE WREN
POLICEMAN	JOHN POTE
MAN ON FIRE ESCAPE	PAT McCULLAGH

Scene 2—Investigation

COMMISSIONER	EDWIN WHITNER
MR. ROSEN	MAX HIRSCH
FIRE DEPARTMENT INSPECTOR	DICK FITZGERALD
BUILDING DEPARTMENT INSPECTOR	TOM HARRIS
TENEMENT HOUSE INSPECTOR	WAYNE NUNN
MR. SCHULTZ	RICHARD KELLER
CAR OWNER	SNITZ MOORE
AUTOMOBILE SALESMAN	ALEXANDER POLAK

Scene 3—Land

A—Trinity Church

(Staged by TAMARIS)

LORD CORNBURY	PETER KING
MINISTER	GEORGE A. RYAN
LEASEHOLDERS	LAWRENCE HAWLEY HUGH BANKS WILLIAM BURBRIDGE ROBERT WARD
ALDERMAN	JAMES J. COYLE
WILLIAM RHINELANDER	ZACK MACCUBBIN
AARON BURR	THURLOW BERGEN

B—The City Grows

LANDOWNER	ROBERT NOACK
VOICE OF TOWN CRIER	ZACK MACCUBBIN
SECOND VOICE	TOM HARRIS
MAN-in-SEARCH-of-HOME	SIDNEY RIGGS
VERY FAT MAN	PHIL BISHOP
ROBERT GOELET	SAM BONNELL
JOHN WENDELL	ROBERT MACK
JOHN JACOB ASTOR	ED. BRANDON
JAMES GORDON BENNETT	ROBERT LINWOOD

Scene 4—Looking Backward

LITTLE MAN	CLARENCE R. CHASE
GUIDE	JOSEPH DIXON
CITIZEN	WAYNE NUNN

A—Why They Came (Irish Family)

MARY	VIRGINIA DALY
IRISH FATHER	EUGENE MacGREGOR
IRISH MOTHER	BEATRICE HENDRICKS
MIKE, THEIR SON	DON STEWART

B—What They Saw (Steve and Joe)

JOE	WILLIAM S. PHILLIPS
STEVE	MICKIE JACOBI

C—What They Got (Cholera)

JEWISH MOTHER	MIRIAM GOLDINA
JEWISH FATHER	MAX HIRSCH
DOCTOR	ZACK MACCUBBIN
SICK WOMAN	LOUISE McGREGOR
HER DAUGHTER	JOAN DANTON
NURSE	JEAN THOMAS
ANOTHER WOMAN	ANNE VOORHEES
HER SON	ROY LeMAY
DOCTOR	ROBERT WARD
DOCTOR	GEORGE A. RYAN
SICK MAN	SAM BONNELL
ORDERLIES	EDWIN WHITNER WILLIAM PARKE
SICK BOY	RICHARD HUETT
REPORTERS	LAWRENCE HAWLEY TOM HARRIS
VOICE OF GERRITT FORBES	ROBERT LINWOOD

Scene 5—Appoint a Committee

ANNOUNCER OF STATISTICS	JOHN POTE
	ZACK MACCUBBIN GEORGE A. RYAN ROBERT WARD
DR. JOHN H. GRISCOM, INSPECTOR OF HEALTH (1855)	HUGH BANKS
MAYOR	PHIL BISHOP
CHAIRMAN OF MAYOR'S COMMITTEE	WILLIAM BURBRIDGE
OTHER COMMITTEE MEMBERS	CHARLES DEIGHAN RICHARD KELLER MILE METRAS
CHARWOMEN	JANET McGUINESS MATHILDE BARING MARION DAY

Scene 6—Renting

LANDLORD	WILLIAM BURBRIDGE
FIRST AGENT	RICHARD KELLER
ITALIAN FAMILY	DAVID RESNIKOFF DOROTHY GAMMON ANE HOWE RICHARD HUETT NANCY SKIDMORE
MAN	PAT McCULLAGH
WOMAN	BEATRICE OLSON
ANOTHER FAMILY	NAT LOSSBERG TOMMI BISSELL ANNE VOORHEES MAY RITCHIE GEORGE BATSON
SECOND AGENT	DICK FITZGERALD
THIRD AGENT	MAX HIRSCH
NEW YORKERS IN SEARCH OF A HOME	PAUL JACCHIA ALMA MAKEE WILLIAM La VAR ANNE ASHLEY
GRANDDAUGHTER	JOAN DANTON
GRANDFATHER	GEORGE COLAS
JEWISH MAN	VLADIMIR PERLOFF
JEWISH WOMAN	MIRIAM GOLDINA
MINISTER	WAYNE NUNN

ACT II

Scene 1—The Law

VOICE OF THE HOUSE	EDWIN WHITNER
ANNOUNCERS OF THE LAW	ED BRANDON ZACK MACCUBBIN
COMMITTEE TO INVESTIGATE HOUSING (1894)	EMILE METRAS
RICHARD WATSON GILDER, CHAIRMAN	SAM BONNELL
ENOCH VREELAND, DEPUTY SUPERINTENDENT OF BUILDING DEPARTMENT	ROBERT LINWOOD
EDITOR OF NEW YORK HERALD	GEORGE A. RYAN
COLONEL S. VAN RENSSELAER CRUGER, COMPTROLLER OF TRINITY CHURCH	PHIL BISHOP
THE VERY REVEREND A. WOODRUFF HALSEY	JAMES J. COYLE
JUDGE PRYOR	WILLIAM PARKE
S.P. NASH, ATTORNEY FOR TRINITY	TOM HARRIS
ROGER FOSTER, ATTORNEY FOR CITY	PETER KING
JUDGE PECKHAM	THURLOW BERGEN
ANNOUNCER OF LAW	WAYNE NUNN

Scene 2—Crosstown

THE LITTLE MAN	CLARENCE R. CHASE
GUIDE	JOSEPH DIXON

A—Street Kids

FRANK	MICKIE JACOBI
SAMMY	ROY LeMAY
SAMMY'S MOTHER	MIRIAM GOLDINA
ANNOUNCERS	CATHERINE HUTH MAVIS WALSH

B—East Side—West Side

MIN	HELENE AMBROSE
JIM, HER HUSBAND	JOHN POTE
MRS. BUTTONKOOPER	EDITH GROOME
TENEMENT HOUSE COMMISSIONER	PETER KING

C—Harlem

A STEVEDORE	ADD BATES
A BOOTBLACK	KERMIT AUGUSTINE

D—Rent Strike

EAST SIDE STRIKERS	DOROTHY GAMMON JOAN DANTON BEATRICE OLSON

BRONX STRIKERS	MARION DAY JANET McGUINESS JEAN THOMAS
ORGANIZER	SAM BONNELL
BROOKLYN STRIKERS	VLADIMIR PERLOFF KATHERINE BERGER

Scene 3—What Price Housing?

LANDLORD	ALEXANDER POLAK
LANDOWNER	WAYNE NUNN
BROKERS	PHIL BISHOP
BUILDING SUPPLY MEN	SAM BONNELL SNITZ MOORE TOM HARRIS
CONTRACTOR	ROBERT LINWOOD
BANKER	JAMES J. COYLE
MORTGAGE COMPANY PRESIDENT	WILLIAM PARKE
FEDERAL TAX COLLECTOR	EMILE METRAS
STATE TAX COLLECTOR	ROBERT MACK
CITY TAX COLLECTOR	DICK FITZGERALD
INSURANCE AGENT	RICHARD KELLER
COAL DEALER	PAUL JACCHIA
RENTING AGENT	MAVIS WALSH
JANITOR	JAMES WILLIAMS
ANNOUNCERS	DON STEWART ROBERT WARD WILLIAM BURBRIDGE JAMES F. KELLY
NATHAN STRAUS, ADMINISTRATOR, U.S. HOUSING AUTHORITY	LAWRENCE HAWLEY

Scene 4—Government Housing

CLERK OF THE SENATE	TOM HARRIS
SENATOR WILLIAM E. BORAH OF IDAHO	EUGENE MacGREGOR
VICE-PRESIDENT JOHN N. GARNER	JAMES F. KELLY
SENATOR ROBERT F. WAGNER OF NEW YORK	ED. BRANDON
SENATOR C.O. ANDREWS OF FLORIDA	EDWIN WHITNER
SENATOR HARRY F. BYRD OF VIRGINIA	JAMES J. COYLE
SENATOR MILLARD E. TYDINGS OF MARYLAND	GEORGE A. RYAN

Scene 5—Looking Forward

HELEN ALFRED, DIRECTOR NATIONAL PUBLIC HOUSING CONFERENCE	DORIS FRANCIS
HON. FIORELLO H. LAGUARDIA, MAYOR, NEW YORK CITY	LEOPOLD BADIA

LANDOWNER	ROBERT NOACK
LANDLORD	ALEXANDER POLAK
MRS. BUTTONKOOPER	EDITH GROOME

TENANTS, MEN AND WOMEN IN SEARCH OF HOMES, ETC.

CLARENCE M. KANE, DAVID RESNIKOFF, RICHARD HUETT, AURELIO TOBIAS, JAMES WILLIAMS, JEAN THOMAS, NANCY SKIDMORE, ANNE VOORHEES, MAVIS WALSH, LOIS GRAY, GEORGE COLAN, WILLIAM LaVAR, PAUL JACCHIA, PAT McCULLAGH, MAY DeLOURIER, MARION DAY, CATHERINE HUTH, ALMA McKEE, MATHILDE BARING, MAY RITCHIE, DOROTHY GAMMON, JOAN DANTON, JANET McGUINESS, VLADIMIR PERLOFF, KATHERINE BERGER.

ORCHESTRA CONDUCTOR—FRED HOFF

STAFF OF THE LIVING NEWSPAPER

MANAGER FOR THE LIVING NEWSPAPER	IRVING MENDELL
MANAGING EDITOR	ARTHUR ARENT
RESEARCH SUPERVISOR	RICHARD J. McMANUS
LIBRARIAN	STEPHEN MADIGAN

★

SCENE TITLES

ACT I

SCENE 1—Fire!

SCENE 2—Investigation

SCENE 3—Land
- A—Trinity Church
- B—The City Grows

SCENE 4—Looking Backward
- A—Why they came (an Irish family)
- B—What they saw (Steve and Joe)
- C—What they got (cholera)

SCENE 5—Appoint a Committee

SCENE 6—Renting

ACT II

SCENE 1—The Law

SCENE 2—Crosstown—1933
- A—Street Kids
- B—East Side—West Side
- C—Harlem
- D—Rent Strike

SCENE 3—What Price Housing?

SCENE 4—Government Housing

SCENE 5—Looking Forward

★

ACT I

Scene 1—Fire!

CHARACTERS

Loudspeaker
A little girl
Two small boys
Two girls
Another girl
Her mother
Her father
Man
Occupants of the tenement
Crowd of onlookers and passersby
Policeman
Fireman
Jewish man (Mr. Rosen)
Man (on fire escape)

★

OVERTURE

Curtain rises on a slum tenement which appears as a cross section of a number of tenements. On stage right, the ground floor of a tenement building represents the entrance to a cellar. Above this is cubicle stage right—a room completely exposed, the upstage walls carrying up to flies; the walls, possibly from a house that has been demolished and is left standing, showing the plaster lines made by the former floors and stairways. Upstage and continuing from right to left is a cross section of a main tenement showing center—two exposed rooms, one over the other, and a narrow stairway to the left leading from the street up to the interior of the house. Continuing upward is the landing of the third floor and a connecting stairway to the fourth floor. The fourth floor shows a hallway with three closed doors—up. There is a balustrade down across the entire hallway. One center rung of the balustrade is out, leaving a wide gap. To the left of this structure stands another small section of a tenement with a fire escape about 24 feet above and one window as an egress to the fire escape. From the railing of the fire escape hangs a vertical ladder, each side of which is attached to the railing by a hook. On left of this is an alley leading up to the street with a view of the neighboring tenement houses, warehouse in need of repair, whole buildings in poor condition, and in the far distance a gas-tank. At entrance to alley is indicted passage to basement of small tenement. Opposite this, in alley stands a rubbish heap.

A ship ladder stairway leads from the street to cubicle stage right and a connecting stairway from this cubicle into the main tenement. Against wall of cubicle stage right is a stationary cot, on top of which is a mattress. Half way down stage in front of building and running across from right to left is a 3 step.

The apron has been built out and joins the stage by a step extending right to left. At each end of the apron a 2 step, down right and down left.

Steps lead from pit on to stage left. The action of the play alternates between the scenes in the tenement structure and those played in front of blacks. The blacks are flown upstage directly behind the 3 step. The scene develops as follows:

As the curtain rises—a SMALL GIRL is seen getting water from the cellar faucet stage right. She then picks up her pail and starts to go up ship ladder stairway. As she reaches the middle of the stairway TWO SMALL BOYS, who have been shooting crap on the bottom step of the stairway to the second floor call her and wave. She waves back and continues on her way up to the top floor. Her walk is slow and indicates that the pail is heavy and that it is a long climb. At the same time in the lower center cubicle TWO GIRLS are lounging. A small victrola is playing a dance record of the period (1924). They are preparing to retire and are sitting at ease previous to going to bed. In the cubicle above is seen a YOUNG GIRL dozing on a chair, her MOTHER, in house dress, preparing a lunch pail for the girl's FATHER who is ready to go to work on his night shift. As the GIRL WITH THE PAIL reaches the third floor, the VOICE OF THE LIVING NEWSPAPER is heard over the microphone.

LOUDSPEAKER

February 1924—This might be 397 Madison Street, New York.[1] It might be 245 Halsey Street, Brooklyn,[2] or Jackson Avenue and 10th Street, Long Island City.[3]

Wisps of smoke appear coming from the third floor, the basement left, and the cellar right. The BOYS sniff, look about, and go back to shooting crap. A moment later dense puffs of smoke appear from cellar right and basement left. A MAN, coughing, comes up from the cellar right. He goes to get water at the faucet and the BOYS run over to question him. They all realize that the building is on fire and one of the boys excitedly starts to run up the stairs. The SMALL ONE, having remained downstairs, yells up to him, "Hey, where are you going?" The FIRST BOY, unheeding, continues on his way up the stairs to warn the occupants on the upper floors. The OTHER BOY starts to follow him up. As the FIRST BOY reaches the third floor, PEOPLE in various modes of attire and dishabille emerge from the various apartments and nearby tenements. The screech of fire sirens and the clang of bells are heard. From this point on the excitement mounts. PEOPLE on the third and fourth floors and in the various cubicles start running, taking with them any personal belongings that they are able to lay hands on, knocking on doors, waking up people in the other apartments.

A CROWD OF ONLOOKERS and PASSERSBY start to gather on stage. In the crowd is a POLICEMAN who bangs his club on the ground and blows his whistle. A FIREMAN appears with a searchlight playing his light all over the structure. A Jewish man (MR. ROSEN)[4] enters right, agitatedly pointing to the building and begging the POLICEMAN to let him go up. The POLICEMAN refuses and holds him back with much difficulty. During the above a MAN comes out of window and appears on the fire escape in tenement left, 24 feet above stage. The CROWD sees him. He puts his foot over the railing of the fire escape. As his foot touches the ladder one hook gives way and it starts swinging crazily, shutting off his means of escape. He tries to clamber back in through the window but a cloud of smoke and flame blasts out, hitting him in the face. He is trapped on the fire escape. As the CROWD sees this, a cry of "look" is heard, over the screaming of sirens and clanging of bells. They rush to a spot directly underneath the fire escape. As they reach this spot they point to the MAN above who has been cowering on the fire escape. They freeze as

BLACKOUT.

(Blacks in)

★

Scene Two—Investigation

Loudspeaker
Man (Mr. Rosen)
Commissioner
Three inspectors
  Fire Department
  Building Department
  Old Building Bureau, Tenement House Department
Mr. Schultz—landlord
Man—car owner
Automobile salesman

★

LOUDSPEAKER

Thirteen persons lost their lives in that fire on Madison Street—four men, two women and seven children. Another man was killed in an unsuccessful attempt to make his way down a flare escape ladder into the yard. When the fire department arrived the building was in flames. Only a few of those inside could be reached . . .[5] What started this fire? Why did it spread so quickly? Why was the death toll so high?

(Lights up. Scene takes place in front of blacks. A man, MR. ROSEN seated down right. He is the one who tried to get back into the burning building. He is dazed and a little cowed, seemingly absorbed in something inside himself, puzzling it out.

Upstage, center on 3 step, are seated in a row the INSPECTORS of the Fire Department, Building Department and the Old Building Bureau of the Tenement House Department.

Downstage, left center conspicuously empty, a chair . . .)

(All attention is focused on ROSEN, rights and the COMMISSIONER, who stands downstage center interrogating him)

COMMISSIONER

(sympathetically but a little worn, as though this has been going on for some time and he has almost despaired of getting an answer)

. . . and now, Mr. Rosen,[6] won't you tell us what happened when you came home?

(no answer. ROSEN just stares ahead, still absorbed, still trying to puzzle it out)

I realize how difficult this is, but we're trying to get at what caused this fire, and you've got to help us. That's how we can prevent more fires, by finding out about these things and correcting them.

(no answer)

(almost pleadingly)

Mr. Rosen . . .

ROSEN

(turns his head, regards COMMISSIONER; then slowly)

They no let me into the house.

(He stares out again)

COMMISSIONER

(gratefully)

Thank you. And then, what happened?

ROSEN

My wife burn up. In bed. My two children burn up, in bed.

(He faces COMMISSIONER)

Sons! Mine! Two!

COMMISSIONER

(eagerly)

And then?

ROSEN

And then . . . They no let me into the house.

(relapses into his brooding)

COMMISSIONER

(giving it up as a bad job)

That's all. Thank you.

(regards ROSEN for a moment—then turns quickly and sharply to FIRE INSPECTOR)

Are you the Fire Inspector?

FIRE INSPECTOR

Yes, sir.

COMMISSIONER

What do you know about this?

FIRE INSPECTOR

The flames started in the cellar.[7]

COMMISSIONER

How?

FIRE INSPECTOR

Probably in a pile of rubbish. We're not sure.

COMMISSIONER

What ignited the rubbish?

FIRE INSPECTOR

Cigarette, maybe. We don't know that, either.

COMMISSIONER

What happened then?

FIRE INSPECTOR

The halls went up and the stairways. That's why they couldn't get out. Then the walls caved in. You couldn't stop it because the wainscoting was made of wood. That carried the flames right up like somebody ran along it with a torch.[8]

COMMISSIONER

Is wooden wainscoting a violation?

FIRE INSPECTOR

(looking at COMMISSIONER then nodding his head in direction of BUILDING DEPARTMENT INSPECTOR)

Well, er . . . maybe you'd better ask the Building Department about that.

COMMISSIONER

(crosses to BUILDING DEPARTMENT INSPECTOR)

Are you the Inspector of the Building Department?

BUILDING DEPARTMENT INSPECTOR

Yes, sir.

COMMISSIONER

When was this house built?

BUILDING DEPARTMENT INSPECTOR

1884. It's an old-law tenement.[9]

COMMISSIONER

What are the old-law tenements?

BUILDING INSPECTOR

Well, most of the brownstones, wooden frame houses, tenements and every building that was put up before the law of 1901.[10]

BUILDING DEPARTMENT INSPECTOR

It said that any building erected after that date had to have certain improvements like a separate water closet for each apartment, adequate fire escapes.[11]

COMMISSIONER

And those already built and still in use?

BUILDING DEPARTMENT INSPECTOR
They had to conform to the new law in certain respects.

COMMISSIONER
What respects?

BUILDING DEPARTMENT INSPECTOR
They had to have fire escapes.[12]

COMMISSIONER
How about wooden wainscoting?[13] Is that a violation?

BUILDING DEPARTMENT INSPECTOR
In a new house, yes.

COMMISSIONER
In an old-law tenement?

BUILDING DEPARTMENT INSPECTOR
No!

COMMISSIONER
Have you recently inspected the premises at 397 Madison Street?

BUILDING DEPARTMENT INSPECTOR
Well, er, that comes under the duties of the Tenement House Department.

COMMISSIONER
(crosses to TENEMENT HOUSE INSPECTOR)

Are you the Tenement House Inspector?

TENEMENT HOUSE INSPECTOR
Yes, sir.

COMMISSIONER
Did you re-examine the premises at 397 Madison Street?

TENEMENT HOUSE INSPECTOR
Yes, sir. About six months ago.[14]

COMMISSIONER
What did you find?

TENEMENT HOUSE INSPECTOR
An adequate number of fire escapes with vertical ladders as required by law.[15]

COMMISSIONER
Is the collection of rubbish in the cellar a violation?

TENEMENT HOUSE INSPECTOR
It is.

COMMISSIONER
Did you find any there?

TENEMENT HOUSE INSPECTOR
No.

COMMISSIONER
But you haven't been there in six months. Why?

TENEMENT HOUSE INSPECTOR
Because we haven't received any complaint.

COMMISSIONER
You mean a house is never inspected unless a complaint has been received?[16]

TENEMENT HOUSE INSPECTOR
Exactly.

COMMISSIONER
(sharply)

But you did receive one six months ago?[17]

TENEMENT HOUSE INSPECTOR
Yes, sir.

COMMISSIONER
(eager to discover a violation)

What was it for?

TENEMENT HOUSE INSPECTOR
Roaches.

COMMISSIONER
Roaches?

TENEMENT HOUSE INSPECTOR
Roaches.

COMMISSIONER
Why must you wait for complaints before an inspection is made? Why don't you have periodic inspections?

TENEMENT HOUSE INSPECTOR
(distinctly enumerating statistics)

We have 224 inspectors to cover 105,000 tenements[18] and apartment houses. It would take our entire staff three years to visit each one of these houses *once.*[19]

COMMISSIONER
I see . . . Just one more thing, Mr. Inspector, in the light of your years of experience in the Department, would you consider this building a firetrap?

TENEMENT HOUSE INSPECTOR
If that building is a firetrap, then so is every old-law tenement in New York city[20]—*and there are 67,000 of them!*[21]

COMMISSIONER
That's all gentlemen. Thank you. My report will state that a fire of undetermined origin broke out in the basement of the house at 397 Madison Street . . . According to your testimony there were no violations and all the laws were scrupulously—

(They all rise and prepare to leave)

LOUDSPEAKER

(breaking in)

Just a moment, Mr. Commissioner, Has *everybody* testified?

COMMISSIONER

Why, yes . . .

LOUDSPEAKER

How about that empty chair? Don't you think there ought to be somebody in it?

(COMMISSIONER shakes head in bewilderment)

Well, you want to get at the bottom of this thing, don't you?

COMMISSIONER

Certainly.

LOUDSPEAKER

And you want to prevent more fires, by finding out about these things and correcting them, don't you?

COMMISSIONER

That's what I'm here for.

LOUDSPEAKER

(with finality)

Then let's call the landlord!

COMMISSIONER

Oh, no, I can't do that!

LOUDSPEAKER

Why not?

COMMISSIONER

The law doesn't allow me to. Only in a clear case of violations are we permitted to call in the landlord.[22] And you heard what they

(nodding to INSPECTORS)

said: There were no violations.

LOUDSPEAKER

Well, that settles it . . . Of course we can't break the law.

(There is a pause, then, insidiously)

But wouldn't you like to know what he's got to say, anyhow . . . just, sort of, off the record?

COMMISSIONER

I certainly would!

LOUDSPEAKER

Fine. I'll call him!

(calling)

Mr. Schultz![23] Mr. Schultz!

(as SCHULTZ appears left)

Would you mind testifying about your house on Madison Street?

SCHULTZ

(a bit suspicious)

No, I wouldn't mind. Where do I go?

LOUDSPEAKER

Right over there, center stage.

(as SCHULTZ comes to chair down left)

Mr. Commissioner, this is Carl Schultz . . . Mr. Schultz, this is the Commissioner.

(SCHULTZ and COMMISSIONER shake hands)

There you are. The witness is yours.

(SCHULTZ starts a bit as he spies ROSEN, then sits on chair. INSPECTORS sit again)

COMMISSIONER

Now, Mr. Schultz, were there any violations in your house?

(SCHULTZ hesitates and looks up at the LOUDSPEAKER for advice)

LOUDSPEAKER

Go on, Carl. It's all off the record!

SCHULTZ

Well, maybe a few. But they were all small and had nothing to do with the fire.

COMMISSIONER

Do you live in that house?

SCHULTZ

(looking up at him)

I do not!

COMMISSIONER

Why not?

SCHULTZ

(slowly)

Well, er, I got to live near my butcher store uptown.

COMMISSIONER

Is that the only reason?

SCHULTZ

(slyly)

That's the only one I tell you about!

COMMISSIONER

I see . . . Now tell me, why did you never renovate that house . . . so it would be a better place to live in, and not such a firetrap?

SCHULTZ

Well, first, I don't have any money. Second, it's not any worse than any other tenement on the block; and third, if I do have the money and do fix it up I have to raise the rent to get my money back. The tenants they have no money to pay and everybody moves out!

(spreading hands to express that)

COMMISSIONER

Did you make any money on your house, Mr. Schultz?

SCHULTZ

Some years yes, some years no.

(shakes head, sadly)

No, it is a bad investment.

LOUDSPEAKER

(suddenly sharp)

Do you want to sell, Mr. Schultz?

SCHULTZ

(A bargaining look comes into his eyes; he becomes cautious)

Sell? Well, maybe!

LOUDSPEAKER

I'll give you just what you paid for it, even though the house today in 1924 . . . is practically worthless.

(SCHULTZ shakes his head, turning it down)

When you bought that house twenty-five years ago it was almost brand new. Today it's just a rubbish heap—a slum. Come on, Mr. Schultz, you can get rid of it without losing a cent!

(SCHULTZ shakes his head again)

Perhaps you don't understand. Let me show you what happens when people try to get rid of something they've used for a long time.

(Spot picks out MAN and automobile SALESMAN, down right)

MAN

I'd like to sell my car.

SALESMAN

What make?

MAN

Dodge.

SALESMAN

What model?

MAN

Sedan.

SALESMAN

What condition?

MAN

It's four years old. Cost me $2300.[24]

SALESMAN

I'll give you five hundred.[25]

MAN

Five hundred! Why, it's only four years old.

SALESMAN

Mister, the minute you bought that car it became second hand. Every day you hold on to it it's worth less. Come around and see me next year, and I'll give you three hundred.[26]

MAN

$500!

SALESMAN

$500! And you'd better grab it before I change my mind.

(BLACKOUT on the TWO MEN)

LOUDSPEAKER

D'you see, Mr. Schultz, that's what happens.

SCHULTZ

(self-satisfied)

Not to me it won't.

LOUDSPEAKER

No matter what you have, furniture, clothing, a bicycle or a yacht—the longer you hold on to it and use it—the lower the price drops.

SCHULTZ

(leans forward)

You know the trouble with that fellow? He didn't invest his money in real estate.

LOUDSPEAKER

In a house, you mean?

SCHULTZ

No. My house is just like you say—rubbish heap, a slum. Ah, but the land it's on. That's different!

LOUDSPEAKER

Oh, *the land*!

SCHULTZ

In a big city like this, land never goes down. If you hold on to it long enough it goes up, all the time! I cannot fix up the apartments, I cannot lower the rents, why? Because the land cost too much! I pay more than it's worth when I buy. I get still more when I sell. Each time rents go up, up, up!

LOUDSPEAKER

But, Mr. Schultz, you're speculating, and if you're successful, the standard of living of six million people[27] goes down. They still have to pay more in rent and do without other things that they need.

SCHULTZ

(rises, almost hysterically)

Speculating? Sure, I am! And so is every other landlord, who expects to make anything out of his investment! I tell you, it's land, land, LAND! *That's where the money is*! And I don't sell mine without a nice big profit!

(There is a pause. For the first time ROSEN looks up. Slowly he rises and crosses to SCHULTZ)

ROSEN

(softly)

And me? What about me?

SCHULTZ

(slowly, earnestly)

Mr. Rosen, believe me, I'm sorry for you. I'll do anything I can to help you . . . But if you can only afford to pay $24 a month you'll have to live in my house or one just like it—and you cannot blame me.

(a pause—even more slowly)

You'll have to go back into history and blame whatever it was that made New York City real estate the soundest and most profitable speculation on the face of the earth.

(HOLD—as they regard each other, and—

BLACKOUT

★

Scene 3—Land

CHARACTERS

Loudspeaker

A—Trinity Church

- Lord Cornbury
- Minister
- Anthony Lispenard, Vestryman
- Abraham Mortier
- Robert Harrison
- William Rhinelander
- Alderman
- Francis Ryerson
- Aaron Burr

B—The City Grows

- Landowner
- Voice of Town Crier
- Second Voice

Tenants of the grass plot

First Tenant	(man)
Second "	(man)
Third "	(man)
Fourth "	(man)
Fifth "	(woman)
Sixth "	(man)
Seventh "	(man)
Eighth "	(woman)
Ninth "	(woman)

Very fat man

Six other men and women

Robert Goelet

John Wendell

John Jacob Astor

James Gordon Bennett

★

A—Trinity Church

LOUDSPEAKER

Back into history! The mad scramble for land begins! . . . Who owned it first? How did they get it? Who bought it? And above all, *who made the profit?*

(Music swells and ends in fanfare. Scene played in front of blacks)

(Light up on CORNBURY, on 2 step down right)

CORNBURY

(reads)

On this, the twentieth of November, in the year of our Lord, 1705, I, Edward Hyde Lord Cornbury, Third Earl of Clarendon and Governor of New York, do hereby grant the lands known as the King's Farm,[28] comprising sixty-three acres, bounded on the east by the Common and the Swamp, and on the west by the Hudson River, to Trinity Church, to own and to improve for the great glory of the Church, and for other pious uses.[29]

(Lights up. MINISTER enters left crosses to CORNBURY; receives deed)

MINISTER

Trinity Church acknowledges with profound gratitude this demonstration of Her Majesty's affection.

(CORNBURY exits. The MINISTER turns to a line of FOUR MEN who have just entered left and stand on apron step. He holds the imaginary deed in his hand. Then, crosses to FIRST MAN in line)

To Anthony Lispenard, Vestryman, the lease on 81 lots for eighty-three years at a rental of $177 per year.[30]

(He tears a small piece from the imaginary document and hands it to LISPENARD, crosses to SECOND MAN)

To Abraham Mortier, the lease on 465 lots for ninety-nine years at a rental of $269 per year.[31]

(same business)

To Robert Harrison, the lease on the land known as the King's Farm. . . .[32]

(same business. He now has none of the deeds remaining. He crosses to FOURTH MAN and spreads his arms to indicate that fact)

LOUDSPEAKER

1794 . . . Trinity Church again petitions the City for more land. William Rhinelander, of Tammany Hall,[33] urges the presiding Alderman to grant the petition.

(During the above the ALDERMAN and RHINELANDER enter right to the accompaniment of fanfare. They stand down right at 2 step)

ALDERMAN

The Common Council of the City of New York will continue to assist religious institutions as in the past . . .

(He reads)

To Trinity Church, in the name of the city; Water Grant covering all the land under water between Chambers and Reade Streets from Washington Street to the North River.[34]

(MINISTER crosses and addresses ALDERMAN)

MINISTER

And the rental? . . .

ALDERMAN

. . . at an annual rental of one shilling per running foot. . . .

MINISTER

. . . to begin? . . .

ALDERMAN

. . . to begin forty-two years from this date, June 10, 1794.[35]

(He hands over the deed and exits. RHINELANDER takes his place beside LISPENARD. MINISTER turns to RHINELANDER)

MINISTER

To William Rhinelander, a part of the water grant, between Chamber and Reade Streets. . . .[36]

RHINELANDER

(interrupting him)

. . . and the rental?

MINISTER

. . . free and clear for the first forty-two years. . . .

RHINELANDER

. . . and thereafter?

MINISTER

. . . and thereafter, one shilling per running foot.[37]

(RHINELANDER accepts and exits right, MINISTER crosses back to FOURTH MAN)

To Francis Ryerson . . .[38]

(tears off part of lease and hands it to him)

LOUDSPEAKER

Suspecting that the annual income of Trinity Church from its property was more than the twelve thousand dollars permitted by law, the City ordered an investigation, Aaron Burr was appointed Chairman.[39]

(Enter BURR left, and stands on 2 step down left)

AARON BURR

It seems to me that the Corporation of Trinity Church is increasing its income in a manner most incompatible with the dignity and piety of the Church. As Chairman of the Committee of Investigation,[40] I—

(The MINISTER stops him, urges him to wait a moment. He then crosses back to MORTIER, whispers to him. MORTIER nods agreement, MINISTER tears off a piece of his lease walks over and proffers it to BURR)

MINISTER

To Aaron Burr, a part of the Mortier lease, with seventy-seven years to run . . .[41]

BURR

At the same rental?

MINISTER

At the same rental.

(BURR accepts the lease)

LOUDSPEAKER

The investigation was dropped. . . .[42]

(Music—gesture)

BLACKOUT

★

B—*The City Grows*

(Enter down left the LANDOWNER. He carries a grass mat, rolled up, under one arm, and under the other, two stanchions. He is dressed in a costume that somehow suggests the period from 1775 to 1850. Spot follows him as he crosses to center. Music)

LOUDSPEAKER

Oh, hello. Who're you?

LANDOWNER

Well, I might be a lot of people. My name might be Rhinelander, Astor, Goelet, Wendell, or—er, Schultz.

LOUDSPEAKER

Schultz?

LANDOWNER

Schultz.

LOUDSPEAKER

That's very interesting. And what do you do for a living, if I may ask?

LANDOWNER

I put my money in the ground.

LOUDSPEAKER

You mean you bury it?

LANDOWNER

No. I invest it.

LOUDSPEAKER

Now we're getting some place! What's that thing under your arm?

LANDOWNER

That's it—land! . . .

(Lights come up as he puts down the stanchions and begins to unroll the grass mat, laying it on the apron step)

. . . and I own it!

LOUDSPEAKER

Looks like you've got quite a lot of it there.

LANDOWNER

(still unrolling it)

Five acres. Just bought it. Cost me $200.

LOUDSPEAKER

Where abouts is your property, Mister?

LANDOWNER

Way uptown—Broadway and Canal Street.

(He picks up one of the stanchions bearing the street markings; this he places beside his grass plot, stage right.)

That's Broadway—and that's Canal . . .

(points—Broadway up—Canal, right angle to Broadway)

The City's down there a couple of miles.

(He places the other stanchion upstage center from grass plot. It reads: "THIS IS MINE. KEEP OFF!"

He stands at a distance, admiring the layout, With a wave of his hand)

There you are!

LOUDSPEAKER

Very pretty. And what are you going to do with it?

LANDOWNER

I'm going to *sit* here on my land, and make a lot of money.

LOUDSPEAKER

How can you make any money just sitting?

LANDOWNER

Watch me.

(He sits down, gets himself comfortable, then begins to whistle, nonchalantly. As he sits there, under his stanchion, the Voice of the Town Crier is heard a long way off. It is followed immediately by a Second Voice (not the Loudspeaker) This is sharp, metallic, unemotional)

VOICE OF TOWN CRIER

(off)

(bell ringing)

Cornwallis defeated at Yorktown! Cornwallis defeated at Yorktown! Eight thousand British surrender to Washington![43] Cornwallis defeated at Yorktown!

SECOND VOICE

(off)

New York City, 1781—population, 18,000[44]

LANDOWNER

18,000! Town's growing up;

(looks off, at the town. Stands up and starts walking around the grass plot)

In a little while it's going to get kind of crowded down there and then I'll—

(He breaks off, then starts whistling again. . . . He stands stage right, pleased with himself and the announcement. A MAN enters, left. He is poorly dressed in clothes of the same period. He mops his brow, looking for a place to sit. He sees the green patch and sinks into a small corner, some distance away. He starts to stretch happily as)

LANDOWNER

(pointing to sign)

Hey! Can't you read! Get off!

MAN

Can't I just sit here for a *minute*?

LANDOWNER

(thinking it over doubtfully)

Well, maybe a minute . . . but that's all.

MAN

(sits, then, looking around)

Certainly is nice to get away from all them people. City's growin' too fast . . .

(pats the grass appreciatively)

. . . Certainly is nice out here, real country. Say, you know what! I'd like to build me a house right . . .

(waves his finger and places it in the center of the plot)

here!

LANDOWNER

You don't say! . . . Right here?

(pointing)

Got any money?

MAN

Well—er—no.

LANDOWNER

Then you can't live here.

MAN

But you know, a man's got to have a place to live.

LANDOWNER

Well, well, well.

MAN

You can do without a lot of things, but you've got to have a place to live.

LANDOWNER

That's very interesting. Come around and tell me about it some time . . .

(He shoos him away)

Your minute's up now. You'll have to get off my land,

MAN

(rising)

That's what everybody says—Get off my land! Get off my land! YOU CAN'T LIVE HERE!

LANDOWNER

(crosses left a step)

And they're right, too. If you want to have a place of your own you'll have to buy it, the way I did.

MAN

But I haven't got any money. Mister, I couldn't even buy—this much!

(marks off a tiny segment in one corner. Starts off left)

LANDOWNER

Say . . . Do you work?

MAN

(stops and turns)

Certainly I work.

LANDOWNER

Do you get paid for working?

MAN

(getting angry)

Certainly I get paid for working.

LANDOWNER

(slowly)

How would you like to live on that patch over there in the corner?

(pointing to down left corner)

MAN

(eagerly—pointing to spot)

This one?

LANDOWNER

That's it. But not so much of it.

(gesture, cutting it down)

MAN

This much?

MAN

(marks off smaller piece)

LANDOWNER

No-o

MAN

This much?

LANDOWNER

Well, er —

MAN

(marks off still smaller piece)

This much?

LANDOWNER

Well, er—

MAN

This much?

(marks off very tiny segment at extreme corner)

LANDOWNER

(heartily—as though looking it over)

That's right . . . Now that's a very fine lot. Plenty of air and sunshine, and a good view.

MAN

(stands off a bit and looks it over)

Pretty far away from the stagecoach line . . . and it seems a bit swampy. Must be plenty of mosquitoes around here . . .

(LANDOWNER turns away but keeps an eye on him over his shoulder. MAN pats spot affectionately)

But it's a place to live.

LANDOWNER

Fine. You can live there for twenty years at fifty dollars a year.

MAN

You mean you'll *lease* it to me?

(LANDOWNER nods)

MAN

But fifty dol—Say, how much did this whole thing cost you?

LANDOWNER

Two hundred dollars.

MAN

In twenty years you'll be getting five times that much for just a little piece!

(as LANDOWNER nods)

Not only that—but I'll have to give the piece back.

LANDOWNER

When I bought this place ten years ago I couldn't lease the whole thing for fifty dollars. It was

(looking at LOUDSPEAKER)

too far outside the town. . . . But I've been *sitting* on it.

MAN

Sitting on it! Why?

LANDOWNER

(slowly, to MAN)

Because I figured that some day *you'd* have to have a place to live.

MAN

Well, I guess you were right.

(starts to sit on land)

LANDOWNER

Hey! Fifty dollars, please.

(holds out hand for money as MAN has about seated himself)

MAN

(rising)

All right, all right . . . Here's your money!

(takes pouch from pocket and pours out the silver dollars as LANDOWNER pockets them)

VOICE OF TOWN CRIER

(bell ringing)

Thomas Jefferson elected President! Thomas Jefferson of Virginia, the third President of the United States! Jefferson elected![45]

SECOND VOICE

New York City, 1800. Population reaches 79,216.[46]

(LANDOWNER and MAN are seated contentedly)

LANDOWNER

Seventy-nine thousand! Not bad. Not bad at all.

(whistles happily. Rises. Enter SECOND, THIRD, and FOURTH TENANTS right. They look around, see plot and are about to sit down)

Hey!

(points to sign significantly)

SECOND TENANT (MAN)

Can't I just—?

LANDOWNER

No.

THIRD TENANT (MAN)

Do you suppose you could—?

LANDOWNER

No.

FOURTH TENANT (MAN)

But the town's overcrowded!

LANDOWNER

Is it?

SECOND TENANT (MAN)

There's no place to live!

LANDOWNER

Well, well, well.

THIRD TENANT (MAN)

And a man's got to have a place to live.

LANDOWNER

That's right. It'll cost you a hundred dollars a year.

SECOND TENANT

A hundred a year!

(MAN beckons to FOURTH TENANT and whispers in his ear)

FOURTH TENANT

(excitedly, to LANDOWNER)

Say, he says he's only paying you fifty!

LANDOWNER

(grinning)

Wait until next year when his lease is up!

SECOND TENANT

A hundred a year!

LANDOWNER

That's right. That's what we're all getting for property in this select residential neighborhood.

(as the MEN stand hesitating, TWO MEN enter, right. They stop to look at the land. They are interested in it. They are about to approach the LANDOWNER)

THIRD TENANT

(hurriedly)

Here you are. Here's my hundred.

SECOND TENANT

(same)

One hundred dollars, yes sir.

FOURTH TENANT

(counting his while handing it over)

One hundred, yes sir!

(They all hand the money over; the two MEN change their minds and walk, off, as)

VOICE OF TOWN CRIER

(bell ringing)

The Canal is finished! The Erie Canal! 363 miles from Buffalo to Albany![47]

SECOND VOICE

1845! The Great Immigration begins.[48] New York's population reaches 696,115.[49]

(The FOUR TENANTS are now seated on the carpet. There is still plenty of room for more. The first sounds of building (off) is heard)

LANDOWNER

696,000! Did you hear that! It won't be long now . . .

(From this point action speeds up. TEN MEN and WOMEN enter right and left—five from each side. One is about to sit)

Hey!

(points to sign)

FIFTH TENANT (WOMAN)

But—!

LANDOWNER

I know. It's crowded.

SIXTH TENANT (MAN)

But—!

LANDOWNER

I know. You can do without a lot of things.

SEVENTH TENANT (WOMAN)

But—!

LANDOWNER

But you can't do without a place to live! . . . Two hundred dollars, please.

EIGHTH TENANT

(without any hesitation whatsoever)

Two hundred. Here you are!

(EIGHTH TENANT starts to pay)

LANDOWNER

(looks at him in amazement, having expected an argument; then seeing how easy it is)

Two hundred and fifty dollars is my price.

FIFTH, SIXTH, SEVENTH, EIGHTH TENANTS

Two fifty!

(They rush up, pay him and tumble to the carpet)

LANDOWNER

Three hundred!

(shrugs shoulders as if to say. "Take it or leave it." THREE MORE PEOPLE pay—LANDOWNER points out their spots, and they sit.

LANDOWNER crosses down and looks over his land for more space to sell. By this time the TENANTS are sitting in restricted, cramped positions. They can hardly move. Their arms are pressed close to their sides. In these positions they are all engaged in going through some part of their daily routine. For instance, one is shaving; another is reading a newspaper; another is trying to eat; a fourth is washing himself. Still another is attempting to tie his shoe lace . . . Needless to say, all these activities must be cramped and hemmed in or the point of the scene is lost. They continue right through the scene until the blackout. The remaining THREE PROSPECTIVE TENANTS stand down stage)

LANDOWNER

(to the PROSPECTS)

Sorry, folks, that's all there is . . . all rented and busy as a beehive, that's what we are.

(The PROSPECTS start to exit)

LANDOWNER

(He calls the last man who is very fat. FAT MAN stays behind as others exit)

Say—wait a minute! . . .

(His roving eye has lighted on a few blades of green grass still visible at the far end of the carpet. He bends down to see it, then, with a slight push, he forces all in the first row to topple over)

. . . There you are, sir, the last parcel! Almost missed it, I did.

(as FAT MAN bends down to look at it)

It is a little small, but right in the heart of the business section. The lucky man who rents this won't have to walk far to work . . . It'll cost you ten dollars a square foot for this.

VERY FAT MAN

I'll take it.

(He hands over the money, kneels down, looks at it. He backs away to get a running start, then runs and jumps on to his spot. He bumps the TENANTS who are annoyed. Then, Music)

Home! Sweet Home!

LANDOWNER

Thank you folks. Thank you very much indeed.

(TENANTS on carpet continue their activities. LANDOWNER crosses down, center)

LANDOWNER

(to LOUDSPEAKER, jingling money in pocket)

Not bad, eh?

LOUDSPEAKER

How much is your property worth now, Mister?

LANDOWNER

Oh, about forty thousand dollars.

LOUDSPEAKER

That's a lot of money! To what do you attribute your success?

LANDOWNER

Well, I had faith in the development and growth of the city.

LOUDSPEAKER

I see. Tell me, Mister: who developed it? Who made it grow?

LANDOWNER

The people. Everybody. Me, too.

LOUDSPEAKER

No, not you. You just sat. Remember? . . . That city was developed through the industry of 696,000 people.

(suddenly)

Look at them! They built the city! What did you do?

LANDOWNER

(slowly)

I remembered that they had to have a place to live in while they were building it. . . . And don't forget, I didn't break any laws! Everything was honest and above board! All the smartest people of my generation were doing it!

LOUDSPEAKER

For instance?

LANDOWNER

For instance, Robert Goelet!

(fanfare. Spot on GOELET, on 3 step left)

GOELET

Before 1850 I bought a farm running from 14th Street to 47th Street and Fifth Avenue.[50] I advised my descendants to keep on buying uptown lots ahead of the crowd. . . .[51] They did, and when my grandsons died, their combined fortune was in the neighborhood of 140 million dollars![52]

LANDOWNER

140 million! That makes me feel pretty small!

(fanfare. Spot on WENDELL on 3 step right)

WENDELL

My family made fifty million dollars in New York real estate.

LANDOWNER

That's John Wendell.

WENDELL

To make it we followed four cardinal rules: never to mortgage, never to sell, never to repair, and never to forget that Broadway moved uptown at the rate of ten blocks in ten years![53]

LANDOWNER

And here's the Granddaddy of us all—John Jacob Astor!

(fanfare. Spot on ASTOR, on 3 step, center)

ASTOR

In my lifetime I invested two million dollars in Manhattan real estate. When I died in 1848, it was worth about twenty million! . . . I never failed to foreclose when I could and I didn't believe in coddling my tenants when they couldn't pay the rent![54]

LANDOWNER

Thank you, gentlemen.

(bows to them. Lights out on the THREE MEN. to LOUDSPEAKER)

You see, the best people, the founders of some of our greatest American families.

(crosses down)

Everybody did it! That is, everybody who was smart enough! And nobody thought it was wrong. *Nobody*, do you hear!

(Spot on BENNETT at 2 step down right)

BENNETT

Well, not exactly *nobody*.

LANDOWNER

(unenthusiastically)

Oh, hello!

(to LOUDSPEAKER)

This is James Gordon Bennett of the "Herald" . . .

(They bow)

He's got a lot of crazy ideas.

BENNETT

John Jacob Astor died today. He left a will disposing of property worth twenty million dollars among his various descendants. . . . Now if I had been an associate of Mr. Astor the first idea I would have put into his head was this: at least one-half of his immense property—belongs to the people of the City of New York. During the last fifty years of this man's life, his property has been augmented and increased in value by the aggregate intelligence, industry, enterprise and commerce of the citizens of New York. It is therefore as plain as two and two make four, that at least half of his immense estate, has accrued to him by the industry of the community![55]

(BENNETT exits)

LANDOWNER

Crazy as a bedbug! Everybody's out of step but Jim Bennett!

(starts off)

Well, so long!

LOUDSPEAKER

Hey, where are you going now?

LANDOWNER

Up the line a ways. Just bought a piece of property way uptown—around Fourteenth Street.

LOUDSPEAKER

But what about those people? Look at them!

LANDOWNER

Oh, them! They're all right! They'll be here when I come back on rent day!

LOUDSPEAKER

They will? Why?

LANDOWNER

Because a man's got to have a place to live!

(pause)

So long!

(picks up signs and crosses off. TENANTS remain and as music starts, they go into their own individual occupations as—)

BLACKOUT

★

Scene 4—Looking Backward

CHARACTERS

Loudspeaker
Little Man
Guide
Citizen, Man
Tenants of the HOUSE

A—Why they came (Irish Family)
- Father
- Mother
- Daughter (Mary, 18)
- Son (Mike, 25)

B—What they saw (Steve and Joe)
- Steve (14)
- Joe (17)

C—What they got (Cholera)
- *Jewish Family*
  - Mother
  - Father
  - Doctor

Third Floor Landing
- Patient—Woman
- Her Daughter
- Doctor
- Nurse

Stage Right Cubicle
- Doctor
- Mother
- Boy

First Orderly
Second Orderly
Man
Emaciated Man
First Newspaper Reporter
Second Newspaper Reporter
Voice of Gerritt Forbes, City Inspector, New York

★

(The stage is dark. Music. There is a pause)

LITTLE MAN

Hey! Give me some light!

(LITTLE MAN comes down the aisle of the theatre, left. Spot follows him as he comes up stairway from pit to stage left.

Scene is played in front of blacks.)

LOUDSPEAKER

What is it?

LITTLE MAN

I'd like some information.

LOUDSPEAKER

What about?

LITTLE MAN

Housing.

LOUDSPEAKER

What are you doing up there in those clothes?

LITTLE MAN

What's the matter with them?

LOUDSPEAKER

The matter with them? Why, they look like 1938. The scene we just finished was 1845.

LITTLE MAN

Oh that. Say, I'm no actor. I just came from down—

(pointing to seat in orchestra)

LOUDSPEAKER

Well, what do you want?

LITTLE MAN

Information. Every time something happens that I don't understand I'm going to stop the show and ask questions.

LOUDSPEAKER

And who's going to answer them?

LITTLE MAN

You are.

LOUDSPEAKER

I see . . . Now tell me, Mister, what makes you so curious about housing?

LITTLE MAN

Well, it's like this: every time there's a new housing development in New York, in Brooklyn, Queens or New Jersey, I dash right out there, get myself interviewed and fill out an application for an apartment.

LOUDSPEAKER

And then what happens?

LITTLE MAN

I wait.

LOUDSPEAKER

I see. And then?

LITTLE MAN

And then, after two or three years, I get tired of waiting and I read about another new development.

LOUDSPEAKER

What happens then?

LITTLE MAN

I dash right out, get myself interviewed and fill out an application. Hillside, Boulevard Gardens, Knickerbocker Village, First Houses—[56] I've seen 'em all—and I'm still waiting.

LOUDSPEAKER

And that makes you curious?

LITTLE MAN

That started it. So I went down to see the Tenement House Commissioner. He told me the Living Newspaper was doing a show on Housing and I ought to see it. . . . So here I am.

LOUDSPEAKER

So I see . . . Well, what's the first question?

LITTLE MAN

It's this: Why didn't I ever get rooms in any of those developments?

LOUDSPEAKER

Because, without exception, they were swamped with applications long before they opened their doors. There are 1,750,000 people living in old-law tenements in New York City today,[57] and if they all wanted to get into a model housing development like, say, "First Houses" their chances are about 3,600 to one.[58]

LITTLE MAN

3,600 to one! . . .

(whistles—a pause)

Now you say, my troubles started about a hundred years ago when land began to go up. . . .

LOUDSPEAKER

That's what we've been showing.

LITTLE MAN

Tell me, at that time, didn't anybody *say* anything about it?

LOUDSPEAKER

Sure. Everybody said it was a shame.

LITTLE MAN

Well, didn't they *do* anything?

LOUDSPEAKER

Those were the good old days when nobody did anything about anything.

LITTLE MAN

They just let it ride . . .?

LOUDSPEAKER

They just let it ride.

LITTLE MAN

(starts to cross right, then stops)

O.K. Now, let's see some of the houses these people

(turns toward LOUDSPEAKER at right)

lived in. And for the love of Mike, let's see some people—not landlords, *people*!

LOUDSPEAKER

All right, where do you want to go?

LITTLE MAN

Well, let's see. What year are we in now?

LOUDSPEAKER

Any one you like.

LITTLE MAN

(thinking)

Um-m—let's make it 1850. Now, I'd like to take a walk around the town and get acquainted. Got a map?

LOUDSPEAKER

Sure.

(to PROJECTIONIST)

Hey, Dave, let's have a look at New York about 1850.

(Screen comes down directly in front of blacks; projection of map[59] LITTLE MAN starts to cross up to screen—looks it over then starts to cross down center, nods approvingly to LOUDSPEAKER but seems a bit puzzled because he does not recognize the neighborhood)

LITTLE MAN

Don't you think I need a guide? I might get lost.

LOUDSPEAKER

Anything you say.

(spot on a MAN sprawled out, asleep on 2 step down left. He is dressed in period of 1850)

There you are.

LITTLE MAN

He's asleep.

LOUDSPEAKER

Wake him up.

LITTLE MAN

(doubtfully)

Sure?

(crosses gingerly, stops, then swings around)

Say, just in case we both get lost—where am I now?

LOUDSPEAKER

You are standing beside a brook on what is now the Hotel Astor.[60]

(projection on screen)

LITTLE MAN

You don't say . . .

(to himself)

That means when I come back here, I walk down to Forty-second, take the 7th Avenue Subway home and—

LOUDSPEAKER

—and add eighty-eight years on the way.

(as LITTLE MAN crosses back to wake GUIDE)

And you'd better watch out for Indians!

LITTLE MAN

Indians?

LOUDSPEAKER

You never can tell.

LITTLE MAN

Oh well—

(crosses to 2 step down left quickly, shakes GUIDE)

Hey, wake up!

GUIDE

(stretching and rubbing his eyes)

Huh?

LITTLE MAN

I'd like to have a look at the town. How about it?

(as GUIDE stares at him)

You live here, don't you?

GUIDE

(shaking his head)

Not me. Too noisy . . . It's all right for a visit, maybe, hut I couldn't *live* here . . .

(He gets up)

I know the town pretty well, though. I'll take you. We'll just go down Broadway. Come on!

(They start striding in place in front of screen to indicate walking through the neighborhood projected. Music. Projection changes.)

That's the Leeds Farm,[61]

LITTLE MAN

Leeds Farm?

LOUDSPEAKER

Thirty-fourth Street and Broadway to you.

(THEY stride again and projection changes)

GUIDE

That's the Madison Farm,[62] best cows in the whole county.

LITTLE MAN

Madison, eh?

LOUDSPEAKER

(softly)

Twenty-third and Broadway—where the Flatiron Building is.

(They stride again; projection changes)

GUIDE

That's a quiet little spot called Union Place.[63]

LITTLE MAN

Union *Place*?

LOUDSPEAKER

Union *Square*!

(They stride again; projection changes)

GUIDE

Now we're really in the city. This is the New Bowery; number 40. It's a converted stable—about thirty people live there now.[64]

LITTLE MAN

Did they make much of an alteration?

GUIDE

Sure—whitewashed the whole place.

(grabs LITTLE MAN)

Look out! That buggy almost ran you down. Traffic's certainly terrible here. They don't give a hoot about the pedestrians.

(They stride again; projection changes)

That's Bleecker Street. Pretty smart neighborhood. . . . Only the swells live here.[65]

(LITTLE MAN backs up downstage to look at projection)

LITTLE MAN

You'd never think it to look at it now.

GUIDE

Huh?

LITTLE MAN

Skip it . . . I was just talking to myself . . . let's have a look at a tenement.

GUIDE

All right. We'll turn east into Cherry Street.[66]

(They stride again . . . projection changes, they stop)

This is Gotham Court—at 36–38 Cherry Street.

(projection of Gotham Court—front view)

LOUDSPEAKER

Gotham Court: thirty-five feet front, 240 feet deep. Five stories high,[67] twenty-four apartments to a floor. The windows open on an alley eight feet wide[68]—Want to hear some more?

(LITTLE MAN nods; projection changes to view of court (Gotham Court)[69]

The Chairman of the Council of Hygiene and Public Health of the Citizens' Association of New York will now read his report!

(spot picks out MAN on 2 step down right)

CITIZEN

(reading)

Gotham Court, housing 126 families, is entered at the sides from alleys eight feet wide and, by reason of the vicinity of another tenement of equal height, the rooms are so dark that on a cloudy day it is impossible to read or sew without artificial light. It has not one room which can in any way be thoroughly ventilated. The vaults and sewers which are to carry off the filth of the one hundred and twenty-six families have grated openings in the alleys through which the noisome and deadly odors poison the dank air of the house and the courts. The water closets for the whole vast establishment are a range of underground stalls without doors, accessible not only from the building, hut even from the street.[70] We have found . . .

(Projection off; screen away)

LITTLE MAN

(unable to stand anymore)

That's enough!

(BLACKOUT on CITIZEN. GUIDE exits)

LITTLE MAN

(turns toward LOUDSPEAKER)

What happened after he handed in that report?

LOUDSPEAKER

Everybody said it was a shame and something ought to be done about it.

LITTLE MAN

Did they do anything?

LOUDSPEAKER

No.[71]

LITTLE MAN

What about the people who live here?

LOUDSPEAKER

Why don't you go in and have a look?

LITTLE MAN

Me?

LOUDSPEAKER

Certainly.

LITTLE MAN

O.K. but if anything happens you can trace me through my social security number.

(pats his wallet. Crosses and sits on 2 step down left. Blacks away. Music)

BLACKOUT

★

Scene A—Why They Came (Irish Family)

(Upper center cubicle lights up—FATHER, MOTHER, MARY (18).

The FATHER is seated at the table, reading his paper. Some distance away, MARY is struggling with a skirt over her head. The MOTHER passes around the table silently, laying out the dishes for dinner)

(There is a pause . . .)

MARY

(finally getting her skirt down and adjusting it)

All right, Pa. You can put your paper down now.

(He does)

What's in it, anyhow?

FATHER

I don't know. I wasn't reading it.

MOTHER

(without looking up)

Paper cost a cent.

FATHER

I know, Ma. I'll read it later.

(to DAUGHTER)

Where you going?

(MIKE enters—stands left of door)

MARY

Back to the store. Have to work tonight.

(sniffs)

What's that smell?

MOTHER

(as FATHER picks up paper again)

Toilet. Drain's all stopped up.

MARY

Well, why doesn't somebody go down and fix 'em?

MOTHER

Your father fixed it twice today.

MARY

What's the matter with the landlord? What do we pay rent for?

MOTHER

Ask your father.

FATHER

(as they all turn to him, puts down his paper)

Let's eat.

MARY

(putting on her coat)

I can't. I'll be late.

(starts toward door)

FATHER

Watch out for that broken step on the way down. . . .

MOTHER

And come straight home. . . .

FATHER

Of course she will. She always does.

(He begins to eat, reading his paper. MARY has just reached the door when MIKE bars the way)

MIKE

(easily, in a low voice)

What you goin' to do in the store tonight?

MARY

Work.

MIKE

Didn't know it was open—tonight.

MARY

Well it is.

MIKE

You wouldn't be foolin' your big brother, now, would you?

(as she just looks at him—a bit louder)

I said, you wouldn't be fool—

MARY

(fearfully)

Ssssh!

(She looks at FATHER to see if he has heard)

FATHER

(to MOTHER, without looking up from paper) I see where Frank Conolly died yesterday. . . .

MIKE

(grabbing her by the wrist)

Would you?

MARY

Honest, Mike, I got to get back. I got to!

FATHER

That makes the third funeral in that house this week . . .

MOTHER

(covertly watching MARY and MIKE)

What did he die of?

FATHER

Paper doesn't say . . .

MARY

(in a whisper, struggling to free her arm)

I got to work, Mike, I swear. I ain't lyin' to you! You believe me, don't you, Mike?

MOTHER

(still watching them)

That's funny. . . .

FATHER

It just says he died. . . .

MARY

Don't you?

MIKE

Been seein' anything of that boy next door lately?

MARY

No, Mike. I haven't seen him. Honest I haven't.

MIKE

(giving her arm a twist)

Have you?

MARY

(afraid to cry out)

No. Mike! MIKE!

FATHER

(looking up from paper)

I thought you were in a hurry.

MARY

(crosses to FATHER)

I am. Good-bye, Pop . . .

(kisses him—looks at MOTHER—then exits)

MOTHER

(sits at table as MIKE crosses up and puts hat on)

Where are you going, son?

MIKE

I'll just make sure she gets there.

(Exits. Pause as MARY and MIKE go down the narrow stairway left and off)

FATHER

I know what's in your mind, Kate . . . hut you're all wrong; Mary's a good girl. Wish they were all like her.

MOTHER

Don't take cream long to get sour in this neighborhood,

(a pause)

Tom, we've got to move.

FATHER

But I've told you so many times. . . .

MOTHER

I don't care. We've got to move.

(rising)

How long can four grown-up people live in one room? How long, Tom?

FATHER

But we've no place to go. I've spent the last four Sundays walking up and down Cherry Street, Oliver, Catherine, Madison![72] There isn't a flat to let in any of them. And even if there were, they'd be no better than this for what we can afford to pay!

MOTHER

(softly)

Tom, is this what we left Ireland for? Is this what we gave up a cottage and green grass and the good hot sun for?

FATHER

There's no famine here, Kate. Plenty of potatoes and bread and meat, if you can afford to pay for 'em. And I've been working steady a whole year . . . a whole year.

MOTHER

Sure, but where does it all go? To the landlord, to the butcher! Mary was right . . . What *do* we pay rent for, anyhow?

FATHER

Because we've got to have a place to live—

MOTHER

Does it have to be here?

(no answer)

Does it have to be here where your own daughter's got to take her clothes off in front of your eyes, in a place that smells so you can't even eat!

(suddenly pointing)

Look! Roaches!

(as FATHER rises and stamps on them)

I scrub and I clean and nothing happens. Just filth and vermin and garbage, and, and . . . I tell you, I can't stand it!

(she falls back onto the chair, weeping)

★

Scene B—What They Saw (Steve and Joe)

(Light comes up on cubicle stage right. STEVE (14) and JOE (17). JOE is at a mirror fixing his tie. STEVE stares out as though looking through a window)

JOE

Hey, kid, where's Pop!

STEVE

(staring out)

Out.

JOE

I know he's out! Where is he?

STEVE

Looking for a job.

JOE

Is he still sore at me?

STEVE

Yeah.

JOE

What'd he say?

STEVE

He said if he sees you around here, he'll throw you out.

JOE

What else?

STEVE

He said I should keep away from you.

JOE

Oh, he did?

STEVE

He said you're no damn good and if he thought I'd turn out like you he'd crack my skull.

JOE

Well, he don't have to worry. I'm clearing outta' here.

STEVE

Where'll you go, Joe?

JOE

Never mind.

STEVE

But where will you go, Joe?

JOE

(putting on coat)

Nonna your business. You're too young.

STEVE

Joe, can I go with you?

JOE

No!

STEVE

Aw, Joe.

JOE

No!

(sniffs)

That toilet stinks. Go on down and fix it.

STEVE

(still staring out)

Guy across the hall fixed it.

JOE

Well, it's busted again. Go on!

STEVE

Wait a minute, will you, Joe.

(suddenly, leaning forward, in a hushed voice)

She's just come in again.

JOE

Who?

STEVE

You know.

JOE

(looks out window, then goes back to mirror)

What do you know about it?

STEVE

I'm not so dumb.

JOE

Get away from that window!

(Enter MARY, left. Stands at entrance to alley)

STEVE

(staring, fascinated)

There's a fellow with her I never seen before.

JOE

Get away from that window!

STEVE

(excited)

Look, Joe, she's—

JOE

Get away from that window!

STEVE

(swings around, his voice shrill, defiant)

I won't! You're only my brother and you can't make me!

JOE

(starting for him)

I can't, eh?

STEVE

If you touch me, I'll tell Pop, that's what I'll do!

JOE

(coming closer)

What'll you tell him?

(no answer)

What'll you tell him?

STEVE

This ain't the first time I looked out of that window.

JOE

What's that?

STEVE

I said it's not the first time I looked out of that window.

JOE

What else will you tell him?

(STEVE looks away, not answering. JOE grabs him)

STEVE

You'll see—

JOE

What else will you tell him?

STEVE

I'll tell him who else I saw.

JOE

Who else did you see?

STEVE

You know who else I saw! You know—

JOE

Who?

STEVE

You!

(a pause. JOE stands rooted)

JOE

Why, you—

(He punches him in the face. STEVE sinks to the floor. JOE takes a final, fleeting look toward STEVE and exits. . . . We follow him as he comes down the steps, whistling happily. He crosses stage. MARY steps out of the shadow of alley and greets him)

MARY

(putting her hand on his arm)

Joe

JOE

(without enthusiasm)

Hello, Mary.

MARY

Glad to see me, Joe?

JOE

(doubtfully)

Sure.

MARY

I had a hard time getting away tonight.

JOE

Yeah?

MARY

Mike knows about us, Joe, and I think Mom does.

JOE

(defiantly)

What if they do?

MARY

(interrupting)

I don't care about them. Kiss me, Joe.

(He does, then—putting her arm through his both cross downstage)

Where're we going tonight?

JOE

No place. I'm leavin' here—for good.

MARY

(shocked)

Leaving?

JOE

That's right. Leavin'. I'm sick of this place and the old man kickin' me around.

MARY

Oh!

(There is a pause, as the idea sinks in, then)

When do we go?

JOE

(backing away a step—looking right at her)

We? I can't have no woman hanging around! I got things to do!

MARY

(unbelievingly)

You're going away and leave me? *Here*?

(He looks at her, hut he doesn't answer)

Joe—you've got to take me with you!

(He looks away. As he still doesn't answer, her mood changes; she grows a little dazed)

Where you goin', Joe?

JOE

I don't know.

MARY

How you goin' to live?

JOE

(looking at her again)

I ain't worried. There's ways.

(suddenly turning on MARY)

I can't take you with me, Mary. I just can't—anyhow, you got a job.

MARY

Sure, I got a job. You know what else I got? I got a pain, Joe, right here.

(putting hand on chest)

It comes from not havin' any fun and workin' all day and livin' and eatin' and sleepin' in the same room with three other people, every one of 'em watchin' me every minute, afraid I'm goin' to go bad on 'em! It comes from a lot of things—I don't know what they are—only I feel sick . . . and tired . . . and hopeless. . . . AND I DON'T WANT TO GO BACK IN THERE—WITHOUT YOU!

(crosses to him and puts arm on his slowly)

Take me with you, Joe.

JOE

I can't. I haven't got the money.

(as she looks down—pause—He looks at her—then, pointedly)

Now, if I could lay my hands on some. . . .

MARY

(looks at him. Then quickly . . .)

Mom's just got enough for supper, and Mike wouldn't give it to me even if he had any.

(She begins to get an idea. A pause—he starts off. Crosses in front of her left, and looking at her . . .)

JOE

Good-bye, Mary.

MARY

Joe!

(She puts her arm out and stops him. He swings around slowly)

I think I know maybe where I could find some. . . .

JOE

Where?

MARY

Will you take me with you?

(crossing a step to him)

JOE

Well. . . .

MARY

(insistent)

Will you?

JOE

Yeah—

(He nods, MARY, not able to come out with it)

MARY

No. . . . No. . . .

(backing away).

JOE

(twisting her arm)

Where is it?

MARY

(looking down)

The old man at the store where I work . . . he keeps a lot of money hidden under . . .

JOE

Ssssh!

(looking up at house—a pause)

Come on.

(crosses left—looks around)

Come on.

MARY

(stands there—looks at him)

Yeah,

(starts left—looks back at house over shoulder)

come on.

(Then she runs out with him)

BLACKOUT

★

(Spot picks up LITTLE MAN on 2 step down left)

LOUDSPEAKER

Want to see some more?

LITTLE MAN

(doubtfully)

Well. . . .

LOUDSPEAKER

Why don't you try that room downstairs?

LITTLE MAN

Do you think I'd better?

LOUDSPEAKER

Go on!

(as LITTLE MAN nods his head)

BLACKOUT

★

Scene C—What They Got (Cholera)

(Lights go on in lower center cubicle, on a Jewish family—FATHER, MOTHER. A crib—music)

JEWISH MOTHER

He hasn't moved for a long time now.

JEWISH FATHER

It's good. Sleep is good.

JEWISH MOTHER

How white his face is.

(leans over crib)

Such a good baby. Never cries.

JEWISH FATHER

With a mother like you he should cry.

JEWISH MOTHER

Max—I'm afraid . . .

(suddenly)

Where is the Doctor? You said he was coming right away.

FATHER

Soon, He'll be here soon.

MOTHER

Well, where is he? Why isn't he here now? How many times—

FATHER

Maybe we should send him to the hospital?

MOTHER

Hospital? Do you want to kill him?

FATHER

Maybe it's better there. In the hospital you can get a doctor right away.

MOTHER

(at crib, suddenly)

Look, Max—he can't breathe! . . . Where is the doctor? Where is he?

FATHER

(sits down, wearily)

He's coming.

MOTHER

Coming! Coming! When is he coming? When it's too late?

FATHER

He's upstairs.

MOTHER

Upstairs! So go up and get him!

FATHER

Other people are sick.

MOTHER

Other people—He's worrying about other people—when your own baby is—

(as he leans forward wearily in his chair)

Max! What's the matter with you?

(He just shakes his head, tired. She, desperately, looking from the FATHER to the BABY)

Where is the doctor? Where is he? Max!

(He opens his eyes and looks at her)

FATHER

(in a dazed manner)

Sick . . . everybody- sick . . . the baby . . . the whole house . . .

(He gasps and sinks down. MOTHER turns, sees him sink—screams)

BLACKOUT

★

(Spot up on third floor landing. PATIENT, (woman) held up by her daughter is being examined by DOCTOR in hot spot, with NURSE standing by. DOCTOR is giving symptoms[73])

DOCTOR

CHOLERA!

(tips face back)

Usual cyanotic color of skin . . .

(picks up hand)

Fingernails . . .

(looks into mouth)

and mucous membrane.

(as he releases her hand)

Eyes sunken . . .

NURSE

Pulse . . .

DOCTOR

(after holding wrist a few counts)

Rapid and weak.

NURSE

Respiration . . .

BLACKOUT

★

(Lights up in stage right cubicle.

BOY on bed, DOCTOR at head of bed, bent over, head against chest. MOTHER at foot of bed. DOCTOR looks up)

DOCTOR

Respiration rapid and irregular. Heart feeble.

(PATIENT groans and turns toward side of bed)

Bring the pan.

(The MOTHER brings a pan, and kneels by the side of bed. DOCTOR helps BOY to raise up slightly, and holds his head over the pan. The BOY retches into the pan. Lights dim out)

(The spot comes up in the lower center cubicle. JEWISH FATHER is still in a state of collapse. DOCTOR is examining him. JEWISH MOTHER is standing by)

MOTHER

Max. My husband . . .

DOCTOR

(examining MAN—head, fingernails, mouth, pulse, heart)

Usual cyanotic color. Eyes sunken. Pulse rapid and weak. I'm afraid it's Cholera. When was he taken sick?

MOTHER

This morning he didn't feel so good.

DOCTOR

Cholera can run its course in a few hours. Put him to bed.

(DOCTOR crosses to BABY)
(abruptly)

This baby is dead.

MOTHER

(screams)

BLACKOUT

★

(Lights come up sharply on the right area of third floor landing, catching TWO ORDERLIES coming out of a doorway carrying a stretcher. NURSE stands center of landing, reading chart)

NURSE

Ground floor. Cholera. Baby dead. Male adult. Advanced stages.

(to ORDERLIES)

You're late! I've got twenty cases to go out immediately!

(SECOND ORDERLY dropping front end of stretcher to the floor)

SECOND ORDERLY

Wait a minute.

FIRST ORDERLY

What's the matter?

SECOND ORDERLY

How many does this make for you?

FIRST ORDERLY

I ain't counted.

SECOND ORDERLY

Me neither. Bill, I'm scared.

FIRST ORDERLY

Scared of your luck?

SECOND ORDERLY

Sure I'm scared—scared I'll catch it. Scared I'll—

(An OLD EMACIATED MAN comes out of the door right next to the stairs, third landing and crosses with jerky, painful movements to the NURSE. He holds up the fingers of his hands, and slowly, with effort, moves them in jerky painful movements)

MAN

I can't move my hands. Look! Where's the Doctor?

NURSE

He's busy. Go back to your room. You're sick.

MAN

(turning to the SECOND ORDERLY, who is staring at him)

Doctor!

SECOND ORDERLY

Get away!

MAN

I can't move my hands.

SECOND ORDERLY

For God's sake, let's get out of here!

(He rushes off)

(Dim lights come up on entire stage. MAN comes out of alley left and collapses on top of 3 step. DOCTOR crosses to him. TWO NEWSPAPER REPORTERS enter stage left)

FIRST NEWSPAPER REPORTER

Say, Doc, what's this I hear about a Cholera epidemic?

DOCTOR

Say, who are you, anyway?

FIRST NEWSPAPER REPORTER

I'm from the "Post."

SECOND NEWSPAPER REPORTER

The "Herald."

DOCTOR

(turns away from the OLD MAN, calls to FIRST ORDERLY, who comes down stairs)
(to ORDERLY)

Get back to the hospital[74] and tell them to send men, sedan chairs, stretchers, baskets, anything! This whole house is infected!

(as the ORDERLY stands there, looking at him)

Well, don't stand there! Go on! Hurry! It's Cholera! Cholera!

SECOND NEWSPAPER REPORTER

But, good Lord, everybody says there's no such thing as Cholera in New York!

DOCTOR

Everybody! Who's everybody? It's Cholera. I'm telling you! Over two thousand[75] have died of it already. But the good people who make a living out of these tenements are trying to hush it up.

FIRST NEWSPAPER REPORTER

Well, my paper won't. We'll spread it all over—

DOCTOR

Oh, no, you won't, you're afraid! You're afraid of telling the truth! Afraid to mention that no cases have been reported outside the slums![76] Go on, print it, I dare you! *I DARE YOU*!

HOLD and BLACKOUT

★

LOUDSPEAKER

New York Post, June 12, 1854[77]—*Cholera*—Cholera epidemic spreads in Tenement District. Gerritt Forbes, Health Inspector[78] of New York City says:

(During the following speech which comes over the LOUDSPEAKER, the stage is darkened save for a spot on LITTLE MAN sitting on 2 step down left)

VOICE OF FORBES

Some cause should be assigned for the increase of deaths beyond the increase of population, and none appears as prominent as that of the crowded and filthy state in which a great portion of our population lives. We have serious cause to regret that there are in our city so many mercenary landlords who only contrive, in what manner they can, to stow the greatest number of human beings in the smallest possible space![79]

LOUDSPEAKER

Twenty-five hundred men, women and children lost their lives before that Cholera epidemic ended.[80] Five thousand died in the previous one.[81] This was the third time in twenty years that New York was visited by Cholera.[82]

★

Scene 5—Appoint a Committee

CHARACTERS

Little Man

Loudspeaker

Citizens' Committee

- N.P. Willis
- Dr. James L. Little
- Dr. Alexander Hadden

Man—Announcer of statistics on disease

Mayor

Dr. John H. Griscom, City Inspector, New York

Mayor's Committee of Four

★

LITTLE MAN

(looking toward LOUDSPEAKER)

What happened after that?

LOUDSPEAKER

Nothing.

LITTLE MAN

You mean to say they still went on just *talking* about it.

LOUDSPEAKER

A Citizens' Committee was formed to investigate conditions.

(Lights come up on house, bare and empty)

LITTLE MAN

Again?

LOUDSPEAKER

It consisted of Mr. N. P. Willis and Doctors James L. Little, and Alexander Hadden . . .[83]

(As their names are called lights come up on the THREE MEN in each of the three cubicles, inspecting the furniture and making notes)

LITTLE MAN

Well, what did they do?

LOUDSPEAKER

Well, give them a chance, will you?

(LITTLE MAN starts up impatiently)

Sit down for a minute. You're getting me nervous!

(LITTLE MAN sits down. He takes out a package of cigarettes)

That's right have a smoke.

(LITTLE MAN'S fingers tremble as he lights his cigarette)

You're not worried about anything, are you?

LITTLE MAN

(as though they had kept it a secret from him)

Nobody ever told me there was Cholera in New York!

LOUDSPEAKER

I guess a lot of other people didn't know about it, either.

LITTLE MAN

I thought it only happened in China.

LOUDSPEAKER

Our brand was just as good as any *they* ever had!

LITTLE MAN

Well, at least there isn't any more Cholera in New York today, not even in old-law tenements.

LOUDSPEAKER

That's right. No more Cholera. But look what we've got instead—in old-law tenements. . . . Report by the New York City Housing Authority, Tuberculosis!

(spot on MAN on 2 step down right)

MAN

From 1919 to 1934 the death rate from Tuberculosis was 129 per cent higher in old-law tenements.[84]

LOUDSPEAKER

Diphtheria!

MAN

The death rate from Diphtheria was 97 per cent higher in old-law tenements.[85]

LOUDSPEAKER

Spinal Meningitis!

MAN

The death rate from Spinal Meningitis was one hundred and nineteen per cent higher in old-law tenements—and, the death rate from all causes was ninety-three per cent higher in old-law tenements.[86]

(blackout on MAN)

LITTLE MAN

But I live in an old-law tenement! What I want to know is—

LOUDSPEAKER

Let's go back to 1850 again. Sssh!

(The lights come up on entire stage. MAYOR enters, stage right and crosses to center, down from 3 step. THREE MEN wait for him on top of 3 step)

LITTLE MAN

(pointing to MAYOR)

Who's that?

LOUDSPEAKER

That's the Mayor.

DR. HADDEN

Mr. Mayor, it is a humiliating fact that no complete examples of sanitary renovation can be found in the City of New York. The "Five Points" is a district still full of perpetual fever nests and the breeding place of epidemic diseases! All told, in New York, not a district, not a street has been redeemed from its filthiness.[87]

DR. LITTLE

I saw, between Tenth Avenue and the Hudson River, three large manure yards, a number of fat-boiling establishments and slaughter houses. And to these may be added the dirty conditions of the streets, with gutters running with blood and filth. Scattered through the midst of these, surrounding them on all sides are the crowded and ill-ventilated tenements of the district![88]

WILLIS

Mr. Mayor, I did not dream that human beings within the reach of human aid could be abandoned to the wretchedness which I saw with my own eyes. And all those horrors of want and abandonment lie almost within sound of your own voice as you pass Broadway.[89]

LITTLE MAN

That's enough!

LOUDSPEAKER

Dr. John H. Griscom, Health Inspector of New York presents a city-wide report on Housing.

(Enter DR. GRISCOM stage left, crosses to center)

DR. GRISCOM

Mr. Mayor, in the attempt to raise from the depressed and the poor the necessity of living crowded in single rooms, much aid cannot be found in any legal enactment. The remedy lies with the humane and philanthropic capitalists by whom houses might be erected with all the comforts and conveniences of separate rooms, running water and so forth, which would yield a fair interest on their value and make thousands of people happy! . . . These are my findings and suggestions.[90]

(Hands imaginary document to MAYOR. A Committee of four enter down right on 2 step. MAYOR beckons to COMMITTEE CHAIRMAN, who crosses to him)

LOUDSPEAKER

New York's first comprehensive document on Housing.[91]

(MAYOR takes imaginary document to CHAIRMAN of Committee who catches it and goes back to his group. The COMMITTEE discusses the imaginary document in a sort of gibberish. Music)

COMMITTEE

Document—Survey—Housing—Cholera—Document—Survey—Housing—Cholera—

LOUDSPEAKER

(spacing the figures between the Committee's words)

One month . . . two months . . . three months . . . four months . . . five months . . .

CHAIRMAN OF COMMITTEE

(crosses to MAYOR)

Mr. Mayor, your committee do not profess to be judges of the subject. In other words, we do not think it proper at this time to go into such a measure. We recommend that the paper be returned to its author.[92]

(Committee exits right. As CHAIRMAN exits he tosses paper to MAYOR. MAYOR tosses it to GRISCOM as he is leaving)

LITTLE MAN

Well, I'll be damned.

BLACKOUT

★

Scene 6—Renting

CHARACTERS

Three Charwomen
Little Man
Loudspeaker
Landlord
Apartment Seekers
  First Agent
  Italian Family (5)
Young Couple
  Man
  Woman
Second Agent
Irish Family of five
Young Boy
His Parents
  Father
  Mother
Old Man
His Granddaughter
Third Agent
Jewish Couple
  Man
  Woman
Elderly Man
Group
  Three Women
  One Man

★

(Spots pick up 3 CHARWOMEN, each in one of the cubicles. They are lethargically cleaning and dusting the furniture, sort of ballet style. Music)

LITTLE MAN

(still on 2 step down left; after music stops; lights up)

Say, who are they?

LOUDSPEAKER

Why they're sterilizing the place, so we don't have another epidemic. Got to be careful you know.

(Music again as they continue the dusting)

(Eater LANDLORD right and crosses to 3 stop left. Turns and looks up at CHARWOMEN)

LANDLORD

(clapping his hands)

All right, girls, that's enough. There's another place four doors down. Hurry up.

(The CHARWOMEN exit . . . He takes another look around and then, satisfied . . . he hangs a large cardboard sign on the stage left structure; it reads: "TO LET." He turns his back to his property, and waits, expectantly, on 3 step . . . Enter right, the FIRST

AGENT with an ITALIAN FAMILY. He seats them, on the 3 step and crosses to LANDLORD)

FIRST AGENT

I brought you some customers—just off the boat.

LANDLORD

Greenhorns, eh? All one family?

FIRST AGENT

I didn't ask 'em. All I know is they want a place to live.

LANDLORD

Together?

FIRST AGENT

Sure.

LANDLORD

Room three. Third floor.

(FIRST AGENT returns to GROUP; he speaks to them in Italian; they nod happily to AGENT and then to LANDLORD. They cross and follow AGENT upstairs into upper center cubicle.

During the above a young COUPLE has entered left. They read sign and stop. They talk together excitedly)

MAN

(to LANDLORD)

Are you the landlord?

LANDLORD

I am.

MAN

I—er—we'd like to rent a room.

WOMAN

We've just got married.

LANDLORD

Well, you've come to the right place.

MAN

Something light and airy and . . .

WOMAN

(quickly)

And cheap. We can't afford—

LANDLORD

I've got just the thing for you: private entrance, ground floor, and handy to the toilets.

(points to basement)

MAN

Is it light and airy and—

LANDLORD

It's got a window and a stove and it's two dollars a week.

WOMAN

One window?

LANDLORD

One window

WOMAN

Oh!

MAN

(putting his arm around her)

That's all right, darling. We won't be here long.

(A pause as she looks at the building, and then they follow LANDLORD into the lower center cubicle . . .

SECOND AGENT appears with an IRISH FAMILY of five, right. The AGENT leaves them standing, right center below 3 step, and crosses to LANDLORD in cubicle)

IRISH GIRL

(to HUSBAND as SECOND AGENT crosses to LANDLORD)

This is it, Tom—America!

(looks up at structure)

Would you believe they made 'em this big if you didn't see it with your own eyes?

SECOND AGENT

(to LANDLORD)

Got any rooms left?

LANDLORD

Still got a few.

SECOND AGENT

Party of five people down there.

(pointing)

LANDLORD

How many rooms?

SECOND AGENT

One.

LANDLORD

Rent?

SECOND AGENT

(giving him money)

Here you are.

LANDLORD

Fourth floor rear.

(During the above a YOUNG BOY passing has stopped; he hurries off left and returns with his PARENTS. They cross below 3 step.

OLD MAN and GRANDDAUGHTER enter left, and cross to center. THIRD AGENT and JEWISH COUPLE enter right immediately after. FIRST AGENT comes down from upper center cubicle and pushes past them. He exits right)

THIRD AGENT

(calling to LANDLORD in lower center cubicle)

Hello, Landlord! I would like one of your best rooms for my friends over here.

GRANDDAUGHTER

We were here first, Mister.

YOUNG BOY

We were here first!

LANDLORD

(coming out of lower center cubicle with SECOND AGENT; stands on 3 step center)

Just a minute! What's going on hero?

(SECOND AGENT crosses to IRISH FAMILY and they all start up ship stairway to cubicle stage right)

GRANDDAUGHTER

We were here first, and we want a room.

YOUNG BOY

They were not!

GRANDDAUGHTER

We were—weren't we, Grandpa?

OLD MAN

(sitting on 3 step)

I'm tired.

LANDLORD

Never mind. There's room for the both of you. Got the rent?

(An elderly, distinguished looking MAN has entered down loft, and heard the argument)

ELDERLY MAN

Are you renting rooms in this building.

LANDLORD

(sizing him up and observing his clothes)

You're on the wrong street, Mister.

ELDERLY MAN

I don't think so.

LANDLORD

Well, you'll have to wait your turn like everybody else—

ELDERLY MAN

Isn't this one of the tenements where the Cholera epidemic—

LANDLORD

(quickly)

No.

(He looks fearfully at the TENANTS)

You must be thinking of that place around the corner.

(to GRANDFATHER, helping him up)

Just because you were here first I'm going to give you the nicest room in the whole—

ELDERLY MAN

I'm sure this is the place where Cholera—

LANDLORD

Shut up, will you!

MOTHER

(to YOUNG BOY)

You bring us to a Cholera house! You want us to die!

IRISH MAN

Cholera!

(crosses himself)

JEWISH MAN

(to THIRD AGENT)

We go some place else. Give me my money back.

THIRD AGENT

Now, wait—wait!

LANDLORD

(to ELDERLY MAN)

Who the hell are you anyway to be upsettin' honest people with your lies and ruinin' business?

(to TENANTS)

Don't you listen to him. He's probably got a house of his own he wants to rent! And it's probably a damned sight worse than mine!

ELDERLY MAN

This filthy pesthole should be burned to the ground!

(to TENANTS)

If you don't believe me, call a policeman and ask him. He'll tell you all about it!

(defiantly, to LANDLORD)

I say there was Cholera here!

(As the TENANTS start picking up their belongings, apprehensively)

LANDLORD

(desperately)

Wait a minute. Listen. We'd all like to live in a marble palace but we all can't—so we take what God gives us and we're thankful . . .

What if there *was* Cholera here?

Was this the only house in town that had it? Was it?

(as ELDERLY MAN doesn't answer)

Why don't you answer that, my good friend?

(same)

And let me tell you this: We've cleaned this house out! We've scrubbed it! We've washed it! *We've whitewashed it!* Why the whole place is just as fresh and clean as it ever was—look at it!

(The TENANTS start to leave)

LANDLORD

(to TENANTS)

And you—before you go, remember this: If you don't live here, where are you going to live? In the park? In the street? In another place that's no better than mine and maybe a hell of a lot worse? *Are you?*

(A pause, as the TENANTS put down their belongings)

(A group of THREE WOMEN and a MAN enter left and join crowd)

Because, in case you're forgetting, there's one thing you've got to have—all of you—and you've got to make up your mind to it . . . *You've got to have a place to live!. . .*

(pauses)

Yes, sir, you've got to have a place to live!

(There is a pause. . . . Slowly they all pick up their belongings and start climbing the stairs into the structure, as)

SLOW CURTAIN

END OF ACT I

HOUSE LIGHTS

★

ACT II

Scene 1—The Law

CHARACTERS

Voice of the HOUSE
Announcers of the LAW
First Man
Second Man
Committee of Three—Housing Investigation, 1894
Richard Watson Gilder, Chairman
Enoch Vreeland, Deputy Superintendent, Building Department
Another member of committee
Editor, *New York Herald*
Colonel S. Van Rensselaer Cruger, Comptroller of the Rector, Trinity
Very Reverend A. Woodruff Halsey
Trinity "In Court"
Hon. Roger A. Pryor, Judge, "General Term"
S. P. Nash, Attorney for Trinity
Roger Foster, Attorney for City of New York
Hon. Rufus W. Peckham, Judge, "Court of Appeals"
Third Man—*Announcer of the LAW*

★

(Music . . . Curtain up on bare House—one light very dim covers entire structure throughout scene. Music stops . . .)

VOICE OF HOUSE

Well, I'm still here . . . There's been a lot of water under the bridge. We've had a few new Presidents and a Civil War—but I'm still here, You're curious, aren't you? You don't know where I am. Well, I'm here—inside the house. I AM THE HOUSE!

(There is a pause. A spot picks up odd corners of the interior)

Do you see that broken balustrade? That crumbling plaster? And that sink down there under the steps? Do you see that rubbish piled up?

That's me. I haven't changed a bit in all these years! Not a bit. In spite of their laws! LAWS!

(cackling laughter; sardonic)

When you hear the gong strike, the City Fathers will have given birth to a brand new law.

(Gong strikes. Spots come up on TWO MEN who enter right and left, and stand on 2 step, down right and down left. They announce the Law)

1867! A law!

FIRST MAN

It shall be required that no horse, cow, calf, pig, swine, sheep or goat be domiciled in any tenement or lodging house![93]

SECOND MAN

It shall be required that there be a proper fire escape for each tenement,[94] and there shall be one toilet for every twenty occupants.[95]

(Gong strikes)

VOICE OF HOUSE

1879! A law!

FIRST MAN

No windowless rooms![96]

(Gong strikes)

VOICE OF HOUSE

1887! A law!

SECOND MAN

Water on every floor![97]

(Lights out on ANNOUNCERS)

VOICE OF HOUSE

Did you hear that? Fire escapes, a toilet for every twenty occupants, no windowless rooms, and water on every floor! That's what the law says! But I'm still here. And I haven't changed a bit. . . . Oh, well, I guess it's time for another investigation.

(Dim up THREE COMMITTEEMEN right on 3 step. They stare up at the house, notebooks and pencils poised)

What did I tell you? Come on, boys, look me over. But if you don't mind, I guess I'll go back to sleep for a while.

(His voice takes on the quality of a yawn)

. . . If anything exciting happens, just . . . wake . . . me . . . up.

(There is a pause; the COMMITTEE has been looking at the sink on the ground floor and up at the broken balustrade)

LOUDSPEAKER

May 4, 1894[98] . . . As a result of the campaign waged in the New York "Press,"[99] Governor Flower today appointed a Committee to investigate housing conditions in the city. The Chairman is Richard Watson Gilder. (Spot on one of the MEN who steps down)

GILDER

Of the 8441 houses we visited, we found 16,756 windowless rooms[100] . . .

LOUDSPEAKER

That was fifteen years after the law was passed.

GILDER

Only 306 out of over 225,000 people had access to a bathroom. More than five sixths of the buildings had toilets in the yard. More than one fourth of all the apartments had no fire escapes of any kind.[101]

LOUDSPEAKER

That was twenty-seven years after the law was passed.

(Another of the men,—ENOCH VREELAND, comes away from the House; he stands beside GILDER)

VREELAND

I would like to supplement that report.

LOUDSPEAKER

This is Enoch Vreeland, Deputy Superintendent of the Building Department.

VREELAND

The tenements owned by Trinity Church are, without a doubt, among the worst in the city, with a death rate of 32 per thousand as against a general death rate in New York of 24 per thousand.[102]

LOUDSPEAKER

The New York Herald publishes the following reports concerning the Trinity properties made by the Department's Sanitary Inspectors. . . .

EDITOR

(Spot on EDITOR stage right; reads)

Eight families are housed over a shop at 8 Sullivan Street. The apartments are without Croton water or plumbing of any description. . . . At 264 Houston Street is perhaps one of the worst of the Trinity tenements. The waste pipes in the rear house are in such bad condition that sewage has escaped into the cellar, rendering the place a veritable pesthole. It was well-nigh impossible to remain in the cellar a moment owing to the overpowering stench![103]

(EDITOR exits. Enter CRUGER, stage right)

LOUDSPEAKER

Colonel S. Van Rensselaer Cruger, Comptroller of the Rector, Church-wardens and Vestrymen.

(CRUGER crosses up to 3 step)

CRUGER

The situation has been greatly magnified. The defects found by the Inspectors are trivial. . . . A great deal of smoke has been made out of very little fire. This is all I have to say on the subject![104]

(CRUGER moves down stage to apron step)

LOUDSPEAKER

The Very Reverend A. Woodruff Halsey.

(Enter HALSEY, stage right. He crosses up to 3 step)

HALSEY

We take no exception to these charges. A corporation owning between six and seven hundred pieces of property will, in the nature of things, overlook and even mismanage. No doubt some of the houses complained of were in a bad sanitary condition and needed overhauling . . . but that this is true of any considerable number of properties under the care of Trinity—or that Trinity, the Church, is governed by the law of righteousness, and Trinity, the Corporation, by the law of greed—I cannot for a moment believe![105]

(HALSEY moves down stage to apron step)

(Enter stage right, THREE PARTICIPANTS in lawsuit. JUDGE stands on 2 step down right—the ATTORNEYS stand on apron step right, facing JUDGE)

LOUDSPEAKER

The Board of Health orders running water to be supplied to every floor. Trinity refuses. The case is taken to the courts, and Trinity is ordered to comply with the law.[106] But the verdict is set aside until "Exceptions" could be reviewed by the General Term . . . The General Term![107] Stephen P. Nash, Attorney for Trinity, Roger Foster, Attorney for New York.

NASH

The acts of Legislature which impose the duty of supplying water on each floor of the houses described, cannot he sustained as a proper exercise of police power.[108]

FOSTER

The statute is a lawful exercise of the police power both for the protection of the health of the community and protection against fire.[109]

NASH

The legislation under review is a burden imposed upon landlords for the ease and comfort of tenants. It is clearly a violation of constitutional guarantees![110]

FOSTER

It is not a taking of property to compel an owner to improve or alter the condition of his property.[111]

LOUDSPEAKER

Judge Roger A. Pryor renders the decision.

JUDGE PRYOR

The uncontroverted proof is that the lack of water on the various floors is not bad for the health of the tenants. There is no evidence, nor can the Court judicially know, that the presence of water will conduce to the health of the occupants. The required conduct of water up to the floors serves no other purpose than the convenience of the tenants. . . . A conclusion contrary to the present decision would involve that species of socialism under the regime of which the individual disappears and is absorbed by a collective being called "the State" . . . a principle utterly repugnant to the spirit of our political system, and necessarily fatal to our form of liberty. . . . Exceptions sustained and a new trial ordered.[112]

(PECKHAM enters stage left and stands down left on 2 step. NASH and FOSTER cross to left; still on apron step and face PECKHAM)

LOUDSPEAKER

The Court of Appeals—Judge Rufus W. Peckham presiding . . .

NASH

The particular requirement under consideration is that the landlord should carry water up to the upper floors of his tenement in order to save the tenants the necessity of carrying it up themselves. It would be quite as reasonable to require the landlord to furnish the houses with elevators to save the tenants the trouble of carrying up the coal.[113]

FOSTER

Stronger evidence of the need of such a water supply as the Statute requires has been furnished by the extraordinarily filthy, and unhealthy conditions of the defendant's tenement houses. The death rate in these tenements, according to official statistics on file in the office of the plaintiff, is far above the average and higher than in any other tenement houses.[114]

LOUDSPEAKER

The verdict of the Court of Appeals.

PECKHAM

There is scarcely a dissent from the general belief on the part of all who have studied the disease that Cholera is essentially a filth disease. The Legislature cannot in practice enforce a law to make a man wash himself, but when it provides facilities therefor, it has taken a long step toward the accomplishing of that object. That dirt and filth are great promoters of disease, that they breed pestilence and contagion, sickness and death, cannot be denied. We think the act is valid as an exercise of the police power with respect to the public health. The Judgment is reversed.[115]

(Blackout on ACTORS)
(Pause)

VOICE OF THE. HOUSE

Well, folks, I guess it's time to have a few new laws. As long as the Courts say you can enforce 'em, let's write 'em in the books and then you can tear down my poor old carcass and give me a nice decent burial.

(Spot on TWO MEN, Announcers of the Law, who enter right and left. They stand on 2 step down right and down left)

VOICE OF THE HOUSE

1901. The new laws for tenements[116]

FIRST MAN

A separate water closet in each apartment![117]

SECOND MAN

Hallways must be at least three feet wide![118]

FIRST MAN

No room may he less than seventy square feet of floor area![119]

SECOND MAN

No airshafts. Side courts must he at least twelve feet wide![120]

FIRST MAN

Adequate fire escapes![121]

SECOND MAN

Adequate light and air![122]

(Blackout on TWO MEN)

THIRD MAN

(hurrying on, right, stands center in spot)
But—

VOICE OF THE HOUSE

Oh, Lord, I'm afraid of this "but!"

THIRD MAN

—But these laws shall in no way affect any tenements already in existence prior to today's date, April 12, 1901.[123]

(Blackout on THIRD MAN)

(There is a pause)

VOICE OF THE HOUSE

(slowly, very tired)

Well, folks, I'm still here. . . . There's been a lot of water under the bridge, we've had a few new Presidents and the Spanish-American War. . . . But I'm still here. . . . Yeah, I'm still here . . . still here . . .

(Voice fades away)

BLACKOUT

(Blacks in)

★

Scene 2—Crosstown, 1933

CHARACTERS

Little Man
Loudspeaker
Guide

A—Street Kids
Sammy (12)
Frank (13)
Woman—Yiddish accent
Announcers—Statistics on Juvenile Delinquency
First Woman
Second Woman

B—East Side—West Side
Man
Woman (Min)
Mrs. Buttonkooper
Tenement House Commissioner, New York

C—Harlem
First Negro (a stevedore)
Second Negro (a bootblack)

D—Rent Strike
Fourth Floor Hallway
First Woman
Second Woman
Third Woman
Third Floor Landing
Fourth Woman
Fifth Woman
Sixth Woman
Mrs. MacNamara
Upper center cubicle
Tenant League Organizer
Group of Women Strikers

★

LITTLE MAN
(hurrying down the aisle of the theatre)

Hey! . . . Hey!

(He stumbles over somebody's foot . . .)

Pardon me!

(He hurries up stairway from pit to stage left. Follow spot picks him out. Crosses to center on apron step. Scene played in front of blacks)

Here I am, Hey!

LOUDSPEAKER
Oh, hello. Where were you?

LITTLE MAN
Out for a beer. I just caught the end of that last scene. Tell me, why don't we tear down all those old-law tenements? Seems to me if we did that, all our troubles would be over.

LOUDSPEAKER
That's a very good question. Why don't you answer it?

LITTLE MAN
Me?

LOUDSPEAKER
That's right . . . Where do you live?

LITTLE MAN
Eighty-fifth and Amsterdam.

LOUDSPEAKER
In an old-law tenement?

LITTLE MAN
Well, it's a made-over brownstone.

LOUDSPEAKER
That's an old-law tenement, too. Now if we tore down your house, where would you move, Mr.—Mr.—?

LITTLE MAN
Buttonkooper. Angus K. Buttonkooper.

LOUDSPEAKER
Well, Mr. Buttonkooper, where would you move?

LITTLE MAN
Oh, in the neighborhood. Maybe around the corner.

LOUDSPEAKER
In another old-law tenement?

LITTLE MAN
Sure.

LOUDSPEAKER
Why?

LITTLE MAN

Because that's all I can afford!

LOUDSPEAKER

Exactly. Do you know what that means? It means we'd have the same number of people crowding into a smaller number of old-law tenements. And you wouldn't be any better off than you were before.

LITTLE MAN

(trying to interrupt)

But—

LOUDSPEAKER

Statistics show that only one per cent of the people who lived in the slums where Knickerbocker Village now stands could afford to live there after that development was put up![124]

LITTLE MAN

(impatient)

But—

LOUDSPEAKER

While the remaining ninety-nine per cent moved into other old-law tenements in the neighborhood,—around the corner.[125]

LITTLE MAN

(insistently)

But—

LOUDSPEAKER

But what?

LITTLE MAN

(excited)

But suppose we tore 'em all down?

LOUDSPEAKER

Suppose we did. *Where would you live?*

LITTLE MAN

(smiling happily)

In a brand new house!

LOUDSPEAKER

That's great. Why don't you live in one now?

LITTLE MAN

I told you. I can't afford it.

LOUDSPEAKER

Well, what makes you think you would afford it *then*?

LITTLE MAN

(disappointedly, as he sees the point)

Oh! . . .

LOUDSPEAKER

You see, slum clearance is one thing. Building new apartments you can afford to live in to replace them is another.

LITTLE MAN

(thoughtfully)

Oh! . . .

LOUDSPEAKER

Any more questions?

LITTLE MAN

(angry—crosses left and stops short at 2 step down left)

No. I was just wondering . . . How about the rest of the old-law tenements around New York? Are they all as bad as mine? Does the heat go off in all of 'em at ten o'clock and the water stop running just when you want to take a bath? Are the rooms all dark, do the walls crack, and how about the bathrooms? Are they hot as hell in summer and freezing in the winter? Are they all firetraps, is the landlord just as tough, does he refuse to paint, does he come around on the first for his rent.

(getting excited)

do they have roaches, do they have mice, do they have—

LOUDSPEAKER

Hey, wait a minute! One thing at a time.

LITTLE MAN

(finally getting it out)

What I want to know is: am I any worse off than anybody else?

LOUDSPEAKER

Would you like to see for yourself?

LITTLE MAN

I sure would.

LOUDSPEAKER

Fine. How about a trip around New York in 1933?

LITTLE MAN

Wait a minute, wouldn't that sort of be repeating ourselves? We did that in the first act.

LOUDSPEAKER

Let's try it . . . You see, that's the whole point of this Housing business. It repeats itself. It just goes on and on.

LITTLE MAN

Well how are you going to stop it?

LOUDSPEAKER

(correcting him)

How are *we* going to stop it?

LITTLE MAN

(a bit sheepish)

Yeah, how are *we* going to stop it?

LOUDSPEAKER

That'll come later . . . Now, are you ready?

LITTLE MAN

Where am I going?

LOUDSPEAKER

Oh, uptown, downtown, crosstown.

LITTLE MAN

O.K.

(He starts to walk, then stops)

Say, wait a minute. Do I have to go alone? I get kind of lonesome by myself in some of those dark streets.

LOUDSPEAKER

You're not afraid, are you?

LITTLE MAN

(putting on the bravado)

Oh, no, not at all! Just the same it would be kind of nice if . . .

LOUDSPEAKER

All right, all right . . . Who do you want to go with?

LITTLE MAN

Well, let's see now . . .

(He thinks)

Say, do you remember that fellow in the first act who showed me around New York in the old days? I'd like to take him.

LOUDSPEAKER

You can't. He's dead.

LITTLE MAN

Dead?

LOUDSPEAKER

The last time you saw him was in 1850. He can't go on living forever.

LITTLE MAN

(persuasively)

Aw, come on, dig him up. I can't just talk to myself up here!

LOUDSPEAKER

But why do you want to see *him*?

LITTLE MAN

Well, I felt pretty uncomfortable walking around in *his* century. Let's see how he feels walking around in mine.

LOUDSPEAKER

All right. Call him.

LITTLE MAN

(first to right, then to left)

Hey! . . . Hey! . . .

(nothing happens)

LOUDSPEAKER

Why don't you try a little magic?

LITTLE MAN

Magic? . . . All right!

(He goes through the movements of a magician, saying)

Allakazam, allakazam, allakazam, BOOM!

(Spot picks up GUIDE, asleep on 2 step down left)

LITTLE MAN

(shaking his head in wonder at the miracle)

I wish I could get an apartment that way!

(crosses to GUIDE; shakes him)

Hey, you still asleep? . . . Wake up!

(GUIDE wakes)

Remember me? You showed me New York about eighty-five years ago!

(Screen comes down in front of blacks)

GUIDE

Sure.

(They shake hands)

LITTLE MAN

Well, this time I'm going to show it to you! Come on!

(grabs his arm . . . then, to LOUDSPEAKER)

Where are we now?

LOUDSPEAKER

You're standing right in the middle of Times Square *and you'd better watch out!*

(Projection on screen of movie trip around New York, 1938, including crowded sections of the city—Times Square, Herald Square.[126] The honk of an automobile is heard, also noise of crowd . . . GUIDE jumps out of the way. They start striding)

GUIDE

What's this?

LITTLE MAN

Thirty-fourth and Broadway.

GUIDE

Thirty-fourth and Broadway?

LOUDSPEAKER

Remember? The Leeds Farm?[127]

(They stride again. Projection changes to Twenty-third and Broadway)

Twenty-third and Broadway.

GUIDE

Twenty-third and Broad—

LOUDSPEAKER

Madison Farm.[128] Best cows in the whole county!

(They stride again. Projection changes to Fourteenth Street. Soapboxes, etc.)

Union Square![129] Quiet little spot.

(They stride again. Projection changes to Bleecker Street.—slum tenement)

Bleecker Street.

GUIDE

Bleecker!

LOUDSPEAKER

You know, where the swells live.[130]

LITTLE MAN

I thought it would surprise you.

(grabs him)

Look out! That car almost bumped you off!

GUIDE

"Bumped me off?"

LITTLE MAN

Skip it.

GUIDE

Wait a minute. What *is* that thing?

LITTLE MAN

Automobile.

GUIDE

What's that?

LITTLE MAN

Horseless carriage.

GUIDE

Go on, there ain't no such thing.

(They stride again, the GUIDE still looking back at the auto)

Where're we going now?

LITTLE MAN

Downtown, the East Side. Have a look at a slum.

(They stride again. Scene changes to Orchard Street)

GUIDE

Say, what's all this?

LITTLE MAN

Orchard Street. We're going to cross east into Madison and then—hey!

(looking backward at the GUIDE as he talks)
(Moves off; Screen is flown)

BLACKOUT

★

Scene A—Street Kids

(Lights come up. House is empty. A young boy, SAMMY, (12) sits on bottom of 3 step, right. He is repairing the skate on a home-made skooter. The skooter is lying on its side, the BOY bent over it . . . some distance away down center from 3 step stands another boy, FRANK, (13) watching him)

LITTLE MAN

(stumbling over skooter)
(rubbing his shin)

Why don't you he more careful with that thing!

SAMMY

Excuse me—

LITTLE MAN

(to GUIDE)

Let's go.

(They start to walk)

LOUDSPEAKER

Just a moment, Mr. Buttonkooper.

(They stop)

I thought you wanted to see how the other guy lives and what his kids are like!

LITTLE MAN

I do, but—

LOUDSPEAKER

Well, here they are.

LITTLE MAN

But we want to look at a slum!

LOUDSPEAKER

Mr. Buttonkooper, you're looking at the results of one right now . . . Listen!

(They watch BOYS)

FRANK

(watching SAMMY repair skate)

Whatsa matter?

(no answer)

I said, whatsa matter?

SAMMY

(without looking at him)

Skooter's busted.

FRANK

Who busted it?

SAMMY

(calmly)

You did.

FRANK

(a little taken aback)

I did . . . Who told you?

SAMMY

Nobody.

FRANK

(grabs him and swings him around)

Who told you? . . .

SAMMY

(still very calm)

I saw you drop that cobblestone on it.

FRANK

(releases him; SAMMY bends over the skooter as though nothing has happened)

Well, ain't you goin' t' do nothin' about it?

SAMMY

I'm goin'—to fix it.

(There is a pause; SAMMY tinkers with skate) (LITTLE MAN and GUIDE remain standing, stage right, watching)

FRANK

Anybody busted my skooter I'd beat him up. I'd beat him up plenty.

(bends over him)

First I'd give him the knuckles—like this . . .

(rubs his knuckles hard on SAMMY'S head)

. . . then I'd give him the rabbit—like this . . .

(slaps him sharply on the back of the neck)

. . . then I'd stretch his nose . . . like this . . .

(pulls his nose)

. . . and then I'd smack him down—*LIKE THIS*!

(He smacks him across the face, knocking him on his back. Throughout this SAMMY has not uttered a word, nor has he cried out . . . Slowly now he rises, blows his nose to hide the tears and then goes back to his tinkering)

FRANK

(slowly after a pause)

Anybody I did it to would bust me one back—if he wasn't yeller. He'd get up on his two feet and smack me right in the nose—if he wasn't yeller . . .

(SAMMY goes on tinkering)

But ye can't expect nothin' out of a guy that's yeller, kin ya! Kin ya!

SAMMY

(regarding him fearfully)

No.

FRANK

And ya can't expect nothin' out of a guy that has to sleep in the same bed as his big sister, kin ya?

(as SAMMY says nothing)

Ya do, don't ya? Don't ya?

(as he doesn't answer FRANK grabs him by the collar)

SAMMY

(almost crying out)

I got to. We ain't got no more room.

FRANK

(jovially)

Say, what's she like, your sister? Why don't ya introdooce me sometime?

(as he doesn't answer)

. . . I'll bet you get a nice little feel in sometime when she don't know it, eh? . . .

(as SAMMY tries to wriggle loose)

. . . Say, I wouldn't mind changin' places with ya some night—some night when it's nice and cold. You go home and sleep with my old man and I'll go to your house and—and—

(as SAMMY wriggles desperately)

Say, what ya bawlin' for? I was only bein' nice to ya. I was only sayin' that some cold night I was goin' over to your house and maybe do a little sleepin' with your—

(with a tremendous heave SAMMY tears himself loose; then with a cry he throws himself upon FRANK. They roll over on the ground. They are fighting desperately. FRANK on top, SAMMY underneath gone completely berserk. . . . BOTH BOYS freeze. . . . There is a pause)

WOMAN

(Yiddish accent. She has come out of door on fourth floor hallway and leans over balustrade, looking down)

Sammy! . . . What's the matter, Sammy?

SAMMY

(underneath)

Nothin' mom.

WOMAN

Come upstairs for supper.

(as they remain frozen)

Supper!

SAMMY

I'm comin' . . .

(They both rise; SAMMY dusts himself off; he picks up his skooter)

WOMAN

You're all right, Sammy?

SAMMY

(slowly)

Yeah, I'm all right . . .

(without a look at FRANK he picks up his skooter and starts up the ship ladder stairway slowly. FRANK watches him for a moment, spits, then, hands in his pockets, he crosses off left. There is a pause)

(Spot on LITTLE MAN and GUIDE still watching stage right)

GUIDE

Pretty mean little cuss. Are they all like that?

LITTLE MAN

That's what I'd like to know. Is that kid unusual or is it the result of where he lives and what he sees?

(to LOUDSPEAKER)

Come on. Let's have the facts.

LOUDSPEAKER

Seattle, Washington.

(Lights up on TWO WOMEN down right and left. They stand at 2 step down right and down left)

FIRST WOMAN

25% of all juvenile delinquency found in six and one half per cent of the city area—the slums![131]

LOUDSPEAKER

Richmond, Virginia.

SECOND WOMAN

50% of all juvenile delinquency found in eighteen per cent of the city area—the slums.[132]

LOUDSPEAKER

Cleveland, Ohio.

FIRST WOMAN

47% of all juvenile delinquency found in seventeen per cent of the city area—the slums![133]

LOUDSPEAKER

Philadelphia, Pennsylvania.

SECOND WOMAN

46% of all juvenile delinquency found in nine per cent of the city area—the slums![134]

(Lights out on WOMEN)

★

Scene B—East Side—West Side

(Standing before the house, right, LITTLE MAN is jostled by a MAN holding a chair with both his hands. On the chair is piled a breadbox and various other articles. Under his arm he carries a broom. The MAN crosses up to narrow stairway left leading to upper center cubicle)

LITTLE MAN

That's enough.

(to LOUDSPEAKER)

Where's he going?

LOUDSPEAKER

Why don't you follow him and find out?

LITTLE MAN

O.K. I will.

(grabs GUIDE as latter starts off right)

Uh! Uh! You come with me.

(Spot out on LITTLE MAN and GUIDE as they cross center)

(Lights up on upper center cubicle which is cluttered with furniture, chairs, etc. MIN is at stove, trying futilely to polish it. MAN enters and stands holding the chair)

MAN

Where do you want this, Min?

WOMAN (MIN)

(tired)

Oh, drop it any place. The room's so jammed up you can't move anyhow. Drop it and sit on it. Then you'll both be takin' up the same space. That'll save somethin'.

(MAN drops the chair, then bends down and holds up breadbox)

MAN

Where do you want the breadbox?

WOMAN

I'll take it.

(takes box and puts it on stove)

MAN

(leaning on broom)
Where do you want the broom?

WOMAN

(excitedly)

How do I know! You got eyes in your head. Find a place for it! . . . This is the last time I move if I have to rot here!

MAN

(good-humoredly)

How'd you like a place on Fifth Avenue with nine bathrooms and a swimmin' pool?

WOMAN

(crosses, stops center)
(sharply)

How'd you like to go—

(pause, then bit kinder)

—back and get the rest of the stuff!

MAN

Lemme rest a little, will ya? Them three blocks seem plenty far away when you're carrin' a load on your back.

(MAN sits on chair. WOMAN continues cleaning around)

WOMAN

They'll seem further away than that in a year or so when you look up at them tall buildings and say to yourself, "I used to live there."

MAN

What're they goin' to call it, Min?

WOMAN

Knickerbocker Village.

MAN

Knickerbocker Village! Sounds swell. What's the idea of it?

WOMAN

The idea is they want to tear down the slums so poor folks can have a decent place to live.

MAN

Well, why don't we move in?

WOMAN

(looking up from her polishing)

I guess we're *too* poor.[135]

MAN

That don't make sense.

WOMAN

You said it!

(There is a pause)

MAN

(in a different tone)

Hey, Min!

(She turns and regards him for a moment)

Sit down a minute, willya—I want to talk to you. Sit down.

(She shrugs her shoulders, moves chair over, and sits center. He rises and crosses left a step, then turns . . . slowly)

Looks like I won't be any better off in the next few years than I am right now. Right?

(She just looks at him)

Looks like we'll be livin' in this dump or one just like it for a long time to come. Right?

(She continues to look at him)
(slowly)

How about us havin' a kid?

(There is a pause)

WOMAN

(looks away)

No.

MAN

What's the use of us holdin' out and hopin'? Nothin's goin' to change.

WOMAN

(decisively)

No.

MAN

I ain't gettin' any younger, Min. I'd like to see a piece of me and you crawlin' around the house—sort of representin' us after we're gone . . .

(pleadingly, holding her chin)

Min . . .

WOMAN

(softly, but definitely and turning away)

We had two, didn't we?

MAN

(patting her shoulder and turning away)

I know. It ain't your fault. It ain't nobody's fault they died.

WOMAN

Listen to me, Jim. There's nothing wrong with me. And there's no thin' wrong with you—you couldn't heave that coal around the way you do if there was . . .

(suddenly, leaning forward)

What made them kids die, Jim?

MAN

(resignedly)

I guess it was just bound to be, Min.

WOMAN

(rises)

Bound to be—hell! It's the house we lived in! It's the houses we always lived in! It's these walls and these lice and no sun and no air and no decent food and these stinking toilets! That's what it is!

(hysterically)

And you want me to have another kid and have him die before he's a year old! Or maybe if he's lucky, grow up to be a gangster like Peg Leg Lonergan or Two Gun Crowley and die with a cop's slug in his belly! No, I say, NO! . . . NO! Goddamn it, no.

(She stands there. Hold and BLACKOUT on MAN and WOMAN. Spot on LITTLE MAN and GUIDE sitting on 3 step, left. LITTLE MAN heaves a deep sigh and shakes his head despairingly)

GUIDE

You want to know something? What goes on in these houses is pretty much like what I showed you—back in 1850. . . . It's the same story all over again.

LITTLE MAN

Yeah, that's what *he* said.

(points to LOUDSPEAKER)

It repeats itself. It just goes on and on.

GUIDE

Well, isn't anybody going to do anything about it?

LITTLE MAN

Funny, you asking that question. That's just what I keep on asking.

GUIDE

Well, aren't they?

LITTLE MAN

I dunno.

(points to LOUDSPEAKER)

I think he's got something up his sleeve. But he won't spring it yet. . . . How about taking a trip up to Harlem?

GUIDE

Harlem?

LITTLE MAN

Up about a Hundred and Twenty-fifth Street. We'll take a subway.

GUIDE

Subway?

LITTLE MAN

Skip it. I always forget about you being—

(from the audience—)

A WOMAN'S VOICE (MRS. BUTTONKOOPER)

Angus! Angus!

(They stop as spot on WOMAN coming up stairway from pit to stage left)

LITTLE MAN

Oh, hello, dear.

(to GUIDE)

That's Mrs. Buttonkooper.

GUIDE

(takes off hat and makes old-fashioned bow)

How do you do?

MRS. BUTTONKOOPER

Angus, what are you doing up here, and who is that man in the funny suit?

(GUIDE looks at his clothes bewildered)

LITTLE MAN

Oh, him! He died about fifty years ago. We just dug him up.

MRS. BUTTONKOOPER

Will you stop being a fool and get your hat and come with me? Hurry!

LITTLE MAN

But, dearest . . .

MRS. BUTTONKOOPER

Did you hear what I said!

LITTLE MAN

But, darling . . .

MRS. BUTTONKOOPER

Angus K. Buttonkooper! Will you come with me this instant!

LITTLE MAN

(folding his arms, bravely and stamping his foot)

No. Not unless you tell me what it's all about.

MRS. BUTTONKOOPER

(looking around apprehensively)

Do you want everybody to hear?

LITTLE MAN

Certainly. I have no secrets.

MRS. BUTTONKOOPER

(a very loud whisper)

There's a new Housing Development. Williamsburg. They're taking applications![136]

LITTLE MAN

(in a dither of excitement)

Why didn't you say so!

(starts pacing)

What did you stand there talking for! Why didn't you say something! Why didn't you send me a—

(They start toward steps. SPOT on TENEMENT HOUSE COMISSIONER, right)

TENEMENT HOUSE COMMISSIONER

Just a moment, Mr. Buttonkooper.

(They stop)

Remember me? I'm the Tenement House Commissioner.

LITTLE MAN

Can't talk to you now, Mr. Commissioner. I'm too busy.

(They start toward steps again)

TENEMENT HOUSE COMMISSIONER

That's what I want to talk to you about. . . . There's no need for you to rush like that. You see, we've got 1622 apartments in that Williamsburg Development.[137]

LITTLE MAN

(rapturously)

1622 apartments!

TENEMENT HOUSE COMMISSIONER

. . . but we already have 19,000 applications for them.[138]

LITTLE MAN

Nineteen thou—Oh!

(Both stop and gasp)

COMMISSIONER

So you see there's no need to rush!

BLACKOUT ON COMMISSIONER

MRS. BUTTONKOOPER

(sarcastically)

You see! That's what you get when you go galavantin' all over the place and nobody can find you! . . .What are you doing here anyhow?

LITTLE MAN

I'm seeing a show. It's about Housing.

MRS. BUTTONKOOPER

Housing! Will they show us how we can get our hands on a lease for one of those model developments?

LOUDSPEAKER

We're coming to that, Mrs. Buttonkooper. You'll just have to be patient.

LITTLE MAN

(taking her arm—pushing her toward steps)

That's right, dear. You'll just have to be patient. Now go on home and wash the dishes or put the baby to sleep or something. I'll stay here and find out all about everything.

MRS. BUTTONKOOPER

(stops on top step)

I'll do no such thing. The dishes are washed and the baby's asleep. And if you're going to stay here and learn something, then so am I.

(faces front)

LITTLE MAN

All right, if that's the way you feel about it.

MRS. BUTTONKOOPER

That's the way I feel.

LITTLE MAN

But don't look at me up here. You'll make me nervous. . . .

MRS. BUTTONKOOPER

Oh, don't be silly—

LITTLE MAN

(spotting empty seat—pointing to it)

There's a seat. Sit in it.

MRS. BUTTONKOOPER

(looks at him—is about to refuse, then changes her mind)

Wait 'til I get you home!

(goes down steps and sits in seat. LITTLE MAN remains stage center)

On, go on—

LITTLE MAN

Well, where were we?

GUIDE

You said something about a place called Harlem.

LITTLE MAN

Oh, yeah!

(They start walking)

You know, I'm not so familiar with this neighborhood. I don't know just what to show you.

LOUDSPEAKER

How about showing him the "Hot Bed"?

LITTLE MAN

(puzzled)

The "Hot Bed"?

LOUDSPEAKER

That's right. The "Hot Bed."

LITTLE MAN

Where'll I find it?

LOUDSPEAKER

Just walk up Lenox Avenue and turn in any street—135th, 140th, 145th—almost any one will do.

(They walk across stage to right)

★

Scene C—Harlem

(Dim up on stage right cubicle, on TWO NEGROES. SECOND NEGRO asleep on cot. FIRST NEGRO stands in center of cubicle, taking off coat)

FIRST NEGRO

(crosses to bed)

Hey, wake up!

(no response)

Come on there, man, UP!

(He shakes him)

SECOND NEGRO

(rubbing his eyes)

Huh? Whas' a matter?

FIRST NEGRO

Four o'clock. You had all the sleepin' you're goin' to. . . .

SECOND NEGRO

Ain't hardly closed my eyes.

FIRST NEGRO

(sitting on steps leading to main tenement. He takes off his shoes and socks)

Well, you better open 'em pretty quick. I got some fast sleepin' to do. "Aquitania" comes in at twelve o'clock midnight. I gotta be down there and rassle that cargo.

(as SECOND NEGRO doesn't move)

All right, Jack, let your feet hit the floor. I said I got some sleepin' to do!

SECOND NEGRO

I ain't goin' to git up . . .

FIRST NEGRO

You ain't eh?

SECOND NEGRO

I'm sick and I'm goin' to sleep. What you think I pay three dollars a week for this bed for?

FIRST NEGRO

Same reason I do, I expect. You gets your eight hours and I gets mine and Bob, he gets his. And there ain't but twenty-four hours in a day!

(crosses to bed)

Why don't you stop jibin' and get outa that bed.

SECOND NEGRO

Landlady tell me I can sleep as long as I like.

FIRST NEGRO

She did, eh?

(rolls him out of the bed and drops him on the floor)

You can sleep there as long as you like!

SECOND NEGRO

(angry)

What you do that for?

FIRST NEGRO

(getting into bed and lying down)

Don't get sassy, sonny. All I want is what's comin' to me.

SECOND NEGRO

(on floor)

By God, I gotta sleep, I tell you! I gotta pain right here in the middle and I gotta sleep.

(FIRST NEGRO rolls over, turning his back to him)

What kind of thing I gotta put up with anyhow? In the bed, outa the bed! First me, then you, then that other fellow. What kind of thing is this anyhow!

(crawls on floor)

Twelve hours a day, ten bucks a week! Shine, Mister? Shine 'em up black, shine 'em up brown! In the summertime it's white. . . .

Shine, Mister? No, boss, he don't want no shine. . . .

(as he crawls further and sits on top step of ship ladder stairway leading from street)

But I wanna sleep, I gotta sleep, d'you hear?

(He stops, then, as if talking to himself)

Try and get myself a decent room where a man kin lay his head when he's got a sick belly. Landlady tell me white folks live here pay thirty dollars for this flat. Black ones move in—forty-five![139] Same rooms, same busted bannister, same lousy sink!

(claps his hand to his stomach in a spasm of pain)

By God, what kind of thing is this!

(pause . . . then slowly, intensely, reminiscently)

. . . member what my grandpop used to tell me—'bout the old country where he come from . . .

(reciting the words verbatim, as though his grandpop were speaking through his lips)

. . . When a man's got more misery'n he kin stand, and his bones ache and his eyeballs burnin' with fire and there's hot pain runnin' up and down his arms and legs—you know what he do? You know what? . . . He grab his machete, and run out into the clearing where all the planters are stanin' with their whips in their hands and he yell as loud as he can, *AMOK, AMOK*!

(quietly, as FIRST NEGRO sits up in bed to listen)

You know what that mean? It mean I can't work no more! I'm crazy from work and I don't wanta live! I'm going to bust right into you and cut you wide open and keep on cuttin' until I'm dead! Until I'm dead!

(suddenly struck with the idea)

Until I'm dead!

(pause, then suddenly as the idea takes hold and possesses him)

Did you hear, did you hear me?

(FIRST NEGRO gets out of bed)

AMOK! AMOK! AMOK!

(stands swaying, hysterically . . .)
(FIRST NEGRO stands watching him, SECOND NEGRO shrieks and starts for FIRST NEGRO. The latter crosses to him, shakes him hard, then . . .)

FIRST NEGRO

What happens when one of these guys you talkin' about goes out of his head that way?

SECOND NEGRO

He fight until they kill him.

FIRST NEGRO

And then he's dead. And what good is it for him? And what good is he for anybody else?

(slowly)

That ain't the way to do it, all by yourself. This kinda business won't get you nowhere. When you don't like the way things are, and you want to change 'em, don't try to do it all by yourself. You can't. . . . You got to get 'em all together—and then you gotta do somethin'—*TOGETHER*!

(There is a pause)

SECOND NEGRO

(slowly)

Do something? Like what?

FIRST NEGRO

Like this. . . .

(Slowly he turns, facing out; then, addressing an imaginary landlord . . .)

You go to the landlord and say: If you don't stop gougin' us—if you don't fix them rusty pipes and clean up this here house, you know what we're goin' to do? YOU KNOW WHAT!

(pause)

We ain't gonna pay no rent!

SECOND NEGRO

No rent? . . . But they won't let me stay here. They'll kick me out.

FIRST NEGRO

Sure they will—if you do it by yourself. But suppose everybody in this whole house didn't pay the rent until every man had a bed of his own and that sink downstairs was fixed—WOULD YOU GET IT FIXED OR WOULDN'T YOU?

(There is a pause, the SECOND NEGRO regards him for a moment, then, joyously)

SECOND NEGRO

(shouting)

No rent! We ain't gonna pay no rent!

FIRST NEGRO

That's it—no rent!

TWO NEGROES

No rent! No rent!

BLACKOUT

★

Scene D—Rent Strike

(The music comes up)

LOUDSPEAKER

Harlem Rent Strike: New York, October 11, 1936 . . . four thousand march in fight on Harlem rent rise![140] East Side Rent Strike—New York, January 28, 1933—300 Tenants picket landlord.[141]

(Light up fourth floor—THREE WOMEN come out of the three doorways and stand in hallway)

FIRST WOMAN

(pointing to gap in balustrade)

Three dollars a month more rent! Look at that bannister!

SECOND WOMAN

It's been just like this ever since I moved in!

FIRST WOMAN

Some day somebody's going to get hurt.

THIRD WOMAN

Nobody did yet!

FIRST WOMAN

That's right—nobody did yet! So let's not do anything until some kid falls and breaks his skull on the landing down there!

SECOND WOMAN

But what are we going to do?

FIRST WOMAN

Let's just sit back and pray.

THIRD WOMAN

But what can we do about it!

FIRST WOMAN

I'm not sure but I've got an idea. . . .

BLACKOUT

(Music comes up again)

LOUDSPEAKER

Bronx Rent Strike—New York, January 6, 1933—20 families in Charlotte Street tenement picket landlord.[142]

(THREE WOMEN rush down steps and into third floor landing as light comes up. THREE OTHER WOMEN meet them)

FOURTH WOMAN

I'm not going to pay it—that's what!

FIFTH WOMAN

Three dollars a month more beginning October first!

FOURTH WOMAN

What about Mrs. MacNamara— where is she?

(calling)

Mrs. MacNamara!

MRS. MACNAMARA

(stepping out of shadows of landing, right)

Here I am! And I just saw him!

FOURTH WOMAN

Are you going to pay it?

MRS. MACNAMARA

NO!

FIFTH WOMAN

Are you going to move?

MRS. MACNAMARA

NO!

FIFTH WOMAN

What *are* you going to do?

MRS. MACNAMARA

I'll tell you what I'm going to do—I'm going to picket—and so are you—and you –

(to SIXTH WOMAN)

and *you*, too!

SIXTH WOMAN

Picket? We can't picket!

MRS. MACNAMARA

Why not? All you have to do is walk up and down!

SIXTH WOMAN

With signs?

MRS. MACNAMARA

With signs and banners and everything! Sure—if the men can do it—so can we!

BLACKOUT

(Music comes up and continues throughout LOUDSPEAKER'S announcement)

LOUDSPEAKER

Brooklyn rent strike.—January 17, 1933. Two hundred members of the Brooklyn Tenants' League picket the landlord.[143]

(Lights come up on FIVE or SIX WOMEN and TENANTS LEAGUE ORGANIZER in upper center cubicle)

ORGANIZER

Do you know how much it'll cost him to evict each tenant? $25.001—For forty apartments it'll cost him a thousand dollars!

FOURTH WOMAN

A thousand dollars! He'll never spend it!

(There is a pause)

FIRST WOMAN

But is it right for us to stay here without paying rent?

ORGANIZER

Is it right for him to raise rents when there's a housing shortage? For us to be thrown out on the street? Is it?

CHORUS OF VOICES

NO!

(pause)

ORGANIZER

And so, I'm proposing right now that we, members of the Tenants' League, declare a rent strike of all the tenants in this house. That nobody move and nobody pay rent until the landlord—

FOURTH WOMAN

Until the landlord is willing to let us stay for the old rent!

CHORUS OF VOICES

Right!

BLACKOUT

(Blacks in)

★

Scene 3—What Price Housing?

CHARACTERS

Guide
Little Man
Loudspeaker
Landlord
Land Buying
Real Estate Operators
    Landowner
    First Broker—Mr. Salt
    Second Broker—Mr. Spinach
Construction
    First Building Supply Man
    Second Building Supply Man
    Contractor
Finance
    Banker
    Mortgage Company President
Collective
    First Man—Government Taxes

Second Man—State Taxes
Third Man—State Taxes

Operating Expense

Fourth Man—Insurance Agent
Fifth Man—Coal Dealer
Woman—Renting Agent
Sixth Man—Janitor

Announcers—Government Housing Projects

First Man
Second Man
Third Man
Fourth Man

Nathan Straus, Administrator, United States Housing Authority

★

(Spot up on LITTLE MAN and GUIDE sitting on 2 step down right. Scene played in front of blacks)

GUIDE

Say, that's a new one on me! . . .

LITTLE MAN

Is it?

GUIDE

Never had anything like a rent strike in my day! . . . Any good come out of it? Did they get the rent cut? Did they get rid of the roaches? Did they?

LITTLE MAN

Well, er . . .

(looks at LOUDSPEAKER, helplessly)

LOUDSPEAKER

They did. In one case the rent was cut two dollars a month. In another, the landlord was forced to comply with the Multiple Dwelling Laws. In other cases rent increases have been prevented, painting done, drains repaired and roaches exterminated. The City-Wide Tenants' Council has on its record thousands of instances where repairs were made and rent adjusted only after action was taken.[144]

GUIDE

Well, well, well.

LITTLE MAN

(smiling happily)

Well, well, well.

(takes out paper and pencil)

I'll have to make a note of that. City-Wide Tenant's—

(He does)

GUIDE

Then all you've got to do is join the union and all your troubles are over . . .

LITTLE MAN

Well, not exactly. . . . You see—or—Well, you see, all they can do for you is help keep the landlord from raising the rent, and see that he obeys the laws. But they can't give you light and sunshine and a decent place to live! *You need new houses for that!*

(He looks up at the LOUDSPEAKER for approbation)

LOUDSPEAKER

That's telling him, Angus!

(LITTLE MAN smiles)

GUIDE

Well, why haven't you got these new houses; why aren't they building new ones every day to replace the old ones?

(Spot on LANDLORD who enters) left, crosses to center)

LANDLORD

I'll tell you why.

LITTLE MAN

Oh, hello. Who're you?

LANDLORD

I'm the fellow who can answer that question. I'm a landlord.

LITTLE MAN

A landlord. Well, well.

(He introduces him to GUIDE

Mister Guide, I want you to meet a landlord.

(GUIDE bows)

LANDLORD

Now the reason there's no incentive to the commercial builder to build for the low income group is this; there's no money in it.[145] That's simple, isn't it?

LITTLE MAN

(crosses center to LANDLORD)

But why is there no money in it? I don't want a marble palace. All I want is a little light and air, fair-sized rooms, and a few modern plumbing gadgets!

LANDLORD

You got any ideas what goes into the building and operation of a house?

LITTLE MAN

Sure. First, the land has to be bought. . . .

LANDLORD

Uh-huh.

LITTLE MAN

. . . and the contractor and laborers paid. . . .

LANDLORD

That's right.

LITTLE MAN

. . . there's taxes and the janitor, and—and—

LANDLORD

Go on.

LITTLE MAN

. . . and—and—well, I guess that's all.

LANDLORD

You guess that's all! Well, let me show *you* something!

(beckons off)

Hey, come here!

(Light up on FOURTEEN MEN and a WOMAN who enter left and right. Music)

LITTLE MAN

(puzzled)

Say, who are all these people?

LANDLORD

Don't rush me. That's what I'm going to show you.

(to MEN and WOMAN who stand upstage)

Line up over here, where everybody can see you. . . . That's right.

(THREE MEN come to apron step and line up, left—LANDOWNER, center—FIRST BROKER, right, SECOND BROKER, left)
(to LITTLE MAN and GUIDE)

Now, you two get out of the way . . .

(pause)
(LITTLE MAN and GUIDE stand at 2 step down right)

Now, I'm a philanthropic sort of guy, see, and I love my fellow men. So I decide to build a house where they can have light—and air—and—and—what else do you want?

LOUDSPEAKER

A few modern plumbing gadgets!

LANDLORD

A few modern plumbing gadgets. . . . Now I don't want to make anything out of it—much! Just a couple of dollars a year so I don't have to depend on the Old Age Security Act. . . .

(crosses in front of line below apron step)

. . . Now I want to rent my apartments for about seven or eight dollars a room[146]—Remember that, seven or eight dollars a room!—that's for the low-income brackets. . . . So I draw my money out of the bank and I go to work. . . .

(crosses to MAN at end of line, left, who has just begun to whistle. This happens each time—The MAN about to be approached whistles)
(to first in line)

I want to buy a piece of your land on the East Side.[147]

LANDOWNER

You'll have to consult my brokers—Pepper, Salt, Mustard and Cider, 220 Broadway!

(indicates MAN next to him, center. LANDLORD crosses)

LANDLORD

You Mister Pepper?

FIRST BROKER

No, I'm Salt. What can I do for you?

LANDLORD

I'd like to buy a piece of his property.

FIRST BROKER

Where's your broker?

LANDLORD

Do I have to have one, too?

FIRST BROKER

Certainly. I can highly recommend the firm of Beans, Beans, Beans and Spinach.

(indicates MAN next to him, right. LANDLORD crosses)

LANDLORD

You Mister Beans?

SECOND BROKER

No, I'm Spinach. What can I do for you?

LANDLORD

I want to buy a piece of his property. Ask him how much he wants.

SECOND BROKER

(to FIRST BROKER)

How much?

FIRST BROKER

(to LANDOWNER)

How much?

LANDOWNER

(to FIRST BROKER)

Ten dollars a square foot!

FIRST BROKER

(to SECOND BROKER)

Ten fifty a square foot!

SECOND BROKER

(to LANDLORD)

Eleven dollars a square foot!

LANDLORD

(to SECOND BROKER)

But he said ten fifty!

SECOND BROKER

That's my commission!

LANDLORD

(to FIRST BROKER)

And *he* said ten dollars!

FIRST BROKER

That's my commission!

LANDLORD

(doubtfully)

Eleven dollars!

LANDOWNER

(poking FIRST BROKER in the ribs)

Tell him I just sold a small piece for twelve dollars.

FIRST BROKER

(poking SECOND BROKER)

He says he just sold a fairly large piece for sixteen dollars.

SECOND BROKER

(poking LANDLORD)

He says he just sold a square block for nineteen dollars!

LANDLORD

But eleven dollars! That's an awful lot of money! . . . Can't we shave it down just a little?

(He looks at SECOND BROKER who turns to FIRST BROKER, who turns to LANDOWNER)

LANDOWNER

Ten dollars, that's my price.

FIRST BROKER

Ten fifty, that's his price.

SECOND BROKER

Eleven dollars, that's his price.

(THREE MEN step back. After group has spoken they remain frozen in their last positions)

LANDLORD

(a deep sigh)

O.K. I'll take it.

(hands over money to SECOND BROKER)

Well, now I'm a man of property.

LITTLE MAN

What'd it cost you?

(TWO MEN step to apron step; they stand right—FIRST BUILDING SUPPLY MAN, and left—SECOND BUILDING SUPPLY MAN)

LANDLORD

Plenty.

(crosses to MAN right—FIRST BUILDING SUPPLY MAN)

I want to build a house. Four stories high, walkup, plenty of light and air, and—and—

LITTLE MAN

Plumbing gadgets!

LANDLORD

Yeah. How much for the materials?[148]

FIRST BUILDING SUPPLY MAN

Fifteen thousand dollars.

LANDLORD

Fifteen thousand! Too much.

FIRST BUILDING SUPPLY MAN

Why don't you try him?

(indicates left)

There may be a lot of sand in his cement but he's cheap.

LANDLORD

Thanks. I will.

(crosses to MAN, left a little tired)

Want to build a house. Four stories. Light. Air. Gadgets. How much?

SECOND BUILDING SUPPLY MAN

(looks at FIRST BUILDING SUPPLY MAN, inquiringly. FIRST BUILDING SUPPLY MAN holds up fifteen fingers. SECOND BUILDING SUPPLY MAN nods, LANDLORD suspecting something, swings around at FIRST MAN but he's too late)

Fifteen thousand.

LANDLORD

That's what he said.

SECOND BUILDING SUPPLY MAN

Did he? What a coincidence!

LANDLORD

He also said your cement was full of sand.

SECOND BUILDING SUPPLY MAN

That's O.K. So is his.

LANDLORD

(hesitant)

Well, I may as well go back to him. He saw me coming first.

(crosses back)

Here you are. Fifteen thousand.

(hands over money to FIRST BUILDING SUPPLY MAN and crosses to MAN who has come down and stands center, up from apron step)

You a contractor?

CONTRACTOR

Yeah.

LANDLORD

Do I have to repeat it all or did you hear me talking to them?

CONTRACTOR

I heard you.

LANDLORD

How much?

CONTRACTOR

Twenty-four thousand.

LANDLORD

(indignant)

Twenty-four—

CONTRACTOR

That's right. My carpenters get twelve dollars a day.[149]

LANDLORD

Twelve dollars a—

LOUDSPEAKER

Don't let him get away with that one. Sure they get twelve dollars a day. And they probably worked three days last month!

LANDLORD

Oh, well. . . .

(starts counting out money and stops in consternation)

Say, I haven't got enough money!

(CONTRACTOR languidly turns away and starts whistling)

What'll I do?

CONTRACTOR

(stops whistling)

Try the bank.

(Steps up as TWO MEN come down and stand on apron step right and left)

LANDLORD

Thanks.

(crosses to MAN, left—BANKER)

I want a mortgage.

BANKER

Sorry. Got too many!

LANDLORD

What'll I do?

BANKER

Try the Mortgage Company.

LANDLORD

Thanks.

(crosses to MAN, right—MORTGAGE COMPANY PRESIDENT)

I want a mortgage.

MORTGAGE COMPANY PRESIDENT

Sure. We'll float bonds. Six percent.[150]

LANDLORD

Six percent!

MORTGAGE COMPANY PRESIDENT

Plus my commission!

LANDLORD

Your commission! . . . O.K. Give me the money.

(MORTGAGE COMPANY PRESIDENT hands over money. LANDLORD crosses back to CONTRACTOR)

Here you are. Twenty-four thou—

(stops, hears whistling of MAN, standing directly back of CONTRACTOR on 3 step. His hand is outstretched. The COLLECTORS follow FIRST MAN, circling past the LANDLORD, all with their hands outstretched, while he, in bewildered fashion hands them money as they ask for it.)

Who're you?

FIRST MAN

Government, taxes.

(LANDLORD pays him)

LANDLORD

Who're you?

SECOND MAN

State, taxes.

(same business)

LANDLORD

Who're you?

THIRD MAN

City, taxes.

(same business)

LANDLORD

Who're you?

FOURTH MAN

Insurance.

(same business)

LANDLORD

Who're you?

FIFTH MAN

Coal.

(same business)

LANDLORD

Who're you?

WOMAN

Renting Agent.

(same business)

LANDLORD

Who're you?

SIXTH MAN

I'm the Janitor!

(The circle freezes)

LANDLORD

Thank God!

(He goes down and sinks exhausted on apron step center. There is a pause. . . .)

LOUDSPEAKER

Well, now what?

LANDLORD

Wait a minute, will you?

LANDLORD

(He takes out a sign: "APARTMENTS FOR RENT," and hangs it around his neck. LITTLE MAN seeing the sign, rushes to center)

LITTLE MAN

Have you got an apartment to rent?

(LANDLORD still exhausted, nods)

Pretty fair-sized rooms?

LANDLORD

Uh-huh.

LITTLE MAN

—and—er—modern plumbing gadgets?

LANDLORD

Uh-huh.

LITTLE MAN

(suddenly)

Got a three-room apartment left?

LANDLORD

Uh-huh.

LITTLE MAN.

(incredulous)

Did you say, uh-huh?

LANDLORD

Uh-huh.

LITTLE MAN

(beside himself with excitement)

Now lemme get this straight—fair-sized rooms, light, and airy, modern gadgets—*And you've got an apartment for me!*

LANDLORD

Uh-huh.

LITTLE MAN

(same)

For the love of Mike, how much is the rent?

LANDLORD

Twenty-five dollars a room!

(Music)

BLACKOUT AND HOLD

LOUDSPEAKER

Wait a minute! Hold it! Don't blackout on that yet! Bring those lights up—full!

(they come up)

That's better. This scene isn't over yet!

(pause)

Now, Mister Landlord, we know that the conditions you showed us exist. They were a little exaggerated perhaps, hut they exist . . . But we can't just let it go at that. We can't let people walk out of this theatre knowing the disease is there, but believing there's no cure. *There is a cure!*

LANDLORD

What is it?

LOUDSPEAKER

(pause)

You see, every one of those people who had his hand in your pocket while you were building that house, was inspired by the profit motive—the Landowner, the Broker, the Building Supply Man, the Contractor, and you, too, you were all out to get yours—and you did! . . . But there's one thing you've got to stop taking profits on—and that's human misery! *If you can't build cheap houses—and you've just proved that you can't—then let somebody do it who can—and I mean the United States Government—for instance.*

(Enter left, MAN holding in front of him on a large board, a relief model of a housing project. Stands at 2 step, down left)

Chicago, Illinois. . . .

FIRST MAN

Government Housing Project—Jane Addams Houses—$7.38 per room per month![151]. . .

(Exits)

(Enter SECOND MAN, down right, same business)

LOUDSPEAKER

Memphis, Tennessee. . . .

SECOND MAN

Government Housing Project—Dixie Homes—$6.51 per room per month![152]

(Exits)

(Enter THIRD MAN, down left—same business)

LOUDSPEAKER

Detroit. . . .

THIRD MAN

Government Housing Project—Brewster Houses—$5.78 per room per month![153]

(Exits)

(Enter FOURTH MAN, down right—same business)

LOUDSPEAKER

Cleveland. . . .

FOURTH MAN

Government Housing Project—Lekeview Terrace—$5.53 per room per month![154]

(Exits)

LANDLORD

Did they say, "government?"

LANDOWNER

Government?

FIRST BROKER

(to CONTRACTOR)

Did he say, "government?"

LOUDSPEAKER

Yes, I said "government!"

LANDOWNER

But that's socialism!

SECOND BROKER

It's an invasion of private rights!

BANKER

It's contrary to economic laws!

MORTGAGE COMPANY PRESIDENT

By God, it's unconstitutional!

LOUDSPEAKER

It is, is it? . . . Let's hear what Nathan Straus, Administrator, United States Housing Authority has to say about that!

(Enter STRAUS left, crosses to center and stands up from apron step)

STRAUS

There is no reform within my memory that has not been attacked as an invasion of private rights and as contrary to economic laws. There is usually the added comment that it's unconstitutional. . . .

(He bows to MORTGAGE COMPANY PRESIDENT)

. . . We have only to recall the history of the enactment of Workmen's Compensation Laws, of the Income Tax Laws, of the laws creating a Public Service Commission to curb improper practices of the Public Utility Corporations. In every one of these cases we were told that the new legislation was contrary to economic laws, in that it interfered with private initiative. In practically every case we were told that it was unconstitutional. Yet each of these reforms has been written into the laws of our land.[155]

HOLD AND BLACKOUT

★

Scene 4—Government Housing

CHARACTERS

Little Man
Guide
Loudspeaker
United States Senate
Stage right
Group of three Senators
Group of two Senators
Centre
Hon. William E. Borah—Idaho
Robert F. Wagner—New York
Stage left
Hon. C. O. Andrews—Florida
Harry F. Byrd—Virginia
Millard E. Tydings-Maryland
Group of two Senators
Vice-President, John N. Garner
Clerk of Senate

★

(Spot on LITTLE MAN and GUIDE at 2 step down right. Scene played in front of blacks)

LITTLE MAN

(pacing, excitedly)

Five dollars a room, six dollars a room. . . . Lakeview Terrace.[156] . . .

First Houses[157] . . . That's the kind of place I want to live in!

GUIDE

Well, why don't you?

LITTLE MAN

Didn't you hear what he said?

(points to LOUDSPEAKER)

My chances of getting a flat in one of 'em are about three thousand six hundred to one. THREE THOUSAND SIX HUNDRED TO ONE![158]

GUIDE

Well, why don't they build more of 'em?

LITTLE MAN

Why don't they build—

(stops short in amazement, then)

Say, that's right! *Why don't they*?

GUIDE

I don't know. I'm asking *you* . . . You—er still have a Congress, don't you?

LITTLE MAN

Certainly we've got a Congress!

GUIDE

Do they—er—still pass laws?

LITTLE MAN

Certainly they still pass laws!

GUIDE

Well, what're they doing about it?

LITTLE MAN

What are they—say—Seems to me I remember reading something about . . .

(to LOUDSPEAKER)

Hey! What's this about a Housing Bill they passed some time last summer?

(Lights come up on five groups of SENATORS and VICE-PRESIDENT GARNER. The groups stand stage right, center, and stage left—a group of three at

2 step down right, a group of two upstage right; two Senators center, a group of three down left, and a group of two up left.
VICE-PRESIDENT GARNER stands on 2 step down left)

LOUDSPEAKER
February 27, 1937. . . . The Wagner-Steagall Housing Bill is introduced in the Senate![159] The Wagner-Steagall Housing Bill:

(Enter CLERK of SENATE. He stands down left at 2 step)

CLERK
To create a United States Housing Authority, to provide financial assistance to the States and the political subdivisions thereof for the elimination of unsafe and unsanitary housing conditions; for the development of decent, safe and sanitary dwellings for families of low income; and for the reduction of unemployment and the stimulation of business activity. . . . For these purposes there shall be made available, the sum of one billion dollars.[160]

(Exits)

LOUDSPEAKER
Senator William E. Borah of Idaho.

BORAH
(stands left center)

Mr. President . . .

GARNER
Does the Senator from New York yield to the Senator from Idaho?[161]

WAGNER
(stands right center, facing BORAH)

Certainly.

BORAH
Is the Senator going to discuss the question of causes of slums? Why do we have these awful degraded conditions?[162]

LOUDSPEAKER
Senator Robert F. Wagner of New York.

WAGNER
I think it is a very simple matter. It is because of the low incomes received by the individuals who live in the slums. That is the fundamental difficulty. If overnight we could increase their incomes by a more fair distribution of the wealth of the country, we would not have any slums![163]

LOUDSPEAKER
Senator C. O. Andrews of Florida.

ANDREWS
(stands down left)

Mr. President, I should like to ask the Senator from New York where the people who live in the slums come from.[164]

WAGNER
(turning toward ANDREWS)

A great many of them have been here a long time. What does the Senator mean by, "Where do they come from?" Whether they have come from some other country?[165]

ANDREWS
I think we ought not to offer any inducement to people to come in from our country or foreign countries or anywhere else and take advantage of our government in supplying them with homes. For instance, if we examine the birth records in New York, we will find that most of the people there in the slums were not born in New York, but the bright lights have attracted them from everywhere, and that is one reason why there are so many millions in New York without homes![166]

LOUDSPEAKER
Despite his position during the debate, Senator Andrews voted for and supported the Bill in its final form.[167]

BORAH
Mr. President . . .

(Enter CLERK left. He hands GARNER a slip of paper. Three raps of a gavel are heard. CLERK exits)

GARNER
(reads)

The appropriation for the Wagner-Steagall Housing Bill has been reduced from one billion to seven hundred million dollars![168]

LOUDSPEAKER
Senator Harry F. Byrd of Virginia.

BYRD
(stands down left in group with ANDREWS)

Mr. President, I offer an amendment, the purpose of which is to prevent the extravagance which has occurred in other homestead projects built throughout the country. . . . This amendment is presented for the purpose of preventing the expenditure of more than four thousand dollars per family unit.[169]

WAGNER
Those who are *not* in sympathy with our efforts to do something for the one third of the people of the United States who are ill-housed—something to give these unfortunate people who have not sufficient income to

enable them to live in decent quarters a chance for life—will feel that the amendment of the Senator from Virginia ought to be adopted and the bill defeated. I say very candidly to the Senate that if the amendment of the Senator from Virginia is adopted it will kill the bill.[170]

(Enter CLERK down left. He hands GARNER another slip of paper. Three raps of the gavel are heard)

GARNER

(reads)

The appropriation for the Wagner-Steagall Housing Bill has been reduced from seven hundred million to five hundred twenty-six million dollars![171]

(His voice fades and lights dim down as a large screen rises up. Blacks out. The voices of the SENATORS fade but are heard debating in a vague sort of mum bo jumbo pattern under the LOUDSPEAKER. Music)

BYRD

Does the Senator think this low income group about which he is talking—and I am thoroughly in accord with *that*—

WAGNER

If the Senator is in accord with that, he should not suggest this amendment because he may be able to do in Virginia what he suggests, but there will be few areas in the United States where a room can be built for a thousand dollars, and under the Senator's amendment this benefit would be limited to a few localities![172]

LOUDSPEAKER

Senator Millard E. Tydings of Maryland.

TYDINGS

(stands down left in group with ANDREWS and BYRD)

Mr. President, I think the amendment of the Senator from Virginia is liberal. If these people cannot be rehabilitated at four thousand dollars per family, then we had better give up slum clearance![173]

(while debate is going on second series of movies of City appears[174] with running commentary by)

LOUDSPEAKER

(AREAS OF NEW YORK including Brooklyn Bridge)

This is New York City in 1938, considered by many to be the wealthiest city in the world. Skyscrapers, Wall Street, the Empire State. In some part of this area seven million people[175] have a place they call "home."

(PARK AVENUE—and sign "NO DOGS ALLOWED")

Park Avenue where some of America's millionaires have their homes.

(PUSHCARTS)

The same Park Avenue—further along. The rent is much cheaper here. Dogs run all over the place and nobody minds.

(TENEMENTS)

Slums. The lower East Side.

(AIRSHAFT)

Air and sunshine, primary requirements for growing children.

(DIRTY YARD)

To avoid being hit by automobiles children are advised to play in their backyards.

(MAN MERGES FROM CELLAR DOOR)

Yes, he lives down there.

(REAR HOUSE)

See those vertical ladders on the fire escapes? How would you like to climb down one of those in the middle of the night when a fire breaks out?

(BARRED WINDOWS)

Or try to get through these barred windows.

(FIRE SCENE)

And there *are* fires. How many lives were lost in this one? How many people were trapped in the halls? How many old men and women missed their footing on those vertical ladders? How many firemen were killed when the wall caved in?

(DIRTY YARD)

A home with a view.

(TWO WOMEN ENTERING TOILET ROOM)

Out of a sick-bed two flights down.

(OLD-FASHIONED WATER CLOSETS)

Modern plumbing—more modern plumbing.

(GARBAGE CANS AND A DEAD RAT)

Out of the slums of New York City . . . typhus . . . meningitis . . . tuberculosis.

(FAUCET IN YARD)

One faucet for the whole house and that's in the yard.

(GARBAGE CANS)

A million and three quarter[176] people look at these every day of their lives. Garbage . . . filth . . . disease . . . crime . . . slums!

(Voices of SENATORS are raised higher and higher in dispute as one group right shouts: "PASS THE BILL! PASS THE BILL!" The other group left shouts: "POINT OF ORDER." Movies end with projection of hand with gavel in it, descending, then crash of gavel, then)

GARNER

The Wagner-Steagall Housing Bill, with an appropriation of five hundred twenty-six million dollars, is passed![177]

(Blacks come in; Music)

BLACKOUT

★

Scene 5—Looking Forward

CHARACTERS

Loudspeaker
Little Man
Langdon W. Post—Former Tenement House Commissioner, New York City—Voice
Helen Alfred, Secretary and Executive Director, National Public Housing Conference
Hon. Fiorello H. La Guardia, Mayor, New York City
Landowner, 1800—Same as Act I, Scene 3
Landlord, 1938—Same as Act II, Scene 3
Mrs. Buttonkooper
Tenants of the HOUSE—Same as Act I, Scene 1.

★

(After short musical interlude follow spot picks out the LITTLE MAN, down right. He paces agitated, then crosses stage, to center)

LOUDSPEAKER

Hey!

(no answer; he continues pacing)

Hey! What are you doing?

LITTLE MAN

(without stopping)

Arithmetic.

LOUDSPEAKER

Arithmetic?

LITTLE MAN

That's right.

(He stops; leans forward, intently)

I suppose you noticed how they cut that Bill down to half of what Senator Wagner originally asked for.[178]

LOUDSPEAKER

I noticed it.

LITTLE MAN

Of course, 526 million is a lot of money.

LOUDSPEAKER

Of course.

LITTLE MAN

I could do a lot of things with 526 million.

LOUDSPEAKER

Sure you could. But where does the arithmetic come in?

(Blacks in)

LITTLE MAN

Well, I'm taking ten per cent of 526 million—

LOUDSPEAKER

You mean five hundred million—twenty six million goes for maintenance—[179]

LITTLE MAN

All right, five hundred million. Ten per cent of that is fifty million—which is all that any one State can get under the terms of the Bill.[180] Right?

LOUDSPEAKER

Right.

LITTLE MAN

Well, I'm taking that fifty million and trying to fit it into the New York City Housing problem.

LOUDSPEAKER

But you can't do that.

LITTLE MAN

You're telling me!

LOUDSPEAKER

That fifty million is for the whole State.[181] According to Mayor La Guardia the most New York City can hope to get is thirty million.[182]

LITTLE MAN

As I was saying. I'm taking that thirty million and trying to fit it into the New York City Housing problem.

LOUDSPEAKER

That's fine. Before you begin, let me show you what the New York City Housing problem really is—in dollars and cents. This is Langdon Post, former Tenement House Commissioner.

VOICE OF POST

A conservative estimate of the cost of removing the slums in New York City alone is about two billion dollars![183]

LOUDSPEAKER

Two billion dollars! There's your problem in arithmetic, Mr. Buttonkooper. How to make thirty million equal to two billion.

LITTLE MAN

(with paper and pencil)

That's what I'm working on.

LOUDSPEAKER

Well, what's the answer?

LITTLE MAN

A headache.

(He starts pacing again; he stops)

Do you realize that the Wagner Bill at the end of four years will have solved less than two per cent of the Housing problem in New York City?[184] Do you realize that, at that rate it will take us more than two hundred years before every slum in New York has been demolished?[185]—And by that time the ones they're building now will be slums and we'll be back just where we started.

(He crosses down; then, intently)

Remember, *I* want to live in one of those new developments! I don't give a damn about my great-great grandchildren!

(pause, then, more composed)

You know, when I heard all those Senators arguing, I got a funny feeling. I thought maybe I was crazy. . . . Tell me, isn't there anybody else who's taken the trouble to figure this thing out? Doesn't anybody know what the score is?

LOUDSPEAKER

Most of the local Housing authorities have studied the matter.

LITTLE MAN

Well, let's have it! What do they say? Let's hear somebody say something.

LOUDSPEAKER

Helen Alfred, Secretary and Executive Director of the National Public Housing Conference.

(Spot on MISS ALFRED, at 2 step, down right)

MISS ALFRED

The Wagner-Steagall Housing Act lays a permanent foundation for the too long delayed attack on dangerous and unsanitary housing conditions prevalent throughout the country. But in view of the great need for new accommodations, the sum stipulated is pitifully inadequate.[186]

(Light out on MISS ALFRED. Spot on LA GUARDIA, down left.)

LOUDSPEAKER

The Honorable Fiorello H. La Guardia, Mayor of New York City.

LA GUARDIA

The Wagner-Steagall Housing Bill with its provisions for 500 million dollars for rehousing the nation is a step in the right direction, but only a step—*a drop in the bucket!*[187] It is therefore my intention to start a building program aside and apart from, and in addition to the Federal program. . . . I have therefore requested the Board of Estimate to be prepared to act upon a resolution appropriating funds to take care of interest charges and amortization of capital investments for the construction of low rent houses. . . . Remember, slums cannot be wished away, nor even legislated away. THE ANSWER IS BUILDING![188]

(Lights out on LA GUARDIA)

LOUDSPEAKER

Well, there you are. Feel any better?

LITTLE MAN

No—but at least I know that if I'm crazy, I'm in pretty good company! According to all those fellows we're not much better off than we were before. . . .

LOUDSPEAKER

Less than two per cent better, according to your arithmetic.

LITTLE MAN

Well, what are we going to do about it?

(excitedly)

Are we going to take it lying down like mice? *Or, are we men?*

(starts taking off his coat)

LOUDSPEAKER

What are you going to do now?

LITTLE MAN

I'm going to find the guy who's responsible for these slum conditions! I'll tell him something all right, all right!

LOUDSPEAKER

Do you know who it is?

LITTLE MAN

Certainly I know who it is! What do you think I came to see this show for!

(Goes to wings right, and leads out to center, LANDOWNER 1800—Act I. Scene 3)

There you are!

(pointing to tenement)

Do you see that? Look at it! You started all this when you began to speculate in land!

LANDOWNER

All I did was sit. Remember?

LITTLE MAN

Yeah, I remember. And while you sat the town grew up around you. Land values went up, and because people had to have a place to live in, *this* is the result!

LANDOWNER

Well, what are you going to do about it?

LITTLE MAN

(taken aback)

Huh?

LANDOWNER

(belligerently)

I said, what are you going to do about it? Do you think you can take the land away from my descendants and make it public property? *Do you?*

LITTLE MAN

(doubtfully)

No—o.

LANDOWNER

That's all I wanted to know! Good-bye.

(He crosses off, right leaving a bewildered LITTLE MAN, down center)

LOUDSPEAKER

You certainly told him something, all right, all right.

LITTLE MAN

(sheepishly)

He was too quick for me. . . . But there's another guy I'm going to get my hooks into and he won't get away so fast!

(crosses to wings, left, shouting)

Hey, come on out here!

(He emerges, bringing on the LANDLORD of Act 2, Scene 3)

You're to blame for that! You and the high rents you collect every month! Do you know the percentage of income used for rent is higher here than in any other country on the face of the earth?[189]

LANDLORD

Well, what are you going to do about it?

LITTLE MAN

I'll tell you what we're going to do! We're going to march right up to Albany and get some emergency rent laws passed! That'll take care of you all right!

LANDLORD

(calmly)

Is that all?

LITTLE MAN

(a bit shaken by his calm)

Well—er—isn't it enough?

LANDLORD

I don't think so. . . . As I recall, you fellows marched up to Albany in 1920, 1924 and 1926.[190] In each case Emergency Rent Laws were passed.

(suddenly)

Are you paying any less for your apartment today than you did then?

LITTLE MAN

No.

LANDOWNER

That's all I wanted to know! Good bye.

(He crosses off)

LOUDSPEAKER

You certainly got your hooks into him all right.

LITTLE MAN

Let's not talk about it.

LOUDSPEAKER

Of course those emergency rent laws did prevent rents from going still higher.

LITTLE MAN

(explosively)

Sure they did!

LOUDSPEAKER

Well, why didn't you tell him that!

LITTLE MAN

He—er—he was too quick for me.

LOUDSPEAKER

I see . . . Well, what next?

LITTLE MAN

Let's see now . . . there was the Landowner—and the Landlord—and—er—I guess that's all.

LOUDSPEAKER

Isn't there something you've forgotten, Mr. Buttonkooper?

LITTLE MAN

What is it?

LOUDSPEAKER

How about the thing that's made these slum conditions possible for the last hundred and fifty years? The thing that makes people like you and everybody else sit back and say, "Well, this is the way it always has been and this is the way it's always going to be!"

LITTLE MAN

What thing is that?

LOUDSPEAKER

. . . it's called "inertia."

LITTLE MAN

Inertia?

(He looks puzzled)

MRS. BUTTONKOOPER

(rising from seat in audience)

Don't look so surprised, Angus. That's just what it is—inertia!

(Spot picks her up as she comes down aisle and up on stage, left. Stands facing LITTLE MAN)

You know about these conditions and so do I and so does everybody else that lives in 'em—but we don't do anything about it!

LITTLE MAN

By golly, that's right. According to what we've seen here tonight people have been going around for a hundred years or more—taking notes, making surveys—but nobody's ever *done* anything!

MRS. BUTTONKOOPER

That's it . . . What good are all those surveys and speeches to us when we've got to live in a place almost as bad as that twenty-four hours a day! . . . What good are all those new laws that nobody obeys when maybe those kids are going to turn out to be crooks or murderers!—

LITTLE MAN

Sure! And what good are all those Housing Bills that take care of less than two per cent of the trouble. What good are they when we still have this?

(points to tenement)

MRS. BUTTONKOOPER

Look at it—and don't forget—that isn't only New York. It's Philadelphia and Chicago and Boston and St. Louis! . . . According to a man named Roosevelt, it's one third of a nation![191] *One third of a nation is just like that in 1938*!

LITTLE MAN

(pause)

Well, what are we going to do about it?

MRS. BUTTONKOOPER

I don't know yet,—but it seems to me—

(suddenly)

Angus, how much did you say that Wagner Bill was for?

LITTLE MAN

526 million.

MRS. BUTTONKOOPER

526 million—for four years! Why was that bill cut down from a billion dollars, Angus?

LOUDSPEAKER

Because they're trying to balance the budget.

MRS. BUTTONKOOPER

Balance the budget? What with? Human lives? Misery? Disease?

(A whistle is heard as)

LOUDSPEAKER

FLASH.[192] New York, February 24, the cracking walls in three buildings at Avenue C and 12th Street caused all the tenants to flee for their lives. A few minutes after they had abandoned their homes and possessions, two of the buildings collapsed.[193]

LOUDSPEAKER

FLASH, New York, March 9th, thirty men, women and children were forced to flee for their lives when the walls in another old-law tenement at 82 St. Marks Place began to crack. This is the SECOND case of the kind in the last two weeks.[194]

LOUDSPEAKER

FLASH, New York, March 12th, this afternoon at 843 St. Nicholas Avenue, Manhattan, a fire broke out in a FIRE ESCAPELESS three story tenement. Leaping from a second floor window, a woman was impaled on a spiked fence and a three year old child was asphyxiated. Mayor La Guardia visited the scene and promised a thorough investigation.[195]

MRS. BUTTONKOOPER

Say, Mister, how much was the appropriation for the Army and Navy?

LOUDSPEAKER

The appropriation for the Army and Navy for the last four years was three billion, 125 million dollars.[196]

LITTLE MAN

Three billion, 125 million dollars. Why—why—that's more than enough money to clean out every slum in New York!

(pacing excitedly)

Well, what *are* we going to do?

MRS. BUTTONKOOPER

(interrupting)

You know what we're going to do—you and me? We're going to holler. And we're going to keep on hollering until they admit in Washington it's just as important to keep a man alive as it is to kill him!

LITTLE MAN

Will that do any good?

MRS. BUTTONKOOPER

Sure it will. If we do it loud enough!

LITTLE MAN

You think they'll hear us?

MRS. BUTTONKOOPER

They'll hear us all right if we all do it together—you and me and La Guardia and Senator Wagner and the Housing Authorities and the Tenant Leagues and everybody who lives in a place like that!

(pointing to tenement. TENANTS start to fill the tenement as lights come up on it)

LITTLE MAN

(excitedly)

All right, all right, when do we begin?

MRS. BUTTONKOOPER

Right now.

LITTLE MAN

Now?

MRS. BUTTONKOOPER

NOW!

(She crosses down center)
(shouting)

We want a decent place to live in! I want a place that's clean and fit for a man and woman and kids! CAN YOU HEAR ME—YOU IN WASHINGTON OR ALBANY OR WHEREVER YOU ARE! GIVE ME A DECENT PLACE TO LIVE IN! GIVE ME A HOME! A HOME!

LITTLE MAN

Do you think they'll hear us?

MRS. BUTTONKOOPER

And if we don't make them hear us you're going to have just what you've always had—slums—disease—crime—juvenile delinquency . . . and . . . and . . .

(TENANTS start activities as in Act I—Scene 1. Smoke starts to appear and begins to rise. Suddenly the fire sirens are heard. Pandemonium as fire scene is re-enacted. The entire scene builds to a crescendo topped by flames, smoke, and the MAN cowering on the fire escape. Music)

LOUDSPEAKER

Ladies and gentlemen, this might be Boston, New York, St. Louis, Chicago, Philadelphia—but just let's call it, ". . . one third of a nation . . ."

BLACKOUT

★

CURTAIN

HOUSE LIGHTS

Notes

1. New York Times—Feb. 19, 1924.
2. New York Times—Feb. 21, 1924.
3. New York Times—Feb. 24, 1924.
4. Fictional character.
5. N.Y. Times, February 19, 1924.
6. Fictional character.
7. Digest of Report of N.Y. Board of Fire Underwriters on Feb. 19, 1924 Tenement Fire at 397 Madison St., N.Y.—Municipal Reference Library, New York, N.Y.
8. Digest of Report New York Times, February 19, 1924.
9. Report of New York State Board of Housing, Legislative Document (1932) #84—p. 11.
10. Report of N.Y. State Board of Housing. Legislative Document (1932).
11. Ibid, p. 15.
12. N.Y. Times, February 19, 1924.
13. New York City Tenement House Commission—interview by Living News staff with Inspection Department—Ed.
14. New York Times, February 19, 1924.
15. Ibid.
16. New York City Tenement House Department.
17. New York, Times, February 19, 1924.
18. Langdon Post, N.Y. City Tenement House Commissioner.
19. Ibid.
20. N.Y. Times, February 19, 1924.
21. Report of the N.Y. State Board of Housing Legislative Document (1932) #84.
22. New York State Statute Tenement House Act 1909 Section 143.
23. Fictional character—scene creative.
24. Branham's Automobile Reference Book, 1928, p. 56.
25. New York American, June 22, 1924—classified advertisements.
26. Ibid, June 19, 1925.
27. 1935 World Almanac, p. 483, Population New York City—1924.
28. "Memorial History of New York," Wilson, Vol. 1, p. 82.
29. "A History of the Parish of Trinity Church in New York," Dix, p. 139.
30. "History of the Great American Fortunes," by Gustavus Myers, pp. 129–130.
31. "History of the Great American Fortunes," Gustavus Myers—p. 129.
32. "Trinity Break Ye My Commandments," Willis T. Gridley, pp. 134–5.
33. "History of the Great American Fortunes," Gustavus Myers, p. 183.
34. Common Council Minutes, Volume 1, May 13, 1779, p. 354.
35. Ibid.
36. Report of the Comptroller to the Council, New York, Vol. 4. p. 529, Aug. 17, 1807.
37. Ibid.
38. "Trinity Break Ye My Commandments," Willis T. Gridley, pp. 134–5.
39. "History of the Great American Fortunes," Gustavus Myers, p. 129.
40. Ibid.
41. "History of the Great American fortunes," Gustavus Myers, p. 129.
42. Ibid.
43. "Battles of the American Revolution," by Henry P. Carrington, p. 643.
44. "A Century of Population and Growth"—Gov't. Printing office, Washington, DC, 1909.
45. New York Commercial Advertiser, Feb. 17, 1801, et Supra.
46. 1935 World Almanac, p. 483.
47. Encyclopedia Americana, p. 485.
48. "The Tenement House Problem" edited by De Forest & Veiller, Vol. 2., p. 7.
49. World Almanac, 1935, p. 483.
50. "History of the Great American Fortunes"—Gustavus Myees, p. 178.

51. "The Golden Earth"—Arthur Pound, p. 295.
52. "Great American Fortunes"—Gustavus Myers, p. 180.
53. "The Golden Earth"—Arthur Pound, pp. 286–87.
54. "The Life and Ventures of the Original John Jacob Astor"—by Elizabeth L. Gebhard, p. 246.
55. "History of the Great American Fortunes"—Gustavus Myers, p. 148.
56. Opened for tenancy, Hillside, 1935; Boulevard Gardena, 1935: Knickerbocker Village, 1934; First Houses, 1935. New York City Housing Authority.
57. "Housing or Else," p. 8, Langdon W. Post, New York City Housing Authority, 1936.
58. On a basis of four persons to a family, with 120 apartments in "First Houses," the ratio is 3,600 to one.—Ed.
59. Map of New York in 1850, from files of Beseler Lantern Slide Co., 131 E. 23rd St., New York.
60. Hall of Records, New York, N.Y.
61. Hall of Records, New York, N.Y.
62. Valentine's Manual, 1862.
63. Stokes, Iconography A9—Vol. 3, p. 136.
64. "New York And Its Institutions—1609–1872." J. S. Richmond, p. 488.
65. Home of Abraham Van Nest, Bleecker Street—between Charles and Perry, New York, N.Y.—Valentine's Manual—1854, p. 538.
66. Picture from "Slums and Housing," James Ford, Vol. 1, p. 143.
67. "Tenement House Problem,"—edited by De Forest & Veiller, p. 78.
68. "Slums and Housing"—James Ford, Vol. 1, p. 143.
69. Ibid.
70. Report of Council of Hygiene and Public Health of the Citizens' Association . . . 1864—New York City Municipal Library.
71. "Slums and Housing," James Ford, Vol. 1, p. 138.
72. Historian, Immigrants' Industrial Savings Bank, New York, N.Y.
73. Text book of Medicine—edited by Russel L. Cecil, M.D. pp. 262–64. Published by W.B. Saunders—1928.
74. "Slums and Housing," James Ford, Vol, 1. p. 117.
75. Ibid Vol. 1. p. 129
76. "Lost and Found, or Life Among the Poor," by Samuel B. Halliday, pp. 199–201.
77. New York Post, June 12, 1854—first reference to Cholera for that year, under head, "The Cholera and Smallpox on Staten Island." Ed.
78. Mr. Fortes' official city title was "City Inspector." At that time the City Inspection staff took care of all the inspection work necessary. It was in this capacity that Mr. Forbes reported for the Health Department. Librarian, Health Department, New York City.
79. "The Tenement House Problem," edited by De Forest & Veiller, Vol. 1, p. 71.
80. "Slums and Housing"—James Ford, Vol. 1, p. 129.
81. Ibid—Vol. 1, p. 117.
82. Ibid—Vol. 1, p. 93. Epidemics of Cholera in New York City, 1832, 1849, 1854.—Ed.
83. "Slums and Housing"—James Ford—Vol. 1, pp. 142.
84. Report to His Honor Fiorello H. LaGuardia, Mayor of the City of New York by the New York City Housing Authority, Jan. 25, 1937.
85. Ibid.
86. Ibid.
87. "Slums and Housing"—James Ford—Vol. 1. p. 146–148.
88. Ibid, p. 145.
89. Ibid, p. 104.
90. Ibid, p. 108.
91. Ibid, p. 108.
92. "Slums and Housing"—James Ford—Vol. 1, p. 108.
93. Tenement House Law of 1867-N.Y.State Statutes, Chap. 908, Sec. 1, Pt. 6.
94. Ibid, Pt. 8.
95. Ibid, Pt. 5.
96. Tenement House Law of 1879-N.Y.State Statutes, Chap. 504, Sec. 1, Pt. 14.

97. Tenement House Law of 1887—Chapter 84, Section 663.
98. New York Tribune, May 5, 1894.
99. "The Tenement House Problem" edited by DeForest & Veiller, Vol. 1, P.105,
100. Report of Tenement House Committee, authorized by Laws of I894, Transmitted to Legislature, January 17, 1895, pp. 98–116.
101. lbid.
102. The New York Tribune, December 17, 1894.
103. New York Herald, December 12, 1894.
104. New York Herald, December 19, 1894.
105. "The New York Observer," January 24, 1895.
106. New York Supplement, Vol. 17, N.Y. Supreme & Lower Court of Record, 1891–2.
107. Ibid.
108. N.Y. Court of Appeals—Vol. 8, 1895.
109. Ibid.
110. Ibid.
111. Ibid.
112. N.Y. Supplement, Vol. 17, New York Supreme and Lower Courts of Record, 1891–92.
113. N.Y. Court of Appeals—Vol. 8, 1895.
114. Ibid.
115. Ibid.
116. Tenement House Laws of 1901—N.Y. State Statutes.
117. Ibid, Chapter 555, part 75.
118. Ibid, Chapter 334, part 14.
119. Tenement House Laws of 1901—N.Y. State Statutes, Chap. 334, part 70.
120. Tenement House Laws of 1901, N.Y. State Statutes, Chapter 334, part 61.
121. Ibid, Chapter 334, Section 79.
122. Ibid.
123. Ibid.
124. "Building America,"—Special Edition on Housing, June, 1935, p. 21.
125. Ibid.
126. Movies of New York City—shots of street scenes in crowded business also slum neighborhoods. Taken by technical staff, Living Newspaper in co-operation with East Side Tenants' Union, New York.—Ed.
127. Valentine's Manual, 1862—also Hall of Records, New York.
128. Ibid.
129. stokes Iconography, Vol. 3, p. 136.
130. Valentine's Manual, 1854—p. 528.
131. "Slums and Blighted Areas in the United States," Edith Elmer Wood, Federal Emergency Administration of Public Works Housing Bulletin #1, p. 13.
132. Ibid.
133. Ibid.
134. "Slums and Blighted Areas in the United States," Edith Elmer Wood, Federal Emergency Administration of Public Works Housing Bulletin #1, p. 13.
135. Knickerbocker Village rental—$12.50 per room per month. Fred F. French Management Company, New York, N.Y.
136. "Toward the End to be Achieved," the New York City Housing Authority—Its History in Outline, 1937—p. 10.
137. "Toward the End to be Achieved," the New York City Housing Authority—Its History in Outline, 1937—p. 11.
138. By July 12, 1937, 19,000 completed applications for apartments in the Williamsburg Development had been received—N.Y.C. Housing Authority.
139. "Report on Negro Community Housing," Will Thomas Williams, Special Consultant.
140. New York Times, October 11, 1936– tenants in Harlem parade, sponsored by Consolidated Tenants' League, Harlem, N.Y.C.

141. Ibid—January 28, 1933, tenants of "Paradise Alley," Avenue A and 11th Street, N.Y.C.
142. Ibid—January 6, 1933—tenants at 1433 Charlotte St., Bronx, N.Y.
143. New York Times—January 17, 1933, Tenants at 226 Barrett Street, Brooklyn, N.Y.
144. "How Tenant Organization keeps down Rents and Improves Housing Conditions." A table for the month of November, 1937, issued by the City-Wide Tenants' Council, New York, N.Y. December 11, 1937.
145. "A Housing Program for the United States," Nathan Straus, pp. 5 & 6.
146. Average rental for "First Houses"—$6.05. "First Houses" can be considered as a yardstick for low-income rentals in New York City. Booklet—"First Houses,"—New York City Housing Authority, p. 26.
147. Land buying transaction based on figures estimated by Real Estate Board of New York, 12 East 41st Street, N.Y.C., in a survey made October 1, 1936—data furnished by National Association of Builders, Owners and Managers.
148. Average costs of material in 1936–37, furnished by Caldwell Wingate, Builders, 101 Park Ave., New York.
149. Carpenters and Joiners District Council, 130 Madison Ave., New York.
150. New York State Mortgage Commission.
151. Congressional Record, August 13, 1937.
152. Ibid.
153. Congressional Record, August 13, 1937.
154. Ibid.
155. "A Housing Program for the United States"—Nathan Straus, p. 12.
156. Congressional Record—August 13, 1937.
157. Average rental for "First Houses" $6.05 per room, per month—booklet, "First Houses," p. 26, New York City Housing Authority.
158. Based on figures from New York City Housing Authority.
159. New York Times, February 25, 1937.
160. Ibid.
161. Congressional Record—Senate, August 2, 1937, p. 10358.
162. Ibid.
163. Ibid.
164. Congressional Record—Senate, Aug. 2, 1937, pp. 10368–9.
165. Ibid.
166. Ibid.
167. Ibid, August 6, 1937, p. 8373.
168. New York Times, July 23, 1937.
169. Congressional Record-Senate Aug. 4, 1937, pp. 10548–55.
170. Ibid.
171. N.Y. Times—Aug. 17, 1932.
172. Congressional Record—Senate, Aug. 4, 1937, pp.10548–55.
173. Ibid.
174. Movies consist of shots taken by N.Y. City Housing Authority and those taken "on location" by Director and Technical Staff ". . . one third of a nation . . ." Winter 1937. Continuity by Living Newspaper technical staff. Ed.
175. N.Y. City Health Dep't. Quarterly Bulletin—1937.
176. "Housing or Else," p. 8 Langdon W. Post, New York City Housing Authority—1936.
177. New York Times, August 22, 1937.
178. Original appropriation Wagner-Steagall Bill, $1,000,000,000.—Ed.
179. Wagner-Steagall Act as passed,—Ed.
180. Wagner-Steagall Act as passed.—Ed.
181. Ibid.
182. New York Post, January 27, 1938.
183. Letter to Living Newspaper from Langdon W. Post—Dec. 10, 1937
184. Thirty million dollars is one and one-half per cent of two billion dollars.—Ed.
185. At rate of thirty million dollars in four years, it will take 356 years for the total appropriation to equal two billion dollars.—Ed.

186. Interview with Miss Alfred, Dec. 7, 1937.
187. Speech made at conference of Mayors, Washington, DC, Nov. 17, 1937.
188. New York Post, January 27, 1938.
189. "Yearbook of Labor Statistics"—1935–1936—International Labor Office, League of Nations, Geneva. "American Public Housing through British Eyes," Richard Reiss in, "Housing Officials Yearbook," 1936.
190. New York State Statutes—Municipal Reference Library,
191. Second Inaugural Address. Hon. Franklin D. Roosevelt, President of the United States, Washington, DC, Jan. 20, 1937.
192. News flashes of events that have occurred are used—calamaties that are traceable to bad housing. The three above flashes have been used to date.—Ed.
193. Reported by Research Worker on Living Newspaper Staff, 2–24–38.
194. Daily Mirror, March 9, 1938.
195. New York Sun, March 12, 1938.
196. Foreign Policy report—February 15, 1937, Vol. 12, No. 23, Foreign Policy Association.

Part 5
Systems of Government

THE RISE OF FASCISM, ISOLATIONIST AND INTERVENTIONIST THEATRE

18. *It Can't Happen Here*—Sinclair Lewis and John C. Moffitt

Commentary

Sources

Play

18.1 *IT CAN'T HAPPEN HERE*—SUSAN QUINN

These are not normal times; the people are jumpy and very ready to run after strange gods.
—Franklin Delano Roosevelt, 1935

ON MAY 13, 1935, THE BULLET-RIDDLED BODY of a young father named Charles Poole was discovered in a ditch on a lonely road outside Dearborn, Michigan. The timing of his murder added to its cruelty: His wife was in the hospital when he died, giving birth to the couple's second child. Police were puzzled at first: The Poole murder looked like a gangster killing. But Poole was a family man without vices or known enemies. Like millions of others, he had lost his job, then found work on a WPA project after FDR took office. What could have provoked such violent retribution against a seeming innocent?

Charles Poole was murdered because he broke ranks with an organization called the Black Legion, active in the industrial cities of Ohio, Michigan, and Indiana and claiming the allegiance of 135,000 in Michigan alone. According to their creed, the enemies of the Black Legion were "all aliens, Negroes, Jews and cults and creeds believing in racial equality or owing allegiance to any foreign potentates. These we will fight without fear or favor as long as one foe of American liberty is left alive." The Black Legionnaires claimed to be heirs to the Minutemen, freeing the country of foreign domination.

The Black Legion's leverage came from its ability to provide jobs to desperate men. With the aid of industry leaders opposed to union activity, the legion controlled hiring in certain pockets of the steel and auto industry as well as certain New Deal welfare jobs. Leaders boasted that they ran the entire Federal Emergency Relief Administration in Allen country, Indiana. Indeed, at a time when many were still without work, Black Legion members, even when they came from out of state, all seemed to have jobs. As the investigation proceeded, it became increasingly clear that the Depression was the Black Legion's most powerful recruiting tool.

Around the time the Black Legion arrests were shocking the country, Senator Huey Long of Louisiana reached out to the nation with his "Share Our Wealth" campaign. Huey Long, aka "Kingfish," argued that wealth in America should be taken out of the hands of the few and distributed to the many. He proposed new laws that would use millionaires' incomes to provide every household in America with a "homestead allowance" of $5,000. In the first three months of 1935, Long went on national radio six times. After each broadcast, his office received as many as sixty thousand letters from converts to his cause. Few doubted that Long's timing was linked to presidential ambitions.

The red-nosed, potbellied Huey Long did good things for the poorest people in his state. When Hallie Flanagan visited New Orleans on an inspection tour of Federal Theatre Project units in 1935, she was impressed. "Huey, like Benito [Mussolini]," she wrote in her notebook, "thought in epic sweep. He thought in terms of roads, sea walls, park systems, trade schools, all for his own glory possibly, but also for the people who had never had roads, parks, schools."

Huey Long was famous for getting what he wanted: When he was elected governor, he tore down the governor's mansion, which he considered a hopeless antique, and made his mistress secretary of state. But these were minor infractions compared with his assault on the democratic institutions of the state: He introduced a bill that established a separate police force, answerable only to him, and he required all state workers to contribute 20 percent of their salaries to his coffers. He even kidnapped critics who threatened to expose him.

Long had been an effective campaigner for FDR in 1932, but not long after that the two had parted ways, following a visit in which the Kingfish tried to collect favors from "Frank" for his allegiance. By the time of the 1936 campaign, Roosevelt had come to dislike Huey Long immensely and insisted that no one in his administration have anything to do with him.

On the other hand, FDR tried to stay on the good side of another influential demagogue, the radio priest Father Charles Coughlin. Father Coughlin was the first preacher to make use of mass media as a persuasive tool, and he did it with stunning success. By 1935, he had become one of the most popular men in America, receiving eighty thousand admiring letters a day from those who listened with rapt attention to his *Hour of Power* on the radio.

While Long named the names of his enemies, Coughlin preferred to ascribe all problems to a shadowy conspiracy. Coughlin blamed Jewish international financiers for the Depression and the Communists for everything else. When possible, he combined the two enemies: As a star witness for a congressional committee investigating the Communist threat in 1930, Coughlin explained that "the Hebrew Karl Marx" had invented communism and predicted that the Communists were likely to take over America "by 1933, unless something is done." By the time the 1936 presidential campaign got into full swing, Coughlin was calling FDR the "anti-God." "As I was instrumental in removing Herbert Hoover from the White House," he intoned, "so help me God, I will be instrumental in taking a Communist foe from the chair once occupied by Washington."

Both Long and Coughlin appealed to people for whom the New Deal seemed remote and complicated. According to them, the enemy was centralized power in the hands of a few—in the hands of greedy millionaires, according to Long, or alien money changers, according to Father Coughlin. Ironically, both derived their power from radio, a centralizing force if ever there was one. Like Roosevelt, they were masters of the medium.

Father Coughlin's radio voice was his greatest asset, a "beautiful baritone," according to novelist Wallace Stegner, which "always began in a low rich pitch, speaking slowly, gradually increasing in tempo and vehemence, then soaring to high and passionate tones." Although born in Canada and broadcasting out of Detroit, Coughlin enhanced his appeal with the rolled r's and old-country pronunciations of his Irish ancestors. He was especially popular in states like Massachusetts, which had large Irish Catholic populations.

Long, too, was a gifted radio speaker—some said even better than FDR, whose "fireside chats" had captivated the nation. The question in the Roosevelt camp, as the 1936 election approached, was whether FDR's substance could triumph over the paranoia and anger stirred up by the radio demagogues. Their rise, paralleling the rise of Mussolini and Hitler in Europe and Stalin in the Soviet Union, made many fear that the country might be veering toward totalitarianism.

That summer, while Father Coughlin was packing them in at Madison Square Garden and Huey Long was recruiting for Share Our Wealth over the radio, the novelist Sinclair Lewis put the finishing touches on *It Can't Happen Here*, his fictional account of a 1936 Fascist takeover of America. Leading the charge, in Sinclair Lewis's novel, was a character named Buzz Windrip, a country boy who boasted in his campaign biography that he was not an educated man but had "read the Bible through from kiver to kiver . . . some eleven times." Buzz Windrip was, like Huey Long, a "Professional

Common Man" with "a luminous, ungrudging smile which . . . he turned on and off deliberately like an electric light."

In the Lewis novel, a character named Bishop Prang is a stand-in for Father Coughlin. The bishop's organization of millions operates under the banner of the "League of Forgotten Men" (echoing Roosevelt, who had famously spoken of "the forgotten man"). Bishop comes out foursquare in support of Windrip for president. "And may the Lord guide him and us," the bishop prays on the radio, "across the desert of iniquitous politics and swinishly grasping finance into the golden glory of the Promised Land!"

Up until that juncture, there is more talk than action. But once Windrip, with the endorsement of the bishop, becomes president, the novel takes a frightening turn into the territory of the Black Legion. The soldiers of Windrip's army of Corpos (named for Windrip's ruling Corporative Party) are backed up by a terrorizing militia who claim, like the Black Legionnaires, to be heirs to the original Minutemen.

No doubt Sinclair Lewis, who was famous for accumulating detail from real life, relied heavily on newspaper reports in his creation of the Corpos, the Minute Men, Bishop Prang, and Buzz Windrip. But the most important source for his tale of Fascist horror was the firsthand knowledge his wife, Dorothy Thompson, had acquired as a journalist in Adolf Hitler's Germany.

Dorothy Thompson was among the first to interview Adolf Hitler and to alert the world to the Nazi menace. Within a week of the Nazi takeover, she was writing home to her husband, Sinclair Lewis, about "the chancellor's private army, the S.A. troops, and their picked division, the black-breeched S.S. men" who "broke up opposition meetings, terrorized the streets, staged rows, beat up Social Democratic deputies, and even assaulted leading Catholics."

"You must believe it," she wrote a friend, "because I saw victims with my own eyes . . . They beat them with steel rods, knock their teeth out with revolver butts, break their arms—a favorite trick—give them a liter of castor oil; bring them out of unconsciousness by throwing water in their faces, or mustard in their eyes, urinate on them, make them kneel and kiss the Hakenkreuz [the swastika]." She added: "Not a single newspaper dares to bring out anything of true events."

Because of her bold and early truth telling, Dorothy Thompson was expelled from Germany in 1934.

[. . .]

Had it not been for Dorothy Thompson, Sinclair Lewis would never have written *It Can't Happen Here.* Her detailed knowledge of events in Germany turned up everywhere in his American version of fascism: His torturers used the same methods, right down to the castor oil, his MMs were clearly an American version of the Nazi SS. And the overarching message of the book came from Thompson, who held that Hitler come to power in Germany "because so-called civilized people did not believe that he could."

[. . .]

Not long after Sinclair Lewis created the character of Buzz Windrip, his real-life inspiration ceased to be. On September 8, 1935, a young man dressed in a white linen suit suddenly broke through the phalanx of bodyguards surrounding Senator Huey Long as he left a session of the Louisiana legislature in Baton Rouge. The man in white withdrew a pistol from his pocket and fired it into Long's abdomen at close range. Within thirty hours, the Kingfish was no more.

Sinclair Lewis's story interested Hollywood nonetheless. MGM hired the well-known writer Sidney Howard to adapt *It Can't Happen Here* for the screen. But after spending $200,000 on the script, the studio dropped the project: Executives in the foreign department feared it might lead to a ban on all MGM pictures in Fascist countries. The MGM decision, which so clearly reinforced the point of Lewis's novel, resulted in a doubling of sales of the book, from twenty-five hundred to five thousand a week. It also caught the attention of Hallie Flanagan and her play bureau director, Francis Bosworth. Very soon, they were talking about the possibility of a Federal Theatre production of *It Can't Happen Here*. Then Bosworth made a highly unusual proposal: Instead of mounting one production of *It Can't Happen Here* in New York, why not open the play simultaneously in theatres all around the country?

Hallie Flanagan immediately loved the idea.

[. . .]

As Hallie Flanagan put it in a message to Federal Theatre employees, the plan provided theatres with a chance to do innovative, *American* theatre. "We are committed to the belief that we will not find material for plays or methods of production by imitating the past or by borrowing from abroad," she wrote. "We want to do *It Can't Happen Here* because it is a play by one of our most distinguished American writers. We want to do it because it is a play about American life today, based on the passionate belief in American democracy. The play says that when dictatorship comes to threaten such a democracy it comes in an apparently harmless guise, with parades and promises; but that when such dictatorship arrives the promises are not kept and the parade grounds become encampments. We want to do *It Can't Happen Here* because, like Doremus Jessup [the novel's newspaperman and hero] and his creator Sinclair Lewis, we, as American citizens and as workers in a theatre sponsored by the government of the United States, should like to do what we can to keep alive the 'free, enquiring, critical spirit' which is the center and core of a democracy." Hallie Flanagan's repeated use of the word *American* was clearly aimed at critics like Harrison Grey Fiske, who claimed she was out to "Russianize" the Federal Theatre Project.

[. . .]

The final version of the play called *It Can't Happen Here* opens in Mt. Beulah, a small Vermont town that strongly resembles Sinclair Lewis's own Barnard. A homespun ignoramus named Berzelius "Buzz" Windrip has just been elected president, on the Corporative Party ticket, and the inhabitants of Mt. Beulah are reacting with varying degrees of excitement and skepticism. Doremus Jessup, the sensible editor of the town's newspaper, is thinking this Buzz Windrip might not be so bad: The youth are jobless and unruly, and Windrip is providing them with a new mission, recruiting them to march in his "Corpo" militia. Editor Jessup, a widower, has a woman friend named Lorinda Pike, who writes for the society pages of the paper. Lorinda, like the real-life Dorothy Parker, senses trouble from the start. She doesn't want Jessup to have anything to do with President Buzz Windrip or his Vermont deputies. "Get enough people in uniform and any fool knows what happens next," she declares.

Lorinda's worst fears are realized. When a spirited local grocer confronts and jeers at the "Corpos" parading past his store, he's beaten up and killed. When Jessup's son-in-law decries the murder, he, too, is murdered. Jessup, though terrified at first, realizes he must join the opposition, and he and Lorinda, along with his widowed daughter and a few sensible townspeople, begin a furious underground effort to distribute anti-Corpo literature. Jessup is discovered, arrested, and beaten with a metal fishing rod (offstage), then sent to a concentration camp. The final scene takes place at the Canadian border, as the anti-Corpo conspirators attempt to escape the country and join the opposition government in exile. The editor Jessup and his companion, Lorinda, make it through, as does his grandson, but Jessup's daughter is discovered.

There were several different versions of what would happen next, during the frenetic writing and rewriting. But in the final version, Jessup's daughter, Mary, avenges her slain husband by shooting the corporal who murdered him. A border guard then shoots and kills Mary. The curtain goes down on Mary saying final words of farewell to her son and to her father, Doremus, who lives on to fight the Corpos another day.

[. . .]

On October 27, 1936, *It Can't Happen Here* opened simultaneously on twenty-one different stages in twenty-one different versions, each reflecting local sensibilities and capabilities. On that night and subsequent nights, one thousand theatre people all around the country were working onstage and backstage, and twenty thousand were in the audience, watching a play that raised timely questions about totalitarianism. "Through a subtle twist in emphasis in a time of emergency," Brooks Atkinson wrote, "the code of political morals which is popularly looked upon as American might prepare the ground for a Fascist dictatorship. Many of our bullying jingoes are Fascist when they believe that they are defending the faith of the Founding Fathers. The American who hates foreigners and screams 'Red' whenever he encounters a difference of opinion could join in a Fascist dictatorship under the pious impression that he were saving American democracy . . . Americans are easily stampeded into righteousness; they dote on evangelism—for a year or two. And a sincere man with a magnetic personality might make a Fascist dictatorship sound holy . . .

"Thousands of Americans who do not know what a Fascist dictatorship would mean," Brooks Atkinson concluded, "now have an opportunity to find out, thanks to Mr. Lewis' energetic public spirit and the Federal Theatre's wide facilities."

Every production had its own backstage stories to tell.

[. . .]

The Yiddish production included a scene in which Jessup, the newspaper editor, is imprisoned in a concentration camp, which had been cut from the Adelphi version. "We were beginning to get all the refugees from Austria and Germany—the Jewish refugees—at this time," another audience member recalled. "At the Yiddish theatre opening, there were two or three people that fainted. They were identifying."

[. . .]

Productions by minority companies found ways to make *It Can't Happen Here* relevant to their audiences. The only Spanish-language production, in Tampa, cast Buzz Windrip, Bishop Prang, and the Corpo overlord as non-Spanish types, while the rest of the cast were recent Cuban immigrants. In Seattle, the Negro theatre company took a similar tack: Three white actors were cast in the parts of the Fascist leaders, and the rest of the cast, including the courageous Doremus Jessup and his cohorts, were African Americans. The locale was changed to the black section of Seattle.

[. . .]

It Can't Happen Here wound up playing a total of 260 weeks, or five years, in theatres all around the country. It was seen by more than 316,000 people. "No one agreed on the play," Hallie Flanagan told an audience some months later, "but everyone had to see it. It was called good, bad, savage, mild, American, un-American, Fascist, communist, too far left, too far right, a work of genius, a work of the devil." There was, she conceded, "some mystic connection with the coming election, though whether the play was designed to elect Mr. Roosevelt or to defeat him was a moot question."

Some claimed that the entire undertaking had been aimed at bolstering support for FDR and the New Deal. Harold Lord Varney, writing in the Hearst-controlled *New York American*, complained that *It Can't Happen Here* was "a venomed libel upon the D.A.R., the American Legion, Rotary International, and all of the other non-radical movements" and went on to attack Hallie Flanagan as "a pathetic misfit as director of the Federal Theatre project. In any other administration except the present one it would quickly sound the gong upon her career of government financed leftism."

But a few others saw *It Can't Happen Here* differently. It was, after all, the Republican opposition that had been warning of FDR's dictatorial ways. *It Can't Happen Here*, wrote a Seattle critic, "might be called propaganda against the very government which was the 'angel' for the production of the play." To this critic of the Roosevelt regime, the title of the play could have been changed to *It Is Happening Here*.

18.2 GEN. BUTLER BARES "FASCIST PLOT" TO SEIZE GOVERNMENT BY FORCE

The New York Times, November 21st 1934

Gen. Butler Bares "Fascist Plot"
To Seize Government by Force
Says Bond Salesman, as Representative of Wall St. Group, Asked Him to Lead Army of 500,000 in March on Capital—Those Named Make Angry Denials—Dickstein Gets Charge.

A PLOT OF WALL STREET INTERESTS to overthrow President Roosevelt and establish a Fascist dictatorship, backed by a private army of 500,000 ex-soldiers and others, was charged by Major Gen. Smedley D. Butler, retired Marine Corps officer, who appeared yesterday before the House of Representatives Committee on Un-American Activities, which began hearings on the charges.

Meeting in executive session at the Bar Association, it heard testimony from General Butler and Gerald P. MacGuire, a bond salesman in the Stock Exchange firm of Grayson M.-P. Murphy & Co., 52 Broadway, named by General Butler as having urged him to head the proposed Fascist army.

There were immediate emphatic denials by the purported plotters.

From Philadelphia came word that General Butler had told friends there that General Hugh S. Johnson, former NRA administrator, was scheduled for the rôle of dictator, and that J. P. Morgan & Co. as well as Murphy & Co. were behind the plot.

General Johnson led the chorus of denials. Told of General Butler's charges, he barked:

"He had better be pretty damn careful. Nobody said a word to me about anything of this kind, and if they did I'd throw them out the window. I know nothing about it."

Thomas W. Lamont, partner in the firm of J. P. Morgan & Co., said:

"Perfect moonshine! Too unutterably ridiculous to comment upon!"

Said Colonel Grayson M.-P. Murphy:

"A fantasy! I can't imagine how any one could produce it or any sane person believe it. It is absolutely false so far as it relates to me and my firm, and I don't believe there is a word of truth in it with respect to Mr. MacGuire."

Mr. MacGuire, the alleged intermediary, said:

"It's a joke—a publicity stunt. I know nothing about it. The matter is made out of whole cloth. I deny the story completely."

In Washington, aides of General Douglas MacArthur, Chief of Staff, who was confined to his quarters with a heavy cold, expressed amazement and amusement when told that the "plotters," according to General Butler, had used General MacArthur's name as an alternate for head of the Fascist army if General Butler did not accept.

Another alternate as "the man on the white horse" to head the army, General Butler said, was Hanford MacNider, former national commander of the American Legion.

General Butler's story was that MacGuire approached him first with the Fascist army proposition last Summer, and then arranged for Robert Sterling Clark, a wealthy New Yorker with offices in the Stock Exchange Building, to visit him at Butler's home in Newtown Square, Pa.

Says $3,000,000 Was Subscribed.

MacGuire told him that the financial backers of the movement had subscribed $3,000,000, according to General Butler. He added that he was to assemble his 500,000 men in Washington, probably a year from now, with the expectation that such a show of force would enable it to take over the government peacefully in a few days.

It was hoped that President Roosevelt would "go along" as the King of Italy did with Mussolini, according to the story, but if he did not he, the Vice President and the Secretary of State would be forced to resign after appointing the proposed "dictator" as a new Secretary of State, who under the Constitution would then succeed to the Presidency.

General Butler was quoted as saying that Mr. MacGuire had tossed $18,000 in thousand-dollar bills on the bed of General Butler's hotel room in Newark, N.J., on one occasion, "to pay his expenses" in an unsuccessful effort to persuade him to make a speech in favor of the gold standard before the American Legion in Chicago. He also said that Mr. MacGuire showed him a bank book with deposits of $64,000 to "take care of his (Butler's) expenses" at Chicago and several checks drawn for large amounts by Mr. Clark, Colonel Murphy and John Mills to be placed to Butler's account for expenses at Chicago. Later, General Butler added, Mr. MacGuire told him that the same people who financed "the Chicago propaganda" were going to finance the Fascist "march on Washington."

Representative John W. McCormack of Massachusetts, chairman, and Representative Samuel Dickstein of New York, vice chairman, were the only members of the House committee at yesterday's session. They heard General Butler for about two hours in the morning, Mr. MacGuire an equal period in the afternoon. They also heard Captain Samuel Glazier, in charge of the CCC camp at Elkridge, Md.

According to Representative Dickstein, General Butler in his testimony substantiated most of the statements attributed to him and denied none. Both members said that General Butler made it clear that he had flatly rejected all proposals from the Fascist group.

Thorough Inquiry Planned.

Mr. McCormack announced that the committee would make a thorough investigation of General Butler's charges.

"We have been in possession of certain information for about five weeks and have been investigating it. We will call all the men mentioned in the story, although Mr. Clark is reported to be in Europe."

"From present indications," said Mr. Dickstein, "Butler has the evidence. He's not going to make any serious charges unless he has something to back them up. We'll have men here with bigger names than his."

Mr. Dickstein said that about sixteen persons mentioned by General Butler to the committee would be subpoenaed, and that a public hearing might be held next Monday. Mr. MacGuire was directed to reappear before the committee at 2 o'clock this afternoon.

After testifying before the committee, Mr. MacGuire told reporters that he was a personal friend of General Butler, and had last seen him about six months ago when he went to Philadelphia to sell some bonds. They talked about an adequate military force for the nation and world affairs in general, he said, and never discussed a Fascist army or movement.

Colonel Murphy specifically denied to reporters that he had financed any Fascist plot, and characterized the statement that he had made out a check for General Butler's Chicago expenses as "an absolute lie." He said that he did not know General Butler and had never heard of the reputed Fascist movement until yesterday's charges were published.

Colonel Murphy said that he voted for President Roosevelt in 1932. Newspaper clippings show that the Mr. Clark named by General Butler, made a cash contribution of $10,000 to the Democratic National Committee last year.

18.3 HUEY LONG OBITUARY

New York Times, September 11th 1935

OF HUEY LONG PERSONALLY it is no longer necessary to speak except with charity. His motives, his character, have passed beyond human judgment. People will long talk of his picturesque career and extraordinary individual qualities. He carried daring to the point of audacity. He did not hesitate to flaunt his great personal vainglory in public. This he would probably have defended both as a form of self-confidence, and a means of impressing the public. He had a knack of always getting into the picture, and often bursting out of its frame. There would be no end if one were to try to enumerate all his traits, so distinct and so full of color. He succeeded in establishing a legend about himself—a legend of invincibility—which it will be hard to dissipate.

It is to Senator Long as a public man, rather than as a dashing personality, that the thoughts of Americans should chiefly turn as his tragic death extinguishes the envy. What he did and what he promised to do are full of political instruction and also of warning. In his own State of Louisiana he showed how it is possible to destroy self-government while maintaining its ostensible and legal form. He made himself an unquestioned dictator, though a State Legislature was still elected by a nominally free people, as was also a Governor, who was, however, nothing but a dummy for Huey Long. In reality, Senator Long set up a Fascist government in Louisiana. It was disguised, but only thinly. There was no outward appearance of a revolution, no march of Black Shirts upon Baton Rouge, but the effectual result was to lodge all the power of the State in the hands of one man.

If Fascism ever comes in the United States it will come in something like that way. No one will set himself up as an avowed dictator, but if he can succeed in dictating everything, the name does not matter. Laws and Constitutions guaranteeing liberty and individual rights may remain on the statute books, but the life will have gone out of them. Institutions may be designated as before, but they will have become only empty shells. We thus have an indication of the points at which American vigilance must be eternal if it desires to withstand the subtle inroads of the Fascist spirit. There is no need to be on the watch for a revolutionary leader to rise up and call upon his followers to march on Washington. No such sinister figure is likely to appear. The danger is, as Senator Long demonstrated in Louisiana, that freedom may be done away with in the name of efficiency and a strong paternal government.

Senator Long's career is also a reminder that material for the agitator and the demagogue is always ample in this country. He found it and played upon it skillfully, first of all in what may be called the lower levels of society in Louisiana. Afterward, when he began to swell with national ambition, and cast about for a fetching cry, he found it, or thought he did, in his vague formulas, never worked out, about the "distribution of wealth." For a time he seemed in this way to be about to fascinate and capture a great multitude of followers, or at least endorsers, mainly in the cities of this country. There is reason to believe that his hold upon them was relaxing before his assassination. Many observers thought that he had already passed the peak of his national influence. Be that as it may, the moral of his remarkable adventure in politics remains the same. It is that in the United States we have to re-educate each generation in the fundamentals of self government and in the principles of sound finance. And we must have leaders able to defend the faith that is in them. When such masses of people are all too ready to run after a professed miracle-worker, it is essential that we have trained minds to confront the ignorant, to show to the credulous the error of their ways, and to keep alive and fresh the true tradition of democracy in which this country was cradled and brought to maturity.

18.4 NAZI GARDEN PARTY

New York Times, February 26th 1939

BY THE LAST CENSUS, NEW YORK CITY had 237,000 German-born residents. What percentage of this group has been won to Nazi ideology is a matter of guesswork, but last week the pro-Hitler element demonstrated its ability to hire and fill the city's biggest hall. Madison Square Garden's 19,000 seats were occupied by members of the German-American Bund and the aisles were patrolled by a uniformed "Ordnungsdienst" 3,000 strong. Hundreds of police and detectives were inside the hall, too, and in the streets outside some 1,700 of New York's finest, on foot and on horseback, were massed to prevent a counter-demonstration by anti-Nazis.

In Washington's Name

The rally, billed as an "Americanism" meeting in honor of George Washington's Birthday, was featured by anti-Semitic speeches reminiscent of Berlin and by attacks on President Roosevelt and his Cabinet. Two incidents occurred. Dorothy Thompson, the writer, was temporarily ejected because she laughed at statements which the audience cheered. Isadore Greenbaum, an unemployed plumber's helper, was beaten as he attempted to mount the platform during an address by Fritz Kuhn, the Bund's "Fuehrer"; he was arrested and fined for disorderly conduct.

Outside the hall there were more arrests. The police lines, which Police Commissioner Valentine said were big enough "to stop a revolution," were strained by the task of keeping anti-Nazis away from the Garden. Although there were a number of scuffles, the police accomplished their mission of preventing a violent clash between the Nazis and their foes. There were subsequent protests against the police from local anti-Nazi groups. In Berlin the newspapers declared that the disturbances were "a challenge to Germandom in America." Mayor La Guardia, defending the city's action in permitting and protecting the meeting, said: "It was a contrast between the way we do things here and the way they do things here."

18.5 COUGHLIN IS GERMAN HERO—OTTO D. TOLISCHUS

New York Times, 27th November 1938

The German hero in America for the moment is the Rev. Charles E. Coughlin because of his radio speech representing national socialism as a defensive front against bolshevism. His objection to radio censorship is characterized as the revelation of a "typical case of Jewish terrorism of American public opinion."

At the same time, despite the vast propaganda campaign at home, conducted through the radio, press and thousands of mass meetings throughout the country, to convince the German people of the justice of the recent anti-Jewish excesses and prepare them for even more radical measures, such large sections of the population remain unconvinced that the persuasion is being more and more supplemented with threats.

Following the warning by the Schwarzekorps, the organ of the secret police and Elite Guard, that the "rabble" that objects to anti-Semitic measures will have its "mouth shut" with "a well-built fist under its nose," the Fraenkische Tageszeitung, Julius Streicher's newspaper, today drums such objectors out of the German national community and tells them to get out of the country.

"There are," it says, "still some contemporaries in Germany—if only a small fraction—who live behind the moon and also such who never understood national socialism and never will.

"They snapped up from foreign newspapers and the Strasbourg radio some phrases of 'fairy tales about the poor Jews.' Some old women—there are some in skirts and some in pants—who prattled this idiocy about the Jews and in the end believed it.

"The time has come to make a final stand against such an attitude even if it comes from a very small section of the people. And it must be clearly stated that such contemporaries no longer fit among the German people, that German people which as a whole has shown itself so decent and so great as never before in history.

"These creatures, these friends of Jews and slaves of Jews, deserve no better treatment than the Jews themselves. Since they take the stand for the Jewish murder rabble let them leave our German fatherland with the Jews. Nobody held them back. Let them go where the Jews are still in power."

At the same time Dr. Joseph Goebbels, Propaganda Minister, announced in a second speech in the Reich Kultur Chamber that now that German culture had been cleansed of Jews and German artists stand by the Third Reich with all their heart, "not a few of those who in 1933 left Germany for ideological reasons are begging in urgent letters for permission to return and work again in the new Germany."

18.6 FATHER COUGHLIN PRAISED BY A FASCIST NEWSPAPER

New York Times, January 17th 1939

By The Associated Press.

ROME, Jan. 16.—The Rev. Charles E. Coughlin of Royal Oak, Mich., received fascist praise and thanks today from the Regime Fascista, the newspaper that has led attacks on the Vatican in the dispute over the Italian anti-Semitic measures.

Characterizing the priest as a man who "appreciates our line of conduct," the Regime Fascista said that "Italians cannot fail to express their sympathy to this apostle of Christianity."

The newspaper, which is edited by Roberto Farinacci, former secretary of the fascist party, said that the Vatican had attempted "in vain" to silence the priest's radio talks, which had shown "the peril to humanity and especially to Christianity of the demogogic and provocate words of [President] Roosevelt."

18.7 COVER OF *SOCIAL JUSTICE*

NATIONAL WEEKLY

Social Justice

Founded 1936 by Father Coughlin

Royal Oak, Michigan June 5, 1939 10¢

BOYCOTT FORCES 'WINS' TO CANCEL FR. COUGHLIN

BLAME FOR ACTION PUT ON JEWISH-CONTROLLED ADVERTISING PRESSURE

FATHER COUGHLIN

THIS WEEK'S NEWS THIS WEEK

FROM THE TOWER By Father Coughlin

JEWS DEMAND U. S. CLOSE MAIL TO FR. COUGHLIN

A PROFESSOR'S HOLIDAY SAVES PORTUGAL

Detroit Historical Society

Anti-Semitic Roman Catholic priest and radio personality Charles Coughlin on the front cover of his newspaper *Social Justice* advertising how Jews forced him off radio station 'WINS'.

18.8 18 SEIZED IN PLOT TO OVERTHROW THE U.S.

The New York Times, January 15th 1940

18 SEIZED IN PLOT TO OVERTHROW U.S.; ARMS FOUND HERE

LINKED TO 'TERROR'

J. E. Hoover Says Bombs Seized Were to Blast Important Centers

GUARD MEMBERS INVOLVED

Secret Group Within Christian Front Rounded Up in Raids by Agents of FBI

J. EDGAR HOOVER, CHIEF of the Federal Bureau of Investigation, announced yesterday the arrest of eighteen members of the Christian Front, an anti-Semitic organization, on charges of plotting the overthrow of the Government of the United States. For equipment in this undertaking they were found to possess eighteen cans of cordite, an explosive; twelve Springfield rifles of .30-'06 caliber, 3,500 rounds of .30-'06 ammunition and a small assortment of other arms.

More than half of those seized were either in the New York National Guard—one of them holding the rank of captain—or had served in other branches of the armed forces of the nation, either actively or as reservists. The ammunition for the Springfields was said to have been stolen from National Guard armories and checks were being made to determine if the rifles and other equipment had come from the same source.

Two Named as Principals

Mr. Hoover named as the two principals among the group arrested William Gerald Bishop, head of a secret group within the Christian Front known as "The Sports Club," or "The Country Gentlemen," and John F. Cassidy, whom he named as head of the Christian Front in Brooklyn. The National Guard captain was John T. Prout Jr. of Astoria, Queens, whose command is in the 165th Infantry Regiment.

The FBI chief said that the men had, in conversations among themselves, laid down a program that was to begin with efforts to recruit a larger force, to augment their store of arms and ammunition from the stores of the National Guard, to lay down a campaign of terrorizing Jews and go on to bombings of the Jewish Daily Forward, The Daily Worker, the Cameo Theatre in West Forty-second Street, which shows Russian-made films, and quarters of the American League for Peace and Democracy in Brooklyn.

These conversations, it was charged, also included plans for the blasting of bridges and the seizure of all utility facilities—power plants, telegraph and telephone networks—docks and railway terminals, the United States Custom House, the General Postoffice and the Federal Reserve Bank in order to obtain control of the gold supply.

Dictatorship Aim Charged

"Plans were discussed," said Mr. Hoover, "for the wholesale sabotage and blowing up of all these institutions so that a dictatorship could be set up here, similar to the Hitler dictatorship in Germany, seizing the reins of government in this country as Hitler did in Germany. Their scheme was to spread a reign of terrorism so that the authorities would become thoroughly demoralized."

One of the aims of the group was the eradication of the Jews of the United States, Mr. Hoover said.

The fantastic notion of a program of such size being carried out by eighteen men with twelve rifles and eighteen bombs—in a city with 18,000 well-equipped police and several regiments of United States Army regulars handy—was apparently no part of their thought.

Bishop Addressed as "Fuehrer"

Mr. Hoover said that the Christian Front's "Sports Club" had been carrying on training for this venture in a revolutionary putsch at a rented camp at Narrowsburg, _. _., where it had a rifle range, and that on Jan. 20 courses in bomb-throwing were to have been begun. At the camp, Mr. Hoover reported, the "Sports Club" members addressed Bishop as "Fuehrer" and accorded him the Nazi salute.

Five of the eighteen men from the anti-Semitic Christian Front who were arrested by the FBI in a plot to revolt against the U.S. government.

The men held meetings in the homes of various of their number, and the rifles, ammunition and other weapons making up their arsenal were found in various homes where the arrests were made.

These were as a result of a systematic round-up that began late Saturday. The men were all arrested on charges of seditious conspiracy under Section 6 of the United States Code. They were charged with conspiring to "overthrow and destroy the Government of the United States, to oppose by force of arms the authority of the United States Government, and to seize and take possession of property of the United States." A fine of $5,000 and a prison sentence of six years constitute maximum punishment for the offense.

Christian Front is a name that has been used by a half dozen organizations, and has been applied to a loosely cooperative federation of all of the anti-Semitic and fascist organizations in the country.

Mr. Hoover declined to say whether this Christian Front was affiliated with other anti-Semetic organizations. He pointed out that only one of the defendants was a member of the Bund.

There was no estimate of the actual size of Cassidy's organization, beyond one which gave it "probably 2,000 to 3,000" members.

Cassidy has from time to time advocated violence. As long as a year ago, in a speech in Brooklyn, he declared, "We have tried the pen and now must try the sword," but he qualified his utterances by declaring all advances must be made by "constitutional means."

He was reported to have been a follower of Father Coughlin at one time. He appeared as a speaker on the same platform with the Rev. Edward Lodge Curran of Brooklyn in Prospect Hall, Brooklyn, on Jan. 25, 1939, at a meeting called by the Committee for the Defense of Americans Constitutional Rights, and at that time described himself as the chairman of Christian Americans Citizens Committee on Communism. The meeting was held to cheer the "principles of social justice" exemplified by General Franco in Spain.

It was to Cassidy that Mr. Hoover attributed statements to the effect that the bombs would be used to "blow up the whole God damn Police Department," and the plan to kill twelve Representatives who voted for repeal of the arms embargo "to teach them a lesson."

18.9 WPA POSTER OF *IT CAN'T HAPPEN HERE*

WPA poster for the Detroit Federal Theater's 1936 production of Sinclair Lewis' *It Can't Happen Here.* Lewis' play exhibits national concerns about the rise of fascism both in Europe and the United States.

18.10 PRODUCTION PHOTO FROM *IT CAN'T HAPPEN HERE*

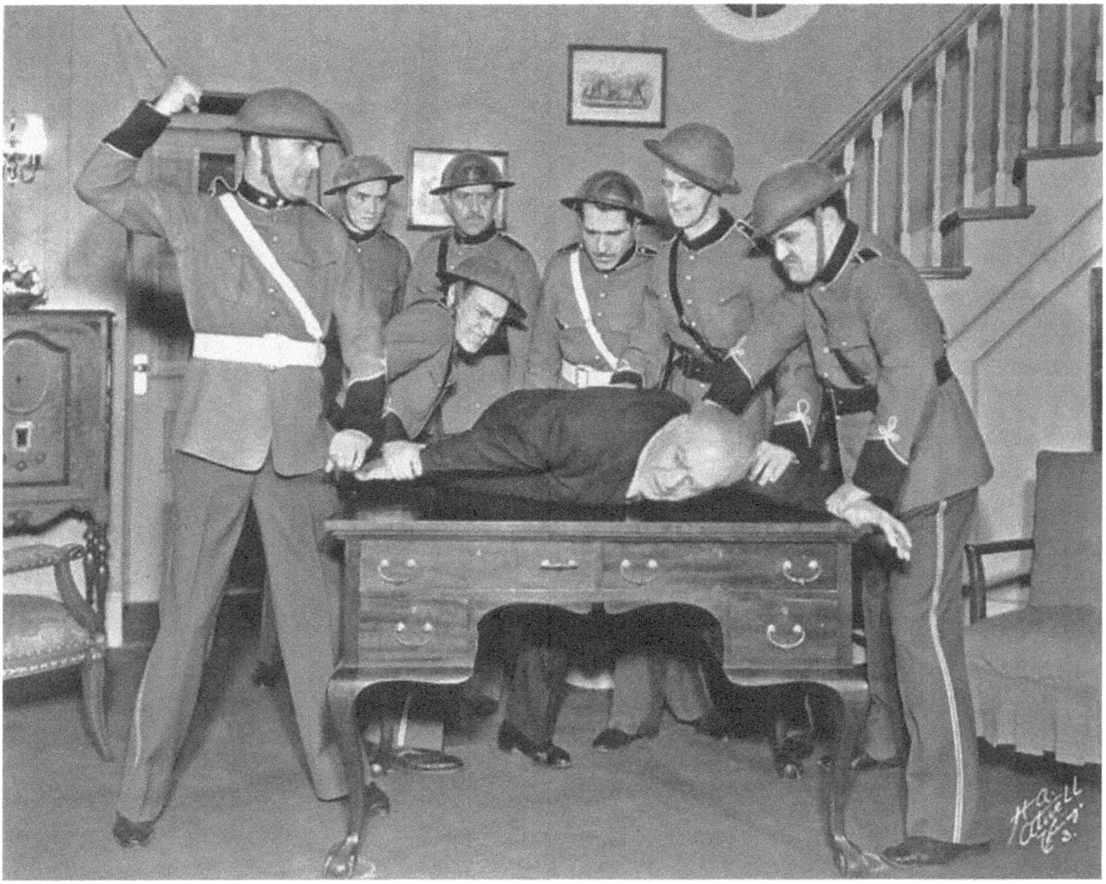

Fascism comes to the United States in the 1936 Cleveland production of *It Can't Happen Here*.

18.11 *IT CAN'T HAPPEN HERE*—SINCLAIR LEWIS AND JOHN C. MOFFITT

LIST OF CHARACTERS

DOREMUS JESSUP. Kindly and liberal New England newspaper editor. In his late fifties.
MARY GREENHILL. His daughter; smart young matron; about 30.
FOWLER GREENHILL. Her husband; competent young doctor, 35.
DAVID GREENHILL. Their son; charming and intelligent; about 10.
LORINDA PIKE. Society editor of Doremus's paper, and his friend. A spinster and an uplifter, yet warmhearted. About 40.
SHAD LEDUE. A tough rustic of about 35. Doremus's hired man, then a Corpo officer.
FRANK TASBROUGH. Pompous, prosperous manufacturer, 55.
EFFINGHAM SWAN. Commissioner for Vermont of the Corpos (troops of the dictator Windrip); cultured, suave, vicious; a good soldier, 40 to 45.
JULIAN FALCK. A recent college graduate; neighbor of Doremus, 24.
HENRY VEEDER and Mrs. VEEDER. Dignified Vermont Farm-couple; about 70.
CLARENCE TUBES. Voluble, amiable rural druggist, 65. In Act I, Scene 1, only.
DAN WILGUS. Doremus's print-shop foreman; gruff, loyal, 50 to 60. In Act II only.
MR. DIMMICK. Secret-service agent posing as a rather dreary insurance salesman. Act II, Scene I, only.
JIM NICKERSON. Corporal of Corpos; small-town tough, but belligerent rather than vicious, 25.
PRIVATE BROWN. A young Corpo.
TWO OR THREE CORPO PRIVATES.

SYNOPSIS OF SCENES

ACT I

SCENE 1: The drugstore of Clarence Tubbs, in Fort Beulah, a small city in Vermont, at three o'clock on an October afternoon.
SCENE 2: The living-room of Doremus Jessup, in Fort Beulah, an hour later.

ACT II

SCENE 1: Doremus's office at the *Daily Informer*, three and a half months later.
SCENE 2: The same, some weeks later.
SCENE 3: Doremus's living-room, some weeks later.

ACT III

Doremus's living-room on a winter evening, a year and a half later.

THE PLACE: A small American city.
THE TIME: Very soon—or never.

ACT I

SCENE 1: *Three in the afternoon, in the old-fashioned drugstore of Clarence Tubbs, in Fort Beulah, a small city in Vermont.*

The set is shallow. Left, halfway up, is the door to the street; down from it, a small show-window, so filled with window-displays that the street is not visible.

Down stage, near the door, is a soda-service table, with three chairs about it. Up right, in the corner, is the el-shaped soda counter. Behind it are old-fashioned wall-fillings of dark wood, and shelves with cigarettes, drug-sundries, etc. Three or four high stools are in front of the counter.

Behind the counter is a narrow door—the entrance to the room for compounding prescriptions.

Against the back wall, center, is a rack of gaudy magazines.

The street door stands open, swung on stage, so that on the street side of it may be seen a printed poster:

Walt Trowbridge
People's Party Candidate

DEFEAT WINDRIP

Fight Dictatorship

A similar poster may be seen on the window, facing into the store.

AT RISE: CLARENCE TUBBS, *a white-haired, kindly but peppery man of 65 or more, proud of having been a Vermont druggist for nearly half a century, is behind the counter, serving* MR. *and* MRS. VEEDER, *a fine old farm couple of about 70.* MRS. VEEDER *is putting wrapped bundles into a string shopping-bag. Off-stage are heard a distant band, not loud, a shuffle of feet, cheers, and like sounds of preparation for a parade.*

CLARENCE. How about some soap, Mrs. Veeder? We got a special, if you take a whole case.

MRS. VEEDER. We couldn't lug it to the car. They won't let us farmers park on Main Street today, because of the parade.

CLARENCE. [*Angrily*] The parade! Buzz Windrip and his marching clubs! Keeping cars off Main Street! Don't know what's happened to Vermont, puttin' up with a thing like that! I'll go to the Mayor.

MRS. VEEDER. Don't know what good it'll do you, Mr. Tubbs.

CLARENCE. People around Fort Beulah won't stand for no monkeying with their rights. My father didn't fight in the Civil War for nothing.

VEEDER. Mine neither!

MRS. VEEDER. Well, I don't know what the world is coming to. Young folks staying up till half-past eleven—thinkin' you're a tyrant if you tell 'em to get in at a decent hour.

VEEDER. At least, the Corpos stand for discipline.

CLARENCE. When it comes to discipline—I believe in freedom. Better let the kids stay up than have 'em bossed all the time.

MRS. VEEDER. My, we certainly would like this fifty dollars a week they say Mr. Windrip is going to give all the old folks, if he's elected president. We could use it, with another winter coming.

CLARENCE. He'll never give it to you—never in a thousand years.

[*Burst of* BAND MUSIC]

VEEDER. There's the Rutland band.

MRS. VEEDER. I sorta like music and uniforms.

CLARENCE. So did my Uncle Cal. He don't now—in the churchyard.

VEEDER. Don't s'pose he does, now.

CLARENCE. Let's see: that was one toothbrush, twenty-three cents; one bottle Ethiopian Wonder Remedy, one dollar; one bottle La Belle Paris perfume, ten cents. That makes—now let me see—

[NICKERSON, *a rustic tough in uniform as a Corpo corporal, rushes in. The Corpo uniforms are rather too competently military for a mere marching club. He pushes the* VEEDER *aside and stands at the counter.*]

NICKERSON. Gimme a pack of Sparks.

CLARENCE. Don't you see I'm awaiting on somebody?

MRS. VEEDER. Oh, don't mind us, Mr. Tubbs.

NICKERSON. [*Tying his shoelace, his foot up on a stool at the counter*] In a hurry—gotta get into the parade. Hustle and shoot the works.

[*The* VERDERS *take down a bright-covered movie magazine from the rack back* C., *and sit at the table to look it over.*]

[*The* BAND MUSIC *has faded out*]

CLARENCE. Don't see no money on the counter.

NICKERSON. Aw, put it on the cuff.

CLARENCE. [*Consulting his account book*] Nosir! Let me tell you, Jim Nickerson, you don't get one cent's worth of credit out of me! You owe me twenty-four dollars and sixteen cents, and you ain't paid a cent now for a month and nine days—ten days—month and nine days it was yesterday—and you got a brand-new second-hand automobile!

NICKERSON. Cut the cackle! I'm here on official business for the Corpos.

CLARENCE. Corpos! Corpos! And just what do you think you Corpos think you're doin'? Drillin'! DRILLIN'! Yes, sir, I heard you. Drillin'! Out behind the old tannery. At night. Drillin'! With uniforms and wooden rifles. What ye doin'? Tryin' to git up some kind of army?

NICKERSON. The Corpos ain't doing anything, except help elect Windrip. But what I came for—You got to tear down those People's Party posters.

CLARENCE. Tear down—Of all the eternal impudence! In my own store!

NICKERSON. Now listen, sweetheart; today Fort Beulah belongs to the Corpos, and not to no damn People's Party. Why, if Commissioner Swan sees those posters—

CLARENCE. See? See? Let him see! He'll see one American that ain't going to knuckle under to Buzz Windrip nor no other dictator! I'm a Walt Trowbridge man!

NICKERSON. [*Crossing to door; angrily*] All right, all right! You won't tear down your seditious posters! Don't blame me if you go out to start your dirty old flivver some morning, and find the tires slashed! [*Exit*]

CLARENCE. [*Sputtering, following* NICKERSON *off*] Dirty old—dirty old—my automobile dirty! [*He re-enters*]

VEEDER. You get some tough boys from back in the hills. [*Rises*]

CLARENCE. [*Crosses back to counter. He is now half laughing at himself.*] I hadn't ought to be so cranky. Guess you have to excuse young fellows like Nickerson, never had no bringing up. But this drilling—Why, I was saying to Mrs. Tubbs, just this morning, when I was shaving, "I don't like this drilling," I says, and says she, "If this man Windrip gets in, she's agoing to take to her bed and never get up."

VEEDER. [*At counter*] These boys nowadays don't get the home training we did. How much is that?

CLARENCE. A dollar and thirty-three cents.

[MR. VEEDER *pays*]

MRS. VEEDER. Bad lot, poor things.

[*Enter* MARY GREENHILL *and* DAVID. MARY *is a smart, very likeable young matron;* DAVID *is agreeable and intelligent. He instantly sits down, excitedly, at the table, in the chair on the* L.]

MARY. [*Crossing nearly to counter*] Hello, Clarence. Why, hello, Mr. Veeder. Why, Mrs. Veeder. Remember me? Mrs. Greenhill, the doctor's wife.

MRS. VEEDER. [*Rising*] Why, how do, Mrs. Greenhill.

VEEDER. Course we remember you! I always read your father's paper. Yessir, Doremus Jessup gets out just as good a newspaper here in Fort Beulah as any they got in Boston.

MRS. VEEDER. This your little boy?

MARY. Yes. Say how do you do, Davy.

DAVY. [*Rising*] How do you do, Mrs. Veeder. [*Plumps down in chair again.*] Mother, can I have a Coney Island Special?

MARY. No, no, dear; it's too rich. [*To* CLARENCE] Strawberry ice cream soda and plain coffee ice cream, please, [*She sits,* R. *of table*] How are you and Mrs. Veeder going to vote?

MRS. VEEDER. We think a lot of Senator Windrip.

VEEDER. Yessir, the country's got to have order and security.

MRS. VEEDER. All the folks down our way are for him.

VEEDER. Yes—that's the only thing I got against him!

MARY. If old-time Vermonters like you approve of him—

VEEDER. He wants to co-ordinate farming and all the industries.

CLARENCE. [*Peppery; bringing to the table the ice cream and ice cream soda which he has been preparing*] Co-ordinate! Co-ordinate! What kind of a word do you call that? My drugstore gets along all right. Don't need no co-ordinating, if 'twa'n't for the dead beats. Dead beats! Lots of 'em in Corpo uniforms, too. How did they buy their uniforms when they don't pay their bills? That's what's wrong! The Corpos has a lot of dead beats! [*Returns to counter*]

MRS. VEEDER. [*Nodding at* DAVID] I guess this young man don't know what a dead beat is.

MARY. Oh yes he does—he's a doctor's son! [*To* MR. VEEDER] Aren't you afraid that if the Corpos get to co-ordinating agriculture, they'll dictate how to run your farm?

VEEDER. [*Laughing, preparing to go*] Why, our farm's been in my family for a hundred years. Anybody tried to dictate to me, I'd just laugh. No ma'am, don't you be afraid. Not in America.

[*Enter* DOREMUS JESSUP. *In his late fifties, editor and owner of the Fort Beulah "Informer," he is humorous, liberal, easy-going, honest. He wears old tweeds and a gay tie. His hair is beginning to be gray.*]

DOREMUS. [*Standing by the table; addressing* MARY *and* DAVID *teasingly*] Going to get out a special!

DAVID. Hello, Grampa!

DOREMUS. [*His hand on* MARY'S *shoulder*] Yessir, a special, Reverend Dana's cat has licked that hard-boiled dog of old man Bennett again!

MARY. [*Fondly, pretending to reprove him. They are more like the warmest of friends than like a father and married daughter living in the same house*] Oh, Father!

VEEDER. How do, Mr. Jessup.

DOREMUS. [*Shaking hands with* MR. VEEDER] Well, well, how are you, Henry? [*To* MRS. VEEDER] Glad to see you in town. [*To* MR. VEEDER] How was the maple sugar this spring?

VEEDER. Fine—fine.

MRS. VEEDER. Henry and I better be getting along.

VEEDER. Come see us, all of you.

DOREMUS. You bet—glad to've seen you—

[*Exeunt* VEEDER *to good-byes from* MARY]

[DOREMUS *strolls back to table; looks down at* MARY'S *ice cream; drawls*] Is that ice cream that I see?

MARY. *That* is ice cream.

DOREMUS. [*Sitting down in chair between* MARY *and* DAVID. *He faces the audience.*] I just wanted to know. Lorinda Pike swore she'd quit, and leave me without a society editor—*and* New England conscience—if I didn't buy her some. . . . Two ice creams, Clarence.

CLARENCE. What kind?

DOREMUS. The most poisonous kind you got.

CLARENCE. And I got it, too! *Corpo* ice cream I call it! [*Starts preparing ice cream*]

[*Enter* DR. FOWLER GREENHILL, *a cheerful, honest, and competent physician of 35*]

FOWLER. Hello, you loafers! [*Kisses* MARY, *pats* DAVID]

MARY. Hello, dear!

DAVID. Hi, Dad!

DOREMUS. Loafer? Me? I'll have you to know I have just composed an editorial *proving* that Senator Berzelius Windrip is a combination of Andy Jackson and Mae West, [CLARENCE *is placing two plates of ice cream in front of* DOREMUS, *and chuckles*] and that if elected president, he won't steal the dome off the Capitol—maybe.

CLARENCE. [*To* FOWLER] What do you think, Doc? [*Goes back of counter*]

FOWLER. [*Crossing to counter*] Don't ask me about politics. I'll leave that to the other fellow. I'm too busy practising medicine.

[FOWLER *hands a prescription to* CLARENCE. MARY *is looking back and up at them. This permits* DOREMUS, *without* MARY'S *seeing it, to give* DAVID *a spoonful from his own ice cream, raising a warning finger*] Fill that, will you please, Clarence, and get it delivered to Ed Moore's.

CLARENCE. Yes *sir!* Ed shall have his elixir if I live.

FOWLER. You'll live to be a hundred.

CLARENCE. Certainly like to. Then I might have a chance to win the argument with my old lady about whether this-here new broccoli is a food or a table-decoration.

FOWLER. Which side you taking?

CLARENCE. I kind of forget! [*Exit to prescription department—small door behind counter*]

[FOWLER *turns to the table*]

MARY. [*To* FOWLER] Going to see the parade?

FOWLER. I've got to make a call. I'll leave the politics to you *liberals!* [*He starts to exit, but halts at sight of* LORINDA PIKE, *just coming in. She is a New England spinster of about 40; acid, tender, brave, shrewd.*] Hello, Aunt Lindy. [*Exit* FOWLER]

DAVID. Hello, Aunt Lindy!

[*At the sound of* FOWLER'S *greeting of* LORINDA, DOREMUS *has risen, to let* LORINDA *have his chair, leaving her ice cream in place, and pushing his own over to the downstage side of the table. He gestures to* LORINDA *to take his chair—which she does—then saunters over to the counter, takes one of the high stools, brings it over—placing it downstage from and to the* R. *of* MARY*—and perches on the stool. All this is during the three speeches following.*]

LORINDA. [*To* DAVID] I'm not *anybody's* Aunt Lindy! . . . Wouldn't mind being yours, though! [*She starts eating her ice cream*]

DOREMUS. Prett' nice grandson I got.

LORINDA. He certainly is. He's a darling. And it's because of all the children like him that you ought to be fighting against dictators like Windrip.

DOREMUS. [*Now perched on his high stool, he lights a cigarette instead of continuing with his ice cream. He answers irritably. Evidently this is an old argument between two good friends*] What's the matter with Windrip? He may not be any Dan'l Webster, but he's a real man of the people.

[DAVID, *bored, goes to explore the soda counter*]

LORINDA. Medicine man—with the loudest holler in the world! All he wants us to do is put ourselves in his hands, and he'll work a miracle.

DOREMUS. [*Serious; sincere*] We *need* a miracle! Unemployment up another two million, stock-market way down, everybody scared of war—the world is filled with trouble.

LORINDA. And a lot of trouble-makers.

MARY. [*To* DOREMUS; *breaking in both because she has some news and because she, too, is bored by the discussion*] Shad Ledue broke another new rake today, and never even tried to repair it. He's the worst hired man ever was. I wish you'd fire him.

LORINDA. I'll wager he did it deliberately.

DOREMUS. Oh, Shad's all right. He's a sort of social experiment of mine. Trying to see whether I can't make him as courteous as a cave-man.

[CLARENCE *re-enters, and is heard thumping a bottle down on the counter, during* LORINDA'S *speech following.*]

LORINDA. Well, you've failed.

DOREMUS. [*Turning on his stool to look across at the counter*] How's Mrs. Tubbs, Clarence?

CLARENCE. She's not so good.

DOREMUS. Sorry to hear that.

CLARENCE. She thinks it's the 'lectric washing-machine. She says it gives her rheumatism. What do you think?

DOREMUS. Well, that's kind of a new theory to me.

CLARENCE. Stands to reason. Now, you take rheumatism. What is it? Electric shocks, that's what it is. And what's the best conductor of electricity? Water, that's what's the best conductor of electricity. And what have you got in a washing-machine—besides the clothes, I mean.

MARY. Soap.

CLARENCE. Eh? Oh yes—yes. Soap, of course. But I mean *water*. And that's how you get rheumatism from an electric washer.

DOREMUS. As logical as Ben Franklin.

[FRANK TASBROUGH, *prosperous, pompous local textile manufacturer, a schoolmate of* DOREMUS, *is entering*]

TASBROUGH. All the intellectuals gathered!

DOREMUS. The great Tasbrough, in person!

TASBROUGH. [*Crosses to the counter; to* CLARENCE] Mr. Tubbs, that English hair-brush you imported for Mrs. Tasbrough is no good. The bristles come out.

CLARENCE. They can't—that's all.

TASBROUGH. Maybe they can't, but they do. Send for it and replace it.

CLARENCE. I'll look it over—

TASBROUGH. [*Ignoring* CLARENCE'S *last speech, he turns to the others; insistent and a little patronising*] I'll buy you all a drink. What you taking?

DOREMUS. Not a thing, thanks. We're all full up.

TASBROUGH. [*Louder*] Come on, come on now, never knew you to pass up anything free, Doremus. I'm buying. What you taking?

DAVID. [*By counter*] Grape-juice with lemon ice cream.

LORINDA. [*Sharply; to* TASBROUGH] We said *nothing*, thank you.

DAVID. Grape juice?

MARY. Be still!
DOREMUS. Da-vy! } [*together, turning on* DAVID]

[DAVID *ducks his head, turtle-wise*]

TASBROUGH. [*Still at the counter, but with his back to it, speaking to* DOREMUS, LORINDA] Well, if you're too good to drink with a poor old capitalist, that it's the fashion for the Treasury Department and every lazy bum on relief to strangle nowadays, I'll buy myself one. [*To* CLARENCE] Bring me a coke. [*To* DOREMUS, *crossing to table*] I see your rag is prett' near admitting Windrip will be elected. [*Sits* L. *of table*]

DOREMUS. Looks like it.

LORINDA. I admit our "rag" isn't doing enough to prevent his election.

TASBROUGH. Lorinda, you're a regular Communist. If you had to run a big textile mill, the way I do, and try to find young machinists that know their business, you'd change your mind. Young folks today simply won't learn.

CLARENCE. [*Taking* TASBROUGH'S *"coke"—i.e. coco-cola—to the table*] Nothing the matter with the young folks. Trouble's with us. [*Returns to counter*]

TASBROUGH. You take my younger daughter. Always wanting to go to Europe. Why, say, I was talking to a fellow the other day, and he told me there wasn't a single factory with an up-to-date assembly line in the whole city of Rome.

DOREMUS. [*Speaking sardonically; nudging* MARY] NO!

LORINDA. You don't mean to say so.

TASBROUGH. Absolutely! I give you my word. And that's why Senator Windrip says, "Keep our dollars at home and reduce taxes." He promises to work up the tourist trade so foreigners will come to see the Grand Canyon and New York and the birthplace of Cal Coolidge, and all them natural wonders.

DOREMUS. Yes, that's good dictator talk.

TASBROUGH. Windrip doesn't want to be any dictator.

LORINDA. That's what *he* says.

TASBROUGH. If you don't believe it, read his own book, "Zero Hour." He says—and mind you, he's the greatest man in the country, but he's so humble—

LORINDA. So's a typhoid germ.

TASBROUGH. He says in "Zero Hour": "I have no desire to be president. My only longing is to serve."

DOREMUS. That's why he's running—because he doesn't *want* to be president.

DAVID. [*By the counter, interrupting*] Grape-juice is very healthy.

TASBROUGH. Tubbs! Give that young man a grape-juice.

MARY. No!

DOREMUS. [*Softly, to* MARY] Oh, let him have it.

MARY. Well, this once.

[DAVID *sits up on high stool at counter, and* CLARENCE *serves him with grape-juice, during the four speeches following.*]

TASBROUGH. Doremus, how'm I going to make cotton fabrics at a decent profit if every mill-hand and railroad roustabout demands hours and wages and God knows what all to suit his own selfish, grasping notions?

DOREMUS. Any more selfish than we are?

TASBROUGH. Yes, sir! You bet they are! And what we got to have is co-ordination, and one strong man as co-ordinator.

DOREMUS. I'll admit a lot of young fellows have straightened up and quit drinking rot-gut since they put on Corpo uniforms.

TASBROUGH. Co-ordination, that's what it is.

DOREMUS. [*Turning to look at and address* DAVID] Hear all that talk, Davy? Don't mean a thing! [*He crosses, perches on a high stool beside* DAVY's *and addresses* DAVY *as one wise old crony to another*] Wish we were on another picnic up in the hills. All these poor deluded folks down here in Fort Beulah, talking politics and dodging traffic, and preachers and editors yelling that two plus two equals four, but up there in the hills, the crickets!

DAVID. I can make a noise like four different kinds of crickets.

DOREMUS. Didn't know there were that many.

DAVID. Well, maybe I did make up a couple.

DOREMUS. Crickets. That's the thing to study. You never heard of a Senator Buzz Cricket trying to get himself elected president of the United States of Cricketeria. Or claiming they got to grab some ant-hills for territories. "Our brave crickets [*Pompously*] have just conquered two billion *pinheads* of territory!"

DAVID. [*Eagerly*] Or—or getting the bumble-bees to fly over 'em and drop bumbles on 'em!

DOREMUS. [*Drily*] Yeah, does kind of make poor ambitious human critters look foolish. Thing for a good Vermonter is to sit up on a hill!

LORINDA. You can't keep sitting on a hill.

TASBROUGH. Good God, Doremus, why don't you take a tumble to yourself? All these years you and your doggone newspaper been having a lot of fun being so doggone liberal. Time for you to take an active stand against all these subversive elements. These are serious times, man. Maybe twenty-eight million on relief and beginning to get ugly, thinking they have a vested right to be supported.

DOREMUS. Yes, these are serious times.

[SHAD LEDUE, *a surly, mean, bulky, quick-witted hillbilly of 30 to 35,* DOREMUS's *man-of-all-work, is entering.* SHAD *is in overalls, and noticeably unshaven. He merely nods to the family, and to* DOREMUS's *greeting, as he crosses to the counter.*] Hello, Shad.

SHAD. [*To* CLARENCE, *in a rough voice*] Gimme package of razor blades. Six'll do.

CLARENCE. [*Slightly sarcastic*] Last you quite some time! [*Chewing a stalk of grass,* SHAD *glances over advertising leaflets on the counter.*]

TASHROUGH. [*Rising, crossing slowly toward counter; continuing to* DOREMUS] All these labor racketeers ganging up with the Communists and trying to tell me how to run my business. [*Drops coins on the counter and turns to exit*] I tell you, Windrip's got to be elected. See you soon.

DOREMUS. So long.

[*Exit* TASBROUGH, *with a not unamiable wave of his hand.*]

DOREMUS. [*To* SHAD, *who stands almost beside the stool on which* DOREMUS *is perched at the counter*] Well, Shad, how you planning to vote?

SHAD. Well now, I'll tell you. I'm going to vote for Buzz Windrip. He's going to fix it so everybody will get twenty-five hundred a year.

DOREMUS. He never promised that.

SHAD. [*Cocksure, smug, slightly patronizing*] Oh yes he has—*secret*. I know these things. Then I'm going to start a chicken farm. I can make a bunch of money out of chickens.

DOREMUS. You didn't have so much luck with *turkeys*, Shad. [*Rises; stands facing* SHAD.] You let the water freeze up on 'em in winter, and I'm afraid they sort of *died*.

SHAD. Them? So what! Heck! There was too few of 'em. I'm not going to waste my time fooling with a couple dozen turkeys. Besides, turkeys is got mean tempers. When I get five-six thousand chickens, to make it worth my while, then I'll show you. [*He starts for the door.*] You bet. Buzz Windrip is O.K.

DOREMUS. Did you get the leaves raked up?

SHAD. [*Halts, turns to look at* DOREMUS, *speaks in a tone of injured virtue.*] I did *not!* How could I rake leaves with a busted rake? [*Exit*]

[DOREMUS *and* MARY *look at each other.* HE *is amused, chuckling.* SHE *is irritated, but also fond of her father.*]

MARY. I don't know whether it's worth the time discharging Shad. [*She rises*] We might just shoot him! . . . Come, David. . . . Good-bye, Aunt Lindy.

DAVID [*Crossing from counter to* MARY, *but looking over his shoulder to cry to* DOREMUS] Good-bye, Grampa.

DOREMUS. [*To* DAVID] Bye, dear. . . . Bye, Mary.

MARY. Bye, Dad.

LORINDA. [*To* DAVID, *as he passes her*] Aren't you going to say good-bye to Aunt Lindy?

DAVID. You betcha! [*Gives* LORINDA *a quick hug.*]

MARY. Good-bye, Clarence.

[*Exeunt* MARY, DAVID.]

[DOREMUS *crosses to table, loungingly, sits in chair just vacated by* MARY.]

LORINDA. We must get back to the office.

DOREMUS. I'm going to work at home, and see the parade.

LORINDA. [*She is still seated—has remained so ever since first sitting at the table.*] That horrible Corpo parade! Hulking young men like Shad, too strong to work. Look here, Doremus, my blind friend. We've just seen the recipe for all dictatorships: timid rich men like Frank Tasbrough, to put up the money, and lumps like Shad Ledue to carry out the dirty work.

DOREMUS. Oh, these Shads aren't dangerous. Their mouths are too big. Folks that have the sense to live in the Vermont hills oughtn't to worry about *them.* And think what's beyond our hills—Ioway cornfields and Oregon forests and an Alaska you could build an empire in. [*Rises, starts for counter, halts to look back at* LORINDA.] Realize how big Texas is? Big as three European countries put together. [*Drops coins, for the sodas, on the counter.*] This isn't any one-horse country that a dictator could get hold of.

CLARENCE. No, sir, and ain't goin' to be. [LORINDA *has arisen.*]

DOREMUS. [*Crossing back to her*] America's too big for *any* one gang to bully, and got too much sense of humor. It can't happen here!

[JULIAN FALCK *is entering. He is a good-looking, well-bred college graduate, son of a rector now dead. He is about* 24. *He wears a neat, worn suit.*]

JULIAN. Hello, everybody.

DOREMUS. Afternoon, young fellow.

CLARENCE. Hello, boy.

LORINDA. Going to march in the Corpo parade?

JULIAN. I am not! I don't care much for the bounding roughneck.

DOREMUS. [*Glancing slyly over* JULIAN'S *shoulder at* CLARENCE] Have a drink, Julian? Purest essence of synthetic cherry.

CLARENCE. [*Slightly indignant*] Tain't no such thing!

JULIAN. Thanks, I only dropped in for a package of cigarettes.

[LORINDA *moves on to the doorway;* DOREMUS *begins to follow her.*]

LORINDA. Good-bye, Julian. Good-bye, Mr. Tubbs.

CLARENCE. [*To* LORINDA] Keep your health now.

JULIAN. Good-bye, Aunt Lindy.

LORINDA. I'm not anybody's—Oh, you're always teasing me, but I love you just the same. [*Exit*]

[DOREMUS, *starting to follow her out, on impulse suddenly turns back, speaks to* JULIAN.]

DOREMUS. Julian, I want to ask a favor of you.

JULIAN. I'll be glad to do it, sir.

DOREMUS. Come have dinner with us, next Sunday. I can guarantee you watermelon pickles.

JULIAN. Be delighted.

DOREMUS. I found an old snapshot of your father, wearing his cassock, that I'd like to give you.

[JULIAN *has moved toward* DOREMUS, *so that they are within arm's-length of each other.*]

JULIAN. [*Earnestly*] Oh, thanks.

DOREMUS. He was about the greatest gentleman I ever knew—so scholarly and yet so gay. He was one of the people who really *do* "serve God with a joyous heart." Sometimes I get kind of lonesome for him. You and I mustn't lose track of each other, Julian.

JULIAN. We won't, sir!

DOREMUS. [*Patting his shoulder*] Bless you—good-bye. [*Exit*]

JULIAN. [*Crossing again to counter*] Coffee milk-shake, please, Mr. Tubbs.

CLARENCE. Coming right up. Got a line on a job yet?

[JULIAN *sits on high stool at the counter;* CLARENCE *prepares milk shake in shaker.*]

JULIAN. [*Bitterly*] I haven't had a thing since the summer hotel closed. My college degree got me the position of bellhop.

CLARENCE. Seems like it's harder on you fellows that done well in college than it is on the bums.

JULIAN. Seems so.

CLARENCE. [*Diffidently*] Excuse me, Julian, but if nothing shows up, and the worst comes to the worst, like the fellow says, you can always sleep here free in the back room. High class running water!

JULIAN. Thanks, old man.

CLARENCE. [*Pouring a glassful from the shaker*] Here y' are. [JULIAN *lays coin on the counter.*] No—this is my treat.

JULIAN. Thanks, Mr. Tubbs, but I don't need that yet.

CLARENCE. Don't mention it—don't mention it. . . . Say, I got to go in and make a prescription for Doc Greenhill. Holler, will you, if anybody comes in?

JULIAN. I'll holler.

[*Exit* CLARENCE, *into the prescription-room.*]

[JULIAN *is clearly hungry. He drinks his milkshake greedily, and pours a second helping from the shaker, making sure that every bit of froth drains into the glass. He is too concentrated to notice the entrance of* EFFINGHAM SWAN.]

[SWAN, *Corpo Commissioner for Vermont, is slim, athletic, suave, literate, brave. He is also cruel, ruthless, contemptuous. He was a young captain in the Great War; since then he has been bored as a Boston stockbroker. He is* 40 *to* 45. *He is in the uniform of a high-ranking Corpo official; military and smart, with breeches and riding-boots but, of course, no side-arms.*]

[*In the doorway, he looks disdainfully at the Trowbridge poster, then speculatively at* JULIAN.]

SWAN. Excuse me.

JULIAN. [*Turning his head, a little startled*] Oh. . . . Mr. Tubbs is filling a prescription.

SWAN. Do you happen to know whether he favors the Corpos? Or is he for Senator Trowbridge?

[SWAN'S *voice is noticeably flexible. It can be lightly amused, earnest, harshly commanding.*]

JULIAN. Clarence says you Corpos want to crush individualism—

SWAN. That's absurd, of course.

JULIAN.—and as a real old New England eccentric, he won't stand for that.

SWAN. Then I shan't waste time on him.

JULIAN. You're a Corpo official, I take it.

SWAN. Commissioner for Vermont.

JULIAN. *Heil!*

SWAN. [*Smiling and extra suave*] No, I don't think we need such childishness. [*Starts for the door, then turns.*] Now let me see. You graduated from some good college, a couple of years ago—your father was a professional man or a merchant of considerable culture—and you have been desperately looking for some kind of job in which you could use at least ten per cent of your college training.

JULIAN. What of it?

SWAN. Don't be offended, Mr.—What is your name?

JULIAN. Julian Falck.

SWAN. My name is Swan. [*They shake hands.*] You see, I've been dealing with a lot of lads from good families who've been ruined by the arguing and experimenting of the last three administrations. The country's gone soft. But Windrip will discipline it, if he has the help of men like you.

JULIAN. You don't really believe the Corpo dogmas—not privately?

SWAN. I do. Sincerely. And so do you!

JULIAN. I do not!

SWAN. Would you rather build your house on a rock, or on the most golden sands?

JULIAN. A metaphor isn't argument.

SWAN. [*Clapping his shoulder*] Good! And now tell me what you've got against the Corpos?

JULIAN. They're a bunch of roughnecks, out for a lark.

SWAN. Plenty of those—thank Heaven! They make the best private soldiers. But the officers—Well, take myself for example. I'm a university man, and that sort of thing—

JULIAN. Obviously, you're different.

SWAN. So are you, Falck. . . . We're recruiting more and more college men. Don't you find it good to be really *needed*, these jobless days—drafted for a man-sized job—with pay! You know they're paying to Corpos who want to stay on after election.

JULIAN. [*Tempted, but still doubtful*] What do they need the Corpos for permanently?

SWAN. Windrip is going to organize a special, highly honored corps, with *authority*, not merely to stop vulgar crime, like drug-traffic, but to prevent bribery, grafting, *treason.* Of course everybody who joins before election will have precedence. You would start as a private, but I assure you that within a few months, you would be an officer.

JULIAN. [*Meditatively*] Officer—

SWAN. Think of it, Falck! Honor, high pay, exciting adventure—and service to your country! It's the chance of a lifetime. Come join us!

JULIAN. Worth looking into.

SWAN. [*Scribbling a note on a page in his memorandum book*] Take this to Fort Beulah headquarters and talk to Major Tanner. Then decide—but decide entirely for yourself, of course.

JULIAN. I'll talk to him.

SWAN. He'll explain anything you want to know.

JULIAN. Would I have to be in this parade?

SWAN. [*His tone changing, but slowly, from cajolery to command*] Parades! They're only the pearl handle on the gun. I'll have to start this one off, but then I'll return to my real job—presenting our side to the leading citizens. I may want you to drive me around. Wait for me at headquarters.

JULIAN. [*Now sold; becoming military*] Very well, sir. [*Starts to exit*]

SWAN. Wait! What's this shoemaker like, next door? One of these sour lovers of humanity that sit and think too much? All shoemakers and tailors do, and so they become Socialists.

JULIAN. Does the Commissioner think that sitting and thinking are bad?

SWAN. Just now? *Terrible!* Time to *act!*

JULIAN. To act!

SWAN. Skip along, then, and I'll size up the laddy next door.

[*Exeunt* SWAN *and* JULIAN, SWAN *murmuring as they go.*] You know, a soldier of peace and not of bloodshed, but with all his glory—

[*The stage is empty for a moment. The* BAND *starts playing a Sousa march, and the noise of confused voices grows louder. A blast of music brings* CLARENCE *out of his den. He sets the filled medicine down on the counter, hastily pastes the prescription in a large ledger, muttering aloud the while.*]

CLARENCE. Corpos! Tell *me* how to run a drugstore! [*He crosses to the door, looks out, and shouts, in a lull of the band-music*] Tin soldiers! Corpos! Want to be dictators! Dictators! [*He spots* NICKERSON *in the crowd.*] Jim Nickerson! Corporal Nickerson! Corpo! Dictator! Dead beat!

[CLARENCE *is pushed back into the store by* NICKERSON *and two or three other* CORPOS, *in uniforms as privates.* CLARENCE *falls back* R, *the others following.*]

NICKERSON You go calling me a dead beat, and you'll get your block knocked off!

CLARENCE. That won't keep you from being one! Buying an automobile and hanging me up!

NICKERSON. You grave-robber!

A CORPO. You old crank!

CLARENCE. You owe everybody in town—all of you!

ANOTHER CORPO. People's Party punk!

CLARENCE. You—you—

[THEY *are interrupted by the swift re-entrance of* SWAN.]

A CORPO. Ten-shun!

[ALL THE CORPOS *stand at attention.*]

SWAN. Too much noise here. [*To* CLARENCE] Noisy old thing, aren't you!

CLARENCE. Who's going to stop me?

SWAN. Belligerent, aren't you!

CLARENCE. Whose place is this?

SWAN. [*Suave and quiet*] Yours, I'm quite sure. So I must ask you to tear clown those [*Indicating them*] People's Party posters.

CLARENCE. You can go right on asking!

SWAN. [*To* NICKERSON] Just tear down those—

[NICKERSON *pulls down the poster on the street door.*]

CLARENCE. Get out of here, you tin soldier! [*Furiously he strikes at* SWAN, *who catches his arm.*]

SWAN. If you will allow me—[*He crosses to* NICKERSON *and, unseen by* CLARENCE, *hands to* NICKERSON *a flexible leather blackjack, taken from his sleeve. . . . To* NICKERSON.] Work on him, will you? Might as well get used to it. [*He crosses to the door, turns, sees* NICKERSON'S *hesitation.*]

NICKERSON. [*Frightened and unwilling*] Aw, gee, Commissioner—

SWAN. Or turn in your uniform! [*Exit*]

CLARENCE. [*Picking up a ginger ale bottle for weapon*] You get out of here! All of you! [*He sees the blackjack in* NICKERSON'S *hand and falls back in horror, at which* ALL THE CORPOS *surround him, their arms rising in blows.*] [BLACKOUT.]

[*The martial music goes on in the darkness.*]

CURTAIN

★

SCENE 2: *An hour later, in the sitting-room of* DOREMUS JESSUP—*with whom live his daughter, son-in-law, and grandson. It is the room of a well-to-do, leisurely, bookish family. All the furniture is good; none of it, except the radio, is new.*

Down R. *is a round table; on the right of it,* DOREMUS'*s favorite armchair—probably a wingchair; other chairs are on the left and upstage sides of the table. Down from the table is a stand with the telephone on it. In the right wall opposite the armchair is a window looking on the street—residence street in a comfortable New England village.*

Up R. *is the street door; convenient to it, a hatrack. Center in the back wall is a fireplace—with another armchair in front of it; to the* R. *of fireplace, a low door leading down to the basement;* L. *of fireplace, bookshelves, and the foot of the stairs leading up to the bedrooms. A couch, slantwise, is to the* L. *of center; about opposite it, in the left wall, door to the dining room—thence to the kitchen. Down* L. *is the radio.*

AT RISE: *Sound of* BAND MUSIC. DOREMUS *and* DAVID *are looking out of the window at the parade.* LORINDA *sits on the couch, correcting proofs.*

DAVID. Gee, they look grand. I love parades.

DOREMUS. Yes, they're kind of fun.

DAVID. Look, Aunt Lindy, there go the Corpo flags.

LORINDA. [*Not answering him; to* DOREMUS] Doremus, I'd think you'd find a better way to spend your time.

DOREMUS. They're a fine-looking body of young men.

LORINDA. That's what you make any dictatorship out of.

DOREMUS. You never heard of the Corpos hurting anybody.

LORINDA. That depends on their leaders. If these boys are made to believe that it's righteous to kill, then they'll kill, and it hurts just as much to be beaten by a fanatic as by a brute.

DAVID. Lookit, lookit, Gramp! Julian's gone in the movies!

DOREMUS. [*Looking out of the window again*] Well! [*Ring at the door.*]

[DOREMUS *opens, to admit* JULIAN, *now in uniform as a Corpo private.*] What's all this? What d' you call this?

JULIAN. I've joined up with the Corpos, Mr. Jessup.

DOREMUS. Surprised to see *you* regimented.

JULIAN. I was sick of being out of everything.

DOREMUS. I can understand that.

JULIAN. Oh—this is Commissioner Swan. [SWAN *steps into the doorway.*]

DOREMUS. Oh—come in—come in.

SWAN. [*Entering*] Very good of you to see me.

DOREMUS. Not at all. Honor to have you. Sit down.

JULIAN. [*To* DOREMUS, *admiringly*] Commissioner Swan wanted to see you more than anybody else in town.

DOREMUS. [*Closing door*] Well!

SWAN. [*Sitting,* L. *of table*] At ease, Falck.

[JULIAN *stands back, attentive.*]

DOREMUS. [*To* SWAN] Understand you're running the whole Vermont campaign for Windrip.

SWAN. [*He is being as winning as possible*] More or less, sir.

VOICE OF TASBROUGH. [*Outside front door*] Hey Doremus!

DOREMUS. [*Opening door again*] Come on in, Frank—best place to watch the parade.

[TASBROUGH *enters.*]

DOREMUS. [*To* SWAN] Commissioner, this is Frank Tasbrough, our leading manufacturer.

[SWAN *rises;* he *and* TASBROUGH *shake hands; meanwhile* DOREMUS *sits in his armchair,* R. *of table.*]

TASBROUGH. [*To* SWAN] I heard you were in town. I suppose you dropped in at my mill to see me.

SWAN. [*Sitting again*] Sorry. Haven't had the chance.

TASBROUGH. Why, it's the biggest single industry in the country, and I've been ordering my employees to vote Corpo.

DOREMUS. [*Sharply*] I don't like that!

SWAN. [*After a quick look at* TASBROUGH, *then at* DOREMUS; *non-commitally*] I see.

TASBROUGH. [*Continuing to* SWAN] There was something I wanted to talk over with you.

LORINDA. I thought so!

[TASBROUGH, *annoyed, looks out of the window.*]

DOREMUS. Oh, Commissioner, our society editor, Miss Pike.

[SWAN *half rises, looking toward* LORINDA *and murmuring* "MISS PIKE."]

LORINDA. [*To* SWAN] Have you come to tell us that Senator Windrip just loves the Common People?

SWAN. I'm a very simple person, Miss Pike, and probably a sentimentalist. To my mind, Senator Windrip has a little of the qualities of Lincoln.

DAVID. [*He has stood back by the window, watching all this. To* SWAN] Are you a general or something?

SWAN. Just a commissioner.

DAVID. Is that a Corpo?

SWAN. Yes, Captain.

DAVID. Aw, I'm not a captain; I'm Dan'l Boone.

DOREMUS. [*Over his shoulder; to* DAVID, *amiably*] Skip out and explore then, Dan'l.

[*Exit* DAVID.]

DOREMUS. [*To* SWAN] Surprised you're not inspecting the parade.

SWAN. I started them off. I'm only in town for three hours. Much more important to talk to you.

DOREMUS. Thanks. Well, my paper has been trying to give both sides a break.—

SWAN. It might surprise you to know how eagerly Boston headquarters has read your summing up of the situation.

DOREMUS. I *am* surprised!

SWAN. There's nothing more important than to have you understand the Corpo ideal of a vigorous and purposeful Youth. [DOREMUS *gestures to* TASBROUGH *to take chair upstage from the table.*] We intend to give them a plan, instead of vague longings to get something for nothing.

TASBROUGH. Relief has produced a lot of slackers.

[*During this last speech,* SHAD LEDUE *has entered through, the basement door, beside the fireplace. He is in overalls. He is carrying an armful of firewood, which he now dumps noisily on the hearth.*]

LORINDA. Shad! Don't be so noisy!

SHAD. Aw, I can't help it! [*Noisily kicks logs.*]

SWAN. Shad?

DOREMUS. Yes—Shad Ledue.

SWAN. [*Consulting his memorandum book*] I see—

DOREMUS. Shad, you pick the most inappropriate times—

[SHAD is scornfully turning back to basement door, when SWAN, rising, stops him with a sharp, military address.]

SWAN. You!

SHAD. [*Snapping to attention*] Yessir.

SWAN. Ever been in the army?

SHAD. Nosir.

SWAN. I believe you've had military training?

SHAD. Militia, sir.

SWAN. Corporal, wasn't it? [*This first word must be said with the last syllable distinct, so that the word will not be confused with "Corpo."*]

SHAD. Yessir.

SWAN. [*Nodding dismissal*] That'll do.

[*Saluting, smirking with satisfaction,* SHAD *exits into basement.*]

LORINDA. Well, I must say!

SWAN. [*Making a check in his note-book*] The way that lout would straighten up under Corpo training would surprise you, ma'am.

LORINDA. It certainly would!

SWAN. [*Crosses toward couch*] We need training. If this nation is not regalvanized into the spirit of '76, any foreign power could walk in and subject us to slavery. We intend to build a wall of steel against European dictatorships.

LORINDA. The Corpos *intend* everything. They tell the industrialists they'll stop all strikes. They tell the workers unions will be sacred. They tell the well-to-do they'll lower taxes. They tell *the* poor they'll have twenty-five hundred a year.

DOREMUS. Now, now, Lindy, it's downright unsporting to remember campaign speeches.

SWAN. [*To* LORINDA] If you'd only listen this afternoon, when our Chief broadcasts from the Little Brown Church in the Vale, in Zenith, with Dr. Prang, the radio pastor. [*Turning toward* DOREMUS.] This afternoon may be as historic as the Battle of Lexington.

DOREMUS. Now that's asking a good deal!

LORINDA. [*Rising, beginning to move toward dining-room door*] Historic? Huh!

SWAN. Please don't go, Miss Pike. We need your feminine touch in politics.

LORINDA. Another demagogue! [*Exit,* L.]

DOREMUS. [*Rising on her last speech, hastening after her*] Now that's not fair! Wait a minute! [*To* SWAN, *passing him*] Don't mind her, Commissioner. I'll go in and coax her. [*Exit,* L., *calling:*] Lindy! Now Lindy—

SWAN. I do hope the dear lady wasn't too offended.

TASBROUGH. [*Rising*] Commissioner, I have a little business I'd like to—

SWAN. Falck, just wait for me outside in the car.

[*Exit* JULIAN. SWAN *sits on couch.* TASBROUGH *crosses and sits beside him.*]

TASBROUGH. [*Confidentially*] You probably know that I've had rather important letters from Corpo headquarters in Chicago, urging me to take an active part in the National Council of Businessmen on behalf of Windrip. Now I wasn't born yesterday—I know what that means—it means *money!* [*He laughs heartily, and slaps* SWAN *on the back, which* SWAN *resents.*] Well, I'm ready to come in with you, since I understand, confidentially, that Windrip's going to put the labor unions in their place.

SWAN [*Very gracious, though he dislikes* TASBROUGH'S *heartiness*] You may take it for granted that one of our chief purposes is to give business a fair deal, and keep the wheels of industry turning in the good old-fashioned American way—forbid all strikes.

TASBROUGH. That's the way I like to hear a man talk! [*He slaps* SWAN *on the knee, and rises.*] So, Commissioner I'm going to make a contribution to the Corpos that will surprise you. [*Crosses to table, sits at it, with his back to* SWAN *and makes out a check.*]

[SWAN *remains seated. While* TASBROUGH *is writing* SHAD *enters, with more wood, dumps it at fireplace, and starts back to basement door. At this entrance,* SWAN *has started scribbling a note, on page from his memorandum book. He beckons to* SHAD *and silently passes the note to him, without* TASBROUGH *seeing.* SHAD *takes the note, delightedly, and exits, just as* TASBROUGH *rises, fanning the wet check, and recrosses to the couch.*]

There you are! One thousand bucks! One thousand bright gold dollars! That'll buy some Corpo Bibles!

SWAN [*Examines the check, rises, hands the check back to* TASBROUGH, *and speaks insolently*] An error, I'm afraid, my dear sir. I'd understood your assessment was *five* thousand.

TASBROUGH. Five thou—

SWAN. Perhaps we'd better not have you as a contributor at all. We don't care to have any one in the inner council who doesn't passionately believe in our ideals.

TASBROUGH. If you think you can bully me—

SWAN. Quite right. We'd rather not have any associates whom we have to bully. Of course it's a little inconvenient—the Corpo troops will soon be augmented to several millions, which means millions of yards of fabric—

TASBROUGH. Well, now—[*Takes out check book again.*]

SWAN. No, not now, my dear Mr. Tasbrough. I really couldn't take a check from you until you have had time to think over our ideals. Then you can communicate with me at my Montpelier headquarters—

TASBROUGH. Oh, well, I'll see what I can do, Commissioner, and write to you. I'll enclose some samples of cotton. See you soon.

[TASBROUGH *is making exit as* MARY *rushes in, at street door.*]

MARY. Oh, Father, Father—Oh, sorry, Mr. Tasbrough; is Father here?

DOREMUS. [*Re-entering from dining-room*] Mary! What is it?

[TASBROUGH *has made exit.* LORINDA *follows* DOREMUS *in.*]

MARY. I've just come from Clarence Tubbs' store. There was some kind of a row. Nobody seems to know what happened. But they say he's injured quite badly.

DOREMUS. [*Crossing to her*] Good God!

MARY. I talked to your reporter, Betts. He thinks maybe the Corpos did it.

SWAN. I'm sure my men had nothing to do with it.

MARY. They're trying to find Fowler.

DOREMUS. Poor Clarence—poor Clarence! I'll have to telephone the A.P. in Boston about this.

LORINDA. [*Crossing to* SWAN] Do you know anything about Mr. Tubbs getting hurt?

SWAN. Oh no, Miss Pike! How could I?

DOREMUS. We may have to ask you help us get to the bottom of it.

SWAN. I shall be glad to.

LORINDA. If you don't, we'll know what your ideals really are.

SWAN. I'll dash right down to headquarters and find out about this unfortunate accident. [*He starts for the door.* DOREMUS *and* LORINDA *glance at each other, worried. Then* SWAN *halts, turns.*] Oh, Mr. Jessup. Why stir up ill feeling by printing any more than a bare announcement of this mishap? You know mob psychology. Hold up the account till I can make a complete investigation.

DOREMUS. I'll think about it. [*Exit* SWAN.]

MARY. Where's Davy? [*Goes to the street door; calls out*] Oh, Davy! Davy!

DOREMUS. [*Crossing to table on her line*] I believe this is the first casualty in the whole election. [*Sits in armchair,* R. *of table.*]

LORINDA. Then it's important.

MARY. [*At the door*] I want you to come in. There are so many strangers in town.

DAVID. [*After entering*] Aw gee, we're just playing Cops and Corpos.

[FOWLER *enters. Exit* DAVID, *upstairs.*]

FOWLER. [*To* MARY] Hello, hon.

MARY. Call your office, quick.

FOWLER. [*Putting hat and physician's bag on table, going to telephone*] O.K. [*On the phone*] Six-five-two. [*To* MARY] What's the trouble?

MARY. Clarence Tubbs has been injured in some kind of row.

FOWLER. [*On phone*] Dr. Greenhill. Anything for me? . . . Yes. I see. [*Hangs up.*] They've got Dr. Strong. I won't need to go.

LORINDA. You do need to. I feel there's something funny about this whole business.

DOREMUS. Maybe you better.

FOWLER, Strong will tend to it.

LORINDA. He's an old pussy-foot. I'm sure the Corpos did it, and that man Swan will cover things up, if you give him the chance.

FOWLER. All right. I'll make sure he doesn't.

[DAVID *appears, on the stairs.*]

DAVID. Come on upstairs, Dad. Got my new airplane working.

FOWLER. [*Taking hat and bag from table*] Got to go start a little trouble, old man. See you later. [*Exit street door.*]

[DAVID *exit, upstairs, followed by* MARY.]

[LORINDA *crosses to the telephone.*]

DOREMUS. What're *you* doing?

LORINDA. I'm certain Swan is unscrupulous. I've got a crazy idea, Doremus, but—[*On the phone*] Get me toll line.

DOREMUS. Who you calling?

LORINDA. Senator Windrip is in Zenith right now, ready to broadcast. He's got to say something on the radio about this—warn his Corpos.

DOREMUS. Preposterous!

LORINDA. I don't care! If this is the first serious trouble in the election, we've got to make it the last. You've got to get a message to Windrip.

DOREMUS. Me? I can't get him! Every politician in Zenith will be on his tail.

LORINDA. [*On the phone*] Toll line? Just a moment. [*Holds receiver out toward* DOREMUS] Here.

DOREMUS. [*Protestingly rising from his chair and taking the receiver; speaking on the phone*] Hold on a second. [*To* LORINDA.] Find out more about it first. [*On phone*] Let it go, operator. [*Hangs up; to* LORINDA] You're just excited.

LORINDA. [*Crossing to couch and sinking down*] Oh, maybe I am. But I can't help wanting to do something. An attack like this one on Clarence is serious.

DOREMUS. [*But he is still casual*] Of course it is. Tell you what I'll do. I'll go down and look into this business myself. Charley Betts and the boys are all right, but they haven't got the old man's experience. [*He has taken his hat from the rack by the door and is prepared to exit.*]

LORINDA. You're going to miss the Windrip broadcast.

DOREMUS. I'll be back in time for most of it. [*Looking back at her*] Let's be practical! [*Exit*]

LORINDA. [*To herself, sadly*] Practical! [*She turns on the radio. When she gets the station, we hear the excited voice of a commentator.*]

COMMENTATOR. The Little Brown Church in the Vale is packed clear to its lofty rafters of gilded cedar with excited listeners, and a crowd of I'd say ten thousand are milling around outside. [*Sound of cheering.*] Senator Windrip is climbing out of his Cadillac. Morena Moretta, the world-famous movie star, is presenting him with a bonquet of California poppies.

[LORINDA *turns off the radio, crosses to the telephone.*]

LORINDA. [*On phone*] Get me toll line. . . . This is Fort Beulah, 67. I want to get a number quick. Get one of the secretaries of Senator Windrip at the Little Brown Church in the Vale in Zenith—you know, that big radio church. It's important. This is Miss Pike of the *"Informer."* Get it, and call me. [*She returns to the radio, turns it on again, then sits on couch to listen.*]

PRANG. [*Voice of the unctuous but forceful pastor heard on the radio*] To the tens of millions who have listened to me on God's own gift, the radio, I want to introduce and commend to you the Corporative candidate for President, Senator Windrip.

WINDRIP. [*Voice on the radio; forceful, dominating, not without culture*] I'm not going to address this radio audience as "my friends," because lots of you are my enemies—I hope so. This is a farmer named Berzelius Windrip, making another political speech—only it isn't political and it isn't a speech! I detest campaign promises that no man under Heaven can carry out. This isn't a campaign—[*Telephone rings*] it's a revolution!

[LORINDA *turns off radio, crosses to telephone, speaks on it.*]

LORINDA. Is this one of Senator Windrip's secretaries? . . . Well, you'll do. You've got to get a message to the Senator. . . . I know he's speaking, but this is a matter of life and death. Write a memo and put it in front of him. It may mean victory or defeat. . . . But you've got to. Uh—uh—this is the secretary of Commissioner Swan, of Vermont. . . . Tell Windrip that his Corpos—I mean, our Corpos—have beaten a man, Clarence Tubbs, a druggist. . . . Clarence T-U-B-B-S, druggist, Fort Beulah, Vermont, in a campaign row. This must stop. Give him that memo. It's vital! [*She hangs up, crosses to the radio, and turns it on again, and again we hear the voice of* WINDRIP.]

WINDRIP. The people are sick to death of political chatter. For a hundred and sixty years the Congress has been discussing—discussing. It's time to ACT—not under a gossiping committee, but under the leadership of one man, whom you can hold responsible. I'm not begging for office, but demanding—demanding!—that I be sanctioned to lead the United States—the last democratic and civilized nation left on earth—into the kind of corporative state that alone can face the raging barbarians. Let me tell you what kind of a fellow Buzz Windrip is. He's a first-class man for anybody to hate. All the milk-and-water reformers, and all the glittering rich folks hate him—yes, and fear him—because he's a farmer, born on the farm, inured to the bone-breaking toil of the farm, and hoping to die on the farm, unless some enemy's bullet lays him low in the marble halls of government.

[*Black-out. A few seconds of darkness are supposed to cover half an hour of Windrip's speech. When the lights and the speaking voice go up again,* DOREMUS *is discovered silting on the couch beside* LORINDA, *both listening to the speech. . . . During the black-out, he enters by the dining-room door, near the couch.*]

So let me sum up the planks of my platform. . . . The President shall determine the size of all courts. He shall enlist all workers in one union, and all business in scientific divisions.

The present political parties and the entire party system shall be abolished, because it is as absurd to have rival gangs in a civil state as in an army at war. AND THIS IS WAR, against all the degenerate countries of Europe, and the Corporative discipline shall not be for the purpose of joining but of opposing ALL forms of dictatorship. And lest any President be tempted, the power of Congress to impeach him shall be facilitated.

One army under one leader! Oh, individualism is a glorious word, and if for the moment we give up a few individual luxuries, it is only so that in the long run we may starve ourselves to greatness!

I would conclude there, but I am able to give you a piece of startling news. Even while I have stood here speaking, in the beautiful little city of Fort Beulah, Vermont, [DOREMUS *and* LORINDA *startled*] Mr. Terence Tubbs, a fine merchant of that place, was seriously injured in a scuffle. My enemies are trying to place the blame upon the Corpos. But I have secret information of what did happen, and it entirely exonerates our gallant marching-clubs. But if any Corpo had been to blame, I would cast him forth, [LORINDA, *irritated, rises to turn off the radio.*] for if any harm be done unto the least of these—

[LORINDA *turns off the radio.*]

LORINDA. Doesn't that sound like dictatorship?

DOREMUS. I'm afraid it's beginning to—though you've got to remember you can't take these speeches literally.

LORINDA. Did you find out about Clarence Tubbs?

DOREMUS. [*Quite placid*] Yes—sure. He's hurt bad, but not fatally, and it positively was not the Corpos—just as Senator Windrip said—gracious, I wonder how he found out about it so soon! Remarkable.

LORINDA. Very!

DOREMUS. Clarence must have got into a scuffle with some strangers. Folks up town were putting it on a Corpo named Jim Nickerson—know him?—kind of a tough egg—somebody had seen Nickerson go into Clarence's store. But I found that Henry Veeder and his wife were right there in the store when Nickerson went in—bought a pack of cigarettes—Veeder remembers it because Clarence made him pay cash—and they were still there when Nickerson went out, so that proves he's innocent, and the Corpos had nothing to do with it. [*Door bell. Starting for the door*] Just goes to show how you mustn't jump to conclusions.

LORINDA. I don't believe you've got the whole story.

DOREMUS. [*Opening the door*] Nonsense! [*Admits* JULIAN FALCK] Back again!

JULIAN. [*Respectful, very friendly*] Letter for you, sir, from Commissioner Swan. [JULIAN *hands over a large envelope, from which* DOREMUS *takes an ornate badge, and a letter.*]

DOREMUS. Letter from Swan? [*Reads aloud*] "Dear Mr. Jessup: We shall be honored if you will accept the enclosed badge as Honorary Corporative Sub-Commissioner for Beulah County. There are no duties involved, except your approval of our endeavors to give strength and purpose to youth." [*Holds up the badge*] Hm! Pretty fancy!

LORINDA. Looks like "The Sons and Daughters of I Will Arise!" [*Sits on couch.*] But it's nothing so funny. It's meant as a bribe, in case there should be any more trouble like the attack on Clarence.

JULIAN. [*Eagerly explaining*] It was an accident. The Commissioner was all broken up about it. He investigated, right away. Clarence got into a scuffle with some fellows from back in the hills—probably Brick MeGee and his gang—*none* of 'em Corpos. That's what happened.

DOREMUS. Prob'ly was . . . Lindy, I ought to accept this appointment. If some of the Corpos tend to be rowdy, all the more reason why I should take part. I can be a good influence.

LORINDA. You can only influence a machine gun from one end of it!

DOREMUS. [*Irritably crosses from couch to table*] Quit making the Corpos out a bunch of Frankensteens! Isn't Julian here one—and we've known him since he was [*Holds out hand a couple of feet from the floor*] so high! [*Sits in armchair; inspects badge again, and pins it on his lapel.*]

LORINDA. [*Looking sadly at* JULIAN] That's what worries me. . . . I can't believe it! A nice boy like you, running around playing soldier. Why don't you get yourself a sweet, wholesome girl?

JULIAN. [*Standing center; speaking almost savagely*] A girl! As though any young man without a rich father can afford to even blow a girl to a soda, these days! They told me if I did well in college, there'd be a good job waiting for me. Well, I got *magna cum laude*, and that was the last thing I got [*Looking toward* DOREMUS] I've begged for a job—any kind of a job—

DOREMUS. You *did* work, Julian.

JULIAN. I've worked exactly four months during the past year! I'm not asking for a cinch, or looking for glory! I'm yelling for a job! And the Corpos will tell me what to do, and they'll feed me. They'll shake off this bungling "Democracy"!

DOREMUS. You mustn't blame it on Democracy!

JULIAN. Anyway, we're going to organize things so we get a living. [*Turning back to* LORINDA] When that happens—I'll stop playing Romeo to an empty balcony!

LORINDA. Don't depend on them. Think out away for yourself.

JULIAN. Think? It's time to *act!* We're not parlor pinks—we're realists. We're behind Buzz Windrip, the Man on Horseback!

[SHAD *suddenly appears from the basement, noisily kicking door open. He wears his cheap and flashy best suit; his hat, with a gaudy band, insolently on the back of his head. He carries a straw suitcase.*]

SHAD. [*Stamping up to* DOREMUS] I want my time. I'm quitting.

DOREMUS. I don't entirely dislike the notion! But it's a little inconvenient. You said you longed to stay with us all winter.

SHAD. Not goin' to try and hold out on my dough, are you?

DOREMUS. [*Leaping up, angrily; taking out billfold*] Certainly not! It's a pleasure!

[*He counts out bills.* SHAD *insolently holds out his hand for them, but* DOREMUS *drops them on the table.* SHAD *scoops them up, glaring. Then he turns to* JULIAN, *pointing to his suitcase, on the floor.*]

SHAD. Take that out to the bus stop.

JULIAN. [*He is a young gentleman of the town thus addressed by a mucker. He doubles up his fist*] Of all the gall! Have I got to—

SHAD. You've got to do a lot of things! Are you a Corpo private?

JULIAN. What's that got to do with it?

SHAD. Commissioner Swan has made me a Sergeant of Corpos, on full time! Take that grip out!

[JULIAN *is furious, but he picks up the suitcase and sullenly trudges out with it.*]

[SHAD *lights a stogie, and airily addresses* DOREMUS *and* LORINDA] You two meant all right. I don't hold no hard feelings. [MARY *is just entering, coming down the stairs, and* SHAD *speaks to her flirtatiously*] Good-bye, cutie! [*Exit*]

[*The others gape after* SHAD.]

DOREMUS. [*After a pause*] Well! Say it!

LORINDA. We don't need to.

[MARY *goes to look out of the window.* DOREMUS *sits in his armchair by the table.*]

DOREMUS. You were right, Lindy. Shad certainly makes you wonder about the Corpos.

[FOWLER *bursts into the room, and addresses himself to* DOREMUS *especially.*]

FOWLER. Dad! There's something rotten about this Clarence Tubbs business. I went to his house. There were Corpos guarding the place. They wouldn't let me in—me, their regular physician! They'd kept out Dr. Strong, too. Told me Dr. Gax was in charge!

DOREMUS. *Gax?*

FOWLER. The worst quack in the state!

DOREMUS. What's he got to do with it?

FOWLER. I sent him in a note, and Gax sent out word that Mrs. Tubbs didn't want me. And the fellow who sent Gax there—the fellow who promised to pay Gax's bill—is Mr. Corpo Commissioner Swan!

DOREMUS. [*Relieved*] Swan's new—doesn't know Gax's reputation.

FOWLER. I don't like it. I saw Gax's face at an upper window. He was laughing at me.

[*Telephone rings.* DOREMUS *rises to answer it.*]

DOREMUS. [*On the phone—casually*] Hello. [*Sharply, unhappily*] *What?* . . . When? . . . All right. [*Hangs up; sits down, faint and miserable.*]

[Pause]

LORINDA. What is it?

DOREMUS. [*Slowly; as to himself*] Clarence is dead.

MARY, LORINDA. Oh—

DOREMUS. [*Still as though to himself; puzzled*] Gax phoned the paper. He said Clarence died of heart failure.

FOWLER. Heart failure—[*He starts for the door.*]

MARY. Where are you going?

FOWLER. Back to the Tubbs house. Dr. Gax won't be there now.

MARY. [*Her hand on his arm; imploring*] Please don't! These awful political rows, and that man Swan—

FOWLER. Think I'm going to stand by and let a thing like this happen?

MARY. But you're so quick-tempered.

FOWLER. Nonsense. Nothing will happen to me.

DOREMUS. Don't go back there now. Look into it later.

FOWLER. [*Angrily*] Yes—give people a chance to forget—is that it?

LORINDA. Better wait. Go to your office.

FOWLER. [*Bitterly*] Sure! I'll go read the ads in the medical journals! [*Exit*]

MARY. [*Running out after him*] Fowler! Listen! Please!

LORINDA. Clarence—a man I was talking to an hour and a half ago! It's begun!

DOREMUS. Then it's up to us to stop it.

LORINDA. Too late. The Corpos are on their way in. The people have waited too long to speak up.

DOREMUS. The press can speak. I can speak! Even if the Corpos do turn violent, one thing can never happen in America—they can't muzzle the press!

[*He is still in his armchair. During his last speech,* LORINDA *has crossed to the window, and she looks out, gloomily.*]

LORINDA. Leaves all faded. Makes me feel old. No more picnics for us this year.

DOREMUS. [*Looking up at her fondly; speaking cheerfully*] Plenty more next year.

LORINDA. Where will we all be, next year? I don't know why, but I'm terribly afraid.

DOREMUS. Buzz Windrip will talk—Swan will talk—but [*Lifting his head proudly*] I've got my newspaper!

LORINDA. [*She turns toward him blindly, hands out*] Terribly afraid!

[*He takes the Corpo badge from his lapel, contemptuously tosses it on the table, and reaches up to pat her hand.*]

DOREMUS. Don't worry, darling.

LORINDA. You've never called me that before!

DOREMUS. Really?

LORINDA. Oh, we're the worst kind of old Yankee lovers! I guess I'm what everybody thinks—a cranky old maid, sticking her nose into everybody's business.

DOREMUS. Nonsense! Whole town knows you're a saint. And now, by golly, you're a saint in armor, and you've aroused me into fighting.

LORINDA. If it isn't too late—oh, my dear, too late!

CURTAIN

★

ACT II

SCENE 1: *Winter, three and a half months later. The office of* DOREMUS JESSUP, *as editor of the Fort Beulah "Daily Informer."*

It also is a shallow set. Up L. *is the one door, opening into a hallway which leads both to the street and to the mechanical department. Down* L. *is* LORINDA*'s desk, with typewriter.*

Down R. IS DOREMUS*'s somewhat larger, flat-topped desk, scattered with proofs, copy-paper, exchanges, a telephone. Pushed back is a typewriter, under which is at present slipped an Associated Press "flimsy." In the top center drawer is a pile of letters, and a revolver.*

The one window is in the right wall, near this desk.

A chair for visitors faces this desk; another such chair stands against the back wall, center. Against the back wall, behind DOREMUS*'s desk, is a steel letter file. On the back wall are old posters, and pasted-up headlines and half-tones.*

AT RISE: DOREMUS, *in shirtsleeves, wearing a green eyeshade, is at his desk, reading a proof.* LORINDA *is at hers, typing.* FRANK TASBROUGH *wanders between them, telling his troubles; and his derby hat, on* DOREMUS*'s desk, is in the way. There is a not-too-loud sound of linotypes, which dies down after the first couple of speeches.*

TASBROUGH. [*At* C., *pacing*]—these Federal inspectors, in Corpo uniforms, putting up a holler about safety devices, all of 'em grafters, with their hands out for a bribe. And making me fire my best men and put Corpos in their place. That's what your President Windrip has done—

LORINDA. Careful! Want to get us in trouble?

TASBROUGH. I'm in trouble enough! Windrip in office only one month, and new taxes every day! Demand we put in more windows for the poor abused workmen—and then tax us on the number of windows! Before election, they were going to do so much for the factory-owners, and what have they done?

DOREMUS. [*Speaking sardonically; his eyes still on his galley-proof*] Don't you approve of their solving unemployment—[*Looks up; speaks irritably*] chasing all the idle into work-camps, and renting 'em out to you for seventy-five cents a day?

TASBROUGH. All they deserve. Ain't they been yelling for *jobs* all these years? Now they got 'em! But even with wages down where they ought to be, I'm not making a decent profit. By Godfrey, I'm losing money!

LORINDA. The women laundry strikers in New Orleans lost their lives!

TASBROUGH. They wouldn't have, if they'd minded their own business, the way I have.

DOREMUS. I'm concerned about President Windrip limiting freedom of speech. [*Sardonically*] My opinion, that's even more important than money!

TASBROUGH. [*Plumping himself into chair by* DOREMUS*'s desk*] Now look here! I'm sick of all this hypocrisy about money! What gives you poetic folks your nice houses, and your motor cars to go out and look at your doggone poetic sunsets? Money! We monied people got to stick together, and we're looking to you to lead the movement against all these taxes. You're supposed to be one of these great liberals. Well, go the whole hog! Denounce the Corpos so hot you'll hear a holler right from Washington, DC

DOREMUS. You were pretty strong for them, before election.

TASBROUGH. So were you. It was your editorials made me vote for Windrip!

DOREMUS. WHAT?

LORINDA. [*Furiously*] You know that's not true!

TASBROUGH. [*Rises, crosses to her*] Absolutely! And I got the right to demand—

LORINDA. Go do your demanding somewhere else. We have to get out a paper. [*Rises, crosses to the letter-file, up* R.]

TASBROUGH. [*Angrily taking his hat from* DOREMUS*'s desk*] All right, but I'm not going to let up till Doremus does his bounden duty, and speaks up for the down-trodden.

LORINDA. The who?

TASBROUGH. [*At the door*] The manufacturers. [*Exit*]

[DOREMUS *and* LORINDA *look at each other, perplexed, then amused.*]

LORINDA. Well, say it!

DOREMUS. Kind of funny! I figure he's actually making almost as much money as he did before election. But guess nobody's happy except the Corpos themselves. [*Rises; lounges against window.*] He's the sixth complainer I've had today.

LORINDA. What did that letter say you were reading before Fathead Tasbrough came in?

DOREMUS. What letter?

LORINDA. You know perfectly well.

DOREMUS. Oh—just a typical kick from some sports fan.

LORINDA. What did you do with it?

DOREMUS. Tore it up, I suppose.

LORINDA. What are you keeping in that top drawer?

DOREMUS. [*Trying to be whimsical*] Well, now, let's see. There's one and a half pair of mittens, and a four-year-old ticket to the County Fair—

LORINDA. Then why is it locked?

DOREMUS. Some private papers.

LORINDA. Let me see 'em.

DOREMUS. Why, Lindy!

LORINDA. Doremus, you've never had secrets from me, before. The cruellest thing that ever happened is your being afraid to trust me. I lie awake nights, imagining every horrible thing. [DOREMUS *takes key from pocket, begins to open top center desk drawer.*] I must know!

[*He opens the drawer. She takes out a letter, begins to read bits of it aloud.*] "Take a shot at you from the bushes, Mr. Editor. . . . Bomb hitched to your starter. . . . A well-wisher." Oh, my dear!

DOREMUS. Some practical joker.

LORINDA. Any others?

DOREMUS. Plenty!

LORINDA. Three days ago, a crowd of masked men dragged the editor of the Sawtray *Argus* into a swamp and beat him, and his own paper reported it as an accident. They weren't practical jokers. [*Sees the revolver in the open drawer and starts to pick it up*] What's that!

DOREMUS. [*Snatching the revolver from the drawer*] Hey sakes a'mighty, be careful! [*He balances the revolver in his hand like one used to it.*] You know, I haven't fired one of these pesky things for ten years, but [*Proudly*] I used to be able to hit a condensed-milk can at thirty yards!

LORINDA. Why did you get it?

DOREMUS. Oh, I dunno—I figured if they tried to start anything, I'd be ready. [*Lays the revolver on the desk.*]

LORINDA. Who are *they?*

DOREMUS. Our Corpo friends.

LORINDA. So you really are worried?

DOREMUS. Yes. Things are getting serious. [*Draws sheet of flimsy from under typewriter.*] Listen. This is an A P dispatch that I just got from Washington. [*Reads aloud*] "One hundred members of Congress have been put under protective arrest!"

LORINDA. [*Aghast*] Congress?

DOREMUS. Yuh.

LORINDA. Then they can't impeach Windrip.

DOREMUS. And he said their power of impeachment would plumb prevent his ever becoming dictator—But there's more here: "Government takes over the American Federation of Labor and the C.I.O. and combines them in one union. All workers are *required* to join. In charge to fix all hours and wages, is the munitions-manufacturer, William Pinto."

LORINDA. [*Crossing* L.] I can't believe it.

DOREMUS. I wish I could get the follow-up of the story. Something's holding it up.

LORINDA. [*Sitting at her desk* L.] National censorship?

DOREMUS. [*Bitterly*] *Protective* censorship! [*Crossing to* C.] Lindy, I don't know what to do. People come and ask my advice, and I don't know—I don't know! I never realized what an editor's position as guardian of the truth could mean, till now—when it's too late. I've failed my people!

LORINDA. You haven't!

DOREMUS. Oh yes I have, my girl! And I want you to do something for me.

LORINDA. Yes?

DOREMUS. Take a little vacation. Let me be alone here for a few weeks, to work things out.

LORINDA. Doremus!

DOREMUS. [*Crossing to her*] You go home—gwan home—I don't want you bothering me!

LORINDA. [*Rising*] I've never in my life heard such a wicked lie! [*She takes hat and coat from hooks on back wall.*] I'm going out and get the D.A.R. news. You can fire me and fire me, and I'll always be back here at my desk at eleven o'clock every single morning! [*At the door, sobbing*] I will! [*Exit, slamming door.*]

DOREMUS. You will not! [*Hurries to the door, and opens it to yell down the corridor after her*] You've never been less than fifteen minutes late in your life! [*He tries to laugh, but ends with a sigh. He returns to his desk, puts the revolver back in the drawer—which he does not lock—sits down, marks a proof, rubs his jaw, and shouts*] Dan! *Dan!* [*Recrosses to the door—reading the proof as he goes—and yells down the hall.*] DAN!

DAN. [*Heard off*] Hold your horses! I'm coming!

[DOREMUS *recrosses to his desk and sits, still absorbed in his proof sheet.*]

[*Enter* DAN WILGUS, *printshop foreman; a lanky New England workman, in his fifties; loyal, gruff, courageous. He is gnawing a corncob, and wearing an inky apron.*]

DOREMUS. Dan—Oh . . . We'll run this editorial, after all. [*He holds out the proof-sheet toward* DAN, *who stands by the desk, but does not take the proof.*]

DAN. We'll do no such thing.

DOREMUS. You make the page up right now, and make this the lead editorial.

DAN. Can't.

DOREMUS. What do you mean: "Can't"?

DAN. I mean I been reading it again, and we're not going to run no such a piece, not in any paper I make up! I've thrown in the type. Talk about Corpo machine guns—want to have 'em turned on us?

DOREMUS. Scared?

DAN. Scared? Me? Remember that editor out in Kansas, two days ago? The Corpos tied him to the press and set fire to it!

[DOREMUS *rises, starts for the door, crossing down from his desk. . . . The two men, so long associated, have the greatest fondness and respect for each other, and express it usually by grumbling.*]

DOREMUS. They didn't burn the printers, did they? . . . Only the editor!

DAN. I wasn't thinking of the editor—I was thinking of the press! [*Follows* DOREMUS *to the door.*] Where d' you suppose you're going?

DOREMUS. [*Hand on the door*] Going out and try to reset this editorial myself!

DAN. All right, all right! [*Snatches proof-sheet from him.*] If you're bound and determined to be a hero, I suppose I'll have to he one too. Nineteen years now you have been having your way!

DOREMUS. Eighteen! [*Starts back for desk.*]

DAN. Seems like eighty!

DOREMUS. [*Standing at desk*] Huh!

DAN. Besides. I may be able to repair a linotype after the Corpos massage it with a crowbar, but not after a liberal intellectual fiddles with it! [*Exit*]

[DOREMUS *sits down, glaring at the door.*

[*In a moment,* DAN *sticks his head in to announce:*] Here's a big Corpo lummox to see you! Don't say I didn't warn you! [*Exit again.*]

[*Enter* DAVID, *wearing imitation Corpo cap, and followed by* MARY.]

DAVID. [*Coming to attention; saluting; to* DOREMUS] Salute, private!

DOREMUS. Mary! What's this the boy's got on? Corpo cap?

MARY. It is silly, but Julian Falck gave it to him.

DAVID. Aw, I like my cap!

DOREMUS. For the last twenty years now, about the only uniform you ever saw in America was the Salvation Army.

MARY. [*To* DAVID] Skip out, dear, and see Mr. Wilgus.

[DAVID *hesitates.*]

DOREMUS. He'll show you some type lice.

DAVID. Okay! [*Exit, cheerfully.*]

DOREMUS. I can't understand how Julian can endure being a Corpo, after the Clarence Tubbs murder.

MARY. [*At* LORINDA'S *desk, nervously fidgeting*] Why, Julian believes that Brick McGee is guilty, and he's not a Corpo, and—Dad!

DOREMUS. What's trouble?

MARY. Commissioner Swan is in town for the day—and he's put Dr. Gax in charge of the County Hospital—

DOREMUS. What?

MARY. —over Fowler's head.

DOREMUS. That's impossible!

MARY. Fowler just phoned me.

DOREMUS. Swan wouldn't dare!

MARY. He has! [*Crosses quickly to* DOREMUS'*s desk.*] Dad, Fowler won't let this pass. You've got to do something.

DOREMUS. I will! I will! [*On the phone*] County Hospital. [*To* MARY, *beside him*] Now you stop worrying. There must be some mistake about this whole thing. [*On phone*] County Hospital? . . . This is Mr. Jessup speaking. I want to talk to Dr. Greenhill. . . . When did he leave? . . . All right—thank you. [*Hangs up; to* MARY] Fowler's on his way here now. We'll straighten this out.

MARY. Dad, I'm afraid. I'm sure all this has something to do with Clarence's death. Fowler's gone on trying to find out about it,

DOREMUS. I know—I know—tell you what you do. You take Davy home now. Let me take care of this. [*Pats her hand, as she leans over desk*] Don't you trust your old dad?

[*Sound of linotypes heard again, not loud.*]

MARY. [*Tired*] I do.

DOREMUS. Good!

MARY. By, Dad!

DOREMUS. By! [MARY *crossing to the door.*] Phone me later.

[*Exit* MARY]

[*For a moment,* DOREMUS *meditates, anxious, growing angry. Then he yanks his typewriter across the desk, to the front of it, tears out a sheet of paper that is already in the machine, feeds in another, and rapidly types about 24 letters and spaces.*

[*Sound of linotypes now louder.*]

[DOREMUS *shouts:*] Dan! DAN!

[DAN *re-enters, closing the door.*]

DAN. [*Casually crossing to the desk, handing* DOREMUS *a galley-proof*] I got your blame editorial reset.

DOREMUS. Throw it away! I got something more important! [*He hands to* DAN *the sheet he has just typed, but absently takes the galley-proof from* DAN *at the same time, and keeps the proof in his hand during the following.*] Set me an eight-column banner head, clean smack across the page; "Corpo Politics Murders the Sick."

DAN. [*Now really agitated*] Have you gone crazy?

DOREMUS. Worse than crazy! Get busy!

[*Sudden and total stoppage of sound of machinery.*]

DAN. What the—Machinery stopped!

[DAN *starts hastily for the door.* DOREMUS *rises, stands at his desk, wondering.* DAN *yanks the door open, revealing—to his astonishment—*SWAN, SHAD, *and several* CORPO PRIVATES *standing there, in uniform, with side arms, all rigid and grim.*]

[SWAN *strolls in, jerking his head at* DAN, *as an order to get out.*]

SWAN. Outside, you!

[DAN *hesitates, then obeys.*]

[SWAN *amiably wanders in, followed by* SHAD *now clean-faced and erect, in uniform as sergeant, with a sort of vulgar smartness, and a hint of menace.*]

DOREMUS. Swan! You have anything to do with that machinery stopping?

SWAN. [*Crossing to desk; suave and insolent*] Almost everything, I should think!

DOREMUS. Then what do you mean by it!

SWAN. [*Now at the desk*] Do be calm, my dear fellow! We're both civilized human beings.

[*He casually sits at desk, in visitor's chair.*]

[DOREMUS *sinks down in his own chair.*]

Surely we should be able to discuss any differences of policy—

[SWAN *has been peering at the galley-proof which* DOREMUS *has all this time been holding in his hand. He suddenly snatches it away—*DOREMUS *too astonished to speak—and reads aloud from it:*]

"Murder by Machine Gun"! Very pretty alliteration. I congratulate you, Doremus.

DOREMUS. [*Recovered; snarling*] My name is Jessup!

SWAN. [*Playfully*] Oh no, it wouldn't be, not between friends, would it, Doremus? I'll call you "Doremus," and you just call me "Commissioner." [*Now sharply, viciously*] Jessup, I came here to stop your vile criticisms of the Corporative Government, but I hadn't expected anything so beastly as this new affront! [*Tears up the galley-proof*] You seem to be asking for a trial. . . . Sergeant Ledue!

SHAD. Yessir.

SWAN. Station a couple of privates by the door. You sit here at the desk and take notes.

[*With gestures,* SHAD *swiftly places* PRIVATES *on guard, and approaches the desk, dragging over the second visitor's chair.*]

DOREMUS. So you and Gax conspire—

SWAN. Conspire? A word out of melodrama, my Doremus!

[SHAD *knocks* DOREMUS*'s left arm aside, in order to take a pad and pencil from under it, and sits by the desk, trying to take notes. His harsh, contemptuous, amused stare,* SWAN*'s sneering mock-civility, and the presence of the guards all begin to intimidate* DOREMUS, *as* SWAN *purrs on.*]

According to a new decree, my friend, I have the power to hold court martial, with myself as judge, prosecutor, and defense—and you'll be simply thrilled to observe how the three of me agree. So now—[*He lakes a gold cigarette-case from his tunic; lights a cigarette.*] Oh, I'm so sorry. Do have a cigarette! [*Holds cigarette case toward* DOREMUS, *though quite out of his grasp.*]

DOREMUS. I don't care much for this cat-and-mouse game! If this is a trial, what are your charges?

SWAN. Charges? Oh, my only aunt! Merely high treason, and incitement to murder, and airy trifles like that—and all so easily got rid of if you would just play along with us. I'd simply adore explaining some of our secret plans. You'd see *such* a new light!

SHAD. Jessup couldn't see a light if it was on the end of his nose.

SWAN. Hush, my dear Sergeant! . . . And of course, Doremus, I do ever so delicately urge you to give me a list of all the people who are secretly opposed to our administration.

DOREMUS. You think I'd become an *informer?*

SWAN. Just so! It could be!

DOREMUS. Oh, don't try to impress me with your Reggie Fortune phrases. I can read, too!

SWAN. Not really! I shouldn't have fancied so, from your proof-reading! But do, I pray you, [*Gravely*] try to show a little more formality at this trial—for curiously enough it *is* a trial!—for *treason!*

[DOREMUS *glances at* SHAD, *whose steady hostile sneer begins to make him realize that he really may be in great danger. His right hand—hidden by the typewriter from* SWAN *and* SHAD*—begins to crumple a galley-proof.*]

One really ought to take you out and shoot you—oh yes, one has the power—but it might he more amusing to keep you here. [SWAN *looks at* SHAD, *and smiles.*] So I announce, as my official decision, that from now on, the editor of this paper is to be Sergeant Ledue!

DOREMUS. [*Incredulous*] Shad? . . . Editor?

SWAN. Why, my dear fellow, I'm picking him because you're old and loving co-workers! [SHAD *guffaws, in a hearty Haw, haw, haw, while* DOREMUS *is too furious to speak.*] We do hope you'll go on writing—playing with the many-colored word—but Sergeant Ledue will tell you precisely what to write, and how to change it afterward. [DOREMUS *leaps up—he has had enough; but* SHAD *rises and pushes him down into the chair again, while the guarding* CORPOS *prepare to move forward. The whole thing terrifies* DOREMUS, *though he still tries to sit up, proudly . . .* SWAN *is talking on, sweetly*] And if the Sergeant ever complains about your work—

[*He is interrupted by* FOWLER GREENHILL, *rushing in, standing over* SWAN'S *chair menacingly. . . .* SHAD*—rising, not too quickly—and the other* CORPOS *move toward* FOWLER.]

FOWLER. Swan, I've had enough! One man is going to protest against your Corpo swinishness!

DOREMUS. Fowler! Let me—

SWAN. [*Very suave*] My dear Doctor, what seems to be the trouble?

FOWLER. I shut up about Clarence Tubbs, to keep myself clear for my work, but now you've taken that away from me. Dr. *Gax!*

SWAN. You're entirely mistaken, my dear Doctor. I've been misrepresented.

FOWLER. I'm going to expose you—

[*Both* DOREMUS *and* SWAN *are now standing, facing* FOWLER.]

DOREMUS. Fowler! Wait! Be quiet now—

FOWLER. [*Still to* SWAN] You murdered Clarence.

SWAN. [*He has been playing for time till his men should be in strategic position. He barks now:*] Grab him! [*The* CORPOS, *including* SHAD, *do so.* SWAN *again speaks casually, to* FOWLER] You have shown a considerable talent for investigating deaths. Now you'll investigate one quite authoritatively. [*To* SHAD] The comrade bores me. Take the swine out in the alley and shoot him.

[SHAD *and the* CORPOS *are too much for the struggling* FOWLER. *They rush him out of the door, while he shouts "You don't dare" and "They'll hang the whole lot of you—"*]

[DOREMUS *slides from the side to the back of his desk and—just as* SWAN *is turning away from the sight of* FOWLER*'s exit—*DOREMUS *yanks open the center top drawer and pulls out the revolver.*

[*But* SWAN *guesses what is up, makes a lightning spring, snatches the revolver from* DOREMUS, *breaks it—the shells scattering on the desk—and drawls:*]

Nasty little gun, Doremus! [*He tucks the revolver into his coat.*]

DOREMUS. [*Sinking into his desk chair*] Swan, you can't do this!

SWAN. Can't?

[*A* CORPO *re-enters the room, stands rigid by the door.*]

DOREMUS. A fine young doctor—

SWAN. A fine young fool, my dear Doremus! [*Telephone rings.* DOREMUS *reaches for it;* SWAN, *after a slight struggle, wrests the instrument from him, and speaks on it, very sweetly.*] Hello . . . Mr. Jessup can't come to the phone at the moment. . . . [SWAN *sits on the edge of the desk, airy and at ease.*] This is just a friend of his. . . . [SWAN *listens to what is being said on the telephone, then turns to* DOREMUS, *simpering:*] It's your daughter. She wants to know about some oddly named man the Corpos have placed over her good husband. Would the name be Gax? [SWAN *speaks again on the telephone.* DOREMUS *starts to rise, vaguely intending to attack* SWAN, *but the* CORPO *at the door takes half a step forward, threateningly, glaring at* DOREMUS, *who collapses into his chair again.* SWAN *on phone:*] Oh yes, your father is here, but he doesn't seem to be feeling very well.

[*Sound of rifles from the alley.* DOREMUS *hides his face in his hands.* SWAN, *as the curtain begins to fall, continues on the telephone, in honeyed tones:*]

No, Mrs. Greenhill, I'm afraid Mr. Jessup won't be able to do anything for your husband.

CURTAIN

★

SCENE 2: *Some weeks after Scene 1. Again* DOREMUS'*s office. But his desk is now occupied by* SHAD, *who has been made a lieutenant, and for* DOREMUS *there is, center against the back wall, facing* L., *a small table. On the wall are large* CORPO *posters.*

AT RISE: SHAD, *in uniform, cap cocked on the back of his head, is seated at* DOREMUS'*s former desk, speaking to* DIMMICK*—an anonymous-looking man of no particular age, size, or expression.*

DIMMICK. Is Mr. Doremus Jessup in?

SHAD. Naw, he's in the composing-room, where he belongs. What d' you want?

DIMMICK. Is this Lieutenant Ledue that I have the pleasure of speaking to?

SHAD. That's me. Who're you?

DIMMICK I hear, sir, that you are not only the new editor here, but in general charge in Fort Beulah.

SHAD. So what?

DIMMICK. Great honor to meet you, sir, Dimmick is my name. I am an insurance representative, from Albany. I would like to interest you—

SHAD. Well, you can't, see? Insurance? Go roll your hoop.

DIMMICK. You don't quite get the idea, sir. The lieutenant doesn't need any insurance. A grateful Government will care for him, with a pension. But I know how the whole district looks to the lieutenant for guidance, and if you could induce a lot of people to take out insurance—and freeze out irresponsible agents—I'd feel it was only my duty to beg the lieutenant to accept ten per cent of my commissions.

SHAD. [*Thoughtful*] Insurance, eh? I hadn't thought of *that!*

DIMMICK. Oh yes, it would come to quite an item.

SHAD. But—ten per cent, and me doing all the work? Think that's fair and square? Is that what you call *honorable?* I wouldn't touch it for less than twenty-five.

DIMMICK. I can see it, now you put it that way. Very well. Twenty-five. And how about my starting in on your hired man, Jessup?

SHAD. [*Guffaws*] Swell idea! My hired man! Go to it. I'll order the old goat to get liberal, and look out for his family. Got a nice daughter, Mary—widow—shame the way he neglects her.

DIMMICK. If the lieutenant would let me have a little time alone with Jessup—

SHAD. Sure. Wait downstairs, and come back here in three minutes. I want to introduce the subject to Jessup tactful. And no monkey-business, mind you, or I'll skin you alive.

DIMMICK. Certainly not, sir. You can look over my books any time.

SHAD. You bet your life I'll look over your books! Now beat it!

DIMMICK. Thank you, sir. [*Exit*]

SHAD. [*Calling*] Jessup. Hey, *Jessup!* [*No answer, and* SHAD *strides to the door and shouts down the hall*] JESSUP!

DOREMUS. [*Heard off*] I'm coming,

[SHAD *returns to his desk, picks up copypaper, clumsily marks it.*

[*Enter* DOREMUS, *cowed and deflated; shabbier titan in II:1; wearing green eyeshade. . . .* SHAD *ignores him.*]

DOREMUS. What about Dan Wilgus, Lieutenant?

SHAD. Hush! I'm thinking. [DOREMUS *stands awaiting his master's pleasure.* SHAD *looks up, grunting:*] I guess that'll do now. Your account of the Corpo Council wasn't enthusiastic enough. What I mean—enthusiastic. You stick around with me, and you'll learn what real guys like to read.

DOREMUS. [*Taking the amended copy from* SHAD] I wanted to ask you about Dan Wilgus.

SHAD. What about him?

DOREMUS. He says you've fired him.

SHAD. We don't need him. He's no good.

DOREMUS. I'm afraid we do. He's about the only experienced printer you've left me.

SHAD. [*Threateningly*] So you don't like the way I run things!

DOREMUS. Yes, but—If we fall down on the posters, Swan'll blame me—he might even blame you.

SHAD. All right then, I'll show you I'm a good guy. You can keep Wilgus. But I don't want you pestering me any more. [*Rises, looks out of the window.*]

DOREMUS. [*Turning away*] Thanks.

SHAD. Say, since I been so nice to you—who handles your insurance?

DOREMUS. Judge Jarvis.

SHAD. There's a fella blew in town peddlin' policies. Fixed me up with coverage on my new coop, real reasonable. Dimmick his name is—from Albany. He's a good friend' of mine, and it won't hurt my feelings none if you do business with him. [SHAD *takes a cigar from a box on desk; throws the stub of an old one on the floor, where it falls at* DOREMUS*'s feet.* DOREMUS *silently sits down at his little table, and begins to revise the piece of copy* SHAD *has handed him. He does not look up, as* SHAD *pompously babbles on.*] I got to go to headquarters. Me and Swan decided I'd keep an eye on headquarters while he's away. Try to get along without me—do a little thinking for yourself, Jessup. But, if anything comes up, you can phone me. [*Knock at door.*] Come in. [*Enter* DIMMICK.] Oh, Jessup, this is my friend Dimmick, and he's one swell insurance agent.

[DOREMUS *merely glances at* DIMMICK; *doesn't think much of him; and looks back at his work.*]

DIMMICK. [*To* DOREMUS, *as in a dreary routine salesman's recital*] Excuse me, but Lieutenant Ledue said you might be interested in some insurance—or no; I shall not call it "insurance," Mr. Jessup, but a bond of hope that pays dividends in happiness.

SHAD. Better take out about ten thousand, Jessup—while you still got some dough left!

DIMMICK. [*Continuing to* DOREMUS] I'd like to analyze your present policies—no charge, no obligation,

SHAD. [*To* DIMMICK] Sure—go ahead. [*To* DOREMUS, *who is still not looking up*] Trouble with you old rams is, you never think of your families. I'll see you later. [*Exit* SHAD.]

DOREMUS. [*To* DIMMICK, *absently, not looking up*] I'm busy, and I've got all the insurance I want.

DIMMICK. Not my kind. I represent an old-line company—founded by George Washington.

DOREMUS. [*Looking up; irritably*] I don't know what kind of a fool scheme—

DIMMICK. [*Bending over* DOREMUS; *suddenly sharp, demanding*] Hush! Listen! I know all about you, and Swan murdering Dr. Greenhill! Good thing for us Shad Ledue is a pompous idiot. Mr. Jessup, I'm an agent of the People's Party!

DOREMUS. [*Aghast*] I don't believe it!

DIMMICK. I'll prove it.

DOREMUS. No one *could* be so foolhardy as to spy for the People's Party!

DIMMICK. You can check up on me through your friend Ed Samson, of the Burlington Paper Company.

DOREMUS. I don't want anything to do with it! There isn't any People's Party any more!

DIMMICK. Don't argue! Senator Trowbridge is in Canada, trying to rally the old America. We're organizing an underground spy system. Want you to take charge in Fort Beulah. Collect all the Corpo atrocities. Distribute propaganda literature—

DOREMUS. [*Rising; hoarsely*] Get out of here! I've got enough trouble—

DIMMICK. Talk to Ed Samson. He knows all about—

DOREMUS. I don't want to know *anything* about it!

DIMMICK. [*Without raising his voice, but relentless*] Every church and synagogue in Chicago has been closed, and their pastors imprisoned.

DOREMUS. I can't help that.

DIMMICK. All Jews have been forbidden to own factories.

DOREMUS. I know.

DIMMICK. The study of all foreign languages is to be forbidden in colleges.

DOREMUS. [*Interested*] I hadn't got *that* information.

DIMMICK. [*Darting to the door, at the sound of steps; then relapsing into feigned ineffectuality*] Quiet. . . . You've always got to think of insurance as an investment.

[LORINDA *enters, goes to her desk.*]

DOREMUS. Good day. Not much use of your staying around.

DIMMICK. Well, I certainly hope you see your way clear to taking out some insurance.

DOREMUS. [*Sitting at his little table again*] Never mind about that.

DIMMICK [*Laying a circular on* DOREMUS'S *desk, then crossing to lay one on* LORINDA'S.] If you change your mind, remember Ed Samson. . . . *Ed Samson.* [*Exit* DIMMICK, *closing door.*]

DOREMUS. [*As* DIMMICK *exits*] Yes, yes, yes! [*He hides the circular in his pocket.*]

LORINDA. I must say you weren't very cordial to him.

DOREMUS. [*Again looking down, intent on his copy*] I don't need any insurance, and it don't pay to get chummy with strangers these days.

LORINDA. [*Looking at circular* DIMMICK *has left*] What's this? "George Washington Insurance Company. . . . Ninety-six sharecroppers shot in Arkansas—"

DOREMUS. [*At the word "sharecroppers," he has raised his head, begun to listen to her. Now he leaps up, crosses to her, snatches the circular from her, tucks it into his pocket, also.*] Be careful! That fellow—claims to be a secret agent of the People's Party!

LORINDA. Oh, is it possible? Think he's real?

DOREMUS. I don't know! May have been sent by the Corpos to trap me.

LORINDA. Did he say Ed Samson would know?

DOREMUS. So he claims.

LORINDA. Why don't you telephone him, and find out?

DOREMUS. I don't want to find out. [*Crosses toward Shad's desk.*] Underground work? I won't touch it. I'm too old for this hero business. What good is an old fool like me to the People? [*Bitterly*] The People!

LORINDA. Don't!

DOREMUS. [*Leaning against the window, half looking out*] Anything happened to me, what'd become of Davy?

LORINDA. I'm not blaming you. I'm glad you're being sensible.

DOREMUS. Yes. "Sensible." That's what we call cowardice, after fifty!

LORINDA. You're not afraid—just dazed. So am I!

DOREMUS. Life could have been pretty decent for us. [*He looks out of the window, his back to her, at her desk.*] Remember how we used to run off to the hills and go picknicking? Can't we take Mary and Davy and run off to Canada, now? I haven't any strength left.

LORINDA. [*Rising, crossing to him*] Find it in the People! There's always strength in the People, if you fight for them. Run away? Do you think we could rest on the hill, and see the People fighting down in the valley?

DOREMUS. It's quiet on the hill.

LORINDA. [*Her hand on his shoulder*] I wish I could give you strength. But I'm frightened too, and lonely. I'm just a cranky old maid. But not in my heart!

DOREMUS. I know how warm that is! [*He kisses her, lightly.*] It will come back—our strength. Some day, some time, we'll fight! [*He looks out of the window; speaks excitedly:*] Look—look—look down there. [LORINDA *and he stare down into the street.*] There's Dimmick now—the secret agent—fellow that's just jumping on the bus that's pulling out for Burlington—for the north. [*Sound of the door opening slowly.*] Hush! Careful! [*Enter* JULIAN. *now in smart uniform as lieutenant of Corpos. He closes the door.* DOREMUS *stares at him and crosses toward him, speaking rather sardonically:*] Ah! Another handsome new lieutenant!

LORINDA. Julian!

[*All three stand center.*]

JULIAN. I saw Shad in the poolroom. He mustn't catch me here.

DOREMUS. What's wrong?

JULIAN. This morning Brick McGee was shot for the murder of Clarence Tubbs. So that's all cleared up! Only I know Brick was innocent!

DOREMUS. Are you sure?

JULIAN. Mr. Jessup, I've had enough. I thought the Corpos would give me a chance to do something with my life. But I'm sick of the lies and the killings.

DOREMUS. Get out of 'em, then.

JULIAN. Once a Corpo, always a Corpo, unless you'd rather be shot.

LORINDA. Julian!

JULIAN. Yes?

LORINDA. Want to risk your life to overthrow the Corpos?

JULIAN. I—I think I might.

LORINDA. Then you've got to be ready for dangerous work—dirty work.

JULIAN. How do you mean?

LORINDA. To betray them. You're young. Stick to the Corpos; learn all the inside stuff. Some day we'll need young men like you on the inside. Will you do it?

DOREMUS. [*To* JULIAN] Yes! Get chummy with the Corpo secret service. Learn who's the traitors to the old America!

LORINDA. And you'll have the greatest chance of us all.

JULIAN. All right! I'll try to do it.

DOREMUS. And now—skip. You better look pretty unfriendly to us, from now on.

JULIAN. I will be! I'll try to. [*Exit, closing door.*]

DOREMUS. [*Somewhat testily, to* LORINDA] All right for you—talking at me over Julian's head.

LORINDA. I did not! [*Sits at her desk*]

DOREMUS. You did so! I know you! Trying to coax me into virtue! You're like all women!

LORINDA. I am not—I mean, thank God I am!

[*A knock.* DOREMUS *opens the door, and admits* HENRY *and* MRS. VEEDER.]

VEEDER. I don't know as you'll remember us—

DOREMUS. [*Glad to see them*] Why sure, sure, Henry! Mrs. Veeder. Come sit down! [*Absent-mindedly, he goes to his old desk, now* SHAD*'s, dragging over for* MRS. VEEDER *the chair from his present little table. Meanwhile:*]

MRS. VEEDER. Real nice office you got here.

DOREMUS. Oh, it's just a small place—

VEEDER. [*As his wife and he sit down, with* DOREMUS *in his old place at the desk, facing them*] Hush, mother—we mustn't waste Mr. Jessup's time. [*To* DOREMUS] I've been a reader of the *Informer* for so many years—almost feel like I belong to it—so I thought I'd come and ask. Our family's been on our farm for a hundred years, but now the Corpos have sort of taken it away from me,

DOREMUS. Taken it away? How?

VEEDER. Well, this is the way it happened. One day a Corpo come to me and said I had to do my part in President Windrip's farm-improvement plan. He said I had to take a $10,000 loan. Mr. Jessup, I didn't need no loan.

MRS. VEEDER. But they made us take it.

VEEDER. Now, now, Mother! [*Continues to* DOREMUS:] Then they said I had to rent the house to them for a Corpo rest-home, and they made me and Mrs. Veeder move out to the shed. They used my crops for food, and when I went down to Corpo headquarters, they said the crops belonged to the Corpos, because they was renting the place.

MRS. VEEDER. They never paid any rent.

VEEDER. Then they took the $10,000 they made me borrow and turned it over to a Corpo contractor, to make over the house into a barracks.

DOREMUS. That beautiful old house?

VEEDER. Yes. And then I got a notice I had to pay the loan back. Well, I didn't have the loan. The man at the bank said the Government owns the bank now, and he had no choice, like they used lo have in the old private banks. He had to act by hard and fast rules.

DOREMUS. We've got to make people understand that—

VEEDER. So they've took my place, because I couldn't pay, and now today they told us we got to pay rent for the shed!

MRS. VEEDER. We're gettin' kind of desperate.

VEEDER. We thought maybe you could give us some advice.

DOREMUS. This has got to change! [*For the first time in the scene, he sounds resolute.*] We've got to act together! We've got—

[*He is interrupted by the hasty entrance of a somewhat agitated* SHAD.]

SHAD. [*Shouting at* DOREMUS] What are you doing at my desk?

DOREMUS. [*Suddenly, completely, crestfallen*] I'm sorry, Shad . . . I forgot.

SHAD. Well, get out. [*He dashes to the desk, elbowing the arisen* DOREMUS *out of the way, and snarls at the* VEEDERS:] What do you folks want? Bellyachin' about something? If you got anything to say, tell me, 'cause I'm the editor.

DOREMUS. I'm afraid it wouldn't interest you, Lieutenant.

SHAD. Well, get them out then. I got some important work.

[*The* VEEDERS *rise and go. As they pass* DOREMUS, *he shakes hands with each of them, using both hands for it; and they look at him with commiseration and an affectionate feeling that now he is one with them in the comradeship of misery.*]

DOREMUS. [*To the* VEEDERS:] Come in some other time. [*They go.* DOREMUS *waits till they have closed the door, then turns on* SHAD *fiercely:*] You don't have to treat my visitors that way!

SHAD. The hell with them! Jessup! Did you buy any insurance from Dimmick?

[DOREMUS *becomes suspicious, cautious.*]

DOREMUS. I didn't decide.

SHAD. What did Dimmick tell you?

DOREMUS. Nothing in particular.

SHAD. Now don't try getting funny with me. You ought to know by this time: I'm onto you. That's why Swan trusts me. So come across. What did you and Dimmick talk about?

DOREMUS. He just asked me if I wanted any insurance.

SHAD. You didn't talk no politics with him?

DOREMUS. Why no.

SHAD. Never mentioned Trowbridge and them traitors in Canada?

DOREMUS. [*Indignant*] Certainly not!

SHAD. That's a good thing for you! You showed some sense, for once. Because Dimmick—You thought he was a friend of mine?

DOREMUS. You said he was.

SHAD. I was just tryin' to see how much taffy you'd swallow. Because, my young friend—Dimmick is a *spy!*

DOREMUS. Oh, no!

SHAD. Oh, yes—for Trowbridge and the People's Party! [SHAD *looks out of the window.* DOREMUS *and* LORINDA *exchange an excited glance.*] I spotted him right away, the minute he came in to see me. Anybody try to fool *me,* he's got a job cut out!

LORINDA. How did you see through him?

SHAD. I use my eyes. I'm an old guide and woodsman! [*Diminuendo*] And when I got to headquarters, there was a report about this fellow—calls himself Dimmick, alias the Reverend John Derby. So we grabbed him.

DOREMUS. [*Anxious*] You have him—already?

SHAD. Well, not exactly, but he's in town, and my men are looking for him. Would you know him if you saw him? [*Sits at desk again.*]

DOREMUS. I'm not sure.

SHAD. Neither am I. I didn't hardly look at him, confound it. Don't know's I can describe him—not real perfect. He say how long he'd be here? Where's he headed?

DOREMUS. Why *yes!* He said something about going down to the quarries, south of town. I'll bet he's down in one of 'em right now, trying to corrupt the quarreymen!

SHAD. Headed south, eh? The quarries! We'll catch him!

DOREMUS. [*Takes up the telephone, still on* SHAD*'s desk; speaks on it:*] Toll line, please. . . . This is the *Informer.* I want a person-to-person call; I want to speak to Edward Samson, the Burlington Paper Company, Burlington.

SHAD. [*Suspicious*] What d' you think you're doing? What you monkeying with my telephone for?

DOREMUS. As I told you, Lieutenant, I didn't promise Dimmick anything, but he got me interested in the idea of more insurance.

SHAD. [*Suspicion allayed*] I'll find a good agent for you.

DOREMUS. Oh, thanks. Meanwhile I want to ask about an old-line company . . . that I used to *know.* [*On the phone*] Hello, Mr. Samson? . . . This is Doremus Jessup. . . . Fine; she's fine, and so is Davy. Say, Ed, I wanted to ask you about the George Washington Insurance Company. Is it reliable? . . . The George Washington Company, I said; I believe Adams and Son once represented it around Boston. . . . Reliable, eh? Thanks, Ed. Drop in and see me. [*Hangs up, and triumphantly strolls toward* LORINDA, *at her desk.*]

SHAD. [*Condescendingly*] So you're going to have some sense, eh, and grab some insurance. How much 're you willing to put in?

DOREMUS. [*Halting, looking back at* SHAD] I'm going to gamble . . . gamble all I've got!

CURTAIN

★

SCENE 3: *A cold evening in early spring; some weeks after Scene 2.*

Again in DOREMUS*'s living-room. The curtains are drawn, the lights on, a low fire in the fireplace.*

DOREMUS *and his fellow-conspirators of the People's Party are preparing propaganda letters and leaflets for distribution . . .* DOREMUS *has become much more purposeful. . . . He wears another green eyeshade.*

AT RISE: LORINDA *and* DOREMUS *sit on the couch, a folding card-table in front of tham, folding circulars and inserting them in envelopes. At the table,* R., *are seated* MARY, *upstage,* MR. VEEDER, L. *of table,* MRS. VEEDER, R., *addressing envelopes.*

JULIAN, *in uniform, sits by the window, checking a list in a notebook. From time to time he cautiously parts the curtains and peeps out.*

On the table in front of DOREMUS *is a small package of sealed envelopes; hidden under the couch-cushions at his right hand is a package of long envelopes. On the table is a copy of a magazine lettered, "The Anthropological Review," in which are concealed mimeographed sheets of propaganda.*

DOREMUS *is chattering casually to* LORINDA *as the curtain goes up.*

DOREMUS.—yes, they had the attack on Windrip printed on tissue paper, and wrapped it around oranges. [*During this speech,* DAN WILGUS *has entered from the basement door, with a box of mimeographed sheets which he puts on the table.*] What about the rest, Dan?

DAN. Coming up. [*Exit into basement.*]

DOREMUS. [*To* LORINDA, *cheerfully*] You about finished?

LORINDA. Yes.

DOREMUS. Better be! I expect Dimmick almost any evening now. Oh! [*With sudden amusement*] I forgot to tell you. Just now Dimmick is a travelling horse-doctor—named Smith!

JULIAN. [*From the window*] I'm afraid not—not any more.

DOREMUS. [*With sudden dismay and grief*] *What?*

JULIAN. We finally got him.

DOREMUS. Oh, dear Lord. . . . What was he, when you caught him?

JULIAN. He was a Corpo—an officer in our motor corps. We found his diary. It seems when Windrip was elected, Mr. Dimmick was a small-town Methodist pastor—very earnest, apparently much given to prayer. Before we shot him he prayed: "Lord forgive them *not,* for they *know* what they do!"

DOREMUS. [*Sighing*] A great soul—a fighter. [*He rises, taking small package of envelopes, goes to the radio, turns it on. There is a snatch of jazz. He turns it off, and crosses toward the table, speaking in a matter-of-fact way*] People's Party report'll be on in a minute now. [*Halts, musing.*] So Dimmick's gone, too. [*To* MR. VEEDER, *tapping him on the shoulder, speaking unemotionally*] Remember, be sure to assort the envelopes so's there's no two with the same handwriting, and don't mail more 'n two or three in any one box.

VEEDER. [*Rising*] I guess my woman and I better start out. Roads bad.

DOREMUS. [*Pointing toward dining-room door,* L.] Careful how you get away from here. Go through the old Falck place. [*Handing the small packages to* MRS. VEEDER] Mrs. Veeder, you better carry the envelopes—safer.

MRS. VEEDER. [*Rising, stooping to hide envelopes in a pocket sewed to the inside of her skirt*] Don't none of ye look now!

[MR. VEEDER *goes to hat rack to put on heavy overcoat and cap;* MRS. VEEDER *follows him, to get her wraps.*]

DOREMUS. You folks getting on all right at your daughter's?

VEEDER. Yes, she's got six children, but she was able to let us have some room in the barn.

MRS. VEEDER. Nice fresh air in the barn!

DOREMUS. You'll have it easy tonight—you'll be home early—not much after one o'clock.

VEEDER. [*Laughs*] Early! Used to think nine o'clock was late!

RADIO. People's Party! People's Party broadcast from Montreal! [DOREMUS *hastens across to turn the radio up louder.* DAN WILGUS *enters, and listens.*] Walt Trowbridge broadcasting on the real state of affairs in the United States. *Nebraska:* Drunken Corpos fired down a residence street in Lincoln yesterday, killing Mrs. Leonard, wife of a Congregational minister, who was reading to her children. *Washington, D.C.:* The Steel Cartel gave a dinner last evening to President Windrip, costing a thousand dollars a plate. *Vermont:* [*In agitation,* DOREMUS *touches* LORINDA'S *shoulder*] Editor Hardington of the [DOREMUS, *startled, groans "Hardington!" He makes the name distinct.*] St. Johnsbury *Bulletin* was murdered in cold blood. This is Walt Trowbridge. With you again at eleven o'clock.

[DOREMUS *turns off the radio.*]

DOREMUS. [*To* LORINDA] Hardington! The jolliest fellow I ever met. I worked with him once. [*Sadly crosses toward the* VEEDERS, *who are coming toward him, in wraps.*]

VEEDER. Used to think good farming was the most important thing a man could do, but now I guess it's even better letting folks know they've lost their freedom. But wouldn't you think they'd know—

[*He is interrupted by a shout from* JULIAN, *who has been peeping through the window curtains.*]

JULIAN. Corpos! Duck!

DOREMUS. Hustle, everybody! [*To the* VEEDERS] Take off your things—stay here—remember, we're visiting!

[VEEDERS *remove wraps, hastily sit in former places at the table.* DOREMUS, LORINDA, JULIAN, MARY, DAN *hide papers under couch-cushions and table-cover, and fold up card-table,* which DAN *carries down into basement—he is followed there, into hiding, by* LORINDA *and* JULIAN. DOREMUS *sits at table.*]

[*During this bustle there is heard a loud ring at the doorbell, then another.* MARY *hastily picks up embroidery, and opens the door—after the others are hidden or in place—on the* CORPOS, JIM NICKERSON *and* BROWN.]

[*As the door opens, talk:*]

VEEDER. Don't know when I've seen an April cold as this one—

DOREMUS. Y-yes, w-winter—more like winter—

MARY. [*At the door, to the* CORPOS] What do you want?

NICKERSON. Don't think much of the Corpos, do you, dearie!

BROWN. [*He is a rather decent type of Corpo*] Aw, let her alone.

DOREMUS. [*Again trying to chatter to the* VEEDERS] Yes sir, winter—just like winter.

MRS. VEEDER. My daughter says she don't know whether it's worth while putting in a garden—

BROWN. [*Standing by* DOREMUS*'s chair*] Sorry to bother you—

DOREMUS. [*Rising; very innocent*] What is it, my friend? [MARY *takes embroidery to chair by fireplace and sits down.*]

NICKERSON. Come to bust all the radios in town. Six times a day now, Walt Trowbridge broadcasting a lot of seditious junk from Canada. We've had orders. [*Crosses to radio.*]

MRS. VEEDER. Oh, dear! I did want to hear the Smoothie Quartet on the Delaware Machine Gun Hour.

NICKERSON. [*Taking tubes out of radio*] Crooners, eh? I guess you old girls have your moments.

DOREMUS. Now, how are we going to hear President Windrip? I can't get along without his straight-from-the-shoulder talks.

BROWN. [*Crossing to radio; speaking quite seriously*] That's it—just because a traitor like Trowbridge broadcasts a lot of lies, decent folks like you and I have to suffer.

NICKERSON. Fault of them seditious Canadians. We're going to lick them, and the Mexicans.

[*During* NICKERSON*'s speech, his back, and that of* BROWN, *are to the table; and* DOREMUS *touches the shoulders of the* VEEDERS *in signal that it is time to go.*]

VEEDER. [*Rising*] I don't know when I've had as good visit as tonight, Mr. Jessup, but guess Lucy and me better be getting home. We won't be in bed till after ten.

DOREMUS. [*Pointing to dining-room door, while* VEEDERS *put their wraps on again*] Better go out the back way—quickest way to your car.

[*Exeunt the* VEEDERS, *with handshakes, and murmurs of "Just had a lovely visit," "Come again soon," "Good night."* DOREMUS *strolls to the couch and sits down.* NICKERSON *finishes with the radio and turns.*]

NICKERSON [*To* DOREMUS] Don't try to fix that now. We'll know if you monkey with it. [*To* BROWN] Come on, Brrrr! I wish it wasn't so cold outside. [*To* DOREMUS] Folks like you and Mrs. Greenhill got no idea what a tough time we boys have, going out nights and smashing radios.

DOREMUS. Yes, we can't appreciate it.

NICKERSON. [*Crossing back toward the couch*] Oh, say, Jessup—you're a newspaperman—maybe *you* can tell me. Prob'ly you heard there's a lot of these seditious pamphlets and papers circulating around. They're giving we boys everlasting hell up at headquarters because we don't find out where the stuff comes from. But how the heck [*Almost pathetically bewildered*] do you *tell* a seditious literature, or who in thunder sent it out?

MARY. Been giving you much trouble?

NICKERSON. Why say, I goes and buys a pair of socks, right in the Corpo Commissary, and there was kind of a lump in one toe, and I pulls it out, and what do you think! It was a tract, that said, "Corpos, Do You Want to Murder Your Own Brothers?" Ain't that a nice thing to ask a poor guy that's just trying to change his socks! Why, it hurt my feelings! Got any idea how you'd spot guys that would send out dirty tracts like them?

DOREMUS. Why yes, I'm certain they're all way back in the hills, in the woods.

BROWN. [*To* NICKERSON] That's what I told you, Jim! We ought to get right out of town, and look for those guys, like they found them Alaska counterfeiters in *Startling Stories*.

NICKERSON. Well, maybe. Thanks, Mr. Jessup. So long.

DOREMUS. [*Most affable*] Good night.

NICKERSON. [*To* MARY, *leering and prancing*] G' night, girlie. Don't look cross at Junior. He just done his duty. [*Exeunt* NICKERSON, BROWN.]

[MARY *glares, but* DOREMUS *laughs at her.*]

DOREMUS. Did Julian put those leaflets in the Corpo socks?

MARY. Um-huh.

DOREMUS. Lord, what nerve! But he's got to be more careful. The rest of us—if they caught us they'd just put us in concentration camp, but Julian, as a Corpo traitor, they'd shoot him. [*Rises, crosses to basement door.*] Well, anyway, that'll be our last Corpo visitation tonight. [*Through basement door*] Okay.

[*From basement enter* LORINDA *and* JULIAN, *the latter now in military overcoat.*]

LORINDA. Don't say "okay."

DOREMUS. "Okay?" I've never used the beastly expression in my life!

LORINDA. You did—just now.

DOREMUS. Really? I *am* getting away from the liberal in a library! [*To* JULIAN] Skip now! Go out the back way and get to Windrip Barracks before Nickerson. Got your leaflets?

JULIAN. [*Tapping his pockets; speaking cheerfully*] Enough treason to seduce a regiment! [*To* LORINDA, MARY] G' night, my lambs! [*Exit, dining-room door.*] [LORINDA *sits at the table, addressing envelopes which have been hidden in a magazine.*]

MARY. [*Shouting through basement door*] Dan!

DAN. [*Off*] Yuh?

MARY. My dynamite ready?

DAN. [*Off*] Right away. [MARY *starts to put on coat.* DOREMUS *rises, goes to her.*]

DOREMUS. Leetle careful, Mary. Might be real dynamite, from your tone o' voice, instead of pamphlets.

MARY. [*Bitterly*] It *will* be real dynamite, pretty soon, if the Corpos hold on. You were so nice to Nickerson and that other Corpo rat. I'd like to slit both their tender young throats!

DOREMUS. [*Sternly, seizing her arm.*] *Stop it!* We're not out to kill, but to prevent their killing.

MARY. [*Not very repentant*] Sorry. I'll try.

[DAN *is entering from the basement, carrying a covered market basket.*]

DAN. [*To* MARY] In the back of the car?

MARY. Yes. [*Exit* DAN, L., *carrying basket.*] [MARY *to* DOREMUS] Orders, chief? Where do I distribute?

DOREMUS. Woodstock. Try to make it through to White River Junction. It's extremely dangerous.

MARY. I know. Corpo patrol tried to stop my car last night; stood out in the road—I almost had to run him down. [*She glances at the stairs. . . . To* LORINDA] You'll keep an eye on Davy? [*To* DOREMUS, *embracing him*] You won't let him read in bed?

DOREMUS. No—no.

DAN. [*Re-entering* L., *making exit to basement; as he crosses, to* MARY] Good luck, girl. [MARY *resolutely crosses to door* L.]

DOREMUS. Good luck! [*Exit* MARY.]

LORINDA. [*Rising*] What's *my* orders?

DOREMUS. [*Taking the package of long envelopes from under couch cushion*] Take these long envelopes. [*Hands them to her.*] They're accusations of leading Corpo sympathizers—to go right into their own mail boxes. [LORINDA *reads some of the names on the envelopes and whistles in slight agitation. She puts on her overcoat and overshoes while they talk.*] Mrs. Veeder wrote 'em at home. Hasn't she a beautiful handwriting?

LORINDA. Yes. She was a schoolteacher.

DOREMUS. *And*—God bless her rocky Vermont soul—as a spy, she's pure poison! Like you!

LORINDA. Thanks!

DOREMUS. Careful of 'em. Wouldn't trust these to anybody but you or myself. I'll put half of 'em in the mailboxes after midnight. But I do so little! Sleeping snug and warm while Mary and you drive through the night.

LORINDA. Sleep? I know you! You sit up and worry yourself sick till you get our "safe" signal.

DOREMUS. No more worry! [*He kisses her lightly.*] You're the real leader here, and I'll never be afraid of anything again! [*Exit* LORINDA, R. DOREMUS *sits disconsolately on the couch.*]

[*Enter* DAN, *from basement, in cap and overcoat.*]

DAN. Well, another day, another dollar. Got the minnie-graphing outfit hid in the apple bin. G' night.

DOREMUS. Night.

DAN. [*Opening front door, then looking back, returning to the couch, and patting* DOREMUS'S *shoulder; speaking comfortingly.*] It's all right, Chief! We'll put it over!

DOREMUS. [*Aroused by this almost to cheerfulness, and patting* DAN'S *arm in return*] You bet we will. Dan! Good night!

[*Exit* DAN, R.]

[DOREMUS *crosses to the front door and bolts it. He has fallen again into despondency.*]

[DAVID *appears on the stairs, in dressing gown and pajamas, watching his grandfather, but silent.*]

[DOREMUS *hangs up his eyeshade on a hook at the right end of the mantelpiece. . . . This hook—or nail—must be long enough to make the hanging-up and, later, taking down of the eyeshade easy. . . . Absorbed, weary,* DOREMUS *sits in the armchair in front of the fireplace. Not till then does he see* DAVID. *He speaks with surprise, but fondly.*]

DOREMUS. What's the idea, young fella? You're supposed to be asleep!

DAVID. [*Slowly coming downstairs*] I was reading "Treasure Island" in bed, and gee, there were pirates creeping around in the dark.

DOREMUS. I'll protect you. I carry cutlasses in my teeth, practically continuously.

DAVID [*Now at the foot of the steps*] Why does mother drive away every night?

DOREMUS. How do you know it's your mother? Maybe it's Aunt Lindy, or me.

DAVID. Because she always hits the curb, and says, "Oh damn!"

DOREMUS. [*Laughs*] I see! Well, better skip up—

DAVID. Please let me stay! I never have anybody to talk to. It isn't any fun at school now.

DOREMUS. All right. Come over by the fireplace. [DAVID *sits on the floor, at* DOREMUS'*s feet. When his grandfather leans his check on his left hand, the boy does the same, with elbow resting on his knee, in unconscious imitation.*] What are they teaching you these days?

DAVID. Oh—how to drill—and "the peace of the world depends on America's ruling the Western hemisphere," and [*He runs the following all together*] "It is right and glorious to serve the cause of country without regard for friendship or ties of kin." . . . Is that true?

DOREMUS. Well, I'll try to explain. . . . You're getting old enough now. . . . Mind you, I don't want you to be a prig.

DAVID. What's a prig?

DOREMUS. [*Gaily*] A prig is a boy that likes to wash his face.

DAVID. Oh, then I'm not a prig!

DOREMUS. [*Slowly, becoming serious*] Maybe I'm wrong to tell you, but I've been thinking about it, these last few days—Boys as young as you have done their part in revolutions, and you might have to take your father's place and mine, too—and it's never too soon to fight for freedom. David.

DAVID. You've never called me "David."

DOREMUS. Maybe it's time now. Davy—David—your father wasn't killed in an automobile accident. . . . The Corpos killed him. [*Pause.*] Do you understand?

DAVID. I knew.

DOREMUS. What?

DAVID. I heard mother and you talking. Long ago. I cried. But I thought maybe you didn't want me to know.

DOREMUS. Oh, that's fine—fine!

DAVID. [*Angrily*] Why do the Corpos do things like killing Daddy?

DOREMUS. Because they hate free people, like your father that want to know the truth! They hate the—oh, the free, inquiring, critical spirit.

DAVID. Free—inquiring—critical spirit?

DOREMUS. That's it. Understand?

DAVID. Well—gee—anyway, it's lots better than "cause-country-thout-regar-friendship." [*He becomes excited again, and cheerful.*] Honest, Grand-dad, I think the professor at school is an awful simp! [*Rising; illustrating*] He salutes and salutes and then spouts all that stuff Mr. Windrip writes!

DOREMUS. Good boy!

DAVID. Why don't you make the Corpos quit?

DOREMUS. We're trying to. That's why we send you to bed early, so we can get out letters about the Corpos. Look. I'll show you. [*He rises, leads* DAVID *to the table, holds up the copy of "The Anthropological Review," and shows that in it are mimeographed sheets.*] We hide these papers, and nights, your mother and Aunt Lindy go out and distribute them.

DAVID. Lookit! Gimme a million of 'em, and I'll go right down Douglas Avenue tomorrow after school, and give 'em to everybody!

DOREMUS. No, no! That's precisely what you musn't do. If the Corpos found 'em, they might send us to concentration camp, so [*Puts finger to lips*] not a word!

DAVID. [*Also finger to lips*] Not a word.

DOREMUS. And you're enlisted against the Corpos?

DAVID. [*Saluting*] Yes, Chief.

DOREMUS. So up to bed.

DAVID. [*Saluting again*] Up to bed!

[DOREMUS *returns the salute, and as* DAVID *marches like a little soldier toward the stairs and up one step,* DOREMUS *follows, with military step.*

[*They are startled and halted by a tremendous KNOCKING at the front door, and the RINGING OF THE DOORBELL.* DOREMUS, *somewhat frightened, puts finger to lips, before going to open the door—while the insistent knocking continues.*

[DOREMUS *unbolts the door, and* SHAD, NICKERSON, BROWN, *and two or three other* CORPOS *burst in—the last of them closing the door.*]

DOREMUS. [*To* SHAD] What's the idea—this time of night?

SHAD. We're having a book-burning on the Green.

DOREMUS. A what?

SHAD. Going to burn all this subversive literature that's corrupting public morals. Got any objections? [*As though he hopes* DOREMUS *may have.*]

DOREMUS. You won't find any subversive literature here.

SHAD. [*Going to bookcase*] The hell we won't! I used to work here! [*Takes a book from the shelf.*] How about this book?

DOREMUS. It's a detective story.

SHAD. "The Murder of Roger Ackroyd." Murder ain't no business for civilians to monkey with. [*He throws the book on the floor, and lakes down one of a set of books.*] How about this fellow Charles Dickens? Wasn't he a Communist?

DOREMUS. Certainly not!

SHAD. [*Throwing volumes from the set on the floor*] Well, I heard about him. I heard he done a lot of complaining about conditions. Guys ought to let conditions alone—leave 'em to the Government.

DOREMUS. But Shad—[SHAD *turns his head angrily, and* DOREMUS *corrects himself*]—uh, Lieutenant; that was a hundred years ago.

SHAD. [*Continuing, unperturbed, to drop various sorts of books on the floor*] Makes no difference. Dead skunk stinks bad 's a live one.

NICKERSON. [*Showing to* SHAD *two books he has found on the mantelpiece*] Found these, Lieut: "Alice in Wonderland" and "Omar something."

SHAD. [*Motioning at the pile on the floor*] Burn 'em—prob'ly seditious.

DOREMUS. "Alice in Wonderland"—they'll laugh at you.

SHAD. I'm going to have a bigger burning than they did at Bellows Falls. Prove this town is twice as literary. [SHAD *glances at and throws more books on the floor.* DOREMUS *stands watching him, not seeing what goes on behind him.*

[MEANWHILE, *at the cue "Alice in Wonderland" in* DOREMUS*'s last speech,* DAVID *has begun to saunter innocently down the stairs, and behind* DOREMUS, *to the table, where* NICKERSON *is now searching.*]

NICKERSON. Any Naked Beauties here? [*No one pays attention to his remark.*

[DAVID *pretends to turn over a couple of magazines, seizes "The Anthropological Review," tucks it under his bathrobe, and strolls toward the stairs.*

[NICKERSON *shouts after him:*] Hey, kid! What you doing with that book?

DAVID. I want something to read before I go to sleep.

[BROWN *has been looking over books on the shelves, so he is near the foot of the stairs. When* DAVID, *in panic now, starts to run upstairs,* BROWN *rushes up, seizes him, and drags him down.*]

BROWN. Come on back down here!

[*"The Anthropological Review" falls from under* DAVID'S *bathrobe.* NICKERSON, *who has also dashed across, picks it up.*

[*Hearing the racket,* DOREMUS *turns about, aghast.*]

DOREMUS. Let the boy go up to bed!

SHAD. [*Turning*] Hey, what's all the roughhouse?

NICKERSON. Say, Lieut, here's what the kid picked out to read himself to sleep—the Anthro-po-some-damn-thing—[SHAD *snatches the magazine from* NICKERSON, *opens it, discovers mimeographed sheets, reads aloud the headings of a couple of them—while* BROWN *holds the squealing* DAVID, *and* DOREMUS *shrinks back toward the armchair in front of the fireplace.*]

SHAD. [*Reading aloud*] "Anti-Semitism [*He pronounces it "se-might-ism"*] Increases." "80,000 in New York Concentration Camps." They ought to be. [*He strides to* DOREMUS, *seizes him by the lapels.*] You traitor! Who's in this with you?

DOREMUS. Nobody!

SHAD. Liar—

DOREMUS. I wrote all that stuff. [SHAD *thrusts* DOREMUS *into the armchair.*]

SHAD. How do I know?

DOREMUS. If there was anybody else in this conspiracy, would I be all alone here—at night?

SHAD. Mary upstairs?

DOREMUS. Weekend with the Sturgises, at Woodstock. [*Bluffing—defiant*] If you don't believe it—phone!

SHAD. That'll keep. [DAVID *breaks away from* BROWN, *wailing, and runs to* DOREMUS. SHAD *contemptuously pushes him away, snarling at* BROWN:] Take the brat upstairs. [BROWN *obeys.*] Nickerson! Go down cellar. You other boys upstairs—kitchen. Look for pieces of paper with writin' or printin' on 'em. Make it snappy! [NICKERSON *and other Corpos obey. One Corpo on guard by front door.*]

[SHAD *to* DOREMUS, *with a dreadful calmness:*] Now, Doremus, old boss, course you know you're going to concentration camp for five years. But if you want to get there all in one piece, you better tell me who's in this with you.

DOREMUS. [*Sunk in chair, head bowed*] All right, if I have to—I worked with Hardington, the St. Johnsbury editor.

SHAD. Him? We shot him yesterday.

DOREMUS. Then I'm all alone. [NICKERSON *appears in basement doorway. He carries a steel fishing rod, speaks cheerfully.*]

NICKERSON. He's guilty, Lieut. I found a whole mimeographing outfit in the cellar—.

SHAD. All right. We'll get busy. No more playing around —got some serious business to do. We're going to give Doremus a workout. He ain't co-operative. I hate to do it, but we got to teach these intellectuals a lesson. [*Casually*] What d' you think you got there?

NICKERSON. I always wanted a steel fish-rod.

SHAD. Now don't you go lootin' private houses—not without you ask me. Well, on the job. Call the boys.

NICKERSON. [*Standing fishing-rod against wall; shouting*] Circus starting, gents! Right this way to the monkey cage! [CORPOS *coming from upstairs and from dining-room.*]

SHAD. [*Addressing* CORPO *by the door*] Too damn bad we didn't bring a whip, or—[*Spies steel fishing-rod, picks it up, swishes it in the air.*] Golly! Wasting money on steel whips, when there's a fish-rod [DOREMUS, *picturing what is going to happen, winces, then sits upright, as defiantly as possible*] like this in prett' near every house! Talk about inventions! I'll get my promotion for this! [*Swishing rod, and with a dreadful casualness pulling a chair away from the table*] Come on. Lay him across the table. [TWO CORPOS *drag* DOREMUS *up from his chair. But* DOREMUS, *struggling, shakes off the* CORPO *holding his right arm.*]

DOREMUS. Shad! Wait! [*The* CORPOS *halt.*]

SHAD [*Chuckling*] I *thought* you'd put up a squawk!

DOREMUS. I'll take my beating gladly. Maybe the other cautious citizens will hear of me now and begin to fight. It was our laziness that let the rats like you come in, but now my blood may wash you out. [*He tears loose from the* OTHER CORPO.] GO on! I am ready! [*He looks away from* SHAD *and marches firmly toward the table, as the curtain falls.*]

CURTAIN

★

ACT III

The Jessup living-room, winter, a year and a half later. There are signs of poverty. The radio, most of the books, some of the pictures are gone. DOREMUS*'s eyeshade still hangs at the* R. *end of the mantel.*

On the wall is a large placard: "All the women in this household have done their patriotic duty by joining the Kitty Windrip Joy through Labor League."

Evidently MARY *and* LORINDA *have gone into the laundry business. Throughout the room are piles of laundry, on chairs and in baskets.*

AT RISE: MARY *is ironing, on a board stretched from a chair-top to the table.* LORINDA *is sorting laundry, on the couch.*

Standing between the table and the front door is FRANK TASBROUGH. *He now wears overalls, a cheap colored shirt, and a mackinaw or canvas jacket. But the hat he holds in his hand is a spotless derby, as of old. Under his arm is a bundle obviously containing not more than one shirt. . . . His voice still booms, but he has learned humility, and he sounds grateful.*

TASBROUGH. I'm awfully obliged to you for washing this. It'll be the first time for half a year that I've had on a clean white shirt.

LORINDA. I know. . . . Not even for funerals, now.

TASBROUGH. Nothing much but funerals, these days.

MARY. Mr. Tasbrough! Won't you come to supper some night?

TASBROUGH. I'd *love* to! In the mill barracks, they just about starve us. They give us lectures instead of hash. [*Something of the old fire, then*] That's what your doggone co-ordination did to me! [*With that, he claps on his pristine derby, in contrast to the rest of his clothes.*] G'by. Thanks a lot. [*Exit*]

LORINDA. [*To* TASBROUGH, *while he is going out*] Come again, if you think it's safe. [*Pause*]

MARY. [*Patiently ironing*] I'm so tired.

LORINDA. [*Crossing to her*] My turn now.

MARY. No. You worked all last night.

LORINDA. Your poor hands.

MARY. It doesn't matter. Besides, it takes my mind off worrying. And I suppose we're lucky. Think of Mr. Tasbrough. And our old Episcopal minister—driving a bus—[*Laughs*] poor darling—he's such a bad driver!

LORINDA. We'll all luckier than your father. Eighteen months in the stockade! [*Takes letter from bosom. Glances at it, during pause*] They couldn't 've beaten him much, do you think? Or he couldn't have written so clearly—that is, for him, I mean. Doremus Jessup always did write the worst hand.

MARY. [*Not listening*] That's so. [*Doorbell*]

LORINDA. [*Opening door*] Oh. It's you. [ENTER SHAD. *He is now a captain. He wears a military greatcoat; no side-arms.*]

SHAD. Hya, girls. [*Crosses to* MARY.] Still making a bluff at working for a living? Got my laundry done?

MARY. Yes.

SHAD. Thought I'd drop in, and save you the trip to my quarters.

MARY. We prefer to have David deliver it.

SHAD. [*Hanging up overcoat, crossing* L., *then lolling on the couch*] Awful sweet and obliging to your old hired man, ain't you! Say, why don't you take a tumble to yourself and be a little friendlier? Not that I care a hoot.

[*Enter* DAVID, L., *with bundle.*]

DAVID. Here's some more laundry from headquarters, mother.

LORINDA. Did you deliver the bundles up on the hill?

DAVID. Yes, Aunt Lindy. But I almost fell down in the snow.

HAD [*To* DAVID] Hya, kid? [DAVID *ignores him and starts for the stairs.*] Where yuh going?

DAVID. I've got to do my homework.

SHAD. Why aren't you at the air-raid lecture for boys?

DAVID. Aunt Lorinda is giving me lessons.

SHAD. What about?

DAVID. Free—inquiring—critical spirit—[*Exit, upstairs*]

SHAD. Free—inquiring—ah, nuts! But the kid'll be a good Corpo yet. Wonderful opportunities the Corpos have brung to the kids of this country. [*Silence*] Well, say something! [*To* MARY] You used to could talk plenty to your dad and the Doc. About tennis. Huh! You do your tennis with a flatiron now! [*Silence*] Still standoffish to the Corpos? Better not be to me. I'm running things here. Swan ain't been here more 'n three-four times all year. I've did all right for myself—Frank Tasbrough sweeping floors in my factory. And I got Mrs. Doc Greenhill washin' my socks—

[MARY *comes toward him, with wrapped package of laundry. He rises.*]

MARY. You came for your laundry, Captain Ledue. Here it is!

SHAD. Oh, showing a little spirit, huh? Let's see how good you done 'em this time. [*Tearing open package—holding up and rumpling a shirt.*] Lousy! You'll wash that again!

[LORINDA *takes over the ironing.*]

MARY. Very well.

SHAD. [*Mimics*] Very well! Very well! Why don't you fight me? Aw, who're you to get excited about?

MARY. Your laundry is eighty-five cents, Captain Ledue.

SHAD. [*Handing her a bill*] All right, here's a buck. [MARY *makes change, at cup on mantelpiece.*] You can keep the change, Mamie!

MARY. [*Throwing the change on the floor*] You get out!

SHAD. You want to do a little time in concentration camp, like your dad, and get beaten—naked?

MARY. [*Frightened*] You can't frighten me.

SHAD. Oh yes I can. I have. You're going to need my protection bad—[*Sound of an aeroplane*] God! Listen!

LORINDA. What's the matter with you?

SHAD. Don't you hear that plane?

LORINDA. [*Suspicious, excited*] It's just the ordinary patrol plane—*isn't it?*

SHAD. I hope so!

MARY. Mr. Shad Ledue—Mr. Captain Ledue—you are scared to death!

SHAD. I am not!

MARY. What is it?

SHAD. I am not—I tell you I ain't scared!

MARY. I'd forgotten what a coward you are, Shad! [LORINDA *and* MARY *stand together, center, arms about each other.*]

SHAD. *You'd* be scared, if you knew what I know—chance o' gettin' bombed any minute—right here—bomb dropped right on the house—the traitors—the cowards [*In a frenzy, he dashes to the front door, opens it, looks out and up, closes door again.*] stealin' army planes and bombing their own comrades—slaughter you right in your own bed, while you're asleep—God!

LORINDA. [*With feigned indifference*] Having nightmares again? *What* planes?

SHAD. I won't tell you nothing! [*The sound of the airplane has died out.*]

LORINDA. [*Crossing to stand between* SHAD *and* MARY] That's because you don't know anything.

SHAD. Oh, I don't, eh?

LORINDA. Commissioner Swan certainly wouldn't take a woodsman like you into his confidence.

SHAD. Oh, he wouldn't, huh—he wouldn't! Well, if you're so smart, I know the whole thing! Revolt—against Windrip—People's Party revolt—bribed by that crook Trowbridge! Half our air-corps 's revolted! They've bombed Omaha—killed General Haik—the hogs—dropping bombs from the sky—dassn't come down and fight like gentlemen. . . . *Revolt!*

LORINDA. Oh, it's come! I wonder if Doremus will see it?

MARY. [*To* SHAD] I'll never be afraid of you again! [*She stalks away, and upstairs.*]

LORINDA. [*Picking up laundry*] You better get out of here, Shad.

SHAD. [*Bewildered; almost human*] I wonder why she hates me so?

LORINDA. Go home!

SHAD. When I was a kid, selling cordwood to her old man, she high-hatted me, and I thought she was a regular movie princess. And I thought this bum little house was so swell! And then she married that sap, Doc Greenhill. And all the while—Mary—God how I wanted her!

LORINDA. This house is still too good for you. [*Exit* LORINDA, *into dining-room.* SHAD *starts to go. At the front door, he hesitates, looks back at the stairs, and licks his lips. He turns back, lays down his bundle of laundry, tosses on a chair the overcoat he has merely swung about his shoulders. He tiptoes across and begins to sneak upstairs. He has gone up only a couple of steps when he stops and grunts in embarrassment at sight of* MARY, *descending. She speaks with contemptuous calmness.*]

MARY. Where are you planning to go?

SHAD. Just—just—Wanted to have a little visit with you, without that nosey old maid butting in.

MARY. Don't you ever get tired of being a stinker?

SHAD. [*He is really shocked*] Ain't you ashamed of yourself, pretending to be a lady and using a word like that! [*Both are downstairs, standing at the foot.*]

MARY. I know worse ones.

SHAD. World going straight to the dogs—women like you acting common. Now you see why I wouldn't marry you!

MARY. *What?*

SHAD. Sure enough. I'd of made you Mrs. Captain Ledue, if you'd acted nice.

MARY. [*Laughing, feeling released and gay*] You're wonderful! . . . Shad, you better get across the border into Canada, quick. I hate to see people killed—even you.

SHAD. Me—killed?

MARY. Oh yes—you'll get killed—if you stay. That was obvious the moment you lost your head and spilled the news about the revolt.

SHAD. I was just kidding. We'd shoot anybody even thought about revolt.

MARY. Let it go. [*She begins to fold up laundry and put away iron and ironing board.*]

SHAD. We will not "let it go"! Look here. You got a chance to quit running the wringer. I've always been that way about you. I've laid awake—

MARY. Please! Let's not hear all that again. I understand. Now that I'm free of you, I confess I didn't treat you any too sympathetically when you were our hired man—in your proper place—

SHAD. So that's what you think of me, huh? Hired man! It just don't pay to treat you nice. I'm not going to marry you. You don't deserve it. But you're going to do what I want.

MARY. Will you kindly stop trying to act like a villain? You look too foolish.

SHAD. [*Seizing her wrist; viciously*] You won't think I'm foolish, before I get through! [*At the front door is a feeble tapping.*]

MARY. If you don't let go, I'll kill you. I mean it! I'll kill you! [*Tapping at the door louder.*] What's that?

SHAD. Somebody at the door. Gwan and answer it. You're safe with me here.

MARY. With you? Am I mad? Whoever is there can't be as bad as you—[*She goes to the door, savagely throws it open. Into the room tumbles a* DOREMUS JESSUP *whom, after eighteen months of concentration camp and a flight through snow, she does not recognize. He is pale, gaunt, ill; seemingly twenty years older. He is in clumsy shoes, prison-uniform of gray denim—a number stamped on the breast—and over it a mangy old overcoat and muffler. A worn fur cap is on his straggly hair, tangled and gone white. At first* MARY *supposed him to be a stray tramp.*] Yes? . . . Oh—Father! Oh, *no!* [*She tenderly leads him into the room. He leans against her, feebly. He can only mutter.*]

DOREMUS Mary—Mary—

SHAD. By God, it *is!* Old Doremus—skipped from prison!

MARY. [*Tenderly taking off her father's cap, unwinding his muffler*] Lorinda! Davy—Davy! [LORINDA *appears in the dining-room door;* DAVID *on the stairs.*]

LORINDA. Who is—Oh, it isn't! [*She flees to* DOREMUS, *helps take off his overcoat.*]

DOREMUS. [*It is more a blurred sound than a word*] L-lindy—

DAVID. [*Frightened*] Mother! Who is it?

MARY. It's your grandfather—

DAVID. Oh, I didn't know him—[*He runs to* DOREMUS, *who puts both hands on his head, not speaking.*]

MARY. [*During the above*] Think he's all right?

LORINDA. It's just the cold—exposure—[*His wraps off, leaning on* MARY, DOREMUS *spies something by the fireplace, and, pitifully smiling, starts toward it.*]

MARY. I'll help you.

LORINDA. No—let him alone. [*By himself, staggering, he reaches the fireplace, and from the right end of the mantel takes down his old green eyeshade. He shakily puts it on, tries to straighten himself, and turning to* MARY, LORINDA, DAVID—*his back to* SHAD—*speaks proudly feebly.*]

DOREMUS. Editor!

SHAD. [*Suddenly barking*] You! Fall in! [*Trembling with reminiscent fear,* DOREMUS *wheels about toward* SHAD, *trying to stand rigid, but trembling.*] Eyes front! Stretch! [DOREMUS *tries to raise his shaky arms up beside his head while* SHAD *guffaws at* MARY *and the others*] Those is concentration-camp commands. Lookit him try to stiffin his skinny old arms!

LORINDA. [*Screaming at* SHAD] You swine! [*She runs to* DOREMUS, *pulls his arms down by his side. She and* MARY *get him into the chair in front of the fireplace. Meanwhile* DAVID *runs to* SHAD, *pummels him with small fists.*]

DAVID. [*To* SHAD] You let him alone!

SHAD. [*Merely pushing him away*] Aw, get out!

LORINDA. [*To* DOREMUS, *now collapsed in the chair*] You're home, dear! You're safe. [*To* MARY] Get him some brandy. There's a little in the sideboard. [MARY *hastens out,* L., *and re-enters instantly with small glass, which she puts to* DOREMUS*'s lips, kneeling by his chair.*]

MARY. [*To* DOREMUS] Try to drink some. [*He sips and, a little recovered, speaks, still feebly.*]

DOREMUS. Be a' right . . . Almost froze . . . People's Party planes . . . bombed Hanover barracks . . . so we could break jail . . . many of us killed.

MARY. We understand.

[SHAD *sits on couch again, looking cynical.*]

LORINDA. Don't try to talk, dear. You're here. That's all that matters.

DOREMUS. Escape?

LORINDA. Yes, we will—indeed we will.

DOREMUS. Canada?

LORINDA. We will, dear. Don't worry.

MARY. [*To* LORINDA] He's exhausted. Let him sleep a while. [*She makes* DOREMUS *comfortable in the chair.*]

[DOREMUS *nods off, in brief slumber.*]

LORINDA. I'll hurry and make some hot soup.

DAVID. Please let me help.

[LORINDA *and* DAVID *exeunt,* L. MARY *starts to follow them.*]

SHAD. [*Rising*] Mamie! I got something important to tell you. [MARY *halts.*] You know what they'll do to your dad, if they catch him.

MARY. I can guess.

SHAD. Oh no you can't! They got a new little trick, with salt fish and no water to drink.

MARY. Oh—

SHAD. He used to laugh at me, but I'm nuts about you. God, Mamie, I am! And if you act sensible and see I'm a good guy, and cut out being so chilly, I'll protect the old duffer, and not give him away. [*Pause*] How about it? [*Pause*] Or do you want your dad to go back and be tortured? Burn sulphur under his finger-nails? [*Long pause*]

MARY. Very well, Shad. You win.

SHAD. Good! I'll show you a swell time. And some day I'll marry you—if you behave.

MARY. [*As sweet as possible*] But if this is a real revolt, there won't be much marriage for any of us.

SHAD. Don't you worry about that, Mamie! If there's going to be any welshing on the damn Corpos, and turning Trowbridge again, old Shad'll beat the whole bunch to it. I'm not no fool! So be sweet to me—aw, be sweet!

MARY. And now—what shall we do with father?

SHAD. May take time before I can smuggle him out. I know the place to hide him—that old wine-closet in the basement—looks like part of the wall. No patrol 'll find him there. [*Chuckling*] Remember how proud Doremus used to be of that hidey-hole? Always was a regular kid, anyway—not much sense, of course—

MARY. [*Interrupting*] We must get him down there, quick! [*Crosses to basement door*]

SHAD. Don't you worry now. I'll protect you and your dad with my life.

MARY. I'm proud of you for your idea about the wine-closet.

SHAD. [*Crossing to basement door; chuckling lovingly*] You better be!

MARY. There's room in it for a cot. . . . If it just weren't so like a cell.

SHAD. I'll fix it up for him. Cut some pictures out of "Naughty Stories" and paste 'em up.

MARY. I don't think he'd care much for those.

SHAD. You don't know these old bucks.

MARY. [*Angrily*] Shad! I want you to distinctly understand—

SHAD. All right, all RIGHT! Scrapping like a wife already! You better remember I hold the old bozo's life right here in my mitt!

MARY. Oh, please, Shad, I do! [*Sound of passing car with SIREN*]

SHAD. There's a squad car. We better hurry and get old Doremus down in his little crib—[*Reaches for, but does not yet touch, the sleeping* DOREMUS.]

MARY. Oh, don't start dragging him around!

SHAD. You got the outside basement door bolted, ain't you?

MARY. Nailed up.

SHAD. See? Nobody can get in or out except by this door, and the old boy'll be as safe as a bug in a rug. [*He lifts* DOREMUS *from the chair.* DOREMUS, *suddenly awakened, is terrified.*]

DOREMUS. Don't—don't—not again—

SHAD. [*Leading* DOREMUS *to the basement door; speaking loudly, in what he regards as genteel amiability.*] Come on, old gentleman, I decided you and me are going to be friends. [*They are passing through the door;* SHAD *is heard off, on the basement stairs:*] Stoop your head now. Be careful. Watch out for that first step. There's a boy! Come on down now! Careful! Nice cellar. You'll like it. There you are—

MARY. [*She has crossed to dining-room door; calls through it:*] David! [*Enter* DAVID, *from dining-room*] Go down in the basement, and help Grandfather get settled. [*Exit* DAVID, *to basement*]

LORINDA. [*Entering from dining-room*] What's happening?

MARY. We're hiding him in the cellar. It's time for the patrol.

LORINDA. I see. . . . What a God's blessing he's here now, all safe, I'll hurry with the soup.

MARY. It was Shad's idea—of all people.

LORINDA. I guess I misjudged Shad. Maybe he has a good heart under the mud.

MARY. [*A bit wildly*] Oh, he *has*—he has to have—now!

LORINDA. Mary! You're not going to—

MARY. I must. For Father—for all of us. [SHAD *enters from the basement; at sight of him, exit* LORINDA *to dining-room.*]

SHAD. [*To* MARY] He'll be all right. Dave 'll watch him. Got a nice horse-blanket over him. It don't smell much. But I got something to say to you, Mame. I'm willing to think about marryin' you, some day—me that could have all the cuties in town. But you certainly got to get over these immoral ideas. A girl of mine coming right out publicly and using a word like "stinker"!

MARY. [*Resigned*] Very well, Shad.

SHAD. I'll learn you the new morality of the streamlined age. I'll teach you—Now what the—[*He halts at sight of* COMMISSIONER SWAN, JULIAN FALCK—*now also a captain*—BROWN, *and* NICKERSON, *all in military greatcoats and wearing revolvers, marching into the room, without knocking.* SWAN *is in a hurry, and in a rage. Except for flashes, he is not suave and playful now, but grim. . . . He carries military gauntlets.*] [SHAD *gasps, and salutes.*] W-why, Commissioner; thought you was in Boston.

SWAN. [*Striding to* SHAD] What you doing here?

SHAD. Just come to get my laundry, sir. [MARY *sits over on couch.*]

SWAN. Where's the fleet of trucks you were to start off for Montpelier?

SHAD. Trucks, sir?

SWAN. You heard me! Where's the gasoline?

SHAD. Gasoline?

SWAN. Yes! Not milk or perfume! Gasoline!

SHAD. I never got any orders, sir.

SWAN. Why didn't you? [*He slaps* SHAD *across the face with his gauntlets.*] Our beautiful military system! If I don't get ten truckloads of gas to Sarason Field tonight, there won't be a Corpo plane in the air—and the rebel planes beginning to bomb New England.

SHAD. [*Indicating* MARY, *on couch, with his thumb*] Please, sir, ought you to let outsiders know how big the revolt is? I've kept it hid, careful.

SWAN. The whole world will know in another forty-eight hours. A thousand bombs will tell them. Of course we'll win, and crush these amateurs but—[*Sharply*] Who's here in the house?

SHAD. Just this woman [*Indicating* MARY] and a lady cooking in the kitchen.

SWAN. [*Pointing to chair* R. *of table*] You sit down, Ledue. [SHAD *obeys*] [SWAN *to* JULIAN] Search.

JULIAN. [*To* BROWN] Upstairs. [*To* NICKERSON] Kitchen. [BROWN *and* NICKERSON *depart.* JULIAN *stands back, while* SWAN, *standing, continues to* SHAD.]

SWAN. This is a crisis. I want all my officers on the job, twenty-four hours a day. Those that aren't—I shall shoot. I come to town, needing you, and I find you lolling in this house. Laundry! I found out at headquarters how much time you've been spending here. Now what's your explanation?

SHAD. I've been at headquarters all day, sir, till just this minute—

SWAN. You had in your charge a tank of ten thousand gallons of gasoline. That tank is empty. To whom did you sell it?

SHAD. Nobody, sir.

SWAN. Mean to tell me you didn't know it was gone?

SHAD. No, I didn't know, sir.

SWAN. So you were merely guilty of carelessness, not theft.

SHAD. Kinda looks that way.

SWAN. So I'll detail only *three* men to shoot you.

SHAD. [*Half-rising, holding the table, in terror*] You're joking, sir.

SWAN. I don't joke with *thieves!* [NICKERSON *is pushing into the room an indignant* LORINDA.]

LORINDA. What do you mean! [*To* SWAN] What's the meaning of this invasion—Mr. Swan? Why am I dragged in here?

SWAN. I want to find out what traitors Ledue is associating with. I'm glad you and Mrs. Greenhill aren't the kind I'll have to shoot. . . . Merely exile to the farm colonies!

MARY. [*Springing up*] No one in this house is a traitor—including Captain Ledue! I have no reason to love him, but he's your most loyal—

SWAN. Dry up.

MARY. *What?*

SWAN. Dry up, you laundress!

JULIAN. [*To* SWAN] If you will permit me, sir, these women are notorious whiners, though I imagine they're loyal. Shall I chase them upstairs?

MARY. Why, Julian!

LORINDA. Julian Falck!

JULIAN. It makes me sick to see lukewarm Corpo females!

[SWAN *suddenly cuts in on* JULIAN. MARY *and* LORINDA, *shocked, glaring at* JULIAN, *stand back.* SHAD *rises and stands at attention as* SWAN *addresses him.*]

SWAN. Ledue, you always were a clumsy crook. Don't I seem to remember that it was in this room, right here, that I first found you—some sort of houseman?

SHAD. Yes, sir.

SWAN. Coming out of that door—[*Indicates basement*] as dreary a lump as I ever saw.

BROWN. If the Commissioner will excuse me, sir, that's the basement where old Doremus Jessup had his underground printing press.

SWAN. So it is. [*To* SHAD] Pardon my interrupting the boresome task of having you shot, for a moment of more amusing recollections. Jessup! An admirable Judas! But his talent for treachery seems merely to have landed him in concentration camp. . . . The historic basement eh? I'll take a look at it. [*He starts for the basement door.*]

MARY. Listen! Don't blame it on us, if you get hurt going down there. The basement's full of cold water. The pipes burst.

SWAN. [*Halting*] Do you suppose that wading in ice water is anything new to me?

LORINDA. [*Very casual*] Of course not. Just be careful the steps don't give way *again*.

SWAN. [*Turning from the door*] Oh, the devil with it. My neck is too valuable to the Government to risk it . . Captain Falck.

JULIAN. Yes, sir.

SWAN. You may have the pleasure of taking Ledue along now. Shoot him in the woods between here and headquarters. I'd hate to stain the shining wintry streets.

[JULIAN *seizes the arm of* SHAD, *who suddenly goes to pieces.*]

SHAD. I'll confess, sir. I did steal the gasoline. But don't shoot *me—please!* I'll tell you where Doremus Jessup is! [MARY *and* LORINDA *stand rigid, expressionless.*]

SWAN. What do you mean?

SHAD. He escaped from Camp Hanover.

JULIAN. The man's lying!

SWAN. [*Ignoring* JULIAN; *much interested; to* SHAD:] Ah. But why should I be interested in Jessup?

SHAD. I've seen him. He told me he's got a secret way to sneak into Canada. He's going to write a book about atrocities in our prison camps.

SWAN. There *are* no Corpo atrocities, you fool!

SHAD. No, sir! But he might make up some.

SWAN. Where *is* Brother Doremus?

SHAD. Right down there in the basement. [*Points*]

SWAN. [*Smiling tenderly; looking from* MARY *to* LORINDA] Oh, this is beautiful—really, this is too beautiful. Such solicitude about my health in the icy water! . . . Falck!

JULIAN. Yes, sir.

SWAN. Drag the old idiot up here.

JULIAN. Yes, sir.

LORINDA. Oh, Julian—Julian—you can't do that—Mr. Jessup that loved you so!

JULIAN. [*To* SWAN] May I speak to this woman, sir?

SWAN. It might be interesting.

JULIAN. [*To* LORINDA] You have apparently forgotten that you and "the man that loved me so" tried to persuade me not to join the Corpos, long ago. [*To* SWAN] Pardon me, sir. [*To* NICKERSON, BROWN] Come on. Lively. [JULIAN *points to basement.* NICKERSON, BROWN *exeunt into it.*]

SHAD. [*To* JULIAN] Juley, you'll find him hidden in a secret cupboard, just behind the woodpile. [*To* SWAN] Shall I go down and show them, sir?

SWAN. You shall not!

SHAD. [*To* JULIAN] You'll notice a yellow plank in the wall. It slides to the right.

JULIAN. Thanks.

SWAN. And Falck—don't forget that Jessup tried to corrupt you once.

JULIAN. I shan't, sir! [*Exit to basement*]

LORINDA. Who can corrupt corruption?

SWAN. Silence.

SHAD. Mr. Commissioner! Am I going to have your pardon, sir?

SWAN. No. But I shall not shoot you—probably.

SHAD. Thank you, sir.

[*They wait, in silence, all looking at the basement door—except* MARY, *who is able to move a couple of steps back toward the couch. Under the cushions of the couch, she has concealed a* REVOLVER. *Out of the basement come* NICKERSON *and* BROWN, *leading a furious and wriggling but silent* DAVID, *and* JULIAN, *leading* DOREMUS, *who still wears the eyeshade. As* DOREMUS *enters, he blinks about the room, uneasy, confused, gaping especially at* SWAN, *then stands waiting.* JULIAN *stands beside him, but does not hold him.*]

SWAN. You don't look well, Mr. Jessup.

SHAD. Haw, haw, haw! He looks terrible!

SWAN. [*To* DOREMUS, *continuing*] But you will look very well, shortly. Are you ready to go? Or are we to be treated to poetic farewells to your loyal family?

DOREMUS. [*Speaking hoarsely, but more strongly than before*] I am ready. For a year now, I have been waiting to die. But I shall go with a great company of ghosts—with John Brown and Nathan Hale. You are not as strong as you think, Commissioner. You can murder lonely men, but you cannot kill the ghosts of freedom.

SWAN. Very pretty, I'm sure; very literary and oratorical; quite up to the gallows tradition. . . . Falck! March him out.

[MARY, *during* DOREMUS*'s speech, has backed clear up to the couch, and leaned against it as though overcome with quiet grief. Now, during* SWAN*'s words "march him out," she scoops the revolver from under the couch cushions, and she is suddenly standing* L., *holding out the revolver with a steady hand, and speaking steadily, sharply.*]

MARY. Hands up, please, all of you! [*All the* CORPOS, *including* SWAN *and* JULIAN, *hastily obey.*] Sorry to be so melodramatic, but revolution's always a bit melodramatic, don't you think? [DOREMUS *has collapsed into a chair in front of fireplace.*] Be careful, Commissioner It would give me pleasure to kill all of you. . . . Eyes front! Stretch! [*The Corpos* ALL *nervously stretch their arms straighter.*] How do you like concentration-camp drill?

JULIAN. [*But with arms still up*] Time for me to come from under cover, I guess, Mary.

MARY. What's all this nonsense?

JULIAN. You didn't trust me?

LORINDA. We can't trust anybody, when it's Doremus Jessup's life.

JULIAN. If you'll look in my left side pocket, you'll find proof.

MARY. Get it, David. [DAVID *takes small notebook from* JULIAN'S *pocket.*] Lindy—what's in it? [DAVID *takes the notebook to* LORINDA, *who examines it.*]

LORINDA. It seems to be a list of Corpo secret agents in Canada. Mary! Julian was always like your brother. We can trust him!

DOREMUS. [*Sitting up fairly straight; speaking strongly*] I know we can!

MARY. Yes! [JULIAN *lowers his hands. If he stands near enough to* DOREMUS, *in his chair, the two shyly pat each other's arms.*] Take their guns, Julian.

JULIAN. It would have been tough to be shot by you! [JULIAN *takes the revolvers from the* CORPOS—SHAD *has none—and puts them in his own pocket.* SWAN *speaks, as his gun is being taken, and for once* SWAN *is quite sincere.*]

SWAN. You too, Falck? I'm sorry for that.

MARY. You can sit, Commissioner. [SWAN *sits by table, trying to smile calmly.*] Julian. You'll take them all across into Canada—in Swan's own car. [JULIAN *has now taken all the revolvers.*]

JULIAN. Right. We must get started. . . . Farewell, Commissioner. Thanks for lending me your Beethoven records and your brass knuckles. I used them both. . . . Mary. Where do we wait for you?

MARY. I have my plans.

DOREMUS. We won't go without you, daughter.

LORINDA. No!

MARY. *Don't argue!* . . . Julian. Go out and start the car. [*Exit* JULIAN]

SWAN. [*All his suavity back; to* MARY] Isn't it a bit dangerous for Captain Falck to steal my car?

MARY. Not very. He's known to be your aide. . . . Lindy! Wrap up Father and Davy.

[*But* DAVID, *running to the hatrack, has his cap and overcoat—not yet buttoned—on before* LORINDA *can help him. She puts on her own wraps, and takes down those of* DOREMUS, *ready to help him, during the following. . . .* DAVID, *his things on, runs to* MARY, *wailing. . . . The* CORPOS *sway a little, hoping for a chance to spring and get the revolver from* MARY.]

DAVID. [*Approaching* MARY *but keeping out of the line of fire*] I won't leave you!

MARY. [*Very cool*] Don't waste time being sentimental, David.

DOREMUS. [*Still in his chair, and trembling, but erect*] We won't go!

MARY. I'm the only one that can hold these people here. It's a question of all our lives. A Corpo patrol may come in any moment.

SWAN. Ah, you realize that, Mrs. Greenhill! If you will stop this mild unpleasantness, I'll let you all go. I give you my word of honor.

MARY. A Corpo? Honor? Don't you know the Corpos have got rid of the inconveniences of personal honor? David. Button up your overcoat. [*He obeys*] Take my purse from the couch. [*He obeys*] There's nearly two hundred dollars in it. You're going to wait for me in Canada, dear. Don't worry if I should be a long time coming. I may have to go a roundabout route. Meantime, keep saying to yourself, "I'm Dr. Fowler Greenhill's son, and Doremus Jessup's grandson. I have to carry on their fight for freedom."

DAVID. Oh, Mummy, Mummy, I want to kiss you! [*He gets almost into the line of fire.* SWAN *becomes tense, ready to spring;* SHAD, NICKERSON, BROWN *sway slightly forward.* MARY *is aware of it; her revolver arm becomes more rigid, though she speaks gently.*]

MARY. It isn't safe now. In Canada we'll have a long kiss, and peace and quiet and lots of fun. Goodbye, dear. Remember everything. *Remember America!*

DAVID. I'll remember! [*He turns from* MARY *blindly, sees his grandfather in the chair, and runs to him.* DOREMUS *puts both hands tenderly on* DAVID'S *shoulders, then slowly rises.* LORINDA *stands behind the chair, with* DOREMUS'*s wraps, but he pays no attention to her. He takes off his eyeshade, looks at it, then holds it up before* DAVID.]

DOREMUS. That's for you, Davy. Some day you'll come home and take it down, and wear it better than I did. [*He reaches out to hang the eyeshade back on the end of the mantelpiece; gently pushes* DAVID *away, and moves slowly toward* MARY.] Mary! I can do it now!

MARY. [*Slightly impatient; not looking at him; gun steady on the Corpos*] What *is* it, Father?

DOREMUS. [*Moving so that he stands to her right, just back of her*] I can't take care of Davy in Canada—and he has to carry on the fight we botched. You go with him, and I'll hold Swan here.

SHAD. Say, will you listen at that!

MARY [*To* DOREMUS, *sharply, still not looking at him*] No! Impossible!

DOREMUS. Do you hear me? I am your father!

MARY. I tell you we can't be sentimental now!

DOREMUS. I am your commanding officer! But all I can do now is clear the way for Davy. Give me that gun! For Davy's sake. [*He slides his hand along her wrist and hand, so that as he seizes, and she releases, the revolver, it remains about where it was. The* CORPOS *sway again, and he commands:*] Don't move! [MARY *crosses to the hatrack and takes her wraps.* LORINDA *drops* DOREMUS'*s coat and cap on the floor.* DAVID *joins the two women,* R. . . . SHAD *moves toward* DOREMUS.] Shad! Better not try it!

SHAD. Aw, you don't dare shoot!

DOREMUS. I warn you!

SHAD. [*Slowly but steadily moving toward* DOREMUS] Put it down, or I'll beat hell out of you. [DOREMUS *shoots, very carefully.* SHAD, *his hands over his belly, crumples, staggers backward to the chair* R. *of the table, and flops into it, dead.*]

DOREMUS. Nasty little gun, Commissioner! . . . Lorinda!

LORINDA. Yes, Doremus.

DOREMUS. Start them going, quickly . . . David—Mary! Don't weep. [LORINDA, MARY, DAVID *move toward door.*]

MARY. [*Tearfully*] Bye, Dad!

DOREMUS. Bye! [*Exeunt, street door,* LORINDA, MARY, DAVID, *sadly, a tiny band of exiles.* DOREMUS *is left alone, moving a bit nearer to* NICKERSON, BROWN, *and the seated* SWAN, *shaky but still dangerous, supporting his gun hand with his left hand.*]

SWAN. [*Sardonically*] Headquarters knows I'm here. Suppose some one came in that door?

DOREMUS. When that door opens, Commissioner Swan, I am going to kill you.

SWAN. But you'll die too, you know.

DOREMUS. I know. But my grandson will be across the border, and I shall live in him. [*He is still holding the revolver on them as*

THE CURTAIN FALLS.

19. *The Skin of Our Teeth*—Thornton Wilder

Commentary

Sources

Play

19.1 EXCERPTS FROM *STAGING THE WAR: AMERICAN DRAMA AND WORLD WAR II*—ALBERT WERTHEIM

IN THORNTON WILDER'S *The Skin of Our Teeth*, history is seen in another light, as the playwright ambitiously and often brilliantly uses the entire sweep of human history to place World War II into a larger context. In many ways, *The Skin of Our Teeth* iterates the theme of human endurance that colored Wilder's prewar *Our Town*. Although Wilder began writing *The Skin of Our Teeth* before Pearl Harbor, he did not complete it until a few weeks after that memorable day. After its pre-Broadway opening at the Schubert Theatre in New Haven (15 October 1942), *The Skin of Our Teeth* made its New York premiere at the Plymouth Theatre on 18 November 1942. The playwright was absent at the opening because he was by then actively involved in the war and stationed overseas as an army intelligence officer. Fifteen years later, in the preface to *Three Plays*, he wrote, "[*The Skin of Our Teeth*] was written on the eve of our entrance into the war and under strong emotion and I think it mostly comes alive under conditions of crisis." It is important, consequently, to consider *The Skin of Our Teeth* not merely (as it is usually seen) as a play about man's ability to retrieve his situation from destruction at the last moment and to begin again, but also as a consideration of the nature of mankind written within the context of the world's most wide-scale, international, and savage war to date, a war in which the playwright himself was actively engaged.

When *Our Town* ran on Broadway, it had been frequently compared with Kaufman and Hart's *The America Way*, which opened eleven months later and which also centered on a typical American family in small-town America. The Kaufman and Hart play had starred Fredric March and his wife, Florence Eldridge. Now, three years later, this onstage and offstage duo, who had made their mark in *The America Way*, were engaged to play the lead characters, Mr. and Mrs. Antrobus, in *The Skin of Our Teeth*, the new play by the author of *Our Town*. Like *The American Way*, *The Skin of Our Teeth* is about the classic American family well known to theatre and radio audiences. But like *Our Town*, it is also about the family of man and the human situation from the beginning of time to the present. Although it can be seen as an extension of the ideas explored in *Our Town*, *The Skin of Our Teeth*, with its pairing of March and Eldridge, also brought to Wilder's new play reminiscences of *The American Way* and of that play's upbeat portrait of American values in the face of rising fascism. When Jed Harris, who had directed *Our Town*, turned down the chance to direct *The Skin of Our Teeth*, Wilder had the good fortune to secure the services of a then young actor-director, Elia Kazan, who was recommended by Wilder's disciple Robert Ardrey and whose sole prior Broadway directing credits were Ardrey's *Casey Jones* (1938) and *Thunder Rock* (1939). Kazan's acting apprenticeship with the politically committed Group Theatre and his experience directing the fanciful *Thunder Rock* (produced by the Group Theatre) may have been the fortuitous combination that unwittingly gave him the appropriate qualifications for directing *The Skin of Our Teeth*.

Starting with Adam and Eve, the repeated survival of mankind by the skin of its teeth is Wilder's large theme, and in the play's successive three acts the Antrobus family, who live in Excelsior, New Jersey, survive first the great ice age glacier, then a version of the biblical deluge, and finally a war of great scope and devastation. At the close of each of the first two acts, the end of the world is imminent, but the beginning of each subsequent act gives proof that the dread event did not take place. In the first act, Wilder nicely uses the fact that, historically, the great glacier did actually stop just shy of New Jersey. Likewise and analogously, in the world as it is represented onstage, the scenery is continually collapsing or disappearing, and the actors miss their lines or become ill. Yet the play itself manages by the skin of its teeth just barely to proceed from act to act, from its beginning to its non-conclusion, as the audience is sent home but told, "This is where you came in. We have to go on for ages and ages yet. You go home. The end of the play isn't written yet" (142). In its way, *The Skin of Our Teeth* is a forerunner of Samuel Beckett's *Waiting for Godot*, in which characters also complain that they do not wish to go on, but do. And like Beckett's drama or Vladimir's song about the dog who came into the kitchen and stole a crust of bread, *The Skin of Our Teeth* perpetually keeps ending and starting over again.

Importantly, in the third act of *The Skin of Our Teeth*, the play's pattern changes: the end of the world is not about to happen but, rather, has just been averted. Calamity is not imminent but has just passed. As in *Our Town*, the miracle of life is that it continues on. Sabina, the Antrobus's maid (famously acted by Tallulah Bankhead), exclaims to the audience, "The whole world's at sixes and sevens, and why the house hasn't fallen down about our ears long ago is a miracle to me"; she follows this by unwittingly quoting from The Book of Common Prayer, "In the midst of life we are in the midst of death, a truer word was never said" (4). For a country embroiled in the global turmoil of World War II, the whole world was indeed at sixes and sevens. Wilder's flying scenery may well have been inspired by the antics of Ole Olsen and Chic Johnson's 1938 slapstick musical comedy *Hellzapoppin'*, which was still running in 1942. But surely in 1942, the collapsing walls and scenery would also bring to mind for those attending a performance of *The Skin of Our Teeth* the destroyed buildings and scenery of wartime Europe, captured so vividly in movie house newsreels and newspaper photographs.

Likewise, refugees fleeing the glacier appear at the Antrobus house. In 1942, the very word *refugees* was highly charged, with hordes of refugees fleeing the Holocaust arriving on American shores. Among the refugees seeking shelter in Excelsior, New Jersey, are Homer, who recites in Greek the opening lines of *The Iliad*, Moses, who recites in Hebrew the opening lines of Genesis (40–41), and a physician. And Miss Somerset, the character who plays the role of the actress playing the role of Sabina, breaks through the fictions of the play and turns to the audience, saying, "Oh I see what this part of the play means now! This means refugees. Oh, I don't like it. I don't like it" (34). Mr. and Mrs. Antrobus react to the immigrants respectively with 1940s American attitudes of welcome and xenophobia:

MRS. ANTROBUS. George, these tramps say that you asked them to come to the house. What does this mean?

ANTROBUS. Just . . . uh . . . These are a few friends, Maggie, I met on the road. But nice, real useful people . . .

MRS. ANTROBUS. NOW, don't ask them in!
George Antrobus, not another soul comes in here over my dead body.

ANTROBUS. Maggie, there's a doctor there. Never hurts to have a good doctor in the house. (36)

Here as elsewhere in *The Skin of Our Teeth*, Wilder brings the entire history of the world into an engaging discourse with the history of World War II to date and with wartime America in 1942.

In act 3 of *The Skin of Our Teeth*, Wilder pointedly cites the eternal source of evil in the world, the evil that Americans were fighting in World War II, and locates it in the character of Henry, the Antrobus son who, we are told early in the play, was once called Cain. Portrayed in the original production by Montgomery Clift, Henry is Wilder's representation of envy, racial prejudice, and greed: the elements eternally present in every human and the source of mankind's ills. As Sabina aptly says, "I don't know how to say it, but the enemy is *Henry*; Henry *is* the enemy. Everybody knows that" (119).

In act 1, Henry is first identified with the envious Cain and the murder of Abel. In act 2, as the embodiment of white racism, Henry, with no cause other than the pleasure of offering violence and with slingshot poised for release, menaces a Negro chair-pusher on Atlantic City's boardwalk (67). In act 3, Henry's seething discontent, arising from a sense of oppression and envy, is figured as a version of the disruptive fascist malady Americans were seeking to extirpate by entering into a war against Hitler, Mussolini, and Hirohito.

Talking in his sleep, Henry sounds like Hitler talking to the Germans about the Jews, "Fellows . . . what have they done for us? . . . Blocked our way at every step. Kept everything in their own hands. And you've stood it. When are you going to wake up" (126). And Henry, as Wilder explains in the stage directions, "*is played, not as a misunderstood or misguided young man, but as a representation of strong unreconciled evil*" (127). As father and son square off, their speeches resonate with the ideological oppositions that set Allies against Axis, even as Wilder looks ahead to a peacetime when the victors will attempt to reconcile with Nazis and fascists, bringing them back into the fold of humanity:

> ANTROBUS. You're the last person I wanted to see. . . . I wish I were back at war still, because it's easier to fight you than to live with you. War's a pleasure—do you hear me?—War's a pleasure compared to what faces us now: trying to build up a peacetime with you in the middle of it.
>
> HENRY. I'm not going to be a part of any peacetime of yours. . . .
>
> ANTROBUS. Henry, let's try again.
>
> HENRY. Try what? Living *here?*—Speaking polite downtown to all the old men like you? Standing like a sheep at the street corner until the red light turns green? Being a good boy and a good sheep, like all the stinking ideas you get out of your books? Oh no, I'll make a world, and I'll show you.
>
> ANTROBUS. How can you make a world for people to live in, unless you've first put order in yourself? Mark my words: I shall continue fighting you until my last breath as long as you mix up your idea of liberty with your idea of hogging everything for yourself. (128–129)

Greed, anti-intellectualism, jealousy, and Oedipal anger are the dominant elements in the venomous brew of evil that seems to course through Henry's veins. By extension, those same elements seem, in 1942, to characterize the forces against which the Allies were fighting.

Wilder's audiences, seeing *The Skin of Our Teeth* while World War II was at its height and two and a half years before it was to be over, were given, in the third act, a foretaste of the peacetime that was to come in 1945 as Sabina opens the act, shouting, "Mrs. Antrobus! Gladys! Where are you? The war's over. The war's over! You can come out. The peace treaty's been signed!" (104). As *Our Town* had assured an audience prior to American entry into World War II that individual lives are lost in war but that life continues and wars fade into history, *The Skin of Our Teeth* assures an American audience, now actively embroiled in the war, that mankind will endure and survive this war, even as it has every other war and every other cataclysm.

By envisioning the peacetime beyond current events, Wilder's play asserts itself as a comedy in the way Shakespeare's *The Winter's Tale* and *The Tempest* are comedies, projecting the world as it can be after tragedy. Mr. Antrobus reveals to his wife and to Wilder's audience, "But during the war,—in the middle of all that blood and dirt and hot and cold—every day and night, I'd have moments, Maggie, when I *saw* the things that we could do when it was over. When you're at war you think about a better life; when you're at peace you think about a more comfortable one. . . . All I ask is the chance to build new worlds and God has always given us that. . . . Maggie, you and I will remember in peacetime all the resolves that were so clear to us in the days of war" (135, 140). Thus well before World War II has ended, Wilder writes *The Skin of Our Teeth* to prophesy that the forces of good will prevail and that a brave new postwar world should be informed by lessons learned during war and tragedy. At the same time, Wilder makes clear that the forces of ill will and evil, the Henrys and the Calibans, never die and are with us, creating havoc from generation to generation.

19.2 LETTER TO SYBIL COLEFAX—THORNTON WILDER

from Thornton Wilder

The MacDowell Colony
Peterborough, N.H.
June 14, 1940

Dear, dear Sibyl:

What times, what things to live through! The mind cannot grasp a small part of the agony undergone, and of the further disasters possible.

Your word months ago that you were sure it would be a long war terrified me, but now I draw comfort from it. Long enough to sustain the best we know, and long enough for America to help.

A few days ago I received a letter from Lynn and Alfred asking me to telegraph the President and my Senator in answer to President Conant's (of Harvard) appeal to expedite the means whereby material could be sent abroad; I had already sent off the telegrams. All too slowly the formalities in Washington are unrolling to some effectiveness.

The Middle West remains obstinately "isolationist," but even that is thawing with a swiftness unprecedented among us—but can it be swift enough to match the acceleration of historical action as we see it taking place abroad.

Each day seems more in crisis than the last—in a few minutes I go back to the "main house" to see what has happened today—and so, each night and each morning.

June 17.

Waiting, Waiting.

And now the news of France's capitulation.

All I can do is send to you my love and a thousand thoughts you can divine, and over here to exert myself in every way I know to make people realize that our aid and participation is essential—to some I can put it (for it is no less true) as pure self-interest; to others and to myself I put it Humitarianism = Civilization. A civilization without instinctive brother-participation with the Thing-France and the Thing-England is no civilization.

Let the thought of me enter as a whisper into your dejected moments and as a voice into your moments of courage, fortitude and hope.

Ever affectionately

Thornton

19.3 THE STRENGTH OF A DEMOCRACY UNDER SIEGE—REX STOUT AND THORNTON WILDER

THIS IS A TRANSCRIPT OF AN INTERVIEW broadcast on the "Speaking of Liberty" program on NBC Radio on 30 October 1941. Transcribed by Drew Eisenhauer.

Rex Stout: Good evening, friends of liberty. Our guest today makes me feel at least as old as the Declaration of Independence. Not that Thornton Wilder is aged or ancient; he may easily have three or four more Pulitzer Prizes left in him. But it is fitting to introduce him not only as the author of *Our Town* and other recent contributions but also that sensational bestseller, *The Bridge at San Luis Rey*. And how long ago, how far off, that seems in the world we inhabit today. It probably seems even further off to Mr. Wilder than to you or me, for he has just been closer to the bombs and the Blitz, having returned from London on the Clipper so recently that he's still blinking at the lights in New York. Aren't you, Mr. Wilder?

Thornton Wilder: I am. It's hard to get used to them, Mr. Stout. In London if you see the smallest chink of light in the window you get all stirred up with civic indignation.

RS: Is the blackout the first thing that struck your attention after your arrival in England, or what was it?

TW: Well, a number of things struck me in quick succession—the fact that there was less destruction in London than I had feared, and the sort of eagerness with which the English wish to show the damage and discuss it, a sort of possessive pride. The wonderful nightly experience of the blackout—pinpoint spots of red, green, and yellow light moving about in the darkness.

Nothing groping about it, nothing furtive or alarming. I can only describe it by saying that suddenly the great city feels like a forest.

RS: Give me some first impressions.

TW: Well, I noticed how well everybody looked.

RS: In spite of raids and food rations?

TW: Yes, they looked many times better than when I last saw them in '39.

RS: Better? How do you explain that?

TW: Chiefly by psychological reasons. This war is being waged directly against every man, woman, and child. As a result, everyone is filled with their resistance and their resolve. It gives new meaning and new weight to everything they do. They walk with decision. They hold their heads up with decision. A thousand small worries and small discontents fall away from them.

RS: You make it sound . . . but I'm ahead of myself. How did you manage to get to England?

TW: Your question is very much to the point, Mr. Stout. It's very hard to get a passport for England these days. John Dos Passos and I were invited to be the American delegates to the seventeenth annual congress of the PEN Club held in London, September 10th. This particular . . .

RS: Excuse me Mr. Wilder. To announce for those who haven't heard of it, the PEN Club is an international society of writers.

TW: This particular congress was attended by representatives from twenty-three countries. It lasted for three days and following the meetings every aid was put at our disposal and we were encouraged to make a brief tour of the country and inquire about various aspects of military and civilian defense.

RS: You were allowed to travel around England anywhere?

TW: It requires a number of permits to go to some districts. The authorities were unfailingly considerate. They arranged for us to go wherever we wanted.

RS: What did you see?

TW: We visited some of the cities that had suffered most, various headquarters for civilian defense, an airplane factory, the headquarters of the Free French, and a bomber command from which planes set out to drop bombs on military objectives in enemy country when weather permits.

RS: What impressed you most, Mr. Wilder?

TW: All the striking impressions could be summed up for me in one: I felt that very suddenly I was obtaining a larger view of the whole war and its meaning.

RS: Larger? How larger?

TW: I thought that when I went to England that I was completely convinced of the fact that the whole world has this one task before it—to collect itself toward the elimination of dictatorships.

RS: Oh, you were? I am. Nearly everyone is.

TW: I know. But the trip to England showed me that I had realized only a small part of that necessity. My conviction with regard to the kind of resistance that had to be made was nowhere near deep enough or lively enough.

RS: What deepened your convictions? Seeing the destruction the Nazis had done in England?

TW: Yes, but that was only a small part of it. To a certain extent destruction is a thing one's imagination can picture beforehand. I wanted to see those things which advance report and anticipatory imagination could not furnish you. However, in regard to the bombing, I will say that I was completely convinced that a great deal of the destruction had been clearly directed against the civilian population. There is a district in Scotland where the obvious military objective has been all but disregarded in order to concentrate on the homes and the workers that supply them.

RS: As a deliberate tactic? What do the British think?

TW: They think that Hitler imagined that it would be quicker and easier to demoralize the civilian population than to accomplish a widespread destruction of industrial and military objectives.

RS: And he guessed wrong?

TW: Yes. Instead of demoralization there was heightened effectiveness and heightened morale. However, Mr. Stout, it was not a view of the bombed cities that chiefly enlarged my realization of the meaning of the war.

RS: What was it? The army they've got, or are getting?

TW: No, though that was impressive also. One of the most striking aspects of that was the work of the home guard. The home guard began under ridicule, drilling with broomsticks and founded by civilians.

RS: Something like the air raid wardens here in New York?

TW: Possibly. I haven't seen that yet of course. By the time I saw it, the home guard of England had grown into an immense thing two million strong, organized and trained with extraordinary skill. And as I was told many times by enthusiastic guardsmen, armed with rifles from the United States. You're to realize that late afternoons after work and on Saturdays and Sundays these men below or above military age are out in the field defending bridges, shooting imaginary parachute troops, learning every advantage that can be obtained from their own knowledge of the network of roads, and progressively educating themselves through a series of disciplines, exercises, problems, and strategies.

RS: Then what impressed you most was not the army of the soldiers, but the army of people?

TW: Yes. I knew of course that the English people had undergone their ordeal with extraordinary courage but I wanted to know what kind of courage it was. Was it mere stoic fortitude and endurance, or was it exalted defiance or was it a grim resolution to wait and retaliate?

RS: Did you find an answer that satisfied you?

TW: Oh, I think to find an answer would take many more months than I had. But here are some of the elements of the answer. In the first place, no one talks cant, no emotional jargon, no patriotic rhetoric. The Britishers discuss all the dangers they've been through and all the lives and destinies that are at stake. They discuss all this in the same even tone of voice and unemphatic way that we discuss the ordinary events of daily life. Imagine for a moment hearing a woman say things like this, in the same tone of voice in which she would describe transplanting tulip bulbs in the garden: "My eldest son was reported dead in Libya; we have just received word from him in Italy where he is a prisoner. He has just undergone a tense operation and writes that if they take any more of his uniform out of him they'll have enough to make a pair of trousers. And my second son, who lost a leg in Norway, is the happiest man alive. He's just been approved fit to serve again as an air pilot."

RS: Yes. How do they talk about the enemy? Also without rhetoric?

TW: Yes. The German is merely "Jerry" and Hitler is, in the same tone of voice, Hitler. This doesn't mean that there is any condoning of the enemy's crimes or any relaxation of the resolve to eliminate them from the earth. It is as though they had attained some large historic viewpoint to regard these as ordeals which have been laid upon their shoulders by destiny itself. All the more impressive therefore become one's glimpses of the Germans as they've been seen in some encounters with the British.

RS: You mean the way they fight?

TW: When they've been taken prisoner. Some British airmen told me that on several occasions they had approached German officers who had been brought down. On the necessity of arresting them they had tried to accord them the courtesy they wish to show towards a skilled opponent and an officer.

RS: I gather something happened?

TW: More than once. The sullen German officers seemed to accept the courtesy, but it turned out that they were merely waiting for the moment to get near enough to the Englishmen to spit in their faces. But returning to the even temper of the people, what I call their guarded equanimity.

RS: But how do you explain it? Merely the well-known Anglo-Saxon reserve?

TW: No. It seems to come from a powerful sense of community responsibility, the responsibility of each individual to his neighbor. Each one conceals his or her own trepidation or concern in order to protect the welfare of the group. For example, during those nineteen successive nights when the greater part of the population of London took shelter underground, or in the lower parts of their houses, inhabitants of that prosperous part of London which is Mayfair remained in the city. They are people who could easily have gone into the safer provinces but they chose to remain where they were to show that they could suffer these things shoulder to shoulder with the whole city's population.

RS: Then you feel that all classes have been drawn together by what they're going through?

TW: Yes, and all types. Let me tell you a story that seems very significant to me. A friend of mine caught in an early afternoon raid descended to a shelter in the neighborhood of St. Martin's in the Fields. The company there consisted of everything from a bishop to some old apple-sellers. The crash and bang, the whistle of high explosives, continued while everyone carried on lively conversation. There were two soldiers laughing and talking, lighting each other's cigarettes. And suddenly one of the soldiers fainted. The shelter marshal brought some water, poured it in his face and he was soon himself. I asked my friend particularly how the company behaved. He said that on the one hand there was no ostentatious ignoring of the incident nor any exaggerated sympathetic concern on the other. The young man on coming to himself did not feel he had to exhibit shame or embarrassment. All realized that there are tricks that one's subconscious plays on even the stoutest heart and one need not apologize for them.

RS: That seems merely elementary humanity, Mr. Wilder, but I suppose you're right that the common peril and the common consciousness of a dangerous and ugly job that cannot be shirked does make people see more clearly and understand more deeply. But I certainly don't believe that war has always done that to all people. Do you?

TW: No, I don't think so. It seems to me that this deep and unified attitude could only be produced by a realization of the extent of the enemy's conception of war. The Germans first showed us what total war can be. The Germans have arranged a world in which they try to harness every energy of every citizen to some aspect of the war activity. That is total war. What began as a grievance was whipped up by government authorities to crusade and hysteria and finally directed by spying and force. How can a democracy oppose such methods without also stooping to hysteria and finally to brutal coercion? The English have shown that a democracy can collect itself into one mind and one will and that one will is not imposed upon it from the governors and is not maintained through either oratory or hypodermics nor through police. It rises instinctively from the people. That deep sense of responsibility from neighbor to neighbor is the finest thing a democracy can show. It is wonderful in wartime; it will be still more wonderful in peace. The Nazi spirit with its contempt for the human being as anything else but a tool has clarified for all of us just what a democracy is. A democracy has greater things to do than to organize itself towards a total war. But when it sees itself threatened with extinction, it can do that too. Our great danger is that we may underestimate the power that drives the Nazis on. They are in a condition which in the days of witchcraft they used to call a state of possession. It may still have a long cruel course to run. To oppose it the rest of the world must also present a unified state of mind as formidable in degree even though it's different in kind. It is hard in a democracy for individuals to abandon temporarily some of those liberties which they have taken five thousand years to acquire. But when the extinction of democracy itself is threatened, democracy too can collect itself to make a total war. When democracy has been saved from this menace we shall have learned better how to apply it to our own country.

RS: If we don't, we're sunk. Like all living things democracy grows or it dies. Thank you, Mr. Wilder. Ladies and gentlemen, our guest today was Thornton Wilder. This is Rex Stout saying good-bye until next week.

19.4 PLAYBILL COVER FOR *THE SKIN OF OUR TEETH*—DON FREEMAN

Cover of the playbill for the 1942 Plymouth Theatre production of *Skin of our Teeth*.

19.5 *THE SKIN OF OUR TEETH*—THORNTON WILDER

Preface

The Skin of Our Teeth begins, also, by making fun of old-fashioned playwriting; but the audience soon perceives that he is seeing "two times at once." The Antrobus family is living both in prehistoric times and in a New Jersey commuters' suburb today. Again, the events of our homely daily life—this time the family life—are depicted against the vast dimensions of time and place. It was written on the eve of our entrance into the war and under strong emotion and I think it mostly comes alive under conditions of crisis. It has been often charged with being a bookish fantasia about history, full of rather bloodless schoolmasterish jokes. But to have seen it in Germany soon after the war, in the shattered churches and beer halls that were serving as theatres, with audiences whose price of admission meant the loss of a meal and for whom it was of absorbing interest that there was "a recipe for grass soup that did not cause the diarrhea," was an experience that was not so cool. I am very proud that this year it has received a first and overwhelming reception in Warsaw. The play is deeply indebted to James Joyce's *Finnegan's Wake*. I should be very happy if, in the future, some author should feel similarly indebted to any work of mine. Literature has always more resembled a torch race than a furious dispute among heirs.

Thornton Wilder

Characters (in the order of their appearance)

ANNOUNCER
SABINA
MR. FITZPATRICK
MRS. ANTROBUS
DINOSAUR
MAMMOTH
TELEGRAPH BOY
GLADYS
HENRY
MR. ANTROBUS
DOCTOR
PROFESSOR
JUDGE
HOMER
MISS E. MUSE
T. MUSE
MISS M. MUSE
TWO USHERS
TWO DRUM MAJORETTES
FORTUNE LETTER
TWO CHAIR PUSHERS
SIX CONVEENERS
BROADCAST OFFICIAL
DEFEATED CANDIDATE
MR. TREMAYNE
HESTER
IVY
FRED BAILEY

Act I. Home, Excelsior, New Jersey.
Act II. Atlantic City Boardwalk.
Act III. Home, Excelsior, New Jersey.

★

ACT I

A projection screen in the middle of the curtain. The first lantern slide; the name of the theatre, and the words: NEWS EVENTS OF THE WORLD. An ANNOUNCER'S *voice is heard.*

ANNOUNCER:

The management takes pleasure in bringing to you—The News Events of the World:

Freeport, Long Island.

- *Slide of the sun appearing above the horizon.*

The sun rose this morning at 6:32 a.m. This gratifying event was first reported by Mrs. Dorothy Stetson of Freeport, Long Island, who promptly telephoned the Mayor.

The Society for Affirming the End of the World at once went into a special session and postponed the arrival of that event for TWENTY-FOUR HOURS.

All honor to Mrs. Stetson for her public spirit.

New York City:

- *Slide of the front doors of the theatre in which this play is playing; three cleaning* women *with mops and pails.*

The X Theatre. During the daily cleaning of this theatre a number of lost objects were collected as usual by Mesdames Simpson, Pateslewski, and Moriarty.
Among these objects found today was a wedding ring, inscribed: To Eva from Adam. Genesis II: 18.
The ring will be restored to the owner or owners, if their credentials are satisfactory.

Tippchatchee, Vermont:

- *Slide representing a glacier.*

The unprecedented cold weather of this summer has produced a condition that has not been yet satisfactorily explained. There is a report that a wall of ice is moving southward across these countries. The disruption of communications by the cold wave now crossing the country has rendered exact information difficult, but little credence is given to the rumor that the ice had pushed the Cathedral of Montreal as far as St. Albans, Vermont.
For further information see your daily papers.

Excelsior, New Jersey:

- Slide of a modest suburban home.

The home of Mr. George Antrobus, the inventor of the wheel. The discovery of the wheel, following so closely on the discovery of the lever, has centered the attention of the country on Mr. Antrobus of this attractive suburban residence district. This is his home, a commodious seven-room house, conveniently situated near a public school, a Methodist church, and a firehouse; it is right handy to an A. and P.

- *Slide of* MR. ANTROBUS *on his front steps, smiling and lifting his straw hat. He holds a wheel.*

Mr. Antrobus, himself He comes of very old stock and has made his way up from next to no riling.

It is reported that he was once a gardener, but left that situation under circumstances that have been variously reported.

Mr. Antrobus is a veteran of foreign wars, and bears a number of scars, front and back.

- *Slide of* MRS. ANTROBUS, *holding some roses.*

This is Mrs. Antrobus, the charming and gracious president of the Excelsior Mothers' Club.

Mrs. Antrobus is an excellent needlewoman; it is she who invented the apron on which so many interesting changes have been rung since.

- *Slide of the* FAMILY *and* SABINA.

Here we see the Antrobuses with their two children, Henry and Gladys, and friend. The friend in the rear, is Lily Sabina, the maid.

I know we all want to congratulate this typical American family on its enterprise. We all wish Mr. Antrobus a successful future. Now the management takes you to the interior of this home for a brief visit.

Curtain rises. Living room of a commuter's home. SABINA *—straw-blonde, over-ranged—is standing by the window back center, a feather duster under her elbow.*

SABINA:

Oh, oh, oh! Six o'clock and the master not home yet.

Pray God nothing serious has happened to him crossing the Hudson River. If anything happened to him, we would certainly be inconsolable and have to move into a less desirable residence district.

The fact is I don't know what'll become of us. Here it is the middle of August and the coldest day of the year. It's simply freezing; the dogs are sticking to the sidewalks; can anybody explain that? No.

But I'm not surprised. The whole world's at sixes and sevens, and why the house hasn't fallen down about our ears long ago is a miracle to me.

A fragment of the right wall leans precariously over the stage. SABINA *looks at it nervously and it slowly rights itself.*

Every night this same anxiety as to whether the master will get home safely: whether he'll bring home anything to eat. In the midst of life we are in the midst of death, a truer word was never said.

The fragment of scenery flies up into the lofts, SABINA *is struck dumb with surprise, shrugs her shoulders and starts dusting* MR. ANTROBUS' *chair, including the under side.*

Of course, Mr. Antrobus is a very fine man, an excellent husband and father, a pillar of the church, and has all the best interests of the community at heart. Of course, every muscle goes tight every time he passes a policeman; but what I think is that there are certain charges that ought not to be made, and I think I may add, ought not to be allowed to be made; we're all human; who isn't?

She dusts MRS. ANTROBUS' *rocking chair.*

Mrs. Antrobus is as fine a woman as you could hope to see. She lives only for her children; and if it would be any benefit to her children she'd see the rest of us stretched out dead at her feet without turning a hair,—that's the truth. If you want to know anything more about Mrs. Antrobus, just go and look at a tigress, and look hard.

As to the children—

Well, Henry Antrobus is a real, clean-cut American boy. He'll graduate from High School one of these days, if they make the alphabet any easier.—Henry, when he has a stone in his hand, has a perfect aim; he can hit anything from a bird to an older brother—Oh! I didn't mean to say that!—but it certainly was an unfortunate accident, and it was very hard getting the police out of the house.

Mr. and Mrs. Antrobus' daughter is named Gladys. She'll make some good man a good wife some day, if he'll just come down off the movie screen and ask her.

So here we are!

We've managed to survive for some time now, catch as catch can, the fat and the lean, and if the dinosaurs don't trample us to death, and if the grasshoppers don't eat up our garden, we'll all live to see better days, knock on wood.

Each new child that's born to the Antrobuses seems to them to be sufficient reason for the whole universe's being set in motion; and each new child that dies seems to them to have been spared a whole world of sorrow, and what the end of it will be is still very much an open question.

We've rattled along, hot and cold, for some time now—

A portion of the wall above the door, right, flies up into the air and disappears.

—and my advice to you is not to inquire into why or whither, but just enjoy your ice cream while it's on your plate,—that's my philosophy.

Don't forget that a few years ago we came through the depression by the skin of our teeth! One more tight squeeze like that and where will we be?

This is a cue line. SABINA *looks angrily at the kitchen door and repeats:*

. . . we came through the depression by the skin of our teeth; one more tight squeeze like that and where will we be?

Flustered, she looks through the opening in the right wall; then goes to the window and reopens the Act.

Oh, oh, oh! Six o'clock and the master not home yet. Pray God nothing has happened to him crossing the Hudson. Here it is the middle of August and the coldest day of the year. It's simply freezing; the dogs are sticking. One more tight squeeze like that and where will we be?

VOICE:

Offstage.

Make up something! Invent something!

SABINA:

Well . . . uh . . . this certainly is a fine American home . . . and—uh . . . everybody's very happy . . . and—uh . . .

Suddenly flings pretense to the winds and coming down stage says with indignation:

I can't invent any words for this play, and I'm glad I can't. I hate this play and every word in it.

As for me, I don't understand a single word of it, anyway,—all about the troubles the human race has gone through, there's a subject for you.

Besides, the author hasn't made up his silly mind as to whether we're all living back in caves or in New Jersey today, and that's the way it is all the way through.

Oh—why can't we have plays like we used to have—*Peg o' My Heart*, and *Smilin' Thru*, and *The Bat*—good entertainment with a message you can take home with you?

I took this hateful job because I had to. For two years I've sat up in my room living on a sandwich and a cup of tea a day, waiting for better times in the theatre. And look at me now: I—I who've played *Rain* and *The Barretts of Wimpole Street* and *First Lady*—God in Heaven!

The STAGE MANAGER *puts his head out from the hole in the scenery.*

MR. FITZPATRICK:
Miss Somerset!! Miss Somerset!

SABINA:
Oh! Anyway!—nothing matters! It'll all be the same in a hundred years.

Loudly.

We came through the depression by the skin of our teeth,—that's true!—one more tight squeeze like that and where will we be?

Enter MRS. ANTROBUS, *a mother.*

MRS. ANTROBUS:
Sabina, you've let the fire go out.

SABINA:

In a lather.

One-thing-and-another; don't-know-whether-my-wits-are-upside-or-down; might-as-well-be-dead-as-alive-in-a-house-all-sixes-and-sevens. . . .

MRS. ANTROBUS:
You've let the fire go out. Here it is the coldest day of the year right in the middle of August, and you've let the fire go out.

SABINA:
Mrs. Antrobus, I'd like to give my two weeks' notice, Mrs. Antrobus. A girl like I can get a situation in a home where they're rich enough to have a fire in every room, Mrs. Antrobus, and a girl don't have to carry the responsibility of the whole house on her two shoulders. And a home without children, Mrs. Antrobus, because children are a thing only a parent can stand, and a truer word was never said; and a home, Mrs. Antrobus, where the master of the house don't pinch decent, self-respecting girls when he meets them in a dark corridor. I mention no names and make no charges. So you have my notice, Mrs. Antrobus. I hope that's perfectly clear.

MRS. ANTROBUS:
You've let the fire go out!—Have you milked the mammoth?

SABINA:
I don't understand a word of this play.—Yes, I've milked the mammoth.

MRS. ANTROBUS:
Until Mr. Antrobus comes home we have no food and we have no fire. You'd better go over to the neighbors and borrow some fire.

SABINA:
Mrs. Antrobus! I can't! I'd die on the way, you know I would. It's worse than January. The dogs are sticking to the sidewalks. I'd die.

MRS. ANTROBUS:
Very well, I'll go.

SABINA:

Even more distraught, coming forward and sinking on her knees.

You'd never come back alive; we'd all perish; if you weren't here, we'd just perish. How do we know Mr. Antrobus'll be back? We don't know. If you go out, I'll just kill myself.

MRS. ANTROBUS:
Get up, Sabina.

SABINA:
Every night it's the same thing. Will he come back safe, or won't he? Will we starve to death, or freeze to death, or boil to death or will we be killed by burglars? I don't know why we go on living. I don't know why we go on living at all. It's easier being dead.

She flings her arms on the table and buries her head in them. In each of the succeeding speeches she flings her head up—and sometimes her hands—then quickly buries her head again.

MRS. ANTROBUS:
The same thing! Always throwing up the sponge, Sabina. Always announcing your own death. But give you a new hat—or a plate of ice cream—or a ticket to the movies, and you want to live forever.

SABINA:
You don't care whether we live or die; all you care about is those children. If it would be any benefit to them you'd be glad to see us all stretched out dead.

MRS. ANTROBUS:
Well, maybe I would.

SABINA:
And what do they care about? Themselves—that's all they care about.

Shrilly.

They make fun of you behind your back. Don't tell me: they're ashamed of you. Half the time, they pretend they're someone else's children. Little thanks you get from them.

MRS. ANTROBUS:
I'm not asking for any thanks.

SABINA:

And Mr. Antrobus—you don't understand *him.* All that work he does—trying to discover the alphabet and the multiplication table. Whenever he tries to learn anything you fight against it.

MRS. ANTROBUS:

Oh, Sabina, I know you.

When Mr. Antrobus raped you home from your Sabine hills, he did it to insult me.

He did it for your pretty face, and to insult me.

You were the new wife, weren't you?

For a year or two you lay on your bed all day and polished the nails on your hands and feet:

You made puff-balls of the combings of your hair and you blew them up to the ceiling.

And I washed your underclothes and I made you chicken broths.

I bore children and between my very groans I stirred the cream that you'd put on your face.

But I knew you wouldn't last.

You didn't last.

SABINA:

But it was I who encouraged Mr. Antrobus to make the alphabet. I'm sorry to say it, Mrs. Antrobus, but you're not a beautiful woman, and you can never know what a man could do if he tried. It's girls like I who inspire the multiplication table.

I'm, sorry to say it, but you're not a beautiful woman, Mrs. Antrobus, and that's the God's truth.

MRS. ANTROBUS:

And you didn't last—you sank to the kitchen. And what do you do there? *You let the fire go out!*

No wonder to you it seems easier being dead.

Reading and writing and counting on your fingers is all very well in their way,—but I keep the home going.

MRS. ANTROBUS:

—There's that dinosaur on the front lawn again—Shoo! Go away. Go away.

The baby dinosaur puts his head in the window.

DINOSAUR:

It's cold.

MRS. ANTROBUS:

You go around to the back of the house where you belong.

DINOSAUR:

It's cold.

The DINOSAUR *disappears.* MRS. ANTROBUS *goes calmly out.*

SABINA *slowly raises her head and speaks to the audience. The central portion of the center wall rises, pauses, and disappears into the loft.*

SABINA:

Now that you audience are listening to this, too, I understand it a little better.

I wish eleven o'clock were here; I don't want to be dragged through this whole play again.

The TELEGRAPH BOY *is seen entering along the back wall of the stage from the right. She catches sight of him and calls:*

Mrs. Antrobus! Mrs. Antrobus! Help! There's a strange man coming to the house. He's coming up the walk, help!
Enter MRS. ANTROBUS *in alarm, but efficient.*

MRS. ANTROBUS:

Help me quick!

They barricade the door by piling the furniture against it.

Who is it? What do you want?

TELEGRAPH BOY:

A telegram for Mrs. Antrobus from Mr. Antrobus in the city.

SABINA:

Are you sure, are you sure? Maybe it's just a trap!

MRS. ANTROBUS:

I know his voice, Sabina. We can open the door.

Enter the TELEGRAPH BOY, *12 years old, in uniform. The* DINOSAUR *and* MAMMOTH *slip by him into the room and settle down front right.*

I'm sorry we kept you waiting. We have to be careful, you know.

To the ANIMALS.

Hm! . . . Will you be quiet?

They nod.

Have you had your supper?

They nod.

Are you *ready* to come in?

They nod.

Young man, have you any fire with you? Then light the grate, will your

He nods, produces something like a briquet; and kneels by the imagined fireplace, footlights center. Pause.

What are people saying about this cold weather?

He makes a doubtful shrug with his shoulders.

Sabina, take this stick and go and light the stove.

SABINA:
Like I told you, Mrs. Antrobus; two weeks. That's the law. I hope that's perfectly clear.

Exit.

MRS. ANTROBUS:
What about this cold weather?

TELEGRAPH BOY:
Lowered eyes.

Of course, I don't know anything . . . but they say there's a wall of ice moving down from the North, that's what they say. We can't get Boston by telegraph, and they're burning pianos in Hartford.

. . . It moves everything in front of it, churches and post offices and city halls.

I live in Brooklyn myself.

MRS. ANTROBUS:
What are people doing about it?

TELEGRAPH BOY:
Well . . . uh . . . Talking, mostly.

Or just what you'd do a day in February.

There are some that are trying to go South and the roads are crowded; but you can't take old people and children very far in a cold like this.

MRS. ANTROBUS:
—What's this telegram you have for me?

TELEGRAPH BOY:
Fingertips to his forehead.

If you wait just a minute; I've got to remember it.

The ANIMALS *have left their corner and are nosing him. Presently they take places on either side of him, leaning against his hips, like heraldic beasts.*

This telegram was flashed from Murray Hill to University Heights! And then by puffs of smoke from University Heights to Staten Island.

And then by lantern from Staten Island to Plainfield, New Jersey. What hath God wrought!

He clears his throat.

"To Mrs. Antrobus, Excelsior, New Jersey:

My dear wife, will be an hour late. Busy day at the office. Don't worry the children about the cold just keep them warm burn everything except Shakespeare."

Pause.

MRS. ANTROBUS:
Men!—He knows I'd burn ten Shakespeares to prevent a child of mine from having one cold in the head. What does it say next?

Enter SABINA.

TELEGRAPH BOY:
"Have made great discoveries today have separated em from en."

SABINA:
I know what that is, that's the alphabet, yes it is. Mr. Antrobus is just the cleverest man. Why, when the alphabet's finished, we'll be able to tell the future and everything.

TELEGRAPH BOY:
Then listen to this: "Ten tens make a hundred semi-colon consequences far-reaching."

Watches for effect.

MRS. ANTROBUS:
The earth's turning to ice, and all he can do is to make up new numbers.

TELEGRAPH BOY:
Well, Mrs. Antrobus, like the head man at our office said: a few more discoveries like that and we'll be worth freezing.

MRS. ANTROBUS:
What does he say next?

TELEGRAPH BOY:
I . . . I can't do this last part very well.

He clears his throat and sings.

"Happy w'dding ann'vers'ry to you, Happy ann'vers'ry to you—"

The ANIMALS *begin to howl soulfully;* SABINA *screams with pleasure.*

MRS. ANTROBUS:
Dolly! Frederick! Be quiet.

TELEGRAPH BOY:
Above the din.

"Happy w'dding ann'vers'ry, dear Eva; happy w'dding ann'vers'ry to you."

MRS. ANTROBUS:
Is that in the telegram? Are they singing telegrams now?

Nods

The earth's getting so silly no wonder the sun turns cold.

SABINA:
Mrs. Antrobus, I want to take back the notice I gave you. Mrs. Antrobus, I don't want to leave a house that gets such interesting telegrams and I'm sorry for anything I said. I really am.

MRS. ANTROBUS:
Young man, I'd like to give you something for all this trouble; Mr. Antrobus isn't home yet and I have no money and no food in the house—

TELEGRAPH BOY:
Mrs. Antrobus . . . I don't like to . . . appear to . . . ask for anything, but . . .

MRS. ANTROBUS:
What is it you'd like?

TELEGRAPH BOY:
Do you happen to have an old needle you could spare? My wife just sits home all day thinking about needles.

SABINA:
Shrilly.

We only got two in the house. Mrs. Antrobus, you know we only got two in the house.

MRS. ANTROBUS:
After a look at SABINA *taking a needle from her collar.*

Why yes, I can spare this.

TELEGRAPH BOY:
Lowered eyes.

Thank you, Mrs. Antrobus. Mrs. Antrobus, can I ask you something else? I have two sons of my own; if the cold gets worse, what should I do?

SABINA:
I think we'll all perish, that's what I think. Cold like this in August is just the end of the whole world.

Silence.

MRS. ANTROBUS:
I don't know. After all, what does one do about anything? Just keep as warm as you can. And don't let your wife and children see that you're worried.

TELEGRAPH BOY:
Yes. . . . Thank you, Mrs. Antrobus. Well, I'd better be going.—Oh, I forgot! There's one more sentence in the telegram. "Three cheers have invented the wheel."

MRS. ANTROBUS:
A wheel? What's a wheel?

TELEGRAPH BOY:
I don't know. That's what it said. The sign for it is like this. Well, goodbye.

The WOMEN *see him to the door, with goodbyes and injunctions to keep warm.*

SABINA:
Apron to her eyes, wailing.

Mrs. Antrobus, it looks to me like all the nice men in the world are already married; I don't know why that is.

Exit.

MRS. ANTROBUS:
Thoughtful; to the ANIMALS.

Do you ever remember hearing tell of any cold like this in August?

The ANIMALS *shake their heads.*

From your grandmothers or anyone?

They shake their heads.

Have you any suggestions?

They shake their heads.

She pulls her shawl around, goes to the front door and opening it an inch calls:

HENRY. GLADYS. CHILDREN. Come right in and get warm. No, no, when mama says a thing she means it.
Henry! HENRY. Put down that stone. You know what happened last time.

Shriek.

HENRY! Put down that stone!
Gladys! Put down your dress!! Try and be a lady.

The CHILDREN *bound in and dash to the fire. They take off their winter things and leave them in heaps on the floor.*

GLADYS:
Mama, I'm hungry. Mama, why is it so cold?

HENRY:
At the same time.

Mama, why doesn't it snow? Mama, when's supper ready?
Maybe, it'll snow and we can make snowballs.

GLADYS:
Mama, it's so cold that in one more minute I just couldn't of stood it.

MRS. ANTROBUS:
Settle down, both of you, I want to talk to you.

She draws up a hassock and sits front center over the orchestra pit before the imaginary fire. The CHILDREN *stretch out on the floor, leaning against her lap. Tableau by Raphael. The* ANIMALS *edge up and complete the triangle.*

It's just a cold spell of some kind. Now listen to what I'm saying:

When your father comes home I want you to be extra quiet.

He's had a hard day at the office and I don't know but what he may have one of his moods.

I just got a telegram from him very happy and excited, and you know what that means. Your father's temper's uneven; I guess you know that.

Shriek.

Henry! Henry!

Why—why can't you remember to keep your hair down over your forehead? You must keep that scar covered up. Don't you know that when your father sees it he loses all control over himself? He goes crazy. He wants to die.

After a moment's despair she collects herself decisively, wets the hem of her apron in her mouth and starts polishing his forehead vigorously.

Lift your head up. Stop squirming. Blessed me, sometimes I think that it's going away—and then there it is: just as red as ever.

HENRY:

Mama, today at school two teachers forgot and called me by my old name. They forgot, Mama. You'd better write another letter to the principal, so that he'll tell them I've changed my name. Right out in class they called me: Cain.

MRS. ANTROBUS:

Putting her hand on his mouth, too late; hoarsely.

Don't say it.

Polishing feverishly.

If you're good they'll forget it. Henry, you didn't hit anyone . . . today, did you?

HENRY:

Oh . . . no-o-o!

MRS. ANTROBUS:

Still working, not looking at Gladys.

And, Gladys, I want you to be especially nice to your father tonight. You know what he calls you when you're good—his little angel, his little star. Keep your dress down like a little lady. And keep your voice nice and low. Gladys Antrobus!! What's that red stuff you have on your face?

Slaps her.

You're a filthy detestable child!

Rises in real, though temporary, repudiation and despair.

Get away from me, both of you! I wish I'd never seen sight or sound of you. Let the cold come! I can't stand it. I don't want to go on.

She walks away.

GLADYS:

Weeping.

All the girls at school do, Mama.

MRS. ANTROBUS:

Shrieking.

I'm through with you, that's all!—Sabinal Sabina!—Don't you know your father'd go crazy if he saw that paint on your face? Don't you know your father thinks you're perfect? Don't you know he couldn't live if he didn't think you were perfect?—Sabina!

Enter SABINA.

SABINA:

Yes, Mrs. Antrobus!

MRS. ANTROBUS:

Take this girl out into the kitchen and wash her face with the scrubbing brush.

MR. ANTROBUS:

Outside, roaring.

"I've been working on the railroad, all the livelong day . . . etc."

The ANIMALS *start running around in circles, bellowing.* SABINA *rushes to the window.*

MRS. ANTROBUS:

Sabina, what's that noise outside?

SABINA:

Oh, it's a drunken tramp. It's a giant, Mrs. Antrobus. We'll all be killed in our beds, I know it!

MRS. ANTROBUS:

Help me quick. Quick. Everybody.

Again they stack all the furniture against the door. MR. ANTROBUS *pounds and bellows.*

Who is it? What do you want?—Sabina, have you any boiling water ready?—Who is it?

MR. ANTROBUS:

Broken-down camel of a pig's snout, open this door.

MRS. ANTROBUS:

God be praised! It's your father.—Just a minute, George! —Sabina, clear the door, quick. Gladys, come here while I clean your nasty face!

MR. ANTROBUS:

She-bitch of a goat's gizzard, I'll break every bone in your body. Let me in or I'll tear the whole house down.

MRS. ANTROBUS:

Just a minute, George, something's the matter with the lock.

MR. ANTROBUS:

Open the door or I'll tear your livers out. I'll smash your brains on the ceiling, and Devil take the hindmost.

MRS. ANTROBUS:

Now, you can open the door, Sabina. I'm ready.

The door is flung open. Silence, MR. ANTROBUS—*face of a Keystone Comedy Cop—stands there in fur cap and blanket. His arms are full of parcels, including a large stone wheel with a center in it. One hand carries a railroad man's lantern. Suddenly he bursts into joyous roar.*

MR. ANTROBUS:

Well, how's the whole crooked family?

Relief. Laughter. Tears. Jumping up and down. ANIMALS *cavorting.* ANTROBUS *throws the parcels on the ground. Hurls his cap and blanket after them. Heroic embraces. Melee of* HUMANS *and* ANIMALS, SABINA *included.*

I'll be scalded and tarred if a man can't get a little welcome when he comes home. Well, Maggie, you old gunny-sack, how's the broken down old weather hen?—Sabina, old fish-bait, old skunkpot.—And the children,—how've the little smellers been?

GLADYS:

Papa, Papa, Papa, Papa, Papa.

MR. ANTROBUS:

How've they been, Maggie?

MRS. ANTROBUS:

Well, I must say, they've been as good as gold. I haven't had to raise my voice once. I don't know what's the matter with them.

ANTROBUS:

Kneeling before GLADYS.

Papa's little weasel, eh?—Sabina, there's some food for you.—Papa's little gopher?

GLADYS:

Her arm around his neck.

Papa, you're always teasing me.

ANTROBUS:

And Henry? Nothing rash today, I hope. Nothing rash?

HENRY:

No, Papa.

ANTROBUS:

Roaring.

Well that's good, that's good—I'll bet Sabina let the fire go out.

SABINA:

Mr. Antrobus, I've given my notice. I'm leaving two weeks from today. I'm sorry, but I'm leaving.

ANTROBUS:

Roar.

Well, if you leave now you'll freeze to death, so go and cook the dinner.

SABINA:

Two weeks, that's the law.

Exit.

ANTROBUS:

Did you get my telegram?

MRS. ANTROBUS:

Yes.—What's a wheel?

He indicates the wheel with a glance. HENRY *is rolling it around the floor. Rapid, hoarse interchange:* MRS. ANTROBUS: *What does this cold weather mean? It's below freezing.* ANTROBUS: *Not before the children!* MRS. ANTROBUS: *Shouldn't we do something about it?—start off, move?* ANTROBUS: *Not before the children!!! He gives* HENRY *a sharp slap.*

HENRY:

Papa, you hit me!

ANTROBUS:

Well, remember it. That's to make you remember today. Today. The day the alphabet's finished; and the day that we *saw* the hundred—the hundred, the hundred, the hundred, the hundred, the hundred—there's no end to 'em.

I've had a day at the office!

Take a look at that wheel, Maggie—when I've got that to rights: you'll see a sight.

There's a reward there for all the walking you've done.

MRS. ANTROBUS:

How do you mean?

ANTROBUS:

On the hassock looking into the fire; with awe.

Maggie, we've reached the top of the wave. There's not much more to be done. We're there!

MRS. ANTROBUS:

Cutting across his mood sharply.

And the ice?

ANTROBUS:

The ice!

HENRY:

Playing with the wheel.

Papa, you could put a chair on this.

ANTROBUS:

Broodingly.

Ye-e-s, any booby can fool with it now,—but I thought of it first.

MRS. ANTROBUS:

Children, go out in the kitchen. I want to talk to your father alone.

The CHILDREN *go out.*

ANTROBUS *has moved to his chair up left. He takes the goldfish bowl in his lap; pulls the canary cage down to the level of his face. Both the* ANIMALS *put their paws up on the arm of his chair.* MRS. ANTROBUS *faces him across the room like a judge.*

MRS. ANTROBUS:

Well?

ANTROBUS:

Shortly.

It's cold.—How things been, eh? Keck, keck, keck.—And you, Millicent?

MRS. ANTROBUS:

I know it's cold.

ANTROBUS:

To the canary.

No spilling of sunflower seed, eh? No singing after lights-out, y'know what I mean?

MRS. ANTROBUS:

You can try and prevent us freezing to death, can't you? You can do something: We can start moving. Or we can go on the animals' backs?

ANTROBUS:

The best thing about animals is that they don't talk much.

MAMMOTH:

It's cold.

ANTROBUS:

Eh, eh, eh! Watch that!—

—By midnight we'd turn to ice. The roads are full of people now who can scarcely lift a foot from the ground. The grass out in front is like iron,—which reminds me, I have another needle for you.—The people up north—where are they?

Frozen . . . crushed . . .

MRS. ANTROBUS:

Is that what's going to happen to us?—Will you answer me?

ANTROBUS:

I don't know. I don't know anything. Some say that the ice is going slower. Some say that it's stopped. The sun's growing cold. What can I do about that? Nothing we can do but burn everything in the house, and the fenceposts and the barn. Keep the fire going. When we have no more fire, we die.

MRS. ANTROBUS:

Well, why didn't you say so in the first place?

MRS. ANTROBUS *is about to march off when she catches sight of two* REFUGEES, *men, who have, appeared against the back wall of the theatre and who are soon joined by others.*

REFUGEES:

Mr. Antrobus! Mr. Antrobus Mr. An-nn-tro-bus!

MRS. ANTROBUS:

Who's that? Who's that calling you?

ANTROBUS:

Clearing his throat guiltily.

Hm—let me see.

Two REFUGEES *come up to the window.*

REFUGEE:

Could we warm our hands for a moment, Mr. Antrobus. It's very cold, Mr. Antrobus.

ANOTHER REFUGEE:

Mr. Antrobus, I wonder if you have a piece of bread or something that you could spare.

Silence. They wait humbly. MRS. ANTROBUS *stands rooted to the spot. Suddenly a knock at the door, then another hand knocking in short rapid blows.*

MRS. ANTROBUS:

Who are these people? Why, they're all over the front yard.

What have they come here for?

Enter SABINA.

SABINA:

Mrs. Antrobus! There are some tramps knocking at the back door.

MRS. ANTROBUS:
George, tell these people to go away. Tell them to move right along. I'll go and send them away from the back door. Sabina, come with me.

She goes out energetically.

ANTROBUS:
Sabina! Stay here! I have something to say to you.

He goes to the door and opens it a crack and talks through it.

Ladies and gentlemen! I'll have to ask you to wait a few minutes longer. It'll be all right . . . while you're waiting you might each one pull up a stake of the fence. We'll need them all for the fireplace. There'll be coffee and sandwiches in a moment.

SABINA *looks out door over his shoulder and suddenly extends her arm pointing, with a scream.*

SABINA:
Mr. Antrobus, what's that??—that big white thing? Mr. Antrobus, it's ICE. It's ICE!!

ANTROBUS:
Sabina, I want you to go in the kitchen and make a lot of coffee. Make a whole pail full.

SABINA:
Pail full!!

ANTROBUS:
With gesture.

And sandwiches . . . piles of them . . . like this.

SABINA:
Mr. An . . . !!

Suddenly she drops the play, and says in her own person as MISS SOMERSET, *with surprise.*

Oh, I *see* what this part of the play means now! This means refugees.

She starts to cross to the proscenium.

Oh, I don't like it. I don't like it.

She leans against the proscenium and bursts into tears.

ANTROBUS:
Miss Somerset!

Voice of the STAGE MANAGER

Miss Somerset!

SABINA:
Energetically, to the audience.

Ladies and gentlemen! Don't take this play serious. The world's not coming to an end. You know it's not. People exaggerate! Most people really have enough to eat and a roof over their heads. Nobody actually starves—you can always eat grass or something. That ice-business—why, it was a long, long time ago. Besides they were only savages. Savages don't love their families—not like we do.

ANTROBUS *AND* STAGE MANAGER:
Miss Somerset!!

There is renewed knocking at the door.

SABINA:
All right. I'll say the lines, but I won't think about the play.

Enter MRS. ANTROBUS.

SABINA:
Parting thrust at the audience.

And I advise *you* not to think about the play, either. *Exit* SABINA.

MRS. ANTROBUS:
George, these tramps say that you asked them to come to the house. What does this mean?

Knocking at the door.

ANTROBUS:
Just . . . uh. . . . There are a few friends, Maggie, I met on the road. Real nice, real useful people. . . .

MRS. ANTROBUS:
Back to the door.

Now, don't you ask them in!

George Antrobus, not another soul comes in here over my dead body.

ANTROBUS:
Maggie, there's a doctor there. Never hurts to have a good doctor in the house. We've lost a peck of children, one way and another. You can never tell when a child's throat will get stopped up. What you and I have seen—!!!

He puts his fingers an his throat, and imitates diphtheria.

MRS. ANTROBUS:
Well, just one person then, the Doctor. The others can go right along the road.

ANTROBUS:
Maggie, there's an old man, particular friend of mine—

MRS. ANTROBUS:
I won't listen to you—

ANTROBUS:
It was he that really started off the A.B.C.'s.

MRS. ANTROBUS:
I don't care if he perishes. We can do without reading or writing. We can't do without food.

ANTROBUS:

Then let the ice come! Drink your coffee!! I don't want any coffee if I can't drink it with some good people.

MRS. ANTROBUS:

Stop shouting. Who else is there trying to push us off the cliff?

ANTROBUS:

Well, there's the man . . . who makes all the laws. Judge Moses!

MRS. ANTROBUS:

Judges can't help us now.

ANTROBUS:

And if the ice melts? . . . and if we pull through? Have you and I been able to bring up Henry? What have we done?

MRS. ANTROBUS:

Who are those old women?

ANTROBUS:

Coughs.

Up in town there are nine sisters. There are three or four of them here. They're sort of music teachers . . . and one of them recites and one of them—

MRS. ANTROBUS:

That's the end. A singing troupe! Well, take your choice, live or die. Starve your own children before your face.

ANTROBUS:

Gently.

These people don't take much. They're used to starving. They'll sleep on the floor.

Besides, Maggie, listen: no, listen:

Who've we got in the house, but Sabina? Sabina's always afraid the worst will happen. Whose spirits can she keep up? Maggie, these people never give up. They think they'll live and work forever.

MRS. ANTROBUS:

Walks slowly to the middle of the room.

All right, let them in. Let them in. You're master here.

Softly.

—But these animals must go. Enough's enough. They'll soon be big enough to push the walls down, anyway. Take them away.

ANTROBUS:

Sadly.

All right. The dinosaur and mammoth—! Come on, baby, come on Frederick. Come for a walk. That's a good little fellow.

DINOSAUR:

It's cold.

ANTROBUS:

Yes, nice cold fresh air. Bracing.

He holds the door open and the ANIMALS *go out. He beckons to his friends. The* REFUGEES *are typical elderly out-of-works from the streets of New York today.* JUDGE MOSES *wears a skull cap.* HOMER *is blind beggar with a guitar. The seedy crowd shuffles in and waits humbly and expectantly.*

ANTROBUS *introduces them to his wife who bows to each with a stately bend of her head.*

Make yourself at home, Maggie, this the doctor . . . m . . . Coffee'll be here in a minute. . . . Professor, this is my wife. . . . And: . . . Judge . . . Maggie, you know the Judge.

An old blind man with a guitar.

Maggie, you know . . . you know Homer?—Come right in, Judge.—

Miss Muse—are some of your sisters here? Come right in. . . . Miss E. Muse; Miss T. Muse, Miss M. Muse.

MRS. ANTROBUS:

Pleased to meet you.

Just . . . make yourself comfortable. Supper'll be ready in a minute.

She goes out, abruptly.

ANTROBUS:

Make yourself at home, friends. I'll be right back.

He goes out.

The refugees *stare about them in awe. Presently several voices start whispering "Homer! Homer!" All take it up.* HOMER *strikes a chord or two on his guitar, then starts to speak:*

HOMER:

Μῆνιν ἄειδε, θεά, Πηληῑάδεω 'Αχιλῆος, οὐλομένην, ἤμυρί' 'Αχαιοῖς ἄλγε' ἔθηκεν, π αλλάς δ' ἰφθίμονς ψνχάς—

HOMER*'s face shows be is lost in thought and memory and the words die away on his lips. The* refugees *likewise nod in dreamy recollection. Soon the whisper "Moses, Moses!" goes around. An aged Jew parts his beard and recites dramatically:*

MOSES:

Be·re·shit ba·ra e·lo·him; et ha·sha·ma·yim ve·'et ha·'a·retz. Ve·ha·'a·retz ha·ye·tah to·hu va·vo·hu, ve·cho·shech al-pe·nei te·ho·vm; Ve·ru·ach e·lo·him, me·ra·che·fet al-pe·nei ham·ma·yim.

The same dying away of the words take place, and on the part of the REFUGEES *the same retreat into recollection. Some of them murmur, "Yes, yes."*

The mood is broken by the abrupt entrance of MR. *and* MRS. ANTROBUS *and* SABINA *bearing platters of sandwiches and a pail of coffee.* SABINA *stops and stares at the guests.*

MR. ANTROBUS:
Sabina, pass the sandwiches.

SABINA:
I thought I was working in a respectable house that had respectable guests. I'm giving my notice, Mr. Antrobus: two weeks, that's the law.

MR. ANTROBUS:
Sabina! Pass the sandwiches.

SABINA:
Two weeks, that's the law.

MR. ANTROBUS:
There's the law. That's Moses.

SABINA:
Stares.

The Ten Commandments—FAUGH!!—(*To Audience*) That's the worst line I've ever had to say on any stage.

ANTROBUS:
I think the best thing to do is just not to stand on ceremony, but pass the sandwiches around from left to right.—Judge, help yourself to one of these.

MRS. ANTROBUS:
The roads are crowded, I hear?

THE GUESTS:
All talking at once.

Oh, ma'am, you can't imagine. . . . You can hardly put one foot before you . . . people are trampling one another.

Sudden silence.

MRS. ANTROBUS:
Well, you know what I think it is,—I think it's sun-spots!

THE GUESTS:
Discreet hubbub.

Oh, you're right, Mrs. Antrobus . . . that's what it is. . . . That's what I was saying the other day.

Sudden silence.

ANTROBUS:
Well, I don't believe the whole world's going to turn to ice.

All eyes are fixed on him, waiting.

I can't believe it. Judge! Have we worked for nothing? Professor! Have we just failed in the whole thing?

MRS. ANTROBUS:
It is certainly very strange—well fortunately on both sides of the family we come of very hearty stock.—Doctor, I want you to meet my children. They're eating their supper now. And of course I want them to meet you.

MISS M. MUSE:
How many children have you, Mrs. Antrobus?

MRS. ANTROBUS:
I have two,—a boy and a girl.

MOSES:
Softly.

I understood you had two sons, Mrs. Antrobus.

MRS. ANTROBUS *in blind suffering; she walks toward the foot lights.*

MRS. ANTROBUS:
In a low voice.

Abel, Abel, my son, my son, Abel, my son, Abel, Abel, my son.

The REFUGEES *move with few steps toward her as though in comfort murmuring words in Greek, Hebrew, German, et cetera.*

A piercing shriek from the kitchen,—SABINA*'s voice.*

All heads turn.

ANTROBUS:
What's that?

SABINA *enters, bursting with indignation, pulling on her gloves.*

SABINA:
Mr. Antrobus—that son of yours, that boy Henry Antrobus—I don't stay in this house another moment! —He's not fit to live among respectable folks and that's a fact.

MRS. ANTROBUS:
Don't say another word, Sabina. I'll be right back.

Without waiting for an answer she goes past her into the kitchen.

SABINA:
Mr. Antrobus, Henry has thrown a stone again and if he hasn't killed the boy that lives next door, I'm very much mistaken. He finished his supper and went out to play; and I heard such a fight; and then I saw it. I saw it with my own eyes. And it looked to me like stark murder.

MRS. ANTROBUS *appears at the kitchen door, shielding* henry *who follows her. When she steps aside, we see on* henry*'s forehead a large ochre and scarlet scar in the shape* *of a C.* MR. ANTROBUS *starts toward him. A pause.* HENRY *is heard saying under his breath:*

HENRY:
He was going to take the wheel away from me. He started to throw a stone at me first.

MRS. ANTROBUS:
George, it was just a boyish impulse. Remember how young he is.

Louder, in an urgent wail.

George, he's only four thousand years old.

SABINA:
And everything was going along so nicely!

Silence; ANTROBUS goes *back to the fireplace.*

ANTROBUS:
Put out the fire! Put out all the fires.

Violently.

No wonder the sun grows cold.

He starts stamping on the fireplace.

MRS. ANTROBUS:
Doctor! Judge! Help me!—George, have you lost your mind?

ANTROBUS:
There is no mind. We'll not try to live.

To the guests.

Give it up. Give up trying,

MRS. ANTROBUS *seizes him.*

SABINA:
Mr. Antrobus! I'm downright ashamed of you.

MRS. ANTROBUS:
George, have some more coffee—Gladys! Where's Gladys gone?

GLADYS *steps in, frightened.*

GLADYS:
Here I am, mama.

MRS. ANTROBUS:
Go upstairs and bring your father's slippers. How could you forget a thing like that, when you know how tired he is?

ANTROBUS *sits in his chair. He covers his face with his hands,* MRS. ANTROBUS *turns to the* REFUGEES:

Can't some of you sing? It's your business in life to sing, isn't it? Sabina!

Several of the women clear their throats tentatively, and with frightened faces gather around homer*'s guitar. He establishes a few chords. Almost inaudibly they start singing, led by* SABINA: *"Jingle Bells."* MRS. ANTROBUS *continues to* ANTROBUS *in a low voice, while taking off his shoes:*

George, remember all the other times. When the volcanoes came right up in the front yard.

And the time the grasshoppers ate every single leaf and blade of grass, and all the grain and spinach you'd grown with your own hands. And the summer there were earthquakes every night.

ANTROBUS:
Henry! Henry!

Puts his hand on his forehead.

Myself, All of us, we're covered with blood.

MRS. ANTROBUS:
Then remember all the times you were pleased with him and when you were proud of yourself.—Henry! Henry! Come here and recite to your father the multiplication table that you do so nicely.

HENRY *kneels on one knee beside his father and starts whispering the multiplication table.*

HENRY:
Finally.

Two times six is twelve; three times six is eighteen—I don't think I know the sixes.

Enter GLADYS *with the slippers.* MRS. ANTROBUS *makes stern gestures to her: Go in there and do your best. The* GUESTS *are now singing "Tenting Tonight."*

GLADYS:
Putting slippers on his feet.

Papa . . . papa . . . I was very good in school today. Miss Conover said right out in class that if all the girls had as good manners as Gladys Antrobus, that the world would be a very different place to live in.

MRS. ANTROBUS:
You recited a piece at assembly, didn't you? Recite it to your father.

GLADYS:
Papa, do you want to hear what I recited in class?

Fierce directorial glance from her mother.

"THE STAR" by Henry Wadsworth LONGFELLOW.

MRS. ANTROBUS:
Wait!!! The fire's going out. There isn't enough wood! Henry, go upstairs and bring down the chairs and start breaking up the beds.

Exit HENRY. *The singers return to "Jingle Bells," still very softly.*

GLADYS:

Look, Papa, here's my report card. Lookit. Conduct A! Look, Papa. Papa, do you want to hear the Star, by Henry Wadsworth Longfellow? Papa, you're not mad at me, are you?—I know it'll get warmer. Soon it'll be just like spring, and we can go to a picnic at the Hibernian Picnic Grounds like you always like to do, don't you remember? Papa, just look at me once.

Enter HENRY *with some chairs.*

ANTROBUS:

You recited in assembly, did you?

She nods eagerly.

You didn't forget it?

GLADYS:

No!!! I was perfect.

Pause. Then ANTROBUS *rises, goes to the front door and opens it. The* REFUGEES *draw back timidly; the song stops; he peers out of the door, then closes it.*

ANTROBUS:

With decision, suddenly.

Build up the fire. It's cold. Build up the fire. We'll do what we can. Sabina, get some more wood. Come around the fire, everybody. At least the young ones may pull through. Henry, have you eaten something?

HENRY:

Yes, papa.

ANTROBUS:

Gladys, have you had some supper?

GLADYS:

I ate in the kitchen, papa.

ANTROBUS:

It you do come through this—what'll you be able to do? What do you know? Henry, did you take a good look at that wheel?

HENRY:

Yes, papa.

ANTROBUS:

Sitting down in his chair.

Six times two are—

HENRY:

—twelve; six times three are eighteen; six times four are—Papa, it's hot and cold. It makes my head all funny. It makes me sleepy.

ANTROBUS:

Gives him a cuff.

Wake up. I don't care if your head is sleepy. Six times four are twenty-four. Six times five are—

HENRY:

Thirty. Papa!

ANTROBUS:

Maggie, put something into Gladys' head on the chance she can use it.

MRS. ANTROBUS:

What do you mean, George?

ANTROBUS:

Six times six are thirty-six.
Teach her the beginning of the Bible.

GLADYS:

But, Mama, it's so cold and close.

HENRY *has all but drowsed off. His father slaps him sharply and the lesson goes on.*

MRS. ANTROBUS:

"In the beginning God created the heavens and the earth; and the earth was waste and void; and the darkness was upon the face of the deep—"

The singing starts up again louder. SABINA *has returned with wood.*

SABINA:

After placing wood on the fireplace comes down to the footlights and addresses the audience:

Will you please start handing up your chairs? We'll need everything for this fire. Save the human race.—Ushers, will you pass the chairs up here? Thank you.

HENRY:

Six times nine are fifty-four; six times ten are sixty.

In the back of the auditorium the sound of chairs being ripped up can be heard. USHERS *rush down the aisles with chairs and hand them over.*

GLADYS:

"And God called the light Day and the darkness he called Night."

SABINA:

Pass up your chairs, everybody. Save the human race.

CURTAIN

★

ACT II

Toward the end of the intermission, though with the houselights still up, lantern slide projections begin to appear on the curtain. Timetables for trains leaving Pennsylvania Station for Atlantic City. Advertisements of Atlantic City hotels, drugstores, churches, rug merchants; fortune tellers, Bingo parlors.

When the house-lights go down, the voice of an ANNOUNCER *is heard.*

ANNOUNCER:

The Management now brings you the News Events of the World. Atlantic City, New Jersey:

Projection of a chrome postcard of the waterfront, trimmed in mica with the legend: FUN AT THE BEACH.

This great convention city is playing host this week to the anniversary convocation of that great fraternal order,—the Ancient and Honorable Order of Mammals, Subdivision Humans. This great fraternal, militant and burial society is celebrating on the Boardwalk, ladies and gentlemen, its six hundred thousandth Annual Convention.

It has just elected its president for the ensuing term,—

Projection of MR. *and* MRS. ANTROBUS *posed as they will be shown a few moments later.*

Mr. George Antrobus of Excelsior, New Jersey. We show you President Antrobus and his gracious and charming wife, every inch a mammal. Mr. Antrobus has had a long and chequered career. Credit has been paid to him for many useful enterprises including the introduction of the lever, of the wheel and the brewing of beer. Credit has been also extended to President Antrobus's gracious and charming wife for many practical suggestions, including the hem, the gore, and the gusset; and the novelty of the year,—frying in oil. Before we show you Mr. Antrobus accepting the nomination, we have an important announcement to make. As many of you know, this great celebration of the Order of the Mammals has received delegations from the other rival Orders,—or shall we say: esteemed concurrent Orders: the WINGS, the FINS, the SHELLS, and so on. These Orders are holding their conventions also, in various parts of the world, and have sent representatives to our own, two of a kind.

Later in the day we will show you President Antrobus broadcasting his words of greeting and congratulation to the collected assemblies of the whole natural world.

Ladies and Gentlemen! We give you President Antrobus!

The screen becomes a transparency. MR. ANTROBUS *stands beside a pedestal;* MRS. ANTROBUS *is seated wearing a corsage of orchids.* ANTROBUS *wears an untidy Prince Albert; spats; from a red rosette in his buttonhole hangs a fine long purple ribbon of honor. He wears a gay lodge hat,—something between a fez and a legionnaire's cap.*

ANTROBUS:

Fellow-mammals, fellow-vertebrates, fellow-humans, I thank you. Little did my dear parents think,—when they told me to stand on my own two feet,—that I'd arrive at this place.

My friends, we have come a long way.

During this week of happy celebration it is perhaps not fitting that we dwell on some of the difficult times we have been through. The dinosaur is extinct—

Applause.

—the ice has retreated; and the common cold is being pursued by every means within our power.

MRS. ANTROBUS *sneezes, laughs prettily, and murmurs: "I beg your pardon."*

In our memorial service yesterday we did honor to all our friends and relatives who are no longer with us, by reason of cold, earthquakes, plagues and . . . and . . .

Coughs.

differences of opinion.

As our Bishop so ably said . . . uh . . . so ably said. . . .

MRS. ANTROBUS:

Closed lips.

Gone, but not forgotten.

ANTROBUS:

"They are gone, but not forgotten."

I think I can say, I think I can prophesy with complete . . . uh . . . with complete . . .

MRS. ANTROBUS:

Confidence.

ANTROBUS:

Thank you, my dear,—With complete lack of confidence, that a new day of security is about to dawn.

The watchword of the closing year was: Work. I give you the watchword for the future: Enjoy Yourselves.

MRS. ANTROBUS:

George, sit down!

ANTROBUS:
Before I close, however, I wish to answer one of those unjust and malicious accusations that were brought against me during this last electoral campaign.

Ladies and gentlemen, the charge was made that at various points in my career I leaned toward joining some of the rival orders,—that's a lie.

As I told reporters of the *Atlantic City Herald*, I do not deny that a few months before my birth I hesitated between . . . uh . . . between pinfeathers and gill-breathing,—and so did many of us here,—but for the last million years I have been viviparous, hairy and diaphragmatic.

Applause. Cries of "Good old Antrobus," "The Prince chap!" "Georgie," etc.

ANNOUNCER:
Thank you. Thank you very much, Mr. Antrobus.

Now I know that our visitors will wish to hear a word from that gracious and charming mammal, Mrs. Antrobus, wife and mother,—Mrs. Antrobus!

mrs. antrobus *rises, lays her program on her chair, bows and says:*

MRS. ANTROBUS:
Dear friends, I don't really think I should say anything. After all, it was my husband who was elected and not I. Perhaps, as president of the Women's Auxiliary Bed and Board Society,—I had some notes here, oh, yes, here they are:—I should give a short report from some of our committees that have been meeting in this beautiful city.

Perhaps it may interest you to know that it has at last been decided that the tomato is edible. Can you all hear me? The tomato is edible.

A delegate from across the sea reports that the thread woven by the silkworm gives a cloth . . . I have a sample of it here . . . can you see it? smooth, elastic. I should say that it's rather attractive,—though personally I prefer less shiny surfaces. Should the windows of a sleeping apartment be open or shut? I know all mothers will follow our debates on this matter with close interest. I am sorry to say that the most expert authorities have not yet decided. It does seem to me that the night air would be bound to be unhealthy for our children, but there are many distinguished authorities on both sides. Well, I could go on talking forever,—as Shakespeare says: a woman's work is seldom done; but I think I'd better join my husband in saying thank you, and sit down. Thank you.

She sits down.

ANNOUNCER:
Oh, Mrs. Antrobus!

MRS. ANTROBUS:
Yes?

ANNOUNCER:
We understand that you are about to celebrate a wedding anniversary. I know our listeners would like to extend their felicitations and hear a few words from you on that subject.

MRS. ANTROBUS:
I have been asked by this kind gentleman . . . yes, my friends, this Spring Mr. Antrobus and I will be celebrating our five thousanth wedding anniversary.

I don't know if I speak for my husband, but I can say that, as for me, I regret every moment of it.

Laughter of confusion.

I beg your pardon. What I *mean* to say is that I do not regret one moment of it. I hope none of you catch my cold. We have two children. We've always had two children, though it hasn't always been the same two. But as I say, we have two fine children, and we're very grateful for that. Yes, Mr. Antrobus and I have been married five thousand years. Each wedding anniversary reminds me of the times when there were no weddings. We had to crusade for marriage. Perhaps there are some women within the sound of my voice who remember that crusade and those struggles; we fought for it, didn't we? We chained ourselves to lampposts and we made disturbances in the Senate,—anyway, at last we women got the ring.

A few men helped us, but I must say that most men blocked our way at every step: they said we were unfeminine.

I only bring up these unpleasant memories, because I see some signs of backsliding from that great victory.

Oh, my fellow mammal, keep hold of that.

My husband says that the watchword for the year is Enjoy Yourselves. I think that's open to misunderstanding. My watchword for the year is: Save the Family. It's held together for over five thousand years: Save it! Thank you.

ANNOUNCER:
Thank you, Mrs. Antrobus.

The transparency disappears.

We had hoped to show you the Beauty Contest that took place here today.

President Antrobus, an experienced judge of pretty girls, gave the title of Miss Atlantic City 1942, to Miss Lily-Sabina Fairweather, charming hostess of our Boardwalk Bingo Parlor.

Unfortunately, however, our time is up, and I must take you to some views of the Convention City and conveeners,—enjoying themselves.

A burst of music; the curtain rises.

The Boardwalk. The audience is sitting in the ocean. A handrail of scarlet card stretches across the front of the stage. A ramp—also with scarlet hand rail—descends to the right corner of the orchestra pit where a great scarlet beach umbrella or a cabana stands. Front and right stage left are benches facing the sea; attached to each bench is a streetlamp.

The only scenery is two cardboard cut-outs six feet high, representing shops at the back of the stage. Reading from left to right they are: SALT WATER TAFFY: FORTUNE TELLER; then the blank space; BINGO PARLOR; TURKISH BATH. They have practical doors, that of the Fortune Teller's being hung with bright gypsy curtains.

By the left proscenium and riskissing from the orchestra pit is the weather signal; it is like the mast of a ship with cross bars. From time to time black discs are hung on it to indicate the storm and hurricane warnings. Three roller chairs, pushed by melancholy NEGROES *file by empty. Throughout the act they traverse the stage in both directions.*

From time to time, CONVEENERS, *dressed like* MR. ANTROBUS, *cross the stage. Some walk sedately by; others engage in inane horseplay. The old gypsy* FORTUNE TELLER *is seated at the door of her shop, smoking a corncob pipe.*

From the Bingo Parlor comes the voice of the CALLER.

BINGO CALLER:

A-Nine; B-Nine. C-Twenty-six; C-Twenty-six. A-Four; A-Four. B-Twelve.

CHORUS:

Back-stage.

Bingo!!!

The front of the Bingo Parlor shudders, rises a few feet in the air and returns to the ground trembling.

FORTUNE TELLER:

Mechanically to the unconscious back of a passerby, pointing with her pipe.

Bright's disease! Your partner's deceiving you in that Kansas City deal. You'll have six grandchildren. Avoid high places.

She rises and shouts after another:

Cirrhosis of the liver!

SABINA *appears at the door of the Bingo Parlor. She hugs about her a blue raincoat that almost conceals her red bathing suit. She tries to catch the* FORTUNE TELLER'S *attention.*

SABINA:

Ssssst! Esmeralda! Ssssst!

FORTUNE TELLER:

Keck!

SABINA:

Has President Antrobus come along yet?

FORTUNE TELLER:

No, no, no. Get back there. Hide yourself.

SABINA:

I'm afraid I'll miss him. Oh, Esmeralda, if I fail in this, I'll die; I know I'll die. President Antrobus!!! And I'll be his wife! If it's the last thing I'll do, I'll be Mrs. George Antrobus.—Esmeralda, tell me my future.

FORTUNE TELLER:

Keck!

SABINA:

All right, I'll tell *you* my future.

Laughing dreamily and tracking it out with one finger on the palm of her hand.

I've won the Beauty Contest in Atlantic City, well, I'll win the Beauty Contest of the whole world. I'll take President Antrobus away from that wife of his. Then I'll take every man away from his wife. I'll turn the whole earth upside down.

FORTUNE TELLER:

Keck!

SABINA:

When all those husbands just think about me they'll get dizzy. They'll faint in the streets. They'll have to lean against lampposts—Esmeralda, who was Helen of Troy?

FORTUNE TELLER:

Furiously.

Shut your foolish mouth. When Mr. Antrobus comes along you can see what you can do. Until then,—go away.

SABINA *laughs. As she returns to the door of her Bingo Parlor a group of* CONVEENERS *rush over and smother her with attentions: "Oh, Miss Lily, you know me. You've known me for years."*

SABINA:

Go away, boys, go away. I'm after bigger fry than you are.—Why, Mr. Simpson!! How *dare* you!! I expect that even you nobodies must have girls to amuse you; but where you find them and what you do with them, is of absolutely no interest to me.

Exit. The CONVEENERS *squeal with pleasure and stumble in after her.*

The FORTUNE TELLER *rises, puts her pipe down on the stool, unfurls her voluminous skirts, gives a sharp wrench to her bodice and strolls towards the audience, swinging her hips like a young woman.*

FORTUNE TELLER:

I tell the future. Keck. Nothing easier. Everybody's future is in their face. Nothing easier.

But who can tell your past,—eh? Nobody!

Your youth,—where did it go? It slipped away while you weren't looking. While you were asleep. While you were drunk? Puh! You're like our friends, Mr. and Mrs. Antrobus; you lie awake nights trying to know your past. What did it mean? What was it trying to say to you?

Think! Think! Split your heads. I can't tell the past and neither can you. If anybody tries to tell you the past, take my word for it, they're charlatans! Charlatans! But I can tell the future.

She suddenly barks at a passing chair-pusher.

Apoplexy!

She returns to the audience.

Nobody listens—Keck! I see a face among you now—I won't embarrass him by pointing him out, but, listen, it may be you: Next year the watchsprings inside you will crumple up. Death by regret,—Type Y. It's the corners of your mouth. You'll decide that you should have lived for pleasure, but that you missed it. Death by regret,—Type Y. . . . Avoid mirrors. You'll try to be angry,—but no!—no anger.

Far forward, confidentially.

And now what's the immediate future of our friends, the Antrobuses? Oh, you've seen it as well as I have, keck,—that dizziness of the head; that Great Man dizziness? The inventor of beer and gunpowder. The sudden fits of temper and then the long stretches of inertia? "I'm a sultan; let my slave-girls fan me?"

You know as well as I what's coming, Rain. Rain. Rain in floods. The deluge. But first you'll see shameful things—shameful things. Some of you will be saying: "Let him drown. He's not worth saying. Give the whole thing up." I can see it in your faces. But you're wrong. Keep your doubts and despairs to yourselves.

Again there'll be the narrow escape. The survival of a handful. From destruction,—total destruction.

She points sweeping with her band to the stage.

Even of the animals, a few will be saved: two of a kind, male and female, two of a kind.

The heads of CONVEENERS *appear about the stage and in the orchestra pit, jeering at her.*

CONVEENERS:

Charlatan! Madam Kill-joy! Mrs. Jeremiah! Charlatan!

FORTUNE TELLER:

And you! Mark my words before it's too late. Where'll you be?

CONVEENERS:

The croaking raven. Old dust and ashes. Rags, bottles, sacks.

FORTUNE TELLER:

Yes, stick out your tongues. You can't stick your tongues out far enough to lick the death-sweat from your foreheads. It's too late to work now—bail out the flood with your soup spoons. You've had your chance and you've lost.

CONVEENERS:

Enjoy yourselves!!!

They disappear. The FORTUNE TELLER *looks off left and puts her finger on her lip.*

FORTUNE TELLER:

They're coming—the Antrobuses. Keck. Your hope. Your despair. Your selves.

Enter from the left, MR. *and* MRS. ANTROBUS *and* GLADYS.

MRS. ANTROBUS:

Gladys Antrobus, stick your stummick in.

GLADYS:

But it's easier this way.

MRS. ANTROBUS:

Well, it's too bad the new president has such a clumsy daughter, that's all I can say. Try and be a lady.

FORTUNE TELLER:

Aijah! That's been said a hundred billion times.

MRS. ANTROBUS:

Goodness! Where's Henry? He was here just a minute ago. Henry!

Sudden violent stir. A roller-chair appears from the left. About it are dancing in great excitement HENRY *and a* NEGRO CHAIR-PUSHER.

HENRY:

Slingshot in band.

I'll put your eye out. I'll make you yell, like you never yelled before.

NEGRO:

At the same time.

Now, I warns you. I warns you. If you make me mad, you'll get hurt.

ANTROBUS:

Henry! What is this? Put down that slingshot.

MRS. ANTROBUS:

At the same time.

Henry! HENRY! Behave yourself.

FORTUNE TELLER:

That's right, young man. There are too many people in the world as it is. Everybody's in the way, except one's self.

HENRY:

All I wanted to do was—have some fun.

NEGRO:

Nobody can't touch my chair, nobody, without I allow 'em to. You get clean away from me and you get away fast.

He pushes his chair off, muttering.

ANTROBUS:

What were you doing, Henry?

HENRY:

Everybody's always getting mad. Everybody's always trying to push you around. I'll make him sorry for this; I'll make him sorry.

ANTROBUS:

Give me that slingshot.

HENRY:

I won't. I'm sorry I came to this place. I wish I weren't here. I wish I weren't anywhere.

MRS. ANTROBUS:

Now, Henry, don't get so excited about nothing, I declare I don't know what we're going to do with you. Put your slingshot in your pocket, and don't try to take hold of things that don't belong to you.

ANTROBUS:

After this you can stay home. I wash my hands of you.

MRS. ANTROBUS:

Come now, let's forget all about it. Everybody take a good breath of that sea air and calm down.

A passing CONVEENER *bows to* ANTROBUS *who nods to him.*

Who was that you spoke to, George?

ANTROBUS:

Nobody, Maggie. Just the candidate who ran against me in the election.

MRS. ANTROBUS:

The man who ran against you in the election!!

She turns and waves her umbrella after the disappearing CONVEENER.

My husband didn't speak to you and he never will speak to you.

ANTROBUS:

Now, Maggie.

MRS. ANTROBUS:

After those lies you told about him in your speeches! Lies, that's what they were.

GLADYS AND HENRY:

Mama, everybody's looking at you. Everybody's laughing at you.

MRS. ANTROBUS:

If you must know, my husband's a SAINT, a downright SAINT, and you're not fit to speak to him on the street.

ANTROBUS:

Now, Maggie, now, Maggie, that's enough of that.

MRS. ANTROBUS:

George Antrobus, you're a perfect worm. If you won't stand up for yourself, I will.

GLADYS:

Mama, you just act awful in public.

MRS. ANTROBUS:

Laughing.

Well, I must say I enjoyed it. I feel better. Wish his wife had been there to hear it. Children, what do you want to do?

GLADYS:

Papa, can we ride in one of those chairs? Mama, I want to ride in one of those chairs.

MRS. ANTROBUS:

No, sir. If you're tired you just sit where you are. We have no money to spend on foolishness.

ANTROBUS:

I guess we have money enough for a thing like that. It's one of the things you do at Atlantic City.

MRS. ANTROBUS:

Oh, we have? I tell you it's a miracle my children have shoes to stand up in. I didn't think I'd ever live to see them pushed around in chairs.

ANTROBUS:
We're on a vacation, aren't we? We have a right to some treats, I guess. Maggie, some day you're going to drive me crazy.

MRS. ANTROBUS:
All right, go. I'll just sit here and laugh at you. And you can give me my dollar right in my hand. Mark my words, a rainy day is coming. There's a rainy day ahead of us. I feel it in my bones. Go on, throw your money around. I can starve. I've starved before. I know how.

A CONVEENER *puts his head through Turkish Bath window, and says with raised eyebrows:*

CONVEENER:
Hello, George. How are ya? I see where you brought the WHOLE family along.

MRS. ANTROBUS:
And what do you mean by that?

CONVEENER *withdraws head and closes window.*

ANTROBUS:
Maggie, I tell you there's a limit to what I can stand. God's Heaven, haven't I worked *enough*? Don't I get *any* vacation? Can't I even give my children so much as a ride in a roller-chair?

MRS. ANTROBUS:
Putting out her hand for raindrops.

Anyway, it's going to rain very soon and you have your broadcast to make.

ANTROBUS:
Now, Maggie, I warn you. A man can stand a family only just so long. I'm warning you.

Enter SABINA *from the Bingo Parlor. She wears a flounced red silk bathing suit, 1905. Red stockings, shoes, parasol. She bows demurely to* ANTROBUS *and starts down the ramp.* ANTROBUS *and the* CHILDREN *stare at her.* ANTROBUS *bows gallantly.*

MRS. ANTROBUS:
Why, George Antrobus, how can you say such a thing! You have the best family in the world.

ANTROBUS:
Good morning, Miss Fairweather.

SABINA *finally disappears behind the beach umbrella or in a cabana in the orchestra pit.*

MRS. ANTROBUS:
Who on earth was that you spoke to, George?

ANTROBUS:
Complacent; mock-modest.

Hm . . . m . . . just a . . . solambaka keray.

MRS. ANTROBUS:
What? I can't understand you.

GLADYS:
Mama, wasn't she beautiful?

HENRY:
Papa, introduce her to me.

MRS. ANTROBUS:
Children, will you be quiet while I ask your father a simple question?—Who did you say it was, George?

ANTROBUS:
Why-uh . . . a friend of mine. Very nice refined girl.

MRS. ANTROBUS:
I'm waiting.

ANTROBUS:
Maggie, that's the girl I gave the prize to in the beauty contest,—that's Miss Atlantic City 1942.

MRS. ANTROBUS:
Hm! She looked like Sabina to me.

HENRY:
At the railing.

Mama, the life-guard knows her, too. Mama, he knows her well.

ANTROBUS:
Henry, come here.—She's a very nice girl in every way and the sole support of her aged mother.

MRS. ANTROBUS:
So was Sabina, so was Sabina; and it took a wall of ice to open your eyes about Sabina.—Henry, come over and sit down on this bench.

ANTROBUS:
She's a very different matter from Sabina. Miss Fairweather is a college graduate, Phi Beta Kappa.

MRS. ANTROBUS:
Henry, you sit here by mama. Gladys—

ANTROBUS:
Sitting.

Reduced circumstances have required her taking a position as hostess in a Bingo Parlor; but there isn't a girl with higher principles in the country.

MRS. ANTROBUS:
Well, let's not talk about it.—Henry, I haven't seen a whale yet.

ANTROBUS:
She speaks seven languages and has more culture in her little finger than you've acquired in a lifetime.

MRS. ANTROBUS:
Assumed amiability.

All right, all right, George. I'm glad to know there are such superior girls in the Bingo Parlors.—Henry, what's that?

Pointing at the storm signal, which has one black disk.

HENRY:
What is it, Papa?

ANTROBUS:
What? Oh, that's the storm signal. One of those black disks means bad weather; two means storm; three means hurricane; and four means the end of the world.

As they watch it a second black disk rolls into place

MRS. ANTROBUS:
Goodness! I'm going this very minute to buy you all some raincoats.

GLADYS:
Putting her cheek against her father's shoulder.

Mama, don't go yet. I like sitting this way. And the ocean coming in and coming in. Papa, don't you like it?

MRS. ANTROBUS:
Well, there's only one thing I lack to make me a perfectly happy woman: I'd like to see a whale.

HENRY:
Mama, we saw two. Right out there. They're delegates to the convention. I'll find you one.

GLADYS:
Papa, ask me something. Ask me a question.

ANTROBUS:
Well . . . how big's the ocean?

GLADYS:
Papa, you're teasing me. It's—three-hundred and sixty million square-miles—and—it—covers—three-fourths—of—the—earth's—surface—and—its—deepest-place—is—five—and—a—half—miles—deep—and—its—average—depth—is—twelve—thousand-feet. No, Papa, ask me something hard, real hard.

MRS. ANTROBUS:
Rising.

Now I'm going off to buy those raincoats. I think that bad weather's going to get worse and worse. I hope it doesn't come before your broadcast. I should think we have about an hour or so.

HENRY:
I hope it comes and zzzzzz everything before it. I hope it—

MRS. ANTROBUS:
Henry!—George, I think . . . maybe, it's one of those storms that are just as bad on land as on the sea. When you're just as safe and safer in a good stout boat.

HENRY:
There's a boat out at the end of the pier.

MRS. ANTROBUS:
Well, keep your eye on it. George, you shut your eyes and get a good rest before the broadcast.

ANTROBUS:
Thundering Judas, do I have to be told when to open and shut my eyes? Go and buy your raincoats.

MRS. ANTROBUS:
Now, children, you have ten minutes to walk around. Ten minutes. And, Henry: control yourself. Gladys, stick by your brother and don't get lost.

They run off.

MRS. ANTROBUS:
Will you be all right, George?

CONVEENERS *suddenly stick their heads out of the Bingo Parlor and Salt Water Taffy store, and voices rise from the orchestra pit.*

CONVEENERS:
George. Geo-r-r-rge! George! Leave the old hen-coop at home, George, Do-mes-ticated Georgie!

MRS. ANTROBUS:
Shaking her umbrella.

Low common oafs! That's what they are. Guess a man has a right to bring his wife to a convention, if he wants to.

She starts off.

What's the matter with a family, I'd like to know. What else have they got to offer?

Exit. ANTROBUS *has closed his eyes. The* FORTUNE TELLER *comes out of her shop and goes ever to the left proscenium. She leans against it watching* SABINA *quizzically.*

FORTUNE TELLER:
Heh! Here she comes!

SABINA:
Loud whisper.

What's he doing?

FORTUNE TELLER:

Oh, he's ready for you. Bite your lips, dear, take a long breath add come on up.

SABINA:

I'm nervous. My whole future depends on this. I'm nervous.

FORTUNE TELLER:

Don't be a fool. What more could you want? He's forty-five. His head's a little dizzy. He's just been elected president. He's never known any other woman than his wife. Whenever he looks at her he realizes that she knows every foolish thing he's ever done.

SABINA:

Still whispering.

I don't know why it is, but every time I start one of these I'm nervous.

The FORTUNE TELLER *stands in the center of the stage watching the following:*

FORTUNE TELLER:

You make me tired.

SABINA:

First tell me my fortune.

The FORTUNE TELLER *laughs drily and makes the gesture of brushing away a nonsensical question.* sabina *coughs and says:*

Oh, Mr. Antrobus,—dare I speak to you for a moment?

ANTROBUS:

What?—Oh, certainly, certainly, Miss Fairweather.

SABINA:

Mr. Antrobus . . . I've been so unhappy. I've wanted . . . I've wanted to make sure that you don't think that I'm the kind of girl who goes out for beauty contests.

FORTUNE TELLER:

That's the way!

ANTROBUS:

Oh, I understand. I understand perfectly.

FORTUNE TELLER:

Give it a little more. Lean on it.

SABINA:

I knew you would. My mother said to me this morning: Lily, she said, that fine Mr. Antrobus gave you the prize because he saw at once that you weren't the kind of girl who'd go in for a thing like that. But, honestly, Mr. Antrobus, in this world, honestly, a good girl doesn't know where to turn.

FORTUNE TELLER:

Now you've gone too far.

ANTROBUS:

My dear Miss Fairweather!

SABINA:

You wouldn't know how hard it is. With that lovely wife and daughter you have. Oh, I think Mrs. Antrobus is the finest woman I ever saw. I wish I were like her.

ANTROBUS:

There, there. There's . . . uh . . . room for all kinds of people in the world, Miss Fairweather.

SABINA:

How wonderful of you to say that. How generous!—Mr. Antrobus, have you a moment free? . . . I'm afraid I may be a little conspicuous here . . . could you come down, for just a moment, to my beach cabana . . . ?

ANTROBUS:

Why-uh . . . yes, certainly . . . for a moment . . . just for a moment.

SABINA:

There's a deck chair there. Because: you know you do look tired. Just this morning my mother said to me; Lily, she said, I hope Mr. Antrobus is getting a good rest. His fine strong face has deep deep lines in it. Now isn't it true, Mr. Antrobus: you work too hard?

FORTUNE TELLER:

Bingo!

She goes into her shop.

SABINA:

Now you will just stretch out. No, I shan't say a word, not a word. I shall just sit there,—privileged. That's what I am.

ANTROBUS:

Taking her hand.

Miss Fairweather . . . you'll . . . spoil me.

SABINA:

Just a moment. I have something I wish to say to the audience.—Ladies and gentlemen, I'm not going to play this particular scene tonight. It's just a shore scene and we're going to skip it. But I'll tell you what takes place and then we can continue the play from there on. Now in this scene—

ANTROBUS:

Between his teeth.

But, Miss Somerset!

SABINA:

I'm sorry. I'm sorry. But I have to skip it. In this scene, I talk to Mr. Antrobus, and at the end of it he decides to leave his wife, get a divorce at Reno and marry me. That's all.

ANTROBUS:

Fitz!—Fitz!

SABINA:

So that now I've told you we can jump to the end of it,—where you say:

Enter in fury MR. FITZPATRICK, *the stage manager.*

MR. FITZPATRICK:

Miss Somerset, we insist on your playing this scene.

SABINA:

I'm sorry, Mr. Fitzpatrick, but I can't and I won't. I've told the audience all they need to know and now we can go on.

Other ACTORS *begin to appear on the stage, listening.*

MR. FITZPATRICK:

And why can't you play it?

SABINA:

Because there are some lines in that scene that would hurt some people's feelings and I don't think the theatre is a place where people's feelings ought to be hurt.

MR. FITZPATRICK:

Miss Somerset, you can pack up your things and go home. I shall call the understudy and I shall report you to Equity.

SABINA:

I sent the understudy up to the corner for a cup of coffee and if Equity tries to penalize me I'll drag the case right up to the Supreme Court. Now listen, everybody, there's no need to get excited.

MR. FITZPATRICK AND ANTROBUS:

Why can't you play it . . . what's the matter with the scene?

SABINA:

Well, if you must know, I have a personal guest in the audience tonight. Her life hasn't been exactly a happy one. I wouldn't have my friend hear some of these lines for the whole world. I don't suppose it occurred to the author that some other women might have gone through the experience of losing their husbands like this. Wild horses wouldn't drag from me the details of my friend's life, but . . . well, they'd been married twenty years, and before he got rich, why, she'd done the washing and everything.

MR. FITZPATRICK:

Miss Somerset, your friend will forgive you. We must play this scene.

SABINA:

Nothing, nothing will make me say some of those lines . . . about "a man outgrows a wife every seven years" and . . . and that one about "the Mohammedans being the only people who looked the subject square in the face." Nothing.

MR. FITZPATRICK:

Miss Somerset! Go to your dressing room, I'll read your lines.

SABINA:

Now everybody's nerves are on edge,

MR. ANTROBUS:

Skip the scene.

MR. FITZPATRICK *and the other* ACTORS *go off.*

SABINA:

Thank you. I knew you'd understand. We'll do just what I said. So Mr. Antrobus is going to divorce his wife and marry me. Mr. Antrobus, you say: "It won't be easy to lay all this before my wife."

The ACTORS *withdraw.* ANTROBUS *walks about, his hand to his forehead mattering:*

ANTROBUS:

Wait a minute. I can't get back into it as easily as all that. "My wife is a very obstinate woman." Hm . . . then you say . . . hm . . . Miss Fairweather, I mean Lily, it won't be easy to lay all this before my wife. It'll hurt her feelings a little.

SABINA:

Listen, George: *other* people haven't got feelings. Not in the same way that we have,—we who are presidents like you and prize-winners like me. Listen, other people haven't got feelings; they just imagine they have. Within two weeks they go back to playing bridge and going to the movies.

Listen, dear: everybody in the world except a few people like you and me are just people of straw. Most people have no insides at all. Now that you're president you'll see that. Listen, darling, there's a kind of secret society at the top of the world,—like you and me,—that know this. The world was made for us. What's life anyway? Except for two things, pleasure and power, what is life? Boredom! Foolishness. You know it is. Except for those two things, life's nau-se-at-ing. So,—come here!

She moves close. They kiss.

So.

Now when your wife comes, it's really very simple; just tell her.

ANTROBUS:
Lily, Lily: you're a wonderful woman.

SABINA:
Of course I am.

They enter the cabana, and it hides them from view. Distant roll of thunder. A third black disk appears on the weather signal. Distant thunder is heard. MRS. ANTROBUS *appears carrying parcels. She looks about, seats herself on the bench left, and fans herself with her handkerchief Enter* GLADYS *right, followed by two* CONVEENERS. *She is wearing red stockings.*

MRS. ANTROBUS:
Gladys!

GLADYS:
Mama, here I am.

MRS. ANTROBUS:
Gladys Antrobus!!! Where did you get those dreadful things?

GLADYS:
Wha-a-t? Papa liked the color.

MRS. ANTROBUS:
You go back to the hotel this minute!

GLADYS:
I won't. I won't. Papa liked the color.

MRS. ANTROBUS:
All right. All right. You stay here. I've a good mind to let your father see you that way. You stay right here.

GLADYS:
I . . . I don't want to stay if . . . if you don't think he'd like it.

MRS. ANTROBUS:
Oh . . . it's all one to me. I don't care what happens. I don't care if the biggest storm in the whole world comes. Let it come.

She folds her hands.

Where's your brother?

GLADYS:
In a small voice.

He'll be here.

MRS. ANTROBUS:
Will he? Well, let him get into trouble. I don't care. I don't know where your father is, I'm sure.

Laughter from the cabana.

GLADYS:
Leaning over the rail.

I think he's . . . Mama, he's talking to the lady in the red dress.

MRS. ANTROBUS:
Is that so?

Pause.

We'll wait till he's through. Sit down here beside me and stop fidgeting . . . what are you crying about?

Distant thunder. She covers GLADYS'S *stockings with a raincoat.*

GLADYS:
You don't like my stockings.

Two CONVEENERS *rush in with a microphone on a standard and various paraphernalia. The* FORTUNE TELLER *appears at the door of her shop. Other characters gradually gather.*

BROADCAST OFFICIAL:
Mrs. Antrobus Thank God we've found you at last. Where's Mr. Antrobus? We've been hunting everywhere for him. It's about time for the broadcast to the conventions of the world.

MRS. ANTROBUS:
Calm.

I expect he'll be here in a minute.

BROADCAST OFFICIAL:
Mrs. Antrobus, if he doesn't show up in time, I hope you will consent to broadcast in his place. It's the most important broadcast of the year.

SABINA *enters from cabana followed by* ANTROBUS.

MRS. ANTROBUS:
No, I shan't. I haven't one single thing to say.

BROADCAST OFFICIAL:
Then won't you help us find him, Mrs. Antrobus? A storm's coming up. A hurricane. A deluge!

SECOND CONVEENER:
Who has sighted ANTROBUS *over the rail.*

Joe! Joe! Here he is.

BROADCAST OFFICIAL:
In the name of God, Mr. Antrobus, you're on the air in five minutes. Will you kindly please come and test the instrument? That's all we ask. If you just please begin the alphabet slowly.

ANTROBUS, *with set face, comes ponderously up the ramp. He stops at the point where his waist is level with the stage and speaks authoritatively to the* OFFICIALS.

ANTROBUS:
I'll be ready when the time comes, until then, move away. Go away. I have something I wish to say to my wife.

BROADCAST OFFICIAL:
Whimpering.

Mr. Antrobus! This is the most important broadcast of the year.

The OFFICIALS *withdraw to the edge of the stage.* SABINA *glides up the ramp behind* ANTROBUS.

SABINA:
Whispering.

Don't let her argue. Remember arguments have nothing to do with it.

ANTROBUS:
Maggie, I'm moving out of the hotel. In fact, I'm moving out of everything. For good. I'm going to marry Miss Fair-weather. I shall provide generously for you and the children. In a few years you'll be able to see that it's all for the best. That's all I have to say.

BROADCAST OFFICIAL:	**BINGO ANNOUNCER:**
Mr. Antrobus! I hope you'll be ready. This is the most important broadcast of the year.	A—nine; A—nine. D—forty-two; D—forty-two. C—thirty; C—thirty. B—seventeen; B—seventeen. C—forty; C—forty.
GLADYS:	**CHORUS:**
What did Papa say, Mama? I didn't hear what papa said.	Bingo!!

BROADCAST OFFICIAL:
Mr. Antrobus. All we want to do is test your voice with the alphabet.

ANTROBUS:
Go away. Clear out.

MRS. ANTROBUS:
Composedly with lowered eyes.

George, I can't talk to you until you wipe those silly red marks off your face.

ANTROBUS:
I think there's nothing to talk about. I've said what I have to say.

SABINA:
Splendid!!

ANTROBUS:
You're a fine woman, Maggie, but . . . but a man has his own life to lead in the world.

MRS. ANTROBUS:
Well, after living with you for five thousand years I guess I have a right to a word or two, haven't I?

ANTROBUS:
To SABINA.

What can I answer to that?

SABINA:
Tell her that conversation would only hurt her feelings. It's-kinder-in-the-long-run-to-do-it-short-and-quick.

ANTROBUS:
I want to spare your feelings in every way I can, Maggie.

BROADCAST OFFICIAL:
Mr. Antrobus, the hurricane signal's gone up. We could begin right now.

MRS. ANTROBUS:
Calmly, almost dreamily.

I didn't marry you because you were perfect. I didn't even marry you because I loved you. I married you because you gave me a promise.

She takes off her ring and looks at it.

That promise made up for your faults. And the promise I gave you made up for mine. Two imperfect people got married and it was the promise that made the marriage.

ANTROBUS:
Maggie, . . . I was only nineteen.

MRS. ANTROBUS:
She puts her ring back on her finger.

And when our children were growing up, it wasn't a house that protected them; and it wasn't our love, that protected them—it was that promise.

And when that promise is broken—this can happen!

With a sweep of the hand she removes the raincoat from GLADYS' *stockings.*

ANTROBUS:

Stretches out his arm, apoplectic.

Gladys!! Have you gone crazy? Has everyone gone crazy?

Turning on SABINA.

You did this. You gave them to her.

SABINA:
I never said a word to her.

ANTROBUS:
To GLADYS.

You go back to the hotel and take those horrible things off.

GLADYS:
Pert.

Before I go, I've got something to tell you,—it's about Henry.

MRS. ANTROBUS:
Claps her hands peremptorily.

Stop your noise,—I'm taking her back to the hotel, George, Before I go I have a letter . . . I have a message to throw into the ocean.

Fumbling in her handbag.

Where is the plagued thing? Here it is.

She flings something—invisible to us—far over the heads of the audience to the back of the auditorium.

It's a bottle. And in the bottle's a letter. And in the letter is written all the things that a woman knows.

It's never been told to any man and it's never been told to any woman, and if it finds its destination, a new time will come. We're not what books and plays say we are. We're not what advertisements say we are. We're not in the movies and we're not on the radio.

We're not what you're all told and what you think we are:

We're ourselves. And if any man can find one of us he'll learn why the whole universe was set in motion. And if any man harm any one of us, his soul—the only soul he's got—had better be at the bottom of that ocean,—and that's the only way to put it. Gladys, come here. We're going back to the hotel.

She drags GLADYS *firmly off by the hand, but* GLADYS *breaks away and comes down to speak to her father.*

SABINA:
Such goings-on. Don't give it a minute's thought.

GLADYS:
Anyway, I think you ought to know that Henry hit a man with a stone. He hit one of those colored men that push the chairs and the man's very sick, Henry ran away and hid and some policemen are looking for him very hard. And I don't care a bit if you don't want to have anything to do with mama and me, because I'll never like you again and I hope nobody ever likes you again,—so there!

She runs off. ANTROBUS *starts after her.*

ANTROBUS:
I . . . I have to go and see what I can do about this.

SABINA:
You stay right here. Don't you go now while you're excited. Gracious sakes, all these things will be forgotten in a hundred years. Come, now, you're on the air. Just say anything,—it doesn't matter what. Just a lot of birds and fishes and things.

BROADCAST OFFICIAL:
Thank you, Miss Fairweather. Thank you very much. Ready, Mr. Antrobus.

ANTROBUS:
Touching the microphone.

What is it, what is it? Who am I talking to?

BROADCAST OFFICIAL:
Why, Mr. Antrobus! To our order and to all the other orders.

ANTROBUS:
Raising his head.

What are all those birds doing?

BROADCAST OFFICIAL:
Those are just a few of the birds. Those are the delegates to our convention,—two of a kind.

ANTROBUS:
Pointing into the audience.

Look at the water. Look at them all. Those fishes jumping. The children should see this!—There's Maggie's whales!! Here are your whales, Maggie!!

BROADCAST OFFICIAL:
I hope you're ready, Mr. Antrobus.

ANTROBUS:
And look on the beach! You didn't tell me these would be here!

SABINA:
Yes, George. Those are the animals.

BROADCAST OFFICIAL:
Busy with the apparatus.

Yes, Mr. Antrobus, those are the vertebrates. We hope the lion will have a word to say when you're through. Step right up, Mr. Antrobus, we're ready. We'll just have time before the storm.

Pause. In a hoarse whisper:

They're waiting.

It has grown dark. Soon after he speaks a high whistling noise begins. Strange veering lights start whirling about the stage. The other characters disappear from the stage.

ANTROBUS:
Friends. Cousins. Four score and ten billion years ago our forefather brought forth upon this planet the spark of life,—

He is drowned out by thunder. When the thunder stops the FORTUNE TELLER *is seen standing beside him.*

FORTUNE TELLER:
Antrobus, there's not a minute to be lost. Don't you see the four disks on the weather signal? Take your family into that boat at the end of the pier.

ANTROBUS:
My family? I have no family Maggie! Maggie! They won't come.

FORTUNE TELLER:
They'll come.—Antrobus! Take these animals into that boat with you. All of them,—two of each kind.

SABINA:
George, what's the matter with you? This is just a storm like any other storm.

ANTROBUS:
Maggie!

SABINA:
Stay with me, we'll go . . .

Losing conviction.

This is just another thunderstorm,—isn't it? Isn't it?

ANTROBUS:
Maggie!!!

MRS. ANTROBUS *appears beside him with* GLADYS.

MRS. ANTROBUS:
Matter-of-fact.

Here I am and here's Gladys.

ANTROBUS:
Where've you been? Where have you been? Quick, we're going into that boat out there.

MRS. ANTROBUS:
I know we are. But I haven't found Henry.

She wanders off into the darkness calling "Henry!"

SABINA:
Low urgent babbling, only occasionally raising her voice.

I don't believe it. I don't believe it's anything at all. I've seen hundreds of storms like this.

FORTUNE TELLER:
There's no time to lose. Go. Push the animals along before you. Start a new world. Begin again.

SABINA:
Esmeralda! George! Tell me,—is it really serious?

ANTROBUS:
Suddenly very busy.

Elephants first. Gently, gently.—Look where you're going.

GLADYS:
Leaning over the ramp and striking an animal on the back.

Stop it or you'll be left behind!

ANTROBUS:
Is the Kangaroo there? *There* you are! Take those turtles in your pouch, will you?

To some other animals, pointing to his shoulder.

Here! You jump up here. You'll be trampled on.

GLADYS:
To her father, pointing below.

Papa, look,—the snakes!

MRS. ANTROBUS:
I can't find Henry. Hen-ry!

ANTROBUS:
Go along. Go along. Climb on their backs.—Wolves! Jackals,—whatever you are,—tend to your own business!

GLADYS:
Pointing, tenderly.

Papa,—look.

SABINA:
Mr. Antrobus—take me with you. Don't leave me here. I'll work. I'll help. I'll do anything.

THREE CONVEENERS *cross the stage, marching with a banner.*

CONVEENERS:
George! What are you scared of?—George! Fellas, it looks like rain.—"Maggie, where's my umbrella?"—George, setting up for Barnum and Bailey.

ANTROBUS:

Again catching his wife's hand.

Come on now, Maggie,—the pier's going to break any minute.

MRS. ANTROBUS:

I'm not going a step without Henry. Henry!

GLADYS:

On the ramp.

Mama! Papa! Hurry. The pier's cracking, Mama. It's going to break.

MRS. ANTROBUS:

Henry! Cain! CAIN!

HENRY *dashes into the stage and joins his mother.*

HENRY:

Here I am, Mama.

MRS. ANTROBUS:

Thank God!—now come quick.

HENRY:

I didn't think you wanted me.

MRS. ANTROBUS:

Quick!

She pushes him down before her into the aisle.

SABINA:

All the ANTROBUSES *are now in the theater aisle.* SABINA *stands at the tap of the ramp.*

Mrs. Antrobus, take me. Don't you remember me? I'll work. I'll help. Don't leave me here!

MRS. ANTROBUS:

Impatiently, but as though it were of no importance.

Yes, yes. There's a lot of work to be done. Only hurry.

FORTUNE TELLER:

Now dominating the stage. To SABINA *with grim smile.*

Yes, go—back to the kitchen with you.

SABINA:

Half-down the ramp. To FORTUNE TELLER.

I don't know why my life's always being interrupted—just when everything's going fine!!

She dashes up the aisle.

Now the CONVENEERS *emerge doing a serpentine dance on the stage. They jeer at the* FORTUNE TELLER.

CONVEENERS:

Get a canoe—there's not a minute to be lost! Tell me my future, Mrs. Croaker.

FORTUNE TELLER:

Paddle in the water, boys—enjoy yourselves.

VOICE FROM THE BINGO PARLOR:

A—nine; A—nine. C—twenty-four, C—twenty-four.

CONVEENERS:

Rags, bottles, and sacks.

FORTUNE TELLER:

Go back and climb on your roofs. Put rags in the cracks under your doors.—Nothing will keep out the flood. You've had your chance. You've had your day. You've failed. You've lost.

VOICE FROM THE BINGO PARLOR:

B—fifteen. B—fifteen.

FORTUNE TELLER:

Shading her eyes and looking out to sea.

They're safe. George Antrobus! Think it over! A new world to make. Think it over!

CURTAIN

★

ACT III

Just before the curtain rises, two sounds are heard from the stage: a cracked bugle call.

The curtain rises on almost total darkness. Almost all the flats composing the walls of MR. ANTROBUS*'s house, as of Act I, are up, but they lean helter-skelter against one another, leaving irregular gaps. Among the flats missing are two in the back wall, leaving the frames of the window and door crazily out of line. Off stage, back right, some red Roman fire is burning. The bugle call is repeated. Enter* SABINA *through the tilted door. She is dressed as a Napoleonic camp follower, "la fille du regiment," in begrimed reds and blues.*

SABINA:
Mrs. Antrobus! Gladys! Where are you?

The war's over. The war's over. You can come out. The peace treaty's been signed.

Where are they?—Hmpf! Are they dead, too? Mrs. Annnntrobus! Glaaaadys! Mr. Antrobus'll be here this afternoon. I just saw him downtown. Huuuurry and put things in order. He says that now that the war's over we'll all have to settle down and be perfect.

Enter MR. FITZPATRICK, *the stage manager, followed by the whole company, who stand waiting at the edges of the stage.* MR. FITZPATRICK *tries to interrupt* SABINA.

MR. FITZPATRICK:
Miss Somerset, we have to stop a moment.

SABINA:
They may be hiding out in the back—

MR. FITZPATRICK:
Miss Somerset! We have to stop a moment.

SABINA:
What's the matter?

MR. FITZPATRICK:
There's an explanation we have to make to the audience.—Lights, please.

To the actor who plays MR. ANTROBUS,

Will you explain the matter to the audience?

The lights go up. We now see that a balcony or elevated runway has been erected at the back of the stage, back of the wall of the Antrobus house. From its extreme right and left ends ladder-like steps descend to the floor of the stage.

ANTROBUS:
Ladies and gentlemen, an unfortunate accident has taken place back stage. Perhaps I should say *another* unfortunate accident.

SABINA:
I'm sorry. I'm sorry.

ANTROBUS:
The management feels, in fact, we all feel that you are due an apology. And now we have to ask your indulgence for the most serious mishap of all. Seven of our actors have . . . have been taken ill. Apparently, it was something they ate. I'm not exactly clear what happened.

All the ACTORS *start to talk at once.* ANTROBUS *raises his hand.*

Now, now—not all at once. Fitz, do you know what it was?

MR. FITZPATRICK:
Why, it's perfectly clear. These seven actors had dinner together, and they ate something that disagreed with them.

SABINA:
Disagreed with them!!! They have ptomaine poisoning. They're in Bellevue Hospital this very minute in agony. They're having their stomachs pumped out this very minute, in perfect agony.

ANTROBUS:
Fortunately, we've just heard they'll all recover.

SABINA:
It'll be a miracle if they do, a downright miracle. It was the lemon on meringue pie.

ACTORS:
It was the fish . . . it was the canned tomatoes . . . it was the fish.

SABINA:
It was the lemon meringue pie. I saw it with my own eyes; it had blue mould all over the bottom of it.

ANTROBUS:
Whatever it was, they're in no condition to take part in this performance. Naturally, we haven't enough understudies to fill all those roles; but we do have a number of splendid volunteers who have kindly consented to help us out. These friends have watched our rehearsals, and they assure me that they know the lines and the business very well. Let me introduce them to you—my dresser, Mr. Tremayne,—himself a distinguished Shakespearean actor for many years; our wardrobe mistress, Hester; Miss Somerset's maid, Ivy; and Fred Bailey, captain of the ushers in this theatre.

These persons bow modestly, IVY *and* HESTER *are colored girls.*

Now this scene takes place near the end of the act. And I'm sorry to say we'll need a short rehearsal, just a short run-through. And as some of it takes place in the auditorium, we'll have to keep the curtain up. Those of you who wish can go out in the lobby and smoke some more. The rest of you can listen to us, or . . . or just talk quietly among yourselves, as you choose. Thank you. Now will you take it over, Mr. Fitzpatrick?

MR. FITZPATRICK:
Thank you.—Now for those of you who are listening perhaps I should explain that at the end of this act, the men have come back from the War and the family's settled down in the house. And the author wants to show the hours of the night passing by over their heads, and the planets crossing the sky . . . uh . . . over their heads.

And he says—this is hard to explain—that each of the hours of the night is a philosopher, or a great thinker. Eleven o'clock, for instance, is Aristotle. And nine o'clock is Spinoza. Like that. I don't suppose it means anything. It's just a kind of poetic effect.

SABINA:
Not mean anything! Why, it certainly does. Twelve o'clock goes by saying those wonderful things. I think it means that when people are asleep they have all those lovely thoughts, much better than when they're awake.

IVY:
Excuse me, I think it means,—excuse me, Mr. Fitzpatrick—

SABINA:
What were you going to say, Ivy?

IVY:
Mr. Fitzpatrick, you let my father come to a rehearsal; and my father's a Baptist minister, and he said that the author meant that—just like the hours and stars go by over our heads at night, in the same way the ideas and thoughts of the great men are in the air around us all the time and they're working on us, even when we don't know it.

MR. FITZPATRICK:
Well, well, maybe that's it. Thank you, Ivy. Anyway,—the hours of the night are philosophers. My friends, are you ready? Ivy, can you be eleven o'clock? "This good estate of the mind possessing its object in energy we call divine." Aristotle.

IVY:
Yes, sir. I know that and I know twelve o'clock and I know nine o'clock.

MR. FITZPATRICK:
Twelve o'clock? Mr. Tremayne, the Bible.

TREMAYNE:
Yes.

MR. FITZPATRICK:
Ten o'clock? Hester,—Plato?

She nods eagerly.

Nine o'clock, Spinoza,—Fred?

BAILEY:
Yes, *sir.*

FRED BAILEY *picks up a great gilded cardboard numeral IX and starts up the steps to the platform.* MR. FITZPATRICK *strikes his forehead.*

MR. FITZPATRICK:
The planets!! We forgot all about the planets.

SABINA:
O my God! The planets! Are they sick too?

ACTORS *nod.*

MR. FITZPATRICK:
Ladies and gentlemen, the planets are singers. Of course, we can't replace them, so you'll have to imagine them singing in this scene. Saturn sings from the orchestra pit down here. The Moon is way up there. And Mars with a red lantern in his hand, stands in the aisle over there—Tz-tz-tz. It's too bad; it all makes a very fine effect. However! Ready—nine o'clock: Spinoza.

BAILEY:
Walking slowly across the balcony, left to right.

"After experience had taught me that the common occurrences of daily life are vain and futile—"

FITZPATRICK:
Louder, Fred. "And I saw that all the objects of my desire and fear—"

BAILEY:
"And I saw that all the objects of my desire and fear were in themselves nothing good nor had save insofar as the mind was affected by them—"

FITZPATRICK:
Do you know the rest? All right. Ten o'clock. Hester. Plato.

HESTER:
"Then tell me, O Critias, how will a man choose the ruler that shall rule over him? Will he not—"

FITZPATRICK:
Thank you. Skip to the end, Hester.

HESTER:
". . . can be multiplied a thousand fold in its effects among the citizens."

FITZPATRICK:
Thank you.—Aristotle, Ivy?

IVY:
"This good estate of the mind possessing its object in energy we call divine. This we mortals have occasionally and it is this energy which is pleasantest and best. But God has it always. It is wonderful in us; but in Him how much more wonderful."

FITZPATRICK:
Midnight. Midnight, Mr. Tremayne. That's right,—you've done it before.—All right, everybody. You know

what you have to do.—Lower the curtain. House lights up. Act Three of The Skin of Our Teeth.

At the curtain descends he is heard saying:

You volunteers, just wear what you have on. Don't try to put on the costumes today.

House lights go down. The Act begins again. The Bugle call. Curtain rises. Enter SABINA.

SABINA:
Mrs. Antrobus! Gladys! Where are you? The war's over.—You've heard all this—

She gabbles the main points.

Where—are—they? Are—they—dead, too, et cetera. I—just—saw—Mr.—Antrobus—down town, et cetera.

Slowing up:

He says that now that the war's over we'll all have to settle down and be perfect. They may be hiding out in the back somewhere, Mrs. An-tro-bus.

She wanders off. It has grown lighter.

A trapdoor is cautiously raised and MRS. ANTROBUS *emerges waist-high and listens. She is disheveled and worn; she wears a tattered dress and a shawl half covers her head. She talks down through the trapdoor.*

MRS. ANTROBUS:
It's getting light. There's still something burning over there—Newark, or Jersey City. What? Yes, I could swear I heard someone moving about up here. But I can't see anybody. I say: I can't see anybody.

She starts to move about the stage. GLADYS' *head appears at the trapdoor. She is holding a* baby.

GLADYS:
Oh, Mama. Be careful.

MRS. ANTROBUS:
Now, Gladys, you stay out of sight.

GLADYS:
Well, let me stay here just a minute. I want the baby to get some of this fresh air.

MRS. ANTROBUS:
All right, but keep your eyes open. I'll see what I can find. I'll have a good hot plate of soup for you before you can say Jack Robinson. Gladys Antrobus! Do you know what I think I see? There's old Mr. Hawkins sweeping the sidewalk in front of his A. and P. store. Sweeping it with a broom. Why, he must have gone crazy, like the others! I see some other people moving about, too.

GLADYS:
Mama, come back, come back.

MRS. ANTROBUS *returns to the trapdoor and listens.*

MRS. ANTROBUS:
Gladys, there's something in the air. Everybody's movement's sort of different. I see some women walking right out in the middle of the street.

SABINA'S VOICE:
Mrs. An-tro-bus!

MRS. ANTROBUS AND GLADYS:
What's that?!!

SABINA'S VOICE:
Glaaaadys! Mrs. An-tro-bus!

Enter SABINA.

MRS. ANTROBUS:
Gladys, that's Sabina's voice as sure as I live.—Sabina! Sabina!—Are you *alive*?!!

SABINA:
Of course, I'm alive. How've you girls been?—*Don't* try and kiss me. I never want to kiss another human being as long as I live. Sh-sh, there's nothing to get emotional about. Pull yourself together, the war's over. Take a deep breath,—the war's over.

MRS. ANTROBUS:
The war's over!! I don't believe you. I don't believe you. I can't believe you.

GLADYS:
Mama!

SABINA:
Who's that?

MRS. ANTROBUS:
That's Gladys and her baby. I don't believe you. Gladys, Sabina says the war's over. Oh, Sabina.

SABINA:
Leaning over the BABY.

Goodness! Are there any babies left in the world! Can it see? And can it cry and everything?

GLADYS:
Yes, he can. He notices everything very well.

SABINA:
Where on earth did you get it? Oh, I won't ask.—Lord, I've lived all these seven years around camp and I've forgotten how to behave.—Now we've got to think about the men coming home.—Mrs. Antrobus, go and wash your face, I'm ashamed of you. Put your best clothes on.

Mr. Antrobus'll be here this afternoon. I just saw him downtown.

MRS. ANTROBUS AND GLADYS:
He's alive!! He'll be here!! Sabina, you're not joking?

MRS. ANTROBUS:
And Henry?

SABINA:

Dryly.

Yes, Henry's alive, too, that's what they say. Now don't stop to talk. Get yourselves fixed up. Gladys, you look terrible. Have you any decent clothes?

SABINA *has pushed them toward the trapdoor.*

MRS. ANTROBUS:

Half down.

Yes, I've something to wear just for this very day. But, Sabina,—who won the war?

SABINA:
Don't stop now,—just wash your face.

A whistle sounds in the distance.

Oh, my God, what's that silly little noise?

MRS. ANTROBUS:
Why, it sounds like . . . it sounds like what used to be the noon whistle at the shoe-polish factory.

Exit.

SABINA:
That's what it is. Seems to me like peacetime's coming along pretty fast—shoe polish!

GLADYS:

Half down.

Sabina, how soon after peacetime begins does the milkman start coming to the door?

SABINA:
As soon as he catches a cow. Give him time to catch a cow, dear.

Exit GLADYS, SABINA *walks about a moment, thinking.*

Shoe polish! My, I'd forgotten what peacetime was like.

She shakes her head, then sits down by the trapdoor and starts talking down the hole.

Mrs. Antrobus, guess what I saw Mr. Antrobus doing this morning at dawn. He was tacking up a piece of paper on the door of the Town Hall. You'll die when you hear: it was a recipe for grass soup, for a grass soup that doesn't give you the diarrhea. Mr. Antrobus is still thinking up new things.—He told me to give you his love. He's got all sorts of ideas for peacetime, he says. No more laziness and idiocy, he says. And oh, yes! Where are his books? What? Well, pass them up. The first thing he wants to see are his books. He says if you've burnt those books, or if the rats have eaten them, he says it isn't worthwhile starting over again. Everybody's going to be beautiful, he says, and diligent, and very intelligent.

A hand reaches up with two volumes.

What language is that? Pu-u-gh,—mold! And he's got such plans for you, Mrs. Antrobus. You're going to study history and algebra—and so are Gladys and I—and philosophy. You should hear him talk:

Taking two more volumes.

Well, these are in English, anyway.—To hear him talk, seems like he expects you to be a combination. Mrs. Antrobus, of a saint and a college professor, and a dance-hall hostess, if you know what I mean.

Two more volumes.

Ugh. German!

She is lying on the floor; one elbow bent, her cheek on her hand, meditatively.

Yes, peace will be here before we know it. In a week or two we'll be asking the Perkinses in for a quiet evening of bridge. We'll turn on the radio and hear how to be big successes with a new toothpaste. We'll trot down to the movies and see how girls with wax faces live—all that will begin again. Oh, Mrs. Antrobus, God forgive me but I enjoyed the war. Everybody's at their best in wartime. I'm sorry it's over. And, oh, I forgot! Mr. Antrobus sent you another message—can you hear me?—

Enter HENRY, *blackened and sullen. He is wearing torn overalls, but has one gaudy admiral's epaulette hanging by a thread from his right shoulder, and there are vestiges of gold and scarlet braid running down his left trouser leg. He stands listening.*

Listen! Henry's never to put foot in this house again, he says. He'll kill Henry on sight, if he sees him.

You don't know about Henry??? Well, where have you been? What? Well, Henry rose right to the top. Top of what? Listen, I'm telling you. Henry rose from corporal to captain, to major, to general.—I don't know how to say it, but the enemy is Henry; Henry is the enemy. Everybody knows that.

HENRY:
He'll kill me, will he?

SABINA:
Who are you? I'm not afraid of you. The war's over.

HENRY:
I'll kill him so fast. I've spent seven years trying to find him; the others I killed were just substitutes.

SABINA:
Goodness! It's Henry!—

He makes an angry gesture.

Oh, I'm not afraid of you. The war's over, Henry Antrobus, and you're not any more important than any other unemployed. You go away and hide yourself, until we calm your father down.

HENRY:
The first thing to do is to burn up those old books; it's the ideas he gets out those old books that . . . that makes the whole world so you can't live in it.

He reels forward and starts kicking the books about, but suddenly falls down in a sitting position.

SABINA:
You leave those books alone!! Mr. Antrobus is looking forward to them a-special.—Gracious sakes, Henry, you're so tired you can't stand up. Your mother and sister'll be here in a minute and we'll think what to do about you.

HENRY:
What did they ever care about me?

SABINA:
There's that old whine again. All you people think you're not loved enough, nobody loves you. Well, you start being lovable and we'll love you.

HENRY:

Outraged.

I don't want anybody to love me.

SABINA:
Then stop talking about it all the time.

HENRY:
I never talk about it. The last thing I want is anybody to pay any attention to me.

SABINA:
I can hear it behind every word you say.

HENRY:
I want everybody to hate me.

SABINA:
Yes, you've decided that's second best, but it's still the same thing.—Mrs. Antrobus! Henry's here. He's so tired he can't stand up.

MRS. ANTROBUS *and* GLADYS, *with her* BABY, *emerge. They are dressed as in Act I.* MRS. ANTROBUS *carries some objects in her apron, and* GLADYS *has a blanket over her shoulder.*

MRS. ANTROBUS AND GLADYS:
Henry! Henry! Henry!

HENRY:

Glaring at them.

Have you anything to eat?

MRS. ANTROBUS:
Yes, I have, Henry. I've been saving it for this very day,—two good baked potatoes. No! Henry! one of them's for your rather. Henry!! Give me that other potato back this minute.

SABINA *sidles up behind him and snatches the other potato away.*

SABINA:
He's so dog-tired he doesn't know what he's doing.

MRS. ANTROBUS:
Now you just rest there, Henry, until I can get your room ready. Eat that potato good and slow, so you can get all the nourishment out of it.

HENRY:
You all might as well know right now that I haven't come back here to live.

MRS. ANTROBUS:
Sh. . . . I'll put this coat over you. Your room's hardly damaged at all. Your football trophies are a little tarnished, but Sabina and I will polish them up tomorrow.

HENRY:
Did you hear me? I don't live here. I don't belong to anybody.

MRS. ANTROBUS:
Why, how can you say a thing like that! You certainly do belong right here. Where else would you want to go? Your forehead's feverish, Henry, seems to me. You'd better give me that gun, Henry. You won't need that any more.

GLADYS:

Whispering.

Look, he's fallen asleep already, with his potato half-chewed.

SABINA:
Puh! The terror of the world.

MRS. ANTROBUS:
Sabina, you mind your own business, and start putting the room to rights.

HENRY *has turned his face to the back of the sofa.* MRS. ANTROBUS *gingerly puts the revolver in her apron pocket, then helps* SABINA. SABINA *has found a rope hanging from the ceiling. Grunting, she hangs all her weight on it, and as she pulls the walls begin to move into their right places.* MRS. ANTROBUS *brings the overturned tables, chairs and hassock into the positions of Act I.*

SABINA:

That's all we do—always beginning again! Over and over again. Always beginning again.

She pulls on the rope and a part of the wall mores into place. She stops, Meditatively:

How do we know that it'll be any better than before? Why do we go on pretending? Some day the whole earth's going to have to turn cold anyway, and until that time all these other things'll be happening, again: it will be more wars and more walls of ice and floods and earthquakes.

MRS. ANTROBUS:

Sabina!! Stop arguing and go on with your work.

SABINA:

All right I'll go on just out of habit, but I won't believe in it.

MRS. ANTROBUS:

Aroused.

Now, Sabina. I've let you talk long enough. I don't want to hear any more of it. Do I have to explain to you what everybody knows,—everybody who keeps a home going? Do I have to say to you what nobody should ever have to say, because they can read it in each other's eyes?

Now listen to me;

MRS. ANTROBUS *takes hold of the rope.*

I could live for seventy years in a cellar and make soup out of grass and bark, without ever doubting that this world has a work to do and will do it.

Do you hear me?

SABINA:

Frightened.

Yes, Mrs. Antrobus.

MRS. ANTROBUS:

Sabina, do you see this house,—216 Cedar Street,—do you see it?

SABINA:

Yes, Mrs. Antrobus.

MRS. ANTROBUS:

Well, just to have known this house is to have seen the idea of what we can do someday if we keep our wits about us. Too many people have suffered and died for my children for us to start reneging now. So we'll start putting this house to rights. Now, Sabina, go and see what you can do in the kitchen.

SABINA:

Kitchen! Why is it that however far I go away, I always find myself back in the kitchen?

Exit.

MRS. ANTROBUS:

Still thinking over her last speech, relaxes and says with a reminiscent smile:

Goodness gracious, wouldn't you know that my father was a parson? It was just like I heard his own voice speaking and he's been dead five thousand years. There! I've gone and almost waked Henry up.

HENRY:

Talking in his sleep, indistinctly.

Fellows . . . what have they done for us? . . . Blocked our way at every step. Kept everything in their own hands. And you've stood it. When are you going to wake up?

MRS. ANTROBUS:

Sh, Henry. Go to sleep. Go to sleep. Go to sleep.—Well, that looks better. Now let's go and help Sabina.

GLADYS:

Mama, I'm going out into the backyard and hold the baby right up in the air. And show him that we don't have to be afraid any more.

Exit GLADYS *to the kitchen.*

MRS. ANTROBUS *glances at* HENRY, *EXITS INTO KITCHEN.* HENRY *thrashes about in his sleep. Enter* ANTROBUS, *his arms full of bundles, chewing the end of a carrot. He has a slight limp. Over the suit of Act I he is wearing an overcoat too long for him, its skirts trailing on the ground. He lets his bundles fall and stands looking about. Presently his attention is fixed on* HENRY, *whose words grow clearer.*

HENRY:

All right! What have you got to lose? What have they done for us? That's right—nothing. Tear everything down. I don't care what you smash. We'll begin again and we'll show 'em.

ANTROBUS *takes out his revolver and holds it pointing downwards. With his back towards the audience he moves toward the footlights.*

HENRY*'s voice grows louder and he wakes with a start. They stare at one another. Then* HENRY *sits up quickly.*

Throughout the following scene HENRY *is played, not as a misunderstood or misguided young man, but as a representation of strong unreconciled evil.*

All right! Do something.

Pause.

Don't think I'm afraid of you, either. All right, do what you were going to do. Do it.

Furiously.

Shoot me, I tell you. You don't have to think I'm any relation of yours. I haven't got any father or any mother, or brothers or sisters. And I don't want any. And what's more I haven't got anybody over me; and I never will have. I'm alone, and that's all I want to be: alone. So you can shoot me.

ANTROBUS:
You're the last person I wanted to see. The sight of you dries up all my plans and hopes. I wish I were back at war still, because it's easier to fight you than to live with you. War's a pleasure—do you hear me?—War's a pleasure compared to what faces us now: trying to build up a peacetime with you in the middle of it.

ANTROBUS *walks up to the window.*

HENRY:
I'm not going to be a part of any peacetime of yours. I'm going a long way from here and make my own world that's fit for a man to live in. Where a man can be free, and have a chance, and do what he wants to do in his own way.

ANTROBUS:
His attention arrested; thoughtfully. He throws the gum out of the window and turns with hope.

. . . Henry, let's try again.

HENRY:
Try what? Living here?—Speaking polite downtown to all the old men like you? Standing like a sheep at the street corner until the red light turns to green? Being a good boy and a good sheep, like all the stinking ideas you get out of your books? Oh, no. I'll make a world, and I'll show you.

ANTROBUS:
Hard.

How can you make a world for people to live in, unless you've first put order in yourself? Mark my words: I shall continue fighting you until my last breath as long as you mix up your idea of liberty with your idea of hogging everything for yourself. I shall have no pity on you. I shall pursue you to the far corners of the earth. You and I want the same thing; but until you think of it as something that everyone has a right to, you are my deadly enemy and I will destroy you.—I hear your mother's voice in the kitchen. Have you seen her?

HENRY:
I have no mother. Get it into your head. I don't belong here. I have nothing to do here. I have no home.

ANTROBUS:
Then why did you come here? With the whole world to choose from, why did you come to this one place: 216 Cedar Street, Excelsior, New Jersey. . . . Well?

HENRY:
What if I did? What if I wanted to look at it once more, to see if—

ANTROBUS:
Oh, you're related, all right—When your mother comes in you must behave yourself. Do you hear me?

HENRY
Wildly.

What is this—must behave yourself. Don't you say must to me.

ANTROBUS:
Quiet!

Enter MRS. ANTROBUS *and* SABINA.

HENRY:
Nobody can say must to me. All my life everybody's been crossing me—everybody, everything, all of you. I'm going to be free, even if I have to kill half the world for it. Right now, too. Let me get my hands on his throat. I'll show him.

He advances toward ANTROBUS. *Suddenly,* SABINA *jumps between them and calls out in her own person:*

SABINA:
Stop! Stop! Don't play this scene. You know what happened last night. Stop the play.

The men fall back, panting. HENRY *covers his face with his hands.*

Last night you almost strangled him. You became a regular savage. Stop it!

HENRY:
It's true. I'm sorry. I don't know what comes over me. I have nothing against him personally. I respect him very much . . . I . . . I admire him. But something comes over

me. It's like I become fifteen years old again. I . . . I . . . listen: my own father used to whip me and lock me up every Saturday night. I never had enough to eat. He never let me have enough money to buy decent clothes. I was ashamed to go downtown. I never could go to the dances. My father and my uncle put rules in the way of everything I wanted to do. They tried to prevent my living at all.—I'm sorry. I'm sorry.

MRS. ANTROBUS:
Quickly.

No, go on. Finish what you were saying. Say it all.

HENRY:
In this scene it's as though I were back in High School again. It's like I had some big emptiness inside me,—the emptiness of being hated and blocked at every turn. And the emptiness fills up with the one thought that you have to strike and fight and kill. Listen, it's as though you have to kill somebody else so as not to end up killing yourself.

SABINA:
That's not true. I knew your father and your uncle and your mother. You imagined all that. Why, they did everything they could for you. How can you say things like that? They didn't lock you up.

HENRY:
They did. They did. They wished I hadn't been born.

SABINA:
That's not true,

ANTROBUS:
In his own person, with self-condemnation, but cold and proud.

Wait a minute. I have something to say, too. It's not wholly his fault that he wants to strangle me in this scene. It's my fault, too. He wouldn't feel that way unless there were something in me that reminded him of all that. He talks about an emptiness. Well, there's an emptiness in me, too. Yes,—work, work, work,—that's all I do. I've ceased to live. No wonder he feels that anger coming over him.

MRS. ANTROBUS:
There! At least you've said it.

SABINA:
We're all just as wicked as we can be, and that's the God's truth.

MRS. ANTROBUS:
Nods a moment, then comes forward; quietly:

Come. Come and put your head under some cold water.

SABINA:
In a whisper.

I'll go with him. I've known him a long while. You have to go on with the play. Come with me.

HENRY *starts out with* SABINA, *but turns at the exit and says to* ANTROBUS:

HENRY:
Thanks. Thanks for what you said. I'll be all right tomorrow. I won't lose control in that place. I promise. *Exeunt* HENRY *and* SABINA.

ANTROBUS *starts toward the front door, fastens it.*

MRS. ANTROBUS: *goes up stage and places the chair dose to table.*

MRS. ANTROBUS:
George, do I see you limping?

ANTROBUS:
Yes, a little. My old wound from the other war started smarting again. I can manage.

MRS. ANTROBUS:
Looking out of the window.

Some lights are coming on,—the first in seven years. People are walking up and down looking at them. Over in Hawkins' open lot they've built a bonfire to celebrate the peace. They're dancing around it like scarecrows.

ANTROBUS:
A bonfire! As though they hadn't seen enough things burning.—Maggie,—the dog died?

MRS. ANTROBUS:
Oh, yes. Long ago. There are no dogs left in Excelsior.—You're back again! All these years. I gave up counting on letters. The few that arrived were anywhere from six months to a year late.

ANTROBUS:
Yes, the ocean's full of letters, along with the other things.

MRS. ANTROBUS:
George, sit down, you're tired.

ANTROBUS:
No, you sit down. I'm tired but I'm restless.

Suddenly, as she comes forward:

Maggie! I've lost it. I've lost it.

MRS. ANTROBUS:
What, George? What have you lost?

ANTROBUS:
The most important thing of all: The desire to begin again, to start building.

MRS. ANTROBUS:
Sitting in the chair right of the table.

Well, it will come back.

ANTROBUS:
At the window.

I've lost it. This minute I feel like all those people dancing around the bonfire—just relief. Just the desire to settle down; to slip into the old grooves and keep the neighbors from walking over my lawn.—Hm. But during the war,—in the middle of all that blood and dirt and hot and cold-every day and night, I'd have moments, Maggie, when I *saw* the things that we could do when it was over. When you're at war you think about a better life; when you're at peace you think about a more comfortable one. I've lost it. I feel sick and tired.

MRS. ANTROBUS:
Listen! The baby's crying.

I hear Gladys talking. Probably she's quieting Henry again.

George, while Gladys and I were living here—like moles, like rats, and when we were at our wits' end to save the baby's life—the only thought we clung to was that you were going to bring something good out of this suffering. In the night, in the dark, we'd whisper about it, starving and sick.—Oh, George, you'll have to get it back again. Think! What else kept us alive all these years? Even now, it's not comfort we want. We can suffer whatever's necessary; only give us back that promise.

Enter SABINA *with a lighted lamp. She is dressed as in Act I.*

SABINA:
Mrs. Antrobus . . .

MRS. ANTROBUS:
Yes, Sabina?

SABINA:
Will you need me?

MRS. ANTROBUS:
No, Sabina, you can go to bed.

SABINA:
Mrs. Antrobus, if it's all right with you, I'd like to go to the bonfire and celebrate seeing the war's over. And, Mrs. Antrobus, they've opened the Gem Movie Theatre and they're giving away a hand-painted soup tureen to every lady, and I thought one of us ought to go.

ANTROBUS:
Well, Sabina, I haven't any money. I haven't seen any money for quite a while.

SABINA:
Oh, you don't need money. They're taking anything you can give them. And I have some . . . some . . . Mrs. Antrobus, promise you won't tell anyone. It's a little against the law. But I'll give you some, too.

ANTROBUS:
What is it?

SABINA:
I'll give you some, too. Yesterday I picked up a lot of . . . of beef-cubes!

MRS. ANTROBUS *turns and says calmly:*

MRS. ANTROBUS:
But, Sabina, you know you ought to give that in to the Center downtown. They know who needs them most.

SABINA:
Outburst.

Mrs. Antrobus, I didn't make this war, I didn't ask for it. And, in my opinion, after anybody's gone through what we've gone through, they have a right to grab what they can find. You're a very nice man, Mr. Antrobus, but you'd have got on better in the world if you'd realized that dog-eat-dog was the rule in the beginning and always will be. And most of all now.

In tears.

Oh, the world's an awful place, and you know it is. I used to think something could be done about it; but I know better now. I hate it. I hate it.

She comes forward slowly and brings six cubes from the bag.

All right. All right. You can have them.

ANTROBUS:
Thank you, Sabina.

SABINA:
Can I have . . . can I have one to go to the movies?

ANTROBUS *in silence gives her one.*

Thank you.

ANTROBUS:
Good night, Sabina.

SABINA:
Mr. Antrobus, don't mind what I say. I'm just an ordinary girl, you know what I mean, I'm just an ordinary girl.

But you're a bright man, you're a very bright man, and of course you invented the alphabet and the wheel, and, my God, a lot of things . . . and if you've got any other plans, my God, don't let me upset them. Only every now and then I've got to go the movies. I mean my nerves can't stand it. But if you have any ideas about improving the crazy old world, I'm really with you. I really am. Because it's . . . it's . . . Good night.

She goes out. ANTROBUS *starts laughing softly with exhilaration.*

ANTROBUS:
Now I remember what three things always went together when I was able to see things most clearly: three things. Three things:

He points to where SABINA *has gone out.*

The voice of the people in their confusion and their need. And the thought of you and the children and this house. And . . . Maggie! I didn't dare ask you: my books! They haven't been lost, have they?

MRS. ANTROBUS:
No. There are some of them right here. Kind of tattered.

ANTROBUS:
Yes.—Remember, Maggie, we almost lost them once before? And when we finally did collect a few torn copies out of old cellars they ran in everyone's head like a fever. They as good as rebuilt the world.

Pauses, book in hand, and looks up.

Oh, I've never forgotten for long at a time that living is struggle. I know that every good and excellent thing in the world stands moment by moment on the razor-edge of danger and must be fought for—whether it's field, or a home, or a country. All I ask is the chance to build new worlds and God has always given us that. And has given us

Opening the book

voices to guide us; and the memory of our mistakes to warn us. Maggie, you and I will remember in peacetime all the resolves that were so clear to us in the days of war. We've come a long ways. We've learned. We're learning. And the steps of our journey are marked for us here.

He stands by the table turning the leaves of a book.

Sometimes out there in the war,—standing all night on a hill—I'd try and remember some of the words in these books. Parts of them and phrases would come back to me. And after a while I used to give names to the hours of the night.

He sits, hunting far a passage in the book.

Nine o'clock I used to call Spinoza, Where is it: "After experience had taught me—"

The back wall has disappeared, revealing the platform. FRED BAILEY *carrying his numeral has started from left to right.* MRS. ANTROBUS *sits by the table sewing.*

BAILEY:
"After experience had taught me that the common occurrences of daily life are vain and futile; and I saw that all the objects of my desire and fear were in themselves nothing good nor bad save insofar as the mind was affected by them; I at length determined to search out whether there was something truly good and communicable to man."

Almost without break HESTER, *carrying a large Roman numeral ten, starts crossing the platform.* GLADYS *appears at the kitchen door and moves towards her mother's chair.*

HESTER:
"Then tell me, O Critias, how will a man choose the ruler that shall rule over him? Will he not choose a man who has first established order in himself, knowing that any decision that has its spring from anger or pride or vanity can be multiplied a thousand fold in its effects upon the citizens?"

HESTER *disappears and* IVY, *as eleven o'clock starts speaking.*

IVY:
"This good estate of the mind possessing its object in energy we call divine. This we mortals have occasionally and it is this energy which is pleasantest and best. But God has it always. It is wonderful in us; but in Him how much more wonderful."

As MR. TREMAYNE *starts to speak,* HENRY *appears at the edge of the scene, brooding and unreconciled, but present.*

TREMAYNE:
"In the beginning, God created the Heavens and the earth; And the Earth was waste and void; And the darkness was upon the face of the deep. And the Lord said let there be light and there was light."

Sudden black-out and silence, except for the last strokes of the midnight bell. Then just as suddenly the lights go up, and SABINA *is standing at the window, as at the opening of the play.*

SABINA:

Oh, oh, oh. Six o'clock and the master not home yet. Pray God nothing serious has happened to him crossing the Hudson River. But I wouldn't be surprised. The whole world's at sixes and sevens, and why the house hasn't fallen down about our ears long ago is a miracle to me.

She comes down to the footlights.

This is where you came in. We have to go on for ages and ages yet.

You go home.

The end of this play isn't written yet.

Mr. and Mrs. Antrobus! Their heads are full of plans and they're as confident as the first day they began,—and they told me to tell you: good night.

20. *Watch on the Rhine*—Lillian Hellman

Commentary

Sources

Play

20.1 HARDSCRABBLE FARM AND *WATCH ON THE RHINE*—RICHARD MOODY

IN EARLY MARCH, 1939, with *Foxes* settled into its long run and with the text published, dedicated to Arthur Kober and Louis Kronenberger, "who have been my good friends," Miss Hellman deserted New York for an isolated village in Cuba. She needed a rest and time to contemplate what had been happening in the world while she had been occupied in the theatre. She could not know, as she said later, that this was to be "the holocaust year of the century," yet she knew from what she had seen in Spain and in Western Europe that "the hurricane was somewhere off the coast and death around the corner." And though there was always a bit of "shame and sorrow at the Liberal's impotence in the face of the hurricane," she ought to become as involved as her friends. Hammett wrote on March 10, 1939, praising Dottie Parker's piece in the *Masses*, and announcing that he was "going to get up and type a long letter to Herbert Biberman on the State of the Nation and how to keep from viewing the future through rose colored testacles [sic]."

Back in New York, late in the spring, she determined to escape the turmoil of the city. She was not by nature an activist or a joiner, and the city was seething with worthy enterprises soliciting her membership and support. Political teamplay was not her meat. In late May, she did, however, moderate a discussion of contemporary problems and the problems of the dramatist, part of the New School's Third American Writers' Congress.

If nature had not prepared her for political involvement, strangely it had prepared her to delight in the 130-acre New York farm she bought in May. On Hardscrabble Road, midway between Pleasantville, Chappaqua, and Briarcliff (between the Saw Mill River and Bronx River Parkways), the farm, half woodland, half open fields, had an eight-acre spring-fed lake, a spacious main residence surrounded by a screen porch, a six-room caretaker's cottage, two guest houses, barns, poultry houses, a stable, rock gardens, orchards, vegetable gardens, and grape arbors. "Hardscrabble Farm," as it was called, provided a happy home for the next thirteen years and the workroom in which her next five plays were written. Her days on the farm were the best of her life, reviving misused land, raising poultry, hunting, trapping turtles, and fishing—Shumlin insisted that "she knew what every goddam fish was planning at the other end of the line"—swimming and tennis, afternoons in the kitchen preparing crab gumbo, turtle soup, or some other New Orleans specialty. She delighted in good food and had once even thought of opening a restaurant. The house was constantly filled with visitors, particularly men, all of whom appeared to have been in love with her at one time or another. They sought her friendship, her artistic and business advice. The happiest years with Hammett were at Hardscrabble, though he was not always there. During the war, he was in the army, having enlisted as a private, and after the war his heavy drinking often became intolerable.

In spite of the relaxed and often zany atmosphere at the farm, she worked well there, as did a number of her guests. Normally she spent three hours at her typewriter in the morning, two to three hours in the afternoon, and again from ten at night until one or two in the morning. When too many helpful guests began invading her sanctuary, she tried writing longhand in bed, but when that didn't work, she posted a warning on her door:

This Room is Used for Work
Do Not Enter Without Knocking
After You Knock, Wait for an Answer
If you get no Answer, go Away and
Don't Come Back
This Means Everybody
This Means You
This Means Night or Day

By Order of the Hellman-Military-Commission-for-Playwrights. Court Martialling Will Take Place in the Barn, and Your Trial Will Not be a Fair One.

The Christmas Court-Martialling Has Now Taken Place! Among those:

Herman Shumlin, former *regisseur.*
Miss Sylvia Hermann, aged three, former daughter of a farmer.
Miss Nora, former dog.
Mr. Samuel Dashiell Hammett, former eccentric.
Mr. Arthur Kober, former itinerant sweet-singer.
Mr. Louis Kronenberger, born in Cincinnati, lynched by me.
Emmy Kronenberger, wife to Kronenberger, died with him.
Mr. Felix Anderson, former butler.
Irene Robinson, former cook and very pretty.

Note: Mr. Max Bernard Hellman, father, is a most constant offender. His age has saved him. This sentimentality may not continue.

Being a Southerner she never much liked fall and winter, but in the spring, "I am like an idiot four-year-old," she once said. "I go around making noises which indicate great contentment with nature. I am in the garden all the time and I get in the way of everyone who is trying to work. I put out seeds on Monday and, one friend says, on Wednesday if plants haven't come up I go out and reseed the whole plot."

From 1939 to 1952, Hardscrabble was home base, and except for brief excursions, she stayed at home base. She lost the farm in 1952, "because," as she later explained, "the hi-jinks of Senator McCarthy and his rivals in the House UnAmerican Activities Committee made it impossible for me to keep it."

On January 10, 1940, she joined Lin Yutang and Edna Ferber as one of the speakers at the Book and Author Luncheon at the Hotel Astor. She welcomed the opportunity to speak her feelings about what was happening in the world: "I am a writer and also a Jew. I want to be sure I can continue to say what I wish without being branded by the malice of people making a living by that malice."

In June she went to the Republican convention in Philadelphia for *PM.* She had been involved with Ralph Ingersoll's paper from the beginning, had suggested the name, and had bought a small share in the enterprise. Her piece, "The Little Men in Philadelphia" (June 25, 1940) did not cover the convention proceedings. After attending a news conference with Senator Vandenburg where "the questions and answers boiled down to simple unspoken cynicism; deals will be arranged and a candidate will be chosen," she roamed about the city talking with a cab driver, two storekeepers, a shoeshine boy and a watermelon boy. None of them would speak out. When you had to earn a living, it was better not to talk politics, it was "not smart to have ideas." She was grieved that "uptown the party of Abraham Lincoln is making deals in a city in which at least three white men and two black men are too suspicious and too tired and too frightened to exercise their primary right of free and easy speech. And I thought that Lincoln might not like that."

She took a brief turn in Hollywood with *The Little Foxes*, "added dialogue by Dorothy Parker, Arthur Kober, and Alan Campbell." According to Kober, their contribution was insignificant, and he preferred to have his name omitted, but Alan Campbell was "a little guy who needed the credit," so the three names appeared. Most of the original text was retained but the action moved out of the house and around the town, with scenes at the bank and at the railroad station. A touching love story was added, with Alexandra and David Hewitt, a handsome young newspaper man. This and the deletion of Regina's references to Horace's fancy women were the only concessions to Hollywood. Produced by Goldwyn, directed by Wyler, with Bette Davis (Regina), Herbert Marshall (Horace), and Teresa Wright (Alexandra), and with the original Hubbard family—Patricia Collinge (Birdie), Dan Duryea (Leo), Charles Dingle (Ben), and Carl Benton Reid (Oscar)—it opened at Radio City Music Hall on August 21, 1941. If some saw shades of nineteenth-century melodrama in *Foxes*, the full program at the Music Hall was like a nineteenth-century hodgepodge evening in the theatre. The Hubbard saga was augmented with a stage show dedicated to the U.S.O., an Hawaiian fantasy featuring "The Cockeyed Mayor of Kaunakaykai," the Rockettes in navy white, swinging a mean hornpipe. Apparently ukuleles and hulas did not reduce the power of the film. The *Times* (August 22, 1941) called it "the most bitingly sinister picture of the year," Bette Davis at "her brittle best, playing one of those Borgias with a cut-glass brilliance, a serene cupidity, a frightening frigidity."

Londoners saw the film of *Foxes* before they saw the play, and when Fay Compton attempted Regina at the Piccadilly Theatre in late October, 1942, the critics found her an inadequate substitute for Bette Davis. She was too much the stock villainess, lacking in Southern charm. Although Emlyn Williams, the director, had not shaped as convincing a family for *Foxes* as he had for *Watch on the Rhine* the previous May (*Watch* opened in London before *Foxes*), one critic advised "those who think the Archbishop of Canterbury goes too far in criticizing the profit-motive in industry should go see it."

Before her brief interlude in Hollywood, she was already well into her next play. Painfully conscious of the rising fury of the hurricane off the coast and the social ills corrupting life at home, she knew she had to use her strong voice in the theatre to shake her audience from their apathy. She returned to the idea of the titled European couple stranded in a midwestern home. She also thought of dramatizing Zola's *Germinal*. Out of its gruesome scenes in the coal mines, its passionate cry for social reform, she might fashion a proletarian documentary to block out the memory of *Days to Come*. This project was abandoned.

Hammett had been instructing her in his own brand of Marxism, beliefs deeply grounded with him, but her irrepressible skepticism never permitted her to subscribe without her fingers crossed. And in 1940 the Hitler hurricane seemed so much more threatening than economic injustice.

The Nazi atrocities, the rumblings of the *Wehrmacht*, the nightmarish horrors of Spain so fiercely remembered, even the dimmer memories, now revived, of Hitler's fair-haired youth first learning their ghastly games, commanded her to raise the danger signals. Smugness, business as usual, the great Atlantic were puny barriers against the Fascist menace.

Knowing what she wanted to say was easier than finding the means. She was not a shouter, though Dorothy Parker once remarked, "When Lillian gets mad, I regret to say she screams." She could not write a screaming play. For her the stage was not a soapbox; she was not a preacher, a propagandist. The play came first; the moral message must be bound to the play.

As with *Foxes*, *Watch on the Rhine* evolved from extensive research: digests of some twenty-five books, pages of preliminary notes, and a series of carefully improved drafts. Although at times she questioned the necessity for so much research, she once said that "I seem to have to do it to be sure I know what I'm talking about."

Her notebook contained lists of possible names: Kabler, Fogler, etc. Items to be checked: "Hamburg speech was '36 or '37?" "Spain during Carlist trouble: Verify." Phrases and words to give the authentic German flavor: "Ten years before (not ago) today." "Depart instead of leave." "I will accompany you." "Not quite very well." "So?" "No?" "Give me fire instead of give me light." A skeletal scenario: "Act One—Anise with mail. Joseph on terrace with breakfast/ Fanny comes down/ David and Marthe/ Teck—Marthe/ All of family/ Sara, David, family; Marthe—Teck/ Maybe Teck and Kurt do not meet until last of act." In another part of the book, Miss Hellman recorded notes for doctoring an early draft: "Say date of play. Anise should not say Balkan nobility. Possible confusion on Emily, who she is. David says 'Mama' too often." Then, "In general: Feel more Sara's coming. 'I'm very excited'—show excitement rather than tell about it. Mention Sara's name more in 1st part. Go back for Bodo's misuse of words." She searched for the means to let the characters show themselves.

On the two earliest drafts, she noted that "Play No. 5" (she was still counting *Dear Queen*) was "started about August 15th [1939] and finished December 27th [1940]," though with two more typed drafts, it was not finally mimeographed for the actors until mid-February, 1941. Even at the earliest stages, she retained only a small part of her original idea, European nobility thrown into an American household. She moved the setting from the Midwest to Washington, DC, made the Europeans villainous, and centered on an heroic anti-Fascist battling for his life, for his family, and above all for freedom.

Apparently there were other notebooks, now misplaced or lost. Miss Hellman showed Margaret Case Harriman (reported in *The New Yorker*, November 8, 1941) "two or three volumes" of 400 to 500 typed, single-spaced pages each with data on contemporary history, local customs, political events, and with long lists of names and biographical sketches of the characters before their appearance in the play. Such notes appeared as "What was he doing in Germany? Scientist? Trade Union Movement? Maybe China? What was going on 1920–1932? Maybe they have only been here about six months? What was he doing here?" As with the *Foxes* research, a detailed history of the period could be written from her notes.

The action begins in the luxurious living room of the Farrelly mansion some twenty miles from Washington on a warm spring morning in 1940. "Four or five generations have furnished this room." Wealth, elegance, and family continuity are immediately evident, and in contrast to the other plays, the scene is contemporary. The morning routine is underway. Anise, the French housekeeper, is sorting mail; Joseph, the handsome Negro butler, is fussing over the breakfast wagon; and Fanny Farrelly, clearly the commanding matron, appears in an elegant dressing gown and orders Joseph to ring the bell. David is not yet down, and he's scheduled to meet the train. Joseph must push the clock ahead and ring the bell; Fanny likes to disturb folks. The first brush strokes on Fanny's portrait reveal another of Miss Hellman's self-assured, strong-minded, and strong-willed females.

As Fanny thumbs through the mail, anxiously asking the time every few minutes, the identity of the expected arrivals is gradually revealed: Miss Sara, a daughter who's not been home in twenty years, is bringing a husband *and* grandchildren. (How much more dramatic anticipation in this opening than in Miss Hellman's first draft with Sara and her family on stage at the opening curtain and with Fanny still asleep!) The stack of mail provides the spark for more family details. Fanny was deeply in love with her husband, Joshua, whose portrait is on the wall. She could not have looked at another man as Birdie Chase's daughter has done. There are legal advertisements for David, invitations to lower-class embassy teas and bills for the count and countess, "the Balkan nobility" who have camped with them for the past six weeks, and a night letter from some woman in Lansing who is pursuing David. Through all this, Joseph has been furiously sounding the bell and now announces that "the sausage cakes is shrinking."

The bell and Fanny's commanding shriek have brought David down. Mother and son greet each other warmly, though David is irritated by the "air-raid alarm." He'll convert the chickenhouse into a playroom, hung with bells, "and you can go into your second childhood in proper privacy." Marthe de Brancovis appears, though not before we learn that David has been flirting with her and that "the Balkans" have been tolerated because her husband, Teck, plays cribbage with Fanny and tells good jokes. Fanny is concerned about accommodating them and the new arrivals.

When Marthe comes in, Fanny adjourns to the terrace for breakfast after informing David, in Marthe's hearing, about the night letter from the Carter woman. She makes her point. Marthe's jealousy is aroused. (In the first versions of the play the affair between Marthe and David—his name was then Gil—received more attention. David had a wife, Emily, who figured prominently and who harbored an intense jealousy. With David unmarried, Fanny has assumed Emily's jealousy. When Miss Hellman abandons characters, she reassigns their attributes.)

David's mind is on Sara and her husband, whom he's never seen. We sense that two sets of refugees, different classes of refugees, are going to disrupt the Farrelly establishment. In this first encounter we grasp little about the involvement of David and Marthe. They first met as children, when David's father was stationed in Paris. We're eager to learn more, when Teck appears. Miss Hellman frequently tantalizes us with such interruptions.

Teck is a good-looking man, continentally slick and smooth, another of Hellman's handsome people. Again the breakfast bell signals Fanny's impatience and helps to clear the stage. As David joins her, Teck and Marthe reveal their situation. Although the "countess" title has worked magic in extending their credit, they are badly in debt and have only $87 in American Express checks. They know something of Sara's husband. He's poor, an engineer, an anti-Nazi, and he left Germany in 1933. They don't know if he is a Jew. Teck has connections with the German Embassy, and in spite of his shaky finances, he still gambles there.

(Miss Hellman was fascinated with gamblers and gambling and with playing for high stakes. One night she won $21,000 at chemin de fer and the next morning ordered two ambulances for the Spanish Loyalists. When she lost $19,000 the next night, she did not cancel the order. In Hollywood she was a regular at the Clover Club. In 1937, Hammett reported that the club was about to abandon chemin de fer when she left town. Although she had arrived too late on the Broadway scene to join the Thanatopsis Inside Straight Club which Heywood Broun, F. P. Adams, Alexander Woollcott, the Marx Brothers, Russel Crouse, and the Gershwins made into one of Broadway's noisiest legends, a later club, with some of the same participants, welcomed her to membership. Morrie Ryskind once commented that he was saddened over the low estate of the arts when he found her on the floor shooting dice. She was also an ardent bridge player. Arthur Kober recalls that during the early days of their marriage, he frequently retired while she was still at the table. One time she was invited to a supper party at a London home. "No sooner was dinner ended," she reported, "than I found myself $700 out of pocket in one of the weirdest crookedest poker games in history." She recouped part of her loss by using her London host—he was "a glamorous aristocrat," and not English—as a model for her portrait of Teck de Brancovis.)

Teck and Marthe are precariously at odds with each other. She distrusts the Nazis and knows that if he should lose when gambling at the Embassy, they would be driven out of the country. The risk does not trouble him; he trusts his skill. He is more disturbed by Marthe's flirtation with their host. For the moment they must maintain their composure and not imperil their comfortable and inexpensive quarters; they join the breakfast table on the terrace. We know, better than the Farrellys, how dangerous this pair could be.

The stage is empty only for a moment before Fanny's plans and our expectancy are dramatically disrupted. Sara Müller and her family march in. Dowdy yet neat, they look like immigrants, each carrying his assigned share of the shabby luggage. Sara and Kurt are sturdy, handsome, and serious. The children are stiff, too heavily dressed, and anxious to behave properly. Joshua, fourteen, named for his grandfather, is the platoon leader. Babette, twelve, fusses over her mother's clothes—she wants her to look her best. Bodo, nine, is the talker, undisturbed that he does not yet command the language; he can always shift to German or French. The children are astounded that they're permitted to sit on the couch, that the door was unlocked. Sara is overjoyed to have her family together in a place like this, though she finds it hard to say so without seeming to be critical of her husband. He understands: "You must enjoy your house, and not be afraid that you hurt me with it. Yes?" Miss Hellman has a good ear.

Anise is the first to discover them, to learn that the later train was too expensive. She calls to the terrace. Fanny's embrace is warm and motherly, her welcome to Kurt straight-forward and honest, no hint that she might have disapproved of him earlier. As the children are introduced, they bow politely. Fanny wonders, as we have, if they are children or "dressed up midgets." No offense intended, and none taken. Fanny informs Sara about the "titled folk." The countess is the former Hortie Randolph—Sara remembers her. The Müller family is adjusting to their new surroundings. Bodo continues chattering, Joshua and Babette laugh when Fanny puts him down: "If you grow up to talk like that, and stay as ugly as you are, you are going to have one of those successful careers on the lecture platform."

After Anise has taken the children to wash for breakfast, Fanny admits that she likes Kurt; her first impression was wrong. She'll remodel the house, and they'll all live together; David has already made inquiries about an engineering job for Kurt. Kurt explains that he's not been an engineer since 1933. He is an anti-Fascist, "and that does not pay well." Sara explains that times have been rough, yet they've lived as they wanted to live: "I don't know the language of rooms like this any more. And I don't want to learn it again." In Germany, Kurt explains, he has gone to work and come home every night; they were as happy as people could be in a starved country that was going to pieces, until 1931, when he saw twenty-seven men murdered in a Nazi street fight. That was the turning point: "I say with Luther, 'Here I stand. I can do nothing else. God help me. Amen.'" Now they've been forced out of Germany for their own safety, but they have not given up the fight.

When the play opened in April, 1941, it carried the blazing effect of a front-page headline. It was just a year after the invasion of Norway and Denmark, less than a year after Hitler had overrun Holland and Belgium, the British had been driven to the beaches at Dunkerque, and France had fallen. Britain was now struggling for its life against the German Luftwaffe; within three months the Nazis would invade Russia. Hitler had never appeared more monstrous and invincible, and those who fought against him more noble, particularly the underground fighters who risked themselves and their families. Kurt Müdler's charismatic command over the audience in 1941 cannot be overestimated.

In the first version of the play, Kurt's activities were more explicitly detailed. He had led a brigade in Spain; his eldest son, then nineteen, had been killed by his side, "fighting for the people." Kurt has been a member of the anti-Nazi underground, "trying to teach the working mass of the German people." One of their closest friends, the night before he was executed, had smuggled out one thousand pieces of paper on which he had written, "Come and see an anti-Nazi die." The Müllers have lived from hand to mouth all over Europe, most recently in Paris, and then in Mexico before entering the United States without a visa. And all over the world he'd discovered that it was "fashionable to be an anti-Fascist, as long as you do it fashionably." By the final version Miss Hellman had eliminated the eldest son, unburdened the play of the revolutionary specifics, and deleted the allusion to the fashionable liberals.

With the political background established, and more compactly than in the early drafts, David and Sara go to the garden to revive their childhood memories, and Kurt is left to face the "Balkan nobility," with some help from Bodo. Bodo is awed by the "splendorous arrangement of the house, the magnificence and sanitary quality of the plumbing," but not impressed with Teck and Marthe; he's met poor counts and countesses before. Teck and Kurt study each other and spar about their accents, wondering if they've met. Kurt breaks the tension. Looking up at the portrait of Joshua, he recites a passage that Joshua once wrote about breakfast on the terrace. This is for Fanny's benefit, and even when he admits that he memorized it the night before, she is pleased. Kurt has won our hearts and Fanny's. He is honest, unpretentious, loving toward his wife and children, and courageously dedicated to the fight against Fascism.

With the family at breakfast, Teck and Marthe speculate on the Müllers. Teck has sharp eyes, sharper than ours. He's seen the bullet scars on Kurt's face, the broken bones in his hands, and fingering the luggage, wonders why such a beat-up brief case should be locked. He could make inquiries at the Embassy, but he hesitates to "ask questions without knowing the value of the answers." When Joseph conveniently appears in the hall, Teck orders him to carry the baggage upstairs. It will be "more comfortable to look at behind closed doors." Teck is a cool, calculating con man in the old tradition, and we sense that Marthe's plea to "leave these people alone" will be ignored. As Teck follows Joseph, we know that Kurt is not safe, even in his mother-in-law's home. This detective-story close to Act I came late in the play's evolution. Originally the act ended with Teck telephoning a Baron Phillip Von Erner to inquire if he knew a Kurt Müller. The present ending is more chilling.

Quickly, yet naturally, a series of threatening questions have unfolded. What will Teck find in the brief case, how will he pursue Kurt, how will Kurt fight back? Will Teck's jealousy, or even Fanny's, shatter the affair between Marthe and David? Can an heroic anti-Fascist survive, even in a free country? These questions are not simply detective questions. Each is enriched with human consequences. Miss Hellman has made us care about what happens to these people.

When the second act opens, the Müllers have adjusted to the new household. Sara is crocheting, Bodo is repairing Anise's heating pad, Joshua is outside with Joseph learning baseball, Fanny and Teck are at cribbage. David, Marthe, Kurt, and, for a moment, Babette are missing. Political conversation appears to have been outlawed, but they skirt the edges. Bodo cannot understand why comfort and plenty exist for some and not for all. Teck probes for more information about Kurt. Did he stay close to the German border because he thought National Socialism would collapse? Sara hopes that day will come; Teck does not. If he thinks that, Joshua wonders if Teck doesn't find it "most difficult to sleep." Sara shuts him up in German and apologizes to Teck. She can no longer tolerate polite politics: "By this time all of us must know where we are and what we have to do. It's an indulgence to sit in a room and discuss your beliefs as if they were a juicy piece of gossip." Babette breaks the tension, running on from the kitchen with a potato pancake she's been cooking. Again Miss Hellman has broken in. The questions are left to simmer under the surface.

Within a few days Teck proposes to collect his $85 cribbage winnings from Fanny and depart. There are too many refugees in the house; no doubt the Müllers will also be moving on. Teck cannot avoid his inquisitorial probing. Fanny corrects him. The Müllers will not ever be leaving. They've come home to see her die and that will take time. "I shall do a fine death. I intend to be a great deal of trouble to everybody. . . . I shall take to my bed early and stay for years. In great pain." Anise is reminded of an earlier exhibition. When Fanny was pregnant with Sara, she began her labor in the middle of a dinner ball for 200 guests, apparently induced by her husband's dancing two waltzes with an English beauty. After being carried to her bedroom, she agonized for three weeks before Sara was born. By the end of Anise's recital, Fanny is ready to expel her from the house. Sara separates them, forcing each to apologize. Miss Hellman enjoys these play-acting scenes, and so does her audience.

The children help to subdue Fanny, assuring her of their love. Bodo loved her "the primary second" he saw her. And Kurt, back from the garden with David where he's been "exchanging misinformation" with the gardener, also helps to break the strain. For a moment family gaiety prevails. Fanny is planning a party for Babbie's birthday tomorrow. That's why Marthe is in town on errands. The mention of Marthe starts a touchy game. Teck has heard that David and Marthe were seen together in a jewelry store. David admits that much, no more. Fanny attempts to ease the embarrassment by asking if Kurt or Teck ever knew Paul Von Seitz? The name came up because Mellie Sewell had heard from Louis Chandler's child's governess that Teck had won quite a bit of money in a poker game at the German Embassy, a game with Sam Chandler, a munitions bootlegger, and Von Seitz's nephew Philip. Kurt has been playing the piano. He stops abruptly at the mention of the German Embassy. Miss Hellman recognized that live music could provide dramatic punctuation; she used it in *Foxes* and would again in later plays. Teck has his eyes on Kurt. Kurt must have known the young Von Seitz; he was the German military attaché in Spain. Kurt does not duck the question. He knew of him, but the side on which he fought was not where he was stationed. These two men do not fear each other. If a showdown comes, neither is going to back away. Miss Hellman does not deal in feeble confrontations. Kurt knows that if his side had won in Spain, the world would now be different. Sara and Fanny share his view, as does Miss Hellman. Sara recalls that Papa said, "For every man who lives without freedom, the rest of us must face the guilt. . . . We are liable in the conscience-balance for the tailor in Lodz, the black man in our South, the peasant in—" Miss Hellman is reminding us what the struggle is all about, what the play is about. Now it's Anise who tries to ease the tension; she's rounding up the children for their baths. Joshua admits that the "tub is a thing of glory," but the event need not be announced so publicly. Bodo is turning the heating pad over to his father. Teck jumps at this opening. Is his father an expert electrician and "as good with the radio?" Kurt, for the first time, puts a cutting edge on his voice: "Count de Brancovis. Make your questions to me, please. Not to my children." Nerves are tightening, but Teck maintains his composure. He's not yet ready for a decisive battle.

Marthe, unwittingly, helps him back away. She's returned with the birthday dresses for Babbie and for Sara. Touched to see Sara looking so happy, Kurt leans down and kisses her tenderly. More than ever we sense the strong bond that holds them together. It's an appropriate moment for Joseph to announce a long-distance call for Kurt. Sara and Teck watch him intently as he leaves the room.

Marthe tries to get their attention back to the dresses. Fanny has also bought one for her. Teck wonders if Fanny also gave her a sapphire bracelet from Barstow's. David has the answer. He gave her the bracelet, and "it is not any business of yours." Teck does not share his view. He orders Marthe upstairs to pack; the time has come for them to leave. Marthe is willing to depart, though not with him, nor with David. She loves David; David does not yet really love her, perhaps because of his mother. She understands maternal management; it led her to a title and her present predicament. She's now a tough girl and she'll survive. If Teck is leaving today—he says he is—we must "make sure we go in different directions, and do not meet again." The refugees are abandoning their sanctuary.

When she has retreated and Kurt returns, Sara and Teck know he's troubled, though he insists that it's nothing important; he must simply go to California for a few weeks. Teck has read the afternoon newspapers; Colonel Max Friedank, chief of the anti-Nazi underground movement, has been captured in Zurich. And at the Embassy he learned that Ebber and Triste were captured with him. "They could not find a man called Gotter." Teck plays his advantage immediately. He would like to have $10,000 before he goes. Blackmail comes easily for Teck, and it's a favored device for Miss Hellman. Morris Ernst, the lawyer, once commented that blackmail was the one indispensable ingredient in her plays.

David rushes at Teck, but Kurt restrains him; the blackmail is not aimed at him and Marthe. Kurt and Teck face each other for a showdown. Kurt knows that Teck has rifled his brief case, admits that his hands have been broken, that they shake when he's afraid, that he's afraid now. He recognizes Teck's power. Teck is willing to wait for the answer while he packs.

Alone with the family, Kurt corroborates Teck's report. He knew he was on the wanted list; he did not know his price had reached $10,000. His brief case contains $23,000, "money gathered from the poor who hate Fascism." If Fanny thinks he was careless to carry so much, wasn't it careless of her "to have in your house a man who opens baggage and blackmails?" Miss Hellman sounds her message again: "Fanny, you must come to understand it is no longer the world you once knew." There's no place for innocent bystanders. Kurt and Sara know that he must return home, use his skill and money to free the new captives. The guards at Sonnenburg can be bribed. It's been done before. Teck will not yet have passed his information to Von Seitz; "he's probably only asked most guarded questions." Sara has the final words before the curtain. She accepts what must be done: "Don't be scared, darling. You'll get back. . . . You'll do a good job, the way you've always done. . . . You'll get home. Don't worry, you'll get home. Yes, you will."

We fear for the Müllers; we cherish their courage. We wish we were like them, knowing in our hearts that we are more like Fanny and David and even Marthe. At no other moment in a Hellman play do we become so passionately involved. What happens to Kurt and Sara is happening to us.

A half-hour later the payoff has not yet been made. Kurt is at the piano, Sara sits quietly on the sofa, David is pacing the terrace. Fanny wonders how bribery can help Kurt. He assures her that though the Fascists are smart, sick, and cruel, they are not supermen. They can be beaten by men "who know what they fight for." Yes, he could abandon the cause, find excuses: his wife, his family. That is not his way.

When Teck appears carrying Kurt's briefcase, David and Fanny explode in anger. He assures them he's touched nothing, he's saving Kurt a trip upstairs, and if they persist in their abuse, he'll raise his price. The "desired list" he got from Von Seitz contains a description of "Gotter" (Kurt) and the record of his subversive activities: border crossings, secret radio broadcasts from Düsseldorf, a raid on a Gestapo chief. Kurt knows Teck and his kind. Fanny and David must try to understand this other world: "All Fascists are not of one mind, one stripe. . . . [Some] come in high places and wish now only to survive. . . . For those last, we may well some day have pity. They are lost men, their spoils are small, their day is gone." We admire, if we cannot share, Kurt's magnanimity.

Teck warns him not to let his "understanding heart" corrupt him; he will not get back if Von Seitz is informed. Kurt knows better. Roumanians, like Teck, might capture him immediately, not the Germans. They'll trail him, hoping to pick up more information before they close in. What's more, the money in his brief case is going with him. He did not touch it when his children were hungry. "If I would not touch it for them, I would not touch it for you." Teck is unconvinced: "You are a brave one, Herr Müller, but you will not get back." Kurt is confident. He promises to send Teck a postcard reporting his arrival.

Frightened by the impasse, Fanny and David agree to supply the money, if they can be sure that Teck will not double-cross them. Understanding their skepticism, Teck will accept $2500 in cash and a postdated check, giving Kurt a month lead time. If Fanny doesn't have that much cash in her safe, he'll settle for what she has, $1500 or $1600. David goes for the checkbook, Fanny for the money.

With the "new world" out of the room Teck feels more comfortable: "We are Europeans, born to trouble and understanding it." Teck may want to play games; Kurt does not. He knows that Teck has his own backlog of troubles: the Budapest oil deal in 1931, his involvement with Fritz Thyssen and with Kessler. Von Seitz would never give him the money, certainly not for a description of a man who has a month to travel; at most the Embassy would reward him with a visa. And he's not going to get the money from Fanny and David. "You are a gambler. But you should not gamble with your life." Teck has pushed the stakes too high.

Kurt quickly drops his glass, strikes Teck on the side of the face, and as he tries to recover, throws him to the floor. After four heavy blows on the head, Teck is quiet. Kurt calmly takes his revolver from his pocket and starts to lift the body. Joshua appears in the doorway. Although stunned by what he sees, he obediently follows his father's command, opening the door and closing it after Kurt has carried the body to the terrace. Sara has been at the window during the struggle. Joshua understands that they must move again. He'll pack and get the children ready. There's no need; only "Papa is going home." Joshua must go upstairs, take Babbie and Bodo to his room, close the door, and stay there until she calls him. He obeys.[1]

Sara calmly and automatically sets the room in order. When Fanny and David return, she's at the telephone booking a flight to Brownsville in the name of Ritter. She assures them that Kurt has done what he had to do; he couldn't take chances with his work to spare them. When Kurt departs, he'll not be coming back. For the rest of her life she'll be alone at night, the dreadful moment in every day. Miss Hellman never lets us forget the human consequences.

Kurt is back onstage. For a thousand years man has been fighting to make a world, so far without success. He has not given up and he alone is responsible for what he's done. "I will do it again. And I will keep my hope that we may make a world in which all men can die in bed." His escape plans are simple. After saying goodbye to the children, he'll pack the body in the trunk of the Farrelly car and drive into Washington. The pistol found in the abandoned car will indicate a quarrel between two Europeans; one was shot, the other disappeared. By that time Kurt will be out of reach.

The final farewell—Sara has brought the children down—is touching and tender. Fanny and David must assume his paternal responsibility for the children; that's his only will. He's robbed them of their childhood, but he had no choice. In a few days they'll know that he's done something bad, yet they will live to see the day when men will cease to steal and lie and kill because "in every town and every village and every mud hut in the world, there is always a man who loves children and who will fight to make a good world for them." Some day he'll come back to them, or they'll come to him, and "I will have ordered an extra big dinner and we will show them what our Germany can be like." As the children give him a final hug and return to their rooms, alone in their sorrow, we wonder when and if that happy reunion will ever occur. It's an overwhelming moment, probably the only time tears cloud our eyes at a Hellman play.

The adult goodbyes are short and simple. Kurt knows that "men who wish to live have the best chance to live," and he wishes to live. Sara knows he speaks for her as well: "Come back for me, darling. If you can." As she hands him the brief case, he assures her he will try. We hear the car starting and moving away, and Sara goes to the children. Fanny and David are given a brief coda before the final curtain. They have been "shaken out of the magnolias," as Fanny says, but they'll manage the rough days ahead. "I'm not put together with flour paste. And neither are you—I am happy to learn."

Watch on the Rhine is a warm and compassionate play, as it is also a play of pith and moment. The Farrellys and Müllers are as blessed with love and nobility as the Hubbards were cursed with hate and avarice. Only Teck could have thrived in the world of *Foxes*. The political challenge does not ring with strident battle alarums, drums, uniforms, and party salutes, yet the terrifying face of Fascism hangs like a gargoyle over the Farrelly household. No longer can the Atlantic and Potomac shield us from the Nazi menace. The message penetrates because these people are "human beings not their ideological ghosts," as Louis Kronenberger put it.

Miss Hellman insisted that she did not consciously write a political document. "Good writers have a good look at the world around them and then they write it down. That's all. . . . Writers should not *see* their work. Writers shouldn't have anything to do with words like betrayal or courage or bigness or smallness or sex or Greek or new or old [or propaganda]. You write it down but you mustn't stand back and see it. You do it and go to bed and leave the big words for other people. It just isn't your business to tell people what you're doing or wanted to do." Because she centered on a minor episode in the current history of death and destruction rather than a major world event, because she shunned preachment and pronouncement, her play overshadowed the other anti-Fascist plays. One critic remarked that by comparison Elmer Rice's *Flight to the West* seemed like "embarrassed stuttering" and Sherwood's *There Shall Be No Night*—from the preceding season—like "boyish cheerleading."

The essential substance of the play remained unaltered from first scenario to final draft, though as always Miss Hellman tightened and sharpened. Early in the development Marthe worked as Teck's ally in the blackmailing scheme, and the first scenario placed the killing before the rise of the curtain on Act III. In an early draft Kurt augmented his anti-Fascist sentiments with extended passages in praise of socialism. Miss Hellman wisely decided to focus on the Fascist threat.

In retrospect, except for those who suffered through the Hitler years, the fierce impact of the play in 1941 cannot be fully sensed. If it appears melodramatic now, it appeared melodramatic then, but with a difference: the world was boiling with melodrama. Cruelty and villainy were not figments of the playwright's imagination, and it was almost impossible for a writer to tell us anything we didn't already know or to dramatize atrocities more effectively than events had already dramatized them. Miss Hellman knew that her fiction must do more than demonstrate the strange and awful truth that screamed from the front pages of every daily paper. She tried, if she did not entirely succeed, to shift from the massive melodrama of life to the heroic human story of one family behaving "like thoroughbreds in an agonizing situation," as one critic remarked, by making us aware of the blinders we still wore, blinders the European had long since discarded, by alerting us to our own vulnerability.

Here was a play of burning intensity for every American who cherished his life and his country, who believed that human decency could prevail. And for those who knew Miss Hellman, here was the expected neatness, precision, and dynamic power; here also were the characters in close-order formation, keenly not crudely differentiated, and all of them breathing with life. At the same time, here was a new Hellman with characters from another mold and with a more skillfully manipulated climactic moment. Certainly there was a firmer plausibility in Teck's destruction than in Martha's suicide or in Horace's heart attack.

Most critics pronounced it her most compelling work. In its unforgettable moments—the Müllers arriving out of the darkness of Europe, Kurt's contempt for the idea that "they" are invincible, Frau Müller letting her husband go back knowing she and the children may never see him again—the awful truth of Fascism was brought close to home. If there was too much aimless wandering in the early scenes, if the Marthe–David love affair seemed superfluous, if too much attention was bestowed on the precocious Bodo, if the final farewells were overextended, these were minor deficiencies. No one could deny its honesty nor escape its fearful message, particularly when supported by the "beautiful direction" of Shumlin[2] and the masterly performances of Lucile Watson (Mrs. Farrelly), Mady Christians (Sara), and Paul Lukas (Kurt). Miss Watson not only gloried in the sure-fire delights of one of Miss Hellman's salty and officious great ladies, she made her a woman as well. Paul Lukas, a native Hungarian who had made some fifty Hollywood movies and had appeared only once before on the American stage in a production of *A Doll's House* with Ruth Gordon, created a truly heroic modern man who, according to Brooks Atkinson, "knew fear a thousand times, but resisted it with modest steadfastness because he believed in the freedom and dignity of man." He was elegant, even in his silences, "one of the great performances in recent years."

Many critics wondered how the play's documentary pertinence might appear a quarter of a century later. Would future readers believe that this was what life in America was like when the Nazi evil began to creep across the ocean? Could we hope that by then they would find it "melodramatic and improbable for all its eloquence"? That day has not arrived.

At a dinner at the Algonquin Hotel on Sunday evening, April 27, 1941, the critics honored her with their highest accolade, the New York Drama Critics' Circle Award. The citation read, "To Lillian Hellman for *Watch on the Rhine*, a vital, eloquent and compassionate play about an American family suddenly awakened to the danger threatening its liberty." When the play opened at the Martin Beck Theatre on April 1, 1941, *The Little Foxes* was still sending back healthy profits from its national tour. Miss Hellman has jumped into the front rank of serious and successful American playwrights.

The following January, while the play was still on the boards, Miss Hellman speculated on changes she might have made. Perhaps, as in *Days to Come*[3] she had one character too many, but she could not determine which one. She thought her anti-Fascist sentiments should have been more pointed, many speeches cleaner, many things said with more depth and understanding. Yet she was certain that she had done her best at the time the play was written. "Within the limitations of my own mind and nature, my own understanding, my own knowledge, it was the best I could do with what I had. If I didn't hope to grow, I would not hope to live."

Two days before the play concluded its Broadway run of 378 performances on Saturday, February 21, 1942, and prepared to go on the road, beginning in Philadelphia the following Monday, a gala farewell was held in the Martin Beck lounge after the performance. The public was invited to contribute a dollar and join Miss Hellman and the cast, the proceeds to go to the Emergency Anti-Fascist Refugee Fund. Since the play had opened, she had been involved with many similar ventures. She was co-chairman of a Dinner-Forum on "Europe Today" at the Hotel Biltmore on October

9, the money to be used to transport outstanding anti-Fascists from French concentration camps to Mexico. In March, 1942, she participated in a dinner honoring Paul Robeson.[4] Her political enterprises were not always so public and solemn. In June, a week before her birthday, she sent a wire to a dozen of her friends: "A birthday present for Lillian Hellman is a blow against Fascism."

In the summer of 1942 an illustrated limited edition of *Watch on the Rhine* was published by the Joint Anti-Fascist Refugee Committee to support their activities. Numbers 1–50, bound in leather, were priced at $50. Everyone involved donated his services, including Rockwell Kent, eleven other artists, and Dorothy Parker.

Miss Parker's foreword, so eloquently echoing Miss Hellman's sentiments, deserves a wider audience than it had:

> The woman who wrote this play and the men who made these drawings give this, their book, to those who earliest fought Fascism. Most of those warriors died; on the stiff plains of Spain, behind the jagged wire of French prison camps, in small echoing rooms of German towns. Few of their names are told, and their numbers are not measured. They wear no clean and carven stones in death. But for them there is an eternal light that will burn with a flame far higher than any beside a tomb.
>
> Many did not die, but they none the less gave their lives. Wherever they are, they bear the battle on. And because they do, death walks behind them daily. No man grows used to that cold follower.
>
> These men, the dead and the living, knew soonest, gave first. Because of them, other men will stand and stretch and stride again, will see their women beside them proud and straight of shoulder, will look in their children's eyes and find no fear. Because of them, the world can go unashamed.
>
> They are brave men who lay down their lives and their liberty that men to come may live and be free. This play, these pictures, more shining than marble, more enduring than brass, stand here to the glory of their courage.
>
> *Dorothy Parker*

During the spring of 1942, Lillian Hellman edited Hammett's screen version of *Watch on the Rhine*. Except for localizing some scenes and supplying more explicit detail for others, the film duplicated the play. At the opening we see the Müllers cross the Mexican border, then in the day coach and at lunch counters on their journey to Washington. These scenes alternate with Fanny in her limousine rushing around Washington to buy tricycles and other necessities for the children. Later the camera tours the Farrelly mansion and the Washington sights, including a view of the Müller children on top of the Washington Monument. It also shows Teck at the German Embassy, talking of spies and anti-Nazis and later procuring a copy of the "wanted" list. But the essentials of the play were not sacrificed to these additions. Apparently at one point the Hays office insisted that the film show some retribution, even if accidental, for Kurt's killing of the count until Miss Hellman wrote to Mr. Breen inquiring if he were aware that it was now national policy to exterminate Nazis. Produced by Hal Wallis at Warner Brothers, directed by Shumlin and with Paul Lukas repeating his stirring performance, it alerted a wider public "to what we are fighting for," and when the critics appraised the 1943–44 film season, it was selected one of the best pictures of the year.

When London saw the play at the end of April, 1942, directed by Emlyn Williams with Anton Walbrook (Kurt), Diana Wynyard (Sara), and Athene Seyler (Fanny), the critics declared that its harrowing message made it "one of the best and most moving plays in years," a shattering reminder that "we are all guilty, and that if it is now too late to undo what has been done, it is by no means too late to re-make, to create again a world in which decent humanity may live, unpursued and undevoured."

Notes

1. Mady Christians, who played Sara, once told me of their difficulties with this scene when they did a command performance in Washington on January 25, 1942, to celebrate President Roosevelt's birthday. This was the President's first public appearance since the war began, except to attend church and address Congress, and the security was unusually tight. The Secret Service chief knew of the gun business and advised Paul Lukas (Kurt) to substitute a wooden prop-revolver. Lukas protested. He would not tolerate such amateurish nonsense. When he was told that Secret Service men would be stationed throughout the house and backstage and though the chief would do his best some men might not get the word that the gun was part of the play, Lukas accepted the wooden gun.
2. The printed text was dedicated to him, with "Thanks and Affection."
3. During the run of *Watch*, Shumlin contemplated a series of special matinees of a reworked *Days to Come*. The project never materialized.
4. George Jean Nathan wrote: "It is a rare committee formed to improve the accommodations of the Negroes at the Ritz-Plaza, or to make Palestine a future Newport for the Jews, or to improve the quality of impoverished Chinese Peasant's chow mein, or to instruct Tom Lamont in the underestimated virtues of the Stalin economy, or to guarantee the right of free speech to Morris Ernst that does not find her name high up on its stationery," (*Theatre Book of the Year, 1943–44.* New York, 1944, p. 296)

20.2 FIRESIDE CHAT 14: ON THE EUROPEAN WAR—FRANKLIN D. ROOSEVELT, SEPTEMBER 3, 1939

MY FELLOW AMERICANS AND MY FRIENDS:

Tonight my single duty is to speak to the whole of America.

Until four-thirty this morning I had hoped against hope that some miracle would prevent a devastating war in Europe and bring to an end the invasion of Poland by Germany.

For four long years a succession of actual wars and constant crises have shaken the entire world and have threatened in each case to bring on the gigantic conflict which is today unhappily a fact.

It is right that I should recall to your minds the consistent and at time successful efforts of your Government in these crises to throw the full weight of the United States into the cause of peace. In spite of spreading wars I think that we have every right and every reason to maintain as a national policy the fundamental moralities, the teachings of religion (and) the continuation of efforts to restore peace—(for) because some day, though the time may be distant, we can be of even greater help to a crippled humanity.

It is right, too, to point out that the unfortunate events of these recent years have, without question, been based on the use of force (or) and the threat of force. And it seems to me clear, even at the outbreak of this great war, that the influence of America should be consistent in seeking for humanity a final peace which will eliminate, as far as it is possible to do so, the continued use of force between nations.

It is, of course, impossible to predict the future. I have my constant stream of information from American representatives and other sources throughout the world. You, the people of this country, are receiving news through your radios and your newspapers at every hour of the day.

You are, I believe, the most enlightened and the best informed people in all the world at this moment. You are subjected to no censorship of news, and I want to add that your Government has no information which it (hesitates to) withholds (from you) or which it has any thought of withholding from you.

At the same time, as I told my Press Conference on Friday, it is of the highest importance that the press and the radio use the utmost caution to discriminate between actual verified fact on the one hand, and mere rumor on the other.

I can add to that by saying that I hope the people of this country will also discriminate most carefully between news and rumor. Do not believe of necessity everything you hear or read. Check up on it first.

You must master at the outset a simple but unalterable fact in modern foreign relations between nations. When peace has been broken anywhere, the peace of all countries everywhere is in danger.

It is easy for you and for me to shrug our shoulders and to say that conflicts taking place thousands of miles from the continental United States, and, indeed, thousands of miles from the whole American Hemisphere, do not seriously affect the Americas—and that all the United States has to do is to ignore them and go about (our) its own business. Passionately though we may desire detachment, we are forced to realize that every word that comes through the air, every ship that sails the sea, every battle that is fought does affect the American future.

Let no man or woman thoughtlessly or falsely talk of America sending its armies to European fields. At this moment there is being prepared a proclamation of American neutrality. This would have been done even if there had been no neutrality statute on the books, for this proclamation is in accordance with international law and in accordance with American policy.

This will be followed by a Proclamation required by the existing Neutrality Act. And I trust that in the days to come our neutrality can be made a true neutrality.

It is of the utmost importance that the people of this country, with the best information in the world, think things through. The most dangerous enemies of American peace are those who, without well-rounded Information on the whole broad subject of the past, the present and the future, undertake to speak with assumed authority, to talk in terms of glittering generalities, to give to the nation assurances or prophecies which are of little present or future value.

I myself cannot and do not prophesy the course of events abroad—and the reason is that because I have of necessity such a complete picture of what is going on in every part of the world, that I do not dare to do so. And the other reason is that I think it is honest for me to be honest with the people of the United States.

I cannot prophesy the immediate economic effect of this new war on our nation but I do say that no American has the moral right to profiteer at the expense either of his fellow citizens or of the men, the women and the children who are living and dying in the midst of war in Europe.

Some things we do know. Most of us in the United States believe in spiritual values. Most of us, regardless of what church we belong to, believe in the spirit of the New Testament—a great teaching which opposes itself to the use of force, of armed force, of marching armies and falling bombs. The overwhelming masses of our people seek peace—peace at home, and the kind of peace in other lands which will not jeopardize our peace at home.

We have certain ideas and certain ideals of national safety and we must act to preserve that safety today and to preserve the safety of our children in future years.

That safety is and will be bound up with the safety of the Western Hemisphere and of the seas adjacent thereto. We seek to keep war from our own firesides by keeping war from coming to the Americas. For that we have historic precedent that goes back to the days of the Administration of President George Washington. It is serious enough and tragic enough to every American family in every state in the Union to live in a world that is torn by wars on other Continents. And those wars today (they) affect every American home. It is our national duty to use every effort to keep (them) those wars out of the Americas.

And at this time let me make the simple plea that partisanship and selfishness be adjourned; and that national unity be the thought that underlies all others.

This nation will remain a neutral nation, but I cannot ask that every American remain neutral in thought as well. Even a neutral has a right to take account of facts. Even a neutral cannot be asked to close his mind or close his conscience.

I have said not once but many times that I have seen war and that I hate war. I say that again and again.

I hope the United States will keep out of this war. I believe that it will. And I give you assurance(s) and reassurance that every effort of your Government will be directed toward that end.

As long as it remains within my power to prevent, there will be no blackout of peace in the United States.

20.3 DES MOINES SPEECH—CHARLES LINDBERGH

Des Moines, Iowa, September 11th 1941

IT IS NOW TWO YEARS SINCE this latest European war began. From that day in September, 1939, until the present moment, there has been an ever-increasing effort to force the United States into the conflict.

That effort has been carried on by foreign interests, and by a small minority of our own people; but it has been so successful that, today, our country stands on the verge of war.

At this time, as the war is about to enter its third winter, it seems appropriate to review the circumstances that have led us to our present position. Why are we on the verge of war? Was it necessary for us to become so deeply involved? Who is responsible for changing our national policy from one of neutrality and independence to one of entanglement in European affairs?

Personally, I believe there is no better argument against our intervention than a study of the causes and developments of the present war. I have often said that if the true facts and issues were placed before the American people, there would be no danger of our involvement.

Here, I would like to point out to you a fundamental difference between the groups who advocate foreign war, and those who believe in an independent destiny for America.

If you will look back over the record, you will find that those of us who oppose intervention have constantly tried to clarify facts and issues; while the interventionists have tried to hide facts and confuse issues.

We ask you to read what we said last month, last year, and even before the war began. Our record is open and clear, and we are proud of it.

We have not led you on by subterfuge and propaganda. We have not resorted to steps short of anything, in order to take the American people where they did not want to go.

What we said before the elections, we say [illegible] and again, and again today. And we will not tell you tomorrow that it was just campaign oratory. Have you ever heard an interventionist, or a British agent, or a member of the administration in Washington ask you to go back and study a record of what they have said since the war started? Are their self-styled defenders of democracy willing to put the issue of war to a vote of our people? Do you find these crusaders for foreign freedom of speech, or the removal of censorship here in our own country?

The subterfuge and propaganda that exists in our country is obvious on every side. Tonight, I shall try to pierce through a portion of it, to the naked facts which lie beneath.

When this war started in Europe, it was clear that the American people were solidly opposed to entering it. Why shouldn't we be? We had the best defensive position in the world; we had a tradition of independence from Europe; and the one time we did take part in a European war left European problems unsolved, and debts to America unpaid.

National polls showed that when England and France declared war on Germany, in 1939, less than 10 percent of our population favored a similar course for America. But there were various groups of people, here and abroad, whose interests and beliefs necessitated the involvement of the United States in the war. I shall point out some of these groups tonight, and outline their methods of procedure. In doing this, I must speak with the utmost frankness, for in order to counteract their efforts, we must know exactly who they are.

The three most important groups who have been pressing this country toward war are the British, the Jewish and the Roosevelt administration.

Behind these groups, but of lesser importance, are a number of capitalists, Anglophiles, and intellectuals who believe that the future of mankind depends upon the domination of the British empire. Add to these the Communistic groups who were opposed to intervention until a few weeks ago, and I believe I have named the major war agitators in this country.

I am speaking here only of war agitators, not of those sincere but misguided men and women who, confused by misinformation and frightened by propaganda, follow the lead of the war agitators.

As I have said, these war agitators comprise only a small minority of our people; but they control a tremendous influence. Against the determination of the American people to stay out of war, they have marshaled the power of their propaganda, their money, their patronage.

Let us consider these groups, one at a time.

First, the British: It is obvious and perfectly understandable that Great Britain wants the United States in the war on her side. England is now in a desperate position. Her population is not large enough and her armies are not strong enough to invade the continent of Europe and win the war she declared against Germany.

Her geographical position is such that she cannot win the war by the use of aviation alone, regardless of how many planes we send her. Even if America entered the war, it is improbable that the Allied armies could invade Europe and overwhelm the Axis powers. But one thing is certain. If England can draw this country into the war, she can shift to our shoulders a large portion of the responsibility for waging it and for paying its cost.

As you all know, we were left with the debts of the last European war; and unless we are more cautious in the future than we have been in the past, we will be left with the debts of the present case. If it were not for her hope that she can make us responsible for the war financially, as well as militarily, I believe England would have negotiated a peace in Europe many months ago, and be better off for doing so.

England has devoted, and will continue to devote every effort to get us into the war. We know that she spent huge sums of money in this country during the last war in order to involve us. Englishmen have written books about the cleverness of its use.

We know that England is spending great sums of money for propaganda in America during the present war. If we were Englishmen, we would do the same. But our interest is first in America; and as Americans, it is essential for us to realize the effort that British interests are making to draw us into their war.

The second major group I mentioned is the Jewish.

It is not difficult to understand why Jewish people desire the overthrow of Nazi Germany. The persecution they suffered in Germany would be sufficient to make bitter enemies of any race.

No person with a sense of the dignity of mankind can condone the persecution of the Jewish race in Germany. But no person of honesty and vision can look on their pro-war policy here today without seeing the dangers involved in such a policy both for us and for them. Instead of agitating for war, the Jewish groups in this country should be opposing it in every possible way for they will be among the first to feel its consequences.

Tolerance is a virtue that depends upon peace and strength. History shows that it cannot survive war and devastations. A few far-sighted Jewish people realize this and stand opposed to intervention. But the majority still do not.

Their greatest danger to this country lies in their large ownership and influence in our motion pictures, our press, our radio and our government.

I am not attacking either the Jewish or the British people. Both races, I admire. But I am saying that the leaders of both the British and the Jewish races, for reasons which are as understandable from their viewpoint as they are inadvisable from ours, for reasons which are not American, wish to involve us in the war.

We cannot blame them for looking out for what they believe to be their own interests, but we also must look out for ours. We cannot allow the natural passions and prejudices of other peoples to lead our country to destruction.

The Roosevelt administration is the third powerful group which has been carrying this country toward war. Its members have used the war emergency to obtain a third presidential term for the first time in American history. They have used the war to add unlimited billions to a debt which was already the highest we have ever known. And they have just used the war to justify the restriction of congressional power, and the assumption of dictatorial procedures on the part of the president and his appointees.

The power of the Roosevelt administration depends upon the maintenance of a wartime emergency. The prestige of the Roosevelt administration depends upon the success of Great Britain to whom the president attached his political future at a time when most people thought that England and France would easily win the war. The danger of the Roosevelt administration lies in its subterfuge. While its members have promised us peace, they have led us to war heedless of the platform upon which they were elected.

In selecting these three groups as the major agitators for war, I have included only those whose support is essential to the war party. If any one of these groups—the British, the Jewish, or the administration—stops agitating for war, I believe there will be little danger of our involvement.

I do not believe that any two of them are powerful enough to carry this country to war without the support of the third. And to these three, as I have said, all other war groups are of secondary importance.

When hostilities commenced in Europe, in 1939, it was realized by these groups that the American people had no intention of entering the war. They knew it would be worse than useless to ask us for a declaration of war at that time. But they believed that this country could be entered into the war in very much the same way we were entered into the last one.

They planned: first, to prepare the United States for foreign war under the guise of American defense; second, to involve us in the war, step by step, without our realization; third, to create a series of incidents which would force us into the actual conflict. These plans were of course, to be covered and assisted by the full power of their propaganda.

Our theaters soon became filled with plays portraying the glory of war. Newsreels lost all semblance of objectivity. Newspapers and magazines began to lose advertising if they carried anti-war articles. A smear campaign was instituted against individuals who opposed intervention. The terms "fifth columnist," "traitor," "Nazi," "anti-Semitic" were thrown ceaselessly at any one who dared to suggest that it was not to the best interests of the United States to enter the war. Men lost their jobs if they were frankly anti-war. Many others dared no longer speak.

Before long, lecture halls that were open to the advocates of war were closed to speakers who opposed it. A fear campaign was inaugurated. We were told that aviation, which has held the British fleet off the continent of Europe, made America more vulnerable than ever before to invasion. Propaganda was in full swing.

There was no difficulty in obtaining billions of dollars for arms under the guise of defending America. Our people stood united on a program of defense. Congress passed appropriation after appropriation for guns and planes and battleships, with the approval of the overwhelming majority of our citizens. That a large portion of these appropriations was to be used to build arms for Europe, we did not learn until later. That was another step.

To use a specific example; in 1939, we were told that we should increase our air corps to a total of 5,000 planes. Congress passed the necessary legislation. A few months later, the administration told us that the United States should have at least 50,000 planes for our national safety. But almost as fast as fighting planes were turned out from our factories, they were sent abroad, although our own air corps was in the utmost need of new equipment; so that today, two years after the start of war, the American army has a few hundred thoroughly modern bombers and fighters—less in fact, than Germany is able to produce in a single month.

Ever since its inception, our arms program has been laid out for the purpose of carrying on the war in Europe, far more than for the purpose of building an adequate defense for America.

Now at the same time we were being prepared for a foreign war, it was necessary, as I have said, to involve us in the war. This was accomplished under that now famous phrase "steps short of war."

England and France would win if the United States would only repeal its arms embargo and sell munitions for cash, we were told. And then [illegible] began, a refrain that marked every step we took toward war for many months—"the best way to defend America and keep out of war," we were told, was "by aiding the Allies."

First, we agreed to sell arms to Europe; next, we agreed to loan arms to Europe; then we agreed to patrol the ocean for Europe; then we occupied a European island in the war zone. Now, we have reached the verge of war.

The war groups have succeeded in the first two of their three major steps into war. The greatest armament program in our history is under way.

We have become involved in the war from practically every standpoint except actual shooting. Only the creation of sufficient "incidents" yet remains; and you see the first of these already taking place, according to plan [illegible]—a plan that was never laid before the American people for their approval.

Men and women of Iowa; only one thing holds this country from war today. That is the rising opposition of the American people. Our system of democracy and representative government is on test today as it has never been before. We are on the verge of a war in which the only victor would be chaos and prostration.

We are on the verge of a war for which we are still unprepared, and for which no one has offered a feasible plan for victory—a war which cannot be won without sending our soldiers across the ocean to force a landing on a hostile coast against armies stronger than our own.

We are on the verge of war, but it is not yet too late to stay out. It is not too late to show that no amount of money, or propaganda, or patronage can force a free and independent people into war against its will. It is not yet too late to retrieve and to maintain the independent American destiny that our forefathers established in this new world.

The entire future rests upon our shoulders. It depends upon our action, our courage, and our intelligence. If you oppose our intervention in the war, now is the time to make your voice heard.

Help us to organize these meetings; and write to your representatives in Washington. I tell you that the last stronghold of democracy and representative government in this country is in our house of representatives and our senate.

There, we can still make our will known. And if we, the American people, do that, independence and freedom will continue to live among us, and there will be no foreign war.

20.4 CANTO 73: CAVALCANTI—REPUBLICAN DISPATCHES—EZRA POUND

And then I slept
And, waking in the wasted air,
Saw and heard thus –
He whom I saw seemed like a cavalier,
And I heard this:
"Watching my people die
Does not satisfy
even if they broke their word,
Even if they *deserve*
    to be governed by King Turd.
Roosevelt, Churchill and Eden
    bastards to a man,
Liar, Jew and glutton
    have squeezed the people dry
        like sheep!
At Sarzana I lay still,
    waiting for the call
        from sleep
I am Guido, whom you loved
    as a spirit from above
And for the burning-glass of my mind's reason.
I knew the cleansing fire
Of Venus's third sphere
    already as I rode
        Cavalcanti, the cavalier
(*Not* a mere follower)
    through the squabbling streets
Of our *città dolente*
        (*Firenze*)
    which breeds
Not men, but a vain and touchy
    race of slaves!

Passing through Arimino
    I met a gallant soul
Singing as though her heart would break
        with joy!
A young *contadinella*
– Big-boned girl, but *bella* –
    with a German on each arm;
And she sang,
    she sang of love
        without thought of
            heaven above.
She had led some Canadians
    into a field of mines
Where the *Tempio* of Ixotta
    used to stand.
They were coming in fours and fives
        – I felt a wave of passion
    steal over me again
        as if I were still alive.
That's the way girls are
    in the Romagna.
The Canadians had come
    to 'mop up' German scum,
To pull down the remains
    of Rimini;
They stopped to ask the way
    to the Via Emilia
        of a girl,
    a poor young girl
Raped by the first of that *canaille*.
    – Be'! Bene! soldiers,
        follow me.
    Let's all go together
        to *Via Emilia*! –
She showed them—where to go.
    Her brother had dug the holes
For that mine-field,
    there beside the sea-side.
Towards the sea-side, she
    (big-boned, but a beauty)
Led the boys.

Brave kid! A real cutie!
She played that prank
for love:
acing 'em all for poise!
Death-threats arrived too late,
Defying Fate
she died –
That big-boned girl –
with pride,
hitting the target straight!
To hell with the enemy!
Twenty of them lay dead
The girl dead, too
in the midst of that *canaille.*
Everyone *except* the prisoners.
A real hard-case
that kid
Singing, singing
with joy
Along the road that leads
beside the sea.
Gloria della patria!
Gloria! the glory
Of dying for one's land
in the Romagna!
The dead are not all dead,
Myself I have returned
from the third sphere
to see Romagna,
To see the North reborn
among the mountains,
In this 'morte saison'
to see the home-land,
And yet – that girl . . .
what girls,
what boys
wear black!"

20.5 PLAYBILL PHOTOS OF *WATCH ON THE RHINE*

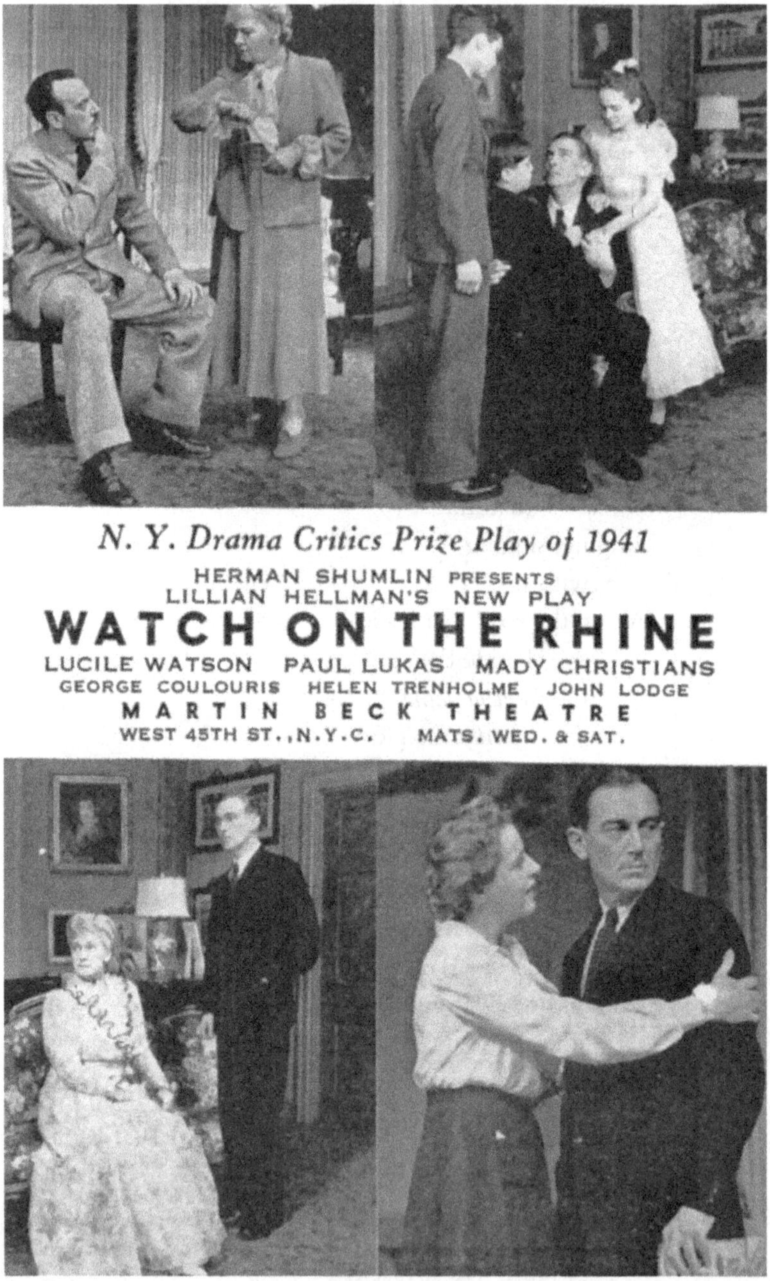

Lillian Hellman's *Watch on the Rhine* at the Martin Beck Theatre, 1941. The play, set in 1940, opened eight months before Pearl Harbor, when there was still a national debate between isolationists and interventionists about how involved the U.S. should be in the war against fascism.

20.6 *WATCH ON THE RHINE*—LILLIAN HELLMAN

(In the order of their appearance)

Anise	Eda Heinemann
Joseph	Frank Wilson
Fanny Farrelly	Lucile Watson
David Farrelly	John Lodge
Marthe de Brancovis	Helen Trenholme
Teck de Brancovis	George Coulouris
Sara Müller	Mady Christians
Joshua Müller	Peter Fernandez
Bodo Müller	Eric Roberts
Babette Müller	Anne Blyth
Kurt Müller	Paul Lukas

Scene

The scene of the play is the living room of the Farrelly country house, about twenty miles from Washington. The time is late spring, 1940.

Act One

Early on a Wednesday morning.

Act Two

Ten days later.

Act Three

A half hour later.

★

ACT ONE

SCENE: *The living room of the Farrelly house, about twenty miles from Washington, D.C., on a warm spring morning.*

Center stage are large French doors leading to an elevated open terrace. On the terrace are chairs, tables, a large table for dining. Some of this furniture we can see; most of it is on the left side of the terrace, beyond our sight. Left stage is an arched entrance, leading to the oval reception hall. We can see the main staircase as it goes off to the back of the hall. Right stage is a door leading to a library. The Farrelly house was built in the early nineteenth century. It has space, simplicity, style. The living room is large. Up stage right is a piano; down stage left, a couch; down stage right, a couch and chairs; up stage a few smaller chairs. Four or five generations have furnished this room and they have all been people of taste. There are no styles, no periods; the room has never been refurnished. Each careless aristocrat has thrown into the room what he or she liked as a child, what he or she brought home when grown up. Therefore the furniture is of many periods: the desk is English, the couch is Victorian, some of the pictures are modern, some of the ornaments French. The room has too many things in it: vases, clocks, miniatures, boxes, china animals. On the right wall is a large portrait of a big kind-faced man in an evening suit of 1900. On another wall is a large, very ugly landscape. The room is crowded. But it is cool and clean and its fabrics and woods are in soft colors.

AT RISE: ANISE, *a thin Frenchwoman of about sixty, in a dark housekeeper's dress, is standing at a table sorting mail. She takes the mail from a small basket, holds each letter to the light, reads each postal card, then places them in piles. On the terrace.* JOSEPH, *a tall, middle-aged Negro butler, wheels a breakfast wagon. As he appears,* FANNY FARRELLY *comes in from the hall. She is a handsome woman of about sixty-three. She has on a fancy, good-looking dressing-gown.*

Left and right are the audience's left and right.

★

FANNY (*stops to watch* ANISE. *Sees* JOSEPH *moving about on terrace. Calls*) Joseph! (*To* ANISE) Morning.

ANISE (*continues examining mail*) Good morning, Madame.

JOSEPH (*comes to terrace door*) Yes'm?

FANNY Everybody down?

JOSEPH No'm. Nobody. I'll get your tea. (*He returns to breakfast wagon on terrace.*)

FANNY Mr. David isn't down yet? But he knows he is to meet the train.

JOSEPH (*comes in from the terrace with the cup of tea*) He's got plenty of time, Miss Fanny. The train ain't in till noon.

FANNY Breakfast is at nine o'clock in this house and will be until the day after I die. Ring the bell.

JOSEPH It ain't nine yet, Miss Fanny. It's eight-thirty.

FANNY Well, put the clocks up to nine and ring the bell.

JOSEPH Mr. David told me not to ring it any more. He says it's got too mean a ring, that bell. It disturbs folks.

FANNY That's what it was put there for. I like to disturb folks.

JOSEPH Yes'm.

FANNY You slept well, Anise. You were asleep before I could dismantle myself.

ANISE I woke several times during the night.

FANNY Did you? Then you were careful not to stop snoring. We must finally get around to rearranging your room. (ANISE *hands her three or four letters*) Even when you don't snore, it irritates me. (FANNY *opens a letter, begins to read it. After a minute*) What time is it?

ANISE It is about eight-thirty. Joseph just told you.

FANNY I didn't hear him. I'm nervous. Naturally. My mail looks dull. (*Reading the letter*) Jenny always tells you a piece of gossip three times, as if it grew fresher with the telling. Did you put flowers in their rooms?

ANISE Certainly.

FANNY David ought to get to the station by eleven-thirty.

ANISE (*patiently*) The train does not draw in until ten minutes past noon.

FANNY But it might come in early. It's been known.

ANISE Never. Not in the Union Station in Washington, the District of Columbia.

FANNY (*irritably*) But it might. It might. Don't argue with me about everything. What time is it?

ANISE It's now twenty-seven minutes before nine. It will be impossible to continue telling you the time every three minutes from now until Miss Sara arrives. I think you are having a nervous breakdown. Compose yourself.

FANNY It's been twenty years. Any mother would be nervous. If your daughter were coming home and you hadn't seen her, and a husband, and grandchildren—

ANISE I do not say that it is wrong to be nervous. I, too, am nervous. I say only that you are.

FANNY Very well. I heard you. I say that I am. (*She goes back to reading her letter. Looks up*) Jenny's still in California. She's lost her lavallière again. Birdie Chase's daughter is still faire l'amouring with that actor. Tawdry, Jenny says it is. An actor. Fashions in sin change. In my day, it was Englishmen. I don't understand infidelity. If you love a man, then why? If you don't love him, then why stay with him? (*Without turning, she points over her head to Joshua Farrelly's portrait*) Thank God, I was in love. I thought about Joshua last night. Three grandchildren. He would have liked that. I hope I will. (*Points to other letters*) Anything in anybody else's mail?

ANISE Advertisements for Mr. David and legal things. For our Count and Countess, there is nothing but what seems an invitation to a lower-class embassy tea and letters asking for bills to get paid.

FANNY That's every morning. (*Thoughtfully*) In the six weeks the Balkan nobility have been with us, they seem to have run up a great many bills.

ANISE Yes. I told you that. Then there was a night-letter for Mr. David.

(*A very loud, very unpleasant bell begins to ring.*)

FANNY (*through the noise*) Really? From whom?

ANISE From her. I took it on the telephone, and—(*Bell drowns out her voice.*)

FANNY Who is "her"? (*Bell becomes very loud*) Go tell him to stop that noise—

ANISE (*goes toward terrace, calling*) Joseph! Stop that bell. Miss Fanny says to stop it.

JOSEPH (*calls*) Miss Fanny said to start it.

FANNY (*shouts out to him*) I didn't tell you to hang yourself with it.

JOSEPH (*appears on terrace*) I ain't hung. Your breakfast is ready. (*Disappears.*)

FANNY (*to* ANISE) Who is "her"?

ANISE That Carter woman from Lansing, Michigan.

FANNY Oh, my. Is she back in Washington again? What did the telegram say?

ANISE It said the long sickness of her dear Papa had terminated in full recovery.

FANNY That's too bad.

ANISE She was returning, and would Mr. David come for dinner a week from Thursday? "Love," it said, "to you and your charming mother." (*To* FANNY) That's you. I think Miss Carter from Lansing, Michigan, was unwise in attending the illness of her Papa.

FANNY I hope so. Why?

ANISE (*shrugs*) There is much winking of the eyes going on between our Countess and Mr. David.

FANNY (*eagerly*) I know that. Anything new happen?

ANISE (*too innocently*) Happen? I don't know what you mean?

FANNY You know damn well what I mean.

ANISE That? Oh, no, I don't think that.

JOSEPH (*appears in the door*) The sausage cakes is shrinking.

FANNY (*rises. To* ANISE) I want everybody down here immediately. Is the car ready? (ANISE *nods*) Did you order a good dinner? (*Shrieks*) David! Oh.

(DAVID FARRELLY, *a pleasant-looking man of thirty-nine, comes in from the entrance hall, almost bumps into* FANNY.)

DAVID Good morning, everybody.

ANISE (*to* FANNY) Everything is excellent. You have been asking the same questions for a week. You have made the kitchen very nervous.

DAVID (*to* JOSEPH) Why did you ring that air-raid alarm again?

JOSEPH Ain't me, Mr. David. I don't like no noise. Miss Fanny told me.

FANNY Good morning, David.

DAVID (*to* JOSEPH) Tell Fred to leave the car. I'll drive to the station.

JOSEPH (*nods*) Yes, sir. (*Exits.*)

DAVID (*to* FANNY, *half amused, half annoyed, as he begins to read his mail*) Mama, I think we'll fix up the chicken-house for you as a playroom. We'll hang the room with bells and you can go into your second childhood in the proper privacy.

FANNY I find it very interesting. You sleep soundly, you rise at your usual hour—although your sister, whom you haven't seen in years, is waiting at the station—

DAVID She is not waiting at the station. (*Laughs*) The train does not come in until ten minutes past twelve.

FANNY (*airily*) It's almost that now.

ANISE (*turns to look at her*) Really, Miss Fanny, contain yourself. It is twenty minutes before nine.

DAVID And I have not slept soundly. And I've been up since six o'clock.

FANNY The Balkans aren't down yet. Where are they?

DAVID I don't know.

ANISE There's nothing in your mail, Mr. David. Only the usual advertisements.

DAVID And for me, that is all that is ever likely to come—here.

ANISE (*haughtily, as she starts toward hall*) I cannot, of course, speak for Miss Fanny. I have never opened a letter in my life.

DAVID I know. You don't have to. For you they fly open.

FANNY (*giggles*) It's true. You're a snooper, Anise. (ANISE *exits.* FANNY *talks as* ANISE *moves out*) I rather admire it. It shows an interest in life. (*She looks up at Joshua's portrait*) You know, I've been lying awake most of the night wondering what Papa would have thought about Sara. He'd have been very pleased, wouldn't he? I always find myself wondering what Joshua would have felt.

DAVID Yes. But maybe it would be just as well if you didn't expect me to be wondering about it, too. I wasn't married to him, Mama. He was just my father.

FANNY My. You got up on the wrong side of the bed. (*She moves past him. Points to the mail which he is still opening*) The bills are for our noble guests. Interesting, how many there are every morning. How much longer are they going to be with us?

DAVID (*without looking at her*) I don't know.

FANNY It's been six weeks. Now that Sara and her family are coming, even this house might be a little crowded—(*He looks up at her. Quickly*) Yes. I know I invited them. I felt sorry for Marthe, and Teck rather amused me. He plays good cribbage, and he tells good jokes. But that's not enough for a lifetime guest. If you've been urging her to stay, I wish you'd stop it. They haven't any money; all right, lend them some—

DAVID I have been urging them to stay?

FANNY I'm not so old I don't recognize flirting when I see it.

DAVID But you're old enough not to be silly.

FANNY I'm not silly. I'm charming.

(MARTHE DE BRANCOVIS, *an attractive woman of thirty-one or thirty-two, enters.*)

MARTHE Good morning, Fanny. Morning, David.

FANNY Good morning, Marthe.

DAVID (*warmly*) Good morning.

MARTHE Fanny, darling, couldn't you persuade yourself to let me have a tray in bed and some cotton for my ears?

DAVID Certainly not. My father ate breakfast at nine; and whatever my father did . . .

FANNY (*carefully, to* DAVID) There was a night-letter for you from that Carter woman in Lansing, Michigan. She is returning and you are to come to dinner next Thursday. (*As she exits on terrace*) C-A-R-T-E-R. (*Pronounces it carefully*) Lansing, Michigan.

DAVID (*laughs*) I know how to spell Carter, but thank you. (FANNY *exits.* DAVID *looks up at* MARTHE) Do you understand my mother?

MARTHE Sometimes.

DAVID Miss Carter was done for your benefit.

MARTHE (*smiles*) That means she has guessed that I would be jealous. And she has guessed right.

DAVID (*looks at her*) Jealous?

MARTHE I know I've no right to be, but I am. And Fanny knows it.

DAVID (*carelessly*) Don't pay any attention to Mama. She has a sure instinct for the women I like, and she begins to hammer away early. Marthe—(*Goes to decanter on side-table*) I'm going to have a drink. I haven't had a drink before breakfast since the day I took my bar examination. (*Pours himself a drink, gulps it down*) What's it going to be like to stand on a station platform and see your sister after all these years? I'm afraid, I guess.

MARTHE Why?

DAVID I don't know. Afraid she won't like me—(*Shrugs*) We were very fond of each other, but it's been a long time.

MARTHE I remember Sara. Mama brought me one day when your father was stationed in Paris. I was about six and Sara about fifteen and you were—

DAVID You were a pretty little girl.

MARTHE Do you really remember me? You never told me before.

FANNY (*yelling from the terrace*) David! Come to breakfast.

DAVID (*as if he had not been listening*) You know, I've never met Sara's husband. Mama did. I think the first day Sara met him, in Munich. Mama didn't like the marriage much in those days—and Sara didn't care, and Mama didn't like Sara not caring. Mama cut up about it, bad.

MARTHE Why?

DAVID Probably because they didn't let her arrange it. Why does Mama ever act badly? She doesn't remember ten minutes later.

MARTHE Wasn't Mr. Müller poor?

DAVID Oh, Mama wouldn't have minded that. If they'd only come home and let her fix their lives for them—(*Smiles*) But Sara didn't want it that way.

MARTHE You'll have a house full of refugees—us and—

DAVID Are you and Teck refugees? I'm not sure I know what you're refugees from.

MARTHE From Europe.

DAVID From what Europe?

MARTHE (*smiles, shrugs*) I don't know. I don't know myself, really. Just Europe. (*Quickly, comes to him*) Sara will like you. I like you. (*Laughs*) That doesn't make sense, does it?

(*On her speech,* TECK DE BRANCOVIS *appears in the hall. He is a good-looking man of about forty-five. She stops quickly.*)

TECK (*to* MARTHE *and* DAVID) Good morning.

(*The bell gives an enormous ring.*)

DAVID (*goes to terrace*) Good morning, Teck. For years I've been thinking they were coming for Mama with a net. I'm giving up hope. I may try catching her myself. (*Disappears, calling*) Mama? Stop that noise.

TECK I wonder if science has a name for women who enjoy noise? (*Goes to table, picks up his mail*) Many mistaken people, Marthe, seem to have given you many charge accounts.

MARTHE The Countess de Brancovis. That still does it. It would be nice to be able to pay bills again—

TECK Do not act as if I refused to pay them. I did not sleep well last night. I was worried. We have eighty-seven dollars in American Express checks. (*Pleasantly, looking at her*) That's all we have, Marthe.

MARTHE (*shrugs*) Maybe something will turn up. It's due.

TECK (*carefully*) David? (*Then, as she turns to look at him*) The other relatives will arrive this morning?

MARTHE Yes.

TECK (*points to porch*) I think Madame Fanny and Mr. David may grow weary of accents and charity guests. Or is the husband of the sister a rich one?

MARTHE No. He's poor. He had to leave Germany in '33.

TECK A Jew?

MARTHE No. I don't think so.

TECK Why did he have to leave Germany?

MARTHE (*still reading*) Oh, I don't know, Teck. He's an anti-Nazi.

TECK A political?

MARTHE No, I don't think so. He was an engineer. I don't know. I don't know much about him.

TECK Did you sleep well?

MARTHE Yes. Why not?

TECK Money does not worry you?

MARTHE It worries me very much. But I just lie still now and hope. I'm glad to be here. (*Shrugs*) Maybe something good will happen. We've come to the end of a road. That's been true for a long time. Things will have to go one way or the other. Maybe they'll go well, for a change.

TECK I have not come to the end of any road.

MARTHE (*looks at him*) No? I admire you.

TECK I'm going into Washington tonight. Phili has a poker game every Wednesday evening. He has arranged for me to join it.

MARTHE (*after a pause*) Have you been seeing Phili?

TECK Once or twice. Why not? Phili and I are old friends. He may be useful. I do not want to stay in this country forever.

MARTHE You can't leave them alone. Your favorite dream, isn't it, Teck? That they will let you play with them again? I don't think they will, and I don't think you should be seeing Phili, or that you should be seen at the Embassy.

TECK (*smiles*) You have political convictions now?

MARTHE I don't know what I have. I've never liked Nazis, as you know, and you should have had enough of them. They seem to have had enough of you, God knows. It would be just as well to admit they are smarter than you are and let them alone.

TECK (*looking at her carefully, after a minute*) That is interesting.

MARTHE What is interesting?

TECK I think you are trying to say something to me. What is it?

MARTHE That you ought not to be at the Embassy, and that it's insane to play cards in a game with Von Seitz with eighty-seven dollars in your pocket. I don't think he'd like your not being able to pay up. Suppose you lose?

TECK I shall try not to lose.

MARTHE But if you do lose and can't pay, it will be all over Washington in an hour. (*Points to terrace*) They'll find out about it, and we'll be out of here when they do.

TECK I think I want to be out of here. I find that I do not like the picture of you and our host.

MARTHE (*carefully*) There is no picture, as you put it, to like or dislike.

TECK Not yet? I am glad to hear that. (*Comes toward her slowly*) Marthe, you understand that I am not really a fool? You understand that it is unwise to calculate me that way?

MARTHE (*slowly, as if it were an effort*) Yes, I understand that. And I understand that I am getting tired. Just plain tired. The whole thing's too much for me. I've always meant to ask you, since you played on so many sides, why we didn't come out any better. I've always wanted to ask you what happened. (*Sharply*) I'm tired, see? And I just want to sit down. Just to sit down in a chair and stay.

TECK (*carefully*) Here?

MARTHE I don't know. Any place—

TECK You have thus arranged it with David?

MARTHE I've arranged nothing.

TECK But you are trying, eh? (*He comes close to her*) I think not. I would not like that. Do not make any arrangements, Marthe. I may not allow you to carry them through. (*Smiles*) Come to breakfast now.

(*He passes her, disappears on the terrace. She stands still and thoughtful. Then she, too, moves to the terrace, disappears.* JOSEPH *appears on the terrace, carrying a tray toward the unseen breakfast table. The stage is empty. After a minute, there are sounds of footsteps in the hall.* SARA MÜLLER *appears in the doorway, comes toward the middle of the room as if expecting to find somebody, stops, looks around, begins to smile. Behind her in the doorway, are three children; behind them,* KURT MÜLLER. *They stand waiting, watching* SARA. SARA *is forty-one or forty-two, a good-looking woman, with a well-bred, serious face. She is very badly dressed. Her dress is too long, her shoes were bought a long time ago and have no relation to the dress, and the belt of her dress has become untied and is hanging down. She looks clean and dowdy. As she looks around the room, her face is gay and surprised. Smiling, without turning, absently, she motions to the children and* KURT. *Slowly, the children come in.* BODO MÜLLER, *a boy of nine, comes first. He is carrying coats. Behind him, carrying two cheap valises, is* JOSHUA MÜLLER, *a boy of fourteen. Behind him is* BABETTE MÜLLER, *a pretty little girl of twelve. They are dressed for a much colder climate. They come forward, look at their mother, then move to a couch. Behind them is* KURT MÜLLER, *a large, powerful,*

German-looking man of about forty-seven. He is carrying a shabby valise and a brief-case. He stands watching SARA. JOSHUA *puts down the valises, goes to his father, takes the valise from* KURT, *puts it neatly near his, and puts the brief-case near* KURT. BABETTE *goes to* SARA, *takes a package from her, places it near the valise. Then she turns to* BODO, *takes the coats he is carrying, puts them neatly on top of the valises. After a second,* KURT *sits down. As he does so, we see that his movements are slow and careful, as if they are made with effort.)*

BABETTE *(points to a couch near which they are standing. She has a slight accent)* Is it allowed?

KURT *(smiles. He has an accent)* Yes. It is allowed. (BABETTE *and* BODO *sit stiffly on the couch.)*

JOSHUA *(nervously. He has a slight accent)* But we did not sound the bell—

SARA *(idly, as she wanders around the room, her face excited)* The door isn't locked. It never was. Never since I can remember.

BODO *(softly, puzzled)* The entrance of the home is never locked. So.

KURT *(looks at him)* You find it curious to believe there are people who live and do not need to watch, eh, Bodo?

BODO Yes, Papa.

KURT *(smiles)* You and I.

JOSHUA *(smiles)* It is strange. But it must be good, I think.

KURT Yes.

SARA Sit back. Be comfortable. I—I wonder where Mama and David—*(Delighted, sees portrait of Joshua Farrelly, points to it)* And that was my Papa. That was the famous Joshua Farrelly. *(They all look up at it. She wanders around the room)* My goodness, isn't it a fine room? I'd almost forgotten—*(Picks up a picture from the table)* And this was my grandmother. *(Very nervously)* Shall I go and say we're here? They'd be having breakfast, I think. Always on the side terrace in nice weather. I don't know. Maybe—*(Picks up another picture)* "To Joshua and Fanny Farrelly. With admiration. Alfonso, May 7, 1910." I had an ermine boa and a pink coat. I was angry because it was too warm in Madrid to wear it.

BODO Alfons von Spanien? Der hat immer Bilder von sich verschenkt. Ein schlectes Zeichen für einen Mann.

JOSHUA Mama told you it is good manners to speak the language of the country you visit. Therefore, speak in English.

BODO I said he seemed always to give his photograph. I said that is a bad flag on a man. Grow fat on the poor people and give pictures of the face. (JOSHUA *sits down.)*

SARA I remember a big party and cakes and a glass of champagne for me. I was ten, I guess—*(Suddenly laughs)* That was when Mama said the first time a king got shot at, he was a romantic, but the fifth time he was a comedian. And when my father gave his lecture in Madrid, he repeated it—right in Madrid. It was a great scandal. You know, Alfonso was always getting shot at or bombed.

BODO *(shrugs)* Certainement.

JOSHUA Certainement? As-tu perdu la tête?

BABETTE Speak in English, please.

KURT *(without turning)* You are a terrorist, Bodo?

BODO *(slowly)* No.

JOSHUA Then since when has it become *natural* to shoot upon people?

BODO Do not give me lessons. It is neither right nor natural to shoot upon people. I know that.

SARA *(looks at* BABETTE, *thoughtfully)* An ermine boa. A boa is a scarf. I should like to have one for you, Babbie. Once, in Prague, I saw a pretty one. I wanted to buy it for you. But we had to pay our rent. *(Laughs)* But I almost bought it.

BABETTE Yes, Mama. Thank you. Tie your sash, Mama.

SARA *(thoughtfully)* Almost twenty years.

BODO You were born here, Mama?

SARA Upstairs. And I lived here until I went to live with your father. *(Looks out beyond terrace)* Your Uncle David and I used to have a garden, behind the terrace. I wonder if it's still there. I like a garden. I've always hoped we'd have a house some day and settle down—*(Stops, nervously, turns to stare at* KURT, *who is looking at her)* I am talking so foolish. Sentimental. At my age. Gardens and ermine boas. I haven't wanted anything—

KURT *(comes toward her, takes her hand)* Sara. Stop it. This is a fine room. A fine place to be. Everything is so pleasant and full of comfort. This will be a good piano on which to play again. And it is all so clean. I like that. Now, you shall not be a baby. You must enjoy your house, and not be afraid that you hurt me with it. Yes?

BABETTE Papa, tie Mama's sash, please.

SARA *(shyly smiles at him as he leans down to tie the belt)* Yes, of course. It's strange, that's all. We've never been in a place like this together—

KURT That does not mean, and should not mean, that we do not remember how to enjoy what comes our way. We are on a holiday.

JOSHUA A holiday? But for how long? And what plans afterward?

KURT *(quietly)* We will have plans when the hour arrives to make them. (ANISE *appears from the hall. She starts into the room, stops, bewildered. The* MÜLLERS *have not seen her. Then, as* SARA *turns,* ANISE *speaks. As she speaks, the children rise.*)

ANISE What? What?

SARA (*softly*) Anise. It's me. It's Sara.

ANISE (*coming forward slowly*) What? (*Then as she approaches* SARA, *she begins to run toward her*) Miss Sara! Miss Sara! (*They reach each other, both laugh happily.* SARA *kisses* ANISE) I would have known you. Yes, I would. I would have known—(*Excited, bewildered, nervous, she looks toward* KURT) How do you do, sir? How do you do? (*Turns toward the children*) How do you do?

JOSHUA Thank you, Miss Anise. We are in good health.

SARA (*very happily*) You look the same. I think you look the same. Just the way I've always remembered. (*To the others*) This is the Anise I have told you about. She was here before I was born.

ANISE But how—Did you just come in? What a way to come home! And after all the plans we've made! But you were to come on the twelve o'clock train, and Mr. David was to meet you—

BABETTE The twelve o'clock train was most expensive. We could not have come with that train. We liked the train we came on. It was most luxurious.

ANISE (*very nervously, very rattled*) But Madame Fanny will have a fit. I will call her—She will not be able to contain herself. She—

SARA (*softly*) I wanted a few minutes. I'm nervous about coming home, I guess.

BODO (*conversationally*) You are French, Madame Anise?

ANISE Yes, I am from the Bas Rhin. (*She looks past* SARA, *and bobs her head idiotically at* KURT) Sara's husband. That is nice. That is nice.

BODO Yes. Your accent is from the North. That is fine country. We were in hiding there once. (BABETTE *quickly pokes him.*)

ANISE Hiding? You—(*Turns nervously to* KURT) But here we stand and talk. You have not had your breakfast, sir!

BASETTE (*simply, eagerly*) It would be nice to have breakfast.

ANISE Yes, of course—I will go and order it. SARA (*to the children*) What would you like for breakfast?

BABETTE (*surprised*) What would we like? Why, Mama, we will have anything that can be spared. If eggs are not too rare or too expensive—

ANISE (*amazed*) Rare? Why—Oh, I—I must call Miss Fanny now. It is of a necessity. (*Excited, rushing toward terrace, calling*) Miss Fanny. Miss Fanny. (*Back to* SARA) Have you forgotten your Mama's nature? She cannot bear not knowing things. Miss Fanny! What a way to come home! After twenty years and nobody at the station—

FANNY'S VOICE Don't yell at me. What is the matter with you?

ANISE (*excitedly, as* FANNY *draws near*) She's here. They're here. Miss Sara. She's here, I tell you. (FANNY *comes up to her, stares at her, then looks slowly around until she sees* SARA.)

SARA (*softly*) Hello, Mama.

FANNY (*after a long pause, softly, coming toward her*) Sara. Sara, darling. You're here. You're really here. (*She reaches her, takes her arms, stares at her, smiles*) Welcome. Welcome. Welcome to your house. (*Slowly*) You're not young, Sara.

SARA (*smiles*) No, Mama. I'm forty-one.

FANNY (*softly*) Forty-one. Of course. (*Presses her arms again*) Oh, Sara, I'm—(*Then quickly*) You look more like Papa now. That's good. The years have helped you. (*Turns to look at* KURT) Welcome to this house, sir.

KURT (*warmly*) Thank you, Madame.

FANNY (*turns to look at* SARA again, *nervously pats her arm. Nods, turns again to stare at* KURT. *She is nervous and chatty*) You are a good-looking man, for a German. I didn't remember you that way. I like a good-looking man. I always have.

KURT (*smiles*) I like a good-looking woman. I always have.

FANNY Good. That's the way it should be.

BODO (*to* SARA) Ist das Grossmama?

FANNY (*looks down*) Yes. I am your grandmother. Also, I speak German, so do not talk about me. I speak languages very well. But there is no longer anybody to speak with. Anise has half forgotten her French, which was always bad; and I have nobody with whom to speak my Italian or German or—Sara, it's very good to have you home. I'm chattering away, I—

JOSHUA Now you have us, Madame. We speak ignorantly, but fluently, in German, French, Italian, Spanish—

KURT And boastfully in English.

BODO There is never a need for boasting. If we are to fight for the good of all men, it is to be accepted that we must be among the most advanced.

ANISE My God.

FANNY (*to* SARA) Are these your *children?* Or are they dressed up midgets?

SARA (*laughs*) These are my children, Mama. This, Babette. (BABETTE *bows*) This, Joshua. (JOSHUA *bows*) This is Bodo. (BODO *bows.*)

FANNY Joshua was named for Papa. You wrote me. (*Indicates picture of Joshua Farrelly*) You bear a great name, young man.

JOSHUA (*smiles, indicates his father*) My name is Müller.

FANNY (*looks at him, laughs*) Yes. You look a little like your grandfather. (*To* BABETTE) And so do you. You are a nice-looking girl. (*To* BODO) You look like nobody.

BODO (*proudly*) I am not beautiful.

FANNY (*laughs*) Well, Sara, well. Three children. You have done well. (*To* KURT) You, too, sir, of course. Are you quite recovered? Sara wrote that you were in Spain and—

BODO Did Mama write that Papa was a great hero? He was brave, he was calm, he was expert, he was resourceful, he was—

KURT (*laughs*) My biographer. And as unprejudiced as most of them.

SARA Where is David? I am so anxious—Has he changed much? Does he . . .

FANNY (*to* ANISE) Don't stand there. Go and get him right away. Go get David. (*As* ANISE *exits*) He's out having breakfast with the titled folk. Do you remember Marthe Randolph? I mean, do you remember Hortie Randolph, her mother, who was my friend? Can you follow what I'm saying? I'm not speaking well today.

SARA (*laughs*) Of course I remember Marthe and Hortie. You and she used to scream at each other.

FANNY Well, Martha, her daughter, married Teck de Brancovis. *Count* de Brancovis. He was fancy when she married him. Not so fancy now, I suspect. Although still chic and tired. You know what I mean, the way they are in Europe. Well, they're here.

SARA What's David like now? I—

FANNY Like? Like? I don't know. He's a lawyer. You know that. Papa's firm. He's never married. You know that, too—

SARA Why hasn't he married?

FANNY Really, I don't know. I don't think he likes his own taste. Which is very discriminating of him. He's had a lot of girls, of course, one more ignorant and silly than the other—(*Goes toward terrace, begins to scream*) And where is he? David! David!

ANISE'S VOICE He's coming, Miss Fanny. He's coming. Contain yourself. He was down at the garage getting ready to leave—

FANNY I don't care where he is. Tell him to come.—David! (*Suddenly points to picture of Joshua*) That's my Joshua. Handsome, eh? We were very much in love. Hard to believe of people nowadays, isn't it?

SARA Kurt and I love each other.

FANNY Oh. You do? I daresay. But there are ways and ways of loving.

SARA How dare you, Mama—

KURT (*laughs*) Ladies, ladies.

SARA (*giggles*) Why, I almost got mad then. You know, I don't think I've been mad since I last saw you.

BODO My! You and Mama must not get angry. Anger is protest. And so you must direction it to the proper channels and then harness it for the good of other men. That is correct, Papa?

FANNY (*peers down at him*) If you grow up to talk like that, and stay as ugly as you are, you are going to have one of those successful careers on the lecture platform. (JOSHUA *and* BABETTE *laugh.*)

JOSHUA (*to* BODO) Ah. It is a great pleasure to hear Grandma talk with you.

BODO (*to* FANNY, *tenderly*) We will not like each other. (KURT *has wandered to the piano. Standing, he touches the keys in the first bars of a Mozart Rondo.*)

FANNY You are wrong. I think we are rather alike; if that is so, let us at least remember to admire each other. (DAVID *comes running in from the entrance hall. At the door he stops, stares at* SARA.)

DAVID (*to* SARA) Sara. Darling—

SARA (*wheels, goes running toward him. She moves into his arms. He leans down, kisses her with great affection*) David. David.

DAVID (*softly*) It's been a long, long time. I got to thinking it would never happen. (*He leans down, kisses her hair. After a minute, he smiles, presses her arm.*)

SARA (*excited*) David, I'm excited. Isn't it strange? To be here, to see each other—But I am forgetting. This is my husband. These are my children. Babette, Joshua, Bodo. (*They all three advance, stand in line to shake hands.*)

BODO (*shaking hand*) How do you do, Uncle David?

DAVID How do you do, Bodo? (DAVID *shakes hands with* JOSHUA) Boys can shake hands. But so pretty a girl must be kissed. (*He kisses* BABETTE. *She smiles, very pleased, and crosses to the side of* SARA.)

BABETTE Thank you. Fix your hairpin, Mama. (SARA *shoves back a falling hairpin.*)

DAVID (*crossing to* KURT) I'm happy to meet you, sir, and to have you here.

KURT Thank you. Sara has told me so much from you. You have a devoted sister.

DAVID (*very pleased*) Have I? Still? That's mighty good to hear. (ANISE *comes in from the library.*)

ANISE Your breakfast is coming. Shall I wash the children, Miss Sara?

JOSHUA (*amazed*) Wash us? Do people wash each other?

SARA No, but the washing is a good idea. Go along now, and hurry. (*All three start for the hall*) And then we'll all have a fine, big breakfast again. (*The children exit.*)

FANNY Again? Don't you usually have a good breakfast?

KURT (*smiles*) No, Madame. Only sometimes.

SARA (*laughs*) Oh, we do all right, usually. (*Very happily, very gaily*) Ah, it's good to be here. (*Puts her arm in* DAVID'S) We were kids. Now we're all grown up! I've got children, you're a lawyer, and a fine one, I bet—

FANNY The name of Farrelly on the door didn't, of course, hurt David's career.

DAVID (*smiles*) Sara, you might as well know Mama thinks of me only as a monument to Papa and a not very well-made monument at that. I am not the man Papa was.

SARA (*to* FANNY, *smiles*) How do you know he's not?

FANNY (*carefully*) I beg your pardon. That is the second time you have spoken disrespectfully of your father. (SARA *and* DAVID *laugh.* FANNY *turns to* KURT) I hope you will like me.

KURT I hope so.

SARA (*pulls him to the couch, sits down with him*) Now I want to hear about you—(*Looks at him, laughs*) I'm awfully nervous about seeing you. Are you, about me?

DAVID Yes. I certainly am.

SARA (*looks around*) I'm like an idiot. I want to see everything right away. The lake, and my old room—and I want to talk and ask questions . . .

KURT (*laughs*) More slow, Sara. It is most difficult to have twenty years in a few minutes.

SARA Yes, I know, but—Oh, well. Kurt's right. We'll say it all slowly. It's just nice being back. Haven't I fine children?

DAVID Very fine. You're lucky. I wish I had them.

FANNY How could you have them? All the women you like are too draughty, if you know what I mean. I'm sure that girl from Lansing, Michigan, would be sterile. Which is as God in his wisdom would have it.

SARA Oh. So you have a girl?

DAVID I have no girl. This amuses Mama.

FANNY He's very attractive to some women. (*To* KURT) Both my children are attractive, whatever else they're not. Don't you think so? (*Points to* DAVID) He's flirting with our Countess now, Sara. You will see for yourself.

DAVID (*sharply*) You are making nervous jokes this morning, Mama. And they're not very good ones.

FANNY (*gaily*) I tell the truth. If it turns out to be a joke, all the better.

SARA (*affectionately*) Ah, Mama hasn't changed. And that's good, too.

FANNY Don't mind me, Sara. I, too, am nervous about seeing you. (*To* KURT) You'll like it here. You are an engineer?

KURT Yes.

FANNY Do you remember the day we met in München? The day Sara brought you to lunch? I thought you were rather a clod and that Sara would have a miserable life. I think I was wrong. (*To* DAVID) You see? I always admit when I'm wrong.

DAVID You are a woman who is noble in all things, at all times.

FANNY Oh, you're mad at me. (*To* KURT) As I say, you'll like it here. I've already made some plans. The new wing will be for you and Sara. The old turkey-house we'll fix up for the children. A nice, new bathroom, and we'll put in their own kitchen, and Anise will move in with them—

SARA That's kind of you, Mama. But—but—we won't make any plans for a while—(*Very quietly*) A good, long vacation; God knows Kurt needs it—

FANNY A vacation? You'll be staying here, of course. You don't have to worry about work—engineers can always get jobs, David says, and he's already begun to inquire—

KURT I have not worked as an engineer since many years, Madame.

DAVID Haven't you? I thought—Didn't you work for Dornier?

KURT Yes. Before '33.

FANNY But you have worked in other places. A great many other places, I should say. Every letter of Sara's seemed to have a new postmark.

KURT (*smiles*) We move most often.

DAVID You gave up engineering?

KURT I gave it up? (*shrugs*) One could say it that way.

FANNY What do you do?

SARA Mama, we—

KURT It is difficult to explain.

DAVID (*after a slight pause*) If you'd rather not.

FANNY No, I—I'm trying to find out something. (*To* KURT) May I ask it, sir?

KURT Let me help you, Madame. You wish to know whether not being an engineer buys adequate breakfasts for my family. It does not. I have no wish to make a mystery of what I have been doing; it is only that it is awkward to place neatly. (*Smiles, motions with his hand*) It sounds so big: it is so small. I am an Anti-Fascist. And that does not pay well.

FANNY Do you mind questions?

SARA Yes.

KURT (*sharply*) Sara. (*To* FANNY) Perhaps I shall not answer them. But I shall try.

FANNY Are you a radical?

KURT You would have to tell me what that word means to you, Madame.

FANNY (*after a slight pause*) That is just. Perhaps we all have private definitions. We all are Anti-Fascists, for example—

SARA Yes. But Kurt works at it.

FANNY What kind of work?

KURT Any kind. Anywhere.

FANNY (*sharply*) I will stop asking questions.

SARA (*very sharply*) That would be sensible, Mama.

DAVID Darling, don't be angry. We've been worried about you, naturally. We knew so little, except that you were having a bad time.

SARA I didn't have a bad time. We never—

KURT Do not lie for me, Sara.

SARA I'm not lying. I didn't have a bad time, the way they mean. I—

FANNY (*slowly*) You had a bad time just trying to live, didn't you? That's obvious, Sara, and foolish to pretend it isn't. Why wouldn't you take money from us? What kind of nonsense—

SARA (*slowly*) We've lived the way we wanted to live. I don't know the language of rooms like this any more. And I don't want to learn it again.

KURT Do not bristle about it.

SARA I'm not bristling. (*To* FANNY) I married because I fell in love. You can understand that.

FANNY (*slowly*) Yes.

SARA For almost twelve years, Kurt went to work every morning and came home every night, and we lived modestly, and happily—(*Sharply*) As happily as peo_ple could in a starved Germany that was going to pieces—

KURT Sara, please. You are angry. I do not like it that way. I will try to find a way to tell you with quickness. Yes. (SARA *turns, looks at him, starts to speak, stops*) I was born in a town called Fürth. (*Pauses. Looks up, smiles*) There is a holiday in my town. We call it Kirchweih. It was a gay holiday with games and music and a hot white sausage to eat with the wine. I grow up, I move away—to school, to work—but always I come back for Kirchweih. It is for me, the great day of the year. (*Slowly*) But after the war, that day begins to change. The sausage is made from bad stuff, the peasants come in without shoes, the children are too sick—(*Carefully*) It is bad for my people, those years, but always I have hope. In the festival of August, 1931, more than a year before the storm, I give up that hope. On that day, I see twenty-seven men murdered in a Nazi street fight. I cannot stay by now and watch. My time has come to move. I say with Luther, "Here I stand. I can do nothing else. God help me. Amen."

SARA It doesn't pay well to fight for what we believe in. But I wanted it the way Kurt wanted it. (*Shrugs*) They don't like us in Europe; I guess they never did. So Kurt brought us home. You've always said you wanted us. If you don't, I will understand.

DAVID Darling, of course we want you—

FANNY (*rises*) I am old. And made of dry cork. And bad-mannered. Please forgive me.SARA (*goes quickly to* FANNY) Shut up, Mama. We're all acting like fools. I'm glad to be home. That's all I know. So damned glad.

DAVID And we're damned glad to have you. Come on. Let's walk to the lake. We've made it bigger and planted the island with blackberries—(*She smiles and goes to him. Together they move out the hall entrance.*)

FANNY (*after a silence*) They've always liked each other. We're going to have Zwetschgen-Knoedel for dinner. You like them?

KURT Indeed.

FANNY I hope you like decent food.

KURT I do.

FANNY That's a good sign in a man.

MARTHE (*coming in from the terrace. Stops in the doorway*) Oh, I'm sorry, Fanny. We were waiting. I didn't want to interrupt the family reunion. I—

FANNY This is my son-in-law, Herr Müller. The Countess de Brancovis.

KURT AND MARTHE (*together*) How do you do?

MARTHE And how is Sara, Herr Müller? I haven't seen her since I was a little girl. She probably doesn't remember me at all. (TECK *comes in from the hall. She turns*) This is my husband, Herr Müller.

KURT How do you do?

TECK How do you do, sir? (KURT *bows. They shake hands*) Would it be impertinent for one European to make welcome another?

KURT (*smiles*) I do not think so. It would be friendly.

BODO (*appears at the hall door*) Papa—(*Sees* TECK *and* MARTHE, *bows*) Oh, good morning. Miss Anise says you are the Count and Countess. Once before we met a Count and Countess. They had a small room bordering on ours in Copenhagen. They were more older than you, and more poor. We shared with them our newspaper.

MARTHE (*laughs*) It wasn't us, but it might have been. What's your name?

TECK (*laughs*) We hope you will be as kind to us.

BODO My name is Bodo. It's a strange name. No? (*To* KURT) Papa, this is the house of great wonders. Each has his bed, each has his bathroom. The arrangement of it, that is splendorous.

FANNY (*laughs*) You are a fancy talker, Bodo.

KURT Oh, yes. In many languages.

BODO (*to* FANNY) Please to correct me when I am wrong. Papa, the plumbing is such as you have never seen. Each implement is placed on the floor, and all are simultaneous in the same room. You will therefore see that being placed most solidly on the floor allows of no rats, rodents or crawlers, and is most sanitary. (*To the others*) Papa will be must interested. He likes to know how each thing of everything is put together. And he is so fond of being clean—

KURT (*laughs. To* FANNY) I am a hero to my children. It bores everybody but me.

TECK It is most interesting, Herr Müller. I thought I had a good ear for the accents of your country. But yours is most difficult to place. It is Bayrisch? Or is it—

BODO That's because Papa has worked in so many—

KURT (*quickly*) German accents are the most difficult to identify. I, myself, when I try, am usually incorrect. It would be particularly difficult with me because I speak other languages. Yours would be Roumanian?

MARTHE (*laughs*) My God, is it that bad?

KURT (*smiles*) I am showing off. I know the Count de Brancovis is Roumanian.

TECK (*heartily*) So? We have met before? I thought so, but I cannot remember—

KURT No, sir. We have not met before. I read your name in the newspapers.

TECK (*to* KURT) Strange. I was sure I had met you. I was in the Paris Legation for many years, and I thought perhaps—

KURT Oh, no. If it is possible to believe, I am the exile who is not famous. (*To* FANNY) I have been thinking with pleasure, Madame Fanny, of breakfast on your porch. (*He points to the picture of Joshua Farrelly*) Your husband once wrote: "I am getting older now and Europe seems far away. Fanny and I will have an early breakfast on the porch and then I shall drive the bays into Washington." (*Remembering*) And then he goes on: "Henry Adams tells me he has been reading Karl Marx. I shall have to tell him my father made me read Marx many years ago and that, since he proposes to exhibit himself to impress me, will spoil Henry's Sunday."

FANNY (*laughs, delighted. Takes* KURT'S *arm*) And so it did. I had forgotten that. I am pleased with you. I shall come and serve you food myself. I had forgotten Joshua ever wrote it. (*They start out of the terrace doors together, followed by* BODO.)

KURT (*as they disappear*) I try to impress you. I learned it last night. (FANNY *laughs. They disappear.*)

TECK (*smiles*) He is a clever man. A quotation from Joshua Farrelly is a sure road to Fanny's heart. Where did you say Herr Müller was from?

MARTHE Germany.

TECK I know that. (*Goes to a valise. He leans over, stares at it, looks at the labels, pushes the lock. The lock opens; he closes it. Then he turns and, as he speaks, picks up the brief-case*) What part of Germany?

MARTHE I don't know. And I never knew you were an expert on accents.

TECK I never knew it either. Are you driving into Washington with David this morning?

MARTHE I was going to. But he may not be going to the office, now that Sara's here. I was to have lunch with Sally Tyne. (TECK *puts down the brief-case*) What are you doing?

TECK Wondering why luggage is unlocked and a shabby brief-case is so carefully locked.

MARTHE You're very curious about Mr. Müller.

TECK Yes. And I do not know why. Something far away . . . I am curious about a daughter of the Farrellys' who marries a German who has bullet scars on his face and broken bones in his hands.

MARTHE (*sharply*) Has he? There are many of them now, I guess.

TECK So there are. But this one is in this house. (*He goes to the bell cord, pulls it. She watches him nervously.*)

MARTHE Is it—is he any business of yours?

TECK What is my business? Anything might be my business now.

MARTHE Yes—unfortunately. You might inquire from your friend Von Seitz. They always know their nationals.

TECK (*pleasantly, ignoring the sharpness with which she has spoken*) Oh, yes, I will do that, of course. But I do not like to ask questions without knowing the value of the answers.

MARTHE Teck. This man is a little German Sara married years ago. I remember Mama talking about it. He was nothing then and he isn't now. They've had a tough enough time already without—

TECK Have you—Have you been sleeping with David?

MARTHE (*stops, stares at him, then simply*) No. I have not been. And that hasn't been your business for a good many years now.

TECK You like him?

MARTHE (*nervously*) What's this for, Teck?

TECK Answer me, please.

MARTHE I—(*She stops.*)

TECK Yes? Answer me.

MARTHE I do like him.

TECK What does he feel about you?

MARTHE I don't know.

TECK But you are trying to find out. You have made plans with him?

MARTHE Of course not. I—

TECK But you will try to make him have plans. I have recognized it. Well, we have been together a long—(JOSEPH *enters,* TECK *stops*) Joseph, Miss Fanny wishes you to take the baggage upstairs.

JOSEPH Yes, sir. I was going to. (*He begins to pick up the baggage.* MARTHE *has turned sharply and is staring at* TECK. *Then she rises, watches* JOSEPH *pick up the baggage, turns again to look at* TECK.)

TECK As I was saying. It is perhaps best that we had this talk.

MARTHE (*she stops, waits for* JOSEPH *to move off. He exits, carrying the valises*) Why did you do that? Why did you tell Joseph that Fanny wanted him to take the baggage upstairs?

TECK Obviously it is more comfortable to look at baggage behind closed doors.

MARTHE (*very sharply*) What kind of silliness is this now? Leave these people alone—(*As he starts to exit*) I won't let you—

TECK What? (*As he moves again, she comes after him.*)

MARTHE I said I won't let you. You are not—

TECK How many times have you seen me angry? (MARTHE *looks up, startled*) You will not wish to see another. Run along now and have lunch with something you call Sally Tyne. But do not make plans with David. You will not be able to carry them out. You will go with me, when I am ready to go. You understand. (*He exits during his speech. The last words come as he goes through the door, and as the curtain falls.*)

★

ACT TWO

SCENE: *The same as Act One, about ten days later. During the act it will begin to grow dark; but the evening is warm and the terrace doors are open.*

AT RISE: SARA *is sitting on the couch, crocheting.* FANNY *and* TECK *are sitting at a small table playing cribbage.* BODO *is sitting near them, at a large table, working on a heating pad. The cord is torn from the bag, the bag is ripped open.* ANISE *sits next to him, anxiously watching him. Outside on the terrace,* JOSHUA *is going through baseball motions, coached by* JOSEPH. *From time to time they move out of sight, reappear, move off again.*

★

FANNY (*playing a card*) One.

BODO (*after a minute, to* TECK) The arrangement of this heating pad grows more complex.

TECK (*smiles, moves on the cribbage board*) And the more wires you remove, the more complex it will grow.

BODO (*points to bag*) Man has learned to make man comfortable. Yet all cannot have the comforts. (*To* ANISE) How much did this cost you?

ANISE It cost me ten dollars. And you have made a ruin of it.

BODO That is not yet completely true. (*To* FANNY) Did I not install for you a twenty-five-cent button-push for your radio?

TECK (*playing a card*) Two and two. (*Moves pegs on the cribbage board.*)

FANNY Yes, you're quite an installer.

BODO (*to* TECK) As I was wishing to tell you, Count de Brancovis, comfort and plenty exist. Yet all cannot have them it. Why?

TECK I do not know. It has worried many men. Why?

ANISE (*to* BODO) Yes, why?

BODO (*takes a deep breath, raises his finger as if about to lecture*) Why? (*Considers a moment, then deflates himself*) I am not as yet sure.

ANISE I thought not.

FANNY (*turns to look at* JOSHUA *and* JOSEPH *on the terrace*) Would you mind doing that dancing some place else?

JOSEPH (*looking in*) Yes'm. That ain't dancing. I'm teaching Josh baseball.

FANNY Then maybe he'd teach you how to clean the silver.

JOSEPH I'm a good silver-cleaner, Miss Fanny.

FANNY But you're getting out of practice.

JOSEPH (*after a moment's thought*) Yes'm. I see what you mean. (*He exits.*)

FANNY (*playing a card*) Three.

JOSHUA It is my fault. I'm crazy about baseball.

BODO Baseball players are among the most exploited people in this country. I read about it.

FANNY You never should have learned to read.

BODO Their exploited condition is foundationed on the fact that—

JOSHUA (*bored*) All right, all right. I still like baseball.

SARA Founded, Bodo, not foundationed.

JOSHUA He does it always. He likes long words. In all languages.

TECK How many languages do you children speak?

BODO Oh, we do not really know any very well, except German and English. We speak bad French and—

SARA And bad Danish and bad Czech.

TECK You seem to have stayed close to the borders of Germany. Did Herr Müller have hopes, as so many did, that National Socialism would be overthrown on every tomorrow?

SARA We have not given up that hope. Have you, Count de Brancovis?

TECK I never had it.

JOSHUA (*pleasantly*) Then it must be most difficult for you to sleep.

TECK I beg your pardon?

SARA Schweig doch, Joshua!

FANNY (*to* TECK) Sara told Joshua to shut up. (*Playing a card*) Twelve.

TECK I have offended you, Mrs. Müller. I am most sorry.

SARA (*pleasantly*) No, sir, you haven't offended me. I just don't like polite political conversations any more.

TECK (*nods*) All of us, in Europe, had too many of them.

SARA Yes. Too much talk. By this time all of us must know where we are and what we have to do. It's an indulgence to sit in a room and discuss your beliefs as if they were a juicy piece of gossip.

FANNY You know, Sara, I find it very pleasant that Kurt, considering his history, doesn't make platform speeches. He hasn't tried to convince anybody of anything.

SARA (*smiles*) Why should he, Mama? You are quite old enough to have your own convictions—or Papa's.

FANNY (*turns to look at her*) I am proud to have Papa's convictions.

SARA Of course. But it might be well to have a few new ones, now and then.

FANNY (*peers over at her*) Are you criticizing me?

SARA (*smiles*) Certainly not.

BABETTE (*comes running in from the right entrance door. She has on an apron and she is carrying a plate. She goes to* FANNY) Eat it while it's hot. Grandma.

(FANNY *peers down, takes the fork, begins to eat.* ANISE *and* BODO *both rise, move to* FANNY, *inspect the plate.*)

FANNY (*to them*) Go away.

ANISE It is a potato pancake.

FANNY And the first good one I've eaten in many, many years. I love a good potato pancake.

BODO I likewise.

BABETTE I am making a great number for dinner. Move away, Bodo.

TECK (*playing a card*) Fifteen and two.

ANISE (*who has followed* BODO *back to the table, leans over to look at the heating pad*) You've ruined it! I shall sue you.

JOSHUA I told you not to let him touch it.

SARA (*laughs*) I remember you were always saying that, Anise—that you were going to sue. That's very French. I was sick once in Paris, and Babbie stayed up for a whole night and day and finished a dress I was making for a woman in the Rue Jacob. I told her to tell the woman she'd done it—I thought perhaps the woman would give her a candy or something—and anyway, I was very proud of her work. But no. The woman admitted the dress was well done, but said she was going to sue because I hadn't done it myself. Fancy that.

FANNY (*slowly*) You sewed for a living?

SARA Not a very good one. But Babbie and I made a little something now and then. Didn't we, darling?

FANNY (*sharply*) Really, Sara, were these—these things necessary? Why couldn't you have written?

SARA (*laughs*) You've asked me that a hundred times in the last week.

JOSHUA (*gently*) I think it is only that Grandma feels sorry for us. Grandma has not seen much of the world.

FANNY Don't you start giving me lectures, Joshua. I'm fond of you. And of you, Babbie. (*To* ANISE) Are there two desserts for dinner? And are they sweet?

ANISE Yes.

FANNY (*turns to* BODO) I wish I were fond of you.

BODO You are. (*Happily*) You are very fond of me.

FANNY (*playing a card*) Twenty-five.

BASETTE This is for you, Grandma. I'm making a bed-jacket. It is nice lace. Papa brought it to me from Spain and I mean for you to have it.

FANNY (*kisses* BABETTE) Thank you, darling. A sequence and three. A pair and five. (*To* TECK, *as they finish the cribbage game*) There. That's two dollars off. I owe you eight-fifty.

TECK Let us carry it until tomorrow. You shall give it to me as a going-away token.

FANNY (*too pleased*) You're going away?

TECK (*laughs*) Ah, Madame Fanny. Do not sound that happy.

FANNY Did I? That's rude of me. When are you going?

TECK In a few days, I think. (*Turns to look at* SARA) We're too many refugees, eh, Mrs. Müller?

SARA (*pleasantly*) Perhaps.

TECK Will you be leaving, also?

SARA I beg your pardon?

TECK I thought perhaps you, too, would be moving on. Herr Müller does not give me the feeling of a man who settles down. Men who have done his work, seldom leave it. Not for a quiet country house.

(*All three children look up.*)

SARA (*very quietly*) What work do you think my husband has done, Count de Brancovis?

TECK Engineering?

SARA (*slowly*) Yes. Engineering.

FANNY (*very deliberately to* TECK) I don't know what you're saying. They shall certainly not be leaving—ever. Is that understood, Sara?

SARA Well, Mama—

FANNY There are no wells about it. You've come home to see me die and you will wait until I'm ready.

SARA (*laughs*) Really, Mama, that isn't the reason I came home.

FANNY It's a good enough reason. I shall do a fine death. I intend to be a great deal of trouble to everybody.

ANISE I daresay.

FANNY I shall take to my bed early and stay for years. In great pain.

ANISE I am sure of it. You will duplicate the disgrace of the birth of Miss Sara.

SARA (*laughs*) Was I born in disgrace?

ANISE It was not your fault. But it was disgusting. Three weeks before you were to come—all was excellent, of course, in so healthy a woman as Madame Fanny—a great dinner was given here and, most unexpectedly, attended by a beautiful lady from England.

FANNY Do be still. You are dull and fanciful—

ANISE Mr. Joshua made the great error of waltzing the beauty for two dances, Madame Fanny being unfitted for the waltz and under no circumstances being the most graceful of dancers.

FANNY (*her voice rising*) Are you crazy? I danced magnificently.

ANISE It is well you thought so. A minute did not elapse between the second of the waltzes and a scream from Madame Fanny. She was in labor. Two hundred people, and if we had left her alone, she would have remained in the ballroom—

FANNY How you invent! How you invent!

ANISE Do not call to me that I am a liar. For three weeks you are in the utmost agony—

FANNY And so I was. I remember it to this day—

ANISE (*to* SARA, *angrily*) Not a pain. Not a single pain. She would lie up there in state, stealing candy from herself. Then, when your Papa would rest himself for a minute at the dinner or with a book, a scream would dismantle the house—it was revolting. (*Spitefully to* FANNY) And now the years have passed I may disclose to you that Mr. Joshua knew you were going through the play-acting—

FANNY (*rises*) He did not. You are a malicious—

ANISE Once he said to me, "Anise, it is well that I am in love. This is of a great strain and her great-uncle Freddie was not right in the head, neither."

FANNY (*screaming*) You will leave this house—You are a liar, a woman of—

SARA Mama, sit down.

ANISE I will certainly leave this house. I will—

SARA (*sharply*) Both of you. Sit down. And be still.

ANISE She has intimated that I lie—

FANNY (*screaming*) Intimated! Is that what I was doing—(ANISE *begins to leave the room*) All right. I beg your pardon. I apologize.

(ANISE *turns*.)

SARA Both of you. You are acting like children.

BODO Really, Mama. You insult us.

ANISE I accept your apology. Seat yourself.

(*They both sit down.*)

FANNY (*after a silence*) I am unloved.

BABETTE I love you, Grandma.

FANNY Do you, Babbie?

JOSHUA And I.

FANNY (*nods, very pleased. To* BODO) And you?

BODO I loved you the primary second I saw you.

FANNY You are a charlatan.

ANISE As for me, I am fond of all the living creatures. It is true that the children cause me greater work, which in turn more greatly inconveniences the feet. However, I do not complain. I believe in children.

FANNY Rather like believing in the weather, isn't it? (DAVID *and* KURT *come in from the terrace. Both are in work clothes, their sleeves rolled up*) Where have you been?

DAVID Oh, we've been helping Mr. Chabeuf spray the fruit trees.

ANISE Mr. Chabeuf says that Herr Müller has the makings of a good farmer. From a Frenchman that is a large thing to say.

KURT (*who has looked around the room, looked at* TECK, *strolled over to* BODO) Mr. Chabeuf and I have an excellent time exchanging misinformation. My father was a farmer. I have a wide knowledge of farmer's misinformation.

FANNY This is good farm land. Perhaps, in time—

DAVID (*laughs*) Mama would give you the place, Kurt, if you guaranteed that your great-grandchildren would die here.

KURT (*smiles*) I would like to so guarantee.

TECK A farmer. That is very interesting. Abandon your ideals, Herr Müller?

KURT Ideals? (*Carefully*) Sara, heisst das auf deutsch "Ideale"?

SARA Yes.

KURT Is that what I have now? I do not like the word. It gives to me the picture of a small, pale man at a seaside resort. (*To* BODO) What are you doing?

BODO Preparing an elderly electric pad for Miss Anise. I am confused.

KURT (*wanders toward the piano*) So it seems.

BODO Something has gone wrong with the principle on which I have been working. It is probably that I will ask your assistance.

KURT (*bows to him*) Thank you. Whenever you are ready. (*Begins to pick out notes with one hand.*)

FANNY We shall have a little concert tomorrow evening. In honor of Babbie's birthday. (*To* KURT) Kurt, you and I will play "The Clock Symphony." Then Joshua and I will play the duet we've learned, and Babbie will sing. And I shall finish with a Chopin Nocturne.

DAVID (*laughs*) I thought you'd be the last on the program.

TECK Where is Marthe?

FANNY She'll be back soon. She went into town to do an errand for me. (*To* DAVID) Did you buy presents for everybody?

DAVID I did.

SARA (*smiles, to* BABETTE) We always did that here. If somebody had a birthday, we all got presents. Nice, isn't it?

DAVID (*to* ANISE) I shall buy you an electric pad. You will need it.

ANISE Indeed.

FANNY Did you buy me a good present?

DAVID Pretty good. (*Pats* BABETTE*'s head*) The best present goes to Babbie; it's her birthday.

FANNY Jewelry?

DAVID No, not jewelry.

FANNY Oh. Not jewelry.

DAVID Why?

FANNY (*too casually*) I just asked you.

TECK (*gets up*) It was a natural mistake, David. You see, Mrs. Mellie Sewell told your mother that she had seen you and Marthe in Barstow's. And your mother said you were probably buying her a present, or one for Babbie.

DAVID (*too sharply*) Yes.

TECK (*laughs*) Yes what?

DAVID (*slowly*) Just yes.

FANNY (*too hurriedly*) Mellie gets everything wrong. She's very anxious to meet Marthe because she used to know Francie Cabot, her aunt. Marthe's aunt, I mean, not Mellie's.

SARA (*too hurriedly*) She really came to inspect Kurt and me. But I saw her first. (*She looks anxiously at* DAVID, *who has turned his back on the room and is facing the terrace*) You were lucky to be out, David.

DAVID Oh, she calls every Saturday afternoon, to bring Mama all the Washington gossip of the preceding week. She gets it all wrong, you understand, but that doesn't make any difference to either Mama or her. Mama then augments it, wits it up, Papa used to say—

FANNY Certainly. I sharpen it a little. Mellie has no sense of humor.

DAVID So Mama sharpens it a little, and delivers it tomorrow afternoon to old lady Marcy down the road. Old lady Marcy hasn't heard a word in ten years, so she unsharpens it again, and changes the names. By Wednesday afternoon—

TECK (*smiles*) By Wednesday afternoon it will not be you who were in Barstow's, and it will be a large diamond pin with four sapphires delivered to Gaby Deslys.

DAVID (*turns, looks at him*) Exactly.

FANNY (*very nervously*) Francie Cabot, Marthe's aunt, you understand—(*To* KURT) Did you ever know Paul von Seitz, a German?

KURT I have heard of him.

FANNY (*speaking very rapidly*) Certainly. He was your Ambassador to somewhere, I've forgotten. Well, Francie Cabot married him. I could have. Any American, not crippled, whose father had money—He was crazy about me. I was better-looking than Francie. Well, years later when he was your Ambassador—my father was, too, as you probably know—not your Ambassador, of course, ours—but I am talking about Von Seitz.

DAVID (*laughs to* KURT) You can understand how it goes. Old lady Marcy is not entirely to blame.

FANNY Somebody asked me if I didn't regret not marrying him. I said, "Madame, je le regrette tous les jours et j'en suis heureuse chaque soir." (FANNY *turns to DAVID*) That means I regret it every day and am happy about it every night. You understand what I meant, by night? Styles in wit change so.

DAVID I understood it, Mama.

JOSHUA We, too, Grandma.

BABETTE (*approvingly*) It was most witty.

BODO I do not know that I understood. You will explain to me, Grandma?

SARA Later.

FANNY (*turns to look at* TECK) You remember the old Paul von Seitz?

TECK (*nods*) He was stationed in Paris when I first was there.

FANNY Of course. I always forget you were a diplomat.

TECK It is just as well.

FANNY There's something insane about a Roumanian diplomat. Pure insane. I knew another one, once. He wanted to marry me, too.

SARA (*laughs*) All of Europe.

FANNY Not all. Some. Naturally. I was rich, I was witty, my family was of the best. I was handsome, unaffected—

DAVID And noble and virtuous and kind and elegant and fashionable and simple—it's hard to remember everything you were. I've often thought it must have been boring for Papa to have owned such perfection.

FANNY (*shrieks*) What! Your father bored with me! Not for a second of our life—

DAVID (*laughs*) Oh God, when will I learn?

BODO Do not shriek, Grandma. It is an unpleasant sound for the ear.

FANNY Where was I? Oh, yes. What I started out to say was—(*She turns, speaks carefully to* TECK) Mellie Sewell told me, when you left the room, that she had heard from Louis Chandler's child's governess that you had won quite a bit of money in a poker game with Sam Chandler and some Germans at the Embassy. (KURT, *who has been playing the piano, stops playing very abruptly.* TECK *turns to look at him*) That's how I thought of Von Seitz. His nephew Philip was in on the game.

DAVID (*looks at* TECK) It must have been a big game. Sam Chandler plays in big games.

TECK Not big enough.

DAVID Have you known Sam long?

TECK For years. Every Embassy in Europe knew him.

DAVID (*sharply*) Sam and Nazis must make an unpleasant poker game. (KURT *begins to play a new melody.*)

TECK (*who has not looked away from* KURT) I do not play poker to be amused.

DAVID (*irritably*) What's Sam selling now?

TECK Bootleg munitions. He always has.

DAVID You don't mind?

TECK Mind? I have not thought about it.

FANNY Well, you ought to think about it. Sam Chandler has always been a scoundrel. All the Chandlers are. They're cousins of mine. Mama used to say they never should have learned to walk on two feet. They would have been more comfortable on four.

TECK Do you know the young Von Seitz, Herr Müller? He was your military attaché in Spain.

KURT He was the German government attaché in Spain. I know his name, of course. He is a famous artillery expert. But the side on which I fought was not where he was stationed, Count de Brancovis.

ANISE (BABETTE *and* JOSHUA *begin to hum the song* KURT *is playing.* SARA *begins to hum*) It is time for the bath and the change of clothes. I will give you five more minutes—

FANNY What is the song?

TECK It was a German soldier's song. They sang it as they straggled back in '18. I remember hearing it in Berlin. Were you there then, Herr Müller?

KURT (*the playing and the humming continue*) I was not in Berlin.

TECK But you were in the war, of course?

KURT Yes. I was in the war.

FANNY You didn't think then you'd live to see another war.

KURT Many of us were afraid we would.

FANNY What are the words?

SARA The Germans in Spain, in Kurt's Brigade, wrote new words for the song.

KURT This was what you heard in Berlin, in 1918.

(*Begins to sing.*)

"Wir zieh'n Heim, wir zieh'n Heim,
Mancher kommt nicht mit,
Mancher ging verschütt,
Aber Freunde sind wir stets."

(*in English.*)

"We come home. We come home.
Some of us are gone, and some of us are lost, but we are friends:
Our blood is on the earth together.
Some day. Some day we shall meet again.
Farewell."

(*Stops singing*) At a quarter before six on the morning of November 7th, 1936, eighteen years later, five hundred Germans walked through the Madrid streets on their way to defend the Manzanares River. We felt good that morning. You know how it is to be good when it is needed to be good? So we had need of new words to say that. I translate with awkwardness, you understand. (*Begins to sing.*)

"And so we have met again.
The blood did not have time to dry.
We lived to stand and fight again.
This time we fight for people.
This time the bastards will keep their hands away.
Those who sell the blood of other men, this time,
They keep their hands away.
For us to stand.
For us to fight.
This time no farewell, no farewell."

(*Music dies out. There is silence for a minute*) We did not win. (*Looks up, gently*) It would have been a different world if we had.

SARA Papa said so years ago. Do you remember, Mama? "For every man who lives without freedom, the rest of us must face the guilt."

FANNY Yes. "We are liable in the conscience-balance for the tailor in Lodz, the black man in our South, the peasant in—" (*Turns to* TECK. *Unpleasantly*) Your country, I think.

ANISE (*rises*) Come. Baths for everybody. (*To* BODO) Gather the wires. You have wrecked my cure.

BODO If you would allow me a few minutes more—

ANISE Come along. I have been duped for long enough. Come Joshua. Babette. Baths.

JOSHUA (*starts out after* ANISE. BABETTE *begins to gather up her sewing*) My tub is a thing of glory. But I do not like it so prepared for me and so announced by Miss Anise. (*He exits.*)

BODO (*to* ANISE) You are angry about this. I do not blame you with my heart or my head. I admit I have failed. But Papa will repair it, Anise. Will you not, Papa? In a few minutes—

TECK (*to* BODO) Your father is an expert electrician?

BODO Oh yes, sir.

TECK And as good with radio—

(BODO *begins to nod.*)

KURT (*sharply*) Count de Brancovis. Make your questions to me, please. Not to my children.

(*The others look up, surprised.*)

TECK (*pleasantly*) Very well, Herr Müller.

ANISE (*as she exits with* BODO) Nobody can fix it. You have made a pudding of it.

BODO (*as he follows her*) Do not worry. In five minutes tonight, you will have a pad far better—(*As* BODO *reaches the door he bumps into* MARTHE *who is carrying large dress boxes*) Oh. Your pardon. Oh, hello. (*He disappears.*)

MARTHE (*gaily*) Hello. (*To* FANNY) I waited for them. I was afraid they wouldn't deliver this late in the day. (*To* SARA) Come on, Sara. I can't wait to see them.

SARA What?

MARTHE Dresses. From Fanny. A tan linen, and a dark green with wonderful buttons, a white net for Babbie, and a suit for you, and play dresses for Babbie, and a dinner dress in gray to wear for Babbie's birthday—gray should be good for you, Sara—all from Savitt's. We sneaked the measurements, Anise and I—

SARA (*she goes toward* FANNY) How nice of you, Mama. How very kind of you. And of you, Marthe, to take so much trouble—(*She leans down, kisses* FANNY) You're a sweet woman, Mama.

DAVID That's the first time Mama's ever heard that word. (*He takes the boxes from* MARTHE, *puts them near the staircase,* MARTHE *smiles at him, touches his hand, as* TECK *watches them.*)

FANNY (*giggles*) I have a bottom sweetness, if you understand what I mean.

DAVID I have been too close to the bottom to see it.

FANNY That should be witty. I don't know why it isn't.

(BABETTE *goes over to stare at the boxes.*)

SARA From Savitt's. Extravagant of you. They had such lovely clothes. I remember my coming-out dress—(*Goes to* KURT) Do you remember the black suit with the braid, and the Milan hat? Not the first day we met, but the picnic day? (*He smiles up at her*) Well, they were from Savitt's. That was over twenty years ago—I've known you a long time. Me, in an evening dress. Now you'll have to take me into Washington. I want to show off. Next week, and we'll dance, maybe—(*Sees that he is not looking at her*) What's the matter, darling? (*No answer. Slowly he turns to look at her*) What's the matter, Kurt? (*Takes his arms, very unhappily*) What have I done? It isn't that dresses have ever mattered to me, it's just that—

KURT Of course, they have mattered to you. As they should. I do not think of the dresses. (*Draws her to him*) How many years have I loved that face?

SARA (*her face very happy*) So?

KURT So. (*He leans down, kisses her, as if it were important.*)

SARA (*pleased, unembarrassed*) There are other people here.

MARTHE (*slowly*) And good for us to see.

TECK Nostalgia?

MARTHE No. Nostalgia is for something you have known.

(FANNY *coughs.*)

BABETTE (*comes to* FANNY) Grandma, is it allowed to look at my dresses?

FANNY Of course, child. Run along.

BABETTE (*picks up the boxes, goes toward the hall entrance, stops near* FANNY) I love dresses, I have a great fondness for materials and colors. Thank you, Grandma. (*She runs out of the room.*)

(JOSEPH *appears in the doorway.*)

JOSEPH There is a long-distance operator with a long-distance call for Mr. Müller. She wants to talk with him on the long-distance phone.

KURT Oh—Excuse me, please—

(KURT *rises quickly.* SARA *turns sharply to look at him.* TECK *looks up.* KURT *goes quickly out.* TECK *watches him go.* SARA *stands staring after him.*)

MARTHE (*laughs*) I feel the same way as Babbie. Come on, Sara. Let's try them on.

(SARA *does not turn.*)

TECK You also have a new dress?

MARTHE (*looks at him*) Yes. Fanny was kind to me, too.

TECK You are a very generous woman, Madame Fanny. Did you also give her a sapphire bracelet from Barstow's?

FANNY I beg your—

DAVID (*slowly*) No. I gave Marthe the bracelet. And I understand that it is not any business of yours.

(FANNY *rises.* SARA *turns.*)

FANNY Really, David—

DAVID Be still, Mama.

TECK (*after a second*) Did you tell him that, Marthe?

MARTHE Yes.

TECK (*looks up at her*) I shall not forgive you for that. (*Looks at* DAVID) It is a statement which no man likes to hear from another man. You understand that? (*Playfully*) That is the type of thing about which we used to play at duels in Europe.

DAVID (*comes toward him*) We are not so musical comedy here. And you are not in Europe.

TECK Even if I were, I would not suggest any such action. I would have reasons for not wishing it.

DAVID It would be well for you not to suggest *any* action. And the reason for *that* is you might get hurt.

TECK (*slowly*) That would not be my reason. (*To* MARTHE) Your affair has gone far enough—

MARTHE (*sharply*) It is not an affair—

TECK I do not care what it is. The time has come to leave here. Go upstairs and pack your things. (*She does not move.* DAVID *turns toward her*) Go on, Marthe.

MARTHE (*to* DAVID) I am not going with him. I told you that.

DAVID I don't want you to go with him.

FANNY (*carefully*) Really, David, aren't you interfering in all this a good deal—

DAVID (*carefully*) Yes, Mama. I am.

TECK (*to* MARTHE) When you are speaking to me, please say what you have to say to me.

MARTHE (*comes to him*) You are trying to frighten me. But you are not going to frighten me any more. I will say it to you: I am not going with you. I am never going with you again.

TECK (*softly*) If you do not fully mean what you say, or if you might change your mind, you are talking unwisely, Marthe.

MARTHE I know that.

TECK Shall we talk about it alone?

MARTHE You can't make me go, can you, Teck?

TECK No, I can't make you.

MARTHE Then there's no sense talking about it.

TECK Are you in love with him?

MARTHE Yes.

FANNY (*sharply*) Marthe! What is all this?

MARTHE (*sharply*) I'll tell *you* about it in a minute.

DAVID You don't have to explain anything to anybody.

TECK (*ignores him*) Is he in love with you?

MARTHE I don't think so. You won't believe it, because you can't believe anything that hasn't got tricks to it, But David hasn't much to do with this. I told you I would leave some day, and I remember where I said it—(*Slowly*)—and why I said it.

TECK I also remember. But I did not believe you. I have not had much to offer you these last years. But if now we had some money and could go back—

MARTHE No. I don't like you, Teck. I never have.

TECK And I have always known it.

FANNY (*stiffly*) I think your lack of affections should be discussed with more privacy. Perhaps—

DAVID Mama—

MARTHE There is nothing to discuss. Strange. I've talked to myself about this scene for almost fifteen years. I knew a lot of things to say to you and I used to lie awake at night or walk along the street and say them. Now I don't want to. I guess you only want to talk that way, when you're not sure what you can do. When you're sure, then what's the sense of saying it? "This is why and this is why and this—" (*Very happily*) But when you know you can do it, you don't have to say anything; you can just go. And I'm going. There is nothing you can do. I would like you to believe that now.

TECK Very well, Marthe. I think I made a mistake. I should not have brought you here. I believe you now.

MARTHE (*after a pause, she looks at* DAVID) I'll move into Washington, and—

DAVID Yes. Later. But I'd like you to stay here for a while, with us, if you wouldn't mind.

SARA It would be better for you, Marthe—

FANNY It's very interesting that I am not being consulted about this. (*To* MARTHE) I have nothing against you, Marthe. I am sorry for you, but I don't think—

MARTHE Thank you, Sara, David. But I'd rather move in now. (*Turns, comes toward* FANNY) But perhaps I have something against you. Do you remember my wedding?

FANNY Yes.

MARTHE Do you remember how pleased Mama was with herself? Brilliant Mama, handsome Mama—everybody thought so, didn't they? A seventeen-year-old daughter, marrying a pretty good title, about to secure herself in a world that Mama liked—she didn't ask me what I liked. And the one time I tried to tell her, she frightened me—(*Looks up*) Maybe I've always been frightened. All my life.

TECK Of course.

MARTHE (*to* FANNY, *as if she had not heard* TECK) I remember Mama's face at the wedding—it was *her* wedding, really, not mine.

FANNY (*sharply*) You are very hard on your mother.

MARTHE Nineteen hundred and twenty-five. No, I'm not hard on her. I only tell the truth. She wanted a life for me, I suppose. It just wasn't the life I wanted for myself. (*Sharply*) And that's what you have tried to do. With your children. In another way. Only Sara got away. And that made you angry—until so many years went by that you forgot.

FANNY I don't usually mind people saying anything they think, but I find that—

MARTHE I don't care what you mind or don't mind. I'm in love with your son—

FANNY (*very sharply*) That's unfortunate—

MARTHE And I'm sick of watching you try to make him into his father. I don't think you even know you do it any more and I don't think he knows it any more, either. And that's what's most dangerous about it.

FANNY (*very angrily*) I don't know what you are talking about.

DAVID I think you do. (*Smiles*) You shouldn't mind hearing the truth—and neither should I.

FANNY (*worried, sharply*) David! What does all this nonsense mean? I—

MARTHE (*to* FANNY) Look. That pretty world Mama got me into was a tough world, see? I'm used to trouble. So don't try to interfere with me, because I won't let you. (*She goes to* DAVID) Let's just have a good time. (*He leans down, takes both her hands, kisses them. Then slowly, she turns away, starts to exit. To* TECK) You will also be going today?

TECK Yes.

MARTHE Then let us make sure we go in different directions, and do not meet again. Good-bye, Teck.

TECK Good-bye, Marthe. You will not believe me, but I tried my best, and I am now most sorry to lose you.

MARTHE Yes. I believe you. (*She moves out. There is silence for a minute.*)

FANNY Well, a great many things have been said in the last few minutes.

DAVID (*crosses to bell cord. To* TECK) I will get Joseph to pack for you.

TECK Thank you. Do not bother. I will ring for him when I am ready. (KURT *comes in from the study door.* SARA *turns, stares at him, waits. He does not look at her*) It will not take me very long. (*He starts for the door, looking at* KURT.)

SARA What is it, Kurt?

KURT It is nothing of importance, darling—(*He looks quickly at* TECK, *who is moving very slowly.*)

SARA Don't tell me it's nothing. I know the way you look when—

KURT (*sharply*) I said it was of no importance. I must get to California for a few weeks. That is all.

SARA I—

TECK (*turns*) It is in the afternoon newspaper, Herr Müller. (*Points to paper on table*) I was waiting to find the proper moment to call it to your attention. (*He moves toward the table, as they all turn to watch him. He picks up the paper, turns it over, begins to read*) "Zurich, Switzerland: The Zurich papers today reprinted a despatch from the *Berliner Tageblatt* on the capture of Colonel Max Freidank. Freidank is said—(SARA *begins to move toward him*)—to be the chief of the Anti-Nazi Underground Movement. Colonel Friedank has long been an almost legendary figure. The son of the famous General Freidank, he was a World War officer and a distinguished physicist before the advent of Hitler." That is all.

SARA Max—

KURT Be still, Sara.

TECK They told me of it at the Embassy last night. They also told me that with him they had taken a man who called himself Ebber, and a man who called himself Triste. They could not find a man called Gotter. (*He starts again toward the door*) I shall be a lonely man without Marthe. I am also a very poor one. I should like to have ten thousand dollars before I go.

DAVID (*carefully*) You will make no loans in this house.

TECK I was not speaking of a loan.

FANNY (*carefully*) God made you not only a scoundrel but a fool. That is a dangerous combination.

DAVID (*suddenly leaps toward* TECK) Damn you, you—

KURT (*suddenly pounds on the top of the piano, as* DAVID *almost reaches* TECK) Leave him alone. (*Moves quickly to stop* DAVID) Leave him alone! *David! Leave him alone!*

DAVID (*angrily to* KURT) Keep out of it. (*Starts toward* TECK *again*) I'm beginning to see what Marthe meant. Blackmailing with your wife—You—

KURT (*very sharply*) He is not speaking of his wife. Or you. He means me. (*Looks at* TECK) Is that correct?

(SARA *moves toward* KURT. DAVID *draws back, bewildered.*)

TECK Good. It was necessary for me to hear you say it. You understand that?

KURT I understand it.

SARA (*frightened, softly*) Kurt—

DAVID What is all this about? What the hell are you talking about?

TECK (*sharply for the first time*) Be still. (*To* KURT) At your convenience. Your hands are shaking, Herr Müller.

KURT (*quietly*) My hands were broken; they are bad when I have fear.

TECK I am sorry. I can understand that. It is not pleasant. (*Motions toward* FANNY *and* DAVID) Perhaps you would like a little time to—I will go and pack, and be ready to leave. We will all find that more comfortable, I think. You should get yourself a smaller gun, Herr Müller. That pistol you have been carrying is big and awkward.

KURT You saw the pistol when you examined our bags?

TECK You knew that?

KURT Oh, yes. I have the careful eye, through many years of needing it. And then you have not the careful eye. The pistol was lying to the left of a paper package and when you leave, it is to the right of the package.

SARA Kurt! Do you mean that—

KURT (*sharply*) Please, darling, do not do that.

TECK It is a German Army Luger?

KURT Yes.

TECK Keep it in your pocket, Herr Müller. You will have no need to use it. And, in any case, I am not afraid of it. You understand that?

KURT (*slowly*) I understand that you are not a man of fears. That is strange to me, because I am a man who has so many fears.

TECK (*laughs, as he exits*) Are you? That is most interesting. (*He exits.*)

DAVID (*softly*) What is this about, Kurt?

KURT He knows who I am and what I do and what I carry with me.

SARA (*carefully*) What about Max?

KURT The telephone was from Mexico, Ilse received a cable. Early on the morning of Monday, they caught Ebber and Triste. An hour after they took Max in Berlin. (*She looks up at him, begins to shake her head. He presses her arm*) Yes. It is hard.

FANNY (*softly*) You said he knew who you were and what you carried with you. I don't understand.

KURT I am going to tell you: I am an outlaw. I work with many others in an illegal organization. I have so worked for seven years. I am on what is called a desired list. But I did not know I was worth ten thousand dollars. My price has risen.

DAVID (*slowly*) And what do you carry with you?

KURT Twenty-three thousand dollars. It has been gathered from the pennies and the nickels of the poor who do not like Fascism, and who believe in the work we do. I came here to bring Sara home and to get the money. I had hopes to rest here for a while, and then—

SARA (*slowly*) And I had hopes someone else would take it back and you would stay with us—(*Shakes her head, then*) Max is not dead?

KURT No. The left side of his face is dead. (*Softly*) It was a good face.

SARA (*to* FANNY *and* DAVID, *as if she were going to cry*) It was a very good face. He and Kurt—in the old days—(*To* KURT) After so many years. If Max got caught, then nobody's got a chance. Nobody. (*She suddenly sits down.*)

DAVID (*points upstairs*) He wants to sell what he knows to you? Is that right?

KURT Yes.

FANNY Wasn't it careless of you to leave twenty-three thousand dollars lying around to be seen?

KURT No, it was not careless of me. It is in a locked briefcase. I have thus carried money for many years. There seemed no safer place than Sara's home. It was careless of you to have in your house a man who opens baggage and blackmails.

DAVID (*sharply*) Yes. It was very careless.

FANNY But you said you knew he'd seen it—

KURT Yes. I knew it the first day we were here. What was I to do about it? He is not a man who steals. This is a safer method. I knew that it would come some other way. I have been waiting to see what the way would be. That is all I could do.

DAVID (*to* FANNY) What's the difference? It's been done (*To* KURT) If he wants to sell to you, he must have another buyer. Who?

KURT The Embassy. Von Seitz, I think.

DAVID You mean he has told Von Seitz about you and—

KURT No. I do not think he has told him anything. As yet. It would be foolish of him. He has probably only asked most guarded questions.

DAVID But you're here. You're in this country. They can't do anything to you. They wouldn't be crazy enough to try it. Is your passport all right?

KURT Not quite.

FANNY Why not? Why isn't it?

KURT (*wearily, as if he were bored*) Because people like me are not given visas with such ease. And I was in a hurry to bring my wife and my children to safety. (*Sharply*) Madame Fanny, you must come to understand it is no longer the world you once knew.

DAVID It doesn't matter. You're a political refugee. We don't turn back people like you. People who are in danger. You will give me your passport and tomorrow morning I'll see Barens. We'll tell him the truth—(*Points to the door*) Tell de Brancovis to go to hell. There's not a damn thing he or anybody else can do.

SARA (*looks up at* KURT, *who is staring at her*) You don't understand, David.

DAVID There's a great deal I don't understand. But there's nothing to worry about.

SARA Not much to worry about as long as Kurt is in this house. But he's not going to—

KURT The Count has made the guess that—

SARA That you will go back to get Ebber and Triste and Max. Is that right, Kurt? Is that right?

KURT Yes, darling, I will try. They were taken to Sonnenburg. Guards can be bribed—It has been done once before at Sonnenburg. We will try for it again. I must go back, Sara. I must start.

SARA Of course, you must go back. I guess I was trying to think it wouldn't come. But—(*To* FANNY *and* DAVID) Kurt's got to go back. He's got to go home. He's got to buy them out. He'll do it, too. You'll see. (*She stops, breathes*) It's hard enough to get back. Very hard. But if they knew he was coming—They want Kurt bad. Almost as much as they wanted Max—And then there are hundreds of others, too—(*She gets up, comes to him. He holds her, puts his face in her hair. She stands holding him, trying to speak without crying. She puts her face down on his head*) Don't be scared, darling. You'll get back. You'll see. You've done it before—you'll do it again. Don't be scared. You'll get Max out all right. (*Gasps*) And then you'll do his work, won't you? That's good. That's fine, You'll do a good job, the way you've always done. (*She is crying very hard. To* FANNY) Kurt doesn't feel well. He was wounded and he gets tired—(*To* KURT) You don't feel well, do you? (*Slowly. She is crying too hard now to be heard clearly*) Don't be scared, darling. You'll get home. Don't worry, you'll get home. Yes, you will.

(*The curtain falls.*)

★

ACT THREE

SCENE: *The same. A half hour later.*

AT RISE: FANNY *is sitting in a chair.* KURT *is at the piano, his head resting on one hand. He is playing softly with the other hand.* SARA *is sitting very quietly on the couch.* DAVID *is pacing on the terrace.*

★

FANNY (*to* DAVID) David, would you stop that pacing, please? (DAVID *comes in*) And would you stop that one-hand piano playing? Either play, or get up.

(KURT *gets up, crosses to the couch, sits.* SARA *looks at him, gets up, crosses to the decanters, begins to make a drink.*)

SARA (*to* DAVID) A drink?

DAVID What? Yes, please. (*To* KURT) Do you intend to buy your friends out of jail?

KURT I intend to try.

FANNY It's all very strange to me. I thought things were so well run that bribery and—

KURT (*smiles*) What a magnificent work Fascists have done in convincing the world that they are men from legends.

DAVID They have done very well for themselves—unfortunately.

KURT Yes. But not by themselves. Does it make us all uncomfortable to remember that they came in on the shoulders of the most powerful men in the world? Of course, And so we would prefer to believe they are men from the planets. They are not. Let me reassure you. They are smart, they are sick, and they are cruel. But given men who know what they fight for—(*Shrugs*) I will console you. A year ago last month, at three o'clock in the morning, Freidank and I, with two elderly pistols, raided the home of the Gestapo chief in Konstanz, got what we wanted, and the following morning Friedank was eating his breakfast three blocks away, and I was over the Swiss border.

FANNY (*slowly*) You are brave men.

KURT *I* do not tell you the story to prove we are remarkable, but to prove they are *not*.

(SARA *brings him a drink. Gives one to* DAVID.)

SARA (*softly, touching* KURT'S *shoulder*) Kurt loves Max.

KURT Always since I came here I have a dream: that he will come into this room some day. How he would like it here, eh, Sara? He loves good food and wine, and you have books—(*Laughs happily*) He is fifty-nine years of age. And when he was fifty-seven, he carried me on his back, seven miles across the border. I had been hurt—That takes a man, does it not?

FANNY (to KURT) You look like a sick man to me.

KURT No. I'm only tired. I do not like to wait. It will go. It is the waiting that is always most bad for me.

DAVID (*points upstairs*) Damn him! He's doing it deliberately.

KURT It is then the corruption begins. Once in Spain I waited for two days until the planes would exhaust themselves. I think then why must our side fight always with naked hands. The spirit and the hands. All is against us but ourselves.

SARA You will not think that when the time comes. It will go.

KURT Of a certainty.

FANNY But does it have to go on being your hands?

KURT For each man, his own hands. He has to sleep with them.

DAVID (*uncomfortably, as if he did not like to say it*) That's right. I guess it's the way all of us should feel. But—but you have a family. Isn't there somebody else who hasn't a wife and children—

KURT Each could have his own excuse. Some love for the first time, some have bullet holes, some have fear of the camps, some are sick, many are getting older. (*Shrugs*) Each could find a reason. And many find it. My children are not the only children in the world, even to me.

FANNY That's noble of you, of course. But they are your children, nevertheless. And Sara, she—

SARA Mama—

KURT (*after a slight pause*) One means always in English to insult with that word noble?

FANNY Of course not, I—

KURT It is not noble. It is the way I must live. Good or bad, it is what I am. (*Turns deliberately to look at* FANNY) And what I am is not what you wanted for your daughter, twenty years ago or now.

FANNY You are misunderstanding me.

KURT (*smiles*) For our girl, too, we want a safe and happy life. And it is thus I try to make it for her. We each have our way. I do not convert you to mine.

DAVID You are very certain of your way.

KURT (*smiles*) I seem so to you? Good.

(JOSEPH *appears in the hall doorway. He is carrying valises and overcoats.*)

JOSEPH What'll I do with these, Miss Fanny?

FANNY They're too large for eating, aren't they? What were you thinking of doing with them?

JOSEPH I mean, it's Fred's day off.

DAVID All right. You drive him into town.

JOSEPH Then who's going to serve at dinner?

FANNY (*impatiently*) Belle can do it alone tonight.

JOSEPH No she can't. Belle's upstairs packing with Miss Marthe. My, there's quite a lot of departing, ain't there?

FANNY (*very impatiently*) All right, then cook can bring in dinner.

JOSEPH I wouldn't ask her to do that, if I were you. She's mighty mad: the sink pipe is leaking again. You just better wait for your dinner till I get back from Washington.

FANNY (*shouting*) We are not cripples and we were eating dinner in this house before you arrived to show us how to use the knife and fork. (JOSEPH *laughs*) Go on. Put his things in the car. I'll ring for you when he's ready.

JOSEPH You told me the next time you screamed to remind you to ask my pardon.

FANNY You call that screaming?

JOSEPH Yes'm.

FANNY Very well. I ask your pardon. (*Waves him away*) Go on!

JOSEPH Yes'm. (*Exits.*)

(TECK *appears in the door. He is carrying his hat and the brief-case we have seen in Act One.* SARA, *seeing the brief-case, looks startled, looks quickly at* KURT. KURT *watches* TECK *as he comes toward him.* TECK *throws his hat on a chair, comes to the table at which* KURT *is sitting, puts the brief-case on the table.* KURT *puts out his hand, puts it on the brief-case, leaves it there.*)

TECK (*smiles at the gesture*) Nothing has been touched, Herr Müller. I brought it from your room, for your convenience.

FANNY (*angrily*) Why didn't you steal it? Since you do not seem to—

TECK That would have been very foolish of me, Madame Fanny.

KURT Very.

TECK I hope I have not kept you waiting too long. I wanted to give you an opportunity to make any explanations—

DAVID (*angrily*) Does your price include listening to this tony conversation?

TECK (*turns to look at him*) My price will rise if I have to spend the next few minutes being interrupted by your temper. I will do my business with Herr Müller. And you will understand, I will take from you no interruptions, no exclamations, no lectures, no opinions of what I am or what I am doing.

KURT (*quietly*) You will not be interrupted.

TECK (*sits down at table with* KURT) I have been curious about you, Herr Müller. Even before you came here. Because Fanny and David either knew very little about you, which was strange, or wouldn't talk about you, which was just as strange. Have you ever had come to you one of those insistent half-memories of some person or some place?

KURT (*quietly, without looking up*) You had such a half-memory of me?

TECK Not even a memory, but something. The curiosity, of one European for another, perhaps.

KURT A most sharp curiosity. You lost no time examining—(*Pats the* case)—this. You are an expert with locks?

TECK No, indeed. Only when I wish to be.

FANNY (*angrily, to* TECK) I would like you out of this house as quickly as—

TECK (*turns to her*) Madame Fanny, I have just asked Mr. David not to do that. I must now ask you. (*Leans forward to* KURT) Herr Müller, I got one of the desired lists from Von Seitz, without, of course, revealing anything to him. As you probably know, they are quite easy to get. I simply told him that we refugees move in small circles and I might come across somebody on it. If, however, I have to listen to any more of this from any of you, I shall go immediately to him.

KURT (*to* DAVID *and* FANNY) Please allow the Count to do this in his own way. It will be best.

TECK (*takes a sheet of paper from his pocket*) There are sixty-three names on this list. I read them carefully, I narrow the possibilities and under "G" I find Gotter. (*Begins to read*) "Age, forty to forty-five. About six feet. One hundred seventy pounds. Birthplace unknown to us. Original occupation unknown to us, although he seems to know Munich and Dresden. Schooling unknown to us. Family unknown to us. No known political connections. No known trade-union connections. Many descriptions, few of them in agreement and none of them of great reliability. Equally unreliable, though often asked for, were Paris, Copenhagen, Brussels police descriptions. Only points on which there is agreement: married to a foreign woman, either American or English; three children; has used name of Gotter, Thomas Bodmer, Karl Francis. Thought to have left Germany in 1933, and to have joined Max Freidank shortly after. Worked closely with Freidank, perhaps directly under his orders. Known to have crossed border in 1934—February, May, June, October. Known to have again crossed border with Max Friedank in 1935—August, twice in October, November, January—"

KURT (*smiles*) The report is unreliable. It would have been impossible for God to have crossed the border that often.

TECK (*looks up, laughs. Then looks back at list*) "In 1934, outlaw radio station announcing itself as Radio European, begins to be heard. Station was located in Düsseldorf: the house of a restaurant waiter was searched, and nothing was found. Radio heard during most of 1934 and 1935. In an attempt to locate it, two probable Communists killed in the tool-house of a farm near Bonn. In three of the broadcasts, Gotter known to have crossed border immediately before and after. Radio again became active in early part of 1936. Active attempt made to locate Freidank. Gotter believed to have then appeared in Spain with Madrid Government army, in one of the German brigades, and to have been a brigade commander under previously used name of Bodmer. Known to have stayed in France the first months of 1938. Again crossed German border some time during week when Hitler's Hamburg radio speech interrupted and went off the air." (*Looks up*) That was a daring deed, Herr Müller. It caused a great scandal. I remember. It amused me.

KURT It was not done for that reason.

TECK "Early in 1939, informer in Konstanz reported Gotter's entry, carrying money which had been exchanged in Paris and Brussels. Following day, home of Konstanz Gestapo chief raided for spy list by two men—" (KURT *turns to look at* FANNY *and* DAVID, *smiles*) My God, Herr Müller, that job took two good men.

SARA (*angrily*) Even you admire them.

TECK Even I. Now I conclude a week ago that you are Gotter, Karl Francis—

KURT Please. Do not describe me to myself again.

TECK And that you will be traveling home—(*Points to brief-case*)—with this. But you seem in no hurry, and so I must wait. Last night when I heard that Freidank has been taken, I guess that you will now be leaving. Not for California. I will tell you free of charge, Herr Müller, that they have got no information from Freidank or the others.

KURT Thank you. But I was sure they would not. I know all three most well. They will take what will be given them.

TECK (*looks down. Softly*) There is a deep sickness in the German character, Herr Müller. A pain-love, a death-love—

DAVID (*very angrily*) Oh, for God's sake, spare us *your* moral judgments.

FANNY (*very sharply*) Yes. They are sickening. Get on!

KURT Fanny and David are Americans and they do not understand our world—as yet. (*Turns to* DAVID *and* FANNY) All Fascists are not of one mind, one stripe. There are those who give the orders, those who carry out the orders, those who watch the orders being carried out. Then there are those who are half in, half hoping to come in. They are made to do the dishes and clean the boots. Frequently they come in high places and wish now only to survive. They come late: some because they did not jump in time, some because they were stupid, some because they were shocked at the crudity of the *German* evil, and preferred their own evils, and some because they were fastidious men. For those last, we may well some day have pity. They are lost men, their spoils are small, their day is gone. (*To* TECK) Yes?

TECK (*slowly*) Yes. You have the understanding heart. It will get in your way some day.

KURT (*smiles*) I will watch it.

TECK We are both men in trouble, Herr Müller. The world, ungratefully, seems to like your kind even less than it does mine. (*Leans forward*) Now. Let us do business. You will not get back if Von Seitz knows you are going.

KURT You are wrong. Instead of crawling a hundred feet an hour in deep night, I will walk across the border with as little trouble as if I were a boy again on a summer walking trip. There are many men they would like to have. I would be allowed to walk directly to them—until they had all the names and all the addresses. (*Laughs, points his finger at* TECK) *Roumanians* would pick me up ahead of time. *Germans* would not.

TECK (*smiles*) Still the national pride?

KURT Why not? For that which is good.

FANNY (*comes over, very angrily, to* TECK) I have not often in my life felt what I feel now. Whatever you are, and however you became it, the picture of a man selling the lives of other men—

TECK Is very ugly, Madame Fanny. I do not do it without some shame, and therefore I must sink my shame in large money. (*Puts his hand on the brief-case*) The money is here. For ten thousand, you go back to save your friends, nobody will know that you go, and I will give you my good wishes. (*Slowly, deliberately,* KURT *begins to shake his head,* TECK *waits, then carefully*) No?

KURT This money is going home with me. It was not given to me to save my life, and I shall not so use it. It is to save the lives and further the work of more than I. It is important to me to carry on that work and to save the lives of three valuable men, and to do that with all speed. But—(*Sharply*) Count de Brancovis, the first morning we arrived in this house, my children wanted their breakfast with great haste. That is because the evening before we had been able only to buy milk and buns for them. If I would not touch this money for them, I would not touch it for you. (*Very sharply*) It goes back with me. The way it is. And if it does not get back, it is because I will not get back.

(*There is a long pause.* SARA *gets up, turns away.*)

TECK Then I do not think you will get back. You are a brave one, Herr Müller, but you will not get back.

KURT (*as if he were very tired*) I will send to you a postal card and tell you about my bravery.

DAVID (*coming toward* KURT) Is it true that if this swine talks, you and the others will be—

SARA (*very softly*) Caught and killed. Of course. If they're lucky enough to get killed quickly. (*Quietly, points to the table*) You should have seen his hands in 1935.

FANNY (*violently, to* DAVID) We'll give him the money. For God's sake, let's give it to him and get him out of here.

DAVID (*to* SARA) Do you want Kurt to go back?

SARA Yes. I do.

DAVID All right. (*Goes to her, lifts her face*) You're a good girl.

KURT That is true. Brave and good, my Sara. She is everything. She is handsome and gay and—(*Puts his hand over his eyes.* SARA *turns away.*)

DAVID (*after a second, comes to stand near* TECK) If we give you the money, what is to keep you from selling to Von Seitz?

TECK I do not like your thinking I would do that. But—

DAVID (*tensely*) Look here. I'm sick of what you'd like or wouldn't like. And I'm sick of your talk. We'll get this over with now, without any more fancy talk from you, or as far as I am concerned, you can get out of here without my money and sell to any buyer you can find. I can't take much more of you at any cost.

TECK (*smiles*) It is your anger which delays us. I was about to say that I understood your fear that I would go to Von Seitz, and I would suggest that you give me a small amount of cash now and a check dated a month from now. In a month, Herr Müller should be nearing home, and he can let you know. And if you should not honor the check because Herr Müller is already in Germany, Von Seitz will pay a little something for a reliable description. I will take my chance on that. You will now say that I could do that in any case—and that is the chance you will take.

DAVID (*looks at* KURT, *who does not look up*) Is a month enough? For you to get back?

KURT (*shrugs*) I do not know.

DAVID (*to* TECK) Two months from today. How do you want the cash and how do you want the check?

TECK *One month from today*. That I will not discuss. One month. Please decide now.

DAVID (*sharply*) All right. (*To* TECK) How do you want it?

TECK Seventy-five hundred dollars in a check. Twenty-five hundred in cash.

DAVID I haven't anywhere near that much cash in the house. Leave your address and I'll send it to you in the morning.

TECK (*laughs*) Address? I have no address, and I wish it now. Madame Fanny has cash in her sitting-room safe.

FANNY Have you investigated that, too?

TECK (*laughs*) No. You once told me you always kept money in the house.

DAVID (*to* FANNY) How much have you got upstairs?

FANNY I don't know. About fifteen or sixteen hundred.

TECK Very well. That will do. Make the rest in the check.

DAVID Get it, Mama, please. (*He starts toward the library door.* FANNY *starts for the hall exit.*)

FANNY (*turns, looks carefully at* TECK) Years ago, I heard somebody say that being Roumanian was not a nationality, but a profession. The years have brought no change.

KURT (*softly*) Being a Roumanian aristocrat is a profession.

(FANNY *exits. After her exit, there is silence,* KURT *does not look up,* SARA *does not move.*)

TECK (*awkwardly*) The new world has left the room. (*Looks up at them*) I feel less discomfort with you. We are Europeans, born to trouble and understanding it.

KURT My wife is not a European.

TECK Almost. (*Points upstairs*) They are young. The world has gone well for most of them. For us—(*Smiles*) The three of us—we are like peasants watching the big frost. Work, trouble, ruin—(*Shrugs*) But no need to call curses at the frost. There it is, it will be again, always—for us.

SARA (*gets up, moves to the window, looks out*) You mean my husband and I do not have angry words for you. What for? We know how many there are of you. They don't, yet. My mother and brother feel shocked that you are in their house. For us—we have seen you in so many houses.

TECK I do not say you *want* to understand me, Mrs. Müller. I say only that you do.

SARA Yes. You are not difficult to understand.

KURT (*slowly gets up, stands stiffly. Then he moves toward the decanter table*) A whiskey?

TECK No, thank you. (*He turns his head to watch* KURT *move. He turns back.*)

KURT Sherry?

TECK (*nods*) Thank you, I will.

KURT (*as he pours*) You, too, wish to go back to Europe.

TECK Yes.

KURT But they do not much want you. Not since the Budapest oil deal of '31.

TECK You seem as well informed about me as I am about you.

KURT That must have been a conference of high comedy, that one. Everybody trying to guess whether Kessler was working for Fritz Thyssen, and what Thyssen *really* wanted—and whether this "National Socialism" was a smart blind of Thyssen's, and where was Wolff—I should like to have seen you and your friends. It is too bad: you guessed an inch off, eh?

TECK More than an inch.

KURT And Kessler has a memory? (*Almost playfully*) I do not think Von Seitz would pay you money for a description of a man who has a month to travel. But I think he would pay you in a visa and a cable to Kessler. I think you want a visa almost as much as you want money. Therefore, I conclude you will try for the money here, and the visa from Von Seitz. (*He comes toward the table carrying the sherry glass*) I cannot get anywhere near Germany in a month and you know it. (*He is about to place the glass on the table*) I have been bored with this talk of paying you money. If they are willing to try you on this fantasy, I am not. Whatever made you think I would take such a chance? Or *any* chance? You are a gambler. But you should not gamble with your life.

(TECK *has turned to stare at him, made a half motion as if to rise. As he does so, and on the words, "gamble with your life,"* KURT *drops the glass, hits* TECK *in the face. Struggling,* TECK *makes a violent effort to rise.* KURT *throws himself on* TECK, *knocking him to the floor. As* TECK *falls to the floor,* KURT *hits him on the side of the head. At the fourth* blow, TECK *does not move.* KURT *rises, takes the gun from his pocket, begins to lift* TECK *from the floor. As he does so,* JOSHUA *appears in the hall entrance. He is washed and ready for dinner. As he reaches the door, he stops, sees the scene, stands quietly as if he were waiting for orders.* KURT *begins to balance* TECK, *to balance himself. To* JOSHUA)

Hilf mir. (JOSHUA *comes quickly to* KURT) Mach die Tür auf! (JOSHUA *runs toward the doors, opens them, stands waiting*) Bleib da! Mach die Tür zu!

(KURT *begins to move out through the terrace. When he is outside the doors,* JOSHUA *closes them quickly, stands looking at his mother.*)

SARA There's trouble.

JOSHUA Do not worry. I will go up now. I will pack. In ten minutes all will be ready. I will say nothing. I will get the children ready—(*He starts quickly for the hall, turns for a second to look toward the terrace doors. Then almost with a sob*) This was a nice house.

SARA (*softly*) We're not going this time, darling. There's no need to pack.

JOSHUA (*stares at her, puzzled*) But Papa—

SARA Go upstairs, Joshua. Take Babbie and Bodo in your room, and close the door. Stay there until I call you. (*He looks at her,* SARA *sits down*) There's nothing to be frightened of, darling. Papa is all right. (*Then very softly*) Papa is going home.

JOSHUA To Germany?

SARA Yes.

JOSHUA Oh. Alone?

SARA Alone. (*Very softly*) Don't say anything to the children. He will tell them himself.

JOSHUA I won't.

SARA (*as he hesitates*) I'm all right. Go upstairs now.

(*He moves slowly out, she watches him, he disappears. For a minute she sits quietly. Then she gets up, moves to the terrace doors, stands with her hands pressed against them. Then she crosses, picks up the overturned chair, places it by the table, picks up the glass, puts it on the table. As if without knowing what she is doing, she wipes the table with her handkerchief.*)

(FANNY *comes in from hall. After a second,* DAVID *comes in from library. Stops, looks around room.*)

DAVID Where is he? Upstairs?

SARA No. They went outside.

FANNY Outside? They went outside. What are they doing, picking a bouquet together?

SARA (*without turning*) They just went outside.

DAVID (*looks at her*) What's the matter, Sara? (SARA *shakes her head. Goes to the desk, opens the telephone book, looks at a number, begins to dial the telephone.*)

FANNY Eleven hundred, eleven hundred and fifty, twelve, twelve-fifty—

DAVID For God's sake, stop counting that money.

FANNY All right. I'm nervous. And I don't like to think of giving him too much.

SARA It's very nice of you and Mama. All that money—(*Into the telephone*) Hello. What time is your next plane? Oh. To—South. To El Paso, or—Brownsville. Yes.

DAVID (*to* FANNY) Is Joseph ready?

FANNY I don't know. I told him I'd call him.

SARA To Brownsville? Yes. Yes. That's all right. At what time? Yes. No. The ticket will be picked up at the airport. (DAVID *begins to cross to the bell cord. She looks up*) No. David. Don't call Joseph. *David! Please!* (*He draws back, stares at her. Looking at him, she goes on with the conversation*) Ritter. R-I-T-T-E-R. From Chicago. Yes. Yes. (*She hangs up, walks away.*)

DAVID Sara! What's happening? What is all this? (*She does not answer*) Where is Kurt? What—(*He starts for the terrace door.*)

SARA David. *Don't go out.*

FANNY (*rises*) Sara! What's happening—

SARA For seven years now, day in, day out, men have crossed the German border. They are always in danger. They always may be going in to die. Did you ever see the face of a man who never knows if this day will be the last day? (*Softly*) Don't go out on the terrace, David. Leave Kurt alone.

FANNY (*softly*) Sara! What is—

SARA (*quietly*) For them, it may be torture, and it may be death. Some day, when it's all over, maybe there'll be a few of them left to celebrate. There aren't many of Kurt's age left. He couldn't take a chance on them. They wouldn't have liked it. (*Suddenly, violently*) He'd have had a bad time trying to explain to them that because of this house and this nice town and my mother and my brother, he took chances with their work and with their lives. (*Quietly*) Sit down, Mama. I think it's all over now. (*To* DAVID) There's nothing you can do about it. It's the way it had to be.

DAVID Sara—

FANNY Do you mean what I think you—(*She sits down.*)

SARA (*she turns, looks out toward the doors. After a pause*) He's going away tonight and he's never coming back any more. (*In a sing-song*) Never, never, never. (*She looks down at her hands, as if she were very interested in them*) I don't like to be alone at night. I guess everybody in the world's got a time they don't like. Me, it's right before I go to sleep. And now it's going to be for always. All the rest of my life. (*She looks up as* KURT *comes in from the terrace*) I've told them. There is an eight-thirty plane going as far south as Brownsville. I've made you a reservation. In the name of Ritter.

KURT (*stands looking at her*) Liebe Sara! (*Then he goes to the table at which* FANNY *is sitting. To* FANNY) It is hard for you, eh? (*He pats her hand*) I am sorry.

FANNY (*without knowing why, she takes her hand away*) Hard? I don't know. I—I don't—I don't know what I want to say.

KURT (*looks at the hand she has touched, then turns to look at* DAVID) Before I come in, I stand and think. I say, I will make Fanny and David understand. I say, how can I? Does one understand a killing? No. To hell with it, I say. I do what must be done. I have long sickened of words when I see the men who live by them. What do you wish to make them understand, I ask myself. Wait. Stand here. Just stand here. What are you thinking? Say it to them just as it comes to you. And this is what came to me. When you kill in a war, it is not so lonely; and I remember a cousin I have not seen for many years; and a melody comes back and I begin to make it with my fingers; a staircase in a house in Bonn years ago; an old dog who used to live in our town; Sara in a hundred places—Shame on us. Thousands of years and we cannot yet make a world. Like a child I am. I have stopped a man's life. (*Points to the place on the couch where he had been sitting opposite* TECK) I sit here. I listen to him. You will not believe —but I pray that I will not have to touch him. Then I know I will have to, I know that if I do not, it is only that I pamper myself, and risk the lives of others. I want you from the room. I know what I must do. (*Loudly*) All right. Do I now pretend sorrow? Do I now pretend it is not I who act thus? No. I do it. I have done it. I will do it again. And I will keep my hope that we may make a world in which all men can die in bed. I have a great hate for the violent. They are the sick of the world. (*Softly*) Maybe I am sick now, too.

SARA You aren't sick. Stop that. It's late. You must go soon.

KURT (*he puts out his hands, she touches them*) I am going to say good-bye now to my children. Then I am going to take your car—(*Motions with his head*) I will take him with me. After that, it is up to you. Two ways: You can let me go and keep silent. I believe I can hide him and the car. At the end of two days, if they have not been found, you will tell as much of the truth as is safe for you to say. Tell them the last time you saw us we were on our way to Washington. You did not worry at the absence, we might have rested there. Two crazy foreigners fight, one gets killed, you know nothing of the reason. I will have left the gun, there will be no doubt who did the killing. If you will give me those two days, I think I will be far enough away from here. If the car is found before then—(*Shrugs*) I will still try to move with speed. And all that will make you, for yourselves, part of a murder. For the world, I do not think you will be in bad trouble. (*He pauses*) There is another way. You can call your police. You can tell them the truth. I will not get home. (*To* SARA) I wish to see the children now. (*She goes out into the hall and up the stairs. There is silence.*)

FANNY What are you thinking, David?

DAVID I don't know. What are you thinking?

FANNY Me? Oh, I was thinking about my Joshua. I was thinking that a few months before he died, we were sitting out there. (*Points to terrace*) He said, "Fanny, the Renaissance American is dying, the Renaissance man is dying." I said what do you mean, although I knew what he meant, I always knew. "A Renaissance man," he said, "is a man who wants to know. He wants to know how fast a bird will fly, how thick is the crust of the earth, what made Iago evil, how to plow a field. He knows there is no dignity to a mountain, if there is no dignity to man. You can't put that in a man, but when it's *really* there, and he will fight for it, put your trust in him."

DAVID (*gets up, smiles, looks at* FANNY) You're a smart woman sometimes. (SARA *enters with* JOSHUA. *To* KURT) Don't worry about things here. My soul doesn't have to be so nice and clean. I'll take care of it. You'll have your two days. And good luck to you.

FANNY You go with my blessing, too. I like you. (BODO *enters.*)

SARA See? I come from good stock. (KURT *looks at* DAVID. *Then he begins to smile. Nods to* DAVID. *Turns, smiles at* FANNY.)

FANNY Do you like me?

KURT I like you, Madame, very much.

FANNY Would you be able to cash that check?

KURT (*laughs*) Oh, no.

FANNY Then take the cash. I, too, would like to contribute to your work.

KURT (*slowly*) All right. Thank you. (*He takes the money from the table, puts it in his pocket.*)

BODO (*to* KURT) You like Grandma? I thought you would, with time. I like her, too. Sometimes she dilates with screaming, but—Dilates is correct? (BABETTE *enters.* JOSHUA *stands away from the others, looking at his father.* KURT *turns to look at him.*)

JOSHUA Alles in Ordnung?

KURT Alles in Ordnung.

BODO What? What does that mean, all is well? (*There is an awkward silence.*)

BABETTE (*as if she sensed it*) We are all clean for dinner. But nobody else is clean. And I have on Grandma's dress to me—

FANNY (*very nervously*) Of course. And you look very pretty. You're a pretty little girl, Babbie.

BODO (*looks around the room*) What is the matter? Everybody is acting like such a ninny. I got that word from Grandma.

KURT Come here. (*They look at him. Then slowly* BABETTE *comes toward him, followed by* BODO. JOSHUA *comes more slowly, to stand at the side of* KURT'S *chair*) We have said many good-byes to each other, eh? We must now say another. (*As they stare at him, he smiles, slowly, as if it were difficult*) This time, I leave you with good people to whom I believe you also will be good. (*Half playfully*) Would you allow me to give away my share in you, until I come back?

BABETTE (*slowly*) If you would like it.

KURT Good. To your mother, her share. My share, to Fanny and David. It is all I have to give. (*Laughs*) There. I have made a will, eh? Now. We will not joke. I have something to say to you. It is important for me to say it.

JOSHUA (*softly*) You are talking to us as if we were children.

KURT (*turns to look at him*) Am I, Joshua? I wish you were children. I wish I could say love your mother, do not eat too many sweets, clean your teeth—(*Draws* BODO *to him*) I cannot say these things. You are not children. I took it all away from you.

BABETTE We have had a most enjoyable life, Papa.

KURT (*smiles*) You are a gallant little liar. And I thank you for it. I have done something bad today—

FANNY (*shocked, sharply*) Kurt—

SARA Don't, Mama. (BODO *and* BABETTE *have looked at* FANNY *and* SARA, *puzzled. Then they have turned again to look at* KURT.)

KURT It is not to frighten you. In a few days, your mother and David will tell you.

BODO You could not do a bad thing.

BABETTE (*proudly*) You could not.

KURT (*shakes his head*) Now let us get straight together. The four of us. Do you remember when we read "Les Misérables"? Do you remember that we talked about it afterward and Bodo got candy on Mama's bed?

BODO I remember.

KURT Well. He stole bread. The world is out of shape we said, when there are hungry men. And until it gets in shape, men will steal and lie and—(*A little more slowly*)—kill. But for whatever reason it is done, and whoever does it—you understand me—it is all bad. I want you to remember that. Whoever does it, it is bad. (*Then very gaily*) But you will live to see the day when it will not have to be. All over the world, in every place and every town, there are men who are going to make sure it will not have to be. They want what I want: a childhood for every child. For my children, and I for theirs. (*He picks* BODO *up, rises*) Think of that. It will make you happy. In every town and every village and every mud hut in the world, there is always a man who loves children and who will fight to make a good world for them. And now good-bye. Wait for me. I shall try to come back for you. (*He moves toward the hall, followed by* BABETTE, *and more slowly, by* JOSHUA) Or you shall come to me. At Hamburg, the boat will come in. It will be a fine, safe land—I will be waiting on the dock. And there will be the three of you and Mama and Fanny and David. And I will have ordered an extra big dinner and we will show them what our Germany can be like—(*He has put* BODO *down. He leans down, presses his face in* BABETTE*'s hair. Tenderly, as her mother has done earlier, she touches his hair.*)

JOSHUA Of course. That is the way it will be. Of course. But—but if you should find yourself delayed—(*Very slowly*) Then I will come to you. Mama.

SARA (*she has turned away*) I heard you, Joshua.

KURT (*he kisses* BABETTE) Gute Nacht, Liebling!

BABETTE Gute Nacht, Papa. Mach's gut!

KURT (*leans to kiss* BODO) Good night, baby.

BODO Good night, Papa. Mach's gut! (BABETTE *runs up the steps. Slowly* BODO *follows her.*)

KURT (*kisses* JOSHUA) Good night, son.

JOSHUA Good night, Papa. Mach's gut! (*He begins to climb the steps.* KURT *stands watching them, smiling. When they disappear, he turns to* DAVID.)

KURT Good-bye, and thank you.

DAVID Good-bye, and good luck.

KURT (*he moves to* FANNY) Good-bye. I have good children, eh?

FANNY Yes, you have. (KURT *kisses her hand.*)

KURT (*slowly, he turns toward* SARA) Men who wish to live have the best chance to live. I wish to live. I wish to live with you. (*She comes toward him.*)

SARAH For twenty years. It is as much for me today—(*Takes his arms*) Just once, and for all my life. (*He pulls her toward him*) Come back for me, darling. If you can. (*Takes brief case from table and gives it to him.*)

KURT (*simply*) I will try. (*He turns*) Good-bye, to you all. (*He exits. After a second, there is the sound of a car starting. They sit listening to it. Gradually the noise begins to go off into the distance. A second later,* JOSHUA *appears.*)

JOSHUA Mama—(*She looks up. He is very tense*) Bodo cries. Babette looks very queer. I think you should come.

SARA (*gets up, slowly*) I'm coming.

JOSHUA (*to* FANNY *and* DAVID. *Still very tense*) Bodo talks so fancy, we forget sometimes he is a baby. (*He waits for* SARA *to come up to him. When she reaches him, she takes his hand, goes up the steps, disappears.* FANNY *and* DAVID *watch them.*)

FANNY (*after a minute*) Well, here we are. We're shaken out of the magnolias, eh?

DAVID Yes. So we are.

FANNY Tomorrow will be a hard day. But we'll have Babbie's birthday dinner. And we'll have music afterward. You can be the audience. I think you'd better go up to Marthe now. Be as careful as you can. She'd better stay here for a while. I daresay I can stand it.

DAVID (*turns, smiles*) Even your graciousness is ungracious, Mama.

FANNY I do my best. Well, I think I shall go and talk to Anise. I like Anise best when I don't feel well. (*She begins to move off.*)

DAVID Mama. (*She turns*) We are going to be in for trouble. You understand that?

FANNY I understand it very well. We will manage. You and I. I'm not put together with flour paste. And neither are you—I am happy to learn.

DAVID Good night, Mama. (*As she moves out, the curtain falls.*)

Part 6
Queer Theory and Psychoanalytic Theory

PERFORMING THE CLOSET: CODED GAY DRAMAS

THE RISE OF U.S. PSYCHOANALYSIS AND FREUD ONSTAGE

21. *Summer and Smoke*—Tennessee Williams

Commentary

Sources

Play

21.1 FROM *SUMMER AND SMOKE* TO *THE ECCENTRICITIES OF A NIGHTINGALE*: THE EVOLUTION OF THE QUEER ALMA—JOHN M. CLUM

ALMA There's not much to do in this town after dark, but there are resorts on the lake that offer all kinds of after-dark entertainment. There's one called Moon Lake Casino. It's under new management, now, but I don't suppose its character has changed.
YOUNG MAN What was its character?
ALMA Gay, very gay.

(*Summer and Smoke*, 255–56)

"GAY, VERY GAY" IS AN APPROPRIATE TERM FOR the once Victorian Alma Winemiller to use to describe the tawdry Moon Lake Casino, which once horrified the prime minister's daughter but where she now feels quite at home. In its original sense, "gay" certainly seems a euphemism for an establishment where, according to John Buchanan, "anything goes" (195) including weekly cock fights. However, the Alma Winemiller of the final scene of *Summer and Smoke* is more than capable of a bit of camp irony. And her creator had already proven in his previous play, *A Streetcar Named Desire*, that he was a master of the codes and subterfuge of gay camp. Surely by the late forties Williams was aware of the double meaning of "gay" and the assumptions that could be made about a place where "anything goes," even without the possibility of an allusion to the gay Cole Porter. The playful appearance of that now highly charged word shows Williams signalling some members of his audience that there are gay connotations to *Summer and Smoke*.

As if to underscore the gay double entendre with which I began, Williams has Miss Alma invoke Oscar Wilde at the Moon Lake Casino as she and John Buchanan argue about the relative merits of flesh and the spirit:

ALMA . . . To me—well, that is the secret, the principle back of existence—the ever-lasting struggle and aspiration for more than our human limits have placed in our reach. . . . Who was that said that—oh, so beautiful thing! "All of us are in the gutter, but some of us are looking at the stars!"
JOHN Mr. Oscar Wilde.
ALMA (somewhat taken aback) Well, regardless of who said it, it's still true. Some of us are looking at the stars! (She looks up raptly and places her hand over his.)

(*Summer and Smoke*, 197–98)

Oscar Wilde's aphorism is truer than Miss Alma is ready to apprehend at this point in the play. In Williams's world all of us are mired in the flesh, specifically guts and groin, in the same neighborhood and symbolically linked as death and desire, but his most troubled characters try to link flesh and spirit or deny the flesh in a quest for spiritual transcendence. At the beginning of *Summer and Smoke*, Alma Winemiller cannot link spirit and flesh (like Brick Pollitt, who, in *Cat on a Hot Tin Roof*, is described as an "ass-aching Puritan,") but moves from one to the other as her beloved John Buchanan moves in the opposite direction. In the exchange I quote, the linking of spirit and flesh comes through the words of a gay poet, Oscar Wilde, whose best work problematized the relationship of flesh and spirit. Alma may be "taken aback" at her spiritual principle springing from what she would see as a polluted source, but for her it's "still true." Alma does not yet see the irony in the physical act of placing her hand on John's as she voices Wilde's epigraph.

In many ways, Tennessee Williams is the true successor to Oscar Wilde in gay literature. Like Wilde, Williams made it impossible for his audience and his critics to separate author from creation. He was the poet as performer, the playwright as celebrity. As Wilde became a scandalous figure, a living embodiment of the unspeakable vice of homosexuality, his name a trope for homosexuality; so Williams, half a century later, would become a figure of depravity, as his works would be considered shocking and dirty, his sexuality a justification for the vicious assaults of homophobic critics in the fifties and sixties. As Wilde became in his performances on and off stage and in his later plays the epitome of high camp, so Williams was able to put on the very straight, and often strait-laced, American stage the playful, deconstructive gay language of camp which explodes any unitary or even binary reading of his work. As Oscar Wilde's Salomé placed a male body as the object of the gaze and created a subject that could be read as female (or, in an appropriately camp reading, male and female), so Williams's female characters elude conventional gendered categories.

In his fine book, *Communists, Cowboys, and Queers*, David Savran has cogently defined what a "camp" reading of Williams's work would entail: a "camp" reading of Williams will not simply "reverse" gender because it will be based on the assumption that genders and sexualities are not produced in opposition and therefore cannot be "simply" reversed. Rather, a "camp" reading will pay particular attention to problems of coding and language, to innuendo and gossip; it will make elaborate substitutions and delight in the capriciousness of spoken and performative languages. It will also frequently and pointedly transpose genders, producing transvestite subjects based on its recognition that all gender is masquerade and all costume is a form of drag.

Paying homage to Oscar Wilde in this symbolically freighted, ostensibly heterosexual exchange signals the gay interpretive community that there is a gay code operative in the play, but it is a code that expands rather than limits the possibilities of interpretation.

Throughout *Summer and Smoke* literature is connected with homosexuality in sometimes comic, sometimes complex ways. Alma Winemiller belongs to a literary society which seems at first a comically pathetic refuge for the least sexual citizens of the town, promoting the notion of a disembodied, ideal literature as a corollary to their sexual frustration and/or repression. Yet the meeting of the literary society (scene three of *Summer and Smoke*) keeps veering toward gayness as it links the solace, escape, and expression literature offers the misfits of Glorious Hill with the sense of community coded gay literature offered gay men in the pre-Stonewall era.

As Rosemary, "a wistful older girl with a long neck and thick-lensed glasses," prepares to read her paper on the poetry of William Blake, Mrs. Bassett blurts out:

> MRS. BASSETT Insane, insane, that man was a mad fanatic!
>
> . . .
>
> I've read up on him and know what I'm talking about. He traveled around with that Frenchman who took a shot at him and landed them both in jail! Brussels, Brussels! . . . That's where it happened, fired a gun at him in a drunken stupor, and later one of them died of T.B. in the gutter! All right. I'm finished. I won't say anything more. Go on with your paper, Rosemary. There's nothing like contact with culture.
>
> (*Summer and Smoke*, 174, 173–74)

In this hilarious moment of cultural semi-literacy, Mrs. Bassett turns Blake into Verlaine and Rimbaud, the turbulent male lovers of nineteenth-century French poetry. For her, poets are to be judged by the purity of their own lives. These notorious homosexuals suggest all that is wrong with "contact with culture." Mrs. Bassett's contact with culture seems inescapably to be a contact with gayness even when the victim of her cultural semi-literacy is William Blake. Blake gets another gay reading when, after Mrs. Bassett's outburst, Alma reads one of Blake's "loveliest lyric poems," which she calls "Love's Secret." What Alma reads is a conflation of two poems, one of which has been shortened, revised, and gender-bent:

I told my love,
I told my love,
I told him all my heart.
Trembling, cold in ghastly fear
Did my love depart.
No sooner had he gone from me
than a stranger passing by,
Silently, invisibly,
Took him with a sigh!

(*Summer and Smoke*, 175)

In essence, Alma creates a new poem out of bits and pieces of Blake filtered through her own desire and imagination. The poem is on one hand an augury of what will happen to Alma in both *Summer and Smoke* and, more so, in its companion piece, *Eccentricities of a Nightingale.* In changing the gender of the pronouns and rewriting the poem to give it a more personal meaning, Alma publicly gives the kind of revision many gay men have privately given to heterosexual literature.

After Alma's reading of the poem has earned an ovation from the community of art lovers, Mrs. Bassett rejoins, "Honey, you're right. That isn't the man I meant. I was thinking about the one who wrote about 'the bought red lips'" (175). This comic undercutting of Alma's rewriting of Blake's lament of lost love by a reference to bought sex does not in Williams provide the contrast Mrs. Bassett sees, but an embrace of the tawdry and the spiritual that will be Alma's fate.

This scene of the literary meeting encapsulates the complex, playful presentation of homosexuality in Williams's major works. Mrs. Bassett, like a number of critics of the fifties and sixties, looks for examples of the corrupting force of homosexuality in the oddest literary places, but it turns up there in a beautiful form acceptable to the moral police. One cannot forget that the title of *Summer and Smoke* comes from the work of gay poet Hart Crane, for whom Williams felt the greatest admiration and a particularly strong personal identification. I begin with literary allusions in *Summer and Smoke*, because here we see Williams hinting at a potential gay reading of the play by placing it in the context of gay literature.

[. . .]

Williams claimed that Miss Alma Winemiller was his favorite character. To quote his 1973 *Playboy* interview:

> Alma of *Summer and Smoke* is my favorite—because I came out so late and so did Alma, and she had the greatest struggle, you know? . . . I didn't even masturbate until I was 27. I only

> had spontaneous orgasms and wet dreams. But I was never frigid like Miss Alma, not even now, when I most need it. But Miss Alma grew up in the shadow of the rectory, and so did I . . . Her man fell in love with someone else and Miss Alma turned to a life of profligacy. I've been profligate, but, being a puritan, I naturally tend to exaggerate guilt.

This sort of statement demonstrates the problem of the relationship of Williams and his plays. He constantly linked himself to his characters, making a non-biographical reading difficult. Rather than disappear behind or within his characters, Williams wanted his audience to be aware of his intensely personal identification with his heroines. He invites one to see his women as himself in drag, but such a "transvestite reading" would be far too simplistic.

The Miss Alma whom Williams refers to in his *Playboy* statement is clearly that of *Summer and Smoke*, the Alma who loses John to her "childish" pupil, Nellie, after confessing her love for John. Alma and John, in the schematized action of Summer and Smoke, reverse positions, making any relationship impossible. As Alma moves from the prudish, repressed semi-hysteric to a woman who recognized the needs of the flesh, John, whose sense of a person could be summed up by his anatomy chart, comes to appreciate the spiritual qualities Alma represented to him. As John enters the conventional world of marriage and community position, Alma seeks out one-night stands with travelling salesmen at the very nightspot John used to frequent. The flesh carries one to "the kindness of strangers" while the spirit leads one to an unfulfilling marriage. John's Nellie (and how playful was that choice of names!) is the daughter of the shameless woman who was known to her sexual profligacy. As Nellie becomes the object of John's affection, Alma takes the role of Nellie's profligate mother.

In the Prologue, Alma tells us her name means soul and that the statue is named eternity, and John tells of hitting his diseased, dying mother in an early battle with death (129, 130). There's a richer play bursting to come out of this shell. Two things flesh the story out. One is Alma's inexorable move from prim, repressed spinster to sexual creature who asks for what she wants sexually. That is, Alma takes the male role of initiator of sex both with John and with the travelling salesman, a position hardly in line with the postwar American sex/gender system. Alma tells John, "the tables have turned with a vengeance" (247). They have, and not only in terms of spirit and flesh. Alma has taken John's active sexual role as John does the bidding of Nellie. But there is another dimension suggested by Williams's comparison of Alma's and his "coming out." Coming out is a gay term, naming the moment when a lesbian or gay man not only privately acknowledges her or his sexuality, but decides to live it before the world, to witness to her or his homosexuality. "Coming out" had a very different meaning in 1948 from what it had when Williams gave his *Playboy* interview in 1973. Before gay liberation it meant coming out in the gay subculture, living one's sexuality but, while the sun is up, protecting oneself through silence and subterfuge. Williams's characters are more in the post-Stonewall mold, living for their desire for men. Alma comes to define herself through her desire for men, the desire Williams shares with Alma. The playwright who spent his childhood in a rectory identifies with the sexual liberation of the minister's daughter.

21.2 SEX BEHAVIOR OF THE AMERICAN MALE—JAMES R. MILLER

IF THE LAWS OF THIS LAND were rigidly enforced, 95 per cent of all men and boys would be jailed as sex offenders. Well over half of them are guilty of premarital intercourse, and almost a third could be charged with homosexuality. Few of them could deny conduct—in or out of marriage—that the law defines as unnatural, immoral, abnormal, or indecent.

These are a few of the facts of our sex lives which we will be learning in the year 1948. For in January, Alfred C. Kinsey, professor of zoology at Indiana University, is publishing his long-awaited *Sexual Behavior in the Human Male.*[1] Astonishing as it may seem, this book will be the first thorough examination of the behavior bound up with the very origin of life, a subject which fascinates us for most of our days, and which determines many of our moral values.

Dr. Kinsey's book is the result of nine years of study, during which he and a group of associates have interviewed 12,000 Americans and recorded the details, casual and intimate, of their sexual behavior. His 700-page volume is only the beginning of a lifetime work that ultimately will cover also female sexual behavior, the sex problem in marital life, and a half-dozen other related subjects. But it is a tremendous beginning. Without moral judgment, he tells us far more than we have ever known before about sex. It is possible that what he has done will illumine, and perhaps sweep away, more illusions, superstitions, and hypocrisies than any single work in modern times.

Dr. Kinsey has established beyond question the fact that popular beliefs and assumptions about sex bear little resemblance to actual practice. He has proved that our sex laws, written and unwritten, are generally unrealistic and unenforceable. He demonstrates that our concepts of "normal" and "abnormal" sex behavior are rooted in ignorance—and violated in secrecy.

Readers may be disposed to question Dr. Kinsey's conclusions—until they learn how thorough and scrupulous has been his survey. For the moment, let us proceed with the assurance that he got his facts from an impressive variety of persons—the rich, the middle class, the poor; the young, the middle-aged, the old; professional people, white-collar workers, and laborers; the married, the single, the previously-married; Protestants, Catholics, and Jews; Negroes and whites; people of a dozen nationalities; farmers and city-dwellers; men and women in every state in the union.

Since there is no such thing as an "average" American male, Dr. Kinsey does not try to describe him. He deals, instead, with sex practices in specific social groups. For each group he makes plausible generalizations, and then, putting all these together, draws some conclusions about the male population as a whole.

Thus, as you read this preview of Dr. Kinsey's conclusions, you are looking into the lives of your friends and acquaintances, your wives, your husbands, your own children. What's more important, you are learning much about yourself.

The subject of primary interest in sexual behavior is intercourse. Dr. Kinsey breaks this down into its main social manifestations: premarital intercourse, marital intercourse, and extramarital intercourse.

Primitives, Asiatics, most Europeans—most of the world's people, in fact—look upon premarital intercourse as desirable, inevitable, or tolerable. But the Anglo-American culture, morally derived from Old Testament codes, condemns it roundly. It is sinful, and it is quite literally against the law. Faced with the question of whether it exists in our culture, we either admit that it does (somewhat) or insist that it doesn't (much). Faced with the question of whether to indulge in it, few hesitate. Despite Scriptures, lectures, pretenses, and laws, premarital intercourse is sought and practiced by 67 per cent of all male college graduates, 84 per cent of all male high school graduates, and 98 per cent of all male grade school graduates—or 90 per cent of all men by the time they are 25. Moreover, of the total *pre*-adolescent population (usually thought uninterested in or incapable of intercourse), 22 per cent try it.

In our society the only kind of sex activity fully approved is marital intercourse. It is legal only if practiced according to conventional ideas of what is normal and natural. It has recently been allowed as conversational and editorial matter because we now realize its tremendous importance to marital happiness.

Perhaps our chief misconception about marital intercourse is that it accounts for most of the total sex picture. From the standpoint of the male, at least, it does not. The fact is that more than half (54.1 per cent) of the sexual outlet of American males is accounted for by premarital and extramarital intercourse, masturbation, nocturnal emissions, homosexuality, and animal contacts. As for married men, marital intercourse accounts for 82 per cent of their total outlet.

How often do married couples have intercourse? Here are the general figures, according to age groups: At age 20—3.9 times per week; at age 30—2.9 times; at age 40—2.2 times; at age 50—1.8 times; at age 60—0.9 times.

It is no longer news that marital happiness often depends on a sound sexual adjustment between man and wife. Related to this are Dr. Kinsey's findings on sex techniques and habits. In our society, for example, 70 per cent of husbands subscribe to the "conventional" method of intercourse. That does not prove, however, that this is always the most desirable or the most natural method. In other cultures, such as that of some Pacific islanders, it is almost unheard of.

Likewise, trouble may arise from differences in attitude between husbands and wives of different social and educational levels. On upper levels, 90 per cent of married couples approve of nudity; on lower levels, only 43 per cent. Obviously, a husband from one level and a wife from another (the one condoning certain practices and the other abhorring them) can run into very real tragedy.

Incidentally, some practices, usually considered rare, turn out to be surprisingly common. Nevertheless, they are interpreted in most states as illegal, because "unnatural," and there are married couples who are serving time in prisons for them today.

We accept marital intercourse. We frown on premarital intercourse. But we really take a stand on extramarital intercourse. Theoretically, marriage precludes it. We assume love and loyalty between man and wife and/or the ability to police each other.

How does it work out? Well, as loyal and loving husbands, a great many males are good policemen. Seventy-five per cent of them admit they would like to have extramarital intercourse. And 50 per cent of them have it. Husbands on the lower social economic levels generally have more such experiences early in marriage and fewer later. Husbands on the upper levels reverse the pattern. Extramarital intercourse is usually sporadic—a week or month of it over a period of a year or two. On any level, not more than 8 to 15 per cent is supplied by prostitution.

Dr. Kinsey has already found that there is much less extramarital intercourse among wives, and he suggests some reasons for the difference. His interviews show that men are far more desirous of sexual variety, and that they are exposed and respond to many more sexual stimuli. (Women dress, move, and generally behave in a way that proclaims their sex from adolescence on; innumerable ads, films, songs, and books are aimed straight at the male libido).

There are other reasons for the difference, but the point is that extramarital intercourse is a commonplace. And we immediately want to know how it affects marriage. The answer to that will be a part of Dr. Kinsey's third book. Meanwhile, he makes some highly tentative but provocative observations. Extramarital intercourse may very well wreck marriages, but some marriages may have survived extramarital intercourse when 1) it was unknown to the marriage partner, and 2) it created no important emotional involvement between the unmarried parties.

Obviously, our sex behavior is not limited to intercourse. To see it whole—and as it is—we must look also at such practices as homosexuality, masturbation, and petting.

There is probably only one thing the average American man demands of other men—namely, that they be, unequivocally, males. A man may get away with being a drunk, a cheat, a home-wrecker, a killer, even a Communist, but let him step over the line on sex and he faces ostracism. The language of contempt has been enlarged for him by a dozen words. He is ridiculed, avoided, and persecuted to the end of his days.

Nevertheless, according to Dr. Kinsey, from one-third to a half of American males are or have been homosexual to some degree at one time or another, and men or women exclusively homosexual are far more numerous than is commonly supposed. We may wonder, therefore, whether they may be justly considered abnormal, queer, or, above all, immoral. The truth is that in the preadolescent period, when all of us begin some kind of sex activity, it begins, as often as not, with members of the same sex.

It is popular to believe that all "normal" people outgrow this sort of practice, but that is only an arbitrary way of defining "normal." Of all the men Dr. Kinsey interviewed, over 40 per cent admitted they had reacted to homosexual stimuli. And 37 per cent (almost two out of every five men) admitted having had such relations *after* adolescence. These ranged, of course, from the rare to the occasional to the exclusively homo-sexual.

It will surprise many to know that only a small percentage of male homosexuals exhibit any of the effeminate characteristics commonly attributed to them. And it may sober others to learn that although there are a fair number of male homosexuals on the highest and lowest social-economic levels the greatest percentage is found on the middle level where they are most loudly and manfully despised.

[. . .]

We have seen something of how the human male behaves in his sex life. Clearly, he is unwilling or unable to behave according to conventional standards that make everything but marital intercourse and solitary masturbation illegal. We may account for this in part by looking at some of the forces Dr. Kinsey calls "factors affecting sex outlet."

The Freudians and their opponents have not yet settled the question of whether sex is an instinctive drive that asserts itself in infancy. Dr. Kinsey doesn't try to settle it either, but he does show that sex activity starts early and has usually gathered terrific momentum before our laws and moral codes are brought to bear on it. Some boys have been known to have erections *and* sexual climax at the ages of three or four. Almost all children begin some kind of sex play with other boys and girls between the ages of eight and ten. And 95 per cent of U.S. males enter adolescence between the ages of 11 and 15. From 16 to 45, fully 99 per cent of them have regular sex activity—intercourse, masturbation, nocturnal emissions, petting, homosexual experience, or animal contacts. And more than three-quarters of them average between one and 6.5 outlets per week for the rest of their sex lives. But variations are enormous. Some have only one or two outlets per year, some have as many as 30 per week. It is little wonder that we have a variety of attitudes as to the importance of sex activity.

As a society we are trying hardest to regulate the sex behavior of young people. But apparently we do not understand how difficult that is. Contrary to popular belief, the male is sexually most active not in his twenties and thirties, but in late adolescence. That single fact is loaded with trouble. The average boy, too young for approved sexual experience (in marriage) but bursting with sexual energy, breaks the rules. We may ponder the fact that most societies have much the same kinds of boys—and very different kinds of rules for them.

In discussing this age group Dr. Kinsey casts light on the well-known "sex conservation" theory. In general, he finds, the boys who begin sex activity earliest maintain a higher level of performance as adults—and last longest. The form and to a lesser degree the amount of our sex activity, for both young or old, are profoundly influenced by our social level. Measuring social level in terms of a man's formal education, his occupation and the occupation of his parents, Dr. Kinsey finds it reflected consistently in sex patterns. A man on the lower level has the greatest total sexual outlet and favors its simplest forms. He thinks of his behavior as "natural." He begins intercourse early. He may have intercourse with dozens of girls and kiss none of them. He doesn't confuse sex activity with love. Thus, he rarely has intercourse with the girl he plans to marry. He wants her to be a virgin.

A man on the upper level generally has less total outlet, but more variety of form. He may pet with dozens of girls and have intercourse with none. He fears or disapproves of "going the limit." He associates sex with love, and often has intercourse with his fiancee. There is in his sex activity far more experiment, elaboration, and refinement of technique—things the lower-level man would consider foolish, time-wasting, or even perverted.

On all levels, religion influences sex patterns. The sexually least active males are the Orthodox Jews, the devout Catholics, and the devout Protestants, in that order. The most active, interestingly, are the non-devout Catholics, Protestants, and Jews, in *that* order.

"Crimes against public morals"

A glance at random into the statute books of a few States scattered from coast to coast discloses that the sex practices admitted by so many of Dr. Kinsey's 12 000 subjects are, quite literally, against the law.

What Dr. Kinsey calls "premarital intercourse" is in legal language the crime of *fornication.* Generally it has to be habitual ("cohabitation") to be criminal, but if it is, the penalties can be severe. The courts of Massachusetts may jail the transgressor for three years and fine him $300. For a single act, the punishment in that state is only three months and $30.

"Extramarital intercourse" is the crime of *adultery*, for which penalties tend to be even stiffer. In California, for instance, the fine is $1,000, the jail term one year. In New York, where fornication is not a crime, adultery may mean six months in jail and a fine of $250. Neither act is a crime in Nevada, although adultery is accepted as grounds for divorce.

Lumped together as the crime of *sodomy* are such practices as homosexuality, animal contact, oral contact, or dual masturbation. In some states, lawmakers could not bring themselves even to describe these acts in literal terms. Such phrases as "abominable and detestable," "infamous crime against nature," or "unnatural and lascivious act" occur again and again—a lavishness with adjectives most unusual in legal English. Penalties for sodomy are extremely severe. In Nevada, the sentence may be life imprisonment. In New York, it is twenty years. In California oral contact may mean fifteen years, while for sodomy, say, with an animal, the maximum penalty is ten years.

The antiquity of some of these laws is perhaps most apparent in Mississippi, where one may be fined $25 for "keeping a stallion or jack within 100 yards of a church or highway or in open view of any public place."

Note

1. W. B. Saunders Co., Philadelphia & London, to whom the author is indebted for permission to quote data.

21.3 MAXIMUM PUNISHMENTS FOR CERTAIN SEX CRIMES IN THE U.S.A.—JAMES R. MILLER

February 1948

	ADULTERY	FORNICATION	SEDUCTION	SODOMY
Ala.	1st conviction—$100 and/or 6 months; 2nd—$300 and/or 1 year; 3rd—2 years	Same as adultery	1–10 years	2–10 years
Ariz.	3 years	No crime; cohabitation—3 years	1–5 years	1–5 years
Ark.	1st conviction—$20–$100; 2nd—$100 and/or 1 years 3rd—1–3 years	Same as adultery	1–10 years and $5000	5–21 years
Cal.	1 year and/or $1000	No crime	5 years and/or $5000	1–10 years; oral perversion—15 years
Colo.	1st offense—$200 or 6 mos.; 2nd—double; 3rd—treble	Same as adultery	10 years	1 year to life
Conn.	5 years	$100 and/or 6 mos.	5 years and $1000	30 years
Del.	1 year and/or $500*	No crime	No crime	$1000 and 3 years
D.C.	$500 and/or 1 year	$100 or 6 mos.	3 years and/or $200	No crime
Fla.	2 years or $500	3 mos. or $30; with a minor, 10 years or $2000	no crime	20 years
Ga.	$1000 or 1 year	Same as adultery	2–20 years	Life; bestiality—5–20 years
Idaho	$100-$1000 or 3 mos.–3 yrs.	$300 or 6 mos	No crime	5 years
Ill.	1st conviction—$500 or 1 year; 2nd—double; 3rd—treble	Same as adultery	$1000–$5000 and/or 1 year	1–10 years
Ind.	$500 and/or 6 mos.	Same as adultery	6 mos.—5 years and $100–$500	$100–$1000 and/or 2–14 years
Iowa	3 years or 1 year and $300	No crime	5 years or $1000 and 1 year	10 years
Kan.	6 mos and/or $500	$500-$1000 or 30 days-3 mos.	No crime	10 years
Ky.	$20–$50	Same as adultery	1–5 years	2–5 years
La.	No crime	No crime	No crime	$2000 and/or 5 years

21.3 Maximum Punishments for Certain Sex Crimes in the U.S.A.—continued

	ADULTERY	FORNICATION	SEDUCTION	SODOMY
Me.	5 years or $1000	$100 and 60 days; cohabitation—$300 or 5 years	No crime	1–10 years
Md.	$10	No crime	No crime	1–10 years
Mass.	2–3 years or $500	3 mos. or $30; cohabitation—3 years or $300	2½–3 years and/or $1000	20 years
Mich.	4 years and/or $2000*	No crime	5 years or $2500	15 years
Minn.	2 years or $300	90 days or $100	5 years and/or $1000	20 years
Miss.	$500 and 6 mos.	Same as adultery	5 years	10 years
Mo.	1 year and/or $1000	Same as adultery	2–5 years or $1000 and 1 year	2 years
Mont.	$500 and/or 6 mos.	Same as adultery	5 years and/or $5000	5 years
Neb.	1 year	$100 and 6 mos.	6 mos .–5 years	20 years
Nev.	No crime	No crime; cohabitation—6 mos.–1 year and/or $500-$1000	No crime	5 years–life
N.H.	1 year and $500 or 3 years	$50 or 6 mos.	No crime	No crime
N J.	$1000 and/or 3 years	$50 and/or 6 mos.	$2000 and/or 7 years	$1000 and/or 21 years
N.M.	No crime	No crime	1–3 years and/or $1000–$3000	1 year and/or $100
N.Y.	6 mos. and/or $250	No crime	5 years and/or $1000	20 years
N.C.	Punishable as misdemeanor at common law	Same as adultery	5 years	5–60 years
N.D.	1–3 years and/or $500	$100 and/or 30 days	1–5 years and/or $1000	1–10 years
Ohio	$200 and 3 mos.	Same as adultery	6 mos.-3 years	1–20 years
Okla.	5 years and/or $500	No crime	1–5 years and/or $1000	10 years
Ore.	3 mos.–2 years or $200–$1000	$50–$500 or 1 mo.–5 years	3 mos.–5 years or $500–$1000	1–15 years
Pa.	1 year and/or $500	$100	$1000 and/or 3 years	10 years and/or $5000

21.3 Maximum Punishments for Certain Sex Crimes in the U.S.A.—continued

	ADULTERY	FORNICATION	SEDUCTION	SODOMY
R.I.	1 year or $500	$10	5 years	7–20 years
S.C.	$100–$500 and/or 6 mos.–1 year	Same as adultery	Misdemeanor punishable at discretion of court	5 years and/or $500
S.D.	5 years and/or $500	No crime	1–5 years and/or $1000	10 years
Tenn.	No crime	No crime	No crime	5–15 years
Tex.	$100–$1000	$50–$500	2–10 years	2–15 years
Utah	3 years	6 mos. or $100	No crime	3–20 years
Vt.	5 years and/or $1000	No crime	No crime	No crime
Va.	$20	Same as adultery	2–10 years	1–3 years
Wash.	2 years or $1000	No crime	1–5 years and/or $1000	10 years
W.Va.	$20	Same as adultery	No crime	1–10 years
Wis.	1–3 years or $200–$1000	6 mos. and/or $100; with a chaste minor, 4 years and/or $200	1–5 years	1–5 years
Wyo.	$100 and 3 mos.	Same as adultery	12 mos.–5 years	12 mos.–5 years

*Applies also to unmarried person.

21.4 REHEARSAL PHOTO FROM *SUMMER AND SMOKE*

Margo Jones and Tennessee Williams at rehearsal of *Summer and Smoke*

Source: Photo © John Springer Collection/Corbis

21.5 *SUMMER AND SMOKE*—TENNESSEE WILLIAMS

Characters

ALMA as a child
JOHN as a child
REV. WINEMILLER, her father
MRS. WINEMILLER, her mother
ALMA WINEMILLER
JOHN BUCHANAN, JR.
DR. BUCHANAN, his father
ROSA GONZALES
PAPA GONZALES, her father
NELLIE EWELL
MRS. BASSETT
ROGER DOREMUS
MR. KRAMER
ROSEMARY
VERNON
DUSTY

Scenes

PART ONE
A SUMMER
PROLOGUE: The Fountain

SCENE 1	The same
SCENE 2	The Rectory Interior & Doctor's Office
SCENE 3	The Rectory Interior
SCENE 4	The Doctor's Office
SCENE 5	The Rectory Interior
SCENE 6	The Arbor

PART TWO
A WINTER

SCENE 7	The Rectory & Doctor's Office
SCENE 8	The Doctor's Office
SCENE 9	The Rectory & Doctor's Office
SCENE 10	The Fountain
SCENE 11	The Doctor's Office
SCENE 12	The Fountain

The entire action of the play takes place in Glorious Hill, Mississippi. The time is the turn of the Century through 1916.

Author's Production Notes

As the concept of a design grows out of reading a play I will not do more than indicate what I think are the most essential points.

First of all—*The Sky.*

There must be a great expanse of sky so that the entire action of the play takes place against it. This is true of interior as well as exterior scenes. But in fact there are no really interior scenes, for the walls are omitted or just barely suggested by certain necessary fragments such as might be needed to hang a picture or to contain a doorframe.

During the day scenes the sky should be a pure and intense blue (like the sky of Italy as it is so faithfully represented in the religious paintings of the Renaissance) and costumes should be selected to form dramatic color contrasts to this intense blue which the figures stand against. (Color harmonies and other visual effects are tremendously important.)

In the night scenes, the more familiar constellations, such as Orion and the Great Bear and the Pleiades, are clearly projected on the night sky, and above them, splashed across the top of the cyclorama, is the nebulous radiance of the Milky Way. Fleecy cloud forms may also be projected on this cyclorama and made to drift across it.

So much for *The Sky*.

Now we descend to the so-called interior sets of the play. There are two of these "interior" sets, one being the parlor of an Episcopal Rectory and the other the home of a doctor next door to the Rectory. The architecture of these houses is barely suggested but is of an American Gothic design of the Victorian era. There are no actual doors or windows or walls. Doors and windows are represented by delicate frameworks of Gothic design. These frames have strings of ivy clinging to them, the leaves of emerald and amber. Sections of wall are used only where they are functionally required. There should be a fragment of wall in back of the Rectory sofa, supporting a romantic landscape in a gilt frame. In the doctor's house there should be a section of wall to support the chart of anatomy. Chirico has used fragmentary walls and interiors in a very evocative way in his painting called "Conversation among the Ruins." We will deal more specifically with these interiors as we come to them in the course of the play.

Now we come to the main exterior set which is a promontory in a park or public square in the town of Glorious Hill. Situated on this promontory is a fountain in the form of a stone angel, in a gracefully crouching position with wings lifted and her hands held together to form a cup from which water flows, a public drinking fountain. The stone angel of the fountain should probably be elevated so that it appears in the background of the interior scenes as a symbolic figure (Eternity) brooding over the course of the play. *This entire exterior set may be on an upper level, above that of the two fragmentary interiors.* I would like all three units to form an harmonious whole like one complete picture rather than three separate ones. An imaginative designer may solve these plastic problems in a variety of ways and should not feel bound by any of my specific suggestions.

There is one more set, a very small exterior representing an arbor, which we will describe when we reach it.

Everything possible should be done to give an unbroken fluid quality to the sequence of scenes.

There should be no curtain except for the intermission. The other divisions of the play should be accomplished by changes of lighting.

Finally, the matter of music. One basic theme should recur and the points of recurrence have been indicated here and there in the stage directions.

Rome, March, 1948.

Summer and Smoke was first produced by Margo Jones at her theater in Dallas, Texas. It was later produced and directed by Miss Jones in New York, opening at the Music Box Theater, October 6, 1948, with Margaret Phillips and Tod Andrews in the two leading roles; incidental music by Paul Bowles and setting by Jo Mielziner.

★

CAST OF THE NEW YORK PRODUCTION

ALMA as a child	ARLEME MCQUADE
JOHN as a child	DONALD HASTINGS
REV. WINEMILLER	RAYMOND VAN SICKLE
MRS. WINEMILLER	MAMA ANN DEIGHTON
ALMA WINEMILLER	MARGARET PHILLIPS
JOHN BUCHANAN, Jr.	TOD ANDREWS
DR. BUCHANAN	RALPH THEDORE
ROSA GONZALES	MONICA BOYAR
PAPA GONZALES	SID CASSEL
NELLIE EWELL	ANNE JACKSON
MRS. BASSETT	BETTY GREENE LITTLE
ROGER DOREMUS	EARL MONTGOMERY
MR. KRAMER	RAY WALSTON
ROSEMARY	ELLEN JAMES
VERNON	SPENCER JAMES
DUSTY	WILLIAM LAYTON
A GIRL	HILDY PARKS

★

PART ONE

A Summer

Prologue

In the park near the angel of the fountain. At dusk of an evening in May, in the first few years of this Century.

Alma, as a child of ten, comes into the scene. She wears a middy blouse and has ribboned braids. She already has the dignity of an adult; there is a quality of extraordinary delicacy and tenderness or spirituality in her, which must set her distinctly apart from other children. She has a habit of holding her hands, one cupped under the other in a way similar to that of receiving the wafer at Holy Communion. This is a habit that will remain with her as an adult. She stands like that in front of the stone angel for a few moments; then bends to drink at the fountain.

While she is bent at the fountain, John, as a child, enters. He shoots a pea-shooter at Alma's bent-over back. She utters a startled cry and whirls about. He laughs.

JOHN: Hi, Preacher's daughter, [*He advances toward her.*] I been looking for you.

ALMA [*hopefully*]: You have?

JOHN: Was it you that put them handkerchiefs on my desk? [*Alma smiles uncertainly.*] Answer up!

ALMA: I put a box of handkerchiefs on your desk.

JOHN: I figured it was you. What was the idea, Miss Priss?

ALMA: You needed them.

JOHN: Trying to make a fool of me?

ALMA: Oh, no!

JOHN : Then what was the idea?

ALMA: You have a bad cold and your nose has been running all week. It spoils your appearance.

JOHN: You don't have to look at me if you don't like my appearance.

ALMA: I like your appearance.

JOHN [*coming closer*]: Is that why you look at me all the time?

ALMA: I—don't!

JOHN: Oh, yeh, you do. You been keeping your eyes on me all the time. Every time I look around I see them cat eyes of yours looking at me. That was the trouble today when Miss Blanchard asked you where the river Amazon was. She asked you twice and you still didn't answer because you w' lookin' at me. What's the idea? What've'y' got an y' mind anyhow? Answer up!

ALMA: I was only thinking how handsome you'd be if your face wasn't dirty. You know why your face is dirty? Because you don't use a handkerchief and you wipe your nose on the sleeve of that dirty old sweater.

JOHN [*indignantly*]: Hah!

ALMA: That's why I put the handkerchiefs on your desk and I wrapped them up so nobody would know what they were. It isn't my fault that you opened the box in front of everybody!

JOHN: What did you think I'd do with a strange box on my desk? Just leave it there till it exploded or something? Sure I opened it up. I didn't expect to find no—*handkerchiefs!*—in it . . .

ALMA [*in a shy trembling voice*]: I'm sorry that you were embarrassed. I honestly am awfully sorry that you were embarrassed. Because I wouldn't embarrass you for the world!

JOHN: Don't flatter yourself that I was embarrassed. I don't embarrass that easy.

ALMA: It was stupid and cruel of those girls to laugh.

JOHN: Hah!

ALMA: They should all realize that you don't have a mother to take care of such things for you. It was a pleasure to me to be able to do something for you, only I didn't want you to know it was me who did it.

JOHN: Hee-haw! Ho-hum! Take 'em back! [*He snatches out the box and thrusts it toward her.*]

ALMA: *Please* keep them.

JOHN: What do I want with them?

[*She stares at him helplessly. He tosses the box to the ground and goes up to the fountain and drinks. Something in her face mollifies him and she sits down at the base of the fountain with a manner that does not preclude a more friendly relation. The dark gathers deeper.*]

ALMA: Do you know the name of the angel?

JOHN: Does she have a name?

ALMA: Yes, I found out she does. It's carved in the base but it's all worn away so you can't make it out with your eyes.

JOHN: Then how do you know it?

ALMA: You have to read it with your fingers. I did and it gave me cold shivers! *You* read it and see if it doesn't give *you* cold shivers! Go on! Read it with your fingers!

JOHN: Why don't you tell me and save me the trouble?

ALMA: I'm not going to tell you.

[*John grins indulgently and turns to the pediment, crouching before it and running fingers along the worn inscription.*]

JOHN: E?

ALMA: Yes, E is the first letter!

JOHN: T?

ALMA: Yes!

JOHN: E?

ALMA: E!

JOHN: K?

ALMA: No, no, not K!—*R!* [*He slowly straightens up.*]

JOHN: Eternity?

ALMA: *Eternity!*—Didn't it give you the cold shivers?

JOHN: Nahh.

ALMA: Well, it did me!

JOHN: Because you're a preacher's daughter. Eternity. What is eternity?

ALMA [*in a hushed wondering* voice]: It's something that goes on and on when life and death and time and everything else is all through with.

JOHN: There's no such thing.

ALMA: There is. It's what people's souls live in when they have left their bodies. My name is Alma and Alma is Spanish for soul. Did you know that?

JOHN: Hee-haw! Ho-hum! Have you ever seen a dead person?

ALMA: No.

JOHN: I have. They made me go in the room when my mother was dying and she caught hold of my hand and wouldn't let me go—and so I screamed and hit her.

ALMA: Oh, you didn't do that.

JOHN [*somberly*]: Uh-huh. She didn't look like my mother. Her face was all ugly and yellow and—terrible—bad-smelling! And so I hit her to make her let go of my hand. They told me that I was a devil!

ALMA: You didn't know what you were doing.

JOHN: My dad is a doctor.

ALMA: I know.

JOHN: He wants to send me to college to study to be a doctor but I wouldn't be a doctor for the world. And have to go in a room and watch people dying! . . . Jesus!

ALMA: You'll change your mind about that.

JOHN: Oh, no, I won't. I'd rather *be* a devil, like they called me and go to South America on a boat! . . . Give me one of them handkerchiefs. [*She brings them eagerly and humbly to the fountain. He takes one: out and wets it at the fountain and scrubs hit face with it.*] Is my face clean enough to suit you now?

ALMA: Yes!—Beautiful!

JOHN: *What!*

ALMA: I said "Beautiful"!

JOHN : Well—let's—kiss each other.

[*Alma turns away.*]

JOHN: Come on, let's just try it!

[*He seizes her shoulders and gives her a quick rough kiss. She stands amazed with one hand cupping the other.*

[*The voice of a child in the distance calls "Johnny! Johnny!"*

[*He suddenly snatches at her hair-ribbon, jerks it loose and then runs off with a mocking laugh.*

[*Hurt and bewildered, Alma turns back to the stone angel, for comfort. She crouches at the pediment and touches the inscription with her fingers. The scene dims out with music.*]

★

Scene One

Before the curtain rises a band is heard playing a patriotic anthem, punctuated with the crackle or fireworks.

The scene is the same as for the Prologue. It is the evening of July 4th in a year shortly before the first World War. There is a band concert and a display of fireworks in the park. During the scene the light changes from faded sunlight to dusk. Sections of roof, steeples, weather-vanes, should have a metallic surface that catches the mellow light on the backdrop; when dusk has fallen the stars should be visible.

As the curtain rises, the Rev. and Mrs. Winemiller come in and sit on the bench near the fountain. Mrs. Winemiller was a spoiled and selfish girl who evaded the responsibilities of later life by slipping into a state of perverse childishness. She is known as Mr. Winemiller's "Cross."

MR. WINEMILLER [*suddenly rising*]: There is Alma, getting on the bandstand! [*Mrs. Winemiller is dreamily munching popcorn.*]

AN ANNOUNCER'S VOICE [*at a distance*]: The Glorious Hill Orchestra brings you Miss Alma Winemiller. The Nightingale of the Delta, singing . . . "La Golondrina."

MR. WINEMILLER [*sitting back dawn again*]: This is going to provoke a lot of criticism.

[*The song commences. The voice is not particularly strong, but it has great purity and emotion. John Buchanan comes along. He is now a Promethean figure, brilliantly and restlessly alive in a stagnant society. The excess of his power has not yet found a channel. If it remains without one, it will burn him up. At present he is unmarked by the dissipations in which he relieves his demoniac unrest; he has the fresh and shining look of an epic hero. He walks leisurely before the Winemillers' bench, negligently touching the crown of his hat but not glancing at them; climbs the steps to the base of the fountain, then turns and looks in the direction of the singer. A look of interest touched with irony appears on his face. A couple, strolling in the park, pass behind the fountain.*]

THE GIRL: Look who's by the fountain!

THE MAN: Bright as a new silver dollar!

JOHN: Hi, Dusty! Hi, Pearl!

THE MAN: How'd you make out in that floating crap game?

JOHN: I floated with it as far as Vicksburg, then sank.

THE GIRL: Everybody's been calling: "Johnny, Johnny—where's Johnny?"

[*John's father, Dr. Buchanan, comes on from the right, as Rev. and Mrs. Winemiller move off the scene to the left, toward the band music. Dr. Buchanan is an elderly man whose age shows in his slow and stiff movements. He walks with a cane. John sees him coming, but pretends not to and starts to walk off.*]

DR. BUCHANAN: John!

JOHN [*slowly turning around, as the couple move off*]: Oh! Hi. Dad. . . . [*They exchange a long look.*] I—uh—meant to wire you but I must've forgot. I got tied up in Vicksburg Friday night and just now got back to town. Haven't been to the house yet. Is everything . . . going okay? [*He takes a drink of water at the fountain.*]

DR. BUCHANAN [*slowly, in a voice hoarse with emotion*]: There isn't any room in the medical profession for wasters, drunkards and lechers. And there isn't any room in my house for wasters—drunkards—lechers! [*A child is heard calling "I sp-yyyyyy!" in the distance.*] I married late in life. I brought over five hundred children into this world before I had one of my own. And by God it looks like I've given myself the rottenest one of the lot. . . . [*John laughs uncertainly.*] You will find your things at the Alhambra Hotel.

JOHN: Okay. If that's how you want it.

[*There is a pause. The singing comes through on the music. John tips his hat diffidently and starts away from the fountain. He goes a few feet and his father suddenly calls after him.*]

DR. BUCHANAN: John! [*John pauses and looks back.*] Come here.

JOHN: Yes, Sir? [*He walks back to his father and stands before him.*]

DR. BUCHANAN [*hoarsely*]: Go to the Alhambra Hotel and pick up your things and—bring them back to the house.

JOHN [*gently*]: Yes, Sir. If that's how you want it. [*He diffidently extends a hand to touch his father's shoulder.*]

DR. BUCHANAN [*brushing the hand roughly off*]: You! . . . You Infernal *whelp,* you!

[*Dr. Buchanan turns and goes hurriedly away, John looks after him with a faint, affectionate smile, then sits down on the steps with an air of relief, handkerchief to forehead, and a whistle of relief. Just then the singing at the bandstand ends and there is the sound of applause. Mrs. Winemiller comes in from the left, followed by her husband.*]

MRS. WINEMILLER: Where is the ice cream man?

MR. WINEMILLER: Mother, hush! [*He sees his daughter approaching.*] Here we are, Alma!

[*The song ends. There is applause. Then the band strikes up the Santiago Waltz.*

[*Alma Winemiller enters. Alma had an adult quality as a child and now, in her middle twenties, there is something prematurely spinsterish about her. An excessive propriety and self-consciousness is apparent in her nervous laughter; her voice and gestures belong to years of church entertainments, to the position of hostess in a rectory. People her own age regard her as rather quaintly and humorously affected. She has grown up mostly in the company of her elders. Her true nature is still hidden even from herself. She is dressed in pale yellow and carries a yellow silk parasol.*

[*As Alma passes in front of the fountain, John slaps his hands resoundingly together a few times. She catches her breath in a slight laughing sound, makes as if to retreat, with a startled "oh!," but then goes quickly to her parents. The applause from the crowd continues.*]

MR. WINEMILLER: They seem to want to hear you sing again, Alma.

[*She turns nervously about, touching her throat and her chest. John grins, applauding by the fountain. When the applause dies out, Alma sinks faintly on the bench.*]

ALMA: Open my bag, Father. My fingers have frozen stiff! [*She draws a deep labored breath.*] I don't know what came over me—absolute panic! Never, never again, it isn't worth it—the tortures that I go through!

MR. WINEMILLER. [*anxiously*]: You're having one of your nervous attacks?

ALMA: My heart's beating so! It seemed to be in my *throat* the whole time I was singing! [*John laughs audibly from the fountain.*] Was it noticeable. Father?

MR. WINEMILLER: You sang extremely well, Alma. But you know how I feel about this, it was contrary to my wishes and I cannot imagine why you wanted to do it, especially since it seemed to upset you so.

ALMA: I don't see how anyone could object to my singing at a patriotic occasion. If I had just sung well! But I barely got through it. At one point I thought that I wouldn't. The words flew out of my mind. Did you notice the pause? Blind panic! They really never came back, but I went on singing—I think I must have been improvising the lyric! Whew! Is there a handkerchief in it?

MRS. WINEMILLER [*suddenly*]: Where is the ice cream man?

ALMA [*rubbing her fingers together*]: Circulation is slowly coming back . . .

MR. WINEMILLER: Sit back quietly and take a deep breath, Alma.

ALMA: Yes, my handkerchief—now . . .

MRS. WINEMILLER: Where is the ice cream man?

MR. WINEMILLER: Mother, there isn't any ice cream man.

ALMA: No, there isn't any ice cream man, Mother. But on the way home Mr. Doremus and I will stop by the drug store and pick up a pint of ice cream.

MR. WINEMILLER: Are you intending to stay here?

ALMA: Until the concert is over. I promised Roger I'd wait for him.

MR. WINEMILLER: I suppose you have noticed who is by the fountain?

ALMA: *Shhh!*

MR. WINEMILLER: Hadn't you better wait on a different bench?

ALMA: This is where Roger will meet me.

MR. WINEMILLER: Well, Mother, we'll run along now. [*Mrs. Winemiller has started vaguely toward the fountain, Mr. Winemiller firmly restraining her.*] This way, this way, Mother! [*He takes her arm and leads her off.*]

MRS. WINEMILLER [*calling back, in a high, childish voice*]: Strawberry. Alma. Chocolate, chocolate and strawberry mixed! Not vanilla!

ALMA [*faintly*]: Yes, yes, Mother—vanilla . . .

MRS. WINEMILLER [*furiously*]: I said *not* vanilla. [*shouting*] Strawberry!

MR. WINEMILLER [*fiercely*]: Mother! We're attracting attention. [*He propels her forcibly away.*]

[*John laughs by the fountain. Alma moves her parasol so that it shields her face from him. She leans back, closing her eyes. John notices a firecracker by the fountain. He leans over negligently to pick it up. He grins and lights it and tosses it toward Alma's bench. When it goes off she springs up with a shocked cry, letting the parasol drop.*]

JOHN [*jumping up as if outraged*]: Hey! Hey, you! [*He looks off to the right. Alma sinks back weakly on the bench. John solicitously advances.*] Are you all right?

ALMA: I can't seem to—catch my breath! Who threw it?

JOHN: Some little rascal.

ALMA: Where?

JOHN: He ran away quick when I hollered!

ALMA: There ought to be an ordinance passed in this town forbidding firecrackers.

JOHN: Dad and I treated fifteen kids for burns the last couple of days. I think you need a little restorative, don't you? [*He takes out a flask.*] Here!

ALMA: What is it?

JOHN: Apple-jack brandy.

ALMA: No thank you.

JOHN: Liquid dynamite.

ALMA: I'm sure.

[*John laughs and returns it to his pocket. He remains looking down at her with one foot on the end of her bench. His steady, smiling look into her face is disconcerting her.*

[*In Alma's voice and manner there is a delicacy and elegance, a kind of "airiness," which is really natural to her as it is, in a less marked degree, to many Southern girls. Her gestures and mannerisms are a bit exaggerated but in a graceful way. It is understandable that she might be accused of "putting on airs" and of being "affected" by the other young people of the town. She seems to belong to a more elegant age, such as the Eighteenth Century in France. Out of nervousness and self-consciousness she has a habit of prefacing and concluding her remarks with a little breathless laugh. This will be indicated at points, but should be used more freely than indicated; however, the characterization must never be stressed to the point of making her at all ludicrous in a less than sympathetic way.*]

ALMA: You're—home for the summer? [*John gives an affirmative grunt.*] Summer is not the pleasantest time of year to renew an acquaintance with Glorious Hill—is it? [*John gives an indefinite grunt. Alma laughs airily.*] The Gulf wind has failed us this year, disappointed us dreadfully this summer. We used to be able to rely on the Gulf wind to cool the nights off for us, but this summer has been an exceptional season. [*He continues to grin disconcertingly down at her; she shows her discomfiture in flurried gestures.*]

JOHN [*slowly*]: Are you—disturbed about something?

ALMA: That firecracker was a shock.

JOHN: You should be over that shock by now.

ALMA: I don't get over shocks quickly.

JOHN: I see you don't.

ALMA: You're planning to stay here and take over some of your father's medical practice?

JOHN: I haven't made up my mind about anything yet.

ALMA: I hope so, we all hope so. Your father was telling me that you have succeeded in isolating the germ of that fever epidemic that's broken out at Lyon.

JOHN: Finding something to kill it is more of a trick.

ALMA: You'll do that! He's so positive that you will. He says that you made a special study of barter—bacter . . .

JOHN: Bacteriology!

ALMA: Yes! At Johns Hopkins! That's in Boston, isn't it?

JOHN: No. Baltimore.

ALMA: Oh, Baltimore. Baltimore, Maryland. Such a beautiful combination of names. And bacteriology—isn't that something you do with a microscope?

JOHN: Well—partly. . . .

ALMA: I've looked through a telescope, but never a microscope. What . . . what do you—see?

JOHN: A—universe, Miss Alma.

ALMA: What kind of a universe?

JOHN: Pretty much the same kind that you saw through the lens of a telescope—a mysterious one. . . .

ALMA: Oh, yes. . . .

JOHN: Part anarchy—and part order!

ALMA: The footprints of God!

JOHN: But not God.

ALMA [*ecstatically*]: To be a doctor! And deal with these mysteries under the microscope lens . . . I think it is more religious than being a priest! There is so much suffering in the world it actually makes one sick to think about it, and most of us are so helpless to relieve it. . . . But a physician! Oh, my! With his magnificent gifts and training what a joy it must be to know that he is equipped and appointed to bring relief to all of this fearful suffering—and fear! And it's an expanding profession, it's a profession that is continually widening its horizons. So many diseases have already come under scientific control but the commencement is just—beginning! I mean there is so much more that is yet to be done, such as mental afflictions to be brought under control. . . . And with your father's example to inspire you! Oh, my!

JOHN: I didn't know you had so many ideas about the medical profession.

ALMA: Well, I am a great admirer of your father, as well as a patient. It's such a comfort knowing that he's right next door, within arm's reach as it were!

JOHN: Why? Do you have fits?

ALMA: Fits? [*She throws back her head with a peal of gay laughter.*] Why no, but I do have attacks!—of nervous heart trouble. Which can be so alarming that I run straight to your father!

JOHN: At two or three in the morning?

ALMA: Yes, as late as that, even . . . occasionally. He's very patient with me.

JOHN: But does you no good?
ALMA: He always reassures me.
JOHN: Temporarily?
ALMA: Yes . . .
JOHN: Don't you want more than that?
ALMA: What?
JOHN: It's none of my business.
ALMA: What were you going to say?
JOHN: You're Dad's patient. But I have an idea . . .
ALMA: Please go on! [*John laughs a little.*] Now you have to go on! You can't leave me up in the air! What were you going to tell me?
JOHN: Only that I suspect you need something more than a little temporary reassurance.
ALMA: *Why?* Why? You think it's more serious than . . .?
JOHN: You're swallowing air.
ALMA: I'm what?
JOHN: You're swallowing air, Miss Alma.
ALMA: I'm swallowing air?
JOHN: Yes, you swallow air when you laugh or talk. It's a little trick that hysterical women get into.
ALMA [*uncertainly*]: Ha-ha . . . I
JOHN: You swallow air and it presses on your heart and gives you palpitations. That isn't serious in itself but it's a symptom of something that is. Shall I tell you frankly?
ALMA: Yes!
JOHN: Well, what I think you have is a *doppelganger!* You have a *doppelganger* and the *doppelganger* is badly irritated.
ALMA: Oh, my goodness! I have an irritated *doppelganger!* [*She tries to laugh, but is definitely uneasy.*] How awful that sounds! What exactly *is* it?
JOHN: It's none of *my* business. You are not *my* patient.
ALMA: But that's downright wicked of you! To tell me I have something awful-sounding as that, and then refuse to let me know what it is! [*She tries to laugh again, unsuccessfully.*]
JOHN: I shouldn't have said anything! I'm not your doctor. . . .
ALMA: Just how did you arrive at this—diagnosis of my case? [*She laughs.*] But of course you're teasing me. Aren't you? . . . There the Gulf wind is stirring! He's actually moving the leaves of the palmetto! And listen to them complaining. . . .

[*As if brought in by this courier from the tropics, Rosa Gonzales enters and crosses to the fountain. Her indolent walk produces a sound and an atmosphere like the Gulf wind on the palmettos, a whispering of silk and a slight rattle of metallic ornaments. She is dressed in an almost outrageous finery, with lustrous feathers on her hat, greenish blue, a cascade of them, also diamond and emerald earrings.*]

JOHN [*sharply*]: *Who is that?*
ALMA: I'm surprised that you don't know.
JOHN: I've been away quite a while.
ALMA: That's the Gonzales girl. . . . Her father's the owner of the gambling casino on Moon Lake. [*Rosa drinks at the fountain and wanders leisurely off.*] She smiled at you, didn't she?
JOHN: I thought she did.
ALMA: I hope that you have a strong character. [*He places a foot on the end of the bench.*]
JOHN: Solid rock.
ALMA [*nervously*]: The pyrotechnical display is going to be brilliant.
JOHN: The what?
ALMA: The fireworks.
JOHN: Aw!
ALMA: I suppose you've lost touch with most of your *old* friends here.
JOHN [*laconically*]: Yeah.
ALMA: You must make some *new* ones! I belong to a little group that meets every ten days. I think you'd enjoy them, too. They're voting people with—intellectual and artistic interests. . . .
JOHN [*sadly*]: Aw, I see . . . intellectual. . . .
ALMA: You must come!—sometime—I'm going to remind you of it. . . .
JOHN: Thanks. Do you mind if I sit down?
ALMA: Why, certainly not, there's room enough for two! Neither of us are—terribly large in diameter! [*She laughs shrilly.*]

[*A voice is heard calling: "Goodbye, Nellie!" and another answers: "Goodbye!" Nellie Ewell enters—a girl of sixteen with a radiantly fresh healthy quality.*]

ALMA: Here comes someone much nicer! One of my adorable little vocal pupils, the youngest and prettiest one with the least gift for music.
JOHN: I know that one.
ALMA: Hello, there, Nellie dear!
NELLIE: Oh, Miss Alma, your singing was so beautiful it made me cry.
ALMA: It's sweet of you to fib so. I sang terribly.
NELLIE: You just being modest, Miss Alma. Hello, Dr. John! Dr. John?
JOHN: Yeah?
NELLIE: That book you gave me is too full of long words.
JOHN: Look 'em up in the dictionary, Nellie.
NELLIE: I did, but you know how dictionaries are. You look up one long word and it gives you another and you look up that one and it gives you the long word you looked up in the first place. [*John laughs.*] I'm coming over tomorrow for you to explain it all to me. [*She laughs and goes off.*]

ALMA: What book is she talking about?

JOHN: A book I gave her about the facts of nature. She came over to the office and told me her mother wouldn't tell her anything and she had to know because she'd fallen in love.

ALMA: Why the precocious little—imp! [*She laughs.*]

JOHN: What sort of a mother has she?

ALMA: Mrs. Ewell's the merry widow of Glorious Hill. They say that she goes to the depot to meet every train in order to make the acquaintance of traveling salesmen. Of course she is ostracized by all but a few of her own type of women in town, which is terribly hard for Nellie. It isn't fair to the child. Father didn't want me to take her as a pupil because of her mother's reputation, but I feel that one has a duty to perform toward children in such—circumstances. . . . And I always say that life is such a mysteriously complicated thing that no one should really presume to judge and condemn the behavior of anyone else!

[*There is a faraway "puff" and a burst of golden light over their heads. Both look up. There is a long-drawn "Ahhh . . ." from the invisible crowd. This is an effect that will be repeated at intervals during the scene.*]

There goes the first sky-rocket! Oh, look at it burst into a million stars!

[*John leans way back to look up and allows his knees to spread wide apart so that one of them is in contact with Alma's. The effect upon her is curiously disturbing.*]

JOHN [*after a moment*]: Do you have a chill?

ALMA: Why, no!—no. Why?

JOHN: You're shaking.

ALMA: Am I?

JOHN: Don't you feel it?

ALMA: I have a touch of malaria lingering on.

JOHN: You have malaria?

ALMA: Never severely, never really severely. I just have touches of it that come and go. [*She laughs airily.*]

JOHN [*with a gentle grin*]: Why do you laugh that way?

ALMA: What way?

[*John imitates her laugh. Alma laughs again in embarrassment.*]

JOHN: Yeah. That way.

ALMA: I do declare, you haven't changed in the slightest. It used to delight you to embarrass me and it still does!

JOHN: I guess I shouldn't tell you this, but I heard an imitation of you at a party.

ALMA: Imitation? Of what?

JOHN: You.

ALMA: I?—I? Why, *what* did they imitate?

JOHN: You singing at a wedding.

ALMA: My voice?

JOHN: Your gestures and facial expression!

ALMA: How mystifying!

JOHN: No, I shouldn't have told you. You're upset about it.

ALMA: I'm not in the least upset, I am just mystified.

JOHN: Don't you know that you have a reputation for putting on airs a little—for gilding the lily a bit?

ALMA: I have no idea what you are talking about.

JOHN: Well, some people seem to have gotten the idea that you are just a little bit—affected!

ALMA: Well, well, well, well. [*She tries to conceal her hurt.*] That may be so, it may seem so to some people. But since I am innocent of any such attempt at affectation, I really don't know what I can do about it.

JOHN: You have a rather fancy way of talking.

ALMA: Have I?

JOHN: Pyrotechnical display instead of fireworks, and that sort of thing.

ALMA: So?

JOHN: And how about that accent?

ALMA: Accent? This leaves me quite speechless! I have sometimes been accused of having a put-on accent by people who disapprove of good diction. My father was a Rhodes scholar at Oxford, and while over there he fell into the natural habit of using the long A where it is correct to use it. I suppose I must have picked it up from him, but it's entirely unconscious. Who gave this imitation at this party you spoke of?

JOHN [*grinning*]: I don't think she'd want that told.

ALMA: Oh, it was a *she* then?

JOHN: You don't think a man could do it?

ALMA: No, and I don't think a lady would do it either!

JOHN: I didn't think it would have made you so mad, or I wouldn't have brought it up.

ALMA: Oh, I'm not mad. I'm just mystified and amazed as I always am by unprovoked malice in people. I don't understand it when it's directed at me and I don't understand it when it is directed at anybody else. I just don't understand it, and perhaps it is better not to understand it. These people who call me affected and give these unkind imitations of me—I wonder if they stop to think that I have had certain difficulties and disadvantages to cope with—which may be partly the cause of these peculiarities of mine—which they find so offensive!

JOHN: Now, Miss Alma, you're making a mountain out of a mole-hill!

ALMA: I wonder if they stop to think that my circumstances are somewhat different from theirs? My father and I have a certain—cross—to bear!

JOHN: What cross?

ALMA: Living next door to us, you should know what cross.

JOHN: Mrs. Winemiller?

ALMA: She had her breakdown while I was still in high school. And from that time on I have had to manage the Rectory and take over the social and household duties that would ordinarily belong to a minister's wife, not his daughter. And that may have made me seem strange to some of my more critical contemporaries. In a way it may have—deprived me of—my youth. . . .

[Another rocket goes up. Another "Ahhh . . ." from the crowd.]

JOHN: You ought to go out with young people.

ALMA: I am not a recluse. I don't fly around here and there giving imitations of other people at parties. But I am not a recluse by any manner of means. Being a minister's daughter I have to be more selective than most girls about the—society I keep. But I do go out now and then. . . .

JOHN: I have seen you in the public library and the park, but only two or three times have I seen you out with a boy and it was always someone like this Roger Doremus.

ALMA: I'm afraid that you and I move in different circles. If I wished to be as outspoken as you are, which is sometimes just an excuse for being rude—I might say that I've yet to see you in the company of a—well, a—reputable young woman. You've heard unfavorable talk about me in your circle of acquaintances and I've heard equally unpleasant things about you in mine. And the pity of it is that you are preparing to be a doctor. You're intending to practice your father's profession here in Glorious Hill. [*She catches her breath in a sob.*] Most of us have no choice but to lead useless lives! But you have a gift for scientific research! You have a chance to serve humanity. Not just to go on enduring for the sake of endurance, but to serve a noble, humanitarian cause, to relieve human suffering. And what do you do about it? Everything that you can to alienate the confidence of nice people who love and respect your father. While he is devoting himself to the fever at Lyon you drive your automobile at a reckless pace from one disorderly roadhouse to another! You say you have seen two things through the microscope, anarchy and order? Well, obviously *order* is not the thing that impressed you . . . conducting yourself like some overgrown schoolboy who wants to be known as the wildest fellow in town! And you—a gifted young doctor—*Magna cum Laude!* [*She turns aside, touching her eyelids with a handkerchief.*] You know what I call it? I call it a *desecration!* [*She sobs uncontrollably. Then she springs up from the bench. John catches her hand.*]

JOHN: You're not going to run off, are you?

ALMA: Singing in public always—always upsets me!—Let go of my hand. [*He holds on to it, grinning up at her in the deepening dusk. The stars are coming out in the cyclorama with its leisurely floating cloud-forms. In the distance the band is playing "La Golondrina."*] Please let go of my hand.

JOHN: Don't run off mad.

ALMA: Let's not make a spectacle of ourselves.

JOHN: Then sit back down.

[A skyrocket goes up. The crowd "Ahhh . . . s."]

ALMA: You threw that firecracker and started a conversation just in order to tease me as you did as a child. You came to this bench in order to embarrass me and to hurt my feelings with the report of that vicious—imitation! No, let go of my hand so I can leave, now. You've succeeded in your purpose. I *was* hurt, I *did* make a fool of myself as you intended! So let me go now!

JOHN: You're attracting attention! Don't you know that I really *like* you, Miss Alma?

ALMA: No, you don't.

[Another skyrocket.]

JOHN: Sure I do. A lot. Sometimes when I come home late at night I look over at the Rectory. I see something white at the window. Could that be you, Miss Alma? Or, is it your *doppelganger*, looking out of the window that faces my way?

ALMA: Enough about *doppelganger*—whatever that is!

JOHN: There goes a nice one, Roman candle they call it!

[This time the explosion is in back of them. A Roman candle shoots up puffs of rainbow-colored light in back of the stone angel of the fountain. They turn in profile to watch it.]

JOHN [*counting the puffs of light*]: Four—five—six—that's all? No—seven! [*There is a pause. Alma sits down slowly.*]

ALMA [*vaguely*]: Dear me . . . [*She fans herself.*]

JOHN: How about going riding?

ALMA: [*too eagerly*]: When . . . now?

[Rosa Gonzales has wandered up to the fountain again. John's attention drifts steadily toward her and away from Alma.]

JOHN [*too carelessly*]: Oh . . . some afternoon.

ALMA: Would you observe the speed limit?

JOHN: Strictly with you, Miss Alma.

ALMA: Why then, I'd be glad to—John.

[John has risen from the bench and crosses to the fountain.]

JOHN: And wear a hat with a plume!

ALMA: I don't have a hat with a plume!

JOHN: Get one!

[*Another skyrocket goes up, and there is another long "Ahhh . . ." from the crowd. John saunters up to the fountain. Rosa has lingered beside it. As he passes her he whispers something. She laughs and moves leisurely off. John takes a quick drink at the fountain, then follows Rosa, calling back "Good night" to Alma. There is a sound of laughter in the distance. Alma sits motionless for a moment, then touches a small white handkerchief to her lips and nostrils. Mr. Doremus comes in, carrying a French horn case. He is a small man, somewhat like a sparrow.*]

ROGER: *Whew!* Golly! Moses!—Well, how did it go, Miss Alma?

ALMA: How did—what—go?

ROGER [*annoyed*]: My solo on the French horn.

ALMA [*slowly, without thinking*]: I paid no attention to it. [*She rises slowly and takes his arm.*] I'll have to hand on your arm—I'm feeling so dizzy!

[*The scene dims out. There is a final skyrocket and a last "Ahhh . . ." from the crowd in the distance. Music is heard, and there is light on the angel.*]

*

Scene Two

Inside the Rectory, which is lighted, Mrs. Winemiller comes in and makes her way stealthily to the love seat, where she seats herself. Opening her parasol, she takes out a fancy white-plumed hat which she had concealed there. Rising, she turns to the mirror on the wall over the love seat and tries on the hat. She draws a long, ecstatic breath as she places it squarely on her head. At that moment the telephone rings. Startled, she snatches off the hat, hides it behind the center table and quickly resumes her seat. The telephone goes on ringing. Alma comes in to answer it.

ALMA: Hello. . . . Yes, Mr. Gillam. . . . She did? . . . Are you sure? . . . How shocking! . . . [*Mrs. Winemiller now retrieves the hat, seats herself in front of Alma and puts the hat on.*] Thank you, Mr. Gillam . . . the hat is here.

[*Mr. Winemiller comes in. He is distracted.*]

MR WINEMILLER: Alma! Alma, your mother . . . !

ALMA [*coming in*]: I know, Father, Mr. Gillam just phoned. He told me she picked up a white plumed bat and he pretended not to notice in order to save you the embarrassment, so I—I told him to just charge it to us.

MR WINEMILLER: That hat looks much too expensive.

ALMA: It's fourteen dollars. Yon pay six of it, Father, and I'll pay eight. [*She gives him the parosol.*]

MR. WINEMILLLER: What an insufferable cross we have to bear. [*He retires despairingly from the room.*]

[*Alma goes over to her mother and seats her in a chair at the table.*]

ALMA: I have a thousand and one things to do before my club meeting tonight, so you work quietly on your picture puzzle or I shall take the hat back, plume and all.

MRS. WINEMILLER [*throwing a piece of the puzzle on the floor*]: The pieces don't fit! [*Alma picks up the piece and puts it on the table.*] The pieces don't fit!

[*Alma stands for a moment in indecision. She reaches for the phone, then puts it down. Then she takes it up again, and gives a number. The telephone across the way in the doctor's office rings and that part of the scene lights up. John comes in.*]

JOHN [*answering the phone*]: Hello?

ALMA: John! [*She fans herself rapidly with a palm leaf clutched in her free hand and puts on a brilliant, strained smile as if she were actually in his presence.*]

JOHN: Miss Alma?

ALMA: You recognized my voice?

JOHN: I recognized your laugh.

ALMA: Ha-ha! How are you, you stranger you?

JOHN: I'm pretty well, Miss Alma, How're you doing?

ALMA: Surviving, just surviving! Isn't it fearful?

JOHN: Uh-huh.

ALMA: You seem unusually laconic. Or perhaps I should say more than usually laconic.

JOHN: I had a big night and I'm just recovering from it.

ALMA: Well, sir, I have a bone to pick with you!

JOHN: What's that, Miss Alma? [*He drains a glass of bromo.*]

ALMA: The time of our last conversation on the Fourth of July, you said you were going to take me riding in your automobile.

JOHN: Aw. Did I say that?

ALMA: Yes indeed you did, sir! And all these hot afternoons I've been breathlessly waiting and hoping that you would remember that promise. But now I know how insincere you are. Ha-ha! Time and again the four-wheeled phenomenon flashes by the Rectory and I have yet to put my—my quaking foot in it!

[*Mrs. Winemiller begins to mock Alma's speech and laughter.*]

JOHN: What was that, Miss Alma? I didn't understand you.

ALMA: I was just reprimanding you, sir! Castigating you verbally! Ha-ha!

MRS. WINEMILLER [*grimacing*]: Ha-ha.

JOHN: What about, Miss Alma? [*He leans back and puts his feet on table.*]

ALMA: Never mind. I know how busy you are! [*She whispers.*] Mother, *hush!*

JOHN: I'm afraid we have a bad connection.

ALMA: I hate telephones. I don't know why but they always make the laugh as if someone were poking me in the ribs! I swear to goodness they do!

JOHN: Why don't you just go to your window and I'll go to mine and we can holler across?

ALMA: The yard's so wide I'm afraid it would crack my voice! And I've got to sing at somebody's wedding tomorrow.

JOHN: You're going to sing at a wedding?

ALMA: Yes. "The Voice that Breathed o'er Eden!" And I'm as hoarse as a frog! [*Another gale of laughter almost shakes her off her feet.*]

JOHN: Better come over and let me give you a gargle.

ALMA: Nasty gargles—I hate them!

MRS. WINEMILLER [*mockingly*]: Nasty gargles—I hate them!

ALMA: Mother, shhh!—please! As you no doubt have gathered, there is some interference at this end of the line! What I wanted to say is—you remember my mentioning that little club I belong to?

JOHN: Aw! Aw, yes! Those intellectual meetings!

ALMA: Oh, now, don't call it that. It's just a little informal gathering every Wednesday and we talk about the new books and read things out loud to each other!

JOHN: Serve any refreshments?

ALMA: Yes, we serve refreshments!

JOHN: Any liquid refreshments?

ALMA: Both liquid and solid refreshments.

JOHN: Is this an invitation?

ALMA: Didn't I promise I'd ask you? It's going to be tonight!—at eight at my house, at the Rectory, so all you'll have to do is cross the yard!

JOHN: I'll try to make it, Miss Alma.

ALMA: Don't say try as if it required some Herculean effort! All you have to do is . . .

JOHN: Cross the yard! Uh-huh—reserve me a seat by the punch bowl.

ALMA: That gives me an idea! We *will* have punch, fruit punch, with claret in it. Do you like claret?

JOHN: I just dote on claret.

ALMA: Now you're being sarcastic! Ha-ha-ha!

JOHN: Excuse me, Miss Alma, but Dad's got to use this phone.

ALMA: I won't hang up till you've said you'll come without fail!

JOHN: I'll be there, Miss Alma. You can count on it.

ALMA: An revoir, then! Until eight.

JOHN: G'bye, Miss Alma.

[*John hangs up with an incredulous grin. Alma remains holding the phone with a dazed smile until the office interior has dimmed slowly out.*]

MRS. WINEMILLER: Alma's in love—in love. [*She waltzes mockingly.*]

ALMA [*sharply*]: Mother, you are wearing out my patience! Now I am expecting another music pupil and I have to make preparations for the club meeting so I suggest that you . . . [*Nellie rings the bell.*] Will you go up to your room? [*Then she calls sweetly.*] Yes, Nellie, coming, Nellie. All right, stay down here then. But keep your attention on your picture puzzle or there will be no ice cream for you after supper!

[*She admits Nellie, who is wildly excited over something. This scene should be played lightly and quickly.*]

NELLIE: Oh, Miss Alma!

[*She rushes past Alma in a distracted manner, throws herself on the sofa and hugs herself with excited glee.*]

ALMA: What is it, Nellie? Has something happened at home? [*Nellie continues her exhilaration.*] Oh, now, Nellie, stop that! Whatever it is, it can't be *that* important!

NELLIE [*blurting out suddenly*]: Miss Alma, haven't you ever had—*crushes?*

ALMA: What?

NELLIE: Crushes?

ALMA: Yes—I suppose I have. [*She sits down.*]

NELLIE: Did you know that I used to have a crush on *you*, Miss Alma?

ALMA: No, Nellie.

NELLIE: Why do you think that I took singing lessons?

ALMA: I supposed it was became you wished to develop your voice.

NELLIE [*cutting in*]: Oh, you know, and I know, I never had any voice. I had a crush on you though. Those were the days when I had crushes on girls. Those days are all over, and now I have crushes on boys. Oh, Miss Alma, you know about Mother, how I was brought up so nobody nice except you would have anything to do with us—Mother meeting the trains to pick up the traveling salesmen and bringing them home to drink and play poker—all of them acting like pigs, pigs, pigs!

MRS. WINEMILLER [*mimicking*]: Pigs, pigs, pigs!

NELLIE: Well, I thought I'd always hate men. Loathe and despise them. But last night—Oh!

ALMA: Hadn't we better run over some scales until you are feeling calmer?

NELLIE [*cutting in*]: I'd heard them downstairs for hours but didn't know who it was—fallen asleep—when all of a sudden my door banged open. He'd thought it was the bathroom!

ALMA [*nervously*]: Nellie, I'm not sure I want to hear any more of this story.

NELLIE [*interrupting*]: Guess who it was?

ALMA: I couldn't possibly guess.

NELLIE: Someone you know. Someone I've seen you with.

ALMA: Who?

NELLIE: The wonderfullest person in all the big wide world! When he saw it was me he came and sat down on the bed and held my hand and we talked and talked until Mother came up to see what had happened to him. You should have heard him bawl her out. Oh, he laid the law down! He said she ought to send me off to a girl's school because she wasn't fit to bring up a daughter! Then she started to bawl him out. You're a fine one to talk, she said, you're not fit to call yourself a doctor. [*Alma rises abruptly.*]

ALMA: John Buchanan?

NELLIE: Yes, of course, Dr. Johnny.

ALMA: Was—with—your—mother?

NELLIE: Oh, he wasn't her beau! He had a girl with him, and Mother had somebody else!

ALMA: Who—did—he—have?

NELLIE: Oh, some loud tacky thing with a Z in her name!

ALMA: Gonzales? Rosa Gonzales?

NELLIE: Yes, that was it! [*Alma sits slowly back down.*] But him! Oh, Miss Alma! He's the *wonderfullest* person that I . . .

ALMA: [*interrupting*]: Your mother was right! He isn't fit to call himself a doctor! I hate to disillusion you, but this wonderfullest person is pitiably weak.

[*Someone calls "Johnny" outside.*]

NELLIE [*in hushed excitement*]: Someone is calling him now!

ALMA: Yes, these people who shout his name in front of his house are of such a character that the old doctor cannot permit them to come inside the door. And when they have brought him home at night, left him sprawling on the front steps, sometimes at daybreak—it takes two people, his father and the old cook, one pushing and one pulling, to get him upstairs. [*She sits down.*] All the gifts of the gods were showered on him. . . . [*The call of "Johnny" is repeated.*] But all he cares about is indulging his senses! [*Another call of "Johnny."*]

NELLIE: Here he comes down the steps! [*Alma crosses toward the window.*] Look at him jump!

ALMA: Oh.

NELLIE: Over the banisters. Ha-ha!

ALMA: Nellie, don't lean out the window and have us caught spying.

MRS. WINEMILLER [*suddenly*]: Show Nellie how *you* spy on him! Oh, she's a good one at spying. She stands behind the curtain and *peeks* around it, and . . .

ALMA [*frantically*]: *Mother!*

MRS. WINEMILLR: She spies on him. Whenever he comes in at night she rushes downstairs to watch him out of this window!

ALMA [*interrupting her*]: Be still!

MRS. WINEMILLER [*going right on*]: She called him just now and had a fit on the telephone! [*The old lady cackles derisively. Alma snatches her cigarette from her and crushes it under her foot.*] Alma's in love! Alma's in love!

ALMA [*interrupting*]: Nellie, Nellie, please go.

NELLLIE: [*with a startled giggle*]: All right, Miss Alma, I'm going. [*She crosses quickly to the door, looking back once with a grin.*] Good night, Mrs. Winemiller!

[*Nellie goes out gaily, leaving the door slightly open. Alma rushes to it and slams it shut. She returns swiftly to Mrs. Winemiller, her hands clenched with anger.*]

ALMA: If ever I hear you say such a thing again, if ever you dare to repeat such a thing in my presence or anybody else's—then it will be the last straw! You understand me? Yes, you understand me! You act like a child, but you have the devil in you. And God will punish you—yes! I'll punish you too. I'll take your cigarettes from you and give you no more. I'll give you no ice cream either. Because I'm tired of your malice. Yes, I'm tired of your malice and your self-indulgence. People wonder why I'm tied down here! They pity me—think of me as an old maid already! In spite of I'm young. Still young! It's you—it's you, you've taken my youth away from me! I wouldn't say that—I'd try not even to think it—if you were just kind, just simple! But I could spread my life out like a rug for you to step on and you'd step on it, and not even say "Thank you, Alma!" Which is what you've done always—and now you dare to tell a disgusting lie about me—in front of that girl!

MRS. WINEMLLLER: Don't you think I hear you go to the window at night to watch him come in and . . .

ALMA: Give me that plumed hat, Mother! It goes back now, it goes back!

MRS. WINEMILLER: *Fight! Fight!*

[*Alma snatches at the plumed hat. Mrs. Winenmiller snatches too. The hat is torn between them. Mrs. Winemiller retains the hat. The plume comes loose in Alma's hand. She stares at it a moment with a shocked expression.*]

ALMA [*sincerely*]: Heaven have mercy upon us!

★

Scene Three

Inside the Rectory.

The meeting is in progress, having just opened with the reading of the minutes by Alma. She stands before the green plush sofa and the others. This group includes Mr. Doremus, Vernon, a willowy younger man with an open collar and Byronic locks, the widow Bassett, and a wistful older girl with a long neck and thick-lensed glasses.

ALMA [*reading*]: Our last meeting which fell on July fourteenth . . .

MRS. BASSETT: Bastille Day!

ALMA: Pardon me?

MRS. BASSETT: It fell on Bastille Day! But, honey, that was the meeting before last.

ALMA: You're perfectly right. I seem to be on the wrong page. . . . [*She drops the papers.*]

MRS. BASSETT: Butterfingers!

ALMA: Here we are! July twenty-fifth! Correct?

MRS. BASSETT: Correct! [*A little ripple of laughter goes about the circle.*]

ALMA [*continuing*]: It was debated whether or not we ought to suspend operations for the remainder of the summer as the departure of several members engaged in the teaching profession for their summer vacations . . .

MRS. BASSETT: Lucky people!

ALMA: . . . had substantially contracted our little circle.

MRS. BASSETT: Decimated our ranks! [*There is another ripple of laughter.*]

[*John appears outside the door-frame and rings the bell.*]

ALMA [*with agitation*]: Is that—is that—the doorbell?

MRS. BASSETT: It sure did sound like it to me.

ALMA: Excuse me a moment. I think it may be . . .

[*She crosses to the door-frame and makes the gesture of opening the door. John steps in, immaculately groomed and shining, his white linen coat over his arm and a white Panama hat in his hand. He is a startling contrast to the other male company, who seem to be outcasts of a state in which he is a prominent citizen.*]

ALMA [*shrilly*]: Yes, it is—our guest of honor! Everybody, this is Dr. John Buchanan, Jr.

JOHN [*easily glancing about the assemblage*]: Hello, everybody.

MRS. BASSETT: I never thought he'd show up. Congratulations, Miss Alma.

JOHN: Did I miss much?

ALMA: Not a thing! Just the minutes—I'll put you on the sofa. Next to me. [*She laughs breathlessly and makes an uncertain gesture. He settles gingerly on the sofa. They all stare at him with a curious sort of greediness.*] Well, now! we are completely assembled!

MRS. BASSETT [*eagerly*]: Vernon has his verse play with him tonight!

ALMA [*uneasily*]: Is that right, Vernon? [*Obviously, it is. Vernon has a pile of papers eight inches thick on his knees. He raises them timidly with downcast eyes.*]

ROGER [*quickly*]: We decided to put that off till cooler weather. Miss Rosemary is supposed to read us a paper tonight on William Blake.

MRS. BASSETT: Those dead poets can keep!

[*John laughs.*]

ALMA [*excitedly jumping up*]: Mrs. Bassett, everybody! This is the way I feel about the verse play. It's too important a thing to read under any but ideal circumstances. Not only atmospheric—on some cool evening with music planned to go with it!—but everyone present so that nobody will miss it! Why don't we . . .

ROGER: Why don't we take a standing vote on the matter?

ALMA: Good, good, perfect!

ROGER: All in favor of putting the verse play off till cooler weather, stand up!

[*Everybody rises but Rosemary and Mrs. Bassett. Rosemary starts vaguely to rise, but Mrs. Bassett jerks her arm.*]

ROSEMARY: Was this a vote?

ROGER: Now, Mrs. Bassett, no rough tactics, please!

ALMA: Has everybody got fans? John, you haven't got one!

[*She looks about for a fan for him. Not seeing one, she takes Roger's out of his hand and gives it to John. Roger is non-plussed. Rosemary gets up with her paper.*]

ROSEMARY: The poet—William Blake.

MRS. BASSETT: Insane, insane, that man was a mad fanatic! [*She squints her eyes tight shut and thrusts her thumbs into her ears. The reactions range from indignant to conciliatory.*]

ROGER: Now, Mrs. Bassett!

MRS. BASSETT: This is a free country. I can speak my opinion. And I have *read up* on him. Go on, Rosemary. I wasn't criticizing your paper. [*But Rosemary sits down, hurt.*]

ALMA: Mrs. Bassett is only joking, Rosemary.

ROSEMARY: No, I don't want to read it if she feels that strongly about it.

MRS. BASSETT: Not a bit, don't be silly! I just don't see why we should encourage the writings of people like that who have already gone into a drunkard's grave!

VARIOUS VOICES [*exclaiming*]: Did he? I never heard that about him. Is that true?

ALMA: Mrs. Bassett is mistaken about that. Mrs. Bassett, you have confused Blake with someone else.

MRS. BASSETT [*positively*]: Oh, no, don't tell me. I've read up on him and know what I'm talking about. He traveled around with that Frenchman who took a shot at him and landed them both in jail! Brussels, Brussels!

ROGER [*gaily*]: Brussels sprouts!

MRS. BASSETT: That's where it happened, fired a gun at him in a drunken stupor, and later one of them died of T.B. in the gutter! All right. I'm finished. I won't say anything more. Go on with your paper, Rosemary. There's nothing like contact with culture!

[*Alma gets up.*]

ALMA: Before Rosemary reads her paper on Blake, I think it would be a good idea, since some of us aren't acquainted with his work, to preface the critical and biographical comments with a reading of one of his loveliest lyric poems.

ROSEMARY: I'm not going to read anything at all! Not I!

ALMA: Then let me read it then. [*She takes a paper from Rosemary.*] . . . This is called "Love's Secret."

[*She clears her throat and waits for a hush to settle. Rosemary looks stonily at the carpet. Mrs. Bassett looks at the ceiling. John coughs.*]

Never seek to tell thy love,
Love that never told can be,
For the gentle wind doth move
Silently, invisibly.

I told my love, I told my love,
I told him all my heart.
Trembling, cold in ghastly fear
Did my love depart.

No sooner had he gone from me
Than a stranger passing by,
Silently, invisibly,
Took him with a sigh!

[*There are various effusions and enthusiastic applause.*]

MRS. BASSETT: Honey, you're right. That isn't the man I meant. I was thinking about the one who wrote about "the bought red lips." Who was it that wrote about the "bought red lips"?

[*John has risen abruptly. He signals to Alma and points to his watch. He starts to leave.*]

ALMA [*springing up*]: *John!*

JOHN [*calling back*]: I have to call on a patient!

ALMA: Oh, John!

[*She calls after him so sharply that the group is startled into silence.*]

ROSEMARY [*interpreting this as a cue to read her paper*]: "The poet, William Blake, was born in 1757 . . ."

[*Alma suddenly rushes to the door and goes out after John.*]

ROGER: Of poor but honest parents.

MRS. BASSETT: No supercilious comments out of you, sir. Go on Rosemary. [*She speaks loudly.*] She has a beautiful *voice!*

[*Alma returns inside, looking stunned.*]

ALMA: Please excuse the interruption, Rosemary. Dr. Buchanan had to call on a patient.

MRS. BASSETT [*archly*]: I bet I know who the patient was. Ha-ha! That Gonzales girl whose father owns Moon Lake Casino and goes everywhere with two pistols strapped on his belt. Johnny Buchanan will get himself shot in that crowd!

ALMA: Why, Mrs. Bassett, what gave you such an idea? I don't think that John even knows that Gonzales girl!

MRS. BASSETT: He knows her, all right. In the Biblical sense of the word, if you'll excuse me!

ALMA: No, I will not excuse you! A thing like that is inexcusable!

MRS. BASSETT: Have you fallen for him, Miss Alma? Miss Alma has fallen for the young doctor! They tell me he has lots of new lady patients!

ALMA: Stop it! [*She stamps her foot furiously and crushes the palm leaf fan between her clenched hands.*] I won't have malicious talk here! You drove him away from the meeting after I'd bragged so much about how bright and interesting you all were! You put your worst foot forward and simpered and chattered and carried on like idiots, idiots! What am I saying? I—I—please excuse me!

[*She rushes out the inner door.*]

ROGER: I move that the meeting adjourn.

MRS. BASSETT: I second the motion.

ROSEMARY: I don't understand. What happened?

MRS. BASSETT: Poor Miss Alma!

ROGER: She hasn't been herself lately. . . .

[*They all go out. After a moment Alma reenters with a tray of refreshments, looks about the deserted interior and bursts into hysterical laughter. The light dims out.*]

★

Scene Four

In the doctor's office.

John has a wound on his arm which he is bandaging with Rosa's assistance.

JOHN: Hold that end. Wrap it around. Pull it tight.

[*There is a knock at the door. They look up silently. The knock is repeated.*]

I better answer before they wake up the old man.

[*He goes out. A few moments later he returns followed by Alma. He is rolling down his sleeve to conceal the bandage. Alma stops short at the sight of Rosa.*]

Wait outside, Rosa. In the hall. But be quiet!

[*Rosa gives Alma a challenging look as she withdraws from the lighted area. John explains about Rosa.*]

A little emergency case.

ALMA: The patient you had to call on. [*John grins.*] I want to see your father.

JOHN: He's asleep. Anything I can do?

ALMA: No, I think not. I have to see your father.

JOHN: It's 2 A.M., Miss Alma.

ALMA: I know, I'm afraid I'll have to see him.

JOHN: What's the trouble?

[*The voice of John's father is heard, calling from above.*]

DR. BUCHANAN: John! What's going on down there?

JOHN [*at the door*]: Nothing much, Dad. Somebody got cut in a flight.

DR. BUCHANAN: I'm coming down.

JOHN: No. Don't! Stay in bed! [*He rolls up his sleeve to show Alma the bandaged wound. She gasps and touches her lips.*] I've patched him up, Dad. You sleep!

[JOHN *executes the gesture of closing a door quietly on the hall.*]

ALMA: You've been in a brawl with that—woman! [*John nods and rolls the sleeve back down. Alma sinks faintly into a chair.*]

JOHN: Is your *doppelganger* cutting up again?

ALMA: It's your father I want to talk to.

JOHN: Be reasonable, Miss Alma. You're not that sick.

ALMA: Do you suppose I would come here at two o'clock in the morning if I were not seriously ill?

JOHN: It's no telling what you would do in a state of hysteria. [*He puts some powders in a glass of water.*] Toss that down, Miss Alma.

ALMA: What is it?

JOHN: A couple of little white tablets dissolved in water.

ALMA: What kind of tablets?

JOHN: You don't trust me?

ALMA: You are not in any condition to inspire much confidence. [*John laughs softly. She looks at him helplessly for a moment, then bursts into tears. He draws up a chair beside hers and puts his arm gently about her shoulders.*] I seem to be all to pieces.

JOHN: The intellectual meeting wore you out.

ALMA: You made a quick escape from it.

JOHN: I don't like meetings. The only meetings I like are between two people.

ALMA: Such as between yourself and the lady outside?

JOHN: Or between you and me.

ALMA: [*nervously*]: Where is the . . .?

JOHN: Oh. You've decided to take it?

ALMA: Yes, if you . . .

[*She sips and chokes. He gives her his handkerchief. She touches her lips with it.*]

JOHN: Bitter?

ALMA: Awfully bitter.

JOHN: It'll make you sleepy.

ALMA: I do hope so. I wasn't able to sleep.

JOHN: And you felt panicky?

ALMA: Yes. I felt walled in.

JOHN: You started hearing your heart?

ALMA: Yes, like a drum!

JOHN: It scared you?

ALMA: It always does.

JOHN: Sure. I know.

ALMA: I don't think I will be able to get through the summer.

JOHN: You'll get through, Miss Alma.

ALMA: How?

JOHN: One day will come after another and one night will come after another till sooner or later the summer will be all through with and then it will be fall, and you will be saying "I don't see how I'm going to get through the fall."

ALMA: Oh . . .

JOHN: That's right. Draw a deep breath!

ALMA: Ah . . .

JOHN: Good. Now draw another!

ALMA: Ah . . .

JOHN: Better? Better?

ALMA: A little.

JOHN: Soon you'll be much better. [*He takes out a big silver watch and holds her wrist.*] Did y' know that time is one side of the four-dimensional continuum we're caught in?

ALMA: What?

JOHN: Did you know space is curved, that it turns back onto itself like a soap-bubble, adrift in something that's even less than space? [*He laughs a little as he replaces the watch.*]

ROSA [*faintly from outside*]: Johnny!

JOHN [*looking up as if the cry came from there*]: Did you know that the Magellanic clouds are a hundred thousand light years away from the earth? No? [*Alma shakes her head slightly.*] That's something to think about when you worry over your heart, that little red fist that's got to keep knocking, knocking against the big black door.

ROSA [*more distinctly*]: Johnny!

[*She opens the door a crack.*]

JOHN: Calla de la boca! [*The door closes and he speaks to Alma.*] There's nothing wrong with your heart but a little functional disturbance, like I told you before. You want me to check it? [*Alma nods mutely. John picks up his stethoscope.*]

ALMA: The lady outside, I hate to keep her waiting.

JOHN: Rosa doesn't mind waiting. Unbutton your blouse.

ALMA: Unbutton . . .?

JOHN: The blouse.

ALMA: Hadn't I better—better come back in the morning, when you father will be able to . . . ?

JOHN: Just as you please, Miss Alma. [*She hesitates. Then begins to unbutton her blouse. Her fingers fumble.*] Fingers won't work?

ALMA [*breathlessly*]: They are just as if frozen!

JOHN [*smiling*]: Let me. [*He leans over her.*] Little pearl buttons . . .

ALMA: If your father discovered that woman in the house . . .

JOHN: He won't discover it.

ALMA: It would distress him terribly.

JOHN: Are you going to tell him?

ALMA: Certainly not! [*He laughs and applies the stethoscope to her chest.*]

JOHN: Breathe! . . . Out! . . . Breathe! . . . Out!

ALMA: Ah . . .

JOHN: Um-hmmm . . .

ALMA: What do you hear?

JOHN: Just a little voice saying—"Miss Alma is lonesome!" [*She rises and turns her back to him.*]

ALMA: If your idea of helping a patient is to ridicule and insult . . .

JOHN: My idea of helping you is to tell you the truth. [*Alma looks up at him. He lifts her hand from the chair arm.*] What is this stone?

ALMA: A topaz.

JOHN: Beautiful stone . . . Fingers still frozen?

ALMA: A little. [*He lifts her hand to his mouth and blows his breath on her fingers.*]

JOHN: I'm a poor excuse for a doctor, I'm much too selfish. But let's try to think about you.

ALMA: Why should you bother about me? [*She sits down.*]

JOHN: You know I like you and I think you're worth a lot of consideration.

ALMA: Why?

JOHN: Because you have a lot of feeling in your heart, and that's a rare thing. It makes you too easily hurt. Did I hurt you tonight?

ALMA: You hurt me when you sprang up from the sofa and rushed from the Rectory in such—in such mad haste that you left your coat behind you!

JOHN: I'll pick up the coat sometime.

ALMA: The time of our last conversation you said you would take me riding in your automobile sometime, but you forgot to.

JOHN: I didn't forget. Many's the time I've looked across at the Rectory and wondered if it would be worth trying, you and me . . .

ALMA: You decided it wasn't?

JOHN: I went there tonight, but it wasn't you and me . . . Fingers warm now?

ALMA: Those tablets work quickly. I'm already feeling drowsy. [*She leans back with her eyes nearly shut.*] I'm beginning to feel almost like a water lily. A water lily on a Chinese lagoon.

[*A heavy iron bell strikes three.*]

ROSA: *Johnny?*

[*Alma starts to rise.*]

ALMA: I *must* go.

JOHN: I will call for you Saturday night at eight o'clock.

ALMA: What?

JOHN: I'll give you this box of tablets but watch how you take them. Never more than one or two at a time.

ALMA: Didn't you say something else a moment ago?

JOHN: I said I would call for you at the Rectory Saturday night.

ALMA: Oh . . .

JOHN: Is that all right? [*Alma nods speechlessly. She remains with the box resting in the palm of her hand as if not knowing it was there. John gently closes her fingers on the box.*]

ALMA: Oh! [*She laughs faintly.*]

ROSA [*outside*]: *Johnny!*

JOHN: Do you think you can find your way home, Miss Alma?

[*Rosa steps back into the office with a challenging look. Alma catches her breath sharply and goes out the side door.*

John reaches above him and turns out the light. He crosses to Rosa by the anatomy chart and takes her roughly in his arms. The light lingers on the chart as the interior dims out.]

★

Scene Five

In the Rectory.

Before the light comes up a soprano voice is heard singing "From the Land of the Sky Blue Waters."

As the curtain rises, Alma gets up from the piano. Mr. and Mrs. Winemiller, also, are in the lighted room.

ALMA: What time is it, Father? [*He goes on writing. She raises her voice.*] What time is it, Father?

MR. WINEMILLER: Five of eight. I'm working on my sermon.

ALMA: Why don't you work in the study?

MR. WINEMILLER: The study is suffocating. So don't disturb me.

ALMA: Would there be any chance of getting Mother upstairs if someone should call?

MR. WINEMILLER: Are you expecting a caller?

ALMA: Not expecting. There is just a chance of it.

MR. WINEMILLER: Whom are you expecting?

ALMA: I said I wasn't expecting anyone, that there was just a possibility . . .

MR. WINEMILLER: Mr. Doremus? I thought that this was his evening with his mother?

ALMA: Yes, it is his evening with his mother.

MR. WINEMILLER: Then who is coming here, Alma?

ALMA: Probably no one. Probably no one at all.

MR. WINEMILLER: This is all very mysterious.

MRS. WINEMILLER: That tall boy next door is coming to see her, that's who's coming to see her.

ALMA: If you will go upstairs, Mother, I'll call the drug store and ask them to deliver a pint of fresh peach ice cream.

MRS. WINEMILLER: I'll go upstairs when I'm ready—good and ready, and you can put that in your pipe and smoke it, Miss Winemiller!

[*She lights a cigarette. Mr. Winemiller turns slowly away with a profound sigh.*]

ALMA: I may as well tell you who might call, so that if he calls there will not be any unpleasantness about it. Young Dr. John Buchanan said he might call.

MRS. WINEMILLER: See!

MR. WINEMILLER: You can't be serious.

MRS. WINEMILLER: Didn't I tell you?

ALMA: Well, I am.

MR. WINEMILLER: That young man might come here?

ALMA: He asked me if he might and I said, yes, if he wished to. But it is now after eight so it doesn't look like he's coming.

MR. WINEMILLER: If he does come you will go upstairs to your room and I will receive him.

ALMA: If he does come I'll do no such thing, Father.

MR. WINEMILLER: You must be out of your mind.

ALMA: I'll receive him myself. You may retire to your study and Mother upstairs. But if he comes I'll receive him. I don't judge people by the tongues of gossips. I happen to know that he has been grossly misjudged and misrepresented by old busybodies who're envious of his youth and brilliance and charm!

MR. WINEMILLER: If you're not out of your senses, then I'm out of mine.

ALMA: I daresay we're all a bit peculiar, Father. . . .

MR. WINEMILLER: Well, I have had one almost insufferable cross to bear and perhaps I can bear another. But if you think I'm retiring into my study when this young man comes, probably with a whiskey bottle in one hand and a pair of dice in the other, you have another think coming. I'll sit right here and look at him until he leaves. [*He turns back to his sermon.*]

[*A whistle is heard outside the open door.*]

ALMA [*speaking quickly*]: As a matter of fact I think I'll walk down to the drug store and call for the ice cream myself. [*She crosses to the door, snatching up her hat, gloves and veil.*]

MRS. WINEMILLER: There she goes to him! Ha-ha! [*Alma rushes out.*]

MR. WINEMILLER [*looking up*]: Alma! Alma!

MRS. WINEMILLER: Ha-ha-haaaaa!

MR. WINEMILLER: Where is Alma?—Alma! [*He rushes through the door.*] Alma!

MRS. WINEMILLER: Ha-ha! Who got fooled? Who got fooled! Ha-haaa! Insufferable cross yourself, you old windbag . . .

[*The curtain comes down.*]

★

Scene Six

A delicately suggested arbor, enclosing a table and two chairs. Over the table is suspended a torn paper lantern. This tiny set may be placed way downstage in front of the two interiors, which should be darkened out, as in the fountain scenes. In the background, as it is throughout the play, the angel of the fountain is dimly visible.

Music from the nearby pavilion of the Casino can be used when suitable for background.

John's voice is audible before he and Alma enter.

JOHN [*from the darkness*]: I don't understand why we can't go in the casino.

ALMA: You do understand. You're just pretending not to.

JOHN: Give me one reason.

ALMA [*coming into the arbor*]: I am a minister's daughter.

JOHN: That's no reason. [*He follows her in. He wears a white linen suit, carrying the coat over his arm.*]

ALMA: You're a doctor. That's a better reason. You can't any more afford to be seen in such places than I can—less!

JOHN [*bellowing*]: Dusty!

DUSTY [*from the darkness*]: Coming!

JOHN: What are you fishing in that pocketbook for?

ALMA: Nothing.

JOHN: What have you got there?

ALMA: Let go!

JOHN: Those sleeping tablets I gave you?

ALMA: Yes.

JOHN: What for?

ALMA: I need one.

JOHN: *Now*?

ALMA: Yes.

JOHN: Why?

ALMA: Why? Because I nearly died of heart failure in your automobile. What possessed you to drive like that? A demon?

[*Dusty enters.*]

JOHN: A bottle of vino rosso.

DUSTY: Sure. [*He withdraws.*]

JOHN: Hey! Tell Shorty I want to hear the "Yellow Dog Blues."

ALMA: Please give me back my tablets.

JOHN: You want to turn into a dope-fiend taking this stuff? I said take one when you need one.

ALMA: I need one now.

JOHN: Sit down and stop swallowing air. [*Dusty returns with a tall wine bottle and two thin-stemmed glasses.*] When does the cockfight start?

DUSTY: 'Bout ten o'clock, Dr. Johnny.

ALMA: When does *what start?*

JOHN: They have a cock-fight here every Saturday night. Ever seen one?

ALMA: Perhaps in some earlier incarnation of mine.

JOHN: When you wore a brass ring in your nose?

ALMA: Then maybe I went to exhibitions like that.

JOHN: You're going to see one tonight.

ALMA: Oh, no, I'm not.

JOHN: That's what we came here for.

ALMA: I didn't think such exhibitions were legal.

JOHN: This is Moon Lake Casino where anything goes.

ALMA: And you're a frequent patron?

JOHN: I'd say constant.

ALMA: Then I'm afraid you must be serious about giving up your medical career.

JOHN: You bet I am! A doctor's life is walled in by sickness and misery and death.

ALMA: May I be so presumptuous as to inquire what you'll do when you quit?

JOHN: You may be so presumptious as to inquire.

ALMA: But you won't tell me?

JOHN: I haven't made up my mind, but I've been thinking of South America lately.

ALMA [*sadly*]: Oh . . .

JOHN: I've heard that cantinas are lots more fun saloons, and senoritas are caviar among females.

ALMA: Dorothy Sykes' brother went to South America and was never heard of again. It takes a strong character to survive in the tropics. Otherwise it's a quagmire.

JOHN: You think my character's weak?

ALMA: I think you're confused, just awfully, awfully confused, as confused as I am—but in a different way . . .

JOHN [*stretching out his legs*]: Hee-haw, ho-hum.

ALMA: You used to say that as a child—to signify your disgust!

JOHN [*grinning*]: Did I?

ALMA [*sharply*]: Don't sit like that!

JOHN: Why not?

ALMA: You look so indolent and worthless.

JOHN: Maybe I am.

ALMA: If you must go somewhere, why don't you choose a place with a bracing climate?

JOHN: Parts of South America are as cool as a cucumber.

ALMA: I never knew that.

JOHN: Well, now you do.

ALMA: Those Latins all dream in the sun—and indulge their senses.

JOHN: Well, it's yet to be proven that anyone on this earth is crowned with so much glory as the one that uses his senses to get all he can in the way of—satisfaction.

ALMA: Self-satisfaction?

JOHN: What other kind is there?

ALMA: I will answer that question by asking you one. Have you ever seen, or looked at a picture, of a Gothic cathedral?

JOHN: Gothic cathedrals? What about them?

ALMA: How everything reaches up, how everything seems to be straining for something out the reach of stone—or human—fingers? . . . The immense stained windows, the great arched doors that are five or six times the height of the tallest man—the vaulted ceiling and all the delicate spires—all reaching up to something beyond attainment! To me—well, that is the secret, the principle back of existence—the everlasting struggle and aspiration for more than our human limits have placed in our reach. . . . Who was that said that

—oh, so beautiful thing!—"All of us are in the gutter, but some of us are looking at the stars!"

JOHN: Mr. Oscar Wilde.

ALMA [*somewhat taken aback*]: Well, regardless of who said it, it's still true. Some of us are looking at the stars! [*She looks up raptly and places her hand over his.*]

JOHN: It's no fun, holding hands with gloves on, Miss Alma.

ALMA: That's easily remedied. I'll just take the gloves off. [*Music is heard.*]

JOHN: Christ! [*He rises abruptly and lights a cigarette*] Rosa Gonzales is dancing in the Casino.

ALMA: You *are* unhappy. You hate me for depriving you of the company inside. Well, you'll escape by and by. You'll drive me home and come back out by yourself. . . . I've only gone out with three young men at all seriously, and with each one there was a desert between us.

JOHN: What do you mean by a desert?

ALMA: Oh—wide, wide stretches of uninhabitable ground.

JOHN: Maybe you made it that way by being stand-offish.

ALMA: I made quite an effort with one or two of them.

JOHN: What kind of an effort?

ALMA: Oh, I—tried to entertain them the first few times. I would play and sing for them in the Rectory parlor.

JOHN: With your father in the next room and the door half open?

ALMA: I don't think that was the trouble.

JOHN: What was the trouble?

ALMA: I—I didn't have my heart in it. [*She laughs uncertainly.*] A silence would fall between us. You know, a silence?

JOHN: Yes, I know a silence.

ALMA: I'd try to talk and he'd try to talk and neither would make a go of it.

JOHN: The silence would fall?

ALMA: Yes, the enormous silence.

JOHN: Then you'd go back to the piano?

ALMA: I'd twist my ring. Sometimes I twisted it so hard that the band cut my finger! He'd glance at his watch and we'd both know that the useless undertaking had come to a close. . . .

JOHN: You'd call it quits?

ALMA: Quits is—what we'd call it. . . . One or two times I was rather sorry about it.

JOHN: But you didn't have your heart in it?

ALMA: None of them really engaged my serious feelings.

JOHN: You do have serious feelings—of that kind?

ALMA: Doesn't everyone—sometimes?

JOHN: Some women are cold. Some women are what is called frigid.

ALMA: Do I give that impression?

JOHN: Under the surface you have a lot of excitement, a great deal more than any other woman I have met. So much that you have to carry these sleeping pills with you. The question is why? [*He leans over and lifts her veil.*]

ALMA: What are you doing that for?

JOHN: So that I won't get your veil in my mouth when I kiss you.

ALMA [*faintly*]: Do you want to do that?

JOHN [*gently*]: Miss Alma. [*He takes her arms and draws her to her feet.*]
Oh, Miss Alma, Miss Alma! [*He kisses her.*]

ALMA [*in a low, shaken voice*]: Not "Miss" any more. Just Alma.

JOHN [*grinning gently*]: "Miss" suits you better, Miss Alma. [*He kisses her again. She hesitantly touches his shoulders, but not quite to push him away. John speaks softly to her.*] Is it so hard to forget you're a preacher's daughter?

ALMA: There is no reason for me to forget that I am a minister's daughter. A minister's daughter's no different from any other young lady who tries to remember that she *is* a lady.

JOHN: This lady stuff, is that so important?

ALMA: Not to the sort of girls that you may be used to bringing to Moon Lake Casino. But suppose that some day . . . [*She crosses out of the arbor and faces away from him.*] suppose that some day you—*married. . . .* The woman that you selected to be your wife, and not only your wife but—the mother of your children! [*She catches her breath at the thought.*] Wouldn't you want that woman to be a lady? Wouldn't you want her to be somebody that you, as her husband, and they as her precious children—could look up to with very deep respect? [*There is a pause.*]

JOHN: There's other things between a man and a woman besides respect. Did you know that, Miss Alma?

ALMA: Yes . . .

JOHN: There's such a thing as intimate relations.

ALMA: Thank you for telling me that. So plainly.

JOHN: It may strike you as unpleasant. But it does have a good deal to do with—connubial felicity, as you'd call it. There are some women that just give in to a man as a sort of obligation imposed on them by the—cruelty of nature! [*He finishes his glass and pours another.*] And there you are.

ALMA: There *I* am?

JOHN: I'm speaking generally.

ALMA: Oh.

[*Hoarse shouts go up from the Casino.*]

JOHN: The cock-fight has started!

ALMA: Since you have spoken so plainly, I'll speak plainly, too. There are some women who turn a possibly beautiful thing into something no better than the coupling of beasts!—but love is what you bring to it.

JOHN: You're right about that.

ALMA: Some people bring just their bodies. But there are some people, there are some women, John—who can bring their hearts to it, also—who can bring their souls to it!

JOHN [*derisively*]: Souls again, huh?—those Gothic cathedrals you dream of!

[*There is another hoarse prolonged shout from the Casino.*]

Your name is Alma and Alma is Spanish for soul. Some time I'd like to show you a chart of the human anatomy that I have in the office. It shows what our insides are like, and maybe you can show me where the beautiful soul is located on the chart. [*He drains the wine bottle.*] Let's go watch the cock-fight.

ALMA: No! [*There is a pause.*]

JOHN: I know something else we could do. There are rooms above the Casino. . . .

ALMA [*her back stiffening*]: I'd heard that you made suggestions like that to girls that you go out with, but I refused to believe such stories were true. What made you think I might be amenable to such a suggestion?

JOHN: I counted your pulse in the office the night you ran out because you weren't able to sleep.

ALMA: The night I was ill and went to your father for help.

JOHN: It was me you went to.

ALMA: It was you father, and you wouldn't call your father.

JOHN: Fingers frozen stiff when I . . .

ALMA [*rising*]: Oh! I want to go home. But I won't go with you. I will go in a taxi! [*She wheels about hysterically.*] Boy! Boy! Call a taxi!

JOHN: I'll call one for you, Miss Alma.—Taxi! [*He goes out of the arbor.*]

ALMA [*wildly*]: *You're not a gentleman!*

JOHN [*from the darkness*]: Taxi!

ALMA: *You're not a gentleman!*

[*As he disappears she makes a sound in her throat like a hurt animal. The light fades out of the arbor and comes up more distinctly on the stone angel of the fountain.*]

★

PART TWO

A Winter

Scene Seven

The sky and the southern constellations, almost imperceptibly moving with the earth's motion, appear on the great cyclorama.

The Rectory interior is lighted first, disclosing Alma and Roger Doremus seated on the green plush sofa under the romantic landscape in its heavy gilt frame. On a tiny table beside them is a cut glass pitcher of lemonade with cherries and orange slices in it, like a little aquarium of tropical fish. Roger is entertaining Alma with a collection of photographs and postcards, mementoes of his mother's trip to the Orient. He is enthusiastic about them and describes them in phrases his mother must have assimilated from a sedulous study of literature provided by Cook's Tour. Alma is less enthusiastic; she is preoccupied with the sounds of a wild party going on next door at the doctor's home. At present there is Mexican music with shouts and stamping.

Only the immediate area of the sofa is clearly lighted; the foundation is faintly etched in light and the night sky walls the interior.

ROGER: And this is Ceylon, the pearl of the Orient!

ALMA: And who is this fat young lady?

ROGER: That is Mother in a hunting costume.

ALMA: The hunting costume makes her figure seem bulky. What was your mother hunting?

ROGER [*gaily*]: Heaven knows what she was hunting! But she found Papa.

ALMA: Oh, she met your father on this Oriental tour?

ROGER: Ha-ha!—yes. . . . He was returning from India with dysentery and they met on the boat.

ALMA [*distastefully*]: Oh . . .

ROGER: And here she is on top of a ruined temple!

ALMA: How did she get up there?

ROGER: Climbed up, I suppose.

ALMA: What an active woman.

ROGER: Oh, yes, active—is no word for it! Here she is on an elephant's back in Burma.

ALMA: Ah!

ROGER: You're looking at it upside down, Miss Alma!

ALMA: Deliberately—to tease you. [*The doorbell rings.*] Perhaps that's your mother coming to fetch you home.

ROGER: It's only ten-fifteen. I never leave till ten-thirty.

[*Mrs. Bassett comes in.*]

ALMA: Mrs. Bassett!

MRS. BASSETT: I was just wondering who I could turn to when I saw the Rectory light and I thought to myself, Grace Bassett, you trot yourself right over there and talk to Mr. Winemiller!

ALMA: Father has retired.

MRS. BASSETT: Oh, what a pity. [*She sees Roger.*] Hello, Roger! . . . I saw that fall your mother took this morning. I saw her come skipping out of the Delta Planters' Bank and I thought to myself, now isn't that remarkable, a woman of her age and weight so light on her feet? And just at that very moment—*down she went!* I swear to goodness I thought she had broken her hip! Was she bruised much?

ROGER: Just shaken up, Mrs. Bassett.

MRS. BASSETT: Oh, how lucky! She certainly must be made out of India rubber! [*She turns to Alma.*] Alma—Alma, if it is not too late for human intervention, your father's the one right person to call up old Dr. Buchanan at the fever clinic at Lyon and let him know!

ALMA: About—what?

MRS. BASSETT: You must be stone-deaf if you haven't noticed what's been going on next door since the old doctor left to fight the epidemic. One continual orgy! Well, not five minutes ago a friend of mine who works at the County Courthouse called to inform me that young Dr. John and Rosa Gonzales have taken a license out and are going to be married tomorrow!

ALMA: Are you—quite certain?

MRS. BASSETT: Certain? I'm always certain before I speak!

ALMA: Why would he—do such a thing?

MRS. BASSETT: August madness! They say it has something to do with the falling stars. Of course it might also have something to do with the fact that he lost two or three thousand dollars at the Casino which he can't pay except by giving himself to Gonzales' daughter. [*She turns to Alma.*] Alma, What are you doing with that picture puzzle?

ALMA [*with a faint, hysterical laugh*]: The pieces don't fit.

MRS. BASSETT [*to Roger*]: I shouldn't have opened my mouth.

ALMA: Will both of you please go!

[*Roger goes out.*]

MRS. BASSETT: I knew this was going to upset you. Good night, Alma. [*She leaves. Alma suddenly springs up and seizes the telephone.*]

ALMA: Long distance. . . . Please get me the fever clinic at Lyon. . . . I want to speak to Dr. Buchanan.

[*The light in the Rectory dims out and light comes on in the doctor's office. Rosa's voice is heard calling.*]

ROSA: *Johnny!*

[*The offstage calling of John's name is used throughout the play as a cue for theme music.*

[*John enters the office interior. He is dressed, as always, in a white linen suit. His face has a look of satiety and confusion. He throws himself down in a swivel chair at the desk.*

[*Rosa Gonzales comes in. She is dressed in a Flamenco costume and has been dancing. She crosses and stands before the anatomy chart and clicks her castanets to catch his attention, but he remains looking up at the roofless dark. She approaches him.*]

ROSA: *You have blood on your face!*

JOHN: You bit my ear.

ROSA: Ohhh . . . [*She approaches him with exaggerated concern.*]

JOHN: You never make love without scratching or biting or something. Whenever I leave you I have a little blood on me. Why is that?

ROSA: Because I know I can't hold you.

JOHN: I think you're doing a pretty good job of it. Better than anyone else. Tomorrow we leave here together and Father or somebody else can tell old Mrs. Arbuckle her eighty-five years are enough and she's got to go now on the wings of carcinoma. Dance, Rosa! [*Accordion music is heard. She performs a slow and joyless dance around his chair. John continues while she dances.*] Tomorrow we leave here together. We sail out of Galveston, don't we?

ROSA: You say it but I don't believe it.

JOHN: I have the tickets.

ROSA: Two pieces of paper that you can tear in two.

JOHN: We'll go all right, and live on fat remittances from your Papa! Ha-ha!

ROSA: Ha-ha-ha!

JOHN: Not long ago the idea would have disgusted me, but not now. [*He catches her by the wrist.*] Rosa! Rosa Gonzales! Did anyone ever slide downhill as fast as I have this summer? Ha-ha! Like a greased pig. And yet every evening I put on a clean white suit. I have a dozen. Six in the closet and six in the wash. And there isn't sign of depravity in my face. And yet all summer I've sat around here like *this*, remembering last night, anticipating the next one! The trouble with me is, I should have been *castrated*! [*He flings his wine glass at the anatomy chart. She stops dancing.*]

Dance, Rosa! Why don't you dance? [*Rosa shakes her head dumbly.*] What is the matter, Rosa? Why don't you go on dancing? [*The accordion continues; he thrusts an arm savagely over her head in the Flamenco position.*]

ROSA [*suddenly weeping*]: *I can't dance any more!* [*She throws herself to the floor, pressing her weeping face to his knees. The voice of her father is heard, bellowing, in the next room.*]

GONZALES: *The sky is the limit!*

[*John is sobered.*]

JOHN: Why does your father want me for a son-in-law?

ROSA [*sobbing*]: *I want you*—I, *I want you!*

JOHN [*raising her from the floor*]: Why do you?

ROSA [*clinging to him*]: Maybe because—I was born in Piedras Negras, and grew up in a one room house with a dirt floor, and all of us had to sleep in that one room, five Mexicans and three geese and a little game-cock named Pepe! Ha-ha! [*She laughs hysterically.*] Pepe was a good fighter! That's how Papa began to make money, winning bets on Pepe! Ha-ha! We all slept in the one room. And in the night, I would hear the love-making. Papa would grunt like a pig to show his passion. I thought to myself, how dirty it was, to be Mexicans and all have to sleep in one room with a dirt floor and not smell good because there was not any bathtub! [*The accordion continues.*]

JOHN: What has that got to do with . . .?

ROSA: Me wanting you? You're tall! You smell good! And, oh, I'm so glad that you never grunt like a pig to show your passion! [*She embraces him convulsively.*] Ah, but *quien sabe!* Something might happen tonight, and I'll wind up with some dark little friend of Papa's.

GONZALES [*imperiously*]: Rosa! Rosa!

ROSA: Si, si, Papa, aqui estoy!

GONZALES [*entering unsteadily*]: The gold beads . . . [*He fingers a necklace of gold beads that Rosa is wearing.*] Johnny . . . [*He staggers up to John and catches him in a drunken embrace.*] Listen! When my girl Rosa was little she see a string a gold bead and she want those gold bead so bad that she cry all night for it. I don't have money to buy a string a gold bead so next day I go for a ride up to Eagle Pass and I walk in a dry good store and I say to the man: "Please give me a string a gold bead." He say: "Show me the money," and I say: "Here is the money!" And I reach down to my belt and I pull out—not the money—but this! [*He pulls out a revolver.*] Now—now I have money, but I still have this! [*laughing*] She got the gold bead. Anything that she want I get for her with this [*He pulls out a roll of bills.*] or this! [*He waves the revolver.*]

JOHN [*pushing Gonzales away*]: Keep your stinking breath out of my face, Gonzales!

ROSA: Dejalo, dejalo, Papa!

GONZALES [*moving unsteadily to the couch, with Rosa supporting him*]: Le doy la tierra y si tierra no basta—le doy el cielo! [*He collapses onto the couch.*] The sky is the limit!

ROSA [*to John*]: Let him stay there. Come on back to the party.

[*Rosa leaves the room. John goes over to the window facing the Rectory and looks across. The light comes up in the Rectory living room as Alma enters, dressed in a robe. She goes to the window and looks across at the doctor's house. As Alma and John stand at the windows looking toward each other through the darkness, music is heard. Slowly, as if drawn by the music, John walks out of his house and crosses over to the Rectory. Alma remains motionless at the window until John enters the room, behind her. The music dies away and there is a murmur of wind. She slowly turns to face John.*]

JOHN: I took the open door for an invitation. The Gulf wind is blowing tonight . . . cools things off a little. But my head's on fire. . . . [*Alma says nothing. John moves a few step towards her.*] The silence? [*Alma sinks onto the love seat, closing her eyes.*] Yes, the enormous silence. [*He goes over to her.*] I will go in a minute, but first I want you to put your hands on my face. . . . [*He crouches beside her.*] Eternity and Miss Alma have such cool hands. [*He buries his face in her lap. The attitude suggests a stone* Pieta. *Alma's eyes remain closed.*]

[*On the other side of the stage Dr. Buchanan enters his house and the light builds a little as he looks around in the door of his office. The love theme music fades out and the Mexican music comes up strongly, with a definitely ominous quality, as Rosa enters the office from the other side.*]

ROSA: Johnny! [*She catches sight of Dr. Buchanan and checks herself in surprise.*] Oh! I thought you were Johnny! . . . But you are Johnny's father. . . . I'm Rosa Gonzales!

DR. BUCHANAN: I know who you are. What's going on in my house?

ROSA [*nervously*]: John's giving a party because we're leaving tomorrow. [*defiantly*] Yes! Together! I hope you like the idea, but if you don't, it don't matter, because *we* like the idea and my father likes the idea.

GONZALES [*drunkenly, sitting up on the couch*]: The sky is the limit!

[*Dr. Buchanan slowly raises his silver-headed cane in a threatening gesture.*]

DR. BUCHANAN: Get your—swine out of—my house! [*He strikes Gonzales with his cane.*]

GONZALES [*staggering up from the couch in pain and surprise*]: Aieeeee!

ROSA [*breathlessly, backing against the chart of anatomy*]: No! No, Papa!

DR. BUCHANAN [*striking at the chest of the bull-like man with his cane*]: Get your swine out, I said! Get them out of my house!

[*He repeats the blow. The drunken Mexican roars with pain and surprise. He backs up and reaches under his coat.*]

ROSA [*wildly and despairingly*]: No, no, no, no, no, no!

[*She covers her face against the chart of anatomy. A revolver is fired. There is a burst of light. The cane drops. The music stops short. Everything dims out but a spot of light on Rosa standing against the chart of anatomy with closed eyes and her face twisted like that of a tragic mask.*]

ROSA [*senselessly*]: Aaaaaahhhhhh . . . Aaaaaahhhhhh . . .

[*The theme music is started faintly and light disappears from everything but the wings of the stone angel.*]

★

Scene Eight

The doctor's office.

The stone angel is dimly visible above.

John is seated in a hunched position at the table. Alma enters with a coffee tray. The sounds of a prayer come through the inner door.

JOHN: What is that mumbo-jumbo your father is spouting in there?

ALMA: A prayer.

JOHN: Tell him to quit. We don't want that worn-out magic.

ALMA: You may not want it, but it's not a question of what you want any more. I've made you some coffee.

JOHN: I don't want any.

ALMA: Lean back and let me wash your face off, John. [*She presses a towel to the red marks on his face.*] It's such a fine face, a fine and sensitive face, that has power in it that shouldn't wasted.

JOHN: Never mind that. [*He pushes her hand away.*]

ALMA: You have to go in to see him.

JOHN: I couldn't. He wouldn't want me.

ALMA: This happened because of his devotion to you.

JOHN: This happened because some meddlesome Mattie called him back here tonight. Who was it did that?

ALMA: I did.

JOHN: It *was* you then!

ALMA: I phoned him at the fever clinic in Lyon as soon as I learned what you were planning to do. I wired him to come here and stop it.

JOHN: You brought him here to be shot.

ALMA: You can't put the blame on anything but your weakness.

JOHN: *You* call me weak?

ALMA: Sometimes it takes a tragedy like this to make a weak person strong.

JOHN: You—white-blooded spinster! You so right people, pious pompous mumblers, preachers and preacher's daughter, all muffled up in a lot of worn-out magic! And I was supposed to minister to your neurosis, give you tablets for sleeping and tonics to give you the strength to go on mumbling your worn-out mumbo-jumbo!

ALMA: Call me whatever you want, but don't let your father hear your drunken shouting. [*She tries to break away from him.*]

JOHN: Stay here! I want you to look at something. [*He turns her about.*] This chart of anatomy, look!

ALMA: I've seen it before. [*She turns away.*]

JOHN: You've never dared to look at it.

ALMA: Why should I?

JOHN: You're scared to.

ALMA: You must be out of your senses.

JOHN: You talk about weakness but can't even look at a picture of human insides.

ALMA: They're not important.

JOHN: That's your mistake. You think you're stuffed with rose-leaves. Turn around and look at it, it may do you good!

ALMA: How can you behave like this with your father dying and you so . . .

JOHN: Hold still!

ALMA: . . . so much to blame for it!

JOHN: No more than you are!

ALMA: At least for this little while . . .

JOHN: Look here!

ALMA: . . . you could feel some shame!

JOHN [*with crazy, grinning intensity*]: Now listen here to the anatomy lecture! This upper story's the brain which is hungry for something called truth and doesn't get much but keeps on feeling hungry! This middle's the belly which is hungry for food. This part down here is the sex which is hungry for love because it is sometimes lonesome. I've fed all three, as much of all three as I could or as much as I wanted—You've fed none—nothing. Well—maybe your belly a little—watery subsistence—But love or truth, nothing but—nothing but hand-me-down notions!—attitudes!—poses [*He releases her.*] Now you can go. The anatomy lecture is over.

ALMA: So that is your high conception of human desires. What you have here is not the anatomy of a beast, but a man. And I—I reject your opinion of where love is, and the kind of truth you believe the brain to be seeking!—There is some thing not shown on the chart.

JOHN: You mean the part that Alma is Spanish for, do you?

ALMA: Yes, that's not shown on the anatomy chart! But it's there, just the same, yes, there! Somewhere, not seen, but there. And it's *that* that I loved you with—that! Not what you mention!—Yes, did love you with, John, did nearly *die* of when you hurt me! [*He turns slowly to her and speaks gently.*]

JOHN: I wouldn't have made love to you.

ALMA [*uncomprehendingly*]: What?

JOHN: The night at the Casino—I wouldn't have made love to you. Even if you had consented to go upstairs. I couldn't have made love to you. [*She stares at him as if anticipating some unbearable hurt.*] Yes, yes! Isn't that funny? I'm more afraid of your soul than you're afraid of my body. You'd have been as safe as the angel of the fountain—because I wouldn't feel *decent* enough to touch you. . . .

[*Mr. Winemiller comes in.*]

MR. WINEMILLER: He's resting more easily now.

ALMA: Oh . . . [*She nods her head. John reaches for his coffee cup.*] It's cold. I'll heat it.

JOHN: It's all right.

MR. WINEMILLER: Alma, Dr. John wants you.

ALMA: I . . .

MR. WINEMILLER: He asked if you would sing for him.

ALMA: I—couldn't—now.

JOHN: Go in and sing to him, Miss Alma!

[*Mr. Winemiller withdraws through the outer door. Alma looks back at John hunched over the coffee cup. He doesn't return her look. She passes into the blurred orange space beyond the inner door, leaving it slightly open. After a few minutes her voice rises softly within, singing. John suddenly rises. He crosses to the door, shoves it slowly open and enters.*]

JOHN [*softly and with deep tenderness*]: Father?

[*The light dims out in the house, but lingers on the stone angel.*]

★

Scene Nine

The cyclorama is the faint blue of a late afternoon in autumn. There is band-music—a Sousa march, in the distance. As it grows somewhat louder, Alma enters the Rectory interior in a dressing gown and with her hair hanging loose. She looks as if she had been through a long illness, the intensity drained, her pale face listless. She crosses to the window frame but the parade is not in sight so she returns weakly to the sofa and sits down closing her eyes with exhaustion.

The Rev. and Mrs. Winemiller enter the outer door frame of the Rectory, a grotesque-looking couple. Mrs. Winemiller has on her plumed hat, at a rakish angle, and a brilliant scarf about her throat. Her face wears a roguish smile that suggests a musical comedy pirate. One hand holds the minister's arm and with the other she is holding an ice cream cone.

MR. WINEMILLER: Now you may let go of my arm, if you please! She was on her worst behavior. Stopped in front of the White Star Pharmacy on Front Street and stood there like a mule; wouldn't budge till I bought her an ice cream cone. I had it wrapped in tissue paper because she had promised me that she wouldn't eat it until we got home. The moment I gave it to her she tore off the paper and walked home licking it every step of way!—just—just to humiliate me! [*Mrs. Winemiller offers him the half-eaten cone, saying "Lick?"*]

MR. WINEMILLER: No, thank you!

ALMA: Now, now, children.

[*Mr. Winemiller's irritation shifts to Alma.*]

MR. WINEMILLER: Alma! Why don't you get dressed? It hurts me to see you sitting around like this, day in, day out, like an invalid when there is nothing particularly wrong with you. I can't read your mind. You may have had some kind of disappointment, but you must not make it an excuse for acting as if the world had come to an end.

ALMA: I have made the beds and washed the breakfast dishes and phoned the market and sent the laundry out and peeled the potatoes and shelled the peas and set the table for lunch. What more do you want?

MR. WINEMILLER [*sharply*]: I want you to either get dressed or stay in your room. [*Alma rises indifferently, then her father speaks suddenly.*] At night you get dressed. Don't you? Yes, I heard you slipping out of the house at two in the morning. And that was not the first time.

ALMA: I don't sleep well. Sometimes I have to get up and walk for a while before I am able to sleep.

MR. WINEMILLER: What am I going to tell people who ask about you?

ALMA: Tell them I've changed and you're waiting to see in what way.

[*The band music becomes a little louder.*]

MR. WINEMILLER: Are you going to stay like this indefinitely?

ALMA: Not indefinitely, but you may wish that I had.

MR. WINEMILLER: Stop twisting that ring! Whenever I look at you you're twisting that ring. Give me that ring! I'm going to take that ring off your finger! [*He catches her wrist. She breaks roughly away from him.*]

MRS. WINEMILLER [*joyfully*]: Fight! Fight!

MR. WINEMILLER: Oh, I give up!

ALMA: That's better. [*She suddenly crosses to the window as the band music gets louder.*] Is there a parade in town?

MRS. WINEMILLER: Ha-ha—yes! They met him at the station with a great big silver loving-cup!

ALMA: Who? Who did they . . .?

MRS. WINEMILLER: That boy next door, the one you watched all the time!

ALMA: Is that true, Father?

MR. WINEMILLER [*unfolding his newspaper*]: Haven't you looked at the papers?

ALMA: No, not lately.

MR. WINEMILLER [*wiping his eyeglasses*]: These people are grasshoppers, just as likely to jump one way as another. He's finished the work his father started, stamped out the fever and gotten all the glory. Well, that's how it is in this world. Years of devotion and sacrifice are overlooked an' forgotten while someone young an' lucky walks off with the honors!

[*Alma has crossed slowly to the window. The sun brightens and falls in a shaft through the frame.*]

ALMA [*suddenly crying out*]: *There he is!* [*She staggers away from the window. There is a roll of drums and then silence. Alma now speaks faintly.*] What . . . happened? Something . . . struck me! [*Mr. Winemiller catches her arm to support her.*]

MR. WINEMILLER: Alma . . . I'll call a doctor.

ALMA: No, no don't. Don't call anybody to help me. I want to die!

[*She collapses on the sofa.*]

[*The band strikes up again and recedes down the street. The Rectory interior dims out. Then the light is brought up in the doctor's office. John enters, with his loving-cup. He is sprucely dressed and his whole manner suggests a new-found responsibility. While he is setting the award on the table, removing his coat and starched collar, Nellie Ewell appears in the door behind him. She stands by the anatomy chart and watches him until he discovers her presence. Nellie has abruptly grown up, and wears very adult clothes, but has lost none of her childish impudence and brightness. John gives a startled whistle as he sees her. Nellie giggles.*]

JOHN: High heels, feathers . . . and paint!

NELLIE: Not paint!

JOHN: Natural color?

NELLIE: Excitement.

JOHN: Over what?

NELLIE: Everything! You! You here! Didn't you see me at the depot? I shouted and waved my arm off! I'm home for Thanksgiving.

JOHN: From where?

NELLIE: Sophie Newcombe's [*He remains staring at her unbelieving. At last she draws a book from under her arm.*] Here is that nasty book you gave me last summer when I was pretending such ignorance of things!

JOHN: Only pretending?

NELLIE: Yes. [*He ignores the book. She tosses it on the table.*] . . . Well? [*John laughs uneasily and sits on the table.*] Shall I go now, or will you look at my tongue? [*She crosses to him, sticking out her tongue.*]

JOHN: Red as a berry!

NELLIE: Peppermint drops! Will you have one? [*She holds out a sack.*]

JOHN: Thanks. [*Nellie giggles as he takes one.*] What's the joke, Nellie?

NELLIE: They make your mouth so sweet!

JOHN: So?

NELLIE: I always take one when I hope to be kissed.

JOHN [*after a pause*]: Suppose I took you up on that?

NELLIE: I'm not scared. Are you?

[*He gives her a quick kiss. She clings to him, raising her hand to press his head against her own. He breaks free after a moment and turns the light back on.*]

JOHN [*considerably impressed*]: Where did you learn such tricks?

NELLIE: I've been away to school. But they didn't teach me to love.

JOHN: Who are you to be using that long word?

NELLIE: That isn't a long word!

JOHN: No? [*He turns away from her.*] Run along Nellie before we get into trouble.

NELLIE: Who's afraid of trouble, you or me?

JOHN: I am. Run along! Hear me?

NELLIE: Oh, I'll go. But I'll be back for Christmas!

[*She laughs and runs out. He whistles and wipes his forehead with a handkerchief.*]

⋆

Scene Ten

An afternoon in December. At the fountain in the park. It is very windy.

Alma enters. She seems to move with an effort against the wind. She sinks down on the bench.

A widow with a flowing black veil passes across the stage and pauses by Alma's bench. It is Mrs. Bassett.

MRS. BASSETT: Hello Alma.

ALMA: Good afternoon, Mrs. Bassett.

MRS. BASSETT: Such wind, such wind!

ALMA: Yes, it nearly swept me off my feet. I had to sit down to catch my breath for a moment.

MRS. BASSETT: I wouldn't sit too long if I were you.

ALMA: No, not long.

MRS. BASSETT: It's good to see you out again after illness.

ALMA: Thank you.

MRS BASSETT: Our poor little group broke up after you dropped out.

ALMA [*insincerely*]: What a pity.

MRS. BASSETT: You should have come to the last meeting.

ALMA: Why, what happened?

MRS. BASSETT: Vernon read his verse play!

ALMA: Ah, how was it received?

MRS. BASSETT: Maliciously, spitefully and vindictively torn to pieces, the way children tear the wings of butterflies. I think next Spring we might reorganize. [*She throws up her black-gloved hands in a deploring gesture.*]

[*Nellie Ewell appears. She is dressed very fashionably and carrying a fancy basket of Christmas packages.*]

NELLIE: Miss Alma!

MRS. BASSETT [*rushing off*]: Goodbye!

NELLIE: Oh, there you are!

ALMA: Why Nellie . . . Nellie Ewell!

NELLIE: I was by the Rectory. Just popped in for a second; the holidays are so short that every minute is precious. They told me you'd gone to the park.

ALMA: This is the first walk I've taken in quite a while.

NELLIE: You've been ill!

ALMA: Not ill, just not very well. How you've grown up, Nellie.

NELLIE: It's just my clothes. Since I went off to Sophie Newcombe I've picked out my own clothes, Miss Alma. When Mother had jurisdiction over my wardrobe, she tried to keep me looking like a child!

ALMA: Your voice is grown-up, too.

NELLIE: They're teaching me diction, Miss Alma. I'm learning to talk like you, long A's and everything, such as "cahn't" and "bahth" and "lahf" instead of "laugh." Yesterday I slipped. I said I "lahfed and lahfed till I nearly died laughing." Johnny was so amused at me!

ALMA: Johnny?

NELLIE: Your nextdoor neighbor!

ALMA: Oh! I'm sure it must be a very fashionable school.

NELLIE: Oh yes, they're preparing us to be young ladies in society. What a pity there's no society here to be young lady in . . . at least not for me, with Mother's reputation!

ALMA: You'll find other fields to conquer.

NELLIE: What's this I hear about *you*?

ALMA: I have no idea, Nellie.

NELLIE: That you've quit teaching singing and gone into retirement.

ALMA: Naturally I had to stop teaching while I was ill and as for retiring from the world . . . it's more a case of the world retiring from me.

NELLIE: I know somebody whose feelings you've hurt badly.

ALMA: Why, who could that be, Nellie?

NELLIE: Somebody who regards you as an angel!

ALMA: I can't think who might hold me in such esteem.

NELLIE: Somebody who says that you refused to see him.

ALMA: I saw nobody. For several months. The long summer wore me out so.

NELLIE: Well, anyhow, I'm going to give you your present. [*She hands her a small package from the basket.*]

ALMA: Nellie, you shouldn't have given me anything.

NELLIE: I'd like to know why not!

ALMA: I didn't expect it.

NELLIE: After the trouble you took with my horrible voice?

ALMA: It's very sweet of you, Nellie.

NELLIE: Open it!

ALMA: Now?

NELLIE: Why, sure.

ALMA: It's so prettily wrapped I hate to undo it.

NELLIE: I love to wrap presents and since it was for you, I did a specially dainty job of it.

ALMA [*winding the ribbon about her fingers*]: I'm going to save this ribbon. I'm going to keep this lovely paper too, with the silver stars on it. And the sprig of holly . . .

NELLIE: Let me pin it on your jacket, Alma.

ALMA: Yes, do. I hardly realized that Christmas was coming . . . [*She unfolds the paper, revealing a lace handkerchief and a card.*] What an exquisite handkerchief.

NELLIE: I hate to give people handkerchiefs, it's so unimaginative.

ALMA: I love to get them.

NELLIE: It comes from Maison Blanche!

ALMA: Oh, does it really?

NELLIE: Smell it!

ALMA: Sachet *Roses*! Well, I'm just more touched and pleased than I can possibly tell you!

NELLIE: The card!

ALMA: Card?

NELLIE: You dropped it. [*She snatches up the card and hands it to Alma.*]

ALMA: Oh, how clumsy of me! Thank you, Nellie. "Joyeux Noel . . . to Alma . . . from Nellie and . . . [*She looks up slowly.*] *John?*"

NELLIE: He helped me wrap presents last night and when we came to yours we started talking about you. Your ears must have burned!

[*The wind blows loudly. Alma bends stiffly forward.*]

ALMA: You mean you—spoke well of me?

NELLIE: "Well of"! We raved, simply raved! Oh, he told me the influence you'd had on him!

ALMA: Influence?

NELLIE: He told me about the wonderful talks he'd had with you last summer when he was mixed up and how you inspired him and you more than anyone else was responsible for his pulling himself together, after his father was killed, and he told me about . . . [*Alma rises stiffly from the bench.*] Where are you going, Miss Alma?

ALMA: To drink at the fountain.

NELLIE: He told me about how you came in the house that night like an angel of mercy!

ALMA [*laughing harshly by the fountain*]: This is the only angel in Glorious Hill. [*She bends to drink.*] Her body is stone and her blood is mineral water.

[*The wind is louder.*]

NELLIE: How penetrating the wind is!

ALMA: I'm going home, Nellie. You run along and deliver your presents now. . . . [*She starts away.*]

NELLIE: But wait till I've told you the wonderfullest thing I . . .

ALMA: I'm going home now. Goodbye.

NELLIE: Oh—Goodbye, Miss Alma.

[*She snatches up her festive basket and rushes in the other direction with a shrill giggle as the wind pulls at her skirts. The lights dim out.*]

★

Scene Eleven

An hour later. In John's office.

The interior is framed by the traceries of Victorian architecture and there is one irregular section of wall supporting the anatomy chart. Otherwise the stage is open to the cyclorama.

In the background mellow golden light touches the vane of a steeple (a gilded weathercock). Also the wings of the stone angel. A singing wind rises and falls throughout scene.

John is seated at a white enameled table examining a slide through a microscope.

[*A bell tolls the hours of five as Alma comes hesitantly in. She wears a russet suit and a matching hat with a plume. The light changes, the sun disappearing behind a cloud, fading from the steeple and the stone angel till the bell stops tolling. Then it brightens again.*]

ALMA: No greetings? No greetings at all?

JOHN: Hello, Miss Alma.

ALMA [*speaking with animation to control her panic*]: How white it is here, such glacial brilliance! [*She covers her eyes, laughing.*]

JOHN: New equipment.

ALMA: Everything new but the chart.

JOHN: The human anatomy's always the same old thing.

ALMA: And such a tiresome one! I've been plagued with sore throats.

JOHN: Everyone has here lately. These Southern homes are all improperly heated. Open grates aren't enough.

ALMA: They burn the front of you while your back is freezing!

JOHN: Then you go into another room and get chilled off.

ALMA: Yes, yes, chilled to the bone.

JOHN: But it never gets quite cold enough to convince the damn fools that a furnace is necessary so they go on building without them.

[*There is the sound of wind.*]

ALMA: Such a strange afternoon.

JOHN: Is it? I haven't been out.

ALMA: The Gulf wind is blowing big, white—what do they call them? cumulus?—clouds over! Ha-ha! It seemed determined to take the plume off my hat, like that fox terrier we had once named Jacob, snatched the plume off a hat and dashed around and around the back yard with it like a trophy!

JOHN: I remember Jacob. What happened to him?

ALMA: Oh, Jacob. Jacob was such a mischievous thief. We had to send him out to some friends in the country. Yes, he ended his days as—a country squire! The tales of his exploits . . .

JOHN: Sit down, Miss Alma.

ALMA: If I'm disturbing you . . .?

JOHN: No—I called the Rectory when I heard you were sick. Your father told me you wouldn't see a doctor.

ALMA: I needed a rest, that was all. . . . You were out of town mostly. . . .

JOHN: I was mostly in Lyon, finishing up Dad's work in the fever clinic.

ALMA: Covering yourself with sudden glory!

JOHN: Redeeming myself with good works.

ALMA: It's rather late to tell you how happy I am, and also how proud. I almost feel as your father might have felt—if . . . And—are you—happy now, John?

JOHN [*uncomfortably, not looking at her*]: I've settled with life on fairly acceptable terms. Isn't that all a reasonable person can ask for?

ALMA: He can ask for much more than that. He can ask for the coming true of his most improbable dreams.

JOHN: It's best not ask for too much.

ALMA: I disagree with you. I say, ask for all, but be prepared to get nothing! [*She springs up and crosses to the window. She continues.*] No, I haven't been well. I've thought many times of something you told me last summer, that I have a *doppelganger.* I looked that up and I found that it means another person inside me, another self, and I don't know whether to thank you or not for making me conscious of it!—I haven't been well. . . . For a while I thought I was dying, that that was the change that was coming.

JOHN: When did you have that feeling?

ALMA: August. September. But now the Gulf wind has blown that feeling away like a cloud of smoke, and I know now I'm not dying, that it isn't going to turn out to be that simple. . . .

JOHN: Have you been anxious about your heart again? [*He retreats to a professional manner and takes out a silver watch, putting his fingers on her wrist.*]

ALMA: And now the stethoscope? [*He removes the stethoscope from the table and starts to loosen her jacket. She looks down at his bent head. Slowly, involuntarily, her gloved hands lift and descend on the crown of his head. He gets up awkwardly. She suddenly leans toward him and presses her mouth to his.*] Why don't you say something? Has the cat got your tongue?

JOHN: Miss Alma, what can I say?

ALMA: You've gone back to calling me "Miss Alma" again.

JOHN: We never really got past that point with each other.

ALMA: Oh, yes, we did. We were so close that we almost breathed together!

JOHN [*with embarrassment*]: I didn't know that.

ALMA: No? Well, I did, I knew it. [*Her hand touches his face tenderly.*] You shave more carefully now? You don't have those little razor cuts on your chin that you dusted with gardenia talcum. . . .

JOHN: I shave more carefully now.

ALMA: So that explains it! [*Her fingers remain on his face, moving gently up and down it like a blind person reading Braille. He is intensely embarrassed and gently removes her hands from him.*] Is it—impossible now?

JOHN: I don't think I know what you mean.

ALMA: You know what I mean, all right So be honest with me. One time I said "no" to something. You may remember the time, and all that demented howling from the cock-fight? But now I have changed my mind, or the girl who said "no," she doesn't exist any more, she died last summer—suffocated in smoke from something on fire inside her. No, she doesn't live now, but she left me her ring—You see? This one you admired, the topaz ring set in pearls. . . . And she said to me when she slipped this ring on my finger—"Remember I died empty-handed, and so make sure that your hands have *something in them!"* [*She drops her gloves. She clasps his head again in her hands.*] I said, "But what about pride?"—She said, "Forget about pride whenever it stands between you and what you must have!" [*He takes hold of her wrists.*] And then I said, "But what if he doesn't want me?" I don't know what she said then. I'm not sure whether she said anything or not—her lips stopped moving—yes, I think she stopped breathing! [*He gently removes her craving hands from his face.*] No? [*He shakes his head in dumb suffering.*] Then the answer is "no"!

JOHN [*forcing himself to speak*]: I have a respect for the truth, and I have a respect for you—so I'd better speak honestly if you want me to speak. [*Alma nods slightly.*] You've won the argument that we had between us.

ALMA: What—argument?

JOHN: The one about the chart.

ALMA: Oh—the chart!

[*She turns from him and wanders across to the chart. She gazes up at it with closed eyes, and her hands clasped in front of her.*]

JOHN: It shows that we're not a package of rose leaves, that every interior inch of us is taken up with something ugly and functional and no room seems to be left for anything else in there.

ALMA: No . . .

JOHN: But I've come around to your way of thinking, that something else is in there, an immaterial something—as thin as smoke—which all of those ugly machines combine to produce and that's their whole reason for being. It can't be seen so it can't be shown on the chart. But it's there, just the same, and knowing it's there—why, then the whole thing—this—this unfathomable experience of ours—takes on a new value, like some—some wildly romantic work in a laboratory! Don't you see?

[*The wind comes up very loud, almost like a choir of voices. Both of them turn slightly, Alma raising a hand to her plumed head as if she were outdoors.*]

ALMA: Yes, I see! Now that you no longer want it to be otherwise you're willing to believe that a spiritual bond can exist between us two!

JOHN: Can't you believe that I am sincere about it?

ALMA: Maybe you are. But I don't want to be talked to like some incurably sick patient you have to comfort. [*A harsh and strong note comes into her voice.*] Oh, I suppose I am sick, one of those weak and divided people who slip like shadows among you solid strong ones. But sometimes, out of necessity, we shadowy people take on strength of our own. I have that now. You needn't try to deceive me.

JOHN: I wasn't.

ALMA: You needn't try to comfort me. I haven't come here on any but equal terms. You said, let's talk truthfully. Well, let's do! Unsparingly, truthfully, even shamelessly, then! It's no longer a secret that I love you. It never was. I loved you as long ago as the time I asked you to read the stone angel's name with your fingers. Yes, I remember the long afternoons of our childhood, when I had to stay indoors to practice my music—and heard your playmates calling you, "Johnny, Johnny!" How it went through me, just to hear your name called! And how I—rushed to the window to watch you jump the porch railing! I stood at a distance, halfway down the block, only to keep in sight of your torn red sweater, racing about the vacant lot you played in. Yes, it had begun that early, this affliction of love, and has never let go of me since, but kept on growing. I've lived next door to you all the days of my life, a weak and divided person who stood in adoring awe of your singleness, of your strength. And that is my story! Now I wish *you* would tell me—why didn't it happen between us? Why did I fail? Why did you come almost close enough—and no closer?

JOHN: Whenever we've gotten together, the three or four times that we have . . .

ALMA: As few as that?

JOHN: It's only been three or four times that we've—come face to face. And each of those times—we seemed to be trying to find something in each other without knowing what it was that we wanted to find. It wasn't a body hunger although—I acted as if I thought it might be the night I wasn't a gentleman—at the Casino—it wasn't the physical you that I really wanted!

ALMA: I know, you've already . . .

JOHN: You didn't have that to give me.

ALMA: Not at that time.

JOHN: You had something else to give.

ALMA: What did I have?

[*John strikes a match. Unconsciously he holds his curved palm over the flame of the match to warm it. It is a long kitchen match and it makes a good flame. They both stare at it with a sorrowful understanding that is still perplexed. It is about to burn his fingers. She leans forward and blows it out, then she puts on her gloves.*]

JOHN: You couldn't name it and I couldn't recognize it. I thought it was just a Puritanical ice that glittered like flame. But now I believe it *was* flame, mistaken for ice. I still don't understand it, but I know it was there, just as I know that your eyes and your voice are the two most beautiful things I've ever known—and also the warmest, although they don't seem to be set in your body at all. . . .

ALMA: You talk as if my body had ceased to exist for you, John, in spite of the fact that you've just counted my pulse. Yes, that's it! You tried to avoid it, but you've told me plainly. The tables have turned, yes, the tables have turned with a vengeance! You've come around to my old way of thinking and I to yours like two people exchanging a call on each other at the same time, and each one finding the other one gone out, the door locked against him and no one to answer the bell! [*She laughs.*] I came here to tell you that being a gentleman doesn't seem so important to me any more, but you're telling me I've got to remain a lady. [*She laughs rather violently.*] The tables have turned with a vengeance!—The air in here smells of ether—It's making me dizzy . . .

JOHN: I'll open a window.

ALMA: Please.

JOHN: There now.

ALMA: Thank you, that's better. Do you remember those little white tablets you gave me? I've used them all up and I'd like to have some more.

JOHN: I'll write the prescription for you. [*He bends to write.*]

[*Nellie is in the waiting room. They hear her voice.*]

ALMA: Someone is waiting in the waiting room, John. One of my vocal pupils. The youngest and prettiest one with the least gift for music. The one that you helped wrap up this handkerchief for me. [*She takes it out and touches her eyes with it.*]

[*The door opens, first a crack. Nellie peers in and giggles. Then she throws the door wide open with a peal of merry laughter. She has holly pinned on her jacket. She rushes up to John and hugs him with childish squeals.*]

NELLIE: I've been all over town just shouting, shouting!

JOHN: Shouting what?

NELLIE: Glad tidings!

[*John looks at Alma over Nellie's shoulder.*]

JOHN: I thought we weren't going to tell anyone for a while.

NELLIE: I couldn't stop myself. [*She wheels about.*] Oh, Alma, has he told *you*?

ALMA [*quietly*]: He didn't need to, Nellie. I guessed . . . from the Christmas card with your two names written on it!

[*Nellie rushes over to Alma and hugs her. Over Nellie's shoulder Alma looks at John. He makes a thwarted gesture as if he wanted to speak. She smiles desperately and shakes her head. She closes her eyes and bites her lips for a moment. Then she releases Nellie with a laugh of exaggerated gaiety.*]

NELLIE: So Alma you were really the first to know!

ALMA: I'm proud of that, Nellie.

NELLIE: See on my finger! This was the present I couldn't tell you about!

ALMA: Oh, what a lovely, lovely solitaire! But solitaire is such a wrong name for it. Solitaire means single and this means *two*! It's blinding. Nellie! Why it . . . hurts my eyes!

[*John catches Nellie's arm and pulls her to him. Almost violently Alma lifts her face; it is bathed in tears. She nods gratefully to John for releasing her from Nellie's attention. She picks up her gloves and purse.*]

JOHN: Excuse her, Miss Alma. Nellie's still such a child.

ALMA [*with a breathless laugh*]: I've got to run along now.

JOHN: Don't leave your prescription.

ALMA: Oh, yes, where's my prescription?

JOHN: On the table.

ALMA: I'll take it to the drug store right away!

[*Nellie struggles to free herself from John's embrace, which keeps her from turning to Alma.*]

NELLIE: Alma, don't go! Johnny, let go of me, Johnny! You're hugging me so tight I can't breathe!

ALMA: Goodbye.

NELLIE: Alma! Alma, you know you're going to sing at the wedding! The very first Sunday in Spring!—which will be Palm Sunday! "The Voice that Breathed o'er Eden."

[*Alma has closed the door. John shuts his eyes tight with a look of torment. He rains kisses on Nellie's forehead and throat and lips. The scene dims out with music.*]

★

Scene Twelve

In the park near the angel of the fountain. About dusk.

Alma enters the lighted area and goes slowly up to the fountain and bends to drink. Then she removes a small white package from her pocketbook and starts to unwrap it. While she is doing this, a Young Man comes along. He is dressed in a checked suit and a derby. He pauses by the bench. They glance at each other.

A train whistles in the distance. The Young Man clears his throat. The train whistle is repeated. The Young Man crosses toward the fountain, his eyes on Alma. She hesitates, with the unwrapped package in her hand. Then she crosses toward the bench and stands hesitantly in front of it. He stuffs his hands in his pockets and whistles. He glances with an effect of unconcern back over his shoulder.

Alma pushes her veil back with an uncertain gesture. His whistle dies out. He sways back and forth on his heels as the train whistles again. He suddenly turns to the fountain and bends to drink. Alma slips the package back into her purse. As the young man straightens up, she speaks in a barely audible voice.

ALMA: The water—is—cool.

THE YOUNG MAN [*eagerly*]: Did you say something?

ALMA: I said, the water is cool.

THE YOUNG MAN: Yes, it sure is, it's nice and cool!

ALMA: It's always cool.

THE YOUNG MAN: Is it?

ALMA: Yes. Yes, even in summer. It comes from deep underground.

THE YOUNG MAN: That's what keeps it cool.

ALMA: Glorious Hill is famous for its artesian springs.

THE YOUNG MAN: I didn't know that.

[*The Young Man jerkily removes his hands from his pockets. She gathers confidence before the awkwardness of his youth.*]

ALMA: Are you a stranger in town?

THE YOUNG MAN: I'm a traveling salesman.

ALMA: Ah, you're a salesman who travels! [*She laughs gently.*] But you're younger than most of them are, and not so fat!

THE YOUNG MAN: I'm just starting out. I travel for Red Goose shoes.

ALMA: Ah! The Delt's your territory?

THE YOUNG MAN: From the Peabody Lobby to Cat-Fish Row in Vicksburg.

[*Alma leans back and looks at him under half-closed lids, perhaps a little suggestively.*]

ALMA: The life of a traveling salesman is interesting . . . but lonely.

THE YOUNG MAN: You're right about that. Hotel bedrooms are lonely.

[*There is a pause. Far away the train whistles again.*]

ALMA: All rooms are lonely where there is only one person. [*Her eyes fall shut.*]

THE YOUNG MAN [*gently*]: You're tired, aren't you?

ALMA: I? Tired? [*She starts to deny it; then laughs faintly and confesses the truth.*] Yes . . . a little . . . But I shall rest now. I've just now taken one of my sleeping tablets.

THE YOUNG MAN: So early?

ALMA: Oh, it won't put me to sleep. It will just quiet my nerves.

THE YOUNG MAN: What are you nervous about?

ALMA: I won an argument this afternoon.

THE YOUNG MAN: That's nothing to be nervous over. You ought to be nervous if you *lost* one.

ALMA: It wasn't the argument that I wanted to win. . . .

THE YOUNG MAN: Well, I'm nervous too.

ALMA: What over?

THE YOUNG MAN: It's my first job and I'm scared of not making good.

[*That mysteriously sudden intimacy that sometimes occurs between strangers more completely than old friends or lovers moves them both. Alma hands the package of tablets to him.*]

ALMA: Then you must take one of my tablets.

THE YOUNG MAN: Shall I?

ALMA: Please take one!

THE YOUNG MAN: Yes, I shall.

ALMA: You'll be surprised how infinitely merciful they are. The prescription number is 96814. I think of it as the telephone number of God! [*They both laugh. He places one of the tablets on his tongue and crosses to the fountain to wash it down.*]

THE YOUNG MAN [*to the stone figure*]: Thanks, angel. [*He gives her a little salute, and crosses back to Alma.*]

ALMA: Life is full of little mercies like that, not big mercies but comfortable *little* mercies. And so we are able to keep on going. . . . [*She has leaned back with half-closed eyes.*]

THE YOUNG MAN [*returning*]: You're falling asleep.

ALMA: Oh no, I'm not. I'm just closing my eyes. You know what I feel like now? I feel like a water-lily.

THE YOUNG MAN: A water-lily?

ALMA: Yes, I feel like a water-lily on a Chinese lagoon. Won't you sit down? [*The Young Man does.*] My name is Alma. Spanish for soul! What's yours?

THE YOUNG MAN: Ha-ha! Mine's Archie Kramer. Mucho gusto, as they say in Spain.

ALMA: Usted habla Espanol, senor?

THE YOUNG MAN: Un poquito! Usted habla Espanol, senorita?

ALMA: Me tambien. Un poquito!

THE YOUNG MAN [*delightedly*]: Ha . . . ha . . . ha! Sometimes un poquito is plenty! [*Alma laughs . . . in a different way than she has ever laughed before, a little wearily, but quite naturally. The Young Man leans toward her confidentially.*] What's there to do in this town after dark?

ALMA: There's not much to do in this town after dark, but there are resorts on the lake that offer all kinds of after-dark entertainment. There's one called Moon Lake Casino. It's under new management, now, but I don't suppose its character has changed.

THE YOUNG MAN: What was its character?

ALMA: Gay, very gay, Mr. Kramer. . . .

THE YOUNG MAN: Then what in hell are we sitting here for? Vamonos!

ALMA: Como no, senor!

THE YOUNG MAN: Ha-ha-ha! [*He jumps up.*] I'll call a taxi. [*He goes off shouting "Taxi."*]

[*Alma rises from the bench. As she crosses to the fountain the grave mood of the play is reinstated with a phrase of music. She faces the stone angel and raises her gloved hand in a sort of valedictory salute. Then she turns slowly about toward the audience with her hand still raised in a gesture of wonder and finality as . . . the curtain falls.*]

22. *The Iceman Cometh*—Eugene O'Neill

Commentary

Sources

Play

22.1 O'NEILL'S CRITIQUE OF PSYCHOLOGICAL DISCOURSE AND *ICEMAN*—JOEL PFISTER

IN 1927 O'NEILL WROTE TO Joseph Wood Krutch that he had never "thought" of his *Strange Interlude* characters "in any Freudian sense," and that he was "no great student of psycho-analysis." Although he acknowledged that his play was "full of psycho-analytic ideas," he attributed their origin, not to Freud, but to the "age-old" insight of authors:

> Any artist who was a good psychologist and had had a varied and sensitive experience with life and all sorts of people could have written *Strange Interlude* without ever having heard of Freud, Jung, Adler & Co. This doesn't apply in my case, of course. I'm simply making this statement because it seems to me that there is a tendency now to read psycho-analysis into an author's work where ordinary psychology offers a sufficient explanation—let alone imagination and intuition. All the author's pet thunder will be stolen if it keeps up!

What Volosinov viewed as the ideological agenda of Freudianism is discernible in O'Neill's tendency to conceptualize the psychological as outside of historical change. Also discounting the influence of psycho-analysis on *Desire Under the Elms*, he insisted: "Playwrights are either intuitively keen analytical psychologists or they aren't good playwrights. . . . Freud only means certain conjectures and explanations about truths of the emotional past of mankind that every dramatist has clearly sensed ever since real drama began. . . . I respect Freud's work tremendously—but I'm not an addict! Whatever of Freudianism is in *Desire* must have walked in 'through my unconscious.'" The psychology that was well represented in the mass culture and the high culture of the twenties undoubtedly sauntered in through his conscious and unconscious mind.

O'Neill expressed some interest in the theories of behaviorism and he also attributed his insights into psychology to his knowledge of Irish literature and culture, but his principal brief against psychoanalysis was that the dramatist—his profession—got there first. His wish to distance his art from psychoanalysis was not generally directed at the latter's specific insights. Rather, O'Neill focuses on the professional *authority* psychoanalysis had culturally produced for itself, a fully credentialed "scientific" expertise that by implication makes psychological dramatists seem like unaccredited psychologists who first consult case studies and then dramatize them for the stage (which is precisely what Eric Bentley, in 1962, would suggest that O'Neill had done). Krutch's reviews of *Strange Interlude* in 1928 elaborated the distinction O'Neill hoped to establish in 1927. Where O'Neill's psychological drama achieved its power by exalting emotions as "cosmically important," Freud's psychoanalysis subverts human nature by making emotions seem "petty." As if looking ahead to *Mourning*, Krutch praised O'Neill's tragic neurotics for having "assume[d] the importance of figures in Greek or Elizabethan tragedy."

O'Neill's defensiveness about psychoanalysis and its capacity to steal his "pet thunder" also surfaces in a sketch for a play (1930) he never wrote: "Play of the psycho-therapeutist to whom a creative artist—genius or of great talent—man or woman comes in torture and half-pleads, half-challenges to have his devils cast out—the haunting ghosts of his past." The suicidal artist transfers "his horrible bitterness, his blasphemies against life, his sins of lust and cruelty" to the therapist, whom it "breaks."

In the concluding scene "the artist has mercy on the doctor and kills him to free him (as he had wished to do with himself) and all his ghosts come back, the ghost of the doctor added."

The therapist cannot withstand the psychological "thunder" sustained by the subjective artist who "half-challenges" him with it. The artist, through the revelation of his disturbances, proves himself even "deeper" than the therapist he destroys. Also noteworthy in this sketch is O'Neill's decision not to use psychoanalytic vocabulary (repression, projection, symptom, oedipus complex, etc.), selecting instead "age-old terms like "bitterness," "sins," "lust," and "cruelty." Three years later, with the non-"psychological" *Ah, Wilderness!* in mind, O'Neill confessed to Saxe Commins that his "unconscious had been rebelling for a long time against creation in the medium of the modern, involved, complicated, warped & self-poisoned psyche and demanded a counter-statement of simplicity and peace that tragedy troubles but does not poison." In this atypical statement, O'Neill reveals that at times he comprehended his modern "medium" of depth as an aberrant depth rather than as the age-old depth in us all.

O'Neill also turned his critical eye on psychological discourse in *The Iceman Cometh* (1939). Hickey converts Harry Hope's barroom pipe-dreamers into a psychological community, a transformation O'Neill goes to great lengths to dramatize as an abusive exercise of power. I do not wish to suggest that the salesman Hickey be viewed either literally or biographically as a pop psychologist; but there are, notwithstanding, intriguing correspondences between his sales rhetoric and the pronouncements of pop psychologists, like Dr. Louis Bisch, who "sold" the public on being "psychiatric-minded."

"I want neurotics to realize what they *really* are," wrote Bisch with evangelical zeal, "not what others would have them believe they are." Similarly, Hickey advised his barroom "boys and girls": "I know from my own experience it's bitter medicine, facing yourself in the mirror with the old false whiskers off" (3:629). Just as Hickey proselytized on behalf of "honesty is the best policy—honesty with yourself" (3:610), Bisch explained: "You may be puzzled over yourself because you are not thoroughly honest with yourself." Bisch's *Be Glad You're Neurotic* could easily have printed a reassurance like the one Hickey offered the pipe-dreamers who grew increasingly restive with his brand of self-scrutiny: "All I want is to see you happy" (3:616). Seabury's *Unmasking Our Minds* outlines the therapeutic advantages of "look [ing] below the surface at last." By the same token, Hickey represents unmasking as the therapeutic means of freeing oneself "from guilt and lying hopes" (3:680).

He who unmasks others holds power over others. Oppenheim's *Behind Your Front* touted psychological reading as an exercise of power when he predicted that his reader would want to "use this little book as a sort of x-ray on his friends." Hickey's account of his own X-ray sales technique describes equally well what he does in Hope's bar: "It was like a game, sizing people up quick, spotting what their pet pipe dreams were" (3:696). Hickey's "sizing up" eschews reference to the professional psychoanalytic terminology promoted by pop psychology's best selling salesmen. Isidor Schneider picked up on this in his 1946 review of *Iceman* for the *New Masses*, in which he attributed its "incredible impact" to "the fact that, unlike O'Neill's previous psychoanalytic plays, which were like caricatures in their literal Freudianism, what is applied in *The Iceman Cometh* is an assimilated knowledge that is used deftly and not stuck on like labels." The same can be said of O'Neill's final dramas, *Long Day's Journey* and *A Moon for the Misbegotten* (1943).

Just after completing *Iceman,* O'Neill wrote Macgowan:

> You would find if I did not build up the complete picture of the group as it now is in the first part—the atmosphere of the place, the humour and friendship and human warmth and *deep inner contentment* of the bottom—you would not be so interested in these people and you would find the impact of what follows a lot less profoundly disturbing. You wouldn't feel the same sympathy and understanding for them, or be so moved by what Hickey does to them.

Along the same line, O'Neill's original sketch for the play is based on the motif that "man desperately needs friendships." Hickey employs the language of social cohesion (gang, governor, Old Scout), but in fact disintegrates this community of boozy pipe-dreamers by turning their gaze inward and unmasking their alibis. The unmasking of Hope's hangers-on succeeds by threatening their sense of self-legitimacy and by playing on their feelings of inadequacy. O'Neill shows that this psychological invasion secures its authority by infantalizing the pipe-dreamers. Hickey, bringing to mind psychoanalytic premises about the determinative influence of childhood on adults, repeatedly labels them "kids" or "boys and girls." He shatters community, civility, and sociability by producing (aggressive) psychological subjects.

Larry, stunned by the destructive wake of the salesman's "Reform wave" (3:652), casts forth the saving lifeline of the story: "The lie of a pipe dream is what gives life to the whole misbegotten mad lot of us, drunk or sober" (3:569–70). Even Hickey confirms this when his ruthless unmasking of the others is disclosed as a denial of his hatred for his wife, Evelyn (his "pipe dream"): "Do you suppose I give a damn about life now? Why, you bonehead, I haven't got a single damned lying hope or pipe dream left!" (3:703). Here again, O'Neill-the-dramatist is competing with a psychological discourse premised on the therapeutic and transformative benefits of unmasking. By implication, age-old drama is more humane and sympathetic in its acceptance of the compulsive pipe dreams that enable one to go on living, mad, drunk, or sober. Age-old tragedy is thus deeper than professional psychological discourse because it grasps that denial, in certain ways, can be at once life-sustaining and tragic. "*I* don't write this as a piece of playwrighting," O'Neill wrote to Macgowan. "*They do it. They have to.* Each of them! In just that way! It is tragically, pitifully important to them to do this! They *must* tell these lies as a first step in taking up life again." This statement is infused with the religious spirit of forgiveness as well as the spirit of hope that one finds in religion, such as the Catholic faith that guided O'Neill as a boy. Pipe dreams bring hope to Hope's bar. As Nietzsche, the philosopher who most influenced O'Neill, once wrote: "The erroneousness of a concept does not for me constitute an objection to it; the question is—to what extent is it advantageous to life."

The binary opposition *Iceman* leaves us with is pipe dreams (the dramatist's depth) versus unmasking (the pop psychologists' depth). Yet O'Neill's early draft notes focus on another theme too, as Virginia Floyd points out: the characters' opening "discourses on anarchism and the corruption of capitalism summarize O'Neill's solid statements: neither 'ism' is able to provide followers with sufficient hope for the present; *as a consequence* they retreat into a world of 'tomorrow' pipe dreams" (emphasis supplied). In an interview he gave during the rehearsals of the Guild production of *Iceman* in 1946, O'Neill implicitly linked pipe dreams to what one might now label the concept of ideology (the American Pipe Dream): "This American Dream stuff gives me a pain . . . If it exists, as we tell the whole world, why don't we make it work in one small hamlet of the United States?" O'Neill refused to have *Iceman* produced at the outset of World War II because he felt its focus on pipe dreams would be inappropriate for the American war effort, perhaps meaning its propaganda campaign. But O'Neill's final version of his play mutes his disgust with the American Pipe Dream. O'Neill underplays the social reasons for why these fallen pipe-dreamers have no wish to go outside.

Arthur Miller has argued that the new social dramatist "must be an even deeper psychologist than those of the past" by recognizing "the futility of isolating the psychological life of man." O'Neill isolates the psychological life of men and women in the final draft of *Iceman*. Hope's pipe-dreamers live in a psychological space built on the foundation of "swapping lies" (3:699). Within the world of Hope's bar, the "isms" are not the problem; living is, seemingly because "life" universally produces ambivalence that necessitates denial. The denial theme is, by implication, valued as deeper than the social theme of political alienation. Personal pipe dreams are not only defended compassionately as therapeutic substitutes for the practice of unmasking; they also function, albeit less visibly in the play, as therapeutic replacements for a disappointing world in which systemic social change is deemed so impossible that it does not qualify as a serious dramatic issue.

Brecht had no desire to isolate the psychological life of his characters and had little use for the notion that human emotions, by their fixed nature, foreclose the possibility of structural social and political change. "Emotions, instincts, impulses are generally presented as being deeper, more eternal, less easily influenced by society than by ideas," he wrote in 1938, having fled Nazi Germany, "but this is in no way true. The emotions are neither common to all humanity nor incapable of alteration." Brecht understood that the cultural categories through which psychology, the emotions, and subjectivities are organized and produced must be scrutinized as historical and political, and that if we don't recognize these categories as social in nature, we simply accept them as nature.

Of course this understanding was never foreign to O'Neill, even as he staged depth from the 1920s to the 1940s. Through Hickey, *Iceman* dramatized the subtly coercive power of psychological discourse to determine concepts of selfhood and to recast social relations. On one level *Iceman* can be read as O'Neill's self-reflexive critique of the psychological dramatist—he who *presumes* to know and to tell us who we really are, down *deep*.

But on another level *Iceman* performs an ideological maneuver quite similar to that of some of O'Neill's overtly pop psychological plays. In 1939, the year O'Neill wrote *Iceman*, Frank O'Hara's *Today in American Drama* speculated that *Strange Interlude* and *Mourning Becomes Electra* would soon be perceived, not as modern, but as "museum pieces." It makes sense that O'Neill's dramatization of pop psychological depth would seem dated by the end of the thirties, a decade that saw a resurgence of realism and naturalism. No doubt it occurred to O'Neill that some of the 1930s realists and naturalists who made *Strange Interlude* seem unreal had learned from his own early work. With *Iceman* and *Long Day's Journey*, he returned with consummate skill to the realism and naturalism that had seemed thin and superficial to him in his pop modernist phase, and he infused his writing with the depth he popularized in the 1920s. *Iceman* draws on some of his early experiments in naturalism: the bar in *The Long Voyage Home* (1917); the drunken reveries in *The Moon of the Caribees*

(1917); the repartee in the saloon in *"Anna Christie."* The preoccupations and "insights" of *Iceman* and *Long Day's Journey* are often just as pop psychological as those of *Strange Interlude* and *Mourning*, but O'Neill used his extraordinary expertise as a dramatic portraitist to make it appear that this psychology was indeed what was most human—most real—about his characters.

Yet the apparent humanity of his characters is given remarkably attenuated agency. The possibilities for action in *Iceman* and *Long Day's Journey* (as in *Strange Interlude* and *Mourning*) fall within a narrow, therapeutic register—characters are fated to contend interminably with denial, ambivalence, obsession, and their own sense of being psychologically determined. Despite O'Neill's sharp critique of Hickey's ruthless psychological unmasking, the playwright's own dramatic, aesthetic, intellectual, and ideological investment is still very much in what I have termed psychological capital. Even Hickey's psychological unmasking of pipe dreams turns out to be "psychological"—a neurotic *symptom* of his own denial, a classic case of projection.

Although Isidor Schneider lauded O'Neill's ability in *Iceman* to portray characters whose Freudian complexes are "not stuck on like labels," his *New Masses* review also disarmingly stepped outside the play's ideological bubble to observe that both the play's author and its mainstream reviewers seem peculiarly oblivious to "the purposeful world outside and the undefeated people moving vigorously and freely in it, those who have the will to struggle, to forgive, to endure, who do without the paralysis and the pipe dream." Schneider sensed that O'Neill deployed his naturalism and realism to make "depth" seem not only more real, more natural, and more *eternally* human than in any other of his plays, but also far more significant—as the subject of human drama—than any staging of characters as social actors whose life-saving investment is not in denial but in changing the world. He found the implications of O'Neill's "therapeutic" antipolitics to be undeniably political.

22.2 LETTERS FROM EUGENE O'NEILL

To Lawrence Langner

Tao House
Danville
Contra Costa County
California

August the 11th 1940

Dear Lawrence, Many thanks for your letter regarding *The Iceman Cometh.* I'm damned pleased you liked it so well. Personally, I love it! And I'm sure my affection is not wholly inspired by nostalgia for the dear dead days "on the bottom of the sea," either! I have a confident hunch that this play, as drama, is one of the best things I've ever done. In some ways, perhaps *the* best. What I mean is, there are moments in it that suddenly strip the secret soul of a man stark naked, not in cruelty or moral superiority, but with an understanding compassion which sees him as a victim of the ironies of life and of himself. Those moments are for me the depth of tragedy, with nothing more that can possibly be said.

To Eugene O'Neill Jr (excerpt)

Tao House
Danville
Contra Costa County
California

August the 28th 1941

. . . In the past two years I've written two plays I'm really enthusiastic about: *The Iceman Cometh* and *Long Day's Journey Into Night*. They will rank among the finest things I've ever done, I know. But they—particularly the second—are emphatically not plays I want produced or published at this crisis-preoccupied time. They could not be understood. Not their real meaning or truth. *The Iceman Cometh* might be a big success, if done well, but it would be for its least significant merits and its finest values would be lost, or dismissed because the present psychology would not want to face them . . .

To Norman Pearson

Tao House
Danville
Contra Costa County
California

July the 30th 1942

Dear Norman Pearson: I'm immensely gratified that *The Iceman Cometh* made such an impression on you. As I wrote you, I cannot be becomingly modest about this play. It is as deeply moving to me as it is ever likely to be to anyone, and I unhesitatingly give myself a pat on the back for it.

I'm delighted to know you found it satisfies every demand both as a tensely-developing dramatic story and as a life symbol. This, of course, has been my intent in many plays, but it did not always come off. Even in titles I have tried for that double meaning—which explains why many people, without realizing the reason, find a lot of them so striking. They hit the subconscious as well as the conscious.

What you say of the wholeness of each character—the life story in each—is another thing I like about this play. *The Iceman Cometh* is, I think, the only play with seventeen fine parts. Which makes casting a problem. It needs seventeen fine actors! It can't ever have them in our theatre because fine actors won't play small parts, however good, and no management could afford their salaries, anyway. So the best I can hope for—as many times before in my experience—is that the parts are strong enough to "carry" mediocre acting and make it look good.

Yes, I am particularly proud of the picture one gets of the women who never appear—the living influence even of those who are dead. Parritt's mother, Hickey's wife, Hope's wife and at the last even Jimmy Tomorrow's wife makes a brief but illuminating entrance in his speech about her. They are all characters of the play to me.

Well, now you've read the play, I know you will understand my refusal to produce it in these times. It is not only my poor health, which might be wrecked by the strain and land me in a hospital again. It's that I know what is important to me in the play could not be seen or heard now. It might well succeed on its outer story and dramatic structure values, but its inner life would be suppressed or ignored. Would have to be—indeed, perhaps ought to be, because now we need an unquestioning faith in all pipe dreams, however irrational, lest we be defeated in spirit and thrown into the sty of final "realistic" opportunism, where God is a murderous blind hog, and there is no dream, and The Iceman cometh like a thief in the night, and we wearily welcome him because there is no longer a kick in any booze whatever.

Again, my gratitude for your appreciation. It means a lot. Very sincerely, Eugene O'Neil

---

22.3 REVIEW OF *THE ICEMAN COMETH*—ISIDOR SCHNEIDER

New Masses, October 29th 1946

"The Iceman Cometh"

O'Neill's world is a **stagnant** ***puddle of decay, in which "sinful" man must*** **flounder and** ***die.***

WITH THE EXCEPTION of three prostitutes whose role is subsidiary and less important than that of the offstage women characters—two wives and a mother, one long deceased and hypocritically lamented, one freshly murdered and one betrayed into jail—the characters of Eugene O'Neill's *The Iceman Cometh* are all men, and, with two exceptions, they are all incurable alcoholics.

They include the Harvard graduate son of a jailed stock market racketeer; an ex-anarchist who has rejected anarchism as merely another form of the power drive which his comrades oppose and envy in its established forms and who has sunk into apathetic cynicism mitigated by "philosophy"; another anarchist so sodden in drink that when he emerges for brief intervals out of his coma it is only to yammer an inarticulate hatred of workers as "slaves"; a jobless publicity man who drinks, so he tells himself, to blot out his wife's infidelity; a Boer general and a British captain who observe a fuzzy truce over the whiskey bottle; a Negro who recalls former great days as operator of a gambling house when he was able to pay big protection money to the police and stand generous treats to rum hounds; a young sot who takes the earnings of one of the three "tarts," as they insist on being called, while he and she nurse the "pipe dream" of eventual marriage and a Jersey farm on which they will settle down to bask in curative Nature; an ex-carnival hand whose "pipe dream" is to return to glory as short-change artist in a cashier's cage; and a dismissed cop whose "pipe dream" is to get to the right higher-ups whose influence will restore him to the Force.

The one sober man among the habitues is an Italian bartender quietly making his pile and adding to it by the earnings of his "stable" of two "tarts." The completing figure is the owner of the joint, Harry Hope, himself an alcoholic, on whose befuddled generosity the rest live. He is a former small-time Tammany politician mourning a wife dead twenty years, grief for whom has presumably kept him from stirring out of the place ever since. Two outsiders intrude upon this snug nest of boozy torpor. One is an entirely new figure, a youth who is the son of the arrested woman leader of a West Coast anarchist group and former sweetheart of the ex-anarchist philosopher. The youth has come to the older man for help in a personal crisis. He has come in the belief and hope that the older man is his father and that he will get from him the stern but obligated direction that he craves, as do all orphans whether their parents are missing through death or illegitimacy.

The other outsider is an old attraction, a free-spending salesman named Hickman—Hickey, for short. Twice a year, on his return from sales trips but particularly on the occasion of Harry Hope's birthday, such as tonight, Hickey stands unlimited treat to the bums and entertains them with drummer's jokes culminating in a description of the probable assignation of his wife with the iceman.

The scene opens in the small hours of the night with the bums asleep or yawning over the saloon tables, waiting for Hickey. Never before has he been so late and from the desultory remarks about it a conversation flares up in which, one after the other, they reveal themselves. Among other things it gradually becomes clear that the youth has betrayed his mother to the police and has come to his hoped-for father in the belief that he too has nursed a vengeful hate for the woman, a hate that has been the other side of their dependent love. He has come either to be justified in their mutual hate for her or to be condemned in their mutual love for her. If the latter, the youth wants to be ordered to atone, by suicide, for the living prison death he has inflicted on his mother. By the time Hickey arrives the various self-revelations are almost complete; only a few additional strokes are needed to fill out or correct the pictures.

BUT the Hickey who arrives is a changed man and the good time they have been waiting for turns out an ordeal. Hickey provides drinks and food on a more lavish scale than ever before but he himself will not take a drop; and in place of his drummer's hilarity he gives them sermons. He explains that he no longer needs the stupefaction of liquor to bring him peace. He has achieved serenity by facing out the conflict within himself, by surrendering his "pipe dream" and accepting reality. The process was hard and agonizing, he admits, but it made a new man of him. The contentment he has reached through it is so satisfying that he feels the salesman's compulsion with a good thing in his hand to sell it to the others.

Under Hickey's prodding the drunks, one by one, go through the torment of "facing themselves," acquiring in the process a thorough hatred of Hickey, one another and themselves. The usually rowdy banquet becomes a lugubrious confessional and a recriminatory free-for-all.

The five-cent rot-gut whiskey they have been swilling suddenly loses its kick. Even the birthday champagne tastes flat. Their own desire for it is gone; and when they try, deliberately, to drink themselves into insensibility, the liquor has no effect.

But through this they arrive at the final stages of self-revelation. It turns out that the jobless publicity man has driven his wife into the arms of a lover to justify an already settled alcoholism; that it was an act of treachery to his people that makes it unsafe for the Boer general to live in South Africa; that it was the British captain's embezzlement of regimental funds that makes it similarly advisable for him to live at a distance; that the Negro hates the white trash here, and the white world in general; that Harry Hope hated his "beloved" wife for her nagging efforts to keep him sober and push his political career, and his twenty-year immurement in the dive is to shut out all reminders of the ambitions she had for him.

Hickey gets them at last, all except the ex-anarchist philosopher, to put their pipe dreams to the test. They go out, some in clothes redeemed for them from the pawnshop by Hickey, to get jobs; Harry Hope to take that walk around the ward that he has been promising himself for twenty years; and the young sot and his tart to get married and look for that farm in Jersey. But the sortie into the world outside is brief and despairing. Each returns miserable and licked. The "tarts" finally concede that they are "whores," the bartender that he is a "pimp," and the young sot and his tart that they are not an engaged couple but "whore" and "pimp."

At this point Hickey in a long and jarringly explicit speech anounces that he has killed his wife to be free of the sense of guilt which her loving patience and unfailing forgiveness of his drunken adulteries has brought to an unbearable intensity. Death was the iceman into whose arms he has finally pushed her. As the police, whom he himself has summoned, take him away, the ex-anarchist philosopher can no longer maintain his indifference. He understands that he alone resisted Hickey's call to face oneself because he is the worst failure among them and has the least courage. In his agony he says the word that frees the youth to kill himself. The sound of the body, crashing offstage, sends the distraught philosopher rushing out of the room.

With Hickey gone, and his counsel pitched outside as the ravings of a murderous lunatic, the rest return to their drink. They swallow it with revived need and the drink itself recovers its kick. The cozy anesthesia returns; the pipe dreams are efficacious again.

THIS drink-numbed guilt is what the play is about. To me the most astonishing thing about the play is that the critics, along with O'Neill, have been trying to read universal significance into this confined thing; have taken this tiny, special, remote and unrepresentative puddle of life as the basis for a judgment of humanity. They have ignored a setting overwhelmingly larger, filled with characters overwhelmingly different— the purposeful world outside and the undefeated people moving vigorously and freely in it, those who have the will to struggle, to forgive, to endure, who do without the paralysis and the pipe dream.

Curiously enough this is implied all through the play itself, and it is another revelation of the extent to which artists are unaware of much in their own work that O'Neill has been unable to read his own implications. The knowledge and the value of the working world outside is implied in the very content of the "pipe dreams" of the derelicts. The content is work, security and love, which in the world outside are not surrendered, are at least struggled for if not yet wholly won. The ex-publicity man, the ex-Harvard law student, the ex-policeman, the ex-carnival hand, even the Boer general and the British captain all go out in at least a pretense of finding work. The young sot makes one last effort to dignify his shabby love.

And in another, and tangential way, the values of the outer world intrude even in the consciousness of the one man who profits in the puddle world. Forced to concede that he is a "pimp," the bartender seeks to win some social sanction, in the puddle world at least, by trying to reason the youth and the philosopher into a co-career in pimping. And he is rejected. In these and other ways, the O'Neill who wrote the play contradicts the O'Neill commenting on it.

The simple fact is that the play is far too restricted in its range and in the very special nature of its personal conflicts to serve as social commentary or as a judgment upon life or upon any large reality of life. What the play comes to is a reduced and thereby intensified reconsideration of the problem that has obsessed O'Neill throughout the second phase of his work, the problem of sin and self-punishment. That problem has pressed with a double weight upon him, the weight of his Catholic original-sin-and-life-long-penitence-superstition and the different but, to him, equally oppressive Freudian concept of the guilt sense born of secret hostility to those supposedly beloved and admired. The undeniable impact of the play comes from the fact that, unlike O'Neill's previous psychoanalytic plays, which were like caricatures in their literal Freudianism, what is applied in *The Iceman Cometh* is an asimilated knowledge that is used deftly and not stuck on like labels.

Critics have sought to explain what is effective in the play either as the appeal of O'Neill's compassion or as the operation of his supposedly fabulous sense of "theater." Neither of these seem to me to satisfy as explanations. For if what O'Neill says of humanity were what he actually felt, and not the evasive rationalization that it seems to me, then he could not have put compassion into the play. The compassion is there but it arises out of O'Neill's confining himself to an essentially simple human ordeal, the ordeal of guilt.

On the other hand, if the impact of the play is to be attributed to O'Neill's sense of theater how is one to account for such defiance of sure-fire theater as a playing time that far exceeds the supposed endurance of the modern Western audience; a long first act which is almost continuous exposition and, to use the critical adjective, "static," and therefore "bad theater"; and finally, in the last act, that supposedly fatal piece of "bad theater" the longer-than-five-minute speech—a fifteen-minute speech, in fact, and a rather poor one as well. Here is enough "bad theater" to counteract any "good theater," if one looks to play-carpentering know-how to account for O'Neill's dramatic effect.

The fact of the matter is that as in greater plays, such as the Greek tragedies and the Elizabethan tragedies, *The Iceman Cometh* draws its power from the conflict in the conscience. That remains today, as it always has been, the supreme source of dramatic conflict. It is given here in a peculiarly restricted and a peculiarly muddy form which has kept it from having any large or clear significance; but it is packed full within its particular limitations; it concentrates great force in its small area.

But because it represses and leaves mutilated its potential social inferences the play offers nothing to take away as a philosophical conclusion. No later statements, sweet or bitter, about humanity that O'Neill can make can put into the play what is not there. Actually O'Neill's best opportunity for a philosophical statement is evaded. The philosophical ex-anarchist, who is the most articulate character in the play and, more than any other, O'Neill's spokesman, should offer some concluding statement—as the audience expects him to—when he realizes the utter hollowness of his philosophy of apathy. But instead he runs off the stage, silent. Even as commentary the running off has no significance, for he has been running off all through the play. And at that point it becomes O'Neill's evasion. For at that climax, where some conclusion about life should be uttered, nothing is said except that the drinks have recovered their kick. The only conclusion that can be drawn is that chronic alcoholics feel best when drunk or, to extend it, that those who cannot live without an excessive load of illusions must have an excessive load of illusions.

As a production there is nothing the American theater has recently put on that equals this Theater Guild offering. Here the Guild functions as an established theater should. The performance has the suppleness, the ease, the conviction of ensemble acting somewhat comparable to the great Russian companies. It would be pointless to single out individual renditions and grade them. For instance, James Barton as Hickey seemed to give the least assured performance but a reading of the script published concurrently with the opening of the play shows his part to be the one written with the least assurance, and shows that, in fact, Barton made up in the performance for special difficulties in the role. Finally, one must pay tribute to the magnificent sets designed by Robert Edmond Jones.

22.4 GAIN IN MENTAL ILLS SEEN

New York Times, August 16th 1946

8,000,000 Americans Afflicted, Health Service Reports

THE UNITED STATES PUBLIC HEALTH SERVICE forecast today an increase in mental ailments but said it now has the machinery to "work toward elimination of mental or nervous illnesses" among citizens of this country.

"An increase of mental cases out of proportion to the increase of total population is forecast," a statement from the service said, "since the incidence of mental disease rises with age, and the number of Americans aged 65 and over is expected to double in the next forty years."

The statement included an estimate that 8,000,000 Americans are suffering from some form of mental or nervous illness now. It added that the "blueprint" for a broad drive against such afflictions is provided in the new National Mental Health Act.

The statement was issued at the opening of the first meeting of the National Advisory Mental Health Council.

22.5 PRODUCTION PHOTO FROM *THE ICEMAN COMETH*

Harry Hope's saloon and its despairing pipe-dreaming patrons in the 1946 production of Eugene O'Neill's *The Iceman Cometh*. Though written in 1939, O'Neill refused to produce *Iceman* during the war when, he wrote, "we need[ed] an unquestioning faith in all pipe dreams, however irrational, lest we be defeated." The play was eventually produced in 1946, when Congress passed the National Mental Health Act to help counter the drastic postwar increase in mental illnesses. People, perhaps, had lost their pipe dreams and discovered, as O'Neill put it, "God is a murderous blind hog, and there is no dream, and The Iceman cometh like a thief in the night, and we wearily welcome him because there is no longer a kick in any booze whatever" (*Selected Letters* 532).

Source: Photo by Vandamm Studio © Billy Rose Theatre Division, the New York Public Library for the Performing Arts

22.6 *THE ICEMAN COMETH*—EUGENE O'NEILL

CHARACTERS

HARRY HOPE, proprietor of a saloon and rooming house*
ED MOSHER, Hope's brother-in-law, one-time circus man*
PAT McGLOIN, one-time Police Lieutenant*
WILLIE OBAN, a Harvard Law School alumnus*
JOE MOTT, one-time proprietor of a Negro gambling house
PIET WETJOEN ("THE GENERAL"), one-time leader of a Boer commando*
CECIL LEWIS ("THE CAPTAIN"), one-time Captain of British infantry*
JAMES CAMERON ("JIMMY TOMORROW"), one-time Boer War correspondent*
HUGO KALMAR, one-time editor of Anarchist periodicals
LARRY SLADE, one-time Syndicalist-Anarchist*
ROCKY PIOGGI, night bartender*
DON PARRITT*
PEARL*
MARGIE* } street walkers
CORA
CHUCK MORELLO, day bartender*
THEODORE HICKMAN (HICKEY), a hardware salesman
MORAN
LIEB

*Roomers at Harry Hope's.

SCENES

ACT ONE

Scene—Back room and a section of the bar at Harry Hope's—early morning in summer, 1912.

ACT TWO

Scene—Back room, around midnight of the same day.

ACT THREE

Scene—Bar and a section of the back room—morning of the following day.

ACT FOUR

Scene—Same as Act One. Back room and a section of the bar—around 1:30 A.M. of the next day.

★

Harry Hope's is a Raines-Law hotel of the period, a cheap ginmill of the five-cent whiskey, last-resort variety situated on the downtown West Side of New York. The building, owned by Hope, is a narrow five-story structure of the tenement type, the second floor a flat occupied by the proprietor. The renting of rooms on the upper floors, under the Raines-Law loopholes, makes the establishment legally a hotel and gives it the privilege of serving liquor in the back room of the bar after closing hours and on Sundays, provided a meal is served with the booze, thus making a back room legally a hotel restaurant. This food provision was generally circumvented by putting a property sandwich in the middle of each table, an old desiccated ruin of dust-laden bread and mummified ham or cheese which only the drunkest yokel from the sticks ever regarded as anything but a noisome table decoration. But at Harry Hope's, Hope being a former minor Tammanyite and still possessing friends, this food technicality is ignored as irrelevant, except during the fleeting alarms of reform agitation. Even Hope's back room is not a separate room, but simply the rear of the barroom divided from the bar by drawing a dirty black curtain across the room.

★

ACT ONE

SCENE—*The back room and a section of the bar of Harry Hope's saloon on an early morning in summer, 1912. The right wall of the back room is a dirty black curtain which separates it from the bar. At rear, this curtain is drawn back from the wall so the bartender can get in and out. The back room is crammed with round tables and chairs placed so close together that it is a difficult squeeze to pass between them. In the middle of the rear wall is a door opening on a hallway. In the left corner, built out into the room, is the toilet with a sign "This is it" on the door. Against the middle of the left wall is a nickel-in-the-slot phonograph. Two windows, so glazed with grime one cannot see through them, are in the left wall, looking out on a backyard. The walls and ceiling once were white, but it was a long time ago, and they are now so splotched, peeled, stained and dusty that their color can best be described as dirty. The floor, with iron spittoons placed here and there, is covered with sawdust. Lighting comes from single wall brackets, two at left and two at rear.*

There are three rows of tables, from front to back. Three are in the front line. The one at left-front has four chairs; the one at center-front, four; the one at right-front, five. At rear of, and half between, front tables one and two is a table of the second row with five chairs. A table, similarly placed at rear of front tables two and three, also has five chairs. The third row of tables, four chairs to one and six to the other, is against the rear wall on either side of the door.

At right of this dividing curtain is a section of the barroom, with the end of the bar seen at rear, a door to the hall at left of it. At front is a table with four chairs. Light comes from the street windows off right, the gray subdued light of early morning in a narrow street. In the back room, Larry Slade and Hugo Kalmar are at the table at left-front, Hugo in a chair facing right, Larry at rear of table facing front, with an empty chair between them. A fourth chair is at right of table, facing left. Hugo is a small man in his late fifties. He has a head much too big for his body, a high forehead, crinkly long black hair streaked with gray, a square face with a pug nose, a walrus mustache, black eyes which peer nearsightedly from behind thick-lensed spectacles, tiny hands and feet. He is dressed in threadbare black clothes and his white shirt is frayed at collar and cuffs, but everything about him is fastidiously clean. Even his flowing Windsor tie is neatly tied. There is a foreign atmosphere about him, the stamp of an alien radical, a strong resemblance to the type Anarchist as portrayed, bomb in hand, in newspaper cartoons. He is asleep now, bent forward in his chair, his arms folded on the table, his head resting sideways on his arms.

Larry Slade is sixty. He is tall, raw-boned, with coarse straight white hair, worn long and raggedly cut. He has a gaunt Irish face with a big nose, high cheekbones, a lantern jaw with a week's stubble of beard, a mystic's meditative pale-blue eyes with a gleam of sharp sardonic humor in them. As slovenly as Hugo is neat, his clothes are dirty and much slept in. His gray flannel shirt, open at the neck, has the appearance of having never been washed. From the way he methodically scratches himself with his long-fingered, hairy hands, he is lousy and reconciled to being so. He is the only occupant of the room who is not asleep. He stares in front of him, an expression of tired tolerance giving his face the quality of a pitying but weary old priest's.

All four chairs at the middle table, front, are occupied. Joe Mott sits at left front of the table, facing front. Behind him, facing right-front, is Piet Wetjoen ("The General"). At center of the table, rear, James Cameron ("Jimmy Tomorrow") sits facing front. At right of table, opposite Joe, is Cecil Lewis ("The Captain").

Joe Mott is a Negro, about fifty years old, brown-skinned, stocky, wearing a light suit that had once been flashily sporty but is now about to fall apart. His pointed tan buttoned shoes, faded pink shirt and bright tie belong to the same vintage. Still, he manages to preserve an atmosphere of nattiness and there is nothing dirty about his appearance. His face is only mildly negroid in type. The nose is thin and his lips are not noticeably thick. His hair is crinkly and he is beginning to get bald. A scar from a knife slash runs from his left cheekbone to jaw. His face would be hard and tough if it were not for its good nature and lazy humor. He is asleep, his nodding head supported by his left hand.

Piet Wetjoen, the Boer, is in his fifties, a huge man with a bald head and a long grizzled beard. He is slovenly dressed in a dirty shapeless patched suit, spotted by food. A Dutch farmer type, his once great muscular strength has been debauched into flaccid tallow. But despite his blubbery mouth and sodden bloodshot blue eyes, there is still a suggestion of old authority lurking in him like a memory of the drowned. He is hunched forward, both elbows on the table, his hands on each side of his head for support.

James Cameron ("Jimmy Tomorrow") is about the same size and age as Hugo, a small man. Like Hugo, he wears threadbare black, and everything about him is clean. But the resemblance ceases there. Jimmy has a face like an old well-bred, gentle bloodhound's, with folds of flesh hanging from each side of his mouth, and big brown friendly guileless eyes, more bloodshot than any bloodhound's ever were. He has mouse-colored thinning hair, a little bulbous nose, buck teeth in a small rabbit mouth. But his forehead is fine, his eyes are intelligent and there once was a competent ability in him. His speech is educated, with the ghost of a Scotch rhythm in it. His manners are those of a gentleman. There is a quality about him of a prim, Victorian old maid, and at the same time of a likable, affectionate boy who has never grown up. He sleeps, chin on chest, hands folded in his lap.

Cecil Lewis ("The Captain") is as obviously English as Yorkshire pudding and just as obviously the former army officer. He is going on sixty. His hair and military mustache are white, his eyes bright blue, his complexion that of a turkey. His lean figure is still erect and square-shouldered. He is stripped to the waist, his coat, shirt, undershirt, collar and tie crushed up into a pillow on the table in front of him, his head sideways on this pillow, facing front, his arms dangling toward the floor. On his lower left shoulder is the big ragged scar of an old wound.

At the table at right, front, Harry Hope, the proprietor, sits in the middle, facing front, with Pat McGloin on his right and Ed Mosher on his left, the other two chairs being unoccupied.

Both McGloin and Mosher are big paunchy men. McGloin has his old occupation of policeman stamped all over him. He is in his fifties, sandy-haired, bullet-headed, jowly, with protruding ears and little round eyes. His face must once have been brutal and greedy, but time and whiskey have melted it down into a good-

humored, parasite's characterlessness. He wears old clothes and is slovenly. He is slumped sideways on his chair, his head drooping jerkily toward one shoulder.

Ed Mosher is going on sixty. He has a round kewpie's face—a kewpie who is an unshaven habitual drunkard. He looks like an enlarged, elderly, bald edition of the village fat boy—a sly fat boy, congenitally indolent, a practical joker, a born grafter and con merchant. But amusing and essentially harmless, even in his most enterprising days, because always too lazy to carry crookedness beyond petty swindling. The influence of his old circus career is apparent in his get-up. His worn clothes are flashy; he wears phony rings and a heavy brass watch-chain (not connected to a watch). Like McGloin, he is slovenly. His head is thrown back, his big mouth open.

Harry Hope is sixty, white-haired, so thin the description "bag of bones" was made for him. He has the face of an old family horse, prone to tantrums, with balkiness always smoldering in its wall eyes, waiting for any excuse to shy and pretend to take the bit in its teeth. Hope is one of those men whom everyone likes on sight, a softhearted slob, without malice, feeling superior to no one, a sinner among sinners, a born easy mark for every appeal. He attempts to hide his defenselessness behind a testy truculent manner, but this has never fooled anyone. He is a little deaf, but not half as deaf as he sometimes pretends. His sight is failing but is not as bad as he complains it is. He wears five-and-ten-cent-store spectacles which are so out of alignment that one eye at times peers half over one glass while the other eye looks half under the other. He has badly fitting store teeth, which click like castanets when he begins to fume. He is dressed in an old coat from one suit and pants from another.

In a chair facing right at the table in the second line, between the first two tables, front, sits Willie Oban, his head on his left arm outstretched along the table edge. He is in his late thirties, of average height, thin. His haggard, dissipated face has a small nose, a pointed chin, blue eyes with colorless lashes and brows. His blond hair, badly in need of a cut, clings in a limp part to his skull. His eyelids flutter continually as if any light were too strong for his eyes. The clothes he wears belong on a scarecrow. They seem constructed of an inferior grade of dirty blotting paper. His shoes are even more disreputable, wrecks of imitation leather, one laced with twine, the other with a bit of wire. He has no socks, and his bare feet show through holes in the soles, with his big toes sticking out of the uppers. He keeps muttering and twitching in his sleep.

As the curtain rises, Rocky, the night bartender, comes from the bar through the curtain and stands looking over the back room. He is a Neapolitan-American in his late twenties, squat and muscular, with a flat, swarthy face and beady eyes. The sleeves of his collarless shirt are rolled up on his thick, powerful arms and he wears a soiled apron. A tough guy but sentimental, in his way, and good-natured. He signals to Larry with a cautious "Sstt" and motions him to see if Hope is asleep. Larry rises from his chair to look at Hope and nods to Rocky. Rocky goes back in the bar but immediately returns with a bottle of bar whiskey and a glass. He squeezes between the tables to Larry.

ROCKY—(*in a low voice out of the side of his mouth*) Make it fast. (*Larry pours a drink and gulps it down. Rocky takes the bottle and puts it on the table where Willie Oban is.*) Don't want de Boss to get wise when he's got one of his tightwad buns on. (*He chuckles with an amused glance at Hope.*) Jees, ain't de old bastard a riot when he starts dat bull about turnin' over a new leaf? "Not a damned drink on de house," he tells me, "and all dese bums got to pay up deir room rent. Beginnin' tomorrow," he says. Jees, yuh'd tink he meant it! (*He sits down in the chair at Larry's left.*)

LARRY—(*grinning*) I'll be glad to pay up—tomorrow. And I know my fellow inmates will promise the same. They've all a touching credulity concerning tomorrows. (*a half-drunken mockery in his eyes*) It'll be a great day for them, tomorrow—the Feast of All Fools, with brass bands playing! Their ships will come in, loaded to the gunwales with cancelled regrets and promises fulfilled and clean slates and new leases!

ROCKY—(*cynically*) Yeah, and a ton of hop!

LARRY—(*leans toward him, a comical intensity in his low voice*) Don't mock the faith! Have you no respect for religion, you unregenerate Wop? What's it matter if the truth is that their favoring breeze has the stink of nickel whiskey on its breath, and their sea is a growler of lager and ale, and their ships are long since looted and scuttled and sunk on the bottom? To hell with the truth! As the history of the world proves, the truth has no bearing on anything. It's irrelevant and immaterial, as the lawyers say. The lie of a pipe dream is what gives life to the whole misbegotten mad lot of us, drunk or sober. And that's enough philosophic wisdom to give you for one drink of rot-gut.

ROCKY—(*grins kiddingly*) De old Foolosopher, like Hickey calls yuh, ain't yuh? I s'pose you don't fall for no pipe dream?

LARRY—(*a bit stiffly*) I don't, no. Mine are all dead and buried behind me. What's before me is the comforting fact that death is a fine long sleep, and I'm damned tired, and it can't come too soon for me.

ROCKY—Yeah, just hangin' around hopin' you'll croak, ain't yuh? Well, I'm bettin' you'll have a good long wait. Jees, somebody'll have to take an axe to croak you!

LARRY—(*grins*) Yes, it's my bad luck to be cursed with an iron constitution that even Harry's booze can't corrode.

ROCKY—De old anarchist wise guy dat knows all de answers! Dat's you, huh?

LARRY—(*frowns*) Forget the anarchist part of it. I'm through with the Movement long since. I saw men didn't want to be saved from themselves, for that would mean they'd have to give up greed, and they'll never pay that price for liberty. So I said to the world, God bless all here, and may the best man win and die of gluttony! And I took a seat in the grandstand of philosophical detachment to fall asleep observing the cannibals do their death dance. (*He chuckles at his own fancy—reaches over and shakes Hugo's shoulder.*) Ain't I telling him the truth, Comrade Hugo?

ROCKY—Aw, fer Chris' sake, don't get dat bughouse bum started!

HUGO—(*raises his head and peers at Rocky blearily through his thick spectacles—in a guttural declamatory tone*) Capitalist swine! Bourgeois stool pigeons! Have the slaves no right to sleep even? (*Then he grins at Rocky and his manner changes to a giggling, wheedling playfulness, as though he were talking to a child.*) Hello, leedle Rocky! Leedle monkey-face! Vere is your leedle slave girls? (*with an abrupt change to a bullying tone*) Don't be a fool! Loan me a dollar! Damned bourgeois Wop! The great Malatesta is my good friend! Buy me a trink! (*He seems to run down, and is overcome by drowsiness. His head sinks to the table again and he is at once fast asleep.*)

ROCKY—He's out again. (*more exasperated than angry*) He's lucky no one don't take his cracks serious or he'd wake up every mornin' in a hospital.

LARRY—(*regarding Hugo with pity*) No. No one takes him seriously. That's his epitaph. Not even the comrades any more. If I've been through with the Movement long since, it's been through with him, and, thanks to whiskey, he's the only one doesn't know it.

ROCKY—I've let him get by wid too much. He's goin' to pull dat slave-girl stuff on me once too often. (*His manner changes to defensive argument.*) Hell, yuh'd tink I wuz a pimp or somethin'. Everybody knows me knows I ain't. A pimp don't hold no job. I'm a bartender. Dem tarts, Margie and Poil, dey're just a side line to pick up some extra dough. Strictly business, like dey was fighters and I was deir manager, see? I fix the cops for dem so's dey can hustle widout gettin' pinched. Hell, dey'd be on de Island most of de time if it wasn't fer me. And I don't beat dem up like a pimp would. I treat dem fine. Dey like me. We're pals, see? What if I do take deir dough? Dey'd on'y trow it away. Tarts can't hang on to dough. But I'm a bartender and I work hard for my livin' in dis dump. You know dat, Larry.

LARRY—(*with inner sardonic amusement—flatteringly*) A shrewd business man, who doesn't miss any opportunity to get on in the world. That's what I'd call you.

ROCKY—(*pleased*) Sure ting. Dat's me. Grab another ball, Larry. (*Larry pours a drink from the bottle on Willie's table and gulps it down. Rocky glances around the room.*) Yuh'd never tink all dese bums had a good bed upstairs to go to. Scared if dey hit the hay dey wouldn't be here when Hickey showed up, and dey'd miss a coupla drinks. Dat's what kept you up too, ain't it?

LARRY—It is. But not so much the hope of booze, if you can believe that. I've got the blues and Hickey's a great one to make a joke of everything and cheer you up.

ROCKY—Yeah, some kidder! Remember how he woiks up dat gag about his wife, when he's cockeyed, cryin' over her picture and den springin' it on yuh all of a sudden dat he left her in de hay wid de iceman? (*He laughs.*) I wonder what's happened to him. Yuh could set your watch by his periodicals before dis. Always got here a coupla days before Harry's birthday party, and now he's on'y got till tonight to make it.

I hope he shows soon. Dis dump is like de morgue wid all dese bums passed out. (*Willie Oban jerks and twitches in his sleep and begins to mumble. They watch him.*)

WILLIE—(*blurts from his dream*) It's a lie! (*miserably*) Papa! Papa!

LARRY—Poor devil. (*then angry with himself*) But to hell with pity! It does no good. I'm through with it!

ROCKY—Dreamin' about his old man. From what de old-timers say, de old gent sure made a pile of dough in de bucket-shop game before de cops got him. (*He considers Willie frowningly.*) Jees, I've seen him bad before but never dis bad. Look at dat get-up. Been playin' de old reliever game. Sold his suit and shoes at Solly's two days ago. Solly give him two bucks and a bum outfit. Yesterday he sells de bum one back to Solly for four bits and gets dese rags to put on. Now he's through. Dat's Solly's final edition he wouldn't take back for nuttin'. Willie sure is on de bottom. I ain't never seen no one so bad, except Hickey on de end of a coupla his bats.

LARRY—(*sardonically*) It's a great game, the pursuit of happiness.

ROCKY—Harry don't know what to do about him. He called up his old lady's lawyer like he always does when Willie gets licked. Yuh remember dey used to send down a private dick to give him the rush to a cure, but de lawyer tells Harry nix, de old lady's off of Willie for keeps dis time and he can go to hell.

LARRY—(*watches Willie, who is shaking in his sleep like an old dog*) There's the consolation that he hasn't far to go! (*As if replying to this, Willie comes to a crisis of jerks and moans. Larry adds in a comically intense, crazy whisper*) Be God, he's knocking on the door right now!

WILLIE—(*suddenly yells in his nightmare*) It's a Goddamned lie! (*He begins to sob.*) Oh, Papa! Jesus! (*All the occupants of the room stir on their chairs but none of them wakes up except Hope.*)

ROCKY—(*grabs his shoulder and shakes him*) Hey, you! Nix! Cut out de noise! (*Willie opens his eyes to stare around him with a bewildered horror.*)

HOPE—(*opens one eye to peer over his spectacles—drowsily*) Who's that yelling?

ROCKY—Willie, Boss. De Brooklyn boys is after him.

HOPE—(*querulously*) Well, why don't you give the poor feller a drink and keep him quiet? Bejees, can't I get a wink of sleep in my own back room?

ROCKY—(*indignantly to Larry*) Listen to that blind-eyed, deef old bastard, will yuh? He give me strict orders not to let Willie hang up no more drinks, no matter—

HOPE—(*mechanically puts a hand to his ear in the gesture of deafness*) What's that? I can't hear you. (*then drowsily irascible*) You're a cockeyed liar. Never refused a drink to anyone needed it bad in my life! Told you to use your judgment. Ought to know better. You're too busy thinking up ways to cheat me. Oh, I ain't as blind as you think. I can still see a cash register, bejees!

ROCKY—(*grins at him affectionately now—flatteringly*) Sure, Boss. Swell chance of foolin' you!

HOPE—I'm wise to you and your sidekick, Chuck. Bejees, you're burglars, not barkeeps! Blind-eyed, deef old bastard, am I? Oh, I heard you! Heard you often when you didn't think. You and Chuck laughing behind my back, telling people you throw the money up in the air and whatever sticks to the ceiling is my share! A fine couple of crooks! You'd steal the pennies off your dead mother's eyes!

ROCKY—(*winks at Larry*) Aw, Harry, me and Chuck was on'y kiddin'.

HOPE—(*more drowsily*) I'll fire both of you. Bejees, if you think you can play me for an easy mark, you've come to the wrong house. No one ever played Harry Hope for a sucker!

ROCKY—(*to Larry*) No one but everybody.

HOPE—(*his eyes shut again—mutters*) Least you could do—keep things quiet—(*He falls asleep.*)

WILLIE—(*pleadingly*) Give me a drink, Rocky. Harry said it was all right. God, I need a drink.

ROCKY—Den grab it. It's right under your nose.

WILLIE—(*avidly*) Thanks. (*He takes the bottle with both twitching hands and tilts it to his lips and gulps down the whiskey in big swallows.*)

ROCKY—(*sharply*) When! When! (*He grabs the bottle.*) I didn't say, take a bath! (*showing the bottle to Larry—indignantly*) Jees, look! He's killed a half pint or more! (*He turns on Willie angrily, but Willie has closed his eyes and is sitting quietly, shuddering, waiting for the effect.*)

LARRY—(*with a pitying glance*) Leave him be, the poor devil. A half pint of that dynamite in one swig will fix him for a while—if it doesn't kill him.

ROCKY—(*shrugs his shoulders and sits down again*) Aw right by me. It ain't my booze. (*Behind him, in the chair at left of the middle table, Joe Mott, the Negro, has been waking up.*)

JOE—(*his eyes blinking sleepily*) Whose booze? Gimme some. I don't care whose. Where's Hickey? Ain't he come yet? What time's it, Rocky?

ROCKY—Gettin' near time to open up. Time you begun to sweep up in de bar.

JOE—(*lazily*) Never mind de time. If Hickey ain't come, it's time Joe goes to sleep again. I was dreamin' Hickey come in de door, crackin' one of dem drummer's jokes, wavin' a big bankroll and we was all goin' be drunk for two weeks. Wake up and no luck. (*Suddenly his eyes open wide.*) Wait a minute, dough. I got idea.

Say, Larry, how 'bout dat young guy, Parritt, came to look you up last night and rented a room? Where's he at?

LARRY—Up in his room, asleep. No hope in him, anyway, Joe. He's broke.

JOE—Dat what he told you? Me and Rocky knows different. Had a roll when he paid you his room rent, didn't he, Rocky? I seen it.

ROCKY—Yeah. He flashed it like he forgot and den tried to hide it quick.

LARRY—*(surprised and resentful)* He did, did he?

ROCKY—Yeah, I figgered he don't belong, but he said he was a friend of yours.

LARRY—He's a liar. I wouldn't know him if he hadn't told me who he was. His mother and I were friends years ago on the Coast. *(He hesitates—then lowering his voice)* You've read in the papers about that bombing on the Coast when several people got killed? Well, the one woman they pinched, Rosa Parritt, is his mother. They'll be coming up for trial soon, and there's no chance for them. She'll get life, I think. I'm telling you this so you'll know why if Don acts a bit queer, and not jump on him. He must be hard hit. He's her only kid.

ROCKY—*(nods—then thoughtfully)* Why ain't he out dere stickin' by her?

LARRY—*(frowns)* Don't ask questions. Maybe there's a good reason.

ROCKY—*(stares at him—understandingly)* Sure. I get it. *(then wonderingly)* But den what kind of a sap is he to hang on to his right name?

LARRY—*(irritably)* I'm telling you I don't know anything and I don't want to know. To hell with the Movement and all connected with it! I'm out of it, and everything else, and damned glad to be.

ROCKY—*(shrugs his shoulders—indifferently)* Well, don't tink I'm interested in dis Parritt guy. He's nuttin' to me.

JOE—Me neider. If dere's one ting more'n anudder I cares nuttin' about, it's de sucker game you and Hugo call de Movement. *(He chuckles—reminiscently)* Reminds me of damn fool argument me and Mose Porter has de udder night. He's drunk and I'm drunker. He says, "Socialist and Anarchist, we ought to shoot dem dead. Dey's all no-good sons of bitches." I says, "Hold on, you talk 's if Anarchists and Socialists was de same." "Dey is," he says. "Dey's both no-good bastards." "No, dey ain't," I says. "I'll explain the difference. De Anarchist he never works. He drinks but he never buys, and if he do ever get a nickel, he blows it in on bombs, and he wouldn't give you nothin'. So go ahead and shoot him. But de Socialist, sometimes, he's got a job, and if he gets ten bucks, he's bound by his religion to split fifty-fifty wid you. You say—how about my cut, Comrade? And you gets de five. So you don't shoot no Socialists while I'm around. Dat is, not if dey got anything. Of course, if dey's broke, den dey's no-good bastards, too." *(He laughs, immensely tickled.)*

LARRY—*(grins with sardonic appreciation)* Be God, Joe, you've got all the beauty of human nature and the practical wisdom of the world in that little parable.

ROCKY—*(winks at Joe)* Sure, Larry ain't de on'y wise guy in dis dump, hey, Joe? *(At a sound from the hall he turns as Don Parritt appears in the doorway. Rocky speaks to Larry out of the side of his mouth.)* Here's your guy. *(Parritt comes forward. He is eighteen, tall and broad-shouldered but thin, gangling and awkward. His face is good-looking, with blond curly hair and large regular features, but his personality is unpleasant. There is a shifting defiance and ingratiation in his light-blue eyes and an irritating aggressiveness in his manner. His clothes and shoes are new, comparatively expensive, sporty in style. He looks as though he belonged in a pool room patronized by would-be sports. He glances around defensively, sees Larry and comes forward.)*

PARRITT—Hello, Larry. *(He nods to Rocky and Joe.)* Hello. *(They nod and size him up with expressionless eyes.)*

LARRY—*(without cordiality)* What's up? I thought you'd be asleep.

PARRITT—Couldn't make it. I got sick of lying awake. Thought I might as well see if you were around.

LARRY—*(indicates the chair on the right of table)* Sit down and join the bums then. *(Parritt sits down. Larry adds meaningfully)* The rules of the house are that drinks may be served at all hours.

PARRITT—*(forcing a smile)* I get you. But, hell, I'm just about broke. *(He catches Rocky's and Joe's contemptuous glances—quickly)* Oh, I know you guys saw—You think I've got a roll. Well, you're all wrong. I'll show you. *(He takes a small wad of dollar bills from his pocket.)* It's all ones. And I've got to live on it till I get a job. *(then with defensive truculence)* You think I fixed up a phony, don't you? Why the hell would I? Where would I get a real roll? You don't get rich doing what I've been doing. Ask Larry. You're lucky in the Movement if you have enough to eat. *(Larry regards him puzzledly.)*

ROCKY—*(coldly)* What's de song and dance about? We ain't said nuttin'.

PARRITT—*(lamely—placating them now)* Why, I was just putting you right. But I don't want you to think I'm a tightwad. I'll buy a drink if you want one.

JOE—*(cheering up)* If? Man, when I don't want a drink, you call de morgue, tell dem come take Joe's body away, 'cause he's sure enuf dead. Gimme de bottle quick, Rocky, before he changes his mind! (*Rocky passes him the bottle and glass. He pours a brimful drink and tosses it down his throat, and hands the bottle and glass to Larry.*)

ROCKY—I'll take a cigar when I go in de bar. What're you havin'?

PARRITT—Nothing. I'm on the wagon. What's the damage? (*He holds out a dollar bill.*)

ROCKY—Fifteen cents. (*He makes change from his pocket.*)

PARRITT—Must be some booze!

LARRY—It's cyanide cut with carbolic acid to give it a mellow flavor. Here's luck! (*He drinks.*)

ROCKY—Guess I'll get back in de bar and catch a coupla winks before opening-up time. (*He squeezes through the tables and disappears, right-rear, behind the curtain. In the section of bar at right, he comes forward and sits at the table and slumps back, closing his eyes and yawning.*)

JOE—(*stares calculatingly at Parritt and then looks away—aloud to himself, philosophically*) One-drink guy. Dat well done run dry. No hope till Harry's birthday party. 'Less Hickey shows up. (*He turns to Larry.*) If Hickey comes, Larry, you wake me up if you has to bat me wid a chair. (*He settles himself and immediately falls asleep.*)

PARRITT—Who's Hickey?

LARRY—A hardware drummer. An old friend of Harry Hope's and all the gang. He's a grand guy. He comes here twice a year regularly on a periodical drunk and blows in all his money.

PARRITT—(*with a disparaging glance around*) Must be hard up for a place to hang out.

LARRY—It has its points for him. He never runs into anyone he knows in his business here.

PARRITT—(*lowering his voice*) Yes, that's what I want, too. I've got to stay under cover, Larry, like I told you last night.

LARRY—You did a lot of hinting. You didn't tell me anything.

PARRITT—You can guess, can't you? (*He changes the subject abruptly.*) I've been in some dumps on the Coast, but this is the limit. What kind of joint is it, anyway?

LARRY—(*with a sardonic grin*) What is it? It's the No Chance Saloon. It's Bedrock Bar, The End of the Line Café, The Bottom of the Sea Rathskeller! Don't you notice the beautiful calm in the atmosphere? That's because it's the last harbor. No one here has to worry about where they're going next, because there is no farther they can go. It's a great comfort to them. Although even here they keep up the appearances of life with a few harmless pipe dreams about their yesterdays and tomorrows, as you'll see for yourself if you're here long.

PARRITT—(*stares at him curiously*) What's your pipe dream, Larry?

LARRY—(*hiding resentment*) Oh, I'm the exception. I haven't any left, thank God. (*shortly*) Don't complain about this place. You couldn't find a better for lying low.

PARRITT—I'm glad of that, Larry. I don't feel any too damned good. I was knocked off my base by that business on the Coast, and since then it's been no fun dodging around the country, thinking every guy you see might be a dick.

LARRY—(*sympathetically now*) No, it wouldn't be. But you're safe here. The cops ignore this dump. They think it's as harmless as a graveyard. (*He grins sardonically.*) And, be God, they're right.

PARRITT—It's been lonely as hell. (*impulsively*) Christ, Larry, I was glad to find you. I kept saying to myself, "If I can only find Larry. He's the one guy in the world who can understand—" (*He hesitates, staring at Larry with a strange appeal.*)

LARRY—(*watching him puzzledly*) Understand what?

PARRITT—(*hastily*) Why, all I've been through. (*looking away*) Oh, I know you're thinking, This guy has a hell of a nerve. I haven't seen him since he was a kid. I'd forgotten he was alive. But I've never forgotten you, Larry. You were the only friend of Mother's who ever paid attention to me, or knew I was alive. All the others were too busy with the Movement. Even Mother. And I had no Old Man. You used to take me on your knee and tell me stories and crack jokes and make me laugh. You'd ask me questions and take what I said seriously. I guess I got to feel in the years you lived with us that you'd taken the place of my Old Man. (*embarrassedly*) But, hell, that sounds like a lot of mush. I suppose you don't remember a damned thing about it.

LARRY—(*moved in spite of himself*) I remember well. You were a serious lonely little shaver. (*then resenting being moved, changes the subject*) How is it they didn't pick you up when they got your mother and the rest?

PARRITT—(*in a lowered voice but eagerly, as if he wanted this chance to tell about it*) I wasn't around, and as soon as I heard the news I went under cover. You've noticed my glad rags. I was staked to them—as a disguise, sort of. I hung around pool rooms and gambling joints and hooker shops, where they'd never look for a Wobblie, pretending I was a sport. Anyway, they'd grabbed everyone important, so I suppose they didn't think of me until afterward.

LARRY—The papers say the cops got them all dead to rights, that the Burns dicks knew every move before it was made, and someone inside the Movement must have sold out and tipped them off.

PARRITT—(*turns to look Larry in the eyes—slowly*) Yes, I guess that must be true, Larry. It hasn't come out who it was. It may never come out. I suppose whoever it was made a bargain with the Burns men to keep him out of it. They won't need his evidence.

LARRY—(*tensely*) By God, I hate to believe it of any of the crowd, if I am through long since with any connection with them. I know they're damned fools, most of them, as stupidly greedy for power as the worst capitalist they attack, but I'd swear there couldn't be a yellow stool pigeon among them.

PARRITT—Sure. I'd have sworn that, too, Larry.

LARRY—I hope his soul rots in hell, whoever it is!

PARRITT—Yes, so do I.

LARRY—(*after a pause—shortly*) How did you locate me? I hoped I'd found a place of retirement here where no one in the Movement would ever come to disturb my peace.

PARRITT—I found out through Mother.

LARRY—I asked her not to tell anyone.

PARRITT—She didn't tell me, but she'd kept all your letters and I found where she'd hidden them in the flat. I sneaked up there one night after she was arrested.

LARRY—I'd never have thought she was a woman who'd keep letters.

PARRITT—No, I wouldn't, either. There's nothing soft or sentimental about Mother.

LARRY—I never answered her last letters. I haven't written her in a couple of years—or anyone else. I've gotten beyond the desire to communicate with the world—or, what's more to the point, let it bother me any more with its greedy madness.

PARRITT—It's funny Mother kept in touch with you so long. When she's finished with anyone, she's finished. She's always been proud of that. And you know how she feels about the Movement. Like a revivalist preacher about religion. Anyone who loses faith in it is more than dead to her; he's a Judas who ought to be boiled in oil. Yet she seemed to forgive you.

LARRY—(*sardonically*) She didn't, don't worry. She wrote to denounce me and try to bring the sinner to repentance and a belief in the One True Faith again.

PARRITT—What made you leave the Movement, Larry? Was it on account of Mother?

LARRY—(*starts*) Don't be a damned fool! What the hell put that in your head?

PARRITT—Why, nothing—except I remember what a fight you had with her before you left.

LARRY—(*resentfully*) Well, if you do, I don't. That was eleven years ago. You were only seven. If we did quarrel, it was because I told her I'd become convinced the Movement was only a beautiful pipe dream.

PARRITT—(*with a strange smile*) I don't remember it that way.

LARRY—Then you can blame your imagination—and forget it. (*He changes the subject abruptly.*) You asked me why I quit the Movement. I had a lot of good reasons. One was myself, and another was my comrades, and the last was the breed of swine called men in general. For myself, I was forced to admit, at the end of thirty years' devotion to the Cause, that I was never made for it. I was born condemned to be one of those who has to see all sides of a question. When you're damned like that, the questions multiply for you until in the end it's all question and no answer. As history proves, to be a worldly success at anything, especially revolution, you have to wear blinders like a horse and see only straight in front of you. You have to see, too, that this is all black, and that is all white. As for my comrades in the Great Cause, I felt as Horace Walpole did about England, that he could love it if it weren't for the people in it. The material the ideal free society must be constructed from is men themselves and you can't build a marble temple out of a mixture of mud and manure. When man's soul isn't a sow's ear, it will be time enough to dream of silk purses. (*He chuckles sardonically—then irritably as if suddenly provoked at himself for talking so much*) Well, that's why I quit the Movement, if it leaves you any wiser. At any rate, you see it had nothing to do with your mother.

PARRITT—(*smiles almost mockingly*) Oh, sure, I see. But I'll bet Mother has always thought it was on her account. You know her, Larry. To hear her go on sometimes, you'd think she was the Movement.

LARRY—(*stares at him, puzzled and repelled—sharply*) That's a hell of a way for you to talk, after what happened to her!

PARRITT—(*at once confused and guilty*) Don't get me wrong. I wasn't sneering, Larry. Only kidding. I've said the same thing to her lots of times to kid her. But you're right. I know I shouldn't now. I keep forgetting she's in jail. It doesn't seem real. I can't believe it about her. She's always been so free. I—But I don't want to think of it. (*Larry is moved to a puzzled pity in spite of himself. Parritt changes the subject.*) What have you been doing all the years since you left—the Coast, Larry?

LARRY—(*sardonically*) Nothing I could help doing. If I don't believe in the Movement, I don't believe in anything else either, especially not the State. I've refused to become a useful member of its society. I've been a philosophical drunken bum, and proud of it. (*Abruptly his tone sharpens with resentful warning.*) Listen to me. I hope you've deduced that I've my own reason for answering the impertinent questions of a stranger, for that's all you are to me. I have a strong hunch you've come here expecting something of me. I'm warning you, at the start, so there'll be no misunderstanding, that I've nothing left to give, and I want to be left alone, and I'll thank you to keep your life to yourself. I feel you're looking for some answer to something. I have no answer to give anyone, not even myself. Unless you can call what Heine wrote in his poem to morphine an answer. (*He quotes a translation of the dosing couplet sardonically.*)

"Lo, sleep is good; better is death; in sooth,
The best of all were never to be born."

PARRITT—(*shrinks a bit frightenedly*) That's the hell of an answer. (*then with a forced grin of bravado*) Still, you never know when it might come in handy. (*He looks away. Larry stares at him puzzledly, interested in spite of himself and at the same time vaguely uneasy.*)

LARRY—(*forcing a casual tone*) I don't suppose you've had much chance to hear news of your mother since she's been in jail?

PARRITT—No. No chance. (*He hesitates—then blurts out*) Anyway, I don't think she wants to hear from me. We had a fight just before that business happened. She bawled me out because I was going around with tarts. That got my goat, coming from her. I told her, "You've always acted the free woman, you've never let anything stop you from—" (*He checks himself—goes on hurriedly*) That made her sore. She said she wouldn't give a damn what I did except she'd begun to suspect I was too interested in outside things and losing interest in the Movement.

LARRY—(*stares at him*) And were you?

PARRITT—(*hesitates—then with intensity*) Sure I was! I'm no damned fool! I couldn't go on believing forever that gang was going to change the world by shooting off their loud traps on soapboxes and sneaking around blowing up a lousy building or a bridge! I got wise it was all a crazy pipe dream! (*appealingly*) The same as you did, Larry. That's why I came to you. I knew you'd understand. What finished me was this last business of someone selling out. How can you believe anything after a thing like that happens? It knocks you cold! You don't know what the hell is what! You're through! (*appealingly*) You know how I feel, don't you, Larry? (*Larry stares at him, moved by sympathy and pity in spite of himself, disturbed, and resentful at being disturbed, and puzzled by something he feels about Parritt that isn't right. But before he can reply, Hugo suddenly raises his head from his arms in a half-awake alcoholic daze and speaks.*)

HUGO—(*quotes aloud to himself in a guttural declamatory style*) "The days grow hot, O Babylon! 'Tis cool beneath thy villow trees!" (*Parritt turns startledly as Hugo peers muzzily without recognition at him. Hugo exclaims automatically in his tone of denunciation*) Gottammed stool pigeon!

PARRITT—(*shrinks away—stammers*) What? Who do you mean? (*then furiously*) You lousy bum, you can't call me that! (*He draws back his fist.*)

HUGO—(*ignores this—recognizing him now, bursts into his childish teasing giggle*) Hello, leedle Don! Leedle monkey-face. I did not recognize you. You have grown big boy. How is your mother? Where you come from? (*He breaks into his wheedling, bullying tone.*) Don't be a fool! Loan me a dollar! Buy me a trink! (*As if this exhausted him, he abruptly forgets it and plumps his head down on his arms again and is asleep.*)

PARRITT—(*with eager relief*) Sure, I'll buy you a drink, Hugo. I'm broke, but I can afford one for you. I'm sorry I got sore. I ought to have remembered when you're soused you call everyone a stool pigeon. But it's no damned joke right at this time. (*He turns to Larry, who is regarding him now fixedly with an uneasy expression as if he suddenly were afraid of his own thoughts—forcing a smile*) Gee, he's passed out again. (*He stiffens defensively.*) What are you giving me the hard look for? Oh, I know. You thought I was going to hit him? What do you think I am? I've always had a lot of respect for Hugo. I've always stood up for him when people in the Movement panned him for an old drunken has-been. He had the guts to serve ten years in the can in his own country and get his eyes ruined in solitary. I'd like to see some of them here stick that. Well, they'll get a chance now to show—(*hastily*) I don't mean—But let's forget that. Tell me some more about this dump. Who are all these tanks? Who's that guy trying to catch pneumonia? (*He indicates Lewis.*)

LARRY—(*stares at him almost frightenedly—then looks away and grasps eagerly this chance to change the subject. He begins to describe the sleepers with sardonic relish but at the same time showing his affection for them.*) That's Captain Lewis, a onetime hero of the British Army. He strips to display that scar on his back he got from a native spear whenever he's completely plastered. The bewhiskered bloke opposite him is General Wetjoen, who led a commando in the War. The two of them met when they came here to work in the Boer War spectacle at the St. Louis Fair and they've been bosom pals ever since. They dream the hours away in happy dispute over the brave days in South Africa when they tried to murder each other. The little guy between them was in it, too, as correspondent for some English paper. His nickname here is Jimmy Tomorrow. He's the leader of our Tomorrow Movement.

PARRITT—What do they do for a living?

LARRY—As little as possible. Once in a while one of them makes a successful touch somewhere, and some of them get a few dollars a month from connections at home who pay it on condition they never come back. For the rest, they live on free lunch and their old friend, Harry Hope, who doesn't give a damn what anyone does or doesn't do, as long as he likes you.

PARRITT—It must be a tough life.

LARRY—It's not. Don't waste your pity. They wouldn't thank you for it. They manage to get drunk, by hook or crook, and keep their pipe dreams, and that's all they ask of life. I've never known more contented men. It isn't often that men attain the true goal of their heart's desire. The same applies to Harry himself and his two cronies at the far table. He's so satisfied with life he's never set foot out of this place since his wife died twenty years ago. He has no need of the outside world at all. This place has a fine trade from the Market people across the street and the waterfront workers, so in spite of Harry's thirst and his generous heart, he comes out even. He never worries in hard times because there's always old friends from the days when he was a jitney Tammany politician, and a friendly brewery to tide him over. Don't ask me what his two pals work at because they don't. Except at being his lifetime guests. The one facing this way is his brother-in-law, Ed Mosher, who once worked for a circus in the ticket wagon. Pat McGloin, the other one, was a police lieutenant back in the flush times of graft when everything went. But he got too greedy and when the usual reform investigation came he was caught red-handed and thrown off the Force. (*He nods at Joe.*) Joe here has a yesterday in the same flush period. He ran a colored gambling house then and was a hell of a sport, so they say. Well, that's our whole family circle of inmates, except the two barkeeps and their girls, three ladies of the pavement that room on the third floor.

PARRITT—(*bitterly*) To hell with them! I never want to see a whore again! (*As Larry flashes him a puzzled glance, he adds confusedly*) I mean, they always get you in dutch. (*While he is speaking Willie Oban has opened his eyes. He leans toward them, drunk now from the effect of the huge drink he took, and speaks with a mocking suavity.*)

WILLIE—Why omit me from your Who's Who in Dypsomania, Larry? An unpardonable slight, especially as I am the only inmate of royal blood. (*to Parritt—ramblingly*) Educated at Harvard, too. You must have noticed the atmosphere of culture here. My humble contribution. Yes, Generous Stranger—I trust you're generous—I was born in the purple, the son, but unfortunately not the heir, of the late world-famous Bill Oban, King of the Bucket Shops. A revolution deposed him, conducted by the District Attorney. He was sent into exile. In fact, not to mince matters, they locked him in the can and threw away the key. Alas, his was an adventurous spirit that pined in confinement. And so he died. Forgive these reminiscences. Undoubtedly all this is well known to you. Everyone in the world knows.

PARRITT—(*uncomfortably*) Tough luck. No, I never heard of him.

WILLIE—(*blinks at him incredulously*) Never heard? I thought everyone in the world—Why, even at Harvard I discovered my father was well known by reputation, although that was some time before the District Attorney gave him so much unwelcome publicity. Yes, even as a freshman I was notorious. I was accepted socially with all the warm cordiality that Henry Wadsworth Longfellow would have shown a drunken Negress dancing the can can at high noon on Brattle Street. Harvard was my father's idea. He was an ambitious man. Dictatorial, too. Always knowing what was best for me. But I did make myself a brilliant student. A dirty trick on my classmates, inspired by revenge, I fear. (*He quotes*) "Dear college days, with pleasure rife! The grandest gladdest days of life!" But, of course, that is a Yale hymn, and they're given to rah-rah exaggeration at New Haven. I was a brilliant student at Law School, too. My father wanted a lawyer in the family. He was a calculating man. A thorough knowledge of the law close at hand in the house to help him find fresh ways to evade it. But I discovered the loophole of whiskey and escaped his jurisdiction. (*abruptly to Parritt*) Speaking of whiskey, sir, reminds me—and, I hope, reminds you—that when meeting a Prince the customary salutation is "What'll you have?"

PARRITT—(*with defensive resentment*) Nix! All you guys seem to think I'm made of dough. Where would I get the coin to blow everyone?

WILLIE—(*sceptically*) Broke? You haven't the thirsty look of the impecunious. I'd judge you to be a plutocrat, your pockets stuffed with ill-gotten gains. Two or three dollars, at least. And don't think we will question how you got it. As Vespasian remarked, the smell of all whiskey is sweet.

PARRITT—What do you mean, how I got it? (*to Larry, forcing a laugh*) It's a laugh, calling me a plutocrat, isn't it, Larry, when I've been in the Movement all my life.

(*Larry gives him an uneasy suspicious glance, then looks away, as if avoiding something he does not wish to see.*)

WILLIE—(*disgustedly*) Ah, one of those, eh? I believe you now, all right! Go away and blow yourself up, that's a good lad. Hugo is the only licensed preacher of that gospel here. A dangerous terrorist, Hugo! He would as soon blow the collar off a schooner of beer as look at you! (*to Larry*) Let us ignore this useless youth, Larry. Let us join in prayer that Hickey, the Great Salesman, will soon arrive bringing the blessed bourgeois long green! Would that Hickey or Death would come! Meanwhile, I will sing a song. A beautiful old New England folk ballad which I picked up at Harvard amid the debris of education. (*He sings in a boisterous baritone, rapping on the table with his knuckles at the indicated spots in the song.*)

"Jack, oh, Jack, was a sailor lad
And he came to a tavern for gin.
He rapped and he rapped with a (*rap, rap, rap*)
But never a soul seemed in."

(*The drunks at the tables stir. Rocky gets up from his chair in the bar and starts back for the entrance to the back room. Hope cocks one irritable eye over his specs. Joe Mott opens both of his and grins. Willie interposes some drunken whimsical exposition to Larry.*) The origin of this beautiful ditty is veiled in mystery, Larry. There was a legend bruited about in Cambridge lavatories that Waldo Emerson composed it during his uninformative period as a minister, while he was trying to write a sermon. But my own opinion is, it goes back much further, and Jonathan Edwards was the author of both words and music. (*He sings*)

"He rapped and rapped, and tapped and tapped
Enough to wake the dead
Till he heard a damsel (*rap, rap, rap*)
On a window right over his head."

(*The drunks are blinking their eyes now, grumbling and cursing. Rocky appears from the bar at rear, right, yawning.*)

HOPE—(*with fuming irritation*) Rocky! Bejees, can't you keep that crazy bastard quiet? (*Rocky starts for Willie.*)

WILLIE—And now the influence of a good woman enters our mariner's life. Well, perhaps "good" isn't the word. But very, very kind. (*He sings*)

"Oh, come up," she cried, "my sailor lad,
And you and I'll agree,
And I'll show you the prettiest (*rap, rap, rap*)
That ever you did see."

(*He speaks.*) You see, Larry? The lewd Puritan touch, obviously, and it grows more marked as we go on. (*He sings*)

"Oh, he put his arm around her waist,
He gazed in her bright blue eyes
And then he—"

(*But here Rocky shakes him roughly by the shoulder.*)

ROCKY—Piano! What d'yuh tink dis dump is, a dump?

HOPE—Give him the bum's rush upstairs! Lock him in his room!

ROCKY—(*yanks Willie by the arm*) Come on, Bum.

WILLIE—(*dissolves into pitiable terror*) No! Please, Rocky! I'll go crazy up in that room alone! It's haunted! I—(*He calls to Hope*) Please, Harry! Let me stay here! I'll be quiet!

HOPE—(*immediately relents—indignantly*) What the hell you doing to him, Rocky? I didn't tell you to beat up the poor guy. Leave him alone, long as he's quiet. (*Rocky lets go of Willie disgustedly and goes back to his chair in the bar.*)

WILLIE—(*huskily*) Thanks, Harry. You're a good scout. (*He closes his eyes and sinks back in his chair exhaustedly, twitching and quivering again.*)

HOPE—(*addressing McGloin and Mosher, who are sleepily awake—accusingly*) Always the way. Can't trust nobody. Leave it to that Dago to keep order and it's like bedlam in a cathouse, singing and everything. And you two big barflies are a hell of a help to me, ain't you? Eat and sleep and get drunk! All you're good for, bejees! Well, you can take that "I'll-have-the-same" look off your maps! There ain't going to be no more drinks on the house till hell freezes over! (*Neither of the two is impressed either by his insults or his threats. They grin hangover grins of tolerant affection at him and wink at each other. Harry fumes*) Yeah, grin! Wink, bejees! Fine pair of sons of bitches to have glued on me for life! (*But he can't get a rise out of them and he subsides into a fuming mumble. Meanwhile, at the middle table, Captain Lewis and General Wetjoen are as wide awake as heavy hangovers permit. Jimmy Tomorrow nods, his eyes blinking. Lewis is gazing across the table at Joe Mott, who is still chuckling to himself over Willie's song. The expression on Lewis's face is that of one who can't believe his eyes.*)

LEWIS—(*aloud to himself with a muzzy wonder*) Good God! Have I been drinking at the same table with a bloody Kaffir?

JOE—(*grinning*) Hello, Captain. You comin' up for air? Kaffir? Who's he?

WETJOEN—(*blurrily*) Kaffir, dot's a nigger, Joe. (*Joe stiffens and his eyes narrow. Wetjoen goes on with heavy jocosity.*) Dot's joke on him, Joe. He don't know you. He's still plind drunk, the ploody Limey chentleman! A great mistake I missed him at the pattle of Modder River. Vit mine rifle I shoot damn fool Limey officers py the dozen, but him I miss. De pity of it! (*He chuckles and slaps Lewis on his bare shoulder.)* Hey, wake up, Cecil, you ploody fool! Don't you know your old friend, Joe? He's no damned Kaffir! He's white, Joe is!

LEWIS—*(light dawning—contritely)* My profound apologies, Joseph, old chum. Eyesight a trifle blurry, I'm afraid. Whitest colored man I ever knew. Proud to call you my friend. No hard feelings, what? *(He holds out his hand.)*

JOE—*(at once grins good-naturedly and shakes his hand)* No Captain, I know it's mistake. Youse regular, if you is a Limey. *(then his face hardening)* But I don't stand for "nigger" from nobody. Never did. In de old days, people calls me "nigger" wakes up in de hospital. I was de leader ob de Dirty Half-Dozen Gang. All six of us colored boys, we was tough and I was de toughest.

WETJOEN—*(inspired to boastful reminiscence)* Me, in old days in Transvaal, I vas so tough and strong I grab axle of ox wagon mit full load and lift like feather.

LEWIS—*(smiling amiably)* As for you, my balmy Boer that walks like a man, I say again it was a grave error in our foreign policy ever to set you free, once we nabbed you and your commando with Cronje. We should have taken you to the London zoo and incarcerated you in the baboons' cage. With a sign: "Spectators may distinguish the true baboon by his blue behind."

WETJOEN—*(grins)* Gott! To dink, ten better Limey officers, at least, I shoot clean in the mittle of forehead at Spion Kopje, and you I miss! I neffer forgive myself! *(Jimmy Tomorrow blinks benignantly from one to the other with a gentle drunken smile.)*

JIMMY—*(sentimentally)* Now, come, Cecil, Piet! We must forget the War. Boer and Briton, each fought fairly and played the game till the better man won and then we shook hands. We are all brothers within the Empire united beneath the flag on which the sun never sets. *(Tears come to his eyes. He quotes with great sentiment, if with slight application)* "Ship me somewhere east of Suez—"

LARRY—*(breaks in sardonically)* Be God, you're there already, Jimmy. Worst is best here, and East is West, and tomorrow is yesterday. What more do you want?

JIMMY—*(with bleery benevolence, shaking his head in mild rebuke)* No, Larry, old friend, you can't deceive me. You pretend a bitter, cynic philosophy, but in your heart you are the kindest man among us.

LARRY—*(disconcerted—irritably)* The hell you say!

PARRITT—*(leans toward him—confidentially)* What a bunch of cuckoos!

JIMMY—*(as if reminded of something—with a pathetic attempt at a brisk, no-more-nonsense air)* Tomorrow, yes. It's high time I straightened out and got down to business again. *(He brushes his sleeve fastidiously.)* I must have this suit cleaned and pressed. I can't look like a tramp when I—

JOE—*(who has been brooding—interrupts)* Yes, suh, white folks always said I was white. In de days when I was flush, Joe Mott's de only colored man dey allows in de white gamblin' houses. "You're all right, Joe, you're white," dey says. *(He chuckles.)* Wouldn't let me play craps, dough. Dey know I could make dem dice behave. "Any odder game and any limit you like, Joe," dey says. Man, de money I lost! *(He chuckles—then with an underlying defensiveness)* Look at de Big Chief in dem days. He knew I was white. I'd saved my dough so I could start my own gamblin' house. Folks in de know tells me, see de man at de top, den you never has trouble. You git Harry Hope give you a letter to de Chief. And Harry does. Don't you, Harry?

HOPE—*(preoccupied with his own thoughts)* Eh? Sure. Big Bill was a good friend of mine. I had plenty of friends high up in those days. Still could have if I wanted to go out and see them. Sure, I gave you a letter. I said you was white. What the hell of it?

JOE—*(to Captain Lewis who has relapsed into a sleepy daze and is listening to him with an absurd strained attention without comprehending a word)* Dere. You see, Captain. I went to see de Chief, shakin' in my boots, and dere he is sittin' behind a big desk, lookin' as big as a freight train. He don't look up. He keeps me waitin' and waitin', and after 'bout an hour, seems like to me, he says slow and quiet like dere wasn't no harm in him, "You want to open a gamblin' joint, does you, Joe?" But he don't give me no time to answer. He jumps up, lookin' as big as two freight trains, and he pounds his fist like a ham on de desk, and he shouts, "You black son of a bitch, Harry says you're white and you better be white or dere's a little iron room up de river waitin' for you!" Den he sits down and says quiet again, "All right. You can open. Git de hell outa here!" So I opens, and he finds out I'se white, sure 'nuff, 'cause I run wide open for years and pays my sugar on de dot, and de cops and I is friends. *(He chuckles with pride.)* Dem old days! Many's de night I come in here. Dis was a first-class hangout for sports in dem days. Good whiskey, fifteen cents, two for two bits. I t'rows down a fifty-dollar bill like it was trash paper and says, "Drink it up, boys, I don't want no change." Ain't dat right, Harry?

HOPE—*(caustically)* Yes, and bejees, if I ever seen you throw fifty cents on the bar now, I'd know I had delirium tremens! You've told that story ten million times and if I have to hear it again, that'll give me D.T.s anyway!

JOE—(*chuckling*) Gittin' drunk every day for twenty years ain't give you de Brooklyn boys. You needn't be scared of me!

LEWIS—(*suddenly turns and beams on Hope*) Thank you, Harry, old chum. I will have a drink, now you mention it, seeing it's so near your birthday. (*The others laugh.*)

HOPE—(*puts his hand to his ear—angrily*) What's that? I can't hear you.

LEWIS—(*sadly*) No, I fancied you wouldn't.

HOPE—I don't have to hear, bejees! Booze is the only thing you ever talk about!

LEWIS—(*sadly*) True. Yet there was a time when my conversation was more comprehensive. But as I became burdened with years, it seemed rather pointless to discuss my other subject.

HOPE—You can't joke with me! How much room rent do you owe me, tell me that?

LEWIS—Sorry. Adding has always baffled me. Subtraction is my forte.

HOPE—(*snarling*) Arrh! Think you're funny! Captain, bejees! Showing off your wounds! Put on your clothes, for Christ's sake! This ain't no Turkish bath! Lousy Limey army! Took 'em years to lick a gang of Dutch hayseeds!

WETJOEN—Dot's right, Harry. Gif him hell!

HOPE—No lip out of you, neither, you Dutch spinach! General, hell! Salvation Army, that's what you'd ought t'been General in! Bragging what a shot you were, and, bejees, you missed him! And he missed you, that's just as bad! And now the two of you bum on me! (*threateningly*) But you've broke the camel's back this time, bejees! You pay up tomorrow or out you go!

LEWIS—(*earnestly*) My dear fellow, I give you my word of honor as an officer and a gentleman, you shall be paid tomorrow.

WETJOEN—Ve swear it, Harry! Tomorrow vidout fail!

McGLOIN—(*a twinkle in his eye*) There you are, Harry. Sure, what could be fairer?

MOSHER—(*with a wink at McGloin*) Yes, you can't ask more than that, Harry. A promise is a promise—as I've often discovered.

HOPE—(*turns on them*) I mean the both of you, too! An old grafting flatfoot and a circus bunco steerer! Fine company for me, bejees! Couple of con men living in my flat since Christ knows when! Getting fat as hogs, too! And you ain't even got the decency to get me upstairs where I got a good bed! Let me sleep on a chair like a bum! Kept me down here waitin' for Hickey to show up, hoping I'd blow you to more drinks!

McGLOIN—Ed and I did our damnedest to get you up, didn't we, Ed?

MOSHER—We did. But you said you couldn't bear the flat because it was one of those nights when memory brought poor old Bessie back to you.

HOPE—(*his face instantly becoming long and sad and sentimental—mournfully*) Yes, that's right, boys. I remember now. I could almost see her in every room just as she used to be—and it's twenty years since she—(*His throat and eyes fill up. A suitable sentimental hush falls on the room.*)

LARRY—(*in a sardonic whisper to Parritt*) Isn't a pipe dream of yesterday a touching thing? By all accounts, Bessie nagged the hell out of him.

JIMMY—(*who has been dreaming, a look of prim resolution on his face, speaks aloud to himself*) No more of this sitting around and loafing. Time I took hold of myself. I must have my shoes soled and heeled and shined first thing tomorrow morning. A general spruce-up. I want to have a well-groomed appearance when I—(*His voice fades out as he stares in front of him. No one pays any attention to him except Larry and Parritt.*)

LARRY—(*as before, in a sardonic aside to Parritt*) The tomorrow movement is a sad and beautiful thing, too!

McGLOIN—(*with a huge sentimental sigh—and a calculating look at Hope*) Poor old Bessie! You don't find her like in these days. A sweeter woman never drew breath.

MOSHER—(*in a similar calculating mood*) Good old Bess. A man couldn't want a better sister than she was to me.

HOPE—(*mournfully*) Twenty years, and I've never set foot out of this house since the day I buried her. Didn't have the heart. Once she'd gone, I didn't give a damn for anything. I lost all my ambition. Without her, nothing seemed worth the trouble. You remember, Ed, you, too, Mac—the boys was going to nominate me for Alderman. It was all fixed. Bessie wanted it and she was so proud. But when she was taken, I told them, "No, boys, I can't do it. I simply haven't the heart. I'm through." I would have won the election easy, too. (*He says this a bit defiantly.*) Oh, I know there was jealous wise guys said the boys was giving me the nomination because they knew they couldn't win that year in this ward. But that's a damned lie! I knew every man, woman and child in the ward, almost. Bessie made me make friends with everyone, helped me remember all their names. I'd have been elected easy.

McGLOIN—You would, Harry. It was a sure thing.

MOSHER—A dead cinch, Harry. Everyone knows that.

HOPE—Sure they do. But after Bessie died, I didn't have the heart. Still, I know while she'd appreciate my grief, she wouldn't want it to keep me cooped up in here all my life. So I've made up my mind I'll go out soon.

Take a walk around the ward, see all the friends I used to know, get together with the boys and maybe tell 'em I'll let 'em deal me a hand in their game again. Yes, bejees, I'll do it. My birthday, tomorrow, that'd be the right time to turn over a new leaf. Sixty. That ain't too old.

McGLOIN—(*flatteringly*) It's the prime of life, Harry.

MOSHER—Wonderful thing about you, Harry, you keep young as you ever was.

JIMMY—(*dreaming aloud again*) Get my things from the laundry. They must still have them. Clean collar and shirt. If I wash the ones I've got on any more, they'll fall apart. Socks, too. I want to make a good appearance. I met Dick Trumbull on the street a year or two ago. He said, "Jimmy, the publicity department's never been the same since you got—resigned. It's dead as hell." I said, "I know. I've heard rumors the management were at their wits' end and would be only too glad to have me run it for them again. I think all I'd have to do would be go and see them and they'd offer me the position. Don't you think so, Dick?" He said, "Sure, they would, Jimmy. Only take my advice and wait a while until business conditions are better. Then you can strike them for a bigger salary than you got before, do you see?" I said, "Yes, I do see, Dick, and many thanks for the tip." Well, conditions must be better by this time. All I have to do is get fixed up with a decent front tomorrow, and it's as good as done.

HOPE—(*glances at Jimmy with a condescending affectionate pity—in a hushed voice*) Poor Jimmy's off on his pipe dream again. Bejees, he takes the cake! (*This is too much for Larry. He cannot restrain a sardonic guffaw. But no one pays any attention to him.*)

LEWIS—(*opens his eyes, which are drowsing again—dreamily to Wetjoen*) I'm sorry we had to postpone our trip again this April, Piet. I hoped the blasted old estate would be settled up by then. The damned lawyers can't hold up the settlement much longer. We'll make it next year, even if we have to work and earn our passage money, eh? You'll stay with me at the old place as long as you like, then you can take the *Union Castle* from Southampton to Cape Town. (*sentimentally, with real yearning*) England in April. I want you to see that, Piet. The old veldt has its points, I'll admit, but it isn't home—especially home in April.

WETJOEN—(*blinks drowsily at him—dreamily*) Ja, Cecil, I know how beautiful it must be, from all you tell me many times. I vill enjoy it. But I shall enjoy more ven I am home, too. The veldt, ja! You could put England on it, and it would look like a farmer's small garden. Py Gott, there is space to be free, the air like vine is, you don't need booze to be drunk! My relations vill so surprised be. They vill not know me, it is so many years. Dey vill be so glad I haf come home at last.

JOE—(*dreamily*) I'll make my stake and get my new gamblin' house open before you boys leave. You got to come to de openin'. I'll treat you white. If you're broke, I'll stake you to buck any game you chooses. If you wins, dat's velvet for you. If you loses, it don't count. Can't treat you no whiter dan dat, can I?

HOPE—(*again with condescending pity*) Bejees, Jimmy's started them off smoking the same hop. (*But the three are finished, their eyes closed again in sleep or a drowse.*)

LARRY—(*aloud to himself—in his comically tense, crazy whisper*) Be God, this bughouse will drive me stark, raving loony yet!

HOPE—(*turns on him with fuming suspicion*) What? What d'you say?

LARRY—(*placatingly*) Nothing, Harry. I had a crazy thought in my head.

HOPE—(*irascibly*) Crazy is right! Yah! The old wise guy! Wise, hell! A damned old fool Anarchist I-Won't-Worker! I'm sick of you and Hugo, too. Bejees, you'll pay up tomorrow, or I'll start a Harry Hope Revolution! I'll tie a dispossess bomb to your tails that'll blow you out in the street! Bejees, I'll make your Movement move! (*The witticism delights him and he bursts into a shrill cackle. At once McGloin and Mosher guffaw enthusiastically.*)

MOSHER—(*flatteringly*) Harry, you sure say the funniest things! (*He reaches on the table as if he expected a glass to be there—then starts with well-acted surprise.*) Hell, where's my drink? That Rocky is too damned fast cleaning tables. Why, I'd only taken one sip of it.

HOPE—(*his smiling face congealing*) No, you don't! (*acidly*) Any time you only take one sip of a drink, you'll have lockjaw and paralysis! Think you can kid me with those old circus con games?—me, that's known you since you was knee-high, and, bejees, you was a crook even then!

McGLOIN—(*grinning*) It's not like you to be so hardhearted, Harry. Sure, it's hot, parching work laughing at your jokes so early in the morning on an empty stomach!

HOPE—Yah! You, Mac! Another crook! Who asked you to laugh? We was talking about poor old Bessie, and you and her no-good brother start to laugh! A hell of a thing! Talking mush about her, too! "Good old Bess." Bejees, she'd never forgive me if she knew I had you two bums living in her flat, throwing ashes and cigar butts on her carpet. You know her opinion of you, Mac. "That Pat McGloin is the biggest drunken grafter that ever disgraced the police force," she used to say to me. "I hope they send him to Sing Sing for life."

McGLOIN—(*unperturbed*) She didn't mean it. She was angry at me because you used to get me drunk. But Bess had a heart of gold underneath her sharpness. She knew I was innocent of all the charges.

WILLIE—(*jumps to his feet drunkenly and points a finger at McGloin—imitating the manner of a cross-examiner—coldly*) One moment, please. Lieutenant McGloin! Are you aware you are under oath? Do you realize what the penalty for perjury is? (*purringly*) Come now, Lieutenant, isn't it a fact that you're as guilty as hell? No, don't say, "How about your old man?" I am asking the questions. The fact that he was a crooked old bucket-shop bastard has no bearing on your case. (*with a change to maudlin joviality*) Gentlemen of the Jury, court will now recess while the D.A. sings out a little ditty he learned at Harvard. It was composed in a wanton moment by the Dean of the Divinity School on a moonlight night in July, 1776, while sobering up in a Turkish bath. (*He sings*)

"Oh, come up," she cried, "my sailor lad,
And you and I'll agree.
And I'll show you the prettiest (*rap, rap, rap on table*)
That ever you did see."

(*Suddenly he catches Hope's eyes fixed on him condemningly, and sees Rocky appearing from the bar. He collapses back on his chair, pleading miserably*) Please, Harry! I'll be quiet! Don't make Rocky bounce me upstairs! I'll go crazy alone! (*to McGloin*) I apologize, Mac. Don't get sore. I was only kidding you. (*Rocky, at a relenting glance from Hope, returns to the bar.*)

McGLOIN—(*good-naturedly*) Sure, kid all you like, Willie. I'm hardened to it. (*He pauses—seriously*) But I'm telling you some day before long I'm going to make them reopen my case. Everyone knows there was no real evidence against me, and I took the fall for the ones higher up. I'll be found innocent this time and reinstated. (*wistfully*) I'd like to have my old job on the Force back. The boys tell me there's fine pickings these days, and I'm not getting rich here, sitting with a parched throat waiting for Harry Hope to buy a drink. (*He glances reproachfully at Hope.*)

WILLIE—Of course, you'll be reinstated, Mac. All you need is a brilliant young attorney to handle your case. I'll be straightened out and on the wagon in a day or two. I've never practiced but I was one of the most brilliant students in Law School, and your case is just the opportunity I need to start. (*darkly*) Don't worry about my not forcing the D.A. to reopen your case. I went through my father's papers before the cops destroyed them, and I remember a lot of people, even if I can't prove—(*coaxingly*) You will let me take your case, won't you, Mac?

McGLOIN—(*soothingly*) Sure I will and it'll make your reputation, Willie. (*Mosher winks at Hope, shaking his head, and Hope answers with identical pantomime, as though to say, "Poor dopes, they're off again!"*)

LARRY—(*aloud to himself more than to Parritt—with irritable wonder*) Ah, be damned! Haven't I heard their visions a thousand times? Why should they get under my skin now? I've got the blues, I guess. I wish to hell Hickey'd turn up.

MOSHER—(*calculatingly solicitous—whispering to Hope*) Poor Willie needs a drink bad, Harry—and I think if we all joined him it'd make him feel he was among friends and cheer him up.

HOPE—More circus con tricks! (*scathingly*) You talking of your dear sister! Bessie had you sized up. She used to tell me, "I don't know what you can see in that worthless, drunken, petty-larceny brother of mine. If I had my way," she'd say, "he'd get booted out in the gutter on his fat behind." Sometimes she didn't say behind, either.

MOSHER—(*grins genially*) Yes, dear old Bess had a quick temper, but there was no real harm in her. (*He chuckles reminiscently.*) Remember the time she sent me down to the bar to change a ten-dollar bill for her?

HOPE—(*has to grin himself*) Bejees, do I! She coulda bit a piece out of a stove lid, after she found it out. (*He cackles appreciatively.*)

MOSHER—I was sure surprised when she gave me the ten spot. Bess usually had better sense, but she was in a hurry to go to church. I didn't really mean to do it, but you know how habit gets you. Besides, I still worked then, and the circus season was going to begin soon, and I needed a little practice to keep my hand in. Or, you never can tell, the first rube that came to my wagon for a ticket might have left with the right change and I'd be disgraced. (*He chuckles.*) I said, "I'm sorry, Bess, but I had to take it all in dimes. Here, hold out your hands and I'll count it out for you, so you won't kick afterwards I short-changed you." (*He begins a count which grows more rapid as he goes on.*) Ten, twenty, thirty, forty, fifty, sixty, seventy, eighty, ninety, a dollar. Ten, twenty, thirty, forty, fifty, sixty—You're counting with me, Bess, aren't you?—eighty, ninety, two dollars. Ten, twenty—Those are pretty shoes you got on, Bess—forty, fifty, seventy, eighty, ninety, three dollars. Ten, twenty, thirty—What's on at the church tonight, Bess?—fifty, sixty, seventy, ninety, four dollars. Ten, twenty, thirty, fifty, seventy, eighty, ninety—That's a swell new hat, Bess, looks very becoming—six dollars. (*He chuckles.*) And so on. I'm bum at it now for lack of practice, but in those days I could have short-changed the Keeper of the Mint.

HOPE—(*grinning*) Stung her for two dollars and a half, wasn't it, Ed?

MOSHER—Yes. A fine percentage, if I do say so, when you're dealing to someone who's sober and can count. I'm sorry to say she discovered my mistakes in arithmetic just after I beat it around the corner. She counted it over herself. Bess somehow never had the confidence in me a sister should. (*He sighs tenderly.*) Dear old Bess.

HOPE—(*indignant now*) You're a fine guy bragging how you short-changed your own sister! Bejees, if there was a war and you was in it, they'd have to padlock the pockets of the dead!

MOSHER—(*a bit hurt at this*) That's going pretty strong, Harry. I always gave a sucker some chance. There wouldn't be no fun robbing the dead. (*He becomes reminiscently melancholy.*) Gosh, thinking of the old ticket wagon brings those days back. The greatest life on earth with the greatest show on earth! The grandest crowd of regular guys ever gathered under one tent! I'd sure like to shake their hands again!

HOPE—(*acidly*) They'd have guns in theirs. They'd shoot you on sight. You've touched every damned one of them. Bejees, you've even borrowed fish from the trained seals and peanuts from every elephant that remembered you! (*This fancy tickles him and he gives a cackling laugh.*)

MOSHER—(*overlooking this—dreamily*) You know, Harry, I've made up my mind I'll see the boss in a couple of days and ask for my old job. I can get back my magic touch with change easy, and I can throw him a line of bull that'll kid him I won't be so unreasonable about sharing the profits next time. (*with insinuating complaint*) There's no percentage in hanging around this dive, taking care of you and shooing away your snakes, when I don't even get an eye-opener for my trouble.

HOPE—(*implacably*) No! (*Mosher sighs and gives up and closes his eyes. The others, except Larry and Parritt, are all dozing again now. Hope goes on grumbling.*) Go to hell or the circus, for all I care. Good riddance, bejees! I'm sick of you! (*then worriedly*) Say, Ed, what the hell you think's happened to Hickey? I hope he'll turn up. Always got a million funny stories. You and the other bums have begun to give me the graveyard fantods. I'd like a good laugh with old Hickey. (*He chuckles at a memory.*) Remember that gag he always pulls about his wife and the iceman? He'd make a cat laugh! (*Rocky appears from the bar. He comes front, behind Masher's chair, and begins pushing the black curtain along the rod to the rear wall.*)

ROCKY—Openin' time, Boss. (*He presses a button at rear which switches off the lights. The back room becomes drabber and dingier than ever in the gray daylight that comes from the street windows, off right, and what light can penetrate the grime of the two backyard windows at left. Rocky turns back to Hope—grumpily*) Why don't you go up to bed, Boss? Hickey'd never turn up dis time of de mornin'!

HOPE—(*starts and listens*) Someone's coming now.

ROCKY—(*listens*) Aw, dat's on'y my two pigs. It's about time dey showed. (*He goes back toward the door at left of the bar.*)

HOPE—(*sourly disappointed*) You keep them dumb broads quiet. I don't want to go to bed. I'm going to catch a couple more winks here and I don't want no damn-fool laughing and screeching. (*He settles himself in his chair, grumbling*) Never thought I'd see the day when Harry Hope's would have tarts rooming in it. What'd Bessie think? But I don't let 'em use my rooms for business. And they're good kids. Good as anyone else. They got to make a living. Pay their rent, too, which is more than I can say for—(*He cocks an eye over his specs at Mosher and grins with satisfaction.*) Bejees, Ed, I'll bet Bessie is doing somersaults in her grave! (*He chuckles. But Mosher's eyes are closed, his head nodding, and he doesn't reply, so Hope closes his eyes. Rocky has opened the barroom door at rear and is standing in the hall beyond it, facing right. A girl's laugh is heard.*)

ROCKY—(*warningly*) Nix! Piano! (*He comes in, beckoning them to follow. He goes behind the bar and gets a whiskey bottle and glasses and chairs. Margie and Pearl follow him, casting a glance around. Everyone except Larry and Parritt is asleep or dozing. Even Parritt has his eyes closed. The two girls, neither much over twenty, are typical dollar street walkers, dressed in the usual tawdry get-up. Pearl is obviously Italian with black hair and eyes. Margie has brown hair and hazel eyes, a slum New Yorker of mixed blood. Both are plump and have a certain prettiness that shows even through their blobby make-up. Each retains a vestige of youthful freshness, although the game is beginning to get them and give them hard, worn expressions. Both are sentimental, feather-brained, giggly, lazy, good-natured and reasonably contented with life. Their attitude toward Rocky is much that of two maternal, affectionate sisters toward a bullying brother whom they like to tease and spoil. His attitude toward them is that of the owner of two performing pets he has trained to do a profitable act under his management. He feels a proud proprietor's affection for them, and is tolerantly lax in his discipline.*)

MARGIE—(*glancing around*) Jees, Poil, it's de Morgue wid all de stiffs on deck. (*She catches Larry's eye and smiles affectionately.*) Hello, Old Wise Guy, ain't you died yet?

LARRY—(*grinning*) Not yet, Margie. But I'm waiting impatiently for the end. (*Parritt opens his eyes to look at the two girls, but as soon as they glance at him he closes them again and turns his head away.)*

MARGIE—*(as she and Pearl come to the table at right, front, followed by Rocky)* Who's de new guy? Friend of yours, Larry? *(Automatically she smiles seductively at Parritt and addresses him in a professional chant.)* Wanta have a good time, kid?

PEARL—Aw, he's passed out. Hell wid him!

HOPE—*(cocks an eye over his specs at them—with drowsy irritation)* You dumb broads cut the loud talk. *(He shuts his eye again.)*

ROCKY—*(admonishing them good-naturedly)* Sit down before I knock yuh down. *(Margie and Pearl sit at left, and rear, of table, Rocky at right of it. The girls pour drinks. Rocky begins in a brisk, business-like manner but in a lowered voice with an eye on Hope.)* Well, how'd you tramps do?

MARGIE—Pretty good. Didn't we, Poil?

PEARL—Sure. We nailed a coupla all-night guys.

MARGIE—On Sixth Avenoo. Boobs from de sticks.

PEARL—Stinko, de bot' of 'em.

MARGIE—We thought we was in luck. We steered dem to a real hotel. We figgered dey was too stinko to bother us much and we could cop a good sleep in beds that ain't got cobble stones in de mattress like de ones in dis dump.

PEARL—But we was outa luck. Dey didn't bother us much dat way, but dey wouldn't go to sleep either, see? Jees, I never hoid such gabby guys.

MARGIE—Dey got onta politics, drinkin' outa de bottle. Dey forgot we was around. "De Bull Moosers is de on'y reg'lar guys," one guy says. And de other guy says, "You're a God-damned liar! And I'm a Republican!" Den dey'd laugh.

PEARL—Den dey'd get mad and make a bluff dey was goin' to scrap, and den dey'd make up and cry and sing "School Days." Jees, imagine tryin' to sleep wid dat on de phonograph!

MARGIE—Maybe you tink we wasn't glad when de house dick come up and told us all to git dressed and take de air!

PEARL—We told de guys we'd wait for dem 'round de corner.

MARGIE—So here we are.

ROCKY—*(sententiously)* Yeah. I see you. But I don't see no dough yet.

PEARL—*(with a wink at Margie—teasingly)* Right on de job, ain't he, Margie?

MARGIE—Yeah, our little business man! Dat's him!

ROCKY—Come on! Dig! *(They both pull up their skirts to get the money from their stockings. Rocky watches this move carefully.)*

PEARL—*(amused)* Pipe him keepin' cases, Margie.

MARGIE—*(amused)* Scared we're holdin' out on him.

PEARL—Way he grabs, yuh'd tink it was him done de woik. *(She holds out a little roll of bills to Rocky.)* Here y'are, Grafter!

MARGIE—*(holding hers out)* We hope it chokes yuh. *(Rocky counts the money quickly and shoves it in his pocket.)*

ROCKY—*(genially)* You dumb baby dolls gimme a pain. What would you do wid money if I wasn't around? Give it all to some pimp.

PEARL—*(teasingly)* Jees, what's the difference—? *(hastily)* Aw, I don't mean dat, Rocky.

ROCKY—*(his eyes growing hard—slowly)* A lotta difference, get me?

PEARL—Don't get sore. Jees, can't yuh take a little kiddin'?

MARGIE—Sure, Rocky, Poil was on'y kiddin'. *(soothingly)* We know yuh got a reg'lar job. Dat's why we like yuh, see? Yuh don't live offa us. Yuh're a bartender.

ROCKY—*(genially again)* Sure, I'm a bartender. Everyone knows me knows dat. And I treat you goils right, don't I? Jees, I'm wise yuh hold out on me, but I know it ain't much, so what the hell, I let yuh get away wid it. I tink yuh're a coupla good kids. Yuh're aces wid me, see?

PEARL—You're aces wid us, too. Ain't he, Margie?

MARGIE—Sure, he's aces. *(Rocky beams complacently and takes the glasses back to the bar. Margie whispers)* Yuh sap, don't yuh know enough not to kid him on dat? Serve yuh right if he beat yuh up!

PEARL—*(admiringly)* Jees, I'll bet he'd give yuh an awful beatin', too, once he started. Ginnies got awful tempers.

MARGIE—Anyway, we wouldn't keep no pimp, like we was reg'lar old whores. We ain't dat bad.

PEARL—No. We're tarts, but dat's all.

ROCKY—*(rinsing glasses behind the bar)* Cora got back around three o'clock. She woke up Chuck and dragged him outa de hay to go to a chop suey joint. *(disgustedly)* Imagine him standin' for dat stuff!

MARGIE—*(disgustedly)* I'll bet dey been sittin' around kiddin' demselves wid dat old pipe dream about gettin' married and settlin' down on a farm. Jees, when Chuck's on de wagon, dey never lay off dat dope! Dey give yuh an earful every time yuh talk to 'em!

PEARL—Yeah. Chuck wid a silly grin on his ugly map, de big boob, and Cora gigglin' like she was in grammar school and some tough guy'd just told her babies wasn't brung down de chimney by a boid!

MARGIE—And her on de turf long before me and you was! And bot' of 'em arguin' all de time, Cora sayin' she's scared to marry him because he'll go on drunks again. Just as dough any drunk could scare Cora!

PEARL—And him swearin', de big liar, he'll never go on no more periodicals! An' den her pretendin'—But it gives me a pain to talk about it. We ought to phone de booby hatch to send round de wagon for 'em.

ROCKY—(*comes back to the table—disgustedly*) Yeah, of all de pipe dreams in dis dump, dey got de nuttiest! And nuttin' stops dem. Dey been dreamin' it for years, every time Chuck goes on de wagon. I never could figger it. What would gettin' married get dem? But de farm stuff is de sappiest part. When bot' of 'em was dragged up in dis ward and ain't never been nearer a farm dan Coney Island! Jees, dey'd think dey'd gone deef if dey didn't hear de El rattle! Dey'd get D.T.s if dey ever hoid a cricket choip! I hoid crickets once on my cousin's place in Joisey. I couldn't sleep a wink. Dey give me de heebie-jeebies. (*with deeper disgust*) Jees, can yuh picture a good bar-keep like Chuck diggin' spuds? And imagine a whore hustlin' de cows home! For Christ sake! Ain't dat a sweet picture!

MARGIE—(*rebukingly*) Yuh oughtn't to call Cora dat. Rocky. She's a good kid. She may be a tart, but—

ROCKY—(*considerately*) Sure, dat's all I meant, a tart.

PEARL—(*giggling*) But he's right about de damned cows, Margie. Jees, I bet Cora don't know which end of de cow has de horns! I'm goin' to ask her. (*There is the noise of a door opening in the hall and the sound of a man's and woman's arguing voices.*)

ROCKY—Here's your chance. Dat's dem two nuts now. (*Cora and Chuck look in from the hallway and then come in. Cora is a thin peroxide blonde, a few years older than Pearl and Margie, dressed in similar style, her round face showing more of the wear and tear of her trade than theirs, but still with traces of a doll-like prettiness. Chuck is a tough, thick-necked, barrel-chested Italian-American, with a fat, amiable, swarthy face. He has on a straw hat with a vivid band, a loud suit, tie and shirt, and yellow shoes. His eyes are clear and he looks healthy and strong as an ox.*)

CORA—(*gaily*) Hello, bums. (*She looks around.*) Jees, de Morgue on a rainy Sunday night! (*She waves to Larry—affectionately*) Hello, Old Wise Guy! Ain't you croaked yet?

LARRY—(*grins*) Not yet, Cora. It's damned tiring, this waiting for the end.

CORA—Aw, gwan, you'll never die! Yuh'll have to hire someone to croak yuh wid an axe.

HOPE—(*cocks one sleepy eye at her—irritably*) You dumb hookers, cut the loud noise! This ain't a cathouse!

CORA—(*teasingly*) My, Harry! Such language!

HOPE—(*closes his eyes—to himself with a gratified chuckle*) Bejees, I'll bet Bessie's turning over in her grave! (*Cora sits down between Margie and Pearl. Chuck takes an empty chair from Hope's table and puts it by hers and sits down. At Larry's table, Parritt is glaring resentfully toward the girls.*)

PARRITT—If I'd known this dump was a hooker hangout, I'd never have come here.

LARRY—(*watching him*) You seem down on the ladies.

PARRITT—(*vindictively*) I hate every bitch that ever lived! They're all alike! (*catching himself guiltily*) You can understand how I feel, can't you, when it was getting mixed up with a tart that made me have that fight with Mother? (*then with a resentful sneer*) But what the hell does it matter to you? You're in the grandstand. You're through with life.

LARRY—(*sharply*) I'm glad you remember it. I don't want to know a damned thing about your business. (*He closes his eyes and settles on his chair as if preparing for sleep. Parritt starts at him sneeringly. Then he looks away and his expression becomes furtive and frightened.*)

CORA—Who's de guy wid Larry?

ROCKY—A tightwad. To hell wid him.

PEARL—Say, Cora, wise me up. Which end of a cow is dehorns on?

CORA—(*embarrassed*) Aw, don't bring dat up. I'm sick of hearin' about dat farm.

ROCKY—You got nuttin' on us!

CORA—(*ignoring this*) Me and dis overgrown tramp has been scrappin' about it. He says Joisey's de best place, and I says Long Island because we'll be near Coney. And I tells him, How do I know yuh're off of periodicals for life? I don't give a damn how drunk yuh get, the way we are, but I don't wanta be married to no soak.

CHUCK—And I tells her I'm off de stuff for life. Den she beefs we won't be married a month before I'll trow it in her face she was a tart. "Jees, Baby," I tells her. "Why should I? What de hell yuh tink I tink I'm marryin', a voigin? Why should I kick as long as yuh lay off it and don't do no cheatin' wid de iceman or nobody?" (*He gives her a rough hug.*) Dat's on de level, Baby. (*He kisses her.*)

CORA—(*kissing him*) Aw, yuh big tramp!

ROCKY—(*shakes his head with profound disgust*) Can yuh tie it? I'll buy a drink. I'll do anything. (*He gets up.*)

CORA—No, dis round's on me. I run into luck. Dat's why I dragged Chuck outa bed to celebrate. It was a sailor. I rolled him. (*She giggles.*) Listen, it was a scream. I've run into some nutty souses, but dis guy was de nuttiest. De booze dey dish out around de Brooklyn Navy Yard must be as turrible bug-juice as Harry's. My dogs was givin' out when I seen dis guy holdin' up a lamppost, so I hurried to get him before a cop did. I says, "Hello, Handsome, wanta have a good time?" Jees, he was paralyzed! One of dem polite jags. He tries to bow to me, imagine, and I had to prop him up or he'd fell on his nose. And what d'yuh tink he said? "Lady," he says, "can yuh kindly tell me de nearest way to de Museum of Natural History?" (*They all laugh.*) Can yuh imagine! At two A.M. As if I'd know where de dump was anyway. But I says, "Sure ting, Honey Boy, I'll be only too glad." So I steered him into a side street where it was dark and propped him against a wall and give him a frisk. (*She giggles.*) And what d'yuh tink he does? Jees, I ain't lyin', he begins to laugh, de big sap! He says, "Quit ticklin' me." While I was friskin' him for his roll! I near died! Den I toined him 'round and give him a push to start him. "Just keep goin'," I told him. "It's a big white building on your right. You can't miss it." He must be swimmin' in de North River yet! (*They all laugh.*)

CHUCK—Ain't Uncle Sam de sap to trust guys like dat wid dough!

CORA—(*with a business-like air*) I picked twelve bucks offa him. Come on, Rocky. Set 'em up. (*Rocky goes back to the bar. Cora looks around the room.*) Say, Chuck's kiddin' about de iceman a minute ago reminds me. Where de hell's Hickey?

ROCKY—Dat's what we're all wonderin'.

CORA—He oughta be here. Me and Chuck seen him.

ROCKY—(*excited, comes back from the bar, forgetting the drinks*) You seen Hickey? (*He nudges Hope.*) Hey, Boss, come to! Cora's seen Hickey. (*Hope is instantly wide awake and everyone in the place, except Hugo and Parritt, begins to rouse up hopefully, as if a mysterious wireless message had gone round.*)

HOPE—Where'd you see him, Cora?

CORA—Right on de next corner. He was standin' dere. We said, "Welcome to our city. De gang is expectin' yuh wid deir tongues hangin' out a yard long." And I kidded him, "How's de iceman, Hickey? How's he doin' at your house?" He laughs and says, "Fine." And he says, "Tell de gang I'll be along in a minute. I'm just finishin' figurin' out de best way to save dem and bring dem peace."

HOPE—(*chuckles*) Bejees, he's thought up a new gag! It's a wonder he didn't borry a Salvation Army uniform and show up in that! Go out and get him, Rocky. Tell him we're waitin' to be saved! (*Rocky goes out, grinning.*)

CORA—Yeah, Harry, he was only kiddin'. But he was funny, too, somehow. He was different, or somethin'.

CHUCK—Sure, he was sober, Baby. Dat's what made him different. We ain't never seen him when he wasn't on a drunk, or had de willies gettin' over it.

CORA—Sure! Gee, ain't I dumb?

HOPE—(*with conviction*) The dumbest broad I ever seen! (*then puzzledly*) Sober? That's funny. He's always lapped up a good starter on his way here. Well, bejees, he won't be sober long! He'll be good and ripe for my birthday party tonight at twelve. (*He chuckles with excited anticipation—addressing all of them*) Listen! He's fixed some new gag to pull on us. We'll pretend to let him kid us, see? And we'll kid the pants off him. (*They all say laughingly,* "Sure, Harry," "Righto," "That's the stuff," "We'll fix him," *etc., etc., their faces excited with the same eager anticipation. Rocky appears in the doorway at the end of the bar with Hickey, his arm around Hickey's shoulders.*)

ROCKY—(*with an affectionate grin*) Here's the old son of a bitch! (*They all stand up and greet him with affectionate acclaim,* "Hello, Hickey!" *etc. Even Hugo comes out of his coma to raise his head and blink through his thick spectacles with a welcoming giggle.*)

HICKEY—(*jovially*) Hello, Gang! (*He stands a moment, beaming around at all of them affectionately. He is about fifty, a little under medium height, with a stout, roly-poly figure. His face is round and smooth and big-boyish with bright blue eyes, a button nose, a small, pursed mouth. His head is bald except for a fringe of hair around his temples and the back of his head. His expression is fixed in a salesman's winning smile of self-confident affability and hearty good fellowship. His eyes have the twinkle of a humor which delights in kidding others but can also enjoy equally a joke on himself. He exudes a friendly, generous personality that makes everyone like him on sight. You get the impression, too, that he must have real ability in his line. There is an efficient, businesslike approach in his manner, and his eyes can take you in shrewdly at a glance. He has the salesman's mannerisms of speech, an easy flow of glib, persuasive convincingness. His clothes are those of a successful drummer whose territory consists of minor cities and small towns—not flashy but conspicuously spic and span. He immediately puts on an entrance act, places a hand affectedly on his chest, throws back his head, and sings in a falsetto tenor*) "It's always fair weather, when good fellows get together!" (*changing to a comic bass and another tune*) "And another little drink won't do us any harm!" (*They all roar with laughter at this burlesque which his personality makes really funny. He waves his hand in a lordly manner to Rocky.*) Do your duty, Brother Rocky. Bring on the rat poison! (*Rocky grins and goes behind the bar to get drinks amid an approving cheer from the crowd. Hickey comes forward to shake hands with Hope—with affectionate heartiness*) How goes it, Governor?

HOPE—(*enthusiastically*) Bejees, Hickey, you old bastard, it's good to see you! (*Hickey shakes hands with Mosher and McGloin; leans right to shake hands with Margie and*

Pearl; moves to the middle table to shake hands with Lewis, Joe Mott, Wetjoen and Jimmy; waves to Willie, Larry and Hugo. He greets each by name with the same affectionate heartiness and there is an interchange of "How's the kid?" "How's the old scout?" "How's the boy?" "How's everything?" *etc., etc. Rocky begins setting out drinks, whiskey glasses with chasers, and a bottle for each table, starting with Larry's table. Hope says)* Sit down, Hickey. Sit down. (*Hickey takes the chair, facing front, at the front of the table in the second row which is half between Hope's table and the one where Jimmy Tomorrow is. Hope goes on with excited pleasure.*) Bejees, Hickey, it seems natural to see your ugly, grinning map. (*with a scornful nod to Cora*) This dumb broad was tryin' to tell us you'd changed, but you ain't a damned bit. Tell us about yourself. How've you been doin'? Bejees, you look like a million dollars.

ROCKY—(*coming to Hickey's table, puts a bottle of whiskey, a glass and a chaser on it—then hands Hickey a key*) Here's your key, Hickey. Same old room.

HICKEY—(*shoves the key in his pocket*) Thanks, Rocky. I'm going up in a little while and grab a snooze. Haven't been able to sleep lately and I'm tired as hell. A couple of hours good kip will fix me.

HOPE—(*as Rocky puts drinks on his table*) First time I ever heard you worry about sleep. Bejees, you never would go to bed. (*He raises his glass, and all the others except Parritt do likewise.*) Get a few slugs under your belt and you'll forget sleeping. Here's mud in your eye, Hickey. (*They all join in with the usual humorous toasts.*)

HICKEY—(*heartily*) Drink hearty, boys and girls! (*They all drink, but Hickey drinks only his chaser.*)

HOPE—Bejees, is that a new stunt, drinking your chaser first?

HICKEY—No, I forgot to tell Rocky—You'll have to excuse me, boys and girls, but I'm off the stuff. For keeps. (*They stare at him in amazed incredulity.*)

HOPE—What the hell—(*then with a wink at the others, kiddingly*) Sure! Joined the Salvation Army, ain't you? Been elected President of the W.C.T.U.? Take that bottle away from him, Rocky. We don't want to tempt him into sin. (*He chuckles and the others laugh.*)

HICKEY—(*earnestly*) No, honest, Harry. I know it's hard to believe but—(*He pauses—then adds simply*) Cora was right, Harry. I have changed. I mean, about booze. I don't need it any more. (*They all stare, hoping it's a gag, but impressed and disappointed and made vaguely uneasy by the change they now sense in him.*)

HOPE—(*his kidding a bit forced*) Yeah, go ahead, kid the pants off us! Bejees, Cora said you was coming to save us! Well, go on. Get this joke off your chest! Start the service! Sing a God-damned hymn if you like. We'll all join in the chorus. "No drunkard can enter this beautiful home." That's a good one. (*He forces a cackle.*)

HICKEY—(*grinning*) Oh, hell, Governor! You don't think I'd come around here peddling some brand of temperance bunk, do you? You know me better than that! Just because I'm through with the stuff don't mean I'm going Prohibition. Hell, I'm not that ungrateful! It's given me too many good times. I feel exactly the same as I always did. If anyone wants to get drunk, if that's the only way they can be happy, and feel at peace with themselves, why the hell shouldn't they? They have my full and entire sympathy. I know all about that game from soup to nuts. I'm the guy that wrote the book. The only reason I've quit is—Well, I finally had the guts to face myself and throw overboard the damned lying pipe dream that'd been making me miserable, and do what I had to do for the happiness of all concerned—and then all at once I found I was at peace with myself and I didn't need booze any more. That's all there was to it. (*He pauses. They are staring at him, uneasy and beginning to feel defensive. Hickey looks round and grins affectionately—apologetically*) But what the hell! Don't let me be a wet blanket, making fool speeches about myself. Set 'em up again, Rocky. Here. (*He pulls a big roll from his pocket and peels off a ten-dollar bill. The faces of all brighten.*) Keep the balls coming until this is killed. Then ask for more.

ROCKY—Jees, a roll dat'd choke a hippopotamus! Fill up, youse guys. (*They all pour out drinks.*)

HOPE—That sounds more like you, Hickey. That water-wagon bull—Cut out the act and have a drink, for Christ's sake.

HICKEY—It's no act, Governor. But don't get me wrong. That don't mean I'm a teetotal grouch and can't be in the party. Hell, why d'you suppose I'm here except to have a party, same as I've always done, and help celebrate your birthday tonight? You've all been good pals to me, the best friends I've ever had. I've been thinking about you ever since I left the house—all the time I was walking over here—

HOPE—Walking? Bejees, do you mean to say you walked?

HICKEY—I sure did. All the way from the wilds of darkest Astoria. Didn't mind it a bit, either. I seemed to get here before I knew it. I'm a bit tired and sleepy but otherwise I feel great. (*kiddingly*) That ought to encourage you, Governor—show you a little walk around the ward is nothing to be so scared about. (*He winks at the others. Hope stiffens resentfully for a second. Hickey goes on.*) I didn't make such bad time either for a fat guy, considering it's a hell of a ways, and

I sat in the park a while thinking. It was going on twelve when I went in the bedroom to tell Evelyn I was leaving. Six hours, say. No, less than that. I'd been standing on the corner some time before Cora and Chuck came along, thinking about all of you. Of course, I was only kidding Cora with that stuff about saving you. (*then seriously*) No, I wasn't either. But I didn't mean booze. I meant save you from pipe dreams. I know now, from my experience, they're the things that really poison and ruin a guy's life and keep him from finding any peace. If you knew how free and contented I feel now. I'm like a new man. And the cure for them is so damned simple, once you have the nerve. Just the old dope of honesty is the best policy—honesty with yourself, I mean. Just stop lying about yourself and kidding yourself about tomorrows. (*He is staring ahead of him now as if he were talking aloud to himself as much as to them. Their eyes are fixed on him with uneasy resentment. His manner becomes apologetic again.*) Hell, this begins to sound like a damned sermon on the way to lead the good life. Forget that part of it. It's in my blood, I guess. My old man used to whale salvation into my heinie with a birch rod. He was a preacher in the sticks of Indiana, like I've told you. I got my knack of sales gab from him, too. He was the boy who could sell those Hoosier hayseeds building lots along the Golden Street! (*taking on a salesman's persuasiveness*) Now listen, boys and girls, don't look at me as if I was trying to sell you a goldbrick. Nothing up my sleeve, honest. Let's take an example. Any one of you. Take you, Governor. That walk around the ward you never take—

HOPE—(*defensively sharp*) What about it?

HICKEY—(*grinning affectionately*) Why, you know as well as I do, Harry. Everything about it.

HOPE—(*defiantly*) Bejees, I'm going to take it!

HICKEY—Sure, you're going to—this time. Because I'm going to help you. I know it's the thing you've got to do before you'll ever know what real peace means. (*He looks at Jimmy Tomorrow*) Same thing with you, Jimmy. You've got to try and get your old job back. And no tomorrow about it! (*as Jimmy stiffens with a pathetic attempt at dignity—placatingly*) No, don't tell me, Jimmy. I know all about tomorrow. I'm the guy that wrote the book.

JIMMY—I don't understand you. I admit I've foolishly delayed, but as it happens, I'd just made up my mind that as soon as I could get straightened out—

HICKEY—Fine! That's the spirit! And I'm going to help you. You've been damned kind to me, Jimmy, and I want to prove how grateful I am. When it's all over and you don't have to nag at yourself any more, you'll be grateful to me, too! (*He looks around at the others.*) And all the rest of you, ladies included, are in the same boat, one way or another.

LARRY—(*who has been listening with sardonic appreciation—in his comically intense, crazy whisper*) Be God, you've hit the nail on the head, Hickey! This dump is the Palace of Pipe Dreams!

HICKEY—(*grins at him with affectionate kidding*) Well, well! The Old Grandstand Foolosopher speaks! You think you're the big exception, eh? Life doesn't mean a damn to you any more, does it? You're retired from the circus. You're just waiting impatiently for the end—the good old Long Sleep! (*He chuckles.*) Well, I think a lot of you, Larry, you old bastard. I'll try and make an honest man of you, too!

LARRY—(*stung*) What the devil are you hinting at, anyway?

HICKEY—You don't have to ask me, do you, a wise old guy like you? Just ask yourself. I'll bet you know.

PARRITT—(*is watching Larry's face with a curious sneering satisfaction*) He's got your number all right, Larry! (*He turns to Hickey.*) That's the stuff, Hickey. Show the old faker up! He's got no right to sneak out of everything.

HICKEY—(*regards him with surprise at first, then with a puzzled interest*) Hello. A stranger in our midst. I didn't notice you before, Brother.

PARRITT—(*embarrassed, his eyes shifting away*) My name's Parritt. I'm an old friend of Larry's. (*His eyes come back to Hickey to find him still sizing him up—defensively*) Well? What are you staring at?

HICKEY—(*continuing to stare—puzzledly*) No offense, Brother. I was trying to figure—Haven't we met before some place?

PARRITT—(*reassured*) No. First time I've ever been East.

HICKEY—No, you're right. I know that's not it. In my game, to be a shark at it, you teach yourself never to forget a name or a face. But still I know damned well I recognized something about you. We're members of the same lodge—in some way.

PARRITT—(*uneasy again*) What are you talking about? You're nuts.

HICKEY—(*dryly*) Don't try to kid me, Little Boy. I'm a good salesman—so damned good the firm was glad to take me back after every drunk—and what made me good was I could size up anyone. (*frowningly puzzled again*) But I don't see—(*suddenly breezily good-natured*) Never mind. I can tell you're having trouble with yourself and I'll be glad to do anything I can to help a friend of Larry's.

LARRY—Mind your own business, Hickey. He's nothing to you—or to me, either. (*Hickey gives him a keen inquisitive glance. Larry looks away and goes on sarcastically.*) You're keeping us all in suspense. Tell us more about how you're going to save us.

HICKEY—(*good-naturedly but seeming a little hurt*) Hell, don't get sore, Larry. Not at me. We've always been good pals, haven't we? I know I've always liked you a lot.

LARRY—(*a bit shamefaced*) Well, so have I liked you. Forget it, Hickey.

HICKEY—(*beaming*) Fine! That's the spirit! (*looking around at the others, who have forgotten their drinks*) What's the matter, everybody? What is this, a funeral? Come on and drink up! A little action! (*They all drink.*) Have another. Hell, this is a celebration! Forget it, if anything I've said sounds too serious. I don't want to be a pain in the neck. Any time you think I'm talking out of turn, just tell me to go chase myself! (*He yawns with growing drowsiness and his voice grows a bit muffled.*) No, boys and girls, I'm not trying to put anything over on you. It's just that I know now from experience what a lying pipe dream can do to you—and how damned relieved and contented with yourself you feel when you're rid of it. (*He yawns again.*) God, I'm sleepy all of a sudden. That long walk is beginning to get me. I better go upstairs. Hell of a trick to go dead on you like this. (*He starts to get up but relaxes again. His eyes blink as he tries to keep them open.*) No, boys and girls, I've never known what real peace was until now. It's a grand feeling, like when you're sick and suffering like hell and the Doc gives you a shot in the arm, and the pain goes, and you drift off. (*His eyes close.*) You can let go of yourself at last. Let yourself sink down to the bottom of the sea. Rest in peace. There's no farther you have to go. Not a single damned hope or dream left to nag you. You'll all know what I mean after you—(*He pauses—mumbles*) Excuse—all in—got to grab forty winks—Drink up, everybody—on me—(*The sleep of complete exhaustion overpowers him. His chin sags to his chest. They stare at him with puzzled uneasy fascination.*)

HOPE—(*forcing a tone of irritation*) Bejees, that's a fine stunt, to go to sleep on us! (*then fumingly to the crowd*) Well, what the hell's the matter with you bums? Why don't you drink up? You're always crying for booze, and now you've got it under your nose, you sit like dummies! (*They start and gulp down their whiskies and pour another. Hope stares at Hickey.*) Bejees, I can't figure Hickey. I still say he's kidding us. Kid his own grandmother, Hickey would. What d'you think, Jimmy?

JIMMY—(*unconvincingly*) It must be another of his jokes, Harry, although—Well, he does appear changed. But he'll probably be his natural self again tomorrow—(*hastily*) I mean, when he wakes up.

LARRY—(*staring at Hickey frowningly—more aloud to himself than to them*) You'll make a mistake if you think he's only kidding.

PARRITT—(*in a low confidential voice*) I don't like that guy, Larry. He's too damned nosy. I'm going to steer clear of him. (*Larry gives him a suspicious glance, then looks hastily away.*)

JIMMY—(*with an attempt at open-minded reasonableness*) Still, Harry, I have to admit there was some sense in his nonsense. It is time I got my job back—although I hardly need him to remind me.

HOPE—(*with an air of frankness*) Yes, and I ought to take a walk around the ward. But I don't need no Hickey to tell me, seeing I got it all set for my birthday tomorrow.

LARRY—(*sardonically*) Ha! (*then in his comically intense, crazy whisper*) Be God, it looks like he's going to make two sales of his peace at least! But you'd better make sure first it's the real McCoy and not poison.

HOPE—(*disturbed—angrily*) You bughouse I-Won't-Work harp, who asked you to shove in an oar? What the hell d'you mean, poison? Just because he has your number—(*He immediately feels ashamed of this taunt and adds apologetically*) Bejees, Larry, you're always croaking about something to do with death. It gets my nanny. Come on, fellers, let's drink up. (*They drink. Hope's eyes are fixed on Hickey again.*) Stone cold sober and dead to the world! Spilling that business about pipe dreams! Bejees, I don't get it. (*He bursts out again in angry complaint*) He ain't like the old Hickey! He'll be a fine wet blanket to have around at my birthday party! I wish to hell he'd never turned up!

MOSHER—(*who has been the least impressed by Hickey's talk and is the first to recover and feel the effect of the drinks on top of his hangover—genially*) Give him time, Harry, and he'll come out of it. I've watched many cases of almost fatal teetotalism, but they all came out of it completely cured and as drunk as ever. My opinion is the poor sap is temporarily bughouse from overwork. (*musingly*) You can't be too careful about work. It's the deadliest habit known to science, a great physician once told me. He practiced on street corners under a torchlight. He was positively the only doctor in the world who claimed that rattlesnake oil, rubbed on the prat, would cure heart failure in three days. I remember well his saying to me, "You are naturally delicate, Ed, but if you drink a pint of bad whiskey before breakfast every evening, and never work if you can help it, you may live to a ripe old age. It's staying sober and working that cuts men off in their prime." (*While he is talking, they turn to him with eager grins. They are longing to laugh, and as he finishes they roar. Even Parritt laughs. Hickey sleeps on like a dead man, but Hugo, who had passed into his customary coma again, head on table, looks up through his thick spectacles and giggles foolishly.*)

HUGO—(*blinking around at them. As the laughter dies he speaks in his giggling, wheedling manner, as if he were playfully teasing children.*) Laugh, leedle bourgeois monkey-faces! Laugh like fools, leedle stupid peoples! (*His tone suddenly changes to one of guttural soapbox denunciation and he pounds on the table with a small fist.*) I vill laugh, too! But I vill laugh last! I vill laugh at you! (*He declaims his favorite quotation.*) "The days grow hot, O Babylon! 'Tis cool beneath thy villow trees!" (*They all hoot him down in a chorus of amused jeering. Hugo is not offended. This is evidently their customary reaction. He giggles good-naturedly. Hickey sleeps on. They have all forgotten their uneasiness about him now and ignore him.*)

LEWIS—(*tipsily*) Well, now that our little Robespierre has got the daily bit of guillotining off his chest, tell me more about your doctor friend, Ed. He strikes me as the only bloody sensible medico I ever heard of. I think we should appoint him house physician here without a moment's delay. (*They all laughingly assent.*)

MOSHER—(*warming to his subject, shakes his head sadly*) Too late! The old Doc has passed on to his Maker. A victim of overwork, too. He didn't follow his own advice. Kept his nose to the grindstone and sold one bottle of snake oil too many. Only eighty years old when he was taken. The saddest part was that he knew he was doomed. The last time we got paralyzed together he told me: "This game will get me yet, Ed. You see before you a broken man, a martyr to medical science. If I had any nerves I'd have a nervous breakdown. You won't believe me, but this last year there was actually one night I had so many patients, I didn't even have time to get drunk. The shock to my system brought on a stroke which, as a doctor, I recognized was the beginning of the end." Poor old Doc! When he said this he started crying. "I hate to go before my task is completed, Ed," he sobbed. "I'd hoped I'd live to see the day when, thanks to my miraculous cure, there wouldn't be a single vacant cemetery lot left in this glorious country." (*There is a roar of laughter. He waits for it to die and then goes on sadly.*) I miss Doc. He was a gentleman of the old school. I'll bet he's standing on a street corner in hell right now, making suckers of the damned, telling them there's nothing like snake oil for a bad burn. (*There is another roar of laughter. This time it penetrates Hickey's exhausted slumber. He stirs on his chair, trying to wake up, managing to raise his head a little and force his eyes half open. He speaks with a drowsy, affectionately encouraging smile. At once the laughter stops abruptly and they turn to him startledly.*)

HICKEY—That's the spirit—don't let me be a wet blanket—all I want is to see you happy—(*He slips back into heavy sleep again. They all stare at him, their faces again puzzled, resentful and uneasy.*)

(*Curtain*)

*

ACT TWO

SCENE—*The back room only. The black curtain dividing it from the bar is the right wall of the scene. It is getting on toward midnight of the same day.*

The back room has been prepared for a festivity. At center, front, four of the circular tables are pushed together to form one long table with an uneven line of chairs behind it, and chairs at each end. This improvised banquet table is covered with old table cloths, borrowed from a neighboring beanery, and is laid with glasses, plates and cutlery before each of the seventeen chairs. Bottles of bar whiskey are placed at intervals within reach of any sitter. An old upright piano and stool have been moved in and stand against the wall at left, front. At right, front, is a table without chairs. The other tables and chairs that had been in the room have been moved out, leaving a clear floor space at rear for dancing. The floor has been swept clean of sawdust and scrubbed. Even the walls show evidence of having been washed, although the result is only to heighten their splotchy leprous look. The electric light brackets are adorned with festoons of red ribbon. In the middle of the separate table at right, front, is a birthday cake with six candles. Several packages, tied with ribbon, are also on the table. There are two necktie boxes, two cigar boxes, a fifth containing a half dozen handkerchiefs, the sixth is a square jeweler's watch box.

As the curtain rises, Cora, Chuck, Hugo, Larry, Margie, Pearl and Rocky are discovered. Chuck, Rocky and the three girls have dressed up for the occasion. Cora is arranging a bouquet of flowers in a vase, the vase being a big schooner glass from the bar, on top of the piano. Chuck sits in a chair at the foot (left) of the banquet table. He has turned it so he can watch her. Near the middle of the row of chairs behind the table, Larry sits, facing front, a drink of whiskey before him. He is staring before him in frowning, disturbed meditation. Next to him, on his left, Hugo is in his habitual position, passed out, arms on table, head on arms, a full whiskey glass by his head. By the separate table at right, front, Margie and Pearl are arranging the cake and presents, and Rocky stands by them. All of them, with the exception of Chuck and Rocky, have had plenty to drink and show it, but no one, except Hugo, seems to be drunk. They are trying to act up in the spirit of the occasion but there is something forced about their manner, an undercurrent of nervous irritation and preoccupation.

CORA—(*standing back from the piano to regard the flower effect*) How's dat, Kid?

CHUCK—(*grumpily*) What de hell do I know about flowers?

CORA—Yuh can see dey're pretty, can't yuh, yuh big dummy?

CHUCK—(*mollifyingly*) Yeah, Baby, sure. If yuh like 'em, dey're aw right wid me. (*Cora goes back to give the schooner of flowers a few more touches.*)

MARGIE—(*admiring the cake*) Some cake, huh, Poil? Lookit! Six candles. Each for ten years.

PEARL—When do we light de candles, Rocky?

ROCKY—(*grumpily*) Ask dat bughouse Hickey. He's elected himself boss of dis boithday racket. Just before Harry comes down, he says. Den Harry blows dem out wid one breath, for luck. Hickey was goin' to have sixty candles, but I says, Jees, if de old guy took dat big a breath, he'd croak himself.

MARGIE—(*challengingly*) Well, anyways, it's some cake, ain't it?

ROCKY—(*without enthusiasm*) Sure, it's aw right by me. But what de hell is Harry goin' to do wid a cake? If he ever et a hunk, it'd croak him.

PEARL—Jees, yuh're a dope! Ain't he, Margie?

MARGIE—A dope is right!

ROCKY—(*stung*) You broads better watch your step or—

PEARL—(*defiantly*) Or what?

MARGIE—Yeah! Or what? (*They glare at him truculently.*)

ROCKY—Say, what de hell's got into youse? It'll be twelve o'clock and Harry's boithday before long. I ain't lookin' for no trouble.

PEARL—(*ashamed*) Aw, we ain't neider, Rocky. (*For the moment this argument subsides.*)

CORA—(*over her shoulder to Chuck—acidly*) A guy what can't see flowers is pretty must be some dumbbell.

CHUCK—Yeah? Well, if I was as dumb as you—(*then mollifyingly*) Jees, yuh got your scrappin' pants on, ain't yuh? (*grins good-naturedly*) Hell, Baby, what's eatin' yuh? All I'm tinkin' is, flowers is dat louse Hickey's stunt. We never had no flowers for Harry's boithday before. What de hell can Harry do wid flowers? He don't know a cauliflower from a geranium.

ROCKY—Yeah, Chuck, it's like I'm tellin' dese broads about de cake. Dat's Hickey's wrinkle, too. (*bitterly*) Jees, ever since he woke up, yuh can't hold him. He's taken on de party like it was his boithday.

MARGIE—Well, he's payin' for everything, ain't he?

ROCKY—Aw, I don't mind de boithday stuff so much. What gets my goat is de way he's tryin' to run de whole dump and everyone in it. He's buttin' in all over de place, tellin' everybody where dey get off. On'y he don't really tell yuh. He just keeps hintin' around.

PEARL—Yeah. He was hintin' to me and Margie.

MARGIE—Yeah, de lousy drummer.

ROCKY—He just gives yuh an earful of dat line of bull about yuh got to be honest wid yourself and not kid yourself, and have de guts to be what yuh are. I got sore. I told him dat's aw right for de bums in his dump. I hope he makes dem wake up. I'm sick of listenin' to dem hop demselves up. But it don't go wid me, see? I don't kid myself wid no pipe dream. (*Pearl and Margie exchange a derisive look. He catches it and his eyes narrow.*) What are yuh grinnin' at?

PEARL—(*her face hard—scornfully*) Nuttin'.

MARGIE—Nuttin'.

ROCKY—It better be nuttin'! Don't let Hickey put no ideas in your nuts if you wanta stay healthy! (*then angrily*) I wish de louse never showed up! I hope he don't come back from de delicatessen. He's gettin' everyone nuts. He's ridin' someone every minute. He's got Harry and Jimmy Tomorrow run ragged, and de rest is hidin' in deir rooms so dey won't have to listen to him. Dey're all actin' cagey wid de booze, too, like dey was scared if dey get too drunk, dey might spill deir guts, or somethin'. And everybody's gettin' a prize grouch on.

CORA—Yeah, he's been hintin' round to me and Chuck, too. Yuh'd tink he suspected me and Chuck hadn't no real intention of gettin' married. Yuh'd tink he suspected Chuck wasn't goin' to lay off periodicals—or maybe even didn't want to.

CHUCK—He didn't say it right out or I'da socked him one. I told him, "I'm on de wagon for keeps and Cora knows it."

CORA—I told him, "Sure, I know it. And Chuck ain't never goin' to trow it in my face dat I was a tart, neider. And if yuh tink we're just kiddin' ourselves, we'll show yuh!"

CHUCK—We're goin' to show him!

CORA—We got it all fixed. We've decided Joisey is where we want de farm, and we'll get married dere, too, because yuh don't need no license. We're goin' to get married tomorrow. Ain't we, Honey?

CHUCK—You bet, Baby.

ROCKY—(*disgusted*) Christ, Chuck, are yuh lettin' dat bughouse louse Hickey kid yuh into—

CORA—(*turns on him angrily*) Nobody's kiddin' him into it, nor me neider! And Hickey's right. If dis big tramp's goin' to marry me, he ought to do it, and not just shoot off his old bazoo about it.

ROCKY—(*ignoring her*) Yuh can't be dat dumb, Chuck.

CORA—You keep outa dis! And don't start beefin' about crickets on de farm drivin' us nuts. You and your crickets! Yuh'd tink dey was elephants!

MARGIE—(*coming to Rocky's defense—sneeringly*) Don't notice dat broad, Rocky. Yuh heard her say "tomorrow," didn't yuh? It's de same old crap.

CORA—(*glares at her*) Is dat so?

PEARL—(*lines up with Margie—sneeringly*) Imagine Cora a bride! Dat's a hot one! Jees, Cora, if all de guys you've stayed wid was side by side, yuh could walk on 'em from here to Texas!

CORA—(*starts moving toward her threateningly*) Yuh can't talk like dat to me, yuh fat Dago hooker! I may be a tart, but I ain't a cheap old whore like you!

PEARL—(*furiously*) I'll show yuh who's a whore! (*They start to fly at each other, but Chuck and Rocky grab them from behind.*)

CHUCK—(*forcing Cora onto a chair*) Sit down and cool off, Baby.

ROCKY—(*doing the same to Pearl*) Nix on de rough stuff, Poil.

MARGIE—(*glaring at Cora*) Why don't you leave Poil alone, Rocky? She'll fix dat blonde's clock! Or if she don't, I will!

ROCKY—Shut up, you! (*disgustedly*) Jees, what dames! D'yuh wanta gum Harry's party?

PEARL—(*a bit shamefaced—sulkily*) Who wants to? But nobody can't call me a ——.

ROCKY—(*exasperatedly*) Aw, bury it! What are you, a voigin? (*Pearl stares at him, her face growing hard and bitter. So does Margie.*)

PEARL—Yuh mean you tink I'm a whore, too, huh

MARGIE—Yeah, and me?

ROCKY—Now don't start nuttin'!

PEARL—I suppose it'd tickle you if me and Margie did what dat louse, Hickey, was hintin' and come right out and admitted we was whores.

ROCKY—Aw right! What of it? It's de truth, ain't it?

CORA—(*lining up with Pearl and Margie—indignantly*) Jees, Rocky, dat's a fine hell of a ting to say to two goils dat's been as good to yuh as Poil and Margie! (*to Pearl*) I didn't mean to call yuh dat, Poil. I was on'y mad.

PEARL—(*accepts the apology gratefully*) Sure, I was mad, too, Cora. No hard feelin's.

ROCKY—(*relieved*) Dere. Dat fixes everything, don't it?

PEARL—(*turns on him—hard and bitter*) Aw right, Rocky. We're whores. You know what dat makes you, don't you?

ROCKY—(*angrily*) Look out, now!

MARGIE—A lousy little pimp, dat's what!

ROCKY—I'll loin yuh! (*He gives her a slap on the side of the face.*)

PEARL—A dirty little Ginny pimp, dat's what!

ROCKY—(*gives her a slap, too*) And dat'll loin you! (*But they only stare at him with hard sneering eyes.*)

MARGIE—He's provin' it to us, Poil.

PEARL—Yeah! Hickey's convoited him. He's give up his pipe dream!

ROCKY—(*furious and at the same time bewildered by their defiance*) Lay off me or I'll beat de hell—

CHUCK—(*growls*) Aw, lay off dem. Harry's party ain't no time to beat up your stable.

ROCKY—(*turns to him*) Whose stable? Who d'yuh tink yuh're talkin' to? I ain't never beat dem up! What d'yuh tink I am? I just give dem a slap, like any guy would his wife, if she got too gabby. Why don't yuh tell dem to lay off me? I don't want no trouble on Harry's boithday party.

MARGIE—(*a victorious gleam in her eye—tauntingly*) Aw right, den, yuh poor little Ginny. I'll lay off yuh till de party's over if Poil will.

PEARL—(*tauntingly*) Sure, I will. For Harry's sake, not yours, yuh little Wop!

ROCKY—(*stung*) Say, listen, youse! Don't get no wrong idea—(*But an interruption comes from Larry who bursts into a sardonic laugh. They all jump startledly and look at him with unanimous hostility. Rocky transfers his anger to him.*) Who de hell yuh laughin' at, yuh half-dead old stew bum?

CORA—(*sneeringly*) At himself, he ought to be! Jees, Hickey's sure got his number!

LARRY—(*ignoring them, turns to Hugo and shakes him by the shoulder—in his comically intense, crazy whisper*) Wake up, Comrade! Here's the Revolution starting on all sides of you and you're sleeping through it! Be God, it's not to Bakunin's ghost you ought to pray in your dreams, but to the great Nihilist, Hickey! He's started a movement that'll blow up the world!

HUGO—(*blinks at him through his thick spectacles—with guttural denunciation*) You, Larry! Renegade! Traitor! I vill have you shot! (*He giggles.*) Don't be a fool! Buy me a trink! (*He sees the drink in front of him, and gulps it down. He begins to sing the Carmagnole in a guttural basso, pounding on the table with his glass.*) "Dansons la Carmagnole! Vive le son! Vive le son! Dansons la Carmagnole! Vive le son des canons!"

ROCKY—Can dat noise!

HUGO—(*ignores this—to Larry, in a low tone of hatred*) That bourgeois svine, Hickey! He laughs like good fellow, he makes jokes, he dares make hints to me so I see what he dares to think. He thinks I am finish, it is too late, and so I do not vish the Day come because it vill not be my Day. Oh, I see what he thinks! He thinks lies even vorse, dat I—(*He stops abruptly with a guilty look, as if afraid he was letting something slip—then revengefully*) I vill have him hanged the first one of all on de first lamppost! (*He changes his mood abruptly and peers around at Rocky and the others—giggling again*) Vhy you so serious, leedle monkey-faces? It's all great joke, no? So ve get drunk, and ve laugh like hell, and den ve die, and de pipe dream vanish! (*A bitter mocking contempt creeps into his tone.*) But be of good cheer, leedle stupid peoples! "The days grow hot, O Babylon!" Soon, leedle proletarians, ve vill have free picnic in the cool shade, ve vill eat hot dogs and trink free beer beneath the villow trees! Like hogs, yes! Like beautiful leedle hogs! (*He stops startledly, as if confused and amazed at what he has heard himself say. He mutters with hatred*) Dot Gottamned liar, Hickey. It is he who makes me sneer. I want to sleep. (*He lets his head fall forward on his folded arms again and closes his eyes. Larry gives him a pitying look, then quickly drinks his drink.*)

CORA—(*uneasily*) Hickey ain't overlookin' no bets, is he? He's even give Hugo de woiks.

LARRY—I warned you this morning he wasn't kidding.

MARGIE—(*sneering*) De old wise guy!

PEARL—Yeah, still pretendin' he's de one exception, like Hickey told him. He don't do no pipe dreamin'! Oh, no!

LARRY—(*sharply resentful*) I—! (*Then abruptly he is drunkenly good-natured, and you feel this drunken manner is an evasive exaggeration.*) All right, take it out on me, if it makes you more content. Sure, I love every hair of your heads, my great big beautiful baby dolls, and there's nothing I wouldn't do for you!

PEARL—(*stiffly*) De old Irish bunk, huh? We ain't big. And we ain't your baby dolls! (*Suddenly she is mollified and smiles.*) But we admit we're beautiful. Huh, Margie?

MARGIE—(*smiling*) Sure ting! But what would he do wid beautiful dolls, even if he had de price, de old goat? (*She laughs teasingly—then pats Larry on the shoulder affectionately.*) Aw, yuh're aw right at dat, Larry, if yuh are full of bull!

PEARL—Sure. Yuh're aces wid us. We're noivous, dat's all. Dat lousy drummer—why can't he be like he's always been? I never seen a guy change so. You pretend to be such a fox, Larry. What d'yuh tink's happened to him?

LARRY—I don't know. With all his gab I notice he's kept that to himself so far. Maybe he's saving the great revelation for Harry's party. (*then irritably*) To hell with him! I don't want to know. Let him mind his own business and I'll mind mine.

CHUCK—Yeah, dat's what I say.

CORA—Say, Larry, where's dat young friend of yours disappeared to?

LARRY—I don't care where he is, except I wish it was a thousand miles away! (*Then, as he sees they are surprised at his vehemence, he adds hastily*) He's a pest.

ROCKY—(*breaks in with his own preoccupation*) I don't give a damn what happened to Hickey, but I know what's gonna happen if he don't watch his step. I told him, "I'll take a lot from you, Hickey, like everyone else in dis dump, because yuh've always been a grand guy. But dere's tings I don't take from you nor nobody, see? Remember dat, or you'll wake up in a hospital—or maybe worse, wid your wife and de iceman walkin' slow behind yuh."

CORA—Aw, yuh shouldn't make dat iceman crack, Rocky. It's aw right for him to kid about it but—I notice Hickey ain't pulled dat old iceman gag dis time. (*excitedly*) D'yuh suppose dat he did catch his wife cheatin'? I don't mean wid no iceman, but wid some guy.

ROCKY—Aw, dat's de bunk. He ain't pulled dat gag or showed her photo around because he ain't drunk. And if he'd caught her cheatin' he'd be drunk, wouldn't he? He'd have beat her up and den gone on de woist drunk he'd ever staged. Like any other guy'd do. (*The girls nod, convinced by this reasoning.*)

CHUCK—Sure! Rocky's got de right dope, Baby. He'd be paralyzed. (*While he is speaking, the Negro, Joe, comes in from the hallway. There is a noticeable change in him. He walks with a tough, truculent swagger and his good-natured face is set in sullen suspicion.*)

JOE—(*to Rocky—defiantly*) I's stood tellin' people dis dump is closed for de night all I's goin' to. Let Harry hire a doorman, pay him wages, if he wants one.

ROCKY—(*scowling*) Yeah? Harry's pretty damned good to you.

JOE—(*shamefaced*) Sure he is. I don't mean dat. Anyways, it's all right. I told Schwartz, de cop, we's closed for de party. He'll keep folks away. (*aggressively again*) I want a big drink, dat's what!

CHUCK—Who's stoppin' yuh? Yuh can have all yuh want on Hickey.

JOE—(*has taken a glass from the table and has his hand on a bottle when Hickey's name is mentioned. He draws his hand back as if he were going to refuse—then grabs it defiantly and pours a big drink.*) All right, I's earned all de drinks on him I could drink in a year for listenin' to his crazy bull. And here's hopin' he gets de lockjaw! (*He drinks and pours out another.*) I drinks on him but I don't drink wid him. No, suh, never no more!

ROCKY—Aw, bull! Hickey's aw right. What's he done to you?

JOE—(*sullenly*) Dat's my business. I ain't buttin' in yours, is I? (*bitterly*) Sure, you think he's all right. He's a white man, ain't he? (*His tone becomes aggressive.*) Listen to me, you white boys! Don't you get it in your heads I's pretendin' to be what I ain't, or dat I ain't proud to be what I is, get me? Or you and me's goin' to have trouble! (*He picks up his drink and walks left as far away from them as he can get and slumps down on the piano stool.*)

MARGIE—(*in a low angry tone*) What a noive! Just because we act nice to him, he gets a swelled nut! If dat ain't a coon all over!

CHUCK—Talkin' fight talk, huh? I'll moider de nigger! (*He takes a threatening step toward Joe, who is staring before him guiltily now.*)

JOE—(*speaks up shamefacedly*) Listen, boys, I's sorry. I didn't mean dat. You been good friends to me. I's nuts, I guess. Dat Hickey, he gets my head all mixed up wit' craziness. (*Their faces at once clear of resentment against him.*)

CORA—Aw, dat's aw right, Joe. De boys wasn't takin' yuh serious. (*then to the others, forcing a laugh*) Jees, what'd I say, Hickey ain't overlookin' no bets. Even Joe. (*She pauses—then adds puzzledly*) De funny ting is, yuh can't stay sore at de bum when he's around. When he forgets de bughouse preachin', and quits tellin' yuh where yuh get off, he's de same old Hickey. Yuh can't help likin' de louse. And yuh got to admit he's got de right dope—(*She adds hastily*) I mean, on some of de bums here.

MARGIE—(*with a sneering look at Rocky*) Yeah, he's coitinly got one guy I know sized up right! Huh, Poil?

PEARL—He coitinly has!

ROCKY—Cut it out, I told yuh!

LARRY—(*is staring before him broodingly. He speaks more aloud to himself than to them.*) It's nothing to me what happened to him. But I have a feeling he's dying to tell us, inside him, and yet he's afraid. He's like that damned kid. It's strange the queer way he seemed to recognize him. If he's afraid, it explains why he's off booze. Like that damned kid again. Afraid if he got drunk, he'd tell—(*While he is speaking, Hickey comes in the doorway at rear. He looks the same as in the previous act, except that now his face beams with the excited expectation of a boy going to a party. His arms are piled with packages.*)

HICKEY—(*booms in imitation of a familiar Polo Grounds bleacherite cry—with rising volume*) Well! Well!! Well!!! (*They all jump startledly. He comes forward, grinning.*) Here I am in the nick of time. Give me a hand with these bundles, somebody. (*Margie and Pearl start taking them from his arms and putting them on the table. Now that he is present, all their attitudes show the reaction Cora has expressed. They can't help liking him and forgiving him.*)

MARGIE—Jees, Hickey, yuh scared me outa a year's growth, sneakin' in like dat.

HICKEY—Sneaking? Why, me and the taxi man made enough noise getting my big surprise in the hall to wake the dead. You were all so busy drinking in words of wisdom from the Old Wise Guy here, you couldn't hear anything else. (*He grins at Larry.*) From what I heard, Larry, you're not so good when you start playing Sherlock Holmes. You've got me all wrong. I'm not afraid of anything now—not even myself. You better stick to the part of Old Cemetery, the Barker for the Big Sleep—that is, if you can still let yourself get away with it! (*He chuckles and gives Larry a friendly slap on the back. Larry gives him a bitter angry look.*)

CORA—(*giggles*) Old Cemetery! That's him, Hickey. We'll have to call him dat.

HICKEY—(*watching Larry quizzically*) Beginning to do a lot of puzzling about me, aren't you, Larry? But that won't help you. You've got to think of yourself. I couldn't give you my peace. You've got to find your own. All I can do is help you, and the rest of the gang, by showing you the way to find it. (*He has said this with a simple persuasive earnestness. He pauses, and for a second they stare at him with fascinated resentful uneasiness.*)

ROCKY—(*breaks the spell*) Aw, hire a church!

HICKEY—(*placatingly*) All right! All right! Don't get sore, boys and girls. I guess that did sound too much like a lousy preacher. Let's forget it and get busy on the party. (*They look relieved.*)

CHUCK—Is dose bundles grub, Hickey? You bought enough already to feed an army.

HICKEY—(*with boyish excitement again*) Can't be too much! I want this to be the biggest birthday Harry's ever had. You and Rocky go in the hall and get the big surprise. My arms are busted lugging it. (*They catch his excitement. Chuck and Rocky go out, grinning expectantly. The three girls gather around Hickey, full of thrilled curiosity.*)

PEARL—Jees, yuh got us all het up! What is it, Hickey?

HICKEY—Wait and see. I got it as a treat for the three of you more than anyone. I thought to myself, I'll bet this is what will please those whores more than anything. (*They wince as if he had slapped them, but before they have a chance to be angry, he goes on affectionately.*) I said to myself, I don't care how much it costs, they're worth it. They're the best little scouts in the world, and they've been damned kind to me when I was down and out! Nothing is too good for them. (*earnestly*) I mean every word of that, too—and then some! (*then, as if he noticed the expression on their faces for the first time*) What's the matter? You look sore. What—? (*Then he chuckles.*) Oh, I see. But you know how I feel about that. You know I didn't say it to offend you. So don't be silly now.

MARGIE—(*lets out a tense breath*) Aw right, Hickey. Let it slide.

HICKEY—(*jubilantly, as Chuck and Rocky enter carrying a big wicker basket*) Look! There it comes! Unveil it, boys. (*They pull off a covering burlap bag. The basket is piled with quarts of champagne.*)

PEARL—(*with childish excitement*) It's champagne! Jees, Hickey, if you ain't a sport! (*She gives him a hug, forgetting all animosity, as do the other girls.*)

MARGIE—I never been soused on champagne. Let's get stinko, Poil.

PEARL—You betcha my life! De bot' of us! (*A holiday spirit of gay festivity has seized them all. Even Joe Mott is standing up to look at the wine with an admiring grin, and Hugo raises his head to blink at it.*)

JOE—You sure is hittin' de high spots, Hickey. (*boastfully*) Man, when I runs my gamblin' house, I drinks dat old bubbly water in steins! (*He stops guiltily and gives Hickey a look of defiance.*) I's goin' to drink it dat way again, too, soon's I make my stake! And dat ain't no pipe dream, neider! (*He sits down where he was, his back turned to them.*)

ROCKY—What'll we drink it outa, Hickey? Dere ain't no wine glasses.

HICKEY—(*enthusiastically*) Joe has the right idea! Schooners! That's the spirit for Harry's birthday! (*Rocky and Chuck carry the basket of wine into the bar. The three girls go back and stand around the entrance to the bar, chatting excitedly among themselves and to Chuck and Rocky in the bar.*)

HUGO—(*with his silly giggle*) Ve vill trink vine beneath the villow trees!

HICKEY—(*grins at him*) That's the spirit, Brother—and let the lousy slaves drink vinegar! (*Hugo blinks at him startledly, then looks away.*)

HUGO—(*mutters*) Gottamned liar! (*He puts his head back on his arms and closes his eyes, but this time his habitual pass-out has a quality of hiding.*)

LARRY—(*gives Hugo a pitying glance—in a low tone of anger*) Leave Hugo be! He rotted ten years in prison for his faith! He's earned his dream! Have you no decency or pity?

HICKEY—(*quizzically*) Hello, what's this? I thought you were in the grandstand. (*then with a simple earnestness, taking a chair by Larry, and putting a hand on his shoulder*) Listen, Larry, you're getting me all wrong. Hell, you ought to know me better. I've always been the best-natured slob in the world. Of course, I have pity. But now I've seen the light, it isn't my old kind of pity—the kind yours is. It isn't the kind that lets itself off easy by encouraging some poor guy to go on kidding himself with a lie—the kind that leaves the poor slob worse off because it makes him feel guiltier than ever—the kind that makes his lying hopes nag at him and reproach him until he's a rotten skunk in his own eyes. I know all about that kind of pity. I've had a bellyful of it in my time, and it's all wrong! (*with a salesman's persuasiveness*) No, sir. The kind of pity I feel now is after final results that will really save the poor guy, and make him contented with what he is, and quit battling himself, and find peace for the rest of his life. Oh, I know how you resent the way I have to show you up to yourself. I don't blame you. I know from my own experience it's bitter medicine, facing yourself in the mirror with the old false whiskers off. But you forget that, once you're cured. You'll be grateful to me when all at once you find you're able to admit, without feeling ashamed, that all the grandstand foolosopher bunk and the waiting for the Big Sleep stuff is a pipe dream. You'll say to yourself, I'm just an old man who is scared of life, but even more scared of dying. So I'm keeping drunk and hanging on to life at any price, and what of it? Then you'll know what real peace means, Larry, because you won't be scared of either life or death any more. You simply won't give a damn! Any more than I do!

LARRY—(*has been staring into his eyes with a fascinated wondering dread*) Be God, if I'm not beginning to think you've gone mad! (*with a rush of anger*) You're a liar!

HICKEY—(*injuredly*) Now, listen, that's no way to talk to an old pal who's trying to help you. Hell, if you really wanted to die, you'd just take a hop off your fire escape, wouldn't you? And if you really were in the grandstand, you wouldn't be pitying everyone. Oh, I know the truth is tough at first. It was for me. All I ask is for you to suspend judgment and give it a chance. I'll absolutely guarantee—Hell, Larry, I'm no fool. Do you suppose I'd deliberately set out to get under everyone's skin and put myself in dutch with all my old pals, if I wasn't certain, from my own experience, that it means contentment in the end for all of you? (*Larry again is staring at him fascinatedly. Hickey grins.*) As for my being bughouse, you can't crawl out of it that way. Hell, I'm too damned sane. I can size up guys, and turn 'em inside out, better than I ever could. Even where they're strangers like that Parritt kid. He's licked, Larry. I think there is only one possible way out you can help him to take. That is, if you have the right kind of pity for him.

LARRY—(*uneasily*) What do you mean? (*attempting indifference*) I'm not advising him, except to leave me out of his troubles. He's nothing to me.

HICKEY—(*shakes his head*) You'll find he won't agree to that. He'll keep after you until he makes you help him. Because he has to be punished, so he can forgive himself. He's lost all his guts. He can't manage it alone, and you're the only one he can turn to.

LARRY—For the love of God, mind your own business! (*with forced scorn*) A lot you know about him! He's hardly spoken to you!

HICKEY—No, that's right. But I do know a lot about him just the same. I've had hell inside me. I can spot it in others. (*frowning*) Maybe that's what gives me the feeling there's something familiar about him, something between us. (*He shakes his head.*) No, it's more than that. I can't figure it. Tell me about him. For instance, I don't imagine he's married, is he?

LARRY—No.

HICKEY—Hasn't he been mixed up with some woman? I don't mean trollops. I mean the old real love stuff that crucifies you.

LARRY—(*with a calculating relieved look at him—encouraging him along this line*) Maybe you're right. I wouldn't be surprised.

HICKEY—(*grins at him quizzically*) I see. You think I'm on the wrong track and you're glad I am. Because then I won't suspect whatever he did about the Great Cause. That's another lie you tell yourself, Larry, that the good old Cause means nothing to you any more. (*Larry is about to burst out in denial but Hickey goes on.*) But you're all wrong about Parritt. That isn't what's got him stopped. It's what's behind that. And it's a woman. I recognize the symptoms.

LARRY—(*sneeringly*) And you're the boy who's never wrong! Don't be a damned fool. His trouble is he was brought up a devout believer in the Movement and now he's lost his faith. It's a shock, but he's young and he'll soon find another dream just as good. (*He adds sardonically*) Or as bad.

HICKEY—All right. I'll let it go at that, Larry. He's nothing to me except I'm glad he's here because he'll help me make you wake up to yourself. I don't even like the guy, or the feeling there's anything between us. But you'll find I'm right just the same, when you get to the final showdown with him.

LARRY—There'll be no showdown! I don't give a tinker's damn—

HICKEY—Sticking to the old grandstand, eh? Well, I knew you'd be the toughest to convince of all the gang, Larry. And, along with Harry and Jimmy Tomorrow, you're the one I want most to help. (*He puts an arm around Larry's shoulder and gives him an affectionate hug.*) I've always liked you a lot, you old bastard! (*He gets up and his manner changes to his bustling party excitement—glancing at his watch*) Well, well, not much time before twelve. Let's get busy, boys and girls. (*He looks over the table where the cake is.*) Cake all set. Good. And my presents, and yours, girls, and Chuck's, and Rocky's. Fine. Harry'll certainly be touched by your thought of him. (*He goes back to the girls.*) You go in the bar, Pearl and Margie, and get the grub ready so it can be brought right in. There'll be some drinking and toasts first, of course. My idea is to use the wine for that, so get it all set. I'll go upstairs now and root everyone out. Harry the last. I'll come back with him. Somebody light the candles on the cake when you hear us coming, and you start playing Harry's favorite tune, Cora. Hustle now, everybody. We want this to come off in style. (*He bustles into the hall. Margie and Pearl disappear in the bar. Cora goes to the piano. Joe gets off the stool sullenly to let her sit down.*)

CORA—I got to practice. I ain't laid my mits on a box in Gawd knows when. (*With the soft pedal down, she begins gropingly to pick out "The Sunshine of Paradise Alley."*) Is dat right, Joe? I've forgotten dat has-been tune. (*She picks out a few more notes.*) Come on, Joe, hum de tune so I can follow. (*Joe begins to hum and sing in a low voice and correct her. He forgets his sullenness and becomes his old self again.*)

LARRY—(*suddenly gives a laugh—in his comically intense, crazy tone*) Be God, it's a second feast of Belshazzar, with Hickey to do the writing on the wall!

CORA—Aw, shut up, Old Cemetery! Always beefin'! (*Willie comes in from the hall. He is in a pitiable state, his face pasty, haggard with sleeplessness and nerves, his eyes sick and haunted. He is sober. Cora greets him over her shoulder kiddingly*) If it ain't Prince Willie! (*then kindly*) Gee, kid, yuh look sick. Git a coupla shots in yuh.

WILLIE—(*tensely*) No, thanks. Not now. I'm tapering off. (*He sits down weakly on Larry's right.*)

CORA—(*astonished*) What d'yuh know? He means it!

WILLIE—(*leaning toward Larry confidentially—in a low shaken voice*) It's been hell up in that damned room, Larry! The things I've imagined! (*He shudders.*) I thought I'd go crazy. (*with pathetic boastful pride*) But I've got it beat now. By tomorrow morning I'll be on the wagon. I'll get back my clothes the first thing. Hickey's loaning me the money. I'm going to do what I've always said—go to the D.A.'s office. He was a good friend of my Old Man's. He was only assistant, then. He was in on the graft, but my Old Man never squealed on him. So he certainly owes it to me to give me a chance. And he knows that I really was a brilliant law student. (*self-reassuringly*) Oh, I know I can make good, now I'm getting off the booze forever. (*moved*) I owe a lot to Hickey. He's made me wake up to myself—see what a fool—It wasn't nice to face but—(*with bitter resentment*) It isn't what he says. It's what you feel behind—what he hints—Christ, you'd think all I really wanted to do with my life was sit here and stay drunk. (*with hatred*) I'll show him!

LARRY—(*masking pity behind a sardonic tone*) If you want my advice, you'll put the nearest bottle to your mouth until you don't give a damn for Hickey!

WILLIE—(*stares at a bottle greedily, tempted for a moment—then bitterly*) That's fine advice! I thought you were my friend! (*He gets up with a hurt glance at Larry, and moves away to take a chair in back of the left end of the table, where he sits in dejected, shaking misery, his chin on his chest.*)

JOE—(*to Cora*) No, like dis. (*He beats time with his finger and sings in a low voice*) "She is the sunshine of Paradise Alley." (*She plays.*) Dat's more like it. Try it again. (*She begins to play through the chorus again. Don Parritt enters from the hall. There is a frightened look on his face. He slinks in furtively, as if he were escaping from someone. He looks relieved when he sees Larry and comes and slips into the chair on his right. Larry pretends not to notice his coming, but he instinctively shrinks with repulsion. Parritt leans toward him and speaks ingratiatingly in a low secretive tone.*)

PARRITT—Gee, I'm glad you're here, Larry. That damned fool, Hickey, knocked on my door. I opened up because I thought it must be you, and he came busting in and made me come downstairs. I don't know what for. I don't belong in this birthday celebration. I don't know this gang and I don't want to be mixed up with them. All I came here for was to find you.

LARRY—(*tensely*) I've warned you—

PARRITT—(*goes on as if he hadn't heard*) Can't you make Hickey mind his own business? I don't like that guy, Larry. The way he acts, you'd think he had something on me. Why, just now he pats me on the shoulder, like he was sympathizing with me, and says, "I know how it is, Son, but you can't hide from yourself, not even here on the bottom of the sea. You've got to face the truth and then do what must be done for your own peace and the happiness of all concerned." What did he mean by that, Larry?

LARRY—How the hell would I know?

PARRITT—Then he grins and says, "Never mind, Larry's getting wise to himself. I think you can rely on his help in the end. He'll have to choose between living and dying, and he'll never choose to die while there is a breath left in the old bastard!" And then he laughs like it was a joke on you. (*He pauses. Larry is rigid on his chair, staring before him. Parritt asks him with a sudden taunt in his voice*) Well, what do you say to that, Larry?

LARRY—I've nothing to say. Except you're a bigger fool than he is to listen to him.

PARRITT—(*with a sneer*) Is that so? He's no fool where you're concerned. He's got your number, all right! (*Larry's face tightens but he keeps silent. Parritt changes to a contrite, appealing air.*) I don't mean that. But you keep acting as if you were sore at me, and that gets my goat. You know what I want most is to be friends with you, Larry. I haven't a single friend left in the world. I hoped you—(*bitterly*) And you could be, too, without it hurting you. You ought to, for Mother's sake. She really loved you. You loved her, too, didn't you?

LARRY—(*tensely*) Leave what's dead in its grave.

PARRITT—I suppose, because I was only a kid, you didn't think I was wise about you and her. Well, I was. I've been wise, ever since I can remember, to all the guys she's had, although she'd tried to kid me along it wasn't so. That was a silly stunt for a free Anarchist woman, wasn't it, being ashamed of being free?

LARRY—Shut your damned trap!

PARRITT—(*guiltily but with a strange undertone of satisfaction*) Yes, I know I shouldn't say that now. I keep forgetting she isn't free any more. (*He pauses.*) Do you know, Larry, you're the one of them all she cared most about? Anyone else who left the Movement would have been dead to her, but she couldn't forget you. She'd always make excuses for you. I used to try and get her goat about you. I'd say, "Larry's got brains and yet he thinks the Movement is just a crazy pipe dream." She'd blame it on booze getting you. She'd kid herself that you'd give up booze and come back to the Movement—tomorrow! She'd say, "Larry can't kill in himself a faith he's given his life to, not without killing himself." (*He grins sneeringly.*) How about it, Larry? Was she right? (*Larry remains silent. He goes on insistently.*) I suppose what she really meant was, come back to her. She was always getting the Movement mixed up with herself. But I'm sure she really must have loved you, Larry. As much as she could love anyone besides herself. But she wasn't faithful to you, even at that, was she? That's why you finally walked out on her, isn't it? I remember that last fight you had with her. I was listening. I was on your side, even if she was my mother, because I liked you so much; you'd been so good to me—like a father. I remember her putting on her high-and-mighty free-woman stuff, saying you were still a slave to bourgeois morality and jealousy and you thought a woman you loved was a piece of private property you owned. I remember that you got mad and you told her, "I don't like living with a whore, if that's what you mean!"

LARRY—(*bursts out*) You lie! I never called her that!

PARRITT—(*goes on as if Larry hadn't spoken*) I think that's why she still respects you, because it was you who left her. You were the only one to beat her to it. She got sick of the others before they did of her. I don't think she ever cared much about them, anyway. She just had to keep on having lovers to prove to herself how free she was. (*He pauses—then with a bitter repulsion*) It made home a lousy place. I felt like you did about it. I'd get feeling it was like living in a whorehouse—only worse, because she didn't have to make her living—

LARRY—You bastard! She's your mother! Have you no shame?

PARRITT—(*bitterly*) No! She brought me up to believe that family-respect stuff is all bourgeois, property-owning crap. Why should I be ashamed?

LARRY—(*making a move to get up*) I've had enough!

PARRITT—(*catches his arm—pleadingly*) No! Don't leave me! Please! I promise I won't mention her again! (*Larry sinks back in his chair.*) I only did it to make you understand better. I know this isn't the place to—Why didn't you come up to my room, like I asked you? I kept waiting. We could talk everything over there.

LARRY—There's nothing to talk over!

PARRITT—But I've got to talk to you. Or I'll talk to Hickey. He won't let me alone! I feel he knows, anyway! And I know he'd understand, all right—in his way. But I hate his guts! I don't want anything to do with him! I'm scared of him, honest. There's something not human behind his damned grinning and kidding.

LARRY—(*starts*) Ah! You feel that, too?

PARRITT—(*pleadingly*) But I can't go on like this. I've got to decide what I've got to do. I've got to tell you, Larry!

LARRY—(*again starts up*) I won't listen!

PARRITT—(*again holds him by the arm*) All right! I won't. Don't go! (*Larry lets himself be pulled down on his chair. Parritt examines his face and becomes insultingly scornful.*) Who do you think you're kidding? I know damned well you've guessed—

LARRY—I've guessed nothing!

PARRITT—But I want you to guess now! I'm glad you have! I know now, since Hickey's been after me, that I meant you to guess right from the start. That's why I came to you. (*hurrying on with an attempt at a plausible frank air that makes what he says seem doubly false*) I want you to understand the reason. You see, I began studying American history. I got admiring Washington and Jefferson and Jackson and Lincoln. I began to feel patriotic and love this country. I saw it was the best government in the world, where everybody was equal and had a chance. I saw that all the ideas behind the Movement came from a lot of Russians like Bakunin and Kropotkin and were meant for Europe, but we didn't need them here in a democracy where we were free already. I didn't want this country to be destroyed for a damned foreign pipe dream. After all, I'm from old American pioneer stock. I began to feel I was a traitor for helping a lot of cranks and bums and free women plot to overthrow our government. And then I saw it was my duty to my country—

LARRY—(*nauseated—turns on him*) You stinking rotten liar! Do you think you can fool me with such hypocrite's cant! (*then turning away*) I don't give a damn what you did! It's on your head—whatever it was! I don't want to know—and I won't know!

PARRITT—(*as if Larry had never spoken—falteringly*) But I never thought Mother would be caught. Please believe that, Larry. You know I never would have—

LARRY—(*his face haggard, drawing a deep breath and closing his eyes—as if he were trying to hammer something into his own brain*) All I know is I'm sick of life! I'm through! I've forgotten myself! I'm drowned and contented on the bottom of a bottle. Honor or dishonor, faith or treachery are nothing to me but the opposites of the same stupidity which is ruler and king of life, and in the end they rot into dust in the same grave. All things are the same meaningless joke to me, for they grin at me from the one skull of death. So go away. You're wasting breath. I've forgotten your mother.

PARRITT—(*jeers angrily*) The old foolosopher, eh? (*He spits out contemptuously*) You lousy old faker!

LARRY—(*so distracted he pleads weakly*) For the love of God, leave me in peace the little time that's left to me!

PARRITT—Aw, don't pull that pitiful old-man junk on me! You old bastard, you'll never die as long as there's a free drink of whiskey left!

LARRY—(*stung—furiously*) Look out how you try to taunt me back into life, I warn you! I might remember the thing they call justice there, and the punishment for—(*He checks himself with an effort—then with a real indifference that comes from exhaustion*) I'm old and tired. To hell with you! You're as mad as Hickey, and as big a liar. I'd never let myself believe a word you told me.

PARRITT—(*threateningly*) The hell you won't! Wait till Hickey gets through with you! (*Pearl and Margie come in from the bar. At the sight of them, Parritt instantly subsides and becomes self-conscious and defensive, scowling at them and then quickly looking away.*)

MARGIE—(*eyes him jeeringly*) Why, hello, Tightwad Kid. Come to join de party? Gee, don't he act bashful, Poil?

PEARL—Yeah. Especially wid his dough. (*Parritt slinks to a chair at the left end of the table, pretending he hasn't heard them. Suddenly there is a noise of angry, cursing voices and a scuffle from the hall. Pearl yells*) Hey, Rocky! Fight in de hall! (*Rocky and Chuck run from behind the bar curtain and rush into the hall. Rocky's voice is heard in irritated astonishment,* "What de hell?" *and then the scuffle stops and Rocky appears holding Captain Lewis by the arm, followed by Chuck with a similar hold on General Wetjoen. Although these two have been drinking they are both sober, for them. Their faces are sullenly angry, their clothes disarranged from the tussle.*)

ROCKY—(*leading Lewis forward—astonished, amused and irritated*) Can yuh beat it? I've heard youse two call each odder every name yuh could think of but I never seen you—(*indignantly*) A swell time to stage your first bout, on Harry's boithday party! What started de scrap?

LEWIS—(*forcing a casual tone*) Nothing, old chap. Our business, you know. That bloody ass, Hickey, made some insinuation about me, and the boorish Boer had the impertinence to agree with him.

WETJOEN—Dot's a lie! Hickey made joke about me, and this Limey said yes, it was true!

ROCKY—Well, sit down, de bot' of yuh, and cut out de rough stuff. (*He and Chuck dump them down in adjoining chairs toward the left end of the table, where, like two sulky boys, they turn their backs on each other as far as possible in chairs which both face front.*)

MARGIE—(*laughs*) Jees, lookit de two bums! Like a coupla kids! Kiss and make up, for Gawd's sakes!

ROCKY—Yeah. Harry's party begins in a minute and we don't want no soreheads around.

LEWIS—(*stiffly*) Very well. In deference to the occasion, I apologize, General Wetjoen—provided that you do also.

WETJOEN—(*sulkily*) I apologize, Captain Lewis—because Harry is my goot friend.

ROCKY—Aw, hell! If yuh can't do better'n dat—! (*Mosher and McGloin enter together from the hall. Both have been drinking but are not drunk.*)

PEARL—Here's de star boarders. (*They advance, their heads together, so interested in a discussion they are oblivious to everyone.*)

McGLOIN—I'm telling you, Ed, it's serious this time. That bastard, Hickey, has got Harry on the hip. (*As he talks, Margie, Pearl, Rocky and Chuck prick up their ears and gather round. Cora, at the piano, keeps running through the tune, with soft pedal, and singing the chorus half under her breath, with Joe still correcting her mistakes. At the table, Larry, Parritt, Willie, Wetjoen and Lewis sit motionless, staring in front of them. Hugo seems asleep in his habitual position.*) And you know it isn't going to do us no good if he gets him to take that walk tomorrow.

MOSHER—You're damned right. Harry'll mosey around the ward, dropping in on everyone who knew him when. (*indignantly*) And they'll all give him a phony glad hand and a ton of good advice about what a sucker he is to stand for us.

McGLOIN—He's sure to call on Bessie's relations to do a little cryin' over dear Bessie. And you know what that bitch and all her family thought of me.

MOSHER—(*with a flash of his usual humor—rebukingly*) Remember, Lieutenant, you are speaking of my sister! Dear Bessie wasn't a bitch. She was a God-damned bitch! But if you think my loving relatives will have time to discuss you, you don't know them. They'll be too busy telling Harry what a drunken crook I am and saying he ought to have me put in Sing Sing!

McGLOIN—(*dejectedly*) Yes, once Bessie's relations get their hooks in him, it'll be as tough for us as if she wasn't gone.

MOSHER—(*dejectedly*) Yes, Harry has always been weak and easily influenced, and now he's getting old he'll be an easy mark for those grafters. (*then with forced reassurance*) Oh, hell, Mac, we're saps to worry. We've heard Harry pull that bluff about taking a walk every birthday he's had for twenty years.

McGLOIN—(*doubtfully*) But Hickey wasn't sicking him on those times. Just the opposite. He was asking Harry what he wanted to go out for when there was plenty of whiskey here.

MOSHER—(*with a change to forced carelessness*) Well, after all, I don't care whether he goes out or not. I'm clearing out tomorrow morning anyway. I'm just sorry for you, Mac.

McGLOIN—(*resentfully*) You needn't be, then. Ain't I going myself? I was only feeling sorry for you.

MOSHER—Yes, my mind is made up. Hickey may be a lousy, interfering pest, now he's gone teetotal on us, but there's a lot of truth in some of his bull. Hanging around here getting plastered with you, Mac, is pleasant, I won't deny, but the old booze gets you in the end, if you keep lapping it up. It's time I quit for a while. (*with forced enthusiasm*) Besides, I feel the call of the old carefree circus life in my blood again. I'll see the boss tomorrow. It's late in the season but he'll be glad to take me on. And won't all the old gang be tickled to death when I show up on the lot!

McGLOIN—Maybe—if they've got a rope handy!

MOSHER—(*turns on him—angrily*) Listen! I'm damned sick of that kidding!

McGLOIN—You are, are you? Well, I'm sicker of your kidding me about getting reinstated on the Force. And whatever you'd like, I can't spend my life sitting here with you, ruining my stomach with rotgut. I'm tapering off, and in the morning I'll be fresh as a daisy. I'll go and have a private chin with the Commissioner. (*with forced enthusiasm*) Man alive, from what the boys tell me, there's sugar galore these days, and I'll soon be ridin' around in a big red automobile—

MOSHER—(*derisively—beckoning an imaginary Chinese*) Here, One Lung Hop! Put fresh peanut oil in the lamp and cook the Lieutenant another dozen pills! It's his gowed-up night!

McGLOIN—(*stung—pulls back a fist threateningly*) One more crack like that and I'll—!

MOSHER—(*putting up his fists*) Yes? Just start—! (*Chuck and Rocky jump between them.*)

ROCKY—Hey! Are you guys nuts? Jees, it's Harry's boithday party! (*They both look guilty.*) Sit down and behave.

MOSHER—(*grumpily*) All right. Only tell him to lay off me. (*He lets Rocky push him in a chair, at the right end of the table, rear.*)

McGLOIN—(*grumpily*) Tell him to lay off me. (*He lets Chuck push him into the chair on Mosher's left. At this moment Hickey bursts in from the hall, bustling and excited.*)

HICKEY—Everything all set? Fine! (*He glances at his watch.*) Half a minute to go. Harry's starting down with Jimmy. I had a hard time getting them to move! They'd rather stay hiding up there, kidding each other along. (*He chuckles.*) Harry don't even want to remember it's his birthday now! (*He hears a noise from the stairs.*) Here they come! (*urgently*) Light the candles! Get ready to play, Cora! Stand up, everybody! Get that wine ready, Chuck and Rocky! (*Margie and Pearl light the candles on the cake. Cora gets her hands set over the piano keys, watching over her shoulder. Rocky and Chuck go in the bar. Everybody at the table stands up mechanically. Hugo is the last, suddenly coming to and scrambling to his feet. Harry Hope and Jimmy Tomorrow appear in the hall outside the door. Hickey looks up from his watch.*) On the dot! It's twelve! (*like a cheer leader*) Come on now, everybody, with a Happy Birthday, Harry! (*With his voice leading they all shout* "Happy Birthday, Harry!" *in a spiritless chorus. Hickey signals to Cora, who starts playing and singing in a whiskey soprano "She's the Sunshine of Paradise Alley." Hope and Jimmy stand in the doorway. Both have been drinking heavily. In Hope the effect is apparent only in a bristling, touchy, pugnacious attitude. It is entirely different from the usual irascible beefing he delights in and which no one takes seriously. Now he really has a chip on his shoulder. Jimmy, on the other hand, is plainly drunk, but it has not had the desired effect, for beneath a pathetic assumption of gentlemanly poise, he is obviously frightened and shrinking back within himself. Hickey grabs Hope's hand and pumps it up and down. For a moment Hope appears unconscious of this handshake. Then he jerks his hand away angrily.*)

HOPE—Cut out the glad hand, Hickey. D'you think I'm a sucker? I know you, bejees, you sneaking, lying drummer! (*with rising anger, to the others*) And all you bums! What the hell you trying to do, yelling and raising the roof? Want the cops to close the joint and get my license taken away? (*He yells at Cora who has stopped singing but continues to play mechanically with many mistakes.*) Hey, you dumb tart, quit banging that box! Bejees, the least you could do is learn the tune!

CORA—(*stops—deeply hurt*) Aw, Harry! Jees, ain't I—(*Her eyes begin to fill.*)

HOPE—(*glaring at the other girls*) And you two hookers, screaming at the top of your lungs! What d'you think this is, a dollar cathouse? Bejees, that's where you belong!

PEARL—(*miserably*) Aw, Harry—(*She begins to cry.*)

MARGIE—Jees, Harry, I never thought you'd say that—like yuh meant it. (*She puts her arm around Pearl—on the verge of tears herself*) Aw, don't bawl, Poil. He don't mean it.

HICKEY—(*reproachfully*) Now, Harry! Don't take it out on the gang because you're upset about yourself. Anyway, I've promised you you'll come through all right, haven't I? So quit worrying. (*He slaps Hope on the back encouragingly. Hope flashes him a glance of hate.*)

Be yourself, Governor. You don't want to bawl out the old gang just when they're congratulating you on your birthday, do you? Hell, that's no way!

HOPE—(*looking guilty and shamefaced now—forcing an unconvincing attempt at his natural tone*) Bejees, they ain't as dumb as you. They know I was only kidding them. They know I appreciate their congratulations. Don't you, fellers? (*There is a listless chorus of* "Sure, Harry," "Yes," "Of course we do," *etc. He comes forward to the two girls, with Jimmy and Hickey following him, and pats them clumsily.*) Bejees, I like you broads. You know I was only kidding. (*Instantly they forgive him and smile affectionately.*)

MARGIE—Sure we know, Harry.

PEARL—Sure.

HICKEY—(*grinning*) Sure. Harry's the greatest kidder in this dump and that's saying something! Look how he's kidded himself for twenty years! (*As Hope gives him a bitter, angry glance, he digs him in the ribs with his elbow playfully.*) Unless I'm wrong, Governor, and I'm betting I'm not. We'll soon know, eh? Tomorrow morning. No, by God, it's *this* morning now!

JIMMY—(*with a dazed dread*) *This* morning?

HICKEY—Yes, it's today at last, Jimmy. (*He pats him on the back.*) Don't be so scared! I've promised I'll help you.

JIMMY—(*trying to hide his dread behind an offended, drunken dignity*) I don't understand you. Kindly remember I'm fully capable of settling my own affairs!

HICKEY—(*earnestly*) Well, isn't that exactly what I want you to do, settle with yourself once and for all? (*He speaks in his ear in confidential warning.*) Only watch out on the booze, Jimmy. You know, not too much from now on. You've had a lot already, and you don't want to let yourself duck out of it by being too drunk to move—not this time! (*Jimmy gives him a guilty, stricken look and turns away and slumps into the chair on Mosher's right.*)

HOPE—(*to Margie—still guiltily*) Bejees, Margie, you know I didn't mean it. It's that lousy drummer riding me that's got my goat.

MARGIE—I know. (*She puts a protecting arm around Hope and turns him to face the table with the cake and presents.*) Come on. You ain't noticed your cake yet. Ain't it grand?

HOPE—(*trying to brighten up*) Say, that's pretty. Ain't ever had a cake since Bessie—Six candles. Each for ten years, eh? Bejees, that's thoughtful of you.

PEARL—It was Hickey got it.

HOPE—(*his tone forced*) Well, it was thoughtful of him. He means well, I guess. (*His eyes, fixed on the cake, harden angrily.*) To hell with his cake. (*He starts to turn away. Pearl grabs his arm.*)

PEARL—Wait, Harry. Yuh ain't seen de presents from Margie and me and Cora and Chuck and Rocky. And dere's a watch all engraved wid your name and de date from Hickey.

HOPE—To hell with it! Bejees, he can keep it! (*This time he does turn away.*)

PEARL—Jees, he ain't even goin' to look at our presents.

MARGIE—(*bitterly*) Dis is all wrong. We gotta put some life in dis party or I'll go nuts! Hey, Cora, what's de matter wid dat box? Can't yuh play for Harry? Yuh don't have to stop just because he kidded yuh!

HOPE—(*rouses himself—with forced heartiness*) Yes, come on, Cora. You was playing it fine. (*Cora begins to play halfheartedly. Hope suddenly becomes almost tearfully sentimental.*) It was Bessie's favorite tune. She was always singing it. It brings her back. I wish—(*He chokes up.*)

HICKEY—(*grins at him—amusedly*) Yes, we've all heard you tell us you thought the world of her, Governor.

HOPE—(*looks at him with frightened suspicion*) Well, so I did, bejees! Everyone knows I did! (*threateningly*) Bejees, if you say I didn't—

HICKEY—(*soothingly*) Now, Governor. I didn't say anything. You're the only one knows the truth about that. (*Hope stares at him confusedly. Cora continues to play. For a moment there is a pause, broken by Jimmy Tomorrow who speaks with muzzy, self-pitying melancholy out of a sentimental dream.*)

JIMMY—Marjorie's favorite song was "Loch Lomond." She was beautiful and she played the piano beautifully and she had a beautiful voice. (*with gentle sorrow*) You were lucky, Harry. Bessie died. But there are more bitter sorrows than losing the woman one loves by the hand of death—

HICKEY—(*with an amused wink at Hope*) Now, listen, Jimmy, you needn't go on. We've all heard that story about how you came back to Cape Town and found her in the hay with a staff officer. We know you like to believe that was what started you on the booze and ruined your life.

JIMMY—(*stammers*) I—I'm talking to Harry. Will you kindly keep out of—(*with a pitiful defiance*) My life is not ruined!

HICKEY—(*ignoring this—with a kidding grin*) But I'll bet when you admit the truth to yourself, you'll confess you were pretty sick of her hating you for getting drunk. I'll bet you were really damned relieved when she gave you such a good excuse. (*Jimmy stares at him strickenly. Hickey pats him on the back again—with sincere sympathy*) I know how it is, Jimmy. I—(*He stops abruptly and for a second he seems to lose his self-assurance and become confused.*)

LARRY—(*seizing on this with vindictive relish*) Ha! So that's what happened to you, is it? Your iceman joke finally came home to roost, did it? (*He grins tauntingly.*) You should have remembered there's truth in the old superstition that you'd better look out what you call because in the end it comes to you!

HICKEY—(*himself again—grins to Larry kiddingly*) Is that a fact, Larry? Well, well! Then you'd better watch out how you keep calling for that old Big Sleep! (*Larry starts and for a second looks superstitiously frightened. Abruptly Hickey changes to his jovial, bustling, master-of-ceremonies manner.*) But what are we waiting for, boys and girls? Let's start the party rolling! (*He shouts to the bar*) Hey, Chuck and Rocky! Bring on the big surprise! Governor, you sit at the head of the table here. (*He makes Harry sit down on the chair at the end of the table, right. To Margie and Pearl*) Come on, girls, sit down. (*They sit side by side on Jimmy's right. Hickey bustles down to the left end of table.*) I'll sit here at the foot. (*He sits, with Cora on his left and Joe on her left. Rocky and Chuck appear from the bar, each bearing a big tray laden with schooners of champagne which they start shoving in front of each member of the party.*)

ROCKY—(*with forced cheeriness*) Real champagne, bums! Cheer up! What is dis, a funeral? Jees, mixin' champagne wid Harry's redeye will knock yuh paralyzed! Ain't yuh never satisfied? (*He and Chuck finish serving out the schooners, grab the last two themselves and sit down in the two vacant chairs remaining near the middle of the table. As they do so, Hickey rises, a schooner in his hand.*)

HICKEY—(*rapping on the table for order when there is nothing but a dead silence*) Order! Order, Ladies and Gents! (*He catches Larry's eyes on the glass in his hand.*) Yes, Larry, I'm going to drink with you this time. To prove I'm not teetotal because I'm afraid booze would make me spill my secrets, as you think. (*Larry looks sheepish. Hickey chuckles and goes on.*) No, I gave you the simple truth about that. I don't need booze or anything else any more. But I want to be sociable and propose a toast in honor of our old friend, Harry, and drink it with you. (*His eyes fix on Hugo, who is out again, his head on his plate—to Chuck, who is on Hugo's left*) Wake up our demon bomb-tosser, Chuck. We don't want corpses at this feast.

CHUCK—(*gives Hugo a shake*) Hey, Hugo, come up for air! Don't yuh see de champagne? (*Hugo blinks around and giggles foolishly.*)

HUGO—Ve will eat birthday cake and trink champagne beneath the villow tree! (*He grabs his schooner and takes a greedy gulp—then sets it back on the table with a grimace of distaste—in a strange, arrogantly disdainful tone, as if he were rebuking a butler*) Dis vine is unfit to trink. It has not properly been iced.

HICKEY—(*amusedly*) Always a high-toned swell at heart, eh, Hugo? God help us poor bums if you'd ever get to telling us where to get off! You'd have been drinking our blood beneath those willow trees! (*He chuckles. Hugo shrinks back in his chair, blinking at him, but Hickey is now looking up the table at Hope. He starts his toast, and as he goes on he becomes more moved and obviously sincere.*) Here's the toast, Ladies and Gents! Here's to Harry Hope, who's been a friend in need to every one of us! Here's to the old Governor, the best sport and the kindest, biggest-hearted guy in the world! Here's wishing you all the luck there is, Harry, and long life and happiness! Come on, everybody! To Harry! Bottoms up! (*They have all caught his sincerity with eager relief. They raise their schooners with an enthusiastic chorus of* "Here's how, Harry!" "Here's luck, Harry!" *etc., and gulp half the wine down, Hickey leading them in this.*)

HOPE—(*deeply moved—his voice husky*) Bejees, thanks, all of you. Bejees, Hickey, you old son of a bitch, that's white of you! Bejees, I know you meant it, too.

HICKEY—(*moved*) Of course I meant it, Harry, old friend! And I mean it when I say I hope today will be the biggest day in your life, and in the lives of everyone here, the beginning of a new life of peace and contentment where no pipe dreams can ever nag at you again. Here's to that, Harry! (*He drains the remainder of his drink, but this time he drinks alone. In an instant the attitude of everyone has reverted to uneasy, suspicious defensiveness.*)

ROCKY—(*growls*) Aw, forget dat bughouse line of bull for a minute, can't yuh?

HICKEY—(*sitting down—good-naturedly*) You're right, Rocky, I'm talking too much. It's Harry we want to hear from. Come on, Harry! (*He pounds his schooner on the table.*) Speech! Speech! (*They try to recapture their momentary enthusiasm, rap their schooners on the table, call* "Speech," *but there is a hollow ring in it. Hope gets to his feet reluctantly, with a forced smile, a smoldering resentment beginning to show in his manner.*)

HOPE—(*lamely*) Bejees, I'm no good at speeches. All I can say is thanks to everybody again for remembering me on my birthday. (*bitterness coming out*) Only don't think because I'm sixty I'll be a bigger damned fool easy mark than ever! No, bejees! Like Hickey says, it's going to be a new day! This dump has got to be run like other dumps, so I can make some money and not just split even. People has got to pay what they owe me! I'm not running a damned orphan asylum for bums and crooks! Nor a God-damned hooker shanty, either! Nor an Old Men's Home for lousy Anarchist tramps that ought to be in jail! I'm sick of being played for a sucker! (*They stare at him with stunned, bewildered hurt. He goes on in a sort of furious desperation, as if he hated himself for every word he said, and yet couldn't stop.*) And don't think you're kidding me right now, either! I know damned well you're giving me the laugh behind my back, thinking to yourselves, The old, lying, pipe-dreaming faker, we've heard his bull about taking a walk around the ward for years, he'll never make it! He's yellow, he ain't got the guts, he's scared he'll find out—(*He glares around at them almost with hatred.*) But I'll show you, bejees! (*He glares at Hickey.*) I'll show you, too, you son of a bitch of a frying-pan-peddling bastard!

HICKEY—(*heartily encouraging*) That's the stuff, Harry! Of course you'll try to show me! That's what I want you to do! (*Harry glances at him with helpless dread—then drops his eyes and looks furtively around the table. All at once he becomes miserably contrite.*)

HOPE—(*his voice catching*) Listen, all of you! Bejees, forgive me. I lost my temper! I ain't feeling well! I got a hell of a grouch on! Bejees, you know you're all as welcome here as the flowers in May! (*They look at him with eager forgiveness. Rocky is the first one who can voice it.*)

ROCKY—Aw, sure, Boss, you're always aces wid us, see?

HICKEY—(*rises to his feet again. He addresses them now with the simple, convincing sincerity of one making a confession of which he is genuinely ashamed.*) Listen, everybody! I know you are sick of my gabbing, but I think this is the spot where I owe it to you to do a little explaining and apologize for some of the rough stuff I've had to pull on you. I know how it must look to you. As if I was a damned busybody who was not only interfering in your private business, but even sicking some of you on to nag at each other. Well, I have to admit that's true, and I'm damned sorry about it. But it simply had to be done! You must believe that! You know old Hickey. I was never one to start trouble. But this time I had to—for your own good! I had to make you help me with each other. I saw I couldn't do what I was after alone. Not in the time at my disposal. I knew when I came here I wouldn't be able to stay with you long. I'm slated to leave on a trip. I saw I'd have to hustle and use every means I could. (*with a joking boastfulness*) Why, if I had enough time, I'd get a lot of sport out of selling my line of salvation to each of you all by my lonesome. Like it was fun in the old days, when I traveled house to house, to convince some dame, who was sicking the dog on me, her house wouldn't be properly furnished unless she bought another wash boiler. And I could do it with you, all right. I know every one of you, inside and out, by heart. I may have been drunk when I've been here before, but old Hickey could never be so drunk he didn't have to see through people. I mean, everyone except himself. And, finally, he had to see through himself, too. (*He pauses. They stare at him, bitter, uneasy and fascinated. His manner changes to deep earnestness.*) But here's the point to get. I swear I'd never act like I have if I wasn't absolutely sure it will be worth it to you in the end, after you're rid of the damned guilt that makes you lie to yourselves you're something you're not, and the remorse that nags at you and makes you hide behind lousy pipe dreams about tomorrow. You'll be in a today where there is no yesterday or tomorrow to worry you. You won't give a damn what you are any more. I wouldn't say this unless I knew, Brothers and Sisters. This peace is real! It's a fact! I know! Because I've got it! Here! Now! Right in front of you! You see the difference in me! You remember how I used to be! Even when I had two quarts of rotgut under my belt and joked and sang "Sweet Adeline," I still felt like a guilty skunk. But you can all see that I don't give a damn about anything now. And I promise you, by the time this day is over, I'll have every one of you feeling the same way! (*He pauses. They stare at him fascinatedly. He adds with a grin*) I guess that'll be about all from me, boys and girls—for the present. So let's get on with the party. (*He starts to sit down.*)

LARRY—(*sharply*) Wait! (*insistently—with a sneer*) I think it would help us poor pipe-dreaming sinners along the sawdust trail to salvation if you told us now what it was happened to you that converted you to this great peace you've found. (*more and more with a deliberate, provocative taunting*) I notice you didn't deny it when I asked you about the iceman. Did this great revelation of the evil habit of dreaming about tomorrow come to you after you found your wife was sick of you? (*While he is speaking the faces of the gang have lighted up vindictively, as if all at once they saw a chance to revenge themselves. As he finishes, a chorus of sneering taunts begins, punctuated by nasty, jeering laughter.*)

HOPE—Bejees, you've hit it, Larry! I've noticed he hasn't shown her picture around this time!

MOSHER—He hasn't got it! The iceman took it away from him!

MARGIE—Jees, look at him! Who could blame her?

PEARL—She must be hard up to fall for an iceman!

CORA—Imagine a sap like him advisin' me and Chuck to git married!

CHUCK—Yeah! He done so good wid it!

JIMMY—At least I can say Marjorie chose an officer and a gentleman.

LEWIS—Come to look at you, Hickey, old chap, you've sprouted horns like a bloody antelope!

WETJOEN—Pigger, py Gott! Like a water buffalo's!

WILLIE—(*sings to his Sailor Lad tune*)

> "Come up," she cried, "my iceman lad,
> And you and I'll agree—"

(*They all join in a jeering chorus, rapping with knuckles or glasses on the table at the indicated spot in the lyric.*)

> "And I'll show you the prettiest (*rap, rap, rap*)
> That ever you did see!"

(*A roar of derisive, dirty laughter. But Hickey has remained unmoved by all this taunting. He grins good-naturedly, as if he enjoyed the joke at his expense, and joins in the laughter.*)

HICKEY—Well, boys and girls, I'm glad to see you getting in good spirits for Harry's party, even if the joke is on me. I admit I asked for it by always pulling that iceman gag in the old days. So laugh all you like. (*He pauses. They do not laugh now. They are again staring at him with baffled uneasiness. He goes on thoughtfully.*) Well, this forces my hand, I guess, your bringing up the subject of Evelyn. I didn't want to tell you yet. It's hardly an appropriate time. I meant to wait until the party was over. But you're getting the wrong idea about poor Evelyn, and I've got to stop that. (*He pauses again. There is a tense stillness in the room. He bows his head a little and says quietly*) I'm sorry to tell you my dearly beloved wife is dead. (*A gasp comes from the stunned company. They look away from him, shocked and miserably ashamed of themselves, except Larry who continues to stare at him.*)

LARRY—(*aloud to himself with a superstitious shrinking*) Be God, I felt he'd brought the touch of death on him! (*Then suddenly he is even more ashamed of himself than the others and stammers*) Forgive me, Hickey! I'd like to cut my dirty tongue out! (*This releases a chorus of shamefaced mumbles from the crowd.* "Sorry, Hickey." "I'm sorry, Hickey." "We're sorry, Hickey.")

HICKEY—(*looking around at them—in a kindly, reassuring tone*) Now look here, everybody. You mustn't let this be a wet blanket on Harry's party. You're still getting me all wrong. There's no reason—You see, I don't feel any grief. (*They gaze at him startledly. He goes on with convincing sincerity.*) I've got to feel glad, for her sake. Because she's at peace. She's rid of me at last. Hell, I don't have to tell you—you all know what I was like. You can imagine what she went through, married to a no-good cheater and drunk like I was. And there was no way out of it for her. Because she loved me. But now she is at peace like she always longed to be. So why should I feel sad? She wouldn't want me to feel sad. Why, all that Evelyn ever wanted out of life was to make me happy. (*He stops, looking around at them with a simple, gentle frankness. They stare at him in bewildered, incredulous confusion.*)

(*Curtain*)

★

ACT THREE

SCENE—*Barroom of Harry Hope's, including a part of what had been the back room in Acts One and Two. In the right wall are two big windows, with the swinging doors to the street between them. The bar itself is at rear. Behind it is a mirror, covered with white mosquito netting to keep off the flies, and a shelf on which are barrels of cheap whiskey with spiggots and a small show case of bottled goods. At left of the bar is the doorway to the hall. There is a table at left, front, of barroom proper, with four chairs. At right, front, is a small free-lunch counter, facing left, with a space between it and the window for the dealer to stand when he dishes out soup at the noon hour. Over the mirror behind the bar are framed photographs of Richard Croker and Big Tim Sullivan, flanked by framed lithographs of John L. Sullivan and Gentleman Jim Corbett in ring costume.*

At left, in what had been the back room, with the dividing curtain drawn, the banquet table of Act Two has been broken up, and the tables are again in the crowded arrangement of Act One. Of these, we see one in the front row with five chairs at left of the barroom table, another with five chairs at left-rear of it, a third back by the rear wall with five chairs, and finally, at extreme left-front, one with four chairs, partly on and partly off stage, left.

It is around the middle of the morning of Hope's birthday, a hot summer day. There is sunlight in the street outside, but it does not hit the windows and the light in the back-room section is dim.

Joe Mott is moving around, a box of sawdust under his arm, strewing it over the floor. His manner is sullen, his face set in gloom. He ignores everyone. As the scene progresses, he finishes his sawdusting job, goes behind the lunch counter and cuts loaves of bread. Rocky is behind the bar, wiping it, washing glasses, etc. He wears his working clothes, sleeves rolled up. He looks sleepy, irritable and worried. At the barroom table, front, Larry sits in a chair, facing right-front. He has no drink in front of him. He stares ahead, deep in harried thought. On his right, in a chair facing right, Hugo sits sprawled forward, arms and head on the table as usual, a whiskey glass beside his limp hand. At rear of the front table at left of them, in a chair facing left, Parritt is sitting. He is staring in front of him in a tense, strained immobility.

As the curtain rises, Rocky finishes his work behind the bar. He comes forward and drops wearily in the chair at right of Larry's table, facing left.

ROCKY—Nuttin' now till de noon rush from de Market. I'm goin' to rest my fanny. (*irritably*) If I ain't a sap to let Chuck kid me into workin' his time so's he can take de mornin' off. But I got sick of arguin' wid 'im. I says, "Aw right, git married! What's it to me?" Hickey's got de bot' of dem bugs. (*bitterly*) Some party last night, huh? Jees, what a funeral! It was jinxed from de start, but his tellin' about his wife croakin' put de K.O. on it.

LARRY—Yes, it turned out it wasn't a birthday feast but a wake!

ROCKY—Him promisin' he'd cut out de bughouse bull about peace—and den he went on talkin' and talkin' like he couldn't stop! And all de gang sneakin' upstairs, leavin' free booze and eats like dey was poison! It didn't do dem no good if dey thought dey'd shake him. He's been hoppin' from room to room all night. Yuh can't stop him. He's got his Reform Wave goin' strong dis mornin'! Did yuh notice him drag Jimmy out de foist ting to get his laundry and his clothes pressed so he wouldn't have no excuse? And he give Willie de dough to buy his stuff back from Solly's. And all de rest been brushin' and shavin' demselves wid de shakes—

LARRY—(*defiantly*) He didn't come to my room! He's afraid I might ask him a few questions.

ROCKY—(*scornfully*) Yeah? It don't look to me he's scared of yuh. I'd say you was scared of him.

LARRY—(*stung*) You'd lie, then!

PARRITT—(*jerks round to look at Larry—sneeringly*) Don't let him kid you, Rocky. He had his door locked. I couldn't get in, either.

ROCKY—Yeah, who d'yuh tink yuh're kiddin', Larry? He's showed you up, aw right. Like he says, if yuh was so anxious to croak, why wouldn't yuh hop off your fire escape long ago?

LARRY—(*defiantly*) Because it'd be a coward's quitting, that's why!

PARRITT—He's all quitter, Rocky. He's a yellow old faker!

LARRY—(*turns on him*) You lying punk! Remember what I warned you—!

ROCKY—(*scowls at Parritt*) Yeah, keep outta dis, you! Where d'yuh get a license to butt in? Shall I give him de bum's rush, Larry? If you don't want him around, nobody else don't.

LARRY—(*forcing an indifferent tone*) No. Let him stay. I don't mind him. He's nothing to me. (*Rocky shrugs his shoulders and yawns sleepily.*)

PARRITT—You're right, I have nowhere to go now. You're the only one in the world I can turn to.

ROCKY—(*drowsily*) Yuh're a soft old sap, Larry. He's a no-good louse like Hickey. He don't belong. (*He yawns.*) I'm all in. Not a wink of sleep. Can't keep my peepers open. (*His eyes close and his head nods. Parritt gives him a glance and then gets up and slinks over to slide into the chair on Larry's left, between him and Rocky. Larry shrinks away, but determinedly ignores him.*)

PARRITT—(*bending toward him—in a low, ingratiating, apologetic voice*) I'm sorry for riding you, Larry. But you get my goat when you act as if you didn't care a damn what happened to me, and keep your door locked so I can't talk to you. (*then hopefully*) But that was to keep Hickey out, wasn't it? I don't blame you. I'm getting to hate him. I'm getting more and more scared of him. Especially since he told us his wife was dead. It's that queer feeling he gives me that I'm mixed up with him some way. I don't know why, but it started me thinking about Mother—as if she was dead. (*with a strange undercurrent of something like satisfaction in his pitying tone*) I suppose she might as well be. Inside herself, I mean. It must kill her when she thinks of me—I know she doesn't want to, but she can't help it. After all, I'm her only kid. She used to spoil me and made a pet of me. Once in a great while, I mean. When she remembered me. As if she wanted to make up for something. As if she felt guilty. So she must have loved me a little, even if she never let it interfere with her freedom. (*with a strange pathetic wistfulness*) Do you know, Larry, I once had a sneaking suspicion that maybe, if the truth was known, you were my father.

LARRY—(*violently*) You damned fool! Who put that insane idea in your head? You know it's a lie! Anyone in the Coast crowd could tell you I never laid eyes on your mother till after you were born.

PARRITT—Well, I'd hardly ask them, would I? I know you're right, though, because I asked her. She brought me up to be frank and ask her anything, and she'd always tell me the truth. (*abruptly*) But I was talking about how she must feel now about me. My getting through with the Movement. She'll never forgive that. The Movement is her life. And it must be the final knockout for her if she knows I was the one who sold—

LARRY—Shut up, damn you!

PARRITT—It'll kill her. And I'm sure she knows it must have been me. (*suddenly with desperate urgency*) But I never thought the cops would get her! You've got to believe that! You've got to see what my only reason was! I'll admit what I told you last night was a lie—that bunk about getting patriotic and my duty to my country. But here's the true reason, Larry—the only reason! It was just for money! I got stuck on a whore and wanted dough to blow in on her and have a good time! That's all I did it for! Just money! Honest! (*He has the terrible grotesque air, in confessing his sordid baseness, of one who gives an excuse which exonerates him from any real guilt.*)

LARRY—(*grabs him by the shoulder and shakes him*) God damn you, shut up! What the hell is it to me? (*Rocky starts awake.*)

ROCKY—What's comin' off here?

LARRY—(*controlling himself*) Nothing. This gabby young punk was talking my ear off, that's all. He's a worse pest than Hickey.

ROCKY—(*drowsily*) Yeah, Hickey—Say, listen, what d'yuh mean about him bein' scared you'd ask him questions? What questions?

LARRY—Well, I feel he's hiding something. You notice he didn't say what his wife died of.

ROCKY—(*rebukingly*) Aw, lay off dat. De poor guy—What are yuh gettin' at, anyway? Yuh don't tink it's just a gag of his?

LARRY—I don't. I'm damned sure he's brought death here with him. I feel the cold touch of it on him.

ROCKY—Aw, bunk! You got croakin' on de brain, Old Cemetery. (*Suddenly Rocky's eyes widen.*) Say! D'yuh mean yuh tink she committed suicide, 'count of his cheatin' or someting?

LARRY—(*grimly*) It wouldn't surprise me. I'd be the last to blame her.

ROCKY—(*scornfully*) But dat's crazy! Jees, if she'd done dat, he wouldn't tell us he was glad about it, would he? He ain't dat big a bastard.

PARRITT—(*speaks up from his own preoccupation—strangely*) You know better than that, Larry. You know she'd never commit suicide. She's like you. She'll hang on to life even when there's nothing left but—

LARRY—(*stung—turns on him viciously*) And how about you? Be God, if you had any guts or decency—! (*He stops guiltily.*)

PARRITT—(*sneeringly*) I'd take that hop off your fire escape you're too yellow to take, I suppose?

LARRY—(*as if to himself*) No! Who am I to judge? I'm done with judging.

PARRITT—(*tauntingly*) Yes, I suppose you'd like that, wouldn't you?

ROCKY—(*irritably mystified*) What de hell's all dis about? (*to Parritt*) What d'you know about Hickey's wife? How d'yuh know she didn't—?

LARRY—(*with forced belittling casualness*) He doesn't. Hickey's addled the little brains he's got. Shove him back to his own table, Rocky. I'm sick of him.

ROCKY—(*to Parritt, threateningly*) Yuh heard Larry? I'd like an excuse to give yuh a good punch in de snoot. So move quick!

PARRITT—(*gets up—to Larry*) If you think moving to another table will get rid of me! (*He moves away—then adds with bitter reproach*) Gee, Larry, that's a hell of a way to treat me, when I've trusted you, and I need your help. (*He sits down in his old place and sinks into a wounded, self-pitying brooding.*)

ROCKY—(*going back to his train of thought*) Jees, if she committed suicide, yuh got to feel sorry for Hickey, huh? Yuh can understand how he'd go bughouse and not be responsible for all de crazy stunts he's stagin' here. (*then puzzledly*) But how can yuh be sorry for him when he says he's glad she croaked, and yuh can tell he means it? (*with weary exasperation*) Aw, nuts! I don't get nowhere tryin' to figger his game. (*his face hardening*) But I know dis. He better lay off me and my stable! (*He pauses—then sighs.*) Jees, Larry, what a night dem two pigs give me! When de party went dead, dey pinched a coupla bottles and brung dem up deir room and got stinko. I don't get a wink of sleep, see? Just as I'd drop off on a chair here, dey'd come down lookin' for trouble. Or else dey'd raise hell upstairs, laughin' and singin', so I'd get scared dey'd get de joint pinched and go up to tell dem to can de noise. And every time dey'd crawl my frame wid de same old argument. Dey'd say, "So yuh agreed wid Hickey, do yuh, yuh dirty little Ginny? We're whores, are we? Well, we agree wid Hickey about you, see! Yuh're nuttin' but a lousy pimp!" Den I'd slap dem. Not beat 'em up, like a pimp would. Just slap dem. But it don't do no good. Dey'd keep at it over and over. Jees, I get de earache just thinkin' of it! "Listen," dey'd say, "if we're whores we gotta right to have a reg'lar pimp and not stand for no punk imitation! We're sick of wearin' out our dogs poundin' sidewalks for a double-crossin' bartender, when all de thanks we get is he looks down on us. We'll find a guy who really needs us to take care of him and ain't ashamed of it. Don't expect us to work tonight, 'cause we won't, see? Not if de streets was blocked wid sailors! We're goin' on strike and yuh can like it or lump it!" (*He shakes his head.*) Whores goin' on strike! Can yuh tie dat? (*going on with his story*) Dey says, "We're takin' a holiday. We're goin' to beat it down to Coney Island and shoot the chutes and maybe we'll come back and maybe we won't. And you can go to hell!" So dey put on deir lids and beat it, de bot' of dem stinko. (*He sighs dejectedly. He seems grotesquely like a harried family man, henpecked and browbeaten by a nagging wife. Larry is deep in his own bitter preoccupation and hasn't listened to him. Chuck enters from the hall at rear. He has his straw hat with the gaudy band in his hand and wears a Sunday-best blue suit with a high stiff collar. He looks sleepy, hot, uncomfortable and grouchy.*)

CHUCK—(*glumly*) Hey, Rocky. Cora wants a sherry flip. For her noives.

ROCKY—(*turns indignantly*) Sherry flip! Christ, she don't need nuttin' for her noive! What's she tink dis is, de Waldorf?

CHUCK—Yeah, I told her, what would we use for sherry, and dere wasn't no egg unless she laid one. She says, "Is dere a law yuh can't go out and buy de makings, yuh big tramp?" (*resentfully puts his straw hat on his head at a defiant tilt*) To hell wid her! She'll drink booze or nuttin'! (*He goes behind the bar to draw a glass of whiskey from a barrel.*)

ROCKY—(*sarcastically*) Jees, a guy oughta give his bride anything she wants on de weddin' day, I should tink! (*As Chuck comes from behind the bar, Rocky surveys him derisively.*) Pipe de bridegroom, Larry! All dolled up for de killin'! (*Larry pays no attention.*)

CHUCK—Aw, shut up!

ROCKY—One week on dat farm in Joisey, dat's what I give yuh! Yuh'll come runnin' in here some night yellin' for a shot of booze 'cause de crickets is after yuh! (*disgustedly*) Jees, Chuck, dat louse Hickey's coitinly made a prize coupla suckers outa youse.

CHUCK—(*unguardedly*) Yeah. I'd like to give him one sock in de puss—just one! (*then angrily*) Aw, can dat! What's he got to do wid it? Ain't we always said we was goin' to? So we're goin' to, see? And don't give me no argument! (*He stares at Rocky truculently. But Rocky only shrugs his shoulders with weary disgust and Chuck subsides into complaining gloom.*) If on'y Cora'd cut out de beefin'. She don't gimme a minute's rest all night. De same old stuff over and over! Do I really want to marry her? I says, "Sure, Baby, why not?" She says, "Yeah, but after a week yuh'll be tinkin' what a sap you was. Yuh'll make dat an excuse to go off on a periodical, and den I'll be tied for life to a no-good soak, and de foist ting I know yuh'll have me out hustlin' again, your own wife!" Den she'd bust out cryin', and I'd get sore. "Yuh're a liar," I'd say. "I ain't never taken your dough 'cept when I was drunk and not workin'!" "Yeah," she'd say, "and how long will yuh stay sober now? Don't tink yuh can kid me wid dat water-wagon bull! I've heard it too often." Dat'd make me sore and I'd say, "Don't call me a liar. But I wish I was drunk right now, because if I was, yuh wouldn't be keepin' me awake all night beefin'. If yuh opened your yap, I'd knock de stuffin' outa yuh!" Den she'd yell, "Dat's a sweet way to talk to de goil yuh're goin' to marry." (*He sighs explosively.*) Jees, she's got me hangin' on de ropes! (*He glances with vengeful yearning at the drink of whiskey in his hand.*) Jees, would I like to get a quart of dis redeye under my belt!

ROCKY—Well, why de hell don't yuh?

CHUCK—(*instantly suspicious and angry*) Sure! You'd like dat, wouldn't yuh? I'm wise to you! Yuh don't wanta see me get married and settle down like a reg'lar guy! Yuh'd like me to stay paralyzed all de time, so's I'd be like you, a lousy pimp!

ROCKY—(*springs to his feet, his face hardened viciously*) Listen! I don't take dat even from you, see!

CHUCK—(*puts his drink on the bar and clenches his fists*) Yeah? Wanta make sometin' of it? (*jeeringly*) Don't make me laugh! I can lick ten of youse wid one mit!

ROCKY—(*reaching for his hip pocket*) Not wid lead in your belly, yuh won't!

JOE—(*has stopped cutting when the quarrel started—expostulating*) Hey, you, Rocky and Chuck! Cut it out! You's ole friends! Don't let dat Hickey make you crazy!

CHUCK—(*turns on him*) Keep outa our business, yuh black bastard!

ROCKY—(*like Chuck, turns on Joe, as if their own quarrel was forgotten and they became natural allies against an alien*) Stay where yuh belong, yuh doity nigger!

JOE—(*snarling with rage, springs from behind the lunch counter with the bread knife in his hand*) You white sons of bitches! I'll rip your guts out! (*Chuck snatches a whiskey bottle from the bar and raises it above his head to hurl at Joe. Rocky jerks a short-barreled, nickel-plated revolver from his hip pocket. At this moment Larry pounds on the table with his fist and bursts into a sardonic laugh.*)

LARRY—That's it! Murder each other, you damned loons, with Hickey's blessing! Didn't I tell you he'd brought death with him? (*His interruption startles them. They pause to stare at him, their fighting fury suddenly dies out and they appear deflated and sheepish.*)

ROCKY—(*to Joe*) Aw right, you. Leggo dat shiv and I'll put dis gat away. (*Joe sullenly goes back behind the counter and slaps the knife on top of it. Rocky slips the revolver back in his pocket. Chuck lowers the bottle to the bar. Hugo, who has awakened and raised his head when Larry pounded on the table, now giggles foolishly.*)

HUGO—Hello, leedle peoples! Neffer mind! Soon you vill eat hot dogs beneath the villow trees and trink free vine—(*abruptly in a haughty fastidious tone*) The champagne vas not properly iced. (*with guttural anger*) Gottamned liar, Hickey! Does that prove I vant to be aristocrat? I love only the proletariat! I vill lead them! I vill be like a Gott to them! They vill be my slaves! (*He stops in bewildered self-amazement—to Larry appealingly*) I am very trunk, no, Larry? I talk foolishness. I am so trunk, Larry, old friend, am I not, I don't know vhat I say?

LARRY—(*pityingly*) You're raving drunk, Hugo. I've never seen you so paralyzed. Lay your head down now and sleep it off.

HUGO—(*gratefully*) Yes. I should sleep. I am too crazy trunk. (*He puts his head on his arms and closes his eyes.*)

JOE—(*behind the lunch counter—brooding superstitiously*) You's right, Larry. Bad luck come in de door when Hickey come. I's an ole gamblin' man and I knows bad luck when I feels it! (*then defiantly*) But it's white man's bad luck. He can't jinx me! (*He comes from behind the counter and goes to the bar—addressing Rocky stiffly*) De bread's cut and I's finished my job. Do I get de drink I's earned? (*Rocky gives him a hostile look but shoves a bottle and glass at him. Joe pours a brimful drink—sullenly*) I's finished wid dis dump for keeps. (*He takes a key from his pocket and slaps it on the bar.*) Here's de key to my room. I ain't comin' back. I's goin' to my own folks where I belong. I don't stay where I's not wanted. I's sick and tired of messin' round wid white men. (*He gulps down his drink—then looking around defiantly he deliberately throws his whiskey glass on the floor and smashes it.*)

ROCKY—Hey! What de hell—!

JOE—(*with a sneering dignity*) I's on'y savin' you de trouble, White Boy. Now you don't have to break it, soon's my back's turned, so's no white man kick about drinkin' from de same glass. (*He walks stiffly to the street door—then turns for a parting shot—boastfully*) I's tired of loafin' 'round wid a lot of bums. I's a gamblin' man. I's gonna get in a big crap game and win me a big bankroll. Den I'll get de okay to open up my old gamblin' house for colored men. Den maybe I comes back here sometime to see de bums. Maybe I throw a twenty-dollar bill on de bar and say, "Drink it up," and listen when dey all pat me on de back and say, "Joe, you sure is white." But I'll say, "No, I'm black and my dough is black man's dough, and you's proud to drink wid me or you don't get no drink!" Or maybe I just says, "You can all go to hell. I don't lower myself drinkin' wid no white trash!" (*He opens the door to go out—then turns again.*) And dat ain't no pipe dream! I'll git de money for my stake today, somehow, somewheres! If I has to borrow a gun and stick up some white man, I gets it! You wait and see! (*He swaggers out through the swinging doors.*)

CHUCK—(*angrily*) Can yuh beat de noive of dat dinge! Jees, if I wasn't dressed up, I'd go out and mop up de street wid him!

ROCKY—Aw, let him go, de poor old dope! Him and his gamblin' house! He'll be back tonight askin' Harry for his room and bummin' me for a ball. (*vengefully*) Den I'll be de one to smash de glass. I'll loin him his place! (*The swinging doors are pushed open and Willie Oban enters from the street. He is shaved and wears an expensive, well-cut suit, good shoes and clean linen. He is absolutely sober, but his face is sick, and his nerves in a shocking state of shakes.*)

CHUCK—Another guy all dolled up! Got your clothes from Solly's, huh, Willie? (*derisively*) Now yuh can sell dem back to him again tomorrow.

WILLIE—(*stiffly*) No, I—I'm through with that stuff. Never again. (*He comes to the bar.*)

ROCKY—(*sympathetically*) Yuh look sick, Willie. Take a ball to pick yuh up. (*He pushes a bottle toward him.*)

WILLIE—(*eyes the bottle yearningly but shakes his head—determinedly*) No, thanks. The only way to stop is to stop. I'd have no chance if I went to the D.A.'s office smelling of booze.

CHUCK—Yuh're really goin' dere?

WILLIE—(*stiffly*) I said I was, didn't I? I just came back here to rest a few minutes, not because I needed any booze. I'll show that cheap drummer I don't have to have any Dutch courage—(*guiltily*) But he's been very kind and generous staking me. He can't help his insulting manner, I suppose. (*He turns away from the bar.*) My legs are a bit shaky yet. I better sit down a while. (*He goes back and sits at the left of the second table, facing Parritt, who gives him a scowling, suspicious glance and then ignores him. Rocky looks at Chuck and taps his head disgustedly. Captain Lewis appears in the doorway from the hall.*)

CHUCK—(*mutters*) Here's anudder one. (*Lewis looks spruce and clean-shaven. His ancient tweed suit has been brushed and his frayed linen is clean. His manner is full of a forced, jaunty self-assurance. But he is sick and beset by katzenjammer.*)

LEWIS—Good morning, gentlemen all. (*He passes along the front of bar to look out in the street.*) A jolly fine morning, too. (*He turns back to the bar.*) An eye-opener? I think not. Not required, Rocky, old chum. Feel extremely fit, as a matter of fact. Though can't say I slept much, thanks to that interfering ass, Hickey, and that stupid bounder of a Boer. (*His face hardens.*) I've had about all I can take from that fellow. It's my own fault, of course, for allowing a brute of a Dutch farmer to become familiar. Well, it's come to a parting of the ways now, and good riddance. Which reminds me, here's my key. (*He puts it on the bar.*) I shan't be coming back. Sorry to be leaving good old Harry and the rest of you, of course, but I can't continue to live under the same roof with that fellow. (*He stops, stiffening into hostility as Wetjoen enters from the hall, and pointedly turns his back on him. Wetjoen glares at him sneeringly. He, too, has made an effort to spruce up his appearance, and his bearing has a forced swagger of conscious physical strength. Behind this, he is sick and feebly holding his booze-sodden body together.*)

ROCKY—(*to Lewis—disgustedly putting the key on the shelf in back of the bar*) So Hickey's kidded the pants offa you, too? Yuh tink yuh're leavin' here, huh?

WETJOEN—(*jeeringly*) Ja! Dot's vhat he kids himself.

LEWIS—(*ignores him—airily*) Yes, I'm leaving, Rocky. But that ass, Hickey, has nothing to do with it. Been thinking things over. Time I turned over a new leaf, and all that.

WETJOEN—He's going to get a job! Dot's what he says!

ROCKY—What at, for Chris' sake?

LEWIS—(*keeping his airy manner*) Oh, anything. I mean, not manual labor, naturally, but anything that calls for a bit of brains and education. However humble. Beggars can't be choosers. I'll see a pal of mine at the Consulate. He promised any time I felt an energetic fit he'd get me a post with the Cunard—clark in the office or something of the kind.

WETJOEN—Ja! At Limey Consulate they promise anything to get rid of him vhen he comes there tronk! They're scared to call the police and have him pinched because it vould scandal in the papers make about a Limey officer and chentleman!

LEWIS—As a matter of fact, Rocky, I only wish a post temporarily. Means to an end, you know. Save up enough for a first-class passage home, that's the bright idea.

WETJOEN—He's sailing back to home, sveet home! Dot's biggest pipe dream of all. What leetle brain the poor Limey has left, dot isn't in whiskey pickled, Hickey has made crazy! (*Lewis' fists clench, but he manages to ignore this.*)

CHUCK—(*feels sorry for Lewis and turns on Wetjoen—sarcastically*) Hickey ain't made no sucker outa you, huh? You're too foxy, huh? But I'll bet you tink yuh're goin' out and land a job, too.

WETJOEN—(*bristles*) I am, ja. For me, it is easy. Because I put on no airs of chentleman. I am not ashamed to vork vith my hands. I vas a farmer before the war ven ploody Limey thieves steal my country. (*boastfully*) Anyone I ask for job can see vith one look I have the great strength to do work of ten ordinary mens.

LEWIS—(*sneeringly*) Yes, Chuck, you remember he gave a demonstration of his extraordinary muscles last night when he helped to move the piano.

CHUCK—Yuh couldn't even hold up your corner. It was your fault de damned box almost fell down de stairs.

WETJOEN—My hands vas sweaty! Could I help dot my hands slip? I could de whole veight of it lift! In old days in Transvaal, I lift loaded oxcart by the axle! So vhy shouldn't I get job? Dot longshoreman boss, Dan, he tell me any time I like, he take me on. And Benny from de Market he promise me same.

LEWIS—You remember, Rocky, it was one of those rare occasions when the Boer that walks like a man—spelled with a double o, by the way—was buying drinks and Dan and Benny were stony. They'd bloody well have promised him the moon.

ROCKY—Yeah, yuh big boob, dem boids was on'y kiddin' yuh.

WETJOEN—(*angrily*) Dot's lie! You vill see dis morning I get job! I'll show dot bloody Limey chentleman, and dot liar, Hickey! And I need vork only leetle vhile to save money for my passage home. I need not much money because I am not ashamed to travel steerage. I don't put on first-cabin airs! (*tauntingly*) Und *I can* go home to my country! Vhen I get there, they vill let *me* come in!

LEWIS—(*grows rigid—his voice trembling with repressed anger*) There was a rumor in South Africa, Rocky, that a certain Boer officer—if you call the leaders of a rabble of farmers officers—kept advising Cronje to retreat and not stand and fight—

WETJOEN—And I vas right! I vas right! He got surrounded at Poardeberg! He had to surrender!

LEWIS—*(ignoring him)* Good strategy, no doubt, but a suspicion grew afterwards into a conviction among the Boers that the officer's caution was prompted by a desire to make his personal escape. His countrymen felt extremely savage about it, and his family disowned him. So I imagine there would be no welcoming committee waiting on the dock, nor delighted relatives making the veldt ring with their happy cries—

WETJOEN—*(with guilty rage)* All lies! You Gottamned Limey—*(trying to control himself and copy Lewis' manner)* I also haf heard rumors of a Limey officer who, after the war, lost all his money gambling vhen he vas tronk. But they found out it vas regiment money, too, he lost—

LEWIS—*(loses his control and starts for him)* You bloody Dutch scum!

ROCKY—*(leans over the bar and stops Lewis with a straight-arm swipe on the chest)* Cut it out! *(At the same moment Chuck grabs Wetjoen and yanks him back.)*

WETJOEN—*(struggling)* Let him come! I saw them come before—at Modder River, Magersfontein, Spion Kopje—waving their silly swords, so afraid they couldn't show off how brave they vas!—and I kill them vith my rifle so easy! *(vindictively)* Listen to me, you Cecil! Often vhen I am tronk and kidding you I say I am sorry I missed you, but now, py Gott, I am sober, and I don't joke, and I say it!

LARRY—*(gives a sardonic guffaw—with his comically crazy, intense whisper)* Be God, you can't say Hickey hasn't the miraculous touch to raise the dead, when he can start the Boer War raging again! *(This interruption acts like a cold douche on Lewis and Wetjoen. They subside, and Rocky and Chuck let go of them. Lewis turns his back on the Boer.)*

LEWIS—*(attempting a return of his jaunty manner, as if nothing had happened)* Well, time I was on my merry way to see my chap at the Consulate. The early bird catches the job, what? Good-bye and good luck, Rocky, and everyone. *(He starts for the street door.)*

WETJOEN—Py Gott, if dot Limey can go, I can go! *(He hurries after Lewis. But Lewis, his hand about to push the swinging doors open, hesitates, as though struck by a sudden paralysis of the will, and Wetjoen has to jerk back to avoid bumping into him. For a second they stand there, one behind the other, staring over the swinging doors into the street.)*

ROCKY—Well, why don't yuh beat it?

LEWIS—*(guiltily casual)* Eh? Oh, just happened to think. Hardly the decent thing to pop off without saying good-bye to old Harry. One of the best, Harry. And good old Jimmy, too. They ought to be down any moment. *(He pretends to notice Wetjoen for the first time and steps away from the door—apologizing as to a stranger)* Sorry. I seem to be blocking your way out.

WETJOEN—*(stiffly)* No. I vait to say good-bye to Harry and Jimmy, too. *(He goes to right of door behind the lunch counter and looks through the window, his back to the room. Lewis takes up a similar stand at the window on the left of door.)*

CHUCK—Jees, can yuh beat dem simps! *(He picks up Cora's drink at the end of the bar.)* Hell, I'd forgot Cora. She'll be trowin' a fit. *(He goes into the hall with the drink.)*

ROCKY—*(looks after him disgustedly)* Dat's right, wait on her and spoil her, yuh poor sap! *(He shakes his head and begins to wipe the bar mechanically.)*

WILLIE—*(is regarding Parritt across the table from him with an eager, calculating eye. He leans over and speaks in a low confidential tone.)* Look here, Parritt. I'd like to have a talk with you.

PARRITT—*(starts—scowling defensively)* What about?

WILLIE—*(his manner becoming his idea of a crafty criminal lawyer's)* About the trouble you're in. Oh, I know. You don't admit it. You're quite right. That's my advice. Deny everything. Keep your mouth shut. Make no statements whatever without first consulting your attorney.

PARRITT—Say! What the hell—?

WILLIE—But you can trust me. I'm a lawyer, and it's just occurred to me you and I ought to cooperate. Of course I'm going to see the D.A. this morning about a job on his staff. But that may take time. There may not be an immediate opening. Meanwhile it would be a good idea for me to take a case or two, on my own, and prove my brilliant record in law school was no flash in the pan. So why not retain me as your attorney?

PARRITT—You're crazy! What do I want with a lawyer?

WILLIE—That's right. Don't admit anything. But you can trust me, so let's not beat about the bush. You got in trouble out on the Coast, eh? And now you're hiding out. Any fool can spot that. *(lowering his voice still more)* You feel safe here, and maybe you are, for a while. But remember, they get you in the end. I know from my father's experience. No one could have felt safer than he did. When anyone mentioned the law to him, he nearly died laughing. But—

PARRITT—You crazy mutt! *(turning to Larry with a strained laugh)* Did you get that, Larry? This damned fool thinks the cops are after me!

LARRY—(*bursts out with his true reaction before he thinks to ignore him*) I wish to God they were! And so should you, if you had the honor of a louse! (*Parritt stares into his eyes guiltily for a second. Then he smiles sneeringly.*)

PARRITT—And you're the guy who kids himself he's through with the Movement! You old lying faker, you're still in love with it! (*Larry ignores him again now.*)

WILLIE—(*disappointedly*) Then you're not in trouble, Parritt? I was hoping—But never mind. No offense meant. Forget it.

PARRITT—(*condescendingly—his eyes on Larry*) Sure. That's all right, Willie. I'm not sore at you. It's that damned old faker that gets my goat. (*He slips out of his chair and goes quietly over to sit in the chair beside Larry he had occupied before—in a low, insinuating, intimate tone*) I think I understand, Larry. It's really Mother you still love—isn't it?—in spite of the dirty deal she gave you. But hell, what did you expect? She was never true to anyone but herself and the Movement. But I understand how you can't help still feeling—because I still love her, too. (*pleading in a strained, desperate tone*) You know I do, don't you? You must! So you see I couldn't have expected they'd catch her! You've got to believe me that I sold them out just to get a few lousy dollars to blow in on a whore. No other reason, honest! There couldn't possibly be any other reason! (*Again he has a strange air of exonerating himself from guilt by this shameless confession.*)

LARRY—(*trying not to listen, has listened with increasing tension*) For the love of Christ will you leave me in peace! I've told you you can't make me judge you! But if you don't keep still, you'll be saying something soon that will make you vomit your own soul like a drink of nickel rotgut that won't stay down! (*He pushes back his chair and springs to his feet.*) To hell with you! (*He goes to the bar.*)

PARRITT—(*jumps up and starts to follow him—desperately*) Don't go, Larry! You've got to help me! (*But Larry is at the bar, back turned, and Rocky is scowling at him. He stops, shrinking back into himself helplessly, and turns away. He goes to the table where he had been before, and this time he takes the chair at rear facing directly front. He puts his elbows on the table, holding his head in his hands as if he had a splitting headache.*)

LARRY—Set 'em up, Rocky. I swore I'd have no more drinks on Hickey, if I died of drought, but I've changed my mind! Be God, he owes it to me, and I'd get blind to the world now if it was the Iceman of Death himself treating! (*He stops, startledly, a superstitious awe coming into his face.*) What made me say that, I wonder. (*with a sardonic laugh*) Well, be God, it fits, for Death was the Iceman Hickey called to his home!

ROCKY—Aw, forget dat iceman gag! De poor dame is dead. (*pushing a bottle and glass at Larry*) Gwan and get paralyzed! I'll be glad to see one bum in dis dump act natural. (*Larry downs a drink and pours another.*)

(*Ed Mosher appears in the doorway from the hall. The same change which is apparent in the manner and appearance of the others shows in him. He is sick, his nerves are shattered, his eyes are apprehensive, but he, too, puts on an exaggeratedly self-confident bearing. He saunters to the bar between Larry and the street entrance.*)

MOSHER—Morning, Rocky. Hello, Larry. Glad to see Brother Hickey hasn't corrupted you to temperance. I wouldn't mind a shot myself. (*As Rocky shoves a bottle toward him he shakes his head.*) But I remember the only breath-killer in this dump is coffee beans. The boss would never fall for that. No man can run a circus successfully who believes guys chew coffee beans because they like them. (*He pushes the bottle away.*) No, much as I need one after the hell of a night I've had—(*He scowls.*) That drummer son of a drummer! I had to lock him out. But I could hear him through the wall doing his spiel to someone all night long. Still at it with Jimmy and Harry when I came down just now. But the hardest to take was that flannel-mouth, flatfoot Mick trying to tell me where I got off! I had to lock him out, too. (*As he says this, McGloin comes in the doorway from the hall. The change in his appearance and manner is identical with that of Mosher and the others.*)

McGLOIN—He's a liar, Rocky! It was me locked him out! (*Mosher starts to flare up—then ignores him. They turn their backs on each other. McGloin starts into the back-room section.*)

WILLIE—Come and sit here, Mac. You're just the man I want to see. If I'm to take your case, we ought to have a talk before we leave.

McGLOIN—(*contemptuously*) We'll have no talk. You damned fool, do you think I'd have your father's son for my lawyer? They'd take one look at you and bounce us both out on our necks! (*Willie winces and shrinks down in his chair. McGloin goes to the first table beyond him and sits with his back to the bar.*) I don't need a lawyer, anyway. To hell with the law! All I've got to do is see the right ones and get them to pass the word. They will, too. They know I was framed. And once they've passed the word, it's as good as done, law or no law.

MOSHER—God, I'm glad I'm leaving this madhouse! (*He pulls his key from his pocket and slaps it on the bar.*) Here's my key, Rocky.

McGLOIN—(*pulls his from his pocket*) And here's mine. (*He tosses it to Rocky.*) I'd rather sleep in the gutter than pass another night under the same roof with that loon, Hickey, and a lying circus grifter! (*He adds darkly*) And if that hat fits anyone here, let him put it on! (*Mosher turns toward him furiously but Rocky leans over the bar and grabs his arm.*)

ROCKY—Nix! Take it easy! (*Mosher subsides. Rocky tosses the keys on the shelf—disgustedly*) You boids gimme a pain. It'd soive you right if I wouldn't give de keys back to yuh tonight. (*They both turn on him resentfully, but there is an interruption as Cora appears in the doorway from the hall with Chuck behind her. She is drunk, dressed in her gaudy best, her face plastered with rouge and mascara, her hair a bit disheveled, her hat on anyhow.*)

CORA—(*comes a few steps inside the bar—with a strained bright giggle*) Hello, everybody! Here we go! Hickey just told us, ain't it time we beat it, if we're really goin'. So we're showin' de bastard, ain't we, Honey? He's comin' right down wid Harry and Jimmy. Jees, dem two look like dey was goin' to de electric chair! (*with frightened anger*) If I had to listen to any more of Hickey's bunk, I'd brain him. (*She puts her hand on Chuck's arm.*) Come on, Honey. Let's get started before he comes down.

CHUCK—(*sullenly*) Sure, anyting yuh say, Baby.

CORA—(*turns on him truculently*) Yeah? Well, I say we stop at de foist reg'lar dump and yuh gotta blow me to a sherry flip—or four or five, if I want 'em!—or all bets is off!

CHUCK—Aw, yuh got a fine bun on now!

CORA—Cheap skate! I know what's eatin' you, Tightwad! Well, use my dough, den, if yuh're so stingy. Yuh'll grab it all, anyway, right after de ceremony. I know you! (*She hikes her skirt up and reaches inside the top of her stocking.*) Here, yuh big tramp!

CHUCK—(*knocks her hand away—angrily*) Keep your lousy dough! And don't show off your legs to dese bums when yuh're goin' to be married, if yuh don't want a sock in de puss!

CORA—(*pleased—meekly*) Aw right, Honey. (*looking around with a foolish laugh*) Say, why don't all you barflies come to de weddin'? (*But they are all sunk in their own apprehensions and ignore her. She hesitates, miserably uncertain.*) Well, we're goin', guys. (*There is no comment. Her eyes fasten on Rocky—desperately*) Say, Rocky, yuh gone deef? I said me and Chuck was goin' now.

ROCKY—(*wiping the bar—with elaborate indifference*) Well, good-bye. Give my love to Joisey.

CORA—(*tearfully indignant*) Ain't yuh goin' to wish us happiness, yuh doity little Ginny?

ROCKY—Sure. Here's hopin' yuh don't moider each odder before next week.

CHUCK—(*angrily*) Aw, Baby, what d'we care for dat pimp? (*Rocky turns on him threateningly, but Chuck hears someone upstairs in the hall and grabs Cora's arm.*) Here's Hickey comin'! Let's get outa here! (*They hurry into the hall. The street door is heard slamming behind them.*)

ROCKY—(*gloomily pronounces an obituary*) One regular guy and one all-right tart gone to hell! (*fiercely*) Dat louse Hickey oughta be croaked! (*There is a muttered growl of assent from most of the gathering. Then Harry Hope enters from the hall, followed by Jimmy Tomorrow, with Hickey on his heels. Hope and Jimmy are both putting up a front of self-assurance, but Cora's description of them was apt. There is a desperate bluff in their manner as they walk in, which suggests the last march of the condemned. Hope is dressed in an old black Sunday suit, black tie, shoes, socks, which give him the appearance of being in mourning. Jimmy's clothes are pressed, his shoes shined, his white linen immaculate. He has a hangover and his gently appealing dog's eyes have a boiled look. Hickey's face is a bit drawn from lack of sleep and his voice is hoarse from continual talking, but his bustling energy appears nervously intensified, and his beaming expression is one of triumphant accomplishment.*)

HICKEY—Well, here we are! We've got this far, at least! (*He pats Jimmy on the back.*) Good work, Jimmy. I told you you weren't half as sick as you pretended. No excuse whatever for postponing—

JIMMY—I'll thank you to keep your hands off me! I merely mentioned I would feel more fit tomorrow. But it might as well be today, I suppose.

HICKEY—Finish it now, so it'll be dead forever, and you can be free! (*He passes him to clap Hope encouragingly on the shoulder.*) Cheer up, Harry. You found your rheumatism didn't bother you coming downstairs, didn't you? I told you it wouldn't. (*He winks around at the others. With the exception of Hugo and Parritt, all their eyes are fixed on him with bitter animosity. He gives Hope a playful nudge in the ribs.*) You're the damnedest one for alibis, Governor! As bad as Jimmy!

HOPE—(*putting on his deaf manner*) Eh? I can't hear—(*defiantly*) You're a liar! I've had rheumatism on and off for twenty years. Ever since Bessie died. Everybody knows that.

HICKEY—Yes, we know it's the kind of rheumatism you turn on and off! We're on to you, you old faker! (*He claps him on the shoulder again, chuckling.*)

HOPE—(*looks humiliated and guilty—by way of escape he glares around at the others.*) Bejees, what are all you bums hanging round staring at me for? Think you was watching a circus! Why don't you get the hell out of here and 'tend to your own business, like Hickey's told you? (*They look at him reproachfully, their eyes hurt. They fidget as if trying to move.*)

HICKEY—Yes, Harry, I certainly thought they'd have had the guts to be gone by this time. (*He grins.*) Or maybe I did have my doubts. (*Abruptly he becomes *sincerely sympathetic and earnest.*) Because I know exactly what you're up against, boys. I know how damned yellow a man can be when it comes to making himself face the truth. I've been through the mill, and I had to face a worse bastard in myself than any of you will have to in yourselves. I know you become such a coward you'll grab at any lousy excuse to get out of killing your pipe dreams. And yet, as I've told you over and over, it's exactly those damned tomorrow dreams which keep you from making peace with yourself. So you've got to kill them like I did mine. (*He pauses. They glare at him with fear and hatred. They seem about to curse him, to spring at him. But they remain silent and motionless. His manner changes and he becomes kindly bullying.*) Come on, boys! Get moving! Who'll start the ball rolling? You, Captain, and you, General. You're nearest the door. And besides, you're old war heroes! You ought to lead the forlorn hope! Come on, now, show us a little of that good old battle of Modder River spirit we've heard so much about! You can't hang around all day looking as if you were scared the street outside would bite you!

LEWIS—(*turns with humiliated rage—with an attempt at jaunty casualness*) Right you are, Mister Bloody Nosey Parker! Time I pushed off. Was only waiting to say good-bye to you, Harry, old chum.

HOPE—(*dejectedly*) Good-bye, Captain. Hope you have luck.

LEWIS—Oh, I'm bound to, Old Chap, and the same to you. (*He pushes the swinging doors open and makes a brave exit, turning to his right and marching off outside the window at right of door.*)

WETJOEN—Py Gott, if dot Limey can, I can! (*He pushes the door open and lumbers through it like a bull charging an obstacle. He turns left and disappears off rear, outside the farthest window.*)

HICKEY—(*exhortingly*) Next? Come on, Ed. It's a fine summer's day and the call of the old circus lot must be in your blood! (*Mosher glares at him, then goes to the door. McGloin jumps up from his chair and starts moving toward the door. Hickey claps him on the back as he passes.*) That's the stuff, Mac.

MOSHER—Good-bye, Harry. (*He goes out, turning right outside.*)

McGLOIN—(*glowering after him*) If that crooked grifter has the guts—(*He goes out, turning left outside. Hickey glances at Willie who, before he can speak, jumps from his chair.*)

WILLIE—Good-bye, Harry, and thanks for all your kindness.

HICKEY—(*claps him on the back*) That's the way, Willie! The D.A.'s a busy man. He can't wait all day for you, you know. (*Willie hurries to the door.*)

HOPE—(*dully*) Good luck, Willie. (*Willie goes out and turns right outside. While he is doing so, Jimmy, in a sick panic, sneaks to the bar and furtively reaches for Larry's glass of whiskey.*)

HICKEY—And now it's your turn, Jimmy, old pal. (*He sees what Jimmy is at and grabs his arm just as he is about to down the drink.*) Now, now, Jimmy! You can't do that to yourself. One drink on top of your hangover and an empty stomach and you'll be oreyeyed. Then you'll tell yourself you wouldn't stand a chance if you went up soused to get your old job back.

JIMMY—(*pleads objectly*) Tomorrow! I will tomorrow! I'll be in good shape tomorrow! (*abruptly getting control of himself—with shaken firmness*) All right. I'm going. Take your hands off me.

HICKEY—That's the ticket! You'll thank me when it's all over.

JIMMY—(*in a burst of futile fury*) You dirty swine! (*He tries to throw the drink in Hickey's face, but his aim is poor and it lands on Hickey's coat. Jimmy turns and dashes through the door, disappearing outside the window at right of door.*)

HICKEY—(*brushing the whiskey off his coat—humorously*) All set for an alcohol rub! But no hard feelings. I know how he feels. I wrote the book. I've seen the day when if anyone forced me to face the truth about my pipe dreams, I'd have shot them dead. (*He turns to Hope—encouragingly*) Well, Governor, Jimmy made the grade. It's up to you. If he's got the guts to go through with the test, then certainly you—

LARRY—(*bursts out*) Leave Harry alone, damn you!

HICKEY—(*grins at him*) I'd make up my mind about myself if I was you, Larry, and not bother over Harry. He'll come through all right. I've promised him that. He doesn't need anyone's bum pity. Do you, Governor?

HOPE—(*with a pathetic attempt at his old fuming assertiveness*) No, bejees! Keep your nose out of this, Larry. What's Hickey got to do with it? I've always been going to take this walk, ain't I? Bejees, you bums want to keep me locked up in here 's if I was in jail! I've stood it long enough! I'm free, white and twenty-one, and I'll do as I damned please, bejees! You keep your nose out, too, Hickey! You'd think you was boss of this dump, not me. Sure, I'm all right! Why shouldn't I be? What the hell's to be scared of, just taking a stroll around my own ward? (*As he talks he has been moving toward the door. Now he reaches it.*) What's the weather like outside, Rocky?

ROCKY—Fine day, Boss.

HOPE—What's that? Can't hear you. Don't look fine to me. Looks 's if it'd pour down cats and dogs any minute. My rheumatism—(*He catches himself.*)

No, must be my eyes. Half blind, bejees. Makes things look black. I see now it's a fine day. Too damned hot for a walk, though, if you ask me. Well, do me good to sweat the booze out of me. But I'll have to watch out for the damned automobiles. Wasn't none of them around the last time, twenty years ago. From what I've seen of 'em through the window, they'd run over you as soon as look at you. Not that I'm scared of 'em. I can take care of myself. (*He puts a reluctant hand on the swinging door.*) Well, so long—(*He stops and looks back—with frightened irascibility*) Bejees, where are you, Hickey? It's time we got started.

HICKEY—(*grins and shakes his head*) No, Harry. Can't be done. You've got to keep a date with yourself alone.

HOPE—(*with forced fuming*) Hell of a guy, you are! Thought you'd be willing to help me across the street, knowing I'm half blind. Half deaf, too. Can't bear those damned automobiles. Hell with you! Bejees, I've never needed no one's help and I don't now! (*egging himself on*) I'll take a good long walk now I've started. See all my old friends. Bejees, they must have given me up for dead. Twenty years is a long time. But they know it was grief over Bessie's death that made me—(*He puts his hand on the door.*) Well, the sooner I get started—(*Then he drops his hand—with sentimental melancholy*) You know, Hickey, that's what gets me. Can't help thinking the last time I went out was to Bessie's funeral. After she'd gone, I didn't feel life was worth living. Swore I'd never go out again. (*pathetically*) Somehow, I can't feel it's right for me to go, Hickey, even now. It's like I was doing wrong to her memory.

HICKEY—Now, Governor, you can't let yourself get away with that one any more!

HOPE—(*cupping his hand to his ear*) What's that? Can't hear you. (*sentimentally again but with desperation*) I remember now clear as day the last time before she—It was a fine Sunday morning. We went out to church together. (*His voice breaks on a sob.*)

HICKEY—(*amused*) It's a great act, Governor. But I know better, and so do you. You never did want to go to church or any place else with her. She was always on your neck, making you have ambition and go out and do things, when all you wanted was to get drunk in peace.

HOPE—(*falteringly*) Can't hear a word you're saying. You're a God-damned liar, anyway! (*then in a sudden fury, his voice trembling with hatred*) Bejees, you son of a bitch, if there was a mad dog outside I'd go and shake hands with it rather than stay here with you! (*The momentum of his fit of rage does it. He pushes the door open and strides blindly out into the street and as blindly past the window behind the free-lunch counter.*)

ROCKY—(*in amazement*) Jees, he made it! I'd a give yuh fifty to one he'd never—(*He goes to the end of the bar to look through the window—disgustedly*) Aw, he's stopped. I'll bet yuh he's comin' back.

HICKEY—Of course, he's coming back. So are all the others. By tonight they'll all be here again. You dumbbell, that's the whole point.

ROCKY—(*excitedly*) No, he ain't neider! He's gone to de coib. He's lookin' up and down. Scared stiff of automobiles. Jees, dey ain't more'n two an hour comes down dis street, de old boob! (*He watches excitedly, as if it were a race he had a bet on, oblivious to what happens in the bar.*)

LARRY—(*turns on Hickey with bitter defiance*) And now it's my turn, I suppose? What is it I'm to do to achieve this blessed peace of yours?

HICKEY—(*grins at him*) Why, we've discussed all that, Larry. Just stop lying to yourself—

LARRY—You think when I say I'm finished with life, and tired of watching the stupid greed of the human circus, and I'll welcome closing my eyes in the long sleep of death—you think that's a coward's lie?

HICKEY—(*chuckling*) Well, what do you think, Larry?

LARRY—(*with increasing bitter intensity, more as if he were fighting with himself than with Hickey*) I'm afraid to live, am I?—and even more afraid to die! So I sit here, with my pride drowned on the bottom of a bottle, keeping drunk so I won't see myself shaking in my britches with fright, or hear myself whining and praying: Beloved Christ, let me live a little longer at any price! If it's only for a few days more, or a few hours even, have mercy, Almighty God, and let me still clutch greedily to my yellow heart this sweet treasure, this jewel beyond price, the dirty, stinking bit of withered old flesh which is my beautiful little life! (*He laughs with a sneering, vindictive self-loathing, staring inward at himself with contempt and hatred. Then abruptly he makes Hickey again the antagonist.*) You think you'll make me admit that to myself?

HICKEY—(*chuckling*) But you just did admit it, didn't you?

PARRITT—(*lifts his head from his hands to glare at Larry—jeeringly*) That's the stuff, Hickey! Show the old yellow faker up! He can't play dead on me like this! He's got to help me!

HICKEY—Yes, Larry, you've got to settle with him. I'm leaving you entirely in his hands. He'll do as good a job as I could at making you give up that old grandstand bluff.

LARRY—(*angrily*) I'll see the two of you in hell first!

ROCKY—(*calls excitedly from the end of the bar*) Jees, Harry's startin' across de street! He's goin' to fool yuh, Hickey, yuh bastard! (*He pauses, watching—then worriedly*) What de hell's he stoppin' for? Right in de middle of de street! Yuh'd tink he was paralyzed or somethin'! (*disgustedly*) Aw, he's quittin'! He's turned back! Jees, look at de old bastard travel! Here he comes! (*Hope passes the window outside the free-lunch counter in a shambling, panic-stricken run. He comes lurching blindly through the swinging doors and stumbles to the bar at Larry's right.*)

HOPE—Bejees, give me a drink quick! Scared me out of a year's growth! Bejees, that guy ought to be pinched! Bejees, it ain't safe to walk in the streets! Bejees, that ends me! Never again! Give me that bottle! (*He slops a glass full and drains it and pours another—to Rocky, who is regarding him with scorn—appealingly*) You seen it, didn't you, Rocky?

ROCKY—Seen what?

HOPE—That automobile, you dumb Wop! Feller driving it must be drunk or crazy. He'd run right over me if I hadn't jumped. (*ingratiatingly*) Come on, Larry, have a drink. Everybody have a drink. Have a cigar, Rocky. I know you hardly ever touch it.

ROCKY—(*resentfully*) Well, dis is de time I do touch it! (*pouring a drink*) I'm goin' to get stinko, see! And if yuh don't like it, yuh know what yuh can do! I gotta good mind to chuck my job, anyways. (*disgustedly*) Jees, Harry, I thought yuh had some guts! I was bettin' yuh'd make it and show dat four-flusher up. (*He nods at Hickey—then snorts*) Automobile, hell! Who d'yuh tink yuh're kiddin'? Dey wasn' no automobile! Yuh just quit cold!

HOPE—(*feebly*) Guess I ought to know! Bejees, it almost killed me!

HICKEY—(*comes to the bar between him and Larry, and puts a hand on his shoulder—kindly*) Now, now, Governor. Don't be foolish. You've faced the test and come through. You're rid of all that nagging dream stuff now. You know you can't believe it any more.

HOPE—(*appeals pleadingly to Larry*) Larry, you saw it, didn't you? Drink up! Have another! Have all you want! Bejees, we'll go on a grand old souse together! You saw that automobile, didn't you?

LARRY—(*compassionately, avoiding his eyes*) Sure, I saw it, Harry. You had a narrow escape. Be God, I thought you were a goner!

HICKEY—(*turns on him with a flash of sincere indignation*) What the hell's the matter with you, Larry? You know what I told you about the wrong kind of pity. Leave Harry alone! You'd think I was trying to harm him, the fool way you act! My oldest friend! What kind of a louse do you think I am? There isn't anything I wouldn't do for Harry, and he knows it! All I've wanted to do is fix it so he'll be finally at peace with himself for the rest of his days! And if you'll only wait until the final returns are in, you'll find that's exactly what I've accomplished! (*He turns to Hope and pats his shoulder—coaxingly*) Come now, Governor. What's the use of being stubborn, now when it's all over and dead? Give up that ghost automobile.

HOPE—(*beginning to collapse within himself—dully*) Yes, what's the use—now? All a lie! No automobile. But, bejees, something ran over me! Must have been myself, I guess. (*He forces a feeble smile—then wearily*) Guess I'll sit down. Feel all in. Like a corpse, bejees. (*He picks a bottle and glass from the bar and walks to the first table and slumps down in the chair, facing left-front. His shaking hand misjudges the distance and he sets the bottle on the table with a jar that rouses Hugo, who lifts his head from his arms and blinks at him through his thick spectacles. Hope speaks to him in a flat, dead voice.*) Hello, Hugo. Coming up for air? Stay passed out, that's the right dope. There ain't any cool willow trees—except you grow your own in a bottle. (*He pours a drink and gulps it down.*)

HUGO—(*with his silly giggle*) Hello, Harry, stupid proletarian monkey-face! I vill trink champagne beneath the villow—(*with a change to aristocratic fastidiousness*) But the slaves must ice it properly! (*with guttural rage*) Gottamned Hickey! Peddler pimp for nouveau-riche capitalism! Vhen I lead the jackass mob to the sack of Babylon, I vill make them hang him to a lamppost the first one!

HOPE—(*spiritlessly*) Good work. I'll help pull on the rope. Have a drink, Hugo.

HUGO—(*frightenedly*) No, thank you. I am too trunk now. I hear myself say crazy things. Do not listen, please. Larry vill tell you I haf never been so crazy trunk. I must sleep it off. (*He starts to put his head on his arms but stops and stares at Hope with growing uneasiness.*) Vhat's matter, Harry? You look funny. You look dead. Vhat's happened? I don't know you. Listen, I feel I am dying, too. Because I am so crazy trunk! It is very necessary I sleep. But I can't sleep here vith you. You look dead. (*He scrambles to his feet in a confused panic, turns his back on Hope and settles into the chair at the next table which faces left. He thrusts his head down on his arms like an ostrich hiding its head in the sand. He does not notice Parritt, nor Parritt him.*)

LARRY—(*to Hickey with bitter condemnation*) Another one who's begun to enjoy your peace!

HICKEY—Oh, I know it's tough on him right now, the same as it is on Harry. But that's only the first shock. I promise you they'll both come through all right.

LARRY—And you believe that! I see you do! You mad fool!

HICKEY—Of course, I believe it! I tell you I know from my own experience!

HOPE—*(spiritlessly)* Close that big clam of yours, Hickey. Bejees, you're a worse gabber than that nagging bitch, Bessie, was. *(He drinks his drink mechanically and pours another.)*

ROCKY—*(in amazement)* Jees, did yuh hear dat?

HOPE—*(dully)* What's wrong with this booze? There's no kick in it.

ROCKY—*(worriedly)* Jees, Larry, Hugo had it right. He does look like he'd croaked.

HICKEY—*(annoyed)* Don't be a damned fool! Give him time. He's coming along all right. *(He calls to Hope with a first trace of underlying uneasiness.)* You're all right, aren't you, Harry?

HOPE—*(dully)* I want to pass out like Hugo.

LARRY—*(turns to Hickey—with bitter anger)* It's the peace of death you've brought him.

HICKEY—*(for the first time loses his temper)* That's a lie! *(But he controls this instantly and grins.)* Well, well, you did manage to get a rise out of me that time. I think such a hell of a lot of Harry—*(impatiently)* You know that's damned foolishness. Look at me. I've been through it. Do I look dead? Just leave Harry alone and wait until the shock wears off and you'll see. He'll be a new man. Like I am. *(He calls to Hope coaxingly)* How's it coming, Governor? Beginning to feel free, aren't you? Relieved and not guilty any more?

HOPE—*(grumbles spiritlessly)* Bejees, you must have been monkeying with the booze, too, you interfering bastard! There's no life in it now. I want to get drunk and pass out. Let's all pass out. Who the hell cares?

HICKEY—*(lowering his voice—worriedly to Larry)* I admit I didn't think he'd be hit so hard. He's always been a happy-go-lucky slob. Like I was. Of course, it hit me hard, too. But only for a minute. Then I felt as if a ton of guilt had been lifted off my mind. I saw what had happened was the only possible way for the peace of all concerned.

LARRY—*(sharply)* What was it happened? Tell us that! And don't try to get out of it! I want a straight answer! *(vindictively)* I think it was something you drove someone else to do!

HICKEY—*(puzzled)* Someone else?

LARRY—*(accusingly)* What did your wife die of? You've kept that a deep secret, I notice—for some reason!

HICKEY—*(reproachfully)* You're not very considerate, Larry. But, if you insist on knowing now, there's no reason you shouldn't. It was a bullet through the head that killed Evelyn. *(There is a second's tense silence.)*

HOPE—*(dully)* Who the hell cares? To hell with her and that nagging old hag, Bessie.

ROCKY—Christ. You had de right dope, Larry.

LARRY—*(revengefully)* You drove your poor wife to suicide? I knew it! Be God, I don't blame her! I'd almost do as much myself to be rid of you! It's what you'd like to drive us all to—*(Abruptly he is ashamed of himself and pitying.)* I'm sorry, Hickey. I'm a rotten louse to throw that in your face.

HICKEY—*(quietly)* Oh, that's all right, Larry. But don't jump at conclusions. I didn't say poor Evelyn committed suicide. It's the last thing she'd ever have done, as long as I was alive for her to take care of and forgive. If you'd known her at all, you'd never get such a crazy suspicion. *(He pauses—then slowly)* No, I'm sorry to have to tell you my poor wife was killed. *(Larry stares at him with growing horror and shrinks back along the bar away from him. Parritt jerks his head up from his hands and looks around frightenedly, not at Hickey, but at Larry. Rocky's round eyes are popping. Hope stares dully at the table top. Hugo, his head hidden in his arms, gives no sign of life.)*

LARRY—*(shakenly)* Then she—was murdered.

PARRITT—*(springs to his feet—stammers defensively)* You're a liar, Larry! You must be crazy to say that to me! You know she's still alive! *(But no one pays any attention to him.)*

ROCKY—*(blurts out)* Moidered? Who done it?

LARRY—*(his eyes fixed with fascinated horror on Hickey—frightenedly)* Don't ask questions, you dumb Wop! It's none of our damned business! Leave Hickey alone!

HICKEY—*(smiles at him with affectionate amusement)* Still the old grandstand bluff, Larry? Or is it some more bum pity? *(He turns to Rocky—matter-of-factly)* The police don't know who killed her yet, Rocky. But I expect they will before very long. *(As if that finished the subject, he comes forward to Hope and sits beside him, with an arm around his shoulder—affectionately coaxing)* Coming along fine now, aren't you, Governor? Getting over the first shock? Beginning to feel free from guilt and lying hopes and at peace with yourself?

HOPE—*(with a dull callousness)* Somebody croaked your Evelyn, eh? Bejees, my bets are on the iceman! But who the hell cares? Let's get drunk and pass out. *(He tosses down his drink with a lifeless, automatic movement—complainingly)* Bejees, what did you do to the booze, Hickey? There's no damned life left in it.

PARRITT—*(stammers, his eyes on Larry, whose eyes in turn remain fixed on Hickey)* Don't look like that, Larry! You've got to believe what I told you! It had nothing to do with her! It was just to get a few lousy dollars!

HUGO—*(suddenly raises his head from his arms and, looking straight in front of him, pounds on the table frightenedly with his small fists)* Don't be a fool! Buy me a trink! But no more vine! It is not properly iced! *(with guttural rage)* Gottamned stupid proletarian slaves! Buy me a trink or I vill have you shot! (*He collapses into abject begging.*) Please, for Gott's sake! I am not trunk enough! I cannot sleep! Life is a crazy monkey-face! Always there is blood beneath the villow trees! I hate it and I am afraid! (*He hides his face on his arms, sobbing muffledly.*) Please, I am crazy trunk! I say crazy things! For Gott's sake, do not listen to me! (*But no one pays any attention to him. Larry stands shrunk back against the bar. Rocky is leaning over it. They stare at Hickey. Parritt stands looking pleadingly at Larry.*)

HICKEY—(*gazes with worried kindliness at Hope*) You're beginning to worry me, Governor. Something's holding you up somewhere. I don't see why—You've faced the truth about yourself. You've done what you had to do to kill your nagging pipe dreams. Oh, I know it knocks you cold. But only for a minute. Then you see it was the only possible way to peace. And you feel happy. Like I did. That's what worries me about you, Governor. It's time you began to feel happy—

(*Curtain*)

★

ACT FOUR

SCENE—*Same as Act One—the back room with the curtain separating it from the section of the barroom with its single table at right of curtain, front. It is around half past one in the morning of the following day. The tables in the back room have a new arrangement. The one at left, front, before the window to the yard, is in the same position. So is the one at the right, rear, of it in the second row. But this table now has only one chair. This chair is at right of it, facing directly front. The two tables on either side of the door at rear are unchanged. But the table which was at center, front, has been pushed toward right so that it and the table at right, rear, of it in the second row, and the last table at right in the front row, are now jammed so closely together that they form one group.*

Larry, Hugo and Parritt are at the table at left, front. Larry is at left of it, beside the window, facing front. Hugo sits at rear, facing front, his head on his arms in his habitual position, but he is not asleep. On Hugo's left is Parritt, his chair facing left, front. At right of table, an empty chair, facing left. Larry's chin is on his chest, his eyes fixed on the floor. He will not look at Parritt, who keeps staring at him with a sneering, pleading challenge.

Two bottles of whiskey are on each table, whiskey and chaser glasses, a pitcher of water.

The one chair by the table at right, rear, of them is vacant.

At the first table at right of center, Cora sits at left, front, of it, facing front. Around the rear of this table are four empty chairs. Opposite Cora, in a sixth chair, is Captain Lewis, also facing front. On his left, McGloin is facing front in a chair before the middle table of his group. At right, rear, of him, also at this table, General Wetjoen sits facing front. In back of this table are three empty chairs.

At right, rear, of Wetjoen, but beside the last table of the group, sits Willie. On Willie's left, at rear of table, is Hope. On Hope's left, at right, rear, of table, is Mosher. Finally, at right of table is Jimmy Tomorrow. All of the four sit facing front.

There is an atmosphere of oppressive stagnation in the room, and a quality of insensibility about all the people in this group at right. They are like wax figures, set stiffly on their chairs, carrying out mechanically the motions of getting drunk but sunk in a numb stupor which is impervious to stimulation.

In the bar section, Joe is sprawled in the chair at right of table, facing left. His head rolls forward in a sodden slumber. Rocky is standing behind his chair, regarding him with dull hostility. Rocky's face is set in an expression of tired, callous toughness. He looks now like a minor Wop gangster.

ROCKY—(*shakes Joe by the shoulder*) Come on, yuh damned nigger! Beat it in de back room! It's after hours. (*But Joe remains inert. Rocky gives up.*) Aw, to hell wid it. Let de dump get pinched. I'm through wid dis lousy job, anyway! (*He hears someone at rear and calls*) Who's dat? (*Chuck appears from rear. He has been drinking heavily, but there is no lift to his jag; his manner is grouchy and sullen. He has evidently been brawling. His knuckles are raw and there is a mouse under one eye. He has lost his straw hat, his tie is awry, and his blue suit is dirty. Rocky eyes him indifferently.*) Been scrappin', huh? Started off on your periodical, ain't yuh? (*For a second there is a gleam of satisfaction in his eyes.*)

CHUCK—Yeah, ain't yuh glad? (*truculently*) What's it to yuh?

ROCKY—Not a damn ting. But dis is someting to me. I'm out on my feet holdin' down your job. Yuh said if I'd take your day, yuh'd relieve me at six, and here it's half past one A.M. Well, yuh're takin' over now, get me, no matter how plastered yuh are!

CHUCK—Plastered, hell! I wisht I was. I've lapped up a gallon, but it don't hit me right. And to hell wid de job. I'm goin' to tell Harry I'm quittin'.

ROCKY—Yeah? Well, I'm quittin', too.

CHUCK—I've played sucker for dat crummy blonde long enough, lettin' her kid me into woikin'. From now on I take it easy.

ROCKY—I'm glad yuh're gettin' some sense.

CHUCK—And I hope yuh're gettin' some. What a prize sap you been, tendin' bar when yuh got two good hustlers in your stable!

ROCKY—Yeah, but I ain't no sap now. I'll loin dem, when dey get back from Coney. (*sneeringly*) Jees, dat Cora sure played you for a dope, feedin' yuh dat marriage-on-de-farm hop!

CHUCK—(*dully*) Yeah. Hickey got it right. A lousy pipe dream. It was her pulling sherry flips on me woke me up. All de way walkin' to de ferry, every ginmill we come to she'd drag me in to blow her. I got tinkin', Christ, what won't she want when she gets de ring on her finger and I'm hooked? So I tells her at de ferry, "Kiddo, yuh can go to Joisey, or to hell, but count me out."

ROCKY—She says it was her told you to go to hell, because yuh'd started hittin' de booze.

CHUCK—(*ignoring this*) I got tinkin', too, Jees, won't I look sweet wid a wife dat if yuh put all de guys she's stayed wid side by side, dey'd reach to Chicago. (*He sighs gloomily.*) Dat kind of dame, yuh can't trust 'em. De minute your back is toined, dey're cheatin' wid de iceman or someone. Hickey done me a favor, makin' me wake up. (*He pauses—then adds pathetically*) On'y it was fun, kinda, me and Cora kiddin' ourselves—(*Suddenly his face hardens with hatred.*) Where is dat son of a bitch, Hickey? I want one good sock at day guy—just one!—and de next buttin' in he'll do will be in de morgue! I'll take a chance on goin' to de Chair—!

ROCKY—(*starts—in a low warning voice*) Piano! Keep away from him, Chuck! He ain't here now, anyway. He went out to phone, he said. He wouldn't call from here. I got a hunch he's beat it. But if he does come back, yuh don't know him, if anyone asks yuh, get me? (*As Chuck looks at him with dull surprise he lowers his voice to a whisper.*) De Chair, maybe dat's where he's goin'. I don't know nuttin', see, but it looks like he croaked his wife.

CHUCK—(*with a flash of interest*) Yuh mean she really was cheatin' on him? Den I don't blame de guy—

ROCKY—Who's blamin' him? When a dame asks for it—But I don't know nuttin' about it, see?

CHUCK—Is any of de gang wise?

ROCKY—Larry is. And de boss ought to be. I tried to wise de rest of dem up to stay clear of him, but dey're all so licked, I don't know if dey got it. (*He pauses—vindictively*) I don't give a damn what he done to his wife, but if he gets de Hot Seat I won't go into no mournin'!

CHUCK—Me, neider!

ROCKY—Not after his trowin' it in my face I'm a pimp. What if I am? Why de hell not? And what he's done to Harry. Jees, de poor old slob is so licked he can't even get drunk. And all de gang. Dey're all licked. I couldn't help feelin' sorry for de poor bums when dey showed up tonight, one by one, lookin' like pooches wid deir tails between deir legs, dat every-one'd been kickin' till dey was too punch-drunk to feel it no more. Jimmy Tomorrow was de last. Schwartz, de copper, brung him in. Seen him sittin' on de dock on West Street, lookin' at de water and cryin'! Schwartz thought he was drunk and I let him tink it. But he was cold sober. He was tryin' to jump in and didn't have de noive, I figgered it. Noive! Jees, dere ain't enough guts left in de whole gang to battle a mosquito!

CHUCK—Aw, to hell wid 'em! Who cares? Gimme a drink. (*Rocky pushes the bottle toward him apathetically.*) I see you been hittin' de redeye, too.

ROCKY—Yeah. But it don't do no good. I can't get drunk right. (*Chuck drinks. Joe mumbles in his sleep. Chuck regards him resentfully.*) Dis doity dinge was able to get his snootful and pass out. Jees, even Hickey can't faze a nigger! Yuh'd tink he was fazed if yuh'd seen him come in. Stinko, and he pulled a gat and said he'd plug Hickey for insultin' him. Den he dropped it and begun to cry and said he wasn't a gamblin' man or a tough guy no more; he was yellow. He'd borrowed de gat to stick up someone, and den didn't have de guts. He got drunk panhandlin' drinks in nigger joints, I s'pose. I guess dey felt sorry for him.

CHUCK—He ain't got no business in de bar after hours. Why don't yuh chuck him out?

ROCKY—(*apathetically*) Aw, to hell wid it. Who cares?

CHUCK—(*lapsing into the same mood*) Yeah. I don't.

JOE—(*suddenly lunges to his feet dazedly—mumbles in humbled apology*) Scuse me, White Boys. Scuse me for livin'. I don't want to be where I's not wanted. (*He makes his way swayingly to the opening in the curtain at rear and tacks down to the middle table of the three at right, front. He feels his way around it to the table at its left and gets to the chair in back of Captain Lewis.*)

CHUCK—(*gets up—in a callous, brutal tone*) My pig's in de back room, ain't she? I wanna collect de dough I wouldn't take dis mornin', like a sucker, before she blows it. (*He goes rear.*)

ROCKY—(*getting up*) I'm comin', too. I'm trough woikin'. I ain't no lousy bartender. (*Chuck comes through the curtain and looks for Cora as Joe flops down in the chair in back of Captain Lewis.*)

JOE—(*taps Lewis on the shoulder—servilely apologetic*) If you objects to my sittin' here, Captain, just tell me and I pulls my freight.

LEWIS—No apology required, old chap. Anybody could tell you I should feel honored a bloody Kaffir would lower himself to sit beside me. (*Joe stares at him with sodden perplexity—then closes his eyes. Chuck comes forward to take the chair behind Cora's, as Rocky enters the back room and starts over toward Larry's table.*)

CHUCK—(*his voice hard*) I'm waitin', Baby. Dig!

CORA—(*with apathetic obedience*) Sure. I been expectin' yuh. I got it all ready. Here. (*She passes a small roll of bills she has in her hand over her shoulder, without looking at him. He takes it, glances at it suspiciously, then shoves it in his pocket without a word of acknowledgment. Cora speaks with a tired wonder at herself rather than resentment toward him.*) Jees, imagine me kiddin' myself I wanted to marry a drunken pimp.

CHUCK—Dat's nuttin', Baby. Imagine de sap I'da been, when I can get your dough just as easy widout it!

ROCKY—(*takes the chair on Parritt's left, facing Larry—dully*) Hello, Old Cemetery. (*Larry doesn't seem to hear. To Parritt*) Hello, Tightwad. You still around?

PARRITT—(*keeps his eyes on Larry—in a jeeringly challenging tone*) Ask Larry! He knows I'm here, all right, although he's pretending not to! He'd like to forget I'm alive! He's trying to kid himself with that grandstand philosopher stuff! But he knows he can't get away with it now! He kept himself locked in his room until a while ago, alone with a bottle of booze, but he couldn't make it work! He couldn't even get drunk! He had to come out! There must have been something there he was even more scared to face than he is Hickey and me! I guess he got looking at the fire escape and thinking how handy it was, if he was really sick of life and only had the nerve to die! (*He pauses sneeringly. Larry's face has tautened, but he pretends he doesn't hear. Rocky pays no attention. His head has sunk forward, and he stares at the table top, sunk in the same stupor as the other occupants of the room. Parritt goes on, his tone becoming more insistent.*) He's been thinking of me, too, Rocky. Trying to figure a way to get out of helping me! He doesn't want to be bothered understanding. But he does understand all right! He used to love her, too. So he thinks I ought to take a hop off the fire escape! (*He pauses. Larry's hands on the table have clinched into fists, as his nails dig into his palms, but he remains silent. Parritt breaks and starts pleading.*) For God's sake, Larry, can't you say something? Hickey's got me all balled up. Thinking of what he must have done has got me so I don't know any more what I did or why. I can't go on like this! I've got to know what I ought to do—

LARRY—(*in a stifled tone*) God damn you! Are you trying to make me your executioner?

PARRITT—(*starts frightenedly*) Execution? Then you do think—?

LARRY—I don't think anything!

PARRITT—(*with forced jeering*) I suppose you think I ought to die because I sold out a lot of loudmouthed fakers, who were cheating suckers with a phony pipe dream, and put them where they ought to be, in jail? (*He forces a laugh.*) Don't make me laugh! I ought to get a medal! What a damned old sap you are! You must still believe in the Movement! (*He nudges Rocky with his elbow.*) Hickey's right about him, isn't he, Rocky? An old no-good drunken tramp, as dumb as he is, ought to take a hop off the fire escape!

ROCKY—(*dully*) Sure. Why don't he? Or you? Or me? What de hell's de difference? Who cares? (*There is a faint stir from all the crowd, as if this sentiment struck a responsive chord in their numbed minds. They mumble almost in chorus as one voice, like sleepers talking out of a dully irritating dream,* "The hell with it!" "Who cares?" *Then the sodden silence descends again on the room. Rocky looks from Parritt to Larry puzzledly. He mutters*) What am I doin' here wid youse two? I remember I had someting on my mind to tell yuh. What—? Oh, I got it now. (*He looks from one to the other of their oblivious faces with a strange, sly, calculating look—ingratiatingly*) I was tinking how you was bot' reg'lar guys. I tinks, ain't two guys like dem saps to be hangin' round like a coupla stew bums and wastin' demselves. Not dat I blame yuh for not woikin'. On'y suckers woik. But dere's no percentage in bein' broke when yuh can grab good jack for yourself and make someone else woik for yuh, is dere? I mean, like I do. So I tinks, Dey're my pals and I ought to wise up two good guys like dem to play my system, and not be lousy barflies, no good to demselves or nobody else. (*He addresses Parritt now—persuasively*) What yuh tink, Parritt? Ain't I right? Sure, I am. So don't be a sucker, see? Yuh ain't a bad-lookin' guy. Yuh could easy make some gal who's a good hustler, an' start a stable. I'd help yuh and wise yuh up to de inside dope on de game. (*He pauses inquiringly. Parritt gives no sign of having heard him. Rocky asks impatiently*) Well, what about it? What if dey do call yuh a pimp? What de hell do you care—any more'n I do.

PARRITT—(*without looking at him—vindictively*) I'm through with whores. I wish they were all in jail—or dead!

ROCKY—(*ignores this—disappointedly*) So yuh won't touch it, huh? Aw right, stay a bum! (*He turns to Larry.*) Jees, Larry, he's sure one dumb boob, ain't he? Dead from de neck up! He don't know a good ting when he sees it. (*oily, even persuasive again*) But how about you, Larry? You ain't dumb. So why not, huh? Sure, yuh're old, but dat don't matter. All de hustlers tink yuh're aces. Dey fall for yuh like yuh was deir uncle or old man or someting. Dey'd like takin' care of yuh. And de cops 'round here, dey like yuh, too. It'd be a pipe for yuh, 'specially wid me to help yuh and wise yuh up. Yuh wouldn't have to worry where de next drink's comin' from, or wear doity clothes. (*hopefully*) Well, don't it look good to yuh?

LARRY—(*glances at him—for a moment he is stirred to sardonic pity*) No, it doesn't look good, Rocky. I mean, the peace Hickey's brought you. It isn't contented enough, if you have to make everyone else a pimp, too.

ROCKY—(*stares at him stupidly—then pushes his chair back and gets up, grumbling*) I'm a sap to waste time on yuh. A stew bum is a stew bum and yuh can't change him. (*He turns away—then turns back for an afterthought.*) Like I was sayin' to Chuck, yuh better keep away from Hickey. If anyone asks yuh, yuh don't know nuttin', get me? Yuh never even hoid he had a wife. (*His face hardens.*) Jees, we all ought to git drunk and stage a celebration when dat bastard goes to de Chair.

LARRY—(*vindictively*) Be God, I'll celebrate with you and drink long life to him in hell! (*then guiltily and pityingly*) No! The poor mad devil—(*then with angry self-contempt*) Ah, pity again! The wrong kind! He'll welcome the Chair!

PARRITT—(*contemptuously*) Yes, what are you so damned scared of death for? I don't want your lousy pity.

ROCKY—Christ, I hope he don't come back, Larry. We don't know nuttin' now. We're on'y guessin', see? But if de bastard keeps on talkin'—

LARRY—(*grimly*) He'll come back. He'll keep on talking. He's got to. He's lost his confidence that the peace he's sold us is the real McCoy, and it's made him uneasy about his own. He'll have to prove to us—(*As he is speaking Hickey appears silently in the doorway at rear. He has lost his beaming salesman's grin. His manner is no longer self-assured. His expression is uneasy, baffled and resentful. It has the stubborn set of an obsessed determination. His eyes are on Larry as he comes in. As he speaks, there is a start from all the crowd, a shrinking away from him.*)

HICKEY—(*angrily*) That's a damned lie, Larry! I haven't lost confidence a damned bit! Why should I? (*boastfully*) By God, whenever I made up my mind to sell someone something I knew they ought to want, I've sold 'em! (*He suddenly looks confused—haltingly*) I mean—It isn't kind of you, Larry, to make that kind of crack when I've been doing my best to help—

ROCKY—(*moving away from him toward right—sharply*) Keep away from me! I don't know nuttin' about yuh, see? (*His tone is threatening but his manner as he turns his back and ducks quickly across to the bar entrance is that of one in flight. In the bar he comes forward and slumps in a chair at the table, facing front.*)

HICKEY—(*comes to the table at right, rear, of Larry's table and sits in the one chair there, facing front. He looks over the crowd at right, hopefully and then disappointedly. He speaks with a strained attempt at his old affectionate jollying manner.*) Well, well! How are you coming along, everybody? Sorry I had to leave you for a while, but there was something I had to get finally settled. It's all fixed now.

HOPE—(*in the voice of one reiterating mechanically a hopeless complaint*) When are you going to do something about this booze, Hickey? Bejees, we all know you did something to take the life out of it. It's like drinking dishwater! We can't pass out! And you promised us peace. (*His group all join in in a dull, complaining chorus,* "We can't pass out! You promised us peace!")

HICKEY—(*bursts into resentful exasperation*) For God's sake, Harry, are you still harping on that damned nonsense! You've kept it up all afternoon and night! And you've got everybody else singing the same crazy tune! I've had about all I can stand—That's why I phoned—(*He controls himself.*) Excuse me, boys and girls. I don't mean that. I'm just worried about you, when you play dead on me like this. I was hoping by the time I got back you'd be like you ought to be! I thought you were deliberately holding back, while I was around, because you didn't want to give me the satisfaction of showing me I'd had the right dope. And I did have! I know from my own experience. (*exasperatedly*) But I've explained that a million times! And you've all done what you needed to do! By rights you should be contented now, without a single damned hope or lying dream left to torment you! But here you are, acting like a lot of stiffs cheating the undertaker! (*He looks around accusingly.*) I can't figure it—unless it's just your damned pigheaded stubbornness! (*He breaks—miserably*) Hell, you oughtn't to act this way with me! You're my old pals, the only friends I've got. You know the one thing I want is to see you all happy before I go—(*rousing himself to his old brisk, master-of-ceremonies manner*) And there's damned little time left now. I've made a date for two o'clock. We've got to get busy right away and find out what's wrong. (*There is a sodden silence. He goes on exasperatedly.*) Can't you appreciate what you've got, for God's sake? Don't you know you're free now to be yourselves, without having to feel remorse or guilt, or lie to yourselves about reforming tomorrow? Can't you see there is no tomorrow now? You're rid of it forever! You've killed it! You don't have to care a damn about anything any more! You've finally got the game of life licked, don't you see that? (*angrily exhorting*) Then why the hell don't you get pie-eyed and celebrate? Why don't you laugh and sing "Sweet Adeline"? (*with bitterly hurt accusation*) The only reason I can think of is, you're putting on this rotten half-dead act just to get back at me! Because you hate my guts! (*He breaks again.*) God, don't do that, gang! It makes me feel like hell to think you hate me. It makes me feel you suspect I must have hated you. But that's a lie! Oh, I know I used to hate everyone in the world who wasn't as rotten a bastard as I was! But that was when I was still living in hell—before I faced the truth and saw the one possible way to free poor Evelyn and give her the peace she'd always dreamed about. (*He pauses. Everyone in the group stirs with awakening dread and they all begin to grow tense on their chairs.*)

CHUCK—(*without looking at Hickey—with dull, resentful viciousness*) Aw, put a bag over it! To hell wid Evelyn! What if she was cheatin'? And who cares what yuh did to her? Dat's your funeral. We don't give a damn, see? (*There is a dull, resentful chorus of assent,* "We don't give a damn." *Chuck adds dully*) All we want outa you is keep de hell away from us and give us a rest. (*a muttered chorus of assent*)

HICKEY—(*as if he hadn't heard this—an obsessed look on his face*) The one possible way to make up to her for all I'd made her go through, and get her rid of me so I couldn't make her suffer any more, and she wouldn't have to forgive me again! I saw I couldn't do it by killing myself, like I wanted to for a long time. That would have been the last straw for her. She'd have died of a broken heart to think I could do that to her. She'd have blamed herself for it, too. Or I couldn't just run away from her. She'd have died of grief and humiliation if I'd done that to her. She'd have thought I'd stopped loving her. (*He adds with a strange impressive simplicity*) You see, Evelyn loved me. And I loved her. That was the trouble. It would have been easy to find a way out if she hadn't loved me so much. Or if I hadn't loved her. But as it was, there was only one possible way. (*He pauses—then adds simply*) I had to kill her. (*There is a second's dead silence as he finishes—then a tense indrawn breath like a gasp from the crowd, and a general shrinking movement.*)

LARRY—(*bursts out*) You mad fool, can't you keep your mouth shut! We may hate you for what you've done here this time, but we remember the old times, too, when you brought kindness and laughter with you instead of death! We don't want to know things that will make us help send you to the Chair!

PARRITT—(*with angry scorn*) Ah, shut up, you yellow faker! Can't you face anything? Wouldn't I deserve the Chair, too, if I'd—It's worse if you kill someone and they have to go on living. I'd be glad of the Chair! It'd wipe it out! It'd square me with myself!

HICKEY—(*disturbed—with a movement of repulsion*) I wish you'd get rid of that bastard, Larry. I can't have him pretending there's something in common between him and me. It's what's in your heart that counts. There was love in my heart, not hate.

PARRITT—(*glares at him in angry terror*) You're a liar! I don't hate her! I couldn't! And it had nothing to do with her, anyway! You ask Larry!

LARRY—(*grabs his shoulder and shakes him furiously*) God damn you, stop shoving your rotten soul in my lap! (*Parritt subsides, hiding his face in his hands and shuddering.*)

HICKEY—(*goes on quietly now*) Don't worry about the Chair, Larry. I know it's still hard for you not to be terrified by death, but when you've made peace with yourself, like I have, you won't give a damn. (*He addresses the group at right again—earnestly*) Listen, everybody. I've made up my mind the only way I can clear things up for you, so you'll realize how contented and carefree you ought to feel, now I've made you get rid of your pipe dreams, is to show you what a pipe dream did to me and Evelyn. I'm certain if I tell you about it from the beginning, you'll appreciate what I've done for you and why I did it, and how damned grateful you ought to be—instead of hating me. (*He begins eagerly in a strange running narrative manner.*) You see, even when we were kids, Evelyn and me—

HOPE—(*bursts out, pounding with his glass on the table*) No! Who the hell cares? We don't want to hear it. All we want is to pass out and get drunk and a little peace! (*They are all, except Larry and Parritt, seized by the same fit and pound with their glasses, even Hugo, and Rocky in the bar, and shout in chorus,* "Who the hell cares? We want to pass out!")

HICKEY—(*with an expression of wounded hurt*) All right, if that's the way you feel. I don't want to cram it down your throats. I don't need to tell anyone. I don't feel guilty. I'm only worried about you.

HOPE—What did you do to this booze? That's what we'd like to hear. Bejees, you done something. There's no life or kick in it now. (*He appeals mechanically to Jimmy Tomorrow.*) Ain't that right, Jimmy?

JIMMY—(*More than any of them, his face has a wax-figure blankness that makes it look embalmed. He answers in a precise, completely lifeless voice, but his reply is not to Harry's question, and he does not look at him or anyone else.*) Yes. Quite right. It was all a stupid lie—my nonsense about tomorrow. Naturally, they would never give me my position back. I would never dream of asking them. It would be hopeless. I didn't resign. I was fired for drunkenness. And that was years ago. I'm much worse now. And it was absurd of me to excuse my drunkenness by pretending it was my wife's adultery that ruined my life. As Hickey guessed, I was a drunkard before that. Long before. I discovered early in life that living frightened me when I was sober. I have forgotten why I married Marjorie. I can't even remember now if she was pretty. She was a blonde, I think, but I couldn't swear to it. I had some idea of wanting a home, perhaps. But, of course, I much preferred the nearest pub. Why Marjorie married me, God knows. It's impossible to believe she loved me. She soon found I much preferred drinking all night with my pals to being in bed with her. So, naturally, she was unfaithful. I didn't blame her. I really didn't care. I was glad to be free—even grateful to her, I think, for giving me such a good tragic excuse to drink as much as I damned well pleased. (*He stops like a mechanical doll that has run down. No one gives any sign of having heard him. There is a heavy silence. Then Rocky, at the table in the bar, turns grouchily as he hears a noise behind him. Two men come quietly forward. One, Moran, is middle-aged. The other, Lieb, is in his twenties. They look ordinary in every way, without anything distinctive to indicate what they do for a living.*)

ROCKY—(*grumpily*) In de back room if yuh wanta drink. (*Moran makes a peremptory sign to be quiet. All of a sudden Rocky senses they are detectives and springs up to face them, his expression freezing into a wary blankness. Moran pulls back his coat to show his badge.*)

MORAN—(*in a low voice*) Guy named Hickman in the back room?

ROCKY—Tink I know de names of all de guys—?

MORAN—Listen, you! This is murder. And don't be a sap. It was Hickman himself phoned in and said we'd find him here around two.

ROCKY—(*dully*) So dat's who he phoned to. (*He shrugs his shoulders.*) Aw right, if he asked for it. He's de fat guy sittin' alone. (*He slumps down in his chair again.*) And if yuh want a confession all yuh got to do is listen. He'll be tellin' all about it soon. Yuh can't stop de bastard talkin'. (*Moran gives him a curious look, then whispers to Lieb, who disappears rear and a moment later appears in the hall doorway of the back room. He spots Hickey and slides into a chair at the left of the doorway, cutting off escape by the hall. Moran goes back and stands in the opening in the curtain leading to the back room. He sees Hickey and stands watching him and listening.*)

HICKEY—(*suddenly bursts out*) I've got to tell you! Your being the way you are now gets my goat! It's all wrong! It puts things in my mind—about myself. It makes me think, if I got balled up about you, how do I know I wasn't balled up about myself? And that's plain damned foolishness. When you know the story of me and Evelyn, you'll see there wasn't any other possible way out of it, for her sake. Only I've got to start way back at the beginning or you won't understand. (*He starts his story, his tone again becoming musingly reminiscent.*) You see, even as a kid I was always restless. I had to keep on the go. You've heard the old saying, "Ministers' sons are sons of guns." Well, that was me, and then some. Home was like a jail. I didn't fall for the religious bunk. Listening to my old man whooping up hell fire and scaring those Hoosier suckers into shelling out their dough only handed me a laugh, although I had to hand it to him, the way he sold them nothing for something. I guess I take after him, and that's what made me a good salesman. Well, anyway, as I said, home was like jail, and so was school, and so was that damned hick town. The only place I liked was the pool rooms, where I could smoke Sweet Caporals, and mop up a couple of beers, thinking I was a hell-on-wheels sport. We had one hooker shop in town, and, of course, I liked that, too. Not that I hardly ever had entrance money. My old man was a tight old bastard. But I liked to sit around in the parlor and joke with the girls, and they liked me because I could kid 'em along and make 'em laugh.

Well, you know what a small town is. Everyone got wise to me. They all said I was a no-good tramp. I didn't give a damn what they said. I hated everybody in the place. That is, except Evelyn. I loved Evelyn. Even as a kid. And Evelyn loved me. (*He pauses. No one moves or gives any sign except by the dread in their eyes that they have heard him. Except Parritt, who takes his hands from his face to look at Larry pleadingly.*)

PARRITT—I loved Mother, Larry! No matter what she did! I still do! Even though I know she wishes now I was dead! You believe that, don't you? Christ, why can't you say something?

HICKEY—(*too absorbed in his story now to notice this—goes on in a tone of fond, sentimental reminiscence*) Yes, sir, as far back as I can remember, Evelyn and I loved each other. She always stuck up for me. She wouldn't believe the gossip—or she'd pretend she didn't. No one could convince her I was no good. Evelyn was stubborn as all hell once she'd made up her mind. Even when I'd admit things and ask her forgiveness, she'd make excuses for me and defend me against myself. She'd kiss me and say she knew I didn't mean it and I wouldn't do it again. So I'd promise I wouldn't. I'd have to promise, she was so sweet and good, though I knew darned well—(*A touch of strange bitterness comes into his voice for a moment.*) No, sir, you couldn't stop Evelyn. Nothing on earth could shake her faith in me. Even I couldn't. She was a sucker for a pipe dream. (*then quickly*) Well, naturally, her family forbid her seeing me. They were one of the town's best, rich for that hick burg, owned the trolley line and lumber company. Strict Methodists, too. They hated my guts. But they couldn't stop Evelyn. She'd sneak notes to me and meet me on the sly. I was getting more restless. The town was getting more like a jail. I made up my mind to beat it. I knew exactly what I wanted to be by that time. I'd met a lot of drummers around the hotel and liked 'em. They were always telling jokes. They were sports. They kept moving. I liked their life. And I knew I could kid people and sell things. The hitch was how to get the railroad fare to the Big Town. I told Mollie Arlington my trouble. She was the madame of the cathouse. She liked me. She laughed and said, "Hell, I'll stake you, Kid! I'll bet on you. With that grin of yours and that line of bull, you ought to be able to sell skunks for good ratters!" (*He chuckles.*) Mollie was all right. She gave me confidence in myself. I paid her back, the first money I earned. Wrote her a kidding letter, I remember, saying I was peddling baby carriages and she and the girls had better take advantage of our bargain offer. (*He chuckles.*) But that's ahead of my story. The night before I left town, I had a date with Evelyn. I got all worked up, she was so pretty and sweet and good. I told her straight, "You better forget me, Evelyn, for your own sake. I'm no good and never will be. I'm not worthy to wipe your shoes." I broke down and cried. She just said, looking white and scared, "Why, Teddy? Don't you still love me?" I said, "Love you? God, Evelyn, I love you more than anything in the world. And I always will!" She said, "Then nothing else matters, Teddy, because nothing but death could stop my loving you. So I'll wait, and when you're ready you send for me and we'll be married. I know I can make you happy, Teddy, and once you're happy you won't want to do any of the bad things you've done any more." And I said, "Of course, I won't, Evelyn!" I meant it, too. I believed it. I loved her so much she could make me believe anything. (*He sighs. There is a suspended, waiting silence. Even the two detectives are drawn into it. Then Hope breaks into dully exasperated, brutally callous protest.*)

HOPE—Get it over, you long-winded bastard! You married her, and you caught her cheating with the iceman, and you croaked her, and who the hell cares? What's she to us? All we want is to pass out in peace, bejees! (*A chorus of dull, resentful protest from all the group. They mumble, like sleepers who curse a person who keeps awakening them,* "What's it to us? We want to pass out in peace!" *Hope drinks and they mechanically follow his example. He pours another and they do the same. He complains with a stupid, nagging insistence*) No life in the booze! No kick! Dishwater. Bejees, I'll never pass out!

HICKEY—(*goes on as if there had been no interruption*) So I beat it to the Big Town. I got a job easy, and it was a cinch for me to make good. I had the knack. It was like a game, sizing people up quick, spotting what their pet pipe dreams were, and then kidding 'em along that line, pretending you believed what they wanted to believe about themselves. Then they liked you, they trusted you, they wanted to buy something to show their gratitude. It was fun. But still, all the while I felt guilty, as if I had no right to be having such a good time away from Evelyn. In each letter I'd tell her how I missed her, but I'd keep warning her, too. I'd tell her all my faults, how I liked my booze every once in a while, and so on. But there was no shaking Evelyn's belief in me, or her dreams about the future. After each letter of hers, I'd be as full of faith as she was. So as soon as I got enough saved to start us off, I sent for her and we got married. Christ, wasn't I happy for a while! And wasn't she happy! I don't care what anyone says, I'll bet there never was two people who loved each other more than me and Evelyn. Not only then but always after, in spite of everything I did—(*He pauses—then sadly*) Well, it's all there, at the start, everything that happened afterwards. I never could learn to handle temptation. I'd want to reform and mean it. I'd promise Evelyn, and I'd wall paperpromise myself, and I'd believe it. I'd tell her, it's the last time. And she'd say, "I know it's the last time, Teddy. You'll never do it again." That's what made it so hard. That's what made me feel such a rotten skunk—her always forgiving me. My playing around with women, for instance. It was only a harmless good time to me. Didn't mean anything. But I'd know what it meant to Evelyn. So I'd say to myself, never again. But you know how it is, traveling around. The damned hotel rooms. I'd get seeing things in the wallpaper. I'd get bored as hell. Lonely and homesick. But at the same time sick of home. I'd feel free and I'd want to celebrate a little. I never drank on the job, so it had to be dames. Any tart. What I'd want was some tramp I could be myself with without being ashamed—someone I could tell a dirty joke to and she'd laugh.

CORA—(*with a dull, weary bitterness*) Jees, all de lousy jokes I've had to listen to and pretend was funny!

HICKEY—(*goes on obliviously*) Sometimes I'd try some joke I thought was a corker on Evelyn. She'd always make herself laugh. But I could tell she thought it was dirty, not funny. And Evelyn always knew about the tarts I'd been with when I came home from a trip. She'd kiss me and look in my eyes, and she'd know. I'd see in her eyes how she was trying not to know, and then telling herself even if it was true, he couldn't help it, they tempt him, and he's lonely, he hasn't got me, it's only his body, anyway, he doesn't love them, I'm the only one he loves. She was right, too. I never loved anyone else. Couldn't if I wanted to. (*He pauses.*) She forgave me even when it all had to come out in the open. You know how it is when you keep taking chances. You may be lucky for a long time, but you get nicked in the end. I picked up a nail from some tart in Altoona.

CORA—(*dully, without resentment*) Yeah. And she picked it up from some guy. It's all in de game. What de hell of it?

HICKEY—I had to do a lot of lying and stalling when I got home. It didn't do any good. The quack I went to got all my dough and then told me I was cured and I took his word. But I wasn't, and poor Evelyn—But she did her best to make me believe she fell for my lie about how traveling men get things from drinking cups on trains. Anyway, she forgave me. The same way she forgave me every time I'd turn up after a periodical drunk. You all know what I'd be like at the end of one. You've seen me. Like something lying in the gutter that no alley cat would lower itself to drag in—something they threw out of the D.T. ward in Bellevue along with the garbage, something that ought to be dead and isn't! (*His face is convulsed with self-loathing.*) Evelyn wouldn't have heard from me in a month or more. She'd have been waiting there alone, with the neighbors shaking their heads and feeling sorry for her out loud. That was before she got me to move to the outskirts, where there weren't any next-door neighbors. And then the door would open and in I'd stumble—looking like what I've said—into her home, where she kept everything so spotless and clean. And I'd sworn it would never happen again, and now I'd have to start swearing again this was the last time. I could see disgust having a battle in her eyes with love. Love always won. She'd make herself kiss me, as if nothing had happened, as if I'd just come home from a business trip. She'd never complain or bawl me out. (*He bursts out in a tone of anguish that has anger and hatred beneath it*) Christ, can you imagine what a guilty skunk she made me feel! If she'd only admitted once she didn't believe any more in her pipe dream that some day I'd behave! But she never would. Evelyn was stubborn as hell. Once she'd set her heart on anything, you couldn't shake her faith that it had to come true—tomorrow! It was the same old story, over and over, for years and years. It kept piling up, inside her and inside me. God, can you picture all I made her suffer, and all the guilt she made me feel, and how I hated myself! If she only hadn't been so damned good—if she'd been the same kind of wife I was a husband. God, I used to pray sometimes she'd—I'd even say to her, "Go on, why don't you, Evelyn? It'd serve me right. I wouldn't mind. I'd forgive you." Of course, I'd pretend I was kidding—the same way I used to joke here about her being in the hay with the iceman. She'd have been so hurt if I'd said it seriously. She'd have thought I'd stopped loving her. (*He pauses—then looking around at them*) I suppose you think I'm a liar, that no woman could have stood all she stood and still loved me so much—that it isn't human for any woman to be so pitying and forgiving. Well, I'm not lying, and if you'd ever seen her, you'd realize I wasn't. It was written all over her face, sweetness and love and pity and forgiveness. (*He reaches mechanically for the inside pocket of his coat.*) Wait! I'll show you. I always carry her picture. (*Suddenly he looks startled. He stares before him, his hand falling back—quietly*) No, I'm forgetting I tore it up—afterwards. I didn't need it any more. (*He pauses. The silence is like that in the room of a dying man where people hold their breath, waiting for him to die.*)

CORA—(*with a muffled sob*) Jees, Hickey! Jees! (*She shivers and puts her hands over her face.*)

PARRITT—(*to Larry in a low insistent tone*) I burnt up Mother's picture, Larry. Her eyes followed me all the time. They seemed to be wishing I was dead!

HICKEY—It kept piling up, like I've said. I got so I thought of it all the time. I hated myself more and more, thinking of all the wrong I'd done to the sweetest woman in the world who loved me so much. I got so I'd curse myself for a lousy bastard every time I saw myself in the mirror. I felt such pity for her it drove me crazy. You wouldn't believe a guy like me, that's knocked around so much, could feel such pity. It got so every night I'd wind up hiding my face in her lap, bawling and begging her forgiveness. And, of course, she'd always comfort me and say, "Never mind, Teddy, I know you won't ever again." Christ, I loved her so, but I began to hate that pipe dream! I began to be afraid I was going bughouse, because sometimes I couldn't forgive her for forgiving me. I even caught myself hating her for making me hate myself so much. There's a limit to the guilt you can feel and the forgiveness and the pity you can take! You have to begin blaming someone else, too. I got so sometimes when she'd kiss me it was like she did it on purpose to humiliate me, as if she'd spit in my face! But all the time I saw how crazy and rotten of me that was, and it made me hate myself all the more. You'd never believe I could hate so much, a good-natured, happy-go-lucky slob like me. And as the time got nearer to when I was due to come here for my drunk around Harry's birthday, I got nearly crazy. I kept swearing to her every night that this time I really wouldn't, until I'd made it a real final test to myself—and to her. And she kept encouraging me and saying, "I can see you really mean it now, Teddy. I know you'll conquer it this time, and we'll be so happy, dear." When she'd say that and kiss me, I'd believe it, too. Then she'd go to bed, and I'd stay up alone because I couldn't sleep and I didn't want to disturb her, tossing and rolling around. I'd get so damned lonely. I'd get thinking how peaceful it was here, sitting around with the old gang, getting drunk and forgetting love, joking and laughing and singing and swapping lies. And finally I knew I'd have to come. And I knew if I came this time, it was the finish. I'd never have the guts to go back and be forgiven again, and that would break Evelyn's heart because to her it would mean I didn't love her any more. (*He pauses.*) That last night I'd driven myself crazy trying to figure some way out for her. I went in the bedroom. I was going to tell her it was the end. But I couldn't do that to her. She was sound asleep. I thought, God, if she'd only never wake up, she'd never know! And then it came to me—the only possible way out, for her sake. I remembered I'd given her a gun for protection while I was away and it was in the bureau drawer. She'd never feel any pain, never wake up from her dream. So I—

HOPE—(*tries to ward this off by pounding with his glass on the table—with brutal, callous exasperation*) Give us a rest, for the love of Christ! Who the hell cares? We want to pass out in peace! (*They all, except Parritt and Larry, pound with their glasses and grumble in chorus:* "Who the hell cares? We want to pass out in peace!" *Moran, the detective, moves quietly from the entrance in the curtain across the back of the room to the table where his companion, Lieb, is sitting. Rocky notices his leaving and gets up from the table in the rear and goes back to stand and watch in the entrance. Moran exchanges a glance with Lieb, motioning him to get up. The latter does so. No one notices them. The clamor of banging glasses dies out as abruptly as it started. Hickey hasn't appeared to hear it.*)

HICKEY—(*simply*) So I killed her. (*There is a moment of dead silence. Even the detectives are caught in it and stand motionless.*)

PARRITT—(*suddenly gives up and relaxes limply in his chair—in a low voice in which there is a strange exhausted relief*) I may as well confess, Larry. There's no use lying any more. You know, anyway. I didn't give a damn about the money. It was because I hated her.

HICKEY—(*obliviously*) And then I saw I'd always known that was the only possible way to give her peace and free her from the misery of loving me. I saw it meant peace for me, too, knowing she was at peace. I felt as though a ton of guilt was lifted off my mind. I remember I stood by the bed and suddenly I had to laugh. I couldn't help it, and I knew Evelyn would forgive me. I remember I heard myself speaking to her, as if it was something I'd always wanted to say: "Well, you know what you can do with your pipe dream now, you damned bitch!" (*He stops with a horrified start, as if shocked out of a nightmare, as if he couldn't believe he heard what he had just said. He stammers*) No! I never—!

PARRITT—(*to Larry—sneeringly*) Yes, that's it! Her and the damned old Movement pipe dream! Eh, Larry?

HICKEY—(*bursts into frantic denial*) No! That's a lie! I never said—! Good God, I couldn't have said that! If I did, I'd gone insane! Why, I loved Evelyn better than anything in life! (*He appeals brokenly to the crowd.*) Boys, you're all my old pals! You've known old Hickey for years! You know I'd never—(*His eyes fix on Hope.*) You've known me longer than anyone, Harry. You know I must have been insane, don't you, Governor?

HOPE—(*at first with the same defensive callousness—without looking at him*) Who the hell cares? (*Then suddenly he looks at Hickey and there is an extraordinary change in his expression. His face lights up, as if he were grasping at some dawning hope in his mind. He speaks with a groping eagerness.*) Insane? You mean—you went really insane? (*At the tone of his voice, all the group at the tables by him start and stare at him as if they caught his thought. Then they all look at Hickey eagerly, too.*)

HICKEY—Yes! Or I couldn't have laughed! I couldn't have said that to her! (*Moran walks up behind him on one side, while the second detective, Lieb, closes in on him from the other.*)

MORAN—(*taps Hickey on the shoulder*) That's enough, Hickman. You know who we are. You're under arrest. (*He nods to Lieb, who slips a pair of handcuffs on Hickey's wrists. Hickey stares at them with stupid incomprehension. Moran takes his arm.*) Come along and spill your guts where we can get it on paper.

HICKEY—No, wait, Officer! You owe me a break! I phoned and made it easy for you, didn't I? Just a few minutes! (*to Hope—pleadingly*) You know I couldn't say that to Evelyn, don't you, Harry—unless—

HOPE—(*eagerly*) And you've been crazy ever since? Everything you've said and done here—

HICKEY—(*for a moment forgets his own obsession and his face takes on its familiar expression of affectionate amusement and he chuckles.*) Now, Governor! Up to your old tricks, eh? I see what you're driving at, but I can't let you get away with—(*Then, as Hope's expression turns to resentful callousness again and he looks away, he adds hastily with pleading desperation*) Yes, Harry, of course, I've been out of my mind ever since! All the time I've been here! You saw I was insane, didn't you?

MORAN—(*with cynical disgust*) Can it! I've had enough of your act. Save it for the jury. (*addressing the crowd, sharply*) Listen, you guys. Don't fall for his lies. He's starting to get foxy now and thinks he'll plead insanity. But he can't get away with it. (*The crowd at the grouped tables are grasping at hope now. They glare at him resentfully.*)

HOPE—(*begins to bristle in his old-time manner*) Bejees, you dumb dick, you've got a crust trying to tell us about Hickey! We've known him for years, and every one of us noticed he was nutty the minute he showed up here! Bejees, if you'd heard all the crazy bull he was pulling about bringing us peace—like a bughouse preacher escaped from an asylum! If you'd seen all the damned-fool things he made us do! We only did them because—(*He hesitates—then defiantly*) Because we hoped he'd come out of it if we kidded him along and humored him. (*He looks around at the others.*) Ain't that right, fellers? (*They burst into a chorus of eager assent:* "Yes, Harry!" "That's it, Harry!" "That's why!" "We knew he was crazy!" "Just to humor him!")

MORAN—A fine bunch of rats! Covering up for a dirty, cold-blooded murderer.

HOPE—(*stung into recovering all his old fuming truculence*) Is that so? Bejees, you know the old story, when Saint Patrick drove the snakes out of Ireland they swam to New York and joined the police force! Ha! (*He cackles insultingly.*) Bejees, we can believe it now when we look at you, can't we, fellers? (*They all growl assent, glowering defiantly at Moran. Moran glares at them, looking as if he'd like to forget his prisoner and start cleaning out the place. Hope goes on pugnaciously.*) You stand up for your rights, bejees, Hickey! Don't let this smart-aleck dick get funny with you. If he pulls any rubber-hose tricks, you let me know! I've still got friends at the Hall! Bejees, I'll have him back in uniform pounding a beat where the only graft he'll get will be stealing tin cans from the goats!

MORAN—(*furiously*) Listen, you cockeyed old bum, for a plugged nickel I'd—(*controlling himself, turns to Hickey, who is oblivious to all this, and yanks his arm*) Come on, you!

HICKEY—(*with a strange mad earnestness*) Oh, I want to go, Officer. I can hardly wait now. I should have phoned you from the house right afterwards. It was a waste of time coming here. I've got to explain to Evelyn. But I know she's forgiven me. She knows I was insane. You've got me all wrong, Officer. I want to go to the Chair.

MORAN—Crap!

HICKEY—(*exasperatedly*) God, you're a dumb dick! Do you suppose I give a damn about life now? Why, you bone-head, I haven't got a single damned lying hope or pipe dream left!

MORAN—(*jerks him around to face the door to the hall*) Get a move on!

HICKEY—(*as they start walking toward rear—insistently*) All I want you to see is I was out of my mind afterwards, when I laughed at her! I was a raving rotten lunatic or I couldn't have said—Why, Evelyn was the only thing on God's earth I ever loved! I'd have killed myself before I'd ever have hurt her! (*They disappear in the hall. Hickey's voice keeps on protesting.*)

HOPE—(*calls after him*) Don't worry, Hickey! They can't give you the Chair! We'll testify you was crazy! Won't we, fellers? (*They all assent. Two or three echo Hope's* "Don't worry, Hickey." *Then from the hall comes the slam of the street door. Hope's face falls—with genuine sorrow*) He's gone. Poor crazy son of a bitch! (*All the group around him are sad and sympathetic, too. Hope reaches for his drink.*) Bejees, I need a drink. (*They grab their glasses. Hope says hopefully*) Bejees, maybe it'll have the old kick, now he's gone. (*He drinks and they follow suit.*)

ROCKY—*(comes forward from where he has stood in the bar entrance—hopefully)* Yeah, Boss, maybe we can get drunk now. *(He sits in the chair by Chuck and pours a drink and tosses it down. Then they all sit still, waiting for the effect, as if this drink were a crucial test, so absorbed in hopeful expectancy that they remain oblivious to what happens at Larry's table.)*

LARRY—*(his eyes full of pain and pity—in a whisper, aloud to himself)* May the Chair bring him peace at last, the poor tortured bastard!

PARRITT—*(leans toward him—in a strange low insistent voice)* Yes, but he isn't the only one who needs peace, Larry. I can't feel sorry for him. He's lucky. He's through, now. It's all decided for him. I wish it was decided for me. I've never been any good at deciding things. Even about selling out, it was the tart the detective agency got after me who put it in my mind. You remember what Mother's like, Larry. She makes all the decisions. She's always decided what I must do. She doesn't like anyone to be free but herself. *(He pauses, as if waiting for comment, but Larry ignores him.)* I suppose you think I ought to have made those dicks take me away with Hickey. But how could I prove it, Larry? They'd think I was nutty. Because she's still alive. You're the only one who can understand how guilty I am. Because you know her and what I've done to her. You know I'm really much guiltier than he is. You know what I did is a much worse murder. Because she is dead and yet she has to live. For a while. But she can't live long in jail. She loves freedom too much. And I can't kid myself like Hickey, that she's at peace. As long as she lives, she'll never be able to forget what I've done to her even in her sleep. She'll never have a second's peace. *(He pauses—then bursts out)* Jesus, Larry, can't you say something? *(Larry is at the breaking point. Parritt goes on.)* And I'm not putting up any bluff, either, that I was crazy afterwards when I laughed to myself and thought, "You know what you can do with your freedom pipe dream now, don't you, you damned old bitch!"

LARRY—*(snaps and turns on him, his face convulsed with detestation. His quivering voice has a condemning command in it.)* Go! Get the hell out of life, God damn you, before I choke it out of you! Go up—!

PARRITT—*(His manner is at once transformed. He seems suddenly at peace with himself. He speaks simply and gratefully.)* Thanks, Larry. I just wanted to be sure. I can see now it's the only possible way I can ever get free from her. I guess I've really known that all my life. *(He pauses—then with a derisive smile)* It ought to comfort Mother a little, too. It'll give her the chance to play the great incorruptible Mother of the Revolution, whose only child is the Proletariat. She'll be able to say: "Justice is done! So may all traitors die!" She'll be able to say: "I am glad he's dead! Long live the Revolution!" *(He adds with a final implacable jeer)* You know her, Larry! Always a ham!

LARRY—*(pleads distractedly)* Go, for the love of Christ, you mad tortured bastard, for your own sake! *(Hugo is roused by this. He lifts his head and peers uncomprehendingly at Larry. Neither Larry nor Parritt notices him.)*

PARRITT—*(stares at Larry. His face begins to crumble as if he were going to break down and sob. He turns his head away, but reaches out fumblingly and pats Larry's arm and stammers)* Jesus, Larry, thanks. That's kind. I knew you were the only one who could understand my side of it. *(He gets to his feet and turns toward the door.)*

HUGO—*(looks at Parritt and bursts into his silly giggle)* Hello, leedle Don, leedle monkey-face! Don't be a fool! Buy me a trink!

PARRITT—*(puts on an act of dramatic bravado—forcing a grin)* Sure, I will, Hugo! Tomorrow! Beneath the willow trees! *(He walks to the door with a careless swagger and disappears in the hall. From now on, Larry waits, listening for the sound he knows is coming from the backyard outside the window, but trying not to listen, in an agony of horror and cracking nerve.)*

HUGO—*(stares after Parritt stupidly)* Stupid fool! Hickey make you crazy, too. *(He turns to the oblivious Larry—with a timid eagerness)* I'm glad, Larry, they take that crazy Hickey avay to asylum. He makes me have bad dreams. He makes me tell lies about myself. He makes me want to spit on all I have ever dreamed. Yes, I am glad they take him to asylum. I don't feel I am dying now. He vas selling death to me, that crazy salesman. I think I have a trink now, Larry. *(He pours a drink and gulps it down.)*

HOPE—*(jubilantly)* Bejees, fellers, I'm feeling the old kick, or I'm a liar! It's putting life back in me! Bejees, if all I've lapped up begins to hit me, I'll be paralyzed before I know it! It was Hickey kept it from—Bejees, I know that sounds crazy, but he was crazy, and he'd got all of us as bughouse as he was. Bejees, it does queer things to you, having to listen day and night to a lunatic's pipe dreams—pretending you believe them, to kid him along and doing any crazy thing he wants to humor him. It's dangerous, too. Look at me pretending to start for a walk just to keep him quiet. I knew damned well it wasn't the right day for it. The sun was broiling and the streets full of automobiles. Bejees, I could feel myself getting sunstroke, and an automobile damn near ran over me. *(He appeals to Rocky, afraid of the result, but daring it.)* Ask Rocky. He was watching. Didn't it, Rocky?

ROCKY—(*a bit tipsily*) What's dat, Boss? Jees, all de booze I've mopped up is beginning to get to me. (*earnestly*) De automobile, Boss? Sure, I seen it! Just missed yuh! I thought yuh was a goner. (*He pauses—then looks around at the others, and assumes the old kidding tone of the inmates, but hesitantly, as if still a little afraid.*) On de woid of a honest bartender! (*He tries a wink at the others. They all respond with smiles that are still a little forced and uneasy.*)

HOPE—(*flashes him a suspicious glance. Then he understands—with his natural testy manner*) You're a bartender, all right. No one can say different. (*Rocky looks grateful.*) But, bejees, don't pull that honest junk! You and Chuck ought to have cards in the Burglars' Union! (*This time there is an eager laugh from the group. Hope is delighted.*) Bejees, it's good to hear someone laugh again! All the time that bas—poor old Hickey was here, I didn't have the heart—Bejees, I'm getting drunk and glad of it! (*He cackles and reaches for the bottle.*) Come on, fellers. It's on the house. (*They pour drinks. They begin rapidly to get drunk now. Hope becomes sentimental.*) Poor old Hickey! We mustn't hold him responsible for anything he's done. We'll forget that and only remember him the way we've always known him before—the kindest, biggest-hearted guy ever wore shoe leather. (*They all chorus hearty sentimental assent:* "That's right, Harry!" "That's all!" "Finest fellow!" "Best scout!" *etc. Hope goes on.*) Good luck to him in Matteawan! Come on, bottoms up! (*They all drink. At the table by the window Larry's hands grip the edge of the table. Unconsciously his head is inclined toward the window as he listens.*)

LARRY—(*cannot hold back an anguished exclamation*) Christ! Why don't he—!

HUGO—(*beginning to be drunk again—peers at him*) Vhy don't he what? Don't be a fool! Hickey's gone. He vas crazy. Have a trink. (*then as he receives no reply—with vague uneasiness*) What's matter vith you, Larry? You look funny. What you listen to out in backyard, Larry? (*Cora begins to talk in the group at right.*)

CORA—(*tipsily*) Well, I thank Gawd now me and Chuck did all we could to humor de poor nut. Jees, imagine us goin' off like we really meant to git married, when we ain't even picked out a farm yet!

CHUCK—(*eagerly*) Sure ting, Baby. We kidded him we was serious.

JIMMY—(*confidently—with a gentle, drunken unction*) I may as well say I detected his condition almost at once. All that talk of his about tomorrow, for example. He had the fixed idea of the insane. It only makes them worse to cross them.

WILLIE—(*eagerly*) Same with me, Jimmy. Only I spent the day in the park. I wasn't such a damned fool as to—

LEWIS—(*getting jauntily drunk*) Picture my predicament if I *had* gone to the Consulate. The pal of mine there is a humorous blighter. He would have got me a job out of pure spite. So I strolled about and finally came to roost in the park. (*He grins with affectionate kidding at Wetjoen.*) And lo and behold, who was on the neighboring bench but my old battlefield companion, the Boer that walks like a man—who, if the British Government had taken my advice, would have been removed from his fetid kraal on the veldt straight to the baboon's cage at the London Zoo, and little children would now be asking their nurses: "Tell me, Nana, is that the Boer General, the one with the blue behind?" (*They all laugh uproariously. Lewis leans over and slaps Wetjoen affectionately on the knee.*) No offense meant, Piet, old chap.

WETJOEN—(*beaming at him*) No offense taken, you tamned Limey! (*Wetjoen goes on—grinningly*) About a job, I felt the same as you, Cecil. (*At the table by the window Hugo speaks to Larry again.*)

HUGO—(*with uneasy insistence*) What's matter, Larry? You look scared. What you listen for out there? (*But Larry doesn't hear, and Joe begins talking in the group at right.*)

JOE—(*with drunken self-assurance*) No, suh, I wasn't fool enough to git in no crap game. Not while Hickey's around. Crazy people puts a jinx on you. (*McGloin is now heard. He is leaning across in front of Wetjoen to talk to Ed Mosher on Hope's left.*)

McGLOIN—(*with drunken earnestness*) I know you saw how it was, Ed. There was no good trying to explain to a crazy guy, but it ain't the right time. You know how getting reinstated is.

MOSHER—(*decidedly*) Sure, Mac. The same way with the circus. The boys tell me the rubes are wasting all their money buying food and times never was so hard. And I never was one to cheat for chicken feed.

HOPE—(*looks around him in an ecstasy of bleery sentimental content*) Bejees, I'm cockeyed! Bejees, you're all cockeyed! Bejees, we're all all right! Let's have another! (*They pour out drinks. At the table by the window Larry has unconsciously shut his eyes as he listens. Hugo is peering at him frightenedly now.*)

HUGO—(*reiterates stupidly*) What's matter, Larry? Why you keep eyes shut? You look dead. What you listen for in backyard? (*Then, as Larry doesn't open his eyes or answer, he gets up hastily and moves away from the table, mumbling with frightened anger*) Crazy fool! You vas crazy like Hickey! You give me bad dreams, too. (*He shrinks quickly past the table where Hickey had sat to the rear of the group at right.*)

ROCKY—(*greets him with boisterous affection*) Hello, dere, Hugo! Welcome to de party!

HOPE—Yes, bejees, Hugo! Sit down! Have a drink! Have ten drinks, bejees!

HUGO—*(forgetting Larry and bad dreams, gives his familiar giggle)* Hello, leedle Harry! Hello, nice, leedle, funny monkey-faces! *(warming up, changes abruptly to his usual declamatory denunciation)* Gottamned stupid bourgeois! Soon comes the Day of Judgment! *(They make derisive noises and tell him to sit down. He changes again, giggling good-naturedly, and sits at rear of the middle table.)* Give me ten trinks, Harry. Don't be a fool. *(They laugh. Rocky shoves a glass and bottle at him. The sound of Margie's and Pearl's voices is heard from the hall, drunkenly shrill. All of the group turn toward the door as the two appear. They are drunk and look blowsy and disheveled. Their manner as they enter hardens into a brazen defensive truculence.)*

MARGIE—*(stridently)* Gangway for two good whores!

PEARL—Yeah! And we want a drink quick!

MARGIE—*(glaring at Rocky)* Shake de lead outa your pants, Pimp! A little soivice!

ROCKY—*(his black bullet eyes sentimental, his round Wop face grinning welcome)* Well, look who's here! *(He goes to them unsteadily, opening his arms.)* Hello, dere, Sweethearts! Jees, I was beginnin' to worry about yuh, honest! *(He tries to embrace them. They push his arms away, regarding him with amazed suspicion.)*

PEARL—What kind of a gag is dis?

HOPE—*(calls to them effusively)* Come on and join the party, you broads! Bejees, I'm glad to see you! *(The girls exchange a bewildered glance, taking in the party and the changed atmosphere.)*

MARGIE—Jees, what's come off here?

PEARL—Where's dat louse, Hickey?

ROCKY—De cops got him. He'd gone crazy and croaked his wife. *(The girls exclaim, "Jees!" But there is more relief than horror in it. Rocky goes on.)* He'll get Matteawan. He ain't responsible. What he's pulled don't mean nuttin'. So forget dat whore stuff. I'll knock de block off anyone calls you whores! I'll fill de bastard full of lead! Yuh're tarts, and what de hell of it? Yuh're as good as anyone! So forget it, see? *(They let him get his arms around them now. He gives them a hug. All the truculence leaves their faces. They smile and exchange maternally amused glances.)*

MARGIE—*(with a wink)* Our little bartender, ain't he, Poil?

PEARL—Yeah, and a cute little Ginny at dat! *(They laugh.)*

MARGIE—And is he stinko!

PEARL—Stinko is right. But he ain't got nuttin' on us. Jees, Rocky, did we have a big time at Coney!

HOPE—Bejees, sit down, you dumb broads! Welcome home! Have a drink! Have ten drinks, bejees! *(They take the empty chairs on Chuck's left, warmly welcomed by all. Rocky stands in back of them, a hand on each of their shoulders, grinning with proud proprietorship. Hope beams over and under his crooked spectacles with the air of a host whose party is a huge success, and rambles on happily.)* Bejees, this is all right! We'll make this my birthday party, and forget the other. We'll get paralyzed! But who's missing? Where's the Old Wise Guy? Where's Larry?

ROCKY—Over by de window, Boss. Jees, he's got his eyes shut. De old bastard's asleep. *(They turn to look. Rocky dismisses him.)* Aw, to hell wid him. Let's have a drink. *(They turn away and forget him.)*

LARRY—*(torturedly arguing to himself in a shaken whisper)* It's the only way out for him! For the peace of all concerned, as Hickey said! *(snapping)* God damn his yellow soul, if he doesn't soon, I'll go up and throw him off!—like a dog with its guts ripped out you'd put out of misery! *(He half rises from his chair just as from outside the window comes the sound of something hurtling down, followed by a muffled, crunching thud. Larry gasps and drops back on his chair, shuddering, hiding his face in his hands. The group at right hear it but are too preoccupied with drinks to pay much attention.)*

HOPE—*(wonderingly)* What the hell was that?

ROCKY—Aw, nuttin'. Someting fell off de fire escape. A mattress, I'll bet. Some of dese bums been sleepin' on de fire escapes.

HOPE—*(his interest diverted by this excuse to beef—testily)* They've got to cut it out! Bejees, this ain't a fresh-air cure. Mattresses cost money.

MOSHER—Now don't start crabbing at the party, Harry. Let's drink up. *(Hope forgets it and grabs his glass, and they all drink.)*

LARRY—*(in a whisper of horrified pity)* Poor devil! *(A long-forgotten faith returns to him for a moment and he mumbles)* God rest his soul in peace. *(He opens his eyes—with a bitter self-derision)* Ah, the damned pity—the wrong kind, as Hickey said! Be God, there's no hope! I'll never be a success in the grandstand—or anywhere else! Life is too much for me! I'll be a weak fool looking with pity at the two sides of everything till the day I die! *(with an intense bitter sincerity)* May that day come soon! *(He pauses startledly, surprised at himself—then with a sardonic grin)* Be God, I'm the only real convert to death Hickey made here. From the bottom of my coward's heart I mean that now!

HOPE—*(calls effusively)* Hey there, Larry! Come over and get paralyzed! What the hell you doing, sitting there? *(Then as Larry doesn't reply he immediately forgets him and turns to the party. They are all very drunk now, just a few drinks ahead of the passing-out stage, and hilariously happy about it.)* Bejees, let's sing! Let's celebrate! It's my birthday party! Bejees, I'm oreyeyed! I want to sing!

(He starts the chorus of "She's the Sunshine of Paradise Alley," and instantly they all burst into song. But not the same song. Each starts the chorus of his or her choice. Jimmy Tomorrow's is "A Wee Dock and Doris"; Ed Mosher's, "Break the News to Mother"; Willie Oban's, the Sailor Lad ditty he sang in Act One; General Wetjoen's, "Waiting at the Church"; McGloin's, "Tammany"; Captain Lewis's, "The Old Kent Road"; Joe's, "All I Got Was Sympathy"; Pearl's and Margie's, "Everybody's Doing It"; Rocky's, "You Great Big Beautiful Doll"; Chuck's, "The Curse of an Aching Heart"; Cora's, "The Oceana Roll"; while Hugo jumps to his feet and, pounding on the table with his fist, bellows in his guttural basso the French Revolutionary "Carmagnole." A weird cacophony results from this mixture and they stop singing to roar with laughter. All but Hugo, who keeps on with drunken fervor.)

HUGO—

Dansons la Carmagnole!
Vive le son! Vive le son!
Dansons la Carmagnole!
Vive le son des canons!

(They all turn on him and howl him down with amused derision. He stops singing to denounce them in his most fiery style.) Capitalist svine! Stupid bourgeois monkeys! *(He declaims)* "The days grow hot, O Babylon!" *(They all take it up and shout in enthusiastic jeering chorus)* "'Tis cool beneath thy willow trees!" *(They pound their glasses on the table, roaring with laughter, and Hugo giggles with them. In his chair by the window, Larry stares in front of him, oblivious to their racket.)*

(Curtain)

23. *Death of a Salesman*—Arthur Miller

Commentaries

Sources

Play

23.1 ON SOCIAL PLAYS—ARTHUR MILLER

A GREEK LIVING IN THE CLASSICAL PERIOD would be bewildered by the dichotomy implied in the very term "social play." Especially for the Greek, a drama created for public performance had to be "social." A play to him was by definition a dramatic consideration of the way men ought to live. But in this day of extreme individualism even that phrase must be further defined. When we say "how men ought to live," we are likely to be thinking of psychological therapy, of ridding ourselves individually of neurotic compulsions and destructive inner tendencies, of "learning how to love" and thereby gaining "happiness."

It need hardly be said that the Greek dramatist had more than a passing interest in psychology and character on the stage. But for him these were means to a larger end, and the end was what we isolate today as social. That is, the relations of man as a social animal, rather than his definition as a separated entity, was the dramatic goal. Why this should have come to be is a large historical question which others are more competent to explain, as several already have. For our purposes it will be sufficient to indicate one element in the life of classical Greece that differs so radically from anything existing in the modern world as to throw a bright light on certain of our attitudes which we take for granted and toward which we therefore are without a proper perspective.

The Greek citizen of that time thought of himself as belonging not to a "nation" or a "state" but to a *polis*. The polis were small units, apparently deriving from an earlier tribal social organization, whose members probably knew one another personally because they were relatively few in number and occupied a small territory. In war or peace the whole people made the vital decisions, there being no profession of politics as we know it; any man could be elected magistrate, judge, even a general in the armed forces. It was an amateur world compared to our stratified and specialized one, a world in which everyone knew enough about almost any profession to practice it, because most things were simple to know. The thing of importance for us is that these people were *engaged*, they could not imagine the good life excepting as it brought each person into close contact with civic matters. They were avid argufiers. Achilles was blessed by the gods with the power to fight well and make good speeches. The people had a special sense of pride in the polis and thought that it in itself distinguished them from the barbarians outside who lived under tyrannies.

The preoccupation of the Greek drama with ultimate law, with the Grand Design, so to speak, was therefore an expression of a basic assumption of the people, who could not yet conceive, luckily, that any man could long prosper unless his polis prospered. The individual was at one with his society; his conflicts with it were, in our terms, like family conflicts the opposing sides of which nevertheless shared a mutuality of feeling and responsibility. Thus the drama written for them, while for us it appears wholly religious, was religious for them in a more than mystical way. Religion is the only way we have any more of expressing our genuinely social feelings and concerns, for in our bones we as a people do not otherwise believe in our oneness with a larger group. But the religiousness of the Greek drama of the classical time was more worldly; it expressed a social concern, to be sure, but it did so on the part of a people already unified on earth rather than the drive of a single individual toward personal salvation. The great gap we feel between religious or "high" emotion and the emotions of daily life was not present in their mass affairs. The religious expression was not many degrees higher for them than many other social expressions, of which their drama is the most complete example.

It is necessary to add that as the polis withered under the impact of war and historical change, as commerce grew and a differentiation of interest separated man from man, the Greek drama found it more and more difficult to stand as a kind of universal mass statement or prayer. It turned its eye inward, created more elaborated characterizations, and slowly gave up some of its former loftiness. Men, as H. D. F. Kitto has said in *The Greeks*, replaced Man in the plays. Nevertheless, to the end the Greek drama clearly conceived its right function as something far wider than a purely private examination of individuality for the sake of the examination or for art's sake. In every dramatic hero there is the idea of the Greek people, their fate, their will, and their destiny.

In today's America the term "social play" brings up images which are historically conditioned, very recent, and, I believe, only incidentally pertinent to a fruitful conception of the drama. The term indicates to us an attack, an arraignment of society's evils such as Ibsen allegedly invented and was later taken up by left-wing playwrights whose primary interest was the exposure of capitalism for the implied benefit of socialism or communism. The concept is tired and narrow, but its worst effect has been to confuse a whole generation of playwrights, audiences, and theater workers.

If one can look at the idea of "social drama" from the Greek viewpoint for one moment, it will be clear that there can be only either a genuinely social drama or, if it abdicates altogether, its true opposite, the antisocial and ultimately antidramatic drama.

To put it simply, even oversimply, a drama rises in stature and intensity in proportion to the weight of its application to all manner of men. It gains its weight as it deals with more and more of the whole man, not either his subjective or his social life alone, and the Greek was unable to conceive of man or anything else except as a whole. The modern playwright, at least in America, on the one hand is importuned by his most demanding audience to write importantly, while on the other he is asked not to bring onto the stage images of social function, lest he seem like a special pleader and therefore inartistic. I am not attempting a defense of the social dramas of the thirties, most of which were in fact special pleadings and further from a consideration of the whole man than much of the antisocial drama is. I am trying only to project a right conception of what social drama was and what it ought to be. It is, I think, the widest concept of drama available to us thus far.

When, however, a contemporary dramatist is drawn for but a moment toward a concept of form even remotely Greek, certain lacks become evident—a certain abyss even begins to appear around him. When you are writing in the name of a people unified in a self-conscious and rather small band, when you yourself as a writer are not an individual entrepreneur offering wares to a hostile marketplace but a member of a group who is in other ways no different from the rest—when, in short, the dramatic form itself is regarded as inevitably a social expression of the deepest concerns of all your fellow men—your work is bound to be liberated, freed of even the hypothesis of partisanship, if only because partisanship cannot thrive where the idea of wholeness is accepted. Thus in such a situation what we call social matters become inseparable from subjective psychological matters, and the drama is once again whole and capable of the highest reach.

If one considers our own drama of the past forty years in comparison with that of classical Greece, one elemental difference—the difference which seems to me to be our crippling hobble—will emerge. The single theme to which our most ambitious plays can be reduced is frustration. In all of them, from O'Neill's through the best of Anderson, Sidney Howard, and the rest, the underlying log jam, so to speak, the unresolvable paradox, is that, try as he will, the individual is doomed to frustration when once he gains a consciousness of his own identity. The image is that of the individual scratching away at a wall beyond which stands society, his fellow men. Sometimes he pounds at the wall, sometimes he tries to scale it or even blow it up, but at the end the wall is always there, and the man himself is dead or doomed to defeat in his attempt to live a human life.

The tragic victory is always denied us because, I believe, the plays cannot project with any conviction what the society, in the playwrights' views at any rate, has failed to prove. In Greece the tragic victory consisted in demonstrating that the polis—the whole people—had discovered some aspect of the Grand Design which also was the right way to live *together.* If the American playwrights of serious intent are in any way the subconscience of the country, our claims to have found that way are less than proved. For when the Greek thought of the right way to live it was a whole concept; it meant a way to live that would create citizens who were brave in war, had a sense of responsibility to the polis in peace, and were also developed as individual personalities.

It has often seemed to me that the Soviet Russians have studied classical Greece and have tried to bridge with phraseology profound differences between their social organization and that of Greece, while demanding of their writers what in effect is a Greek social drama. The word "cosmopolitan," as Kitto points out, was invented in Greece when the small polis were disintegrating, and when the drama itself was beginning to turn inward, away from the largest questions of social fate to the fate of individuals alone. It was invented to describe a new kind of man, a man whose allegiance was not primarily to his society, his polis, but to others of like mind anywhere in the world. With it goes an intimation—or more—of skepticism, of self-removal, that presages the radical separation of man from society which the American drama expresses ultimately through themes of frustration. To supplant the polis and allegiance to it, the Soviets have a thousand kinds of social organizations, and, for all one knows, the individual Russian might well feel a sense of connection with civic affairs which the West does not afford its citizens. The crucial difference, however, is that only the most theoretical Russian can trace the effects, if any, of his personality upon the policies of his country, while the Greek could literally see what he had done when he made his speech and swayed or failed to sway his fellow men.

Thus the Russian drama after the Revolution, much as ours, is a drama of frustration, the inability of industrialized men to see themselves spiritually completed through the social organization. But in the Soviet case the frustration is not admitted; it is talked away in large phrases having to do with a victory of the people through tragic sacrifice. The fact remains, however, that nowhere in the world where industrialized economy rules—where specialization in work, politics, and social life is the norm—no where has man discovered a means of connecting himself to society except in the form of a truce with it. The best we have been able to do is to speak of a "duty" to society, and this implies sacrifice or self-deprivation. To think of an individual fulfilling his subjective needs through social action, to think of him as living most completely when he lives most socially, to think of him as doing this, not as a social worker acting out of conscientious motives, but naturally, without guilt or sense of oddness—this is difficult for us to imagine, and when we can, we know at the same time that only a few, perhaps a blessed few, are so constructed as to manage it.

As with Greece, so with us—each great war has turned men further and further away from preoccupation with Man and drawn them back into the family, the home, the private life and the preoccupation with sexuality. It has happened, however, that at the same time our theater has exhausted the one form that was made to express the private life—prose realism. We are bored with it; we demand something more, something "higher," on the stage, while at the same time we refuse, or do not know how, to live our private lives excepting as ego-centers. I believe it is this paradox that underlies the kind of struggle taking place in the drama today—a struggle at one and the same time to write of private persons privately and yet lift up their means of expression to a poetic—that is, a social—level. You cannot speak in verse of picayune matters—at least not on the stage—without sounding overblown and ridiculous, and so it should be. Verse reaches always toward the general statement, the wide image, the universal moment, and it must be based upon wide concepts—it must speak not merely of men but of Man. The language of dramatic verse is the language of a people profoundly at one with itself; it is the most public of public speech. The language of prose is the language of the private life, the kind of private life men retreat to when they are at odds with the world they have made or been heirs to.

The social drama, then—at least as I have always conceived it—is the drama of the whole man. It seeks to deal with his differences from others not *per se*, but toward the end that, if only through drama, we may know how much the same we are, for if we lose that knowledge we shall have nothing left at all. The social drama to me is only incidentally an arraignment of society. *A Streetcar Named Desire* is a social drama; so is *The Hairy Ape*, and so are practically all O'Neill's other plays. For they ultimately make moot, either weakly or with full power, the ancient question, how are we to live? And that question is in its Greek sense, its best and most humane sense, not merely a private query.

The social drama, as I see it, is the main stream and the antisocial drama a bypass. I can no longer take with ultimate seriousness a drama of individual psychology written for its own sake, however full it may be of insight and precise observation. Time is moving; there is a world to make, a civilization to create that will move toward the only goal the humanistic, democratic mind can ever accept with honor. It is a world in which the human being can live as a naturally political, naturally private, naturally engaged person, a world in which once again a true tragic victory may be scored.

But that victory is not really possible unless the individual is more than theoretically capable of being recognized by the powers that lead society. Specifically, when men live, as they do under any industrialized system, as integers who have no weight, no *person*, excepting as either customers, draftees, machine tenders, ideologists, or whatever, it is unlikely (and in my opinion impossible) that a dramatic picture of them can really overcome the public knowledge of their nature in real life. In such a society, be it communistic or capitalistic, man is not tragic, he is pathetic. The tragic figure must have certain innate powers which he uses to pass over the boundaries of the known social law—the accepted mores of his people—in order to test and discover necessity. Such a quest implies that the individual who has moved onto that course must be somehow recognized by the law, by the mores, by the powers that design—be they anthropomorphic gods or economic and political laws—as having the worth, the innate value, of a whole people asking a basic question and demanding its answer. We are so atomized socially that no character in a play can conceivably stand as our vanguard, as our heroic questioner. Our society—and I am speaking of every industrialized society in the world—is so complex, each person being so specialized an integer, that the moment any individual is dramatically characterized and set forth as a hero, our common sense reduces him to the size of a complainer, a misfit. For deep down we no longer believe in the rules of the tragic contest; we no longer believe that some ultimate sense can in fact be made of social causation, or in the possibility that any individual can, by a heroic effort, make sense of it. Thus the man that is driven to question the moral chaos in which we live ends up in our estimate as a possibly commendable but definitely odd fellow, and probably as a compulsively driven neurotic. In place of a social aim which called an all-around excellence—physical, intellectual, and moral—the ultimate good, we have set up a goal which can best be characterized as "happiness"—namely, staying out of trouble. This concept is the end result of the truce which all of us have made with society. And a truce implies two enemies. When the truce is broken it means either that the individual has broken out of his ordained place as an integer, or that the society has broken the law by harming him unjustly—that is, it has not left him alone to be a peaceful integer. In the heroic and tragic time the act of questioning the-way-things-are implied that a quest was being carried on to discover an ultimate law or way of life which would yield excellence; in the present time the quest is that of a man made unhappy by rootlessness and, in every important modern play, by a man who is essentially a victim. We have abstracted from the Greek drama its air of doom, its physical destruction of the hero, but its victory escapes us. Thus it has even become difficult to separate in our minds the ideas of the pathetic and of the tragic. And behind this melting of the two lies the overwhelming power of the modern industrial state, the ignorance of each person in it of anything but his own technique as an economic integer, and the elevation of that state to a holy, quite religious sphere.

What, after all, are our basic social aims as applied to the individual? Americans are often accused of worshiping financial success, but this is, first of all, not an American monopoly, and, second, it does not as a concept make clear what is causing so much uneasiness and moral pain. My own belief, at any rate, is that America has merely arrived first at the condition that awaits every country that takes her economic road without enforcing upon every development of industrial technique certain quite arbitrary standards of value.

The deep moral uneasiness among us, the vast sense of being only tenuously joined to the rest of our fellows, is caused, in my view, by the fact that the person has value as he fits into the pattern of efficiency, and for that alone. The reason *Death of a Salesman*, for instance, left such a strong impression was that it set forth unremittingly the picture of a man who was not even especially "good" but whose situation made clear that at bottom we are alone, valueless, without even the elements of a human person, when once we fail to fit the patterns of efficiency. Under the black shadow of that gigantic necessity, even the drift of some psychoanalytic practice is toward the fitting-in, the training of the individual whose soul has revolted, so that he may once again "take his place" in society—that is, do his "work," "function," in other words, accommodate himself to a scheme of things that is not at all ancient but very new in the world. In short, the absolute value of the individual human being is believed in only as a secondary value; it stands well below the needs of efficient production. We have finally come to serve the machine. The machine must not be stopped, marred, left dirty, or outmoded. Only men can be left marred, stopped, dirty, and alone. Our pity for the victim is mixed, I think. It is mixed with an air of self-preserving superiority—we, thank God, know how to fit in, therefore this victim, however pitiful, has himself to thank for his fate. We believe, in other words, that to fit into the patterns of efficiency is the ultimate good, and at the same time we know in our bones that a crueler concept is not easy to arrive at.

Nor may the exponents of socialism take heart from this. There is no such thing as a capitalist assembly line or drygoods counter. The disciplines required by machines are the same everywhere and will not be truly mitigated by old-age pensions and social-security payments. So long as modern man conceives of himself as valuable only because he fits into some niche in the machine-tending pattern, he will never know anything more than a pathetic doom.

The implications of this fact spread throughout our culture, indeed, throughout the culture of the industrialized parts of the world. Be it in music, literature, drama, or whatever, the value of a work is, willy nilly, equated with its mass "acceptance," i.e., its efficiency. All the engines of economic law are, like the mills of the gods, working toward that same end. The novel of excellence that could once be published without financial loss if it sold two or three thousand copies can no longer be published, because the costs of production require that every book sell at least ten, twelve, or fifteen thousand copies. The play that might have been produced at a decent profit if it could fill half a house for a few months can no longer be produced, for the costs of production require a play to draw packed houses from the first night.

When one has the temerity to suggest that the Greek theater was subsidized, that so much of the world's great music, art, and literature was stubbornly patronized by people who found honor in helping to bring beauty onto the earth, one is not quite suspect, to be sure, but the suggestion nevertheless has an unreal air, an air of being essentially at odds and possibly in dangerous conflict with some unspoken sense of values. For we do believe that a "good" thing, be it art or toothpaste, proves its goodness by its public acceptance. And at the same time we know, too, that something dark and dreadful lies within this concept.

The problem, then, of the social drama in this generation is not the same as it was for Ibsen, Chekhov, or Shaw. They, and the left-wing playwrights of the thirties who amplified their findings and repeated their forms, were oriented either toward an arraignment of some of the symptoms of efficiency men or toward the ultimate cure by socialism. With the proliferation of machine techniques in the world, and the relative perfection of distributing techniques, in America first and the rest of the world soon, the time will shortly be upon us when the truth will dawn. We shall come to see, I think, that Production for Profit and Production for Use (whatever their relative advantages—and each has its own) leave untouched the problem which the Greek drama put so powerfully before mankind. How are we to live? From what fiat, from what ultimate source are we to derive a standard of values that will create in man a respect for himself, a real voice in the fate of his society, and, above all, an aim for his life which is neither a private aim for a private life nor one which sets him below the machine that was made to serve him?

The social drama in this generation must do more than analyze and arraign the social network of relationships. It must delve into the nature of man as he exists to discover what his needs are, so that those needs may be amplified and exteriorized in terms of social concepts. Thus, the new social dramatist, if he is to do his work, must be an even deeper psychologist than those of the past, and he must be conscious at least of the futility of isolating the psychological life of man lest he fall always short of tragedy, and return, again and again and again, to the pathetic swampland where the waters are old tears and not the generative seas from which new kinds of life arise.

It is a good time to be writing because the audience is sick of the old formulations. It is no longer believed—and we may be thankful for it—that the poor are necessarily virtuous or the rich necessarily decayed. Nor is it believed that, as some writers would put it, the rich are necessarily not decayed and the poor necessarily the carriers of vulgarity. We have developed so democratic a culture that in America neither the speech of a man nor his way of dressing nor even his ambitions for himself inevitably mark his social class. On the stage social rank tells next to nothing about the man any more. The decks are cleared. There is a kind of perverse unity forming among us, born, I think, of the discontent of all classes of people with the endless frustration of life. It is possible now to speak of a search for values, not solely from the position of bitterness, but with a warm embrace of mankind, with a sense that at bottom every one of us is a victim of this misplacement of aims.

The debilitation of the tragic drama, I believe, is commensurate with the fracturing and the aborting of the need of man to maintain a fruitful kind of union with his society. Everything we learn, everything we know or deem valuable for a man to know, has been thrown into the creation of a machine technology. The nuclear bomb, as a way of waging war, is questioned only now—because we have it, because we have invented it: not before both sides knew how to make it. Both sides have the bomb and both sides have the machine. Some day the whole world will have both and the only force that will keep them from destructive use will be a force strange to machine psychology, a force born of will—the will of man to survive and to reach his ultimate, most conscious, most knowing, most fulfilled condition, his fated excellence.

History has given the social drama its new chance. Ibsen and Shaw had to work through three acts to prove in the fourth that, even if we are not completely formed by society, there is little left that society does not affect. The tremendous growth in our consciousness of social causation has won for these writers their victory in this sense: it has given to us a wider consciousness of the causes that form character. What the middle of the twentieth century has taught us is that theirs was not the whole answer. It is not enough any more to know that one is at the mercy of social pressures; it is necessary to understand that such a sealed fate cannot be accepted. Nor is courage alone required now to question this complex, although without courage nothing is possible, including real dramatic writing. It is necessary to know that the values of commerce, values which were despised as necessary but less than noble in the long past, are now not merely perversely dominant everywhere but claimed as positive moral goodness itself. The question must begin to be asked; not whether a new thing will work or pay, not whether it is more efficient than its predecessor, more popular, and more easily accepted; but what it will do to human beings. The first invention of man to create that response in all nations was the atomic bomb. It is the first "improvement" to have dramatized for even the numbest mind the question of value. Over the past decade this nation and this world have been gripped by in inner debate on many levels, a debate raised to consciousness by this all-destroying "improvement." Alongside it is the "improvement" called automation, which will soon displace workers who mass-produce in industry. The conquest of poverty and hunger is the order of the day; the refusal of the dark peoples to live in subjection to the white is already a fact. The world, I think, is moving toward a unity, a unity won not alone by the necessities of the physical developments themselves, but by the painful and confused re-assertion of man's inherited will to survive. When the peace is made, and it will be made, the question Greece asked will once again be a question not reserved for philosophers and dramatists; it will be asked by the man who can live out his life without fear of hunger, joblessness, disease, the man working a few hours a day with a life-span probability of eighty, ninety, or perhaps a hundred years. Hard as it is for most people, the sheer struggle to exist and to prosper affords a haven from thought. Complain as they may that they have no time to think, to cultivate themselves, to ask the big questions, most men are terrified at the thought of not having to spend most of their days fighting for existence. In every sphere, and for a hundred hard reasons, the ultimate questions are once again becoming moot, some because without the right answers we will destroy the earth, others because the peace we win may leave us without the fruits of civilized life. The new social drama will be Greek in that it will face man as a social animal and yet without the petty partisanship of so much of past drama. It will be Greek in that the "men" dealt with in its scenes—the psychology and characterizations—will be more than ends in themselves and once again parts of a whole, a whole that is social, a whole that is Man. The world, in a word, is moving into the same boat. For a time, their greatest time, the Greek people were in the same boat—their polis. Our drama, like theirs, will, as it must, ask the same questions, the largest ones. Where are we going now that we are together? For, like every act man commits, the drama is a struggle against his mortality, and meaning is the ultimate reward for having lived.

23.2 THE COMMODITY COMES HOME TO ROOST: REPRESSION, REGRESSION, AND DEATH IN ARTHUR MILLER'S *DEATH OF A SALESMAN*—LOIS TYSON

SINCE *DEATH OF A SALESMAN*'S New York premiere in 1949, critics have tended to view Arthur Miller's remarkable play in one of two ways: as a psychological drama or as a Marxist critique of capitalist culture. Despite the play's rather obvious psychoanalytic content—the drama is structured by a series of detailed descriptions of the stages in Willy Loman's psychological breakdown—most critics treat the work's psychological dimension in terms of its tragic, rather than psychoanalytic, function. The psychological drama, the argument goes, foregrounds the protagonist's responsibility for his failure as a husband and father and is thematically centered on the scene in which Willy commits adultery in a Boston hotel room. As Giles Mitchell puts it, Willy's failures are "preeminently personal" (394). Similarly, Leonard Moss argues that "Miller's technical apparatus—the colloquial language, the symbolic images, and the dramatized recollections—shapes the pride and blindness of a mentality, not the evil influence of a social condition" (36). The play's Marxist critique of capitalist culture, on the other hand, is said to foreground the protagonist's victimization by an uncaring society obsessed with material success and to center thematically on the scene in which Willy is cold-bloodedly fired by Howard Wagner.

Those critics who have addressed the coexistence of both dimensions in the play have generally done so in order to show how the two are at odds, observing that the psychological drama and the political critique rest on mutually exclusive assumptions and that each reading depends for its strength on the weakness of the other.

This polarization of the play's psychological and political dimensions misunderstands, I believe, the nature of the overarching mythos that, as everyone ironically acknowledges, informs Miller's play: the mythos of the American dream. As this chapter will attempt to show, it is in the American dream—specifically, in its relation to commodity psychology—that the play's psychological and political strands are inextricably entwined. For the American dream serves as the "ore" from which Willy fashions the ideological armor he uses to disguise and deny his psychological problems and those of his family in order to escape the existential inwardness that such a self-awareness would force upon him. This dialectical relationship between the individual psyche and the socius is manifest at those points where the play's psychological and ideological content intersect most clearly: Willy's commodification of personal image; his five so-called memory scenes, which, I will argue, are regressive episodes the structural similarities of which underscore their psychological importance; and the Loman family's sexuality, which is an important, though critically neglected, aspect of this work. In addition, I will suggest that the intersection of psychology and ideology can be observed, in more speculative terms, in the rather one-sided reading of Willy Loman that has dominated the critical literature and in the playwright's own apparent emotional investment in his protagonist, which is revealed in the interaction of the play's realist and expressionist episodes.

Certainly, the most obvious example of Willy's ideological armor, and the one that informs all the psychological events that structure the play, is his commodification of personal image. For him, the road to the American dream is paved with a winning personality: "That's the wonder, the wonder of this country," the protagonist tells his young sons, "that a man can end with diamonds here on the basis of being liked!" (79; act 2). Because, as Willy observes, a rich man is always well liked, being well liked, he concludes, must be how poor men become wealthy. For this reason, he believes that being well liked is the necessary and sufficient currency for purchasing success in the business world. Of course, Willy's logic depends on a very superficial view of what it means to be well liked. Because he substitutes form for content—"It's not what you say, it's how you say it" (58; act 1)—he mistakes the image of popularity for the reality, ignoring, for example, the obvious fact that, for some rich men, being "well liked" is not the source of their wealth but its effect. (As Charley next door says of the financial scoundrel J. P. Morgan, "with his pockets on he was very well liked" [90; act 2.]) But superficial is Willy's middle name: for him, success and the image of success are one. He "regularly confuses labels with reality," implying, for example, "that a punching bag is good because, as he says, 'It's got Gene Tunney's signature on it'" (Weales 133). It's the image of success Willy tries to project by joking with his customers and by exaggerating his sales prowess, and it's the image of success—the appearance of being well liked—that he teaches his sons is the necessary and sufficient commodity to ensure their future success in the business world, the world that Willy is certain will fulfill his dreams.

As Biff observes, however, Willy "had the wrong dreams" (132; Requiem). We must wonder, although the question is rarely raised, why the protagonist chose—and why, at all costs, he clings to—his dream of business success when his ability and his pleasure clearly lie in working with his hands. The answer can be found in the American dream's promise to remediate Willy's ontological insecurity, his lack of "any unquestionable self-validating certainties" (Laing 39), which has apparently plagued him since his abandonment in early childhood by his father and older brother Ben. The early loss of these two role models, with whose idealized memory Willy could never compete, has left him, in his own words, feeling "kind of temporary about [him]self" (46; act 1) or, in psychoanalytic terms, narcissistically wounded—humiliated by his own powerlessness. The resulting need for a reassuring father explains the otherwise mystifying importance for Willy of the Dave Singleman story: the old salesman, whose popularity and resourcefulness allowed him to make a good living even at the age of eighty-four, fits Willy's idealized image of his own father. The protagonist's obsession with image throughout the play underscores this insecurity, for it bespeaks the narcissist, the man who must continually bolster the surface of his personality by finding its positive reflection in the world around him because that surface has no firm ground of its own to support it from within.

Narcissism also explains why Willy refuses to relinquish, no matter what the cost to himself or his family, the personal image of the successful salesman he has manufactured from the ideological fabric of the American dream. It is not merely shame he fears, but the loss of a coherent self, for an idealized self-image is the sine qua non of the narcissist's identity. Such a shaky structure requires the kind of ego reinforcement Willy desires: the admiration of financially successful, powerful men like his brother, the admiration one receives for achieving the American dream's rags-to-riches metamorphosis. Thus, Willy's failure to see the obvious unscrupulous underside of Ben's financial success, like the rest of his apparent moral confusion concerning his and his sons' success-oriented ethics, is the result, not of an "ignorance of the world and . . . a naiveté so colossal as to amount to a kind of innocence" (Mitchell 406), but of selective perception. The protagonist's overwhelming psychological need for ontological reassurance doesn't permit him to see anything that might inhibit his pursuit of the business success that promises to supply that reassurance.

The only place Willy was ever able to market his personal image successfully was in his home. As we see in his memories of his boys' high-school days, Willy's young sons, Biff and Happy, adored their father. They believed all his stories about his popularity, his sales achievements, and the business of his own that he would have someday so that he'd be able to stay home with his family instead of spending his work-week on the road as he had done all his life. In their eyes, he was the success he pretended to be, and their belief in him helped him to deny the reality of his small sales commissions. If young Biff and Happy kept their father's image shining for him, Linda, Willy's wife, always kept it in good repair by helping her husband deny unpleasant realities. As we can see in the following memory scene, which closely resembles her behavior in the play's present-tense action as well, Linda refused to acknowledge any of Willy's weaknesses and wouldn't let him acknowledge them either:

WILLY: . . . My God, if business don't pick up I don't know what I'm gonna do!

LINDA: Well, next week you'll do better.

WILLY: Oh, I'll knock 'em dead next week. I'll go to Hartford. I'm very well liked in Hartford. You know, the trouble is, Linda, people don't seem to take to me. . . .

LINDA: Oh, don't be foolish.

WILLY: I know it when I walk in. They seem to laugh at me. . . . I talk too much. . . .

LINDA: You don't talk too much, you're just lively.

WILLY: *smiling*, Well, I figure, what the hell, life is short, a couple of jokes. . . .

(30–31; act 1)

If Linda provides "the spiritual glue that holds together [Willy's] rickety frame" (Schlueter and Flanagan 59), it's nevertheless a service of dubious value she performs. By functioning, in effect, as a manic defense against the physical and psychological realities that continually threaten to invade her husband's awareness, Linda prevents him from challenging his own self-delusions and thereby helps preclude the possibility of his psychological growth.

That we must rely on Willy's memories for much of what we know of Linda is one of the reaons why she is such a problematic character. Certainly, when she speaks for herself in the present, she reveals that she is aware of her husband's faults and simply loves him in spite of them. Nevertheless, I think the tendency of some readers to idealize her—to believe, for example, that "she is just too good for Willy and thus too good for the play" (Welland 49)—ignores the role Linda's own desire may play in her collusion with Willy's project to escape existential inwardness. At best, of course, she wants to maintain Willy's self-delusion because she believes it would be more disastrous for him to face the truth about himself; at worst, however, her purpose is to keep the truth about the severity of her husband's psychological problems hidden from herself so that she, too, can avoid the existential inwardness such a realization might force upon her. In either case, by helping Willy deny the physical and psychological realities of his life, Linda exacerbates her husband's problems.

It is Willy's struggle with those realities, brought to the fore by the double trauma of mounting pressures at the office and Biff's visit home, that constitutes the five expressionistic episodes in which he seems to remember or imagine events from his past. However, these episodes are not a function simply of memory or imagination. They are, rather, psychological regressions, which, in pathological cases like Willy's, involve "a full hallucinatory cathexis of the perceptive system" (Freud *Interpretation of Dreams* 496). As D. W. Winnicott explains, regression involves not the imagining but the "*reliving* of dream and memory situations" (288, my emphasis) which opens the psyche to new possibilities. Although, in the therapeutic encounter, the regressed subject relives early childhood episodes, Winnicott's description of regression closely parallels, and illuminates, Willy Loman's behavior.

Like Winnicott's patients, Willy has developed a "false self" (Winnicott 281)—his successful-salesman persona—to defend against what Winnicott calls an "original environmental-failure situation" (287), in this case, Willy's childhood loss of father and older brother. The existence of this false self "results in [a] sense of futility" (292), which the protagonist recurrently manifests throughout the play. Furthermore, regression can involve a return either to a pleasant past experience, such as Willy's happy times with his young family, or to a painful episode from the past, such as his initial falling-out with Biff in the Boston hotel room. Most important for our understanding of the protagonist, "regression is distinct from the other defence organizations in that it carries with it . . . a new opportunity for an unfreezing of the [failure] situation and a chance for spontaneous recovery" (Winnicott 283). Because regression involves a return to the experience that lies at the bottom of a current conflict, as it does in each of Willy's five regressive episodes, it allows the regressed person to become aware of the concrete source of a heretofore baffling psychological condition. Recovery, in this context, means the acquisition of a new attitude toward oneself and one's problems based on the insight gained during the regression. Thus, in offering the opportunity to live an authentic relationship to one's conflicts, regression always offers the opportunity to acquire or deepen existential inwardness. From this perspective, Willy's five regressive episodes represent five opportunities for him to alter his course, both psychologically and existentially, and it is significant that his response, in each case, is the same. For, as we shall see, the pattern formed by his responses to regression reveals a systematic, if only partly conscious, effort on Willy's part to eschew the existential inwardness increasingly pressed upon him by the accumulated refuse of his psyche.

The first three regressive episodes follow roughly the same pattern: each time Willy is confronted with a traumatic reality in the present, he regresses to a time when his American-dream fantasies could still convince him and his family that he was the success he wanted to be. Thus, as we see in his first regression, which occurs shortly after his return home from his aborted attempt to drive to New England (20–34; act 1), the protagonist tries to escape the present reality of having been taken off salary and put on straight commission by regressing to a time when his young sons, still in high school, polished his car and hung on his every word, a time when he could still look to the future with hope. In his second regression, which occurs during and after his card game with Charley later that night (38–46; act 1), Willy tries to escape his present pain over Biff's life as a drifter and his own inability to help his son by regressing to a time when he was able to show off his boys' high-spiritedness and filial devotion in front of his brother Ben: he imagines sending the boys off to steal sand from a nearby construction site in order to rebuild the front stoop. In his third regression, which occurs in Howard Wagner's office (77–83; act 1), the protagonist tries to escape the present trauma of being fired by regressing to a time when he had the opportunity to superintend Ben's Alaskan timberland: "God, timberland! Me and my boys in those grand outdoors!" (78; act 1).

None of these three visions of the past, however, provides the escape Willy seeks. For it is during such regressive experiences that repressed conflicts tend to erupt. Thus, his first regressive vision of his happy young family is inevitably interrupted by the memory that Biff had been an irresponsible boy and a petty thief whose behavior was often wild and selfish:

> BERNARD: *entering on the run,* Where is [Biff]? If he doesn't study!
> WILLY : *moving to the forestage, with great agitation,* You'll give him the answers!
> BERNARD: I do, but I can't on a Regents! That's a state exam! They're liable to arrest me!
> WILLY: Where is he? I'll whip him, I'll whip him!
> LINDA: And he'd better give back that football, Willy, it's not nice.
> WILLY: Biff! Where is he? Why is he taking everything?
> LINDA: He's too rough with the girls, Willy. All the mothers are afraid of him!
> WILLY: I'll whip him.
>
> (33–34; act 1)

Similarly, Willy's second pleasant regression is interrupted by his fear that he didn't raise his sons right. He imagines telling Ben, "Sometimes I'm afraid that I'm not teaching them the right kind of—Ben, how should I teach them?" (46; act 1). Finally, Willy's third regressive episode is interrupted by the memory that he'd refused the opportunity to manage Ben's Alaskan timber-land: Linda's repetition of his story about the successful Dave Singleman convinced him to keep his job.

In terms of Willy's psychological experience, readers' concern over whether or not the past events he recalls are accurately reported according to some standard of objective reality is irrelevant. What matters is that the conflicts' emergence reveals Willy's experience of them; it is subjective reality that is revelatory here. For these eruptions of repressed conflicts are a product of Willy's present psychological state as well as a reflection of his former condition. During a traumatic period, conflicts that have been long buried tend to surface and demand attention or discharge. This is, of course, why regression often functions as a tool of psychological growth: it brings forward into consciousness, and allows the subject the opportunity to work on, conflicts that have heretofore inhabited the unconscious.

In Willy's case, however, the opportunity is never taken: the play does not dramatize the protagonist's "progression to enlightment" (Jackson 17). Instead of using the knowledge offered by his regressive episodes to achieve what George S. Klein terms "active reversal," Willy relies on commodity psychology to repress the conflicts anew: he clings to the American-dream myths and fantasies he used to deny and submerge the conflicts in the first place. Thus, when his pleasant picture of his sons' adoration is interrupted by his memory of Biff's misconduct, he defines the boy's behavior as spiritedness, which, we may recall, is the basis upon which Willy believes socioeconomic success is founded: "There's nothing the matter with [Biff]! . . . He's got spirit, personality. Loaded with it. Loaded!" (34; act 1). Similarly, when self-doubt about his parenting interrupts his vision of showing off his boys for Ben, he imagines receiving Ben's reassurance that he was raising them to be "outstanding, manly chaps" (46; act 1), perfectly suited to fulfill their father's dreams of *success*. And when the memory of his refusal to accept an outdoor job from Ben interrupts his vision of receiving the job offer, Willy remembers Biff's Ebbets Field game—evidence that Biff had what it takes to be a success in Willy's competitive world and that he had therefore made the right decision in turning down Ben's offer.

Even Willy's fourth regressive episode, in which he relives the unhappy time young Biff discovered him in a Boston hotel room with another woman (102–14; act 2), does not "ope[n] the salesman's eyes" (Szondi 23) and force him to recognize "his own responsibility for what has happened to his family" (Welland 47), for the protagonist refuses to accept the painful awakening this regression offers him. As Willy recalls, young Biff flunked his high-school math course and rushed off to Boston to ask his father to pressure the math teacher into giving him the four points he needed to pass. As Bernard later explains to Willy, Biff was ready to make up the credit in summer school, if he had to, so that he could go to college in the fall. It wasn't until Biff's ill-fated trip to see his father that he gave up on his own future. Although Bernard doesn't give Willy this information until later in act 2, it is clear in the fourth regression that Willy's knowledge of his role in Biff's failure is the repressed conflict that is erupting here. When Biff first arrived at Willy's hotel room he was very eager for his father to talk to the math teacher: "If he saw the kind of man you are, and you just talked to him in your way," Biff told his father, "I'm sure he'd come through for me" (111; act 2). It wasn't until Willy's lover came laughing out of the bathroom in her slip—and Biff realized that his father was having an affair—that the boy stubbornly refused to carry out any of Willy's plans for him. Willy represses his awareness of his role in Biff's difficulties, however, telling himself that Biff's flunking the math course is the source of his son's problems, an excuse he uses even when the adult Bernard confronts him with the truth. It is noteworthy that Willy's awareness of the importance of the hotel incident is itself an attempt to sidestep the real issue: his failure as a parent in general. As Biff later admits, his father had so raised his expectations of success—and provided so little real basis for them—that, because instant success didn't come his way, he "stole [himself] out of every good job since high school" (124; act 2). Willy's immediate flight from the restaurant where this regression occurs, to buy seeds for the plot of sterile land behind his house—an obvious escape into a time before the hotel episode occurred—underscores his repression of the psychological insight this regression provides.

It is part of the nature of conflict, however, that repression merely increases its force. Therefore, Willy's conflicts get more out of control with every attempt he makes to deny and resubmerge them. In this context, his decision to kill himself, which occurs during his fifth and final regression at the end of act 2 (119–20, 127–29), is not "an act of affirmation" (Heyen 50), nor an effort to "re-establish his own self-confidence and his family's integrity" (Moss 24), nor, as many critics would have it, a misguided attempt to secure his son's future. Rather, Willy's suicide is his ultimate act of denial. Having bought the seeds he'd run off from the restaurant to get earlier that evening, Willy is now pacing off a garden plot in his backyard. It is noteworthy that planting the garden is an abstract act—not linked, like his behaviors in past regressions, to some significant, specific past event—because Willy wants to avoid the eruptions of repressed content that occurred during his more specific regressions. Unable to face the day's accumulated disappointments, he frantically seeks a way out of his despair, and commodity psychology provides one: he will kill himself in a way that appears to be an accident—in a car wreck—and Biff will collect twenty thousand dollars in life insurance. With this financial backing, Willy reasons, Biff will achieve the business success of which he believes him capable. In both segments of this regression, Willy imagines himself discussing his idea with Ben, and the deeper motive for Willy's intended suicide quickly surfaces: he wants to regain Biff's esteem so that he can regain, in his son's eyes, the personal image that used to impress the boy so much. As Willy tells Ben,

> This [Willy's death] . . . changes all the aspects. Because he thinks I'm nothing, see, and so he spites me. But the funeral—*Straightening up*: Ben, that funeral will be massive! They'll come from Maine, Massachusetts, Vermont, New Hampshire! . . . that boy will be thunder-struck, Ben, because he never realized—I am known . . . and he'll see it with his eyes once and for all.
>
> (119–20; act 2)

The blunt revelations and accusations with which Biff interrupts his father's imaginary conversation with Ben—Biff's claims that Willy raised him to be the thief he is and that he and Happy, like their father, are failures who lie about their success—seem to have no lasting effect on Willy. The only thing the protagonist takes from this experience is the fact that Biff cries to him, that Biff loves him. "That boy . . . is going to be magnificent!" (126; act 2) is Willy's final response to his interaction with Biff, and he returns immediately, his suicide project unchanged, to his conversation with Ben.

"Can you imagine that magnificence with twenty thousand dollars in his pocket?" Willy asks Ben during the second half of his final regression (128; act 2). This vision of Biff holds such charm for Willy, as does every success Biff has ever had, because Willy feels it is his own success he is experiencing in Biff's success. This is something other than healthy parental pride in a son who makes good, pride in one's success as a father—Charley's pride in his son, not Willy's, is of this kind. Willy's pride is projection, a very personal and intense form of vicarious experience. And if he can just keep this vision intact until he kills himself, Willy will not have to face the repressed awareness of his failed life that keeps threatening to break through into his consciousness and overwhelm him. Thus, the protagonist's self-destruction is a last-ditch act of repression; the twenty thousand dollars in life-insurance money intended for Biff provides both his excuse for killing himself and the fantasy he needs in order to keep self-knowledge at bay until he can accomplish it. The conflicts that constitute his psyche have come to such an impasse that ordinary forms of denial and avoidance are nothing but ineffective stopgap measures. The only way to shut *this* psyche off is to kill it. Like all his other defenses, Willy's suicide draws on the same American dream in which personal and financial success are at once wed in and transcended by sign-exchange value. For as we have seen, Willy's suicide is grounded in his vision of the increased status a showy funeral and a life-insurance legacy will purchase for him in the eyes of Biff, who has long been the repository of his father's sign-exchange value.

The play's psychological and political dimensions are fused even more clearly in the Loman family's sexuality. As Walter Davis puts it, human sexuality is primarily a matter of meanings (*Inwardness and Existence* 80–87 and passim): through one's sexuality one enacts one's conscious and unconscious attitudes and motives toward others and thereby reveals, as Merleau-Ponty put it, one's "manner of being towards the world" (158). In the Lomans' case, not only are the family's sexual attitudes compatible with the commodifying ideology of the American dream, but, like that dream, the family's sexual mores help them disguise and deny their own psychology and thereby avoid existential inwardness. In order to see how the Lomans' apparently diverse sexual natures achieve a single, ideologically saturated psychological end, we must first briefly review some key elements in the sexual characterization of each family member.

To begin with, Willy's extramarital affair, a natural focal point for any consideration of his sexuality, reveals neither "the hollowness of [Willy's] affection for Linda" (Aarnes 96), nor his unhappiness over "his failure to impress her" (Hayman 51), nor the paucity of Linda's comprehension of Willy (B. Parker). For the source of the protagonist's infidelity cannot be circumscribed by his relationship to his wife but lies in the merger of his sexual and professional identities. As we can see in the following scene, Willy's memory of his inadequacy in business is replaced by the memory of his lover:

> WILLY: [to Linda] . . . I get so lonely—especially when business is bad and there's nobody to talk to. I get the feeling that I'll never sell anything again, that I won't make a living for you, or a business, a business for the boys. . . . *The Woman primps at the "mirror."* There's so much I want to make for—

THE WOMAN: Me? You didn't make me, Willy. I picked you.
WILLY: *pleased,* You picked me?
THE WOMAN: . . . I've been sitting at that desk watching all the salesmen go by, day in, day out. But you've got such a sense of humor, and we do have such a good time together, don't we?
WILLY: Sure, sure. *He takes her in his arms.* Why do you have to go now?

(31–32; act 1)

Clearly, Willy's strong positive response to The Woman was elicited by her preference for him over the other salesmen who came through her office. Finally, someone in the business world liked him better than his competitors. For Willy, this woman was a commodity the acquisition of which conferred upon him the professional sign-exchange value he was unable to attain otherwise.

For Happy as well, women are commodities used to boost his sign-exchange value. He is not, as Brian Parker suggests, "compulsively competitive in sex and business for no reason at all" (102). Happy uses women to make him feel that he is able to "get" something that he cannot get from his career. Because he covets the attention his father has always lavished on Biff, Happy has invested a good deal of his identity in following in Willy's footsteps, in achieving the business success his father desired for both boys. Happy lives in the town in which he grew up and works in sales: he's one of two assistants to the assistant buyer for a local firm. However, although he makes enough money to support his apartment, car, and social life, he has not achieved the big success—the wealth, power, and prestigious title—that Willy's dreams had reserved for his sons. Therefore, Happy feels disappointed, cheated: a world in which he must take orders from men he "can outbox, outrun, and outlift" (17; act 1) is, he feels, an unjust world. For this reason, he compulsively seduces the fiancées of executives in his firm: he can't have their jobs, so he'll have their women. We can see the connection between Happy's feelings of inadequacy in business and his womanizing when he tells Biff about his struggle to compete with his coworkers and follows immediately with, "But take those two we had tonight. Weren't they gorgeous creatures?" (18; act 1).

For both Willy and Happy, the achievement of financial success is tied to masculine self-image. This is why, as is typical in America, their metaphors for success involve winning fights and killing opponents. "Knocked 'em cold in Providence, slaughtered 'em in Boston," Willy tells his young sons upon returning home from a sales trip (27; act 1), using the same kind of language his brother Ben had used in advising him to go to Alaska: "Screw on your fists and you can fight for a fortune up there" (78; act 2). This link between business success and masculinity is, of course, one reason why both men use women to assuage their egos, to make up for their disappointments in the business world. It is no mere coincidence, then, that Happy abandons his father in the restaurant to pursue women directly upon learning that the plan for a Loman Brothers sporting-goods company is down the drain.

Of course, Happy's sexual pattern has strong Oedipal overtones as well. Raised within a family dynamic in which all Dad's attention was focused on Biff, who was an authority figure for the younger child, it is no wonder that Happy's struggle for identity and recognition early took the form of masculine competitiveness. "I lost weight, Pop, you notice?" (44; act 1) is this character's pathetic boyhood refrain as he undertakes the impossible task of competing with his-brother-the-football-hero for paternal esteem. While Willy frequently embraces Biff, in flashback as in the present, he never touches Happy. And the younger brother must listen to Dad's continual boasting about Biff without ever himself being the object of his father's pride. Happy is, thus, the perpetual bench warmer, the onlooker at the lives of his father and brother, just as Willy had been before him.

The mother's neglect of the younger son adds insult to injury and fans the flame of an already unhealthy Oedipal situation. While Linda frequently addresses Biff using the same language and tone she uses to address Willy—"I know dear" (47; act 1), "Please, dear" (59; act 1), "Thanks, darling" (69; act 2)—she uses such terms for Happy only to express contempt: "You never asked, my dear!" she responds angrily to Happy's remark that he was unaware of his father's demotion to straight commission work (50; act 1). Indeed, Happy barely exists for his mother. She frequently acts as if he were not there, as we see when the brothers return home after the restaurant scene. Although Happy does all of the talking as he and Biff enter the house, Linda ignores him to vent her emotion on Biff: "Linda, *cutting Happy off, violently to Biff*: 'Don't you care whether he lives or dies?" (116; act 2). Only Biff's feelings matter. Only Biff's behavior can change anything. "I'm gonna get married, Mom" (61; act 1) is Happy's new hopeless bid for attention and approval. And it is in his attitude toward marriage and women that we find his Oedipal symptomatology most clearly expressed.

Happy's compulsion to seduce the fiancées of executives he works with is a rather obvious enactment of his Oedipal desire: he wants to compete with his father and brother and, especially, punish his mother for ignoring him. For Happy is a psychologically castrated man who has to use his penis to assert his existence and value. The executives he works with are, like his father and brother, authority figures. They're wealthier and more successful than he is and each has won the (symbolically) exclusive attention of a woman. He can't compete with these men in the marketplace anymore than he could compete with Biff and Willy in the home. So he punishes them by "ruining" their fiancées. Happy can't find a girl "with resistance," a girl "like Mom" (19; act 1) that he could marry, because he doesn't want to. By sticking to his pattern of one "easy" woman after another, he can continue to fulfill two conflicting Oedipal needs simultaneously: he can continue, symbolically, to preserve his mother (no woman can take her place), and he can continue, symbolically, to soil her (to seduce a woman is to seduce his mother).

There is in Biff's psyche, as in his brother's, an important Oedipal layer. However, for young Biff, the Oedipal object was not Linda but Willy, and the relationship between father and son was a symbiotic one: each fulfilled the other's narcissistic and masturbatory phallic projection. For Willy, Biff was, of course, the star athlete, admired by the boys and pursued by the girls, as Willy had never been. For Biff, Willy was the successful businessman, universally respected and given "red-carpet treatment" by everyone everywhere he went, as Biff looked forward to being when the time came for him to take his place in the business world. Father and son saw in each other, and became for each other, an idealized phallus.

The love that bound these two characters resembled that of lovers rather than that of father and son. Linda's reminiscence with Biff certainly sounds like a description of sweethearts: "How you used to talk to him on the phone every night! How lonely he was till he could come home to you!" (51; act 1). Similarly, when Linda reminds young Biff, during Willy's flashback, that there is a cellar full of boys waiting for him, her son responds, "Ah, when Pop comes home they can wait!" (28; act 1). Biff put his father ahead of his pals, as most seventeen-year-old boys put their girlfriends. In fact, Biff put his father ahead of—or in place of—his girlfriends as well. For it was not the young girls Biff dated who received his chivalrous attentions: as we saw earlier, Biff treated the girls too roughly. As Willy's Ebbett's Field flashback reveals, it was Willy who basked in the warmth of Biff's courtly love:

> WILLY: What do they say about you in school, now that they made you captain?
> HAPPY: There's a crowd of girls behind him every time the classes change.
> BIFF: *taking Willy's hand,* This Saturday, Pop, this Saturday—just for you, I'm going to break through for a touchdown.
> HAPPY: You're supposed to pass.
> BIFF: I'm takin' one play for Pop. You watch me, Pop, and when I take off my helmet, that means I'm breakin' out.
>
> (25; act 1)

It was Willy's hand that Biff took, ignoring Happy's comment about the girls at school (Willy's hopeless rivals for Biff's attention), and it was to Willy that Biff dedicated a special touchdown.

Thus, when Biff found his father in a Boston hotel room with another woman, it was not his mother's betrayal for which the boy suffered, it was his own. Willy and Biff, in fact, sounded as if they were having a lovers' quarrel:

> BIFF: *his weeping breaking from him,* Dad . . .
> WILLY: *infected by it,* Oh, my boy . . .
> BIFF: Dad . . .
> WILLY: She's nothing to me, Biff. I was lonely, I was terribly lonely. . . . *grabbing for Biff* . . .
> BIFF: Don't touch me, you—liar!
> WILLY: Apologize for that!
> BIFF: You fake! You phony little fake! You fake! *Overcome, he turns quickly and weeping fully goes out with his suitcase. Willy is left on the floor on his knees.*
>
> (114; act 2)

Biff's outrage at Willy's betrayal of Linda—"You—you gave her Mama's stockings!" (114; act 1)—was a displacement of his outrage at Willy's betrayal of himself, Biff. So deep was Biff's hurt and anger, his sense of personal betrayal, that he rejected the relationship with his father the two had enjoyed until this point. That is, he rejected both his own and Willy's role as idealized phallus. This does not mean, however, that Biff evolved into a delayed Oedipal relationship with his mother. Psychologically, the young man could not free himself of the idealized image of Willy that had always bolstered his own narcissistic identity—he couldn't "kill" the father—and this is why Biff, unable to wholly reject the paternal belief that business success is the only success, has remained vaguely dissatisfied with the outdoor ranch life he loves.

Finally, Linda's sexuality, like her dreams for the family's future, belongs rather to her husband than herself. She is the devoted, sexless wife that "good" women were required to be in the patriarchal society of her time and place; she is the woman, as we saw Happy put it earlier, "with resistance" (19; act 1). Even her frequent use of "dear" and "darling" in addressing her husband bespeaks a motherly, rather than wifely, affection. For as we have seen, she frequently addresses Biff using the same language and tone she uses to address Willy. This is the same motherly caretaking that shows itself in her concern over Biff's remembering to take his comb to his interview with Bill Oliver and over Willy's remembering to take his glasses, handkerchief, and saccharine to his interview with Howard Wagner. Given the dearth of sexual content in Linda's behavior throughout the play, the similarity of her dialogue with her husband and her older son does not suggest the eroticization of her relationship with Biff but the desexualization of her marital discourse.

The Lomans' sexual attitudes intersect in what is known in common parlance as the "good girl/bad girl" view of women. "Good girls" are virgins until marriage; therefore, they are the girls men marry. "Bad girls" do not confine their sexual activity to marriage; therefore, they are the girls men sleep with, hold in contempt, and sooner or later abandon. Obviously, the salesman and his sons enact this attitude in their talk about and behavior toward women. And Linda, who is herself a "good girl" and who calls the women Happy sleeps with his "lousy rotten whores" (117; act 2), certainly concurs with this classification system. The obvious premise underlying "good girl/bad girl" is that sex is "dirty" or evil and that women are marriage commodities whose exchange value is measured by their willingness to put their sexuality in the hands of men. Part of achieving the American dream, from this perspective, must include marriage to a "good girl" like Linda Loman, the kind of girl Willy dreams his sons will bring home—and the kind of girl Happy and Biff are unable to find. This is the pre-1960s sexual attitude associated with the social and political conservatism of post-World War II America, and clearly, it served the patriarchal status quo by maintaining male domination over women physically and psychologically. However, the "good girl/bad girl" classification supports a conservative status quo in a subtler and more powerful manner as well: it masks the psychosexual structures informing relations between the sexes and, in so doing, masks the merger of the psychosexual structures of human consciousness with the ideological structures of the socius.

"Good girl/bad girl" defines Linda's sexless, mindless devotion to Willy as virtue and thereby permits her to ignore her role in Willy's self-delusion and in her self-delusion about him. And "good girl/bad girl" offers the Loman men an excuse for their behavior with women without making any of them responsible for their own psychological subtexts. Their sexuality does not express "their resentment of the role society forces them to play" (Hayman 51). On the contrary, their social role provides them with the psychological escape they seek. Willy doesn't have to ask himself why he cheated on his wife; Happy doesn't have to probe too deeply into his motives for stealing other men's fiancées; Biff doesn't have to wonder why he used to be so rough with the girls who threw themselves at him in high school or why he has always been rather uninterested in women. The rationalization, as we all know, is that "bad girls" don't deserve better treatment—they probably don't even want better treatment—and it is "natural" for men to respond to them as objects to be used. By validating the Loman men's unexamined displacements—displacements of ontological insecurity, of career anxiety, of Oedipal desire, of phallic projection—"good girl/bad girl" helps keep them looking at the surface of their behavior, their motives, the meaning of their lives.

The conservative era during which *Death of a Salesman* was written and in which the play is set is directly related to the sexual attitudes expressed by the Loman family. For the repression of psychosexual awareness is a product of the same unconscious desire that informs the repression of political awareness: the desire to restrict the growth of critical thinking—thinking that examines motives and subtexts—which, as Horkheimer and Adorno were the first to observe, is always a threat to a conservative status quo. A conservative society's restriction of psychosexual awareness (which, as the history of the 1950s and 1980s illustrates, is accompanied by a policy of sexual conservatism on the part of America's political leadership) can be seen as an unconscious symbol of what that society really wants to repress: knowledge of ideology, of how the social/political/economic machinery runs. If we can be kept forever "innocent," forever ignorant of our own psychology and of the ways in which that psychology constitutes and is constituted by the socio-political domain, we will remain, like Willy, in childlike awe of the powers that be, forever seeking access to the realm of the chosen without ever questioning the terms on which that realm exists.

The relationship I have posited between ideology and sexuality might be termed an Althusserian interrogation of Lacan: the question isn't merely, How does psychosexual development mark the individual's programming within the symbolic order? but, How does the individual's psychosexual programming within the symbolic order reproduce the society's conditions of production? In other words, as Miller's play reveals, sexuality hasn't *become* public; it has always *been* public. As we see in the case of the Loman family, unexamined, repressive attitudes toward sexuality are part of the larger symbiotic relationship between the individual psyche and the socius, which finds its most self-destructive expression in the ideological armor of the American dream, the armor Willy has constructed to hide himself and his family from their own psychology.

Considered as a labor to avoid and deny existential possibility, *Death of a Salesman*'s psychological/ideological content—Willy's commodification of personal image, his five regressive episodes, and the Loman family's sexuality—can be seen as a kind of psychological death-work. As a concept applicable to the drama of everyday life, death can be seen as a labor we perform whenever we refuse the Nietzschean daily task of reconquering our humanity. As Walter Davis puts it,

> Insofar as we are dramatic beings defined by certain core conflicts, each day presents a task that will involve some expenditure of energy . . . either to confront or avoid oneself. We mobilize our [psychological] energies to move in one of these directions. Such energy is *bound* to interpretations (selective inattentions) and emotional patterns of behavior which define . . . our field of possible action. Life is the effort to make that situation the emergence of existential possibility. Death is the effort to protect us from same.
>
> (*Get the Guests* n.p.)

This is the real death, the most meaningful death, in *Death of a Salesman*: death seen not as an instinct or a drive but as an effort to avoid existential inwardness. From this perspective, the play's title gains added bite: the death in *Death of a Salesman* no longer refers merely to the way Willy ends his life but to the way he lives it as well.

This kind of death-work should not be wholly unfamiliar to most readers. Few of us can honestly assess our own family histories without seeing the same kind of avoidance and denial we see in Willy. And don't we ourselves regularly practice the kind of death-work that traps us, perhaps unconsciously but certainly not unwillingly, in static careers and interpersonal relationships?

Ironically, I believe it's the ideological familiarity of Willy's death-work that informs many readers' blindness to it. Like Jay Gatsby, Willy Loman is a character whose sympathetic qualities are foregrounded in the criticism, while his weaknesses are often either marginalized or blamed on external forces. And the reason may be, again as in the case of Gatsby, that the protagonist's psychological/ideological project is compatible with those of his critics. As Esther Merle Jackson notes, "the story of Willy Loman" has an "intimate association with our aspirations" (8).

As Christopher Innes observes, "Brooks Atkinson's judgment [in 1947] that Willy represents the homely, decent, kindly virtues of middle class society' . . . was typical" of the critical response of that period (61), and it has remained representative of most of the critical response since that time. Eric Mottram, for example, believes that Willy's failure to succeed in business is based on his failure "to learn that business ethics . . . oppose the traditions he assumed were still in action: the personal ethics of honour, the patriarchal nature of a basically benevolent society and family, and neighborhood relations" (30). As Rita Di Giuseppe puts it, the protagonist can't "follow the praxis of the work ethic" because he is "too noble" (116). These critics don't seem to notice that Willy's personal ethics are, at best, very problematical. Similarly, June Schlueter and James K. Flanagan ignore the difficulties involved in any assessment of Willy's values in their apparent nostalgia for the mythical period they feel the character represents: "Surrounded by high-rise apartment buildings that deflect the sun from the backyard, Willy's little house in Brooklyn stands as a symbol of time past, when the world still had room for vegetable gardens and for salesmen who carried on their trade on the strength of a smile" (57). Harold Bloom, too, believes that Willy "is a good man, who wants only to earn and to deserve the love of his wife and of his sons" (15).

Even among those critics who see Willy's life and death as "a continual commitment to illusion" (Bigsby 120), there is a desire to romanticize this commitment. C. W. E. Bigsby, for example, views Willy's self-delusion as "an attempt to sustain a sense of personal dignity and meaning . . . in a life which seems to consist of little more than a series of contingent events" (117). Similarly, although William Heyen notes that Willy "die[s] lying" (49), he nevertheless calls the decision to commit suicide rather than face the truth about his life "an act of affirmation," a choice of "meaning over meaninglessness," because the character thus chooses, "in effect, to insist that he had lived, to defend his life as it was" (50). And while Gerald Weales observes that much of Willy's behavior is geared to "keep him from questioning the assumptions that lie beneath his failure and his pretence of success" (134), he believes that the play's positive possibility lies only in the protagonist: the possibility "that the individual may finally be able to retain his integrity . . . does not lie in Biff . . . nor in the alternative suggested by Charley and Bernard. It is in Willy's vitality, in his perverse commitment to a pointless dream, in his inability simply to walk away" (135–36).

The desire to see Willy Loman in as positive a light as possible has, I think, also led some readers to distort other aspects of the play in order to support the reading they want to have of the protagonist. As a case in point, Bigsby asserts that Charley does not offer a positive alternative to Willy because Charley believes "that human concerns can play no role in business" and "boasts that his son's success had been a consequence of his own lack of concern" (121). However, Charley does not ignore the role of human concerns in business; he merely rejects the sentimentalization of business—and the trivialization of human concerns—apparent in Willy's attempt to substitute superficial personal interaction for meaningful business service and productivity. Furthermore, Charley's claim that he was an uninterested father, to which Dennis Welland also points as an example of this character's difference from Willy (42), is obviously not to be taken at face value. Charley's oft-quoted "My salvation is that I never took any interest in anything" (89; act 2) is followed immediately with his gift of fifty dollars to Willy and a job offer. Charley continually underplays his concerns—his love for Bernard, of whom he is clearly very proud, and his interest in Willy's well-being, which he shows throughout the play—but he has these concerns nonetheless. Behind the attempt to contrast Charley with Willy in this manner is, I think, the desire to canonize Willy as the repository of familial love in order to romanticize his motives. And it is the romanticization of Willy's motives that leads, for example, Bigsby to say that "Miller's portrait of Bernard—moral, hard-working, successful, attractive–is perhaps in danger of validating the dreams which Willy had for Biff" (122) without recognizing that Willy's dreams for Biff involved the *image* rather than the reality of such values.

Perhaps the most interesting critic to identify with Willy Loman's dream—and therefore to interpret the play in a way that supports the most positive reading possible of this character—is Arthur Miller himself. For Miller, Willy Loman is "a very brave spirit who cannot settle for half but must pursue his dream of himself to the end" (*Essays* 147–48). Willy is a tragic hero, Miller believes, largely because of the "tragic victory" of his death (*Essays* 146):

> Willy Loman is filled with a joy, however brokenhearted, as he approaches his end. . . . he has achieved a very powerful piece of knowledge, which is that he is loved by his son and has been embraced by him and forgiven. In this he is given his existence, so to speak—his fatherhood, for which he has always striven and which until now he could not achieve.
>
> (*Essays* 147)

Thus, although Miller sees Willy's suicide as an error in judgment—due to his obsession with Biff's financial future—the author considers the protagonist's death the result of his newly acquired knowledge concerning his relationship with his son. In addition, Miller points out, Willy has an important kind of self-awareness—he is aware "of his separation from values that endure":

> He was agonized by his awareness of being in a false position, so constantly haunted by the hollowness of all he had placed his faith in, so aware, in short, that he must somehow be filled in his spirit or fly apart, that he staked his very life on the ultimate assertion. That he had not the intellectual fluency to verbalize his situation is not the same thing as saying that he lacked awareness, even an overly intensified consciousness that the life he had made was without form and inner meaning.
>
> (*Essays* 148)

Miller is, I think, correct both about Willy's realization of Biff's love and about the protagonist's awareness of the emptiness in his own spiritual life. However, in both cases, the knowledge Willy achieves dissimulates, both for the character and for his creator, the knowledge he refuses. While Loman does realize that his son loves him, this new knowledge is, as I think I have shown, but a veneer, a gloss Willy uses to avoid and deny a deeper and much more important knowledge concerning his own psychology and that of his family. Similarly, while Willy is aware of the hollowness of his values, this is a knowledge he doesn't want to have. As I have argued, this is an awareness he struggles to repress throughout the play. In fact, it is apparently only Willy's failure to achieve even a modicum of the success he desired for himself and his family that permitted this awareness to come to the surface to begin with. Had Willy achieved any sort of material success—for example, had he been allowed to work in New York, for however little salary—and had Biff had any sort of a steady job with a future, even a job like Happy's, Willy would have been able to continue to repress his awareness of the emptiness of his spiritual life. Perhaps he wouldn't even have found it empty had circumstances allowed him to continue to hope or fantasize or lie about the future.

Miller confesses to his own unawareness of such subtextual elements in the play:

> When I saw the devasting force with which [*Death of a Salesman*] struck its audiences, something within me was shocked and put off. I had thought of myself as rather an optimistic man. I looked at what I had wrought and was forced to wonder whether I knew myself at all if this play which I had written half in laughter and joy, was as morose and as utterly sad as its audiences found it.
>
> (*Essays* 152)

And the playwright describes his experience of artistic creation in terms that suggest the importance of the author's unconscious in the creation of a literary work: "Writing in that form was like moving through a corridor in a dream" (*Essays* 13). The form to which Miller refers is, of course, the almost exclusive use of Willy's very subjective point of view with its focus on the expressionistic memory sequences; and it is apparently this form, which Miller had never used before and would never use again, that produced the dreamlike creative experience so conducive to unconscious production. His retrospective, a year after the play's opening, confirms the notion that something other than the playwright's conscious intention went into the composition of the work: "It may well be that from the moment I read it to my wife and two friends . . . the play cut itself off from me in a way that is incomprehensible. The script suddenly seemed a record of a madness I had passed through, something I ought not admit to at all, let alone read aloud or have produced on the stage" (*Essays* 12).

That Miller is not consciously aware—and, perhaps, does not want to be aware—of the powerful subtext of his play that I have outlined in this chapter is also evident in his use of setting and in the Requiem with which the play closes. For both devices bespeak an attempt to limit his audience's response to the protagonist to a much narrower reading than the play, as a whole, permits. This attempt is especially clear in the stage directions Miller includes at the beginning of the play:

> *A melody is heard, played upon a flute. It is small and fine, telling of grass and trees and the horizon. The curtain rises.*
>
> *Before us is the Salesman's house. We are aware of towering, angular shapes behind it, surrounding it on all sides. Only the blue light of the sky falls upon the house and forestage; the surrounding area shows an angry glow of orange. As more light appears, we see a solid vault of apartment houses around the small, fragile-seeming home.*
>
> (5; act 1)

This description clearly foregrounds Willy's "underdog" elements: the hero has a fight on his hands, and the enemy is an overwhelming environment. If he loses the battle, it will be the fault of social forces bigger than he is. And again, as the curtain falls over Willy's grave, setting reinforces the author's message: "*Only the music of the flute is left on the darkening stage as over the house the hard towers of the apartment buildings rise into sharp focus*" (133; Requiem).

This view of Willy as a tiny boat on a big sea is reinforced by Charley's well-known speech about Willy during the Requiem. Because the other characters simply reiterate the points of view they've held throughout the play—Biff's insistence on telling the truth, Happy's refusal to acknowledge that truth, and Linda's blind devotion to her husband—Charley's apparent change of heart has marked dramatic impact:

> Nobody dast blame this man. You don't understand: Willy was a salesman. And for a salesman, there is no rock bottom to the life. . . . He's a man way out there in the blue, riding on a smile and a shoeshine. And when they start not smiling back—that's an earthquake. And then you get yourself a couple of spots on your hat, and you're finished. Nobody dast blame this man. A salesman is got to dream, boy. It comes with the territory.
>
> (132; Requiem)

Certainly, Charley's comments at this point in the play contradict his earlier view of Willy as a stubborn, foolish man, a salesman who doesn't even know what he can and can't sell (90; act 2). Neil Carson notes, in fact, that Charley's "inconsisten[t] . . . justification for Willy's romantic hopefulness" helps make the Requiem "something of a dramatic *non sequitur*" (57). Why does Miller put such unexpected words in Charley's mouth? Welland believes the explanation is that Charley "doesn't allow his feelings to come through" until Willy's funeral (42). I think, however, that these are Miller's feelings coming through rather than Charley's.

While I certainly agree that Willy is an underdog, I think that Miller uses the setting and the Requiem, not just to make this point, but to cut off other interpretive possibilities. That is, the author focuses on those elements in the protagonist's environment, both at home and at work, that can explain Willy's behavior without recourse to the kind of psychological/ideological subtext revealed, for example, in the regressive episodes. And this focus can be seen, I think, as a diversionary tactic that works to disallow the kind of reading of the play I have offered in this chapter.

It is especially interesting, in this context, to note what seems to be an incongruity in Miller's stage directions at the end of act 2. During the present-tense, realist action of the play, the actors are instructed to observe the set's predrawn wall lines, which indicate the physical boundaries among different rooms and between the house and the yard. When the actors walk through a wall line, it is an indication that they are portraying action occurring in Willy's memory of the past. These are the expressionist episodes of the play, associated with memory, fantasy, dream, imagination, and, as I have argued, regression. Yet as Linda, Charley, Biff, and Happy prepare, just before the Requiem, to go to the cemetery for Willy's funeral, they all "*move toward the audience, through the wall-line of the kitchen*" (130; act 2). Although the Requiem is supposed to take place in real time, as part of the realism of the play's present-tense action, the actors enter the scene through the wall line as if they were entering one of the play's expressionist episodes. Even if Miller deliberately violated the wall line at this point in the play—for example, as an emblem of what has happened to the house of Loman—such an intention would not undermine the unconscious symbolism of this act. Because, as we saw Miller himself suggest, the expressionist episodes are largely a product of the author's unconscious mind, it is especially meaningful that an expressionist stage direction occurs during the realist representation that ushers in the Requiem. And I think it suggests that Miller unconsciously knows the Requiem is a fantasy, his fantasy, in which he, himself, guarantees that Willy dies a tragic hero. Although Miller puts the words in Charley's mouth, it is the playwright himself, who is telling us that "nobody dast blame this man."

Thus, just like many of his critics, Miller romanticizes Willy. Or perhaps more to the point, the author mythologizes him, as Willy himself does, focusing, in Barthes's terms, on the surface of reality, or the appearance of meaning, rather than on its subtext, or the meaning of appearances (143). Perhaps, again like his critics, the author mythologizes his protagonist's psychological/ideological project out of a desire to mythologize a similar project of his own. It is a testimony to the power of the form, then, and to the power of the playwright's conflicted unconscious this form tapped, that the play tells the truth about commodity psychology and the American dream despite the desire of Miller and his critics to hide it.

Works Cited

Aarnes, William. "Tragic Form and the Possibility of Meaning in *Death of a Salesman.*" *Furman Studies* 29 (1983). Rpt. in *Modern Critical Interpretations: Arthur Miller's* Death of a Salesman. Ed. Harold Bloom. New York: Chelsea, 1988. 95–111.

Barthes, Roland. *Mythologies.* 1957. Trans. Annette Lavers. New York: Hill, 1979.

Bigsby, C. W. E. "*Death of a Salesman.*" In *Memoriam: A Critical Introduction to Twentieth Century American Drama 2: Tennessee Williams, Arthur Miller, Edward Albee.* Cambridge University Press, 1984. 135–248. Rpt. in *Modern Critical Interpretations: Arthur Miller's* Death of a Salesman. Ed. Harold Bloom. New York: Chelsea, 1988. 113–28.

Bloom, Harold. Introduction. *Modern Critical Interpretations: Arthur Miller's* Death of a Salesman. Ed. Harold Bloom. New York: Chelsea, 1988. 1–5.

Di Giuseppe, Rita. "The Shadows of the Gods: Tragedy and Commitment in *Death of a Salesman.*" *Quaderni di lingue e letterature* 14 (1989): 109–128.

Davis, Walter A. *Get the Guests: Psychoanalysis—Modern American Drama—The Audience.* Madison, : University of Wisconsin Press, 1994.

——*Inwardness and Existence: Subjectivity in/and Hegel, Heidegger, Marx, and Freud.* Madison, WI: University of Wisconsin Press, 1989

Freud, Sigmund. *The Interpretation of Dreams.* 1900. Rpt. in *The Basic Writings of Sigmund Freud.* Trans. Dr. A. A. Brill, Ed. New York: Modern Library, 1938. 180–549

Hayman, Ronald. *Arthur Miller.* London: Heinemann, 1970.

Heyen, William. "Arthur Miller's *Death of a Salesman* and the American Dream." *American Drama and Theatre in the Twentieth Century.* Ed. Alfred Weber and Siegfried Neuweiler. Gottingen: Vandenhoeck, 1975. Rpt. in *Modern Critical Interpretations: Arthur Miller's* Death of a Salesman. Ed. Harold Bloom. New York: Chelsea, 1988. 47–58

Innes, Christopher. "The Salesman on the Stage: A Study in the Social Influence of Drama." *English Studies in Canada* 3.3 (1977). Rpt. in *Modern Critical Interpretations: Arthur Miller s* Death of a Salesman. Ed. Harold Bloom. New York: Chelsea, 1988. 59–75.

Jackson, Esther Merle. "*Death of a Salesman:* Tragic Myth in the Modern Theatre." *CLA Journal* 7.1 (1963). Rpt. in *Modern Critical Interpretations: Arthur Miller s* Death of a Salesman. Ed. Harold Bloom. New York: Chelsea, 1988. 7–18.

Klein, George S. *Psychoanalytic Theory: An Exploration of Essentials.* New York: International Universities, 1976.

Laing, R. D. "Ontological Insecurity." *The Divided Self.* 1959. Baltimore, MD: Penguin, 1970. 39–61.

Merleau-Ponty, M. *Phenomenology of Perception.* 1945. Trans. Colin Smith. London: Routledge, 1962.

Miller, Arthur. *Death of a Salesman.* 1949. *The Portable Arthur Miller.* Ed. Harold Clurman. New York: Viking, 1971. 3–133.
——*The Theatre Essays of Arthur Miller.* Ed. Robert A. Martin. New York: Penguin, 1978.
Mitchell, Giles. "Living and Dying for the Ideal: A Study of Willy Loman's Narcissism." *Psychoanalytic Review* 77.3 (1990): 391–407.
Moss, Leonard. *Arthur Miller.* Boston, MA: Twayne, 1980.
Mottram, Eric. "Arthur Miller: The Development of a Political Dramatist in America." *American Theatre.* Ed. John Russell Brown and Bernard Harris. London: Arnold, 1967. Rpt. in *Arthur Miller: A Collection of Critical Essays.* Ed. Robert W. Corrigan. Englewood Cliffs, NJ: Prentice-Hall, 1969. 23–57.
Parker, Brian. "Point of View in Arthur Miller's *Death of a Salesman.*" *University of Toronto Quarterly* 35.2 (1966): 144–57. Rpt. in *Arthur Miller: A Collection of Critical Essays.* Ed. Robert W. Corrigan. Englewood Cliffs, NJ: Prentice-Hall, 1969. 95–109.

23.3 MENTAL HEALTH UNIT ESTABLISHED BY U.S.

New York Times, April 15th 1949

SURGEON GENERAL LEONARD A. SCHEELE today announced establishment of the National Institute of Mental Health of the Public Health Service.

Authority for this move was contained in an act of the Seventy-ninth Congress. The institute supplants the Division of Mental Hygiene and will have the same director, Dr. Robert H. Felix. Its aim will be to intensify efforts for the prevention, control and treatment of mental illness, which now accounts for the hospitalization of more than 600,000 patients.

The National Institute of Mental Health will continue the programs under the Mental Health Act of 1946 and will have the aid of the Advisory Mental Health Council set up under that act. This council consists of six authorities in mental health.

Mental health programs have been initiated in twenty-seven states and territories and have been expanded in twenty-four under the provisions of the 1946 act. A training program is also in progress, with grants to support courses in mental health specialties and stipends to graduate students.

Until construction is completed on its buildings in Bethesda, Md., the National Institute of Mental Health will have headquarters in the Federal Security Building in this city.

23.4 LET THE SALESMAN BEWARE—FREDRIC WERTHAM

New York Times, May 15th 1949

ARTHUR MILLER'S "DEATH OF A SALESMAN," which has received the Pulitzer Prize, the Drama Critics Circle award and the Antoinette Perry award, is being published this week in book form. It is the first play to become a Book-of-the-Month Club selection. What follows is a discussion between Mr. Miller and Fredric Wertham, a New York psychiatrist and author of the recent "Show of Violence," of the play's effect on audiences.

"YOU ought to read 'Death of a Salesman,' by Arthur Miller," I told my secretary. "It is really excellent. It is just like the life you see here in the clinic."

My secretary is a matter-of-fact girl. "If it is like what we see here every day in the clinic, why should I read it? Does he say why these people are that way, or what to do about it?"

"It is about the life of a salesman," I said. "That covers a lot of people."

"Well," my secretary retorted, "then I'd rather read about Alexander Botts in The Saturday Evening Post, and enjoy myself."

"You mean William Hazlett Upson's tractor salesman. As a matter of fact, I asked Upson, the sage of Middlebury, about Arthur Miller's play. He has studied salesmen for years. He is an expert on their psychology. He sees them as enthusiastic extroverts who constantly get slapped down and must have more courage than other people or they couldn't go on."

★ ★ ★

THE GREAT Danish critic Georg Brandes expressed the opinion that Shakespeare never wrote a drama for reading. Yet Shakespeare's plays—and nearly all great plays—are read. Dramatic literature has a special appeal that is profound and enduring. Great plays touch upon the point of highest tension, the point where the individual and society meet, clash and unite. I do not believe that there is such a thing as a purely individual tragedy, either in the consultation room or on the stage. That is where questions arose in my mind about Arthur Miller's play.

"Death of a Salesman" is no longer just to play or just a book. It is a phenomenon. What is the basis of its universal success? The people have spoken. But have they listened? I have often wondered what would happen if Coleridge had a chance to answer John Livingston Lowes, or Ibsen, George Jean Nathan. A sort of "Critic Meets the Author." So I resolved to see Arthur Miller.

WHEN I saw 'Death of a Salesman,'" I told him, "there were at least three people right next to me who had tears in their eyes or really wept. Now I suppose that shows the play is realistic. But I think of you as a romantic of realism. Why do you think the people get so much pleasure out of a sad play?"

"I think that there are two reasons for that," Arthur Miller answered. "The first is that the play deals with, at bottom, a kind of insecurity that everyone is aware of but tries to put aside in his daily life. It is the insecurity, first of coming old age and possible uselessness, which is fundamental. But more important, it is the fear that one has lied to one's self over a period of years in relation to one's true identity and what one should be doing in the world. What the play does is to make the individual ask himself whether his rationalizations about himself are not leading him to an ultimate rendezvous with a dreadful reckoning."

"That is just what bothers me," I interrupted him. "The hero of your play has a false dream. He succeeds with it; he fails with it; he dies with it. But why did he have this dream? Isn't it true that he had to have a false dream in our society? You see I raise the question of the social implications of your play. Now there were some authors in the Thirties who tried to put 'social content' in whatever they wrote. They added it like an ingredient. Most of them didn't succeed because they didn't really feel it. They had what I call a 'sour Grapes-of-Wrath complex.' But you are different. You wrote 'Focus' and 'All My Sons.' Let me express the question this way: Here is a man who has a false idea. Here is a man who goes to pieces. Here is a family whose members torment one another. Does your play say why that is so?"

"There are two sources of the false notion of himself that Willy Loman has," Miller said thoughtfully. "One is the need that men have to project for themselves an efficient, successful, praiseworthy personality. This trait is operative in all systems and I think will probably always be so. In the specific American culture of today, this drive takes the form which society prescribes, namely the desirability of being a financial and social success. This is to be attained at all costs.

"Included among the costs is the washing away of the person's peculiar and individual propensities and talents, which in themselves may be healthy and productive, but which do not fit into what is generally conceived to be success. Everything is weighed according to how much it can be exchanged for in terms of money. At the same time there is the official religious ideology which on Sundays denies this kind of equation of humanity in terms of money and power. Between this ideal and the reality of life, the human being is pulled from two directly opposite directions."

"TO MY mind," I answered. "there are two kinds of suffering, the inescapable like death and aging, and the unnecessary which grows out of social conditions The inescapable we have to stand. The unnecessary we should be brave enough *not* to suffer. Your normal people lead such abnormal lives. Do you show us why?"

Arthur Miller replied, "'Social content' is most often little more than the author's disguised opinion. What I attempt to see is the individual in his totality. The social significance of my play is probably this: Man is happiest when he is a giver. The salesman, not as a commercial group, but as a social type engaged in many different careers, is a man who produces nothing, has creative contact with no object, and is in truth the epitome of the taker, the one who deals in objects and gets more out than he could conceivably ever put in."

"In other words," I interrupted. "while we live in a world which says *caveat emptor* (let the buyer beware), the social message of this play is *caveat vendor* (let the salesman beware). But in your play Charlie says: 'The only thing you got in this world is what you can sell'."

"My opinion," said Miller, "is that my meaning could never be stated by any character of my devising as well as it is stated in the tears of the audience. Were my play merely a description of an unavoidable catastrophe, the effect would be totally deadened, and an audience for it could scarcely be found. The play makes the individual realize that his apprehensions about himself are shared by nearly everyone."

"Don't you think," I said, "that the audience, instead of 'having apprehensions about themselves,' should have fears about the social conditions in which these apprehensions grow? To me the great lines of your play, which reminded me of Gorky's 'Lower Depths,' are spoken by the mother: 'He is a human being, and a terrible thing is happening to him. So attention must be paid.' I believe that every great play has a social message, and the message of your play is 'So Attention Must Be Paid'."

Miller remonstrated: "You are leaving out what to me is one of the most important sectors of the play, the character of the older son Biff, who rejects the attitude of life represented by his father and insists that his future stability and sanity lie in production, in achieving a connection with the creation of things rather than attempting to live by manipulation of things. I believe that one of the basic things from which all Willy Lomans suffer is that their inner need to create and to give is contradicted by their way of life. I think that when the audience weeps, they are weeping for themselves."

"Yes," I countered, "but isn't that because they identify themselves with these characters who they think suffer from an inevitable fate? The question is, do they realize that it is up to them not only to sympathize and to deplore the evil that oppresses such families in our society, but to fight it?"

"I could not honestly say what precisely the audience carries away from my play. As a playwright I show the audience something which they have seen every day of their lives, but which they have never recognized. When you call me a romantic of realism, you are right. I believe that great art has always dealt not with the exotic, the peculiar, the rarefied, but really with the commonplace, with the things and the emotions and the objects with which people must live in their daily lives. I believe that my role as an artist is to present the truth of life as close to its entirety as I am able to. I don't want anybody walking out of the theatre and saying: 'That's what *he* thinks!'"

And so we were left with the old problem of participation of art, in art and through art, a problem which "Death of a Salesman" raises more insistently than any other recent play.

★ ★ ★

I SHALL tell my secretary again to read "Death of a Salesman." I shall read to her the lines spoken by the hero's older son Biff: "Why am I trying to become what I don't want to be? . . . When all I want is out there, waiting for me the minute I say I know who I am." I'm only afraid she will answer me: "How do you know that this is not another false dream?"

23.5 PRODUCTION PHOTO FROM *DEATH OF A SALESMAN*

Lee J. Cobb as Willy Loman in Elia Kazan's 1949 production of Arthur Miller's *Death of a Salesman.* New York psychiatrist Fredric Wertham said Miller's play, written at a time when the theories of psychoanalysis were prominently seen on and off stage, was "just like the life you see here in the clinic." Indeed, as Miller put it, "the new social dramatist, if he is to do his work, must be an even deeper psychologist than those of the past" (*Theatre Essays* 62).

Source: Photo by W. Eugene Smith/The LIFE Picture Collection/Getty Images. Illustrator Don Freeman

23.6 NEWS ILLUSTRATION OF *DEATH OF A SALESMAN*

Original caption: "L to R: Arthur Kennedy, Lee J. Cobb and Mildred Dumnock in a symbolical scene in 'Death of a Salesman,' Arthur Miller's new play that tells the story of an ordinary Brooklyn salesman (portrayed by Mr Cobb), who realizes in his middle-age that the high hopes and dreams that he had for himself and his family have been frustrated by reality. The play will open at the Morosco Theatre this Thursday night."

Source: From the *New York Times* February 6th 1949. Permission to reproduce granted by Roy Freeman

23.7 *DEATH OF A SALESMAN*—ARTHUR MILLER

LIST OF CHARACTERS

WILLY LOMAN
LINDA
BIFF
HAPPY
BERNARD
THE WOMAN
CHARLEY
UNCLE BEN
HOWARD WAGNER
JENNY
STANLEY
MISS FORSYTHE
LETTA

SCENE: *The action takes place in* WILLY LOMAN*'s house and yard and in various places he visits in the New York and Boston of today.*

★

Act 1

SCENE: *A melody is heard, played upon a flute. It is small and fine, telling of grass and trees and the horizon. The curtain rises.*

Before us is the Salesman's house. We are aware of towering, angular shapes behind it, surrounding it on all sides. Only the blue light of the sky falls upon the house and forestage; the surrounding area shows an angry glow of orange. As more light appears, we see a solid vault of apartment houses around the small, fragile-seeming home. An air of the dream clings to the place, a dream rising out of reality. The kitchen at center seems actual enough, for there is a kitchen table with three chairs, and a refrigerator. But no other fixtures are seen. At the back of the kitchen there is a draped entrance, which leads to the living room. To the right of the kitchen, on a level raised two feet, is a bedroom furnished only with a brass bedstead and a straight chair. On a shelf over the bed a silver athletic trophy stands. A window opens onto the apartment house at the side.

Behind the kitchen, on a level raised six and a half feet, is the boys' bedroom, at present barely visible. Two beds are dimly seen, and at the back of the room a dormer window. (This bedroom is above the unseen living room.) At the left a stairway curves up to it from the kitchen.

The entire setting is wholly or, in some places, partially transparent. The roof-line of the house is one-dimensional; under and over it we see the apartment buildings. Before the house lies an apron, curving beyond the forestage into the orchestra. This forward area serves as the back yard as well as the locale of all WILLY*'s imaginings and of his city scenes. Whenever the action is in the present the actors observe the imaginary wall-lines, entering the house only through its door at the left. But in the scenes of the past these boundaries are broken, and characters enter or leave a room by stepping "through" a wall onto the forestage.*

From the right, WILLY LOMAN*, the Salesman, enters, carrying two large sample cases. The flute plays on. He hears but is not aware of it. He is past sixty years of age, dressed quietly. Even as he crosses the stage to the doorway of the house, his exhaustion is apparent. He unlocks the door, comes into the kitchen, and thankfully lets his burden down, feeling the soreness of his palms. A word-sigh escapes his lips—it might be*

"Oh, boy, oh, boy." He closes the door, then carries his cases out into the living room, through the draped kitchen doorway.

LINDA, his wife, has stirred in her bed at the right. She gets out and puts on a robe, listening. Most often jovial, she has developed an iron repression of her exceptions to WILLY's behavior—she more than loves him, she admires him, as though his mercurial nature, his temper, his massive dreams and little cruelties, served her only as sharp reminders of the turbulent longings within him, longings which she shares but lacks the temperament to utter and follow to their end.

LINDA (*hearing* WILLY *outside the bedroom, calls with some trepidation*).
Willy!

WILLY. It's all right. I came back.

LINDA. Why? What happened? (*Slight pause.*) Did something happen, Willy?

WILLY. No, nothing happened.

LINDA. You didn't smash the car, did you?

WILLY (*with casual irritation*). I said nothing happened. Didn't you hear me?

LINDA. Don't you feel well?

WILLY. I'm tired to the death. (*The flute has faded away. He sits on the bed beside her, a little numb.*) I couldn't make it. I just couldn't make it, Linda.

LINDA (*very carefully, delicately*). Where were you all day? You look terrible.

WILLY. I got as far as a little above Yonkers. I stopped for a cup of coffee. Maybe it was the coffee.

LINDA. What?

WILLY (*after a pause*). I suddenly couldn't drive any more. The car kept going off onto the shoulder, y'know?

LINDA (*helpfully*). Oh. Maybe it was the steering again. I don't think Angelo knows the Studebaker.

WILLY. No, it's me, it's me. Suddenly I realize I'm goin' sixty miles an hour and I don't remember the last five minutes. I'm—I can't seem to—keep my mind to it.

LINDA. Maybe it's your glasses. You never went for your new glasses.

WILLY. No, I see everything. I came back ten miles an hour. It took me nearly four hours from Yonkers.

LINDA (*resigned*). Well, you'll just have to take a rest, Willy, you can't continue this way.

WILLY. I just got back from Florida.

LINDA. But you didn't rest your mind. Your mind is overactive, and the mind is what counts, dear.

WILLY. I'll start out in the morning. Maybe I'll feel better in the morning. (*She is taking off his shoes.*) These goddam arch supports are killing me.

LINDA. Take an aspirin. Should I get you an aspirin? It'll soothe you.

WILLY (*with wonder*). I was driving along, you understand? And I was fine. I was even observing the scenery. You can imagine, me looking at scenery, on the road every week of my life. But it's so beautiful up there, Linda, the trees are so thick, and the sun is warm. I opened the windshield and just let the warm air bathe over me. And then all of a sudden I'm goin' off the road! I'm tellin' ya, I absolutely forgot I was driving. If I'd've gone the other way over the white line I might've killed somebody. So I went on again—and five minutes later I'm dreamin' again, and I nearly . . . (*He presses two fingers against his eyes.*) I have such thoughts, I have such strange thoughts.

LINDA. Willy, dear. Talk to them again. There's no reason why you can't work in New York.

WILLY. They don't need me in New York. I'm the New England man. I'm vital in New England.

LINDA. But you're sixty years old. They can't expect you to keep traveling every week.

WILLY. I'll have to send a wire to Portland. I'm supposed to see Brown and Morrison tomorrow morning at ten o'clock to show the line. Goddammit, I could sell them! (*He starts putting on his jacket.*)

LINDA (*taking the jacket from him*). Why don't you go down to the place tomorrow and tell Howard you've simply got to work in New York? You're too accommodating, dear.

WILLY. If old man Wagner was alive I'd a been in charge of New York now! That man was a prince, he was a masterful man. But that boy of his, that Howard, he don't appreciate. When I went north the first time, the Wagner Company didn't know where New England was!

LINDA. Why don't you tell those things to Howard, dear?

WILLY (*encouraged*). I will, I definitely will. Is there any cheese?

LINDA. I'll make you a sandwich.

WILLY. No, go to sleep. I'll take some milk. I'll be up right away. The boys in?

LINDA. They're sleeping. Happy took Biff on a date tonight.

WILLY (*interested*). That so?

LINDA. It was so nice to see them shaving together, one behind the other, in the bathroom. And going out together. You notice? The whole house smells of shaving lotion.

WILLY. Figure it out. Work a lifetime to pay off a house. You finally own it, and there's nobody to live in it.

LINDA. Well, dear, life is a casting off. It's always that way.

WILLY. No, no, some people—some people accomplish something. Did Biff say anything after I went this morning?

LINDA. You shouldn't have criticized him, Willy, especially after he just got off the train. You mustn't lose your temper with him.

WILLY. When the hell did I lose my temper? I simply asked him if he was making any money. Is that a criticism?

LINDA. But, dear, how could he make any money?

WILLY (*worried and angered*). There's such an undercurrent in him. He became a moody man. Did he apologize when I left this morning?

LINDA. He was crestfallen, Willy. You know how he admires you. I think if he finds himself, then you'll both be happier and not fight any more.

WILLY. How can he find himself on a farm? Is that a life? A farm hand? In the beginning, when he was young, I thought, well, a young man, it's good for him to tramp around, take a lot of different jobs. But it's more than ten years now and he has yet to make thirty-five dollars a week!

LINDA. He's finding himself, Willy.

WILLY. Not finding yourself at the age of thirty-four is a disgrace!

LINDA. Shh!

WILLY. The trouble is he's lazy, goddammit!

LINDA. Willy, please!

WILLY. Biff is a lazy bum!

LINDA. They're sleeping. Get something to eat. Go on down.

WILLY. Why did he come home? I would like to know what brought him home.

LINDA. I don't know. I think he's still lost, Willy. I think he's very lost.

WILLY. Biff Loman is lost. In the greatest country in the world a young man with such—personal attractiveness, gets lost. And such a hard worker. There's one thing about Biff—he's not lazy.

LINDA. Never.

WILLY (*with pity and resolve*). I'll see him in the morning; I'll have a nice talk with him. I'll get him a job selling. He could be big in no time. My God! Remember how they used to follow him around in high school? When he smiled at one of them their faces lit up. When he walked down the street . . . (*He loses himself in reminiscences.*)

LINDA (*trying to bring him out of it*). Willy, dear, I got a new kind of American-type cheese today. It's whipped.

WILLY. Why do you get American when I like Swiss?

LINDA. I just thought you'd like a change . . .

WILLY. I don't want a change! I want Swiss cheese. Why am I always being contradicted?

LINDA (*with a covering laugh*). I thought it would be a surprise.

WILLY. Why don't you open a window in here, for God's sake?

LINDA (*with infinite patience*). They're all open, dear.

WILLY. The way they boxed us in here. Bricks and windows, windows and bricks.

LINDA. We should've bought the land next door.

WILLY. The street is lined with cars. There's not a breath of fresh air in the neighborhood. The grass don't grow any more, you can't raise a carrot in the back yard. They should've had a law against apartment houses. Remember those two beautiful elm trees out there? When I and Biff hung the swing between them?

LINDA. Yeah, like being a million miles from the city.

WILLY. They should've arrested the builder for cutting those down. They massacred the neighborhood. (*Lost.*) More and more I think of those days, Linda. This time of year it was lilac and wisteria. And then the peonies would come out, and the daffodils. What fragrance in this room!

LINDA. Well, after all, people had to move somewhere.

WILLY. No, there's more people now.

LINDA. I don't think there's more people. I think . . .

WILLY. There's more people! That's what's ruining this country! Population is getting out of control. The competition is maddening! Smell the stink from that apartment house! And another one on the other side . . . How can they whip cheese?

On WILLY*'s last line,* BIFF *and* HAPPY *raise themselves up in their beds, listening.*

LINDA. Go down, try it. And be quiet.

WILLY (*turning to* LINDA, *guiltily*). You're not worried about me, are you, sweetheart?

BIFF. What's the matter?

HAPPY. Listen!

LINDA. You've got too much on the ball to worry about.

WILLY. You're my foundation and my support, Linda.

LINDA. Just try to relax, dear. You make mountains out of molehills.

WILLY. I won't fight with him any more. If he wants to go back to Texas, let him go.

LINDA. He'll find his way.

WILLY. Sure. Certain men just don't get started till later in life. Like Thomas Edison, I think. Or B. F.

Goodrich. One of them was deaf. (*He starts for the bedroom doorway.*) I'll put my money on Biff.

LINDA. And Willy—if it's warm Sunday we'll drive in the country. And we'll open the windshield, and take lunch.

WILLY. No, the windshields don't open on the new cars.

LINDA. But you opened it today.

WILLY. Me? I didn't. (*He stops.*) Now isn't that peculiar! Isn't that a remarkable . . . (*He breaks off in amazement and fright as the flute is heard distantly.*)

LINDA. What, darling?

WILLY. That is the most remarkable thing.

LINDA. What, dear?

WILLY. I was thinking of the Chevvy. (*Slight pause.*) Nineteen twenty-eight . . . when I had that red Chevvy . . . (*Breaks off.*) That funny? I coulda sworn I was driving that Chevvy today.

LINDA. Well, that's nothing. Something must've reminded you.

WILLY. Remarkable. Ts. Remember those days? The way Biff used to simonize that car? The dealer refused to believe there was eighty thousand miles on it. (*He shakes his head.*) Heh! (*To* LINDA.) Close your eyes, I'll be right up. (*He walks out of the bedroom.*)

HAPPY (*to* BIFF). Jesus, maybe he smashed up the car again!

LINDA (*calling after* WILLY). Be careful on the stairs, dear! The cheese is on the middle shelf. (*She turns, goes over to the bed, takes his jacket, and goes out of the bedroom.*)

Light has risen on the boys' room. Unseen, WILLY *is heard talking to himself; "Eighty thousand miles," and a little laugh.* BIFF *gets out of bed, comes downstage a bit, and stands attentively.* BIFF *is two years older than his brother* HAPPY, *well built, but in these days bears a worn air and seems less self-assured. He has succeeded less, and his dreams are stronger and less acceptable than* HAPPY'*s.* HAPPY *is tall, powerfully made. Sexuality is like a visible color on him, or a scent that many women have discovered. He, like his brother, is lost, but in a different way, for he has never allowed himself to turn his face toward defeat and is thus more confused and hard-skinned, although seemingly more content.*

HAPPY (*getting out of bed*). He's going to get his license taken away if he keeps that up. I'm getting nervous about him, y'know, Biff?

BIFF. His eyes are going.

HAPPY. No, I've driven with him. He sees all right. He just doesn't keep his mind on it. I drove into the city with him last week. He stops at a green light and then it turns red and he goes. (*He laughs.*)

BIFF. Maybe he's color-blind.

HAPPY. Pop? Why he's got the finest eye for color in the business. You know that.

BIFF (*sitting down on his bed*). I'm going to sleep.

HAPPY. You're not still sour on Dad, are you, Biff?

BIFF. He's all right, I guess.

WILLY (*underneath them, in the living room*). Yes, sir, eighty thousand miles—eighty-two thousand!

BIFF. You smoking?

HAPPY (*holding out a pack of cigarettes*). Want one?

BIFF (*taking a cigarette*). I can never sleep when I smell it.

WILLY. What a simonizing job, heh!

HAPPY (*with deep sentiment*). Funny, Biff, y'know? Us sleeping in here again? The old beds. (*He pats his bed affectionately.*) All the talk that went across those beds, huh? Our whole lives.

BIFF. Yeah. Lotta dreams and plans.

HAPPY (*with a deep and masculine laugh*). About five hundred women would like to know what was said in this room. (*They share a soft laugh.*)

BIFF. Remember that big Betsy something—what the hell was her name—over on Bushwick Avenue?

HAPPY (*combing his hair*). With the collie dog!

BIFF. That's the one. I got you in there, remember?

HAPPY. Yeah, that was my first time—I think. Boy, there was a pig. (*They laugh, almost crudely.*) You taught me everything I know about women. Don't forget that.

BIFF. I bet you forgot how bashful you used to be. Especially with girls.

HAPPY. Oh, I still am, Biff.

BIFF. Oh, go on.

HAPPY. I just control it, that's all. I think I got less bashful and you got more so. What happened, Biff? Where's the old humor, the old confidence? (*He shakes* BIFF'*s knee.* BIFF *gets up and moves restlessly about the room.*) What's the matter?

BIFF. Why does Dad mock me all the time?

HAPPY. He's not mocking you, he . . .

BIFF. Everything I say there's a twist of mockery on his face. I can't get near him.

HAPPY. He just wants you to make good, that's all. I wanted to talk to you about Dad for a long time, Biff. Something's—happening to him. He—talks to himself.

BIFF. I noticed that this morning. But he always mumbled.

HAPPY. But not so noticeable. It got so embarrassing I sent him to Florida. And you know something? Most of the time he's talking to you.

BIFF. What's he say about me?

HAPPY. I can't make it out.

BIFF. What's he say about me?

HAPPY. I think the fact that you're not settled, that you're still kind of up in the air . . .

BIFF. There's one or two other things depressing him, Happy.

HAPPY. What do you mean?

BIFF. Never mind. Just don't lay it all to me.

HAPPY. But I think if you just got started—I mean—is there any future for you out there?

BIFF. I tell ya, Hap, I don't know what the future is. I don't know—what I'm supposed to want.

HAPPY. What do you mean?

BIFF. Well, I spent six or seven years after high school trying to work myself up. Shipping clerk, salesman, business of one kind or another. And it's a measly manner of existence. To get on that subway on the hot mornings in summer. To devote your whole life to keeping stock, or making phone calls, or selling or buying. To suffer fifty weeks of the year for the sake of a two-week vacation, when all you really desire is to be outdoors, with your shirt off. And always to have to get ahead of the next fella. And still—that's how you build a future.

HAPPY. Well, you really enjoy it on a farm? Are you content out there?

BIFF (*with rising agitation*). Hap, I've had twenty or thirty different kinds of jobs since I left home before the war, and it always turns out the same. I just realized it lately. In Nebraska when I herded cattle, and the Dakotas, and Arizona, and now in Texas. It's why I came home now, I guess, because I realized it. This farm I work on, it's spring there now, see? And they've got about fifteen new colts. There's nothing more inspiring or—beautiful than the sight of a mare and a new colt. And it's cool there now, see? Texas is cool now, and it's spring. And whenever spring comes to where I am, I suddenly get the feeling, my God, I'm not gettin' anywhere! What the hell am I doing, playing around with horses, twenty-eight dollars a week! I'm thirty-four years old, I oughta be makin' my future. That's when I come running home. And now, I get here, and I don't know what to do with myself. (*After a pause.*) I've always made a point of not wasting my life, and everytime I come back here I know that all I've done is to waste my life.

HAPPY. You're a poet, you know that, Biff? You're a—you're an idealist!

BIFF. No, I'm mixed up very bad. Maybe I oughta get married. Maybe I oughta get stuck into something. Maybe that's my trouble. I'm like a boy. I'm not married, I'm not in business, I just— I'm like a boy. Are you content, Hap? You're a success, aren't you? Are you content?

HAPPY. Hell, no!

BIFF. Why? You're making money, aren't you?

HAPPY (*moving about with energy, expressiveness*). All I can do now is wait for the merchandise manager to die. And suppose I get to be merchandise manager? He's a good friend of mine, and he just built a terrific estate on Long Island. And he lived there about two months and sold it, and now he's building another one. He can't enjoy it once it's finished. And I know that's just what I would do. I don't know what the hell I'm workin' for. Sometimes I sit in my apartment—all alone. And I think of the rent I'm paying. And it's crazy. But then, it's what I always wanted. My own apartment, a car, and plenty of women. And still, goddammit, I'm lonely.

BIFF (*with enthusiasm*). Listen, why don't you come out West with me?

HAPPY. You and I, heh?

BIFF. Sure, maybe we could buy a ranch. Raise cattle, use our muscles. Men built like we are should be working out in the open.

HAPPY (*avidly*). The Loman Brothers, heh?

BIFF (*with vast affection*). Sure, we'd be known all over the counties!

HAPPY (*enthralled*). That's what I dream about, Biff. Sometimes I want to just rip my clothes off in the middle of the store and outbox that goddam merchandise manager. I mean I can outbox, outrun, and outlift anybody in that store, and I have to take orders from those common, petty sons-of-bitches till I can't stand it any more.

BIFF. I'm tellin' you, kid, if you were with me I'd be happy out there.

HAPPY (*enthused*). See, Biff, everybody around me is so false that I'm constantly lowering my ideals . . .

BIFF. Baby, together we'd stand up for one another, we'd have someone to trust.

HAPPY. If I were around you . . .

BIFF. Hap, the trouble is we weren't brought up to grub for money. I don't know how to do it.

HAPPY. Neither can I!

BIFF. Then let's go!

HAPPY. The only thing is—what can you make out there?

BIFF. But look at your friend. Builds an estate and then hasn't the peace of mind to live in it.

HAPPY. Yeah, but when he walks into the store the waves part in front of him. That's fifty-two thousand dollars a year coming through the revolving door, and I got more in my pinky finger than he's got in his head.

BIFF. Yeah, but you just said . . .

HAPPY. I gotta show some of those pompous, self-important executives over there that Hap Loman can make the grade. I want to walk into the store the way he walks in. Then I'll go with you, Biff. We'll be together yet, I swear. But take those two we had tonight. Now weren't they gorgeous creatures?

BIFF. Yeah, yeah, most gorgeous I've had in years.

HAPPY. I get that any time I want, Biff. Whenever I feel disgusted. The only trouble is, it gets like bowling or something. I just keep knockin' them over and it doesn't mean anything. You still run around a lot?

BIFF. Naa. I'd like to find a girl—steady, somebody with substance.

HAPPY. That's what I long for.

BIFF. Go on! You'd never come home.

HAPPY. I would! Somebody with character, with resistance! Like Mom, y'know? You're gonna call me a bastard when I tell you this. That girl Charlotte I was with tonight is engaged to be married in five weeks. (*He tries on his new hat.*)

BIFF. No kiddin'!

HAPPY. Sure, the guy's in line for the vice-presidency of the store. I don't know what gets into me, maybe I just have an over-developed sense of competition or something, but I went and ruined her, and furthermore I can't get rid of her. And he's the third executive I've done that to. Isn't that a crummy characteristic? And to top it all, I go to their weddings! (*Indignantly, but laughing.*) Like I'm not supposed to take bribes. Manufacturers offer me a hundred-dollar bill now and then to throw an order their way. You know how honest I am, but it's like this girl, see. I hate myself for it. Because I don't want the girl, and, still, I take it and—I love it!

BIFF. Let's go to sleep.

HAPPY. I guess we didn't settle anything, heh?

BIFF. I just got one idea that I think I'm going to try.

HAPPY. What's that?

BIFF. Remember Bill Oliver?

HAPPY. Sure, Oliver is very big now. You want to work for him again?

BIFF. No, but when I quit he said something to me. He put his arm on my shoulder, and he said, "Biff, if you ever need anything, come to me."

HAPPY. I remember that. That sounds good.

BIFF. I think I'll go to see him. If I could get ten thousand or even seven or eight thousand dollars I could buy a beautiful ranch.

HAPPY. I bet he'd back you. 'Cause he thought highly of you, Biff. I mean, they all do. You're well liked, Biff. That's why I say to come back here, and we both have the apartment. And I'm tellin' you, Biff, any babe you want . . .

BIFF. No, with a ranch I could do the work I like and still be something. I just wonder though. I wonder if Oliver still thinks I stole that carton of basketballs.

HAPPY. Oh, he probably forgot that long ago. It's almost ten years. You're too sensitive. Anyway, he didn't really fire you.

BIFF. Well, I think he was going to. I think that's why I quit. I was never sure whether he knew or not. I know he thought the world of me, though. I was the only one he'd let lock up the place.

WILLY (*below*). You gonna wash the engine, Biff?

HAPPY. Shh!

BIFF looks at HAPPY, who is gazing down, listening. WILLY is mumbling in the parlor.

HAPPY. You hear that?

They listen. WILLY laughs warmly.

BIFF (*growing angry*). Doesn't he know Mom can hear that?

WILLY. Don't get your sweater dirty, Biff!

A look of pain crosses BIFF's face.

HAPPY. Isn't that terrible? Don't leave again, will you? You'll find a job here. You gotta stick around. I don't know what to do about him, it's getting embarrassing.

WILLY. What a simonizing job!

BIFF. Mom's hearing that!

WILLY. No kiddin', Biff, you got a date? Wonderful!

HAPPY. Go on to sleep. But talk to him in the morning, will you?

BIFF (*reluctantly getting into bed*). With her in the house. Brother!

HAPPY (*getting into bed*). I wish you'd have a good talk with him.

The light on their room begins to fade.

BIFF (*to himself in bed*). That selfish, stupid . . .

HAPPY. Sh . . . Sleep, Biff.

Their light is out. Well before they have finished speaking, WILLY's form is dimly seen below in the darkened kitchen. He opens the refrigerator, searches in there, and takes out a bottle of milk. The apartment houses are fading out, and the entire house and surroundings become covered with leaves. Music insinuates itself as the leaves appear.

WILLY. Just wanna be careful with those girls, Biff, that's all. Don't make any promises. No promises of any kind. Because a girl, y'know, they always believe what you tell 'em, and you're very young, Biff, you're too young to be talking seriously to girls.

Light rises on the kitchen. WILLY, talking, shuts the refrigerator door and comes downstage to the kitchen table. He pours milk into a glass. He is totally immersed in himself, smiling faintly.

WILLY. Too young entirely, Biff. You want to watch your schooling first. Then when you're all set, there'll be plenty of girls for a boy like you. (*He smiles broadly at a kitchen chair.*) That so? The girls pay for you? (*He laughs.*) Boy, you must really be makin' a hit.

WILLY *is gradually addressing—physically—a point offstage, speaking through the wall of the kitchen, and his voice has been rising in volume to that of a normal conversation.*

WILLY. I been wondering why you polish the car so careful. Ha! Don't leave the hubcaps, boys. Get the chamois to the hubcaps. Happy, use newspaper on the windows, it's the easiest thing. Show him how to do it, Biff! You see, Happy? Pad it up, use it like a pad. That's it, that's it, good work. You're doin' all right, Hap. (*He pauses, then nods in approbation for a few seconds, then looks upward.*) Biff, first thing we gotta do when we get time is clip that big branch over the house. Afraid it's gonna fall in a storm and hit the roof. Tell you what. We get a rope and sling her around, and then we climb up there with a couple of saws and take her down. Soon as you finish the car, boys, I wanna see ya. I got a surprise for you, boys.

BIFF (*offstage*). Whatta ya got, Dad?

WILLY. No, you finish first. Never leave a job till you're finished—remember that. (*Looking toward the "big trees."*) Biff, up in Albany I saw a beautiful hammock. I think I'll buy it next trip, and we'll hang it right between those two elms. Wouldn't that be something? Just swingin' there under those branches. Boy, that would be . . .

YOUNG BIFF *and* YOUNG HAPPY *appear from the direction* WILLY *was addressing.* HAPPY *carries rags and a pail of water.* BIFF, *wearing a sweater with a block "S," carries a football.*

BIFF (*pointing in the direction of the car offstage*). How's that, Pop, professional?

WILLY. Terrific. Terrific job, boys. Good work, Biff.

HAPPY. Where's the surprise, Pop?

WILLY. In the back seat of the car.

HAPPY. Boy! (*He runs off.*)

BIFF. What is it, Dad? Tell me, what'd you buy?

WILLY (*laughing, cuffs him*). Never mind, something I want you to have.

BIFF (*turns and starts off*). What is it, Hap?

HAPPY (*offstage*). It's a punching bag!

BIFF. Oh, Pop!

WILLY. It's got Gene Tunney's signature on it!

HAPPY *runs onstage with a punching bag.*

BIFF. Gee, how'd you know we wanted a punching bag?

WILLY. Well, it's the finest thing for the timing.

HAPPY (*lies down on his back and pedals with his feet*). I'm losing weight, you notice, Pop?

WILLY (*to* HAPPY). Jumping rope is good too.

BIFF. Did you see the new football I got?

WILLY (*examining the ball*). Where'd you get a new ball?

BIFF. The coach told me to practice my passing.

WILLY. That so? And he gave you the ball, heh?

BIFF. Well, I borrowed it from the locker room. (*He laughs confidentially.*)

WILLY (*laughing with him at the theft*). I want you to return that.

HAPPY. I told you he wouldn't like it!

BIFF (*angrily*). Well, I'm bringing it back!

WILLY (*stopping the incipient argument, to* HAPPY). Sure, he's gotta practice with a regulation ball, doesn't he? (*To* BIFF.) Coach'll probably congratulate you on your initiative!

BIFF. Oh, he keeps congratulating my initiative all the time, Pop.

WILLY. That's because he likes you. If somebody else took that ball there'd be an uproar. So what's the report, boys, what's the report?

BIFF. Where'd you go this time, Dad? Gee we were lonesome for you.

WILLY (*pleased, puts an arm around each boy and they come down to the apron*). Lonesome, heh?

BIFF. Missed you every minute.

WILLY. Don't say? Tell you a secret, boys. Don't breathe it to a soul. Someday I'll have my own business, and I'll never have to leave home any more.

HAPPY. Like Uncle Charley, heh?

WILLY. Bigger than Uncle Charley! Because Charley is not—liked. He's liked, but he's not—well liked.

BIFF. Where'd you go this time, Dad?

WILLY. Well, I got on the road, and I went north to Providence. Met the Mayor.

BIFF. The Mayor of Providence!

WILLY. He was sitting in the hotel lobby.

BIFF. What'd he say?

WILLY. He said, "Morning!" And I said, "Morning!" And I said, "You got a fine city here, Mayor." And then he had coffee with me. And then I went to Waterbury. Waterbury is a fine city. Big clock city, the famous Waterbury clock. Sold a nice bill there. And then Boston—Boston is the cradle of the Revolution. A fine city. And a couple of other towns in Mass., and on to Portland and Bangor and straight home!

BIFF. Gee, I'd love to go with you sometime, Dad.

WILLY. Soon as summer comes.

HAPPY. Promise?

WILLY. You and Hap and I, and I'll show you all the towns. America is full of beautiful towns and fine, upstanding people. And they know me, boys, they know me up and down New England. The finest people. And when I bring you fellas up, there'll be open sesame for all of us, 'cause one thing, boys: I have friends. I can park my car in any street in New England, and the cops protect it like their own. This summer, heh?

BIFF AND HAPPY (*together*). Yeah! You bet!

WILLY. We'll take our bathing suits.

HAPPY. We'll carry your bags, Pop!

WILLY. Oh, won't that be something! Me comin' into the Boston stores with you boys carryin' my bags. What a sensation!

BIFF *is prancing around, practicing passing the ball.*

WILLY. You nervous, Biff, about the game?

BIFF. Not if you're gonna be there.

WILLY. What do they say about you in school, now that they made you captain?

HAPPY. There's a crowd of girls behind him everytime the classes change.

BIFF (*taking* WILLY*'s hand*). This Saturday, Pop, this Saturday—just for you, I'm going to break through for a touchdown.

HAPPY. You're supposed to pass.

BIFF. I'm takin' one play for Pop. You watch me, Pop, and when I take off my helmet, that means I'm breakin' out. Then you watch me crash through that line!

WILLY (*kisses* BIFF). Oh, wait'll I tell this in Boston!

BERNARD *enters in knickers. He is younger than* BIFF, *earnest and loyal, a worried boy.*

BERNARD. Biff, where are you? You're supposed to study with me today.

WILLY. Hey, looka Bernard. What're you lookin' so anemic about, Bernard?

BERNARD. He's gotta study, Uncle Willy. He's got Regents next week.

HAPPY (*tauntingly, spinning* BERNARD *around*). Let's box, Bernard!

BERNARD. Biff! (*He gets away from* HAPPY.) Listen, Biff, I heard Mr. Birnbaum say that if you don't start studyin' math he's gonna flunk you, and you won't graduate. I heard him!

WILLY. You better study with him, Biff. Go ahead now.

BERNARD. I heard him!

BIFF. Oh, Pop, you didn't see my sneakers! (*He holds up a foot for* WILLY *to look at.*)

WILLY. Hey, that's a beautiful job of printing!

BERNARD (*wiping his glasses*). Just because he printed University of Virginia on his sneakers doesn't mean they've got to graduate him, Uncle Willy!

WILLY (*angrily*). What're you talking about? With scholarships to three universities they're gonna flunk him?

BERNARD. But I heard Mr. Birnbaum say . . .

WILLY. Don't be a pest, Bernard! (*To his boys.*) What an anemic!

BERNARD. Okay, I'm waiting for you in my house, Biff.

BERNARD *goes off. The* LOMANS *laugh.*

WILLY. Bernard is not well liked, is he?

BIFF. He's liked, but he's not well liked.

HAPPY. That's right, Pop.

WILLY. That's just what I mean. Bernard can get the best marks in school, y'understand, but when he gets out in the business world, y'understand, you are going to be five times ahead of him. That's why I thank Almighty God you're both built like Adonises. Because the man who makes an appearance in the business world, the man who creates personal interest, is the man who gets ahead. Be liked and you will never want. You take me, for instance. I never have to wait in line to see a buyer. "Willy Loman is here!" That's all they have to know, and I go right through.

BIFF. Did you knock them dead, Pop?

WILLY. Knocked 'em cold in Providence, slaughtered 'em in Boston.

HAPPY (*on his back, pedaling again*). I'm losing weight, you notice, Pop?

LINDA *enters as of old, a ribbon in her hair, carrying a basket of washing.*

LINDA (*with youthful energy*). Hello, dear!

WILLY. Sweetheart!

LINDA. How'd the Chevvy run?

WILLY. Chevrolet, Linda, is the greatest car ever built. (*To the boys.*) Since when do you let your mother carry wash up the stairs?

BIFF. Grab hold there, boy!

HAPPY. Where to, Mom?

LINDA. Hang them up on the line. And you better go down to your friends, Biff. The cellar is full of boys. They don't know what to do with themselves.

BIFF. Ah, when Pop comes home they can wait!

WILLY (*laughs appreciatively*). You better go down and tell them what to do, Biff.

BIFF. I think I'll have them sweep out the furnace room.

WILLY. Good work, Biff.

BIFF (*goes through wall-line of kitchen to doorway at back and calls down*). Fellas! Everybody sweep out the furnace room! I'll be right down!

VOICES. All right! Okay, Biff.

BIFF. George and Sam and Frank, come out back! We're hangin' up the wash! Come on, Hap, on the double! (*He and* HAPPY *carry out the basket.*)

LINDA. The way they obey him!

WILLY. Well, that's training, the training. I'm tellin' you, I was sellin' thousands and thousands, but I had to come home.

LINDA. Oh, the whole block'll be at that game. Did you sell anything?

WILLY. I did five hundred gross in Providence and seven hundred gross in Boston.

LINDA. No! Wait a minute. I've got a pencil. (*She pulls pencil and paper out of her apron pocket.*) That makes your commission . . . Two hundred—my God! Two hundred and twelve dollars!

WILLY. Well, I didn't figure it yet, but . . .

LINDA. How much did you do?

WILLY. Well, I—I did—about a hundred and eighty gross in Providence. Well, no—it came to—roughly two hundred gross on the whole trip.

LINDA (*without hesitation*). Two hundred gross. That's . . . (*She figures.*)

WILLY. The trouble was that three of the stores were half-closed for inventory in Boston. Otherwise I woulda broke records.

LINDA. Well, it makes seventy dollars and some pennies. That's very good.

WILLY. What do we owe?

LINDA. Well, on the first there's sixteen dollars on the refrigerator . . .

WILLY. Why sixteen?

LINDA. Well, the fan belt broke, so it was a dollar eighty.

WILLY. But it's brand new.

LINDA. Well, the man said that's the way it is. Till they work themselves in, y'know.

They move through the wall-line into the kitchen.

WILLY. I hope we didn't get stuck on that machine.

LINDA. They got the biggest ads of any of them!

WILLY. I know, it's a fine machine. What else?

LINDA. Well, there's nine-sixty for the washing machine. And for the vacuum cleaner there's three and a half due on the fifteenth. Then the roof, you got twenty-one dollars remaining.

WILLY. It don't leak, does it?

LINDA. No, they did a wonderful job. Then you owe Frank for the carburetor.

WILLY. I'm not going to pay that man! That goddam Chevrolet, they ought to prohibit the manufacture of that car!

LINDA. Well, you owe him three and a half. And odds and ends, comes to around a hundred and twenty dollars by the fifteenth.

WILLY. A hundred and twenty dollars! My God, if business don't pick up I don't know what I'm gonna do!

LINDA. Well, next week you'll do better.

WILLY. Oh, I'll knock 'em dead next week. I'll go to Hartford. I'm very well liked in Hartford. You know, the trouble is, Linda, people don't seem to take to me.

They move onto the forestage.

LINDA. Oh, don't be foolish.

WILLY. I know it when I walk in. They seem to laugh at me.

LINDA. Why? Why would they laugh at you? Don't talk that way, Willy.

WILLY *moves to the edge of the stage.* LINDA *goes into the kitchen and starts to darn stockings.*

WILLY. I don't know the reason for it, but they just pass me by. I'm not noticed.

LINDA. But you're doing wonderful, dear. You're making seventy to a hundred dollars a week.

WILLY. But I gotta be at it ten, twelve hours a day. Other men—I don't know—they do it easier. I don't know why—I can't stop myself—I talk too much. A man oughta come in with a few words. One thing about Charley. He's a man of few words, and they respect him.

LINDA. You don't talk too much, you're just lively.

WILLY (*smiling*). Well, I figure, what the hell, life is short, a couple of jokes. (*To himself:*) I joke too much! (*The smile goes.*)

LINDA. Why? You're . . .

WILLY. I'm fat. I'm very—foolish to look at, Linda. I didn't tell you, but Christmas time I happened to be calling on F. H. Stewarts, and a salesman I know, as I was going in to see the buyer I heard him say something about—walrus. And I—I cracked him right across the face. I won't take that. I simply will not take that. But they do laugh at me. I know that.

LINDA. Darling . . .

WILLY. I gotta overcome it. I know I gotta overcome it. I'm not dressing to advantage, maybe.

LINDA. Willy, darling, you're the handsomest man in the world . . .

WILLY. Oh, no, Linda.

LINDA. To me you are. (*Slight pause.*) The handsomest.

From the darkness is heard the laughter of a woman. WILLY *doesn't turn to it, but it continues through* LINDA*'s lines.*

LINDA. And the boys, Willy. Few men are idolized by their children the way you are.

Music is heard as behind a scrim, to the left of the house; THE WOMAN, *dimly seen, is dressing.*

WILLY (*with great feeling*). You're the best there is. Linda, you're a pal, you know that? On the road—on the road I want to grab you sometimes and just kiss the life outa you.

The laughter is loud now, and he moves into a brightening area at the left, where THE WOMAN *has come from behind the scrim and is standing, putting on her hat, looking into a "mirror" and laughing.*

WILLY. 'Cause I get so lonely—especially when business is bad and there's nobody to talk to. I get the feeling that I'll never sell anything again, that I won't make a living for you, or a business, a business for the boys. (*He talks through* THE WOMAN*'s subsiding laughter;* THE WOMAN *primps at the "mirror."*) There's so much I want to make for . . .

THE WOMAN. Me? You didn't make me, Willy. I picked you.

WILLY (*pleased*). You picked me?

THE WOMAN (*who is quite proper-looking,* WILLY*'s* age). I did. I've been sitting at that desk watching all the salesmen go by, day in, day out. But you've got such a sense of humor, and we do have such a good time together, don't we?

WILLY. Sure, sure. (*He takes her in his arms.*) Why do you have to go now?

THE WOMAN. It's two o'clock . . .

WILLY. No, come on in! (*He pulls her.*)

THE WOMAN. . . . my sisters'll be scandalized. When'll you be back?

WILLY. Oh, two weeks about. Will you come up again?

THE WOMAN. Sure thing. You do make me laugh. It's good for me. (*She squeezes his arm, kisses him.*) And I think you're a wonderful man.

WILLY. You picked me, heh?

THE WOMAN. Sure. Because you're so sweet. And such a kidder.

WILLY. Well, I'll see you next time I'm in Boston.

THE WOMAN. I'll put you right through to the buyers.

WILLY (*slapping her bottom*). Right. Well, bottoms up!

THE WOMAN (*slaps him gently and laughs*). You just kill me, Willy. (*He suddenly grabs her and kisses her roughly.*) You kill me. And thanks for the stockings. I love a lot of stockings. Well, good night.

WILLY. Good night. And keep your pores open!

THE WOMAN. Oh, Willy!

THE WOMAN *bursts out laughing, and* LINDA*'s laughter blends in.* THE WOMAN *disappears into the dark. Now the area at the kitchen table brightens.* LINDA *is sitting where she was at the kitchen table, but now is mending a pair of her silk stockings.*

LINDA. You are, Willy. The handsomest man. You've got no reason to feel that . . .

WILLY (*coming out of* THE WOMAN*'s dimming area and going over to* LINDA). I'll make it all up to you, Linda, I'll . . .

LINDA. There's nothing to make up, dear. You're doing fine, better than . . .

WILLY (*noticing her mending*). What's that?

LINDA. Just mending my stockings. They're so expensive . . .

WILLY (*angrily, taking them from her*). I won't have you mending stockings in this house! Now throw them out!

LINDA *puts the stockings in her pocket.*

BERNARD (*entering on the run*). Where is he? If he doesn't study!

WILLY (*moving to the forestage, with great agitation*). You'll give him the answers!

BERNARD. I do, but I can't on a Regents! That's a state exam! They're liable to arrest me!

WILLY. Where is he? I'll whip him, I'll whip him!

LINDA. And he'd better give back that football, Willy, it's not nice.

WILLY. Biff! Where is he? Why is he taking everything?

LINDA. He's too rough with the girls, Willy. All the mothers are afraid of him!

WILLY. I'll whip him!

BERNARD. He's driving the car without a license!

THE WOMAN*'s laugh is heard.*

WILLY. Shut up!

LINDA. All the mothers . . .

WILLY. Shut up!

BERNARD (*backing quietly away and out*). Mr. Birnbaum says he's stuck up.

WILLY. Get outa here!

BERNARD. If he doesn't buckle down he'll flunk math! (*He goes off.*)

LINDA. He's right, Willy, you've gotta . . .

WILLY (*exploding at her*). There's nothing the matter with him! You want him to be a worm like Bernard? He's got spirit, personality . . .

As he speaks, LINDA, *almost in tears, exits into the living room.* WILLY *is alone in the kitchen, wilting and staring. The leaves are gone. It is night again, and the apartment houses look down from behind.*

WILLY. Loaded with it. Loaded! What is he stealing? He's giving it back, isn't he? Why is he stealing? What did I tell him? I never in my life told him anything but decent things.

HAPPY *in pajamas has come down the stairs;* WILLY *suddenly becomes aware of* HAPPY*'s presence.*

HAPPY. Let's go now, come on.

WILLY (*sitting down at the kitchen table*). Huh! Why did she have to wax the floors herself? Everytime she waxes the floors she keels over. She knows that!

HAPPY. Shh! Take it easy. What brought you back tonight?

WILLY. I got an awful scare. Nearly hit a kid in Yonkers. God! Why didn't I go to Alaska with my brother Ben that time! Ben! That man was a genius, that man was success incarnate! What a mistake! He begged me to go.

HAPPY. Well, there's no use in . . .

WILLY. You guys! There was a man started with the clothes on his back and ended up with diamond mines!

HAPPY. Boy, someday I'd like to know how he did it.

WILLY. What's the mystery? The man knew what he wanted and went out and got it! Walked into a jungle, and comes out, the age of twenty-one, and he's rich! The world is an oyster, but you don't crack it open on a mattress!

HAPPY. Pop, I told you I'm gonna retire you for life.

WILLY. You'll retire me for life on seventy goddam dollars a week? And your women and your car and your apartment, and you'll retire me for life! Christ's sake, I couldn't get past Yonkers today! Where are you guys, where are you? The woods are burning! I can't drive a car!

CHARLEY *has appeared in the doorway. He is a large man, slow of speech, laconic, immovable. In all he says, despite what he says, there is pity, and, now, trepidation. He has a robe over pajamas, slippers on his feet. He enters the kitchen.*

CHARLEY. Everything all right?

HAPPY. Yeah, Charley, everything's . . .

WILLY. What's the matter?

CHARLEY. I heard some noise. I thought something happened. Can't we do something about the walls? You sneeze in here, and in my house hats blow off.

HAPPY. Let's go to bed, Dad. Come on.

CHARLEY *signals to* HAPPY *to go.*

WILLY. You go ahead, I'm not tired at the moment.

HAPPY (*to* WILLY). Take it easy, huh? (*He exits.*)

WILLY. What're you doin' up?

CHARLEY (*sitting down at the kitchen table opposite* WILLY). Couldn't sleep good. I had a heartburn.

WILLY. Well, you don't know how to eat.

CHARLEY. I eat with my mouth.

WILLY. No, you're ignorant. You gotta know about vitamins and things like that.

CHARLEY. Come on, let's shoot. Tire you out a little.

WILLY (*hesitantly*). All right. You got cards?

CHARLEY (*taking a deck from his pocket*). Yeah, I got them. Someplace. What is it with those vitamins?

WILLY (*dealing*). They build up your bones. Chemistry.

CHARLEY. Yeah, but there's no bones in a heartburn.

WILLY. What are you talkin' about? Do you know the first thing about it?

CHARLEY. Don't get insulted.

WILLY. Don't talk about something you don't know anything about.

They are playing. Pause.

CHARLEY. What're you doin' home?

WILLY. A little trouble with the car.

CHARLEY. Oh. (*Pause.*) I'd like to take a trip to California.

WILLY. Don't say.

CHARLEY. You want a job?

WILLY. I got a job, I told you that. (*After a slight pause.*) What the hell are you offering me a job for?

CHARLEY. Don't get insulted.

WILLY. Don't insult me.

CHARLEY. I don't see no sense in it. You don't have to go on this way.

WILLY. I got a good job. (*Slight pause.*) What do you keep comin' in here for?

CHARLEY. You want me to go?

WILLY (*after a pause, withering*). I can't understand it. He's going back to Texas again. What the hell is that?

CHARLEY. Let him go.

WILLY. I got nothin' to give him, Charley, I'm clean, I'm clean.

CHARLEY. He won't starve. None a them starve. Forget about him.

WILLY. Then what have I got to remember?

CHARLEY. You take it too hard. To hell with it. When a deposit bottle is broken you don't get your nickel back.

WILLY. That's easy enough for you to say.

CHARLEY. That ain't easy for me to say.

WILLY. Did you see the ceiling I put up in the living room?

CHARLEY. Yeah, that's a piece of work. To put up a ceiling is a mystery to me. How do you do it?

WILLY. What's the difference?

CHARLEY. Well, talk about it.

WILLY. You gonna put up a ceiling?

CHARLEY. How could I put up a ceiling?

WILLY. Then what the hell are you bothering me for?

CHARLEY. You're insulted again.

WILLY. A man who can't handle tools is not a man. You're disgusting.

CHARLEY. Don't call me disgusting, Willy.

UNCLE BEN, *carrying a valise and an umbrella, enters the forestage from around the right corner of the house. He is a stolid man, in his sixties, with a mustache and an authoritative air. He is utterly certain of his destiny, and there is an aura of far places about him. He enters exactly as* WILLY *speaks.*

WILLY. I'm getting awfully tired, Ben.

BEN'*s music is heard.* BEN *looks around at everything.*

CHARLEY. Good, keep playing; you'll sleep better. Did you call me Ben?

BEN *looks at his watch.*

WILLY. That's funny. For a second there you reminded me of my brother Ben.

BEN. I only have a few minutes. (*He strolls, inspecting the place.* WILLY *and* CHARLEY *continue playing.*)

CHARLEY. You never heard from him again, heh? Since that time?

WILLY. Didn't Linda tell you? Couple of weeks ago we got a letter from his wife in Africa. He died.

CHARLEY. That so.

BEN. (*chuckling*). So this is Brooklyn, eh?

CHARLEY. Maybe you're in for some of his money.

WILLY. Naa, he had seven sons. There's just one opportunity I had with that man . . .

BEN. I must make a train, William. There are several properties I'm looking at in Alaska.

WILLY. Sure, sure! If I'd gone with him to Alaska that time, everything would've been totally different.

CHARLEY. Go on, you'd froze to death up there.

WILLY. What're you talking about?

BEN. Opportunity is tremendous in Alaska, William. Surprised you're not up there.

WILLY. Sure, tremendous.

CHARLEY. Heh?

WILLY. There was the only man I ever met who knew the answers.

CHARLEY. Who?

BEN. How are you all?

WILLY (*taking a pot, smiling*). Fine, fine.

CHARLEY. Pretty sharp tonight.

BEN. Is Mother living with you?

WILLY. No, she died a long time ago.

CHARLEY. Who?

BEN. That's too bad. Fine specimen of a lady, Mother.

WILLY (*to* CHARLEY). Heh?

BEN. I'd hoped to see the old girl.

CHARLEY. Who died?

BEN. Heard anything from Father, have you?

WILLY (*unnerved*). What do you mean, who died?

CHARLEY (*taking a pot*). What're you talkin' about?

BEN (*looking at his watch*). William, it's half-past eight!

WILLY (*as though to dispel his confusion he angrily stops* CHARLEY'*s hand*). That's my build!

CHARLEY. I put the ace . . .

WILLY. If you don't know how to play the game I'm not gonna throw my money away on you!

CHARLEY (*rising*). It was my ace, for God's sake!

WILLY. I'm through, I'm through!

BEN. When did Mother die?

WILLY. Long ago. Since the beginning you never knew how to play cards.

CHARLEY (*picks up the cards and goes to the door*). All right! Next time I'll bring a deck with five aces.

WILLY. I don't play that kind of game!

CHARLEY (*turning to him*). You ought to be ashamed of yourself!

WILLY. Yeah?

CHARLEY. Yeah! (*He goes out.*)

WILLY (*slamming the door after him*). Ignoramus!

BEN (*as* WILLY *comes toward him through the wall-line of the kitchen*). So you're William.

WILLY (*shaking* BEN'*s hand*). Ben! I've been waiting for you so long! What's the answer? How did you do it?

BEN. Oh, there's a story in that.

LINDA *enters the forestage, as of old, carrying the wash basket.*

LINDA. Is this Ben?

BEN (*gallantly*). How do you do, my dear.

LINDA. Where've you been all these years? Willy's always wondered why you . . .

WILLY (*pulling* BEN *away from her impatiently*). Where is Dad? Didn't you follow him? How did you get started?

BEN. Well, I don't know how much you remember.

WILLY. Well, I was just a baby, of course, only three or four years old . . .

BEN. Three years and eleven months.

WILLY. What a memory, Ben!

BEN. I have many enterprises, William, and I have never kept books.

WILLY. I remember I was sitting under the wagon in—was it Nebraska?

BEN. It was South Dakota, and I gave you a bunch of wild flowers.

WILLY. I remember you walking away down some open road.

BEN (*laughing*). I was going to find Father in Alaska.

WILLY. Where is he?

BEN. At that age I had a very faulty view of geography, William. I discovered after a few days that I was heading due south, so instead of Alaska, I ended up in Africa.

LINDA. Africa!

WILLY. The Gold Coast!

BEN. Principally diamond mines.

LINDA. Diamond mines!

BEN. Yes, my dear. But I've only a few minutes . . .

WILLY. No! Boys! Boys! (YOUNG BIFF *and* HAPPY *appear.*) Listen to this. This is your Uncle Ben, a great man! Tell my boys, Ben!

BEN. Why, boys, when I was seventeen I walked into the jungle, and when I was twenty-one I walked out. (*He laughs.*) And by God I was rich.

WILLY (*to the boys*). You see what I been talking about? The greatest things can happen!

BEN (*glancing at his watch*). I have an appointment in Ketchikan Tuesday week.

WILLY. No, Ben! Please tell about Dad. I want my boys to hear. I want them to know the kind of stock they spring from. All I remember is a man with a big beard, and I was in Mamma's lap, sitting around a fire, and some kind of high music.

BEN. His flute. He played the flute.

WILLY. Sure, the flute, that's right!

New music is heard, a high, rollicking tune.

BEN. Father was a very great and a very wild-hearted man. We would start in Boston, and he'd toss the whole family into the wagon, and then he'd drive the team right across the country; through Ohio, and Indiana, Michigan, Illinois, and all the Western states. And we'd stop in the towns and sell the flutes that he'd made on the way. Great inventor, Father. With one gadget he made more in a week than a man like you could make in a lifetime.

WILLY. That's just the way I'm bringing them up, Ben—rugged, well liked, all-around.

BEN. Yeah? (*To* BIFF.) Hit that, boy—hard as you can. (*He pounds his stomach.*)

BIFF. Oh, no, sir!

BEN (*taking boxing stance*). Come on, get to me! (*He laughs.*)

WILLY. Go to it. Biff! Go ahead, show him!

BIFF. Okay! (*He cocks his fists and starts in.*)

LINDA (*to* WILLY). Why must he fight, dear?

BEN (*sparring with* BIFF). Good boy! Good boy!

WILLY. How's that, Ben, heh?

HAPPY. Give him the left, Biff!

LINDA. Why are you fighting?

BEN. Good boy! (*Suddenly comes in, trips* BIFF, *and stands over him, the point of his umbrella poised over* BIFF*'s eye.*)

LINDA. Look out, Biff!

BIFF. Gee!

BEN (*patting* BIFF*'s knee*). Never fight fair with a stranger, boy. You'll never get out of the jungle that way. (*Taking* LINDA*'s hand and bowing.*) It was an honor and a pleasure to meet you, Linda.

LINDA (*withdrawing her hand coldly, frightened*). Have a nice—trip.

BEN (*to* WILLY). And good luck with your—what do you do?

WILLY. Selling.

BEN. Yes. Well . . . (*He raises his hand in farewell to all.*)

WILLY. No, Ben, I don't want you to think . . . (*He takes* BEN*'s arm to show him.*) It's Brooklyn, I know, but we hunt too.

BEN. Really, now.

WILLY. Oh, sure, there's snakes and rabbits and—that's why I moved out here. Why, Biff can fell any one of these trees in no time! Boys! Go right over to where they're building the apartment house and get some sand. We're gonna rebuild the entire front stoop right now! Watch this, Ben!

BIFF. Yes, sir! On the double, Hap!

HAPPY (*as he and* BIFF *run off*). I lost weight, Pop, you notice?

CHARLEY *enters in knickers, even before the boys are gone.*

CHARLEY. Listen, if they steal any more from that building the watchman'll put the cops on them!

LINDA (*to* WILLY). Don't let Biff . . .

BEN *laughs lustily.*

WILLY. You shoulda seen the lumber they brought home last week. At least a dozen six-by-tens worth all kinds a money.

CHARLEY. Listen, if that watchman . . .

WILLY. I gave them hell, understand. But I got a couple of fearless characters there.

CHARLEY. Willy, the jails are full of fearless characters.

BEN (*clapping* WILLY *on the back, with a laugh at* CHARLEY). And the stock exchange, friend!

WILLY (*joining in* BEN*'s laughter*). Where are the rest of your pants?

CHARLEY. My wife bought them.

WILLY. Now all you need is a golf club and you can go upstairs and go to sleep. (*To* BEN.) Great athlete! Between him and his son Bernard they can't hammer a nail!

BERNARD (*rushing in*). The watchman's chasing Biff!

WILLY (*angrily*). Shut up! He's not stealing anything!

LINDA (*alarmed, hurrying off left*). Where is he? Biff, dear! (*She exits.*)

WILLY (*moving toward the left, away from* BEN). There's nothing wrong. What's the matter with you?

BEN. Nervy boy. Good!

WILLY (*laughing*). Oh, nerves of iron, that Biff!

CHARLEY. Don't know what it is. My New England man comes back and he's bleedin', they murdered him up there.

WILLY. It's contacts, Charley, I got important contacts!

CHARLEY (*sarcastically*). Glad to hear it, Willy. Come in later, we'll shoot a little casino. I'll take some of your Portland money. (*He laughs at* WILLY *and exits.*)

WILLY (*turning to* BEN). Business is bad, it's murderous. But not for me, of course.

BEN. I'll stop by on my way back to Africa.

WILLY (*longingly*). Can't you stay a few days? You're just what I need, Ben, because I—I have a fine position here, but I—well, Dad left when I was such a baby and I never had a chance to talk to him and I still feel—kind of temporary about myself.

BEN. I'll be late for my train.

They are at opposite ends of the stage.

WILLY. Ben, my boys—can't we talk? They'd go into the jaws of hell for me, see, but I . . .

BEN. William, you're being first-rate with your boys. Outstanding, manly chaps!

WILLY (*hanging on to his words*). Oh, Ben, that's good to hear! Because sometimes I'm afraid that I'm not teaching them the right kind of—Ben, how should I teach them?

BEN (*giving great weight to each word, and with a certain vicious audacity*). William, when I walked into the jungle, I was seventeen. When I walked out I was twenty-one. And, by God, I was rich!

(*He goes off into darkness around the right corner of the house.*)

WILLY. . . . was rich! That's just the spirit I want to imbue them with! To walk into a jungle! I was right! I was right! I was right! I was right!

BEN *is gone, but* WILLY *is still speaking to him as* LINDA, *in nightgown and robe, enters the kitchen, glances around for* WILLY, *then goes to the door of the house, looks out and sees him. Comes down to his left. He looks at her.*

LINDA. Willy, dear? Willy?

WILLY. I was right!

LINDA. Did you have some cheese? (*He can't answer.*) It's very late, darling. Come to bed, heh?

WILLY (*looking straight up*). Gotta break your neck to see a star in this yard.

LINDA. You coming in?

WILLY. Whatever happened to that diamond watch fob? Remember? When Ben came from Africa that time? Didn't he give me a watch fob with a diamond in it?

LINDA. You pawned it, dear. Twelve, thirteen years ago. For Biff's radio correspondence course.

WILLY. Gee, that was a beautiful thing. I'll take a walk.

LINDA. But you're in your slippers.

WILLY (*starting to go around the house at the left*). I was right! I was! (*Half to* LINDA, *as he goes, shaking his head.*) What a man! There was a man worth talking to. I was right!

LINDA (*calling after* WILLY). But in your slippers, Willy!

WILLY *is almost gone when* BIFF, *in his pajamas, comes down the stairs and enters the kitchen.*

BIFF. What is he doing out there?

LINDA. Sh!

BIFF. God Almighty, Mom, how long has he been doing this?

LINDA. Don't, he'll hear you.

BIFF. What the hell is the matter with him?

LINDA. It'll pass by morning.

BIFF. Shouldn't we do anything?

LINDA. Oh, my dear, you should do a lot of things, but there's nothing to do, so go to sleep.

HAPPY *comes down the stairs and sits on the steps.*

HAPPY. I never heard him so loud, Mom.

LINDA. Well, come around more often; you'll hear him.

(*She sits down at the table and mends the lining of* WILLY*'s jacket.*)

BIFF. Why didn't you ever write me about this, Mom?

LINDA. How would I write to you? For over three months you had no address.

BIFF. I was on the move. But you know I thought of you all the time. You know that, don't you, pal?

LINDA. I know, dear, I know. But he likes to have a letter. Just to know that there's still a possibility for better things.

BIFF. He's not like this all the time, is he?

LINDA. It's when you come home he's always the worst.

BIFF. When I come home?

LINDA. When you write you're coming, he's all smiles, and talks about the future, and—he's just wonderful. And then the closer you seem to come, the more shaky he gets, and then, by the time you get here, he's arguing, and he seems angry at you. I think it's just that maybe he can't bring himself to—to open up to you. Why are you so hateful to each other? Why is that?

BIFF (*evasively*). I'm not hateful, Mom.

LINDA. But you no sooner come in the door than you're fighting!

BIFF. I don't know why. I mean to change. I'm tryin', Mom, you understand?

LINDA. Are you home to stay now?

BIFF. I don't know. I want to look around, see what's doin'.

LINDA. Biff, you can't look around all your life, can you?

BIFF. I just can't take hold, Mom. I can't take hold of some kind of a life.

LINDA. Biff, a man is not a bird, to come and go with the spring time.

BIFF. Your hair . . . (*He touches her hair.*) Your hair got so gray.

LINDA. Oh, it's been gray since you were in high school. I just stopped dyeing it, that's all.

BIFF. Dye it again, will ya? I don't want my pal looking old. (*He smiles.*)

LINDA. You're such a boy! You think you can go away for a year and . . . You've got to get it into your head now that one day you'll knock on this door and there'll be strange people here . . .

BIFF. What are you talking about? You're not even sixty, Mom.

LINDA. But what about your father?

BIFF (*lamely*). Well, I meant him too.

HAPPY. He admires Pop.

LINDA. Biff, dear, if you don't have any feeling for him, then you can't have any feeling for me.

BIFF. Sure I can, Mom.

LINDA. No. You can't just come to see me, because I love him. (*With a threat, but only a threat, of tears.*) He's the dearest man in the world to me, and I won't have anyone making him feel unwanted and low and blue. You've got to make up your mind now, darling, there's no leeway any more. Either he's your father and you pay him that respect, or else you're not to come here. I know he's not easy to get along with—nobody knows that better than me—but . . .

WILLY (*from the left, with a laugh*). Hey, hey, Biffo!

BIFF (*starting to go out after* WILLY). What the hell is the matter with him? (HAPPY *stops him.*)

LINDA. Don't—don't go near him!

BIFF. Stop making excuses for him! He always, always wiped the floor with you. Never had an ounce of respect for you.

HAPPY. He's always had respect for . . .

BIFF. What the hell do you know about it?

HAPPY (*surlily*). Just don't call him crazy!

BIFF. He's got no character—Charley wouldn't do this. Not in his own house—spewing out that vomit from his mind.

HAPPY. Charley never had to cope with what he's got to.

BIFF. People are worse off than Willy Loman. Believe me, I've seen them!

LINDA. Then make Charley your father, Biff. You can't do that, can you? I don't say he's a great man. Willy Loman never made a lot of money. His name was never in the paper. He's not the finest character that ever lived. But he's a human being, and a terrible thing is happening to him. So attention must be paid. He's not to be allowed to fall into his grave like an old dog. Attention, attention must be finally paid to such a person. You called him crazy . . .

BIFF. I didn't mean . . .

LINDA. No, a lot of people think he's lost his—balance. But you don't have to be very smart to know what his trouble is. The man is exhausted.

HAPPY. Sure!

LINDA. A small man can be just as exhausted as a great man. He works for a company thirty-six years this March, opens up unheard-of territories to their trademark, and now in his old age they take his salary away.

HAPPY (*indignantly*). I didn't know that, Mom.

LINDA. You never asked, my dear! Now that you get your spending money someplace else you don't trouble your mind with him.

HAPPY. But I gave you money last . . .

LINDA. Christmas time, fifty dollars! To fix the hot water it cost ninety-seven fifty! For five weeks he's been on straight commission, like a beginner, an unknown!

BIFF. Those ungrateful bastards!

LINDA. Are they any worse than his sons? When he brought them business, when he was young, they were glad to see him. But now his old friends, the old buyers that loved him so and always found some order to hand him in a pinch—they're all dead, retired. He used to be able to make six, seven calls a day in Boston. Now he takes his valises out of the car and puts them back and takes them out again and he's exhausted. Instead of walking he talks now. He drives seven hundred miles, and when he gets there no one knows him any more, no one welcomes him. And what goes through a man's mind, driving seven hundred miles home without having earned a cent? Why shouldn't he talk to himself? Why? When he has to go to Charley and borrow fifty dollars a week and pretend to me that it's his pay? How long can that go on? How long? You see what I'm sitting here and waiting for? And you tell me he has no character? The man who never worked a day but for your benefit? When does he get the medal for that? Is this his reward—to turn around at the age of sixty-three and find his sons, who he loved better than his life, one a philandering bum . . .

HAPPY. Mom!

LINDA. That's all you are, my baby! (*To* BIFF.) And you! What happened to the love you had for him? You were such pals! How you used to talk to him on the phone every night! How lonely he was till he could come home to you!

BIFF. All right, Mom. I'll live here in my room, and I'll get a job. I'll keep away from him, that's all.

LINDA. No, Biff. You can't stay here and fight all the time.

BIFF. He threw me out of this house, remember that.

LINDA. Why did he do that? I never knew why.

BIFF. Because I know he's a fake and he doesn't like anybody around who knows!

LINDA. Why a fake? In what way? What do you mean?

BIFF. Just don't lay it all at my feet. It's between me and him—that's all I have to say. I'll chip in from now on. He'll settle for half my paycheck. He'll be all right. I'm going to bed. (*He starts for the stairs.*)

LINDA. He won't be all right.

BIFF (*turning on the stairs, furiously*). I hate this city and I'll stay here. Now what do you want?

LINDA. He's dying, Biff.

HAPPY *turns quickly to her, shocked.*

BIFF (*after a pause*). Why is he dying?

LINDA. He's been trying to kill himself.

BIFF (*with great horror*). How?

LINDA. I live from day to day.

BIFF. What're you talking about?

LINDA. Remember I wrote you that he smashed up the car again? In February?

BIFF. Well?

LINDA. The insurance inspector came. He said that they have evidence. That all these accidents in the last year —weren't—weren't—accidents.

HAPPY. How can they tell that? That's a lie.

LINDA. It seems there's a woman . . . (*She takes a breath as:*)

BIFF (*sharply but contained*). What woman?

LINDA (*simultaneously*) . . . and this woman . . .

LINDA. What?

BIFF. Nothing. Go ahead.

LINDA. What did you say?

BIFF. Nothing. I just said what woman?

HAPPY. What about her?

LINDA. Well, it seems she was walking down the road and saw his car. She says that he wasn't driving fast at all, and that he didn't skid. She says he came to that little bridge, and then deliberately smashed into the railing, and it was only the shallowness of the water that saved him.

BIFF. Oh, no, he probably just fell asleep again.

LINDA. I don't think he fell asleep.

BIFF. Why not?

LINDA. Last month . . . (*With great difficulty.*) Oh, boys, it's so hard to say a thing like this! He's just a big stupid man to you, but I tell you there's more good in him than in many other people. (*She chokes, wipes her eyes.*) I was looking for a fuse. The lights blew out, and I went down the cellar. And behind the fuse box—it happened to fall out—was a length of rubber pipe—just short.

HAPPY. No kidding!

LINDA. There's a little attachment on the end of it. I knew right away. And sure enough, on the bottom of the water heater there's a new little nipple on the gas pipe.

HAPPY (*angrily*). That—jerk.

BIFF. Did you have it taken off?

LINDA. I'm—I'm ashamed to. How can I mention it to him? Every day I go down and take away that little rubber pipe. But, when he comes home, I put it back where it was. How can I insult him that way? I don't know what to do. I live from day to day, boys. I tell you, I know every thought in his mind. It sounds so old-fashioned and silly, but I tell you he put his whole life into you and you've turned your backs on him. (*She is bent over in the chair, weeping, her face in her hands.*) Biff, I swear to God! Biff, his life is in your hands!

HAPPY (*to* BIFF). How do you like that damned fool!

BIFF (*kissing her*). All right, pal, all right. It's all settled now. I've been remiss. I know that, Mom. But now I'll stay, and I swear to you, I'll apply myself. (*Kneeling in front of her, in a fever of self-reproach.*) It's just—you see, Mom, I don't fit in business. Not that I won't try. I'll try, and I'll make good.

HAPPY. Sure you will. The trouble with you in business was you never tried to please people.

BIFF. I know, I . . .

HAPPY. Like when you worked for Harrison's. Bob Harrison said you were tops, and then you go and do some damn fool thing like whistling whole songs in the elevator like a comedian.

BIFF (*against* HAPPY). So what? I like to whistle sometimes.

HAPPY. You don't raise a guy to a responsible job who whistles in the elevator!

LINDA. Well, don't argue about it now.

HAPPY. Like when you'd go off and swim in the middle of the day instead of taking the line around.

BIFF (*his resentment rising*). Well, don't you run off? You take off sometimes, don't you? On a nice summer day?

HAPPY. Yeah, but I cover myself!

LINDA. Boys!

HAPPY. If I'm going to take a fade the boss can call any number where I'm supposed to be and they'll swear to him that I just left. I'll tell you something that I hate to say, Biff, but in the business world some of them think you're crazy.

BIFF (*angered*). Screw the business world!

HAPPY. All right, screw it! Great, but cover yourself!

LINDA. Hap, Hap!

BIFF. I don't care what they think! They've laughed at Dad for years, and you know why? Because we don't belong in this nuthouse of a city! We should be mixing cement on some open plain or—or carpenters. A carpenter is allowed to whistle!

WILLY *walks in from the entrance of the house, at left.*

WILLY. Even your grandfather was better than a carpenter. (*Pause. They watch him.*) You never grew up. Bernard does not whistle in the elevator, I assure you.

BIFF (*as though to laugh* WILLY *out of it*). Yeah, but you do, Pop.

WILLY. I never in my life whistled in an elevator! And who in the business world thinks I'm crazy?

BIFF. I didn't mean it like that, Pop. Now don't make a whole thing out of it, will ya?

WILLY. Go back to the West! Be a carpenter, a cowboy, enjoy yourself!

LINDA. Willy, he was just saying . . .

WILLY. I heard what he said!

HAPPY (*trying to quiet* WILLY). Hey, Pop, come on now . . .

WILLY (*continuing over* HAPPY*'s line*). They laugh at me, heh? Go to Filene's, go to the Hub, go to Slattery's, Boston. Call out the name Willy Loman and see what happens! Big shot!

BIFF. All right, Pop.

WILLY. Big!

BIFF. All right!

WILLY. Why do you always insult me?

BIFF. I didn't say a word. (*To* LINDA.) Did I say a word?

LINDA. He didn't say anything, Willy.

WILLY (*going to the doorway of the living room*). All right, good night, good night.

LINDA. Willy, dear, he just decided . . .

WILLY (*to* BIFF). If you get tired hanging around tomorrow, paint the ceiling I put up in the living room.

BIFF. I'm leaving early tomorrow.

HAPPY. He's going to see Bill Oliver, Pop.

WILLY (*interestedly*). Oliver? For what?

BIFF (*with reserve, but trying; trying*). He always said he'd stake me. I'd like to go into business, so maybe I can take him up on it.

LINDA. Isn't that wonderful?

WILLY. Don't interrupt. What's wonderful about it? There's fifty men in the City of New York who'd stake him. (*To* BIFF.) Sporting goods?

BIFF. I guess so. I know something about it and . . .

WILLY. He knows something about it! You know sporting goods better than Spalding, for God's sake! How much is he giving you?

BIFF. I don't know, I didn't even see him yet, but . . .

WILLY. Then what're you talkin' about?

BIFF (*getting angry*). Well, all I said was I'm gonna see him, that's all!

WILLY (*turning away*). Ah, you're counting your chickens again.

BIFF (*starting left for the stairs*). Oh, Jesus, I'm going to sleep!

WILLY (*calling after him*). Don't curse in this house!

BIFF (*turning*). Since when did you get so clean?

HAPPY (*trying to stop them*). Wait a . . .

WILLY. Don't use that language to me! I won't have it!

HAPPY (*grabbing* BIFF, *shouts*). Wait a minute! I got an idea. I got a feasible idea. Come here, Biff, let's talk this over now, let's talk some sense here. When I was down in Florida last time, I thought of a great idea to sell sporting goods. It just came back to me. You and I, Biff—we have a line, the Loman Line. We train a couple of weeks, and put on a couple of exhibitions, see?

WILLY. That's an idea!

HAPPY. Wait! We form two basketball teams, see? Two water-polo teams. We play each other. It's a million dollars' worth of publicity. Two brothers, see? The Loman Brothers. Displays in the Royal Palms—all the hotels. And banners over the ring and the basketball court: "Loman Brothers." Baby, we could sell sporting goods!

WILLY. That is a one-million-dollar idea!

LINDA. Marvelous!

BIFF. I'm in great shape as far as that's concerned.

HAPPY. And the beauty of it is, Biff, it wouldn't be like a business. We'd be out playin' ball again.

BIFF (*enthused*). Yeah, that's . . .

WILLY. Million-dollar . . .

HAPPY. And you wouldn't get fed up with it, Biff. It'd be the family again. There'd be the old honor, and comradeship, and if you wanted to go off for a swim or somethin'—well, you'd do it! Without some smart cooky gettin' up ahead of you!

WILLY. Lick the world! You guys together could absolutely lick the civilized world.

BIFF. I'll see Oliver tomorrow. Hap, if we could work that out . . .

LINDA. Maybe things are beginning to . . .

WILLY (*wildly enthused, to* LINDA). Stop interrupting! (*To* BIFF.) But don't wear sport jacket and slacks when you see Oliver.

BIFF. No, I'll . . .

WILLY. A business suit, and talk as little as possible, and don't crack any jokes.

BIFF. He did like me. Always liked me.

LINDA. He loved you!

WILLY (*to* LINDA). Will you stop! (*To* BIFF.) Walk in very serious. You are not applying for a boy's job. Money is to pass. Be quiet, fine, and serious. Everybody likes a kidder, but nobody lends him money.

HAPPY. I'll try to get some myself, Biff. I'm sure I can.

WILLY. I see great things for you kids, I think your troubles are over. But remember, start big and you'll end big. Ask for fifteen. How much you gonna ask for?

BIFF. Gee, I don't know . . .

WILLY. And don't say "Gee." "Gee" is a boy's word. A man walking in for fifteen thousand dollars does not say "Gee!"

BIFF. Ten, I think, would be top though.

WILLY. Don't be so modest. You always started too low. Walk in with a big laugh. Don't look worried. Start off with a couple of your good stories to lighten things up. It's not what you say, it's how you say it—because personality always wins the day.

LINDA. Oliver always thought the highest of him . . .

WILLY. Will you let me talk?

BIFF. Don't yell at her, Pop, will ya?

WILLY (*angrily*). I was talking, wasn't I?

BIFF. I don't like you yelling at her all the time, and I'm tellin' you, that's all.

WILLY. What're you, takin' over this house?

LINDA. Willy . . .

WILLY (*turning to her*). Don't take his side all the time, goddammit!

BIFF (*furiously*). Stop yelling at her!

WILLY (*suddenly pulling on his cheek, beaten down, guilt ridden*). Give my best to Bill Oliver—he may remember me. (*He exits through the living room doorway.*)

LINDA (*her voice subdued*). What'd you have to start that for? (BIFF *turns away.*) You see how sweet he was as soon as you talked hopefully? (*She goes over to* BIFF.) Come up and say good night to him. Don't let him go to bed that way.

HAPPY. Come on, Biff, let's buck him up.

LINDA. Please, dear. Just say good night. It takes so little to make him happy. Come. (*She goes through the living room doorway, calling upstairs from within the living room.*) Your pajamas are hanging in the bathroom, Willy!

HAPPY (*looking toward where* LINDA *went out*). What a woman! They broke the mold when they made her. You know that, Biff.

BIFF. He's off salary. My God, working on commission!

HAPPY. Well, let's face it: he's no hot-shot selling man. Except that sometimes, you have to admit, he's a sweet personality.

BIFF (*deciding*). Lend me ten bucks, will ya? I want to buy some new ties.

HAPPY. I'll take you to a place I know. Beautiful stuff. Wear one of my striped shirts tomorrow.

BIFF. She got gray. Mom got awful old. Gee, I'm gonna go in to Oliver tomorrow and knock him for a . . .

HAPPY. Come on up. Tell that to Dad. Let's give him a whirl. Come on.

BIFF (*steamed up*). You know, with ten thousand bucks, boy!

HAPPY (*as they go into the living room*). That's the talk, Biff, that's the first time I've heard the old confidence out of you! (*From within the living room, fading off*) You're gonna live with me, kid, and any babe you want just say the word . . . (*The last lines are hardly heard. They are mounting the stairs to their parents' bedroom.*)

LINDA (*entering her bedroom and addressing* WILLY, *who is in the bathroom. She is straightening the bed for him*). Can you do anything about the shower? It drips.

WILLY (*from the bathroom*). All of a sudden everything falls to pieces. Goddam plumbing, oughta be sued, those people. I hardly finished putting it in and the thing . . . (*His words rumble off.*)

LINDA. I'm just wondering if Oliver will remember him. You think he might?

WILLY (*coming out of the bathroom in his pajamas*). Remember him? What's the matter with you, you crazy? If he'd've stayed with Oliver he'd be on top by now! Wait'll Oliver gets a look at him. You don't know the average caliber any more. The average young man today—(*he is getting into bed*)—is got a caliber of zero. Greatest thing in the world for him was to bum around.

BIFF *and* HAPPY *enter the bedroom. Slight pause.*

WILLY (*stops short, looking at* BIFF). Glad to hear it, boy.

HAPPY. He wanted to say good night to you, sport.

WILLY (*to* BIFF). Yeah. Knock him dead, boy. What'd you want to tell me?

BIFF. Just take it easy, Pop. Good night. (*He turns to go.*)

WILLY (*unable to resist*). And if anything falls off the desk while you're talking to him—like a package or something—don't you pick it up. They have office boys for that.

LINDA. I'll make a big breakfast . . .

WILLY. Will you let me finish? (*To* BIFF.) Tell him you were in the business in the West. Not farm work.

BIFF. All right, Dad.

LINDA. I think everything . . .

WILLY (*going right through her speech*). And don't undersell yourself. No less than fifteen thousand dollars.

BIFF (*unable to bear him*). Okay. Good night, Mom. (*He starts moving.*)

WILLY. Because you got a greatness in you, Biff, remember that. You got all kinds of greatness . . . (*He lies back, exhausted.* BIFF *walks out.*)

LINDA (*calling after* BIFF). Sleep well, darling!

HAPPY. I'm gonna get married, Mom. I wanted to tell you.

LINDA. Go to sleep, dear.

HAPPY (*going*). I just wanted to tell you.

WILLY. Keep up the good work. (HAPPY *exits.*) God . . . remember that Ebbets Field game? The championship of the city?

LINDA. Just rest. Should I sing to you?

WILLY. Yeah. Sing to me. (LINDA *hums a soft lullaby.*) When that team came out—he was the tallest, remember?

LINDA. Oh, yes. And in gold.

BIFF *enters the darkened kitchen, takes a cigarette, and leaves the house. He comes downstage into a golden pool of light. He smokes, staring at the night.*

WILLY. Like a young god. Hercules—something like that. And the sun, the sun all around him. Remember how he waved to me? Right up from the field, with the representatives of three colleges standing by? And the buyers I brought, and the cheers when he came out—Loman, Loman, Loman! God Almighty, he'll be great yet. A star like that, magnificent, can never really fade away!

The light on WILLY *is fading. The gas heater begins to glow through the kitchen wall, near the stairs, a blue flame beneath red coils.*

LINDA (*timidly*). Willy dear, what has he got against you?

WILLY. I'm so tired. Don't talk any more.

BIFF *slowly returns to the kitchen. He stops, stares toward the heater.*

LINDA. Will you ask Howard to let you work in New York?

WILLY. First thing in the morning. Everything'll be all right.

BIFF *reaches behind the heater and draws out a length of rubber tubing. He is horrified and turns his head toward* WILLY*'s room, still dimly lit, from which the strains of* LINDA*'s desperate but monotonous humming rise.*

WILLY (*staring through the window into the moonlight*). Gee, look at the moon moving between the buildings!

BIFF *wraps the tubing around his hand and quickly goes up the stairs.*

★

Act 2

SCENE: *Music is heard, gay and bright. The curtain rises as the music fades away.* WILLY, *in shirt sleeves, is sitting at the kitchen table, sipping coffee, his hat in his lap.* LINDA *is filling his cup when she can.*

WILLY. Wonderful coffee. Meal in itself.

LINDA. Can I make you some eggs?

WILLY. No. Take a breath.

LINDA. You look so rested, dear.

WILLY. I slept like a dead one. First time in months. Imagine, sleeping till ten on a Tuesday morning. Boys left nice and early, heh?

LINDA. They were out of here by eight o'clock.

WILLY. Good work!

LINDA. It was so thrilling to see them leaving together. I can't get over the shaving lotion in this house!

WILLY (*smiling*). Mmm . . .

LINDA. Biff was very changed this morning. His whole attitude seemed to be hopeful. He couldn't wait to get downtown to see Oliver.

WILLY. He's heading for a change. There's no question, there simply are certain men that take longer to get—solidified. How did he dress?

LINDA. His blue suit. He's so handsome in that suit. He could be a—anything in that suit!

WILLY *gets up from the table.* LINDA *holds his jacket for him.*

WILLY. There's no question, no question at all. Gee, on the way home tonight I'd like to buy some seeds.

LINDA (*laughing*). That'd be wonderful. But not enough sun gets back there. Nothing'll grow any more.

WILLY. You wait, kid, before it's all over we're gonna get a little place out in the country, and I'll raise some vegetables, a couple of chickens . . .

LINDA. You'll do it yet, dear.

WILLY *walks out of his jacket.* LINDA *follows him.*

WILLY. And they'll get married, and come for a weekend. I'd build a little guest house. 'Cause I got so many fine tools, all I'd need would be a little lumber and some peace of mind.

LINDA (*joyfully*). I sewed the lining . . .

WILLY. I could build two guest houses, so they'd both come. Did he decide how much he's going to ask Oliver for?

LINDA (*getting him into the jacket*). He didn't mention it, but I imagine ten or fifteen thousand. You going to talk to Howard today?

WILLY. Yeah. I'll put it to him straight and simple. He'll just have to take me off the road.

LINDA. And Willy, don't forget to ask for a little advance, because we've got the insurance premium. It's the grace period now.

WILLY. That's a hundred . . .?

LINDA. A hundred and eight, sixty-eight. Because we're a little short again.

WILLY. Why are we short?

LINDA. Well, you had the motor job on the car . . .

WILLY. That goddam Studebaker!

LINDA. And you got one more payment on the refrigerator . . .

WILLY. But it just broke again!

LINDA. Well, it's old, dear.

WILLY. I told you we should've bought a well-advertised machine. Charley bought a General Electric and it's twenty years old and it's still good, that son-of-a-bitch.

LINDA. But, Willy . . .

WILLY. Whoever heard of a Hastings refrigerator? Once in my life I would like to own something outright before it's broken! I'm always in a race with the junkyard! I just finished paying for the car and it's on its last legs. The refrigerator consumes belts like a goddam maniac. They time those things. They time them so when you finally paid for them, they're used up.

LINDA (*buttoning up his jacket as he unbuttons it*). All told, about two hundred dollars would carry us, dear. But that includes the last payment on the mortgage. After this payment, Willy, the house belongs to us.

WILLY. It's twenty-five years!

LINDA. Biff was nine years old when we bought it.

WILLY. Well, that's a great thing. To weather a twenty-five year mortgage is . . .

LINDA. It's an accomplishment.

WILLY. All the cement, the lumber, the reconstruction I put in this house! There ain't a crack to be found in it any more.

LINDA. Well, it served its purpose.

WILLY. What purpose? Some stranger'll come along, move in, and that's that. If only Biff would take this house, and raise a family . . . (*He starts to go.*) Good-by, I'm late.

LINDA (*suddenly remembering*). Oh, I forgot! You're supposed to meet them for dinner.

WILLY. Me?

LINDA. At Frank's Chop House on Forty-eighth near Sixth Avenue.

WILLY. Is that so! How about you?

LINDA. No, just the three of you. They're gonna blow you to a big meal!

WILLY. Don't say! Who thought of that?

LINDA. Biff came to me this morning, Willy, and he said, "Tell Dad, we want to blow him to a big meal." Be there six o'clock. You and your two boys are going to have dinner.

WILLY. Gee whiz! That's really somethin'. I'm gonna knock Howard for a loop, kid. I'll get an advance, and I'll come home with a New York job. Goddammit, now I'm gonna do it!

LINDA. Oh, that's the spirit, Willy!

WILLY. I will never get behind a wheel the rest of my life!

LINDA. It's changing, Willy, I can feel it changing!

WILLY. Beyond a question. G'by, I'm late. (*He starts to go again.*)

LINDA (*calling after him as she runs to the kitchen table for a handkerchief*). You got your glasses?

WILLY (*feels for them, then comes back in*). Yeah, yeah, got my glasses.

LINDA (*giving him the handkerchief*). And a handkerchief.

WILLY. Yeah, handkerchief.

LINDA. And your saccharine?

WILLY. Yeah, my saccharine.

LINDA. Be careful on the subway stairs.

She kisses him, and a silk stocking is seen hanging from her hand. WILLY *notices it.*

WILLY. Will you stop mending stockings? At least while I'm in the house. It gets me nervous. I can't tell you. Please.

LINDA *hides the stocking in her hand as she follows* WILLY *across the forestage in front of the house.*

LINDA. Remember, Frank's Chop House.

WILLY (*passing the apron*). Maybe beets would grow out there.

LINDA (*laughing*). But you tried so many times.

WILLY. Yeah. Well, don't work hard today. (*He disappears around the right corner of the house.*)

LINDA. Be careful!

As WILLY *vanishes,* LINDA *waves to him. Suddenly the phone rings. She runs across the stage and into the kitchen and lifts it.*

LINDA. Hello? Oh, Biff! I'm so glad you called, I just . . . Yes, sure, I just told him. Yes, he'll be there for dinner at six o'clock, I didn't forget. Listen, I was just dying to tell you. You know that little rubber pipe I told you about? That he connected to the gas heater? I finally decided to go down the cellar this morning and take it away and destroy it. But it's gone! Imagine! He took it away himself, it isn't there! (*She listens.*) When? Oh, then you took it. Oh—nothing, it's just that I'd hoped he'd taken it away himself. Oh, I'm not worried, darling, because this morning he left in such high spirits, it was like the old days! I'm not afraid any more. Did Mr. Oliver see you?. . . Well, you wait there then. And make a nice impression on him, darling. Just don't perspire too much before you see him. And have a nice time with Dad. He may have big news too! . . . That's right, a New York job. And be sweet to him tonight, dear. Be loving to him. Because he's only a little boat looking for a harbor. (*She is trembling with sorrow and joy.*) Oh, that's wonderful, Biff, you'll save his life. Thanks, darling. Just put your arm around him when he comes into the restaurant. Give him a smile. That's the boy . . . Good-by, dear. . . . You got your comb? . . . That's fine. Good-by, Biff dear.

In the middle of her speech, HOWARD WAGNER, *thirty-six, wheels in a small typewriter table on which is a wire-recording machine and proceeds to plug it in. This is on the left forestage. Light slowly fades on linda as it rises on* HOWARD. HOWARD *is intent on threading the machine and only glances over his shoulder as* WILLY *appears.*

WILLY. Pst! Pst!

HOWARD. Hello, Willy, come in.

WILLY. Like to have a little talk with you, Howard.

HOWARD. Sorry to keep you waiting. I'll be with you in a minute.

WILLY. What's that, Howard?

HOWARD. Didn't you ever see one of these? Wire recorder.

WILLY. Oh. Can we talk a minute?

HOWARD. Records things. Just got delivery yesterday. Been driving me crazy, the most terrific machine I ever saw in my life. I was up all night with it.

WILLY. What do you do with it?

HOWARD. I bought it for dictation, but you can do anything with it. Listen to this. I had it home last night. Listen to what I picked up. The first one is my daughter. Get this. (*He flicks the switch and "Roll out the Barrel" is heard being whistled.*) Listen to that kid whistle.

WILLY. That is lifelike, isn't it?

HOWARD. Seven years old. Get that tone.

WILLY. Ts, ts. Like to ask a little favor if you . . .

The whistling breaks off, and the voice of HOWARD'S DAUGHTER *is heard.*

HIS DAUGHTER. "Now you, Daddy."

HOWARD. She's crazy for me! (*Again the same song is whistled.*) That's me! Ha! (*He winks.*)

WILLY. You're very good!

The whistling breaks off again. The machine runs silent for a moment.

HOWARD. Sh! Get this now, this is my son.

HIS SON. "The capital of Alabama is Montgomery; the capital of Arizona is Phoenix; the capital of Arkansas is Little Rock; the capital of California is Sacramento . . ." (*and on, and on.*)

HOWARD (*holding up five fingers*). Five years old, Willy!

WILLY. He'll make an announcer some day!

HIS SON (*continuing*). "the capital . . ."

HOWARD. Get that—alphabetical order! (*The machine breaks off suddenly.*) Wait a minute. The maid kicked the plug out.

WILLY. It certainly is a . . .

HOWARD. Sh, for God's sake!

HIS SON. "It's nine o'clock, Bulova watch time. So I have to go to sleep."

WILLY. That really is . . .

HOWARD. Wait a minute! The next is my wife.

They wait.

HOWARD'S VOICE. "Go on, say something." (*Pause.*) "Well, you gonna talk?"

HIS WIFE. "I can't think of anything."

HOWARD'S VOICE. "Well, talk—it's turning."

HIS WIFE (*shyly, beaten*). "Hello." (*Silence.*) "Oh, Howard, I can't talk into this . . ."

HOWARD (*snapping the machine off*). That was my wife.

WILLY. That is a wonderful machine. Can we . . .

HOWARD. I tell you, Willy, I'm gonna take my camera, and my bandsaw, and all my hobbies, and out they go. This is the most fascinating relaxation I ever found.

WILLY. I think I'll get one myself.

HOWARD. Sure, they're only a hundred and a half. You can't do without it. Supposing you wanna hear Jack Benny, see? But you can't be at home at that hour. So you tell the maid to turn the radio on when Jack Benny comes on, and this automatically goes on with the radio . . .

WILLY. And when you come home you . . .

HOWARD. You can come home twelve o'clock, one o'clock, any time you like, and you get yourself a Coke and sit yourself down, throw the switch, and there's Jack Benny's program in the middle of the night!

WILLY. I'm definitely going to get one. Because lots of times I'm on the road, and I think to myself, what I must be missing on the radio!

HOWARD. Don't you have a radio in the car?

WILLY. Well, yeah, but who ever thinks of turning it on?

HOWARD. Say, aren't you supposed to be in Boston?

WILLY. That's what I want to talk to you about, Howard. You got a minute? (*He draws a chair in from the wing.*)

HOWARD. What happened? What're you doing here?

WILLY. Well . . .

HOWARD. You didn't crack up again, did you?

WILLY. Oh, no. No . . .

HOWARD. Geez, you had me worried there for a minute. What's the trouble?

WILLY. Well, tell you the truth, Howard. I've come to the decision that I'd rather not travel any more.

HOWARD. Not travel! Well, what'll you do?

WILLY. Remember, Christmas time, when you had the party here? You said you'd try to think of some spot for me here in town.

HOWARD. With us?

WILLY. Well, sure.

HOWARD. Oh, yeah, yeah. I remember. Well, I couldn't think of anything for you, Willy.

WILLY. I tell ya, Howard. The kids are all grown up, y'know. I don't need much any more. If I could take home—well, sixty-five dollars a week, I could swing it.

HOWARD. Yeah, but Willy, see I . . .

WILLY. I tell ya why, Howard. Speaking frankly and between the two of us, y'know—I'm just a little tired.

HOWARD. Oh, I could understand that, Willy. But you're a road man, Willy, and we do a road business. We've only got a half-dozen salesmen on the floor here.

WILLY. God knows, Howard. I never asked a favor of any man. But I was with the firm when your father used to carry you in here in his arms.

HOWARD. I know that, Willy, but . . .

WILLY. Your father came to me the day you were born and asked me what I thought of the name Howard, may he rest in peace.

HOWARD. I appreciate that, Willy, but there just is no spot here for you. If I had a spot I'd slam you right in, but I just don't have a single solitary spot.

He looks for his lighter. WILLY *has picked it up and gives it to him. Pause.*

WILLY (*with increasing anger*). Howard, all I need to set my table is fifty dollars a week.

HOWARD. But where am I going to put you, kid?

WILLY. Look, it isn't a question of whether I can sell merchandise, is it?

HOWARD. No, but it's business, kid, and everybody's gotta pull his own weight.

WILLY (*desperately*). Just let me tell you a story, Howard . . .

HOWARD. 'Cause you gotta admit, business is business.

WILLY (*angrily*). Business is definitely business, but just listen for a minute. You don't understand this. When I was a boy—eighteen, nineteen—I was already on the road. And there was a question in my mind as to whether selling had a future for me. Because in those days I had a yearning to go to Alaska. See, there were three gold strikes in one month in Alaska, and I felt like going out. Just for the ride, you might say.

HOWARD (*barely interested*). Don't say.

WILLY. Oh, yeah, my father lived many years in Alaska. He was an adventurous man. We've got quite a little streak of self-reliance in our family. I thought I'd go out with my older brother and try to locate him, and maybe settle in the North with the old man. And I was almost decided to go, when I met a salesman in the Parker House. His name was Dave Singleman. And he was eighty-four years old, and he'd drummed merchandise in thirty-one states. And old Dave, he'd go up to his room, y'understand, put on his green velvet slippers—I'll never forget—and pick up his phone and call the buyers, and without ever leaving his room, at the age of eighty-four, he made his living. And when I saw that, I realized that selling was the greatest career a man could want. 'Cause what could be more satisfying than to be able to go, at the age of eighty-four, into twenty or thirty different cities, and pick up a phone, and be remembered and loved and helped by so many different people? Do you know? When he died—and by the way he died the death of a salesman, in his green velvet slippers in the smoker of the New York, New Haven and Hartford, going into Boston—when he died, hundreds of salesmen and buyers were at his funeral. Things were sad on a lotta trains for months after that. (*He stands up,* HOWARD *has not looked at him.*) In those days there was personality in it, Howard. There was respect, and comradeship, and gratitude in it. Today, it's all cut and dried, and there's no chance for bringing friendship to bear—or personality. You see what I mean? They don't know me any more.

HOWARD (*moving away, to the right*). That's just the thing, Willy.

WILLY. If I had forty dollars a week—that's all I'd need. Forty dollars, Howard.

HOWARD. Kid, I can't take blood from a stone, I . . .

WILLY (*desperation is on him now*). Howard, the year Al Smith was nominated, your father came to me and . . .

HOWARD (*starting to go off*). I've got to see some people, kid.

WILLY (*stopping him*). I'm talking about your father! There were promises made across this desk! You mustn't tell me you've got people to see—I put thirty-four years into this firm, Howard, and now I can't pay my insurance! You can't eat the orange and throw the peel away—a man is not a piece of fruit! (*After a pause.*) Now pay attention. Your father—in 1928 I had a big year. I averaged a hundred and seventy dollars a week in commissions.

HOWARD (*impatiently*). Now, Willy, you never averaged . . .

WILLY (*banging his hand on the desk*). I averaged a hundred and seventy dollars a week in the year of 1928! And your father came to me—or rather, I was in the office here—it was right over this desk—and he put his hand on my shoulder . . .

HOWARD (*getting up*). You'll have to excuse me, Willy, I gotta see some people. Pull yourself together. (*Going out.*) I'll be back in a little while.

On HOWARD*'s exit, the light on his chair grows very bright and strange.*

WILLY. Pull myself together! What the hell did I say to him? My God, I was yelling at him! How could I? (WILLY *breaks off, staring at the light, which occupies the chair, animating it. He approaches this chair, standing across the desk from it.*) Frank, Frank, don't you remember what you told me that time? How you put your hand on my shoulder, and Frank . . . (*He leans on the desk and as he speaks the dead man's name he accidentally switches on the recorder, and instantly*)

HOWARD'S SON. ". . . New York is Albany. The capital of Ohio is Cincinnati, the capital of Rhode Island is . . ." (*The recitation continues.*)

WILLY (*leaping away with fright, shouting*). Ha! Howard! Howard! Howard!

HOWARD (*rushing in*). What happened?

WILLY (*pointing at the machine, which continues nasally, childishly, with the capital cities*). Shut it off! Shut it off!

HOWARD (*pulling the plug out*). Look, Willy . . .

WILLY (*pressing his hands to his eyes*). I gotta get myself some coffee. I'll get some coffee . . .

WILLY *starts to walk out.* HOWARD *stops him.*

HOWARD (*rolling up the cord*). Willy, look . . .

WILLY. I'll go to Boston.

HOWARD. Willy, you can't go to Boston for us.

WILLY. Why can't I go?

HOWARD. I don't want you to represent us. I've been meaning to tell you for a long time now.

WILLY. Howard, are you firing me?

HOWARD. I think you need a good long rest, Willy.

WILLY. Howard . . .

HOWARD. And when you feel better, come back, and we'll see if we can work something out.

WILLY. But I gotta earn money, Howard. I'm in no position to . . .

HOWARD. Where are your sons? Why don't your sons give you a hand?

WILLY. They're working on a very big deal.

HOWARD. This is no time for false pride, Willy. You go to your sons and you tell them that you're tired. You've got two great boys, haven't you?

WILLY. Oh, no question, no question, but in the meantime . . .

HOWARD. Then that's that, heh?

WILLY. All right, I'll go to Boston tomorrow.

HOWARD. No, no.

WILLY. I can't throw myself on my sons. I'm not a cripple!

HOWARD. Look, kid, I'm busy this morning.

WILLY (*grasping* HOWARD*'s arm*). Howard, you've got to let me go to Boston!

HOWARD (*hard, keeping himself under control*). I've got a line of people to see this morning. Sit down, take five minutes, and pull yourself together, and then go home, will ya? I need the office, Willy. (*He starts to go, turns, remembering the recorder, starts to push off the table holding the recorder.*) Oh, yeah. Whenever you can this week, stop by and drop off the samples. You'll feel better, Willy, and then come back and we'll talk. Pull yourself together, kid, there's people outside.

HOWARD *exits, pushing the table off left.* WILLY *stares into space, exhausted. Now the music is heard—* BEN*'s music—first distantly, then closer, closer. As* WILLY *speaks,* BEN *enters from the right. He carries valise and umbrella.*

WILLY. Oh, Ben, how did you do it? What is the answer? Did you wind up the Alaska deal already?

BEN. Doesn't take much time if you know what you're doing. Just a short business trip. Boarding ship in an hour. Wanted to say good-by.

WILLY. Ben, I've got to talk to you.

BEN (*glancing at his watch*). Haven't the time, William.

WILLY (*crossing the apron to* BEN). Ben, nothing's working out. I don't know what to do.

BEN. Now, look here, William. I've bought timberland in Alaska and I need a man to look after things for me.

WILLY. God, timberland! Me and my boys in those grand outdoors!

BEN. You've a new continent at your doorstep, William. Get out of these cities, they're full of talk and time payments and courts of law. Screw on your fists and you can fight for a fortune up there.

WILLY. Yes, yes! Linda, Linda!

LINDA *enters as of old, with the wash.*

LINDA. Oh, you're back?

BEN. I haven't much time.

WILLY. No, wait! Linda, he's got a proposition for me in Alaska.

LINDA. But you've got . . . (*To* BEN.) He's got a beautiful job here.

WILLY. But in Alaska, kid, I could . . .

LINDA. You're doing well enough, Willy!

BEN (*To* LINDA). Enough for what, my dear?

LINDA (*frightened of* BEN *and angry at him*). Don't say those things to him! Enough to be happy right here, right now. (*To* WILLY, *while* BEN *laughs.*) Why must everybody conquer the world? You're well liked, and the boys love you, and someday—(*To* BEN)—why, old man Wagner told him just the other day that if he keeps it up he'll be a member of the firm, didn't he, Willy?

WILLY. Sure, sure. I am building something with this firm, Ben, and if a man is building something he must be on the right track, mustn't he?

BEN. What are you building? Lay your hand on it. Where is it?

WILLY (*hesitantly*). That's true, Linda, there's nothing.

LINDA. Why? (*To* BEN.) There's a man eighty-four years old . . .

WILLY. That's right, Ben, that's right. When I look at that man I say, what is there to worry about?

BEN. Bah!

WILLY. It's true, Ben. All he has to do is go into any city, pick up the phone, and he's making his living and you know why?

BEN (*picking up his valise*). I've got to go.

WILLY (*holding* BEN *back*). Look at this boy!

BIFF, *in his high school sweater, enters carrying suitcase.* HAPPY *carries* BIFF*'s shoulder guards, gold helmet, and football pants.*

WILLY. Without a penny to his name, three great universities are begging for him, and from there the sky's the limit, because it's not what you do, Ben. It's who you know and the smile on your face! It's contacts, Ben, contacts! The whole wealth of Alaska passes over the lunch table at the Commodore Hotel, and that's the wonder, the wonder of this country, that a man can end with diamonds here on the basis of being liked! (*He turns to* BIFF.) And that's why when you get out on that field today it's important. Because thousands of people will be rooting for you and loving you. (*To* BEN, *who has again begun to leave.*) And Ben! when he walks into a business office his name will sound out like a bell and all the doors will open to him! I've seen it, Ben, I've seen it a thousand times! You can't feel it with your hand like timber, but it's there!

BEN. Good-by, William.

WILLY. Ben, am I right? Don't you think I'm right? I value your advice.

BEN. There's a new continent at your doorstep, William. You could walk out rich. Rich! (*He is gone.*)

WILLY. We'll do it here, Ben! You hear me? We're gonna do it here!

YOUNG BERNARD *rushes in. The gay music of the Boys is heard.*

BERNARD. Oh, gee, I was afraid you left already!

WILLY. Why? What time is it?

BERNARD. It's half-past one!

WILLY. Well, come on, everybody! Ebbets Field next stop! Where's the pennants? (*He rushes through the wall-line of the kitchen and out into the living room.*)

LINDA (*to* BIFF). Did you pack fresh underwear?

BIFF (*who has been limbering up*). I want to go!

BERNARD. Biff, I'm carrying your helmet, ain't I?

HAPPY. No, I'm carrying the helmet.

BERNARD. Oh, Biff, you promised me.

HAPPY. I'm carrying the helmet.

BERNARD. How am I going to get in the locker room?

LINDA. Let him carry the shoulder guards. (*She puts her coat and hat on in the kitchen.*)

BERNARD. Can I, Biff? 'Cause I told everybody I'm going to be in the locker room.

HAPPY. In Ebbets Field it's the clubhouse.

BERNARD. I meant the clubhouse. Biff!

HAPPY. Biff!

BIFF (*grandly, after a slight pause*). Let him carry the shoulder guards.

HAPPY (*as he gives* BERNARD *the shoulder guards*). Stay close to us now.

WILLY *rushes in with the pennants.*

WILLY (*handing them out*). Everybody wave when Biff comes out on the field. (HAPPY *and* BERNARD *run off.*) You set now, boy?

The music has died away.

BIFF. Ready to go, Pop. Every muscle is ready.

WILLY (*at the edge of the apron*). You realize what this means?

BIFF. That's right, Pop.

WILLY (*feeling* BIFF*'s muscles*). You're comin' home this afternoon captain of the All-Scholastic Championship Team of the City of New York.

BIFF. I got it, Pop. And remember, pal, when I take off my helmet, that touchdown is for you.

WILLY. Let's go! (*He is starting out, with his arm around* BIFF, *when* CHARLEY *enters, as of old, in knickers.*) I got no room for you, Charley.

CHARLEY. Room? For what?

WILLY. In the car.

CHARLEY. You goin' for a ride? I wanted to shoot some casino.

WILLY (*furiously*). Casino! (*Incredulously.*) Don't you realize what today is?

LINDA. Oh, he knows, Willy. He's just kidding you.

WILLY. That's nothing to kid about!

CHARLEY. No, Linda, what's goin' on?

LINDA. He's playing in Ebbets Field.

CHARLEY. Baseball in this weather?

WILLY. Don't talk to him. Come on, come on! (*He is pushing them out.*)

CHARLEY. Wait a minute, didn't you hear the news?

WILLY. What?

CHARLEY. Don't you listen to the radio? Ebbets Field just blew up.

WILLY. You go to hell! (CHARLEY *laughs. Pushing them out.*) Come on, come on! We're late.

CHARLEY (*as they go*). Knock a homer, Biff, knock a homer!

WILLY (*the last to leave, turning to* CHARLEY). I don't think that was funny, Charley. This is the greatest day of his life.

CHARLEY. Willy, when are you going to grow up?

WILLY. Yeah, heh? When this game is over, Charley, you'll be laughing out of the other side of your face. They'll be calling him another Red Grange. Twenty-five thousand a year.

CHARLEY (*kidding*). Is that so?

WILLY. Yeah, that's so.

CHARLEY. Well, then, I'm sorry, Willy. But tell me something.

WILLY. What?

CHARLEY. Who is Red Grange?

WILLY. Put up your hands. Goddam you, put up your hands!

CHARLEY, *chuckling, shakes his head and walks away, around the left corner of the stage.* WILLY *follows him. The music rises to a mocking frenzy.*

WILLY. Who the hell do you think you are, better than everybody else? You don't know everything, you big, ignorant, stupid . . . Put up your hands!

Light rises, on the right side of the forestage, on a small table in the reception room of CHARLEY'*s office. Traffic sounds heard.* BERNARD, *now mature, sits whistling to himself. A pair of tennis rackets and an old overnight bag are on the floor beside him.*

WILLY (*offstage*). What are you walking away for? Don't walk away! If you're going to say something say it to my face! I know you laugh at me behind my back. You'll laugh out of the other side of your goddam face after this game. Touchdown! Touchdown! Eighty thousand people! Touchdown! Right between the goal posts.

(BERNARD *is a quiet, earnest, but self-assured young man.* WILLY'*s voice is coming from right upstage now.* BERNARD *lowers his feet off the table and listens.* JENNY, *his father's secretary, enters.*)

JENNY (*distressed*). Say, Bernard, will you go out in the hall?

BERNARD. What is that noise? Who is it?

JENNY. Mr. Loman. He just got off the elevator.

BERNARD (*getting up*). Who's he arguing with?

JENNY. Nobody. There's nobody with him. I can't deal with him any more, and your father gets all upset every time he comes. I've got a lot of typing to do, and your father's waiting to sign it. Will you see him?

WILLY (*entering*). Touchdown! Touch—(*He sees* JENNY.) Jenny, Jenny, good to see you. How're ya? Workin'? Or still honest?

JENNY. Fine. How've you been feeling?

WILLY. Not much any more, Jenny. Ha, ha! (*He is surprised to see the rackets.*)

BERNARD. Hello, Uncle Willy.

WILLY (*almost shocked*). Bernard! Well, look who's here!

(*He comes quickly, guiltily, to* BERNARD *and warmly shakes his hand.*)

BERNARD. How are you? Good to see you.

WILLY. What are you doing here?

BERNARD. Oh, just stopped by to see Pop. Get off my feet till my train leaves. I'm going to Washington in a few minutes.

WILLY. Is he in?

BERNARD. Yes, he's in his office with the accountant. Sit down.

WILLY (*sitting down*). What're you going to do in Washington?

BERNARD. Oh, just a case I've got there, Willy.

WILLY. That so? (*Indicating the rackets.*) You going to play tennis there?

BERNARD. I'm staying with a friend who's got a court.

WILLY. Don't say. His own tennis court. Must be fine people, I bet.

BERNARD. They are, very nice. Dad tells me Biff's in town.

WILLY (*with a big smile*). Yeah, Biff's in. Working on a very big deal, Bernard.

BERNARD. What's Biff doing?

WILLY. Well, he's been doing very big things in the West. But he decided to establish himself here. Very big. We're having dinner. Did I hear your wife had a boy?

BERNARD. That's right. Our second.

WILLY. Two boys! What do you know!

BERNARD. What kind of a deal has Biff got?

WILLY. Well, Bill Oliver—very big sporting-goods man—he wants Biff very badly. Called him in from the West. Long distance, carte blanche, special deliveries. Your friends have their own private tennis court?

BERNARD. You still with the old firm, Willy?

WILLY (*after a pause*). I'm—I'm overjoyed to see how you made the grade, Bernard, overjoyed. It's an encouraging thing to see a young man really—really . . . Looks very good for Biff—very . . . (*He breaks off, then.*) Bernard . . . (*He is so full of emotion, he breaks off again.*)

BERNARD. What is it, Willy?

WILLY (*small and alone*). What—what's the secret?

BERNARD. What secret?

WILLY. How—how did you? Why didn't he ever catch on?

BERNARD. I wouldn't know that, Willy.

WILLY (*confidentially, desperately*). You were his friend, his boyhood friend. There's something I don't understand about it. His life ended after that Ebbets Field game. From the age of seventeen nothing good ever happened to him.

BERNARD. He never trained himself for anything.

WILLY. But he did, he did. After high school he took so many correspondence courses. Radio mechanics; television; God knows what, and never made the slightest mark.

BERNARD (*taking off his glasses*). Willy, do you want to talk candidly?

WILLY (*rising, faces* BERNARD). I regard you as a very brilliant man, Bernard. I value your advice.

BERNARD. Oh, the hell with the advice, Willy. I couldn't advise you. There's just one thing I've always wanted to ask you. When he was supposed to graduate, and the math teacher flunked him . . .

WILLY. Oh, that son-of-a-bitch ruined his life.

BERNARD. Yeah, but, Willy, all he had to do was go to summer school and make up that subject.

WILLY. That's right, that's right.

BERNARD. Did you tell him not to go to summer school?

WILLY. Me? I begged him to go. I ordered him to go!

BERNARD. Then why wouldn't he go?

WILLY. Why? Why! Bernard, that question has been trailing me like a ghost for the last fifteen years. He flunked the subject, and laid down and died like a hammer hit him!

BERNARD. Take it easy, kid.

WILLY. Let me talk to you—I got nobody to talk to. Bernard, Bernard, was it my fault? Y'see? It keeps going around in my mind, maybe I did something to him. I got nothing to give him.

BERNARD. Don't take it so hard.

WILLY. Why did he lay down? What is the story there? You were his friend!

BERNARD. Willy, I remember, it was June, and our grades came out. And he'd flunked math.

WILLY. That son-of-a-bitch!

BERNARD. No, it wasn't right then. Biff just got very angry, I remember, and he was ready to enroll in summer school.

WILLY (*surprised*). He was?

BERNARD. He wasn't beaten by it at all. But then, Willy, he disappeared from the block for almost a month. And I got the idea that he'd gone up to New England to see you. Did he have a talk with you then?

WILLY *stares in silence.*

BERNARD. Willy?

WILLY (*with a strong edge of resentment in his voice*). Yeah, he came to Boston. What about it?

BERNARD. Well, just that when he came back—I'll never forget this, it always mystifies me. Because I'd thought so well of Biff, even though he'd always taken advantage of me. I loved him, Willy, y'know? And he came back after that month and took his sneakers—remember those sneakers with "University of Virginia" printed on them? He was so proud of those, wore them every day. And he took them down in the cellar, and burned them up in the furnace. We had a fist fight. It lasted at least half an hour. Just the two of us, punching each other down the cellar, and crying right through it. I've often thought of how strange it was that I knew he'd given up his life. What happened in Boston, Willy?

WILLY *looks at him as at an intruder.*

BERNARD. I just bring it up because you asked me.

WILLY (*angrily*). Nothing. What do you mean, "What happened?" What's that got to do with anything?

BERNARD. Well, don't get sore.

WILLY. What are you trying to do, blame it on me? If a boy lays down is that my fault?

BERNARD. Now, Willy, don't get . . .

WILLY. Well, don't—don't talk to me that way! What does that mean, "What happened?"

CHARLEY *enters. He is in his vest, and he carries a bottle of bourbon.*

CHARLEY. Hey, you're going to miss that train. (*He waves the bottle.*)

BERNARD. Yeah, I'm going. (*He takes the bottle.*) Thanks, Pop. (*He picks up his rackets and bag.*) Good-by, Willy, and don't worry about it. You know, "If at first you don't succeed . . ."

WILLY. Yes, I believe in that.

BERNARD. But sometimes, Willy, it's better for a man just to walk away.

WILLY. Walk away?

BERNARD. That's right.

WILLY. But if you can't walk away?

BERNARD (*after a slight pause*). I guess that's when it's tough. (*Extending his hand.*) Good-by, Willy.

WILLY (*shaking* BERNARD'*s hand*). Good-by, boy.

CHARLEY (*an arm on* BERNARD'*s shoulder*). How do you like this kid? Gonna argue a case in front of the Supreme Court.

BERNARD (*protesting*). Pop!

WILLY (*genuinely shocked, pained, and happy*). No! The Supreme Court!

BERNARD. I gotta run. 'By, Dad!

CHARLEY. Knock 'em dead, Bernard!

BERNARD *goes off.*

WILLY (*as* CHARLEY *takes out his wallet*). The Supreme Court! And he didn't even mention it!

CHARLEY (*counting out money on the desk*). He don't have to—he's gonna do it.

WILLY. And you never told him what to do, did you? You never took any interest in him.

CHARLEY. My salvation is that I never took any interest in anything. There's some money—fifty dollars. I got an accountant inside.

WILLY. Charley, look . . . (*with difficulty.*) I got my insurance to pay. If you can manage it—I need a hundred and ten dollars.

CHARLEY *doesn't reply for a moment; merely stops moving.*

WILLY. I'd draw it from my bank but Linda would know, and I . . .

CHARLEY. Sit down, Willy.

WILLY (*moving toward the chair*). I'm keeping an account of everything, remember. I'll pay every penny back. (*He sits.*)

CHARLEY. Now listen to me, Willy.

WILLY. I want you to know I appreciate . . .

CHARLEY (*sitting down on the table*). Willy, what're you doin'? What the hell is going on in your head?

WILLY. Why? I'm simply . . .

CHARLEY. I offered you a job. You make fifty dollars a week. And I won't send you on the road.

WILLY. I've got a job.

CHARLEY. Without pay? What kind of a job is a job without pay? (*He rises.*) Now, look, kid, enough is enough. I'm no genius but I know when I'm being insulted.

WILLY. Insulted!

CHARLEY. Why don't you want to work for me?

WILLY. What's the matter with you? I've got a job.

CHARLEY. Then what're you walkin' in here every week for?

WILLY (*getting up*). Well, if you don't want me to walk in here . . .

CHARLEY. I'm offering you a job.

WILLY. I don't want your goddam job!

CHARLEY. When the hell are you going to grow up?

WILLY (*furiously*). You big ignoramus, if you say that to me again I'll rap you one! I don't care how big you are! (*He's ready to fight.*)

Pause.

CHARLEY (*kindly, going to him*). How much do you need, Willy?

WILLY. Charley, I'm strapped. I'm strapped. I don't know what to do. I was just fired.

CHARLEY. Howard fired you?

WILLY. That snotnose. Imagine that? I named him. I named him Howard.

CHARLEY. Willy, when're you gonna realize that them things don't mean anything? You named him Howard, but you can't sell that. The only thing you got in this world is what you can sell. And the funny thing is that you're a salesman, and you don't know that.

WILLY. I've always tried to think otherwise, I guess. I always felt that if a man was impressive, and well liked, that nothing . . .

CHARLEY. Why must everybody like you? Who liked J. P. Morgan? Was he impressive? In a Turkish bath he'd look like a butcher. But with his pockets on he was very well liked. Now listen, Willy, I know you don't like me, and nobody can say I'm in love with you, but I'll give you a job because—just for the hell of it, put it that way. Now what do you say?

WILLY. I—I just can't work for you, Charley.

CHARLEY. What're you, jealous of me?

WILLY. I can't work for you, that's all, don't ask me why.

CHARLEY (*angered, takes out more bills*). You been jealous of me all your life, you damned fool! Here, pay your insurance. (*He puts the money in* WILLY'*s hand.*)

WILLY. I'm keeping strict accounts.

CHARLEY. I've got some work to do. Take care of yourself. And pay your insurance.

WILLY (*moving to the right*). Funny, y'know? After all the highways, and the trains, and the appointments, and the years, you end up worth more dead than alive.

CHARLEY. Willy, nobody's worth nothin' dead. (*After a slight pause.*) Did you hear what I said?

WILLY *stands still, dreaming.*

CHARLEY. Willy!

WILLY. Apologize to Bernard for me when you see him. I didn't mean to argue with him. He's a fine boy. They're all fine boys, and they'll end up big—all of them. Someday they'll all play tennis together. Wish me luck, Charley. He saw Bill Oliver today.

CHARLEY. Good luck.

WILLY (*on the verge of tears*). Charley, you're the only friend I got. Isn't that a remarkable thing? (*He goes out.*)

CHARLEY. Jesus!

CHARLEY *stares after him a moment and follows. All light blacks out. Suddenly raucous music is heard, and a red glow rises behind the screen at right.* STANLEY, *a young waiter, appears, carrying a table, followed by* HAPPY, *who is carrying two chairs.*

STANLEY (*putting the table down*). That's all right, Mr. Loman, I can handle it myself. (*He turns and takes the chairs from* HAPPY *and places them at the table.*)

HAPPY (*glancing around*). Oh, this is better.

STANLEY. Sure, in the front there you're in the middle of all kinds of noise. Whenever you got a party, Mr. Loman, you just tell me and I'll put you back here. Y'know, there's a lotta people they don't like it private, because when they go out they like to see a lotta action around them because they're sick and tired to stay in the house by theirself. But I know you, you ain't from Hackensack. You know what I mean?

HAPPY (*sitting down*). So how's it coming, Stanley?

STANLEY. Ah, it's a dog life. I only wish during the war they'd a took me in the Army. I coulda been dead by now.

HAPPY. My brother's back, Stanley.

STANLEY. Oh, he come back, heh? From the Far West.

HAPPY. Yeah, big cattle man, my brother, so treat him right. And my father's coming too.

STANLEY. Oh, your father too!

HAPPY. You got a couple of nice lobsters?

STANLEY. Hundred percent, big.

HAPPY. I want them with the claws.

STANLEY. Don't worry, I don't give you no mice. (HAPPY *laughs.*) How about some wine? It'll put a head on the meal.

HAPPY. No. You remember, Stanley, that recipe I brought you from overseas? With the champagne in it?

STANLEY. Oh, yeah, sure. I still got it tacked up yet in the kitchen. But that'll have to cost a buck apiece anyways.

HAPPY. That's all right.

STANLEY. What'd you, hit a number or somethin'?

HAPPY. No, it's a little celebration. My brother is—I think he pulled off a big deal today. I think we're going into business together.

STANLEY. Great! That's the best for you. Because a family business, you know what I mean?—that's the best.

HAPPY. That's what I think.

STANLEY. 'Cause what's the difference? Somebody steals? It's in the family. Know what I mean? (*Sotto voce.*) Like this bartender here. The boss is goin' crazy what kinda leak he's got in the cash register. You put it in but it don't come out.

HAPPY (*raising his head*). Sh!

STANLEY. What?

HAPPY. You notice I wasn't lookin' right or left, was I?

STANLEY. No.

HAPPY. And my eyes are closed.

STANLEY. So what's the . . .?

HAPPY. Strudel's comin'.

STANLEY (*catching on, looks around*). Ah, no, there's no . . .

He breaks off as a furred, lavishly dressed girl enters and sits at the next table. Both follow her with their eyes.

STANLEY. Geez, how'd ya know?

HAPPY. I got radar or something. (*Staring directly at her profile.*) Oooooooo . . . Stanley.

STANLEY. I think that's for you, Mr. Loman.

HAPPY. Look at that mouth. Oh, God. And the binoculars.

STANLEY. Geez, you got a life, Mr. Loman.

HAPPY. Wait on her.

STANLEY (*going to the girl's table*). Would you like a menu, ma'am?

GIRL. I'm expecting someone, but I'd like a . . .

HAPPY. Why don't you bring her—excuse me, miss, do you mind? I sell champagne, and I'd like you to try my brand. Bring her a champagne, Stanley.

GIRL. That's awfully nice of you.

HAPPY. Don't mention it. It's all company money. (*He laughs.*)

GIRL. That's a charming product to be selling, isn't it?

HAPPY. Oh, gets to be like everything else. Selling is selling, y'know.

GIRL. I suppose.

HAPPY. You don't happen to sell, do you?

GIRL. No, I don't sell.

HAPPY. Would you object to a compliment from a stranger? You ought to be on a magazine cover.

GIRL (*looking at him a little archly*). I have been.

STANLEY *comes in with a glass of champagne.*

HAPPY. What'd I say before, Stanley? You see? She's a cover girl.

STANLEY. Oh, I could see, I could see.

HAPPY (*to the* GIRL). What magazine?

GIRL. Oh, a lot of them. (*She takes the drink.*) Thank you.

HAPPY. You know what they say in France, don't you? "Champagne is the drink of the complexion"—Hya, Biff!

BIFF *has entered and sits with* HAPPY.

BIFF. Hello, kid. Sorry I'm late.

HAPPY. I just got here. Uh, Miss . . .?

GIRL. Forsythe.

HAPPY. Miss Forsythe, this is my brother.

BIFF. Is Dad here?

HAPPY. His name is Biff. You might've heard of him. Great football player.

GIRL. Really? What team?

HAPPY. Are you familiar with football?

GIRL. No, I'm afraid I'm not.

HAPPY. Biff is quarterback with the New York Giants.

GIRL. Well, that is nice, isn't it? (*She drinks.*)

HAPPY. Good health.

GIRL. I'm happy to meet you.

HAPPY. That's my name. Hap. It's really Harold, but at West Point they called me Happy.

GIRL (*now really impressed*). Oh, I see. How do you do? (*She turns her profile.*)

BIFF. Isn't Dad coming?

HAPPY. You want her?

BIFF. Oh, I could never make that.

HAPPY. I remember the time that idea would never come into your head. Where's the old confidence, Biff?

BIFF. I just saw Oliver . . .

HAPPY. Wait a minute. I've got to see that old confidence again. Do you want her? She's on call.

BIFF. Oh, no. (*He turns to look at the* GIRL.)

HAPPY. I'm telling you. Watch this. (*Turning to the* GIRL.) Honey? (*She turns to him.*) Are you busy?

GIRL. Well, I am . . . but I could make a phone call.

HAPPY. Do that, will you, honey? And see if you can get a friend. We'll be here for a while. Biff is one of the greatest football players in the country.

GIRL (*standing up*). Well, I'm certainly happy to meet you.

HAPPY. Come back soon.

GIRL. I'll try.

HAPPY. Don't try, honey, try hard.

The GIRL *exits.* STANLEY *follows, shaking his head in bewildered admiration.*

HAPPY. Isn't that a shame now? A beautiful girl like that? That's why I can't get married. There's not a good woman in a thousand. New York is loaded with them, kid!

BIFF. Hap, look . . .

HAPPY. I told you she was on call!

BIFF (*strangely unnerved*). Cut it out, will ya? I want to say something to you.

HAPPY. Did you see Oliver?

BIFF. I saw him all right. Now look, I want to tell Dad a couple of things and I want you to help me.

HAPPY. What? Is he going to back you?

BIFF. Are you crazy? You're out of your goddam head, you know that?

HAPPY. Why? What happened?

BIFF (*breathlessly*). I did a terrible thing today, Hap. It's been the strangest day I ever went through. I'm all numb, I swear.

HAPPY. You mean he wouldn't see you?

BIFF. Well, I waited six hours for him, see? All day. Kept sending my name in. Even tried to date his secretary so she'd get me to him, but no soap.

HAPPY. Because you're not showin' the old confidence, Biff. He remembered you, didn't he?

BIFF (*stopping* HAPPY *with a gesture*). Finally, about five o'clock, he comes out. Didn't remember who I was or anything. I felt like such an idiot, Hap.

HAPPY. Did you tell him my Florida idea?

BIFF. He walked away. I saw him for one minute. I got so mad I could've torn the walls down! How the hell did I ever get the idea I was a salesman there? I even believed myself that I'd been a salesman for him! And then he gave me one look and—I realized what a ridiculous lie my whole life has been! We've been talking in a dream for fifteen years. I was a shipping clerk.

HAPPY. What'd you do?

BIFF (*with great tension and wonder*). Well, he left, see. And the secretary went out. I was all alone in the waiting room. I don't know what came over me, Hap. The next thing I know I'm in his office—paneled walls, everything. I can't explain it. I—Hap. I took his fountain pen.

HAPPY. Geez, did he catch you?

BIFF. I ran out. I ran down all eleven flights. I ran and ran and ran.

HAPPY. That was an awful dumb—what'd you do that for?

BIFF (*agonized*). I don't know, I just—wanted to take something, I don't know. You gotta help me, Hap. I'm gonna tell Pop.

HAPPY. You crazy? What for?

BIFF. Hap, he's got to understand that I'm not the man somebody lends that kind of money to. He thinks I've been spiting him all these years and it's eating him up.

HAPPY. That's just it. You tell him something nice.

BIFF. I can't.

HAPPY. Say you got a lunch date with Oliver tomorrow.

BIFF. So what do I do tomorrow?

HAPPY. You leave the house tomorrow and come back at night and say Oliver is thinking it over. And he thinks it over for a couple of weeks, and gradually it fades away and nobody's the worse.

BIFF. But it'll go on forever!

HAPPY. Dad is never so happy as when he's looking forward to something!

WILLY *enters.*

HAPPY. Hello, scout!

WILLY. Gee, I haven't been here in years!

STANLEY *has followed* WILLY *in and sets a chair for him.* STANLEY *starts off but* HAPPY *stops him.*

HAPPY. Stanley!

STANLEY *stands by, waiting for an order.*

BIFF (*going to* WILLY *with guilt, as to an invalid*). Sit down, Pop. You want a drink?

WILLY. Sure, I don't mind.

BIFF. Let's get a load on.

WILLY. You look worried.

BIFF. N-no. (*To* STANLEY.) Scotch all around. Make it doubles.

STANLEY. Doubles, right. (*He goes.*)

WILLY. You had a couple already, didn't you?

BIFF. Just a couple, yeah.

WILLY. Well, what happened, boy? (*Nodding affirmatively, with a smile.*) Everything go all right?

BIFF (*takes a breath, then reaches out and grasps* WILLY'*s hand*). Pal . . . (*He is smiling bravely, and* WILLY *is smiling too.*) I had an experience today.

HAPPY. Terrific, Pop.

WILLY. That so? What happened?

BIFF (*high, slightly alcoholic, above the earth*). I'm going to tell you everything from first to last. It's been a strange day. (*Silence. He looks around, composes himself as best he can, but his breath keeps breaking the rhythm of his voice.*) I had to wait quite a while for him, and . . .

WILLY. Oliver?

BIFF. Yeah, Oliver. All day, as a matter of cold fact. And a lot of—instances—facts, Pop, facts about my life came back to me. Who was it, Pop? Who ever said I was a salesman with Oliver?

WILLY. Well, you were.

BIFF. No, Dad, I was a shipping clerk.

WILLY. But you were practically . . .

BIFF (*with determination*). Dad, I don't know who said it first, but I was never a salesman for Bill Oliver.

WILLY. What're you talking about?

BIFF. Let's hold on to the facts tonight, Pop. We're not going to get anywhere bullin' around. I was a shipping clerk.

WILLY (*angrily*). All right, now listen to me . . .

BIFF. Why don't you let me finish?

WILLY. I'm not interested in stories about the past or any crap of that kind because the woods are burning, boys, you understand? There's a big blaze going on all around. I was fired today.

BIFF (*shocked*). How could you be?

WILLY. I was fired, and I'm looking for a little good news to tell your mother, because the woman has waited and the woman has suffered. The gist of it is that I haven't got a story left in my head, Biff. So don't give me a lecture about facts and aspects. I am not interested. Now what've you got to say to me?

STANLEY *enters with three drinks. They wait until he leaves.*

WILLY. Did you see Oliver?

BIFF. Jesus, Dad!

WILLY. You mean you didn't go up there?

HAPPY. Sure he went up there.

BIFF. I did. I—saw him. How could they fire you?

WILLY (*on the edge of his chair*). What kind of a welcome did he give you?

BIFF. He won't even let you work on commission?

WILLY. I'm out! (*Driving.*) So tell me, he gave you a warm welcome?

HAPPY. Sure, Pop, sure!

BIFF (*driven*). Well, it was kind of . . .

WILLY. I was wondering if he'd remember you. (*To* HAPPY.) Imagine, man doesn't see him for ten, twelve years and gives him that kind of a welcome!

HAPPY. Damn right!

BIFF (*trying to return to the offensive*). Pop, look . . .

WILLY. You know why he remembered you, don't you? Because you impressed him in those days.

BIFF. Let's talk quietly and get this down to the facts, huh?

WILLY (*as though* BIFF *had been interrupting*). Well, what happened? It's great news, Biff. Did he take you into his office or'd you talk in the waiting room?

BIFF. Well, he came in, see, and . . .

WILLY (*with a big smile*). What'd he say? Betcha he threw his arm around you.

BIFF. Well, he kinda . . .

WILLY. He's a fine man. (*To* HAPPY.) Very hard man to see, y'know.

HAPPY (*agreeing*). Oh, I know.

WILLY (*to* BIFF). Is that where you had the drinks?

BIFF. Yeah, he gave me a couple of—no, no!

HAPPY (*cutting in*). He told him my Florida idea.

WILLY. Don't interrupt. (*To* BIFF.) How'd he react to the Florida idea?

BIFF. Dad, will you give me a minute to explain?

WILLY. I've been waiting for you to explain since I sat down here! What happened? He took you into his office and what?

BIFF. Well—I talked. And—and he listened, see.

WILLY. Famous for the way he listens, y'know. What was his answer?

BIFF. His answer was—(*He breaks off, suddenly angry.*) Dad, you're not letting me tell you what I want to tell you!

WILLY (*accusing, angered*). You didn't see him, did you?

BIFF. I did see him!

WILLY. What'd you insult him or something? You insulted him, didn't you?

BIFF. Listen, will you let me out of it, will you just let me out of it!

HAPPY. What the hell!

WILLY. Tell me what happened!

BIFF (*to* HAPPY). I can't talk to him!

A single trumpet note jars the ear. The light of green leaves stains the house, which holds the air of night and a dream. YOUNG BERNARD *enters and knocks on the door of the house.*

YOUNG BERNARD (*frantically*). Mrs. Loman, Mrs. Loman!

HAPPY. Tell him what happened!

BIFF (*to* HAPPY.) Shut up and leave me alone!

WILLY. No, no! You had to go and flunk math!

BIFF. What math? What're you talking about?

YOUNG BERNARD. Mrs. Loman, Mrs. Loman!

LINDA *appears in the house, as of old.*

WILLY (*wildly*). Math, math, math!

BIFF. Take it easy, Pop!

YOUNG BERNARD. Mrs. Loman!

WILLY (*furiously*). If you hadn't flunked you'd've been set by now!

BIFF. Now, look, I'm gonna tell you what happened, and you're going to listen to me.

YOUNG BERNARD. Mrs. Loman!

BIFF. I waited six hours . . .

HAPPY. What the hell are you saying?

BIFF. I kept sending in my name but he wouldn't see me. So finally he . . . (*He continues unheard as light fades low on the restaurant.*)

YOUNG BERNARD. Biff flunked math!

LINDA. No!

YOUNG BERNARD. Birnbaum flunked him! They won't graduate him!

LINDA. But they have to. He's gotta go to the university. Where is he? Biff! Biff!

YOUNG BERNARD. No, he left. He went to Grand Central.

LINDA. Grand—You mean he went to Boston!

YOUNG BERNARD. Is Uncle Willy in Boston?

LINDA. Oh, maybe Willy can talk to the teacher. Oh, the poor, poor boy!

Light on house area snaps out.

BIFF (*at the table, now audible, holding up a gold fountain pen*). . . . so I'm washed up with Oliver, you understand? Are you listening to me?

WILLY (*at a loss*). Yeah, sure. If you hadn't flunked . . .

BIFF. Flunked what? What're you talking about?

WILLY. Don't blame everything on me! I didn't flunk math—you did! What pen?

HAPPY. That was awful dumb, Biff, a pen like that is worth—

WILLY (*seeing the pen for the first time*). You took Oliver's pen?

BIFF (*weakening*). Dad, I just explained it to you.

WILLY. You stole Bill Oliver's fountain pen!

BIFF. I didn't exactly steal it! That's just what I've been explaining to you!

HAPPY. He had it in his hand and just then Oliver walked in, so he got nervous and stuck it in his pocket!

WILLY. My God, Biff!

BIFF. I never intended to do it, Dad

OPERATOR'S VOICE. Standish Arms, good evening!

WILLY (*shouting*). I'm not in my room!

BIFF (*frightened*). Dad, what's the matter? (*He and* HAPPY *stand up.*)

OPERATOR. Ringing Mr. Loman for you!

WILLY. I'm not there, stop it!

BIFF (*horrified, gets down on one knee before* WILLY). Dad, I'll make good, I'll make good. (WILLY *tries to get to his feet.* BIFF *holds him down.*) Sit down now.

WILLY. No, you're no good, you're no good for anything.

BIFF. I am, Dad, I'll find something else, you understand? Now don't worry about anything. (*He holds up* WILLY*'s face.*) Talk to me, Dad.

OPERATOR. Mr. Loman does not answer. Shall I page him?

WILLY (*attempting to stand, as though to rush and silence the* OPERATOR). No, no, no!

HAPPY. He'll strike something, Pop.

WILLY. No, no . . .

BIFF (*desperately, standing over* WILLY). Pop, listen! Listen to me! I'm telling you something good. Oliver talked to his partner about the Florida idea. You listening? He—he talked to his partner, and he came to me . . . I'm going to be all right, you hear? Dad, listen to me, he said it was just a question of the amount!

WILLY. Then you . . . got it?

HAPPY. He's gonna be terrific, Pop!

WILLY (*trying to stand*). Then you got it, haven't you? You got it! You got it!

BIFF (*agonized, holds* WILLY *down*). No, no. Look, Pop. I'm supposed to have lunch with them tomorrow. I'm just telling you this so you'll know that I can still make an impression, Pop. And I'll make good somewhere, but I can't go tomorrow, see.

WILLY. Why not? You simply . . .

BIFF. But the pen, Pop!

WILLY. You give it to him and tell him it was an oversight!

HAPPY. Sure, have lunch tomorrow!

BIFF. I can't say that . . .

WILLY. You were doing a crossword puzzle and accidentally used his pen!

BIFF. Listen, kid, I took those balls years ago, now I walk in with his fountain pen? That clinches it, don't you see? I can't face him like that! I'll try elsewhere.

PAGE'S VOICE. Paging Mr. Loman!

WILLY. Don't you want to be anything?

BIFF. Pop, how can I go back?

WILLY. You don't want to be anything, is that what's behind it?

BIFF (*now angry at* WILLY *for not crediting his sympathy*). Don't take it that way! You think it was easy walking into that office after what I'd done to him? A team of horses couldn't have dragged me back to Bill Oliver!

WILLY. Then why'd you go?

BIFF. Why did I go? Why did I go! Look at you! Look at what's become of you!

Off left, THE WOMAN *laughs.*

WILLY. Biff, you're going to go to that lunch tomorrow, or . . .

BIFF. I can't go. I've got no appointment!

HAPPY. Biff, for . . .!

WILLY. Are you spiting me?

BIFF. Don't take it that way! Goddammit!

WILLY (*strikes* BIFF *and falters away from the table*). You rotten little louse! Are you spiting me?

THE WOMAN. Someone's at the door, Willy!

BIFF. I'm no good, can't you see what I am?

HAPPY (*separating them*). Hey, you're in a restaurant! Now cut it out, both of you! (*The girls enter.*) Hello, girls, sit down.

THE WOMAN *laughs, off left.*

MISS FORSYTHE. I guess we might as well. This is Letta.

THE WOMAN. Willy, are you going to wake up?

BIFF (*ignoring* WILLY). How're ya, miss, sit down. What do you drink?

MISS FORSYTHE. Letta might not be able to stay long.

LETTA. I gotta get up very early tomorrow. I got jury duty. I'm so excited! Were you fellows ever on a jury?

BIFF. No, but I been in front of them! (*The girls laugh.*) This is my father.

LETTA. Isn't he cute? Sit down with us, Pop.

HAPPY. Sit him down, Biff!

BIFF (*going to him*). Come on, slugger, drink us under the table. To hell with it! Come on, sit down, pal.

On BIFF*'s last insistence,* WILLY *is about to sit.*

THE WOMAN (*now urgently*). Willy, are you going to answer the door!

THE WOMAN*'s call pulls* WILLY *back. He starts right, befuddled.*

BIFF. Hey, where are you going?

WILLY. Open the door.

BIFF. The door?

WILLY. The washroom . . . the door . . . where's the door?

BIFF (*leading* WILLY *to the left*). Just go straight down.

WILLY *moves left.*

THE WOMAN. Willy, Willy, are you going to get up, get up, get up, get up?

WILLY *exits left.*

LETTA. I think it's sweet you bring your daddy along.

MISS FORSYTHE. Oh, he isn't really your father!

BIFF (*at left, turning to her resentfully*). Miss Forsythe, you've just seen a prince walk by. A fine, troubled prince. A hardworking, unappreciated prince. A pal, you understand? A good companion. Always for his boys.

LETTA. That's so sweet.

HAPPY. Well, girls, what's the program? We're wasting time. Come on, Biff. Gather round. Where would you like to go?

BIFF. Why don't you do something for him?

HAPPY. Me!

BIFF. Don't you give a damn for him, Hap?

HAPPY. What're you talking about? I'm the one who . . .

BIFF. I sense it, you don't give a good goddam about him. (*He takes the rolled-up hose from his pocket and puts it on the table in front of* HAPPY.) Look what I found in the cellar, for Christ's sake. How can you bear to let it go on?

HAPPY. Me? Who goes away? Who runs off and . . .

BIFF. Yeah, but he doesn't mean anything to you. You could help him—I can't! Don't you understand what I'm talking about? He's going to kill himself, don't you know that?

HAPPY. Don't I know it! Me!

BIFF. Hap, help him! Jesus . . . help him . . . Help me, help me, I can't bear to look at his face! (*Ready to weep, he hurries out, up right.*)

HAPPY (*starting after him*). Where are you going?

MISS FORSYTHE. What's he so mad about?

HAPPY. Come on, girls, we'll catch up with him.

MISS FORSYTHE (*as* HAPPY *pushes her out*). Say, I don't like that temper of his!

HAPPY. He's just a little overstrung, he'll be all right!

WILLY (*off left, as* THE WOMAN *laughs*). Don't answer! Don't answer!

LETTA. Don't you want to tell your father . . .

HAPPY. No, that's not my father. He's just a guy. Come on, we'll catch Biff, and, honey, we're going to paint this town! Stanley, where's the check! Hey, Stanley!

They exit. STANLEY *looks toward left.*

STANLEY (*calling to* HAPPY *indignantly*). Mr. Loman! Mr. Loman!

STANLEY *picks up a chair and follows them off. Knocking is heard off left.* THE WOMAN *enters, laughing.* WILLY *follows her. She is in a black slip; he is buttoning his shirt. Raw, sensuous music accompanies their speech:*

WILLY. Will you stop laughing? Will you stop?

THE WOMAN. Aren't you going to answer the door? He'll wake the whole hotel.

WILLY. I'm not expecting anybody.

THE WOMAN. Whyn't you have another drink, honey, and stop being so damn self-centered?

WILLY. I'm so lonely.

THE WOMAN. You know you ruined me, Willy? From now on, whenever you come to the office, I'll see that you go right through to the buyers. No waiting at my desk anymore, Willy. You ruined me.

WILLY. That's nice of you to say that.

THE WOMAN. Gee, you are self-centered! Why so sad? You are the saddest, self-centeredest soul I ever did see-saw. (*She laughs. He kisses her.*) Come on inside, drummer boy. It's silly to be dressing in the middle of the night. (*As knocking is heard.*) Aren't you going to answer the door?

WILLY. They're knocking on the wrong door.

THE WOMAN. But I felt the knocking. And he heard us talking in here. Maybe the hotel's on fire!

WILLY (*his terror rising*). It's a mistake.

THE WOMAN. Then tell him to go away!

WILLY. There's nobody there.

THE WOMAN. It's getting on my nerves, Willy. There's somebody standing out there and it's getting on my nerves!

WILLY (*pushing her away from him*). All right, stay in the bathroom here, and don't come out. I think there's a law in Massachusetts about it, so don't come out. It may be that new room clerk. He looked very mean. So don't come out. It's a mistake, there's no fire.

The knocking is heard again. He takes a few steps away from her, and she vanishes into the wing. The light follows him, and now he is facing YOUNG BIFF, *who carries a suitcase.* BIFF *steps toward him. The music is gone.*

BIFF. Why didn't you answer?

WILLY. Biff! What are you doing in Boston?

BIFF. Why didn't you answer? I've been knocking for five minutes, I called you on the phone . . .

WILLY. I just heard you. I was in the bathroom and had the door shut. Did anything happen home?

BIFF. Dad—I let you down.

WILLY. What do you mean?

BIFF. Dad . . .

WILLY. Biffo, what's this about? (*Putting his arm around* BIFF.) Come on, let's go downstairs and get you a malted.

BIFF. Dad, I flunked math.

WILLY. Not for the term?

BIFF. The term. I haven't got enough credits to graduate.

WILLY. You mean to say Bernard wouldn't give you the answers?

BIFF. He did, he tried, but I only got a sixty-one.

WILLY. And they wouldn't give you four points?

BIFF. Birnbaum refused absolutely. I begged him, Pop, but he won't give me those points. You gotta talk to him before they close the school. Because if he saw the kind of man you are, and you just talked to him in your way, I'm sure he'd come through for me. The class came right before practice, see, and I didn't go enough. Would you talk to him? He'd like you, Pop. You know the way you could talk.

WILLY. You're on. We'll drive right back.

BIFF. Oh, Dad, good work! I'm sure he'll change it for you!

WILLY. Go downstairs and tell the clerk I'm checkin' out. Go right down.

BIFF. Yes, sir! See, the reason he hates me, Pop—one day he was late for class so I got up at the blackboard and imitated him. I crossed my eyes and talked with a lithp.

WILLY (*laughing*). You did? The kids like it?

BIFF. They nearly died laughing!

WILLY. Yeah? What'd you do?

BIFF. The thquare root of thixthy twee is . . . (WILLY *bursts out laughing;* BIFF *joins.*) And in the middle of it he walked in!

WILLY *laughs and* THE WOMAN *joins in offstage.*

WILLY (*without hesitation*). Hurry downstairs and . . .

BIFF. Somebody in there?

WILLY. No, that was next door.

THE WOMAN *laughs offstage.*

BIFF. Somebody got in your bathroom!

WILLY. No, it's the next room, there's a party . . .

THE WOMAN (*enters, laughing; she lisps this*). Can I come in? There's something in the bathtub, Willy, and it's moving!

WILLY *looks at* BIFF, *who is staring open-mouthed and horrified at* THE WOMAN.

WILLY. Ah—you better go back to your room. They must be finished painting by now. They're painting her room so I let her take a shower here. Go back, go back . . . (*He pushes her.*)

THE WOMAN (*resisting*). But I've got to get dressed, Willy, I can't . . .

WILLY. Get out of here! Go back, go back . . . (*Suddenly striving for the ordinary.*) This is Miss Francis, Biff, she's a buyer. They're painting her room. Go back, Miss Francis, go back . . .

THE WOMAN. But my clothes, I can't go out naked in the hall!

WILLY (*pushing her offstage*). Get outa here! Go back, go back!

(BIFF *slowly sits down on his suitcase as the argument continues offstage.*)

THE WOMAN. Where's my stockings? You promised me stockings, Willy!

WILLY. I have no stockings here!

THE WOMAN. You had two boxes of size nine sheers for me, and I want them!

WILLY. Here, for God's sake, will you get outa here!

THE WOMAN (*enters holding a box of stockings*). I just hope there's nobody in the hall. That's all I hope. (*To* BIFF.) Are you football or baseball?

BIFF. Football.

THE WOMAN (*angry, humiliated*). That's me too. G'night. (*She snatches her clothes from* WILLY, *and walks out.*)

WILLY (*after a pause*). Well, better get going. I want to get to the school first thing in the morning. Get my suits out of the closet. I'll get my valise. (BIFF *doesn't move.*) What's the matter! (BIFF *remains motionless, tears falling.*) She's a buyer. Buys for J. H. Simmons. She lives down the hall—they're painting. You don't imagine—(*He breaks off. After a pause.*) Now listen, pal, she's just a buyer. She sees merchandise in her room and they have to keep it looking just so . . . (*Pause. Assuming command.*) All right, get my suits. (BIFF *doesn't move.*) Now stop crying and do as I say. I gave you an order. Biff, I gave you an order! Is that what you do when I give you an order? How dare you cry! (*Putting his arm around* BIFF.) Now look, Biff, when you grow up you'll understand about these things. You mustn't—you mustn't overemphasize a thing like this. I'll see Birnbaum first thing in the morning.

BIFF. Never mind.

WILLY (*getting down beside* BIFF). Never mind! He's going to give you those points. I'll see to it.

BIFF. He wouldn't listen to you.

WILLY. He certainly will listen to me. You need those points for the U. of Virginia.

BIFF. I'm not going there.

WILLY. Heh? If I can't get him to change that mark you'll make it up in summer school. You've got all summer to . . .

BIFF (*his weeping breaking from him*). Dad . . .

WILLY (*infected by it*). Oh, my boy . . .

BIFF. Dad . . .

WILLY. She's nothing to me, Biff. I was lonely, I was terribly lonely.

BIFF. You—you gave her Mama's stockings! (*His tears break through and he rises to go.*)

WILLY (*grabbing for* BIFF). I gave you an order!

BIFF. Don't touch me, you—liar!

WILLY. Apologize for that!

BIFF. You fake! You phony little fake! You fake! (*Overcome, he turns quickly and weeping fully goes out with his suitcase.* WILLY *is left on the floor on his knees.*)

WILLY. I gave you an order! Biff, come back here or I'll beat you! Come back here! I'll whip you!

STANLEY *comes quickly in from the right and stands in front of* WILLY.

WILLY (*shouts at* STANLEY). I gave you an order . . .

STANLEY. Hey, let's pick it up, pick it up, Mr. Loman. (*He helps* WILLY *to his feet.*) Your boys left with the chippies. They said they'll see you home.

A second waiter watches some distance away.

WILLY. But we were supposed to have dinner together.

Music is heard, WILLY*'s theme.*

STANLEY. Can you make it?

WILLY. I'll—sure, I can make it. (*Suddenly concerned about his clothes.*) Do I—I look all right?

STANLEY. Sure, you look all right. (*He flicks a speck off* WILLY*'s lapel.*)

WILLY. Here—here's a dollar.

STANLEY. Oh, your son paid me. It's all right.

WILLY (*putting it in* STANLEY*'s hand*). No, take it. You're a good boy.

STANLEY. Oh, no, you don't have to . . .

WILLY. Here—here's some more, I don't need it any more. (*After a slight pause.*) Tell me—is there a seed store in the neighborhood?

STANLEY. Seeds? You mean like to plant?

As WILLY *turns,* STANLEY *slips the money back into his jacket pocket.*

WILLY. Yes. Carrots, peas . . .

STANLEY. Well, there's hardware stores on Sixth Avenue, but it may be too late now.

WILLY (*anxiously*). Oh, I'd better hurry. I've got to get some seeds. (*He starts off to the right.*) I've got to get some seeds, right away. Nothing's planted. I don't have a thing in the ground.

WILLY *hurries out as the light goes down.* STANLEY *moves over to the right after him, watches him off. The other waiter has been staring at* WILLY.

STANLEY (*to the waiter*). Well, whatta you looking at?

The waiter picks up the chairs and moves off right. STANLEY *takes the table and follows him. The light fades on this area. There is a long pause, the sound of the flute coming over. The light gradually rises on the kitchen, which is empty.* HAPPY *appears at the door of the house, followed by* BIFF. HAPPY *is carrying a large bunch of long-stemmed roses. He enters the kitchen, looks around for* LINDA. *Not seeing her, he turns to* BIFF, *who is just outside the house door, and makes a gesture with his hands, indicating "Not here, I guess." He looks into the living room and freezes. Inside,* LINDA, *unseen, is seated,* WILLY'*s coat on her lap. She rises ominously and quietly and moves toward* HAPPY, *who backs up into the kitchen, afraid.*

HAPPY. Hey, what're you doing up? (LINDA *says nothing but moves toward him implacably.*) Where's Pop? (*He keeps backing to the right, and now* LINDA *is in full view in the doorway to the living room.*) Is he sleeping?

LINDA. Where were you?

HAPPY (*trying to laugh it off*). We met two girls, Mom, very fine types. Here, we brought you some flowers. (*Offering them to her.*) Put them in your room, Ma.

She knocks them to the floor at BIFF'*s feet. He has now come inside and closed the door behind him. She stares at* BIFF, *silent.*

HAPPY. Now what'd you do that for? Mom, I want you to have some flowers . . .

LINDA (*cutting* HAPPY *off, violently to* BIFF). Don't you care whether he lives or dies?

HAPPY (*going to the stairs*). Come upstairs, Biff.

BIFF (*with a flare of disgust, to* HAPPY). Go away from me! (*To* LINDA.) What do you mean, lives or dies? Nobody's dying around here, pal.

LINDA. Get out of my sight! Get out of here!

BIFF. I wanna see the boss.

LINDA. You're not going near him!

BIFF. Where is he? (*He moves into the living room and* LINDA *follows.*)

LINDA (*shouting after* BIFF). You invite him for dinner. He looks forward to it all day—(BIFF *appears in his parents' bedroom, looks around, and exits*)—and then you desert him there. There's no stranger you'd do that to!

HAPPY. Why? He had a swell time with us. Listen, when I—(LINDA *comes back into the kitchen*)—desert him I hope I don't outlive the day!

LINDA. Get out of here!

HAPPY. Now look, Mom . . .

LINDA. Did you have to go to women tonight? You and your lousy rotten whores!

BIFF *re-enters the kitchen.*

HAPPY. Mom, all we did was follow Biff around trying to cheer him up! (*To* BIFF.) Boy, what a night you gave me!

LINDA. Get out of here, both of you, and don't come back! I don't want you tormenting him any more. Go on now, get your things together! (*To* BIFF.) You can sleep in his apartment. (*She starts to pick up the flowers and stops herself.*) Pick up this stuff, I'm not your maid any more. Pick it up, you bum, you!

HAPPY *turns his back to her in refusal.* BIFF *slowly moves over and gets down on his knees, picking up the flowers.*

LINDA. You're a pair of animals! Not one, not another living soul would have had the cruelty to walk out on that man in a restaurant!

BIFF (*not looking at her*). Is that what he said?

LINDA. He didn't have to say anything. He was so humiliated he nearly limped when he came in.

HAPPY. But, Mom, he had a great time with us . . .

BIFF (*cutting him off violently*). Shut up!

Without another word, HAPPY *goes upstairs.*

LINDA. You! You didn't even go in to see if he was all right!

BIFF (*still on the floor in front of* LINDA, *the flowers in his hand; with self-loathing*). No. Didn't. Didn't do a damned thing. How do you like that, heh? Left him babbling in a toilet.

LINDA. You louse. You . . .

BIFF. Now you hit it on the nose! (*He gets up, throws the flowers in the wastebasket.*) The scum of the earth, and you're looking at him!

LINDA. Get out of here!

BIFF. I gotta talk to the boss, Mom. Where is he?

LINDA. You're not going near him. Get out of this house!

BIFF (*with absolute assurance, determination*). No. We're gonna have an abrupt conversation, him and me.

LINDA. You're not talking to him.

Hammering is heard from outside the house, off right. BIFF *turns toward the noise.*

LINDA (*suddenly pleading*). Will you please leave him alone?

BIFF. What's he doing out there?

LINDA. He's planting the garden!

BIFF (*quietly*). Now? Oh, my God!

BIFF *moves outside,* LINDA *following. The light dies down on them and comes up on the center of the apron as* WILLY *walks into it. He is carrying a flashlight, a hoe, and a handful of seed packets. He raps the top of the hoe sharply to fix it firmly, and then moves to the left, measuring off the distance with his foot. He holds the flashlight to look at the seed packets, reading off the instructions. He is in the blue of night.*

WILLY. Carrots . . . quarter-inch apart. Rows . . . one-foot rows. (*He measures it off.*) One foot. (*He puts down a package and measures off.*) Beets. (*He puts down another package and measures again.*) Lettuce. (*He reads the package, puts it down.*) One foot—(*He breaks off as* BEN *appears at the right and moves slowly down to him.*) What a proposition, ts, ts. Terrific, terrific. 'Cause she's suffered, Ben, the woman has suffered. You understand me? A man can't go out the way he came in, Ben, a man has got to add up to something. You can't, you can't—(BEN *moves toward him as though to interrupt.*) You gotta consider now. Don't answer so quick. Remember, it's a guaranteed twenty-thousand-dollar proposition. Now look, Ben, I want you to go through the ins and outs of this thing with me. I've got nobody to talk to, Ben, and the woman has suffered, you hear me?

BEN (*standing still, considering*). What's the proposition?

WILLY. It's twenty thousand dollars on the barrelhead. Guaranteed, gilt-edged, you understand?

BEN. You don't want to make a fool of yourself. They might not honor the policy.

WILLY. How can they dare refuse? Didn't I work like a coolie to meet every premium on the nose? And now they don't pay off? Impossible!

BEN. It's called a cowardly thing, William.

WILLY. Why? Does it take more guts to stand here the rest of my life ringing up a zero?

BEN (*yielding*). That's a point, William. (*He moves, thinking, turns.*) And twenty thousand—that is something one can feel with the hand, it is there.

WILLY (*now assured, with rising power*). Oh, Ben, that's the whole beauty of it! I see it like a diamond, shining in the dark, hard and rough, that I can pick up and touch in my hand. Not like—like an appointment! This would not be another damned-fool appointment, Ben, and it changes all the aspects. Because he thinks I'm nothing, see, and so he spites me. But the funeral . . . (*Straightening up.*) Ben, that funeral will be massive! They'll come from Maine, Massachusetts, Vermont, New Hampshire! All the old-timers with the strange license plates—that boy will be thunderstruck, Ben, because he never realized—I am known! Rhode Island, New York, New Jersey—I am known, Ben, and he'll see it with his eyes once and for all. He'll see what I am, Ben! He's in for a shock, that boy!

BEN (*coming down to the edge of the garden*). He'll call you a coward.

WILLY (*suddenly fearful*). No, that would be terrible.

BEN. Yes. And a damned fool.

WILLY. No, no, he mustn't, I won't have that! (*He is broken and desperate.*)

BEN. He'll hate you, William.

The gay music of the boys is heard.

WILLY. Oh, Ben, how do we get back to all the great times? Used to be so full of light, and comradeship, the sleigh-riding in winter, and the ruddiness on his cheeks. And always some kind of good news coming up, always something nice coming up ahead. And never even let me carry the valises in the house, and simonizing, simonizing that little red car! Why, why can't I give him something and not have him hate me?

BEN. Let me think about it. (*He glances at his watch.*) I still have a little time. Remarkable proposition, but you've got to be sure you're not making a fool of yourself.

BEN *drifts off upstage and goes out of sight.* BIFF *comes down from the left.*

WILLY (*suddenly conscious of* BIFF, *turns and looks up at him, then begins picking up the packages of seeds in confusion*). Where the hell is that seed? (*Indignantly.*) You can't see nothing out here! They boxed in the whole goddam neighborhood!

BIFF. There are people all around here. Don't you realize that?

WILLY. I'm busy. Don't bother me.

BIFF (*taking the hoe from* WILLY). I'm saying good-by to you, Pop. (WILLY *looks at him, silent, unable to move.*) I'm not coming back any more.

WILLY. You're not going to see Oliver tomorrow?

BIFF. I've got no appointment, Dad.

WILLY. He put his arm around you, and you've got no appointment?

BIFF. Pop, get this now, will you? Everytime I've left it's been a—fight that sent me out of here. Today I realized something about myself and I tried to explain it to you and I—I think I'm just not smart enough to make any sense out of it for you. To hell with whose fault it is or anything like that. (*He takes* WILLY*'s arm.*) Let's just wrap it up, heh? Come on in, we'll tell Mom. (*He gently tries to pull* WILLY *to left.*)

WILLY (*frozen, immobile, with guilt in his voice*). No, I don't want to see her.

BIFF. Come on! (*He pulls again, and* WILLY *tries to pull away.*)

WILLY (*highly nervous*). No, no, I don't want to see her.

BIFF (*tries to look into* WILLY*'s face, as if to find the answer there*). Why don't you want to see her?

WILLY (*more harshly now*). Don't bother me, will you?

BIFF. What do you mean, you don't want to see her? You don't want them calling you yellow, do you? This isn't your fault; it's me, I'm a bum. Now come inside! (WILLY *strains to get away.*) Did you hear what I said to you?

WILLY *pulls away and quickly goes by himself into the house.* BIFF *follows.*

LINDA (*to* WILLY). Did you plant, dear?

BIFF (*at the door, to* LINDA). All right, we had it out. I'm going and I'm not writing any more.

LINDA (*going to* WILLY *in the kitchen*). I think that's the best way, dear. 'Cause there's no use drawing it out, you'll just never get along.

WILLY *doesn't respond.*

BIFF. People ask where I am and what I'm doing, you don't know, and you don't care. That way it'll be off your mind and you can start brightening up again. All right? That clears it, doesn't it? (WILLY *is silent, and* BIFF *goes to him.*) You gonna wish me luck, scout? (*He extends his hand.*) What do you say?

LINDA. Shake his hand, Willy.

WILLY (*turning to her, seething with hurt*). There's no necessity—to mention the pen at all, y'know.

BIFF (*gently*). I've got no appointment, Dad.

WILLY (*erupting fiercely*). He put his arm around . . .?

BIFF. Dad, you're never going to see what I am, so what's the use of arguing? If I strike oil I'll send you a check. Meantime forget I'm alive.

WILLY (*to* LINDA). Spite, see?

BIFF. Shake hands, Dad.

WILLY. Not my hand.

BIFF. I was hoping not to go this way.

WILLY. Well, this is the way you're going. Good-by.

BIFF *looks at him a moment, then turns sharply and goes to the stairs.*

WILLY (*stops him with*). May you rot in hell if you leave this house!

BIFF (*turning*). Exactly what is it that you want from me?

WILLY. I want you to know, on the train, in the mountains, in the valleys, wherever you go, that you cut down your life for spite!

BIFF. No, no.

WILLY. Spite, spite, is the word of your undoing! And when you're down and out, remember what did it. When you're rotting somewhere beside the railroad tracks, remember, and don't you dare blame it on me!

BIFF. I'm not blaming it on you!

WILLY. I won't take the rap for this, you hear?

HAPPY *comes down the stairs and stands on the bottom step, watching.*

BIFF. That's just what I'm telling you!

WILLY (*sinking into a chair at a table, with full accusation*). You're trying to put a knife in me—don't think I don't know what you're doing!

BIFF. All right, phony! Then let's lay it on the line. (*He whips the rubber tube out of his pocket and puts it on the table.*)

HAPPY. You crazy . . .

LINDA. Biff! (*She moves to grab the hose, but* BIFF *holds it down with his hand.*)

BIFF. Leave it there! Don't move it!

WILLY (*not looking at it*). What is that?

BIFF. You know goddam well what that is.

WILLY (*caged, wanting to escape*). I never saw that.

BIFF. You saw it. The mice didn't bring it into the cellar! What is this supposed to do, make a hero out of you? This supposed to make me sorry for you?

WILLY. Never heard of it.

BIFF. There'll be no pity for you, you hear it? No pity!

WILLY (*to* LINDA). You hear the spite!

BIFF. No, you're going to hear the truth—what you are and what I am!

LINDA. Stop it!

WILLY. Spite!

HAPPY (*coming down toward* BIFF). You cut it now!

BIFF (*to* HAPPY). The man don't know who we are! The man is gonna know! (*To* WILLY.) We never told the truth for ten minutes in this house!

HAPPY. We always told the truth!

BIFF (*turning on him*). You big blow, are you the assistant buyer? You're one of the two assistants to the assistant, aren't you?

HAPPY. Well, I'm practically . . .

BIFF. You're practically full of it! We all are! and I'm through with it. (*To* WILLY.) Now hear this, Willy, this is me.

WILLY. I know you!

BIFF. You know why I had no address for three months? I stole a suit in Kansas City and I was in jail. (*To* LINDA, *who is sobbing.*) Stop crying. I'm through with it.

LINDA *turns away from them, her hands covering her face.*

WILLY. I suppose that's my fault!

BIFF. I stole myself out of every good job since high school!

WILLY. And whose fault is that?

BIFF. And I never got anywhere because you blew me so full of hot air I could never stand taking orders from anybody! That's whose fault it is!

WILLY. I hear that!

LINDA. Don't, Biff!

BIFF. It's goddam time you heard that! I had to be boss big shot in two weeks, and I'm through with it!

WILLY. Then hang yourself! For spite, hang yourself!

BIFF. No! Nobody's hanging himself, Willy! I ran down eleven flights with a pen in my hand today. And suddenly I stopped, you hear me? And in the middle of that office building, do you hear this? I stopped in the middle of that building and I saw—the sky. I saw the things that I love in this world. The work and the food and time to sit and smoke. And I looked at the pen and said to myself, what the hell am I grabbing this for? Why am I trying to become what I don't want to be? What am I doing in an office, making a contemptuous, begging fool of myself, when all I want is out there, waiting for me the minute I say I know who I am! Why can't I say that, Willy? (*He tries to make* WILLY *face him, but* WILLY *pulls away and moves to the left.*)

WILLY (*with hatred, threateningly*). The door of your life is wide open!

BIFF. Pop! I'm a dime a dozen, and so are you!

WILLY (*turning on him now in an uncontrolled outburst*). I am not a dime a dozen! I am Willy Loman, and you are Biff Loman!

BIFF *starts for* WILLY, *but is blocked by* HAPPY. *In his fury,* BIFF *seems on the verge of attacking his father.*

BIFF. I am not a leader of men, Willy, and neither are you. You were never anything but a hardworking drummer who landed in the ash can like all the rest of them! I'm one dollar an hour, Willy! I tried seven states and couldn't raise it. A buck an hour! Do you gather my meaning? I'm not bringing home any prizes any more, and you're going to stop waiting for me to bring them home!

WILLY (*directly to* BIFF). You vengeful, spiteful mutt!

BIFF *breaks from* HAPPY. WILLY, *in fright, starts up the stairs.* BIFF *grabs him.*

BIFF (*at the peak of his fury*). Pop! I'm nothing! I'm nothing, Pop. Can't you understand that? There's no spite in it any more. I'm just what I am, that's all.

BIFF'*s fury has spent itself and he breaks down, sobbing, holding on to* WILLY, *who dumbly fumbles for* BIFF'*s face.*

WILLY (*astonished*). What're you doing? What're you doing? (*To* LINDA.) Why is he crying?

BIFF (*crying, broken*). Will you let me go, for Christ's sake? Will you take that phony dream and burn it before something happens? (*Struggling to contain himself he pulls away and moves to the stairs.*) I'll go in the morning. Put him—put him to bed. (*Exhausted,* BIFF *moves up the stairs to his room.*)

WILLY (*after a long pause, astonished, elevated*). Isn't that—isn't that remarkable? Biff—he likes me!

LINDA. He loves you, Willy!

HAPPY (*deeply moved*). Always did, Pop.

WILLY. Oh, Biff! (*Staring wildly.*) He cried! Cried to me. (*He is choking with his love, and now cries out his promise.*) That boy—that boy is going to be magnificent!

BEN *appears in the light just outside the kitchen.*

BEN. Yes, outstanding, with twenty thousand behind him.

LINDA (*sensing the racing of his mind, fearfully, carefully.*) Now come to bed, Willy. It's all settled now.

WILLY (*finding it difficult not to rush out of the house*). Yes, we'll sleep. Come on. Go to sleep, Hap.

BEN. And it does take a great kind of a man to crack the jungle.

In accents of dread, BEN'*s idyllic music starts up.*

HAPPY (*his arm around* LINDA). I'm getting married, Pop, don't forget it. I'm changing everything. I'm gonna run that department before the year is up. You'll see, Mom. (*He kisses her.*)

BEN. The jungle is dark but full of diamonds, Willy.

WILLY *turns, moves, listening to* BEN.

LINDA. Be good. You're both good boys, just act that way, that's all.

HAPPY. 'Night, Pop. (*He goes upstairs.*)

LINDA (*to* WILLY). Come, dear.

BEN (*with greater force*). One must go in to fetch a diamond out.

WILLY (*to* LINDA, *as he moves slowly along the edge of the kitchen, toward the door*). I just want to get settled down, Linda. Let me sit alone for a little.

LINDA (*almost uttering her fear*). I want you upstairs.

WILLY (*taking her in his arms*). In a few minutes, Linda. I couldn't sleep right now. Go on, you look awful tired. (*He kisses her.*)

BEN. Not like an appointment at all. A diamond is rough and hard to the touch.

WILLY. Go on now. I'll be right up.

LINDA. I think this is the only way, Willy.

WILLY. Sure, it's the best thing.

BEN. Best thing!

WILLY. The only way. Everything is gonna be—go on, kid, get to bed. You look so tired.

LINDA. Come right up.

WILLY. Two minutes.

LINDA *goes into the living room, then reappears in her bedroom.* WILLY *moves just outside the kitchen door.*

WILLY. Loves me. (*Wonderingly.*) Always loved me. Isn't that a remarkable thing? Ben, he'll worship me for it!

BEN (*with promise*). It's dark there, but full of diamonds.

WILLY. Can you imagine that magnificence with twenty thousand dollars in his pocket?

LINDA (*calling from her room*). Willy! Come up!

WILLY (*calling into the kitchen*). Yes! Yes. Coming! It's very smart, you realize that, don't you, sweetheart? Even Ben sees it. I gotta go, baby. 'By! 'By! (*Going over to* BEN, *almost dancing.*) Imagine? When the mail comes he'll be ahead of Bernard again!

BEN. A perfect proposition all around.

WILLY. Did you see how he cried to me? Oh, if I could kiss him, Ben!

BEN. Time, William, time!

WILLY. Oh, Ben, I always knew one way or another we were gonna make it, Biff and I.

BEN (*looking at his watch*). The boat. We'll be late. (*He moves slowly off into the darkness.*)

WILLY (*elegiacally, turning to the house*). Now when you kick off, boy, I want a seventy-yard boot, and get right down the field under the ball, and when you hit, hit low and hit hard, because it's important, boy. *He swings around and faces the audience.*) There's all kinds of important people in the stands, and the first thing you know . . . (*Suddenly realizing he is alone.*) Ben! Ben, where do I . . . ? (*He makes a sudden movement of search.*) Ben, how do I . . .?

LINDA (*calling*). Willy, you coming up?

WILLY (*uttering a gasp of fear, whirling about as if to quiet her*). Sh! (*He turns around as if to find his way; sounds, faces, voices, seem to be swarming in upon him and he flicks at them, crying.*) Sh! Sh! (*Suddenly music, faint and high, stops him. It rises in intensity, almost to an unbearable scream. He goes up and down on his toes, and rushes off around the house.*) Shhh!

LINDA. Willy?

There is no answer. LINDA *waits.* BIFF *gets up off his bed. He is still in his clothes.* HAPPY *sits up.* BIFF *stands listening.*

LINDA (*with real fear*). Willy, answer me! Willy!

There is the sound of a car starting and moving away at full speed.

LINDA. No!

BIFF (*rushing down the stairs*). Pop!

As the car speeds off the music crashes down in a frenzy of sound, which becomes the soft pulsation of a single cello string. BIFF *slowly returns to his bedroom. He and* HAPPY *gravely don their jackets.* LINDA *slowly walks out of her room. The music has developed into a dead march. The leaves of day are appearing over everything.* CHARLEY *and* BERNARD, *somberly dressed, appear and knock on the kitchen door.* BIFF *and* HAPPY *slowly descend the stairs to the kitchen as* CHARLEY *and* BERNARD *enter. All stop a moment when* LINDA, *in clothes of mourning, bearing a little bunch of roses, comes through the draped doorway into the kitchen. She goes to* CHARLEY *and takes his arm. Now all move toward the audience, through the wall-line of the kitchen. At the limit of the apron,* LINDA *lays down the flowers, kneels, and sits back on her heels. All stare down at the grave.*

★

Requiem

CHARLEY. It's getting dark, Linda.

LINDA *doesn't react. She stares at the grave.*

BIFF. How about it, Mom? Better get some rest, heh? They'll be closing the gate soon.

LINDA *makes no move. Pause.*

HAPPY (*deeply angered*). He had no right to do that. There was no necessity for it. We would've helped him.

CHARLEY (*grunting*). Hmmm.

BIFF. Come along, Mom.

LINDA. Why didn't anybody come?

CHARLEY. It was a very nice funeral.

LINDA. But where are all the people he knew? Maybe they blame him.

CHARLEY. Naa. It's a rough world, Linda. They wouldn't blame him.

LINDA. I can't understand it. At this time especially. First time in thirty-five years we were just about free and clear. He only needed a little salary. He was even finished with the dentist.

CHARLEY. No man only needs a little salary.

LINDA. I can't understand it.

BIFF. There were a lot of nice days. When he'd come home from a trip; or on Sundays, making the stoop; finishing the cellar; putting on the new porch; when he built the extra bathroom; and put up the garage. You know something, Charley, there's more of him in that front stoop than in all the sales he ever made.

CHARLEY. Yeah. He was a happy man with a batch of cement.

LINDA. He was so wonderful with his hands.

BIFF. He had the wrong dreams. All, all, wrong.

HAPPY (*almost ready to fight* BIFF). Don't say that!

BIFF. He never knew who he was.

CHARLEY (*stopping* HAPPY*'s movement and reply; to* BIFF). Nobody dast blame this man. You don't understand: Willy was a salesman. And for a salesman, there is no rock bottom to the life. He don't put a bolt to a nut, he don't tell you the law or give you medicine. He's a man way out there in the blue, riding on a smile and a shoeshine. And when they start not smiling back—that's an earthquake. And then you get yourself a couple of spots on your hat, and you're finished. Nobody dast blame this man. A salesman is got to dream, boy. It comes with the territory.

BIFF. Charley, the man didn't know who he was.

HAPPY (*infuriated*). Don't say that!

BIFF. Why don't you come with me, Happy?

HAPPY. I'm not licked that easily. I'm staying right in this city, and I'm gonna beat this racket! (*He looks at* BIFF, *his chin set.*) The Loman Brothers!

BIFF. I know who I am, kid.

HAPPY. All right, boy. I'm gonna show you and everybody else that Willy Loman did not die in vain. He had a good dream. It's the only dream you can have—to come out number-one man. He fought it out here, and this is where I'm gonna win it for him.

BIFF (*with a hopeless glance at* HAPPY, *bends toward his mother*). Let's go, Mom.

LINDA. I'll be with you in a minute. Go on, Charley. (*He hesitates.*) I want to, just for a minute. I never had a chance to say good-by.

CHARLEY *moves away, followed by* HAPPY. BIFF *remains a slight distance up and left of* LINDA. *She sits there, summoning herself. The flute begins, not far away, playing behind her speech.*

LINDA. Forgive me, dear. I can't cry. I don't know what it is, but I can't cry. I don't understand it. Why did you ever do that? Help me, Willy, I can't cry. It seems to me that you're just on another trip. I keep expecting you. Willy, dear, I can't cry. Why did you do it? I search and search and I search, and I can't understand it, Willy. I made the last payment on the house today. Today, dear. And there'll be nobody home. (*A sob rises in her throat.*) We're free and clear. (*Sobbing mournfully, released.*) We're free. (BIFF *comes slowly toward her.*) We're free . . . We're free . . .

BIFF *lifts her to her feet and moves out up right with her in his arms.* LINDA *sobs quietly.* BERNARD *and* CHARLEY *come together and follow them, followed by* HAPPY. *Only the music of the flute is left on the darkening stage as over the house the hard towers of the apartment buildings rise into sharp focus and the curtain falls.*

Index